HAWAII HANDBOOK

IS THIS BOOK OUT OF DATE?

In today's world, things change so rapidly that it's impossible for one person to keep up with everything happening in any one place. This is particularly true in Hawaii, where situations are always in flux. Travel books are like automobiles: they require fine tuning and frequent overhauls to keep in shape. Help us keep this book in shape! We require input from our readers so that we can continue to provide the best, most current information available. Please write to let us know about any inaccuracies, new information, or misleading suggestions. Although we try to make our maps as accurate as possible, errors do occur. If you have any suggestions for improvement or places that should be included, please let us know about it.

We especially appreciate letters from female travelers, visiting expatriates, local residents, and hikers and outdoor enthusiasts. We also like hearing from experts in the field as well as from local hotel owners and individuals wishing to accommodate visitors from abroad.

As you travel through the islands, keep notes in the margins of this book. Notes written on the spot are always more accurate than those put down on paper later. Send us your copy after your trip, and we'll send you a fresh one as a replacement. If you take a photograph during your trip which you feel might be included in a future edition, please send it to us. Send only good slide duplicates or glossy black-and-white prints. Drawings and other artwork are also appreciated. If we use your photo or drawing, you'll be mentioned in the credits and receive a free copy of the book. Keep in mind, however, that the publisher cannot return any materials unless you include a self-addressed, stamped envelope. Moon Publications will own the rights on all material submitted. Address your letters to:

J.D. Bisignani
Moon Publications
722 Wall Street
Chico, CA 95928 USA

FREE MOON BOOK FOR CONTRIBUTORS!

For those who send us substantial information, we will send a free copy of the next edition of *Hawaii Handbook* or any other Moon Publications guide they wish. We reserve the right, however, to determine what is "substantial." Thank you for your help.

HAWAII HANDBOOK

J.D. Bisignani

MOON PUBLICATIONS

HAWAII HANDBOOK
First Edition (September 1987)

Please send all comments,
corrections, additions,
amendments and critiques to:

J.D. BISIGNANI
MOON PUBLICATIONS
722 Wall Street
Chico, CA 95928, USA

Published by
Moon Publications
722 Wall Street
Chico, California 95928, USA
tel. (916) 345-5473/5413

Printed by
Colorcraft Ltd., Hong Kong

Library of Congress Cataloging-in-Publication Data

Bisignani, J.D., 1947–
Hawaii Handbook / J.D. Bisignani.
p. cm.
Bibliography: p. 765
Includes index.
ISBN 0-918373-14-X
1. Hawaii–Description and travel–1981–Guide-books.
I. Title.
DU622.B55 1987
919.969'044–dc19 87–17108
CIP

Cover painting by Susan Strangio from an original photograph by J.D. Bisignani.

To Sandy B.,
who from first glance
filled my life with aloha

Love, Dad

ACKNOWLEDGEMENTS

After four years of working on *Hawaii Handbook* I can finally write those two sweet words, "thank you." Sweet because they bring back a flood of memories of all the people who worked on this book, and sweet because they are synonymous with two other words that I've longed to write, "the end."

I want to offer my sincerest gratitude to the following people who helped me with their expertise, energy, advice, and positive criticism. You are all beautiful, and without you, *Hawaii Handbook* could not have been possible. Deke Castleman, my chief editor, whose hand is on every page of this book, sometimes velvet, and sometimes velvet-covered steel, whose main task was to hold the mirror before my eyes and let me *see.* Mark Morris, second editor, who like the gentleman that he is put up with my tantrums, smiled, and got the job done in spite of me. Dave "Hot Wax" Hurst, Moon's production manager, who can lay out a book like old John Henry could lay track. Louise Foote, whom you can all thank for helping you to get around. She drew all the maps in *Hawaii Handbook* and turned her skilled hand to many of the illustrations. Asha Johnson, whose title of typesetter doesn't come close to describing her input into these books. Thanks for your chuckles and sighs as you read my book. It meant more to me than you could ever know. Donna Galassi, Moon's sales manager, one of those rare people who can be business tough but always gracious as she keeps Moon sales rising. Marne Bass, Moon's money man, who has the thankless job of dealing with all of us artist types when we come and ask for our "dough." Bill Dalton, the "full moon" himself, who has the split roll of publisher and author, and who instinctively knows when to run away. My illustrators Diana Lasich, Sue Strangio, Mary Ann Abel, Louise Foote, Debra Fau, and my contributing photographers, Gary Quiring and Bob Cowan, whose remarkable talents graced the pages of *Hawaii Handbook* adding a touch of beauty. These fine people are profiled in the backmatter of this book.

California State University at Chico professors Bob Vivian, Ed Myles, George Benson, and Ellen Walker who provided me with quality interns from their respective departments of Journalism, Geography, Tourism, and English. The following student interns worked in the "trenches" transcribing, in-putting, designing charts, and generally infusing my surroundings with positive energy: Caroline Schoepp, Maureen Cole, Suzanne Booth, Lee Wilkinson, Sally Price, Elena Wilkinson, Bret Lampman, Rich Zimmerman, Craig Nelson, Pat Presley, Leslie Crouch, and Monica "Don't Smile No" Moore.

I would also like to thank the following people for their special help and consideration: Lindy Boyes of the Honolulu HVB; Roger Rose and Elisa Johnston of the Bishop Museum; Lee Wild, Hawaiian Mission Houses Museum; Marilyn Nicholson, State Foundation of Culture and Arts; Janet Hyrne National Car Rental; Glenn Masutani, Hawaiian Pacific Resorts; Bill Gough, Royal Hawaiian Airlines; Lindsey Pollock, Hawaiian Air; Hal Corbett, pilot, Polynesian Air. Also, many thanks to my friends who shared their special Hawaii with me: Donna and Ray Barnett; Jim and John Costello; Dr. Terry and Nancy Carolan; and Nasisu Rehnborg Kahalewai. Bob Nilsen, fellow writer and cycling partner, who nightly rescued me from my computer, and kept me healthy and sane. Finally, to my wife Marlene, who has always been there from beginning to end. To all of you my deepest *aloha.*

CONTENTS

LIST OF MAPS

MAP LEGEND

FREEWAY
MAIN HIGHWAY
SECONDARY ROAD
JEEP TRAIL
FOOT TRAIL
TOWN OR VILLAGE
POINT OF INTEREST
HIGHWAY NUMBER
WATER
MOUNTAIN
STATE OR BEACH PARK
HEIAU
CAMPGROUND
LARGE TOWN OR CITY

All maps are oriented with north at the top of the map unless otherwise indicated.

GRAPHS AND CHARTS

PHOTO AND ILLUSTRATION CREDITS

Photos: All photographs are by the the author except: **Bob Cowan**— 295; **Fritz Craft**— 54, 62, 103, 209, 218, 263; **Hawaii State Archives**— 4, 25, 27, 30, 31, 33, 34, 38, 40, 50, 57, 64, 67, 68, 72, 78, 79, 98, 101, 139, 149, 156, 170, 186, 523, 573, 631; **Hawaii Visitors Bureau**— 3; **Carl Parkes**— 330; **Gary Quiring**— 146, 380.

Illustrations: **Mary Ann Abel**— 69, 331, 374, 403, 450, 452, 459, 576, 582, 619, 642, 753, 756; **John Costello**— 89, 94, 145, 311; **Debra Fau**— 7, 183, 322, 323, 333; **Louise Foote**— 11, 12, 14, 15, 16, 18, 19, 22, 23, 53, 80, 91, 92, 141, 161, 172, 173, 178, 179, 180, 194, 195, 321, 324, 366, 430, 457, 458, 468, 498, 511, 527, 530, 533, 544, 559, 577, 593, 613, 626, 660, 661, 662, 693, 719, 732; **Diana Lasich Harper**— 1, 9, 20, 21, 43, 47, 48, 74, 82, 90, 95, 99, 113, 124, 136, 155, 157, 159, 160, 164, 171, 175, 189, 225, 248, 288, 302, 325, 353, 389, 425, 427, 445, 453, 474, 484, 485, 522, 550, 652, 682, 698, 706; **Mission Houses Museum**— 81, 231; **Susan Strangio**— 106, 134, 137, 165, 176, 181, 182, 411, 418, 431, 442, 596, 653.

INTRODUCTION

The modern geological theory concerning the formation of the Hawaiian Islands is no less fanciful than the Polynesian legends sung about their origins. Science maintains that 30 million years ago Earth was little more than a mudball. While the great continents were being geologically tortured into their rudimentary shapes, the Hawaiian Islands were a mere ooze of bubbling magma 20,000 feet below the surface of the primordial sea. For millions of years this molten rock flowed up from fissures in the sea floor. Slowly, layer upon layer of lava was deposited until an island rose above the surface of the sea. The great weight then sealed the fissure, whose own colossal forces progressively crept in a southwesterly direction, then burst out again and again to build the chain. At the same time the entire Pacific plate was afloat on the giant sea of molten magma, and it slowly glided to the northwest carrying the newly formed islands with it.

In the beginning the spewing crack formed Kure and Midway islands in the extreme northwestern sector of the Hawaiian chain. Today, more than 130 islands, islets, and shoals make up the Hawaiian Islands, stretching 1,500 miles across an expanse of the North Pacific. Geologists maintain that the *hot spot,* now primarily under the Big Island, remains relatively stationary, and the 1,500-mile spread of the Hawaiian Archipelago is only due to a northwest drifting effect of about three to five inches per year. Still, with the center of activity under the Big Island, Mauna Loa and Kilauea volcanoes regularly add more land to the only state in the Union that is literally still growing. About 30 miles southeast of the Big Island is Loihi Sea Mount, waiting 3,000 feet below the waves. Frequent eruptions bring it closer and closer to the surface until one day it will emerge and become the newest Hawaiian Island.

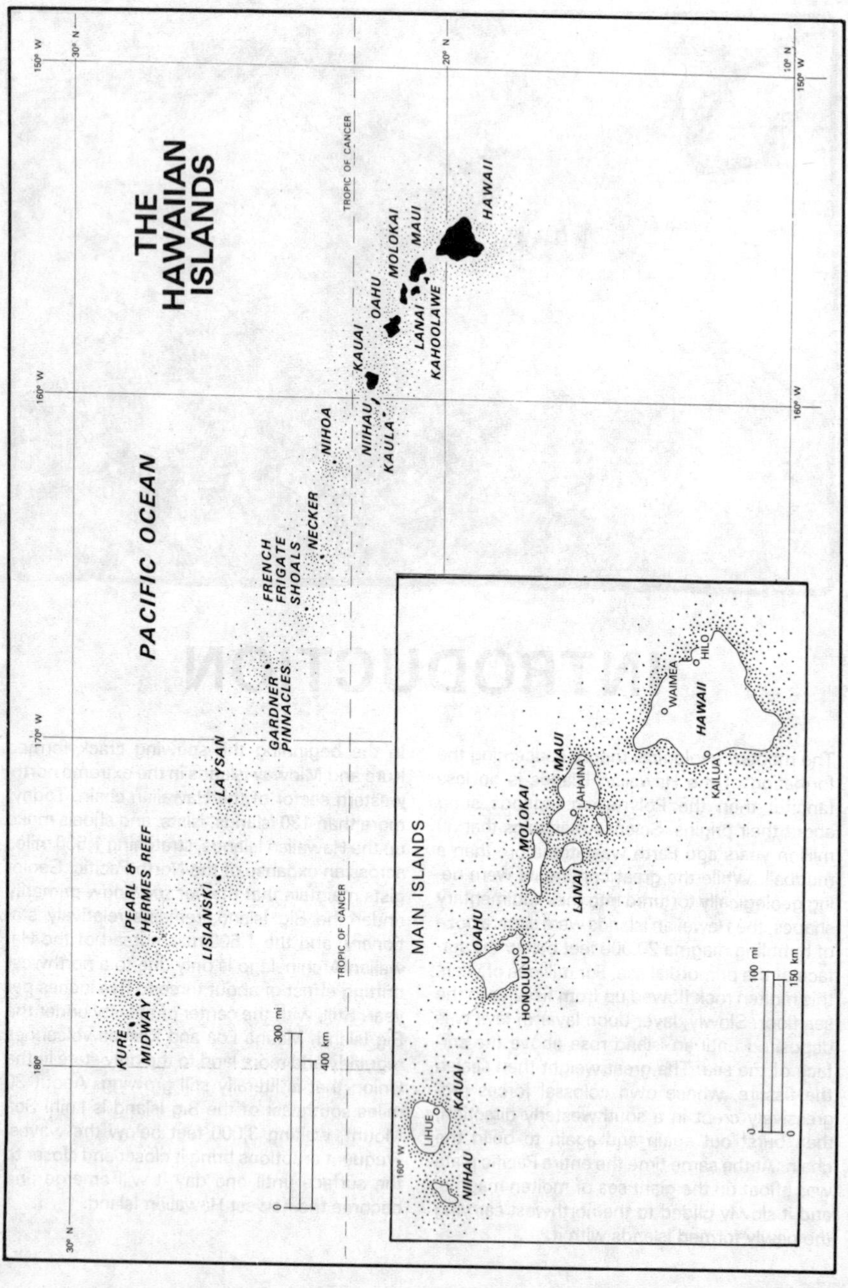
THE HAWAIIAN ISLANDS
PACIFIC OCEAN
TROPIC OF CANCER
30° N
20° N
10° N
180°
170° W
160° W
150° W
KURE
MIDWAY
PEARL & HERMES REEF
LISIANSKI
LAYSAN
GARDNER PINNACLES
FRENCH FRIGATE SHOALS
NECKER
NIHOA
NIIHAU
KAULA
KAUAI
OAHU
MOLOKAI
LANAI
KAHOOLAWE
MAUI
HAWAII
0 300 mi
0 400 km
MAIN ISLANDS
LIHUE
HONOLULU
LAHAINA
KAILUA
WAIMEA
HILO
0 100 mi
0 150 km

THE LAND

The Hawaiian Islands sit right in the middle of the North Pacific just a touch south of the Tropic of Cancer. They take up about as much room as a flower petal floating in a swimming pool. The sea makes life possible on the islands, and the Hawaiian sea is a mostly benign benefactor providing the basics: food, fresh water, and moderate climate. It is also responsible for an endless assortment of pleasure, romance, excitement, and a cultural link between Hawaii and its Polynesian counterparts. The Hawaiian Islands rise dramatically from the sea floor, not with a gradual sloping, but abruptly, like a temple pillar rising straight up from Neptune's kingdom.

Volcanism

The Hawaiian Islands are perfect examples of **shield volcanoes.** These are formed by a succession of gentle submarine eruptions which build an elongated dome much like a turtle shell. As the dome nears the surface of the sea, the eruptions combine with air and become extremely explosive due to the rapid temperature change and increased oxygen. Once above the surface they mellow again and steadily build upon themselves. As the island-mountain mushrooms, its weight seals off the spewing fissure below. Instead of forcing lava upward, it now finds less resistance by moving laterally. Eventually, the giant tube which carried lava to the top of the volcano sinks in upon itself and becomes a caldera. More eruptions occur periodically, but the lava is less dense and could be thought of as icing on a titanic cake. Now the relentless forces of wind and water take over to sculpt the raw lava into deep crevices and cuts that eventually become valleys. The smooth, once-single mountain is transformed into a miniature mountain range, while marinelife builds reefs around the islands, and the rising and falling of the surrounding seas during episodic ice ages combine with eroded soil to add or destroy coastal plains.

Lava flows on the Big Island regularly add more land to the state of Hawaii.

Lava

The Hawaiian Islands are huge mounds of cooled **basaltic lava** skirted by coral reefs, the skeletons of billions of polyps. The main components of Hawaiian lava are silica, iron oxide, magnesia, and lime. Lava flows in two distinct types for which the Hawaiian names have become universal geological terms: *a'a'* and *pahoehoe*. They are easily distinguished in appearance, but in chemical composition they are the same. Their differing appearance is due to the amount of gases contained in the flow when the lava hardens. ***A'a'*** lava is extremely rough, and spiny, and will quickly tear up your shoes if you do much hiking over it. If you have the misfortune to fall down, you'll soon find out why it's called *a'a'*. ***Pahoehoe*** is a billowy, ropy lava that looks like burned pancake batter. Not nearly as dense as *a'a'*, it can form some fantastic shapes and designs.

Lava actually forms molten rivers as it barrels down the steep slopes of the volcanoes. Sometimes these lava rivers crust over while the molten material on the inside continues to drain, until a lava tube is formed. These tubes characteristically have a domed roof and a flat floor and would make a very passable subway tunnel. Some can even measure more than 20 feet in diameter. One of the best examples is the Thurston Lava Tube at Volcanoes National Park on Hawaii. Other lava oddities are **peridots** (green gem-like stones) and clear **feldspar.** Gray lichens that cover older volcanic flows are known as **Hawaiian snow,**

engraving of Hawaii's unique pali *by Barthelme Lauvergue, c. 1836. (Hawaii State Archives)*

and volcanic glass that has been spun into hairlike strands is known as **Pele's hair,** while congealed lava droplets are known as **Pele's tears.**

Lakes And Rivers

Hawaii has very few natural lakes because of the porousness of the lava: water tends to seep into the ground rather than form ponds or lakes. However, *underground* deposits where water has been trapped between porous lava on top and dense subterranean layers below account for many freshwater springs throughout the islands; these are tapped as a primary source for irrigating sugarcane and pineapple. Hawaii's only large natural lakes happen to be on the private island of Niihau, and are therefore seldom seen by the outside world. **Lake Waiau,** at the 13,000-foot level on the Big Island's Mauna Kea, ranks among the highest lakes in the U.S. Honolulu's **Salt Lake,** once Oahu's only natural inland body of water, was bulldozed for land reclamation. No extensive rivers are found in Hawaii except the **Waimea River** on Kauai; none are navigable except for a few miles of the Waimea. The uncountable "streams" and "rivulets" on all the main islands turn from trickles to torrents depending upon the rainfall. The greatest concern is to hikers who can find themselves threatened by a flash flood in a valley that was the height of hospitality only a few minutes before.

Physical Features

Hawaii is the southernmost state in the Union and the most westerly except for a few farflung islands in the Alaskan Aleutians. The Tropic of Cancer runs through the state, and it shares the same latitude as Mexico City, Havana, Calcutta, and Hong Kong. It's the fourth smallest state, larger than Rhode Island, Connecticut, and Delaware. All together its 132 shoals, reefs, islets, and islands constitute 6,450 square miles of land. The eight *major* islands of Hawaii account for over 99% of the total land area, and are home to 100% of the population (except for a manned military installation here and there). They cover about 400 miles of Pacific, and from northwest to southeast include: Niihau (privately owned),

LAND STATISTICS

All figures given are closest approximations

WHERE	SQ. MILES	COASTLINE	ELEVATION (ft)
State	6,450	1,052	
Hawaii	4,038	313	
Mauna Kea			13,796
Mauna Loa			13,677
Kilauea			4,093
Oahu	608	209	
Mt. Kaala			4,020
Tantalus			2,013
Diamond Head			760
Maui	729	149	
Haleakala			10,023
Puu Kukui			5,788
Kauai	553	110	
Kawaikini			5,243
Waialeale			5,148
Molokai	261	106	
Kamakou			4,970
Lanai	140	52	
Lanaihale			3,370
Niihau	73	50	
Paniau			1,281
Kahoolawe	45	36	
Lua Makika			1,477
Northwestern Islands (total)	32	25	
Nihoa			910
Lehua			702

Kauai, Oahu, Molokai, Maui, Lanai, Kahoolawe (uninhabited), and Hawaii, the Big Island. The little-known Northwestern Islands, less than 1 percent of the state's total land mass, are dotted through the North Pacific for over 1,100 miles running from Kure in the far north to Nihoa, about 100 miles off Kauai's north shore. The state has just over 1,000 miles of tidal shoreline, and ranges in elevation from Mauna Loa's 13,796-foot summit to Maro Reef which is often awash.

Tidal Waves

Tsunami, the Japanese word for "tidal wave," ranks up there in causing the worst of horror in human beings. A Hawaiian *tsunami* is actually a seismic sea wave generated by an earthquake that could easily have its origins thousands of miles away in South America or Alaska. Some waves have been clocked at speeds up to 500 miles per hour. The U.S. Geological Service has recently uncovered data that indicates a 1,000-foot-high wall of water crashed into the Hawaiian Islands about 100,000 years ago. They believe a giant undersea landslide about 25 miles south of Lanai was the cause. The wave was about 15 miles wide and when it hit Lanai it stripped land more than

1,200 feet above sea level. It struck the other islands less severely, stripping land up to 800 feet above sea level. The worst *tsunami* in modern times have both struck Hilo on the Big Island: the one in May 1960 claimed 61 lives. Maui also experienced a catastrophic wave that inundated the Hana coast on April I, I946, taking lives and destroying much property. Other waves have inexplicably claimed no lives. The Big Island's Waipio Valley, for example, was a place of royalty that, according to ancient Hawaiian beliefs, was protected by the gods. A giant *tsunami* inundated Waipio in the 1940s catching hundreds of people in its watery grasp. Unbelievably not one person was hurt or killed. After the wave departed many people rushed to the valley floor to gather thousands of fish that were washed ashore. Without warning a second towering wave struck and grabbed the people again. Although giant trees and even boulders were washed out to sea not one person was harmed even the second time around. The safest place, besides high ground well away from beach areas, is out on the open ocean where even an enormous wave is perceived only as a large swell. A tidal wave is only dangerous when it is opposed by land. If you were to count up all the people in Hawaii that have been swept away by a tidal wave in the last 50 years it wouldn't come close to those killed on bicycles in a few Mainland cities in five years.

Earthquakes

Earthquakes are also a concern in Hawaii and offer a double threat because they cause *tsunami.* If you ever feel a tremor and are close to a beach, evacuate as soon as possible. The Big Island, because of its active volcanoes, experiences hundreds of technical earthquakes every year, although 99% can only be felt on very delicate equipment. The last major quake occurred on the Big Island in late November 1975, reaching 7.2 on the Richter Scale, and causing many millions of dollars worth of damage on the island's southern portion. The only loss of life was when a beach collapsed and two campers of a large party were drowned.

Hawaii has an elaborate warning system against natural disasters. You will notice loud speakers high atop poles along many beaches and coastal areas; these warn of *tsunami,* hurricanes, and earthquakes. They are tested at 11:00 a.m. on the first working day of each month. All island telephone books contain a Civil Defense warning and procedures section with which you should acquaint yourself. Note the maps showing which areas have been traditionally inundated by *tsunami* and what procedures to follow in case an emergency occurs.

CLIMATE

Of the wide variety of reasons for visiting Hawaii, most people have at least one in common: the weather! Nowhere on the face of the Earth do human beings feel more physically comfortable than in Hawaii, and a happy body almost always means a happy mind and spirit too. Cooling trade winds, low humidity, high pressure, clear sunny days, negative ionization from the sea, and an almost total lack of industrial pollution combine to make Hawaii *the* most healthful spot in America.

"So Good" Weather

The ancient Hawaiians had words to describe climatic specifics such as rain, wind, fog, and even snow, but they didn't have a general word for *weather.* The reason is that the weather is just about the same throughout the year and depends more on where you are on any given island than on what season it is. The Hawaiians did distinguish between *kau* (summer, May-Oct.) and *hoo'ilo* (winter, Nov.-April), but this distinction included social, religious, and even navigational factors, far beyond a mere distinction of weather variations. The average daytime temperature throughout Hawaii is about 80 degrees F (26 degrees C), with the average winter (Jan.) day registering 78 degrees, and the average summer (Aug.) day raising the thermometer only 7 degrees to 85. Nighttime temperatures drop less than 10 degrees. Altitude, however, does drop temperatures about three degrees for every 1,000 feet; if you intend to visit the mountain peaks of Haleakala, Mauna Loa, and Mauna Kea (all over 10,000 feet), expect the temperature to be at least 30 degrees cooler than sea level. The lowest temperatures ever recorded in Hawaii were atop Haleakala in January 1961 when the mercury dropped well below freezing to a mere 11 degrees; the hottest day occurred in 1931 in the Puna District of the Big Island with a scorching (for Hawaii) 100 degrees.

The Trade Winds

One reason that the Hawaiian temperatures are both constant and moderate is because of the trade winds. These breezes are so prevailing that the northeast sides of the islands are always referred to as **windward,** regardless of where the wind happens to be blowing on any given day. You can count on the *trades* to be blowing on an average of 300 days per year: hardly missing a day during summer, and half the time in winter. They blow throughout the day, but are strong during the heat of the afternoon and weaken at night. Just when you need a cooling breeze, there they are, and when the temperature drops at night, it's as if someone turned down the giant fan. The trade winds are also a factor in keeping down the humidity. They will suddenly disappear, however, usually in winter, and might not resume for a few weeks. The Tropic of Cancer runs through the center of Hawaii, yet its famed oppressively hot and muggy weather is joyfully absent. Honolulu, on the same latitude as sweaty Hong Kong and Havana, has only a 50-60% daily humidity factor.

Kona Winds

Kona means "leeward" in Hawaiian, and when the trades stop blowing these southerly winds often take over. To anyone from Hawaii, "kona wind" is euphemistic for bad weather: bringing in hot sticky air. Luckily they are most common from October to April when they appear roughly half the time. The temperatures drop slightly during the winter so these hot winds are tolerable, and even useful for moderating the thermometer. In the summer they are awful, but luckily again they hardly ever blow during this season. A **kona storm** is another matter. These subtropical low-pressure storms develop west of the Hawaiian Islands, and as they move easterly draw winds up from the south. Usual only in winter, they can cause considerable damage to crops and real estate. There is no real pattern to kona storms—some years they come every few weeks while in other years they don't appear at all.

Rain

Hardly a day goes by where it isn't raining somewhere on *all* the main islands. If this amazes you, just consider each island to be a mini continent: it would virtually be the same as expecting no rain anywhere in North America on any given day. All islands have a windward (northeast, wet) and leeward (southwest, dry) side. It rains much more on the windward side, and much more often during winter than summer. (However kona storms, because they come from the south, hit the islands' leeward sides most often.) Another important rain factor are the mountains, which act like water magnets. Moist winds gather around them and eventually build rain clouds. The ancient Hawaiians used these clouds and the reflected green light on their underbellies to spot land from great distances. Precipitation mostly occurs at and below the 3,000-foot level, thus the upper slopes of taller mountains such as Haleakala are quite dry. The average annual rainfall in the seas surrounding Hawaii is only 25 inches,

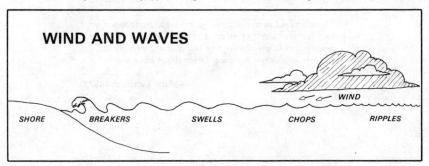

WIND AND WAVES

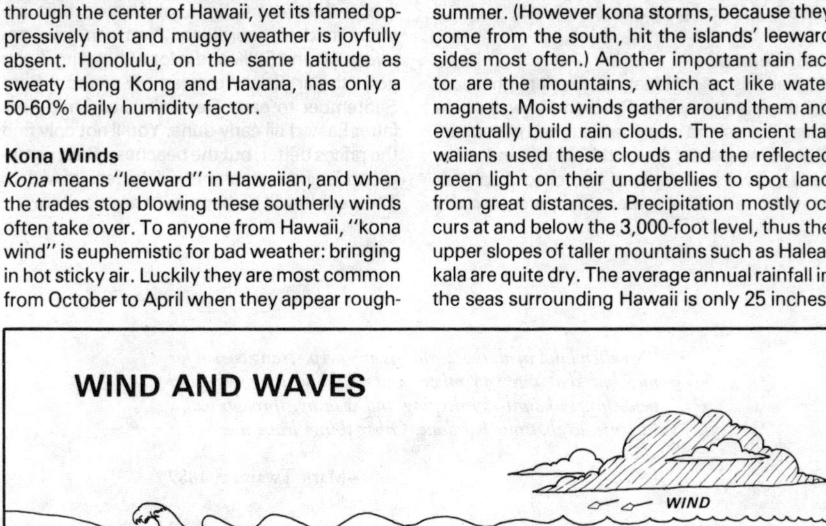

while a few miles inland around the windward slopes of mountains it can be 250 inches! A dramatic example of this phenomenon is seen by comparing Lahaina and Mt. Puu Kukui, only 7 miles distant from each other on West Maui. Hot, arid Lahaina has an annual rainfall of only 17 inches; Puu Kukui can receive close to 40 *feet* of rainfall a year, rivaling Mt. Waialeale on Kauai as the "wettest spot on Earth." Another point to remember is where there's rain there's also an incredible explosion of colorful flowers like an overgrown natural hothouse. You'll find this effect mostly on the windward sides of the islands. Conversely, the best beach weather is on the leeward sides: Kaanapali, Waikiki, Kailua-Kona, Poipu. They all sit in the "rain shadows" of interior mountains, and if it happens to be raining at one leeward beach, just move down the road to the next. One more thing about Hawaiian rains—they aren't very nasty. Much of the time just a light drizzle, they hardly ever last all day. Mostly localized to a relatively small area, you can oftentimes spot them by looking for the rainbows. Rain should never spoil your outings in Hawaii. Just "hang loose brah" and go to the sunshine.

Bad Weather

With all this talk of ideal weather it might seem like there isn't any bad. Read on. When a storm does hit an island it can be bleak and miserable. The worst storms are in the winter and often have the warped sense of humor to drop their heaviest rainfalls on areas that are normally quite dry. It's not infrequent for a storm to dump more than three inches of rain an hour; this can go as high as 10, making Hawaiian rainfalls some of the heaviest on Earth. Hawaii has also been hit with some walloping hurricanes in the last few decades. There haven't been many but they've been destructive. The vast majority of hurricanes originate far to the southeast off the coast of Mexico and Latin America. They mostly pass harmlessly south of Hawaii but some, swept along by kona winds, strike the islands. The most recent and destructive was Hurricane Iwa, which battered the islands in 1982. It had its greatest effect on Niihau, the Poipu Beach area of Kauai, and the leeward coast of Oahu. Iwa carried a destructive price tag of 200 million dollars.

When To Go

The prime tourist season starts two weeks before Christmas and lasts until Easter. It picks up again with summer vacation in early June and ends once more in late August. If possible avoid these times of year. Everything is usually booked solid and prices are inflated. Hotel, airline, and car reservations, which are a must, are often hard to coordinate. You can save between 10 and 50% and a lot of hassling if you go in the artificially created **off season**, from September to early December, and mid-April (after Easter) till early June. You'll not only find the prices better, but the beaches, hikes, campgrounds and restaurants will be less crowded. The people will be happier to see you too.

> *"No alien land in all the world has any deep, strong charm for me, but that one; no other land could so longingly and beseechingly haunt my sleeping and waking, through half a lifetime, as that one has done. Other things leave me, but it abides."*
>
> —Mark Twain, c. 1889

FLORA AND FAUNA

THE MYSTERY OF MIGRATION

Anyone who loves a mystery will be intrigued by the speculation about how plants and animals first came to Hawaii. Most people's idea of an island paradise includes swaying palms, dense mysterious jungles ablaze with wildflowers, and luscious fruits just waiting to be plucked. In fact, for millions of years these were raw and barren islands where no plants grew and no birds sang. Why? Because they are geological orphans that spontaneously popped up in the middle of the Pacific Ocean. The islands, more than 2,000 miles from any continental landfall, were therefore exempted from the normal ecological spread of plants and animals. Even the most tenacious travelers of the fauna and flora kingdom would be sorely tried in crossing the mighty Pacific. Those that made it by pure chance found a totally foreign ecosystem. They had to adapt or perish. The survivors evolved quickly, and many plants and birds became so specialized that they were not only limited to specific islands in the chain but to habitats that frequently encompassed a single isolated valley. It was as if after traveling so far, and finding a niche, they never budged again. Luckily, the soil of Hawaii was virgin and rich; the competition from other plants or animals was non-existent; and the climate was sufficiently varying and nearly perfect for most growing things.

The evolution of plants and animals on the isolated islands was astonishingly rapid. A tremendous change in environment, coupled with a limited gene pool, accelerated natural selection. For example, many plants lost their protective thorns and spines because there were no grazing animals or birds to destroy them. Pre-man Hawaii had no fruits, vegetables, palms, edible land animals, conifers, mangroves, or banyans. Flowers were relatively few. In a land where thousands of orchids now brighten every corner, there were only four native varieties, the least in any of the 50 states. Today, the pre-man plants and animals have the highest rate of extinction anywhere on Earth. By the beginning of this century, native plants below 1,500 feet were almost completely extinct or totally replaced by introduced species. The land and its living things have been greatly transformed by man and his agriculture. This inexorable process began when Hawaii was the domain of its original Polynesian settlers, then greatly accelerated when the land was inundated by Western man.

Plantlife Comes First

Much like the Polynesian settlers who followed, the drifters, castaways, and shanghaied of the plant and animal kingdom were first to reach Hawaii. Botanists say spores and seeds were carried aloft into the upper atmosphere by powerful winds, then made lucky landings on the islands. Some hardy seeds came with the tides and somehow managed to sprout and grow once they hit land. Others were carried on the feathers and feet of migratory birds, while some made the trip in birds' digestive tracts and were ignominiously deposited with their droppings. This chance seeding of Hawaii obviously took a very long time: scientists estimate one plant arrival and establishment every 20,000-30,000 years. By latest count over 1,700 distinct species of *endemic* (only Hawaiian) and *indigenous* (other islands of Polynesia) plants had been catalogued throughout the island chain. It is reasonably certain all of these plants were introduced by only 250 original immigrants, and the 168 different Hawaiian ferns, for example, are the result of approximately 13 colonists. Most of the seeds and spores are believed to have come from Asia and Indonesia, and evidence of this spread can be seen in related plant species common to many Polynesian islands. Other endemic species such as the *koa,* which the Hawaiians put to great use in canoe building, have close relatives only in Australia. No other group of islands between Hawaii and Australia have such trees; the reason remains a mystery. Many plants and grasses came from North and South America and can be identified with common ancestors still there. Some species are so totally Hawaiian relatives are found nowhere else on Earth. This last category either evolved so dramatically they can no longer be recognized, or their common ancestors have long been extinct from the original environment. An outstanding example in this category is the silversword *(ahina ahina),* found in numbers only atop Haleakala on Maui, with a few specimens extant on the volcanoes of the Big Island.

Insects Arrive

No one knows for sure, but it's highly probable the first animal arrivals in Hawaii were insects. Again the theory is most were blown there by ancient hurricanes or drifted there imbedded in floating logs and pieces of wood. Like the plants that preceded them, their success and rapid evolution were phenomenal. A pregnant female had to make the impossible journey, then happen upon a suitable medium in which to deposit her eggs. Here, at least, they would be free from predators and parasites with a good chance of developing to maturity. Again the gene pool was highly restricted and the environment so foreign that amazing evolutionary changes occurred. Biologists feel only 150 original insect species are responsible for the more than 10,000 species that occur in Hawaii today. Of these 10,000, nearly 98% are found nowhere else on Earth. Many are restricted to only one island, and most are dependent on only one plant or fruit. For this reason, when Hawaiian plants become extinct, many insects disappear as well.

It's very probable there were no pests before humans arrived. The first Polynesians introduced flies, lice, and fleas. Westerners brought the indestructible cockroach, mosquito larvae in their ships' stores of water, termites, ants, and all the plant pests that could hitch a ride in the cuttings and fruits intended for planting. Today visitors often note the stringent agricultural controls at airports. Some complain about the inconvenience, but they should know that in the past 50 years over 700 new insect species have become established in Hawaii. Many are innocent enough, though others cause great problems for Hawaii's agriculture.

Land Snails

People have the tendency to ignore snails until they step on one, and then they only find them repulsive. But Hawaiian snails are some of the most remarkable and beautiful in the world. It's one thing to accept the possibility that a few insects or plant spores could have been driven to Hawaii by high winds or on birds' feet, given the fact of their uncountable billions. But how did the snails get there? Snails, after all, aren't known for their nimbleness or speed. Most Hawaiian snails never make it much beyond the tree in which they're born. Yet over 1,000 snail varieties are found in Hawaii, and most are inexplicably found nowhere else. The Polyne-

sians didn't bring them, sea water kills them, and it would have to be a mighty big bird that didn't notice one clinging to its foot. Biologists have puzzled over Hawaiian snails for years. One, J.T. Gulick, wrote in 1858, "These *achatinellinae* (tree snails) never came from Noah's ark." Tree snails are found on Oahu, Maui, Molokai, and Lanai, but not on Kauai. Kauai has its own land dwellers, and the Big Island has land snails that have moved into the trees. Like all the other endemic species, Hawaiian land snails now face extinction. Of the estimated 1,000 species existing when the Europeans came, 600 are now gone forever, and many others are threatened. Agriculture, the demise of native flora, and the introduction of new species add up to a bleak future for the snails.

Indigenous Land Animals

Hawaii before humans had a paucity of higher forms of land animals. There were no amphibians, no reptiles, and except for a profusion of birdlife, insects, and snails, only two other animals were present: the **monk seal** and the **hoary bat,** both highly specialized mammals. The monk seal has close relatives in the Caribbean and Mediterranean, although the Caribbean relatives are now believed to be extinct, making the monk seal one of the only two tropical seals left on Earth. It's believed that the monk seal's ancestors entered the Pacific about 200,000 years ago when the Isthmus of Panama was submerged. When the land rose, no more seals arrived, and the monk seal became indigenous to Hawaii. The main habitat for the Hawaiian monk seal is the outer islands, from the French Frigate Atolls north to Kure Island, but infrequently a seal is spotted on the shores of one of the main islands. Though the seals' existence was known to the native Hawaiians who called them *ilio-holo-i-kauaua* ("dog running in the toughness"), they didn't seem to play much of a role in their folklore or ecosystem. Whalers and traders certainly knew of their existence, hunting them for food and sometimes for skins. This kind of pressure almost wiped out the small seal population in the 18th century. Scientists were largely unaware of the monk seal until early this century. Finally, the seals were recognized as an endangered species and put under the protection of the Hawaiian Islands National Wildlife Refuge where they remain in a touch-and-go battle against extinction. Today it's estimated that only 1,000 individuals are left.

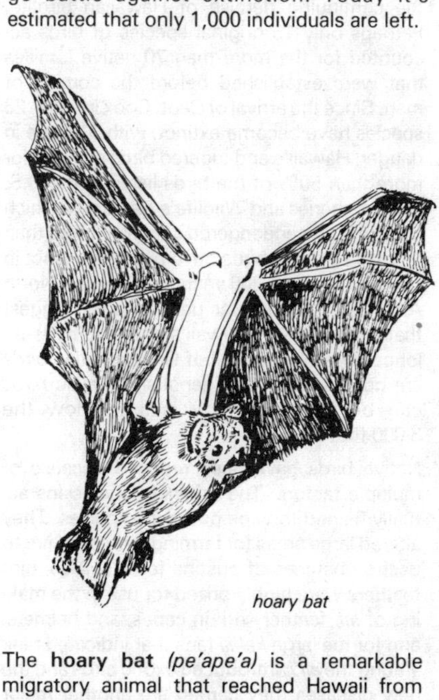

hoary bat

The **hoary bat** *(pe'ape'a)* is a remarkable migratory animal that reached Hawaii from North and South America under its own power. The Hawaiian hoary bat no longer migrates, but its continental relatives still range far and wide. The Hawaiian bat has become somewhat smaller and reddish in color over the years, distinguishing it from its larger, darker brown cousins. The main population is on the Big Island, with a smaller breeding ground on Kauai. The bats normally live at altitudes below 4,000 feet, but some have been observed on Mauna Loa and Mauna Kea above 6,000 feet. Sometimes bats are spotted on the other main islands, but it remains unsure whether they inhabit the islands or simply fly there from their established colonies. The hoary bat is a solitary creature that spends the daylight hours hanging from the branches of trees. It doesn't live in caves like others of its species. Look for them over Hilo Bay on the Big Island at sunset.

BIRDLIFE

One of the great tragedies of natural history is the continuing demise of Hawaiian birdlife. Perhaps only 15 original species of birds accounted for the more than 70 native families that were established before the coming of man. Since the arrival of Capt. Cook in 1778, 23 species have become extinct, with 31 more in danger. Hawaii's endangered birds account for more than 50% of the birds listed in the U.S. Sport Fisheries and Wildlife's *Red Book* (which cites rare and endangered animals). More than 4 times as many birds have become extinct in Hawaii in the last 200 years than in all of North America. These figures unfortunately suggest that a full 40% of Hawaii's endemic birds no longer exist. Almost all of Oahu's native birds are gone and few indigenous Hawaiian birds can be found on any island below the 3,000-foot level.

Native birds have been reduced because of multiple factors. The original Polynesians actually helped to wipe out many species. They altered large areas for farming, and used fire to destroy patches of pristine forests. Also, bird feathers were highly prized for use in the making of *lei,* featherwork in capes, and helmets, and for the large *kahili* fans that indicated rank among the *ali'i.* Introduced exotic birds and the new diseases they carried are another major reason, along with predation by the mongoose and rat—especially upon ground-nesting birds. However, the most damaging factor, by far, is the assault upon the native forests by agriculture and land developers. The vast majority of Hawaiian birds evolved into specialists. They lived in only one small area and ate only a very limited number of plants or insects, which once removed or altered soon killed the birds.

Preservation

Theodore Roosevelt established the Northwest Islands as a National Wildlife Reserve in the early 20th C., and efforts have continued since then to preserve Hawaii's unique avifauna. Many fine organizations are fighting the battle to preserve Hawaii's natural heritage, including: Hawaii Audubon Society, University of Hawaii, U.S. Fish and Wildlife Service, World Wildlife Fund, and Hawaii Department of Natural Resources. While visiting Hawaii make sure to obey all rules regarding the natural environment. Never disturb nesting birds or their habitat while hiking. Be careful with fire

Hawaiian stilt

and never cut any living trees. If you spot an injured or dead bird do not pick it up but make sure to report it to the local office of the U.S. Fish and Wildlife Service. Only through a conscientious effort of all concerned does Hawaii's wildlife stand a chance of surviving.

Hawaiian Honeycreepers

A most amazing family of all the birds on the face of Earth is one known as *drepanididae,* or Hawaiian honeycreepers. There are more than 40 distinct types of honeycreepers, with many more suspected to have become extinct pre-Capt. Cook; they are all believed to have evolved from *a single* ancestral species. The honeycreepers have differing body types. Some look like finches, while others resemble warblers, thrushes, blackbirds, parrots, and even woodpeckers. Their bills range from long pointed honeysuckers to tough hooked nutcrackers. They are the most divergently evolved birds in the world. If Darwin, who studied the birds of the Galapagos Islands, had come to Hawaii, he would have found bird evolution that made the Galapagos seem like child's play.

More Endangered Endemic Birds

Maui is the last home of the **crested honeycreeper** *(akohe'kohe).* It once lived on Molokai but no longer. Its habitat is on the windward slope of Haleakala form the 4,500- to the 6,500-foot level. A rather large bird, averaging about 7 inches, it's predominantly black. Its throat and breast are tipped with gray feathers with a bright orange on its neck and underbelly. A distinctive fluff of feathers forms a crown. It primarily eats *ohia* flowers, and it's believed that the crown feathers gather pollen and help to propigate the *ohia.* The **Maui parrotbill** is another endangered bird found only on the slopes of Haleakala above 5,000 feet. It has an olive-green back and yellow body. Its most distinctive feature is the parrot-like bill it uses to crack branches and pry out larvae. Two endangered waterbirds are the **Hawaiian stilt** *(ae'o)* and the **Hawaiian coot** *(alae ke'oke'o).* The stilt is a 16-inch, very thin, wading bird. It is primarily black with a white belly. Its long stick-like legs are pink. It lives on Maui at Kanaha and Kealia ponds. The adults will pretend to be hurt, putting on an excellent performance of the "broken wing," in order to lure predators away from their nests. The Hawaiian coot is a web-foot water bird that resembles a duck. Found on all the main islands but mostly on Maui and Kauai, its feathers are a dull gray with a white bill and tail feathers. It builds a large floating nest and vigorously defends its young. The **dark-rumped petrel** is slightly different than others in its family that are primarily marine birds. This petrel is found around the Visitor's Center at Haleakala crater about an hour after dusk from May to October.

Survivors

The ***amakihi*** and ***iiwi*** are endemic birds not endangered at the moment. The *amakihi* is one of the most common native birds; yellowish green, it frequents the high branches of the *ohia, koa,* and sandalwood looking for insects, nectar, or fruit. It is less specialized than most other Hawaiian birds, the main reason for its continued existence. The *iiwi* is a bright red bird with a salmon-colored hooked bill. It's found only on Maui, Hawaii, and Kauai in the forests above 2,000 feet. It too feeds on a variety of insects and flowers. The *iiwi* is known for a harsh voice that sounds like a squeaking hinge, but is also capable of a melodious song. Other indigenous birds found throughout the islands are the wedge-tailed shearwater, white-tailed tropic bird, black noddy, American plover, and a large variety of escaped exotic birds.

Nene

The *nene* or Hawaiian goose deserves special mention because it is Hawaii's state bird and is making a comeback from the edge of extinction. The *nene* is found only on the slopes of Mauna Loa and Mauna Kea on the Big Island, and in Haleakala Crater on Maui. It was extinct on Maui until a few birds were returned there in 1957. *Nenes* are raised at the Wildfowl Trust in Slimbridge, England, which placed the first birds at Haleakala, and at the Hawaiian Fish and Game Station at Pohakuloa on Hawaii. By the 1940s less than 50 birds lived in the wild. Now approximately 125 birds are on Haleakala and 500 on the Big Island. Although the birds can be raised successfully in captivity, their life in the wild is still in question. Some ornithologists even debate whether the *nene* ever originally lived on Maui. The *nene* is believed to be a descendant of the Canadian goose, which it resembles. Geese are migratory birds that form strong kinship ties, mating for life. It's speculated that a migrating goose became disabled, and along with its loyal mate remained in Hawaii. The *nene* is smaller than its Canadian cousin, has lost a great deal of webbing in its feet, and is perfectly at home away from water, foraging and nesting on rugged and bleak lava flows. The *nene* is a perfect symbol for Hawaii. Let it be, and it will live.

pueo

The *Pueo*

This Hawaiian owl is found on all the main islands but most frequently on Maui, especially in Haleakala crater. The *pueo* is one of the oldest examples of an *aumakua* (family-protecting spirits) in Hawaiian mythology, an especially benign and helpful guardian called upon in times of fear and war. Old Hawaiian stories abound in which a *pueo* came to the aid of a warrior in distress. A defeated army would often head for a tree in which a *pueo* had alighted. Once there, they were safe from their pursuers under the protection of "the wings of an owl." Many introduced barn owls in Hawaii are easily distinguished from a *pueo* by their distinctive heart-shaped faces. The *pueo* is about 15 inches tall with a mixture of brown and white feathers. The eyes are large, round, and yellow; the legs are heavily feathered unlike a barn owl. *Pueo* chicks are a distinct yellow.

WHALES

It is perhaps their tremendous size and graceful power, coupled with a dancer's delicacy of movement, that render whales so esthetically and emotionally captivating. In fact, many claim that they even feel a spirit-bond to these obviously intelligent mammals that at one time shared dry land with us and then re-evolved into creatures of the great seas. Experts often remark that whales exhibit behavior akin to the highest social virtues. For example, whales rely much more on learned behavior than on instinct, the sign of a highly evolved intelligence. Gentle mothers and protective "escort" males join to teach the young to survive. They display loyalty and bravery in times of distress, and innate gentleness, curiosity, and unmistakable joy for life. Their "songs," especially those of the humpbacks, fascinate scientists who consider them a form of communication unique in the animal kingdom. Hawaii, especially the shallow and warm waters around Maui, is home to migrating humpback whales every year from November to May. Here, they winter, mate, give birth, nurture their young, and joyfully cavort until returning to food-rich northern waters in the spring. It's hoped that mankind can peacefully share the oceans with these magnificent giants forever. If humans can learn to love and spare the whale for the simple reason that they're beautiful creatures and deserve no less, then perhaps we will have taken the first step in saving ourselves.

Evolution And Socialization

Many millions of years ago, for an unknown reason, animals similar to cows were genetically triggered to leave the land and readapt to the sea. Known as cetaceans, this family contains about 80 species of whales, porpoises, and dolphins. Being mammals, cetaceans are warm blooded and maintain a body temperature of 96 degrees, only 2½ degrees less than humans. After a gestation period of about one year, whales give birth to fully formed young, which usually enter the world tail first. The mother whale spins quickly to snap the umbilical cord, then places herself under the newborn and lifts it to the surface where it takes its first breath. A whale must be taught to swim or it would drown like any other air-breathing mammal. The baby whale, nourished by its mother's rich milk, becomes a member of an extended family **pod**, through which it's cared for, socialized and protected by many **nannies.**

Hawaiian Whales And Dolphins

The role of whales and dolphins in Hawaiian culture seems quite limited. Unlike fish, which were intimately known and individually named, only two generic names described them: *kohola,* ("whale"), and *palaoa* ("sperm whale"). Dolphins were all lumped together under one name, *nai'a;* Hawaiians were known to harvest dolphins on occasion by herding them onto a beach. Whale jewelry was worn by the *ali'i.* The most coveted ornament came from a sperm whale's tooth, called a *lei niho palaoa,* which was carved into one large curved pendant. Sperm whales have upwards of 50 teeth, ranging in size from 4 to 12 inches and weighing up to 2 pounds. One whale could provide numerous pendants. The most famous whale in Hawaiian waters is the humpback (for more information see p. 332), but others often sighted include: the sperm, killer, false killer, pilot, Cuvier's, Blainsville, and pygmy killer. There are technically no porpoises, but dolphins include: common, bottlenose, spinner, white-sided, broad- and slender-beaked, rough-toothed, and pygmy killer. The *mahi mahi,* a favorite eating fish found on many menus, is commonly referred to as a dolphin, but is totally unrelated and is a true fish, not a cetacean.

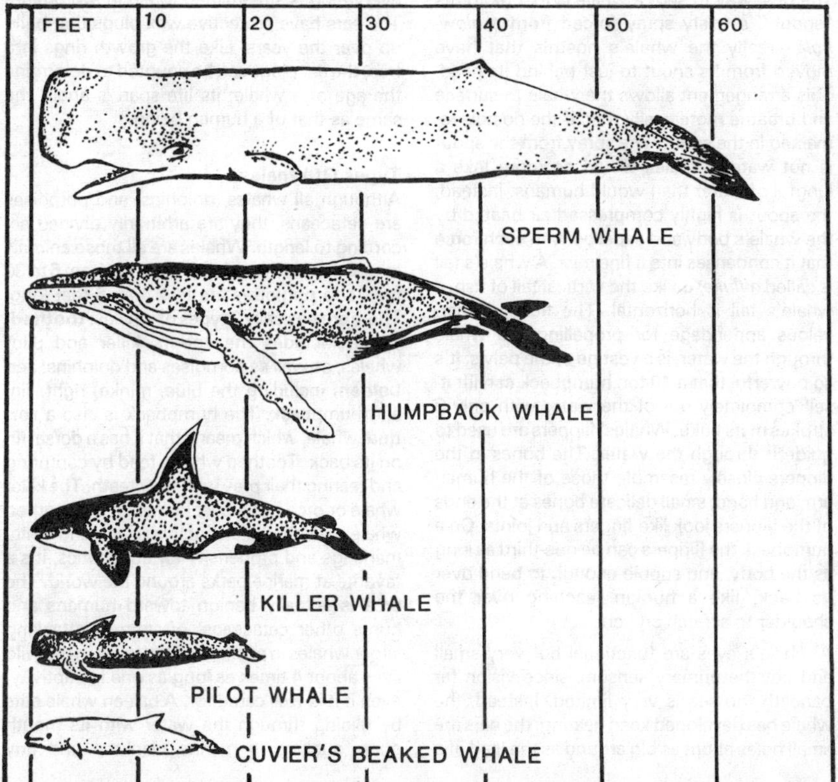

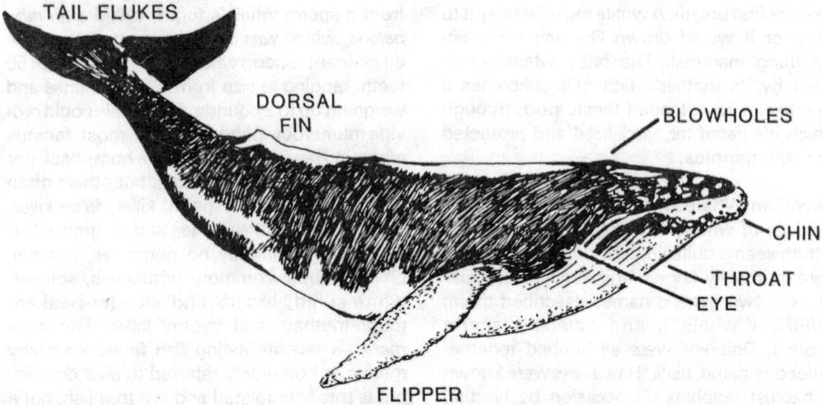

Physiology

The best way to spot a whale is to look for its "spout," a misty spray forced from a *blowhole*—really the whale's nostrils that have moved from its snout to just behind its head. This arrangement allows the whale to surface and breathe more easily than if the nostrils remained in the snout. The spray from the spout is not water. Whales would no more take a lungful of water than would humans. Instead, the spout is highly compressed air heated by the whale's body and expelled with such force that it condenses into a fine mist. A whale's tail is called a *fluke;* unlike the vertical tail of fish, a whale's tail is horizontal. The fluke, a marvelous appendage for propelling the whale through the water, is a vestige of the pelvis. It's so powerful that a 40-ton humpback can lift itself completely out of the water with only 3 strokes of its fluke. Whales' flippers are used to guide it through the water. The bones in the flippers closely resemble those of the human arm and hand; small delicate bones at the ends of the flippers look like fingers and joints. On a humpback the flippers can be one-third as long as the body, and supple enough to bend over its back, like a human reaching over the shoulder to scratch an itch.

A whale's eyes are functional but very small and not the primary sensors, since vision far beneath the sea is very limited. Instead, the whale has developed keen hearing; the ears are small holes about as big around as the lead of a pencil. There are no external ears because everything is streamlined to aid in swimming. The ears have protective wax plugs that build up over the years. Like the growth rings in a tree, the ear plugs can be counted to determine the age of a whale; its life span is about the same as that of a human being.

Types Of Whales

Although all whales, dolphins, and porpoises are cetaceans, they are arbitrarily divided according to length. Whales are all those animals longer than 30 feet; dolphins range from 6 to 30 feet; and porpoises are less than 6 feet long. There are basically 2 types of whales: **toothed,** which includes the sperm, killer and pilot whales, as well as porpoises and dolphins; and **baleen,** including the blue, minke, right, fin, and humpback. The humpback is also a **rorqual** whale, which means that it has a dorsal fin on its back. Toothed whales feed by capturing and tearing their prey with their teeth. The killer whale or orca is the best known of the toothed whales. With its distinctive black-and-white markings and propensity for aquabatics, it's a favorite at marine parks around the world. The orca is actually benign toward humans and hunts other cetaceans, oftentimes attacking larger whales in packs. A killer whale in the wild lives about 4 times as long as one in captivity, even if it is well cared for. A baleen whale eats by gliding through the water with its mouth open, sucking in marine plankton and tiny shrimplike-creatures called krill. The whale then expels the water and captures the food in row after row of a prickly, fingernail-like substance called baleen.

Whaling History

Man has undoubtedly known about whales for many thousands of years. A Minoan palace on the island of Crete depicts whales on a 5,000-year-old mural. The first whalers were probably Norwegians who used stone harpoon heads to capture their prey over 4,000 years ago. Eskimos have long engaged in whaling as a means of survival, and for centuries many peoples living along coastal waters have harpooned migrating whales that ventured close to shore. The Basques had a thriving medieval whaling industry in the 12th C. centered in the Bay of Biscay, until they wiped out all the Biscayan right whales. The height of the classic whaling industry that inspired Melville's *Moby Dick* occurred from 1820 until 1860. The international capital perfectly situated in the center of the winter whaling grounds was Lahaina, Maui. At that time 900 sailing ships roamed the globe in search of whales. Of these, 700 were American, which led the field by moving from coastal to pelagic whaling by bringing their tryworks (blubber pots) aboard ship. Although the killing was great during these years, an unarguably romantic mystique connected with these "old salts." Also, every part of the whale was needed and used: blubber, meat, bone, teeth. Whale oil, the main product, was a superior lighting fuel and lubricant unmatched until petroleum came into general use toward the mid-19th century. Today, every single whale byproduct can be manufactured synthetically and there's absolutely no primary need to go on slaughtering whales.

During the great whaling days, the whales actually had a fighting chance. After all, they were hunted by men in wooden sailing ships that depended upon favorable winds. Once sighted by a sailor perched high in the rigging using a low-powered telescope, a small boat heaved off, and after desperate rowing and dangerous maneuvering the master harpooner threw his shaft by hand. When the whale was dead it took every able-bodied man to haul it in. Today, however, modern methods have wiped out every trace of daring and turned the hunt to technologically assisted slaughter. Low-flying aircraft radio the whales' location to huge factory-ships that track them with radar and sonar. Once the pod is spotted, super-swift launches tear into them firing cannon-propelled harpoons with lethal exploding tips. The killer launches keep firing until every whale in the pod is dead, and the huge factory boat follows behind merely scooping up the lifeless carcasses and hauling them aboard with diesel winches. Many pirate whalers still roam the seas. The worst example perpetrated by these vultures occurred in the Bahamas in 1971. A ship that ironically carried the name of *the* classic conservation group, the *Sierra,* succeeded in wiping out every single humpback whale that wintered in Bahamian waters. Since 1971 not one whale has been sighted in the Bahamas, and whalewatchers lament that they will never return.

A Glimmer Of Hope

A great awakening of consciousness around the world began in the mid-1960s, when people realized that we live in a finite world and our resources must be preserved and conserved. Governments could no longer ignore the mounting documentation that the great whales were disappearing at an alarming rate. Since then world opinion, coupled with benign but aggressive organizations such as Greenpeace, has labored to let the whales live. The **International Whaling Commission** (IWC), a voluntary group of 17 nations, was formed. It sets standards and passes quotas on the number and species of whales that can be killed. Over the last 18 years the blue, right, gray, bowhead, and humpback have become totally protected. Unfortunately, many great whales such as the sperm, sei, and fin are still hunted. Also, the IWC has no power of enforcement except for public opinion and possible voluntary economic sanction. It growls but it has no teeth; all it can really do is wag a finger. Fortunately, the U.S. and most other countries around the world no longer engage in whaling.

The Last Whalers

Unfortunately, the two great offenders are Japan and the USSR. Recently the USSR has shown great signs of heavily modifying its whaling industry. That leaves Japan. The Japanese technically stay within their quotas, but they hire and outfit other nationals to hunt whales for them. Their main argument is that whaling is a traditional industry upon which they rely for food and jobs. This is patently false. Palegic whaling is a new industry to the Japanese hardly more than 100 years old. Also, the Japanese have become meat eaters only within recent memory, and whales are meat, not fish. A vast amount of Japanese whale meat becomes pet food anyway, which is mainly exported. Besides, it's ludicrous for the third most powerful industrialized nation in the world to claim economic hardship if it had to curtail its whaling industry. Their economy is booming and there is little unemployment. The Japanese, extremely touchy on the subject, feel that they're being singled out for ridicule. The only course is to use reasonable persuasion and the affirmation that they have done no wrong or no different from many nations in the past but now the harvesting of the great whales must stop.

PLANTS, FLOWERS, AND TREES

Hawaii's indigenous and endemic plants, flowers, and trees are both fascinating and beautiful, but unfortunately, like everything else that was native, are quickly disappearing. The majority of flora found exotic by visitors was either introduced by the original Polynesians or later by white settlers. The Polynesians who colonized Hawaii brought foodstuffs including coconut, banana, taro, breadfruit, sweet potato, yam, and sugarcane. They also carried along gourds to use as containers, *awa* to make a basic intoxicant, and the *ti* plant to use for offerings or to string into *hula* skirts. Non-Hawaiian settlers over the years have brought mangoes, papaya, passionfruit, pineapples, and all the other tropical fruits and vegetables associated with the islands. Also, most of the flowers, including protea, plumeria, anthuriums, orchids, heleconia, ginger, and most hibiscus have come from every continent on Earth. Tropical America, Asia, Java, India, and China have all yielded their most beautiful and delicate blooms. Hawaii is blessed with state parks, gardens, undisturbed rainforests, private reserves, and commercial nurseries that offer an exhaustive botanical survey of Hawaii. The following is just a sampling of common, native, and introduced flora that adds the dazzling colors and exotic tastes to the landscape. **Note:** For fauna indigenous to a particular island, please refer to the islands' introduction.

ohi'a-lehua

Native Trees

Koa and *ohia* are two native trees still seen on the main islands. Both have been greatly reduced by the foraging of introduced cattle and goats, and through logging and forest fires. The *koa,* a form of acacia, is Hawaii's finest native tree. It can grow to over 70 feet high and has a strong straight trunk which can measure more than 10 feet in circumference. The leaf-like foliage is sickle shaped, and produces an inconspicuous pale yellow flower. The *koa* does best in well-drained soil in deep forest areas, but scruffy specimens will grow on poorer soil. The Hawaiians used *koa* as the main log for their dugout canoes, and elaborate ceremonies were performed when a log was cut and dragged to a canoe shed. *Koa* wood was also preferred as paddles, spears, even surfboards. Today it is still considered an excellent furniture wood. The *ohia* is a survivor, and therefore the most abundant of all the native Hawaiian trees. Coming in a variety of shapes and sizes, it grows as miniature trees in wet bogs or 100-foot giants on the cool dark slopes of higher elevations. This tree is often the first life in new lava flows. The *ohia* produces a tuft-like flower that resembles a natural pom-pom. Considered sacred to Pele, it was said that she would cause a rainstorm if you picked them without the proper prayers. The flowers were fashioned into a *lei* that resembled a feather boa. The strong hard wood was also used in canoe building, favored to make *poi* bowls and especially for temple images.

koa

The Greening Of Hawaii

The first *deliberate* migrants to Hawaii were Polynesians from the Marquesa Islands. Many of these voyages were undertaken when life on the native islands became intolerable. They were prompted mostly by defeat in war, or growing island populations that overtaxed the available food supply. Whatever the reasons, the migrations were deliberate and permanent. The first colonizers were known as "the land seekers" in the old Marquesan language—probably advance scouting parties who provthat the ancient chants which sung of a land to the north were true. Once they discovered Hawaii the return voyage to the southern homeland would be relatively easy. They had the favorable trade winds at their back, plus the certainty of sailing into familiar waters. The follow-up canoes would be laden with women so that the human seed could be propagated, seeds and cuttings of plants necessary for survival, and animals for both consumption and sacrifice.

Not all the plants and animals came at once, but enough were brought to get started. The basic foodplants included taro, banana, coconut, sugarcane, breadfruit, and yams. They also brought the paper mulberry from which *tapa* was made, and the *ti* plant necessary for cooking and making offerings at the *heiau.* Various gourds were grown to be used as bowls, containers, and even as helmets in a Hawaiian style of defensive armor. Arrowroot and turmeric were used in cooking and by the healing *kahuna* as medicines. *Awa* was brought by the high priests to be used in rituals; chewed, the resulting juice was spat into a bowl where it fermented and became a mind-altering intoxicant. Bamboo, the wonder material of natural man, was planted and used for uncountable purposes. The only domesticated animals taken to the new land were pigs, dogs, and chickens. Rats also made the journey but only as stowaways.

In the new land the Polynesians soon found native plants that they incorporated and put to good use. Some included: the *olona,* which made the best-known fiber cord anywhere in the world and later was eagerly accepted by sailing ships as new rigging and as a trade item; *koa,* an excellent hardwood used for the manufacture of highly prized calabashes and the hulls of magnificent sea-going canoes; *kukui* (candlenut), eaten as a tasty nut, strung to make *leis,* or burned as a source of light like a natural candle. For 1,000 years the distinct Hawaiian culture formed in relative isolation. When the white men came they found a people that had become intimately entwined with their environment. The relationship between the Hawaiians and their *aina* (land) was spiritual, physical, and emotional: they were one.

Prickly Pear Cactus

The Hawaiians called them *panini,* which translates as "very unfriendly," undoubtedly because of the sharp spines covering the flat thick leaves. These cactus are typical of those found in Mexico and the southwestern U.S. They were introduced to Hawaii before 1810 and established themselves, coincidentally in conjunction with the cattle being brought in at the time. It is assumed that Don Marin, a Spanish advisor to Kamehameha I, was responsible for importing them. Perhaps the early *paniolo* ("cowboy") felt lonely without them. The *panini* can grow to heights of 15 feet and are now considered a pest, but nonetheless look as if they belong. They develop small delicious pear-shaped fruit. Hikers who decide to pick them should be careful of small yellowish bristles that can burrow under the skin and become irritating. The fruit turns into beautiful 3-inch yellow and orange flowers.

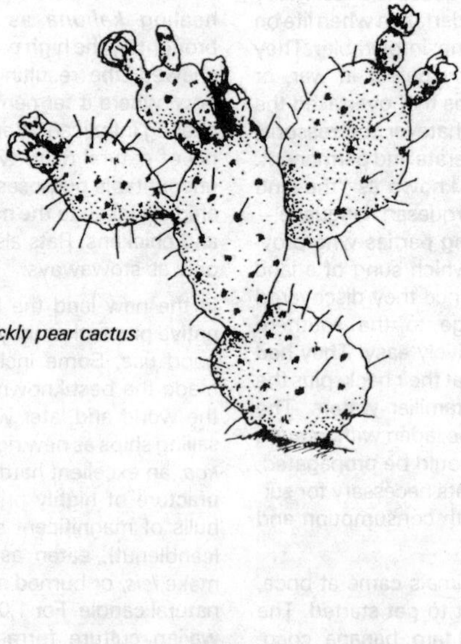

prickly pear cactus

HISTORY

THE ROAD FROM TAHITI

Until the 1820s, when New England missionaries began a phonetic rendering of the Hawaiian language, the past was kept vividly alive only by the sonorous voices of special *kahuna* who chanted the sacred *mele.* The chants were beautiful flowing word pictures that captured the essence of every aspect of life. These *mele* praised the land *(mele aina),* royalty *(mele ali'i),* and life's tender aspects *(mele aloha).* Chants were dedicated to friendship, hardship, and to favorite children. Entire villages sometimes joined together to compose a *mele*—every word was chosen carefully, and the wise old *kapuna* would decide if the words were lucky or unlucky. Some *mele* were bawdy or funny on the surface, but contained secret meanings, often with biting sarcasm, that ridiculed an inept or cruel leader. But the most important chants took the listeners back into the dim past, even before people lived in Hawaii. From these genealogies *(ko'ihonua),* the *ali'i* derived the right to rule, since these chants went back to the gods Wakea and Papa from whom the *ali'i* were directly descended.

The Kumulipo

The great genealogies, finally compiled in the late 1800s by order of King Kalakaua, were collectively known as *The Kumulipo, A Hawaiian Creation Chant,* basically a Polynesian account of Genesis. Other chants related to the beginning of this world, but *The Kumulipo* sums it all up and is generally considered the best. The chant relates that after the beginning of time, there is a period of darkness. The darkness, however, mysteriously brims with spontaneous life; during this period plants and animals are born, as well as Kumulipo, the man, and Po'ele, the woman. In the eighth chant darkness gives way to light and the gods descend to Earth. Wakea is "the sky father" and Papa is "the earth mother," whose union gives birth to the islands of Hawaii. First born is Hawaii, followed by Maui, then Kahoolawe. Apparently, Papa becomes bushed after three consecutive births and decides to vacation in Tahiti. While Papa is away recovering from post-partum depression and working on her tan, Wakea gets lonely, and takes Kaula as his second wife who bears him the island-child of Lanai. Not fully cheered up, but getting the hang of it, Wakea takes a third wife, Hina, who promptly bears the island of Molokai. Meanwhile, Papa gets wind of these shenanigans, returns from Polynesia, and retaliates by taking up with Lua, a young and virile god, and soon gives birth to the island of Oahu. Papa and Wakea finally decide that they really are meant for each other and reconcile to conceive Kauai, Niihau, Kaula, and Nihoa. These two progenitors are the source to which all the *ali'i* ultimately traced their lineage, and from which they derived their god-ordained power to rule.

Basically, there are two major genealogical families: the **Nana'ulu**, who became the royal *ali'i* of Oahu and Kauai; and the **Ulu**, who provided the royalty of Maui and Hawaii. The best sources of information on Hawaiian myth and legend are Martha Beckwith's *Hawaiian Mythology,* and the monumental three-volume opus *An Account of the Polynesian Race* compiled by Abraham Fornander from 1878 to 1885. Fornander, after settling in Hawaii, married an *ali'i* from Molokai and had an illustrious career as a newspaper man, Maui circuit judge, and finally Supreme Court justice. For years Fornander sent scribes to every corner of the kingdom to listen to the elder *kapuna.* They returned with the first-hand accounts and he dutifully recorded them.

Polynesians

Since prehistory, Polynesians have been seafaring people whose origins cannot be completely traced. They seem to have come from Southeast Asia mostly through the gateway of Indonesia, and their racial strain pulls features from all three dominant races: white, negro, and mongoloid. They learned to navigate on tame narrow waterways along Indonesia and New Guinea, then fanned out eastward into the great Pacific. They sailed northeast to the low islands of Micronesia and southwest to Fiji, the New Hebrides (now called Vanuatu), and New Caledonia. Fiji is regarded as the "cradle of Polynesian culture"; carbon dating places humans there as early as 3,500 B.C. Many races blended on Fiji, until finally the negroid became dominant and the Polynesians moved on. Wandering, they discovered and settled Samoa and Tonga, then ranged far east to populate Tahiti, Easter Island, and the Marquesas. Ultimately, they became the masters of the "Polynesian Triangle," which measures more than 5,000 miles on each leg, stretching across both the North and South Pacific studded with islands. The great Maori kingdom of New Zealand is the southern apex of the triangle, with Easter Island marking the point farthest east; Hawaii, farthest north, was last to be settled.

The Polynesians, attuned to every nuance in their environment, noticed that a migratory land bird called the golden plover arrived from the north every year. They reasoned that since the plover was not a seabird, there must be land to the north.

Migrations And Explorations

Ancient legends common throughout the South Pacific speak of a great Polynesian culture that existed on the island of Raiatea about 150 miles north of Tahiti. Here a powerful priesthood held sway in an enormous *heiau* in the Opoa district called Toputapuatea. Kings from throughout Polynesia came here to worship. Human sacrifice was common, as it was believed that the essence of the spirit could be utilized and controlled in this life; therefore the *mana* of Toputapuatea was great. Defeated warriors and commoners were used as living rollers to drag canoes up onto the beach, while corpses were dismembered and hung in trees. The power of the priests of Opoa lasted for many generations, evoking trembling fear in even the bravest warrior just by the mention of their name. Finally, their power waned and Polynesians lost their centralized culture, but the constant coming and going from Raiatea for centuries sharpened the Polynesians' already excellent sailing skills and convinced them that the world was vast, and unlimited opportunities existed to better their lot.

Now explorers, many left to look for the "heavenly homeland to the north." Samoans called it *Savai'i;* Tongans *Hawai;* Rarotongans *Avaiki;* and Society Islanders *Havai'i.* Others abandoned the small islands throughout Polynesia where population pressures exceeded the limits of natural resources, prompting famine. Furthermore, Polynesians were also very warlike among themselves; power struggles between members of a ruling family were common, as were marauders from other islands. So, driven by hunger or warfare, countless refugee Polynesians headed north. Joining them were a few who undoubtedly went for the purely human reason of wanderlust.

The Great Navigators

No one knows exactly when the first Polynesians arrived in Hawaii, but the great *deliberate migrations* from the southern islands seem to have taken place between A.D. 500 and 800, though anthropologists keep pushing the date backward in time as new evidence becomes available. Even before that, however, it's reasonable to assume that the first people to set foot on Hawaii were probably fishermen, or perhaps defeated warriors whose canoes were blown hopelessly northward into unfamiliar waters arriving by a combination of extraordinary good luck and an uncanny ability to sail and navigate by the seat of their pants. With no instruments they could navigate, using the sun by day and the moon and rising stars by night. They could feel the water and determine direction by swells, tides, and currents. The movements of fish and cloud formations were also utilized to give direction. Since their arrival was probably an accident, they were unprepared to settle on the fertile but barren lands, having no stock animals, plant cuttings, or women. Forced to return southward, undoubtedly many lost their lives at sea, but a few wild-eyed stragglers must have made it home where they told tales of a paradise to the north where land was plentiful and the sea bounteous. This is affirmed by ancient navigational chants from Tahiti, Moorea, and Bora Bora, which passing from father to son revealed how to follow the stars to the "heavenly homeland in the north." Possibly a few migrations followed, but it's known that for centuries there was no real reason for a mass exodus, so the chants alone remained and eventually became shadowy legend.

From Where They Came

It's generally agreed that the first planned migrations were from the violent cannibal islands that Spanish explorers called the Marquesas, 11 islands in extreme eastern Polynesia. The islands themselves are harsh and inhospitable, breeding a toughness into these people which enabled them to withstand the hardships of long unsure ocean voyages and years of resettlement. Marquesans were a fiercely independent people whose chiefs could rise from the ranks because of bravery or intelligence. They must have also been a savage-looking lot. Both men and women tatooed themselves in complex blue patterns from head to foot. The warriors carried massive, intricately designed ironwood war clubs and wore carved whale-teeth in slits in

The canoe hull was a log shaped by masterly stone adze work. The sides were planks that were drilled and sewn together with fiber cord.

their earlobes which became stretched to the shoulders. They shaved the sides of their heads with sharks' teeth, tied their hair in two topknots that looked like horns, and rubbed their heavily muscled and tattooed bodies with scented coconut oils. Their cults worshipped mummified ancestors; the bodies of warriors of defeated neighboring tribes were consumed. They were masters at building great double-hulled canoes launched from huge canoe sheds. Two hulls were fastened together to form a catamaran, and a hut in the center provided shelter in bad weather. The average voyaging canoe was 60-80 feet long and could comfortably hold an extended family of about 30 people. These small family bands carried all the staples they would need in the new lands.

The New Lands

For five centuries the Marquesans settled and lived peacefully on the new land, as if Hawaii's *aloha* spirit overcame most of their fierceness. The tribes co-existed in relative harmony, especially since there was no competition for land. Cannibalism died out. There was much coming and going between Hawaii and Polynesia and new people came to settle for hundreds of years. Then, it appears that in the 12th C. a deliberate exodus of warlike Tahitians arrived and subjugated the settled islanders. They came to conquer. This incursion had a terrific significance on the Hawaiian religious and social system. Oral tradition relates that a Tahitian priest, Paao, found the *mana* of the Hawaiian chiefs to be low, signifying that their gods were weak. Paao built a *heiau* at Wahaula on the Big Island, then introduced the warlike god Ku and the rigid *kapu* system through which the new rulers became dominant. Voyages between Tahiti and Hawaii continued for about 100 years and Tahitian customs, legends, and language became the Hawaiian way of life. Then suddenly, for no recorded or apparent reason, the voyages discontinued and Hawaii returned to total isolation. It remained forgotten for almost 500 years until the indomitable English seaman, Capt. James Cook, sighted Oahu on January 18, 1778 and stepped ashore at Waimea on Kauai two days later. At that time Hawaii's isolation was so complete that even the Polynesians had forgotten about it. On an earlier voyage, Tupaia, a high priest from Raiatea, had accompanied Capt. Cook as he sailed throughout Polynesia. Tupaia's knowledge of existing archipelagos throughout the South Pacific was vast, which he demonstrated by naming over 130 islands and drawing a map that included the Tonga group, the Cook Islands, the Marquesas, even tiny Pitcairn, a rock in far eastern Polynesia, where the mutinous crew of the *Bounty* found solace. In mentioning the Marquesas Tupaia said, *"he ma'a te ka'ata,"* which equals "food is man" or simply "cannibals!" But remarkably absent from Tupaia's vast knowledge was the existence of Easter Island, New Zealand, and Hawaii. The next waves of people to Hawaii would be white men, and the Hawaiian world would be changed quickly and forever.

THE WORLD DISCOVERS HAWAII

The late 18th century was an extraordinary time in Hawaiian history. Monumental changes seemed to happen all at once. First, Capt. James Cook, a Yorkshire farm boy, fulfilling his destiny as the all-time greatest Pacific explorer, found Hawaii for the rest of the world. For better or worse, it could no longer be an isolated Polynesian homeland. For the first time in Hawaiian history, a charismatic leader named Kamehameha emerged, and after a long civil war united all the islands into one centralized kingdom. The death of Capt. Cook in Hawaii marked the beginning of a long series of tragic misunderstandings between white man and native. When Kamehameha died, the old religious system of *kapu* came to an end, leaving the Hawaiians in a spiritual vortex. Many takers arrived to fill the void: missionaries after souls, whalers after their prey and a good time, traders and planters after profits and a home. The islands were opened and devoured like ripe fruit, as powerful nations including Russia, Great Britain, France, and the United States yearned to bring this strategic Pacific jewel under their own influence. The 19th C. brought the demise of the Hawaiian people as a dominant political force in their own land and with it the end of Hawaii as a soverign monarchy. An almost bloodless yet bitter military coup followed by a brief period of a Hawaiian Republic ended in annexation by the United States. As the U.S. became completely entrenched politically and militarily, a new social and economic order was founded on the plantation system. Amazingly rapid population growth occurred with the importation of plantation workers from Asia and Europe,which yielded a unique cosmopolitan blend of races like nowhere else on Earth. By the dawning of the 20th C., the face of old Hawaii had been altered forever; the "sacred homeland in the north" was hurled into the modern age. The attack on Pearl Harbor saw a tremendous loss of life and brought Hawaii closer to the U.S. by a baptism of blood. Finally, on August 21, 1959, after 59 years as a "territory," Hawaii officially became the 50th state of the Union.

Captain Cook Sights Hawaii

In 1776 Captain James Cook set sail for the Pacific from Plymouth, England, on his third and final expedition into this still vastly unexplored region of the world. On a fruitless quest for the fabled Northwest Passage across the North American continent, he sailed down the coast of Africa, rounded the Cape of Good Hope, crossed the Indian Ocean, and traveled past New Zealand, Tasmania, the Friendly Islands (where an unsuccessful plot was hatched by the *friendly* natives to murder him), and finally spotted Hawaii. On January 18, 1778 Capt. Cook's 100-foot flagship HMS *Resolution* and its 90-foot companion HMS *Discovery* sighted Oahu. Two days later, they sighted Kauai and went ashore at the village of Waimea on January 20, 1778. Though anxious to get on with his mission, Cook decided to make a quick sortee to investigate this new land and reprovision his ships. He did, however, take time to remark in his diary about the close resemblance of these new-found people to others he had encountered as far south as New Zealand, and marveled at their widespread habitation across the Pacific.

The first trade was some brass medals for a mackerel. Cook also stated that he never before met natives so astonished by a ship, and that they had an amazing fascination for iron which they called *toe,* Hawaiian for "adz."

Capt. James Cook (Hawaii State Archives)

There is even some conjecture that a Spanish ship under one Capt. Gaetano had landed in Hawaii as early as the 16th C., trading a few scraps of iron that the Hawaiians valued even more than the Europeans valued gold. It was also noted that the Hawaiian women gave themselves freely to the sailors with the apparent good wishes of the island men. This was actually a ploy by the *kahuna* to test if the white newcomers were gods or men—gods didn't need women. These sailors proved immediately mortal. Cook, who was also a physician, tried valiantly to keep the 66 men (out of 112) who had measurable cases of V.D. away from the women. The task proved impossible as women literally swarmed the ships; when Cook returned less than a year later, it was logged that signs of V.D. were already apparent on some natives' faces.

Cook was impressed with their swimming and with their well-bred manners. They had happy dispositions and sticky fingers, stealing any object made of metal, especially nails. The first item stolen was a butcher's cleaver. An unidentified native grabbed it, plunged overboard, swam to shore, and waved his booty in triumph. The Hawaiians didn't seem to care for beads and were not at all impressed with a mirror. Cook provisioned his ships by trading chisels for hogs, while common sailors gleefully traded nails for sex. Landing parties were sent inland to fill casks with fresh water. On one such excursion a Mr. Williamson, who was eventually drummed out of the Royal Navy for cowardice, unnecessarily shot and killed a native. After a brief stop on Niihau, the ships sailed away, but both groups were indelibly impressed with the memory of each other.

Cook Returns

Almost a year later, when winter weather forced Cook to return from the coast of Alaska, his discovery began to take on far-reaching significance. Cook had named Hawaii the **Sandwich Islands,** in honor of one of his patrons, John Montague, the Earl of Sandwich. On this return voyage, he spotted Maui on November 26, 1778. After 8 weeks of seeking a suitable harbor it was bypassed, but not before the coastline was duly drawn by Lt. William Bligh, one of Cook's finest and most trusted officers. (Bligh would find his own drama almost 10 years later as commander of the infamous HMS *Bounty.*) The *Discovery* and *Resolution* finally found a safe anchorage at Kealakekua on the Kona coast of the Big Island. It is very lucky for history that on board was Mr. Anderson, ship's chronicler, who left a hand-written record of the strange and tragic events that followed. Even more important were the drawings of John Webber, ship's artist, who rendered invaluable impressions in superb drawings and etchings. Other noteworthy men aboard were George Vancouver, who would himself lead the first British return to Hawaii after Cook's death and introduce many fruits, vegetables, cattle, sheep, and goats, and James Burney, who would become a longstanding leading authority on the Pacific.

The Great God Lono Returns

By all accounts Cook was a humane and just captain, greatly admired by his men. Unlike many other supremacists of that time, he was known to have a respectful attitude to any people he discovered, treating them as equals and recognizing the significance of their cultures. Not known as a violent man, he would use his superior weapons against natives only in an absolute case of self defense. His hardened crew had been at sea facing untold hardship for almost 3 years; returning to Hawaii was truly like re-entering paradise.

A strange series of coincidences sailed with Cook into Kealakekua Bay on January 16, 1779. It was *makahiki* time, a period of rejoicing and festivity dedicated to the fertility god of the earth, Lono. Normal *kapu* days were suspended, and willing partners freely enjoyed each other sexually, along with dancing, feasting, and the islands' version of Olympic games. It was long held in Hawaiian legend that the great god Lono would return to Earth. Lono's image was a small wooden figure perched on a tall mast-like crossbeam; hanging from the crossbeam were long white sheets of *tapa*. Who else could Cook be but Lono, and what else could his ships with their masts and white sails be but his sacred floating *heiau?* This explained the Hawaiians' previous fascination with his ships, but to add to the remarkable coincidence, Kealakekua Harbor happened to be considered Lono's private sacred harbor. Natives from throughout the land prostrated themselves and paid homage to the returning god. Cook was taken ashore and brought to Lono's sacred temple where he was afforded the highest respect. The ships badly needed fresh supplies and the Hawaiians readily gave all they had, stretching their own provisions to the limit. To the sailors delight this included full measures of the *aloha* spirit.

The Fatal Misunderstandings

After an uproarious welcome and generous hospitality for over a month, it became obvious that the newcomers were beginning to overstay their welcome. During the interim a seaman named William Watman died, convincing the Hawaiians that the *haole* were indeed mortals, not gods. Watman was buried at Hikiau Heiau where a plaque commemorates the event to this day. Incidents of petty theft began to increase dramatically. The lesser chiefs indicated it was time to leave by "rubbing the Englishmen's bellies." Inadvertently many *kapu* were broken by the Englishmen, and once-friendly relations became strained. Finally, the ships sailed away on February 4,

1779. After plying terrible seas for only a week, the formast on the *Resolution* was badly damaged, and Cook sailed back into Kealekekua Bay dragging the mast ashore on February 13th. The natives, now totally hostile, hurled rocks at the marines. Orders were given to load muskets with ball; firearms had previously only been loaded with shot and a light charge. Confrontations increased when some Hawaiians stole a small boat and marines set after them capturing the fleeing canoe, which held an *ali'i* named Palea. The Englishmen treated him roughly; to the Hawaiians horror, they even smacked him on the head with a paddle. The Hawaiians then furiously attacked the marines who abandoned the small boat.

Cook Goes Down

Next the Hawaiians stole a small cutter from the *Discovery* that had been moored to a buoy and partially sunk to protect it from the sun. For the first time Capt. Cook became furious. He ordered Capt. Clerk of the *Discovery* to sail to the southeast end of the bay, and to stop any canoe trying to leave Kealakekua. Cook then made a fatal error in judgment. He decided to take nine armed marines ashore in an attempt to convince the venerable King Kalaniopuu to accompany him back aboard ship where he would hold him for ransom in exchange for the cutter. The old king agreed, but his wife prevailed upon him not to trust the *haole*. Kalaniopuu sat down on the beach to think while the tension steadily grew. Meanwhile, a group of marines fired upon a canoe trying to leave the bay and a lesser chief, Nookemai, was killed. The crowd around Cook and his men reached an estimated 20,000, and warriors outraged by the killing of the chief armed themselves with clubs and protective straw-mat armor. One bold warrior advanced on Cook and struck him with his *pahoa*. In retaliation Cook drew a tiny pistol lightly loaded with shot and fired at the warrior. His bullets spent themselves on the straw armor and harmlessly fell to the ground. The Hawaiians went wild. Lt. Molesworth Phillips, in charge of the nine marines, began a withering fire; Cook himself slew two natives. Overpowered by sheer numbers, the marines headed for boats standing offshore, while Lt. Phillips lay wounded. It is believed that Capt. Cook, the greatest seaman ever to enter the Pacific, stood helplessly in knee-deep water instead of making for the boats because he could not swim! Hopelessly surrounded, he was knocked on the head, then countless warriors passed a knife around and hacked and mutilated his lifeless body. A sad Lt. King lamented in his diary, "Thus fell our great and excellent commander."

"The Death of Captain Cook" by John Webber, ship's artist on Cook's third Pacific exploration, c. 1779 (Hawaii State Archives)

The Final Chapter

Captain Clerk, now in charge, settled his men and prevailed upon the Hawaiians to return Cook's body. On the morning of February 16th a grisly piece of charred meat was brought aboard: the Hawaiians, according to their custom, had afforded Cook the highest honor by baking his body in an underground oven to remove the flesh from the bones. On the 17th a group of Hawaiians in a canoe taunted the marines by brandishing Cook's hat. The Englishmen, strained to the limit and thinking that Cook was being desecrated, finally broke. Foaming with blood-lust, they leveled their cannon and muskets on shore and shot anything that moved. It is believed that Kamehameha the Great was wounded in this flurry, along with four *ali'i* and 25 *makaainana* (commoners) killed. Finally on February 21, 1779, the bones of Capt. James Cook's hands, skull, arms, and legs were returned and tearfully buried at sea. A common seaman, one Mr. Zimmerman, summed up the feelings of all who sailed under Cook when he wrote, "...he was our leading star." The English sailed next morning after dropping off their Hawaiian girlfriends who were still aboard.

Captain Clerk, in bad health, carried on with the fruitless search for the Northwest Passage. He died and was buried at the Siberian village of Petropavlovisk. England was at war with upstart colonists in America, so the return of the expedition warranted little fanfare. The *Resolution* was converted into an army transport to fight the pesky Americans; the once proud *Discovery* was reduced to a convict ship ferrying inmates to Botany Bay, Australia. Mrs. Cook, the great captain's steadfast and chaste wife, lived to the age of 93, surviving all her children. She was given a stipend of 200 pounds per year, and finished her days surrounded by Cook's mementos, observing the anniversary of his death to the very end by fasting and reading from the Bible.

THE UNIFICATION OF OLD HAWAII

Hawaii was already in a state of political turmoil and civil war when Cook arrived. In the 1780s the islands were roughly divided into three kingdoms: venerable Kalaniopuu ruled Hawaii and the Hana district of Maui; wily and ruthless warrior-king Kahekili ruled Maui, Kahoolawe, Lanai, and later Oahu; and Kaeo, Kahekili's brother, ruled Kauai. War ravaged the land until a remarkable chief, Kamehameha, rose and subjugated all the islands under one rule. Kamehameha initiated a dynasty that would last for about 100 years, until the independent monarchy of Hawaii forever ceased to be. To add a zing to this brewing political stew, Westerners and their technology were beginning to come in ever-increasing numbers. In 1786, Capt. LaPerouse and his French exploration party landed in what's now LaPerouse Bay, near Lahaina, foreshadowing European attention. In 1786 two American captains, Portlock and Dixon, made landfall in Hawaii. Also, it was known that a fortune could be made on the fur trade between the great Northwest and Canton, China; stopping in Hawaii could make it all feasible. After this was reported, the fate of Hawaii was sealed.

Hawaii under Kamehameha was ready to enter its "golden age." The social order was medieval, with the *ali'i* as knights, owing their military allegiance to the king, and the serf-like *makaainana* paying tribute and working the lands. The priesthood of *kahuna* filled the posts of advisors, sorcerers, navigators, doctors, and historians. This was Polynesian Hawaii at its apex. But like the uniquely Hawaiian silversword, the old culture blossomed, and as soon as it did, it began to wither. Ever since, all that was purely Hawaiian has been supplanted by the relentless foreign influences that began bearing down upon it.

Young Kamehameha

Kamehameha was a man noticed by everyone; there was no doubt he was a force to be reckoned with. He had met Capt. Cook when the *Discovery* unsuccessfully tried to land at Hana on Maui. While aboard, he made a lasting impression, distinguishing himself from the multitude of natives swarming the ships by his royal bearing. Lt. James King, in a diary entry, remarked that Kamehameha was a fierce-looking man, almost ugly, but that he was obviously intelligent, observant, and very good-natured. Kamehameha received his early military training from his uncle Kalaniopuu, the great king of Hawaii and Hana, who fought fierce battles against Alapai, the usurper who stole his hereditary lands. After regaining Hawaii, Kalaniopuu returned to his Hana district and turned his attention to conquering of all Maui. During this period young Kamehameha distinguished himself as a ferocious warrior and earned himself the nickname of "the hard-shelled crab," even though old Kahekili, Maui's king, almost annihilated Kalaniopuu's army at the sand hills of Wailuku.

When the old king neared death he passed on the kingdom to his son Kiwalao. He also, however, empowered Kamehameha as the keeper of the family war god Kukailimoku: Ku of the Bloody Red Mouth, Ku the Destroyer. Oddly enough, Kamehameha had been born not 500 yards from Ku's great *heiau* at Kohala, and had heard the chanting and observed the ceremonies dedicated to this fierce god from his first breath. Soon after Kalaniopuu died, Kamehameha found himself in a bitter war that he did not seek against his two cousins, Kiwalao and his brother Keoua, with the island of Hawaii at stake. The skirmishing lasted nine years until Kamehameha's armies met the two brothers at Mokuohai in an indecisive battle in which Kiwalao was killed. The result was a shaky truce with Keoua, a much embittered enemy. During this fighting, Kahekili of Maui conquered Oahu where he built a house of the skulls and bones of his adversaries as a reminder of his omnipotence. He also extended his will to Kauai by marrying his half brother to a high-ranking chieftess of that island. A new factor would be needed to resolve this stalemate of power—the coming of the *haole*.

The Olowalu Massacre

In 1790 the American merchant ship *Ella Nora,* commanded by Yankee captain Simon Metcalfe, was looking for a harbor after its long voyage from the Pacific Northwest. Following a day behind was the *Fair American,* a tiny ship manned by Metcalfe's son Thomas and a crew of five. Metcalfe, perhaps by necessity, was a stern and humorless man who would broach no interference. While anchored at Olowalu, a beach area about five miles east of Lahaina, some natives slipped close in their canoes and stole a small boat, killing a seaman in the process. Metcalfe decided to trick the Hawaiians by first negotiating a truce and then unleashing full fury upon them. Signaling he was willing to trade, he invited canoes of innocent natives to visit his ship. In the meantime, he ordered that all cannon and muskets be readied with scatter shot. When the canoes were within hailing distance, he ordered his crew to fire at will. Over 100 people were slain; the Hawaiians remembered this killing as "the day of spilled brains." Metcalf then sailed away to Kealakekua Bay and in an unrelated incident succeeded in insulting Kameiamoku, a ruling chief, who vowed to annihilate the next *haole* ship that he saw.

Fate sent him the *Fair American* and young Thomas Metcalfe. The little ship was entirely overrun by superior forces. In the insuing battle, the mate, Isaac Davis, so distinguished himself by open acts of bravery that his life alone was spared. While harbored at Kealakekua, Metcalf sent John Young to reconnoiter. Kamehameha, learning of the capture of the *Fair American,* detained Young so he could not report, and Metcalfe, losing patience, marooned his own man and sailed off to Canton. (Metcalfe never learned of the fate of his son Thomas, and was later killed with another son while trading with the Indians along the Pacific coast.) Kamehameha quickly realized the significance of his two captives and the *Fair American* with its brace of small cannon. He appropriated the ship and made Davis and Young trusted advisors, eventually raising them to the rank of chief. They would all play a significant role in the unification of Hawaii.

Kamehameha The Great

Later in 1790, supported by the savvy of Davis and Young and the cannon from the *Fair American* which he mounted on carts, Kamehameha invaded Maui using Hana as his power base. The island defenders under Kalaniekupule, son of Kahekili who was lingering on Oahu, were totally demoralized, then driven back into the death-trap of Iao Valley. There, Kamehameha's forces annihilated them. No mercy was expected and none given, although mostly commoners were slain with no significant *ali'i* falling to the victors. So many were killed in this sheer-walled, inescapable valley that the battle was called *"ka pani wai"* which means "the damming of the waters"...literally

Kamehameha I as drawn by Louis Choris, ship's artist for the Von Kotzebue expedition, c. 1816. Supposedly the only time that Kamehameha sat to have his portrait rendered. (Hawaii State Archives)

with dead bodies. While Kamehameha was fighting on Maui, his old nemesis Keoua was busy running amok back on Hawaii, again pillaging Kamehameha's lands. The great warrior returned home flushed with victory, but in two battles could not subdue Keoua. Finally, Kamehameha had a prophetic dream in which he was told that Ku would lead him to victory over all the lands of Hawaii if he would build a *heiau* to the war god at Kawaihae. Even before the temple was finished, old Kahekili attempted to invade Waipio, Kamehameha's stronghold. But Kamehameha summoned Davis and Young, and with the *Fair American* and an enormous fleet of war canoes defeated Kahekili at Waimanu. Kahekili had no choice but to accept the indomitable Kamehameha as the king of Maui, although he himself remained the administrative head until his death in 1794.

Now only Keoua remained in the way and he would be defeated not by war, but by the great *mana* of Ku. While Keoua's armies were crossing the desert on the southern slopes of Kilauea, the fire goddesss Pele trumpeted her disapproval and sent a huge cloud of poisonous gas and mud-ash into the air. It descended upon and instantly killed the middle legions of Keoua's armies and their families. The footprints of this ill-fated army remain to this day outlined in the mud-ash as clearly as if they were deliberately encased in wet cement. Keoua's intuition told him that the victorious *mana* of the gods had swung to Kamehameha and that his own fate was sealed. Kamehameha sent word that he wanted Keoua to meet with him at Ku's newly dedicated temple in Kawaihae. Both knew that Keoua must die. The old nemesis came riding proudly in his canoe, gloriously outfitted in the red and gold feathered cape and helmet signifying his exalted rank. When he stepped ashore he was felled by Kamehameha's warriors and his body was ceremoniously laid upon the altar along with 11 others who were slaughtered and dedicated to Ku, Of the Maggot-Dripping Mouth.

Increasing Contact

By the time Kamehameha had won the Big Island, Hawaii was becoming a regular stopover for numerous ships seeking the lucrative sandalwood trade with China. In February 1791, Capt. George Vancouver, still seeking the Northwest Passage, returned to Kealakekua where he was greeted by a throng of 30,000. The captain at once recognized Kamehameha, who was wearing a Chinese dressing gown that he had received in tribute from another chief who in turn had received it directly from the hands of Cook himself. The diary of a crewmember, Thomas Manby, relates that Kamehameha, missing his front teeth, was more fierce-looking than ever as he approached the ship in an elegant double-hulled canoe sporting 46 rowers. The king invited all to a great feast prepared for them on the beach. Kamehameha's appetite matched his tremendous size. It was noted that he ate two sizable fish, a king-size bowl of *poi,* a small pig, and an entire baked dog. Kamehameha personally entertained the Englishmen by putting on a mock battle in which he deftly avoided spears by rolling, tumbling, and catching them in mid-air, all the while hurling his own a great distance. The English reciprocated by firing cannon bursts into the air, creating an impromptu fireworks display. Kamehameha requested from Vancouver a full table setting with which he was provided, but his request for firearms was prudently denied. The captain did, however, leave beef cattle, fowl, and breeding stock of sheep and goats. The ship's naturalist, Archibald Menzies, was the first *haole* to climb Mauna Kea; he also introduced a large assortment of fruits and vegetables. The Hawaiians were cheerful, outgoing, and showed remorse when they indicated that the remainder of Cook's bones had been buried at a temple close to Kealakekua. John Young, by this time firmly entrenched into Hawaiian society, made no request to sail away with Vancouver. During the next two decades of Kamehameha's rule, the French, Russians, English, and Americans discovered the great whaling waters off Hawaii, and their increasing visits shook and finally tumbled the ancient religion and social order of *kapu*.

Finishing Touches

After Keoua was laid to rest it was only a matter of time till Kamehameha consolidated his power over all of Hawaii. In 1794 the old warrior Kahekili of Maui died, and gave Oahu to his son Kalanikupule, while Kauai and Niihau went to his brother Kaeo. Warring between themselves, Kalanikupule was victorious, though he did not possess the grit of his father nor the great *mana* of Kamehameha. He had previously murdered a Capt. Brown who had anchored in Honolulu and seized his ship the *Jackall*. With the aid of this ship, Kalanikupule now determined to attack Kamehameha. However, while enroute, the sailors regained control of their ship and cruised to the Big Island to inform and join with Kamehameha. An army of 16,000 was raised and sailed for Maui, where they met only token resistance, destroyed Lahaina, pillaged the countryside, and vanquished Molokai in one bloody battle. The war canoes next sailed for Oahu and the final showdown. The great army landed at Waikiki, and though defenders fought bravely, giving up Oahu by the inch, they were steadily driven into the surrounding mountains. The beleaguered army made its last stand at Nuuanu Pali, a great precipice in the mountains behind present-day Honolulu. Kamehameha's warriors mercilessly drove the enemy into the great abyss. Kalanikupule, who hid in the mountains, was captured after a few months and sacrificed to Ku, The Snatcher of Lands, thereby ending the struggle for power. Kamehameha put down a revolt on Hawaii in 1796 and the king of Kauai, Kaumuali, accepting the inevitable, recognized Kamehameha as supreme ruler without suffering the hopeless ravages of a needless war. Kamehameha, for the first time in Hawaiian history, was the undisputed ruler of all the islands of "the heavenly homeland in the north."

Capt. George Vancouver (Hawaii State Archives)

Kamehameha's Rule

Kamehameha was as gentle in victory as he was ferocious in battle. His rule lasted until his death on May 8, 1819, under which Hawaii enjoyed a peace unlike the warring islands had ever known before. The king moved his royal court to Lahaina, where in 1803, he built the "Brick Palace," the first permanent building of Hawaii. The benevolent tyrant also enacted the "Law of the Splintered Paddle." This law, which protected the weak from the exploitation of the strong, had its origins when, many years before, a brave defender of a small overwhelmed village broke a paddle over Kamehameha's head and taught the chief—literally in one stroke—about the nobility of the common man.

However, just as Old Hawaii reached its "golden age," its demise was at hand. The relentless waves of *haole* both innocently and determinedly battered the old ways into the ground. With the foreign ships came prosperity and fanciful new goods after which the *ali'i* lusted. The *makaaina* were worked mercilessly to provide sandalwood for the China trade. This was the first "boom" economy to hit the islands, but it set the standard of exploitation that would follow. Kamehameha built an observation tower in Lahaina to watch for ships, many of which were his own, returning laden with riches from the world at large. In the last years of his life Kamehameha returned to his beloved Kona coast where he enjoyed the excellent fishing renowned to this day. He had taken Hawaii from the darkness of warfare into the light of peace. He died true to the religious and moral *kapu* of his youth, the only ones he had ever known, and with him died a unique way of life. Two loyal retainers buried his bones after the baked flesh had been ceremoniously stripped away. A secret burial cave was chosen so that no one could desecrate the remains of the great chief, thereby absorbing his *mana*. The tomb's whereabouts remains unknown, and disturbing the dead remains one of the strictest *kapu* to this day. "The Lonely One's" kingdom would pass to his son, Liholiho, but true power would be in the hands of his beloved but feisty wife Kaahumanu. As Kamehameha's spirit drifted from this Earth, two forces sailing around Cape Horn would forever change Hawaii: the whalers and the missionaries.

MISSIONARIES AND WHALERS

The year 1819 is of the utmost significance in Hawaiian history. It marked the death of Kamehameha, the overthrow of the ancient *kapu* system, the arrival of the first "whaler" in Lahaina, and the departure of Calvinist missionaries from New England determined to convert the heathen islands. Great changes began to rattle the old order to its foundations. With the *kapu* system and all of the ancient gods abandoned (except for the fire goddess Pele of Kilauea), a great void permeated the souls of the Hawaiians. In the coming decades Hawaii, also coveted by Russia, France, and England, was finally consumed by America. The islands had the first American school, printing press, and newspaper *(The Polynesian)* west of the Mississippi. Lahaina, in its heyday, became the world's greatest whaling port, accommodating over 500 ships during its peak years.

The Royal Family

Maui's Hana District provided Hawaii with one of its greatest queens, Kaahumanu, born in 1768 in a cave within walking distance of Hana Harbor. At the age of 17 she became the third of Kamehameha's 21 wives and eventually the love of his life. At first she proved to be totally independent and unmanageable, and was known to openly defy her king by taking numerous lovers. Kamehameha placed a *kapu* on her body and even had her attended by horribly deformed hunchbacks to curb her carnal appetites, but she continued to flaunt his authority. Young Kaahumanu had no love for her great, lumbering, unattractive husband, but (even Capt. Vancouver was pressed into service as a marriage counselor) in time she learned to love him dearly. She in turn became his favorite wife, although she remained childless throughout her life. Kamehameha's first wife was the supremely royal Keopuolani, who so outranked even him that the king himself had to approach her naked and crawling on his belly. Keopuolani produced the royal children Liholiho and Kauikeaouli, who became King Kamehameha II and III, respectively. When

the great Queen Kaahumanu, by ship's artist Louis Choris from the Otto Von Kotzebue expedition, c. 1816 (Hawaii State Archives)

Kamehameha I died in 1819 he appointed Liholiho his successor, but he also had the wisdom to make Kaahumanu the *kuhina nui* or queen regent. Initially, Liholiho was weak and became a drunkard. Later he became a good ruler, but he was always supported by his royal mother Keopuolani and by the ever-formidable Kaahumanu.

Kapu Is *Pau*

Kaahumanu was greatly loved and respected by the people. On public occasions, she donned Kamehameha's royal cloak and spear: so attired and infused with the king's *mana,* she demonstrated that she was the real leader of Hawaii. For six months after Kamehameha's death, Kaahumanu counseled Liholiho on what he must do. The wise *kuhina nui* knew that the old ways were *pau* ("finished") and Hawaii could not hope to function in a rapidly changing world under the *kapu* system. In November 1819, Kaahumanu and Keopuolani prevailed open Liholiho to break two of the oldest and most sacred *kapu:* to eat together with women and to allow women to eat previously forbidden foods, such as bananas and certain fish. Kaahumanu sat with Liholilho, heavily fortified with strong drink, and attended by other high-ranking chiefs and a handful of foreigners, they ate in public. This feast became known as *Ai Noa* ("free eating"), and as the first morsels passed her lips the ancient gods of Hawaii tumbled. Throughout the land revered *heiau* were burned and abandoned and the idols knocked to the ground. Now the people had nothing but their own weakened inner selves to rely on. Nothing and no one could answer their prayers; their spiritual lives were empty and in shambles.

Missionaries

In October 1819 the *Brig Thaddeus* left Boston carrying 14 missionaries bound for Hawaii. On April 4, 1820 they landed at Kailua on the Big Island where Liholiho had moved the royal court. The reverends Bingham and Thurston went ashore and were granted a one-year trial missionary period by King Liholiho. They established themselves on Hawaii and Oahu and from there began the transformation of Hawaii. The missionaries were men of God, but also practical-minded Yankees. They brought education, enterprise, and most importantly, unlike the transient seafarers, a commitment to stay and build. In 1823, Rev. Richards established the first mission in Lahaina, a village of about 2,300 inhabitants.

Rapid Conversions

The year 1823 also marked the death of Keopuolani, who was given a Christian burial. Setting the standard by accepting Christianity, a number of the *ali'i* had followed the queen's lead. Liholiho had sailed off to England where he and his wife contracted measles and died. Their bodies were returned by the British in 1825, on the HMS *Blonde* captained by Lord Byron, cousin of *the* Lord Byron. During these years, Kaahumanu allied herself with Rev. Richards and together they wrote Hawaii's first code of laws based upon the Ten Commandments. Foremost was the condemnation of murder, theft, brawling, and the desecration of the Sabbath by work or play. The early missionaries had the best of intentions, but like all zealots were blinded by the singlemindedness that was also their greatest ally. The destruction of the native beliefs they felt to be abominations was not surgically selective. *Anything* native was felt to be inferior, and they set about to wipe out all traces of the old ways. In their rampage they reduced the Hawaiian culture to ashes, plucking self-will and determination from the hearts of a once-proud people. Moreso than the whalers, they terminated the Hawaiian way of life.

The Early Seamen

A good portion of the common seamen of the early 19th C. were the dregs of the Western world. Many a whoremongering drunkard had awoken from a stupor and found himself on the pitching deck of a ship, discovering to his dismay that he had been "pressed into naval service." For the most part these sailors were a filthy, uneducated, lawless rabble. Their present situation was dim, their future hopeless, and they would live to be 30 if they were lucky and didn't die from scurvy or a thousand other miserable fates. They snatched brief pleasure in every port, and jumped ship at every opportunity, especially in an easy berth like Lahaina. They displayed the worst elements of Western culture—which the Hawaiians naively mimicked. In exchange for *aloha* they gave drunkeness, sloth, and insidious death by disease. By the 1850s the population of native Hawaiians tumbled from the estimated 300,000 reported by Capt. Cook in 1778 to barely 60,000. Common conditions such as colds, flu, venereal disease, and sometimes small pox and cholera decimated the Hawaiians who had no natural immunities to these foreign ailments. By the time the missionaries arrived, *hapahaole* children were common in Lahaina streets. The earliest lawless opportunists had come seeking sandalwood after first filling their holds with furs from the Pacific Northwest. Aided by *ali'i* hungry for manufactured goods and Western finery, they raped Hawaiian forests of this fragrant wood so coveted in China. Next, droves of sailors came in search of the whales. The whalers, decent men at home, left their morals back in the Atlantic and lived by the slogan "no conscience east of the Cape." The delights of Hawaii were just too tempting for most.

William Alexander preaching on Kauai. Drawing by A. Agate, c. 1840 (Hawaii State Archives)

Two Worlds Tragically Collide

The 1820s were a time of confusion and soul-searching for the Hawaiians. When Kamehameha II died the kingdom passed to Kauikeaouli (Kamehameha III), who made his life-long residence in Lahaina. The young king was only 9 years old when the title passed to him, but his power was secure because Kaahumanu was still a vibrant *kuhina nui.* The young prince, moreso than any other, was raised in the cultural confusion of the times. His childhood was spent during the very cusp of the change from old ways to new, and he was often pulled in two directions by vastly differing beliefs. Since he was royal born, according to age-old Hawaiian tradition, he must mate and produce an heir with the highest ranking *ali'i* in the kingdom. This natural mate happened to be his younger sister, the Princess Nahienaena. To the old Hawaiian advisors, this arrangement was perfectly acceptable and encouraged. To the increasingly influential missionaries, incest was an unimaginable abomination in the eyes of God. The problem was compounded by the fact that Kamehameha III and Nahienaena were drawn to each other and were deeply in love. The young king could not stand the mental pressure imposed by conflicting worlds. He became a teenage alcoholic too royal to be restrained by anyone in the kingdom, and his bouts of drunkenness and womanizing were both legendary and scandalous. Meanwhile, Nahienaena was even more pressured because she was a favorite of the missionaries, baptized into the church at age 12. She too vacillated between the old and the new. At times a pious Christian, at others she drank all night and took numerous lovers. As the Prince and Princess grew into their late teens, they became even more attached to each other and hardly made an attempt to keep their relationship from the missionaries. Whenever possible, they lived together in a grass house built for the Princess by her father.

In 1832, the great Kaahumanu died, leaving the king on his own. In 1833, at the age of 18, Kamehameha III announced that the "regency" was over and that all the lands in Hawaii were his, personally, and that he alone was the ultimate law. Almost immediately, however, he decreed that his half sister Kinau would be "premier," signifying that he would leave the actual running of the kingdom in her hands. Kamehameha III fell into total drunken confusion, until one night he attempted suicide. After this episode he seemed to straighten up a bit and mostly kept a low profile. In 1836, Princess Nahienaena was convinced by the missionaries to take a husband. She married Leleiohoku, a chief from the Big Island, but continued to sleep with her brother. It is uncertain who fathered the child, but Nahienaena gave birth to a baby boy in September 1836. The young prince survived for only a few hours, and Nahienaena never recovered from her convalescence. She died in December 1836, and was laid to rest in the mausoleum next to her mother, Keopuolani, on the royal island in Mokuhina Pond, still in existence in modern-day Lahaina. After the death of his sister, Kamehameha III became a sober and righteous ruler. Oftentimes seen paying his respects at the royal mausoleum, he ruled longer than any other king until his death in 1854.

Kamehameha III

The Missionaries Prevail

In 1823, the first mission was established in Lahaina under the pastorage of Rev. Richards and his wife. Within a few years, many of the notable *ali'i* had been, at least in appearance, converted to Christianity. By 1828 the cornerstones for Wainee Church, the first stone church on the island, were laid just behind the palace of Kamehameha III. The struggle between missionaries and whalers centered around public drunkenness and the servicing of sailors by local native girls. The normally god-fearing whalers had signed on for perilous duty that lasted up to 3 years, and when they anchored in Lahaina they demanded their pleasure. The missionaries were instrumental in placing a curfew on sailors and prohibiting native girls from boarding ships which had become customary. These measures certainly did not stop the liaisons between sailor and *wahine,* but it did impose a modicum of social sanction and tolled the end of the wide open days. The sailors were outraged; in 1825 the crew from the *Daniel* attacked the home of the meddler, Rev. Richards. A year later a similar incident occurred. In 1827, confined and lonely sailors from the whaler *John Palmer* fired their cannon at Rev. Richards' newly built home.

Slowly the tensions eased, and by 1836 many sailors were regulars at the Seamen's Chapel, adjacent to the Baldwin Home. Unfortunately, even the missionaries couldn't stop the pesky mosquito from entering the islands through the port of Lahaina. The mosquitos arrived in 1826, from Mexico, aboard the merchant *Wellington.* They were inadvertently carried as larvae in the water barrels and democratically pestered everyone in the islands from that day forward regardless of race, religion, or creed.

Lahaina Becomes A Cultural Center

By 1831, Lahaina was firmly established as a seat of Western influence in Hawaii. That year marked the founding of Lahainaluna School, the first *real* American school west of the Rockies. Virtually a copy of a New England normal school, it attracted the best students, both native and white, from throughout the kingdom. By 1834, Lahainaluna had an operating printing press publishing the islands' first newspaper, *The Torch of Hawaii,* starting a lucrative printing industry centered in Lahaina that dominated not only the islands but also California for many years.

An early native student was David Malo. He was brilliant and well educated, but more importantly, he remembered the "old ways." One of the first Hawaiians to realize his native land was being swallowed up by the newcomers, Malo compiled the first history of pre-contact Hawaii and the resulting book, *Hawaiian Antiquities,* became a reference masterpiece which has yet to be eclipsed. David Malo insisted that the printing be done in Hawaiian, not English. Malo is buried in the mountains above Lahainaluna where, by his own request, he is "high above the tide of foreign invasion." By the 1840s, Lahaina was firmly established as the "whaling capital of the world"; the peak year 1846 saw 395 whaling ships anchored here. A census in 1846 reported that Lahaina was home to 3,445 natives, 112 permanent *haole,* 600 sailors, and over 500 dogs. The populace was housed in 882 grass houses, 155 adobe houses, and 59 relatively permanent stone and wooden framed structures. Lahaina would probably have remained the islands' capital, had Kamehameha III not moved the royal capital to the burgeoning port of Honolulu on the island of Oahu.

REVOLUTIONARY CHANGES

Foreign Influence

By the 1840s Honolulu was becoming the center of commerce in the islands; when Kamehameha III moved the royal court there from Lahaina the ascendant fate of the new capital was guaranteed. In 1843, Lord Paulet, commander of the warship *Carysfort,* forced Kamehameha III to sign a treaty ceding Hawaii to the British. London, however, repudiated this act and Hawaii's independence was restored within a few months when Queen Victoria sent Admiral Thomas as her personal agent of good intentions. The king memorialized the turn of events by a speech in which he uttered the phrase, *"Ua mau ke o ka aina i ka pono,"* ("The life of the land is preserved in righteousness"), now Hawaii's motto. The French used similar bullying tactics to force an unfavorable treaty on the Hawaiians in 1839; as part of these heavyhanded negotiations they exacted a payment of $20,000, and the right for Catholics to enjoy religious freedom in the islands. In 1842 the U.S. recognized and guaranteed Hawaii's independence without a formal treaty, and by 1860 over 80% of the islands' trade was with America.

The Great *Mahele*

In 1840 Kamehameha III ended his autocratic rule and instituted a constitutional monarchy. This brought about the Hawaiian Bill of Rights, but the most far-reaching change was the transition to private ownership of land. Formerly, all land belonged to the ruling chief who gave wedge-shaped parcels called *ahupua'a* to lesser chiefs to be worked for him. The commoners did all the real labor, their produce heavily taxed by the *ali'i.* The fortunes of war, the death of a chief, or the mere whim of a superior could force a commoner off his land. The Hawaiians, however, could not think in terms of "owning" land. No one could *possess* land, one could only *use* land, and its *ownership* was a strange foreign concept. (As a result, naive Hawaiians gave up their lands for a song to unscrupulous traders, which remains an integral unrectified problem to this day.) In 1847 Kamehameha III and his advisers separated the lands of Hawaii into three groupings: crown land (belonging to the king), government land (belonging to the chiefs), and the people's land (the largest parcels). In 1848, 245 *ali'i* entered their land claims in the *Mahele Book* assuring them ownership. In 1850 the commoners were given title in fee simple to the lands they cultivated and lived on as tenants, not including house lots in towns. Commoners without land could buy small *kuleana* (farms) from the government at 50 cents per acre. In 1850, foreigners were also allowed to purchase land in fee simple, and the ownership of Hawaii from that day forward slipped steadily from the hands of its indigenous people.

KING SUGAR

The sugar industry began at Hana, Maui, in 1849. A whaler named George Wilfong hauled 4 blubber pots ashore and set them up on a rocky hill in the middle of 60 acres he had planted in sugar. A team of oxen turned "crushing rollers" and the cane juice flowed down an open trough into the pots, under which an attending native kept a roaring fire burning. Wilfong's methods of refining were crude but the resultant high-quality sugar turned a neat profit in Lahaina. The main problem was labor. The Hawaiians, who had made excellent whalers, were basically indentured workers. They became extremely disillusioned with their contracts, which could last up to 10 years. Most of their wages were eaten up by manufactured commodities sold at the company store, and it didn't take long for them to realize that they were little more than slaves. At every opportunity they either left the area or just refused to work.

Imported Labor

The **Masters and Servants Act of 1850**, which allowed importation of laborers under the contract system, ostensibly guaranteed an endless supply of cheap labor for the plantations. Chinese laborers were imported, but were too enterprising to remain in the fields for a meager $3 per month. They left as soon as opportunity permitted, and went into business as small merchants and retailers. In the meantime, Wilfong had sold out, releasing most of the Hawaiians previously held under contract, and his plantation fell into disuse. In 1860 two Danish brothers, August and Oscar Unna, bought land at Hana to raise sugar. They solved the labor problem by importing Japanese laborers who were extremely hardworking and easily managed. The workday lasted 10 hours, 6 days a week, for a salary of $20 per month with housing and medical care thrown in. Plantation life was very structured with stringent rules governing even bedtimes and lights out. A worker was fined for being late or for smoking on the job. Even the Japanese couldn't function under these circumstances, and improvements in benefits and housing were slowly gained.

Sugar Grows

The demand for "Sandwich Island Sugar" grew as California was populated during the gold rush, and increased dramatically when the American Civil War demanded a constant sup-

Women of many ethnic backgrounds worked the plantations at the turn of the century.

ply. The only sugar plantations on the Mainland were small plots confined to the Confederate states, whose products would hardly be bought by the Union and whose fields, later in the war, were destroyed. By the 1870s it was clear to the planters, still mainly New Englanders, that the U.S. was their market; they tried often to gain closer ties and favorable tariffs. The Americans also planted rumors that the British were interested in annexing Hawaii; this put pressure on the U.S. Congress to pass the long-desired **Reciprocity Act**, which would exempt sugar from import duty. It finally passed in 1875, in exchange for U.S. long-range rights to the strategic naval port of Pearl Harbor, among other concessions. These agreements gave increased political power to a small group of American planters, whose outlooks were similar to the post-Civil War South where a few powerful whites were the virtual masters of a multitude of dark-skinned laborers. Sugar was now big business and the Hana District alone exported almost 3,000 tons per year. All of Hawaii would have to reckon with the "sugar barons."

Changing Society

The sugar plantation system changed life in Hawaii physically, spiritually, politically, and economically. Now boatloads of workers came not only from Japan, but from Portugal, Germany, and even Russia. The white-skinned workers were most often the field foremen *(luna)*. With the immigrants came new religions, new animals and plants, unique cuisines, and a plantation language known as *pidgin* or better yet *da kine.* The Orientals mainly, but also portions of all the other groups including the white plantation owners, intermarried with Hawaiian girls. A new class of people properly termed "cosmopolitan" but more familiarly and aptly known as "locals" was emerging. These were the people of multiple race backgrounds who couldn't exactly say *what* they were but it was clear to all just *who* they were. The plantation owners became the new "chiefs" of Hawaii who could carve up the land and dispense favors. The Hawaiian monarchy was soon eliminated.

A KINGDOM PASSES

The fate of Lahaina's Wainee Church through the years has been a symbol of the political and economic climate of the times. Its construction heralded the beginning of missionary dominance in 1828. It was destroyed by a tornado or "ghost wind" in 1858, just when whaling began to falter. The previously dominant missionaries began losing their control to the merchants and planters. In 1894, Wainee Church was burned to the ground by Royalists supporting the besieged Queen Liliuokalani, then was rebuilt with a grant from H.P. Baldwin in 1897 while Hawaii was a Republic ruled by the sugar planters. It wasn't until 1947 that Wainee was finally completed and remodeled.

The Beginning Of The End

Like the Hawaiian people themselves, the Kamehameha dynasty in the mid-1800s was dying from within. King Kamehameha IV (Alexander Liholiho) ruled from 1854 to 1863; his only child died in 1862. He was succeeded by his older brother Kamehameha V (Lot Kamehameha) who ruled until 1872. With his passing the Kamehameha line ended. William Lunalilo, elected king in 1873 by popular vote, was of royal, but not Kamehameha, lineage. He died after only a year in office, and being a bachelor left no heirs. He was succeeded by David Kalakaua, known far and wide as "The Merry Monarch." He made a world tour and was well received wherever he went. He built Iolani Palace in Honolulu and was personally in favor of closer ties with the U.S., helping push through the Reciprocity Act. Kalakaua died in 1891 and was replaced by his sister Lydia Liliuokalani, last of the Hawaiian monarchs.

The Revolution

When Liliuokalani took office in 1891 the native population was at a low of 40,000 and she felt that the U.S. had too much influence over her homeland. She was known to personally favor the English over the Americans. She attempted to replace the liberal constitution of 1887 (adopted by her pro-American brother) with an autocratic mandate in which she would have much more political and economic control of the islands. When the McKinley Tariff of 1890 brought a decline in sugar profits, she made no attempt to improve the situation. Thus, the planters saw her as a political obstacle to their economic growth; most of Hawaii's American planters and merchants were in favor of a rebellion. She would have to go! A central spokesman and firebrand was Lorrin Thurston, a Honolulu publisher who, with a central core of about 30 men, challenged the Hawaiian monarchy. Although Liliuokalani rallied some support and had a small military potential in her personal guard, the coup was ridiculously easy—it took only one casualty. Capt. John Good shot a Hawaiian policeman in the arm and that did it. Naturally, the conspirators could not have succeeded without some solid assurances from a secret contingent in the U.S. Congress as well as outgoing President Benjamin Harrison who favored Hawaii's annexation. Marines from the *Boston* went ashore to "protect American lives," and on January 17, 1893, the Hawaiian monarchy came to an end.

The provisional government was headed by Sanford B. Dole who became president of the Hawaiian Republic. Liliuokalani actually surrendered not to the conspirators but to U.S. Ambassador John Stevens. She believed that the U.S. government, which had assured Hawaiian independence, would be outraged by the overthrow and would come to her aid. Actually, incoming President Grover Cleveland *was* outraged and Hawaii wasn't immediately

Queen Liliuokalani

annexed as expected. When queried about what she would do with the conspirators if she were reinstated, Liliuokalani said that they would be hung as traitors. The racist press of the times, which portrayed the Hawaiians as half-civilized blood-thirsty heathens, publicized this widely. Since the conspirators were the leading citizens of the land, the queen's words proved untimely. In January 1895, a small, ill-fated counterrevolution headed by Liliuokalani failed, and she was placed under house arrest in Iolani Palace. Forced to abdicate her throne, officials of the Republic insisted that she use her married name (Mrs. John Dominis) to sign the documents. She was also forced to swear allegiance to the new Republic. Liliuokalani went on to write *Hawaii's Story* and also the lyric ballad *Aloha O'e*. She never forgave the conspirators and remained to the Hawaiians "queen" until her death in 1917.

Annexation

The overwhelming majority of Hawaiians opposed annexation and desired to restore the monarchy. But they were prevented from voting by the new Republic because they couldn't meet the imposed property and income qualifications—a transparent ruse by the planters to control the majority. Most *haole* were racist and believed that the "common people" could not be entrusted with the vote because they were childish and incapable of ruling themselves. The fact that the Hawaiians had existed quite well for 1,000 years before the white man even reached Hawaii was never considered. The Philippine theater of the Spanish-American War also prompted annexation. One of the strongest proponents was Alfred Mahon, a brilliant naval strategist who, with support from Theodore Roosevelt, argued that the U.S. military must have Hawaii to be a viable force in the Pacific. In addition, Japan, flushed with victory in its recent war with China, protested the American intention to annex, and in so doing prompted even moderates to support annexation in fear that the Japanese themselves coveted the prize. On July 7, 1898, President McKinley signed the annexation agreement, and this "tropical fruit" was finally put into America's basket.

Sanford B. Dole reads the proclamation inaugurating the Hawaiian Republic on July 4, 1894.

MODERN TIMES

Hawaii entered the 20th C. totally transformed from what it had been. The old Hawaiian language, religion, culture, and leadership were all gone. Western dress, values, education, and recreation were the norm. Native Hawaiians were now unseen citizens who lived in dwindling numbers in remote areas. The plantations, new centers of social order, had a strong Oriental flavor; more than 75% of their work force was Asian. There was a small white middle class, an all-powerful white elite, and a single political party ruled by that elite. Education, however, was always highly prized, and by the turn of the century all racial groups were encouraged to attend school. By 1900, almost 90% of Hawaiians were literate (far above the national norm) and schooling was mandatory for all children between ages 6 and 15. Intermarriage was accepted, and there was a mixing of the races like nowhere else on Earth. The military became increasingly important to Hawaii. It brought in money and jobs, dominating the island economy. The Japanese attack on Pearl Harbor, which began U.S. involvement in World War II, bound Hawaii to America forever. Once the islands had been baptized by blood, the average mainlander felt that Hawaii was American soil. A movement among Hawaiians to become part of the Union began to grow. They wanted a real voice in Washington, not merely a voteless delegate as provided under their territory status. Hawaii became the 50th state in 1959 and the jumbo jet revolution of the 1960s made it easily accessible to growing numbers of tourists from all over the world.

Military History

A few military strategists realized the importance of Hawaii early in the 19th C., but most didn't recognize the advantages until the Spanish-American War. It was clearly an unsinkable ship in the middle of the Pacific from which the U.S. could launch military operations. Troops were stationed at Camp McKinley, at the foot of Diamond Head, the main military compound until it became obsolete in 1907. Pearl Harbor was first surveyed in 1872 by General Schofield. Later a military base named in his honor, Schofield Barracks, was a main military post in central Oahu. It first housed the U.S. 5th Cavalry in 1909 and was heavily bombed by the Japanese at the outset of WW II. Pearl Harbor, first dredged in 1908, was officially opened on December 11, 1911. The first warship to enter was the cruiser *California*. Ever since, the military has been a mainstay of island economy. Unfortunately, there has been long-standing bad blood between locals and military personnel. Each group has tended to look down upon the other.

Pearl Harbor Attack

On the morning of December 7, 1941, the Japanese carrier *Akagi,* flying the battle flag of the famed Admiral Togo of the Russo-Japanese War, received and broadcast over its PA system island music from Honolulu station KGMB. Deep in the bowels of the ship a radio man listened for a much different message, coming thousands of miles from the Japanese mainland. When the ironic poetic message "east wind rain" was received, the attack was launched. At the end of the day, 2,325 U.S. ser-

Honolulu Star-Bulletin 1st EXTRA

8 PAGES—HONOLULU, TERRITORY OF HAWAII, U. S. A., SUNDAY, DECEMBER 7, 1941—8 PAGES ★ PRICE FIVE CENTS

WAR!

(Associated Press by Transpacific Telephone)

SAN FRANCISCO, Dec. 7.—President Roosevelt announced this morning that Japanese planes had attacked Manila and Pearl Harbor.

OAHU BOMBED BY JAPANESE PLANES

SIX KNOWN DEAD. 21 INJURED, AT EMERGENCY HOSPITAL

The Honolulu Star Bulletin *banner headline announces the beginning of U.S. involvement in WW II on Sunday, December 7, 1941.*

vicemen and 57 civilians were dead; 188 planes were destroyed; 18 major warships were sunk or heavily damaged; and the U.S. was in the war. Japanese casualties were ludicrously light and the ignited conflict would rage for 4 years until Japan, through Nagasaki and Hiroshima, was vaporized into total submission. At the end of hostilities, Hawaii would never again be considered separate from America.

Statehood

A number of economic and political reasons explain why the ruling elite of Hawaii desired statehood, but simply, the vast majority of people who lived there, especially after WW II, considered themselves Americans. The first serious mention of making "The Sandwich Islands" a state was in the 1850s under President Franklin Pierce, but wasn't taken seriously until the monarchy was overthrown in the 1890s. For the next 50 years statehood proposals were made repeatedly to Congress, but there was stiff opposition, especially from the southern states. With Hawaii a territory, an import quota system beneficial to Mainland producers could be enacted on produce, especially sugar. Also, there was prejudice against creating a state in a place where the majority of the populace was not white. This situation was illuminated by the infamous Massie Rape case of 1931 (see p. 69), which went down as one of the greatest miscarriages of justice in American history. During WW II, Hawaii was placed under martial law, but no serious attempt to intern the Japanese population was made, as in California. There were simply too many Japanese, who went on to gain respect of the American people by their outstanding fighting record during the war. Hawaii's own 100th Battalion became the famous 442 Regimental Combat Team which gained notoriety by saving the Lost Texas Battalion during the Battle of the Bulge, and went on to be *the* most decorated battalion in all of WW II. When these GIs returned home, *no one* was going to tell them that they were not loyal Americans. Many of these AJAs (Americans of Japanese Ancestry) took advantage of the GI Bill and received higher education. They were from the common people, not the elite, and they rallied grass roots support for statehood. When the vote finally occurred, approximately 132,900 voted in favor of statehood with only 7,800 votes against. Congress passed the Hawaii State Bill on March 12, 1959, and on August 21, 1959, President Eisenhower announced that Hawaii was officially the 50th state.

STATEHOOD!

House Roll Call Results, Page 16; Senate, Page 14

Bill Is Sent To President

10¢

Statehood Booms Isle Stock Prices

Honolulu Star-Bulletin

Stock Final

Special Radio, Phone Lines Flash News

Sirens, Bells Herald Statehood Arrival

Ike Delighted Hawaii Got Statehood

GOVERNMENT

Being the newest state in the Union, Hawaii has had the chance to scrutinize the others, pick their best attributes, and learn from their past mistakes. The government of the State of Hawaii is in essence no different from any other except that it is streamlined and, in theory, more efficient. There are only two levels: state and county. There are no town or city governments to deal with, and added bureaucracy is theoretically eliminated. Unfortunately, some of the state-run agencies, like the centralized Board of Education, have become "red-tape" monsters. Hawaii, in anticipation of becoming a state, drafted a constitution in 1950 and was ready to go when statehood was ratified. Politics and government are taken seriously in the "Aloha State," which consistently turns in the best national voting record per capita. For example, in the election to ratify statehood, hardly a ballot went uncast, with 95% of the voters opting for statehood. In the first state elections that followed, 173,000 of 180,000 registered voters voted. The bill carried every island of Hawaii except for Niihau, where, coincidentally, the majority of people (total population 250, or so) are of relatively pure Hawaiian blood.

State Government

Hawaii's state legislature has 76 members, with 51 elected seats in the House of Representatives, and 25 in the State Senate. Members serve 2- and 4-year terms respectively. All officials come from 76 separate electorates based on population, which sometimes makes for strange political bedfellows. For example, Maui's split 5th Senatorial District and 9th Representative District share one member from each with both Lanai and Molokai. These districts combine some of the island's richest condo and resort communities on Maui's Kaanapali coast with Lanai, where many people are Filipino field workers, and with economically depressed Molokai, where 80% of native Hawaiians live on welfare.

Oahu, which has the largest number of voters, elects 19 of 25 senators and 39.7 of 51 representatives, giving this island a majority in both houses. Maui, in comparison, elects 2.2 state senators and 4 representatives. The state is divided into four administrative counties: the **County of Kauai,** covering Kauai and Niihau; the **City and County of Honolulu,** which encompasses Oahu, and includes all of the Northwestern Hawaiian Islands; the **County of Hawaii,** the Big Island, and the **County of Maui,** administering the islands of Maui, Lanai, Molokai, and uninhabited Kahoolawe, with the county seat at Wailuku on Maui.

Branches Of Government

The **State Legislature** is the collective body of the House of Representatives and the Senate. They meet during a once-yearly legislative session that begins on the third Wednesday of January and lasts for 90 working days. (These sessions are oftentimes extended and special sessions are frequently called.) The Legislature primarily focuses on taxes, new laws, and appropriations. The **Executive Branch** is headed by the governor and lieutenant governor, both elected on a state-wide basis for four years with a two-term maximum. The governor has the right to appoint the heads of 20 state departments outlined in the constitution. The department appointees must be approved by the Senate, and they usually hold office as long as the appointing administration. **The Judiciary** is headed by a state Supreme Court of five justices, an appeals court, and four circuit courts. All are appointed by the governor and serve for 10 years with Senate approval. There are 27 district courts which have local jurisdiction; the judges are appointed for six-year terms by the chief justice of the Supreme Court.

Governor John Waihee III

Special Departments

The Department of Education is headed by a board of 13 non-partisan representatives elected for four-year terms, 10 from Oahu and three from the other islands. The board has the right to appoint the Superintendent of Schools. Many praise the centralized board as a democratic body offering equal educational opportunity to all districts of Hawaii regardless of socio-financial status. Detractors say that the centralized board provides "equal educational mediocrity" to all. The University of Hawaii is governed by a Board of Regents appointed by the governor. They choose the president of the university.

Political History

The politics of Hawaii before WW II was a self-serving yet mostly benevolent oligarchy. The one real political party was Republican controlled by the Hawaiian Sugar Planters Association. The planters felt that, having made Hawaii a paradise, they should rule because they had "right on their side." The Baldwin family of Maui *was* the government, with such supporters as the Rice family, which controlled Kauai, and William (Doc) Hill of Hawaii. These were the preeminent families of the islands; all were represented on the boards of the Big Five corporations that ruled Hawaii economically by controlling sugar, transportation, refining, and utilities. An early native politician was Prince Jonah Kuhio Kalanianaole, a brother to Liliuokalani, who joined with the Republicans to gain perks for himself and for his own people. Nepotism and political hoopla was the order of those days. The Republicans, in coalition with the native Hawaiians, maintained a majority over the large racial groups such as the Japanese and Filipinos who, left to their own devices, would have been Democrats. The Republicans also used unfair literacy laws, land ownership qualifications, and proof of birth in Hawaii to control the large numbers of immigrant workers who could threaten their ruling position. It was even alleged that during elections a pencil

The Hawaii State Seal. The translated motto reads "The life of the land is preserved in righteousness." It was uttered by Kamehameha III in July 1843 when Hawaiian sovereignty was restored by a joint declaration by France and Great Britain after a brief period in which Hawaii was under British rule.

was hung on a string over the Republican ballot: if a person wanted to vote Democratic he would have to pull the string to reach the other side of the voting booth. The tell-tale angle would give him away. He would be unemployed the next day.

The Democrats Rise To Power

The Democrats were plagued with poor leadership and internal factionalism in the early years. Their first real rise to power began in 1935 when the International Longshoremen's and Warehousemen's Union (ILWU) formed a branch in Hilo on the Big Island. In 1937, an incident known as the "Hilo Massacre" occurred when policemen fired on and wounded 25 striking stevedores, which was the catalyst needed to bind labor together. Thereafter, the ILWU, under the leadership of Jack Hall, became a major factor in the Democratic party. Their relationship was strained in later years when the ILWU was linked to Communism, but during the early days, whomever the ILWU supported in the Democratic Party won. The Democrats began to take over after WW II when returning Japanese servicemen became active in politics. The Japanese by this time were the largest ethnic group in Hawaii. A central character during the late 1940s and '50s was Jack Burns. Although a *haole,* this simple man was known to be for "the people" regardless of their ethnic background. During the war as a police captain he made his views clear that he considered the Japanese to be exemplary Americans. The Japanese community never forgot this, and were instrumental in Burns' election as governor, both in 1962 and 1966. The majority of people in the Oriental ethnic groups in Hawaii tend to remain Democrat even after they have climbed the socio-economic ladder. The first special election after statehood saw the governorship go to the previously appointed Republican Governor William Quinn, and the lieutenant governorship to another Republican, James Kealoha, of Hawaiian-Chinese ancestry. The first congressman elected was Japanese-American, Democrat Daniel Inouye. Since then, every governor has been a Democrat and one out of every two political offices is held by a person of Japanese extraction. The present governor is John Waihee III, the first Hawaiian governor in the United States.

OFFICE OF HAWAIIAN AFFAIRS

In 1979, constitutional mandate created the Office of Hawaiian Affairs (OHA). This remarkable piece of legislation, for the first time since the fall of the monarchy in 1893, recognized the special plight of native Hawaiians. For 75 years, no one in government was eager to face the "native question," but since 1979, OHA has opened a Pandora's box of litigation and accusation. For example, in 1983, a presidential commission investigated U.S. involvement in the overthrow of Hawaii's last queen, Liliuokalani, to decide if the federal government owed reparations to her Hawaiian people. After listening to testimony from thousands attesting to personal family loss of land and freedom, complete with old deeds documenting their claims, the commission concluded that the U.S. was guiltless and that native Hawaiians have nothing coming from Uncle Sam. Jaws dropped, and even those opposed to native Hawaiian rights couldn't believe this "whitewash." Governor George Ariyoshi said

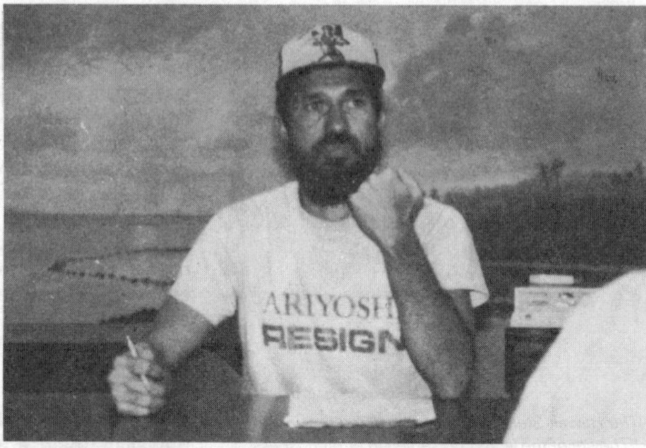

Walter Ritte, grassroots activist

in a newspaper interview, "A recent congressional study did not accurately portray what went on here at the turn of the century...To say that the monarchy was not overthrown...is something that I cannot accept. It is not historically true."

Trouble In Paradise

OHA, as the vanguard of native political activism, has focused on gaining monies guaranteed in the state constitution as recently as 1959 for "ceded lands." They have also been instrumental in regaining disputed Hawaiian lands and have helped in the fight to save the sacred island of Kahoolawe, which is now uninhabited and has been used as a bombing target since WW II. To simply state a complex issue, native Hawaiians have been eligible for benefits from revenues accrued from ceded lands and haven't been receiving them. These lands (1.8 million acres) were crown and government lands belonging to the Hawaiian monarchy and, therefore, to its subjects. When the kingdom was overthrown, the lands passed on to the short-lived Republic, followed by the U.S. Protectorate, and then finally to the state in 1959. No one disputed that these lands belonged to *the people,* who were entitled to money collected from rents and leases. For the last 26 years, however, these tens of millions of dollars have gone into a "general fund" used by various state agencies such as the Department of Transportation and the Department of Land and Natural Resources; the state is extremely reluctant to turn these funds over to what they derisively call an "unconstitutional special interest group." A major fight is expected at the Constitutional Convention scheduled for 1988.

Native Hawaiian Rights

The question has always been, "Just what is a native Hawaiian?" The answer has always been ambiguous. The government has used the "blood quantum" as a measuring stick. This is simply the percentage of Hawaiian blood in a person's ancestry—customarily 50% qualifies a person as *Hawaiian.* The issue is compounded by the fact that no other group of people has been so racially intermarried for so many years. Even though many people have direct ancestry to pre-Republic Hawaiians, they don't have enough "Hawaiianess" to qualify. An overwhelming number of these people fall into the category of "locals": they "feel" Hawaiian, but bloodwise they're not. They suffer all of the negativity of second-class citizens and reap none of the benefits accorded Hawaiians. Those that do qualify according to blood quantum don't have the numbers or the political clout necessary to get results. In fact, many people involved with OHA would not qualify themselves, at least not according to the blood quantum! Strong factionalism within the native Hawaiian movement itself threatens its credibility. Many people that do qualify by the blood quantum view the others as impinging on their rightful claims. The most vocal activists point out that only a coalition of people that have Hawaiian blood, combined with those who "identify" with the movement, will get results. Walter Ritte, a political firebrand and OHA trustee from Molokai, says that "anti-Hawaiian rights" lobbyists such as the tourist industry, airlines, large corporations, etc. are now stronger than the Hawaiians. Ritte advises that the only way the Hawaiian rights movement can win is to become active "political warriors" and vote for legislators that will support their cause. The rhetoric of OHA is reminiscent of the "equal rights movement" of the 1960s.

Obviously compromise is necessary. Perhaps certain social entitlements (such as tuition grants) could be equal for all, whereas money and land entitlements could be granted by percentages equal to the claiming persons actual "blood quantum." OHA members appeal directly to the Hawaiian people and can build political constituencies at a grassroots level. Since they are elected by the people and not appointed by the government (the case with the Hawaiian Home Lands Department and the trustees of the Bishop Estate, two other *supposedly* Hawaiian institutions), the status quo political parties of Hawaii are wary of them. Their candidates may be opposed and defeated in the future. What makes the issue even more ludicrous is that some of the state's most powerful corporate families opposed to Hawaiian rights have direct lineage to not only pre-Republic Hawaiian ancestors, but to Hawaiian royalty! They themselves would receive "entitlements" from the ceded land according to blood quantum, but socio-economically they are the natural enemies of OHA. The problem is difficult and it is improbable that all concerned will get satisfaction. OHA maintains offices at 567 S. King Street, Honolulu 96813. They publish a newspaper entitled *Ka Wai Ola O OHA* (The Living Waters of OHA), which is available upon request.

the hibiscus, Hawaii's state flower

ECONOMY

Hawaii's mid-Pacific location makes it perfect for two primary sources of income: tourism and the military. Tourists come in anticipation of endless golden days on soothing beaches, while the military is provided with the strategic position of an unsinkable battleship. Each nets Hawaii about $4 billion annually, which should keep flowing smoothly into the foreseeable future, increasing proportionally with the times. These revenues mostly remain aloof from the normal ups and downs of the Mainland U.S. economy. Together they make up 60% of the islands' income, and both attract either gung-ho enthusiasts or rabidly negative detractors. The remaining 40% comes in descending proportions from manufacturing, construction, and agriculture (mainly sugar and pineapples). As long as the sun shines and the balance of global power requires a military presence, the economic stability of Hawaii is guaranteed.

TOURISM

"The earthly paradise! Don't you want to go to it? Why, of course!" This was the opening line of *The Hawaiian Guide Book* by Henry Whitney that appeared in 1875. In print for 25 years, it sold for 60 cents during a time when a round-trip sea voyage between San Francisco and Honolulu cost $125. The technique is a bit dated, but the human desires remain the same: some of us seek paradise, all seek escape, some are drawn to play out a drama in a beautiful setting. Tourists have been coming to Hawaii ever since steamship service began in the 1860s. Until WW II, luxury liners carried the financial elite on exclusive voyages to the islands. By the 1920s 10,000 visitors a year were spending almost $5 million dollars—cementing the bond between Hawaii and tourism.

A $25,000 prize offered by James Dole of pineapple fame sparked a trans-Pacific air race in 1927. The success of these aerial daredevils proved that commercial air travel to Hawaii was feasible. Two years later, **Hawaiian Air** was offering regularly scheduled flights between all of the major islands. By 1950 airplanes had captured over 50% of the transportation market, and ocean voyages were relegated to "specialty travel," catering to the elite. By 1960 the large air-buses made their debut; 300,000 tourists arrived on eight designated airlines. The Boeing 747 began operating in 1969. These enormous planes could carry hundreds of passengers at reasonable rates, so travel to Hawaii became possible for the average-income person. In 1970, 2 million arrived, and by 1980 close to 4 million passengers arrived on 22 international air carriers. The first hotel in Honolulu was the **Hawaiian,** built in 1872. It was pre-dated by **Volcano House,** which overlooked Kilauea Crater on the Big Island, and was built in 1866. The coral-pink **Royal Hawaiian,** built in 1927, is Waikiki's graciously aging grand dame, a symbol of days gone by. As late as the 1950s it had Waikiki Beach almost to itself. Only 10,000 hotel units were available in 1960; today there are over 60,000, and thousands of condos as well.

Tourists: Who, When, And Where

Tourism-based income outstripped pineapples and sugar by the mid '60s and the boom was on. Long-time residents could even feel a physical change in air temperature: many trees were removed from Honolulu to build parking lots, and reflected sunlight made Honolulu much hotter and at times unbearable. Even the trade winds, known to moderate temperatures, were not up to that task. So many people from the outlying farming communities were attracted to work in the hotels that there was a *poi* famine in 1967. But for the most part, islanders knew that their economic future was tied to this "non-polluting industry." Most visitors (75%) are Americans, and the largest numbers come from the West Coast. Sun-seeking refugees from frigid Alaska, however, make up the greatest proportional number, according to population figures. The remaining arrivals are in descending order from Japan, Canada, Australia, and England. Europe, as a whole, sends proportionately less visitors than North America or Asia, while the least amount comes from South America. The Japanese market is constantly growing; by the year 1990 over a million Japanese visitors per year are expected. This is particularly beneficial to the tourist market because the average Western tourist spends about $90 per day, while his Japanese counterpart spends just over $200 per day. However, they stay only about 5 days, shorter than the typical visit. Up until very recently the Japanese traveled only in groups and primarily stayed on Oahu. Now the trend is to travel independently, or come with a group and then peel off, with a hefty percentage heading for the Neighbor Islands.

The typical visitor is slightly affluent, about 35, with 20% more women than men. The average age is a touch higher than most vacation areas because it reflects an inflated proportion of retirees heading for Hawaii, especially Honolulu, to fulfill a lifelong "dream" vacation. A typical stay lasts about 12 days, down from a month in the 1950s; a full 50% are repeat visitors. On any given day there are about 70,000 travelers on Oahu, 15,000 on Maui, and about 7,000 each on Kauai and Hawaii. Molokai and Lanai get so few that the figures are hardly counted. In 1964 only 10% of the islands' hotel rooms were on the Neighbor Islands, but by 1966 the figure jumped to 25%, with more than 70% of tourists opting to visit the Neighbor Islands. Today four out of 10 hotel rooms are on the Neighbor Islands and that figure should reach 50% shortly. The overwhelming number of tourists are on package tours, and the largest number of people congregate in Waikiki, which has a 74% average hotel occupancy and attracts two and a half times as many visitors as the Neighbor Islands together. Obviously, Waikiki is still most people's idea of paradise. Those seeking a more intimate experience can have it with a 20-minute flight from Oahu or a direct flight to Hilo (Hawaii) and now Maui and Kauai. Joaquin Miller, the 19th C. poet of the Sierras said, "I tell you my boy, the man who has not seen the Sandwich Islands, in this one great ocean's warm heart, has not seen the world." The times have certainly changed, but the sentiments of most visitors to Hawaii remain consistently the same.

Waikiki growing rice, c. 1920 (Hawaii State Archives)

Tourism-Related Problems

Tourism is both boon and blight to Hawaii. It is the root cause of two problems: one environmental, the other socio-economic. The environmental impact is obvious and best described in the lament of songstress Joni Mitchell's "they paved paradise and put up a parking lot." Simply, tourism can draw too many people to an area and overburden it. In the process, it stresses the very land and destroys the natural beauty that attracted people in the first place. Tourists come to Hawaii for what has been called its "ambient resource": a balanced collage of indulgent climate, invigorating waters, intoxicating scenery, and exotic people all wrapped up neatly in one area which can both soothe and excite at the same time. It is in the best interest of Hawaii to preserve this "resource."

Most point to Waikiki as a prime example of development gone mad. It is super-saturated, and amazingly enough, hotel owners themselves are now trying to keep development in check. Two prime examples of the best and the worst development can be found on Maui's south shore at Kihei and Wailea, less than five miles apart. In the late '60s Kihei experienced a development-inspired "feeding frenzy" that made the real sharks offshore seem to be about as dangerous as Winnie the Pooh. Condos were slapped up as fast as cement would dry and their architecture was as inspired as a stack of shoe boxes. They lined the coast renowned for its beauty, wiping out the view in the process. Anyone who had the bucks built, and now Kihei looks like a high-rise, low-income, federally funded housing project. You can bet those who made a killing building here don't live here. Just down the road, Wailea is a model of what development could and should be. The architecture is tasteful, low rise, nonobtrusive, and done with people and the preservation of the scenery in mind. It's obviously more exclusive, but access points to the beaches are open to everyone and the view is still there for all to enjoy. It points the way for the development of the future.

Changing Lifestyle

Like the land, humans are stressed by tourism. Local people, who once took the "Hawaiian lifestyle" for granted, become displaced and estranged in their own land. Some areas, predominantly along gorgeous beaches that were average- to low-income communities, are now overdeveloped with prices going through the roof. The locals are not only forced to move out, but often must come back as service personnel in the tourist industry and cater to the very people who displaced them. At one time the psychological blow was softened because, after all, the newcomers were merely benign tourists who would stay a short time, spend a wad of money, and leave. Today, condos are being built and a different sort of visitor is arriving. Many condo owners are in the above-average income bracket: well-educated businesspeople and professionals. The average condo owner is a mainlander who purchases one as a second or retirement home. These people are not islanders and have a tough time relating to the locals, who naturally feel resentment. Moreover, since they don't *leave* like normal tourists, they use all community facilities, find those special nooks and crannies for shopping or sunbathing that were once exclusively the domain of locals, and have a say as voters in community governments. The islanders become more and more disenfranchised. Many believe that the new order instigated by tourism is similar to what has always existed in Hawaii: a few from the privileged class being catered to by many from the working class. In a way it's an extension of the plantation system, but instead of carrying pineapples, most islanders find themselves carrying luggage, cocktails, or broiled fish. One argument, however, remains undeniable: whether it's people or pineapples, one has to make a living. The days of a little grass shack on a sunny beach aren't gone, it's just that you need a wallet full of credit cards to afford one.

THE MILITARY

Hawaii is the most militarized state in the Union: all five services are represented. Oahu is the headquarters of CINCPAC (Commander in Chief Pacific), which controls 70% of Earth's surface from California to the east coast of Africa and to both poles. The U.S. military presence dates back to 1887, when Pearl Harbor was given to the Navy as part of the "Sugar Reciprocity Treaty." The sugar planters were given favorable "duty-free" treatment on their sugar, while the U.S. Navy was allowed exclusive rights to one of the best harbors in the Pacific. In 1894, when the monarchy was being overthrown by the sugar planters, the USS *Boston* sent a contingency of marines ashore to "keep order," which really amounted to a show of force, backing the revolution. The Spanish-American War saw U.S. troops billeted at Camp McKinley at the foot of Diamond Head, and Schofield Barracks opened to receive the 5th Cavalry in 1909. Pearl Harbor's flames ignited WW II and there has been no looking back since then.

About 60,000 military personnel are stationed in Hawaii, with a slightly higher number of

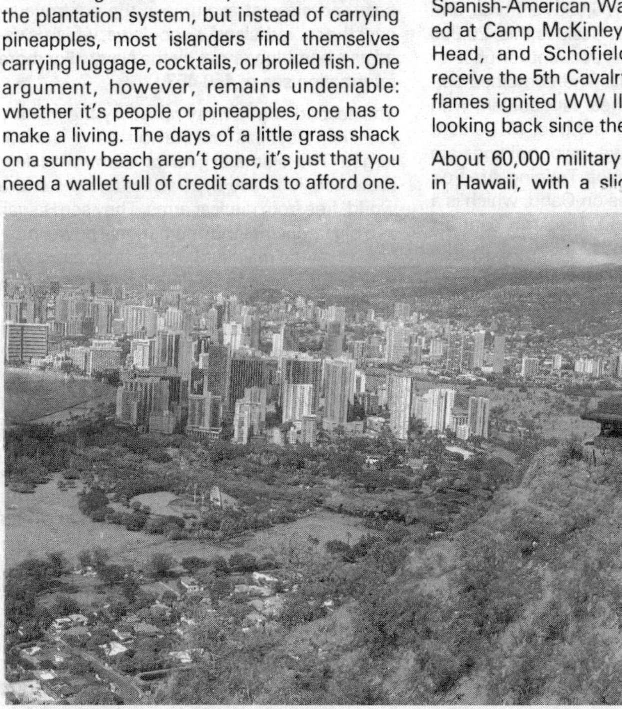

Waikiki growing high-rises, c. 1987

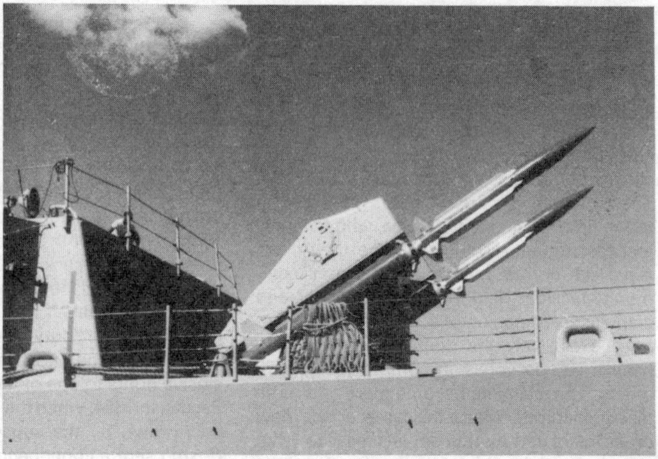

Nuclear missiles stand ready to defend America's unsinkable Battleship Hawaii.

dependents. The Navy and Marines combined have the most personnel with about 36,000 followed by 17,000 Army, 6,000 Air Force, and 1,000 or so Coast Guard. Besides this, 20,000 civilian support personnel account for 65% of all federal jobs in Hawaii. The combined services are one of the largest landholders with over 242,000 acres, accounting for six percent of Hawaiian land. The two major holdings are the 100,000-acre Pohahuloa Training Area on Hawaii and 100,000 acres on Oahu, which is a full 26% of the entire island. The Army controls 71% of the military lands, followed by the Navy at 25% and the remainder goes to the Air Force and a few small installations to the Coast Guard.

The Military Has No *Aloha*

Not everyone is thrilled about the strong military presence in Hawaii. Two factions, native Hawaiians and anti-nuclear groups, are downright angry. Radical contingencies of "native Hawaiian-rights groups" actually consider Hawaii to be an independent country, besieged and "occupied" by the U.S. government. They date their loss of independence to Liliuokalani's overthrow in 1894. The vast majority of ethnic Hawaiians, though they consider themselves Americans, are concerned with loss of their rightful homelands, with no financial reparation, and a continuing destruction and disregard for their traditional religious and historical sites. A long list of grievances is cited by native Hawaiian action groups, but the best and clearest example is the controversy over the sacred island, Kahoolawe, which is used as a bombing target by the Navy. (For more information see p. 450-453.)

The second controversy raised by the military presence focuses on Hawaii as a nuclear target. The ultimate goal of the anti-nuclear protestors is to see the Pacific, and the entire world, free from nuclear arms. They see Hawaii as a big target that the international power merchants on the mainland use as both pawn and watchdog. There is no doubt that Hawaii is a nuclear arsenal and the anti-nuke groups say that if war breaks out the Hawaiian Islands will be reduced to cinders. The military naturally counters that a strong Hawaii is a deterrent to nuclear war and that Hawaii is not only a powerful offensive weapon, but one of the best-defended regions of the world. Unfortunately, when you are on an island there is no place to go: like a boxer in a ring, you can run, but you can't hide. Anyone interested in the nuclear controversy can contact any of the following organizations: cAtholic Action of Hawaii, 1918 University Ave., Honolulu, HI 96822; U.S. Nuclear Free Pacific Network, 942 Market St., Rm. 711, San Francisco, CA 94102; or, *Kahuliau* ("an independent newspaper focusing on Hawaii and Pacific issues"), Box 61337, Honolulu, HI 96822.

SUGAR

Sugarcane *(ko)* was brought to Hawaii by its original settlers and was known throughout Polynesia. Its cultivation was well established and duly noted by Capt. Cook when he first sighted the islands. The native Hawaiians used various strains of sugarcane for food, rituals, and medicine. It was never refined, but the stalk was chewed and juice was pressed from it. It was used as food during famine, and as an ingredient in many otherwise unpalatable medicines, and especially as a love potion. Commercial growing started with a failure on Oahu in 1825, followed by a successful venture a decade later on Kauai. This original plantation, now part of the McBryde Sugar Co., is still productive. The industry received a technological boost in 1850 when a centrifuge, engineered by David Weston of the Honolulu Iron Works, was installed at a plantation on East Maui. It was used to spin the molasses out of the cooked syrup, leaving a crude crystal. Hawaii's biggest market has always been the mainland U.S. Demand rose dramatically during the California Gold Rush of 1849-50, and again a decade later during the American Civil War. At first Hawaiian sugar had a poor reputation that almost killed its export market, but with technological advances it became the best-quality sugar available last century.

Irrigation And Profit Politics

In 1876 the **Reciprocity Treaty** freed Hawaiian sugar from import duty. Now a real fortune could be made. One entrepreneur, **Claus Spreckles,** a sugar-beet magnate from California, became the reigning Sugar King in Hawaii. His state-of-the-art refineries on Maui employed every modern convenience, including electric lighting; he was also instrumental in building marvelous irrigation ditches necessary to grow sugar on once-barren land. The biggest hurdle to commercial sugarcane growing has always been water. One pound of sugar requires one ton of water, or about 250 gallons. A real breakthrough came when the growers reasoned that fresh water in the form of rain must seep through the lava and be stored underground. Fresh water will furthermore float atop heavier salt water and therefore be recoverable by a series of vertical wells and tunnels. By 1898, planters were tapping this underground supply of water and sugar could be produced in earnest as an export crop.

The Plantation System

Sugarcane also produced the plantation system, which was in many ways socially comparable to the pre-Civil War South. It was the main cause of the cosmopolitan mixture of races found in Hawaii today. Workers were in great demand, and the sugar growers scoured the globe looking for likely sources. Importing plantation workers started by liberalizing **The Masters and Servants Act;** this basically allowed the importation of conscripted workers. Even during its heyday, people with consciences felt that this system was no different from slavery. The first conscripts were Chinese, followed by Japanese, and then a myriad of people including other Polynesians, Germans, Norwegians, Spanish, Portuguese, Puerto Ricans, Filipinos, and even a few freed slaves from the southern U.S. (For further coverage see "People.") Today, grown on Oahu, Maui, Kauai, and Hawaii, yearly sugar sales

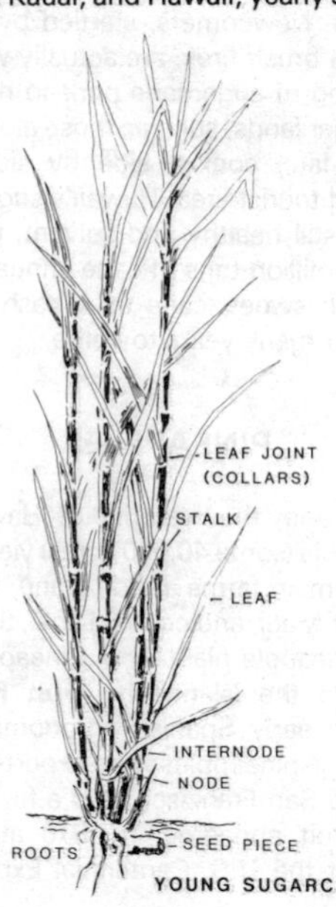

YOUNG SUGARCANE

The majority of plantation workers were of Oriental descent well into this century. (Fritz Craft)

reach $500 million. The state's 330 sugarcane-producing farms, and their attendant refineries, still employ a hefty amount of the islands' workforce. Newcomers, startled by what appear to be brush fires, are actually witnessing the burning of sugarcane prior to harvesting. Some sugar lands, such as those along Kaanapali on Maui, coexist side by side with a developed tourist area. Hawaii's sugarcane industry is still healthy and solvent, producing over nine million tons of cane annually. If profits remain sweet, cane as a cash crop will flourish for many years to come.

PINEAPPLES

Next to cane, the majority of Hawaii's cultivated lands (some 40,000 acres) yield pineapples. The main farms are on Oahu, the northwest tip of Maui, and central Lanai, the world's largest pineapple plantation. Pineapples were brought to the islands by **Don Francisco Marin,** an early Spanish agronomist, in the 1820s. Fresh pineapples were exported as early as 1850 to San Francisco, and a few cases of canned fruit appeared in 1876 at Hawaii's pavilion at the U.S. Centennial Exposition in Philadelphia. Old varieties of pineapples were pithier and pricklier than the modern variety. Today's large, luscious, golden fruits are the "smooth cayenne variety" from Jamaica, introduced by Capt. Kidwell in 1886.

Dole

But Hawaiian pineapple, as we know it, is synonymous with one man, **James Dole,** who actually *made* the industry at the turn of this century. Jim Dole started growing pineapples on a 60-acre homestead in Wahiawa, Oahu. He felt that America was ready to add this fruit to its diet and that "canning" would be the conveyance. By 1903, he was shipping canned fruit from his Iwilei plant and by 1920 pineapples were a familiar item in most American homes. Hawaii was at that time the largest producer in the world. In 1922, Jim Dole bought the entire island of Lanai, whose permanent residents numbered only about 100, and started the world's largest pineapple plantation. (For more information see "Lanai," p. 61.) By all accounts, Jim Dole was an exemplary human being, but he could never learn to "play ball" with the economic powers that ruled Hawaii, namely "The Big Five." They ruined him by 1932 and took control of his **Hawaiian**

Pineapple Company. Today, the Hawaiian pineapple industry is beleagured by competition from Asia, Central America, and the Philippines, resulting in the abandonment of many corporate farms. Hit especially hard was Molokai, where Del Monte shut down its operations in 1982. The other plantations are still reasonably strong, bringing in about 200 million dollars annually, but employment in the pineapple industry has dropped by 25% in the last decade, and there are strong doubts that these jobs will ever return.

OTHER AGRICULTURE

Every major food crop known can be grown in Hawaii because of its amazingly varied climates and rich soil. Farming ventures through the years have produced cotton, sisal, rice, and even rubber trees. Today, Hawaii is a major producer of the Australian macadamia nut, considered by some to be the world's most useful and delicious nut. The islands' fresh exotic fruits are unsurpassed, and juices and nectars made from papaya, passion fruit, and guava are becoming well known worldwide. Dazzling flowers such as protea, carnations, orchids, and anthuriums are also commercially grown. Hawaii has a very healthy livestock industry, headed by the Big Island's quarter-million-acre Parker Ranch, the largest singly owned cattle ranch in the U.S. Also poultry, dairy, and pork are produced on many farms. The only coffee grown in the U.S. is found on the slopes of Mauna Loa in the Kona district of the Big Island. "Kona coffee" is of gourmet quality and well regarded for its aroma and rich flavor. *Pakalolo* (see "Health-Drugs") is the most lucrative cash crop, but no official economic records exist. It's grown by enterprising gardeners on all the islands.

Hawaiian waters are alive with fish, but its commercial fleet is woefully small and obsolete. Fishing revenues amount to only $25 million per year, which is ludicrous in a land where fish is the obvious natural bounty. Native Hawaiians were masters of aquaculture, routinely building fishponds and living from their harvest. Where once there were hundreds of fish ponds, only a handful are in use today. The main aquaculture is growing freshwater prawns; the state is considered the world leader although there are less than 25 prawn farms operating at a yearly value of only $1.5 million. With all of these foodstuffs, unbelievable as it may sound, Hawaii must import much of its food. Hawaii can feed *itself,* but it cannot support the four million hungry tourists that come to sample its superb and diverse cuisine every year.

ECONOMIC POWER

Until statehood, Hawaii was ruled economically by a consortium of corporations known as **The Big Five: C. Brewer and Co.,** sugar, ranching, and chemicals, founded 1826; **Theo. H. Davies & Co.,** sugar, investments, insurance, and transportation, founded 1845; **Amfac Inc.,** originally H. Hackfield Inc. (a German firm that changed its name and ownership during the anti-German sentiment of WW I to American Factors), sugar, insurance, and land development, founded 1849; **Castle and Cooke Inc.,** (Dole) pineapple, food packing, and land development, founded 1851; and, **Alexander and Baldwin Inc.,** shipping, sugar, and pineapple, founded 1895. This economic oligarchy ruled Hawaii with a velvet glove and a steel grip.

With members on all important corporate boards, they controlled all major commerce including banking, shipping, insurance, hotel development, agriculture, utilities, and wholesale and retail merchandising. Anyone trying to buck the system was ground to dust, finding it suddenly impossible to do business in the islands. The Big Five was made up of the islands' oldest and most well-established *haole* families; all included bloodlines from Hawaii's own nobility and *ali'i.* They looked among themselves for suitable husbands and wives, so breaking in from the outside even through marriage was hardly possible. The only time they were successfully challenged prior to statehood was when Sears, Roebuck and Co. opened a store on Oahu. Closing ranks, the Big Five decreed that their steamships would not carry Sears' freight. When Sears threatened to buy its own steamship line, the Big Five relented. Actually, statehood, and more to the point, tourism broke their oligarchy. After 1960 too much money was at stake for Mainland-based corporations to ignore. Eventually the grip of the Big Five was loosened, but they are still enormously powerful and richer than ever, though unlike before, they don't control everything. Now, their power is land. With only five other major landholders, they control 65% of all the privately held land in Hawaii.

Land Ownership

Hawaii, landwise, is a small pie. Its slices are not at all well divided. There are 6,425 square miles of land, 98% of which make up the six main inhabited islands. This figure does not include Niihau, which is privately owned by the Robinson family and inhabited by the last remaining pure-blooded Hawaiians, nor does it include Kahoolawe, the uninhabited Navy bombing target just off Maui's south shore. Of the 4,045,511 acres that make up the inhabited islands 36% is owned by the state, 10% is owned by the federal government, and the remaining 54% is in private hands, but 40 owners with 5,000 or more acres own 75% of all private lands. Moreover, only 10 private concerns own two-thirds of these lands. To be more vivid, Castle and Cooke Inc. owns 99% of Lanai, while 40-60% of Maui, Oahu, Molokai, Kauai, and Hawaii are owned by less than 12 private parties.

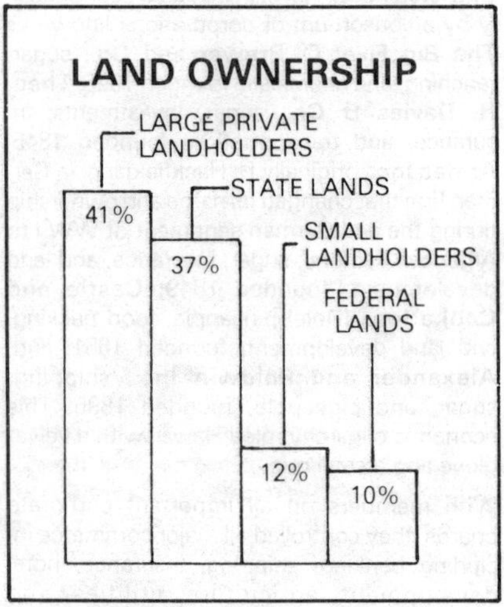

The largest private landowner is the Kamehameha Schools/Bishop Estate which recently lost a Supreme Court battle allowing the State of Hawaii to acquire privately owned land for "the public good." More than in any other state, Hawaiian landowners tend to lease land instead of selling it, and many private homes are on rented ground. This was the case with many homes rented from the Bishop Estate. The state acquired the land and resold it to long-term lease holders. These lands had previously earned a slow but steady profit for native Hawaiians. With land prices going up all the time, only the very rich land developers will be able to purchase long-term leases, and the "people" of Hawaii will become even more land poor.

"The land and industries of Hawaii are owned by old families and large corporations, and Hawaii is only so large."

—Jack London, c. 1916

Jacques Arago, c. 1819 (Hawaii State Archives)

THE PEOPLE

The people of Hawaii are no longer *in* the human race, they've already *won* it. Nowhere else on Earth can you find such a kaleidoscopic mixture of people. Every major race is accounted for, with over 50 ethnic groups adding not only their genes, but their customs, traditions, and outlooks. The modern Hawaiian is the future's "everyman": a blending of all races. Interracial marriage has been long accepted in Hawaii, and people are so mixed that it's already difficult to place them in a specific racial category. Besides the original Hawaiians, themselves a mixed race of Polynesians, people in the islands have multiple ancestor combinations from China, Japan, Korea, the Philippines, England, America, Norway, Russia, Germany, Scotland, Poland, Portugal, and Spain. There are American blacks, whose forebearers came just after the Civil War, Puerto Ricans, a hefty group of American Samoans, a few thousand American Indians, and recent Vietnamese refugees. Hawaii is the most racially integrated state in the Union, and although the newest, it epitomizes the time-honored American ideal of the "melting pot" society.

THE ISSUE OF RACE

This polyracial society should be a model of understanding and tolerance, and in most ways it is, but there are still racial tensions. People tend to identify with one group, and though not openly hostile, they do look disparagingly on others. Some racial barbs maintain that the Chinese are grasping, the Japanese too cold and calculating, the *haoles* materialistic, Hawaiians lackadaisical, Filipinos emotional, etc. In Hawaii this labeling tendency is a bit modified because *people,* as individuals, are not usually discriminated against, but their *group* may be. Another factor is that individuals identify with a group not along strict blood lines, but more by a "feeling of identity." If a white/Japanese man married a Hawaiian/Chinese woman, they would be accepted by all groups concerned. Their children, moreover, would be what they chose to be and more to the point, what they "felt" like.

There are no ghettos as such, but traditional areas where people of similar racial strains live, and where outsiders are made to feel unwelcome. For example, the Wainae district of Oahu is considered a strong "Hawaiian" area where other people may meet with hostility; the Kahala area of Oahu mostly attracts upwardly mobile whites; on the plantation island of Lanai, Japanese managers don't live amongst Filipino workers. Some clubs make it difficult for non-whites to become members; certain Japanese, Chinese, and Filipino organizations attract only members from these ethnic groups; and Hawaiian *Ohana* would question any person seeking to join unless they had some Hawaiian blood. Generally, however, the vast majority of people get along with each other and mix with no discernible problems.

The real catalyst responsible for most racial acceptance is the Hawaiian public school system. Education has always been highly regarded in Hawaii; the classroom has long been integrated. Thanks to a standing tradition of progressive education, democracy and individualism have always been basic maxims taught in the classroom. The racial situation in Hawaii is far from perfect, but it does point the way to the future in which all people can live side by side with respect and dignity.

Who, What, And Where

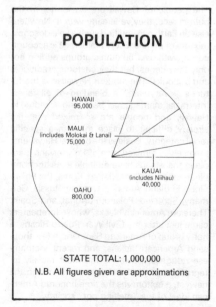

Hawaii has a population of one million, which includes 120,000 permanently stationed military personnel and their dependents. (All numbers used in this section are approximations.) It has the highest ratio of population to immigration in the U.S., and is the only state where whites are not the majority. White people are, however, the fastest growing group, due primarily to immigration from the West Coast. About 60% of Hawaiian residents were born there; 25% were born on the mainland U.S.; and 15% are foreign-born. The average age is 29, and men slightly outnumber the women. This is due to the large concentration of predominantly male military personnel, and to the substantial numbers of older, bachelor, plantation workers that came during the first part of this century and never found wives. The population has grown steadily in recent times, but has fluctuated wildly in the past. In 1876, it reached its lowest ebb with only 55,000 permanent residents. This was the era of large sugar plantations; their constant demand for labor was the primary cause for importing various peoples from around the world, and led to Hawaii's racially integrated society. WW II saw the population swell from 400,000 to 900,000. These 500,000 military personnel left at war's end, but many returned to settle after getting a taste of island living. Of the 1,000,000 people in the islands today, 800,000 live on Oahu, with 400,000 in the Honolulu metropolitan area. The rest are distributed as follows: 93,000 on Hawaii, with 36,000 in Hilo; 63,000 on Maui, the largest concentration around Wailuku/Kahului with 23,000; 40,000 on Kauai, including 230 pure-blood Hawaiians on Niihau; Molokai with 6,000; and Lanai with just over 2,000. The overall population density is 164 people per square mile, equal to that of California, with Honolulu claiming more than 1,400 people per square mile, and Maui the second most densely populated island with only 105 people per square mile. City dwellers outnumber those living in the country by 4 to one. The average household size ranges from just over one person in Honolulu, to 3.1 persons per household throughout the remainder of the state.

POPULATION

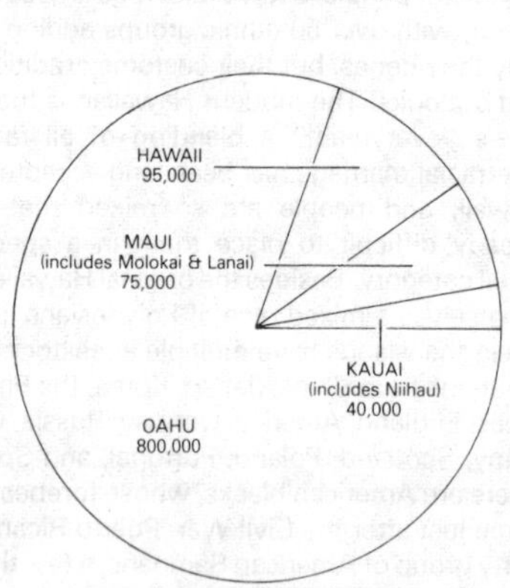

STATE TOTAL: 1,000,000

N.B. All figures given are approximations

THE HAWAIIANS

The drama of the native Hawaiians is a tragedy: it ends in their demise as a viable people. When Capt. Cook discovered Hawaii in 1778, an estimated 300,000 natives were living in harmony with their surroundings; within 100 years a scant 50,000 demoralized and dejected Hawaiians existed almost as wards of the state. Today, although 115,000 people claim varying degrees of Hawaiian blood, experts say that less than 1,000 can lay claim to being pure Hawaiian, and that's stretching it! A resurgence of Hawaiian ethnic pride is sweeping the islands as many people trace their roots and attempt to absorb the finer aspects of their ancestral lifestyle. It's easy to see why they could be bitter over what they've lost, since they're now strangers in their own land, much like American Indians. The overwhelming majority of Hawaiians are of mixed heritage, and the wisest take the best from all worlds. But from the Hawaiian side comes simplicity, love of the land, and acceptance of people. It is the Hawaiian legacy of *aloha* that remains immortal and adds that special elusive quality that "is" Hawaii.

Polynesian Roots

The Polynesians' original root stock is muddled and remains an anthropological mystery. It's believed they were nomadic wanderers who migrated from both the Indian subcontinent and SE Asia through Indonesia, where they learned to sail and navigate on protected waterways. As they migrated they honed their sailing skills until they could take on the Pacific, and absorbed other cultures and races until they coalesced into Polynesians. Abraham Fornander, still considered a major authority on the subject, wrote in his *Account of the Polynesian Race* (1885) that the Polynesians started as a white race, heavily influenced by contact with the Cushite, Chaldeo-Arabian civilization. He estimated their arrival in Hawaii at A.D. 600 based on Hawaiian genealogical chants. Modern science seems to bear this date out, but remains skeptical on his other surmises.

Thousands of years before Europeans even imagined the existence of a Pacific Ocean, Polynesians had populated the far-flung islands of the "Polynesian Triangle" stretching from New Zealand in the south, thousands of miles east to Easter Island, and finally to Hawaii, the northern apex. Similar language, gods, foods, and crafts add credibility to this theory. Other more fanciful versions are all long on conjecture and short on evidence. For example, Atlantis, the most "found" lost continent in history, pops up again, with the Hawaiians the supposed remnants of this advanced civilization. The slim proof is that the Hawaiian *kahuna* were so well versed in the curative arts that they had to be Atlantians. The theory holds that they not only made it to Hawaii, but also to the Philippines where their secret powers have been passed on the the faith healers of today. That the Hawaiians are the "lost tribe of Israel" is another theory, but this too is only wild conjecture.

The "Land Seekers"

The intrepid Polynesians who actually settled Hawaii are believed to have come from the Marquesas Islands, 1,000 miles south of Hawaii and a few hundred miles east. The Marquesans were cannibals known for their tenacity and strength, two attributes that would serve them well. They left their own islands because of war and famine; these migrations went on for centuries. Ships' logs mention Marquesan sea-going canoes setting sail in search of new land as late as the mid-19th century. The first navigator-explorers, advance scouting parties, were referred to as "land seekers." They were led northward by a few terse words sung in a chant that told a general direction and promised some guiding stars (probably recounting the wild adventures of canoes blown far off course that somehow managed to return to the southern islands of Polynesia). The land seekers were familiar with the stars, currents, habits of land birds, and countless other subliminal clues that are overlooked by "civilized" man. After finding Hawaii, they were aided in their voyage home by favorable trade winds and familiar waters. They set sail again in canoes laden with hopeful families and all the foodstuffs necessary to colonize a new land, anticipating a one-way ride with no return. Over the centuries, the fierce Marquesans mellowed into Hawaiians, and formed a new benevolent culture based on the fertility god Lono. Then, in the 12th C., a ferocious army of Tahitians invaded Hawaii and supplanted not only the ruling chiefs but also the gentler gods with their war-god Ku, who demanded human sacrifice. Abruptly, contact with Polynesia stopped. Some say the voyages, always fraught with danger, were no longer necessary. Hawaii was forgotten by the Polynesians, and the Hawaiians became the most rarified race in the world. It was to these people that Capt. Cook in 1778 brought the outside world. Finding Polynesians stretched so far and wide across the Pacific, he declared them to be "the most extensive nation upon earth."

The "Little People" Of Hawaii

The *Mu, Was, Eepas,* and *Waos* are all "little people" of Hawaii, but the most famous are the *Menehune.* As a group they resemble the trolls and leprechauns of Europe, but so many stories concern them that they appear to have actually existed in Hawaii at one time. Even in the late 18th C., an official census noted that King Kaumualii of Kauai had 65 *Menehune,* who were said to live in Wainiha Valley. Fighting among themselves, it's held that the

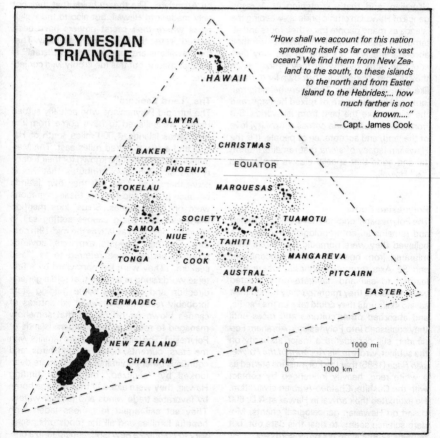

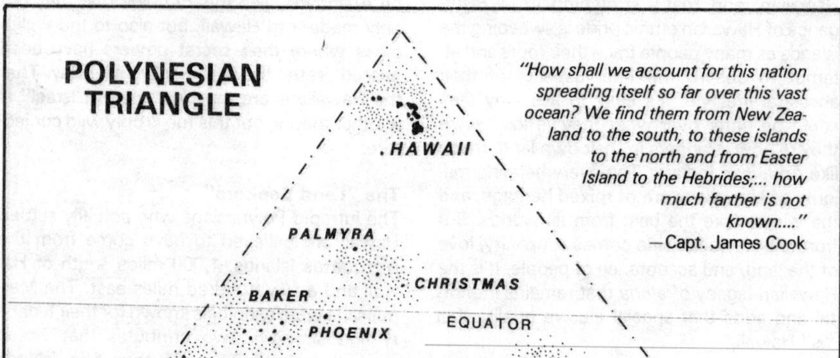

Menuhune drove out the *Mu* and the *Was.* They also differed slightly in appearance. The *Menehune* are about two to three feet tall with hairy, well-muscled bodies. Their red faces have thick noses, protruding foreheads, long eyebrows, and stringy hair. They love to frolic, especially by rolling down hills into the sea, and their favorite foods are shrimp and *poi.* They seldom speak, but their chatter sounds like the low growling of a dog. Nocturnal creatures, *Menehune* are frightened of owls and dogs. The *Mu* are mute, while the *Was* are noted for their loud blustering shouts. The *Mu* were thought to be black skinned and to live deep in the forest on a diet of bananas. All had their specialties, but the *Menehune* were stone masons par excellence. Many feats involving stonework are attributed to the *Menehune.* The most famous is the *"Menehune Ditch"* on Kauai. They finished their monumental tasks in one night, disappearing by daybreak. Even in the 1950s, masons building with stone near Diamond Head insisted that their work was disturbed at night, and a *kahuna* had to be called in to appease the *Menehune.* After that, all went well. In a more scientific vein, the Tahitian word for *Menehune* means "commoner." Many feel that they were non-Polynesian aboriginals who somehow made it to the islands, and co-mingled with Hawaiians until their chiefs became alarmed that their little race would vanish. (Mohikia and Analike are the respective names of a *Menehune* prince and princess who married Hawaiians and whose names have been preserved in legend.) The *Menehune* assembled en masse and supposedly floated away on an island called "Kuaihelani" that descended from the heavens. Some say that they headed for the far-flung outer islands of Necker and Nihoa, where, oddly enough, stone gods found there are unlike any on the other Hawaiian islands. But there the trail grows cold. Today, island mothers warn their misbehaving toddlers that the *Menehune* will come and take them away, but in most stories they are actually pixie-like and benign.

Point Of Contact

When Capt. Cook stepped ashore on Waimea, Kauai, on the morning of Jan. 20, 1778, he discovered a population of 300,000 natives living in perfect harmony with their surroundings. Their agrarian society had flourished in the last thousand years. When they had first arrived, Hawaii was a hostile and wind-blown place where only a few ferns and some wild birds were fit to be eaten. Fish were plentiful, but even the coconut, mainstay of the tropics, was missing. The Polynesians brought their staples of taro and breadfruit, sweet potatoes, coconuts, sugarcane, and bananas. They introduced and cultivated gourds for containers and even as armor, bamboo for a thousand uses, *ti* to wrap offerings and fashion *hula* skirts, paper mulberry to produce the intricate cloth-like *tapa,* and arrowroot and turmeric for flavorings. They also introduced pigs, a barkless dog, and chickens that were all relished as fine food. Also, the ubiquitous rat managed to stow away on their canoes and was transported to the islands.

The Demise Of Hawaiians

The ecological system of Hawaii has always been exceptionally fragile, its people included! When the white man came he found a great people who were large, strong, and virile, but when it came to fighting even minor diseases they proved as delicate as hot-house flowers. To exacerbate the situation, the Hawaiians were totally uninhibited in sex between willing partners. Unfortunately, the white sailors were laden with syphilis, gonorrhea, and all manner of germs and common European diseases. Captain Cook tried desperately to keep the sexually diseased members of his crew away from the Hawaiian women, but it was impossible. The *hospitality* of Hawaiian women was legendary, and promises of "paradise" were actually used as a lure to get sailors for perilous cruises into the Pacific that could last for years. When he returned from the north in less than one year, there were already natives with telltale signs of VD.

Fatal Flaws

Hawaiian women brought VD home, and it spread like wildfire. By the time the missionaries came in 1820 and halted the widespread fornication, native population was only 140,000, half of what it had been only 40 years

Native Hawaiians lived a more and more humble existence as times passed them by. (Fritz Craft, c. 1920)

after initial contact! In 1804 alone, perhaps 100,000 died from *okuu* (either typhoid or cholera). In the next 50 years measles, mumps, influenza, and tuberculosis further ravaged the people. In 1853 a smallpox epidemic ate further into the doomed and weakened Hawaiian race, and leprosy ranged far and wide in the land. In addition, during the whaling years, at least 25% of all able-bodied Hawaiian men sailed away, never to return. By 1880 King Kalakaua had only 48,000 Hawaiian subjects, a cata clysmic decrease of 82% of the original population. Wherever the king went, he would beseech his people, *"Hooulu lahui,"* ("increase the race,") but it was already too late. Nature herself had turned her back on these once-proud people. Many of their marriages were barren and in 1874 when only 1,400 children were born, a full 75% died in infancy. The final coup de grace was intermarriage. With so many inter-racial marriages, the Hawaiians literally bred themselves out of existence.

Painful Adjustments

The old paternalism inherent in the Hawaiian caste system was carried on by the ruling *haole* families of the last century. The remaining Hawaiians looked to the ruling class of whites like they had to their own *ali'i,* and for many years this attitude discouraged self help. Many Hawaiians fervently accepted the Christianity that had supplanted their own religion because it was a haven against a rapidly changing world in which they felt more and more alienated. Though Hawaiians did not make good plantation workers and were branded as lazy, they were actually hard and dedicated workers. Like all people attuned to their environment, they chose to work in the cool of the mornings and late afternoons, and could make no sense of laboring in the intense heat of the day. As fishermen they were unparalleled, and also made excellent cowboys on the ranches, preferring open ranges to the constricting plantation fields.

Hawaiians readily engaged in politics and were impressed with all the hoopla and fanfare. They would attend rallies, perform *hula* and songs, and in most instances sided with the whites against the Orientals. They were known to accept money for their votes and almost considered it the obligation of the leader, whom they regarded as a sort of chief, to grease their palms. Educated Hawaiians tended to become lawyers, judges, policemen, and teachers, and there are still a disproportionate number of Hawaiians, population-wise, in these fields. Hawaiians were racist toward the Japanese and Chinese. However, they would readily intermarry because, true to *aloha,* they accepted "people" even though they might be prejudiced toward their group. In 1910, although the native population was greatly reduced, there were still twice as many full-blooded Hawaiians as mixed bloods. By 1940 mixed-blood Hawaiians were the fastest growing group, and full bloods the fastest declining.

Hawaiians Today

Many Hawaiians moved to the cities and became more and more disenfranchised. Their folk society stressed openness and a giving nature, but downplayed the individual and the ownership of private property. These cultural traits made them easy targets for users and schemers. After repeated unfair treatment, they became either apathetic, or angry. About 116,000 people living in Hawaii have *some* Hawaiian blood. Most surveys reveal that although they number only 12% of the population, they account for almost 50% of the financially destitute families, arrests, and illegitimate births. Niihau, a privately owned island, is home to about 250 pure-blood Hawaiians, the largest concentration *per capita* in the islands. The Robinson family, which owns the island, restricts visitors to invited guests only. The second largest concentration is on Molokai, where 2,700 Hawaiians, living mostly on Hawaiian Homes Lands, make up 45% of the population. The majority, 80,000 or so, live on Oahu, where they are particularly strong in the hotel and entertainment fields. People of Hawaiian extraction are still a delight to meet, and anyone so lucky as to be befriended by one long regards this friendship as the highlight of his travels. The Hawaiians have always given their *aloha* freely and it is we that must accept it as a precious gift.

Aloha *still shows.*

THE CHINESE

Next to Yankees from New England, the Chinese are the oldest migrant group in Hawaii. Since the beginning, their influence has far outshined their meager numbers. They have long been the backbone in the small, privately owned retail trade. They brought to Hawaii, along with their individuality, Confucianism, Taoism, and Buddhism. Though many became Christians, the flavor of their Oriental traditions still lingers. The Chinese population of 57,000 makes up only 6% of the state's total, and the vast majority (52,000) reside on Oahu. Their key to success has been indefatigable hard work, the shrewdness to seize a good opportunity, and above all, an almost fanatical desire to educate their children. As an ethnic group they have the least amount of crime, the highest per capita income, a disproportionate number of professionals, and remain some of Hawaii's most prominent citizens.

The First Chinese

No one knows his name, but a Chinaman is credited with being the first person in Hawaii to refine sugar. This Oriental wanderer tried his hand at crude refining on Lanai in 1802. He failed, but other Chinese were operating sugar mills by 1830. Within 20 years, the plantations desperately needed workers, and the first Chinese laborers were 195 coolies from Amoy who arrived in 1852 under the newly passed Masters and Servants Act. These conscripted laborers were contracted for three to five years, and given $3 per month plus room and board. This was for 12 hours a day, six days per week—even in 1852 absolutely miserable wages. The Chinese almost always left the plantations the minute their contracts expired. They went into business for themselves and promptly monopolized the restaurant and small shop trade.

Bad Feelings

When they left the plantations, they were universally resented, due to prejudice, Chinese xenophobia, and their success in business. The first Chinese peddler in Honolulu was mentioned as early as 1823. The Chinese hated the plantations where they were cruelly treated, and the Chinese Consul in Hawaii was very conservative and sided with the plantation owners, giving his own people no support. When leprosy became epidemic in the islands, it was blamed on the Chinese. The Hawaiians called it *pake* disease, their derisive name for Chinamen (which oddly enough was an endearment in China meaning "uncle"). Although leprosy cannot be blamed solely on the Chinese, a boatload of Chinese immigrants did bring in smallpox in 1880. At the turn of the century, a smallpox epidemic broke out again in Honolulu's Chinatown (half the residents were really Japanese), and it was promptly burnt to the ground by the authorities. Amidst all this negativity, some intrepid souls prospered. The greatest phenomenon was Chun Afong who, with little more than determination, became a millionaire by 1857, raised 16 children, and almost single-handedly created the Chinese bourgeoisie in Hawaii. The Chinese were also responsible for making rice Hawaii's second most important crop from 1867 until 1872. It was Ah In, a Chinaman, who brought in the first water buffalo used to cultivate rice during this period.

The Chinese Exclusion Act

Although reforms on the plantations were forthcoming, the Chinese preferred the retail trade. In 1880 half of all plantation workers were Chinese, by 1900 10%, and by 1959, only 300 Chinese worked on plantations. When the "powers that were" decided that Hawaii needed compliant laborers, not competitive businessmen, the monarchy passed the Chinese Exclusion Act in 1886, forbidding any more Chinese contract laborers from entering Hawaii. Still, 15,000 more Chinese were contracted in the next few years. In 1900 there were about 25,000 Chinese in Hawaii, but

Many believed that the devastating Chinatown fire of 1900 was deliberately allowed to burn in order to displace the Chinese population of Honolulu. (Hawaii State Archives)

because of the Exclusion Act and other prejudices, many sold out and moved away. By 1910 their numbers were reduced to 21,000.

The Chinese Niche

Although most residents considered all the Chinese the same, they were actually quite different. The majority were two distinct ethnic groups from Kwangtung Province in southern China—the Punti made up 75% of the immigrants—and the Hakka made up the remainder. The Hakka had invaded Punti lands over 1,000 years previously and lived in the hills overlooking the Punti villages, never mixing. But in Hawaii, they mixed out of necessity. Few Chinese women came at first, so a Chinaman would gladly accept any Chinese woman as a wife, regardless of her ethnic background. The Chinese were also one of the first groups that willingly intermarried with the Hawaiians, and gained a reputation of being exceptionally caring husbands. By the 1930s, there was still resentment, but the Japanese were receiving most of the negative scrutiny by then, and the Chinese were firmly entrenched in the merchant class. Their thrift, hard work, and family solidarity had paid off. The Chinese accepted the social order and kept a low profile. During Hawaii's turbulent labor movements of the 1930s and '40s, the Chinese community produced *not one* labor leader, radical intellectual, or left-wing politician. When Hawaii became a state, one of the two first senators was Hiram Fong, a racially mixed Chinese. Since statehood, the Chinese community has carried on business as usual, as they continue to rise even further, both economically and socially.

THE JAPANESE

Conjecture holds that a few Japanese castaways, who floated to Hawaii long before Capt. Cook, introduced iron, which the islanders seemed to be familiar with before the white men arrived. Most scholars refute this claim and say Portuguese or Spanish ships lost in the Pacific introduced iron. Nevertheless, shipwrecked Japanese did make it to the islands. The most famous episode involved Jirokichi who, lost at sea for 10 months, was rescued by Capt. Cathcart of Nantucket in 1839. Cathcart brought him to Hawaii where he boarded with prominent families. This adventure-filled episode is recounted in the Japanese classic *Ban Tan* (Stories of the Outside World) written by the scribe Yuten-sei. The first *official* arrivals were a group of ambassadors sent by the *shogun* to negotiate with the U.S. in Washington. They stopped en route at Honolulu in March 1860, only 7 years after Commodore Perry and his famous "Black Ships" had roused Japan from its self-imposed 200-year slumber. A small group of Japanese plantation workers arrived in 1868, though mass migration was politically blocked for almost 20 years, and Japanese laborers didn't start coming in large numbers until 1886. King Kalakaua, among others, proposed that Japanese be brought as contract laborers in 1881; the thinking went that millions of Japanese subsistence farmers held promise as an inexhaustible supply of hard-working, uncomplaining, inexpensive, resolute workers. In 1886, when famine struck Japan, the Japanese government allowed farmers mainly from southern Honshu, Kyushu, and Okinawa to emigrate. Among these were members of Japan's little talked-about untouchable caste, called *eta* or *burakumin* in Japan and *chorinbo* in Hawaii. They gratefully seized this opportunity to better their lot, an impossibility in their homeland.

The Japanese Arrive

The first Japanese migrants were almost all men. Under Robert Irwin, the American agent for recruiting the Japanese, almost 27,000 Japanese came, for which he received a fee of $5 per head. The contract workers received $9 plus room and board, and an additional $6 for a working wife. This pay was for a 26 working-day month at 10 hours per in the fields or 12 hours in a factory. Between 1897-1908, migration was steady with about 70% men and 30% women arriving. Afterwards, the "Gentlemen's Agreement," a euphemism for racism against the "yellow peril," halted most immigration. By 1900 over 60,000 Japanese had arrived, constituting the largest ethnic group. Until 1907 most Japanese longed to return home and faithfully sent back part of their pay to help support their families. Eventually, a full 50% did return to Japan, but the others began to consider Hawaii their home and resolved to settle...if they could get wives! Between 1908 and 1924, "picture brides" arrived whose marriages had been arranged *(omiai)* by family members back home. These women clung to the old ways and reinforced the Japanese ethnic identity. Excellent plantation workers, they set about making their rude camps into model villages. They felt an obligation that extended from person to family, village, and their new country. As peasants, they were imbued with a feeling of a natural social order which they readily accepted...if treated fairly.

Changing Attitudes

Unfortunately some plantation *luna* were brutal, and Japanese laborers were mistreated, exploited, and made to live in indecent conditions on the plantations. In unusual protest, they formed their first trade union under Yasutaro Soga in 1908 and gained better treatment and higher wages. In 1919 an unsuccessful state-wide plantation strike headed by the Federation of Japanese Labor lasted 7 bitter months, earning the lasting mistrust of the establishment. By the 1930s, the Japanese, frustrated at being passed over for advancement because they were non-white, began to move from the plantations and opened retail stores and small businesses. By WW II they owned 50% of retail stores and accounted for 56% of household domestics. Many became small farmers, especially in Kona, where they began to grow coffee. They also accounted for Hawaii's fledgling fishing fleet and would brave the deep waters in their small, seaworthy sampans. Like the Chinese, they were committed to bettering themselves and placed education above all else. Unlike the Chinese, they did not marry outside their own ethnic group and, remained relatively racially intact.

Americans Of Japanese Ancestry (AJAs)

Parents of most Japanese children born in Hawaii before WW II were *issei* (first generation), who considered themselves apart from other Americans and clung to the notion of "We Japanese." They held traditional beliefs of unwavering family loyalty, and to propagate their values and customs they supported Japanese language schools, which 80% of their children attended before the war. This group, who were never "disloyal," were, however, "prideful" in being Japanese. Some diehards even refused to believe that Japan lost WW II and were shamed at their former homeland's unconditional surrender.

Their children, the *nissei* or second generation, were a different breed. In one generation they had become Americans through that basic melting pot called a schoolroom. They put into practice the high Japanese virtues of obligation, duty, and loyalty to the homeland—which was now, unquestionably, America. After Pearl Harbor was bombed, many people were terrified that the Hawaiian Japanese would be disloyal to America and would serve as spies and even as advance combatants for Imperial Japan. The FBI kept close tabs on the Japanese community, and the menace of the "enemy within" prompted the decision to place Hawaii under martial law for the duration of the war. Because of sheer numbers it was impossible to place the Hawaiian Japanese into concentration camps as was done in California, but prejudice and suspicion toward them, especially from Mainland military personnel, was fierce.

AJAs As G.I.s

Although Japanese had formed a battalion during WW I, they were insulted by being considered unacceptable as American soldiers in WW II. Those already in the armed services were relieved of any duty involving weapons. Those that knew better supported the AJAs. One was Jack Burns, a Honolulu policeman, who stated unequivocally that the AJAs were totally trustworthy. They never forgot his support, and thanks to a huge Japanese vote he was elected governor in 1963. Also, it has since been noted that not a single instance of Japanese sabotage, spying, or disloyalty was ever reported in Hawaii. Some American Japanese volunteered to serve in labor battalions, and because of their flawless work and loyalty, it was decided to put out a call for a few hundred volunteers to form a combat unit. Over 10,000 rushed to sign up!

AJAs formed two distinguished units in WW II—the *100th Infantry Battalion* and, later, the *442nd Regimental Combat Team.* They landed in Italy at Salerno and even fought from Guadalcanal to Okinawa. They distinguished themselves as *the* most decorated unit in American military history. They made excellent newspaper copy; their exploits hit front pages around the nation. They were immortalized as the rescuers of a Texas company pinned down during the Battle of the Bulge. These Texans became known as "The Lost Battalion" and have periodic reunions with the AJA G.I.s who risked and lost so much to bring them out to safety.

The Japanese GIs returned as "our boys."

The AJAs Return

The AJAs returned home to a grateful country. In Hawaii, at first, they were accused of being cocky. Actually, they were refusing to revert to the pre-war status of second-class citizens and began to assert their rights as citizens who had defended their country. Many took advantage of the G.I. Bill and received college educations. The "Big 5 Corporations" for the first time accepted former AJA officers as executives, and the "old order" began to wobble. Many Japanese became involved with Hawaiian politics, and the first elected member to Congress was Daniel Inouye, who had lost an arm fighting in the war. Hawaii's former governor, George Ariyoshi, was the country's first Japanese-American ever to reach such high office. Most Japanese, even as they climb the economic ladder, tend to remain Democrats.

Today, one out of every two political offices in Hawaii is held by a Japanese. In one of those weird quirks of fate, it is now the Hawaiian Japanese who are accused by other ethnic groups of engaging in unfair political practices, nepotism, and reverse discrimination. It's often heard that "if you're not Japanese, forget about getting a government job." Many of these accusations against AJAs are undoubtedly motivated by jealousy, but their record of social fairness is not without blemish, and true to their custom of family loyalty, they do stick together. There are now 240,000 people in Hawaii of Japanese ancestry, and making up 25% of the state's population. Heavily into the "professions," they're committed to climbing the social ladder. The AJAs of Hawaii are now indistinguishable from "the establishment," enjoy a higher standard of living than most, and are highly motivated to get the best education possible for their children. AJA men are the least likely to marry outside of their ethnic group.

CAUCASIANS

White people have a distinction from all other ethnic groups in Hawaii—they are all lumped together as one. You can be anything from a Norwegian dock worker to a Greek shipping tycoon, but if your skin is white, you're a *haole*.

What's more, you could have arrived at Waikiki from Missoula, Montana, in the last 24 hours, or your *kamaaina* family can go back 5 generations, but again, if you're white, you're a *haole*. The word *haole* has a floating connotation that depends upon the spirit in which it's used. It can mean everything from a derisive "honky or cracker" to nothing more than "white person." The exact Hawaiian meaning is clouded, but some say it meant "a man of no background," because white men couldn't chant a genealogical *kanaenae* telling the Hawaiians who they were. *Haole* then became euphemized into "foreign white man" and today simply "white person."

White History

Next to Hawaiians, white people have the oldest stake in Hawaii. Settlers in earnest since the missionaries of the 1820s, they were established long before any other migrant group. From last century until statehood old *haole* families owned and controlled everything, and although they were benevolent, philanthropic, and paternalistic, they were also racist. They felt (not without certain justification) that they had "made" Hawaii, and that they had the right to rule. Established *kamaaina* families, many of which made up the boards of the "Big 5" or owned huge plantations, formed an inner social circle closed to the outside except through marriage, and many managed to find mates from among close family acquaintances. Their paternalism, which they accepted with grave responsibility, at first only extended to the Hawaiians, who saw them as replacing their own *ali'i*. Orientals were considered primarily as "instruments of production." These supremacist attitudes tended to drag on until quite recent times. Today, they're responsible for the sometimes sour relations between white and non-white people in the islands. Since the *haole* had the power over all the other ethnic groups for so long, they offended each group at one time or another. Today, all white people are resented to a certain degree for these past acts, although they were in no way involved.

Members of the "Safety Committee" responsible for the overthrow of the monarchy were from respectable kamaaina *families and in effect the ruling caste of Hawaii at the turn of the century. (Hawaii State Archives)*

White Plantation Workers

In the 1880s, the white landowners looked around and felt surrounded and outnumbered by Orientals. Many figured that these people would one day be a political force to be reckoned with, so they tried to import white people for plantation work. Some of the imported workers included: 600 Scandinavians in 1881; 1,400 Germans 1881-85; 400 Poles 1897-98; and 2,400 Russians 1909-12. None worked. Europeans were accustomed to much higher wages and better living conditions than provided on the plantations. Although they were workers, not considered the equals of the ruling elite, they were expected to act like a special class, and were treated preferentially, meaning higher wages for the same job performed by an Oriental. Even so, they proved troublesome, unwilling to work under Oriental conditions, and were especially resentful of Hawaiian *luna*. Most moved quickly to the Mainland, and the Poles and Russians even staged strikes after only months on the job. A contingency of Scots, who first came as mule skinners and gained a reputation for hard work and frugality, became successful plantation managers and supervisors. There were so many on the Hamakua Coast of the Big Island that it was dubbed the "Scotch Coast." The

Germans and Scandinavians were well received and climbed the social ladder rapidly, becoming professionals and skilled workers. The Depression years, not as economically disastrous in Hawaii, brought more whites seeking opportunity. These new folks, many from the U.S. south and west tended to be even more racist towards brown-skinned people and Orientals than the *kamaaina haoles*. They made matters worse and competed more intensely for jobs.

The racial tension generated during this period came to a head in 1931 with the infamous **Massie Rape Case.** Thomas Massie, a naval officer, and his young wife Thalia attended a party at the Officers Club. After drinking and dancing all evening, they got into a row and Thalia rushed out in a huff. A few hours later, Thalia was at home, confused and hysterical, claiming to have been raped by some local men. On the most circumstantial evidence, Joseph Kahahawai and four friends of mixed ethnic background were accused. In a highly controversial trial rife with racial tensions, the verdict ended in a hung jury. While a new trial was being set, Kahahawai and his friends were out on bail. Seeking revenge, Thomas Massie and Grace Fortescue, Thalia's mother, kidnapped Joseph Kahawai with a plan of extracting a confession from him. They were aided by two enlisted men assigned to guard Thalia. While questioning Joseph, they killed him and attempted to dump his body in the sea but were apprehended. Another controversial trial—this time for Mrs. Fortescue, Massie, and the accomplices—followed. Clarence Darrow, the famous lawyer, sailed to Hawaii to defend them. For killing Kahahawai, these people served *one hour* of imprisonment in the judge's private chambers. The other four, acquitted with Joseph Kahahawai, maintain innocence of the rape to this day.

Later, the Massies divorced, and Thalia went on to become a depressed alcoholic who took her own life.

The Portuguese

The last time anyone looked, Portugal was still attached to the European continent, but for some anomalous reason they weren't con-

Portuguese plantation workers maintained their own ethnic identity.

sidered *haole.* This was because they weren't part of the ruling elite, but merely workers, showing that at one time *haole* implied social standing and not just skin color. About 12,000 arrived from 1878-87 and another 6,000 came from 1906-13. They were accompanied during the latter period by 8,000 Spanish, who were considered one in the same. Most of the Portuguese were illiterate peasants from Madeira and the Azores, while Spanish hailed from Andalucia. The majority of Spanish and some Portuguese tended to leave for California as soon as they made passage money. Those that remained were well received because they were white but not *haole* and made a perfect "buffer" ethnic group. Unlike other Europeans, they would take any job, worked hard, and accepted authority. Committed to staying in Hawaii, they rose to be skilled workers and the *luna* class on the plantations. However, the Portuguese spent the least amount on education and became very racist toward Orientals, seeing them as a threat to job security. By 1920 27,000 Portuguese made up 11% of the population. After that they tended to blend with the other ethnic groups and weren't counted separately. Portuguese men married within their ethnic group, but a good portion of Portuguese women married other white men and became closer to the *haole* group, while another large portion chose Hawaiian mates. Although they didn't originate pidgin English (see "Language"), the unique melodious quality of their native tongue did give pidgin that certain lilt it has today. Also, the *ukelele* ("jumping flea") was closely patterned after a Portuguese stringed folk instrument.

The White Population

Today all white people together make up the largest racial, if not ethnic, group in the islands at 33% (about 330,000) of the population. Percentage-wise, they are spread evenly throughout Kauai, Oahu, Maui, and the Big Island, with much smaller percentages on Molokai and Lanai. Numerically, the vast majority (260,000) live on Oahu, in the more fashionable central valley and southeastern sections. Heavy white concentrations are also found on the Kihei and Kaanapali coasts of Maui and the north Kona coast of Hawaii. The white population is also the fastest growing in the islands; most people resettling in Hawaii are white Americans predominantly from the West Coast.

FILIPINOS AND OTHERS

The Filipinos that came to Hawaii brought high hopes of making a fortune and returning home as rich heroes: for most this dream never came true. Filipinos were American nationals since the Spanish-American War of 1898, and as such weren't subject to the immigration laws that curtailed the importation of Oriental workers at the turn of the century. Fifteen families arrived in 1906, but a large number came in 1924 as strike breakers. The majority that came were illiterate Ilocano peasants from the northern Philippines with about 10% Visayans from the central cities. The Visayans were not as hard-working or thrifty, but much more sophisticated. From the first, Filipinos were looked down upon by all the other immigrant groups, considered particularly uncouth by the Japanese. They put the least value on education of any group and, even by 1930, only half could speak rudimentary English, while the majority remained illiterate. They were billeted in the worst housing, performed the most menial jobs, and were the last hired and first fired. One big deterrent keeping Filipinos from becoming a part of mainstream society was that they had no women to marry, and they clung to the idea of returning home. In 1930 there were 30,000 men and only 360 women. This hopeless situation caused a great deal of prostitution and homosexuality, and many of these terribly lonely bachelors would feast and drink on weekends and engage in their gruesome but exciting pastime of cockfighting on Sunday. When some did manage to find wives, their mates were inevitably part Hawaiians.

Tourists often mistake Filipinos for Hawaiians.

Today, there are still plenty of old Filipino bachelors who never managed to get home, and the Sunday cockfight remains a way of life. Filipinos constitute 14% (140,000) of Hawaii's population, with almost 90% living on Oahu. The largest concentration, however, is on Lanai, where 1,100 Filipino pineapple workers make up 50% of that island's population. Many of these men are new arrivals with the same dream held by their countrymen for over 70 years. Many visitors to Hawaii mistake Filipinos for Hawaiians because of their dark skin. This case of mistaken identity irritates Hawaiians and Filipinos alike although some street-wise Filipinos claim to be Hawaiians because being Hawaiian is *in,* and it goes over well with tourists, especially the young women. For the most part, these people are hard-working, dependable laborers who do tough jobs for little recognition. They still remain low man on the social totem pole and have not yet organized to stand up for their rights.

Minor Groups

About 10% of Hawaii's population is made up of a conglomerate of small ethnic groups. Of these, the largest is **Korean** with 14,000 people. About 8,000 Koreans came to Hawaii from 1903-05 when their own government halted emigration. When Japan annexed their homeland in 1910, most Koreans realized that their future lay in Hawaii, and they settled in. During the same period about 6,000 **Puerto Ricans** arrived, but they have become so assimilated that only 4,000 people in Hawaii today consider themselves Puerto Ricans. Two attempts were made last century to import other **Polynesians** to strengthen the dying Hawaiian race, but they were failures. In 1869, only 126 central Polynesian natives could be lured to Hawaii, and from 1878-85, 2,500 Gilbert Islanders arrived. Both groups became immediately disenchanted with Hawaii and could find no tangible reason to remain. They pined away for their own islands and departed for home as soon as possible. Today, however, 12,000 **Samoans** have resettled in Hawaii, and with more on the way are the fastest growing minority in the state. For unexplainable reasons, Samoans and native Hawaiians get along terribly, having the worst racial animosity of any groups. This is a true paradox, especially given the increased ethnic awareness of modern-day Hawaiians. The Samoans ostensibly should represent the archetypal Polynesians that the Hawaiians seek, but it doesn't work that way. Samoans are criticized by Hawaiians for their hot tempers, lingering feuds, and petty jealousies. They're clannish and are often the butt of "dumb" jokes. This racism seems especially ridiculous, but that's the way it is. Just to add a bit of exotic spice to Hawaii's people stew, there are about 10,000 **blacks,** a few thousand **American Indians,** and a smattering of **Vietnamese** refugees.

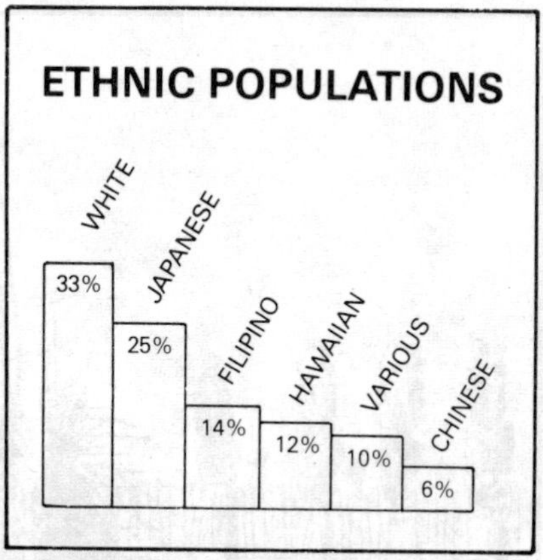

*"In what other land save this one is the commonest form of greeting not 'Good Day,'...but 'Love'? ...*Aloha...*It is the positive affirmation of one's own heart giving."*

—Jack London, 1916

ship's artist Wm. Ellis, c. 1791 (Hawaii State Archives)

RELIGION

The Lord saw fit to keep His island paradise secret from mankind for a few million years, but once we finally arrived we were awfully thankful. Hawaii sometimes appears like a floating tabernacle—everywhere you look there's a church, temple, shrine, or *heiau*. The islands are either very holy, or a powerful lot of sinning's going on to require so many houses of prayer. Actually, it's just America's "right to worship" concept fully employed...in microcosm. Everyone who came to Hawaii brought his own form of devotion. The Polynesian Hawaiians praised the primordial creators, Wakea and Papa, from whom their pantheon of animist-inspired gods sprang. Obviously, to a modern world these old gods would never do. There were simply too many, and belief in them was looked down upon as mere superstition, the folly of semi-civilized pagans. So, the famous missionaries of the 1820s brought Congregational Christianity and the "true path to heaven." Unfortunately, the Catholics, Mormons, Reformed Mormons, Adventists, Episcopalians, Unitarians, Christian Scientists, Lutherans, Baptists, Jehovah's Witnesses, the Salvation Army, and every other major and minor denomination of Christianity that followed in their wake brought their own brand of enlightenment. The Chinese and Japanese established all the major sects of Buddhism, Confucianism, Taoism, and Shintoism. Today, Allah is praised, the Torah is canted in Jewish synagogues, and nirvana is available at a variety of Hindu temples. If the spirit moves you, a Hare Krishna devotee will be glad to point you in the right direction and give you a free flower for only a dollar or two. If the world is still too much with you, you might find peace at a Church of Scientology, or meditate at a Kundalini Yoga institute, or perhaps find relief at a local assembly of Baha'i. Regardless, rejoice because in Hawaii you'll find not only paradise, you might even find salvation.

THE WATERS OF KANE

The Polynesian Hawaiians worshipped nature. They saw its forces manifested in a multiplicity of forms to which they ascribed god-like powers. Daily life was based on this animistic philosophy. Hand-picked and specially trained storytellers chanted the exploits of the gods. These ancient tales, kept alive in a special oral tradition called *moolelo,* were recited only by day. Entranced listeners encircled the chanter and, in respect for the gods and in fear of their wrath, were forbidden to move once the tale was begun. This was serious business where a man's life could be at stake; it was not like the telling of *kaao* which were simple fictions, tall tales of ancient heroes, merely related for amusement and to pass the long nights. Any object, animate or inanimate, could be a god. All could be infused with *mana,* especially a dead body or a respected ancestor. *Ohana* had personal family gods called *aumakua* on whom they called in times of danger or strife. Children of gods, called *kupua,* were thought to live among men, distinguished either for their beauty and strength or for their ugliness and terror. Hawaiian's believed that processions of dead *ali'i* called "Marchers of the Night" wandered through the land of the living, and unless you were properly protected it could mean death if they looked upon you. Simple ghosts known as *akua lapu* merely frightened people. Waterfalls, trees, springs, and a thousand forms of nature were the manifestations of *akua li'i* "little spirits" that could be invoked at any time for help or protection.

Behind all of these beliefs was an innate sense of natural balance and order, and the idea that everything had its opposite. The time of darkness when only the gods lived was *po.* When the great gods descended to Earth and created light, this was *ao,* and man was born. All of these *moolelo* are part of the *Kumulipo,* the great chant that records the Hawaiian version of creation. From the time that the gods descended and touched Earth at Ku Moku on Lanai, the genealogies were kept. Unlike the Bible, they included the noble families of both male and female *ali'i.*

Heiau **And Idols**

The basic *heiau* (temple) was a masterly built and fitted rectangular stone wall that varied in size from as large as a basketball court to the size of a football field. Once the restraining outer walls were built, the interior was backfilled with smaller stones, and the top dressing was expertly laid and then rolled, perhaps with a log, to form a pavement-like surface. All that remains of Hawaii's many *heiau* are the stone platforms. The buildings—made from perishable wood, leaves and grass—have long disappeared. At some dreaded *heiau* humans were sacrificed. Tradition says that this barbaric custom began at *Wahaula Heiau* on the Big Island in the 12th C., introduced by a ferocious Tahitian priest named Paao. Other *heiau,* such as *Puuhonua o Honaunau*, also on the Big Island, were temples of refuge where the weak, widowed, orphaned, and vanquished could find sanctuary. Within *heiau* ceremonies were conducted by the priestly *kahuna.* Offerings of chickens, dogs, fish, fruit, and *tapa* were laid on the *lele,* a huge stone altar, in hopes that the gods would act favorably toward their people. Some buildings held the bones of dead *ali'i,* infused with their *mana.* Other structures were god houses in which idols resided, while others were oracle towers from which prophecies were made. The gods were honored by *ali'i* and *makaainana* alike, but the *kahuna* prayed for the *ali'i,* while the commoners represented themselves. There was a patron god for every aspect of life, especially farming and fishing, but gods could be invoked for everything from weaving to a special god who helped thieves! Men and women had their own gods, with rituals governing birth, cutting the umbilical cord, death, and sickness. Ceremonies, often lasting for many days, were conducted by *kahuna,* many of whom had highly specialized functions. Two of the most interesting were: *kahuna kilikilo,* who could see a person die in a dream and save his life through offerings of white dogs, chickens, *tapa,* and *awa;* and, *kahuna kaula,* semi-hermits who could foretell the future.

All worshiped the gods in the form of idols, which were fashioned from wood, feathers, and stone. Some figures were over 6 feet tall, and crowned with elaborate head pieces. Figures were often pointed at the end so that they could be stuck into the ground. Until eyes, made from pearl shell, were fitted or carved, the idol was dormant. With eyes, it was alive! The hair used was often human hair, and the arms and legs were usually flexed. The mouth was either gaping or formed a figure 8 on its side, and usually lined with glistening dog teeth. Small figures were made of woven basketry expertly covered with red and yellow feathers taken from specific birds by men whose only work was to roam the forests in search of them. It made no difference who or what you were in old Hawaii, the gods were ever-present, and they took a direct and active role in your life.

GREAT GODS

Ku

The progenitors of the gods were Wakea, the "sky father," and Papa, the "earth mother," but the actual gods that were worshipped in Hawaii were Ku, Kane and Kanaloa, and Lono. Ku was a national god who represented the male aspect of nature, and Hina, the Moon Goddess, was its female counterpart. Ku was prayed to at sunrise and Hina at sunset. Ku's maleness was represented with pointed stones, while flat ones symbolized Hina's womanhood. Ku ruled the forest, land, mountains, farming and fishing—his benevolent side. But Ku was better known as the god of war. It was Ku that demanded human sacrifice, especially in times of calamity or in preparation for battle. At times, Ku was represented by an *ohia* log, and a human sacrifice was made in the forest where it was cut and also at the post hole that held it upright at the *heiau*. When Ku was invoked, the strict and serious ceremonies could go on for over a week. The entire *aha* (assembly) kept complete silence and sat ramrod straight with the ieft leg and hand crossed over the right leg and hand in an attitude called *neepu*. At a precise command everyone simultaneously pointed their right hand heavenward. Anyone caught dozing or daydreaming, or who for some reason missed the command, instantly became the main course for Ku's lunch. Kamehameha the Great carried a portable Ku into battle with him at all times, known as Kukailimoku ("the snatcher of lands"). It was held to be true that during battle this effigy, whose gaping mouth gleamed with canine incisors, would cry out in a loud voice and stir Kamehameha's warriors on to victory. After a battle, the slain enemies were taken to the *heiau* and placed upon Ku's altar with their arms encircling two pigs. Now Ku became Kuwahailo ("of the dripping maggot mouth"). With Ku's killing nature appeased, the people would pray for good crops, good fishing, and fertile wives. The scales were balanced and life went on.

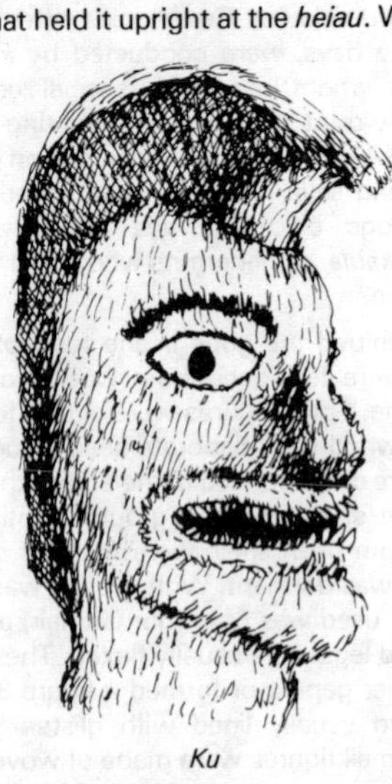

Ku

Kane And Kanaloa

Kane is the Hawaiian word for "man" or "husband," and he was the leading god of worship when the missionaries arrived. God of life, ancestor of all Hawaiians, the Hawaiian creation myth centers around Kane and, the events depicted are amazingly similar to Genesis. Kane comes forward from *po* (darkness) into *ao* (light), and with the help of Ku and Lono, fashions man from clay gathered from the four cardinal points of the compass. Once the body is formed, the gods breathe (some say spit) into the mouth and nostrils and give it life. The man is placed upon a paradise island, *Kalani i hauola,* and a wife is fashioned for him out of his right side. Like Adam and Eve, these two break the law by eating from the forbidden tree and are driven from paradise by the sacred white albatross of Kane.

Kane is a forgiving god, who demands no human sacrifice, because all life is sacred to him. He is a god of a higher order, not usually rendered as an idol. Instead he was symbolized as a single upright male stone that was splashed with oil and wrapped in white *tapa.* Kanaloa, the antithesis of Kane, was represented as a great squid, and often likened to the Christian devil. He warred with Kane and was driven out of heaven along with his minions. Kanaloa became the ruler of the dead, and was responsible for all "black" sorcery and for all poisonous things. Oftentimes however, these two gods were linked together. For example, prayers would be offered to Kane when a canoe was built and to Kanaloa to provided favorable winds. Farmers and diviners often prayed simultaneously to Kane and Kanaloa. Both gods were intimately connected to water and the narcotic beverage *awa.*

Pele

The Hawaiian gods were toppled literally and figuratively in 1819, and began to fade from the minds of men. Two that remained prominent were Madame Pele, Fire Goddess, who resides at Kilauea Volcano on Hawaii, and the demigod Maui who is like Paul Bunyan and Ulysses rolled into one. Many versions account for how Pele wound up living in Kilauea firepit, but they all follow a general outline. It seems that the beautiful young goddess, from a large family of gods, was struck by wanderlust. Tucking her young sister, who was conveniently in the form of an egg, under her armpit, she set out to see the world. Fortune had its ups and downs in store for young Pele. For one, she was ravished by a real swine, Kama pua'a the Pig God. Moreover, she fought desperately with her sister, Namaka o Kahai, over the love of a handsome young chief; Pele's sister stalked her and smashed her bones on the Hana coast of Maui at a spot called *Kaiwi o Pele* (the Bones of Pele). Pulling herself back together, Pele set out to make a love nest for her lover and herself. She chose the firepit at Kilauea Volcano and has long been held responsible for its lava flows along with anything else that deals with heat or fire. Pele can change her form from a withered old woman to a ravishing beauty; her moods can change from gentle to fiery hot. She is traditionally appeased with *ohelo* berries cast into her firepit, but lately she prefers juniper berries in the form of gin. Pele's myth was shattered by the Hawaiian queen Kapiolani, one of the earliest and most fervent converts to Christianity. In the 1820s this brave queen made her way to Kilauea fire pit and defiantly ate the *ohelo* berries sacred to Pele. She then cast stones into the pit and cried in a loud voice, "Jehovah is my god...it is my God not Pele that kindled these fires." Still, stories abound of Pele's continuing powers. Modern-day *kahuna* are always consulted and prayers offered over construction of an *imu,* which falls under Pele's fire domain. It's said by traditional Hawaiians and educated *haole* that when Kilauea erupts, the lava miraculously stops before or circles around a homestead over which proper prayers were made to the fire goddess. In addition, the rangers at Volcanoes National Park receive hundreds of stones every year that were taken as souvenirs and then returned by shaken tourists, who claim bad luck stalked them from the day they removed Pele's sacred stones from her volcano. And, no one who has lived in the islands for any length of time will carry pork over the volcano at night, lest they offend the goddess. She's perhaps still angry with that swine, Kama pua'a.

The Strifes Of Maui

Of all the heroes and mythological figures of Polynesia, Maui is the best known. His "strifes" are like the great Greek epics, and they make excellent tales of daring that elders loved to relate to youngsters around the evening campfire. Maui was abandoned by his mother, "Hina of Fire," when he was an infant. She wrapped him in her hair and cast him upon the sea, where she expected him to die, but he lived and returned home to become her favorite. She knew then that he was a born hero and had strength far beyond that of mortal men. His first exploit was to "lift the sky." In those days the sky hung so low that men had to crawl around on all fours. A seductive young woman approached Maui and asked him to use his great strength to lift the sky. In fine heroic fashion this big boy agreed if the beautiful woman would, euphemistically, "give him a drink from her gourd." He then obliged her by lifting the sky.

The territory of man was small at that time, and Maui then decided that more land was needed, so he conspired to "fish up islands." He descended into the land of the dead and petitioned an ancestress to fashion him a hook out of her jawbone. She obliged, and created the mythical hook *Manai ikalanai.* Maui then secured a sacred bird, the *alae* that he intended to use for bait. He bid his brothers to paddle him far out to sea, and when he arrived at the deepest spot, he lowered *Manai ikalanai* baited with the sacred bird. His sister, Hina of the Sea, placed it into the mouth of "Old One Tooth" who held land fast to the bottom of the waters. Maui then exhorted his brothers to row, but warned them not to look back. They strained at the oars, and slowly a great land mass rose. One brother, overcome by curiosity, looked back, and when he did so, the land shattered into all of the islands of Polynesia.

Maui desired to serve mankind further. People were without fire and the secret was held by the sacred *alae,* who had learned it from Maui's benificent ancestress. She had given Maui her burning fingernails, but he oafishly kept dropping them into streams until all had fizzled out, and he had totally irritated this generous relative. She pursued Maui trying to burn him to a cinder. Maui desperately chanted for rain to put out her scorching fires. When she saw her fires being quenched she hid her fire in the barks of special trees and informed common mud hens where they could be found, but first made them promise never to tell men. Maui learned of this, captured a mud hen, and threatened to wring its neck unless it gave up the secret. The bird tried trickery and told Maui first to rub together the stems of sugarcane, then banana and even *taro.* None worked, and Maui's determined rubbing is why these plants have hollow roots today. Finally, with Maui's hands tightening around the mud hen's neck, the bird confessed that fire could be found in the *hau* tree and also the sandalwood, which Maui named *ili aha* ("fire bark"). Maui then rubbed all the feathers of the mud hen's head for being so deceitful, and that's why their crown is featherless today.

Maui's greatest deed, however, was snaring the sun and exacting a promise that it would go slower across the heavens. The people had complained that there were not enough daylight hours to fish or farm. Maui's mother could not dry her *tapa* cloth because the sun rose and set so quickly. When she asked her son to help, Maui went to his blind grandmother for assistance. She lived on the slopes of Haleakala and was responsible for cooking the sun's bananas that he ate in passing every day. Maui kept stealing his granny's bananas until she agreed to help. She told him to personally weave 16 strong ropes and to make nooses out of his sister's hair. Some say these weavings came from her head, but other versions insists that it was no doubt Hina's pubic hair that had the power to hold "Sunny Boy." Maui positioned himself, and as each of the 16 rays of the sun came across Haleakala, he snared them until the sun was defenseless and had to bargain for his life. Maui agreed to free him if he promised to go more slowly. The sun agreed, and Haleakala ("The House of the Sun") became his home.

Lono And The Makahiki Festival

Lono was a benevolent god of the clouds, harvest, and rain. In a fit of temper he killed his wife, whom he thought to be unfaithful. When he discovered his grave error, he roamed the countryside challenging everyone he met to a boxing match. Boxing later became an event of the *Makahiki,* the Harvest Festival, held in his honor. Lono decided to leave his island home, but promised one day to return on a floating island. Every year at the beginning of *ho'oilo* (winter), starting in October, the *Makahiki* was held. It was a jubilant time of harvest when taxes were collected and most *kapu* were lifted. It ended sometime in February, and then began the New Year. During this time great sporting events included surfing, boxing, sledding, and a form of bowling. At night, people feasted at *luau* to the rhythm of drums and *hula.* Fertility was honored, and willing partners from throughout the land coupled and husbands and wives shared their mates in the tradition of *puna'lua.* Lono's idol was an *akua loa,* a slender 15-foot pole with his small image perched atop. Another pole fastened at the top formed a cross. Hanging from the cross pole were long banners of white *tapa* and it was festooned with the feathers and skins of sea birds. To this image the *kahuna* offered red and white fish, black coconut, and immature *awa.* This image, called "Long God," proceeded in a procession clockwise around the island. It was met at every *ahuapuaa* (land division) by the chief of that region and new *tapa* was offered by the chieftess along with roasted *taro*. The *makaainana* came and offered their produce from sea and land and so the taxes were collected. At the end of the festival a naked man representing the god Kohoali'i ate the eyeball of a fish and one of a human victim and proclaimed the New Year.

It was just during the *Makahiki* that Capt. Cook sailed into Kealakekua Bay! *Kahuna* saw his great "floating islands" and proclaimed the return of Lono. Uncannily, the masts of the sailing ships draped in canvas looked remarkably like Lono's idol. Cook himself was particularly tall and white skinned, and many natives at first sight fell to their knees and worshiped him as "Lono returned."

konane *board, Hawaiian checkers often played during* Makahiki

THE CASTE *(KAPU)* SYSTEM

All was not heavenly in paradise due to horrible wars, but mostly the people lived a quiet and ordered life based on a strict caste society and the *kapu* system. Famine was contained to a regional level. The population was kept in check by herbal birth-control potions, crude abortions, and infanticide, especially of baby girls. The strict caste system was determined by birth, which there was no chance of changing. The highest rank was the ***ali'i,*** the chiefs and royalty. The impeccable genealogies of the *ali'i* were traced back to the gods themselves, and recorded in chants *(mo'o ali'i)* memorized and sung by professionals called *ku'auhau.* Ranking passed from both father and mother, and custom dictated that the first mating of an *ali'i* be with a person of equal rank. After a child was produced, the *ali'i* was free to mate with lesser *ali'i* or even with a commoner. The custom of ***punalua,*** the sharing of mates, was practiced throughout Hawaiian society. Moreover, incest was not only condoned but sanctioned among *ali'i.* To achieve an offspring of the highest rank, *ni'au pi'o* ("coconut leaf looped back on itself"), the parents were required to be full brothers and sisters. These offspring were so sacred that they were considered an *akua* ("living god"), and people of all rank had to literally crawl on their stomachs in their presence. *Ali'i* that ran society were of lesser rank, and they were the real functionaries. The two most important were the land supervisors *(konohiki)* and caste priests *(kahuna).* The *konohiki* were in charge of the *ahua'pua,* pie-shaped land divisions running from mountain to sea. The common people came in contact with these *ali'i* who also collected taxes and ruled as judges amongst the people.

Kahuna were highly skilled people whose advice was sought before any major undertaking such as building a house, hollowing a canoe log, or even offering a prayer. The *mo'o kahuna* were the priests of *Ku* and *Lono,* in charge of praying and following rituals. These powerful *ali'i* kept strict secrets and laws concerning their various functions. The *kahuna* dedicated to *Ku* were severe: it was they that sought human sacrifice. The *kahuna* of Lono were comforting to the people, but were of lesser rank than the *Ku kahuna*. Other *kahuna* were not *ali'i* but commoners. The two most important were the healers *(kahuna lapa'au),* and the black magicians *(kahuna ana'ana),* who could pray a person to death. The *kahuna lapa'au* had a marvelous pharmacopia of herbs and spices that could cure over 250 diseases. They employed baths, massage and used

a royal woman of the Sandwich Isles as drawn by Jacques Arago, c. 1819 (Hawaii State Archives)

various colored stones to outline the human body and accurately pinpoint not only the organs but the internal origins of illness. The *kahuna ana ana* were given a wide berth by the people, who did everything possible to stay on their good side! The *kahuna ana ana* could be hired to cast a love spell over a person or cause his untimely death. They seldom had to send a reminder of payment!

The common people were called the ***maka'ainana,*** "people of the land." They were the farmers, craftsmen, and fishermen. Their land was owned by the *ali'i,* but they were not bound to it. If the local *ali'i* was cruel or unfair, the *maka'ainana* had the right to leave. Very unjust *ali'i* were even put to death by their own people, with no retribution if their accusations proved true. The *maka'ainana* mostly loved their local *ali'i,* and vice versa. *Maka'ainana* who lived close to the *ali'i* and could be counted on as warrior in times of trouble were called *kanaka no lua kaua,* "a man for the heat of battle." They were treated with greater favor than those who lived in the backcountry, *kanaka no hii kua,* whose lesser standing opened them up to discrimination and cruelty. All *maka'ainana* formed extended families ***(ohana)*** and usually lived on the same section of land *(ahuapua'a)* Inland farmers would barter their produce with fishermen, thus all shared equally in the bounty of the land and sea.

A special group ***(kauwa)*** was a landless untouchable caste confined to living on reservations. Their origins were obviously Polynesian, but they appeared to be remnants of castaways that had survived and become perhaps the aboriginals of Hawaii before the main migrations. It was *kapu* for anyone to go onto *kauwa* lands; doing so meant instant death. If a *kauwa* was driven by necessity to leave his lands, he was required to cover his head with *tapa* cloth, with his eyes focused on the ground in a humble manner. If a human sacrifice was needed, the *kahuna* simply summoned a *kauwa* who had no recourse but to mutely comply. Through the years after discovery by Cook, the *kauwa* became obscured as a class and mingled with the remainder of the population. But even to this day, calling someone *kauwa,* which now supposedly only means servant, is still considered a fight-provoking insult.

Kapu And Daily Life

A strict division of labor existed between men and women. Only men were permitted to have anything to do with *taro,* a foodstuff so sacred that it had a greater *kapu* than man himself. Men pounded *poi* and served it to the women. Men were also the fishermen and builders of houses, canoes, irrigation ditches, and walls. Women tended gardens and were responsible for making *tapa* and tending to shore-line fishing. The entire family lived in the common house *(hale noa).* But certain things were *kapu* between the sexes. The primary *kapu* was that women could not enter the *mua* (men's house) nor could they eat with men. Certain foods such as pork and bananas were forbidden to women. It was *kapu* for a man to have intercourse before going fishing, engaging in battle, or attending a religious ceremony. Young boys lived with the women until they underwent circumcision *(pule ipu),* after which they were required to keep the *kapu* of men. *Ali'i* could also declare a *kapu,* and often did so. Certain lands or fishing areas were temporarily made *kapu* so that they could revitalize. Even today, it is *kapu* for anyone to remove all the *opihi* (a type of limpet) from a rock. The great King Kamehameha I even placed a *kapu* on the body of his notoriously unfaithful child bride, Kaahumanu. It didn't work! The greatest *kapu (kapu moe)* was afforded to the highest ranking *ali'i:* anyone coming into their presence had to prostrate themselves. Lesser ranking *ali'i* were afforded the *kapu noho:* lessers had to sit or kneel in their presence. Commoners could not let their shadows fall upon an *ali'i* or enter their house except through a special door. Breaking a *kapu* meant immediate death.

Ghosts

The Hawaiians had countless superstitions and ghost legends, but two of the more interesting involve astral travel of the soul, and the "death marchers." The soul, *uhane,* was considered by Hawaiians to be totally free and independent of its body, *kino.* The soul could separate, leaving the body asleep or very drowsy. This disincorporated soul *(hihi'o)* could visit people, and was considered quite different from a *lapu,* an ordinary spirit of a dead person. A *kahuna* could immediately recognize if a person's *uhane* had left his body, and a special wreath was placed upon his head to protect them and to facilitate reentry. If a person was confronted by an apparition, he could test to see if it was indeed dead or still alive by placing leaves of an *ape* plant upon the ground. If the leaves tore when they were walked upon, the spirit was merely human, but if they remained intact it was a ghost. Also, you could sneak up and startle the vision and if it disappeared it was a ghost, or if no reflection of the face appeared when it drank water from an offered calabash, it was also a ghost. Unfortunately, there were no instructions to follow once you had determined that you indeed had a ghost on your hands. Maybe it was better not to know! Some people would sprinkle salt and water around their houses, but this only kept away evil spirits, not ghosts.

There are also many stories of *kahuna* restoring a soul to a dead body. First they had to catch it and keep it in a gourd. They then placed beautiful *tapa* and fragrant flowers and herbs about the body to make it more enticing. Slowly, they would coax the soul out of the gourd, which reentered the body through the big toe.

Death Marchers

One inexplicable phenomenon that many people attest to is *ka huakai o ka po,* "Marchers of the Night." This march of the dead is fatal if you gaze upon it unless one of the marchers happens to be a friendly ancestor that will protect you. The peak time for "the march" is from 7:30 p.m. till 2:00 a.m. The marchers can be

Punishment of a kapu-*breaker was harsh and swift. (Jacques Arago, Hawaii State Archives)*

dead *ali'i* and warriors, the gods themselves, or the lesser *aumakua*. When the *aumakua* march there is usually chanting and music. *Ali'i* marches are more somber. The entire procession, lit by torches, oftentimes stops at the house of a relative and might even carry them away. When the gods themselves march, there is often thunder, lightning, and heavy seas. The sky is lit with torches, and they walk 6 abreast, 3 gods and 3 goddesses. If you get in the way of a march, remove your clothing and prostrate yourself. If the marching gods or *aumakua* happen to be ones to which you prayed, you might be spared. If it's a march of the *ali'i* you might make it if you lie face upward and feign death. If you *do* see a death march, that last thing that you'll worry about is lying naked on the ground and looking ridiculous.

MISSIONARIES ONE AND ALL

In Hawaii when you say "missionaries," it usually refers to the small determined band of Congregationalists that arrived aboard the *Brig Thaddeus* in 1820 and the "companies or "packets" that reinforced them over the next 40 years. They were sent from Boston by the American Board of Commissioners for Foreign Missions (ABCFM), who learned of the "godless plight" of the Hawaiian people from returning sailors and from the few Hawaiians that had come to America to study. A young man named Opukahaia was instrumental in bringing the missionaries to Hawaii. An orphan befriended by a captain and taken to New England, he studied theology, and was obsessed with the desire to return home to save his people from sure damnation. His widely read accounts of life in Hawaii were the direct cause of the formation of the Pioneer Company to the Sandwich Islands Missions. Unfortunately, Opukahaia died in New England from typhus in 1819, the year before the missionaries sailed. The missionaries' first task was to Christianize and civilize. They met with extreme hostility—not from the natives, but from sailors and traders content with the open debauchery and wanton whoremongering that was the status quo in 1820s Hawaii. Many incidents of direct confrontation between these two factions even included the cannonading of missionary homes by American sea captains who were denied the customary services of island women thanks to the meddlesome "do gooders." Actually, the situation was much closer to the sentiments of James Jarves who wrote, "The missionary was a far more useful and agreeable man than his catechism would indicate; and the trader was not so bad a man as the missionary would make him out to be." The missionary's aim was conversion, but the fortuitous by-product was education that raised the consciousness of every Hawaiian regardless of his religious affiliation.

The American Board of Missions officially ended its support in 1863, and in 40 short years Hawaii was considered a civilized nation well on the road to modernity. Some of Hawaii's finest museums and grandest architecture are part of the missionary legacy. Some of the most notable are: Mokuaikaua Church in Kona,

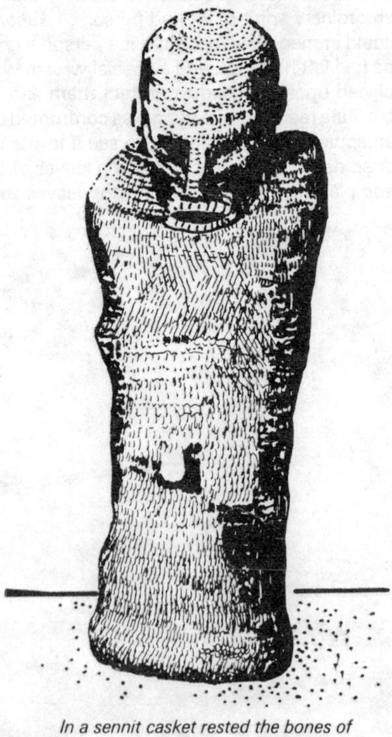

In a sennit casket rested the bones of the dead.

Rev. Hiram Bingham preaching at Waimea (Mission Houses Museum)

Hawaii, the first Christian church founded in 1820; the Lyman House Museum of Hilo; Kawaiahao Church in Honolulu, founded 1821, and next door the superb Mission Houses Museum; Wainee Church, the first stone church in Hawaii, founded in Lahaina in 1828, and the Baldwin Home just down Front Street; Lahainaluna High School and Printing House, the first American school and publishing house west of the Rockies. The churches, but especially the homes and museums, offer not only a glimpse of religious life, but are some of the finest "windows" into 19th C. America. Their collections of artifacts, utensils, and general memorabilia put life and times of 18th C. Yankees in a setting that could hardly be more different than New England.

Bonanza For Missionaries

Although the missionaries were the first, they by no means had the field to themselves. Hot on the same religious trail came the Catholics—French Sacred Hearts led by Father Bachelot who arrived in Honolulu in July 1827 aboard the *La Comete.* Immediately Queen Kaahumanu, who had been converted by the Congregationalists, ordered them to leave. They refused. For the next 10 years the Catholic priests and their converts met with open hostility and persecution which, in true missionary fashion, only strengthened their resolve. The humiliation of a young convert, Juliana Keawahine, who was tied to tree and scourged became a religious rallying point, and after this incident the persecutions stopped. Honolulu's Our Lady of Peace Cathedral was completed in 1843 and Ahuimanu Catholic School, Oahu's counterpart to Lahainaluna, opened for instruction in 1846. Today, Roman Catholicism with 290,000 adherents (29% of the state's total) is the single largest religious group in Hawaii.

The Saints Come Marching In

A strange episode in Hawaii's history involved the Mormons. In 1850, the Latter-Day Saints arrived direct from missionary work in California gold fields. By 1852, George Cannon had already translated the *Book of Mormon* into Hawaiian. The 5 original Mormon missionaries spent every moment traveling and converting the Hawaiians. They had a grand plan of constructing a "City of Joseph" on Lanai, where they managed to gain a large tract of land. In 1858 the Mormon Wars broke out in Utah and the missionaries were called home. One of their band, Walter Murray Gibson, who stayed to manage the fledgling Mormon Church, became one of the most controversial and singularly strange fixtures in Hawaiian politics. When the Mormons returned in 1864, they found that Gibson had indeed carried on the "City of Joseph," but had manipulated all of the deeds and land grants into his personal possession. Furthermore, he had set himself up as an omnipotent grand patriarch and openly denounced the polygamous beliefs of the Mormons of the day. Immediately excommunicated, the Mormons abandoned him to his fate and moved to Oahu where they founded a sugar plantation and temple in Laie. The Mormon Church now has approximately 32,000 members, the largest Protestant denomination in Hawaii. Their settlement at Laie is now home to an impressive Mormon Temple and an island branch of Brigham Young University. Close by, the Mormons also operate the Polynesian Culture Center which is one of the top 5 tourist attractions in all of Hawaii. As for Gibson, he was elected to the legislature in 1876 and became a private counselor to King Kalaukaua. In 1882, he worked himself into the office of "Premier" which he ran like a petty dictator. One of his more visionary suggestions was to import Japanese labor. Two of his most ridiculous were to drive all non-Hawaiians from the islands (excluding himself) and gather all Oceania into one Pacific nation with Hawaii in the lead. By 1887 he and Kalaukaua had so infuriated the sugar planters that Gibson was railroaded out of the islands and Kalaukaua was forced to sign a constitution that greatly limited his power. Gibson died in 1888 and his daughter Talulah sold the lands on Lanai for a song, after she and her husband tried but failed to grow sugarcane.

Non-Christian

By the turn of this century, Shintoism (brought by the Japanese) and Buddhism (brought by both the Japanese and Chinese) were firmly established in Hawaii. The first official Buddhist Temple was Hongpa Hongwanji, established on Oahu in 1889. Buddhist sects combined have about 170,000 parishinoers (17% of the islands' religious total); there are perhaps 50,000 Shintoists. The Hindu religion has 2,000 adherents, with about the same number of Jewish people living throughout Hawaii, though only one synagogue, Temple Emanuel, is on Oahu. About 10,000 people are in new religious movements and lesser-known faiths such as Baha'i and Unitarianism. The largest number of people in Hawaii (300,000) remain unaffiliated.

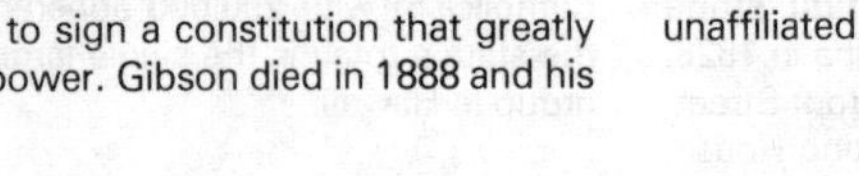

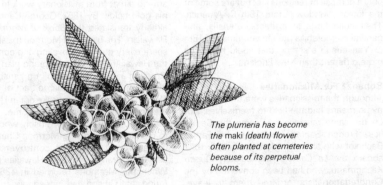

The plumeria has become the maki *(death) flower often planted at cemeteries because of its perpetual blooms.*

THE LANGUAGE

Hawaii is America and people speak English there, but that's not the whole story. On the TV evening news, you hear "Walter Cronkite" English, unless, of course, you happen to tune in a Japanese-language broadcast designed for tourists from that country. You can easily pick up a Chinese-language newspaper, or groove to the music on a Filipino radio station, but let's not confuse the issue. Wherever you happen to travel you will be completely understood in English. However, when you happen to overhear "islanders" speaking, what they're saying will sound somewhat familiar, but you won't be able to pick up all the words, and the beat and melody of the language will be noticeably different. Hawaii, like New England, the Deep South, and the Midwest, has its own linguistic regionalism. All the ethnic peoples who make up Hawaii have enriched the English spoken there with words, expressions, and subtle shades of meaning that are commonly used and understood throughout the islands. The greatest influence on English has come from the Hawaiian language itself, and words such as *aloha, kapu,* and *muumuu* are familiarly used and understood by most Americans. Other immigrants, especially the Chinese, Japanese, and Portuguese, influenced the local dialect to such an extent that the simplified plantation lingo that they spoke has become known as "pidgin." A fun and enriching part of the "island experience" is picking up a few words of Hawaiian and pidgin. English is the official language of the state, business, education, and perhaps even the mind; but pidgin is the language of the people, the emotions, and life, while Hawaiian remains the language of the heart and the soul.

PIDGIN

The dictionary definition of pidgin is: a simplified language with a rudimentary grammar used as a means of communication between people speaking different languages. Hawaiian pidgin is a little more complicated than that. It had its roots during the plantation days when white owners and *luna* had to communicate with recently arrived Chinese, Japanese, and Portuguese laborers. It was designed as a simple language of the here and now, and was primarily concerned with the necessary functions of working, eating, and sleeping. It has an economical noun-verb-object structure (not necessarily in that order). Hawaiian words make up most of pidgin's non-English vocabulary. There is a good smattering of Chinese, Japanese, Samoan, and the distinctive rising inflection is provided by the melodious Mediterranean lilt of the Portuguese. Pidgin is not a stagnant language. It's kept alive by hip new words introduced by people who are "so radical," or especially by slang words introduced by teenagers. It's a colorful English, like "jive" or "ghettoese" spoken by American blacks, and is as regionally unique as the speech of Cajuns from Louisiana's bayous. *Maka'aina* of all socio-ethnic backgrounds can at least understand pidgin. Most islanders are proud of it, while some consider it a low-class jargon. The Hawaiian House of Representatives has given pidgin an official sanction, and most people feel that it adds a real local style and should be preserved.

Pidgin Lives

Pidgin is first learned at school where all students, regardless of background, are exposed to it. The pidgin spoken by young people today is "fo' real" different from that of their parents. It's no longer only plantation talk, but has moved to the streets and picked up some sophistication. At one time there was an academic movement to exterminate it, but that idea died away with the same thinking that insisted on making left-handed people write with their right hand. It is strange, however, that pidgin has become the unofficial language of Hawaii's grassroots movement, when it actually began as a white owner's language which was used to supplant Hawaiian and all other languages brought to the islands. Although hip young *haole* use it all the time, it has gained

CAPSULE PIDGIN

The following are a few commonly used words and expressions that should give you an idea of pidgin. It really can't be written properly, merely approximated, but for now, *"brah, study da kine an' bimbye you be hele on, brah! O.K.? Lesgo."*

an' den—and then?; big deal; so what's next; how boring.

blalah—brother, but actually only refers to a large, heavy-set, good-natured Hawaiian man.

brah—all the bro's in Hawaii are brahs; other; pal. Used to call someone's attention. One of the most common words used even among people who are not acquainted. After a fill-up at a gas station, a person would say "Tanks, brah."

bimbye—after a while; bye and bye. "Bimbye, you learn pidgin."

cockaroach—steal; rip off. If you really want to find out what *cockaroach* means, just leave your camera on your beach blanket when you take a little dip.

da' kine—a catch-all word of many meanings that epitomizes the essence of pidgin. *Da' kine* is easily used as a euphemism for pidgin and is substituted whenever the speaker is at a loss for a word or just wants to generalize. It can mean: you know?; watchamacallit; of that type.

geev um—give it to them; give them hell; go for it. Can be used as an encouragement. If a surfer is riding a great wave, the people on the beach might yell, "Geev um, brah!"

hana ho—again; especially after a concert the audience shouts "hana ho" (one more!).

hele on—right on!; hip; with it; groovy.

howzit?—as in "howzit brah?"; what's happening; how is it going. The most common greeting, used in place of the more formal "How do you do?"

hu hu—angry! "You put the make on the wrong da' kine wahine brah, and you in da' kine trouble, if you get one big Hawaiian blalah plenty hu hu."

kapu—a Hawaiian word meaning forbidden. If *kapu* is written on a gate or posted on a tree it means "No trespassing." *Kapu*-breakers are still very unpopular in the islands.

lesgo—Lets go! Do it!

li'dis an' li'dat—like this or that; a catch-all grouping especially if you want to avoid details; like, ya' know?

lolo buggah—stupid or crazy guy (person). Words to a tropical island song go, "I want to find the lolo who stole my pakalolo (marijuana)."

mo' bettah—real good!; great idea. An island sentiment used to be, "mo'bettah you *come* Hawaii." Now it has subtly changed to, "mo'bettah you *visit* Hawaii."

ono—number one! delicious; great; groovy. "Hawaii is ono, brah!"

pakalolo—literally "crazy smoke"; marijuana; grass; reefer. "Hey, brah! Maui-wowie da' kine ono pakalolo."

pakiki head—stubborn; bull-headed.

pau—a Hawaiian word meaning finished; done; over and done with. *Pau hana* means end of work or quitting time. Once used by plantation workers, now used by everyone.

stink face—basically frowning at someone; using facial expression to show displeassure. Hard looks. What you'll get if you give local people a hard time.

swell head—burned up; angry.

talk story—spinning yarns; shooting the breeze; throwing the bull; a rap session. If you're lucky enough to be around to hear *kapuna* (elders) "talk story," you can hear some fantastic tales in the tradition of old Hawaii.

tita—sister, but only used to describe a fun-loving, down-to-earth country girl.

waddascoops—what's the scoop?; what's up?; what's happening?

some of the connotation of being the language of the non-white locals, and is part of the "us against them" way of thinking. All local people, *haole* or not, do consider pidgin their own island language, and don't really like it when it's used by *malihini* (newcomers). If you're in the islands long enough, you don't have to bother learning pidgin; it'll learn you. There's a book sold all over the islands called *Pidgin to da Max,* written by (you guessed it), a *haole* from Nebraska named Doug Simonson. You might not be able to understand what's being said by locals speaking pidgin (that's usually the idea), but you should be able to feel what's being meant.

HAWAIIAN

The Hawaiian language sways like a palm tree in a gentle wind. Its words are as melodious as a love song. Linguists say that you can learn a lot about people through their language: when you hear Hawaiian you think of gentleness and love, and it's hard to imagine the ferocious side so evident in Hawaii's past. With many Polynesian root words that are easily traced to Indonesian and Malayan, it's evident that Hawaiian is from this same stock. The Hawaiian spoken today is very much different from old Hawaiian. Its greatest metamorphosis occurred when the missionaries began to write it down in the 1820s. There is a movement to re-establish the Hawaiian language, and courses are offered in it at the University of Hawaii. Many scholars have put forth translations of Hawaiian, but there are endless, volatile disagreements in the academic sector about the real meanings of Hawaiian words. Hawaiian is no longer spoken as a language except on Niihau, and the closest tourists will come to it is in place names, street names and in words that have become part of common usage, such as *aloha* and *mahalo.* A few old Hawaiians still speak it at home and there are sermons in Hawaiian at some local churches. Kawaiahao Church in downtown Honolulu is the most famous of these. (See glossary for lists of commonly used Hawaiian words.)

Wiki Wiki Hawaiian

Thanks to the missionaries, the Hawaiian language is rendered phonetically using only

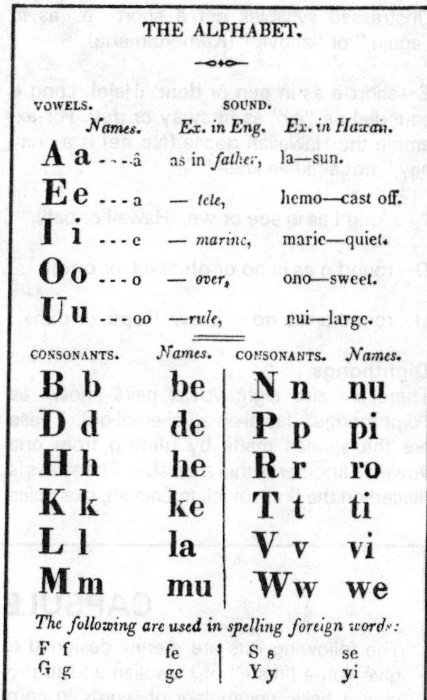

THE ALPHABET.

VOWELS.	Names.	SOUND. Ex. in Eng.	Ex. in Hawaii.
A a	â	as in *father,*	la—sun.
E e	a	— *tele,*	hemo—cast off.
I i	e	— *marine,*	marie—quiet.
O o	o	— *over,*	ono—sweet.
U u	oo	— *rule,*	nui—large.

CONSONANTS.	Names.	CONSONANTS.	Names.
B b	be	N n	nu
D d	de	P p	pi
H h	he	R r	ro
K k	ke	T t	ti
L l	la	V v	vi
M m	mu	W w	we

The following are used in spelling foreign words:

F f	fe	S s	se
G g	ge	Y y	yi

cover page of the first Hawaiian primer

12 letters. They are the five vowels, a-e-i-o-u, sounded as they are in Italian, and seven consonants, h-k-l-m-n-p-w, sounded exactly as they are in English. Sometimes "w" is pronounced as "v," but this only occurs in the middle of a word and always follows a vowel. A consonant is always followed by a vowel, forming two-letter syllables, but vowels are often found in pairs or even triplets. A slight oddity about Hawaiian is the "glottal stop." This is merely an abrupt break in sound in the middle of a word such as "oh-oh" in English, and is denoted with an apostrophe ('). A good example is *ali'i* or even better, the Oahu town of **Ha'iku** which actually means "abrupt break."

Pronunciation Key

For those unfamiliar with the sounds of Italian or a romance language, the vowels are sounded as follows:

A—in stressed syllables, long "a" as in "Ah" (that feels good!). (Hah lay ah kah lah.)

Unstressed syllables get a short "a" as in "again," or "above." (**Kame**ha**meha**).

E—short **e** as in p**e**n or d**e**nt. (Ha**le**). Long **e** sounded as "ay" as in sw**ay** or d**ay**. For example the Hawaiian goose **(Ne ne)** is a "nay nay," not a "knee knee."

I—a long **i** as in **see** or we. (Hawaii or pa**li**).

O—round **o** as in no or **oh**. (koa, or **ono**).

U—round **u** like **do** or **stew**. (kap**u**, or **pu**na).

Diphthongs
There are also eight vowel pairs known as "diphthongs" (ae-ai-ao-au-ei-eu-oi-ou). These are the sounds made by **gliding** from one vowel to another within a syllable. The stress is placed on the first vowel. In English, examples would be **soi**l and **eu**phoria. Common examples in Hawaiian are *lei* (lay) and *heiau*.

Stress
The best way to learn which syllables are stressed in Hawaiian is just by listening closely. It becomes obvious after a while. There are also some vowel sounds that are held longer than others and these can occur at the beginning of a word such as the first "a" in *aina* or in the middle of a word like the first "a" in *lanai*. Again, it's a matter of tuning your ear and paying attention. No one is going to give you a hard time if you mispronounce a word. It's good, however, to pay close attention to the pronunciation of street and place names because many Hawaiian words sound alike and a misplaced vowel here or there could be the difference in getting to where you want to go and getting lost.

CAPSULE HAWAIIAN

The following lists are merely designed to give you a "taste" of Hawaiian and to provide a basic vocabulary of words in common usage which you are likely to hear. Becoming familiar with them is not a strict necessity, but they will definitely enhance your experience and make it more congenial when talking with local people. You'll soon notice that many islanders spice their speech with certain words especially when they're speaking "pidgin," and you too can use them just as soon as you feel comfortable. You might even discover some Hawaiian words that are so perfectly expressive, that they'll become a regular part of your vocabulary. Many Hawaiian words have actually made it into the English dictionary. Place names, historical names, and descriptive terms used throughout the text may not appear in the lists below, but will be sited in the "Glossary" at the back of the book. Also see "Pidgin," "Food," and "Getting Around" for applicable Hawaiian words and phrases in these categories. The definitions given are not exhaustive, but are generally considered the most common.

BASIC VOCABULARY

a'a—rough clinker lava; *a'a* has become the correct geological term to describe this type of lava found anywhere in the world.
ae—yes
akamai—smart; clever; wise.
ali'i—a Hawaiian chief or nobleman.
aloha—the most common greeting in the islands. Can mean both hello and good-bye, welcome or farewell. It also can mean romantic love, affection or best wishes.
aole—no

(continued)

hale—house or building; often combined with other words to name a specific place such as Haleakala (House of the Sun), or Hale Pai at Lahainaluna meaning "printing house."

hana—work; combined with *pau* means end of work or quitting time.

haole—a word that at one time meant foreigner, but now means a white person or Caucasian. Many etymological definitions have been put forth, but none satisfy everyone. Some feel that it signified a person without a background, because the first white men could not chant their genealogies as was common to Hawaiians.

hapai—pregnant. Used by all ethnic groups when a *keiki* is on the way.

hapa—half, as in a mixed blooded person being referred to as *hapa haole*.

heiau—a traditional Hawaiian temple. A platform made of skillfully fitted rocks, upon which structures were built and offerings made to the gods.

holomu—a long ankle length dress that is much more fitted than a *muumuu*, and which is often worn on formal occasions.

hoolaulea—any happy event, but especially a family outing or picnic.

hoomalimali—sweettalk; flattery.

huhu—angry; irritated; mad.

huli huli—barbeque, as in *huli huli* chicken.

hula—a native Hawaiian dance where the rhythm of the islands is captured in swaying hips and the story is told by lyrically moving hands.

hui—a group; meeting; society. Often used to refer to Chinese businessmen or family members who pooled their money to get businesses started.

imu—underground oven filled with hot rocks and used for baking. The main cooking feature at a *luau* used to steam-bake the pork and other succulent dishes. Traditionally the tending of the *imu* was for men only.

ipo—sweetheart; lover; girl or boyfriend.

kalua—roasted underground in an *imu*. A favorite island food is *kalua* pork.

kamaaina—a child of the land; an old timer; a long time island resident of any ethnic background; a resident of Hawaii or native son. Oftentimes hotels and airlines offer discounts called *kamaaina rates* to anyone who can prove island residence.

kane—means man, but actually used to signify a relationship such as husband or boyfriend. Written on a door means "Men's Room."

kapu—forbidden; tabu; Keep out; Do not touch.

kaukau –slang word meaning food or chow; grub. Some of the best eating in Hawaii is from "kaukau wagons," which are trucks from which plate lunches and other morsels are sold.

keiki—child or children; used by all ethnic groups. "Have you hugged your *keiki* to-day?"

kokua—help. As in "Your *kokua* is needed to keep Hawaii free from litter."

kona wind—a muggy sub tropical wind that blows from the south and hits the leeward side of the islands. Usually brings sticky hot weather. One of the few times when air conditioning will be appreciated.

kapuna—a grandparent or old timer; usually means someone who has gained wisdom. The statewide school system now invites *kupuna* to talk to the children about the old ways and methods.

lanai—veranda or porch. You'll pay more for a hotel room if it has a *lanai* with an ocean view.

lei—a traditional garland of flowers or vines. One of Hawaii's most beautiful customs. Given at any auspicious occasion, but especially when arriving or leaving Hawaii.

limu—edible seaweed of various types. Gathered from the shoreline and makes

(continued)

an excellent salad. Used to garnish many island dishes and is a favorite at a *luau*.

lomilomi—traditional Hawaiian massage; also, raw salmon made up into a vinegared salad with chopped onion and spices.

lua—the toilet; the head; the bathroom.

luau—a Hawaiian feast featuring *poi, imu*-baked pork and other traditional foods. Good ones provide some of the best gastronomical delights in the world.

mahalo—thanks; thank you ; "mahalo nui", big thanks or thank you very much.

mahu—a homosexual; often used derisively like "fag" or "queer."

makai—toward the sea. Used by most islanders when giving directions.

malihini—what you are if you have just arrived. A newcomer; a tenderfoot; a recent arrival.

manauahi—free; gratis; extra.

manini—stingy; tight. A Hawaiinized word taken from the name of Don Francisco "Marin" who was instrumental in bringing many fruits and plants to Hawaii. He was known for never sharing any of the bounty from his substantial gardens on Vineyard Street.

mauka—toward the mountains. Used by most islanders when giving directions.

mauna—mountain. Often combined with other words to be more descriptive as *Mauna Kea*, (White Mountain).

moana—the ocean; the sea. Many businesses and hotels as well as place names have *moana* as part of their name.

muumuu—the garment introduced by the missionaries to cover the nakedness of the Hawaiians. A "mother hubbard"; a long dress with a high neckline that has become fashionable attire for almost any occasion in Hawaii.

ohana—a family; the fundamental social division; extended family. Now used to denote a social organization with "grass roots" overtones as in the "Save Kahoolawe Ohana."

okolehau—literally "iron bottom"; a traditional booze made from *ti* root; okole means your "rear end" and "hau" means iron, which was descriptive of the huge blubber pots that it was made in. Also, if you drink too much it'll surely knock you on your *okole*.

ono—delicious; delightful; the best. *Ono ono* means "extra or absolutely" delicious.

opu—belly; stomach.

pahoehoe—smooth ropey lava that looks like spilled and burned pancake batter. *Pahoehoe* is now the correct geological term used to describe this type of lava found anywhere in the world.

pakalolo—"crazy smoke;" marijuana; grass; smoke; dope.

pali— a cliff; precipice. Hawaii's geology makes them quite common. The most famous are the Pali of Oahu where a major battle was fought.

paniolo—a Hawaiian cowboy. Derived from the Spanish *espaniola.* The first cowboys brought in during the early 19th century were Mexicans from California.

pau—finished; done; completed. Often combined into *pau hana* which means end of work or quitting time.

pilau—stink; smells bad; stench.

pilikia—trouble of any kind, big or small; bad times.

pono—righteous or excellent.

poi—a glutinous paste made from the pounded corm of taro which ferments slightly and has a light sour taste. Purplish in color, and a staple at a *luau,* where it is called "one, two, or three finger" poi depending upon the thickness of it.

puka—a hole of any size. *Puka* is used by all island residents and can be employed when talking about a tiny *puka* in a rubber boat or a *puka* (tunnel) through a mountain.

punee— bed; narrow couch. Used by all ethnic groups. To recline on a *punee* on a breezy *lanai* is a true island treat.

(continued)

pupule—crazy; nuts; out of your mind.

pupu— appetizer; a snack; hors d'oeuvres; can be anything from cheese and crackers to *sushi.* Oftentimes, bars or nightclubs offer them free.

tapa—a traditional paper cloth made from beaten bark. Intricate designs were stamped in using beaters, and color was added with natural dyes. The tradition was lost in Hawaii, but is now making a come-back, and provides some of the most beautiful folk art in the islands

tutu—grandmother; granny; older woman. Used by all as a term of respect and endearment.

ukulele—literally *uku* means "flea" and *lele* means "jumping" or "jumping flea." The way the Hawaiians perceived the quick finger movements on the banjo-type Portuguese folk instrument called a *cavaquinha.* The ukelele quickly became synonymous with the islands.

wahine—young woman; female; girl; wife. Used by all ethnic groups. When written on a door means "Women's Room."

wai—fresh water; drinking water.

wela—hot. *"Wela kahao"* is a "hot time" or "making whoopy."

wiki—quickly; fast; in a hurry. Often seen as *wiki wiki* (very fast), as in "Wiki Wiki Messenger Service."

USEFUL PHRASES

aloha ahiahi—Good evening.

aloha au ia oe—I love you!

aloha kakahiaka—Good morning.

aloha nui loa—much love; fondest regards.

hauoli la hanau—Happy Birthday.

hauoli makahiki hau—Happy New Year.

komo mai—please come in; enter; welcome.

mele kalikimaka—Merry Christmas.

okole maluna—bottoms up; salute'; cheers; kampai.

The name is longer than the fish.

ARTS AND CRAFTS

Referring to Hawaii as "paradise" is about as hackneyed as you can get, but when you combine it into "artists' paradise" it's the absolute truth. Something about the place evokes art (or at least personal expression) from most people. The islands are like a magnet: they not only draw artists to them, but they draw art *from* the artists. The list of literary figures that have visited Hawaii and had something inspirational to say reads like a freshman survey in literature: William Dana, Herman Melville, Mark Twain, Robert Louis Stevenson, Jack London, Somerset Maugham, Joaquin Miller, and of course, James Michener.

The inspiration comes from the astounding natural surroundings. The land is so beautiful yet so raw; the ocean's power and rhythm is primal and ever-present; the riotous colors of flowers and fruit leap from the deep-green jungle background. Crystal water beads and pale mists turn the mountains into mystic temples, while rainbows come riding on the crests of waves. The stunning variety of faces begging to be rendered appears as if all the world sent a local delegation to the islands. And in most cases it did! Inspiration is everywhere as is art, good or bad.

Sometimes the artwork is overpowering in itself and in its sheer volume. Though geared to the tourist's market of cheap souvenirs, there is hardly a shop in Hawaii that doesn't sell some item that falls into the general category of "art." You can find everything from carved monkey-face coconut shells to true masterpieces. The Polynesian Hawaiians were master craftsmen, and their legacy still lives in a wide variety of woodcarvings, basketry, and weavings. The *hula* is art in swaying motion, and the true form is rigorously studied and taken very seriously. There is hardly a resort area that doesn't offer the "bump and grind" tourist's *hula* and even these revues are accompanied by proficient local musicians. Nightclubs offer "slack key" balladeers and island music made on *ukeleles,* and Hawaii's own steel guitars spills from many lounges. Vibrant fabrics, which catch the spirit of the islands are rendered into *muumuu* and aloha shirts at countless local factories. They're almost a mandatory purchase! Pottery, heavily influenced by the Japanese, is well developed at numerous kilns. Local artisans fashion delicate jewelry from coral and olivine, while some ply the whaler's legacy of etching, called scrimshaw. There is a fine tradition of quilt making, flower art in *lei,* and street artists working in everything from airbrush to glass. The following is an overview; for local offerings please see "Shopping" in the travel Chapters.

ARTS OF OLD HAWAII

Since everything in old Hawaii had to be fashioned by hand, almost every object was either a work of art or at least a highly refined craft. With the "civilizing" of the natives, most of the "old ways" disappeared, including the old arts and crafts. Most authentic Hawaiian art exists only in museums, but with the resurgence of Hawaiiian *roots,* many old arts are being revitalized, and a few artists are becoming proficient.

Magnificent Canoes

The most respected artisans in old Hawaii were the canoe makers. With little more than a stone adz and a pump drill, they built canoes that could carry 200 people and last for generations—sleek, well proportioned, and infinitely seaworthy. The main hull was usually a gigantic *koa* log, and the gunwale planks were minutely drilled and sewn to the sides with sennit rope. Apprenticeships lasted for years, and a young man knew that he had graduated when one day he was nonchalantly asked to sit down and eat with the master builders. Small family-sized canoes with outriggers were used for fishing, and perhaps carried a spear rack; large ocean-going double-hulled canoes were used for migration and warfare. On these, the giant logs had been adzed to about 2 inches thick. A mainsail woven from pandanus was mounted on a central platform, and the boat was steered by two long paddles. The hull was dyed with plant juices and charcoal, and the entire village helped launch the canoe in a ceremony called "drinking the sea."

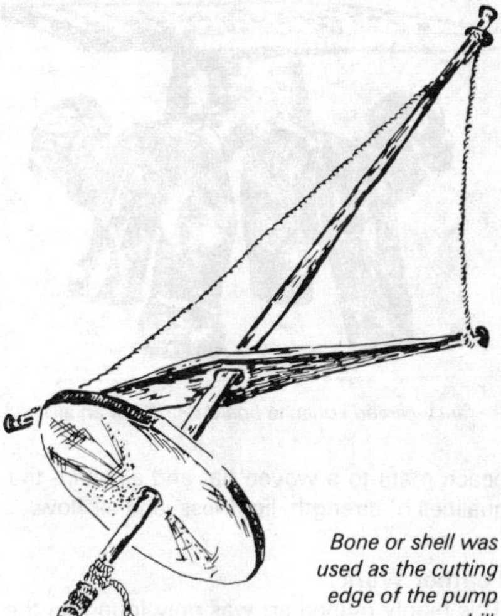

Bone or shell was used as the cutting edge of the pump drill.

Carving And Weaving

Wood was a primary material, and craftsmen turned out well-proportioned and distinctive calabashes. Made mostly from *koa,* the lustre and intricate grain was brought out with hand rubbing. Temple idols were a major product of woodcarving, and a variety of stone artifacts including *poi* pounders, mirrors, fish sinkers, and small idols were turned out. Hawaiians became the *best* basket makers and mat weavers in all of Polynesia. *Ulana* (mats) were made from *lau hala* (pandanus) leaves. Once split, the spine was removed and the leaves stored in large rolls. When needed they were soaked, pounded, and then fashioned into various floor coverings and sleeping mats. Intricate geometrical patterns were woven in, and the edges were rolled and well fashioned. Coconut palms were not used to make mats in old Hawaii, but a wide variety of basketry was made from the aerial root *ie'ie.* The shapes varied according to use. Some were tall and narrow, some were cones, others were flat like trays, while many were woven around gourds and calabashes. A strong tradition of weaving and carving has survived in Hawaii, and the time-tested materials of *lau hala* are still the best, although much is now made from coconut fronds. You can purchase anything from

fancy carved konanae *board worthy of an* ali'i

beach mats to a woven hat and all share the qualities of strength, lightness, and air flow.

Feather Work

This highly refined art was only found on the islands of Tahiti, New Zealand, and Hawaii, while the fashioning of feather helmets and idols was unique to Hawaii alone. Favorite colors were red and yellow, which came only in a very limited number on a few birds such as the *o'o, i'iwi, mamo,* and *apapane*. Professional bird hunters in old Hawaii paid their taxes to *ali'i* in prized feathers. The feathers were fastened to a woven net of *olona* cord and made into helmets, idols, and beautiful flowing capes and cloaks. These resplendent garments were made and worn only by men, especially during battle when a fine cloak became a great trophy of war. Featherwork was also employed in the making of *kahili,* and *lei* which were highly prized by the noble *ali'i* women.

Tapa Cloth

Tapa, cloth made from tree bark, was common throughout Polynesia, and was a woman's art. A few trees such as the *wauke* and *mamaki* produced the best cloth, but a variety of other barks could be utilized. First the raw bark was pounded into a felt-like pulp and beaten together to form strips. The beaters had distinctive patterns that also helped to make the cloth supple. They were then decorated by stamping, using a form of block printing, and dyed with natural colors from plants and sea animals, in shades of gray, purple, pink, and red. They were even painted with natural brushes made from pandanus fruit, with an overall gray color made from charcoal. The *tapa* cloth was sewn together to make bed coverings, and fragrant flowers and herbs were either sewn or pounded in to produce a permanent fragrance. *Tapa* cloth is still available today, but the Hawaiian methods have been lost, and most comes from other areas of Polynesia.

First Western Artists

When Capt. Cook made first contact in 1778, the ship's artists immediately began recording things Hawaiian. John Webber and James Clevely did etchings and pen and inks of Hawaiian people, structures, *heiau* and everyday occurrences that struck them as noteworthy or peculiar. William Ellis, ship's surgeon, also a fair hand at etching, was attracted to portraying native architecture. These three left a priceless and faithful record of what Hawaii was like at the moment of contact. Louis Choris, ship's artist with Otto Von Kotzebue in 1816, painted early portraits of King Kamehameha

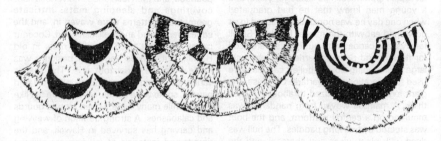

short feather capes for men of rank

and Queen Kaahumanu, the two grandest figures in Hawaii's history. Jacques Arago, aboard the *Uranie* with the French Captain de Freycinet in 1819, recorded some gruesome customs of punishment of *kapu* breakers, and made many drawings of island people. Robert Dampier who sailed on the *Blonde,* the ship that returned King Liholiho's body from England, recorded one of the earliest landscapes of Honolulu, which has continued to be depicted on film by more tourists than almost any other city on Earth. These early artists merely set a trend that continues unabated to this day; artists endeavour to "capture" Hawaii, and they do so with every artistic medium avilable.

Modern Masters

Countless artists working at all levels of accomplishment try to match their skills to the vigor and beauty of the islands. Some have set the standards, and their names have become synonymous with Hawaiian art. Heading this list of luminaries are Huc Luquiens, Madge Tennent, Tadashi Sato, Jean Charlot, and John Kelly. Madge Tennent (1889-1972) was an Englishwoman who came to Hawaii via Samoa after spending years in South Africa and New Zealand. She worked in oils that she applied liberally and in bold strokes. Enamored with the people of Hawaii, her portraits are of a race striking in appearance and noble in character. Her works, along with those of other island artists, are displayed at the Tennent Art Foundation, on the slopes of Punchbowl on Oahu. Huc Luquiens, former chairman of the Art Department at the University of Hawaii, was a master at etching, and especially accomplished in dry point. His works, mainly island landscapes, are displayed in the Hawaiiana Collection of the Honolulu Academy of Arts. Maui-born Tadashi Sato, a superbly accomplished muralist, has produced such famous mosaics as the 30-foot "Aquarius" at the State Capitol in Honolulu, and the 60-foot "Portals of Immortality" at the Maui Memorial Gymnasium in Lahaina. Frenchman Jean Charlot perfected his mural art in Mexico before coming to Hawaii in 1949. He is renowned for his frescoes and became a well-known art critic and the grand old man of Hawaiian art. He died in 1979 at the ripe old age of 90. John M. Kelly was in love with Hawaiian women; his etchings of them are both inspired and technically flawless. Kelly was infinitely patient, rendering his subjects in the minutest detail. These artists are the "Big 5 of Hawaiian Art"; their accomplishments should be seen as an "artistic gauge" of what Hawaii can inspire in an artist. By observing their works you can get an instant "art course" and comparative view of the state of the arts in Hawaii.

Contemporary Artists

The crop of new artists making their mark always seems to be bounteous and their works, heavily influenced by the "feeling of Hawaii," continue to be superb. Every island has art galleries, co-ops, or unofficial art centers. One of the finest groups of island artists can be found at the **Sunday Art Mart,** which recently changed its official name to **Artists of Oahu, Sunday Exhibit.** It's located along the "fence" of the Honolulu Zoo fronting Kapiolani Park. These artists along with others around the islands will be discussed in their respective travel chapters, so check. The following list of artists, with a short description of their work, is by no means exhaustive. It merely shows the wide range of artwork available.

Robert Nelson is a Maui artist who superbly transmits the integrated mystical life of land and sea. His watercolors are often diffused with the strange filtered light found beneath the waves. A conservationist, he has often depicted the gentle frolicking life of the whales that visit Hawaiian waters.

Bill Christian is a master of scrimshaw that he renders on slate. He also produces fine oil paintings of the sea and old salts. A world-class artist, his works are hung in art galleries on Maui as well as in the Smithsonian, and the New Bedford Massachusetts Whaling Museum.

Pegge Hopper is often compared with Madge Tennent. She works in bold colors and strokes. Her subject matter is islanders, especially the delicacy and inner strength of women. Her works are displayed at various galleries, especially on Maui and Oahu, and are often available in limited edition serigraphs.

John Costello, an Oahu artist, specializes in pointalism to captures the waves, women, and flora of Hawaii in a sensitive and mystical way. He co-owns and operates Kaala Art and Rainbow Island T's with his brother Jim in Haleiwa on North Shore Oahu. John's work as well as local artists are showcased in their small shop.

Alapai Hanapi is a traditionalist sculptor who tries to recreate the motifs of his Hawaiian ancestors. He works in wood and stone with tools that he fashions himself. His driving force is "cultural awareness" and through his art he tells of the old ways. He lives simply with his wife and three daughters near an old fish pond on eastern Molokai. His work is known for its simplicity and is available at art shows periodically held throughout the islands.

Joe Mathieu owns and operates Waipio Woodworks along with his four sons in Kukuihaele, Hawaii. They create authentic Hawaiian bowls and calabashes. Their favorite wood is traditional *koa,* but they also use monkey pod, melo, and even guava. His bowls can take 3 years to complete, mostly spent in perfectly drying the wood. In his gallery, all the artists displayed are from Hawaii. He features the work of Edwin Caton, Katherin Merrill who specializes in pottery, and various artists who turn in works ranging from stained glass to *batik.*

Robert "Woody" Woodward's van is his art gallery. He sets up just outside Huggo's Restaurant in Kona, Hawaii. He creates everything from fast $10 island sketches to in-depth canvases of a purely Hawaiian theme. Intimate with his surroundings, his pen and oils say "Kona" to anyone familiar with the area.

The Maui Crafts Guild in Paia, Maui, showcases some of the finest arts and crafts in the islands. All artists, required to use only natural materials, are juried by the other members of the co-op. There's basketwork by Mika, pottery by Vitarelli and Vijay, and free-form ceramics by Karen Jennings. The Crafts Guild also features stained glass, beadwork, silk clothing, jewelry, and delicate shell work. Once Touchstone Ceramics, a kiln is still maintained on the premises. Kathy, the founder of Touchstone, was instrumental in establishing the Maui Crafts Guild.

Hawaiian maiden by John Costello

Al Furtado is a freelance artist working in Honolulu. He specializes in capturing the movement of Hawaiian dance. His depictions are often larger than life with a strong sense of vitality and motion.

Daniel Wang was born in Shanghai where he learned the art of Chinese watercolors. Although born deaf and mute, he speaks loudly, clearly and beautifully through his art. Daniel has a special technique in which the palm of his hand becomes his artistic tool. He feels that he can transmit intense inner emotions directly from his body to the canvas.

The following is a *potpourri* of distinguished artists displayed at various galleries around the islands. Any work bearing their name is authentic island art considered to be superior by fellow artists. Satoru Abe, sculptor; Ruthadell Anderson, weaver; Betty Tseng Yu-ho Ecke, *dsui* painter; Claude Horan, sculptor, ceramics; Erica Karawina, stained glass; Ron Kowalke, painter; Ben Norris, painter; Louis Pohl, printmaker; Mamoru Sato, sculptor; Tadashi Sato, painter; Reuben Tam, painter; Jean Williams, weaver; John Wisnosky, painter; John Young, painter.

ARTS TO BUY

Alohawear

A wild Hawaiian shirt or a bright *muumuu,* especially when worn on the Mainland, has the magical effect of making the wearer "feel" like he is in Hawaii, while at the same time eliciting spontaneous smiles from passers by. Maybe it's the colors, or the vibe that says "hang loose," but nothing says Hawaii like alohawear does. More than a dozen fabric houses in Hawaii turn out distinctive patterns, and dozens of factories create their own designs. Oftentimes these factories have retail outlets, but in any case hundreds of shops sell alohawear.

Aloha shirts were the great idea of a Honolulu Chinese merchant who hand-tailored and sold them to tourists that arrived by ship in the glory days before World War II. They were an instant success. *Muumuus* or "Mother Hubbards" were the idea of missionaries who were scandalized by Hawaiian women running about *au natural,* and insisted on covering their new Christian converts from head to foot. Now the roles are reversed, and it's Mainlanders who come to Hawaii and immediately strip down to as little clothing as possible. Alohawear was at one time exclusively made of cotton or rayon. These materials are still the best for tropical wear, but slowly polyester has crept into the market. No material could possibly be worse than polyester for the island climate—check the label! *Muumuus* now come in various styles and can be worn for the entire spectrum of social occasions in Hawaii. Aloha shirts are still basically cut the same, but the patterns have changed; apart from the original flowers and ferns, modern shirts might depict an island scene giving the impression of a silk-screen painting. A basic, good-quality *muumuu* or aloha shirt starts at about $25, and is guaranteed to be worth its price in good times and happy smiles. The connoisseur might want to purchase *The Hawaiian Shirt, Its Art and History* by R. Thomas Steele. It's illustrated with more than 150 shirts that are now considered works of art by collectors the world over.

Scrimshaw

This art, etching and carving on bone and ivory, has become an island tradition handed down from the times of the great whaling ships. Although scrimshaw can be found throughout Hawaii, the center remains the old whaling capital of Lahaina, Maui. Here, along Front Street numerous shops specialize in scrimshaw. Today, pieces are carved on fossilized walrus ivory, gathered by Eskimos and shipped to Hawaii. It comes in a variety of shades from pure white to *mocha,* depending upon the mineral content of the earth in which it was buried. Elephant ivory or whale bone is no longer used because of ecological considerations, but there is a "gray market" in Pacific walrus tusks. Eskimos can legally hunt the walrus. They then make a few minimal scratches on the tusks, which technically makes them "Native American Art," a form free of most governmental restrictions. The tusks are then sent to Hawaii as art objects, but immediately the superficial scratches are removed, and the ivory is reworked by artisans. Scrimshaw is made into everything from belt buckles to delicate earrings and even into coffee table centerpieces. The prices can go from a few dollars up to thousands.

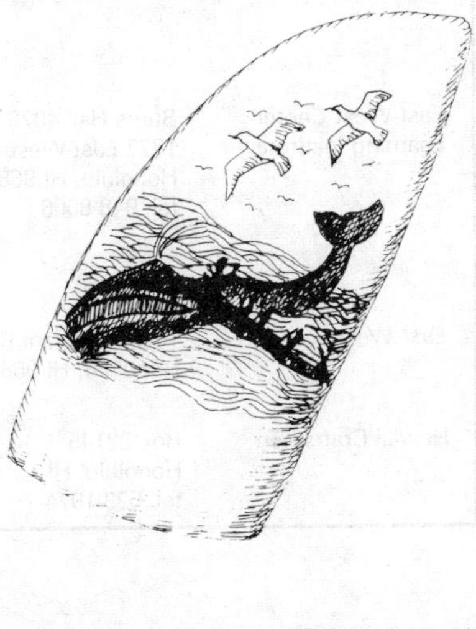

ART INFORMATION

Organization	Address and Telephone	Remarks
Arts Council of Hawaii	Box 50225 Honolulu, HI 96850 tel. 524-7120	A citizen's advocacy group for the arts providing technical assistance and information. Publishes the *Cultural Climate,* newsletter covering the arts of Hawaii. Includes a calendar of events, feature articles and editorials. Membership fee $15, includes newsletter, non-members, $.50 per issue.
Bishop Museum	1355 Kalihi St. Box 19000-A Honolulu, HI 96819 tel. 847-3511	World's best museum covering Polynesia and Hawaii; exhibits, galleries archives, demonstrations of Hawaiian crafts, and a planetarium. On premises, Shop Pacifica has books and publications on Hawaiian art and culture. Shouldn't be missed. See Oahu chapter for details.
Contemporary Arts Center	605 Kapiolani Blvd. Honolulu, HI 96813 tel. 525-8047	Promotes public awareness of contemporary art by providing gallery space, publicity, and exposure for local artists. Also, a permanent collection and monthly exhibitions.
East Hawaii Cultural Center	Box 1312 Hilo, HI 96721	Publishes *The Center Newspaper,* a monthly newsletter of what's happening artistically and culturally, primarily on the Big Island. Good monthly calendar of events: from exhibit openings to movies.
East-West Center Learning Institute	Burns Hall 4076 1777 East-West Rd. Honolulu, HI 96848 tel. 948-8006	At U of H campus. Dedicated to the sharing, exhibiting, and appreciation of arts, culture, and crafts from throughout Asia and the Western world. Their free bi-monthly *Centerviews* includes an event calendar and tropical editorials on the Pacific.
East-West Journal	1633 Kapiolani Blvd. Honolulu, HI 96814	Yearly guide to exhibition galleries featuring the work of locally renowned artists.
Hawaii Craftsmen	Box 22145 Honolulu, HI tel. 523-1974	Increase awareness of Hawaiian crafts through programs, exhibitions, workshops, lectures, and demonstrations.

Honolulu Academy of Arts	900 S. Beretania St. Honolulu, HI 96814 tel. 538-3693	Collects, preserves, and exhibits artworks. Offers public art education programs related to their collections, plus tours, classes, lectures, films, and a variety of publications.
Honolulu Symphony Society	1000 Bishop St. Honolulu, HI 96813 tel. 537-6171	Provides professional-level music, primarily symphonic and concerts
Pacific Handcrafters' Guild	Box 15491 Honolulu, HI 96818 tel. 923-5726	Focuses on developing and preserving handicrafts in Hawaii and the Pacific Sponsors 4 major craft fairs annually
State Foundation on Culture and the Arts	335 Merchant Street Room 202 Honolulu, HI 96813 tel. 548-4145	Preserves Hawaii's cultural and artistic heritage. Publishes *Hawaii Cultural Resource Directory,* listing art organizations, galleries, councils, co-ops, and guilds. Very complete.
University of Hawaii at Manoa Art Gallery	2535 The Mall Honolulu, HI 96822 tel. 948-6888	Showcase for contemporary artworks. Theme changes periodically

Woodcarving

One Hawaiian art that has not died out is woodcarving. Extremely well developed among the old Hawaiians, they almost exclusively used *koa* because of its density, strength, and natural lustre. It was turned into canoes, woodware, and furniture used by the *ali'i. Koa* is becoming increasingly scarce, but many items are still available, although they are pricy. Milo and monkey pod, also excellent woods for carving, have largely replaced *koa*. You can buy *tikis,* bowls, and furniture at numerous shops. Variety stores sell countless inexpensive carved items, such as little hula girls or salad servers, but most of these are imported from Asia or the Philippines.

Weaving

The minute you arrive in Hawaii you should spend $2 for a woven beach mat. This is a necessity, not a frivolous purchase, but the mat won't be made in Hawaii. What is made in Hawaii is *lau hala,* traditional Hawaiian weaving from the leaves *(lau)* of the pandanus *(hala)* tree. These leaves vary greatly in length with the largest being over 6 feet; their thorny spine must be removed before they can be worked. The leaves are cut into strips from one-eighth to one inch wide, then woven; colors range from light tan to dark brown. *Lau hala* makes great purses, mats, and baskets. It makes absolutely superb hats, not to be confused with a palm frond hat. A *lau hala* hat is amazingly supple—when squashed it'll pop back into shape. A good one is expensive ($25), and with proper care will last for years. All *lau hala* should be given a light application of mineral oil on a monthly basis, expecially if it is exposed to the sun. Iron flat items over a damp cloth, and keep purses and baskets stuffed wiith paper when not in use. Palm fronds are widely used in weaving. They too are a great raw material, but not as good as *lau hala.* Almost any item woven from palm makes a good authentic yet inexpensive gift or souvenir.

Gift Items

Jewelry is always an appreciated gift, especially if it's distinctive, and Hawaii has some of the most unique. The sea provides the basic raw materials of pink, gold, and black coral, and it's so beautiful that it holds the same fascination as gems. Harvesting the coral is very dangerous work. The Lahaina beds have one of the best black coral lodes in the islands, but unlike reef coral, these trees grow at depths which are at the outer limits of a scuba diver's capabilities. Only the best risk diving 180 feet after the black coral (at least one diver loses his life per year). Conservationists have placed great pressure to restrict the harvesting of these deep coral, and the state strictly regulates the firms and divers involved. Coral jewelry is on sale at many shops throughout Hawaii, and the value comes from the color and the workmanship. *Puka* (shells with little naturally occurring holes) and *opihi* shells are also made into jewelry. Many times these items are very inexpensive, yet authentic and great purchases. Hanging macrame planters festooned with shells are usually affordable and sold at roadside stands along with shells. Hawaii produces some unique food items appreciated by most people: various sized jars of macadamia nuts and butters, as well as tins of rich, gourmet Kona coffee, the only coffee produced in the U.S. Island fruits of guava, pineapple, passion fruit, and mango are often gift boxed into assortments of jams, jellies, and spicy chutneys. And for that special person in your life, you can bring home island fragrances, perfumes, and colognes with the exotic smells of gardenia, plumeria, and even island ginger. All of the above items are reasonably priced, lightweight, and travel well.

LANGUAGE OF THE *LEI*

The goddess Hiiaka is Pele's youngest sister, and although many gods were depicted wearing flower garlands, the *lei* is most associated with her. Perhaps it was because Hiiaka was the goddess of mercy and protection, qualities which the *lei* seemed to symbolize. Hiiaka traveled throughout the islands destroying evil spirits wherever she found them. In the traditional translation of "The Song of the Islands" by Rev. Samuel Kapu, the last verses read, "We all call to you, answer us O Hiiaka, the woman who travels the seas. This is the conclusion of our song, O wreaths of Hawaii, respond to our call." A special day, May 1, is *Lei* Day in Hawaii. It started in 1928 as a project of Don Blanding, an island poet.

Hardly a more beautiful tradition exists anywhere in the world than placing a flower garland around the neck of someone special. The traditional time to give a *lei* is when someone is arriving or departing the islands, so every airport has *lei* sellers, mostly older women who have a little booth at the entrance to the airport. But *lei* are worn on every occa-

lei *for sale, Honolulu c. 1920 (Hawaii State Archives)*

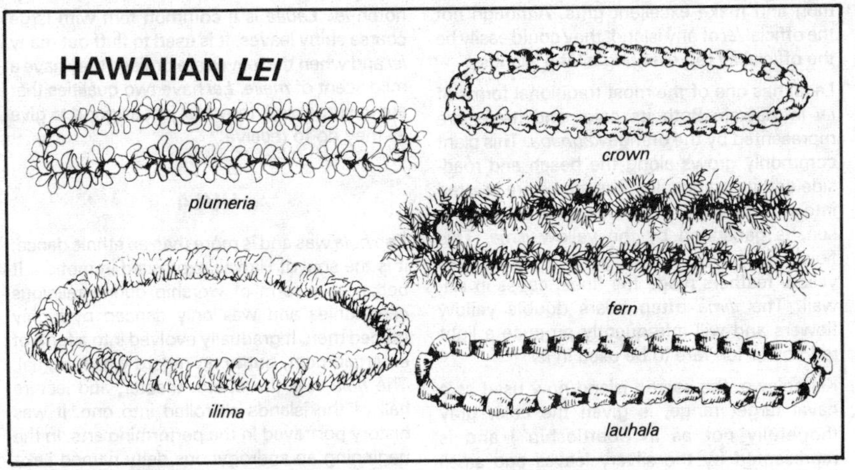

sion, from marriages to funerals, and are as apt to appear around the lovely neck of a *hula* dancer as a floral hat band on the grizzled head of an old *paniolo,* or even draped around his horse's neck. In old Hawaii *lei* were given to the local *ali'i* as a sign of affection. When two warring chiefs sat together and wove a *lei,* it meant the end of hostilities and symbolized the circle of peace.

Lei Making

Any flower or blossom can be strung into a *lei,* but the most common are carnations or the lovely smelling plumeria. *Lei,* like babies, are all beautiful, but special ones are highly prized by those who know what to look for. Of the different stringing styles, the most common is *kui*—stringing the flower through the middle or side. Most "airport-quality" *lei* are of this type. The *humuhumu* style, reserved for making flat *lei,* is made by sewing flowers and ferns to a *ti,* banana, or sometimes to a *hala* leaf. A *humuhumu lei* makes an excellent hatband. The *wili* is the winding together of greenery, ferns, and flowers into short bouquet type lengths. The most traditional form is *hili,* which requires no stringing at all but involves braiding fragrant ferns and leaves such as *maile*. If flowers are interwoven, the *hili* becomes the *haku* style, the most difficult and most beautiful type of *lei*.

The *Lei* Of The Land

Every major island is symbolized by its own *lei* made from a distinctive flower, shell, or fern. Each island has its own official color as well, though it doesn't necessarily correspond to the color of the island's *lei*. The island of Hawaii's *lei* is made from the red (or rare creamy white or orange) *lehua* blossom. The *lehua* tree grows from sea level to 9,000 feet and produces an abundance of tufted flowers. The official color of Hawaii Island, like the lava from its active volcanoes, is red.

Kauai, oldest of the main islands, is represented by the *mokihina lei* and the regal color purple. The *mokihina* tree produces a small cube-like fruit that smells like anise. Green when strung into Kauai's *lei,* they then turn a dark brown and keep their scent for months.

Maui is the pink island; its *lei* is the corresponding small pink rose called the *lokelani*. Not native but imported, in recent years they've fallen prey to a rose beetle. When they're scarce, a substitute *roselani* is used for Maui's *lei*.

Molokai is the silvery green island, and its *lei* is fashioned from the green leaves and small white flowers of the *kukui* tree. After it's shaped and polished, the *kukui* nut makes some of the most permanent and beautiful *lei* for sale in Hawaii. *Kukui* nut *lei* are quite common and make excellent gifts. Although not the official *lei* of any island, they could easily be the official *lei* representing all the islands.

Lanai has one of the most traditional forms of *lei* in Hawaii. Both its color and its *lei* are represented by the orange *kaunaoa.* This plant commonly grows along the beach and roadside and its orange, leafless stems are twisted into strands to form a *lei*. Oahu, the color of the sun, is garlanded by the yellow *ilima*. This flower is reminiscent of the *o'o* bird whose yellow feathers made the finest capes in Hawaii. The *ilima* often bears double yellow flowers and will infrequently produce a light red flower too rare to be used in *lei.*

Kahoolawe, the sacred island now used as a naval target range, is given the color gray (hopefully not as in "battleship") and is represented by the silvery leaves and small white sweet-scented flowers of the *hinahina*. This heliotrope grows on sandy beaches just above the highwater mark, and is a very common plant throughout the Pacific.

Niihau, the Forbidden Island, is home to some of the last remaining pure-blooded Hawaiians, and takes the color white. The island's *lei* is the rare *pupu* shell. This shell is white, less than ½ inch long, and sometimes has brown spots. The shell was the home of a mollusk that died on the offshore reef. These *pupu lei,* considerd fine jewelry, fetch a handsome price. Very cheap facsimiles of *pikake*-shell *lei* are sold everywhere, and most have been imported from the Cook and Society Islands of the South Pacific.

The last island is the semi-submerged volcano of Molokini, just off Maui's south shore. Molokini is represented by the very traditional *lei* made from *limu kala,* a brown coarse seaweed with feathery spiny leaves that makes a boatype *lei*.

Besides these island *lei* two others must be mentioned. A *lei* made from *maile* is perhaps the most traditional of all. *Maile* is an ordinary green leafy vine. Its stiff bone-like inner stem is removed, leaving the leaves and pliable bark intact, which are then twisted into a *lei.* They might be ordinary to look at, but they have a delicious smell that is Hawaii. *Maile* is often used in conjunction with flowers to make topnotch *lei. Lauae* is a common fern with large coarse shiny leaves. It is used to fluff out many *lei* and when the leaves are bruised they have a mild scent of *maile. Lei* have two qualities that are unsurpassed: they feel just as good to give as they do to receive.

HULA

The *hula* was and is more than an ethnic dance; it is the soul of Hawaii expressed in motion. It began as a form of worship during religious ceremonies and was only danced by highly trained men. It gradually evolved into a form of entertainment, but in no regard was it sexual. The *hula* was the opera, theater, and lecture hall of the islands all rolled into one. It was history portrayed in the performing arts. In the beginning an androgynous deity named Laka descended to Earth and taught men how to dance the *hula.* In time the male aspect of Laka departed for the heavens, but the female aspect remained. The female Laka set up her own special *hula heiau* at Haena Point on the Na Pali coast of Kauai, where it still exists. As time went on women were allowed to learn the *hula.* Scholars surmise that men became too busy wresting a living from the land to maintain the art form. Most likely, it was the dance's swaying movements and primal rhythm that attracted the women. And once they began showing off what nature had bestowed upon them, what chief in his right mind was going to tell them to stop?!

Men did retain a type of *hula* for themselves called *lua.* This was a form of martial art employed in hand-to-hand combat. It included paralyzing holds, bone-crunching punches, and thrusting with spears and clubs. It evolved into a ritualized warfare dance called *hula kui.* During the 19th C., the *hula* almost vanished because the missionaries considered it vile and heathen. King Kalakaua is generally regarded as saving it during the 1880s, when he formed his own troupe and encouraged the dancers to learn the old *hula.* Many of the original dances were forgotten, but some were retained and are performed to this day. Although professional dancers were highly trained, everyone took part in the *hula. Ali'i,* commoners, young, and old all danced. The early drawings of ships' artists like Arago, Choris, and Webber all recorded *hula* scenes. Old folks even did it sitting down if their legs were too weak to perform the necessary gyrations.

Hula Training

Only the most beautiful, graceful, and elegant girls were chosen to enter the *hula halau* (school). At one time, the *halau* was a temple in its own right and the girls who entered at the age of 4 or 5 would emerge as accomplished dancers in their early teens to begin a lifelong career of the highest honor. In the *halau,* the *haumana* (pupils) were under the strict and total guidance of the *kumu* (teacher) and many *kapu* were placed upon them. The *hula* was a subordination of gross strength into a sublime coupling of grace and elegance. Once a woman became a proficient and accomplished dancer, her *hula* showed a personal, semi-spontaneous interpretation based upon past experiences. Today, *hula halau* are active on every island, teaching *hula,* and keeping the old ways and culture alive. Performers still spend years perfecting their techniques. They show off their accomplishments during the fierce competition of the Merrie Monarch Festival in Hilo every April. The winning *halau* is praised and recognized throughout the islands.

King Kalakaua is credited with saving the hula *as an art form. (Hawaii State Archives)*

The Special World Of *Hula*

Hawaiian *hula* was never performed in grass skirts; *tapa* or *ti*-leaf skirts were worn. Grass skirts came to Hawaii from the Gilbert Islands, and if you see grass and cellophane skirts in a "hula revue," it's not traditional. Almost every major resort offering entertainment or a *luau* also offers a "hula review." Most times, young island beauties accompanied by local musicians put on a floor show for the tourists. It'll be fun, but it won't be traditional. A *hula* dancer has to learn how to control every part of her/his body including the facial expressions, which help to set the mood. The correct chanting of the *mele* is an integral part of the performance. These story chants, combined with accompanying musical instruments, make the *hula* very much like opera, especially similar in the way the tale unfolds. The hands are extremely important and provide instant background scenery. For example, if the hands are thrust outward in an aggressive manner, this can mean a battle; if they sway gently overhead, they refer to the gods or to creation; they can easily become rain, clouds, the sun, sea, or moon. Watch the hands to get the gist of the story, though in the words of one wise-guy, "You watch the parts you like, and I'll watch the parts I like!" Swaying hips, depending upon their motion, can be a long walk, a canoe ride, or sexual intercourse. The foot motion can portray a battle, a walk, or any kind of conveyance. The overall effect is multi-directional synchronized movement.

Hula Music

Accompaniment is provided by chants called *mele* or *oli* and by a wide variety of basic instruments. The *ipu* is a primary *hula* instrument made of 2 gourds fastened together. It's thumped on a mat and slapped with the hand. In the background is the steady rhythm of the *pahu,* a large bass drum made from a hollowed coconut or breadfruit tree log, and covered

a modern hula *accompanist*

with a sharkskin membrane. Hawaii's largest drum, it was sometimes placed on a pedestal and used in ceremonies at the *heiau*. The *uli uli* is a gourd or coconut filled with shells or pebbles and used like *maracas,* while *ili ili* are merely stones clicked together like *castanets.* The *punui* is a small drum made from a half coconut shell and beaten in counterpoint to the *ipu.* Oftentimes it was played by the *hula* dancer, who had it fastened to her body as a knee drum. The *puili* is a length of bamboo split at one end to look like a whisk, and struck against the body to make a rattling noise, while the *kaekaekee* and *kalau* are bamboo cut to various lengths and struck to make a rudimentary xylophonic sound. Two unique instruments are the *kupee niho ilio,* a dog's tooth rattle worn as an ankle bracelet by men only, now replaced by sea shells, and a *ohe hano ihu,* a nose flute of bamboo that had a few melody holes and was played in accompaniment while the person chanted. Not all of these instruments are actually necessary to perform a *hula.* All that's really needed is a dancer and a chant.

THAT GOOD OLD ISLAND MUSIC

The missionaries usually take a beating when it's recounted how much Hawaiian culture they destroyed while civilizing the natives. However, they seemed to have done one thing right. They taught the Hawaiians the musical scale and immediately opened a door filled with latent and superbly harmonious talent. Before the missionaries, the Hawaiians knew little about melody. Though sonorous, their *mele* were repetitive chants where the emphasis was placed on historical accuracy and not on "making music." The Hawaiians, in short, didn't *sing.* But within a few years of the missionaries' arrival, they were belting out good old Christian hymns and one of their favorite pastimes became group and individual singing.

Early in the 1800s, Spanish *vaqueros* from California were imported to teach the Hawaiians how to be cowboys. With them came guitars and moody ballads. The Hawaiian *paniolo* quickly learned both how to punch cows and to croon away the long lonely nights on the range. Immigrants that came along a little later in the 19th C., especially from Portugal, helped create a Hawaiian-style music. Their biggest influence was a small 4-stringed instrument called a *braga* or *cavaquinho*. One owned by Augusto Dias was the prototype of a home-grown Hawaiian instrument that became known as the *ukulele*. "Jumping flea," the translation of *ukelele,* is an appropriate name devised by the Hawaiians when they saw how nimble the fingers were as they "jumped" over the strings.

The Merry Monarch, King Kalakaua, and Queen Liliuokalani were both patrons of the arts who furthered the Hawaiian musical identity at the turn of the century. Kalakaua revived the *hula* and was also a gifted lyricist and balladeer. He wrote the words to "Hawaii Pono" that became the national anthem of Hawaii and later the state anthem. Liliuokalani wrote the hauntingly beautiful "Aloha Oe," which is often pointed to as the "spirit of Hawaii" in music. Detractors say that its melody is extremely close to the old Christian hymn, "Rock Beside the Sea," but the lyrics are so beautiful and perfectly fitted that this doesn't matter. Just prior to Kalakaua's reign a Prussian bandmaster, Capt. Henri Berger, was invited to head the fledgling Royal Hawaiian Band, which he turned into very respectable orchestra lauded by many visitors to the islands. Berger was open-minded and learned to love Hawaiian music. He collaborated with Kalakaua and other island musicians to incorporate their music into a Western format. He headed the band for 43 years until 1915, and was instrumental in making music a serious pursuit of talented Hawaiians.

Popular Hawaiian Music

Hawaiian music has a unique twang, a special feeling that says the same thing to everyone that hears it: "relax, sit back in the moonlight, watch the swaying palms as the surf sings a lullaby." This special sound is epitomized by the bouncy *ukelele,* the falsetto voice of Hawaiian crooners, and by the smooth ring of the "steel" or "Hawaiian" guitar. The steel guitar is a variation that was originated by Joseph Kekuku in the 1890s. Stories abound of how Joseph Kekuku devised this instrument, some even saying that it wasn't his idea. The most popular versions say that Joe dropped his comb or pocket knife on his guitar strings and liked what he heard. Driven by the faint rhythm of an inner sound, he went to the machine shop at the Kamehameha School and turned out a steel bar for sliding over the strings. To complete the sound he changed the cat-gut strings to steel and raised them so they wouldn't hit the frets. *Voila!*—Hawaiian music as the world knows it today.

Hawaiian guitarists also have a particular form of tuning called "slack key," similar to what some musicians call "open tuning." In effect, the guitar strings are tuned to the key that best suits the singer's voice. Hawaiian music received its biggest boost from a remarkable radio program known as "Hawaii Calls." This program sent out its music from the Banyan Court of the Moana Hotel from 1935 until 1975. At its peak in the mid-1950s, it was syndicated on over 700 radio stations throughout the world. Ironically, Japanese pilots heading for Pearl Harbor, tuned in island music as a signal beam. Some internationally famous classic tunes came out of the '40s and '50s. Jack Pitman composed "Beyond the Reef" in 1948; over 300 artists have recorded it and it has sold well over 12 million records. Other million-sellers include: "Sweet Leilani," "Lovely Hula Hands," "The Crosseyed Mayor of Kaunakakai," "The Hawaiian Wedding Song."

By the 1960s, Hawaiian music began to die. It was just too corny for those turbulent years. Hawaiian music was too light, belonging to the older generation and the good times that followed WW II. One man was instrumental in keeping Hawaiian music alive during this

photo by Fritz Craft, c. 1930

period. Don Ho and his "Tiny Bubbles" became the token Hawaiian musician of the '60s and early '70s. He's persevered long enough to become a legend in his own time, and his Polynesian Extravaganza still packs them in 6 nights a week in Honolulu. Al Harrington, "The South Pacific Man," has another Honolulu "big revue" that draws large crowds. Of this type of entertainment, perhaps the most Hawaiian is Danny Kaleikini who entertains his audience with dances, Hawaiian anecdotes, and tunes on the traditional Hawaiian nose flute. Polynesian revues, and extravaganzas are found at most major resorts throughout the islands.

The Beat Goes On

Beginning in the mid-'70s, all islanders began to assert their cultural identity. One of the unifying factors was the coming of age of "Hawaiian" music. It graduated from the "little grass shack" novelty tune, and began to include sophisticated jazz, rock, and contemporary rhythms. Accomplished musicians whose roots were in traditional island music began to highlight their tunes with this distinctive sound. The best embellish their arrangements with *ukeleles,* steel guitars, and traditional percussion and melodic instruments. Some excellent modern recording artists have

RADIO STATIONS

Station	Dial Number	Remarks
	OAHU	
KCCN	AM 1420	Hawaiian music 24 hours. Indiscriminate selections will either delight or exasperate.
KDEO	AM 940	Country
KDUK	AM 980	Rock. Surfline report at tel. 538-7131
	MAUI	
KHEI	AM 1100	Rock
KUIB	FM 94	Rock
KAIM	AM 870, FM 95.5	
KAOI	FM95	Stereo
	HAWAII	
KBIG	FM 98	Excellent stations, sound like FM with very few commercials
KHLO	AM 850	
KIPA	AM 620	
KKON	AM 790	Contemporary
KPUA	AM 970	Contemporary
KOAST	FM 92.1	Contemporary
	KAUAI	
KIPO	AM 93.5, FM 93.5	Contemporary
KAUI	AM 720	Contemporary

become island institutions. The local people say that you know if the Hawaiian harmonies are good if they give you "chicken skin." Each year special music awards, *Na Hoku Hanohano,* or *Hoku* for short, are given to distinguished island musicians. The following are recent *Hoku* winners considered by their contemporaries to be among the best in Hawaii. If they're playing while you're there, don't miss them. They include: **Brothers Cazimero**, whose "Island in Your Eyes," won Best Contemporary Hawaiian Album. The Brothers are blessed with beautiful harmonic voices, but they are becoming increasingly commercial; **Krush**, whose "More and More," won the *Hoku* for "Best Contemporary Album"; **The Peter Moon Band**, contemporary but 100% quality with a strong traditional sound; **Karen Keawehawai'i** whose "With Love, Karen" won the *Hoku* for "Best Female Vocalist" has a sparkling voice and can be very funny when the mood strikes her; **Henry Kapono**, formerly of **Cecilio and Kapono** keeps a low profile, but is an incredible performer and excellent songwriter. His shows are non-commercial and very special; **Cecilio** is now teamed up with **Maggie Herron**, who are hot together and have a strong following in Honolulu; **The Makaha Sons of Niihau** captured the *Hoku* for "Best Traditional Hawaiian Album," and "Best Group." Their sound, led by Israel Kamakawiwoole, is the best. They shouldn't be missed; **The Beamer Brothers** are excellent performances, and can be seen at various nightspots.

Some top-notch newcomers that are gaining popularity are: Ledward Kaapana; Mango; Oliver Kelly; Ka'eo; Na Leo Pilimehana, whose "Local Boys" recently won a *Hoku* for "Best Single"; Freitas Brothers; Brickwood Galuteria, who won a double *Hoku* for "Best Male Vocalist" and "Most Promising Artist"; and Third Road Delite.

Classical And Chamber Music

A wide assortment of classical and chamber music is offered in Hawaii. The following organizations sponsor concerts throughout the year: Chamber Music Hawaii, 905 Spencer St., No. 404, Honolulu, Hi 96822, (tel. 531-6617); Classical Guitar Society of Hawaii, 1229 D. Waimanu, Honolulu, HI 96814 (tel. 537-6451); The Ensemble Players Guild, Box 50225, Honolulu, HI 96850 (tel. 735-1173); Hawaii Concert Society, Box 663, Hilo, HI 96721 (tel. 935-5831); Honolulu Symphony Society, 1000 Bishop St., Suite 901, Honolulu, HI 96813 (tel. 537-6171); Kauai Concert Assoc., 5867 Haaheo Pl., Kapaa, HI 96746 (tel. 822-7593); Maui Philharmonic Society, 2274 S. Kihei Rd., Kihei, HI 96753 (tel. 879-2962).

FESTIVALS, HOLIDAYS, AND EVENTS

In addition to all the American national holidays, Hawaii celebrates its own festivals, pageants, ethnic fairs, and a multitude of specialized exhibits. They occur throughout the year, some particular to only one island or locality, while others such as Aloha Week and Lei Day are celebrated on all the islands. Some of the smaller local happenings are semi-spontaneous, so there's no *exact* date when they're held. These are some of the most rewarding, because they provide the best times to have fun with the local people. At festival time, everyone is welcome. Check local newspapers and the free island magazines for exact dates of some events.

JANUARY

Early January

Start the New Year off right by climbing to the top of Koko Crater on Oahu for the ***Hauoli Makahiki Hou,*** a great way to focus on the horizons of the coming year and a great hangover remedy. Check with HVB for details. Or, continue the party with the **Sunshine Music Festival** rock concert at Diamond Head Crater.

Thump in the New Year with a traditional Japanese **Mochi Pounding Festival** at Volcano Art Center, Volcanoes National Park, Hawaii.

Sporting Events

January's first Saturday brings the **Hula Bowl Game** to Aloha Stadium, Honolulu. This annual game is a college all-star football classic. Aloha Stadium, tel. 488-7731 for details.

The **Molokai Challenge**, a new biathlon, is held along Molokai's amazing north coast. Watch a 3-mile run and a kayak race against time and the power of the sea.

The **Kauai Loves You Triathlon** is at lovely Hanalei Bay, Kauai. Amateurs and professionals are welcome. Covered by CBS, it can occur in December.

The athletes gear up with the Big Island **Triathlon Invitational** held in late December or early January. This is a 3-day event that ranges all over the island and includes an overnight stay at Volcanoes National Park.

At **The Volcano Wilderness Marathon and Rim Runs,** the truly energetic run 26 miles through the desolate Kau Desert and a 10-mile race around the Caldera Crater Rim. Over 1,000 runners participate.

The grueling **Maui Triathlon**, Kaanapali, Maui, is a very competitive sporting event with world-class athletes running for top prizes.

NFL Pro Bowl at Aloha Stadium, Honolulu, is the annual all-star football game offering the best from both conferences. Aloha Stadium, tel. 488-7731 for details.

Late January

Robert Burns Night at the Ilikai Hotel, Honolulu, is when local and visiting Scots from Canada and the Mainland celebrate the birthday of Scotland's poet Robert Burns.

The **Cherry Blossom Festival** in Honolulu can begin in late January and last through March. The fun includes a Japanese cultural and trade show, tea ceremony, flower arranging, queen pageant, and coronation ball. Check newspapers and free tourist magazines for dates and times of various Japanese cultural events.

The Narcissus Festival in Honolulu's Chinatown starts with the parade and festivities of Chinese New Year which can be anytime from mid-January to early February. The city sparkles with lion dances in the street, fireworks, a beauty pageant, and a coronation ball.

FEBRUARY

Early February

The **Punahou School Carnival,** in Honolulu, with its arts, crafts, and a huge rummage sale, is held at one of Hawaii's oldest and most prestigious high schools. Great ethnic foods and you'd be surprised at what Hawaii's oldest and most established families donate to the rummage sale.

The **Hawaiian Open International Golf Tournament** tees off in Honolulu at the exclusive Waialae Country Club. $500,000 prize money lures the best PGA golfers to this tournament which is beginning its second decade.

February offers everything from the links to skiing at the **Mauna Kea Ski Meet** atop the Big Island's 13,000-foot volcano—weather and snow conditions dictate the exact time, which can vary from early January to March. Skiers from around the world compete in cup skiing, and crosscountry.

Mid To Late February

The **Carole Kai Bed Race** is a fund-raising race of crazies, pushing decorated beds down Front Street in Lahaina, Maui, and at the Kukui Grove Center in Lihue, Kauai. It's held in Honolulu in early March.

The **Haleiwa Sea Spree** on Oahu's North Shore is 4-day action-packed event with surfing championships, outrigger canoe races, and ancient Hawaiian sports. An around-the-island bicycle race tops it off.

Enjoy the authentic western flavor of the **Great Waikoloa Horse Races and Rodeo** at Waikoloa Stables, Waikoloa, Hawaii. Major rodeo events draw skilled *paniolo* from around the islands.

The **Annual Keauhou-Kona Triathlon** at Keauhou Bay, Big Island, equals half the Ironman requirements. Open to athletes unable to enter Ironman, and to anyone in good health, it allows relay team racing for the grueling events.

The **Captain Cook Festival** is held at Waimea, Kauai, the spot where this intrepid Pacific explorer first made contact. Food, entertainment, and a partial marathon add to the fun.

Buffalo's Annual Big Board Surfing Classic at Makaha Beach, Oahu, features the best of the classic board riders along with an authentic cultural event complete with entertainment, crafts, and food. The 2-day competitions are held the last weekend in February and again on the first weekend in March.

MARCH

Early March brings the Annual Maui Marathon along island roads from Wailuku to Lahaina, Maui. For information contact the Valley Isle Road Runners at tel. 242-6042.

The **Kukini Run** follows an ancient trail through Kahakuloa Valley on Maui's northwest coast.

The **Carole Kai Bed Race** heads down Kalakaua Avenue in Waikiki. A free concert is given at the Waikiki Shell the night before. Appearances by Hawaii's name entertainers are part of this fun-filled charity fund-raiser.

Mid March rumbles in with the **Kona Stampede** at Honaunau Arena, Honaunau, Kona, Hawaii. *Paniolo* provide plenty of action during the full range of rodeo events. For information tel. 885-7628.

The more *genteel* **Polo Season** starts in March and lasts until September. International teams come to Dillingham Field, Mokuleia, Oahu, for the competition.

Bagpipes herald late March at the **Hawaiian Highland Gathering,** Richardson's Field, Pearl Harbor, Oahu. Clans gather for Scottish games, competitions, ethnic foods, highland dancing, and pipe bands. Enjoy Scotsmen in kilts and *lei.*

Music And Dance

The **Hawaiian Song Festival and Song Composing Contest** at Kapiolani Park Bandstand in Waikiki determines the year's best Hawaiian song and attracts top-name entertainers.

continued

Honolulu's **Emerald Ball** is an elegant affair sponsored by the Society of the Friendly Sons of St. Patrick which features dinner and dancing to a big-name band. At this time the St. Patrick's Day Parade winds along Kalakaua Ave., in Waikiki.

Competition among secondary grade students of Hawaiian ancestry marks the **Kamehameha School Annual Song Contest** held at the Blaisdell Center Arena, Honolulu. For information call Kamehameha Schools at tel. 842-8211

March For Women

Mid month features feminine beauty, grace, and athletic ability at the **Miss Maui Pageant** at Baldwin High School, Wailuku, Maui; **Miss Kauai Pageant** at the Kauai War Memorial Convention Hall, Lihue; the **Miss Aloha Hawaii Pageant** at Hilo Civic Auditorium, Hilo, Hawaii.

The prestigious **LPGA Women's Kemper Open** chooses one of the islands' best golf courses for this annual event that features the Helene Curtis Pro-Am, and draws the world's best women golfers.

March For The Prince

The end of March is dedicated to Prince Kuhio, a member of the royal family and Hawaii's first delegate to the U.S. Congress. **Prince Kuhio Day** is a state holiday honoring Hawaii's Prince Kuhio held on March 26, his birthday. Celebrations are held at the Prince Kuhio Federal Building, Oahu. Tel. 546-7573 for details.

The **Prince Kuhio Festival** at Lihue, Kauai, features festivities from the era of Prince Kuhio along with canoe races and a royal ball.

The **Prince Kuhio Rodeo** is held at Po'oku Stables, in Princeville, Kauai. Tel. 826-6777 for details.

APRIL

Easter Sunday's **Sunrise Service** at the National Memorial Cemetery of The Pacific, Punchbowl Crater, Honolulu, is a moving ceremony that shouldn't be missed if you're in the islands at that time.

The **Annual Hawaiian Festival of Music** at Waikiki Shell, Honolulu, is a grand and lively music competition of groups from all over the islands and the mainland. This music-lovers' smorgasbord offers everything from symphony, to swing and all beats in between. Tel. 637-6566 for information.

Wesak or Buddha Day is on the closest Sunday to April 8, and celebrates the birthday of Gautama Buddha. Ornate offerings of tropical flowers are placed at temple altars throughout Hawaii. Enjoy the sunrise ceremonies at Kapiolani Park, Honolulu, with Japanese in their best *kimono* along with flower festivals, pageants, and dance programs in many island temples.

Mid To Late April

The **Aloha Basketball Classic** at the Blaisdell Center Arena, Honolulu, brings top college seniors who are invited to Hawaii to participate in charity games made up of 4 teams. Blaisdell Center, tel. 527-5400.

The **Paniolo Ski Meet** is exciting skiing atop the Big Island's Mauna Kea, conditions permitting.

The **Merrie Monarch Festival** in Hilo sways with the best *hula* dancers that the islands' *hula halau* have to offer. Gentle but stiff competition features both ancient and modern dances. The festival runs for a week on a variable schedule from year to year. It's immensely popular with islanders, and hotels, cars, and flights are booked solid. Tel. 935-9168 for information.

The **Kona Sports Festival** Kailua-Kona, Hawaii, is a solid week of sports entertainment and frivolity held toward the end of the month.

MAY

Early May

May 1 is May Day to the communist world, but in Hawaii red is only one of the colors when everyone dons a *lei* for ***Lei* Day**. Festivities abound throughout Hawaii, but there are special "goings on" at Kapiolani Park, Waikiki.

The **Captain Cook Festival** at Kailua-Kona offers Hawaiian games, music, and fishing.

Costumed pageants, canoe races, and a beard-judging contest commemorate times past at the **Lahaina Whaling Spree**, Lahaina, Maui.

The **Pacific Handcrafters Guild Fair** at Ala Moana Park, Honolulu, is a perfect opportunity to see the "state of the arts" in Hawaii when the islands' best artists gather in one spot to sell their creations.

Look skyward on May 5, **Japanese Boys' Day**, and you'll see paper carp *(koi)* flying from rooftops. Carp symbolize the manly virtues of strength and courage. The number of *koi* kites correspond to the number of sons in the family with the largest on top for the eldest, and then down the line.

Mid To Late May

Armed Forces Week brings military open houses, concerts, and displays in and around the islands. Hawaii is the most militarized state in the Union and this fact becomes obvious. Call Military Relations, tel. 438-9761 for details.

Filipino Fiesta is a month-long celebration of the islands' Filipino poulation. Food, various festivities, and a beauty contest are part of the fiesta.

Costumed riders from the annals of Hawaiian history ride again at **Hawaii on Horseback**. Horsemanship and a western flair mark these days held in and around Waimea, and the Parker Ranch on the Big Island.

Annual Western Week at Honokaa on the Big Island is a fun-filled week with a western theme. It includes a cookout, parade, rodeo, and dance.

Memorial Day in Hawaii is special with military services held at Honolulu's, National Memorial Cemetery of the Pacific on the last Monday in May. Tel. 546-3190 for details.

Agricultural exhibits, down-home cooking, entertainment, and fresh produce are presented for 4 weekends starting in late May at the **50th State Fair**, at Aloha Stadium, Honolulu, tel. 536-5492.

JUNE

Early June
The **Kauai County Fair** at the Kauai War Memorial Convention Hall, Lihue, is a typical county fair offering the best in agriculture that the island has to offer.

Hawaii's best artists and craftsmen come to the **Mission Houses Museum Fancy Fair** in Honolulu. Browse while enjoying homemade food and entertainment. Tel. 531-0481 for details.

King Kamehameha Day
June 11 is a state holiday honoring Kamehameha the Great with festivities on all islands. Check local papers for times and particulars. The following are the main events: Oahu holds a *lei*-draping ceremony at King Kamehameha statue at the Civic Center in downtown Honolulu, along with parades complete with floats and pageantry featuring a *ho'olaule'a* (street party) in Waikiki; Kailua-Kona on the Big Island is hospitable with a *ho'olaule'a,* parades, art demonstrations, entertainment, and contests; on Kauai enjoy parades, *ho'olaule'a,* arts, and crafts centered around the Kauai County Building; Maui's Lahaina and Kahului are decked out for parades, and pageants. Also, the Kamehameha Day Invitational Archery Tournament is held at the Kahului Armory and Valley Isle Archers Field Range.

The **Kamehameha Ski Meet** is in early June when bikini-clad contestants add a little extra spice on those bouncy moguls.

Mid To Late June
The Brigham Young University at Laie, Oahu, swings with the **Annual King Kamehameha Traditional Hula And Chant Competition**.

The **Annual Upcountry Fun Fair** at the Eddie Tam Center, Makawao, Maui, is an old-fashioned farm fair right in the heart of Maui's *paniolo* country. Crafts, food, and competitions are part of the fair.

The **Annual Hawaiian Festival Of Music** at the Waikiki Shell, Honolulu, is a repeat of the April festivities, but no less of a music lovers delight as local and Mainland bands compete in mediums from symphony to swing.

Hilo, Hawaii flashes its brilliant colors with the **Annual Hilo Orchid Society Show** at the Hilo Civic Auditorium, and the **Annual Big Island Bonsai Show,** Wailoa Center, Hilo (both sometimes scheduled for early July).

Dancing is part of the **Annual Japan Festival** in Honolulu at Kapiolani Park and the Blaisdell Center. Also, ***Bon Odori,*** the Japanese festival of departed souls, featuring dances and candle-lighting ceremonies are held at numerous Buddhist temples throughout the islands. A special *bon odori* festival is offered at Haleiwa Jodo Mission, Haleiwa, Oahu. These festivities change yearly and can be held anytime from late June to early August.

JULY

The week of the **Fourth of July** offers the all-American sport of rodeo along with parades on every island. Don't miss the following if possible.

July 4 Parker Ranch Rodeo And Horseraces, Paniolo Park, Waimea, Hawaii. The epitome of rodeo by Hawaii's top cowboys, the setting is the Parker Ranch, the largest privately owned ranch in all of America, including Texas, *pardner!* Tel. 885-7655.

Annual Naalehu Rodeo, Naalehu, Hawaii, with rodeo events, motorcycle and dune buggy races, *luau,* food booths, and Hawaiian entertainment.

Makawao Statewide Rodeo at the Oskie Rice Arena, Makawao, Maui, is an old-time upcountry rodeo that can't be beat for fun and entertainment anywhere in the country. Tel. 572-8102.

The **Hawaiian Islands Tall Ships Parade** floats off Oahu on the 4th of July. Tall-masted ships from throughout the islands parade from Koko Head to Sand Island and back to Diamond Head. A rare treat and taste of days gone by.

continued

July Sports
Sporting events throughout July feature races and competitions both on land and in the sea. The **Big Island Marathon** in Hilo is a full and half marathon starting and ending at the Hilo Hawaiian Hotel.

The Tin Man Triathlon, Honolulu, gathers over 1,000 triathletes to swim 800 meters, bike 25 miles and finish with a 10,000-meter (6.2 miles) run around Diamond Head and back to Kapiolani Park in Waikiki. Tel. 533-4262.

Run To The Sun from Kahului, Maui, is a grueling 37.5-mile ultra-marathon from sea level to Maui's 10,000-foot Haleakala. Held in June or August. Tel. 242-6042.

The **Annual Pan Am Windsurfing Pacific Cup** is held at various beaches around Oahu, determined by wind conditions.

Boats from ports around the world sail to Oahu for the **Pan Am Clipper Cup Series.** They navigate a series of triangles off Waikiki, along with one non-stop race from Ala Wai Harbor to Molokai, and an around-the-state non-stop race.

The **Trans Pacific Race** from Los Angeles to Honolulu sails during odd-numbered years. Yachties arrive throughout the month and converge on Ala Wai Yacht basin where "party" is the password. They head off for Hanalei Bay, Kauai, to begin the year's yachting season.

Four-man teams of one pro and 3 amateurs compete in the 54-hole **Mauna Kea Beach Hotel's Annual Pro-Am Golf Tournament** held at the hotel links along the Big Island's Kohala Coast.

Mid To Late July
The **International Festival Of The Pacific** in mid-July features a "Pageant of Nations" in Hilo. Folk dances, complete with authentic costumes from throughout Asia and the Pacific, add a rare excitement to the festivities. Contact the Japanese Chamber of Commerce, tel. 961-6123 for details.

The **Prince Lot Hula Festival** in Honolulu is a great chance for visitors to see "authentic" *hula* from some of the finest *hula halau* in the islands. Held at Moanalua Gardens, tel. 839-5334.

Hundreds of ukulele players from throughout the islands come to the Kapiolani Park Bandstand, Waikiki for, the **Annual Ukulele Festival.**

Take the opportunity to see the "state of the arts" all in one locality. Browse, buy, and eat ethnic foods at various stalls of the **Pacific Handcrafters Fair** at Thomas Square, Honolulu.

The beauty and grace of one of Hawaii's ethnic groups is apparent at the **Miss Hawaii Filipina Pageant,** Naniloa Hotel, Hilo.

The **Annual Honomu Village Fair,** Honomu, Hawaii, starts with a 46-mile Volcano to Honomu team relay race followed by "mountainball," and volleyball. There's plenty of local foods, and arts and crafts.

AUGUST

Early August
Honolulu Zoo Day in Waikiki is a day of family fun where "kids" of all ages get an up-close look at the animals, along with a full day of entertainment.

The **Annual Hanalei Stampede** is held at the Po'oku Stables, Princeville, Kauai.

Recent *hula* graduates from Honolulu's Summer Fun classes perform at the **Hula Festival,** Kapiolani Park, Waikiki. Dancers of all ages, shapes, and sizes perform some amazing bodily gyrations.

Chamber music by nationally acclaimed artists fills the Kapalua Bay Hotel on Maui for the **Kapalua Music Festival,** one of Hawaii's few formal occasions.

The first August weekend is **Establishment Day** with traditional *hula* and *lei* workshops being presented at the Big Island's Puukohala Heiaua where traditional artifacts are also on display.

Mid August
The **Kona Hawaiian Billfish Tournament** in the waters off Kona, Hawaii brings American teams seeking entry to the **Annual Hawaiian International Billfish Tournament,** held about one week later. Contact Peter Fithian, tel. 922-9708.

Hula, artifacts, workshops in *lei*-making, Hawaiian language, and other ancient skills are the focus of **Establishment Day** at Puukohala Heiau on the Big Island. The day is extremely educational and packed with family fun. Puukohala Heiau, tel. 882-7218.

The macadamia nut harvest is celebrated with sporting events, horse racing and a "Harvest Ball" at the **Macadamia Nut Harvest Festival,** Honokaa, Hawaii. Tel. 755-7792.

August 17 is **Admissions Day,** a state holiday recognizing the day that Hawaii became a state.

Late August
The **Hawaiian Open State Tennis Championships** is held at various courts around Honolulu and offers substantial prizes.

At the **Kaui County Fair** gardeners, stockmen, and craftspeople of the "Garden Island" display their wares at the War Memorial Center in Lihue. There is pageantry, great local foods, and terrific bargains to be had.

Terminally cute children from ages 5 to 12 dance for the **Queen Liliuokalani Keiki Hula Competition** at the Kamehameha Schools, Honolulu.

SEPTEMBER

In early September don't miss the **Parker Ranch Round-Up Rodeo,** Paniolo Park, Waimea, Hawaii, or the **Maui County Rodeo,** Makawao, Maui. Call Brenden Balthazar, tel. 572-8102 for details.

Athletes compete in the **Waikiki Rough Water Swim,** a 2-mile open ocean swim from Sans Souci Beach to Duke Kahanamoku Beach. Open to all ages and ability levels. Also, the **Garden Island Marathon And Half Marathon** starts at the Sheraton Hotel, Kapaa, Kauai.

Mid September

The **Annual Seiko Super Tennis Tournament** at Wailea, Maui, is a championship tennis competition with leading professional team players.

The **Million Dollar Golden Marlin Fishing Tournament** catches plenty of fishermen at Kailua-Kona, Hawaii.

The **Hawaii County Fair** at Hilo, Hawaii, is an old-time fair held on the grounds of Hilo Civic Auditorium.

Aloha Week

Late September brings festivities on all of the islands, as everyone celebrates Hawaii's own "intangible quality," *aloha.* There are parades, *luau,* historical pageants, balls, and various entertainment. The spirit of *aloha* is infectious and all are welcomed to join in. Check local papers and tourist literature for happenings near you.

The **Molokai To Oahu Canoe Race** for women (men in October) takes off at the end of September in Hawaiian-stlye canoes from a remote beach on Kauai to Fort DeRussy in Honolulu. In crossing, the teams must navigate the always-rough Kaiwi Channel.

OCTOBER

Early October

A fall show of the best works of Guild members perfect for early-bird Christmas shopping is featured at the **Pacific Handcrafters Guild,** Ala Moana Center Gallery, Honolulu.

The **Maui County Fair** at the fairgrounds in Kahului is the oldest in Hawaii! Tel. 877-3432.

The **Makahiki Festival** at Waimea Falls Park, an 800-acre tropical preserve on Oahu, features Hawaiian games, crafts, and dances reminiscent of the great *makahiki* celebrations of ancient Hawaii.

The **Molokai To Oahu Canoe Race** for men (women in Sept.) navigates Hawaiian-style canoes across the rough Kaiwi Channel from a remote beach on Molokai to Fort DeRussy, Honolulu.

Oktoberfest. Where else would you expect to find German *oompah* bands, succulent *weinerschnitzels unt* beer than in Honolulu? At the Budweiser Warehouse, 99-877 Iwaena St., Halawa Park, from noon until 10:00 p.m.

Mid To Late October

Watch the boys from throughout Oceania smash, clash, and collide in the rough-and-tumble **Pan Am International Rugby Club Tournament** held at Queen Kapiolani Park, Honolulu, during odd-numbered years.

The **Annual Orchid Plant And Flower Show** displays Hawaii's copious and glorious flowers at the Blaisdell Center Exhibition Hall, Honolulu, tel. 527-5400.

The later part of the month is a superb time to visit the world's best museum of Polynesian and Hawaiian culture during the **Bishop Museum Festival.** Arts, crafts, plants, and tours of the museum and planetarium provide a full day of fun and entertainment for the family. Bishop Museum, Honolulu, tel. 847-3511.

When they really "wanna have fun" super-athletes come to the **Ironman World Triathlon Championship** at Kailua-Kona, Hawaii. A 2.4-mile open-ocean swim, followed by a 112-mile bike ride, and topped off with a full marathon is their idea of a good day. Ironman Office, tel. 528-2050.

The **Kapalua International Championship Of Golf,** at Kapalua, Maui, is one of the best pro tournaments, drawing the world's best golfers for one of the world's largest purses. Runs to early November. Kapalua International, tel. 669-4844.

NOVEMBER

Early November

Taste the best and only coffee commercially grown in the U.S. at the **Annual Kona Coffee Festival,** Kailua-Kona, Hawaii. Parades, arts and

continued

crafts, ethnic food and entertainment are part of the festivities.

Na Mele O'Maui Festival, Kaanapali and Lahaina, Maui, is a time when old Hawaii comes alive through art, dances, and music.

At the **Ho'Olaulea In Waianae,** Wainae, Oahu, the military lets down its hair and puts on a display accompanied by top entertainers, food and music in this very ethnic area. All-day event. Army Community Relations, tel. 438-9761.

Mid November
Here's your chance to see polo at the **Michelob Polo Cup And Bar-B-Que,** Olinda Polo Field, Makawao, Maui. Tel. 877-5541.

The **Annual King Kalakaua Keiki Hula Festival** is for children from around the state who come to Kailua-Kona, Hawaii to perform their *hula.* Plenty of fun, but the competition is serious.

November 11, **Veterans Day,** is a National holiday celebrated by a large parade from Fort DeRussy to Queen Kapiolani Park, Waikiki (all islands have a parade). For information, American Legion, tel. 949-1140.

Christmas in November
Hui Noeau Christmas Craft Fair is an annual event offering gifts, decorations, and food for those hungry shoppers. Held at Kaluanui Museum, Makawao, Maui. Tel. 979-2873

Christmas In The Country atop Hawaii's volcano is a delight where merrymakers frolic in the crisp air around a blazing fire, drinking hot toddys. Also, plenty of arts and crafts, food, and Santa for the *keikis.* Volcano Art Center, Hawaii Volcanoes National Park, Hawaii. Tel. 976-7676.

The **YWCA Festival Of Trees** presents Christmas crafts, ornaments, and decorated trees on display and for sale at the YMCA, Hilo, Hawaii, tel. 935-7141.

Quality items are offered by Hawaii's top craftsmen in an open-air bazaar at the **Annual Christmas Fair** of the Mission Houses Museum, Honolulu. Tel. 531-0481.

Late November
The best surfers in the world come to the best surfing beaches on Oahu for the **Hawaiian Pro-Surfing Championships.** Wave action determines sites except for the **Men's Masters** which is always held at Banzai Pipeline, North Shore, Oahu. Big money and national TV coverage bring out the best in everyone. Tel. 926-0611.

The Honolulu Academy of Art, Honolulu, tel. 538-3693, showcases some of Hawaii's finest contemporary artists at its **Artists Of Hawaii Annual Exhibition.**

DECEMBER

Early December
The **Kauai Junior Miss Presentation,** Kauai War Memorial Convention Hall, Lihue, is where young hopefuls get their first taste of the "big time."

The **Hawaii International Film Festival** at the East West Center, Honolulu, screens some of the best art films from the "East," "West," and Oceania. Tel. 944-7203 for details.

Christmas Celebrations
Christmas Fantasyland Of Trees at Honokaa, Hawaii, is an early showing of gaily decorated trees. The right Christmas spirit auctions them off for charity. Tel. 775-0345.

The **Festival Of Trees** is when the business community pitches in and offers gaily decorated trees with the proceeds to charity. It's held at the Coco Palms Hotel Queen's Audience Hall, Lihue, Kauai.

The **Kauai Museum Holiday Festival** is an annual Christmas event known for attracting the island's best in hand-crafted items and home-baked goodies. At the Kauai Museum, Lihue, Kauai, tel. 245-6931.

The **Kamehameha Schools Christmas Concert** is open to everyone and lifts the Christmas spirit at the Blaisdell Center Concert Hall, Honolulu, tel. 842-8211.

The open-air **Pacific Handcrafters Guild Christmas Fair,** Thomas Square, Honolulu, presents the best by the best, just in time for Christmas. Pacific Handcrafters, tel. 923-5726.

Mid To Late December
The **Annual Honolulu Marathon** is an "institution" in marathon races attracting the best runners from around the world. TV coverage. For information, tel. 723-7200.

The people of Hilo celebrate a New England Christmas in memory of the missionaries with **A Christmas Tradition.** Held at the Lyman House Memorial Museum, Hilo, tel. 935-5021.

A Christmas Tradition features the distinctive touches of a New England-style Christmas at the Lyman House Memorial Musem, Hilo, tel. 935-5021.

Bodhi Day is ushered in with ceremonies at Buddhist temples to commemorate Buddha's day of enlightenment. All islands.

The **Christmas Concert** by the Kauai High School Band and Chorus performs a medley of classic, contemporary and Hawaiian Christmas carols and tunes. At the Kauai War Memorial Convention Hall, Lihue, tel. 245-6422.

On **New Years Eve** hold on to your hat, because they do it up big in Hawaii. The merriment and alcohol flow all over the islands. Firecrackers are illegal, but they go off everywhere. Beware of hangovers and "amateur" drunken drivers.

December Sports

At the **Mauna Kea Beach Hotel's Annual Invitational Golf Tournament** men and women play at this fabulous golf course on the Kohala Coast, Hawaii, tel. 882-7222.

The **Kapalua-Betsey Nagelson Tennis Invitational** is a select field of women pros and amateurs. At Kapalua, Maui, Tennis Garden, tel. 669-5677.

The **Annual Rainbow Classic** is an invitational tournament of collegiate basketball teams. Blaisdell Center Arena, Honolulu, tel. 948-7523.

The **Aloha Bowl Game** is collegiate football with top teams from the Mainland coming to Aloha Stadium, Honolulu, tel. 488-7731.

PERFORMING ARTS EVENTS

The following offer top-notch performances at various times throughout the year: **Honolulu Symphony**, tel. 537-6191; **Hawaii Opera Theatre**, tel. 521-6537; **Honolulu Community Theatre**, tel. 734-0274; **Hawaii Performing Arts Company Theatre**, tel. 988-6131.

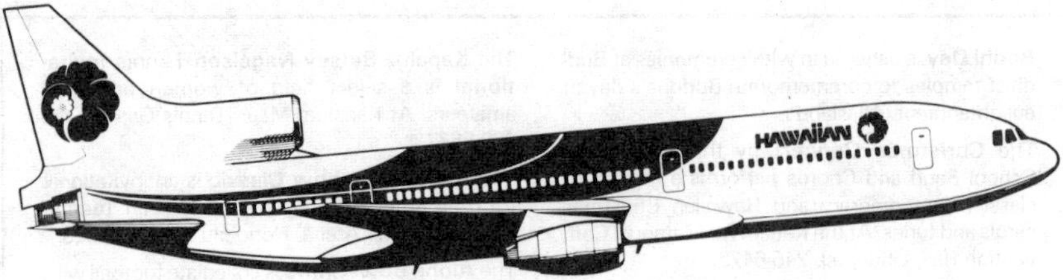

GETTING THERE

With more than four and a half million tourists visiting each year, and double that number of travelers just passing through, Hawaii is one of the easiest places in the world to get to...by plane. About 10 large U.S. airlines (and other small ones) fly to and from the islands; about the same number of foreign carriers, mostly from Asia and Oceania, touch down on a daily basis. In 1978 airlines were "deregulated." In 1984, the reign of the Civil Aeronautics Board (CAB), that controlled exactly which airlines flew where and how much they could charge, ended. Routes, prices, and schedules were thrown open to free competition. Airlines that had previously monopolized preferred destinations found competitors prying loose their strangleholds. Thus, Hawaii is now one of the most hotly contested air markets in the world. The competition between carriers is fierce, and this makes for "sweet deals" and a wide choice of fares for the money-wise traveler. It also makes for pricing chaos. It's impossible to give airline prices that will hold true for more than a month, if that long. But it's comforting to know that flights to Hawaii are cheaper today than they have been in years, and mile for mile are one of the best travel bargains in the industry. What's really important is to be familiar with the alternatives at your disposal, so you can make an informal travel selection. Now more than ever you should work with a sharp travel agent who's on your side.

Brief Airline History

On May 20-21, 1927, the people of the world were mesmerized by the heroic act of Charles Lindbergh, The Lone Eagle, as he safely piloted his sturdy craft *The Sprit of St. Louis* across the Atlantic. With the Atlantic barrier broken, it took only 4 days for Jim Dole, of pineapple fame, to announce an air race from the West Coast to Hawaii. He offered the same first prize of $25,000 that Lindbergh had claimed, and to sweeten the pot he offered $10,500 for second place. The **Dole Air Derby** applied only to civilian flights, though the military was already at work attempting the Pacific crossing. In August 1925, a Navy flying boat took off from near San Francisco, piloted by Commander John Rodgers. The seaplane flew without difficulty across the wide Pacific's expanse, but ran out of gas just north of the Hawaiian islands and had to put down in a stormy sea. Communication devices went dead and the mission was given up as lost. Heroically, Rodgers and his crew made crude sails from the wing's fabric and sailed the plane to within 12 miles of Kauai where they were spotted by an incredulous submarine crew. On June 28, 1927, Army Lieutenants Maitland and Hegenberger successfully flew a Fokker trimotor land plane, *The Bird of Paradise,* from Oakland to Oahu in just under 26 hours. On July 14, 1927, independent of the air derby, two indomitable pilots, Smith and Bronte, flew their *City of Oakland* from its namesake to a forced landing on the shoreline of Molokai. On August 16, 1927, 8 planes lined up in Oakland to start the derby. The first to take off was the *Woolaroc,* piloted by Art Goebel and Bill Davis. It went on to win the race and claim the prize in just over 26 hours. Second place went to the appropriately named *Aloha,* crewed by Martin Jensen and Paul Schluter, coming in 2 hours behind the *Woolaroc*. Unfortunately, two planes were lost in the crossing and two more in the rescue attempt, which accounted for 12 dead. However, most realized that flying to Hawaii was indeed feasible.

WINGS TO HAWAII

There are two categories of airlines that you can take to Hawaii: **domestic,** meaning American owned, and **foreign** owned. An American law, penned at the turn of the century to protect American shipping, says "only" an American carrier can transport you to and from two American cities. In the airline industry, this law is still very much in effect. It means, for example, if you want a *round trip* San Francisco/Honolulu, you *must* fly on a domestic carrier, such as United or Pan Am. If, however, you are flying San Francisco to Tokyo, you are at liberty to fly a "foreign" airline such as Japan Airlines, and you may even have a stopover in Hawaii, but you must continue on to Tokyo or some other foreign city and cannot fly JAL back to San Francisco. Canadians have no problem flying Canadian Pacific, round trip from Toronto to Honolulu because this route does not connect two "American" cities, and so it is with all foreign travel to and from Hawaii. Travel agents all know this, but if you're planning your own trip be aware of this fact and know that if you're "round trip," it must be on a domestic carrier.

Kinds Of Flights

The 3 kinds of flights are the "milk run," direct, and non-stop. Milk runs are the least convenient. On these, you board a carrier, say in your home town, fly it to a gateway city, change planes and carriers, fly on to the West Coast, change again, and then fly to Hawaii. They're a hassle—your bags have a much better chance of getting lost, you waste time in airports, and to top it off, they're not any cheaper. Avoid them if you can. On direct flights you fly from point A to point B without changing planes; it doesn't mean that you don't land in between. Direct flights do land usually once to board and deplane passengers, but you sit cozily on the plane along with your luggage and off you go again. Non-stop is just that, but can cost a bit more. You board and when the doors open again you're in Hawaii. All flights from the West Coast gateway cities are non-stop (God willing) because there is only the Pacific in between!

Travel Agents

At one time people went to a travel agent the same way they went to a barber or beautician ...loyally sticking with one. Most agents are reputable professionals who know what they're doing. They should be members of the American Society of Travel Agents (ASTA), and licensed by the Air Traffic Conference (ATC). Most have the inside track on the best deals, and they'll save you countless hours calling 800 numbers and listening to elevator music while you hold. Unless you require them to make very special arrangements, their services are free—the airlines and hotels that they book you into pay the commission. If you've done business with a travel agent in the past, and were satisfied with his services and prices, by all means stick with him. If no such positive rapport exists, then shop around. Ask friends or relatives for recommendations; if you can't get any endorsements go to the Yellow Pages. Call 2 or 3 travel agents to compare prices. Make sure to give them all equal information and be as precise as possible. Tell them where and when you want to go, how long you want to stay, class you want to travel, and any special requirements. Write down their information. It's amazing how confusing travel plans can be when you have to keep track of flight numbers, times, prices, and all the preparation info. When you compare, don't look only for the cheapest price. Check for convenience in flights, amenities of hotels, and any other fringe benefits that might be included. Then make your choice of agent, and if he's willing to give you individualized service, stick with him from this point on.

Agents become accustomed to offering the same deals to many clients because they're familiar with making the arrangements and they worked well in the past. Sometimes these are indeed the best, but if they don't suit you, don't be railroaded into accepting them. Any good agent will work with you. After all, it's your trip and your money.

Package Tours

As an independent traveler, practical package deals that include flight, car, and lodging only are OK. Agents put these together all the time and they just might be the best, but if they

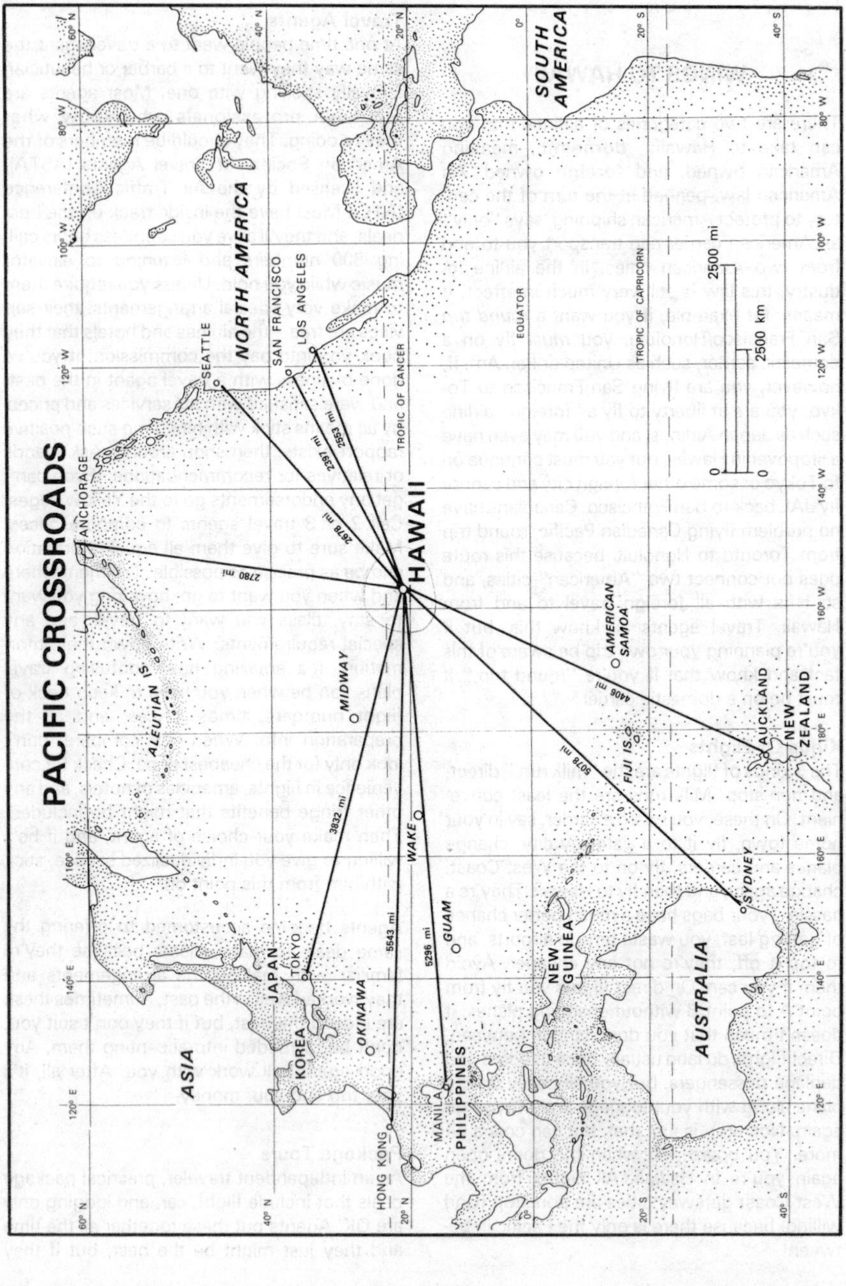
PACIFIC CROSSROADS
HAWAII
NORTH AMERICA
SOUTH AMERICA
ASIA
AUSTRALIA
ANCHORAGE
SEATTLE
SAN FRANCISCO
LOS ANGELES
ALEUTIAN IS.
MIDWAY
WAKE
GUAM
JAPAN
TOKYO
KOREA
OKINAWA
HONG KONG
MANILA
PHILIPPINES
NEW GUINEA
FIJI IS.
AMERICAN SAMOA
AUCKLAND
NEW ZEALAND
SYDNEY
EQUATOR
TROPIC OF CANCER
TROPIC OF CAPRICORN
2780 mi
2678 mi
2391 mi
2553 mi
3832 mi
5543 mi
5296 mi
4406 mi
5078 mi
2500 mi
2500 km

don't suit you make arrangements separately. A **package tour** is totally different. On these you get your hand held by an escort, eat where they want you to eat, go where they want you to go, and watch Hawaii slide by past the window of your bus. For some people, especially older folks or groups, this might be the way, but everyone else should avoid them. You'll see Hawaii best on your own, and if you want a tour you can arrange one there, often cheaper. Once arrrangements have been made with your travel agent, make sure to take all receipts and letters of confirmation (hotel, car) with you to Hawaii. They probably won't be needed, but if they are nothing will work better in getting results.

Fares

There are many categories of airline fares, but only 3 generally apply to the average traveler: 1st class, coach, and excursion (APEX). Traveling **1st class** seats you in the front of the plane, gives you free drinks and movie headsets, a wider choice of meals, more leg room, and access to VIP lounges if they exist. There are no restrictions, payment penalties on advance booking, minimum stays, or rebooking return flights.

Coach, the way that most people fly, is totally adequate. You sit in the plane's main compartment behind 1st class. Your seats are comfortable, but you don't have as much leg room or such a wide choice of meals. Movie headsets and drinks cost you a few dollars, but that's about it. Coach offers many of the same benefits as 1st class and costs about 30% less. You can buy tickets up to takeoff; you have no restrictions on minimum or maximum stays; you receive liberal stopover privileges, and you can cash in your return ticket or change your return date with no penalties.

Excursion or **Advance Payment Excursion (APEX)** fares are the cheapest. You are accommodated on the plane exactly the same as if you were flying coach. There are, however, some restrictions. You must book and pay for your ticket in advance (7-14 days). At the same time, you must book your return flight, and under most circumstances can't change either without paying a penalty. Also, your stopovers are severely limited and you will have a minimum/maximum stay period. Only a limited number of seats on any one plane are set aside for APEX fares, so book as early as you can. Also, if you must change travel plans, you can go to the airport and get on as a stand-by passenger using a discounted ticket even if the airline doesn't have an official stand-by policy. There's always the risk that you won't get on but you do have a chance, as well as priority over an actual stand-by customer.

Stand-by is exactly what its name implies: you go to the airport and wait around to see if any flights going to Hawaii have an empty seat. You can save some money, but cannot have a firm itinerary or limited time. Since Hawaii is such a popular destination stand-bys can wait days before catching a plane. A company called **Stand Bys Ltd.** offers an up-to-the-minute newsletter and an 800 number which gives you information on charter flights that haven't sold out. The service costs $45 per year, but you can save from 15-60% on most tickets. Write Stand Bys Ltd. 26711 Northwestern Hwy., Southfield, MI 48034 (tel. (313)352-4876.)

Tips

Flights from the West Coast take about 5 hours; you gain two hours over PST when you land in Hawaii. From the East Coast it takes about 11 hours and you gain 5 hours over EST. Try to fly Mon. through Thurs., when flights are cheaper and easier to book. Pay for your ticket as soon as your plans are firm. If prices go up there is no charge added, but merely booking doesn't guarantee the lowest price. Make sure that airlines, hotels, and car agencies get your phone number too, not only your travel agent's, in case any problems with availability arise (travel agents are often closed on weekends). It's not necessary, but it's a good idea to call and reconfirm flights 24-72 hours in advance. First-row (bulkhead) seats are good for people who need more leg room, but bad for watching the movie. Airlines will give you special meals (vegetarian, kosher, low cal, low salt) often at no extra charge, but you must notify them in advance. If you're "bumped" from an overbooked flight, you're entitled to a comparable flight to your destination within one hour. If more than an hour elapses, you get denied-boarding compensation which goes up proportionately with the amount of time you're

photo by Fritz Craft

held up. Sometimes this is cash or a voucher for another flight to be used in the future. You don't have to accept what the airlines offer on the spot, if you feel they aren't being fair.

Charters

Charter flights were at one time only for groups or organizations that had memberships in travel clubs. Now they're open to the general public. A charter flight is an entire plane or a "block" of seats purchased at a quantity discount by a charter company and then sold to customers. Because they are bought at wholesale prices, charter fares can be the cheapest available. As in package deals, only take a charter flight if it is a "fly only," or perhaps includes a car. You don't need one that includes a guide and a bus. Most importantly, make sure that the charter company is reputable. They should belong to the same organizations (ASTA and ATC) as most travel agents. If not check the local Chamber of Commerce. More restrictions apply to charters than any others. You must pay in advance. If you cancel after a designated time, you can be penalized severely or lose your money entirely. You can not change departure or return dates and times. However, 10 days before departure the charter company is legally able to cancel, raise the price by 10%, or change time and dates. They must return your money if cancellation occurs, or if changed arrangements are unacceptable to you. Mostly they are on the up and up and flights go smoothly, but there are horror stories. Be careful. Be wise. Investigate!

Traveling With Children

Fares for children 2 to 12 are 50% of the adult fare; children under 2 not occupying a seat travel free. If you're traveling with an infant or active toddler, book your flight well in advance and request the bulkhead seat or first row in any section and a bassinet if available. Many carriers have fold-down cribs with restraints for baby's safety and comfort. Toddlers appreciate the extra space provided by the front-row seats. Be sure to reconfirm and arrive early to assure getting this special seating. On long flights you'll be glad that you took these extra pains. Although most airlines have coloring books, puppets, etc. to keep your child busy, it's always a good idea to bring your own. These can make the difference between a pleasant flight and a harried ordeal. Also, remember to bring baby bottles, formula (if used), diapers, and other necessities as many airlines may not be equipped with exactly what you need. Make all inquiries ahead of time so you're not caught unprepared.

Baggage

You are allowed two free pieces of luggage and a carry-on bag. The two main pieces can weigh up to 70 pounds each with an extra charge levied for extra weight. The largest can have an overall added dimension (height plus width plus length) of 62 inches and the second at 55 inches. Your carry-on must fit under your seat or in the overhead storage compartment. Purses and camera bags are not counted as carry-ons and may be taken aboard. Surfboards and bicycles are about $15 extra. Although they make great mementos, remove all previous baggage tags from your luggage; they can confuse handlers. Attach a sturdy holder with your name and address on the handle, or use a stick-on label on the bag itself. Put your name and address inside the bag, and the address where you'll be staying in Hawaii if possible. Carry your cosmetics, identification, money, prescriptions, tickets, reservations, change of underwear, camera equipment, and perhaps a change of shirt or blouse in your carry-on.

Visas

Entering Hawaii is like entering anywhere else in the U.S. Foreign nationals must have a current passport and proper visa. An ongoing or return air ticket as well as sufficient funds for the proposed stay in Hawaii are also requirements of U.S. Immigration. Canadians do not need a visa or passport, but must have proper identification such as passport, driver's license, or birth certificate.

DOMESTIC CARRIERS

The following are the major domestic carriers to and from Hawaii. The planes used are primarily DC-10s and 747s, with a smaller 727 flown now and again. A list of the gateway cities from which they fly direct and non-stop flights is given, but connecting cities are not. All flights, by all carriers, land at Honolulu International Airport except for limited direct flights to Maui, Kauai, and Hawaii. Only the established companies are listed. Entrepreneurial small airlines such as the now defunct Hawaii Express pop up now and again and specialize in dirt-cheap fares. There is a hectic frenzy to buy their tickets. Business is great for a while, then the established companies lower their fares and the gamblers fold.

United Airlines

Since their first island flight in 1947, United has become "top dog" in flights to Hawaii. Having just bought all of Pan American's Pacific routes, they'll dominate the field even more. Their mainland routes connect over 100 cities to Honolulu. The main gateways are direct flights from San Francisco, Los Angeles, San Diego, Seattle, Portland, Chicago, New York, Denver, and Toronto. They also offer direct flights to Maui from San Francisco, Chicago, Portland, and Los Angeles, San Francisco and Los Angeles to Kauai, and to Kona on the Big Island; with a Los Angeles run to Hilo. United offers a number of packages ranging from a first-class "Classic Hawaii" to their more moderate "Affordable Hawaii." They interline with **Aloha Airlines** and offer special deals with **National Car Rental** among others. They're the "big guys" and they intend to stay that way—their packages are hard to beat. Call 800-652-1211.

Hawaiian Air

One of Hawaii's own domestic airlines has entered the Mainland market. As of now, they operate a daily flight from Los Angeles and San Francisco to Honolulu, and a non-stop Saturday flight from San Francisco to Maui. Hawaiian flies brand-new 325-passenger L-1011s. The "common fare" ticket price includes an ongoing flight to any of the Neighbor Islands, and if leaving from Hawaii, a free flight from a Neighbor Island to the link-up in Honolulu. Hawaiian has plans to expand, but for now they only offer reasonable charter flights from other cities in California. These are available through SunTrips at 800-662-9292. Other charter agents for Hawaiian include **International Travel Arrangers** for the Midwest, and **Conquest Tours** of Toronto for Canada. Hawaiian Airlines' **transpacific** schedule features four weekly flights between Honolulu and points in the South Pacific. Flights depart for Pago Pago, American Samoa, every Tues., Thurs., Fri., and Sunday; Tues. and Fri. flights continue to Apia, Western Samoa, with Thurs. and Sun. flights to Tonga. Return flights are Wed., Fri., Sat., and Monday. Contact Hawaiian Air at 800-367-5320; on Maui 244-9111.

American Airlines

Offers direct flights to Honolulu from Los Angeles, San Francisco, Dallas, and Chicago. They also fly from Los Angeles to Maui. Call 800-252-0421.

Pan American Airlines, now out of business in the Pacific, opened Hawaii to mass air travel with this historic flight on Wednesday, April 17, 1935. The flight from Alameda Airport to Pearl Harbor took 19 hours and 48 minutes.

The Honolulu Advertiser EXTRA

Hawaii's Territorial Newspaper

CLIPPER LANDS AT 8:00

An Early Morning Caller

Thousands See Flight's Start At Golden Gate

Heavily - Laden Ship In Graceful Takeoff from Bay Waters; Routine Job to Crew

By WENDELL BURCH
(United Press by Radio)

ALAMEDA, Cal., April 16—Pan American Airways Oriental Clipper, her four mighty motors humming a challenge to the broad Pacific, swept away from San Francisco Bay at 1:50 p.m. (PST) today for Honolulu on the first leg of a venture which will inaugurate commercial air transport service between the United States and China.

Despite a tremendous load, the great gray airliner lifted gracefully from the waters of the landing basin and pointed out over the Golden Gate while thousands of spectators lining the Alameda rim of the Bay waved and cheered.

The Sikorsky-built ship carried 130 pounds of mail, two tons of mechanical and engineering equipment for Pan American's base in Hawaii, and 1,000 gallons of gasoline and 300 gallons of oil.

FUEL FOR 3,200 MILES

She had fuel enough to fly at least 3,200 miles, though the Great Circle route to Honolulu is only approximately 2,400. Officials said this supply was considerably below the ship's maximum fuel capacity.

Reaches Honolulu At 7:04; Cruises Over Island Until Crowds Arrive At Air Base

Giant Plane Sets New Record for Westbound Hop; Could Easily Have Made Better Time But Delayed Landing for Spectators

At exactly 8 a. m. the 19-ton Pan American Clipper Ship came to a graceful landing at the fleet air base in Pearl Harbor, completing her flight from Alameda Airport to Honolulu in 19 hours and 48 minutes, and bettering the previous record for a westbound crossing of 24 hours and 45 minutes, made by the mass flight of the U. S. navy patrol squadron in January, 1934, by the wide margin of four hours and three minutes.

But the giant plane, commanded by Captain Edwin Musick, reached Honolulu at 7:04 o'clock and could have landed less than ten minutes later. To accommodate the crowds and the welcoming committee Captain Musick circled over the city and kept her aloft until 8 o'clock.

Aided by the trade winds over approximately the last 500 miles the clipper ship came along at speeds ranging from 115 to 160 miles

Advertiser Signs Wood

Here's Log Of Clipper Since Hop From Coast

Receptions Ready Today

Western Airlines
They have a big share of the Hawaii market with numerous connecting flights all over the country. Their gateway cities to Honolulu are Los Angeles, San Francisco, San Diego, Anchorage, and Vancouver. Call 800-227-6105.

Continental
Flights to Honolulu from Los Angeles, Houston, and Chicago. Also offers flights from Australia and New Zealand via Fiji. Connects with Air Micronesia to Guam. Call 800-525-0280.

Northwest Orient
Flies from Los Angeles, San Francisco, and Seattle via Portland. Onward flights to Tokyo, Osaka, Okinawa, Manila, Hong Kong, Taipei, and Seoul. Call 800-225-2525.

Delta Airlines
In 1985, Delta entered the Hawaiian market with non-stop flights to Honolulu from Atlanta and Dallas/Ft. Worth. Call 800-652-1330.

Maui Airlines
One of the newest airlines in Hawaii got off the ground in 1985. At first they offered flights throughout Hawaii, but now they fly only to/from the Micronesian islands of Guam, Saipan, Rota, and Tinian on 17-passenger Twin Otters aircraft. Their regularly scheduled flights are more expensive than the established commuter lines, while their air tours are about average. Call Maui Airlines at 800-367-2920; Maui, 871-6201.

FOREIGN CARRIERS

The following carriers operate throughout Oceania but have no U.S. flying rights. This means that in order to vacation in Hawaii using one of these carriers, your flight must originate or terminate in a foreign city. You can have a stop-over in Honolulu with a connecting flight to a "Neighbor Island." For example, if you've purchased a flight on Japan Airlines from San Francisco to Tokyo, you can stop in Hawaii, but you then must carry on to Tokyo. Failure to do so will result in a stiff fine, and the balance of your ticket will not be refunded.

Canadian Pacific Air
Flights from Canada to Honolulu originate in Vancouver, Edmonton, Toronto, and Calgary. Canadian Pacific also continues on to Fiji and Australia. Call 800-426-7007.

Air New Zealand
Flights link New Zealand, Australia, and Fiji with Los Angeles via Honolulu. They also offer a remarkable APEX fare from Los Angeles to Honolulu, with 11 stopovers throughout Oceania before deplaning in New Zealand. Call 800-262-1234.

Japan Air Lines
The Japanese are the second largest group, next to Americans, to visit Hawaii. JAL flights to Honolulu originate in Tokyo and Osaka. There are no JAL flights to or from the Mainland from Hawaii. Both Japan's **All Nippon**

Airways and Hawaii's **Aloha Airlines** are seeking expansion into this territory through bilateral agreements. Call 800-525-3663.

Philippine Airlines
Flights to and from Los Angeles and San Francisco to Manila via Honolulu. Connections in Manila to most Asian cities. Call 800-227-4600.

Qantas
Multiple weekly flights from San Francisco and Los Angeles to Sydney via Honolulu. Stopovers possible in New Caledonia, New Zealand, Fiji, and Tahiti. Call 800-622-0850.

China Airlines
They maintain routes from Los Angeles to Taipei with stop-overs in Honolulu and Tokyo possible, though not available year-round. Connections from Taipei to most Asian capitals. Call 800-652-1428.

Korean Airlines
Some of the least expensive flights to Asia. Free stop-overs from Los Angeles and San Francisco in both Honolulu and Tokyo on a RT ticket. One-way ticket allows only one stopover. Connections to many Asian cities. Call 800-421-8200.

Singapore Airlines
Flights to and from San Francisco and Los Angeles to Singapore via Honolulu. Free stopover. Nominal fee for additional stop-overs in Taipei and Hong Kong. Call 800-742-3333.

Air Tungaru
Limited flights from Kiribati to Honolulu via Christmas Island and Tarawa. In Hawaii, call 839-4561.

Air Niugini
Weekly flight from Honolulu to Papua New Guinea with connections to Japan, Australia, Hong Kong, Manila, and Singapore. In Hawaii, call 531-5341.

Air Nauru
The South Pacific's richest island offers flights throughout Polynesia including most major islands with connections to Japan, Taipei, Hong Kong, Manila, Singapore, and Australia. In Hawaii, call 531-9766.

South Pacific Island Airways
Grounded for awhile because of lack of sound-muffling "hush kits," SPIA is back in the air. Flights to Honolulu from Guam, Tahiti, American Samoa, Vancouver, and Anchorage. Connecting flights to Port Moresby (Papua New Guinea), Belau, Pago Pago (American Samoa), Tonga, and Saipan. In Hawaii, call 526-0844.

Samoa Airlines
Operates twice-weekly flights to American Samoa from Honolulu. They're also trying for rights to Tonga and Tahiti. In Hawaii call 537-2098.

TRAVEL BY SHIP

At one time Hawaiians lined the pier in Honolulu waiting to greet the cruise ships bringing visitors. It was the only way to get to Hawaii, but that's long since gone. Now only one American company, and a few foreign lines make the crossing.

American Hawaii Cruises
This American cruise ship company operates two 800-passenger ships, the SS *Independence,* and the SS *Constitution*. Primarily, these ships offer similar 7-day itineraries that circumnavigate and call at the four main islands. Their price ranges from $995 for a berth on the economy deck to $2,995 for a suite. (Children under 18 at $99 to share a double cabin.) You board in Honolulu after arriving by plane (arranged by the cruise company). Also, each ship makes one transpacific sailing yearly. One departs Honolulu for San Francisco, Los Angeles, and San Diego in late November, and the other in late December—return to Honolulu in mid-December, the other in mid-January. Each ship is a luxury sea-going hotel and gourmet restaurant; swimming pools, driving ranges, tennis courts, health clubs, movies, and nightclubs are all part of the amenities. For details contact: American Hawaii Cruises, 550 Kearny St., San Francisco, CA 94108, tel. 800-227-3666, from Canada call collect 415-392-9400.

Alternatives

Other companies offering varied cruises are **P&O Lines** which operates the *Sea Princess* through the South Pacific, making port at Honolulu on its way from the West Coast once a year.

Royal Cruise Line out of Los Angeles, or Auckland alternatively, sails the *Royal Odyssey* that docks in Honolulu on its South Pacific and Orient cruise, from $2,200 to $4,000.

The **Nauru Pacific Line** offers freighter/-passenger service from San Francisco to Micronesia via Honolulu, at 6-week intervals year round.

The **Holland America Line** sails the *Rotterdam* on its 108 day Grand Circle cruise, departing Fort Lauderdale, passing around South America and calling at Honolulu as it heads for Asia. Prices are from $20,000 to $70,000. Tel. 800-426-0327.

Society Expeditions offers a 42-day cruise throughout the South Pacific departing from Honolulu. Fares are from $3,000 to $9,000. Tel. 800-426-7794.

Information

Most travel agents can provide information on the above cruise lines. If you're really interested in traveling by ship contact: **Freighter Travel Club of America,** Box 12693, Salem, Oregon USA; **Ford's Freighter Travel Guide,** Box 505, 22151 Clarendon St., Woodland Hills, CA USA.

TOUR COMPANIES

Many tour companies offer packages to Hawaii in large city newspapers every week. They advertise very reasonable air fares, car rentals, and accommodations. Without trying, you can get RT airfare from the West Coast and a week in Hawaii for $400 using one of these companies. The following are tour companies that offer great deals, and have excellent reputations. Others that cover only specific Hawaiian islands are listed in the appropriate chapters. This list is by no means exhaustive.

Student Travel Network

You don't have to be a student to avail yourself of their services. Their main office is at 2500 Wilshire Blvd., no. 920, Los Angeles, CA 90057, tel. 213-380-2184. In Honolulu at 1831 S. King St., Honolulu, HI 96826, tel. 942-7755. STN also maintains offices in San Diego, San Francisco, and Northridge, California, as well as throughout Australia.

Nature Expeditions International

These quality tours have nature as the theme. Their guides are experts in their fields and give personable and attentive service. Contact Nature Expeditions International at 474 Willamette, Box 11496, Eugene, Oregon 97440, tel. 503-484-6529.

SunTrips

This California-based tour and charter company sells vacations all over the world. They're primarily a wholesale company, but will work with the general public. Contact SunTrips, 100 Park Center, Box 18505, San Jose, CA 95158, tel. 800-662-9292.

Pacific Outdoor Adventures

This truly remarkable tour company offers the best in nature tours. The emphasis is on the outdoors with hiking, camping, and kayaking. Prices are very hard to beat. Contact Pacific Outdoor Adventures, P.O. Box 61609, Honolulu, HI 96822, tel. 988-3913.

Island Holiday Tours

An established Hawaii-based company that offers flights with United and American. Contact Island Holiday Tours, 2255 Kuhio Ave., Honolulu, HI 96815, tel. 800-448-6877.

Pleasant Hawaiian Holidays

A California-based company specializing in Hawaii. At 2404 Townsgate Road, West Lake Village, CA 91361, tel. 800-242-9244.

Hawaiian Holidays

An Hawaiian-based company with plenty of experience. Featuring United, Hawaiian Air and National Car Rental. Contact Hawaiian Holidays 2222 Kalakaua Ave, Honolulu, HI 96815, tel. 800-367-5040; in Hawaii, 923-6548.

Council Travel Services
These full-service, budget-travel specialists are a subsidiary of the non-profit Council on International Educational Exchange, and the official U.S. representative to the International Student Travel Conference. They'll custom design trips and programs for everyone from senior citizens to college students. Groups and business travelers are also welcome. However, they deal with Hawaii only as a stopover en route to Asia. For full information, write to the main offices at Council Travel Services, 919 Irving St., No. 102, San Francisco, CA 94122, tel. 415-566-6222.

Bicycle Tours
For those interested in peddling around the Hawaiian Islands contact one of the following for their specialized bike trips. **Island Bicycle Adventures,** 569 Kapahulu Ave., Honolulu, HI 96815, tel. 732-7227. The owners and tour leaders are intimately familiar with bicycle touring on all islands, and are members of the Hawaii Bicycling league. They offer tours to Maui, the Big Island, and Oahu; **Backroads Bicycle Touring,** Box 1626, San Leandro, CA 94577, tel. 415-895-1738 are also experts in the field of bike touring, but at this time only tours to the Big Island are offered. For more information, see "Bicycling" under "Sports."

"O, how my spirit languishes
To step ashore in the
Sanguishes..."
—Robert Louis Stevenson,
1888

GETTING AROUND

Inter-island air travel is highly developed, economical, and ridiculously convenient. You can go almost anywhere at anytime on everything from wide-bodied jets, to single-engine air taxis. But ironically, in an island community complete with its sea history, modern shipping, and port towns, you cannot go between islands on regularly scheduled ships, boats, or floating conveyances of any nature. You can charter a pleasure boat for a tremendous fee, or maybe bum a ride between the Neighbor Islands on a passing yacht, but nothing is available on a regular schedule. A hovercraft that once serviced the islands is now defunct. Periodically, there is a cry to reinstate some sort of coastal and inter-island boat or ferry service. Some say that visitors and islanders alike would enjoy the experience and be able to travel more economically. Others argue the Hawaiian waters are as dangerous and unpredictable as ever, and no evidence of need or enough passengers exist. A few skippers that run pleasure craft between Maui-Molokai-Lanai are willing to take on passengers, but this is a hit-and-miss situation based on space. These special situations will be discussed in the appropriate travel chapters under "Getting Around." For now, inter-island travelers have to be content with seeing the islands from the air only.

By Air

Hawaiians take flying for granted, using planes the way most people use buses. A shopping excursion to Honolulu from a Neighbor Island is commonplace, as is a trip from the city for a picnic at a quiet beach. The longest flight, just over an hour, is from Kauai to Hawaii, including a stopover at one of the islands in between. The moody sea can be uncooperative (no inter-island boats anyway), but the skies above Hawaii are generally clear and perfect for flying. Their infrequent gloomier moments can delay flights, but the major airlines of Hawaii have a perfect safety record ever since Hawaiian Air's maiden flight in 1929. The fares are competitive, schedules convenient, and the service friendly.

Brief History

Little more than a motorized kite, the *Hawaiian Skylark* was the first plane ever to fly in Hawaii.

On New Year's Day, 1911, it circled a Honolulu polo field, where 3,000 spectators, including Liliuokalani, witnessed history. Hawaiians have been soaring above their lovely islands ever since. The first paying customer, Mrs. Newmann, took off on a $15 joy ride in 1913 with a Chinese aviator named Tom Gunn. In February 1920, Charles Fern piloted the first inter-island customer round trip from Honolulu to Maui for $150. He worked for Charles Stoffer, who started the first commercial airline the year before with one Curtiss bi-plane, affectionately known as "Charlie's Crate." For about 10 years sporadic attempts at inter-island service amounted to little more than extended joy rides to deliver the day's newspaper from Honolulu. The James Dole Air Race in 1927 proved that transpacific flight was possible (see p. 114) but inter-island passenger service didn't really begin until Stanley C. Kennedy, a WW I flier and heir to Inter-Island Steam Navigation Co., began Inter-Island Airways in January 1929. For a dozen years he ran Sikorsky Amphibians, considered the epitome of safety. By 1941 he converted to the venerable workhorse, the DC-3, and changed the company name to **Hawaiian Air**.

By 1948, Hawaiian Air was unopposed in the inter-island travel market, because regularly scheduled boats had already become obsolete. However, in 1946 a fledgling airline named Trans-Pacific opened for business. A non-scheduled airline with only one war surplus DC-3, they carried a hunting party of businessmen to Molokai on their maiden flight. By June 1952, they were a regularly scheduled airline in stiff competition with Hawaiian Air and had changed their name to **Aloha Airlines**. Both airlines had their financial glory days and woes over the next decade; by the end of the '60s both were flying inter-island jets. They remained the undisputed champions of the airs until **Mid Pacific** began flying in 1981 and filled the Hawaiian skies with the flak of an airfare war.

A healthy crop of small unscheduled airlines known as "air taxis" always darted about the wings of the large airlines, flying to minor airfields and performing flying services that were uneconomical for the bigger airlines. Most of these tiny, often one-plane "air taxis" were swatted from the air like gnats whenever the economy went sour or tourism went sluggish. They had names like Peacock and Rainbow, and after a brief flash of wing, they were gone.

The Big Inter-island Carriers

Hawaiian Air is not only the oldest airline in Hawaii, it's also the biggest. It flies more aircraft, to more airports, more times a day than any other airline in Hawaii. It services all islands including Molokai and Lanai. Hawaiian Air boasts a top-notch fleet of DC-9 jets for its longer flights, and the modern Dash-7, 4-engine turbo-prop (50 passenger) for its shorter runs. From the Mainland call toll-free, 800-367-5320; Canada, 800-663-3389, B.C. Zenith 2950; Oahu, 537-5100; Maui, 244-9111; Kauai, 245-3671; Hawaii, 935-0811; Molokai, 553-5321; Lanai, 565-6429.

HAWAIIAN® AIRLINES

Interisland Route System Map

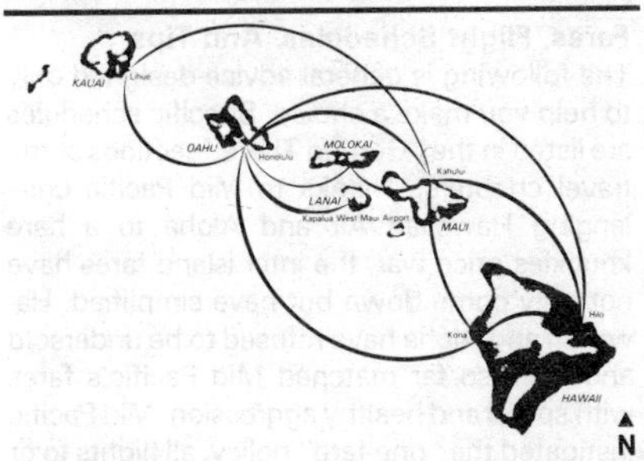

Aloha Airlines, Hawaii's second largest carrier, has numerous flights aboard its fleet of Boeing 737s to the 4 major islands, but none to Lanai and Molokai. From the Mainland, 800-367-5250; Canada, 800-663-9471, Alberta and B.C., 800-663-9396; Oahu, 836-1111; Maui, 244-9071; Hawaii, 935-5771; Kauai, 245-3691.

The newest airline, **Mid Pacific**, uses a fleet of Japanese-built, 60-passenger, YS-11 turboprops and Fokker-28, 85-passenger jets. They fly to the 4 main islands. Tel., mainland, 800-367-7010; Oahu, 836-3313; Maui, 242-4906; Hawaii, 329-8047; Kauai, 245-7775.

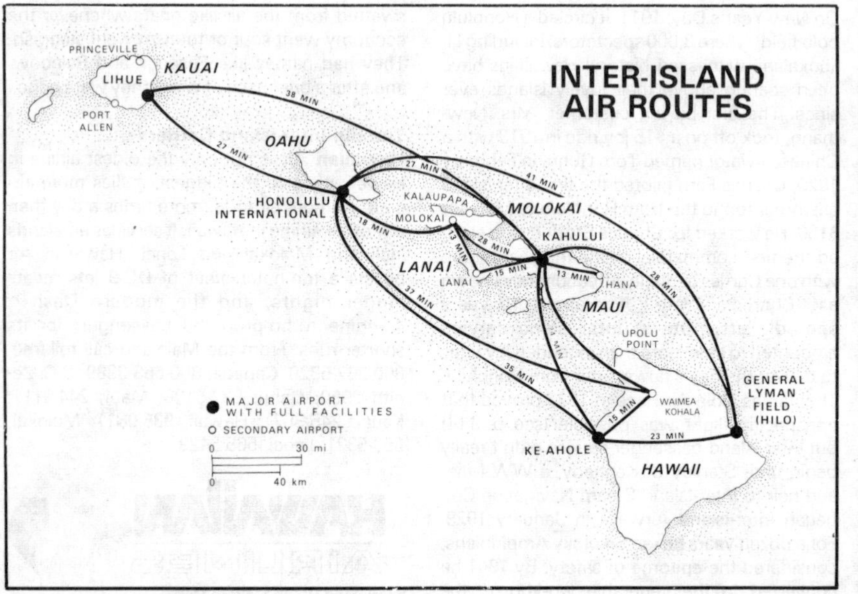

Fares, Flight Schedules, And Tips
The following is general advice designed only to help you make a choice. Specific schedules are listed in the "Getting There" sections of the travel chapters. Thanks to Mid Pacific challenging Hawaiian Air and Aloha to a bare knuckles price war, the inter-island fares have not only come down but have simplified. Hawaiian and Aloha have refused to be undersold and have so far matched Mid Pacific's fares with speed and healthy aggression. Mid Pacific instigated the "one-fare" policy: all flights to or from any island are one price—about $40, but this is only a ball-park figure. The price can change while you're reading this sentence. Hawaiian and Aloha's prices are within $1 of Mid Pacific's. To get you aboard, they all run short-term specials, and give little perks like free drinks. Aloha is squeezed most because they only run jets, and don't have the same leverage to cut prices like Mid Pacific who fly more economical turbo-props and Hawaiian that operates both. Aloha counters this by offering first-class service for more money, including extra leg room, meals, and a free surprise gift. Hawaiian Air, by contrast, gives you a stop-over on Molokai or Lanai if you're flying Honolulu to Maui on a flight scheduled to stop on either island.

Actually, the real choice comes down to scheduling. Does the airline offer a flight to where you want to go when you want to go there? The normal flying hours in Hawaii are 6:00 a.m. to 8:00 p.m., with scores of flights during this time period. Like rush-hour traffic in the Mainland cities, most flights are clustered around 8:00 a.m. and 5:00 p.m., with one leaving from the major airports every 20 minutes or so. All three airlines offer **joint fare**: if you book a round-trip ticket with a specific major Mainland airlines, the Hawaiian inter-island airlines give you a fare reduction (not applicable to charter flights, or stopover flights on non-American carriers). Check with your travel agent to see which airlines are currently offering joint fares. At one time, all three airlines had their own Travel Club—$5 to join gave you special fare reductions. They still exist, but because of the one-fare policy they have no real money savings advantage for the average traveler. Hawaiian Air offered fare reductions to AAA Motor Club members, but this too has no advantage; however, you still save a little bit with both the AAA membership and the Travel Club on flights to Molokai and Lanai.

The budget traveler's ace in the hole was flying "stand-by." You can still wait at the gate to get on a flight if you haven't booked, but it doesn't save money any longer because of the one-fare policy. Stand-by now only comes in handy if you get an uncontrollable urge to travel immediately.

Practical Information

On Oahu, all three inter-island carriers are located at the newly remodeled Inter Island Terminal at Honolulu International Airport. It's to the right or *ewa* of the main terminal as you face it. The baggage allowance is 2 "normal sized" pieces of luggage. Golf bags count as one piece. Oversized and extra bags or boxes are charged $5-10 more. Bicycles and surfboards cost $10 and can't be substituted as luggage. Although 60 minutes is recommended, if you check in under 30 minutes prior to flight time you can lose your seat.

COMMUTER AIRLINES

Hawaii has a good selection of "commuter airlines" offering regularly scheduled flights, air tours, and special flights to small airports that the big carriers don't service. They're so handy and personalized that they might be considered "air taxis." All use smaller aircraft that seat less than 12 people, and fly low enough so that their normal inter-island flights are like an air tour. Stories abound of passengers being invited to ride co-pilot, or of a pilot going out of his way to show off a glimmering coastline or a beautiful waterfall. Many times you get the sense that it's "your" flight and that the airline is doing everything possible to make it memorable.

Fares, Schedules, And Tips

The following is offered merely as general advice to help you make a choice. Specific schedules are listed in the "Getting There" sections of the travel chapters. The commuter airlines are limited in plane size and routes serviced. Among themselves, prices are very competitive, but, except on their specialty runs, they tend to be more expensive than the 3 major inter-island carriers. They're also not as generous on baggage allowance, and you'll be charged more for extra, some of which may not accompany you on the plane.

Princeville Airways flies from Princeville on Kauai to Honolulu, and from Honolulu to Waikaloa on the Big Island. They've also picked up some routes of the now defunct Royal Hawaiian Airlines, and offer limited service to Maui. Their planes are 18-seat Twin Otters, the largest of the commuter airlines. Tel., Mainland, 800-367-7090; on Oahu and Big Island, 800-652-6541; Kauai, 826-6066.

Oahu's **Reeves Aviation** will fly you anywhere you want to go at anytime. They also offer a number of air tours and run regular schedules between Oahu, Maui, and Molokai. They fly Cessna 402s, with 24-hour charter flights to any airport in Hawaii. Tel., on Oahu, 833-9555.

Air Molokai-Tropic Airlines flies variable routes between Molokai, Oahu, Maui, and Lanai. Their fleet includes Cessna 402s and vintage DC-3s. On Oahu call 536-6611; Molokai, 567-6102; other islands, 800-352-3616.

Tiny **Polynesian Air** does charter flights anywhere in the islands, and services Molokai and Lanai. Their flea-hop on Molokai from Kalaupapa to "topside" can't be beat. On Oahu call 836-3838; Molokai, 567-6697.

pilot Hal Corbett (l) of Polynesian Air

Air Tours And Helicopters
Scores of air-tour companies specialize in personalized flights around the islands. These are not economical as travel between islands. Also a growing number of helicopters fly in the islands. They too offer air tours and adventures: Waimea Canyon, Haleakala, and Kilauea when it's spouting lava are some of their more popular sightseeing tours. Many land in remote areas, so you can enjoy your own private waterfall and views. One of the best is **Papillon Helicopters**, tel. Maui, 669-4884; Kauai, 826-6591. Others are listed in "Sightseeing Tours" in the island introductions on which they fly.

Practical information
On Oahu, commuter airlines are located at the small, open-air "Commuter Terminal," at Honolulu International, left of the main terminal as you face it. Commuter airlines allow 2 normal-sized bags, but they are concerned with weight—up to 44 pounds no problem; between 44 and 80 pounds, free, but on a space-available basis; over 80, space-available but you pay extra; some airlines vary. Check-in is 30 minutes prior to departure; if you're not there at least 10 minutes before take-off, your seat can be sold.

CAR RENTALS

Does Hawaii really have more rental cars than pineapples? Oahu's Yellow Pages have 8 pages of listings for car rental agencies; there are over 40 firms on Maui; a few dozen on the Big Island, 20 or so on Kauai, Molokai has a handful, and even Lanai has one or two. You can rent anything from a 60-passenger Scenic-cruiser, to a 60cc moped. Even so, if you visit the islands during a peak tourist frenzy without reserving your wheels in advance, you'll be marooned at the airport.

There's a tremendous field of cars and agencies from which to choose and they're cheaper than anywhere else in America. Special deals come and go like tropical rain showers; swashbuckling price slashings and come-on's are all over the rental car market. A little knowledge combined with some shrewd shopping around can save you a bundle. And renting a car is the best way to see the islands if you're going to be there for a limited time. Outside of Oahu, it simply isn't worth hassling with the poor public transportation system, or relying on your thumb.

Car Rental Categories
When you arrive at any of Hawaii's airports, you'll walk the gauntlet of car rental booths and courtesy phones shoulder to shoulder along the main hallways. Of the 3 categories of car rental agencies in Hawaii, each has its own advantage. The first is the big international firms like National, Hertz, Avis, and Budget. These big guys are familiar, easy to work with, sometimes offer special fly/drive deals with airlines, and live up to their promises. If you want your rental experience to be hassle free, they're the ones. Also, don't be prejudiced against them just because they're so well known; sometimes they offer the best deal.

Hawaii has spawned a good crop of statewide car rental agencies such as Tropical, Robert's, and Holiday Hawaii. These companies and their cars are also reliable, easy to book through a travel agent, and give good service. Their bargain prices and special deals make it worthwhile to price them. The third category is the local entrepreneurial rental agencies. Their deals and cars can range, like rummage-sale treasures, from great finds to pure junk. Some, like Hawaii Rent a Car, El Cheapo, and Molokai U Drive, are reliable and good. These companies have the advantage of being able to cut deals on the spot. If nothing is moving from their lot on the day you arrive, you might get a real bargain. Unfortunately, mixed in this category is a hodge-podge of the fly-by-nights. Some of these are small, but adequate, while others are a rip-off. Their cars are bad, their service is worse, and they have more hidden costs than a Monopoly board.

Requirements
A variety of requirements is imposed on the renter by car agencies, but the most important clauses are common. Some of the worst practices being challenged are: no rentals to people under 25 and over 70, and no rentals to military personnel or Hawaiian residents! Before renting, check if you fulfill the requirements. Gen-

erally, you must be 21, although some agencies rent to 18-year-olds, while others still require you to be 25. You must possess a valid driver's license, with licenses from most countries accepted, but to be safe if you are not American, get an International Driver's License. You should have a major credit card in your name. This is the easiest way, though some companies take a deposit, but it will be very stiff. It could easily be $50 per day on top of your rental fees and sometimes much more, and a credit check on the spot, complete with phone calls to your employer and bank, may be required. If you damage the car, charges will be deducted from your deposit, and the car company itself determines the extent of the damages. Some companies *will not* rent you a car without a major credit card in your name, no matter how much of a deposit you are willing to leave.

When To Rent

On this one, you'll have to make up your own mind, because it's a "bet" that you can either win or lose big. But it's always good to know the odds before you plop down your money. You can reserve your car in advance when you book your air ticket, or play the field when you get there. If you book in advance, you'll obviously have a car waiting for you, but the deal that you made is the deal that you'll get—it may or may not be the best around. On the other hand, if you wait to play the field, you can oftentimes take advantage of excellent on-the-spot deals. Obviously, however, you're betting that cars are available. You might be totally disappointed, and not be able to rent a car at all, or you might make a honey of a deal. If you're arriving during the peak seasons of Christmas, Easter and late summer vacation, *absolutely book your car in advance.* They are all accounted for during this period, and even if you can find a junk from a fly-by-night, they'll price-gouge you mercilessly. If you're going off-peak, you stand a good chance of getting the car you want, at the price you want. It's generally best to book ahead, but the majority of car companies have free 800 numbers, (listed below). At least call them for an opinion of your chances of getting a car when you intend to arrive.

Rates

If you pick up a car rental brochure at a travel agent, notice the price for Hawaii rentals are about the lowest. The two rate options for renting are **mileage**, or **flat rate**. A third type, mileage/minimum, is generally a bad idea unless you plan to do some heavy-duty driving. Mileage rate costs less per day, but you are charged for every mile driven. Mileage rates are best if you drive less than 30 miles per day—even on an island that isn't much! The flat rate is *best* with a fixed daily rate and unlimited mileage. Either rate, you buy the gas; don't buy the cheapest because the poor performance from low octane eats up your savings. Discounts of about 10-15% for weekend, weekly, and monthly rates are available. It's sometimes cheaper to rent a car for the week even if you're only going to use it for 5 days. Both weekly and monthly rates can be split between neighboring islands, but this will only apply if the firm has inter-island offices, and this usually eliminates the small local guys. Extra costs are assessed if you drop off the car at a different spot from where you rented it; a common one is a Hilo pick-up and a Kona drop-off on the Big Island. Don't be surprised if some car companies want an extra fee if you drop your Waikiki rental at the Honolulu Airport, even if they have a facility there. If you keep your car beyond your contract, you'll be charged the highest daily rate unless you notify the rental agency beforehand. **Warning:** Don't keep your car longer than the contract without notifying the company. They are *quick* to send out their repossession specialists. You might find your car gone, a warrant for your arrest, and an extra charge. A simple courtesy call notifying them of your intentions saves a lot of headaches and hassle.

What Wheels To Rent

The super cheap rates on the eye-catcher brochures refer to sub-compact standard shifts. The price goes up with the size of the car and with an automatic transmission. Like options on a new car, the more luxury, the more you pay. If you can drive a standard shift, get one! They're cheaper to rent and operate. Because many Hawaiian roads are twisty affairs, you'll appreciate the down-shifting ability and extra control of a standard shift. Don't pay extra for a/c; you won't need it. AM/FM radios are good to have for entertainment, and for weather and surf conditions. If you have the choice take a car with cloth seats instead of sticky vinyl. The average price of a sub-compact, standard shift, no a/c is $25 per day with a weekly rate of $90 (add about $8 per day—$50 per week—for an automatic) but rates vary widely. Luxury cars are about $10 a day more with a comparable weekly rate. Most of the car companies, local and national, offer *special rates* and deals. National Car Rental, for example, has a special drive/stay package with Hawaiian Pacific Resorts for a room and a car on all major islands. If you fly Hawaiian Air on their new Mainland service, or inter-island, you can get a car with Tropical or Holiday for less than $15 per day. Budget sometimes runs fly/drive specials with United and Western, and Hertz has a truly "Affordable Hawaii" package that gives you an excellent weekly rate if you meet the prerequirements. These deals fluctuate too rapidly to give any hard and fast information except that they are common, so make sure to inquire. Also, peak periods have "black outs" where normal good deals no longer apply.

Insurance
Before signing your car rental agreement, you'll be offered "insurance," for around $8 per day. Since insurance is already built into the contract (don't expect the rental agency to point this out), what you're really buying is a waiver on the deductible ($500-$1,000), in case you crack up the car. If you have insurance at home, you almost always have coverage on a rental car, including your normal deductible, but not all policies are the same, so check with your agent. Also, if you haven't bought their waiver, and you have a mishap, the rental agencies will put a claim against your major credit card on the spot for the amount of deductible, even if you can prove that your insurance will cover. They'll tell you to collect from your insurance because they don't want to be left holding the bag on an across-the-waters claim. If you have a good policy with a small deductible, it's hardly worth paying the extra money even if you do have a claim against you. You'll eventually recover it, but if your own policy is inadequate, buy the insurance.

Driving Tips
Protect your children as you would at home with car seats. Their rental prices vary considerably: Alamo offers them free of charge; National charges $3 per day; Hertz needs 48 hours notice; Dollar gives them free but they're not always available at all locations; and, almost all the agencies can make arrangements if you give them enough notice. Check before you go and if all else fails, bring one from home.

There are few differences between driving in Hawaii and on the Mainland. Just remember that many people on the roads are tourists and can be confused about where they're going. Since many drivers are from somewhere else, there's hardly a "regular style" of driving in the islands. A farmer from Iowa accustomed to poking along on back roads can be sandwiched between a frenetic New Yorker who's trying to drive over his roof and a super-polite but horribly confused Japanese tourist who normally drives on the left.

In Hawaii, drivers don't honk their horns except to say hello, or in an emergency. It's considered rude, and honking to hurry someone might earn you a knuckle sandwich. Hawaiian drivers reflect the climate: they're relaxed and polite. Oftentimes, they'll brake to let you turn left when they're coming at you. They may assume you'll do the same, so be ready, after a perfunctory turn signal, for a driver to turn across your lane. The more rural the area, the more apt this is to happen.

4WDs, Campers, And RVs
For normal touring, it is totally unnecessary to rent 4WDs in Hawaii except on Lanai where they're a must, or if you really want to get off the beaten track. They are expensive ($65 per day), uneconomical, and you simply don't need them. However, if you want one, most car rental agencies have them. Because their numbers are limited, reservations are absolutely necessary.

Some people figure, "why not rent your wheels and accommodations all in one by going for a camper or an RV?" These are available, and with a large network of national, federal, and local parks and campgrounds, they're not a bad idea. You don't really save any money over renting a compact car and a mid-priced room, but you get mobility and cooking facilities thrown into the bargain. Prices vary from island to island and on what kind of rig you want—from a small pickup with camper to a full-fledged motorhome. Expect to pay from $45-$90 per day and a $.06 per mile. The smallest rigs sleep 2 and have basic cooking facilities, an icebox, and no toilet. The amenities, including full bathrooms, increase with size and price of the unit. The largest outfit is **Beach Boy Campers,** with rentals on Hawaii, Maui, Kauai and Oahu. Contact Beach Boy Campers at 1720 Ala Moana Blvd., Suite B2, Honolulu, HI 96815, tel. 955-1849. Another RV rental agency with a good reputation is **Travel Camp,** servicing the Big Island only. Write: Travel Camp, Box 11, Hilo, HI 96720, tel. 935-7406.

B-Y-O Car

Unless you'll be in Hawaii for a bare minimum of 6 months, and spending all your time on one island, don't even think about bringing your own car. It's an expensive proposition, and takes time and plenty of arrangements. From California, it costs at least $600 to Honolulu, with an additional $100 to any other island. It would be better to buy and sell a car there, or lease for an extended period to save on rental costs. If you want to bring your own car write for information to: Director of Finance, Division of Licenses, 1455 S. Beretania St., Honolulu, HI 96814.

AGENCY INFORMATION

The following is a partial list of the car rental agencies operating in Hawaii. The phone numbers given are toll-free 800 numbers when available, or the head-office numbers when not. Remember that 800 numbers sometimes vary according to your area code, so if you can't make connection please call your 800 operator (1-800-555-1212). Local addresses and phone numbers, by island, are listed in the "Getting Around" sections of the travel chapters, as are small local car rental agencies and specialty transport such as bicycles and mopeds.

Car Pick-Up

The vast majority of agencies listed have booths at all of the airport terminal buildings throughout Hawaii. If they don't, they have clearly marked courtesy phones in the lobbies. Just pick it up and they'll give directions on where to wait, and then come to fetch you with their shuttle.

NATIONAL AND INTERNATIONAL AGENCIES

The following rent vehicles on all islands except Molokai and Lanai. (Avis rents cars on Molokai).

National Car Rental, 800-227-7368; Alaska and Hawaii, 800-328-6321. Features GM cars, others available. Drive/stay packages with Hawaiian Pacific Resorts. Equal rates throughout islands. Minimum age 21, will rent without credit card.

Hertz, 800-654-3131. Fly/drive special with United. Also, "Affordable Hawaii," a special that really lives up to its name. Minimum age 18, but must have credit card in your own name or special Hertz voucher.

Avis, 800-331-1212; Alaska and Hawaii, 800-645-6393. Fly/drive packages with American and United. Minimum age 18, but must have major credit card.

Budget (Sears), 800-527-0700. Drive/stay packages with various resorts and tour companies. Fly/drive packages with United and Western. Free coupon books. Minimum age 21.

Dollar, 800-367-7006, also Alaska and Hawaii. Minimum age 21 with major credit card, but manager may make special arrangement on the spot.

Thrifty, 800-331-4200; Alaska and Hawaii, 800-331-9191. No rentals on the Big Island. Fly/drive packages with Continental and Northwest.

American International, 800-527-0202; Alaska and Hawaii, 800-527-0160.

Gray Line, 800-367-5360.

Many tourist areas provide free "jitneys" that run from town to the major hotels.

STATEWIDE AGENCIES

The following are statewide car rental agencies with excellent reputations. Rentals on all major islands. Molokai and Lanai, only when listed.

Holiday, 800-367-2631; Oahu, 836-1974. Fly/drive special with Hawaiian Air. The same founder as Tropical, offering personalized island service and a VIP lounge.

Tropical, 800-367-5140; Oahu, 836-1176; Molokai, 567-6118. Great local company that has hired *tutu* (grandmothers) who spread *aloha* while you wait, but then won't rent to people over 75 years old. Fly/drive with Hawaiian Air. Minimum age 21 with major credit card, 25 without.

Roberts, all islands, 947-3939. Well-established island company that rents to 18-year-olds, with conditions.

Molokai Island U Drive, Molokai only, 567-6156. Good local company.

Oshiro Service U Drive, Lanai only, 565-6952. Jeeps, cars, advice on road conditions. Cheaper junks out back. Excellent and friendly advice from the owner, Glenn Oshiro.

Lanai City Service, Lanai only, 565-6780. A subsidiary of Trilogy Expeditions. Rent Toyotas, Jeeps, pick-ups, and vans.

PUBLIC TRANSPORTATION

There is very limited public transportation in Hawaii except for the exemplary **TheBus** on Oahu. TheBus (tel. 531-1661) can take you just about anywhere that you want to go on Oahu for only $.60. Carrying over 200,000 passengers per day, it's a model of what a bus system should be. The **Hele On Bus Company** (tel. 935-8241 or 961-8343) is a woefully slow bus system that tries to service the Big Island. It's cheap and OK for short hops, but too infrequent and slow for long distances. Travelers say that they consistently make better time hitchhiking between Hilo and Kona than waiting for Hele On to waddle by. The **Blue Shoreline Bus** (tel. 661-3927) is like a convenience shuttle that services the tourist-oriented southwest coast of Maui between Napili and Lahaina. It does the job for its limited area. Another on Maui, the **Gray Line** (tel. 877-5507), runs between Kahului, Kihei, and Lahaina. It's expensive and its service is mostly limited to daytime hours. On Kauai, all that is available is **Aloha Jitney** (tel. 822-9532) and it runs from Nawiliwili Bay, just south of Lihue, for 8 miles to the Coconut Plantation Shopping Center in Waipouli near Kapaa. It runs only from 9:30 a.m. to 4:30 p.m. and is really a service for shoppers. Molokai and Lanai have no public transportation, but as on all the islands, taxis are available. There are novelty pedicabs in Waikiki, many hotel shuttles to and from airports, and convenience buses from some major resorts to nearby beaches and shopping centers, but that's about all the "public transportation" in Hawaii.

Ongoing Public Transportation

For those continuing on to the Mainland and wishing to procure a **Greyhound** "Ameripass" (sorry, not good in Hawaii), this can be done in Hawaii. Write or visit "Greyhound International," 550 Paiea St., Suite 104, Honolulu, HI 96819, tel. 893-1909. Send a $75 money order (for up-to-the-minute prices call any Greyhound terminal) for 7 days unlimited travel in the U.S., with the name of the person using the pass. For $12 per day more, you get an extension if the pass is renewed before the initial 7-day period runs out.

HITCHHIKING

Hitchhiking varies from island to island, both in legality and method of "thumbing a ride." On Oahu, hitchhiking is legal, and you use the tried-and-true style of facing traffic and waving your thumb. But you can only hitchhike from bus stops! Not many people hitchhike and the pickings are reasonably easy, but TheBus is only $.60 for anywhere you want to go and the paltry sum that you save in money is lost in "seeing time." It's semi-legal (the police don't bother you) to hitch on Kauai and Hawaii. Remember that Hawaii is indeed a "big" island; be prepared to take some time getting from one end to the other. Though on Lanai and Molokai hitching is illegal, hardly any policemen are to be seen. If they stop, it will probably be just to warn you, but note that the traffic is light on both islands. On Maui, thumbing a ride is illegal and the police will hassle you. You must learn a new and obviously transparent charade to hitch successfully. Basically: thumb at your side, stand by the road, face traffic, and smile. Everyone knows you're hitching, but that's the game.

You will get a ride eventually, but in comparison to the amount of traffic going by it isn't easy. Two things against you: many of the people are tourists and don't want to bother with hitchhikers and many locals don't want to bother with non-local hitchhikers. When you do get a ride, most of the time it will be from a *haole* who is either a tourist on his own or a recent island resident. If you are just hitchhiking along a well-known beach area, perhaps in your bathing suit and obviously not going far, you can get a ride more easily. Women should exercise caution like everywhere else in the U.S., and avoid hitchhiking alone.

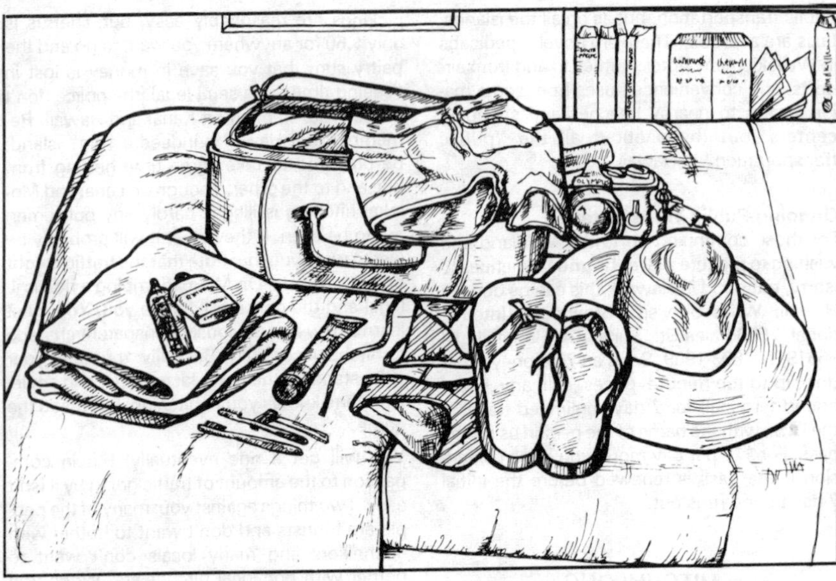

WHAT TO TAKE

It's a snap to pack for a visit to Hawaii. Everything is on your side. The weather is moderate and uniform on the whole, and the style of dress is delightfully casual. The rule of thumb is to pack lightly: few items, and light clothing both in color and weight. What you need depends largely on your itinerary and desires. Are you drawn to the nightlife, the outdoors, or both? If you forget something at home, it won't be a disaster. You can buy everything you need in Hawaii. As a matter of fact, Hawaiian clothing, such as *muumuus* and *aloha* shirts, are some of the best purchases you can make, both in comfort and style. It's quite feasible to bring only one or two changes of clothing with the express purpose of outfitting yourself while there. Prices on bathing suits, bikinis, and summer wear are quite reasonable.

A Matter Of Taste

A grand conspiracy in Hawaii adhered to by tourist, traveler, and resident is to "hang loose" and dress casual. Very rare occasions in Hawaii such as a symphony or a grand ball call for formal dress. Men don't need a suit and tie, and women don't need evening wear. Even the hoity-toity hotels and restaurants don't require them, so go with the flow and dress easy. Nowhere else do a dress shirt and slacks and a simple little dress go so far. During the day around the beach, you won't need more than a bathing suit. You might want a top to put on if you slip into a restaurant for lunch, but that's about it. For getting around during the day or evening, shorts are fine; for going out to dinner a pair of slacks or casual dress will do it.

Alohawear

Best of all, alohawear is all you need for virtually every occasion and for comfort. The classic *muumuu* is large and billowy so the cloth doesn't press against the skin, and *aloha* shirts are made to be worn out of the pants. The best of both are made of cool cotton. Not all *muumuus* are of the "tent persuasion." Some are very fashionable and form-fitted with peek-a-boo slits up the side, down the front, or around the back. *Holomuu* are fitted at the waist with a flowing skirt to the ankles. They're elegant and perfect for "stepping out." You'll notice many island women prefer *holomuu.* The colors are more subdued than those of tourists, and the bodice is fringed with lace. Oftentimes island women wear a flower hatband to set off their ensemble. If the occasion calls for it, men will formalize their outfit by tucking their aloha shirt into their pants. This also means that instead of wearing sandals they'll probably wear shoes. Women in *muumuu* and men in *aloha* shirts can go everywhere and do everything in Hawaii in perfect taste.

Basic Necessities

As previously mentioned, you really have to consider only two modes of dressing in Hawaii: beachwear and casual clothing. The following is designed for the mid-range traveler carrying one suitcase or a backpack. Remember there are laundromats and you'll be spending a considerable amount of time in your bathing suit. Consider the following: one or two pair of light cotton slacks for going out and about, and one pair of jeans for trekking, or better yet, corduroys which can serve both purposes; two to three casual sundresses—*muumuus* are great; three or four pair of shorts for beachwear and for sightseeing; four to five short-sleeved shirts or blouses and one long-sleeved; three to four colored and printed T-shirts; a beach cover-up, short terrycloth-type is best; a brimmed hat for rain and sun—the crushable floppy type is great for purse or daypack; two to three pairs of socks are sufficient, nylons you won't need; two bathing suits, nylon ones dry quickest; plastic bags to hold wet bathing suits and laundry; five to six pair of underwear; towels (optional, because hotels provide them, even for the beach); a first-aid kit (see below), pocket size is sufficient; suntan lotion; insect repellent; a daypack or large beach purse; and don't forget your windbreaker, perhaps a shawl for the evening and a universal jogging suit.

In The Cold And Rain

Two occasions for dressing warm are visiting the top of mountains, and going on boat rides where wind and ocean spray are a factor.You can conquer both with a jogging suit (sweat suit) and a featherweight, water-resistant windbreaker. Haleakala on Maui, or Mauna Kea and Mauna Loa on the Big Island, can be downright chilly. If you're going to camp or trek, you should add another layer, the best being a woolen sweater. Wool is the only fiber that retains most of its warmth-giving properties even if it gets wet. If your hands get cold, put a pair of socks over them. Tropical rain showers can happen at any time, so you might consider a fold-up umbrella.

Shoes

Dressing your feet is hardly a problem. You'll most often wear *zoris* (rubber thongs) for going to and from the beach, leather sandals for strolling and dining, and jogging shoes for trekking and sightseeing. A few discos require leather shoes, but it's hardly worth bringing them just for that. If you plan on heavy-duty trekking, you'll definitely want your hiking boots. Lava, especially *a'a,* is murderous on shoes. Most backcountry trails are rugged and muddy, and you'll need those good old lug soles for traction. If you plan moderate hikes, you might want to bring rubberized ankle supports to complement your jogging shoes. Most drug stores sell them, and the best are a rubberized sock with toe and heel cut out.

Specialty Items

Following is a list of specialty items. They're not necessities but most definitely come in handy. A pair of binoculars really enhances sightseeing—great for watching birds, sweeping panoramas, and almost a necessity if you're going whale watching. A folding Teflon-bottomed travel iron makes up for cotton's one major shortcoming—wrinkles—and you can't always count on hotels having irons. Nylon twine and miniature clothespins are used for drying garments, especially bathing suits. Commercial and hotel laundromats abound, but you can get by with hand washing a few items in the sink. A transistor radio/tape recorder provides news, weather, entertainment, and can be used to record impressions, island music, and a running commentary for your slide show. Hair dryer: although the wind can be relied on to dry, it leaves a bit to be desired in the styling department. An inflatable raft for riding waves, along with flippers, mask, and snorkel, can easily be bought in Hawaii, but don't really weigh that much or take up much space in your luggage.

For The Camper

If you don't want to take it with you, all necessary camping gear can be purchased or rented while in Hawaii. Besides the above, you should consider taking the following: framed backpack or the convertible packs that turn into suitcases, daypack; matches in a waterproof container; all-purpose knife; mess kit; eating utensils; flashlight (remove batteries); candle; nylon cord; and sewing kit (dental floss works as thread). Take a first-aid kit containing Band-Aids, all-purpose antiseptic cream, alcohol swabs, tourniquet string, cotton balls, elastic bandage, razor blade, telfa pads, and a small mirror to view private nooks and crannies. A light sleeping bag is good, although your fleecy jogging suit with a ground pad and covering of a light blanket or even your rain poncho are sufficient. Definitely bring a down sleeping bag for Haleakala or mountainous areas, and in a film container pack a few nails, safety pins, fish hooks, line, and bendable wire. Nothing else does what these do and they're all handy for a million and one uses. See "Camping and Hiking" for more information on what to bring.

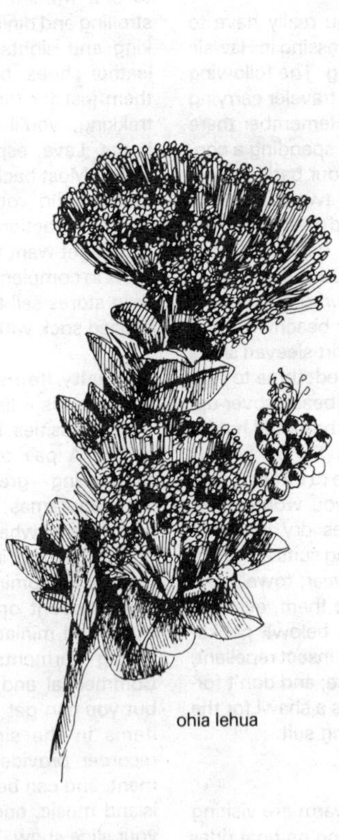

ohia lehua

HEALTH AND WELL BEING

In a recent survey published by *Science Digest,* Hawaii was cited as the healthiest state in the Union in which to live. Indeed, Hawaiian citizens live longer than anywhere else in America: men to 74 years and women to 78. Lifestyle, heredity, and diet help, but more importantly, Hawaii is an oasis in the middle of the ocean, and germs just have a tougher time getting there. There are no cases of malaria, cholera, or yellow fever. Because of a strict quarantine law, rabies is also nonexistent. On the other hand, tooth decay, perhaps because of a wide use of sugar and enzymes present in certain tropical fruits, is 30% above the national average. With the perfect weather, a multitude of outdoor activities, soothing negative ionization from the sea, and a generally relaxed and carefree lifestyle, everyone feels better there. Hawaii is just what the doctor ordered: a beautiful natural health spa with the best air quality in the country.

Pollution In Paradise

Calling Hawaii the healthiest state in America doesn't mean that it has totally escaped pollution. It is the only state, however, in which natural beauty is protected by state law, with a statewide zoning and a general development plan. For example, the absence of billboard advertising is due to the pioneering work of a women's club, "The Outdoor Circle," which was responsible for an anti-billboard law passed in 1927. It's strictly enforced, but unfortunately high-rise and ill-advised development have obscured some of the lovely views that these far-sighted women were trying to preserve. Numerous environmental controversies, including nuclear proliferation and the ill effects of rampant development, rage on the islands.

The most obvious infringements occur on Oahu, with 80% of the islands' population, which places the greatest stress on the environment. An EPA study found that almost 20% of Oahu's wells have unacceptably high concentrations of DBCP and TCP. Because of Hawaii's unique water lenses (fresh water trapped by layers of lava), this fact is particularly onerous. The "Great Oahu Milk Crisis" of 1982 saw dairies shut down when their milk was found to have abnormally high concentrations of hepatachlor, a chemical used in the pineapple industry. When tops of pineapple plants were sold as fodder, the milk became tainted. Widespread concern exists over a 1,500-unit development on the Waianae coast known as West Beach. Environmentalists say that it will not only put a major strain on diminishing water resources, but impinge on one of the last fruitful fishing areas near long-established homes of native Hawaiians. A new freeway known as H-3 will cut across an ecologically sensitive mountain range, and an alternative bio-mass energy plant is denuding the islands of its remaining indigenous *ohia* trees. Just to be pesky, the Mediterranean fruit fly made its appearance and Malathion had to be sprayed. Compared to many states, these conditions are small potatoes, but it lucidly points out the holistic global concept that no place on Earth is immune from the ravages of pollution.

Handling The Sun

A burning issue with most visitors to Hawaii is the sun. Don't become a victim of your own exuberance. People can't wait to strip down and lie on the sand like a beached whale, but the tropical sun will burn you to a cinder if you're not cautious. The burning rays come through easier in Hawaii because of the sun's angle, and you don't feel them as much because there's always a cool breeze. The worst part of the day is from 11:00 a.m. until 3:00 p.m. You'll just have to force yourself to go slowly. Don't worry; you'll be able to flaunt your best souvenir, your golden Hawaiian tan, to your green-with-envy friends when you get home. It's better than showing them a boiled lobster body with peeling skin! If your skin is snowflake white, 15 minutes per side on the first day is plenty. Increase by 15-minute intervals every day, which will allow you a full hour per side by the fourth day. Have faith; this is enough to give you a deep golden uniform tan.

***Haole* Rot**

A peculiar condition caused by the sun is referred to locally as *haole* rot. It's called this because it supposedly affects only white people, but you'll notice some dark-skinned people with the same condition. Basically, the skin becomes mottled with white spots that refuse to tan. You get a blotchy effect, mostly on the shoulders and back. Dermatologists have a fancy name for it, and they'll give you a fancy prescription with a not-so-fancy price tag to cure it. It's common knowledge throughout the islands that Selsun Blue Shampoo has some ingredient that stops the mottling effect. Just wash your hair with it and then make sure to rub the lather over the affected areas, and it should clear up.

Cockroaches And Bugs

Everyone, in varying degrees, has an aversion to vermin and creepy crawlers. Hawaii isn't infested with a wide variety, but it does have its share. Mosquitoes were unknown in the islands until their larvae stowed away in the water barrels of the *Wellington* in 1826 and were introduced at Lahaina. They bred in the tropical climate and rapidly spread to all the islands. They are a particular nuisance in the rainforests. Bring a natural repellent like citronella oil, available in most health stores on the islands, or a commercial product available in all groceries or drug stores. Campers will be happy to have mosquito coils to burn at night as well.

Cockroaches are very democratic insects. They hassle all strata of society equally. They breed well in Hawaii and most hotels are at war with them, trying desperately to keep them from being spotted by guests. One comforting thought is that in Hawaii they aren't a sign of filth or dirty housekeeping. They love the climate like everyone else, and it's a real problem keeping them under control. Many hotels post a little card in each room instructing you to call the desk if you spot a roach; they'll be happy to charge up to your room and annihilate it. Of a number of different roaches in Hawaii, the ones that give most people the jitters are big bombers over 2 inches long. Roaches are after food crumbs and the like, and very infrequently bother with a human. Be aware of this if you rent a room with a kitchenette or condo. If you are in a modest hotel and see a roach, it might make you feel better to know that the millionaire in the $600-a-night suite probably has them too. Bring your own spray if you wish, call the desk if you see them, or just let them be.

Poisonous Plants

A number of plants in Hawaii, mostly imported, contain toxins. In almost every case you have to eat a quantity of them before they'll do you any real harm. The following is a partial list of the most common plants that you'll encounter and the parts to avoid: poinsettia, leaves, stems and sap; oleander, all parts; azalea, all parts; crown flower, juice; lantana, berries; castor bean, all parts; bird of paradise, seeds; coral plant, seeds.

WATER SAFETY

Hawaii has one very sad claim to fame: more people drown here than anywhere else in the world. Moreover, there are dozens of yearly victims of broken necks, backs, and scuba and snorkeling accidents. These statements shouldn't keep you out of the sea, because it is indeed beautiful, benevolent in most cases, and a main reason to go to Hawaii. But if you're foolish, *Moana* will bounce you like a basketball and suck you away for good. The best remedy is to avoid situations you can't handle. Don't let anyone dare you into a situation that makes you uncomfortable. "Macho men" who know nothing about the power of the sea will be tumbled into a Cabbage Patch doll in short order. Ask lifeguards or beach attendants about conditions, and follow their advice. If local people refuse to go in, there's a good reason. Even experts get in trouble in Hawaiian waters. Some beaches, such as Waikiki, are as gentle as a lamb and you would have to tie an anchor around your neck to drown there. Others, especially on the north coasts during the winter months, are frothing giants.

While beachcombing, or especially when walking out on rocks, never turn your back to the sea. Be aware of undertows (the waves drawing back into the sea). They can knock you off your feet. Before entering the water, study it for rocks, breakers, reefs, and riptides. Riptides are powerful currents, like rivers in the sea, that can drag you out. Mostly they peter out not too far from shore, and you can often see their choppy waters on the surface. If caught in a "rip," don't fight to swim directly against it; you'll lose and only exhaust yourself. Swim diagonally across it, while going along with it, and try to stay parallel to the shore. Don't waste all your lung power yelling, and rest by floating.

When body surfing, never ride straight in; come to shore at a 45-degree angle. Remember, waves come in sets. Little ones can be followed by giants, so watch the action awhile instead of plunging right in. Standard procedure is to duck under a breaking wave. You can even survive thunderous oceans using this technique. Don't try to swim through a heavy froth and never turn your back and let it smash you. Don't swim alone if possible, and obey all warning signs. Hawaiians want to entertain you and don't put up signs just to waste money. The last rule is, "If in doubt, stay out."

ship's artist Francis Olmsted, c. 1840 (Hawaii State Archives)

Yikes!

Sharks live in all the oceans of the world. Most mind their own business and stay away from shore. Hawaiian sharks are well fed—on fish—and don't usually bother with unsavory humans. If you encounter a shark, don't panic! Never thrash around because this will trigger their attack instinct. If they come close, scream loudly.

Portuguese men-o-war put out long floating tentacles that sting if they touch you. Don't wash it off with fresh water; this will only aggravate it. Hot salt water will take away the sting, as will alcohol, the drinking or rubbing kind, aftershave, and meat tenderizer (MSG), which can be found in any supermarket or Chinese restaurant. Coral can give you a nasty cut, and it's known for causing infections because it's a living organism. Wash it immediately and apply an antiseptic. Keep it clean and covered, and watch for infection.

Poisonous sea urchins, such as the lacquer-black *wana,* can be beautiful creatures. They are found in shallow tide pools and can only hurt you if you step on them. Their spines will break off, enter your foot and burn like blazes. There are cures. Vinegar and wine poured on the wound will stop the burning. If not available, the Hawaiian method is urine. It might be ignominious to have someone pee on your foot, but it'll put the fire out. The spines will disintegrate in a few days, and there are generally no long-term effects.

Hawaiian reefs also have their share of moray eels. These creatures are ferocious in appearance, but will never initiate an attack. You'll have to poke around in their holes while snorkeling or scuba diving to get them to attack. Sometimes this is inadvertent on the diver's part, so be careful where you stick your hand while underwater.

HAWAIIAN FOLK MEDICINE AND CURES

Hawaiian folk medicine is well developed, and its cures for common ailments have been used effectively for centuries. *Kahuna* were highly regarded for their medicinal skills, and native Hawaiians were by far some of the healthiest people in the world until the coming of the Europeans. Many folk remedies and cures are used to this day and, what's more, they still work! Some of the most common plants and fruits you encounter provide some of the best remedies. When roots, seeds, or special exotic plants are used, the preparation of the medicine is as painstaking as in a modern pharmacy. These prescriptions are exact and take an expert to prepare. They should never be prepared or administered by an amateur.

Lomi Lomi

This traditional Hawaiian massage is of exceptional therapeutic value. It has been practiced since very early times, and is especially useful in cases of fatigue, general body aches, preventive medicine, and sports injuries. When Otto von Kotzebue arrived in 1824, he noted, "...Queen Nomahana, after feasting heartily, turned on her back, whereupon a tall fellow sprang upon her body and kneaded it unmercifully with his knees and fists as if it had been the dough of bread. Digestion was so assisted that the queen resumed her feasting." *Lomi lomi* practitioners must be accredited by the state.

Common Curative Plants

Arrowroot, for diarrhea, is a powerful narcotic used in rituals and medicines. The pepper plant *(Piper methisticum)* is chewed and the juice is spat into a container for fermenting. Used as a medicine in urinary tract infections, rheumatism, and asthma, it also induces sleep and cures headaches. A poultice for wounds is made from the skins of ripe bananas. Peelings have a powerful antibiotic quality and contain vitamins A, B, and C, phosphorous, calcium, and iron. The nectar from the plant was fed to babies as a vitamin juice. Breadfruit sap is used for healing cuts and as a moisturizing lotion. Coconut is used to make moisturizing oil, and the juice was chewed, spat into the hand and used as a shampoo. Guava is a source of vitamins A, B, and C. Hibiscus has been used as a laxative. *Kukui* nut oil is a gargle for sore throats, a laxative, and the flowers are used to cure diarrhea. *Noni* reduces tumors, diabetes, high blood pressure, and the juice is good for diarrhea. Sugarcane sweetens many concoctions, and the juice of toasted cane was a tonic for sick babies. Sweet potato is used as a tonic during pregnancy, and juiced as a gargle for phlegm. Tamarind is a natural laxative and contains the most acid and sugar of any fruit on Earth. Taro has been used for lung infections, thrush, and as suppositories. Yams are good for coughs, vomiting, constipation, and appendicitis.

KUKUI (CANDLENUT)

Reaching heights of 80 feet, the kukui *(candlenut) was a veritable department store to the Hawaiians, who made use of almost every part of this utilitarian giant. Used as a cure-all, its nuts, bark, or flowers were ground into potions and salves and taken as a general tonic, applied to ulcers and cuts as an effective antibiotic, or administered internally as a cure for constipation or asthma attacks. The bark was mixed with water and the resulting juice was used as a dye in tattooing,* tapa *cloth making, canoe painting, and as a preservative for fishnets. The oily nuts were burned as a light source in stone holders, and ground and eaten as a condiment called* inamona. *Polished nuts took on a beautiful sheen and were strung as lei. Lastly, the wood itself was hollowed into canoes and used as fishnet floats.*

Commonly Treated Ailments
For arthritis make a pultice of *koali* and Hawaiian salt; cover the area and keep warm. A bad breath gargle is made from the *hapu'u* fern. The latex from inside the leaves of *aloe* is great for soothing burns and sunburn, as well as for innumerable skin problems. If you get chapped lips or windburned skin use oil from the *hinu honu*. A headache is lessened with *awa* or *ape*. Calm nervousness with *awa* and *lomi lomi,* Hawaiian-style massage. To get rid of a raspy sore throat chew the bark of the root of the *uhaloa*. A toothache is eased by the sticky narcotic juice from the *pua kala* seed, a prickly poppy.

MEDICAL AND EMERGENCY SERVICES

Emergency: Dial 911
The following are hospitals providing emergency room, long-term, and acute care. **Oahu:** Kaiser Foundation Hospital, 1697 Ala Moana Blvd., Honolulu, tel. 949-5811. They have an emergency room and are closest to Waikiki. They demand payment before treatment; Queen's Medical Center, 1301 Punchbowl, Honolulu, tel. 538-9011; St. Francis Hospital, 2230 Liliha, Honolulu, tel. 547-6551. **Maui:** Kula Hospital, 204 Kula Hwy., tel. 878-1221; Maui Memorial, Kaahumanu Ave., Wailuku, tel. 244-9056. **Molokai:** Molokai General, Kaunakakai, tel. 553-5331. **Lanai:** Lanai Community Hospital, Lanai City, tel. 565-6411. **Hawaii:** Hilo Hospital, 1190 Waianenue Ave., Hilo, tel. 961-4211; Kona Hospital, Kailua-Kona, tel. 322-9311. **Kauai:** Wilcox Memorial Hospital, 3420 Kuhio Hwy., Lihue, tel. 245-1100.

ALTERNATIVE MEDICINE

Most ethnic groups that migrated to Hawaii brought their own cures along. The Chinese and Japanese are especially known for their unique and effective medicines, such as herbal medicine, acupuncture and *shiatsu.* Hawaii also has a huge selection of chiropractors and its own form of massage called *lomi lomi*. The Yellow Pages on all islands list holistic practitioners, herbalists, and naturopaths.

Acupuncture

This time-honored Chinese therapy is available throughout the islands. On Oahu contact the Hawaiian Association of Certified Acupuncturists, Box 11202, Honolulu 96828, tel. 941-7771 for referrals to state-licensed acupuncturists throughout the islands.

Massage

All types of massage are available throughout the islands. If you look in the Yellow Pages, you'll find everything from *shiatsu* and *lomi lomi* to "escort services" that masquerade their real profession as massage (for these, see "Sex and Drugs"). It's easy to tell the ads of legitimate massage practitioners offering therapeutic holistic massage. Check listings under "holistic practitioners" as well as "massage."

HELP FOR THE HANDICAPPED

A handicapped or physically disabled person can have a wonderful time in Hawaii; all that's needed is a little pre-planning. The following is general advice that should help with your planning.

Commission On The Handicapped

This commission was designed with the expressed purpose of aiding handicapped people. They are a source of invaluable information and distribute self-help booklets free of charge. Any handicapped person heading to Hawaii should write first or visit their offices on arrival. For a "Handicapped Travelers Guide" to each of the four islands, write or visit the head office at: Commission on the Handicapped, Old Federal Bldg., 335 Merchant St., no. 215, Honolulu, HI 96813, tel. 548-7606; on Maui, 54 High St., Wailuku, Maui, HI 96793, tel. 244-4441; on Kauai, Box 671, Lihue, Kauai 96766, tel. 245-4308; on Hawaii, Box 1641, Hilo, HI 96820, tel. 935-7257.

General Information

The key for a smooth trip is to make as many arrangements ahead of time as possible. Here are some tips concerning transportation and accommodations. Tell the companies concerned of the nature of your handicap in advance so that they can make arrangements to accommodate you. Bring your medical records and notify medical establishments of your arrival if you'll be needing their services. Travel with a friend or make arrangements for an aide on arrival (see below). Bring your own wheelchair if possible and let airlines know if it is battery-powered; boarding inter-island carriers requires steps. No problem. They'll board you early on special lifts, but they must know that you're coming. Many hotels and restaurants accommodate disabled persons, but always call ahead just to make sure.

Oahu Services

At Honolulu International, parking spaces are on the fourth floor of the parking garage near the elevator closest to the inter-island terminal. The **Wiki Wiki Bus** to town has steps. **Medical Services**, 24-hours, Honolulu County Medical Society, tel. 536-6988; airport medical services at tel. 836-3341; visitor information at tel. 836-6417. For getting around, the City of Honolulu has a free curb-to-curb service for disabled persons, called **Handi-Van.** You must make arrangements for a pass 24 hours in advance. For a free handicapped bus pass for disabled but ambulatory people, write, Handi-Van Pass, or Handicapped Bus Pass, 650 S. King St., Honolulu 96813, tel. 524-4626. A private special taxi company is **Handi-Cabs of the Pacific** in Honolulu at tel. 524-3866. **Avis** will rent cars with hand controls, tel. 836-5511. **Grant Wheelchair and Repair of Honolulu,** tel. 533-2794, will do just that and outfit cars with hand controls. For **medical equipment** the following Honolulu establishments rent all kinds of apparatus: **AAA Medical,** tel. 538-7021; **Abbey Rents,** tel. 537-2922; **Medical Supplies,** tel. 845-9522; **Honolulu Orthopedic,** tel. 536-6661. For **medical support and help** the following provide nurses, companions, and health aides—all require advance notice. **Hawaii Center for Independent Living,** tel. 537-1941; **Travel-Well International,** tel. 689-5420; **Voluntary Action Center,** tel. 536-7234.

Maui Services

On arrival at Kahului Airport, parking spaces are directly in front of the main terminal. The restaurant there has steps, so food will be brought to you in the cocktail lounge. No special emergency medical services. Visitor information at tel. 877-6431. There is no centralized medical service, but Maui Memorial Hospital in Wailuku will refer, tel. 244-9056. Getting around can be tough because there is no public transportation on Maui, and no tours or companies to accommodate non-ambulatory handicapped persons. However, both Hertz and Avis rent cars with hand controls. Health care is provided by Maui Center for Independent Living, tel. 242-4966. Medical equipment is available at Crafts Drugs, tel. 877-0111; Hawaiian Rentals, tel. 877-7684; Maui Rents, tel. 877-5827. Special recreation activities referrals are made by Easter Seal Society, tel. 242-9323, or by the Commission on Handicapped, tel. 244-4441.

Kauai Services
At Lihue Airport, parking is available in an adjacent lot and across the street in the metered area. **Emergency services,** tel. 245-3773; visitor info, tel. 245-8183. For medical services, **Kauai Medical Group** at Wilcox Hospital will refer, tel. 245-1500. To get around, arrangements can be made if the following are contacted well in advance: **Office of Elderly Affairs,** tel.245-7230; **Akita Enterprises,** tel. 245-5344. **Avis** will install hand controls on cars, but they need a month's notice. **Holiday** will do the same, tel. 245-6944. There are very few cut curbs on Kauai and none in Lihue. Special **parking permits** (legal anywhere, anytime) are available from the police station in Lihue. Medical equipment rentals are available from: **American Cancer Society,** tel. 245-2942; **Pay n' Save,** tel. 245-6776; **Easter Seals,** tel. 245-6983. For medical support and help contact **Kauai Center for Independent Living,** tel. 245-4034.

Hawaii Services
At Hilo Airport there are no facilities for deplaning non-ambulatory people from propeller planes, only jets and on the jetways. Interisland flights should be arranged only on jets. Ramps and a special elevator provide access in the bi-level terminal. Parking is convenient in designated areas. At Kona boarding and deplaning is possible for the handicapped. Ramps make the terminal accessible. To get around, **Handi-Vans** are available in Hilo, tel. 961-6722. **Kamealoha Unlimited** has specially equipped vans, tel. 966-7244. **Parking permits** are available from Dept. of Finance, tel. 961-8231. Medical help, nurses, and companions are arranged through **Big Island Center for Independent Living,** tel. 935-3777. Doctors are referred by **Hilo Hospital,** tel. 961-4211, and **Kona Hospital,** tel. 322-9311. Medical equipment is available from **Kamealoha Unlimited,** tel. 966-7244; **Medi-Home,** tel. 969-1123; **Pacific Rentall,** tel. 935-2974.

THE HEAVY STUFF

Though the small towns and villages are as safe as you can find anywhere in America, Hawaii isn't all good clean fun. Wherever there's a constant tourist flow, a huge military presence, and high cost of living, there will be those people that mama warned you about. Most of the heavy night action occurs in Waikiki around Kuhio and Kalakaua avenues, with Maui's Front Street a far distant second. Something about the *vibe* exudes sexuality. The land is raw and wild, and the settings are intoxicating. All those glistening bodies under the tropical sun, and the carefree lifestyle are super conducive to you know what! It's long been known as a great place for boy meets girl, or whatever, but there is also "play for pay" if you want it.

Hawaii's sugar and pineapple industries started to flag in the last decade and people had to do something to make ends meet. More than a few began to grow marijuana *(pakalolo),* now counted as one of the biggest cash crops in Hawaii. The *pakalolo* (literally "crazy smoke") is first rate, and will knock your purple socks off even if you aren't wearing any. Theft and minor assaults can be a problem, but they're usually not violent or vicious like in some Mainland cities. Mostly, it's locals with a chip on their shoulder and little prospects, who will ransack your car or make off with your camera. A big Hawaiian or local guy will be obliged to flatten your nose if you look for trouble, but mostly it will be sneak thieves out to make a fast buck. You can go two ways on the "sleaze" scene in Hawaii: ignore it and remain aloof and never see any; or, look for and find it with no trouble. The following is neither a condemnation nor an endorsement of how you should act and what you should do. It's merely the facts and the choice is up to you.

Prostitution—The Way It Was
Ever since the first ship arrived in 1778, Hawaii has known prostitution. At that time, a sailor paid for a woman for the night for one iron nail. Funny, today they'll take a plastic card. Prostitution, rampant until the missionaries arrived in 1819, was indeed a major cause of the tragic population decline of the Hawaiian race. The tradition carried on into this century. Iwilei was a notorious red-light district in Honolulu at the turn of the century. The authorities, many of whom were clientele, not only turned a blind eye to this scene, but semi-legalized it. A policeman was stationed inside the "stockade" and police rules were listed on the 5 entrances. The women were required to have a weekly VD checkup from the Board of Health, and without a current disease-free certificate they couldn't work. Iwilei was even considered by some to be an attraction: when Somerset Maugham passed through the islands in 1916 on his way to Russia as a spy for England, he was taken here as if on a sightseeing tour. The long-established military presence in Hawaii has also helped to keep prostitution a flourishing business. During WW II, troops were entertained by streetwalkers, houses of prostitution, and at dance halls. The consensus of the military commanders is that prostitution is a necessary evil, needed to keep up the morale of the troops.

The Scene Today
The two areas notorious for prostitution today are Kuhio and Kalakaua avenues in Waikiki, which are geared toward the tourist, and Hotel Street in downtown Honolulu, for servicemen and a much rougher trade. All sorts of women solicit on Kuhio and Kalakaua avenues—whites, blacks, and Asians—but the majority are young white women from the Mainland. They cruise along in the old-fashioned style, meeting your eyes and giving you the nod. As long as they keep walking the police won't roust them. They talk business on the street, and then take their john to a nearby backstreet hotel, where he'll be required to pay for the room. Prices vary with the services sought. Rock bottom is $60 for a 15-minute "slam bam." The room might cost another $15.

The prostitutes on Kuhio Avenue number about 300. There was a great influx when Los Angeles cracked down for the 1984 Olympics, and Honolulu inherited many of their displaced streetwalkers. Most hookers prefer Japanese clientele, followed by the general tourist, and lastly, the always broke serviceman. In the terse words of one streetwalker queried about the preference for Japanese, she said, "They're small, clean, fast, and they pay a lot." Sounds like a streetwalker's dream! A Honolulu policemen on his Kuhio Avenue beat said, "I can't do anything if they keep walking. It's a free country. Besides, I'm not here to teach anyone morals...last week a john "fell" out of an 8-story window and a prostitute was found with her throat slit...I'm just on the front lines fighting herpes and AIDS. Just fighting herpes and AIDS, man." The average guy won't have any hassles with the Kuhio Avenue prostitues. Mostly it's a straightforward business transaction, but unlike the days of Iwilei there is absolutely no official control or testing for VD. Hotel Street is as rough as guts. The girls are shabby, the bars and strip joints are shabbier, and the vibe is heavy. Prices are cheaper, but if you visit a Hotel Street hooker, you'd be well advised to wear a condom and a scuba diving wet suit for protection. Women can find male prostitutes on most of the beaches of Honolulu and Waikiki. Mostly these transactions take place during the day. Although many men make a legitimate living as "beach boys" instructing in surfing and the like, many are really prostitutes. It's always up to the woman to decide how far her "lessons" proceed.

Massage Parlors, Etc.
Besides streetwalkers, Honolulu and some of the Neighbor Islands have their share of massage parlors, escort services, and exotic dance joints. Most are in Honolulu, and some will even fly their practitioners to the Neighbor Islands if necessary. For massage parlors and "escort services" you can let your fingers do the walking—14 pages are in the Honolulu Yellow Pages alone. Oddly enough, the "mas-

sage" listing is preceded by one for "marketing" and followed by one for "meat." Many legitimate massage practitioners in Hawaii can offer the best therapeutic massages in a variety of disciplines including, *shiatsu, lomi lomi,* and Swedish. Unfortunately, they share the same listings with the other kind of massage parlors. If the Yellow Pages listing reads something like "Fifi's Playthings—We'll rub it day or night, wherever it is," this should tip you off. Usually, they offer escort services too, for both men and women. The initial cost is about $50 to have an "escort" come to your hotel. Once there, this young man or woman will negotiate his or her own deal for services (about $75). This protects the escort service business, because if you happen to be an undercover vice officer, the "escort" takes the rap and not the business, since of course they had no idea of what was really going on.

Honolulu also has a number of exotic dance clubs, many along Kapiolani Boulevard. Basically, they're strip joints with an extra twist. The dancers themselves are very attractive white women that have been brought over from the Mainland. They can easily make $100 per night dancing, and the majority are not prostitutes, although money, if it's enough, always talks. Their act lasts for 3 songs, and gets raunchier as it goes. They start off like the girl next door in a prom dress, and wind up writhing naked on the floor, gyrating to some imaginary phallic stimulus. If you invite a dancer to have a drink, it'll cost you $10, but it will be a real drink. This gets you nothing but conversation. The patron's drinks aren't as inflated as the scene would suggest, and some think it a bargain for the price of one drink to have a naked woman bumping and grinding just 5 feet away. Working the sexually agitated male crowd are women who can best be described as "lap sitters." They're almost always older Korean women who've been through the mill. They'll charge you $5 for a fake drink called *niko hana* (nothing), and then try to entice you over to a dark corner table, where they'll chisel $20 more, for all you can manage, or are brave enough to do, in a dark corner of a night club. Their chief allies are dim lights and booze. (See "Honolulu Entertainment.")

ILLEGAL DRUGS

The use and availability of illegal, controlled, and recreational drugs is about the same in Hawaii as it is throughout the rest of America. Cocaine is the fastest growing recreational drug, and it's available on the streets of the main cities, especially Honolulu. Although most dealers are small-time, the drug is brought in by organized crime. The underworld here is mostly populated by men of Asian descent, and the Japanese *yakuza* is said recently to be displaying a heightened involvement in Hawaiian organized crime. Cocaine trafficking fans out from Honolulu. However, the most available and commonly used drug in Hawaii is *pakalolo.* There are also three varieties of psychoactive mushrooms that contain the hallucinogen psilocybin. They grow wild, but are considered illegal controlled substances.

Pakalolo Growing

About 10 years ago, mostly *haole* hippies from the Mainland began growing pot in the more remote sections of the islands, such as Puna on Hawaii and around Hana on Maui. They discovered what legitimate planters had known for

200 years: plant a broomstick in Hawaii, treat it right, and it'll grow. *Pakalolo,* after all, is only a weed, and it grows in Hawaii like wildfire. The locals quickly got into the act when they realized that they, too, could grow a "money tree." As a matter of fact, they began resenting the *haole* usurpers, and a quiet and sometimes dangerous feud has been going on ever since. Much is made of the viciousness of the backcountry "growers" of Hawaii. There are tales of booby traps and armed patrols guarding their plants in the hills, but mostly it's a cat and mouse game between the authorities and the growers. If you, as a tourist, are tramping about in the forest and happen upon someone's "patch," don't touch anything. Just back off and you'll be OK. Pot has the largest monetary turnover of any crop in the islands, and as such, is now considered a major source of revenue.

Buying *Pakalolo*

There are all kinds of local names for pot in Hawaii, the most potent being "Kona Gold," "Puna Butter," and "Maui Wowie." Actually, these names are all becoming passe. At one time the best *pakalolo* came from plants grown from Thai and Colombian seeds. Today, the growing is much more sophisticated. The most potent grass is *sinsemilla* (Latin for "without seeds"), the flowering heads of female plants that have not been allowed to be fertilized by males. They waste no energy growing seeds and all of the potent THC stays in the flowers. The next step up is raising plants from "clones." These are *sinsemilla* plants grown in hothouses from proven super-good "mother plants," and then transplanted outside where they all grow large, resiny colas. Today, the generic term for the best pot is "buds."

Prices vary, but if the pot has seeds it's only Colombian or some lesser strain and should sell for about $50 an ounce. If it's Thai Stick or seedless "buds," it will be about $200 an ounce, and the potency will be very high. You can normally buy anything from a quarter ounce ($50) on up. The best time to buy is around Christmas or just before, when the main harvest is in. As you get closer to the summer, *pakalolo* gets a little more scarce and prices tend to rise. You can ask a likely person for pot, but mostly dealers will approach you. Their normal technique is to stroll by, and in a barely audible whisper say, "Buds?"

There's plenty of street dealers hawking in Waikiki on Kuhio Avenue, on Front Street in Lahaina, and on the beaches of the Neighbor Islands. One of the worst-kept secrets in Hawaii is that Waikiki's pedicab drivers can tell you where to score pot. Legend tells of one enterprising pedicabby who wrote the names and prices of drugs on a sign that he placed in the small of his back. If he picked up a rider who seemed a likely candidate, he just lifted his shirt without saying a word and you could peruse his menu. Hawaiian *pakalolo* is sold slightly differently than on the Mainland. The dealers all seem to package it in those heat-sealed "Seal-a-Meal" plastic bags. It's not the good old "baggie," and this makes it hard to check it out. Mostly deals are on the up and up, but you can always get ripped off with counterfeit drugs. If the dealer refuses to let you smell it, or better yet, smoke a bit, don't bother. Smoking

magic mushrooms

pot while in Hawaii is usually cool, but trying to bring it home is a hassle. All passengers leaving Hawaii are open to a thorough "agricultural inspection," and you can bet they're not only looking for illegal papayas. In 1984 there was an uproar involving a particular post office on the Big Island. It turned out that a staggering 80% of the outgoing packages contained *pakalolo*. The authorities are getting wise.

Magic mushrooms are also available in the islands. There are poisonous mushrooms around, so you're much better off letting the experts pick them and sell them to you. If you insist on finding your own, the best time to search is just after a rain shower. Go to a cow pasture and inspect the "cow pies" (manure droppings). The mushrooms will be growing in them. If you crush them, the stem will turn a purplish color in your hands.

THEFT AND HASSLES

From the minute you sit behind the wheel of your rental car, you'll be warned about not leaving valuables unattended and locking your car up tighter than a drum. Signs warning about theft at most major tourist attractions help to fuel your paranoia. Many hotel rooms offer coin-operated safes, so you can lock your valuables away and be able to relax while getting sunburned. Stories abound about purse snatchings and surly locals who are just itching to give you a hard time. Well, they're all true to a degree, but Hawaii's reputation is much worse than the reality. In Hawaii you'll have to observe two golden laws: if you look for trouble, you'll find it; and, a fool and his camera are soon parted.

Crime In Hawaii

The FBI recently compiled some amazing statistics. They compared the crime rates of 10 American cities including Honolulu, Atlanta, Dallas, New Orleans, Miami, Phoenix, and Los Angeles. According to the number of murders, robberies, assaults, and burglaries per 100,000 residents, in every comparison, Honolulu had the lowest rates by far. The islands of Maui, Kauai, and Hawaii display similar statistics showing crime rates lower than most U.S. areas of comparable size and population. Simply stated, Hawaii is safer than most places in America, but it isn't crime free. Population-wise, Chinese and Japanese have the lowest rate of felons; whites and Filipinos have criminals equal to their percentage of population; Hawaiians and part Hawaiian generate twice as many criminals as their population percentage and Samoans contribute 6% of the islands' felons while making up only 1% of the population.

Theft

The majority of theft in Hawaii is of the "sneak thief" variety. If you leave your hotel door unlocked, a camera sitting on the seat of your rental car, or valuables on your beach towel, you'll be inviting a very obliging thief to pad away with your stuff. You'll have to learn to take precautions, but they won't have to be anything like those employed in rougher traveling areas like South America or Southeast Asia, just normal American precautions.

If you must walk alone at night, stay on the main streets in well-lit areas. Always lock your hotel door and windows and place all valuable jewelry in the hotel safe. When you leave your hotel for the beach, there is absolutely no reason to carry all your traveler's cheques, credit cards, or a big wad of money. Just take what you'll need for drinks and lunch. If you're uptight about leaving any money in your beach bag, just stick it in your bathing suit or bikini. American money is just as negotiable if it is damp. Don't leave your camera or portable stereo on the beach unattended. Ask a person nearby to watch them for you while you go for a dip. Most people won't mind at all, and you can repay the favor.

While sightseeing in your shiny new rental car, which immediately brands you as a tourist, again, don't take more than what you'll need for the day. Many people lock valuables away in the trunk, but remember most good car thieves can jimmy it as quickly as you can open it with your key. If you must, for some reason, leave your camera or valuables in your car, lock them in the trunk or consider putting them under the hood. Thieves usually don't look there and on most modern cars, you can only pop the hood with a lever on the inside of the car. It's not failsafe, but it's worth a try.

Campers face special problems because their entire scene is open to thievery. Most campgrounds don't have any real security, but who, after all, wants to fence an old tent or a used sleeping bag? Many tents have zippers that can be secured with a small padlock. If you want to go trekking and are afraid to leave your gear in the campgrounds, take a large green garbage bag with you. Transport your gear down the trail and then walk off through some thick brush. Put your gear in the garbage bag and bury it under leaves and other light camouflage. That's about as safe as you can be. You can also use a variation on this technique instead of leaving your valuables in your rental car.

Hassles

Another self-perpetuating myth about Hawaii is that "the natives are restless." An undeniable animosity exists between locals, especially those with some Hawaiian blood, and *haoles.* Fortunately, this prejudice is directed mostly at the "group" and not at the "individual." The locals are resentful against those *haoles* who came, took their land, and relegated them to second-class citizenship. They realize that this is not the average tourist and they can tell what you are at a glance. Tourists usually are treated with understanding and are given a type of immunity. Besides, Hawaiians are still among the most friendly, giving, and understanding people on Earth.

Haoles who live in Hawaii might tell you stories of their children having trouble at school. They could even mention an unhappy situation at some schools called "beat-up-a-*haole*" day, and you might hear that if you're a *haole* it's not a matter of if you'll be beaten up, but when. Truthfully, most of this depends upon your attitude and your sensitivity. The locals feel infringed upon, so don't fuel these feelings. If you're at a beach park and there is a group of local people in one area, don't crowd them. If you go into a local bar and you're the only one of your ethnic group in sight, you shouldn't have to be told to leave. Much of the hassle involves drinking. Booze brings out the worst prejudice on all sides. If you're invited to a beach party, and the local guys start getting drunk, make this your exit call. Don't wait until it's too late.

Most trouble seems to be directed towards white men. White women are mostly immune from being beaten up, but they have to beware of the violence of sexual abuse and rape. Although plenty of local women marry white men, it's not a good idea to try to pick up a local girl. If you're known in the area and have been properly introduced, that's another story. Also, girls out for the night in bars or discos can be approached if they're not in the company of local guys. If you are with your bikini-clad girlfriend, and a bunch of local guys are, say, drinking beer at a beach park, don't go over and try to be friendly and ask, "What's up?" You (and especially your girlfriend) might not want to know the answer to this question. Maintain your own dignity and self-respect by treating others with dignity and respect. Most times you'll reap what you sow.

"Some were rapacious exploiters, seeking to deceive, loot and leave. Hawaii has known them by the thousands through the years."

—Edward Joesting

Alphonse Pellion, c. 1819
(Hawaii State Archives)

ACCOMMODATION

Hawaii's accommodations won't disappoint anyone. An exceptionally wide range of places to stay varies both in style and in price range. You can camp on totally secluded beaches 3 days down a hiking trail, have a dream vacation at some of the undisputed top resorts in the world, or get a package deal including a week's lodging in plenty of island hotels for less than you would spend at home. If you want to experience the islands as if you lived there, bed and breakfasts are becoming popular and easy to arrange. Condominiums are plentiful and great for extended stays for families who can set up home away from home, or even for a group of friends who want to save money by sharing costs. There are a smattering of youth hostels and YM/WCAs, home exchanges, and if you're a student maybe a summer session at the University of Hawaii to mix education and fun.

Hawaii makes the greater part of its living from visitors, and all concerned desire to keep Hawaiian standards up and vacationers coming back. This means that accommodations in Hawaii are operated by professionals who know the business of pleasing people. This adds up to benefits for you. Rooms in even the more moderate hotels are clean; the standard of services range from adequate to luxurious pampering. With the few tips and advice given below, you should be able to find a place to stay that will match your taste with your pocketbook. For specifics, please refer to "Accommodations" in each of the travel chapters.

HOTELS

Even with the wide variety of other accommodations available, most visitors, at least first-timers, tend to stay in hotels. At one time, hotels were the only places to stay, and characters like Mark Twain were berthed at Kilauea's rude Volcano House, while millionaires and nobility sailed for Waikiki where they stayed in luxury at the Moana Hotel or Royal Hawaiian, which both still stand as vintage reminders of days past. Maui's Pioneer Inn dates from the turn of the century, and if you were Hawaii-bound, these and a handful that haven't survived, were about all that was offered. Today, there are 60,000 hotel rooms statewide, and every year more hotels are built and older ones renovated. They come in all shapes and sizes, from 10-room family-run affairs to high-rise giants. A trend turned some into condominiums, while the Neighbor Islands have learned an aesthetic lesson from Waikiki and build low-rise resorts that don't obstruct the view and blend more readily with the surroundings. Whatever accommodation you want, you'll find it in Hawaii.

Types Of Hotel Rooms

Most readily available and least expensive is a bedroom with bath, the latter sometimes being shared in the more inexpensive hotels. Some hotels also offer a studio, a large sitting room that converts to a bedroom; suites, a bedroom with sitting room; and apartments that have a full kitchen plus at least one bedroom. Kitchenettes are often available, and contain a refrigerator, sink, and stove usually in a small corner nook, or fitted together as one space-saving unit. Kitchenettes cost a bit more, but save a bundle by allowing you to prepare some of your own meals. To get that vacation feeling while keeping costs down, eat breakfast in, pack a lunch for the day, and go out to dinner. If you rent a kitchenette, make sure all the appliances work as soon as you arrive. If they don't, notify the front desk immediately, and if the hotel will not rectify the situation ask to be moved for a reduced rate. Hawaii has cockroaches (see p. 138), so put all food away.

Hotel Rates: add 9% room tax

Every year Hawaiian hotels welcome in the New Year by hiking their rates by about 10%. A room that was $30 this year will be $33 next year, and so on. Hawaii, because of its gigantic tourist flow and tough competition, offers hotel rooms at universally lower rates than most developed resort areas around the world. Package deals, especially to Waikiki, almost throw in a week's lodging for the price of an air ticket. The basic **daily rate** is geared toward double occupancy; singles are hit in the pocketbook. Single rates are cheaper than doubles, but never as low as half the double rate; the most you get off is 40%. **Weekly and monthly** rates will save you approximately 10% off the daily rate. Make sure to ask because this information won't be volunteered. Many hotels will charge for a double and then add an additional charge ($3 to $25) for extra persons. Some hotels, not always the budget ones, let you cram in as many as can sleep on the floor with no additional charge, so again, ask. Others have a policy of **minimum stay,** usually 3 days, but their rates can be cheaper.

Hawaii's **peak season** runs from just before Christmas until after Easter, and then again in early summer. Rooms are at a premium, and peak-season rates are an extra 10% above the normal daily rate. Oftentimes they'll also suspend weekly and monthly rates during peak season. The **off-peak** season is in late summer and fall, when rooms are easy to come by and most hotels offer off-peak rates. Here, subtract about 10% from the normal rate.

Waikiki hotels

In Hawaiian hotels you always pay more for a good view. Terms vary slightly, but usually "ocean front" means your room faces the ocean and mostly your view is unimpeded. "Ocean view" is slightly more vague. It could be a decent view, or it could require standing on the dresser and craning your neck to catch a tiny slice of the sea sandwiched between two skyscrapers. Rooms are also designated and priced upward as **standard, superior,** and **deluxe**. As you go up, this could mean larger rooms with more amenities, or can merely signify a better view.

Plenty of hotels offer the **family plan,** which allows children under a certain age to stay in their parents' room free, if they use the existing bedding. If another bed or crib is required, there is an additional charge. Only a limited number of hotels offer the **American Plan,** where breakfast and dinner are included with the night's lodging. In many hotels, you get a refrigerator and a heating unit to make coffee and tea provided free.

Paying, Deposits, And Reservations

The vast majority of Hawaiian hotels accept foreign and domestic traveler's checks, personal checks preapproved by the management, foreign cash, and most major credit cards. Reservations are always the best policy, and they're easily made through travel agents or directly by contacting the hotel. In all cases, bring documentation of your confirmed reservations with you in case of a mix-up.

Deposits are not always required to make reservations, but they do secure them. Some hotels require the first night's payment in advance. Reservations without a deposit can be legally released if the room is not claimed by 6:00 p.m. Remember too, that letters "requesting reservations" are not the same as "confirmed reservations." In letters, include your dates of stay, type of room you want, and price. Once the hotel answers your letter, "confirm" your reservations with a phone call or follow-up letter and make sure that the hotel sends you a copy of the confirmation. All hotels and resorts have **cancellation requirements** for refunding deposits. The time limit on these can be as little as 24 hours before arrival, to a full 30 days. Some hotels require full **advance payment** for your length of stay especially during peak season, or during times of crowded special events such as the Merrie Monarch Festival in Hilo. Be aware of the time required for a cancellation notice *before* making your reservation deposit, especially when dealing with advance payment. If you have confirmed reservations, especially with a deposit, and there is no room for you, or one that doesn't meet prearranged requirements, you should be given the option of accepting alternate accommodations. You are owed the difference in room rates if there is any. If there is no room whatsoever, the hotel is required to find you one at another comparable hotel and refund your deposit in full.

Amenities

All hotels have some of them, and some hotels have all of them. Air conditioning is available in most, but under normal circumstances you won't need it. Balmy tradewinds flow through louvered windows and doors in many hotels. Casablanca room fans are better. TVs are often included in the rate, but not always. In-room phones are provided, but a service charge is usually tacked on, even for local calls. Swimming pools are very common, even though the hotel may sit right on the beach. There is always a restaurant of some sort, a coffee shop or two, a bar, cocktail lounge, and sometimes a sundries shop. Some hotels also offer tennis courts or golf courses either as part of the premises or affiliated with the hotel; usually an "activities desk" can book you into a variety of daily outings. Plenty of hotels offer laundromats on the premises, and hotel towels can be used at the beach. Bellhops get about $1 per bag, and maid service is free, though maids are customarily tipped $1-$2 per day and a bit more if kitchenettes are involved. Parking is free. Hotels can often arrange special services like babysitters, all kinds of lessons, and often special entertainment activities. A few even have bicycles and some snorkeling equipment to lend. They'll receive and send mail for you, cash your traveler's cheques and take messages.

CONDOMINIUMS

Hawaii was one of the first states struck by the condominium phenomenon; it began in the 1950s and has increased ever since. Now condos are almost as common as hotels, and renting one is just about as easy. Condos, unlike hotel rooms, are privately owned apartments which are normally part of a complex or high-rise. The condo is usually an absentee owner's second or vacation home. An on-premises condo manager rents the vacant apartments, and is responsible for maintenance and security.

Things to Know: add 9% room tax

Staying in a condo has advantages and disadvantages from staying in a hotel.The method of paying for and reserving a condo is just about the same as for a hotel. However, requirements for deposits, final payments, and cancellation charges are much stiffer than in hotels. Make absolutely sure you fully understand all of these requirements when you make your reservations. The main qualitative difference between a condo and a hotel is in amenities. At a condo, you're more on your own. You're temporarily renting an apartment, so there won't be any bellhops, rarely a bar, restaurant, or lounge on the premises, though many times you'll find a sundries store. The main lobby, instead of having that grand entrance feel of many hotels, is more like an apartment house entrance, although there might be a front desk. Condos can be efficiencies (one big room), but mostly they are one- or multiple-bedroom affairs with a complete kitchen. Reasonable housekeeping items should be provided: linens, all furniture, and a fully equipped kitchen. Most have TVs and phones, but remember that the furnishings provided are all up to the owner. You can find brand-new furnishings that are top of the line, right down to "garage sale" bargains. Inquire about the furnishings when you make your reservations. Maid service might be included on a limited basis (for example once weekly), or you might have to pay for it if you require a maid.

Condos usually require a minimum stay, although some will rent on a daily basis, like hotels. Minimum stays when applicable are often three days, but seven is also commonplace, and during peak season, two weeks isn't unheard of. Swimming pools are common, and depending on the "theme" of the condo, you can find saunas, weight rooms, jacuzzis, and tennis courts. Rates are about 10-15% higher than comparable hotels, with hardly any difference between doubles and singles. A nominal extra is charged for more than two people, and condos can normally accommodate 4 to 6 guests. You can find clean, decent condos for as little as $200 per week, all the way up to exclusive apartments for well over $1,000 per week. Their real advantage is for families, friends who want to share, and especially long-term stays where you will always get a special rate. The kitchen facilities save a great deal on dining costs, and it's common to find units with their own mini-washers and dryers. Parking space is ample for guests, and like hotels, plenty of stay/drive deals are offered.

Hotel/Condominium Information

The best source of hotel/condo information is the **Hawaii Visitors Bureau**. While planning your trip either visit one nearby or write to them in Hawaii. (Addresses are given in the "Visitors Bureau" section.) Request a copy of their free and current ***Member Accommodation Guide.*** This handy booklet lists all the hotel/condo members of the HVB. Listings include the addresses, phone numbers, facilities, rates, and general tips. Understand that these are not all of the hotels/condos in Hawaii, just those members of the HVB.

BED AND BREAKFAST

Bed and Breakfasts are hardly a new idea. The Bible talks of the hospitable hosts who opened the gates of their homes and invited the wayfarer in to spend the night. Bed and Breakfasts (B&Bs) have a long tradition in Europe, and were commonplace in Revolutionary America. Now, lodging in a private home is becoming increasingly fashionable throughout America, and Hawaii is no exception. Not only can you *visit* Hawaii, you can *live* there for a time with a host family and share an intimate experience of daily life.

Points To Consider

The beauty of B&Bs is that every one is privately owned, and therefore uniquely different from any other. The range of B&Bs is as wide as the living standards in America. You'll find everything from semi-mansions in the most fashionable residential areas to little grass shacks offered by a down-home fisherman and his family. This means that it's particularly important for you to choose a host family with whom your lifestyle is compatible. Unlike a hotel or a condo, you'll be living *with* a host and most likely his or her family, although your room will be private, with private baths and separate entranceways being quite common. You don't just "check in" to a bed and breakfast. In Hawaii you go through agencies (listed below) which match host and guest. Write to them and they'll send you a booklet with a complete description of the bed and breakfast, its general location, the fees charged, and a good idea of the lifestyle of your host family. With the reservations application they'll include a questionnaire that will basically determine your profile: are you single? children? smoker? etc., as well as arrival and departure dates and all pertinent particulars. Since B&Bs are run by individual families, the times that they will accept guests can vary according to what's happening in their lives. This makes it imperative to write well in advance: three months is good; earlier (six months) is too long and too many things can change. Four weeks is about the minimum time required to make all necessary arrangements. Expect a minimum stay (three days is common) and a maximum stay. Bed and breakfasts are not "long-term" housing, although it's hoped that guest and host will develop a friendship and future stays can be as long as both desire.

Rates and Particulars: add 9% room tax

The B&B you choose can have all of the modern amenities including kitchen facilities, laundry, gorgeous views, TV, and everything else necessary for a comfortable stay thrown in for one price, or it can be a trekker's cabin at the foot of Haleakala with little more than a cot, cook stove, and roof over your head. Generally, you can expect to spend $30-$65 per day, with weekly and monthly discounts. Local phone calls are free. Special rates combine various car rentals, flights, and sightseeing tours. Most agencies require a deposit to make reservations, with a non-refundable cancellation fee because of the work involved. You do, however, get your deposit back, if you notify of cancellation before deadline. Get particulars straight, so that you don't lose money in case of a change of plans.

B&B Agencies

A top-notch B&B agency is **Bed and Breakfast Hawaii,** operated by Evelyn Warner and Al Davis. They've been running this service since 1978. B&B Hawaii has a membership fee of $5 yearly. For this they mail you their "Directory of Homes," a periodic "hot sheet" of new listings, and all pertinent guest applications. Write Bed and Breakfast Hawaii, Box 449, Ka-

a secluded B&B

paa, HI 96746, tel. 822-7771, Oahu, 536-8421. Another B&B agency with a good reputation is **Go Native Hawaii.** They'll send you a directory and all needed information by writing to their Mainland address at Box 13115, Lansing, MI 48901, or in Hawaii at 130 Puhili St., Hilo, HI 96720. Go Native will also accept collect calls from travelers already in Hawaii at tel. 961-2080. An Oahu-based firm with extensive listings is **Bed and Breakfast Pacific Hawaii,** c/o Maria Wilson, 19 Kai Nani Pl., Kailua, HI 96734, tel. 262-6026, or 262-7865. Also operating on Oahu is **Bed and Breakfast Honolulu,** 3242 Kaohinani Dr., Honolulu, HI 96817, tel. 595-6170. Information on B&Bs can also be obtained from the **American Board of Bed and Breakfast Assn.,** Box 23294, Washington, D.C. 20026.

SPECIAL ACCOMMODATIONS

YM/WCAs are quite limited in Hawaii. They vary as far as private room and bath are concerned, so each should be contacted individually. Prices vary too, but expect to pay $15 single. Men or women are accepted at respective Ys unless otherwise stated. Oahu has 5 Ys, and Maui and Kauai each have one. You can get information by writing **YMCA Central Branch,** 401 Atkinson Dr., Honolulu 96814, tel. 941-3344; Maui YMCA, J. Walter Cameron Center, 95 Mahalani St., Wailuku, HI 96793, tel. 244-3153; YMCA of Kauai, Box 1786, Lihue, HI 96766. Call 742-1182 or 742-1200. Refer to "Accommodations" in the travel chapters for particulars on the Ys.

There is only one **American YH** in Hawaii, located in Honolulu and always busy. You can make reservations. **Elderhostel,** 100 Boylston St., Suite 200, Boston MA 02116, offers non-credit courses at Hawaii Loa College, Oahu. The **University of Hawaii** has two 6-week summer sessions beginning late May and again in early July offering reasonable rates in residence halls (mandatory meals), and in apartments on campus along with the course work. For complete information see "Honolulu, Accommodations."

Home Exchanges

One other method of staying in Hawaii, open to homeowners, is to offer the use of their home for a home in Hawaii. This is done by listing your home with an agency that facilitates the exchange and publishes a descriptive directory. To list your home and to find out what is available, write: Vacation Exchange Club, 12006 111 Ave., Youngtown, AZ 85363; or, Interservice Home Exchange, Box 87, Glen Echo, MD 20812.

FOOD AND DRINK

Hawaii is a gastronome's Shangri-La, a sumptuous smorgasbord in every sense of the word. The ethnic groups that have come to Hawaii in the last 200 years have brought their own special enthusiasm and culture, and lucky for all, they didn't forget their cook pots, hearty appetites, and exotic taste buds. The Polynesians who first arrived found a fertile but barren land. Immediately they set about growing their taro, coconuts, and bananas, and raising chickens, pigs, fish, and even dogs, though these were reserved for the nobility. The harvests were bountiful and the islanders thanked the gods with the traditional feast called the *luau.* The underground oven, the *imu,* baked most of the dishes, and participants were encouraged to feast while relaxing on straw mats and enjoying the *hula* and various entertainments. The *luau* is as popular as ever, a treat that's guaranteed to delight anyone with a sense of eating adventure.

The missionaries and sailors came next and their ships' holds carried barrels of ingredients for the puddings, pies, dumplings, gravies, and roasts—the sustaining "American foods" of New England farms. The mid-1800s saw the arrival of boatloads of Chinese and Japanese peasants, who wasted no time making rice instead of bread the staple of the islands. The Chinese added their exotic spices, creating complex Szechuan dishes, as well as workingmen's basics like chop suey. The Japanese introduced *sashimi,* boxed lunches, delicate tempura, and rich, filling noodle soups. The Portuguese brought their luscious Mediterranean dishes with tomatoes and peppers surrounding plump spicy sausages, nutritious bean soups, and mouth-watering sweet treats like *malasadas* and *pao dolce* (sweet bread). Koreans carried crocks of zesty *kimchi,* and quickly fired up barbecue pits for *pulgogi,* a traditional marinated beef cooked over an open fire. Filipinos served up their mouth-watering *adobo* stews of fish, meat or chicken in a rich sauce of vinegar and garlic.

Recently, Thai and Vietnamese restaurants

have been offering their irresistible dishes side by side with fiery burritos from Mexico and elegant marsala cream sauces from France. The ocean breezes of Hawaii not only cool the skin, but on them waft some of the most delectable aromas on Earth, to make the tastebuds thrill and the spirit soar.

Special Note

Nothing is sweeter to the appetite than reclining on a beach and deciding just what dish will make your taste buds laugh tonight. Kick back, close your eyes, and let the smells and tastes of past meals drift into your consciousness. The following should help you decide just exactly what it is that you're in the mood for, and let you know the types of foods available in Hawaii, and their ingredients. Particular restaurants, eateries, stores, and shops will be covered in the travel chapters under "Food," and "Shopping."

HAWAIIAN FOODS

Hawaiian foods, oldest of all island dishes, are wholesome, well prepared, and delicious. All you have to do on arrival is notice the size of some of the local boys (and women) to know immediately that food to them is indeed a happy and serious business. An oft-heard island joke is that "local men don't eat until they're full, they eat until they're tired." Many Hawaiian dishes have become standard fare at a variety of restaurants, eaten one time or another by anyone who spends time in the islands. Hawaiian food in general is called *kaukau,* cooked food is *kapahaki,* and something broiled is called *kaola.* All of these prefixes on a menu will let you know that Hawaiian food is served. Usually inexpensive, they'll definitely fill you and keep you going.

Traditional Favorites

In old Hawaii, although the sea meant life, many more people were farmers than fishermen. They cultivated neat garden plots of taro, sugarcane, breadfruit, and various sweet potatoes *(uala).* They husbanded pigs and barkless dogs *(ilio),* and prized *moa* (chicken) for their feathers and meat, but found eating the eggs repulsive. Their only farming implement was the *o'o,* a sharpened hardwood digging stick. The Hawaiians were the best farmers of Polynesia, and the first thing they planted was taro, a tuberous root that was created by the gods at the same time as man. This main staple of the old Hawaiians was pounded into *poi,* a glutinous purple paste. It comes in liquid consistencies referred to as "one-, two-, or three-finger *poi."* The fewer fingers you need to eat it, the thicker it is. *Poi* is one of the most nutritious carbohydrates known, but people unaccustomed to it find it bland and tasteless,

Hawaiian family eating poi *by A. Plum, c. 1846 (Hawaii State Archives)*

although some of the best, fermented for a day or so, has an acidy bite. *Poi* is made to be eaten *with* something, but locals who love it pop it in their mouths and smack their lips. However, those unaccustomed to it will suffer constipation if they eat too much.

A favorite popular desert is *haupia,* a custard made from coconut. *Limu* is a generic term for edible seaweed, which many people still gather from the shoreline and eat as a salad, or mix with ground *kukui* nuts and salt as a relish. A favorite Hawaiian snack is *opihi,* small shellfish (limpets) that cling to rocks. People gather them, always leaving some for the future. Cut from the shell and eaten raw by all peoples of Hawaii, as testament to their popularity they sell for $150 per gallon in Honolulu. A general term that has come to mean hors d'oeuvres in Hawaii is *pu pu.* Originally the name of a small shellfish, now everyone uses it for any "munchy" that's considered a finger food. A traditional liquor made from *ti* root is *okolehao*. It literally means "iron bottom," reminiscent of the iron blubber pots used to ferment it.

Luau

Thick cookbooks are filled with common Hawaiian dishes, but you can get a good sampling at a well-done *luau.* The central feature is the *imu,* an underground oven. Basically, a shallow hole is dug and lined with stones upon which a roaring fire is kindled. Once the fire dies down and the stones are super-heated, the ashes are swept away and the *imu* is ready for cooking. At one time only men could cook in this fashion; it was *kapu* for women. These restrictions have long been lifted, but men still seem to do most of the pit cooking, while women primarily serve. The main dish at a *luau* is *kalua* pork. *Kalua* refers to any dish baked underground. A whole pig *(pua'a)* is wrapped in *ti* and banana leaves and placed in the hot center. Its stomach cavity is filled with more hot stones; surrounding the pig are little bundles of food wrapped in *ti* leaves. These savory bundles, *lau lau,* contain the side dishes: fish, chicken, *poi,* sweet potatoes, breadfruit, and even bananas. The entire contents are then covered with multiple layers of banana, *ti,* or sometimes ginger leaves and a final coating of

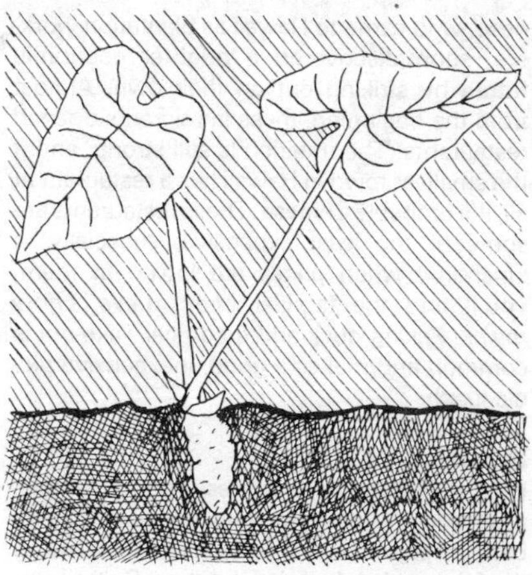

taro

earth. A long tube of bamboo may stick from the *imu* so that water (for steam) can be added. In about 4 hours the coverings are removed and the *luau* begins. You are encouraged to recline on *lau hala* mats placed around the central dining area, although tables and chairs are provided. There are forks and plates also, but traditionally it is proper to use your fingers and a sturdy banana leaf as a plate. Professional *luau* pride themselves on their methods of cooking and their food, and for a fixed price you can gorge yourself like an ancient *ali'i.* All supply entertainment, and exotic drinks flow like the tides. Your biggest problem after one of these extravaganzas will be having the strength to rise up off your *lau hala* mat.

INTERNATIONAL DISHES

Chinese and Japanese cuisines have a strong influence on island cooking, and their well-known spices and ingredients are creatively used in many recipes. Other cuisines, such as Filipino, Korean, and Portuguese are not as well known, but are now becoming standard island fare.

Chinese

Tens of thousands of fortune cookies yield their little springs of wisdom every day to hungry diners throughout Hawaii. The Chinese, who came to Hawaii as plantation workers, soon discovered a brighter economic future by striking out on their own. Almost from the beginning, these immigrants opened restaurants. The tradition is still strong, and if the smallest town in Hawaii has a restaurant at all, it's probably Chinese. These restaurants are some of the least expensive, especially at lunchtime when prices are lower. In them, you'll find the familiar *chop sueys, chow meins,* Peking duck and fried rice. Take-out is common and makes a good, inexpensive picnic lunch.

Japanese

For the uninitiated, Japanese food is simple, aesthetically pleasing, and delicious. *Sushi* bars are plentiful, especially in Honolulu, using the freshest fish from local waters. Some common dishes include: *teriyaki* chicken, fish, or steak, which is grilled in a marinated *shoyu* (soy) sauce base; *tempura,* mouth-sized bites of fish and vegetables dipped in a flour and egg batter and deep fried; *sukiyaki,* vegetables, meat, mushrooms, *tofu,* and vermicelli are brought to your table where you cook them in a prepared stock kept boiling with a little burner. You then dip the morsels into a mixture of egg and *shoyu; shabu shabu,* similar to *sukiyaki* without noodles and the emphasis on beef; *don buri,* ("various ingredients on rice in a bowl"), such as *ten don buri,* battered shrimp on rice; and various dishes of *tofu,* and *miso* soup, which provide some of the highest sources of non-meat protein. Japanese restaurants span the entire economic range, from some of the most elegant and expensive to hole-in-the-wall eateries where the surroundings are basic, but where the food is fit for a *samurai.* Above all, cleanliness is guaranteed.

Filipino

Most people have never sampled Filipino food. This cuisine is spicy with plenty of exotic sauces. The following are a sampling found in most Filipino restaurants: *singang,* sour soup made from fish, shrimp, or vegetables, that has an acidy base from fruits like tamarind; *adobo,* a generic term for anything (chicken and pork are standards) stewed in vinegar and garlic; *lumpia,* a Filipino spring roll; *pancit,* many variations of noodles made into ravioli-like bundles stuffed with pork or other meats; *lechon,* a whole suckling pig stuffed and roasted; *siopao,* a steam-heated dough ball filled with chicken or other tasty ingredients; and *halo halo,* a confection of shaved ice smothered in preserved fruits and canned milk.

Korean

Those who have never dined on Korean dishes are in for a sumptuous treat: *kalbitang,* a beef rib soup in a thin but tasty broth; *pulgogi,* marinated beef and vegetables grilled over an open flame; *pulkalbi,* beef ribs grilled over an open flame; *pibimbap,* a large bowl of rice smothered with beef, chicken, and vegetables that you mix together before eating; *kimchi,* fermented cabbage and hot spices made into a zesty "slaw"; *kimchi chigyae,* stew of *kimchi,* pork vegetables, and spices in a thick soup base.

TROPICAL FRUITS AND VEGETABLES

Some of the most memorable taste treats from the islands require no cooking at all: the luscious tropical and exotic fruits and vegetables sold in markets and roadside stands, or found just hanging on trees, waiting to be picked. Make sure to experience as many as possible. The general rule in Hawaii is that you are allowed to pick fruit on public lands, but it should be limited to personal consumption. The following is a sampling of some of Hawaii's best produce.

Bananas

No tropical island is complete without them. There are over 70 species in Hawaii, with hundreds of variations. Some are for peeling and eating while others are cooked. A "hand" of bananas is great for munching, backpacking, or just picnicking. Available everywhere—and cheap.

Avocados

Brought from South America, avocados were originally cultivated by the Aztecs. They have a buttery consistency and a nutty flavor. Hundreds of varieties in all shapes and colors are available fresh year-round. They have the highest fat content of any fruit next to the olive.

breadfruit

Coconuts

What tropical paradise would be complete without coconuts? Indeed, these were some of the first plants brought by the Polynesians. When children were born, coconut trees were planted for them so they'd have fruit throughout their lifetime. Truly tropical fruits, they know no season. Drinking nuts are large and green, and when shaken you can hear the milk inside. You get about a quart of fluid from each. It takes skill to open one, but a machete can handle anything. Cut the stem end flat so that it will stand, then bore a hole into the pointed end and put in a straw or hollow bamboo. Coconut water is slightly acidic and helps to balance alkaline foods. Spoon meat is a custard-like gel on the inside of drinking nuts. Sprouted coconut meat is also an excellent food. Split open a sprouted nut, and inside is the yellow fruit, like a moist sponge cake. "Millionaire's salad" is made from the heart of a coconut palm. At one time an entire tree was cut down to get to the heart, which is just inside the trunk below the fronds and is like an artichoke heart except that it's about the size of a watermelon. In a downed tree, the heart stays good for about two weeks.

Litchi

Called nuts but really a small fruit with a thin red shell. They have a sweet and juicy white flesh when fresh, and appear like nuts when dried.

Breadfruit

This island staple provides a great deal of carbohydrates, but many people find the baked, boiled, or fried fruit bland. It grows all over the islands and is really thousands of little fruits growing together to form a ball.

Mangos

These are some of the most delicious fruits known to humans. They grow wild all over the islands; the ones on the leeward sides of the islands ripen from April to June, while the ones on the windward sides can last until October. They're found in the wild on trees up to 60 feet tall, and the problem is to stop eating them once you start!

Passionfruit

Known by their island name of *lilikoi,* they make excellent juice and pies. They're a small yellow fruit (similar to lemons but smooth-skinned) mostly available in summer and fall, and many wild ones grow on vines, waiting to be picked. Slice off the stem end, scoop the seedy pulp out with your tongue, and you'll know why they're called "passionfruit."

Guava

These small round yellow fruits are abundant in the wild where they are ripe from early summer to late fall. Considered a pest—so pick all you want. A good source of vitamin C, they're great for juice, jellies, and desserts.

solo papaya

Papaya
This truly tropical fruit has no real season but is mostly available in the summer. They grow on branchless trees and are ready to pick as soon as any yellow appears. Of the many varieties, the "solo papaya," meant to be eaten by one person, is the best. Split them in half, scrape out the seeds and have at them with a spoon.

Macadamia Nuts
The king of nuts was brought from Australia in 1892. Now it's the state's fourth largest agricultural product. Available roasted, candied, or buttered.

FISH AND SEAFOOD

Anyone who loves fresh fish and seafood has come to the right place. Island restaurants specialize in seafood, and it's available everywhere. Pound for pound, seafood is one of the best dining bargains in Hawaii. You'll find it served in every kind of restaurant, and often the fresh catch of the day is proudly displayed on ice in a glass case. The following is a sampling of the best.

Mahi Mahi
This excellent eating fish is one of the most common and least expensive in Hawaii. It's referred to as a "dolphin," but is definitely a fish and not a mammal at all. *Mahi mahi* can weigh 10-65 pounds; the flesh is light and moist, and the fish is broadest at the head. When caught it's a dark olive color, but after a while the skin turns iridescent—blue, green, and yellow. Can be served as a main course, or as a patty in a fish sandwich.

A'u
This true island delicacy is a broadbill swordfish or marlin. It's expensive even in Hawaii because the damn thing's so hard to catch. The meat is moist and white and truly superb. If it's offered on the menu, order it. It'll cost a bit more, but you won't be disappointed.

Ono
Ono means "delicious" in Hawaiian so that should tip you off to the taste of this "wahoo," or king mackerel. *Ono* is regarded as one of the finest eating fishes in the ocean, and its white flakey meat lives up to its name.

Manini
These five-inch fish are some of the most abundant in Hawaii and live in about 10 feet of water. They school and won't bite a hook but are easily taken with spear or net. Not often on a menu, but they're favorites with local people who know best.

Ulua
This member of the "Jack Cravelle" family ranges between 15 and 100 pounds. Its flesh is white and has a steak-like texture. Delicious and often found on the menu.

Fish Potpourri
Uku is a gray snapper that's a favorite with local people. The meat is light and firm and grills well. ***ahi:*** A yellowfin tuna with the distinctive pinkish meat. A great favorite cooked, or uncooked in sushi bars. ***moi:*** This is the Hawaiian word for "king." It has large eyes and a shark-like head. Considered one of the finest eating fishes in Hawaii, it's best during the autumn months.

Some other island seafood found on the menu include *limu,* edible seaweed; *opihi,* small shellfish (limpets) that clings to rocks and is considered one of the best island delicacies, eaten raw; *aloalo,* like tiny lobsters; crawfish, plentiful in taro fields and irrigation ditches; *ahipalaka,* albacore tuna; various octopus (squid or calamari); and shark of various types.

HAWAIIAN GAME FISH

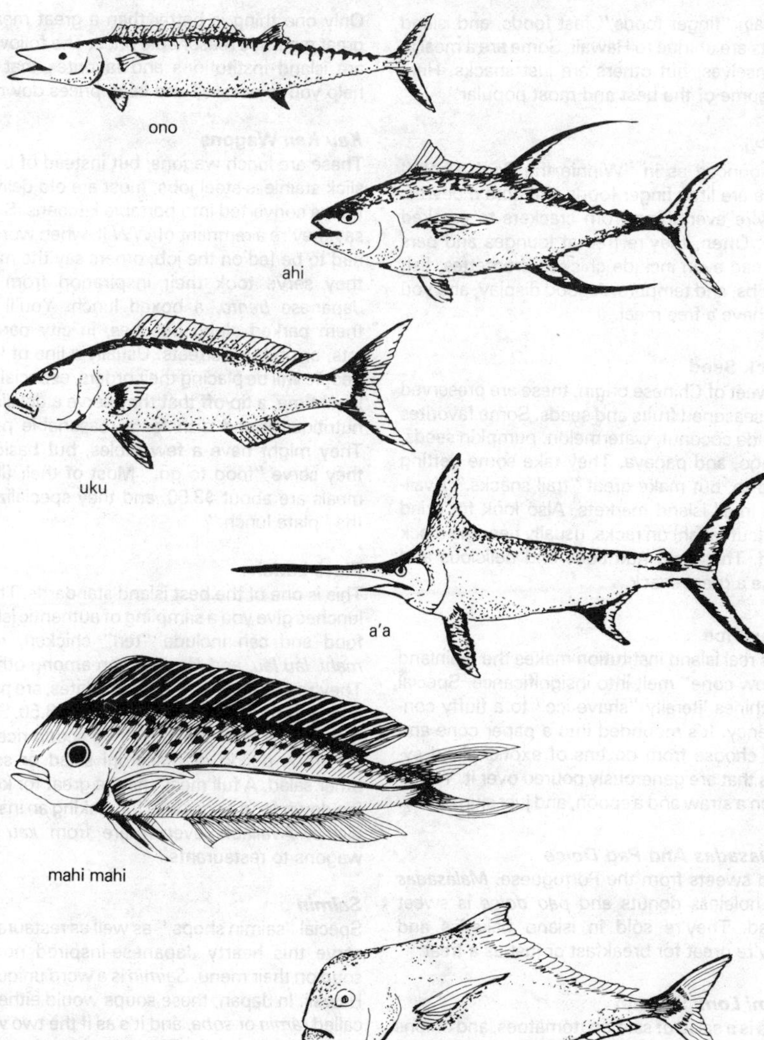

See "deep-sea fishing" p. 177

MUNCHIES AND ISLAND TREATS

Certain "finger foods," fast foods, and island treats are unique to Hawaii. Some are a meal in themselves, but others are just snacks. Here are some of the best and most popular.

Pu Pu

Pronounced as in "Winnie the Pooh Pooh," these are little finger foods and hors d'oevres. They're everything from crackers to cracked crab. Often, they're free at lounges and bars and can even include chicken drumettes, fish kabobs, and tempura. A good display, and you can have a free meal.

Crack Seed

A sweet of Chinese origin, these are preserved and seasoned fruits and seeds. Some favorites include coconut, watermelon, pumpkin seeds, mango, and papaya. They take some getting used to, but make great "trail snacks." Available in all island markets. Also look for dried fish (cuttlefish) on racks, usually near the crack seed. These are nutritious and delicious and make a great snack.

Shave Ice

This real island institution makes the mainland "snow cone" melt into insignificance. Special machines literally "shave ice" to a fluffy consistency. It's mounded into a paper cone and you choose from dozens of exotic island syrups that are generously poured over it. You're given a straw and a spoon, and just slurp away.

Malasadas And *Pao Dolce*

Two sweets from the Portuguese. *Malasadas* are holeless donuts and *pao dolce* is sweet bread. They're sold in island bakeries and they're great for breakfast or just as a treat.

Lomi Lomi Salmon

This is a salad of salmon, tomatoes, and onions with garnish and seasonings. Often accompanies "plate lunches" and featured at buffets and *luau.*

MONEYSAVERS

Only one thing is better than a great meal: a great meal at a reasonable price. The following are island institutions and favorites that will help you to eat well and keep prices down.

Kau Kau Wagons

These are lunch wagons, but instead of being slick stainless steel jobs, most are old delivery trucks converted into portable kitchens. Some say they're a remnant of WW II, when workers had to be fed on the job; others say the meals they serve took their inspiration from the Japanese *bento,* a boxed lunch. You'll see them parked along beaches, in city parking lots, or on busy streets. Usually a line of local people will be placing their orders, especially at lunchtime, a tip-off that they serve a delicious, nutritious island dish for a reasonable price. They might have a few tables, but basically they serve "food to go." Most of their filling meals are about $3.50, and they specialize in the "plate lunch."

Plate Lunch

This is one of the best island standards. These lunches give you a sampling of authentic island food and can include "teri" chicken, *mahi mahi, lau lau,* and *lomi* salmon among others. They're on paper or styrofoam plates, are packed to go, and usually cost less than $3.50. Standard with a plate lunch is "two scoop rice," a generous dollop of macaroni salad or some other salad. A full meal, they're great for keeping down food prices and for making an instant picnic. Available everywhere from *kau kau* wagons to restaurants.

Saimin

Special "saimin shops," as well as restaurants, serve this hearty Japanese-inspired noodle soup on their menu. *Saimin* is a word unique to Hawaii. In Japan, these soups would either be called *ramin* or *soba,* and it's as if the two were combined to *saimin*. These are large bowls of noodle soup, a light broth with meat, chicken, fish or vegetables stirred in. They cost only a

Those really determined to save money can always try this.

few dollars and are big enough for an evening meal. The best place to eat saimin is in a little local hole-in-the-wall shop, run by a family.

Luau And Buffets
As previously mentioned, the *luau* is an island institution. For a fixed price of about $30, you get to gorge yourself on a tremendous variety of island foods. On your *luau* day, skip breakfast and lunch and do belly stretching exercises! Buffets are also quite common in Hawaii, and like *luau* they're "all you can eat" affairs. Offered at a variety of restaurants and hotels, they usually cost $8 and up. The food, however, ranges from quite good to only passable. At lunchtime, they're even cheaper, and they're always advertised in the free tourist literature, which often includes a discount coupon.

Tips
Even some of the island's best restaurants in the fanciest hotels offer "early-bird specials"—the regular menu dinners offered to diners who come in before the usual dinner hour, which is approximately 6:00 p.m. You pay as little as half the normal price, and can dine in luxury on some of the best foods. Often advertised in the "free" tourist books, coupons for reduced meals might also be included: two for one, or limited dinners at a much lower price. Just clip them out. Hawaii has the full contingency of American fast-food chains including Jack in the Box, McDonalds, Shakeys Pizza, Kentucky Fried Chicken, and all the rest.

EXOTIC ISLAND DRINKS

To complement the fine dining in the islands, the bartenders have been busy creating their own tasty concoctions. The full range of beers, wines, and standard drinks is served in Hawaii, but for a real treat you should try some mixed drinks inspired by the islands. Kona coffee is the only coffee grown commercially in America. It comes from the Kona District of the Big Island and it is rich, aromatic, and a truly fine coffee. If it's offered on the menu, have a cup.

Drinking Laws
There are no "state" liquor stores; all kinds of spirits, wines, and beers are available in markets and shops, generally open during normal business hours, seven days a week. The drinking age is 18, and no towns are "dry." Legal hours for serving drinks depend on the type of establishment. Hours generally are: hotels, 6:00 a.m. to 4:00 a.m.; discos, and nightclubs where there is dancing, 10:00 a.m. to 4:00 a.m.; bars, lounges where there is no dancing, 6:00 a.m. to 2:00 a.m. Most restaurants serve alcohol, and in many that don't, you can bring your own.

Beer
A locally brewed beer is "Primo." At one time brewed only in Hawaii, it's also made on the Mainland now. It's a serviceable American brew in the German style, but it lacks that full,

hearty flavor of the European beers. "Maui Lager," a new beer being brewed on Maui, is a different story. It's a rich German-stlye beer made by brothers Klaus and Aloyisius Klink. "Maui Lager" is made in Wailuku, at the Pacific Brewing Co., where tours can be arranged.

Exotic Drinks

To make your experience complete, you must order one of these colorful island drinks. Most look very innocent because they come in pineapples, coconut shells, or tall frosted glasses. They're often garnished with little umbrellas or sparklers, and most have enough fruit in them to give you your vitamins for the day. Rum is used as the basis of many of them. It's been an island favorite since it was introduced by the whalers of last century. Here are some of the most famous: *Mai Tai,* a mixture of light and dark rum, orange curacao, orange and almond flavoring and lemon juice; *Chi Chi,* a simple concoction of vodka, pineapple juice and coconut syrup, real sleeper because it tastes like a milk shake; Blue Hawaii, vodka and blue curacao; Planter's Punch, light rum, grenadine, bitters, and lemon juice. Great thirst quencher; Singapore Sling, a sparkling mixture of gin, cherry brandy, and lemon juice.

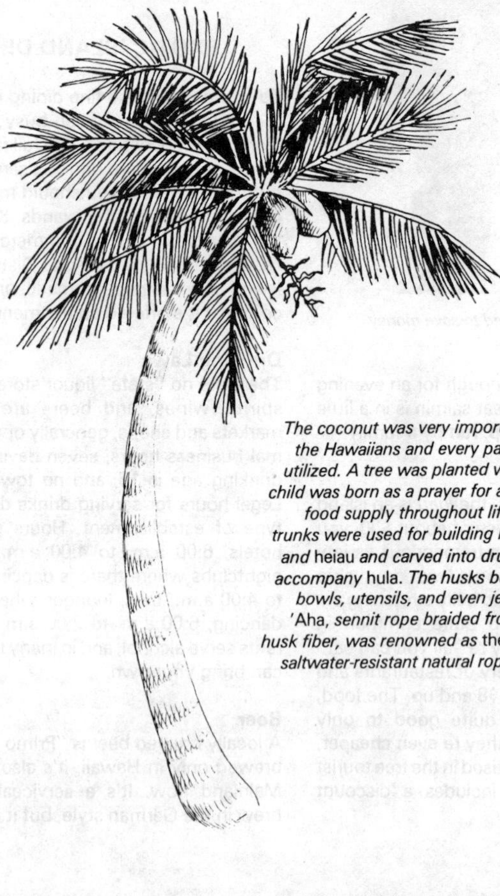

The coconut was very important to the Hawaiians and every part was utilized. A tree was planted when a child was born as a prayer for a good food supply throughout life. The trunks were used for building homes and heiau *and carved into drums to accompany* hula*. The husks became bowls, utensils, and even jewelry.* 'Aha, *sennit rope braided from the husk fiber, was renowned as the most saltwater-resistant natural rope ever made.*

CAMPING AND HIKING

A major aspect of the "Hawaii experience" is found in the simple beauty of nature and the outdoors. Visitors come to Hawaii to luxuriate at resorts and dine in fine restaurants, but everyone heads for the sand and surf, and most are captivated by the lush mountainous interior. What better way to savor this natural beauty than by hiking slowly through it or pitching a tent in the middle of it? Hawaii offers a full range of hiking and camping, and what's more, most of it is easily accessible and free. Camping facilities are located near many choice beaches and amid the most scenic areas in the islands. They range in amenities from full housekeeping cabins to primitive "hike-in" sites. Some restrictions to hiking apply because much of the land is privately owned, so you may require advance permission. But plenty of public access trails along the coast and deep into the interior would fill the itineraries of even the most intrepid trekkers. If you enjoy the great outdoors on the Mainland, you'll be thrilled by these "mini-continents," where in one day you can go from the frosty summits of alpine wonderlands down into baking cactus-covered deserts and emerge through jungle foliage onto a sun-soaked subtropical shore.

Note

Descriptions of individual state, county, and national parks, along with directions on how to get there, are given under "Camping and Hiking" in the respective travel chapters.

NATIONAL PARKS

Hawaii's 2 national parks sit atop volcanoes: **Haleakala National Park** on Maui, and **Hawaii Volcanoes National Park** centered around Kilauea Crater on the Big Island. Camping is free at both, and permits are not required except for cabins and campgrounds inside of Haleakala crater. Get free information by writing to the individual Park Headquarters listed below, or from **National Park Service,** 300 Ala Moana Blvd., Honolulu, HI 96850, tel. 546-7584.

Hawaii Volcanoes National Park

You won't need a permit to camp at the 3 overnight facilities at this amazing national park that spans one of the most active volcanoes in the world, but maybe an offering to Madame Pele would be a good idea. Registration at Park HQ is required if you intend to go trekking into the backcountry where you will need a wilderness permit. There are 3 campgrounds in the park that you can drive to; though they operate on a first-come first-served basis, they're hardly ever filled. All have water, firepits, shelters, tables, and a 7-day limit, but no one counts too closely. Information, including pamphlets, brochures, and maps are available on request from: **Park Headquarters,** Hawaii Volcanoes National Park, Hawaii, HI 96718, tel. 967-7311.

Haleakala National Park

Camping is free at Haleakala National Park on Maui. Permits are not needed to camp at Hosmer Grove, just a short drive from Park HQ, or at Oheo Stream Campground (formerly Seven Sacred Pools) near Kipahulu, along the coastal road 10 miles south of Hana. Camping is on a first-come, first-served basis, and there's an official three-day stay limit, but it's a loose count, especially at Oheo which is almost always empty. The case is much different at the campsites located inside Haleakala crater proper. On the floor of the crater are two primitive tenting campsites for which you'll need a wilderness permit. Because of ecological considerations, only 25 campers per night can stay at each site, and a 3-night, 4-day maximum stay is strictly enforced, with tenting allowed at any one site for only two nights. However, because of the strenuous hike involved, campsites are open most of the time. You must be totally self-sufficient and equipped for cold weather to be comfortable. Also, Paliku, Holua, and another site at Kapalaoa on the south rim offer fully self-contained cabins. To have a chance at getting a cabin you must make reservations, so write well in advance for complete information to: **Haleakala National Park,** Box 537, Makawao, HI 96768, tel. 572-9306.

STATE PARKS

Hawaii's 67 state parks are managed by the Dept. of Land and Natural Resources, through their Division of State Parks with branch offices on each island. These facilities include everything from historical sites like Iolani Palace in downtown Honolulu to wildland parks accessible only by trail. Some are only for looking at, some are restricted to day use, and at 16 or so (which change periodically without notice) there is overnight camping. At 7 of these 16 state parks, there are either A-frames, self-contained cabins, or group accommodations available on a fee basis with reservations necessary. At the others, camping is free, but permits are required. RVs are technically not allowed.

Polihale State Park, Kauai

Permits And Rules

Camping permits, available free, are good for a maximum stay of 5 nights at any one park. A permit to the same person for the same park is again available only after 30 days have elapsed. Campgrounds are open every day on the Neighbor Islands, but closed Wednesday and Thursday on Oahu. Arrive after 2:00 p.m. and check out by 11:00 a.m., except again on Oahu where Wednesday check out is 8:00 a.m. You must be 18 for park permits, and anyone under that age must be accompanied by an adult. Alcoholic beverages are prohibited, along with nude sunbathing and swimming. Plants and wildlife are protected, but reasonable amounts of fruits and seeds may be gathered for personal consumption. Fires are allowed on cook stoves or in designated pits only. Dogs and other pets must be under control at all times, and are not permitted to run around unleashed. Hunting and freshwater fishing are allowed in season with a license, and ocean fishing is permitted except when disallowed by posting. Permits are required for certain trails, pavilions, and remote camps, so check.

Cabins And Shelters

Housekeeping cabins, A-frames, and group lodges are available at 7 state parks throughout the state (see "Camping And Hiking" travel chapters for charts). As with camping, permits are required with the same 5-day maximum stay limitations. Reservations are necessary because of popularity, and a 50% deposit at time of confirmation is required. There is a 3-day cancellation requirement for refunds, with payment made in cash, money order, certified check, or personal check only if the latter is received 30 days before arrival so cashing procedures are possible. The balance is due on arrival; check in is 2:00 p.m., check out 11:00 a.m. Rates for A-frames, a single room with bunks and a picnic table, are a flat $7 per night, with a 4-person maximum. Centrally located is a pavilion with a stove, refrigerator, restroom, and cold showers. Cabins are on a sliding scale of $10 for the 1st person, down to $5 for the 6-person maximum. These are completely furnished down to the utensils, with heaters for cold weather and private baths. Group accommodations (holding 32 to 64 people) are on an inexpensive, but slightly convoluted per-person, per-night basis: the maximum is $8 for the first person, first night, down to $1 for the 64th person after 2 nights. They're broken up into 8-person units which can be rented as such. Each has its own toilet and shower facilities but cooking is in a central mess hall.

State Park Permit Issuing Offices

Permits can be reserved 2 months in advance by writing a letter including your name, address, phone number, number in your party, type of permit requested, and duration of stay. They can be picked up on arrival with proof of identification. Office hours are 8:00 a.m. to 4:15 p.m., Monday through Friday. Usually, camping permits are no problem (Oahu excepted, see "Camping Hiking" Oahu chapter) to secure on the day you arrive, but reserving insures you a space and alleviates anxiety. The permits are available from the following offices: **Oahu,** Division of State Parks, 1151 Punchbowl St., Honolulu 96813, tel. 548-7455; **Hawaii,** Div. of State Parks, 75 Aupuni St., Hilo 96720, tel. 961-7200; **Maui and Molokai,** Div. of State Parks, 54 High St., Wailuku, 96793, tel. 244-4354; **Kauai,** Div. of State Parks, State Bldg., 3060 Eiwa and Hardy Sts., Box 1671, Lihue, 96766, tel. 245-4444. For lodging at **Kokee State Park,** Kauai, write Kokee Lodge, Box 819, Waimea, HI 96796, tel. 335-6061.

COUNTY PARKS

The state of Hawaii is broken up into counties, and the counties control their own parks. Over 100 of these are scattered primarily along the coastlines, and are generally referred to as **beach parks.** Most are for day use only, where visitors fish, swim, snorkel, surf, picnic and sunbathe, but over 36 beach parks have overnight camping. The rules governing their use vary slightly from county to county, but most have about the same requirements as state parks. The main difference is that, along with a use permit, most county parks charge a fee for overnight use. Again, the differences between individual parks are too numerous to mention, but the majority have a central pavilion for cooking, restrooms, and cold-water showers (solar heated at a few), sometimes individual fire pits, picnic tables, and electricity (usually only at the central pavilion). RVs are allowed to park in appropriate spaces.

Fees And Permits

The fees are quite reasonable at $1-2 per night, per person, children about $.50 each. One safety point to consider is that beach parks are open to the general public and most are used with regularity. Quite a few people pass through, and your chances of encountering a hassle or rip-off are slightly higher (see p. 147 for safety tips). To get a permit and pay your fees for use of a county park, either write in advance, or visit one of the following issuing offices. Most will accept reservations months in advance, with offices generally open during normal working hours. For county parks write or visit the Dept. of Parks and Recreation, County Parks: **Oahu,** 650 S. King St., Honolulu, HI 96813, tel. 523-4525; **Maui,** War Memorial Gym, Wailuku HI 96793, tel. 244-5514; **Hawaii,** 25 Aupuni St., Hilo HI 96720, tel. 961-8311; **Kauai,** 4191 Hardy St., Lihue HI 96766, tel. 245-4982, or during off hours at Lihue Police Station, 3060 Umi St., Lihue 96766, tel. 245-6721; **Molokai,** County Bldg., Kaunakakai HI 96748, tel. 553-5141.

EQUIPMENT, INFORMATION, AND SAFETY

Equipment

Like everything else you take to Hawaii, your camping and hiking equipment should be lightweight and durable. Camping equipment size and weight should not cause a problem with baggage requirements on airlines: if it does, it's a tip-off that you're hauling too much. One odd luggage consideration you might make is to bring along a small **styrofoam cooler** packed with equipment. Exchange these for food items when you get to Hawaii; if you intend to car camp successfully and keep food prices down, you'll definitely need a cooler. You can also buy one on arrival for only a few dollars. You'll need a lightweight **tent,** preferably with a rainfly, and a sewn-in floor. This will save you from getting wet and miserable, and will keep out mosquitoes, cockroaches, ants, and Hawaii's few stinging insects. In Haleakala Crater, where you can expect cold and wind, a tent is a must; in fact you won't be allowed to camp without one.

Sleeping bags are a good idea, although you can get along at sea level with only a blanket. Down-filled bags are necessary for Haleakala, Mauna Kea, Mauna Loa, or any high altitude-camping—you'll freeze without one. **Camp stoves** are needed because there's very little wood in some volcanic areas, it's often wet in the deep forest, and open fires are often prohibited. If you'll be car camping, take along a multi-burner stove, and for trekking, a backpacker's stove will be necessary. The grills found only at some campgrounds are popular with many families that go often to the beach parks for an open-air dinner. You can buy a very inexpensive charcoal grill at many variety stores throughout Hawaii. It's a great idea to take along a **lantern**. This will give added safety for car campers. Definitely take a **flashlight**, replacement batteries, and a few small **candles**. A complete **first-aid kit** can be the difference between life and death, and is worth the extra bulk. Hikers, especially those leaving the coastal areas, should take **rain gear**, a plastic ground cloth, utility knife, compass, safety whistle, mess kit, water purification tablets, canteen, nylon twine, and waterproof matches. You can find plenty of stores that sell, and a few stores that rent, camping equipment; see the Yellow Pages under "Camping Equipment," and "Shopping" in the travel chapters.

Safety

There are two things in Hawaii that you must keep your eye on to remain safe: humans and nature. The general rule is, the farther you get away from towns, the safer you'll be from human-induced hassles. If possible, don't hike or camp alone, especially if you're a woman. Don't leave your valuables in your tent, and always carry your money, papers, and camera with you. (See "Theft.") Don't tempt the locals by being overly friendly or unfriendly, and make yourself scarce if they're drinking. While hiking, remember that many trails are well maintained, but trailhead markers are often missing. The trails themselves can be muddy, which can make them treacherously slippery and oftentimes knee-deep. Always bring food

Rugged pali *are found on all islands.*

because you cannot, in most cases, forage from the land. Water in most streams is biologically polluted and will give you bad stomach problems if you drink it without purifying it first, either through boiling or with tablets. For your part, please don't use the streams as a toilet.

Precautions

Always tell a ranger or official of your hiking intentions. Supply an itinerary and your expected route, then stick to it. Twilight is short in the islands, and night sets in rapidly. In June sunrise and sunset are around 6:00 a.m. and 7:00 p.m., in December these occur at 7:00 a.m. and 6:00 p.m. If you become lost at night, stay put, light a fire if possible, and stay as dry as you can. Hawaii is made of volcanic rock which is brittle and crumbly. Never attempt to climb steep *pali* (cliffs). Every year people are stranded and fatalities have occurred on the *pali.* If lost, walk on ridges and avoid the gulches which have more obstacles and make it harder for rescuers to spot you. Be careful of elevation sickness, especially on Haleakala, Mauna Loa, and Mauna Kea. The best cure is to head down as soon as possible.

Heat can cause you to lose water and salt. If you become woozy or weak, rest, take salt, and drink water as you need it. Remember, it takes much more water to restore a dehydrated person than to keep hydrated; take small frequent sips. Be mindful of flash floods. Small creeks can turn into raging torrents with upland rains. Never camp in a dry creek bed. Fog is only encountered at the 1,500- to 5,000-foot level, but be careful of disorientation. Generally, stay within your limits, be careful, and enjoy yourself.

Guide Books

For a well-written and detailed hiking guide complete with maps, check out the *Hiking Hawaii Series* (a book for each island, plus a general book for all the islands) by Robert Smith, published by Wilderness Press, 2440 Bancroft Way, Berkeley, CA 94704. Another book by the same company is *Hawaiian Camping* by Shirley Rizzuto. Geared toward family camping, it's adequate for basic information and listing necessary addresses, but at times it's limited in scope.

Helpful Departments And Organizations
The following will be helpful in providing trail maps, accessibility information, hunting and fishing regulations, and general forest rules. The **Dept. of Land and Natural Resources,** Division of Forestry and Wildlife, 1151 Punchbowl, St., Honolulu, 96813, tel. 548-2861. Their "Recreation Map" (for each island) is excellent and free. The following organizations can provide general information on wildlife, conservation, and organized hiking trips: **Hawaiian Trail and Mountain Club,** Box 2238, Honolulu, 96804. The Trail and Mountain Club meets behind Iolani Palace on Saturdays at 10:00 a.m., and on Sundays at 8:00 a.m. Their hikes are announced in the *Honolulu Star Bulletin* in the "Pulse of Paradise" column; **Hawaiian Audobon Society,** Box 22832, Honolulu 96822; **Sierra Club,** 1212 University Ave., Honolulu, 96826, tel. 946-8494.

Topographical And Nautical Charts
For in-depth topographical maps, write **U.S. Geological Survey,** Federal Center, Denver, CO 80225. In Hawaii, a wide range of topographical maps can be purchased at **Trans-Pacific Instrument Co.,** 1406 Colburn St., Honolulu, HI 96817, tel. 841-7538. For nautical charts, write **National Ocean Survey,** Riverdale, MD 20240.

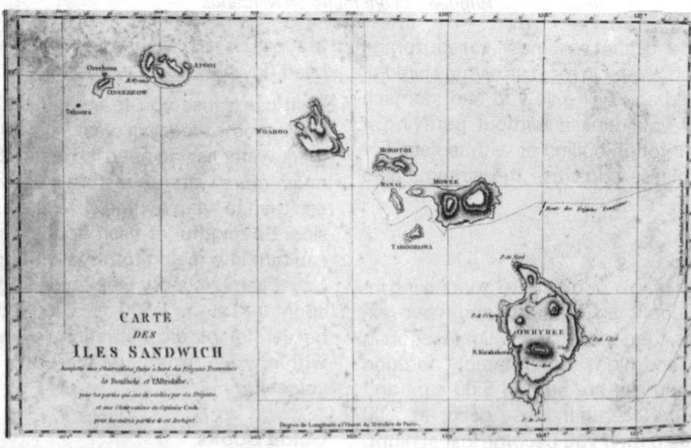

map of the "Sandwich Isles" by Capt. Jean La Perouse, c. 1786 (Hawaii State Archives)

SPORTS AND RECREATION

Hawaii is a playground for young and old with sports, games, and activities galore. Everyone can find something they enjoy, and most activities are free, relatively cheap, or once-in-a-lifetime thrills that are worth the money. The sea is the ideal playground. You can swim, snorkel, scuba, surf, fish, sail, canoe, kayak, sailboard, bodysurf, parasail, cruise, or merely stroll along the shore picking shells or exploring tidepools. Every island offers tennis and golf, along with plenty of horseback riding, hiking, hunting, and freshwater fishing. Spectator sports like baseball, basketball, polo and especially football are popular, and the Kona Coast of the Big Island is a mecca for world-class triathletes. Whatever your desire or physical abilities may be, there'll be some activity that strikes your fancy in Hawaii.

One of the best tonics for relaxation is to play hard at something you thoroughly enjoy, so you're deliciously tired and fulfilled at day's end. For you this might be hooking onto an 800-pound marlin that'll test you to the limit, or perhaps just giving yourself to the sea and floating on gentle waves. Hawaii is guaranteed to thrill the young, invigorate the once young, put a twinkle in your eye and a bounce in your step.

Note

The following sports and activities breakdowns are designed to give you an idea of what's available. They'll all be covered in depth in the travel chapters under "Sports." There you'll also find specific entries for localized sports like horseback riding, jet skiing, water skiing, snow skiing, parasailing, kayaking, and much more. Whatever else you may do in Hawaii, you owe it to yourself to do one thing: enjoy it!

SCUBA AND SNORKELING

If you think that Hawaii is beautiful above the sea, wait until you explore below. The warm tropical waters and coral growth make it a fascinating haven for reef fish and aquatic plantlife. Snorkel and dive sites, varying in dif-

continued on p. 174

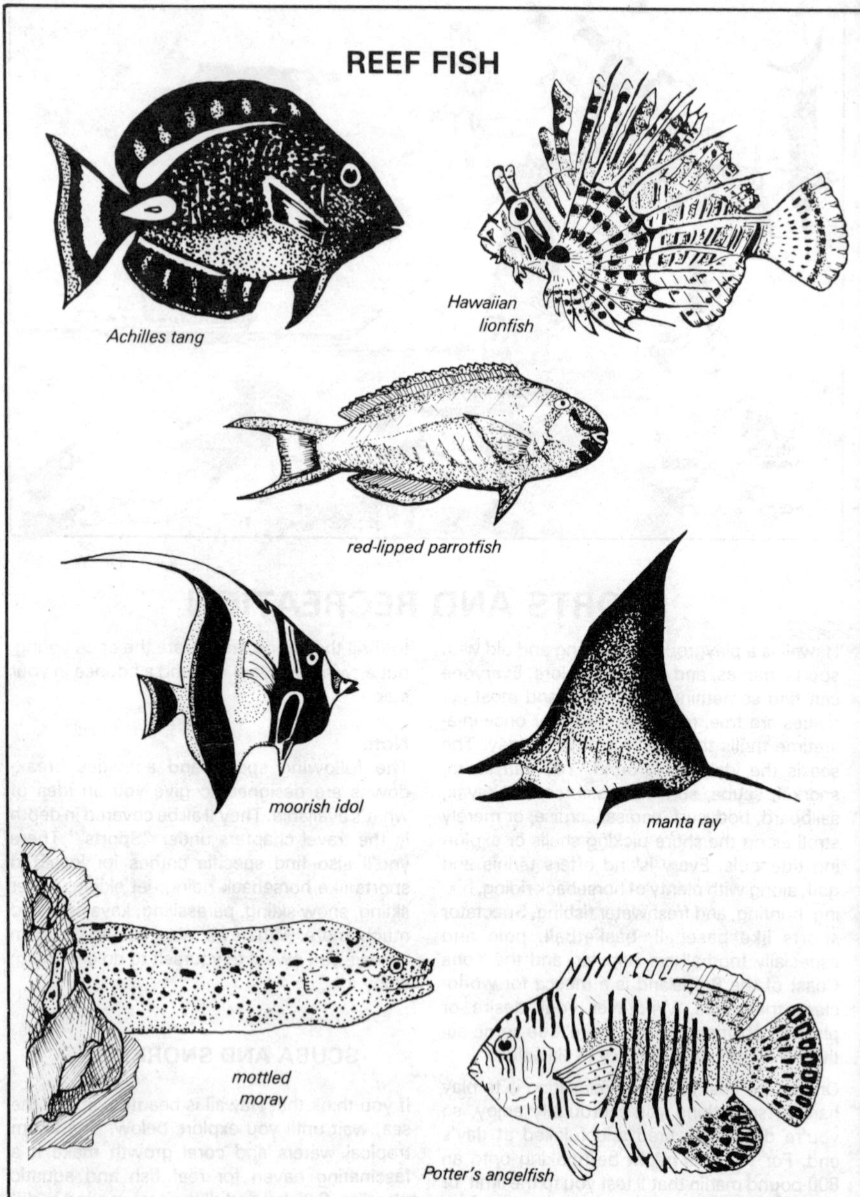
REEF FISH
Achilles tang
Hawaiian lionfish
red-lipped parrotfish
moorish idol
manta ray
mottled moray
Potter's angelfish

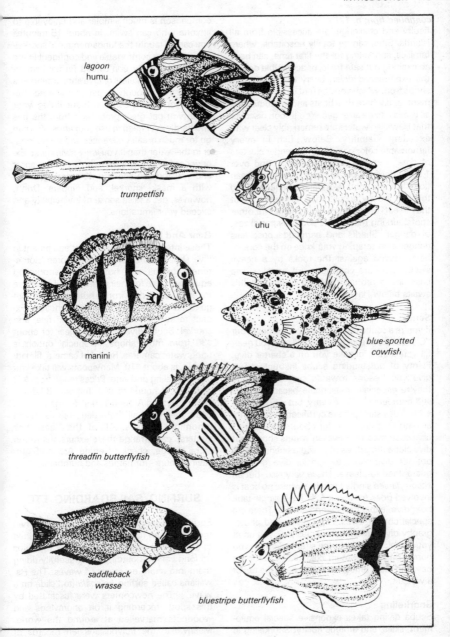

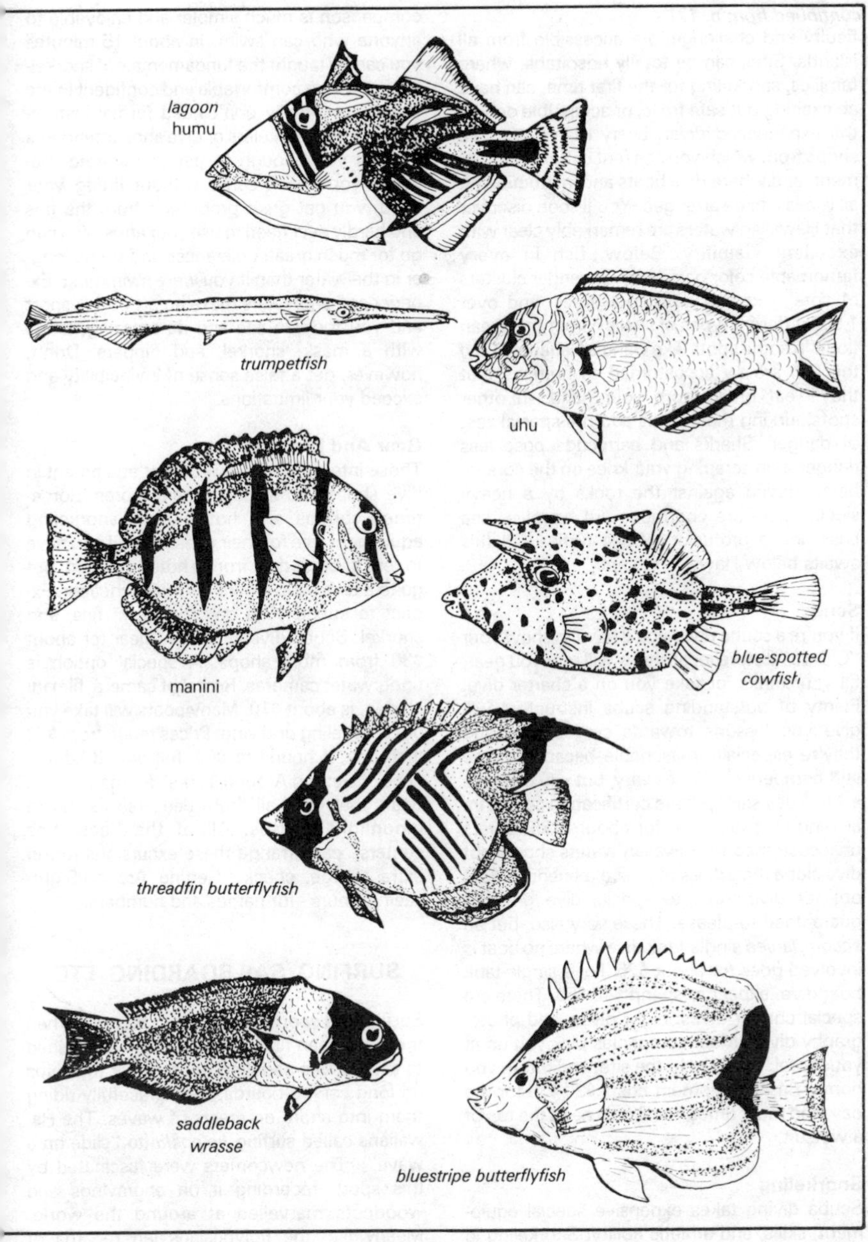
lagoon humu
trumpetfish
uhu
manini
blue-spotted cowfish
threadfin butterflyfish
saddleback wrasse
bluestripe butterflyfish

continued from p. 171
ficulty and challenge, are accessible from all islands. Sites can be totally hospitable where families, snorkeling for the first time, can have an exciting but safe frolic, or accessible only to the experienced diver. Every island has dive shops from which you can rent or buy all equipment, and where dive boats and instruction on all levels can be arranged. You'll soon discover that Hawaiian waters are remarkably clear with excellent visibility. Below, fish in every fathomable color parade by. Lavender clusters of coral, red and gold coral trees, and over 1,500 different types of shells carpet the ocean floor. In some spots (like Oahu's Hanauma Bay) the fish are so accustomed to humans that they'll eat bread from your hand. In other spots, lurking moray eels add the special zest of danger. Sharks and barracuda pose less danger than scraping your knee on the coral or being driven against the rocks by a heavy swell. There are enormous but harmless sea bass and a profusion of sea turtles. All this awaits below Hawaii's waters.

Scuba

If you're a scuba diver you'll have to show your "C Card" before local shops will rent you gear, fill your tanks, or take you on a charter dive. Plenty of outstanding scuba instructors will give you lessons towards certification, and they're especially reasonable because of the stiff competition. Prices vary, but you can take a 4 to 5 day semi-private certification course including all equipment for about $175. Divers unaccustomed to Hawaiian waters should not dive alone regardless of their experience. Most opt for dive tours to special dive grounds guaranteed to please. These vary also, but an *accompanied* single-tank dive where no boat is involved goes for about $25. For a single-tank boat dive, expect to spend $40-$50. There are special charter dives, night dives, and photography dives. Most companies pick you up at your hotel, take you to the site, and return you home. Basic equipment costs $20-$30 for the day, and most times you'll only need the top of a wetsuit.

Snorkeling

Scuba diving takes expensive special equipment, skills, and athletic ability. Snorkeling in comparison is much simpler and enjoyable to anyone who can swim. In about 15 minutes you can be taught the fundamentals of snorkeling, so you're comfortable and confident in the water—you really don't need formal instructions. Other snorkelers or dive shop attendants can tell you enough to get you started. Because you can breathe without lifting your head, you get great propulsion from the fins and hardly ever need to use your arms. You can go for much greater distances and spend longer in the water than if you were swimming. Experienced snorkelers make an art of this sport and you too can see and do amazing things with a mask, snorkel, and flippers. Don't, however, get a false sense of invincibility and exceed your limitations.

Gear And Excursions

Those interested can buy or rent equipment in dive shops and in department stores. Sometimes condos and hotels have snorkeling equipment free for their guests, but if you have to rent it, don't do it from a hotel or condo, but go to a dive shop where it's much cheaper. Expect to spend $7 a day for mask, fins, and snorkel. Scuba divers can rent gear for about $30 from most shops. A special option is underwater cameras. Rental of camera, film included, is about $10. Many boats will take you out snorkeling or diving. Prices range from $30 (half day, 4 hours) to $60 (full day, 8 hours), check "Getting Around/Tours" for many of the boats that do it all, from deep-sea fishing to moonlight cruises. All of the "activities centers" can arrange these excursions for no extra charge, check "Getting Around/Sightseeing Tours" for names and numbers.

SURFING, SAILBOARDING, ETC.

Surfing is a sport indigenous to Hawaii. When the white man first arrived he was astonished to see natives paddling out to meet the ships on long carved boards, then gracefully riding them into shore on crests of waves. The Hawaiians called surfing *he'enalu* (to "slide on a wave"). The newcomers were fascinated by this sport, recording it on engravings and woodcuts marvelled at around the world. Meanwhile, the Polynesians left records of

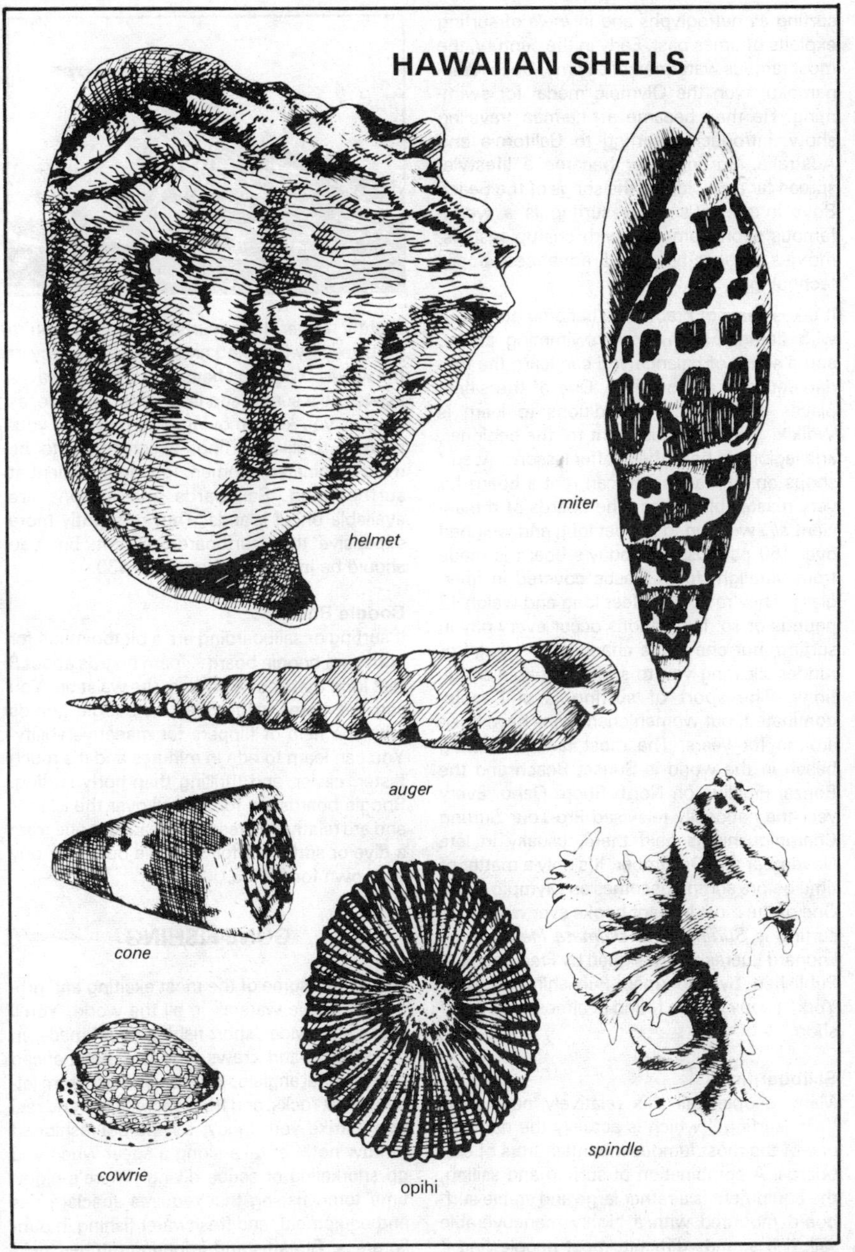
HAWAIIAN SHELLS
miter
helmet
auger
cone
opihi
spindle
cowrie

surfing as petroglyphs and in *mele* of surfing exploits of times past. Early in the century, the most famous waterman of all time, Duke Kahanamoku, won the Olympic medal for swimming. He then became a one-man traveling show, introducing surfing to California and Australia. Surfing later became a lifestyle, spread far and wide by the songs of the Beach Boys in the '60s. Now surfing is a world-famous sport complete with championships, movies, magazines, and advanced board technology.

It takes years of practice to become good, but with determination, good swimming ability, and a sense of balance you can learn the fundamentals in a short time. One of the safest places offering ideal conditions to learn is Waikiki. The sea is just right for the beginner, and legions of beachboys offer lessons. At surf shops on all islands you can rent a board for very reasonable prices. The boards of the ancient *ali'i* were up to 20 feet long and weighed over 150 pounds, but today's board is made from ultralight foam plastic covered in fiberglass. They're about 6 feet long and weigh 12 pounds or so. Innovations occur every day in surfing, but one is the changeable "skeg" or rudder allowing you to surf in variable conditions. The sport of surfing is still male-dominated, but women champions have been around for years. The most famous surfing beach in the world is Sunset Beach and the Bonzai Pipeline on North Shore Oahu. Every year the nationally televised Pro-Tour Surfing Championship is held there, usually in late November and December. It's only a matter of time before surfing becomes an Olympic sport. One of the most brilliant books ever written on surfing is *Surfing, The Ultimate Pleasure,* by Leonard Lueras and designed by Fred Bechlen. Published by Workman Publishing of New York, a copy can be found at almost every surf shop.

Sailboarding

Many people call this relatively new sport "windsurfing," which is actually the name of one of the most famous manufacturers of sailboards. A combination of surfing and sailing, the equipment is a rather large and stable surfboard mounted with a highly maneuverable sail. If it sounds difficult, most people find it

slightly easier than surfing because you're mobilized by the wind and not at the mercy of the waves. You don't have to "read" the waves as well as a surfer, and like riding a bicycle, as long as you keep moving, you can hold your balance. Unlike surfing, which tends to be male-dominated, women, too, are excellent at surfboarding. Sailboards and lessons are available on all islands. They're slightly more expensive then surfboards to rent, but you should be in business for about $30.

Boogie Boards

If surfing or sailboarding are a bit too much for you, try a boogie board—foam boards about 3 feet long that you lie on from the waist up. You can get tremendous rides on boogie boards with the help of flippers for maneuverability. You can learn to ride in minutes and it's much faster, easier, and thrilling than body surfing. Boogie boards are for sale all over the islands and are relatively cheap. You can rent one from a dive or surf shop for a couple bucks, or buy your own for $10-15.

GONE FISHING

Hawaii has some of the most exciting and productive "blue waters" in all the world. You'll find a statewide "sport fishing fleet" made up of skippers and crews who are experienced professional anglers. You can also fish from jetties, piers, rocks, and from shore. If rod and reel don't strike your fancy, try the old-fashioned "throw net," or take along a spear when you go snorkeling or scuba diving. There's nighttime torch fishing that requires special skills and equipment, and freshwater fishing in public areas. Streams and irrigation ditches yield introduced trout, bass, and catfish. While you're at it, you might want to try crabbing for Kona and Samoan crabs, or working low-tide areas after sundown hunting squid (really octopus), a tantalizing island delicacy.

Deep-sea Fishing

Most game fishing boats work the blue waters on the calmer leeward sides of the islands. Some skippers, carrrying anglers who are accustomed to the sea, will also work the much rougher windward coasts and island channels where the fish bite just as well. Trolling is the preferred method of deep-sea fishing; this is done usually in waters of between 1,000-2,000 fathoms (a fathom is 6 feet). The skipper will either "area fish," which means running in a criss-crossing pattern over a known productive area, or "ledge fish," which involves trolling over submerged ledges where the gamefish are known to feed. The most advanced marine technology, available on many boats, sends sonar bleeps searching for fish. On deck, the crew and anglers scan the horizon in the age-old Hawaiian tradition—searching for seabirds clustered in an area, feeding on the very bait-fish pursued to the surface by the huge and aggressive gamefish. "Still fishing," or "bottom fishing" with hand lines, yields some tremendous fish.

The Gamefish

The most thrilling gamefish in Hawaiian waters is marlin, generically known as "billfish" or *a'u* to the locals. The king of them is the blue marlin, with record catches well over 1,000 pounds. There're also striped marlin and sailfish, which often go over 200 pounds. The best times for marlin are during spring, summer, and fall. The fishing tapers off in January and picks up again by late February. "Blues" can be caught year-round, but, oddly enough, when they stop biting it seems as though the striped marlin pick up. Second to the marlin are tuna. *Ahi* (yellowfin tuna) are caught in Hawaiian waters of depths of 100-1,000 fathoms. They can weigh 300 pounds, but between 25 and 100 pounds is common. There's also *aku* (skipjack tuna), and the delicious *ono,* which average between 20 and 40 pounds.

Mahi mahi is another strong, fighting, deep-water gamefish abundant in Hawaii. These delicious fish can weigh up to 70 pounds. Shore fishing and baitcasting yield *papio,* a jack tuna. *Akule,* a scad, (locally called *halalu,)* is a smallish schooling fish that comes close to shore and is great to catch on light tackle. *Ulua* are shore fish and can be found in tidepools. They're excellent eating, average two to three pounds, and are taken at night or with spears. *O'io* are bonefish that come close to shore to spawn. They're caught baitcasting and bottom fishing with cut bait. They're bony, but they're a favorite for fish cakes and *poki. Awa* is a schooling fish that loves brackish water. It can get up to three feet long, and is a good fighter. A favorite for "throw netters," it's even raised commercially in fish ponds. Besides these there are plenty of goatfish, mullet, mackerel, snapper, various sharks, and even salmon. For Hawaiian gamefish, see p. 161.

"Blue Water" Areas

One of the most famous fishing spots in Hawaii is the **Penguin Banks** off the west coast of Molokai and the south coast of Oahu. "Chicken Farm" at the southern tip of the Penguin Banks has great trolling waters for marlin and *mahimahi.* The calm waters off the Waianae Coast of Oahu yield marlin and *ahi.* The Kona Coast of Hawaii with its crystal waters is the most famous marlin grounds in Hawaii. Every year the **Hawaiian International Billfish Tournament** draws anglers from around the world to Kona. The marlin are in 1,000 fathoms of water, but close in on the Kona Coast you can hook *ono* and handline for *onaga* and *kahala.* Maui fishermen usually head for the waters formed by the triangle of Maui, Lanai, and Kahoolawe where they troll for marlin, *mahi,* and *ono,* or bottom fish for snapper. The waters around Kahoolawe are also good. Kauai has excellent fishing waters year around, with *ono, ahi,* and marlin along the ledges. Large schools of *ahi* come to Kauai in the spring, and the fishing is fabulous with 200-pounders not uncommon.

Charter Boats

The charter boats of Hawaii come in all shapes and sizes, but they are all manned by professional, competent crews and captains intimately knowledgeable of Hawaiian waters. Prices vary but expect to spend $50-$60 on a "share basis." The average number of fishermen per boat is 6, and most boats rent all day for $300. You can also arrange half days, and bigger boats with more anglers cost as little as $35 per person. All tackle from 30 to 130 pounds is carried on the boats and is part of the service. Oftentimes soft drinks are supplied, but usually you carry your own lunch. It is customary for the crew to be given any fish that are caught, but naturally this doesn't apply to trophy fish; the crew is also glad to cut off some steaks and fillets for your personal use. Honolulu's Kewalo Basin, only a few minutes from Waikiki, has the largest fleet of charter boats. Pokai Bay also has a fleet and many charter boats sail out of Kaneohe Bay. On the Big Island, Kailua-Kona has the largest concentration of charter boats, with some boats out of Kawaihae. Maui boats come out of Lahaina or Maalaea Bay. Molokai has a small fleet berthed in Kaunakakai Harbor, and on Kauai most boats sail out of Nawiliwili Bay.

FRESHWATER FISH

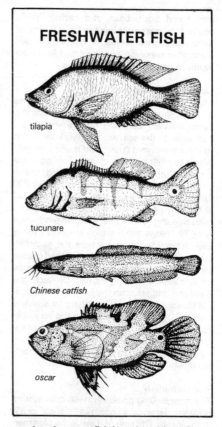

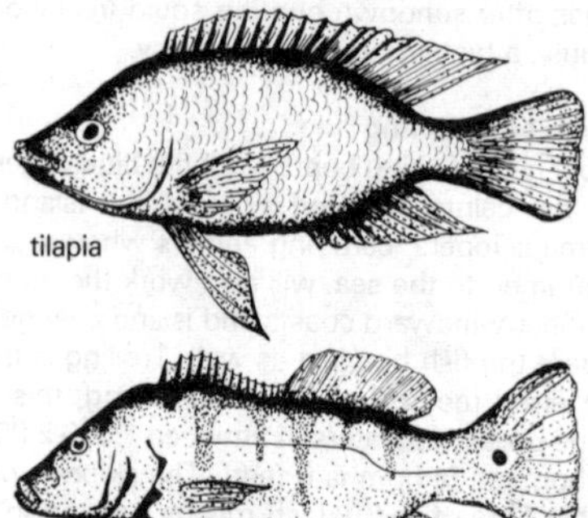

Freshwater Fishing

Due to Hawaii's unique geology, only a handful of natural lakes and rivers are good for fishing. The state maintains 5 "Public Fishing Areas" spread over Kauai, Oahu, and Hawaii (none on Maui, Lanai, or Molokai). Public fishing areas include: on Oahu, **Wahiawa Public Area,** a 300-acre irrigation reservoir primarily for sugarcane located near Wahiawa in central Oahu, and **Nuuanu Resevoir No. 4,** located in the Koolau Mountains above Honolulu; on Kauai, **Kokee Public Fishing Area,** located north of Kekaha, offers 13 miles of stream, 2 miles of irrigation ditches, and a 15-acre reservoir offering only rainbow trout; on Hawaii, **Waiakea Public Area** is a 26-acre pond within the city of Hilo, and **Kohala Reservoir** on the north coast.

Freshwater Fish, And Rules

Hawaii has only one native freshwater gamefish, the *o'opu*. This gobie is an oddball with fused ventral fins. They grow to be 12 inches and are found on all islands, especially Kauai. Introduced species include largemouth and smallmouth bass, bluegills, catfish, *tucunare,* oscar, carp, and *tilapia.* The only trout to survive is the rainbow, found only in the streams of Kauai. The *tucunare* is a tough, fighting, good-tasting gamefish introduced from South America, similar to the oscar, from the same region. Both have been compared to bass, but are of a different family. *Tilapia* are from Africa and have become common in Hawaii's irrigation ditches. They're "mouth breeders" and the young will take refuge in their parents' protective jaws even a few weeks after hatching. Snakehead are eel-like fish that inhabit the reservoirs and are great fighters. Channel catfish can grow to over 20 pounds and bite best after sundown. There's also carp, and with their broad tail and tremendous strength, they're the poor man's gamefish. All of these species are best caught with light spinning tackle, or with a bamboo pole and a trusty old worm.

Fishing licenses are good from July 1 to June 30. Licenses cost: $7.50 for non-residents, $3.50 for tourists good for 30 days, $3.75 for residents and military personnel, $1.50 for children between 9 and 15 years old, and free to senior citizens. Licenses are obtained from Division of Conservation and Resources Enforcement (Oahu, tel. 548-8766) or from most sporting goods stores. For free booklets and information write, Division of Aquatic Resources, 1151 Punchbowl St., Honolulu, HI 96813. All gamefish may be taken year-round, except trout. Trout, only on Kauai, may be taken for 16 days commencing on the first Saturday of August. Thereafter, for the remainder of August and September, trout can be taken only on Sat., Sun. and state holidays.

HUNTING

Most people don't think of Hawaii as a place to hunt, but actually it's quite good. Seven species of introduced game animals are regularly hunted, and 16 species of game birds. Not all species of game animals are open on all islands, but every island offers hunting. Please refer to "Sports" in the travel chapters for full details on hunting on particular islands.

General Hunting Rules

Hunting licenses are mandatory to hunt on public, private, or military land anywhere in Hawaii. They're good for one year beginning July 1. They cost $7.50 residents, $15 nonresident, senior citizens free. Licenses are available from the various offices of the Division of Forestry and Wildlife (see below) and from sporting goods stores. This government organization also sets and enforces the rules, so contact them with any questions. Generally hunting hours are from a half-hour before sunrise to a half-hour after sunset. At times, there are "checking stations," where the hunter must check in before and after hunting.

Rifles must have greater than a 1,200-foot-pound muzzle velocity. Shotguns larger than .20 gauge are allowed, and muzzleloaders must have a .45 caliber bore or larger. Bows must have a minimum draw of 45 pounds for straight bows and 30 pounds for compounds. Arrows must be broadheads. Dogs are permitted only with some birds and game, and smaller caliber rifles and shotguns are permitted with their use, along with spears and knives. Hunters must wear orange safety cloth on front and back no smaller than a 12-inch square. Certain big game species are hunted only by lottery selection; contact the Division of Forestry and Wildlife two months in advance. Guide service is not mandatory, but is advised if you're unfamiliar with hunting in Hawaii. You can hunt on private land only with permission, and you must possess a valid hunting license. Guns and ammunition brought into Hawaii must be registered with the chief of police of the corresponding county within 48 hours of arrival.

feral pig

Game Animals

All game animals have been introduced to Hawaii. Some are adapting admirably and becoming well entrenched, while the existence of others is still precarious. **Axis deer** originated in India and were brought to Lanai and Molokai, where they're doing well. The small herd on Maui is holding its own. Their unique flavor makes them one of the best wild meats, and they're hunted on Molokai and Lanai in March and April, by public lottery. **Feral pigs** are escaped domestic pigs that have gone wild and are found on all islands except Lanai. The stock is a mixture of original Polynesian pigs and all that came later. Hunted with dogs and usually killed with a spear or long knife, pig hunting is not recommended for the timid or tender hearted. These beasts' four-inch tusks and fighting spirit make them tough and dangerous. **Feral goats** come in a variety of colors. Found on all islands except Lanai, they have been known to cause erosion and are considered a pest in some areas, especially on Haleakala. Openly hunted on all islands, their meat when done properly is considered delicious. **Black-tailed deer** come from the Rocky Mountains. Forty were released on Kauai in 1961; the herd is now stabilized at around 400 and they're hunted in October by public lottery. **Mouflon sheep** are native to Corsica and Sardinia. They do well on Lanai and on the windswept slopes of Mauna Loa and Mauna Kea where they're hunted at various times by public lottery. **Feral sheep** haunt the slopes of Mauna Kea and Mauna Loa from 7,000 to 12,000 feet. They travel in flocks and destroy vegetation. It takes determination and a good set of lungs to bag one, especially with a bow and arrow. **Pronghorn antelope** on Lanai, **feral cattle** on the Big Island, and **rock wallaby,** from Australia, who now make their home on Oahu, are not hunted.

Game Birds

A number of game birds are found on most of the islands. Bag limits and hunting seasons vary, so check with the Division of Forestry and Wildlife for details. **Ring-necked pheasant** are one of the best game birds, and found on all the islands. The **kalij pheasant** from Nepal is found only on the Big Island, where the **green pheasant** is also prevalent with some found on Oahu and Maui. **Francolins,** gray and black, from India and the Sudan, are similar to

Gambel's quail

gray francolin

partridges. They are hunted on all islands with dogs and are great roasted. There are also **chukar** from Tibet, found on the slopes of all islands; a number of **quail,** including the Japanese and California varieties; **doves;** and the **wild Rio Grande turkey** which is found on all islands except Kauai and Oahu (although a few of the "featherless variety" have been known to walk the streets of Waikiki).

Information

Hunting rules and regulations are always subject to change. Also, environmental considerations often change bag limits and seasons. Make sure to check with the Division of Forestry and Wildlife for the most current information. Request "Rules Regulating Game Bird Hunting, Field Trails and Commercial Shooting Preserves," "Rules Regulating Game Mammal Hunting," and "Hunting in Hawaii." Direct inquiries to: Dept. of Land and Natural Resources, Division of Forestry and Wildlife Office, 1151 Punchbowl St., Honolulu 96813, tel. 548-2861; on Maui, 54 S. High St., P.O. Box 1015, Wailuku, 96793, tel. 244-4352; on Hawaii, Box 4849, Hilo 96720, tel. 961-7221; on Lanai, 338 8th St., Lanai City 96763, tel. 565-6688; on Kauai, 3060 Eiwa St., Box 1671, Lihue 96766, tel. 245-4444; on Molokai, Puu Kapeelua Ave., Hoolehua 96729, tel. 553-5415.

GOLF AND TENNIS

People addicted to chasing that little white ball around the links are going to be delighted with Hawaii. You can golf every day of the year on over 60 golf courses scattered around the state. Many are open to the public, and are built along some of the most spectacular scenery in the world where the pounding surf, or flower-dappled mountains form the backdrop. Many courses have pros and pro shops, and a profusion of hotels offer "golfing specials." You'll find everything from Lanai's 9-hole Cavendish Golf Course, where you put your money in an envelope on the honor system, to the Mauna Kea Beach Golf Club, one of the most exclusive and exciting golf courses in the world. Master builders such as Robert Trent Jones have laid out links in the islands where major tournaments, such as the Kemper Open, are yearly events. Fees range from as little as $2.50 for some little 9-holers up to $50 and more at the more exclusive resorts.

Tennis courts are found on every island of Hawaii and enjoyed by locals and visitors on a year-round basis. County courts are open to the public, as are some hotel and private courts where fees range from complimentary to about $6 for non-hotel guests. Most courts are of laykold or plexipave asphalt. Many of the hotel, and some public courts are lighted.

Note: Golf and tennis charts and listings appear under "Sports" in the travel chapters.

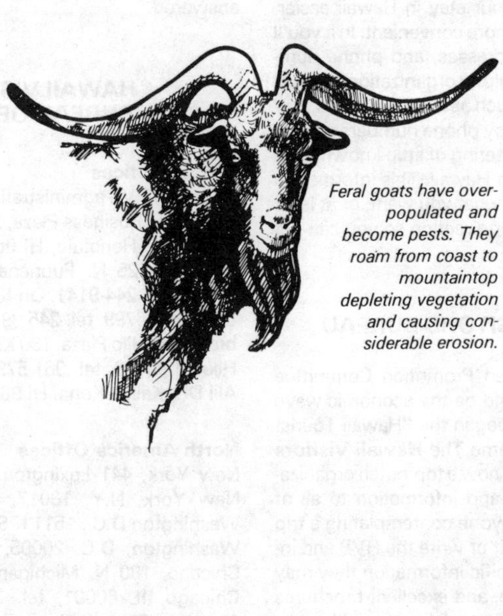

Feral goats have overpopulated and become pests. They roam from coast to mountaintop depleting vegetation and causing considerable erosion.

FACTS, FIGURES AND INFORMATION

This entire chapter is dedicated to the practical side of travel, the "nuts and bolts" you'll need to know to make your stay in Hawaii easier, more efficient, and more convenient. In it you'll find the names, addresses, and phone numbers of useful and helpful organizations and offices. Information, such as business hours, currency, and emergency phone numbers are listed, as well as a smattering of little-known facts and tidbits related to Hawaii. This information should help you get what you want, or at least point you in the right direction so you can get started. Good luck!

HAWAII VISITORS BUREAU

In 1903 the Hawaiian Promotion Committee thought tourism could be the economic wave of the future. They began the "Hawaii Tourist Bureau" which became The **Hawaii Visitors Bureau.** The **HVB** is now a top-notch organization providing help and information to all of Hawaii's visitors. Anyone contemplating a trip to Hawaii should visit or write the HVB and inquire about any specific information they may require. Their advice, and excellent brochures on virtually every facet of living, visiting, or simply enjoying Hawaii, are free. The material offered is too voluminous to list, but for basics, request individual island brochures (including maps), and ask for their copies of "Member Accommodation Guide," and "Member Restaurant Guide." Allow 2-3 weeks for requests to be answered.

HAWAII VISITORS BUREAU OFFICES

Hawaii Offices

The main HVB administration office is on Oahu at Waikiki Business Plaza, 2270 Kalakaua Ave. Suite 801, Honolulu, HI 96815, tel. 923-1811. On Maui, 25 N. Puunene Ave., Kahului, HI 96732, tel. 244-9141. On Kauai, 3016 Umi St., Lihue HI 96799, tel. 245-3971. Hawaii has two branches: Hilo Plaza, 180 Kinoole St. Suite 104, Hilo HI 96720, tel. 961-5797, and 75-5719 W. Alii Dr., Kailua-Kona, HI 96740, tel. 329-7787.

North America Offices

New York, 441 Lexington Ave. Room 1407, New York, N.Y. 10017, tel. 212-986-9203. Washington D.C., 1511 K St. N.W., Suite 415, Washington, D.C. 20005, tel. 202-393-6752. Chicago, 180 N. Michigan Ave. Suite 1031, Chicago, IL 60601, tel. 312-236-0632. Los Angeles, Central Plaza, 3440 Wilshire Blvd. Room 502, Los Angeles, CA 90010, tel. 213-385-5301. San Francisco, 50 California St., Suite 450, San Francisco, CA 94111, tel. 415-392-8173.

Foreign Offices

Canada 4915 Cedar Crescent, Delta, B.C., Canada V4M 1J9.

United Kingdom c/o Hewland Brook Hart Ltd., 15 Albemarle St., London W1X 4QL, England.

Australia c/o Walshes World, 92 Pitt St., Sydney, N.S.W. 2000.

Japan, 630 Shin Kokusai Bldg., 4-1 Marunouchi 3-chome, Chiyoda-ku, Tokyo 100.

Indonesia, c/o Odner Hotels, Kartika Plaza Hotel, Jl. M.H. Thamrin No. 10, Jakarta.

Hong Kong, c/o Pacific Leisure, Suite 904, Tung Ming Bldg., 40 Des Voeux Rd., Central Hong Kong.

Philippines, c/o Philippine Leisure Inc., Peninsula Hotel Arcade, Ayala Ave., Metro Manila.

Korea, c/o Pacific Leisure, 1&2 Hong-Ik Bldg., 198-1 Kwanhoon-Dong, Chongno-ku, Seoul 110.

Singapore, c/o Pacific Leisure, # 03-01 UOL Bldg., 96 Somerset Rd., Singapore 0923.

Thailand, c/o Pacific Leisure, 542/1 Ploenchit Rd., Bangkok.

Other offices are found through Pacific Leisure in Kuala Lumpur, Penang, and Taipei.

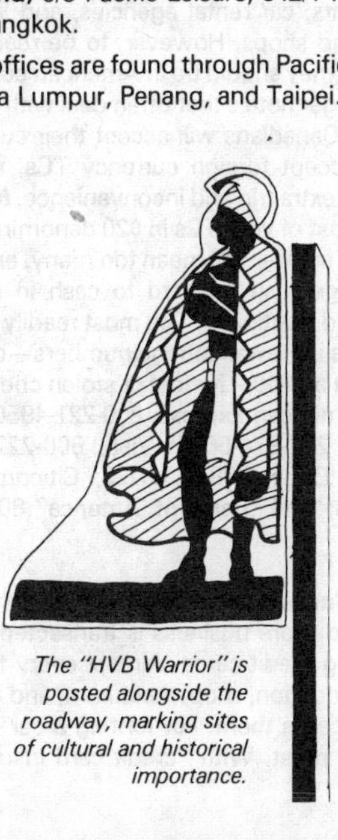

The "HVB Warrior" is posted alongside the roadway, marking sites of cultural and historical importance.

FOREIGN CONSULATES

All of the foreign Consulates and diplomatic offices are located in Honolulu. Most major European, Asian, and Oceanic nations, along with many South American countries, have delegates in Honolulu. They are all listed under "Consulates" in the Oahu Yellow Pages. The following are only some of the phone numbers for foreign consulates in Hawaii.

Australia, 524-5050; Japan, 536-2226; Nauru, 523-7821; Micronesia, 836-4775; France, 923-2666; Germany, 847-4411; India, 947-2618; Indonesia, 524-4300; Korea, 595-6109; New Zealand, 922-3853; Philippines, 595-6316; Thailand, 524-3888; W. Samoa, 734-3233.

TELEPHONES

Area Code: 808

The telephone system on all the main islands is modern, and comparable to any systems on the Mainland. You can "direct dial" from Hawaii to the Mainland and 70 foreign countries. Undersea cables and satellite communications insure top-quality phone service. Public telephones are found at hotels, street booths, restaurants, most public buildings, and at some beach parks. It is common to have a phone in most hotel rooms and condominiums, though a service charge is usually collected, even on local calls. The **area code** for all islands is **808**.

Rates

Like everywhere else in the U.S. it's cheaper to make long-distance calls on weekdays in the evenings. Rates go down at 5:00 p.m. and again at 11:00 p.m. until 8:00 a.m. the next morning. From Fri. at 5:00 p.m. until Mon. morning at 8:00 a.m., rates are also cheapest. Local calls from public telephones (anywhere on the same island is a local call) cost 20 cents. Calling between islands is a toll call, and the price depends on when and from where you call and for how long you speak. Emergency calls are always free. For directory assistance: local, 1-411; inter-island, 1-555-1212; Mainland, 1-area code-555-1212; toll free, 1-800-555-1212.

Helpful Numbers

Police—Fire—Ambulance: On Oahu, Maui, and Kauai dial 911 from any phone. Lanai, police 565-6525, fire 565-6766, ambulance, 565-6411; Molokai, police, 553-5355, fire 553-5401, ambulance 553-5911; Hawaii, police (Hilo) 935-3311, fire 961-6022, ambulance 961-6022; all no charge.

Coast Guard Rescue: Oahu, 536-4336; Maui, 244-5256; Kauai, 245-4521; Hawaii, 935-6370.

Civil defense: In case of natural disaster such as hurricanes or *tsunami* call Oahu 523-4121; Maui, 244-7721; Kauai, 245-4001; Hawaii, 935-0031.

Crisis and self-help centers: Oahu, 521-4555; Maui, 244-7407; Kauai, 245-7838; Hawaii, 329-9111.

Consumer protection: If you encounter problems finding accommodations, bad service, or downright rip-offs try the following all on Oahu: Chamber of Commerce, 531-411; Hawaii Hotel Association, 923-0407; Office of Consumer Protection, 548-2540.

OTHER PRACTICALITIES

Time Zones

There is no "daylight savings time" observed in Hawaii. When daylight savings time is not in effect on the Mainland, Hawaii is two hours behind the West Coast, four hours behind the Midwest, and five hours behind the East Coast. Hawaii, being just east of the International Date Line, is almost a full day behind most Asian and Oceanic cities. Hours behind these countries and cities are: Japan, 19 hours; Singapore, 18 hours; Sydney, 20 hours; New Zealand, 22 hours; Fiji, 22 hours.

Electricity

The same electrical current applies in Hawaii as on the U.S. Mainland and is uniform throughout the islands. The system functions on 110 volts, 60 cycles of alternating current (AC). Appliances from Japan will work, but there is some danger of burn out, while those requiring normal European 220 current won't work.

MONEY AND FINANCES

Currency

U.S. currency is among the drabbest in the world. It's all the same size and color; those unfamiliar with it should spend some time getting acquainted so that they don't make costly mistakes. U.S. coinage in use is: \$.01, \$.05, \$.10, \$.25, \$.50, and \$1 (uncommon); paper currency is \$1, \$2, (uncommon), \$5, \$10, \$20, \$50, \$100. Bills larger than \$100 are not in common usage.

Banks

Full-service banks tend to open slightly earlier than Mainland banks, at 8:30 a.m. Mon. through Friday. Closing is at 3:00 p.m., except for late hours on Fri. when most banks remain open until 6:00 p.m. Of most value to travelers, banks sell and cash traveler's cheques, give cash advances on credit cards, and exchange and sell foreign currency.

Traveler's Cheques

TCs are accepted throughout Hawaii at hotels, restaurants, car rental agencies, and in most stores and shops. However, to be readily acceptable they should be in American currency. Some larger hotels that often deal with Japanese and Canadians will accept their currency. Banks accept foreign currency TCs, but it'll mean an extra trip and inconvenience. It's best to get most of your TCs in \$20 denominations; anything smaller will mean too many, and anything larger can be hard to cash in smaller shops and boutiques. The most readily acceptable TCs in Hawaii (phone numbers—call collect if not an 800—for lost or stolen checks) include: American Express, 800-221-4950; MasterCard, 212-974-5696; Visa, 800-227-6830; Thomas Cook, 808-523-0722; Citicorp, 516-352-6000; and, Bank of America, 800-227--3460.

Credit Cards

More and more business is transacted in Hawaii using credit cards. Almost every form of accommodation, shop, restaurant, and amusement accepts them. For renting a car they're almost a must. With "credit card insurance"

MEASUREMENTS

Distance, weights, and measures

Hawaii like all of the U.S., employs the "English method" of measuring weights and distances. Basically, dry weights are in ounces and pounds; liquid measures are in ounces, quarts and gallons; and distances are measured in inches, feet, yards and miles. The metric system, based on units of 10, is known but is not in general use. The following conversion charts should be helpful.

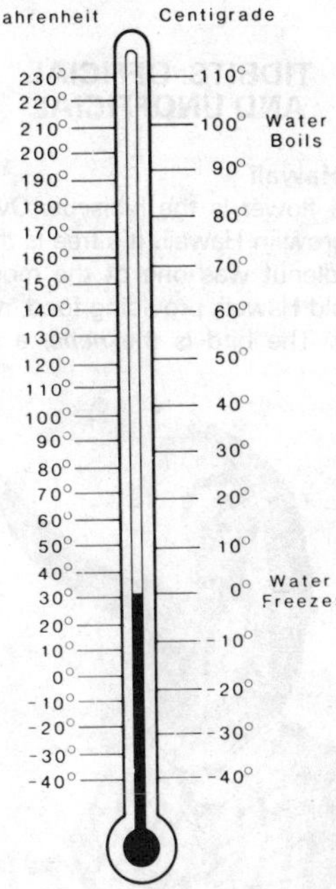

1 inch = 2.54 centimeters (cm)
1 foot = .3048 meters (m)
1 mile = 1.6093 kilometers (km)
1 km = .6214 miles
1 nautical mile = 1.852 km
1 fathom = 1.8288 m
1 chain = 20.1168 m
1 furlong = 201.168 m
1 acre = .4047 hectares (ha)
1 sq km = 100 ha
1 sq mile = 2.59 sq km
1 ounce = 28.35 grams
1 pound = .4536 kilograms (kg)
1 short ton = .90718 metric ton
1 short ton = 2000 pounds
1 long ton = 1.016 metric tons
1 long ton = 2240 pounds
1 metric ton = 1000 kg
1 quart = .94635 liters
1 U.S. gallon = 3.7854 liters
1 Imperial gallon = 4.5459 liters

To compute Centigrade temperatures, subtract 32 from Fahrenheit and divide by 1.8. To go the other way, multiply Centigrade by 1.8 and add 32.

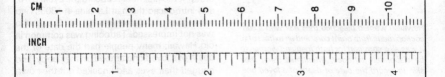

readily available, they're as safe as TCs and sometimes even more convenient. Write down the numbers of your cards in case they're stolen. Don't rely on them completely because there are some establishments that won't accept them, or perhaps won't accept the kind that you carry. The most readily accepted credit cards are MasterCard and Visa, followed by American Express, Diners Club, and Carte Blanche. Most banks will give you cash advances on your credit cards for a fee.

TIDBITS: OFFICIAL AND UNOFFICIAL

Official Hawaii

The state flower is the hibiscus. Over 5,000 species grow in Hawaii. It's tree is the *kukui.* This candlenut was one of the most useful trees of old Hawaii, providing food, medicine, and light. The bird is the *nene,* a modified goose that came to Hawaii eons ago and adapted to the rugged terrain, becoming a permanent resident and losing its instinct for migration. The humpback whale that visits Hawaii every year was made the official mammal in 1979. The nickname is "The Aloha State." The motto, *Ua mau ke ea o ka aina i ka pono,* ("The life of the land is perpetuated in righteousness,") came from King Kamehameha III, when in 1843 Hawaii was restored to self sovereignty after briefly being seized by the British. The anthem, "Hawaii Pono," was written by the "Merry Monarch," King Kalakaua, and put to music by the royal bandmaster, Henri Berger, in 1876. "Hawaii Pono," at one time was the anthem of the Kingdom of Hawaii and later the Territory before becoming the official state anthem.

Hawaiian women bleached their hair with a concoction made from burnt coral and an extract of ti. *It was also common for both men and women to be elaborately tattooed, oftentimes using their skin to record the date of death of a loved one. Both practices were first reported by Otto Von Kotzebue in 1816.*

Little-known Facts

The Hawaiian Islands stretch 1,600 miles from Kure Atoll in the north to the Big Island in the south. South Point (Ka Lae) on the Big Island is the southernmost point of the U.S. The islands are 25 million years old and are entirely made from volcanic activity. There's about as much land mass as New Jersey. Haleakala on Maui is the world's largest inactive volcano, while Hawaii's Mauna Loa is the world's largest active volcano, and Kilauea is *the* most active volcano in the world. Kauai's Mount Waialeale is the wettest spot on Earth, receiving over 600 inches of rain per year. Honolulu's Iolani Palace is the only "Royal Palace" in the U.S. Hawaii had the first company (C. Brewer), American School (Lahainaluna), newspaper *(Sandwich Island Gazette)*, bank (First Hawaiian) and church (Pukoo, Molokai) west of the Rocky Mountains.

Tidbits

American captains Shaler and Cleveland brought the first horses aboard the *Lydia Byrd,* and introduced them at Lahaina in 1803. Two were given to Kamehameha the Great who was not impressed. Tattooing was common in old Hawaii; many people had the date of the death of a loved one tattooed on their body, and gouged their eyes and knocked out their own teeth as a sign of mourning. The greatest insult was to inlay a spittoon with the teeth of a defeated enemy. The name of the channel between Maui and Kahoolawe, *Kealaikahiki,* means "the way to Tahiti." Voyagers got their bearings here for the long voyage south. "It will happen when Boki comes back" means something is impossible. Boki was a chief who sailed away in 1829 looking for sandalwood. He never returned. Only 20 of the 500 who sailed with him made it back to Hawaii.

POST OFFICE

Post offices are located in all major towns and cities. Most larger hotels also offer limited postal services. Normal business hours are 8:00 or 8:30 a.m. until 4:30 or 5:00 p.m., Mon. through Fri., Sat. from 8:00 a.m. until noon.

Receiving Mail

The simplest way to receive mail is to have it sent to your lodgings if you're there long enough to receive it. Have it addressed to you in care of your hotel or condo; include the room number if you know it. It'll be in your box at the front desk. If you plan frequent moves, or a multiple-island itinerary with short stays on each island, have mail sent "General Delivery" to a post office in a town you plan to visit. The P.O. will hold your mail in "general delivery" for 30 days. It takes about 5 days for a first-class letter to arrive in Hawaii from the Mainland. It's a good idea to notify the postmaster of the P.O. where you will be receiving mail of when you expect to be there to pick it up. The third method is to have mail sent to you c/o American Express, 2222 Kalakaua Ave., Honolulu, HI 96815 (Hyatt Regency, Waikiki). This service is free for American Express card holders (sometimes charge a small fee for others). They also forward mail for a $3 fee. You must visit Honolulu to pick up your mail, or phone them and send money to have it forwarded. Most people find this too awkward.

Zip Codes And Main P.Os.

The first three zip code digits, 967, are the same for all of Hawaii (except Honolulu is 968). The last two digits designate the particular post office. The following are the zip codes for the main P.Os. in Hawaii: Oahu, Honolulu (downtown, 3600 Aolele St.) 96820, Waikiki 96815; Kauai, Lihue 96766; Maui, Lahaina 96761, Kihei, 96753, Kahului, 96732; Molokai, Kaunakakai, 96748; Lanai, 96763; Hawaii, Hilo 96720, Kailua 96740.

LARGEST CITIES/TOWNS

Island	Town/City	Pop.
Oahu	Aiea	33,000
	Honolulu	400,000
	Kailua	36,000
	Kaneohe	30,000
	Pearl City	43,000
	Wahiawa	17,000
	Waipahu	30,000
Maui	Kahulwi	13,000
	Kihei	5,700
	Lahaina	7,300
	Wailuki	10,300
Hawaii	Captain Cook	2,100
	Hilo	35,300
	Kailua-Kona	4,900
Kauai	Hanamalu	3,300
	Kapaa	4,500
	Kekaha	3,300
	Lihue	4,100
Molokai	Kaunakakai	2,300
Lanai	Lanai City	2,100
Nihau		250

NEWSPAPERS

Hawaii's two main English-language dailies are *The Honolulu Star Bulletin,* and *The Honolulu Advertiser.* The *Bulletin* has a circulation of just over 100,000, while the *Advertiser* is just under that figure. The Japanese-English *Hawaii Hochi* has a circulation of 10,000, and the Chinese *United Chinese Press* sells 1,000 per day. All are published on Oahu and available on other islands.

Weeklies And Magazines

There's a stampede of weeklies in Hawaii; all major islands have at least one and Oahu has at least six. On Kauai look for the *Kauai Times* and the slightly smaller *Garden Island*. The *Maui News,* published in Wailuku, reaches about 16,000 on Maui. The Big Island offers the *Hawaii Tribune Herald* out of Hilo with a circulation of 20,000, and *West Hawaii Today,* published in Kailua, reaches 6,000. All of these papers are great to see "what's happening" and to clip out money-saving coupons for restaurants, rentals, and amusements. A few military newspapers are printed on Oahu, along with the *Hawaii Times,* a Japanese-English paper reaching about 10,000 readers.

Over 20 magazines are published in Hawaii, but the ones with most general interest are *Honolulu, Hawaii Business,* and *Waikiki Beach Press* (free).

Tourist Publications And Free Literature

On every island, at airports, hotel lobbies, shopping malls, and along the main streets are racks filled with free magazines, pamphlets, and brochures. Sometimes the sheer volume is overwhelming, but most have up-to-the-minute information on "what's happening," and many money-saving coupons. They're also loaded with maps and directions to points of interest. The best, published in a convenient narrow format, are *This Week...Oahu, Maui, Kauai, Big Island,* published weekly. *Spotlight,* published weekly for the main islands, is also good, offering information with a strong emphasis on sightseeing. *Guide to...* all major islands is in normal magazine format, with good maps. There are also regional magazines such as *Maui Gold* and Harry Lyon's *Kona Coast,* that are well worth checking out.

The first Hawaiian coin was a one-cent copper issued by Kamehameha III in 1847. By 1883, when King Kalakaua issued this akahi dala, *the monetary system was in conformity with that of the United States.*

OAHU

INTRODUCTION

It is the destiny of certain places on Earth to be imbued with an inexplicable magnetism to draw people whose visions and desires combine at just the right moment to create a dynamism so strong that it becomes history. The result for these certain places is greatness...and Oahu is one of these. It is difficult to separate Oahu from its vibrant metropolis, Honolulu, whose massive political, economic, and social muscle dominates the entire state, let alone its home island. But to look at Honolulu *as* Oahu is to look only upon the face of a great sculpture, ignoring the beauty and subtleness of the whole. Just the words "Honolulu, Waikiki, Pearl Harbor" conjure up visions common to people the world over. Immediately imaginations flush with palm trees swaying, a healthy tan, bombs dropping with infamy, and a golden moon rising romantically over coiled lovers on a white-sand beach. Oahu is called the "Gathering Place," and to itself it has indeed gathered the noble memories of old Hawaii, the vibrancy of a bright-eyed fledgling state, and the brawny power so necessary for the future. On this amazing piece of land adrift in the great ocean, 800,000 people live; 4 times that number visit yearly, and as time passes Oahu remains strong as one of those certain places.

OVERVIEW

Oahu is partly a tropical garden, bathed by soft showers and sunshine, and swaying with a gentle but firm rhythm. You can experience this feeling all over the island, even in pockets of downtown Honolulu and Waikiki. However, it's other side is brash—dominated by the con-

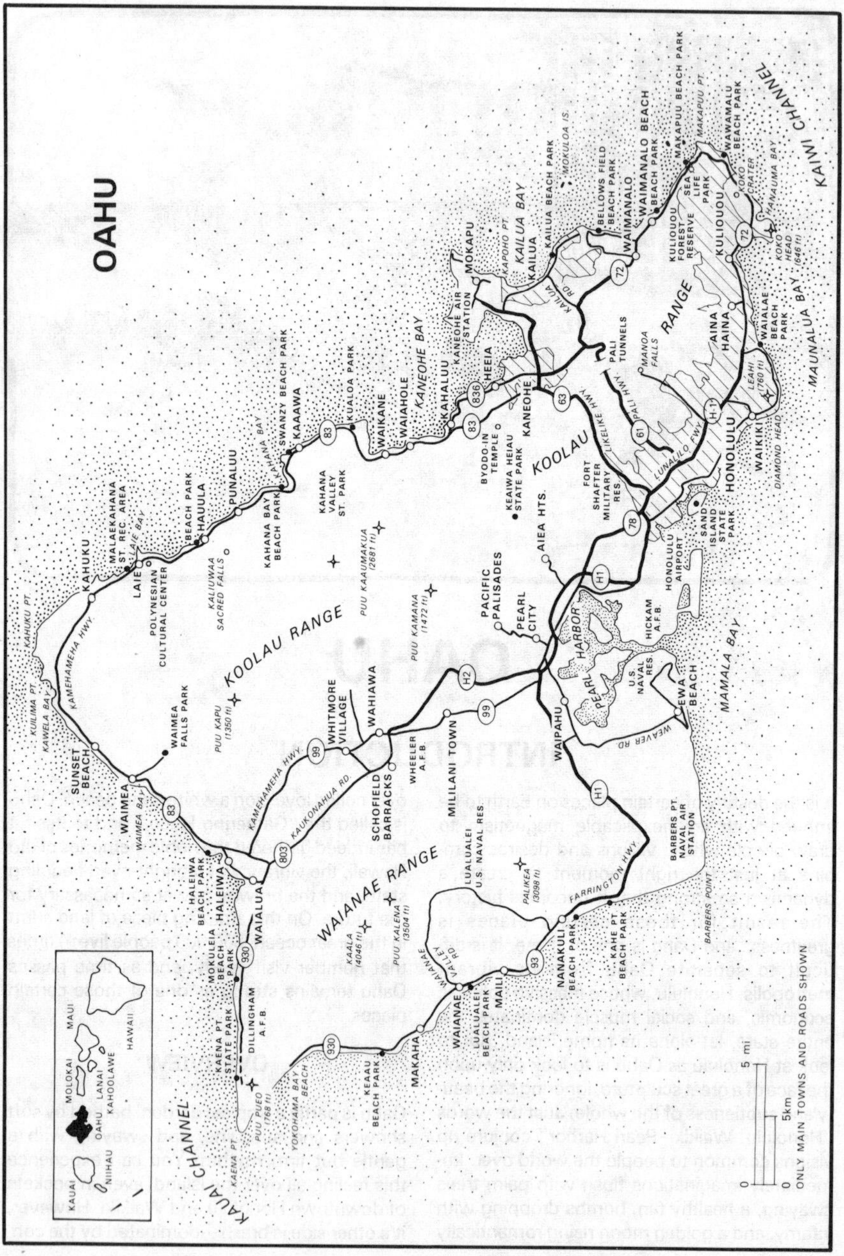
OAHU
KOOLAU RANGE
WAIANAE RANGE
KOOLAU
RANGE
KAUAI CHANNEL
KAIWI CHANNEL
MAMALA BAY
MAUNALUA BAY
KANEOHE BAY
KAILUA BAY
WAIMEA BAY
KAWELA BAY
LAIE BAY
KAHANA BAY
HANAUMA BAY
KAHUKU PT.
KUILIMA PT.
KAENA PT.
KAPOHO PT.
MAKAPUU PT.
BARBERS POINT
DIAMOND HEAD
KOKO HEAD (646 ft)
KOKO CRATER
LEAHI (760 ft)
MOKULOA IS.
KAMEHAMEHA HWY.
FARRINGTON HWY.
LIKELIKE HWY.
PALI HWY.
LUNALILO FWY.
KAUKONAHUA RD.
WEAVER RD.
KAILUA RD.
WAIANAE VALLEY RD.
SUNSET BEACH
WAIMEA
WAIMEA FALLS PARK
KAHUKU
MALAEKAHANA ST. REC. AREA
LAIE
POLYNESIAN CULTURAL CENTER
KALIUWAA SACRED FALLS
BEACH PARK
HAUULA
PUNALUU
KAHANA BAY BEACH PARK
KAHANA VALLEY ST. PARK
SWANZY BEACH PARK
KAAAWA
KUALOA PARK
WAIKANE
WAIAHOLE
KAHALUU
HEEIA
KANEOHE AIR STATION
MOKAPU
KAILUA
KAILUA BEACH PARK
BELLOWS FIELD BEACH PARK
WAIMANALO
WAIMANALO BEACH
MAKAPUU BEACH PARK
SEA LIFE PARK
WAWAMALU BEACH PARK
KULIOUOU FOREST RESERVE
KULIOUOU
AINA HAINA
WAIALAE BEACH PARK
PALI TUNNELS
MANOA FALLS
KANEOHE
BYODO-IN TEMPLE
KEAIWA HEIAU STATE PARK
FORT SHAFTER MILITARY RES.
HONOLULU
WAIKIKI
SAND ISLAND STATE PARK
HONOLULU AIRPORT
HICKAM A.F.B.
AIEA HTS.
PACIFIC PALISADES
PEARL CITY
PEARL HARBOR
U.S. NAVAL RES.
EWA BEACH
BARBERS PT. NAVAL AIR STATION
WAIPAHU
MILILANI TOWN
WAHIAWA
WHITMORE VILLAGE
SCHOFIELD BARRACKS
WHEELER A.F.B.
PUU KAPU (1350 ft)
PUU KAAUMAKUA (2681 ft)
PUU KAMANA (1472 ft)
PALIKEA (3098 ft)
PUU KALENA (3504 ft)
KAAA (4046 ft)
PUU PUEO (1768 ft)
LUALUALEI U.S. NAVAL RES.
LUALUALEI BEACH PARK
NANAKULI BEACH PARK
KAHE PT. BEACH PARK
WAIANAE
MAILI
MAKAHA
KEAAU BEACH PARK
YOKOHAMA BAY BEACH
KAENA PT. STATE PARK
DILLINGHAM A.F.B.
MOKULEIA BEACH PARK
WAIALUA
HALEIWA
HALEIWA BEACH PARK
83
99
803
930
93
H1
H2
H-1
78
61
63
836
72
KAUAI
NIIHAU
OAHU
MOLOKAI
LANAI
KAHOOLAWE
MAUI
HAWAII
0 5 mi
0 5km
ONLY MAIN TOWNS AND ROADS SHOWN

fidence of a major American city perched upon the Pacific Basin whose music is a pounding staccato jack-hammer, droning bulldozer, and mechanical screech of the ever-building crane. The vast majority of first-time and return visitors land at Honolulu International, and spend at least a few days on Oahu, usually in Waikiki. People are amazed at the diversity of experiences the island has to offer. Besides the obvious (and endless) beach activities, are museums, botanical gardens, a fantastic zoo and aquarium, night clubs, extravagant shows, free entertainment, cultural classes, theaters, sporting events, major university, historical sights galore, an exotic cosmopolitan atmosphere, back-country trekking, and an abundance of camping—all easily accessible via terrific public transportation. Finally, to sweeten the pot, Oahu can easily be the least expensive island to visit.

Waikiki

Loosely, this world-famous beach is a hunk of land bordered by the **Ala Wai Canal** and running eastward to **Diamond Head.** Early last century these 2 golden miles were little more than a string of dirty beaches backed by a mosquito-infested swamp. Until 1901, when the Moana Hotel was built, only Hawaii's few remaining *ali'i* and a handful of wealthy *kamaaina* families had homes here. Now, over 125 hotels and condos provide more than 35,000 rooms, and if you placed a $20 bill on the ground, it would barely cover the land that it could buy! This hyper-active area will delight and disgust you, excite and overwhelm you, but never bore you. Waikiki gives you the feeling that you've arrived *someplace.* Besides lolling on the beach and walking the gauntlet of restaurants, hotels, malls, and street merchants, you can visit the **Waikiki Aquarium** or **Honolulu Zoo.** Then, ever-present Diamond Head, that monolith of frozen lava so symbolic of Hawaii, is a few minutes' drive and a leisurely stroll to its summit. Head eastward around the bulge passing exclusive residential areas and you quickly find a string of secluded beaches. Around this tip you pass **Koko Head Crater,** a trekker's haven, **Hanauma Bay,** an underwater conservation park renowned for magnificent family-class snorkeling, **Sea Life Park,** an extravaganza of the deep, and the sleepy village of **Waimanalo Beach.** Nearby, at **Bellow's Beach** is camping, where it's hard to believe the city's just 10 miles back.

Downtown Honolulu

Head for downtown and give yourself a full day to catch all the sights. It's as if a huge grappling hook, attached to the heart of a Mainland city, hauled it down to the sea. But don't get the idea that it's not unique, because it is! You'll find a delightful mixture of quaintly historic and future-shock new, exotic and ordinary. The center is **Iolani Palace,** only royal palace in America, heralded by the gilded statue of Kamehameha I. In an easy walking radius is the **State Capitol** and attendant government buildings. Chrome and glass skyscrapers holding the offices of Hawaii's economically mighty shade small stone and wooden structures from last century: **Mission Houses Museum, Kawaiiahao Church,** and **St. Andrews Cathedral.** Down at the harbor **Aloha Tower** greets the few passenger ships that still make port; nearby is the floating museum ship, **Falls of Clyde,** a nostalgic reminder of simpler times. Hotel Street takes you to **Chinatown,** an old and not always venerable section, filled with alleyways housing tiny temples, herbalists, aromatic markets, inexpensive eateries, rough night spots, dives, and the strong, distinctive flavor of transplanted Asia. If the hustle and bustle gets to be too much, head for **Foster Botanical Gardens.** Or hop a special London bus for the serenity of the **Bishop Museum and Planetarium,** undoubtedly *the best* Polynesian cultural and anthropological museum in the world.

Pearl Harbor

Hawaii's only interstate, H-1, runs west of city center to Pearl Harbor. You can't help noticing the huge military presence throughout the area, and it becomes clear why Hawaii is considered *the* most militarized state in the Union. The attraction here, which shouldn't be missed, is the **USS *Arizona* Memorial.** The museum, visitors center, and tours, operated jointly by the U.S. Navy and the National Park Service, are both excellent and free.

Heading For the Hills

Behind the city is the **Koolau Range.** As you

head for these beckoning hills, you can sidetrip over to the **University of Hawaii,** with its attendant **East West Center,** while passing through Manoa Valley, epitome of the "good life" in Hawaii. Route 61 takes you up and over **Nuuanu Pali** to Oahu's windward side. En route you'll pass **Punchbowl,** an old crater holding the dead from WW II, Korean and Vietnam wars in the **National Cemetery of the Pacific.** As you climb, the road passes the **Royal Mausoleum,** final resting place for some of Hawaii's last kings, queens, and nobility. Then comes **Queen Emma's Summer Palace,** a Victorian home of gentility and lace. Next **Nuuanu Pali,** where Kamehameha drove 16,000 Oahu warriors over the cliff, sealing his dominance of the island kingdom with their blood. The view is hauntingly beautiful, as the mountains drop suddenly to the coast of windward Oahu.

Windward Oahu

On the windward side, **Kailua** and **Kaneohe** have become suburban bedroom communities for Honolulu; this entire coast has few tourist accommodations, so it remains relatively uncrowded. The beaches are excellent, with beach parks and camping spots one after another, and the winds make this side off the island perfect for sailboarding. North of Kaneohe is **Valley of the Temples,** where a Christian cross sits high on a hill, and Buddha rests calmly in **Byodoin Temple.** Just up Rt. 83, the coastal highway, comes **Waiahole,** Oahu's outback, where tiny farms and *taro* patches dot the valleys, and local folks move with the slow beat of bygone days, then a quick succession of beaches, many rarely visited by more than a passing fishermen. **Punaluu Town** follows, offering some of the only accommodations along this coast, and a lovely walk to **Kahuwaa,** the Sacred Falls. In **Laie** is the **Polynesian Cultural Center,** operated by the Mormon Church. **B.Y.U.** is here too, along with a solid Mormon Temple that's open to visitors.

Northern Tip

North Shore is famous for magnificent surf. From **Sunset Beach** to **Haleiwa,** world-class surfers come to be challenged by the liquid thunder of the **Banzai Pipeline** and **Waimea Bay.** Art shops, boutiques, tiny restaurants, and secluded hideaways line these sun-drenched miles. At the far western end is **Dillingham Airfield** where you can take a glider or air tour of the island. The road ends with a very rugged jeep trail leading to **Kaena Point,** renowned for the most monstrous surf on the North Shore.

Northwest

The northwestern end of the island is the **Waianae Coast.** The towns of **Maili, Waianae, and Makaha** are considered the last domain of the locals of Oahu. This coastal area has escaped development so far, and it's one of the few places on the island where ordinary people can afford to live near the beach. Sometimes an attitude of resentment spills over against tourists; mostly though, lovely people with good hearts live here, who will treat you as nicely as you're willing to treat them. World-class surfing beaches along this coast are preferred by many of the best-known surfers from Hawaii. Many work as lifeguards in the beach parks, and they all congregate for the annual surfing championships held in Makaha. Here is a perfect chance to mingle with the people and soak up some of the last real *aloha* left on Oahu.

THE LAND

When Papa, the Hawaiian earth mother, returned from vacationing in Tahiti, she was less than pleased. She had learned through a gossiping messenger that her husband, Wakea, had been playing around. Besides simple philandering, he'd been foolish enough to impregnate Hina, a lovely young goddess who bore him island children. Papa, scorned and furious, showed Wakea that two could play the same game by taking a handsome young lover, Lua. Their brief interlude yielded the man-child Oahu, sixth of the great island children. Geologically, Oahu is the second oldest main island after Kauai. It emerged from beneath the waves as hissing lava a few million years after Kauai, and cooled a little quicker than Papa's temper to form Hawaii's third largest island.

Land Facts

Oahu has a total land area of 608 square miles, and measured from its farthest points is 44 miles long by 30 miles wide. The 112-mile coastline holds the two largest harbors in the state, **Honolulu** and **Pearl**. The **Koolau Mountains** run north-south for almost the entire length of the island, dramatically creating windward and leeward Oahu. The **Waianae Range** is smaller, confined to the northwestern section of the island. It too runs north-south, dividing the **Waianae Coast** from the massive **Leilehua Plateau** of the interior. **Mount Ka'ala,** at 4,020 feet in the northern portion of the Koolau's, is Oahu's highest peak. The huge Leilehua Plateau is still covered in pineapple and sugarcane, and lies between the two mountain ranges running all the way from Waialua on the north shore to Ewa, just west of Pearl Harbor. At its widest point, around Schofield Barracks, it's more than six miles across.

Oahu's most impressive natural features were formed after the heavy volcanic activity ceased and erosion began to sculpt the island. The most obvious is the wall-like cliffs of the **Pali**—mountain heads eroded by winds from the east, valleys cut by streams from the west. Perfect examples of these eroded valleys are **Nuuanu** and **Kalihi**. Other impressive examples are **Diamond Head, Koko Head,** and **Punchbowl,** three "tuff-cone" volcanoes that occurred after the heavy volcanic activity of early Oahu. A tuff cone is volcanic ash cemented together to form solid rock. Diamond Head is the most dramatic, formed after a minor eruption about 100,000 years ago and rising 760 feet from its base.

Oahu has the state's longest stream, **Kaukonahua,** that begins atop Puu Kaaumakua at 2,681 feet in the central Koolaus and runs westward for over 30 miles through the Leilehua Plateau. En route, it bypasses the **Wahiawa Reservoir** which, at 302 acres, forms the second largest body of fresh water in Hawaii. Oahu's tallest waterfalls are **Kaliuwaa** (Sacred Falls), just west of Punaluu, that drop for 80 feet, and **Waihee Falls,** in the famous Waimea Park on the North Shore, that have a sheer drop of over 40 feet. The main water concern is that usage is outstripping supply, and major municipal water shortages are expected by the year 2000 unless conservation measures and new technology are employed.

The Climate

Oahu, like all the Hawaiian islands, has equitable weather year round with the average daily temperature about 80 degrees F. The mountainous interior experiences about the same temperatures as the coastal areas because of the small difference in elevation. However, the **Pali** is known for strong, chilly winds that rise up the mountainside from the coast. Precipitation is the biggest differentiating factor in the climate of Oahu. Generally, the entire leeward coast, from Makaha to Koko Head, is dry. Rain falls much more frequently and heavily in the Koolau Mountains and along

the pali from the windward side

AVERAGE MAXIMUM/MINIMUM TEMPERATURE AND RAINFALL

Island	Town		Jan.	Mar.	May	June	Sept.	Nov.
Oahu	Honolulu	high	80	82	84	85	82	81
		low	60	62	68	70	71	68
		rain	4	2	0	0	0	4
	Kaneohe	high	80	80	80	82	82	80
		low	67	62	68	70	70	68
		rain	5	5	2	0	2	5
	Waialua	high	79	79	81	82	82	80
		low	60	60	61	63	62	61
		rain	2	1	0	0	1	3

N.B. Rainfall in inches; temperature in F°

the windward coast. Although rain can occur at any time of year, it is more plentiful in winter. Huge surf also pummels the North Shore during this period, closing off many beaches to the neophyte, but making them absolutely perfect for expert surfers. The maxim throughout the islands is *don't let rain spoil your day.* If it's raining, simply move on to the next beach, or around to the other side of the island where it'll probably be dry. You can most often depend on the beaches of Waikiki and Waianae to be sunny and bright.

FAUNA

You would think that with Oahu's dense human population, little room would be left for animals. In fact, they are environmentally stressed, but they do survive. The interior mountain slopes are home to **wild pigs,** and a small population of **feral goats** survives along in the Waianae Range. Migrating **whales** pass by, especially along the leeward coast where they can be observed from lookouts ranging from Waikiki to Koko Head. Half a dozen introduced game birds are found around the island, but Oahu's real animal wealth is its indigenous birdlife.

National Wildlife Refuges

Two areas at opposite ends of the island have been set aside as national wildlife refuges (NWR): **James Campbell NWR,** above the town of Kahuku on the extreme northern tip; and, **Pearl Harbor NWR,** at the harbor entrance. Both were established in the mid '70s, and managed by the U.S. Fish and Wildlife Service. They serve mainly as wetland habitats for the endangered Hawaiian gallinule ***(alae'ula),*** stilt ***(aeo),*** and coot ***(alae ke'oke'o).*** Clinging to existence, these birds should have a future as long as their nesting grounds remain undisturbed. These refuges also attract a wide variety of other birds, mostly introduced species such as **cattle egrets, herons,** a few species of **doves, munia, cardinals,** and the **common finch.** Much of the area within the refuges are natural marshlands, but ponds, complete with water-regulating pumps and dikes, have been built. The general public is not admitted to these areas without permission from the refuge managers. For more information, and to arrange a visit, contact Refuge Manager, Hawaiian and Pacific Islands NWR, U.S. Fish and Wildlife Service, Federal Bldg., Room 5302, Box 50167, Honolulu, HI 96850.

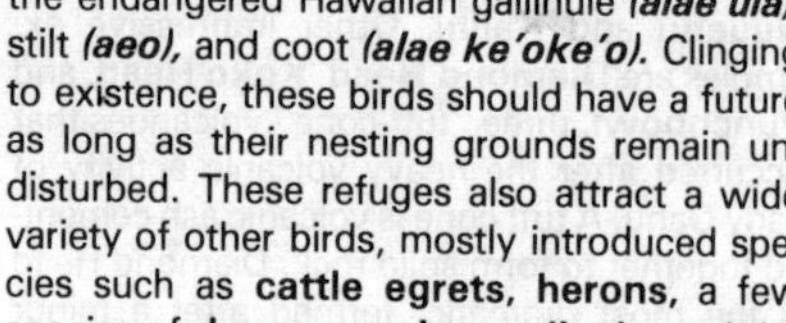

Hawaiian coot

Birds

The shores around Oahu, including those off Koko Head and Sand Island, but especially on the tiny islets of Moku Manu and Manana on the windward side, are home to thriving colonies of marine birds. On these diminutive islands it's quite easy to spot a number of birds from the **tern** family including the white, gray, and sooty tern. All have a distinctive screeching voice, and an approximate wingspan of 30 inches. Part of their problem is that they have little fear of humans. Along with the terns are **shearwaters.** These birds have a normal wingspan of about 36 inches, and make a series of moans and wails, oftentimes while in flight. For some reason they're drawn to bright city lights where they fall prey to house cats and automobiles. Sometimes Moku Manu even attracts an enormous **Laysan albatross** with its seven-foot wingspan. **Tropicbirds** with their lovely streamer-like tails are quite often seen along the windward coast.

To catch a glimpse of exotic birds on Oahu you don't have to head for the sea or the hills. The city streets and beach parks are constantly aflutter with wings. Black **myna birds** with their sassy yellow eyes are common mimics around town. **Sparrows,** introduced to Hawaii through Oahu in the 1870s, are everywhere, while **munia,** first introduced as cage birds from Southeast Asia, have escaped and are generally found anywhere around the island. Another escaped cage bird from Asia is the **bulbul,** a natural clown that perches on any likely city roost and draws attention to itself with loud calls and generally ridiculous behavior.

If you're lucky, you can also catch a glimpse of the Hawaiian owl ***(pueo)*** in the mountainous areas of Waianae and the Koolaus. Also, along trails and deep in the forest from Tantalus to the Waianae Range you can sometimes see elusive native birds like the ***elepaio, amakihi,*** and the fiery red but very rare ***i'iwi.***

Oahu also is home to a number of game birds mostly found in the dry upland forests. These include two varieties of **dove,** the **Japanese quail,** both the **green** and **ring-necked pheasant,** and **Erkel's francolin.** Hunting of these birds occurs year round and information can be had by contacting the Oahu branch of the Division of Forestry and Wildlife.

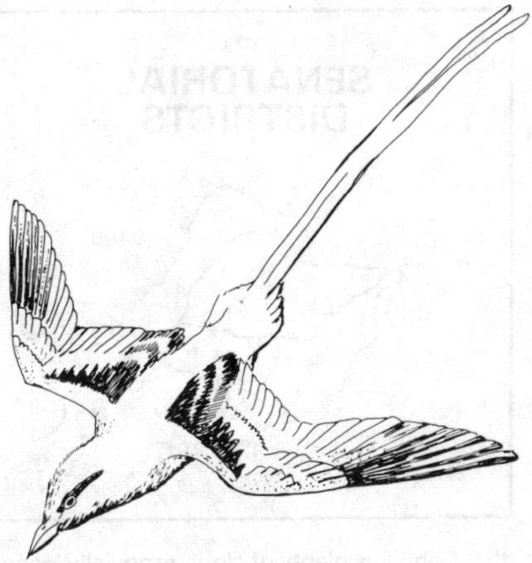

tropicbird

GOVERNMENT

Oahu has been the center of government for about 150 years, since King Kamehameha III permanently established the royal court there in the 1840s. In 1873-74, King David Kalakaua built Iolani Palace as the central showpiece of the island kingdom. Liliuokalani, the last Hawaiian monarch, lived after her dethronement in the nearby residence, Washington Place. While Hawaii was a territory, and for a few years after it became a state, the palace was used as the capital building, the governor residing in Washington Place. Modern Oahu, besides being the center of state government, governs itself as the **City and County of Honolulu.** The county not only covers the entire island of Oahu, but all the far-flung Northwestern islands, except for Midway, which is under federal jurisdiction.

State Representation

Oahu has four times as many people as the other islands combined. Nowhere is this more evident than in the representation of Oahu in the State House and Senate. Oahu claims 19 of the 25 state senators, and 39.7 of the 51 state representatives. (The 0.7 state representative covers the split district of the north Waianae area of Oahu, and the north shore of Kauai chips in with the remainder 0.3 of the representative). These lopsided figures make it obvious

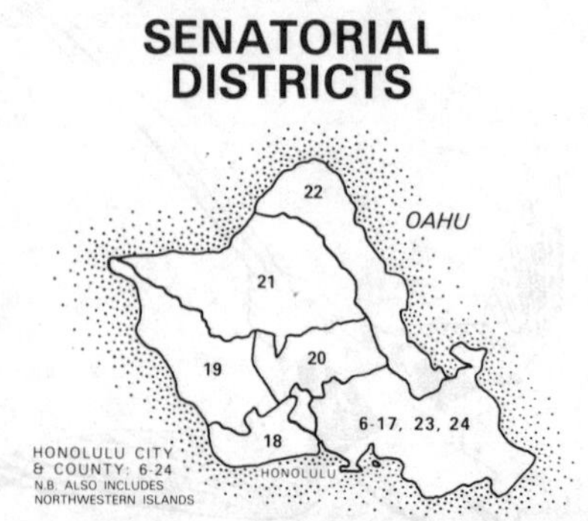

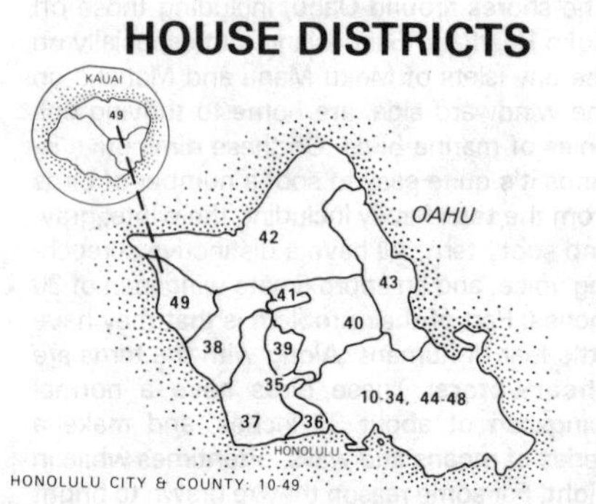

that Oahu has plenty of clout, especially Honolulu urban districts which elect more than 50% of Oahu's representatives.

Frequent political battles ensue, since what's good for the city and county of Honolulu isn't always good for the rest of the state. More often than not, the political moguls of Oahu, backed by huge business interests, prevail. The Oahu state senators are overwhelmingly Democratic, except for 3 Republicans, all from the Honolulu urban districts. State representation is similar: only 9 are Republicans, all from urban Honolulu or the suburban communities around Kailua.

ECONOMY

Economically, Oahu also dwarfs the rest of the islands combined. It generates income from government spending, tourism, and agriculture. A huge military presence, an international airport that receives the lion's share of visitors, and unbelievably, half of the state's best arable lands keep Oahu in the economic catbird seat. The famous Big 5 all maintain their corporate offices in downtown Honolulu from which they oversee vast holdings throughout Hawaii and the Mainland. Located in about the same spots as when their founders helped to overthrow the monarchy, things are about the same as then, except that they're going strong, while the old royalty of Hawaii has vanished.

Military And Government Spending

Hawaii is the most militarized state in the Union, and Oahu is the most militarized island in the state. It all started in 1872, when General Schofield declared Pearl Harbor an essential base for maintaining military strength in the Pacific. Shortly after the turn of the century, Pearl was dredged by the Navy, and the Army was firmly ensconced at Schofield Barracks; Hawaii's military fate was sealed.

All 4 branches of the Armed Forces are represented on the island, and Camp H.M. Smith, overlooking Pearl Harbor, is HQ for CINCPAC, Commander in Chief, Pacific. CINCPAC oversees the largest strategic area in the world, ranging from both poles, and from the west of South America across the entire Pacific to the Bay of Bengal. A full 25% of Oahu is owned or controlled by the military; largest landholder is the Army, with over 100,000 acres. Much of this land, used for maneuvers, is off-limits to the public. Besides Pearl, so obviously dominated by battleship gray, the largest military lands are around Schofield Barracks, and the Kahuku-Kawailoa Training Area. About 62,000 military personnel, and at least that same number of their dependents, live on Oahu, which accounts for over 99% of the servicemen and women based in the state. Moreover, a corps of 20,000 civilians works directly for the armed services, with many more employed indirectly, from providing essential services to entertainment. Non-military government spending chips into the pot, and together the amount of money generated is astronomical.

Tourism
The flow of visitors to Oahu has remained unabated ever since tourism outstripped sugar and pineapples in the early 1960s, becoming Hawaii's top money-maker. Of the nearly 5 million people that visit the state yearly, two-thirds stay on Oahu; almost all the rest, en route to the Neighbor Islands, at least pass through. Hotels directly employ over 15,000 workers, half the state's total, not including all the shop assistants, waiters and waitresses, taxi drivers, and everyone else needed to insure a carefree vacation. Of Hawaii's 58,000 hotel rooms, Oahu claims 34,000. The visitor industry generates over $2 billion of yearly revenue, and this is only the amount that can be directly related to the hotel and restaurant trades. With the flow of visitors seemingly endless, Oahu has a bright economic future.

handbiller "assisting" tourists in Waikiki

Agriculture
You'd think that with all the people living on Oahu, coupled with the constant land development, there'd hardly be any room left for things to grow. But that's not the case. The land is productive, though definitely stressed. It is startling that in downtown Honolulu and Waikiki, so many trees were removed to build parking lots that the asphalt becomes overheated from the lack of shade, allowing temperatures, once moderated by the trade winds, to rise demonstrably. Changing times and attitudes led to a *"poi* famine" that hit Oahu in 1967 because very few people were interested in the hard work of farming this staple. However, with half the state's best arable land, Oahu manages to produce a considerable amount of sugarcane, pineapples, and the many products of diversified agriculture. Sugar lands account for 33,000 acres, most owned by the James Campbell Estate, located around Ewa, north and west of Pearl Harbor, with some acreage around Waimea and Waialua on the north shore. Pineapples cover 11,500 acres, with the biggest holdings in the Leilehua Plateau belonging to Dole, a subsidiary of Castle and Cook. In the hills, entrepreneurs raise *pakalolo,* which has become the state's most productive cash crop. Oahu is also a huge agricultural consumer, demanding more than 4 times as much vegetables, fruits, meats, and poultry to feed its citizens and visitors than the remainder of the state combined.

THE PEOPLE

For most visitors, regardless of where they've come from, Oahu (especially Honolulu) will be the first place they've ever encountered such an integrated multi-racial society. Various countries may be cosmopolitan, but nowhere will you meet so many individuals from such a diversity of ethnic groups, and mixes of these groups. You could be driven to your hotel by a Chinese-Portuguese cab driver, checked in by a Japanese-Hawaiian clerk, served lunch by a Korean waiter, serenaded by a Hawaiian-Italian-German musician, while an Irish-English-Filipino-French chambermaid tidies your room. This racial symphony is evident throughout Hawaii, but it's more apparent on Oahu where the large population creates more opportunity for a racial hodge-podge. The warm feeling you get almost immediately upon arrival is that everyone belongs.

Population Figures
Oahu's 800,000 residents account for 80% of the state's population. All these people are on an island comprising only 10% of the state's land total, which adds up to nearly 1,600 people per square mile, 8 times that of California. Sections of Waikiki can have a combined pop-

ulation of permanent residents and visitors as high as 90,000 per square mile, making cities like Tokyo, Hong Kong, and New York seem quite roomy by comparison. The good news is that Oahu *expects* all these people and knows how to accommodate them comfortably.

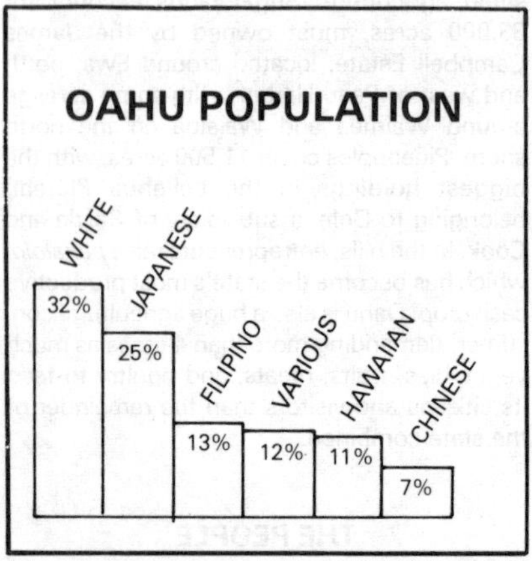

About 400,000 people live in greater Honolulu, generally considered the built-up area from Ewa to Koko Head. The next most populous urban centers after Honolulu are the Kailua-Kaneohe area with about 100,000 residents, followed by Pearl City and Waipahu with a combined total of about 75,000 or so. With all of these people, and such a finite land resource, real estate on the island is sky high. A typical one-family home sells for $180,000, while a condo averages about $110,000. And around plenty of prime real estate, these figures would barely cover the down payment!

So where is everybody? Of the major ethnic groups you'll find the Hawaiians clustered around Waianae and on the windward coast near Waiahole; the whites tend to be in Wahiawa, around Koko Head, in Waikiki, and in Kailua-Kaneohe; those of Japanese ancestry prefer the valleys heading toward the Pali, including Kalihi, Nuuanau, and Tantalus; Filipinos live just east of the airport, in downtown Honolulu, around Barbers Point, and in Wahiawa; and the Chinese are in Chinatown and around the Diamond Head area. Of the minor ethnic groups the highest concentration of blacks is in the Army towns around Schofield Barracks; Samoans live along with the Hawaiians in Waianae, and the windward coastal towns, though the heaviest concentration is in downtown Honolulu not far from Aloha Tower; and Koreans and Vietnamese are scattered here and there, but mostly in Honolulu.

SHOPPING

You can't come to Oahu and *not* shop. Even if the idea of it doesn't thrill you, the lure of almost endless shops offering every imaginable kind of merchandise will sooner or later tempt even the most "big-waste-of-time" mumbler through their doors. So why fight it? And if you're the other type, who feels as though a day without shopping is like being marooned on a deserted island, have no fear of rescue, because everywhere on the horizon is "a sale, a sale!" You can use "much much more" as either an aspersion or a tribute when describing Oahu, and nowhere does this qualifier fit better than when describing its shopping. Over a dozen major and minor shopping centers and malls are in Honolulu and Waikiki alone! Population centers around the island, including those in the interior, the south shore, windward shore, and north shore, all have shopping centers in varying degrees—at the very least, a parking lot rimmed with a half-dozen shops that can provide immediate necessities. On the Neighbor Islands, a major shopping mall is usually found only in the island's main city, with mom 'n' pop stores and small superettes taking up the slack. On Oahu, you've got these too, but you're never very far from some serious shopping centers. The tourist trade fosters the sale of art and artifacts, jewelry and fashions, and numerous boutiques selling these are strung around the island like a shell necklace. Food costs, in supermarkets, tend to be reasonable because Oahu is the main distribution center, and with all the competition, prices in general seem to be lower. If your trip to Hawaii includes a stop on Oahu, do most of your shopping here, because of the cut-rate prices and much greater availability of goods. When most Hawaiians go on a shopping spree, they head for Oahu.

King's Village, Waikiki

Note
The following listings are general; refer to "Shopping" in the travel sections for listings of specific shops, stores, and markets.

Honolulu Shopping Centers
Since it serves as the main terminal for TheBus, you could make a strong case that **Ala Moana Shopping Center** is the heart of shopping on Oahu. At one time billed as the largest shopping center in the country, today it settles for being the largest in the state, with its hundreds of stores covering 50 acres. It's on Ala Moana Blvd., just across from the Ala Moana Beach Park. **The Ward Warehouse** is just a few blocks west of the Ala Moana Center, at 1050 Ala Moana Blvd. The **Ward Center**, on Ala Moana across from Ward Warehouse, is a relatively new shopping center that's gaining a reputation for some exclusive shops.

Waikiki Shopping
Shopping in Waikiki is as easy as falling off a surfboard. In 2 or 3 blocks of Kuhio and Kalakaua avenues are no less than 7 shopping centers. If that's not enough, there are hundreds of independent shops, plus plenty of street vendors. Main shopping centers include **Royal Hawaiian Shopping Center**, the **Waikiki Shopping Plaza**, the **International Market Place**, an open-air shopping bazaar across from the Moana Hotel at 2330 Kalakaua Ave., open daily from 9:00 a.m. until the vendors get tired at night. The **Hyatt Regency Shopping Center** is located on the first three floors of the Hyatt Regency Hotel, at 2424 Kalakaua Ave., tel. 922-5522. The **King's Village** is at 131 Kaiulani Ave., the **Waikiki Trade Center** is on the corner of Seaside and Kuhio avenues, and the **Rainbow Bazaar** is a unique mall located at the Hilton Hawaiian Hotel, at 2005 Kalia Road.

Around The Island
Heading east from Waikiki on Rt. 72, the first shopping is the **Niu Shopping Center** on your left, about 4 miles before Hanauma Bay. The **Time Supermarket** is known for good prices. Also on the left is the **Koko Marina Shopping Center**, just before Hanauma Bay, with a Liberty House, a few art galleries, and **Foodland Supermarket. Kailua** and **Kaneohe** bedroom communities have shopping malls. Numerous shops are found on the North Shore from Haleiwa to Waimea, including surf, art, boutiques and plenty of fast food and restaurants. The **Pearlridge Center** in Pearl City at the corner of the Kamehameha Hwy. and Waimano Home Rd. is a full shopping complex with over 90 stores. The **Waianae Mall** at 86-120 Farrington Hwy. serves the Waianae coast with a supermarket, drug store, fast foods, and sporting goods.

Food Shopping
Around the island plenty of mom 'n' pop gro-

cery stores provide fertile ground for a cultural exchange, but they're expensive. Oahu's large supermarkets include **Times, Safeway, Foodland, and Star Markets.** Preference is highly individual, but Times has a good reputation for fresh vegetables and good prices. Japanese **Holiday Mart** has stores around the island. They've got some bargains in their general merchandise departments, but because they try to be everything, their food section suffers, especially the fruits and vegetables.

A **Floating Farmer's Market** appears at different times and places around Honolulu. For example, on Wednesday mornings from 9:45 to 10:45 a.m., it's across the street from the main library at 478 S. King St., in downtown Honolulu. The vendors are mostly Filipino, who drive up in small battered trucks and sell wonderful fresh vegetables from their home plots at very reasonable prices. Big shots who bring in fruits and vegies from California and the like have been trying to weed these little guys out. The Honolulu Dept. of Parks regulates the time and place for the market, and you can get information at tel. 527-6060.

Chinatown offers the **People's Open Market** at the Cultural Plaza, located at the corner of Mauna Kea and Beretania streets. Besides produce, you'll find fresh fish, meats, and poultry; the **Oahu Fish Market** is in the heart of Chinatown along King Street. The shops are run down but clean, and sell everything from octopus to *kimchi.*

Health Food Stores

Brown rice and *tofu* eaters can keep that special sparkle in their eyes with no problem on Oahu—some excellent health food stores. Most have a snack bar where you can get a delicious and nutritious meal for bargain prices (see "Food" in the various travel sections.) **Down to Earth,** 2525 S. King St., tel. 947-7678, is an old standby where you can't go wrong; great stuff at great prices. **Celestial Natural Foods,** at the Haleiwa Shopping Plaza on the North Shore, tel. 637-6729, is also top notch. **Kailua Health Foods** at 124 Oneawa in Kailua, tel. 261-0353, is small but well stocked, especially with detoxification products. **Earth Seed,** also in Kailua at 354 Uluniu St., tel. 261-9141, has a good stock of merchandise and also features the Little Kitchen Restaurant, for sit-down vegetarian dinners. **Vim and Vigor** is a small chain of health food stores with locations around the island; the main one is at the Ala Moana Center, tel. 955-3600, and others at Pearlridge Center, and the Kahala and Kamehameha centers.

Sundries

ABC has over a dozen mini-marts in and around Waikiki. Their prices are generally high, but they do have some good bargains on suntan lotions, sunglasses, and beach mats. The cheapest place to buy **film** is at **Sears, Woolworths,** and **Longs Drugs.** All have good selections, cheap prices, and stores all over the island. **Francis Camera Shop** in the Ala Moana Center, tel. 946-2879, is extremely well stocked with accessories. For a large selection of military surplus and camping goods try the **Big 88** at 330 Sand Island Access Rd., tel. 845-1688. If gadgetry fascinates you, head for **Shirokiya Department Store** at the Ala Moana and Pearlridge centers and in Waikiki. Besides everything else, they have a wonderful selection of all the jim-jicks and doohickeys that Nippon has to offer. The atmosphere is somewhat like a trade fair. Those who can't imagine a tour with anything on their feet but Birkenstock's can have their tootsies accommodated, but they won't be entirely happy. If you get a sole blowout, **Birkenstock Footprints** at Ala Moana Center, tel. 531-6014, will re-sole them for $14, but they want a full week to do it. For one-day service, they'll refer you to a shoemaker, **Joe Pacific** at the Ala Moana Center, tel. 946-2998, but he wants a toe-twisting $25 for the service!

Bookstores

Oahu has plenty of excellent bookstores. In Honolulu, try the **Upstart Crow and Co.** at 1050 Ala Moana, Ward Warehouse, tel. 533-1761, and 1200 Ala Moana, Ward Center, tel. 536-4875. If you get fatigued perusing the bestsellers, you can always sit down and have a delicious coffee and pastry in their coffee shop. **Honolulu Book Shops** has 3 locations at the Ala Moana Center, tel. 941-2274, in downtown Honolulu at 1001 Bishop St., tel. 537-6224, and at the Pearlridge Center at tel. 487-1548. **Waldenbooks** is at the Pearlridge

Center, tel. 488-9488, Kahala Mall, tel. 737-9550, and Waikiki Shopping Plaza, tel. 922-4154. For a fine selection of Hawaiiana try the **Bishop Museum and Planetarium Bookshop,** at the Bishop Museum, 1525 Bernice St., tel. 847-3511, and at the **Mission Houses Museum** in downtown Honolulu at 553 S. King St., tel. 531-0481.

Three women, Rachel McMahan, Janice Beam, and Kathryn Decker, have shopped their fingers to the bone for you and have written a small but definitive book entitled *The Shopping Bag.* It describes shops all over Oahu from art supplies to toys and sporting goods.

Arts And Crafts

The following are a few of many art shops and boutiques, just to get you started. An excellent place to find original arts and crafts at reasonable prices is along **The Fence** surrounding the Honolulu Zoo fronting Kapiolani Park. Island artists come here every weekend from 10:00 a.m. to 4:00 p.m. to display and sell their artwork. The **Honolulu Academy of Arts** at 900 S. Beretania, open Tues. to Sat. 10:00 a.m. to 4:30 p.m., Sun. 1:00-5:00 p.m., is not only great to visit (free), but has a fine gift shop that specializes in Asian art. The same high-quality and authentic handicrafts are available in both the **Hawaiian Mission Houses Museum** and **Bishop Museum** gift shops (see "Bookstores" above). For Oriental art try **Gallery Mikado** and **Garakuta-Do,** both in Waikiki's Eaton Square Complex. **Rainbow Island Tees and Ka'Ala Art,** tel. 637-7533, is a great one-stop shop for fine arts, pop art, and handicrafts, all by aspiring island artists. If you get tired of browsing have a delicious ice cream from their stand. Owned and operated by Jim and John Costello, these two transplanted Mainlanders have lived on the North Shore for years and are willing to dispense advice and wisdom. Located in Haleiwa on your right as you enter the west side of town, just past the large shell stand. Also in Haleiwa, the **Fettig Art Gallery,** tel. 637-4933, is the oldest gallery on the North Shore, featuring works by Beverly Fettig and various island artists. The **Punaluu Gallery,** tel. 237-8325, is the oldest gallery on the windward coast. It's been there over 30 years and is operated by Dorothy Zoller. It's well known for local art at fair prices. Dorothy is a local historian who loves meeting people, and will even open her gallery at night if you call ahead.

Flea Markets And Swap Meets

These are the cheapest places to find treasures. Three operate successfully on Oahu and have a regular following. **The Honolulu Flea Market,** at 1789 Kapiolani Blvd., tel. 943-1791, is open weekdays 10:00 a.m. to 6:00 p.m., Sat. and Sun. 8:30 a.m. to 5:00 p.m. A profusion of stalls in an old warehouse, selling everything from jewelry to papayas. **Aloha Flea Market,** tel. 732-2437, is at Aloha Stadium every Sat. and Sun. morning. Biggest flea market on Oahu selling everything from bric-a-brac to real heirlooms and treasures. **Kam Swap Meet,** tel. 488-5822, Kam Drive-In Theater, 98-850 Moanalua Rd., Pearl City, is open Wed., Thurs., Sat., and Sun. mornings. Regular stall holders to housewives cleaning out the garage offer great fun and bargains.

GETTING THERE

The old adage of "all roads leading to Rome" applies almost perfectly to Oahu, though instead of being cobblestones, they're sea lanes and air routes. Except for a handful of passenger ships still docking at Honolulu Harbor, and some limited *non-stop* flights to Maui and the Big Island, all other passengers to and from Hawaii are routed through **Honolulu International Airport**. These flights include *direct* flights to the Neighbor Islands, which means stopping over at Honolulu International and continuing on the same plane, or more likely changing to an inter-island carrier whose fare is included in the original price of the flight. Types of flights and carriers are fully explained in the "Getting There" chapter in the general "Introduction."

Honolulu International Airport

The state's only international airport is one of the busiest in the entire country, with hundreds of flights to and from cities around the world arriving and departing daily. In a routine year, over 15 million passengers utilize this facility. The two terminals (directions given as you face the main entranceway) are: the **main**

terminal, accommodating all international and Mainland flights, with a small wing at the far left end of the ground floor for a few commuter airlines; and the **inter-island terminal** in a separate building at the far right end of the main terminal. The ground floor of the main terminal is mostly for arriving passengers, and contains the baggage claim area, lockers and long-term storage, car rental agencies, and international and domestic arrival doors which are kept separate. The second floor is for departing passengers, with most activity centered here, including ticket counters, shops, lounges, baggage handlers, and the entrance to most of the gates. From both levels you can board taxis and TheBus to downtown Honolulu and Waikiki. International carriers usually park on the right side of the main terminal and use gates 26 through 31, while gates 6 through 31, on the left, are used by domestic carriers. The peak hours for the airport are 7:00-11:00 a.m. and 5:00-7:00 p.m.

The **inter-island terminal** services flights aboard Hawaiian, Aloha, and Mid-Pacific Airlines to and from Honolulu. It has its own snack bars, car rental booths, transportation to and from the city, lounges, information windows, and restrooms. It is only a leisurely 5-min. stroll between the 2 terminals, which is fine if you don't have much baggage; if you do, there are plenty of shuttles every few minutes. If you are at the small commuter airlines terminal at the opposite end of the complex, shuttles ($.50) come regularly, but if you need one in a hurry just ask at the ticket booths there to summon one for you.

Services, Information, Tips

The main **information booth** is located on the second level just near the central escalators. Besides general information, they have good maps of the airport, Oahu, Honolulu, and Waikiki. Also, inquiry booths lined up along the ground level and at the inter-island terminal are also friendly and helpful, but not always stocked with as many maps as the main information booth.

The **lost and found** is located on the ground level of the main terminal, and at the inter-island terminal. The **post office** is across the street from the main entranceway toward the inter-island terminal.

Lockers are located on both levels of the main terminal and at the inter-island terminal, with a **baggage storage room** only on the ground floor of the main terminal. Locker rental is $1 for a 24-hour period, with a refundable $5 key deposit. Normally a 3-day cycle, you can rent lockers for a month or longer, but you must prepay and leave a deposit. If your deposit isn't large enough even though you prepaid, they may open your locker 3 days before your time is up and put your gear into the storage room where you'll be charged $2 per item per 24-hour period, which is the normal price. Liability for lockers and storage room is $500 per bag. The baggage storage accepts no personal checks, no prepayments, and no pets or perishables. You *must* have your claim ticket to retrieve your belongings. The service is well run, efficient, and unfriendly.

Money can be a hassle at the airport, especially getting change which is a downright rip-off, and very bad public relations for visitors. The **foreign currency exchange** is on the second floor of the main terminal along the concourse behind the United ticket window. Here, and at a few smaller exchanges on the ground floor, the charge is one percent per transaction on foreign currency, and the same on TCs no matter where they're from, with a minimum charge of $1.50. Unfortunately, no one will give you change, putting you at the mercy of $1 bill-change machines located throughout the airport. These machines happily dispense $.85 for every $1 you put in, so if you want to make a phone call, or the like, you're out of luck. The snack bars will only change money for you with a purchase. For a state that prides itself on the *aloha* spirit and depends on good relations with its visitors, this is a ridiculously poor way of greeting people, or giving them a last impression before they return home.

To refresh and relax, you might visit the **Shower Tree,** on the second floor behind the United counter, next to the hairdresser. You can have a shower for $7.50, which includes soap, towel, shampoo, deodorant, and hair-

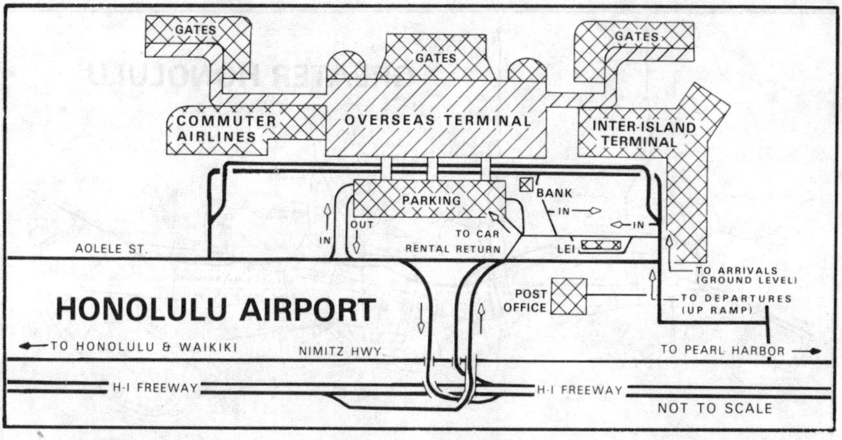

dryers; an 8-hour sleep in a private little room and a shower for $18.72; or a rest at $3 per hour. If this seems a bit pricy, just use the public bathrooms for a quick wash, then choose any one of three small gardens near the central concourse to take a little nap. If you're there just for a short snooze, airport security won't bother you.

Airport Transportation

Car rental agencies are lined up at booths on the ground floor of both terminals. Many courtesy phones for car rental agencies not at the airport are located in and around the baggage claim area; call for free vans to pick you up and take you to their nearby facility. This procedure even saves the hassle of maneuvering through heavy airport traffic—you usually wait at the island in the middle of the road just outside the baggage claim area. Make sure to specify the number of the area where you'll wait.

If you're driving to the airport to pick up or drop off someone, you should know about **parking.** If you want to park on the second level of the parking garage for departures, you must either take the elevator up to the fourth floor, or down to ground level, and from there cross the pedestrian bridge. There's no way to get across on levels 2 and 3.

Public transportation to downtown Honolulu, especially Waikiki, is abundant. Moreover, some hotels have courtesy phones near the baggage claim area; if you're staying there, they'll send a van to fetch you. Current charges for taxis, vans, TheBus, and limos are posted just outside the baggage claim area, so you won't have to worry about being overcharged.

Taxis to Waikiki cost about $12, not counting bags. **Gray Line** runs a small bus or van to Waikiki for about $5 with no baggage charge. **Terminal Transportation,** tel. 926-4747, offers hotel pickup and a ride to the airport, including 2 standard pieces of luggage, for $4 adult, $2 child. **Em's Airport Shuttle,** tel. 545-1266, offers similar service from Waikiki every half hour from 6:00 a.m. to 10:00 p.m.

You can take **TheBus** (no. 8 and no. 20) to Waikiki via the Ala Moana Terminal, from which you can get buses all over the island. If you're heading north pick up bus no. 20, 51, or 52 just outside the airport. TheBus only costs $.60 (exact change), but you are allowed only one carry-on bag that must be small enough to be held on your lap.

GETTING AROUND

Touring Oahu is especially easy, since almost every normal (and not so normal) mode of conveyance is readily available. You can rent

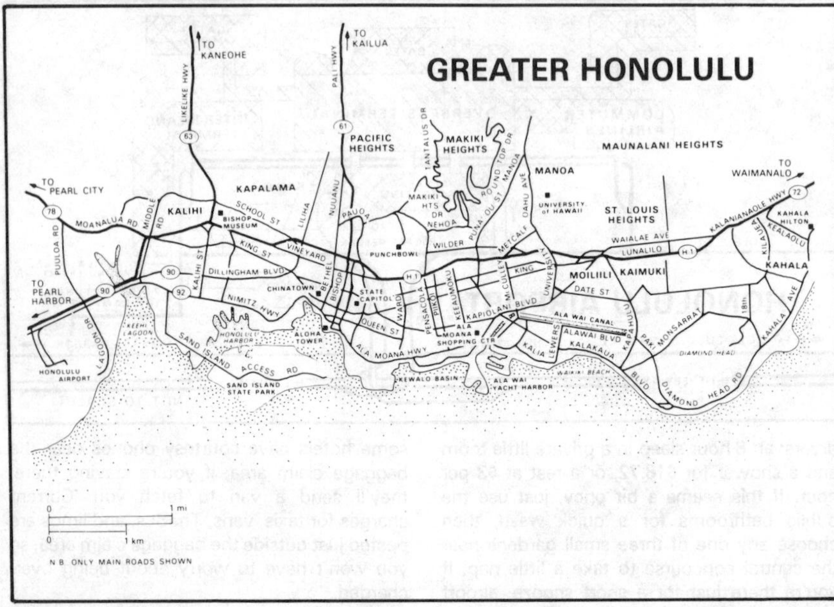

anything from a moped to a pedicab, and the competition is very stiff, which helps keep prices down. A few differences separate Oahu from the other islands. To begin with is a *model* public transportation system called TheBus—not only efficient, but very inexpensive. Also, Oahu is the only island that has a true expressway system, though along with it rush hour and traffic jams. A large part of Oahu's business is processing people, even if it's only to send them on to another island! The agencies operating these businesses on the island are masters at moving people down the road. With the huge volume of tourists that visit every year, it's amazing how smoothly it works. The following is a cross-section of what's available and should help you to decide how you want to get around. Have fun!

Tips And Procedures

Every reputable national, state, and island-wide car rental agency is here, along with some car rental hucksters, that'll hook you and land you like a *mahi mahi* if you're not careful. Most of the latter are located along the main tourist drags of Waikiki. The rule of thumb is, if their deal sounds to good to be true, it is. The competition is so fierce between the reputable agencies, however, that their deals are equally as good. Always check with your travel agency for big savings in fly/drive or stay/drive packages. Make sure your car comes with a flat daily rate and unlimited mileage. One of the hooks to lure you into renting a "bargain" car is to whack you with a mileage charge. Extra benefits from many firms include a free *Drive Guide* that has good maps and lists the island's main attractions; oftentimes you receive a booklet of coupons that entitle you to free or reduced prices on services, admissions, dining, and entertainment. Eight full pages of car rental agencies grace the Honolulu Yellow Pages, from firms that rent Mercedes convertibles down to low-budget operations with a few dented and dated Datsuns. Don't get the impression that the backyard firms are all rip-offs. You can get some great deals, but you have to choose wisely and be willing to settle for a less than prestigious car.

Reserving a car on Oahu is doubly important because of the huge turnover that can occur at any time. Be aware of **drop-off charges;** for example, if you rent in Waikiki and leave the car at the airport, you'll be charged. It's convenient to rent a car at the airport. But it's also convenient to take an inexpensive shuttle to and from Waikiki (see below) and rent there. Many of the firms have offices in Waikiki, and you can even rent a car from your hotel desk and have it delivered to you. This saves the obvious hassle of dealing with traffic and unfamiliar roads during arrival and departure, and avoids drop-off fees, but you don't always get the cheapest rates.

Agencies

Car rental agencies include: **National,** one of the best, airport location at 2965 N. Nimitz Hwy., tel. 836-2655, in Waikiki at 2160 Kalakaua Ave., tel. 922-6461, or toll free at 800-227-7368; **Avis,** at the airport tel. 836-5531, in Waikiki at tel. 836-5543, or 800-331-1212; **Hertz,** with 11 locations around the island, and at the airport tel. 836-2511, or toll free at 800-654-8200; **Budget,** at the airport at tel. 836-1700, with locations in Waikiki, call central reservations at tel. 922-3600, or toll free at 800-527-0700.

Smaller but good firms include: **Sears,** accepting Sears credit cards, central reservations tel. 922-3805; **Thrifty,** airport tel. 836-2388, Waikiki tel. 923-7383, toll free 800-367-22-77; **Aloha Funway Rentals,** airport tel. 834-1016, Waikiki tel. 942-9696; **Tropical,** airport tel. 836-1041, Waikiki tel. 922-2385; **Holiday,** airport tel. 836-1974, Waikiki tel. 926-2752.

Cheaper firms offer bargain rates, and older cars. Many of these rent without a major credit card, but with a stiff deposit. Sometimes they even rent to those under 21, but you'll have to show reservations at a major hotel. Some where you usually make out all right are: **Mal-Mat,** at 1111 Kapiolani Blvd., tel. 533-3986; **Alpert's Used Car Rentals,** tel. 955-4370; **Hawaii Discount,** tel. 536-1861; **AAA Rents,** 524-8060.

If you're after a luxury car or a convertible try: **Convertibles Honolulu,** tel. 595-6170; and **Convertible Rentals,** featuring Mustangs, tel. 923-4131.

4WDs, Campers, Mopeds

If you're into 4WDs try: **Odyssey Rentals,** tel. 947-8036; **United Car Rental,** tel. 922-4605; or **Aloha Funway Rentals,** tel. 834-1016.

Campers and RVs can be rented from **Beach Boy Campers,** at 1720 Ala Moana, tel. 955-6381.

Motorcycles and mopeds are available from: **Aloha Funway Rentals,** tel. 942-9696; **Continental Rent a Bike,** 923-7533; **Sunshine Moped Rentals,** tel. 923-6083; and **Odyssey Rentals,** tel. 947-8036.

Bicycles

Peddling around Oahu can be both fascinating and frustrating. The roads are well paved, but the shoulders are often torn up. Traffic in and around Honolulu is horrifying, and the only way to avoid it is by leaving very early in the morning. TheBus has no facilities for transporting your bike out of town, so an early departure is your only alternative. Once you leave the city, traffic, especially on the secondary interior roads, isn't too bad. Unfortunately, all of the coastal roads are heavily trafficked. You're better off renting a **cruiser** or **mountain bike,** which allow for the sometimes poor road conditions and open up the possibilities of off-road biking. Even experienced mountain bikers should be careful on Oahu trails, which are often extremely muddy and rutted. Peddling around Waikiki, although congested, is usually safe, and a fun way of seeing the sights. Always lock your bike, and take your bike bag.

Great views with only half the flats to worry about.

For info on biking on Oahu, contact **Hawaii Bicycling League,** Box 4403, Honolulu, HI 96813. This non-profit corporation sponsors rides all over Oahu almost every weekend. Non-members are always welcome. The rides are multiple-level ability and are listed in the Hawaii Bicycling League's monthly newsletter, *SPOKE-N-WORDS.* If you're into cycling and want a unique look at Oahu, don't miss these rides. See "Sightseeing Tours/Bicycling" p. 208-209 for more info.

For bicycle rentals try: good old **Aloha Funway Rentals, tel. 942-9696; The Bike Way,** at 655 Kapiolani Blvd., tel. 538-7433. For sales and repairs try: **The Bike Shop,** featuring Fuji, Mongoose, and Schwinn, at 1149 S. King St., tel. 531-7071; **McCully Bicycle,** featuring Specialized, Miyata, and Takara, at 1018 McCully St., tel. 955-6329; and **The Bike Way,** featuring Bianchi, and Univega at 655 Kapiolani, tel. 538-7433.

TheBus

If Dorothy and her mates had TheBus to get them down the Yellow Brick Road, she might have chosen to stay in Oz and forget about Kansas. TheBus, TheBus, ThewonderfulBus is the always-coming, slow-moving, go-everywhere friend of the budget traveler. Operated by Mass Transit Lines (MTL) Inc., it could serve as a model of efficiency and economy in any city of the world. What makes it more amazing is that it all came together by chance, beginning as an emergency service in 1971. These brown, yellow, and orange coaches go up and down both the windward and leeward coasts, through the interior, while passing through all of the major and most of the minor towns in between, and most often stopping near the best sights.

The **direction** in which TheBus travels is posted after the number and the name of the town. They are designated as EB (east-bound toward Diamond Head) and WB (west-bound toward the airport). The **fare** is only $.60, paid in *exact* change upon entering. Even putting a $1 bill into the box and not expecting change is unacceptable. Students under age 19 and over 6 are charged $.25, while kids under 5 that can sit on their parent's lap aren't charged at all. Adult **monthly bus passes,** good at any time and on all routes, are $15, students $7.50, and senior citizens over age 65 are free. But they (seniors) must furnish proof of age and the processing period takes 3-4 weeks. Passes are available at Foodland and Emjay stores, Pioneer Federal Banks, all city halls, U. of Hawaii (adult passes only), and at the MTL Bus Pass office at 725 Kapiolani Boulevard.

Transfers are free and are issued upon request when entering TheBus, but you can only use them for ongoing travel in the same direction, and on a different line (numbered bus). They are also timed and dated. For example, you can take no. 8 from Waikiki to the Ala Moana Terminal, get off and do some fast shopping, then use your transfer on no. 20 to continue on to Pearl Harbor.

Circling the island is a terrific way to see the sights and meet people all along the way. The circle route takes about 4 hours if you stay on, but you can use the transfer system to give yourself a reasonable tour of the sights that strike your fancy. The **circle island** bus is no. 52, but remember there are two no. 52s, going in different directions. The buses are labeled: **no. 52 Wahiawa Kaneohe,** going inland to Wahiawa, north to Haleiwa, along the north shore, down the windward coast to Kaneohe and back over the Pali to Honolulu; **no. 52 Kaneohe Wahiawa** follows the same route but in the opposite direction. If you'll be taking this bus to Pearl Harbor, be absolutely sure to take no. 52 Wahiawa Kaneohe, because if you took the other, you'd have to circle the entire island before arriving at Pearl!

Get full information on TheBus by writing to **MTL Inc.**, TheBus, 1585 Kapiolani St. Honolulu 96813, tel. 942-3702, or by visiting the information booth at the Ala Moana Terminal where you can pick up fliers and maps. An excellent, inexpensive little guide is *Hawaii Bus and Travel Guide* by Milly Singletary, available in most bookstores. The following are some popular destinations and their bus numbers, all originating from the Ala Moana Terminal: Airport, no. 8 Airport, no. 20; Arizona Memorial, Pearl Harbor, no. 20, 50, 51, 52 Wahiawa, (not 52 Kaneohe); Bishop Museum, no. 2 School; Chinatown, no. 1, 2, 3, 4, 6, 8, 9, 11, 12, 50, 52 Wahiawa; Fisherman's Wharf, no. 8 Airport, 20, 52 Kaneohe; Hanauma Bay, no. 1, 57, beach bus weekends; Honolulu (downtown), no. 1, 2, 3, 4, 9, 11, 12; Pali Lookout, not serviced; Polynesian Culture Center, both no. 52s, then a shuttle; Queen Emma palace, no. 4; Sea Life Park, no. 57; Waikiki Beach, no. 2, 4, 8, 14, 20. A special "beach bus," an old battered green clunker, operates from June through August and runs from Waikiki to Waimanalo Beach stopping at Hanauma Bay and Sandy Beach. It has racks for surfboards and leaves every hour (11:00 a.m. to 4:00 p.m.) from the corner of Monsarrat and Kalakaua avenues.

Taxis

The law says that taxis are not allowed to cruise around looking for fares, so you can't hail them. But they do and you can, and most policemen have more important things to do than monitor cabs. Best is to summon one from your hotel or a restaurant. All are radio-dispatched, they're usually there in a flash. The fares, posted on the taxi doors, are set by law and are fair, but still expensive for the budget traveler. The rates do change, but expect about $1.50 for the flag fall, and then $.25 for each additional 1/6 mile. The airport to Waikiki is about $15. You pay extra for bags. Of the many taxi companies, ones with good reputations are: **SIDA**, a cooperative of owner-drivers, at tel. 836-0011; **Aloha State Taxi**, tel. 847-3566; **Charley's**, tel. 955-2211; **Discount Taxi**, 841-033. If you need some special attention like a Rolls Royce limo, try: **Silver Cloud Limousines**, tel. 941-2901; for the handicapped and people in wheelchairs, **Handicabs**, tel. 524-3866. For **Pedicabs**, see p. 272.

SIGHTSEEING TOURS

Guided land tours are much more of a luxury than a necessity on Oahu. Because of the excellent bus system and relatively cheap rental cars, you spend a lot of money for a narration and to be spared the hassle of driving. If you've come in a group and don't intend on renting a car, they also may be worth it. Sea cruises and air tours are equally luxurious, but provide glimpses of this beautiful island you'd normally miss. The following partial list of tour companies should get you started.

Land Tours

If you're going to take a land tour, you must have the right attitude, or it'll be a disaster. Your tour leader, usually driving the van or bus, is part instructor, comedian, and cheerleader. There's enough "corn" in his jokes to impress an Iowa hog. On the tour, you're expected to become part of one big happy family, and most importantly, to be a good sport. Most guides are quite knowledgeable about Oahu and its history, and they honestly try to do a good job. But they've done it a million times before, and their performance can be as stale as week-old bread. The larger the tour vehicle and the shorter the miles covered, the worse it is likely to be. If you still want a tour, take a full-day jaunt in a small van: you get to know the other people and the guide, who'll tend to give you a more in-depth presentation. Tips are cheerfully accepted. Also, be aware that some tours get kickbacks from stores and restaurants they take you to, where you don't always get the best bargains. Most companies offer free hotel pickup and delivery. Lunch or dinner is not included unless specified, but if the tour includes a major tourist spot like Waimea Falls Park or the Polynesian Culture Center, admission is usually included.

About 8 different tours offered by most companies are variations on the same theme; since the prices are regulated, the cost is fairly uniform. The more popular are the **circle-island tour**, including stops at Diamond Head, Hanauma Bay, the windward and north shores,

Waimea Falls, and perhaps the Mormon Temple and Dole Pineapple Plantation, for about $40, and half for children. A **night tour** to the Polynesian Culture Center, including admission and dinner show, costs $50. **Picnic tours,** and tours to **Byodoin Temple,** go for around $35. Tours to **Punchbowl** and the **Arizona Memorial** are around $20. A small tour worth considering is the **snorkel and swim** at Hanauma Bay, including transport to this underwater park, about 4 hours exploring, and your snorkel gear, for under $15.

Some reputable companies include: **Akamai Tours,** tel. 922-6485; **Polynesian Adventure Tours,** tel. 922-0888; **Robert's Hawaii Tours,** tel. 947-3939, and **Gray Line Hawaii Ltd.,** tel. 922-5094 (large coaches accommodating 30 or more as well as smaller vans); **Transhawaiian Tours,** tel. 735-6467; **Charley's Tours,** tel. 955-3381; **E Noa Tours,** 941-6608; and **Four Wheel Drive Tours,** tel. 623-7021 (touring the rough road to Kaena Point).

The following are special tours that you should seriously consider. **Diplomat's Passport to Polynesia,** operated by the Bishop Museum, tel. 847-3511, leaves King's Alley daily at 8:30 a.m. in its red double-decker bus. For under $15, you get a wonderful narration of the history of Honolulu, plus admission to the *Falls of Clyde,* a floating maritime museum, the Bishop Museum and Planetarium, and the Mission Houses Museum. You save money and get a mini-seminar on Hawaii and Hawaiiana at the same time. **Walking Tour of Chinatown,** tel. 533-3181, by the Chinese Chamber of Commerce, leaves every Tues. at 9:30 a.m. from in front of their offices at 42 N. King Street. You get a narrated 3-hour tour of Chinatown for about $3, and an optional Chinese lunch for around $4. **Walking Tour of Honolulu, the 1800s,** tel. 531-0481, is a 2-hour tour led by a very knowledgeable volunteer from the Mission Houses Museum, who is probably a member of the Cousin's Society and a descendant of one of the original Congregationalist missionaries to Hawaii. You're led on a wonderfully anecdoted walk through the historical buildings of central Honolulu for only $5 or so, every Wed. and Fri. at 9:30 a.m., beginning from TheBus stop in front of the capitol. Reserve!

Oahu By Bicycle

Free rides and tips for cycling are offered by the **Hawaiian Bicycling League** (see "Bicycles-Getting Around" for information). Also, **Island Bicycle Adventures,** 569 Kapahulu Ave., Honolulu, HI 96815, tel. 732-7227, offers guided rides to Oahu, Maui, and the Big Island. These tours are led by Ken Reilly, Roberta Baker, and Frank and Laura Smith, all effective cycling instructors. They run three extensive tours: Maui Magic, 5 days touring Maui, $495; Hawaii Highlights, 10 days on the Big Island, $795, Oahu Explorer, a 2-day leisurely circuit, $159. Good quality KHS 12-speeds are provided at an additional $10 p/pd. Helmets, insurance, and

Dillingham Airfield

all accommodations and meals are included in the price. Write for full details and deposit and refund information to the above address.

Oahu By Air

When you soar above Oahu, you realize just how beautiful this island actually is, and considering that the better part of a million people live in this relatively small space, it's amazing just how much undeveloped land still exists in the interior and even along the coast. The following are some air tours worth considering. Remember that small, one- or 2-plane operations come and go as quickly as cloud bursts. They're all licensed and regulated for safety, but if business is bad, the propellers stop spinning.

Novel air tours are offered from Dillingham Airfield, up on the northwest section of Oahu, a few miles down the Farrington Hwy. from Waialua. Up here you can soar silently above the coast with **Glider Rides,** tel. 677-3404, an outfit offering one- or 2-passenger, piloted rides infinitely more exciting than the company's name. A plane tows you aloft and you circle in a 5-mile radius with a view that can encompass 80 miles on a clear day. The rides are available daily, first-come first-served, from 10:00 a.m. to 5:00 p.m. Cost is around $30 single, $40 double, and flights, depending upon air currents, last about 20 minutes. **Surf Air Tours,** tel. 637-7003, offers plane rides along the north shore for a reasonable $29 per person that lasts a half hour, while a one-hour cirlce island tour costs $49. The aircraft are very dependable Cessna 172s or 206s, and the pilots narrate while positioning the plane so that you can take some good photos. The operation is professional, but low-key, like taking a spin with a guy in his private plane.

Islands in the Sky gives one-day flying extravaganzas that cover all the main islands except the Big Island, offered by the most reputable island-based airline, **Hawaiian Air,** tel. 537-5100. For about $200 they fly you to the 7 islands, and include a breakfast, lunch, and ground excursion to Hana on Maui and the Fern Grotto on Kauai. It's a long full day, and one to remember.

Panorama Air Tours, tel. 836-2122 or 800-367-2671, have tailor-made tours of Oahu and an all-encompassing "flightsee Hawaii tour" similar to Hawaiian Air for about the same price. They fly smaller 2-engined aircraft, and include the Big Island, Maui, and Kauai with a ground stop on each.

Helicopter companies rev up their choppers to flightsee you around the island starting at $25 for a short trip over Waikiki. Prices rise from there as you head for the north shore. Chopper companies include: **Hawaii Pacific Helicopters,** tel. 836-1561; **Kenai Air Hawaii,** tel. 836-2071; and **Royal Helicopters,** tel. 941-4683.

Aga Waikiki dinner sail is as romantic as ever. (Fritz Craft, c. 1930)

Sails And Dinner Cruises

If you're taking a tour at all, your best bet is a sail or dinner cruise. They're touristy, but a lot of fun, and actually good value. Many times money-saving coupons for them are found in the free tourist magazines, and plenty of street buskers in Waikiki give special deals. The latter are mostly on the up and up, but make sure that you know exactly what you're getting. Most of these cruises depart from the Kewalo Basin Marina, near Fisherman's Wharf, at 5:30 p.m. and cruise Waikiki toward Diamond Head before returning about 2 hours later. On board are a buffet, open all-you-can-guzzle bar, live entertainment, and dancing. Costs vary but expect to spend about $40 per person. For cruises to Pearl Harbor and the Arizona Memorial see p. 245, and snorkeling and fishing charters p. 218-219, 223.

Some of the better dinner sails and cruises follow. **Royal Hawaiian Holidays** is a tour-booking company that can get you on a variety of cruises from a lunch to dinner sail. Prices are as low as $18, tel. 926-0623. The *Manu Kai* of the Hyatt Regency, tel. 922-9292, ext. 75145, takes hotel guests and the general public for a snorkel, sail, or cocktail cruise aboard this lovely 35-footer. **Aikane Catamarans**, tel. 538-3680, is an established company with a number of boats sporting a thatched roof and Polynesian Review. **Windjammer Cruises** tel. 521-0036, sails a 3-deck, 285-foot, 4-masted fake sailing ship called the *Rella Mae* from Kewalo Basin. It looks good, but the sails are only for show. If you're sitting on Waikiki Beach and you see a rainbow-colored sail, it belongs to **Rainbow Cruises,** tel. 955-3348.

For something different try the **No Booze Cruise,** tel. 944-8033, sailing from Hula Kai Pier no. 11 aboard the *Adventure V* at 5:15 p.m. on Fri. evening, and offers worship on the water on Sundays at 7:40 a.m. Live Christian music, soft drinks, and popcorn. Small fee on Fri., and donation on Sunday. The **International Society for Krishna Consciousness** offers free rides on its *Jaludata,* along with free love feasts on Sun. at 4:30 p.m. For information, *Hare Krishna, hare rama,* call 595-3947. The *Ani Ani* belongs to **Glass Bottom Boats Hawaii,** tel. 537-1958, doing one-hour cruises along Waikiki; 3 cruises in the morning and 3 in the afternoon run on the hour, beginning at 9:30 a.m. and 1:30 p.m. Cost is under $10.

ACCOMMODATIONS

The innkeepers of Oahu would be personally embarrassed if you couldn't find adequate lodging on their island. So long as Oahu has to suffer the "slings and arrows" of development gone wild, at least you can find all kinds, qualities, and prices of places in which to spend your vacation. Of the nearly 60,000 rooms available in Hawaii, 35,000 are on Oahu, 30,000 in Waikiki alone! Some are living landmarks, historical mementos of the days when only millionaires came by ship to Oahu, dallying as if it were their own private hideaway. When the jumbo jets began arriving in the early '60s, Oahu, especially Waikiki, began to build frantically. The result was hotel skyscrapers that grew faster than bamboo in a rainforest. These monoliths, which offered the *average family* a place to stay, marked a tremendous change in social status of visitors to Oahu. The runaway building continued unabated for 2 decades, until the city politicians, supported by the hotel keepers themselves, cried "Enough!" and the activity finally slowed down. Now a great deal of money is put into refurbishings and remodelings of what's already built. Visitors can find breathtakingly beautiful hotels that are the best in the land, next door to more humble inns that can satisfy most anyone's taste and pocketbook. On Oahu, you may not get your own private beach with swaying palms and *hula* girls, but it's easy and affordable to visit one of the world's most exotic and premier vacation resorts.

What, Where And How Much

At almost anytime of year, bargains, plenty of them, include **fly/drive/stay deals,** or any combination thereof, designed to attract visitors, while keeping the prices down. You don't even have to look hard to find RT airfare, room, and rental car for a week from the Mainland's West Coast, all for around $500 based on double occupancy. Oahu's rooms are found in all manners and sorts of hotels, condos, and private homes. Some venerable old inns along **Waikiki Beach** were the jewels of the city when only a few palms obscured the views of Diamond Head. However, most of Waikiki's hotels are relatively new high-rises. In Waikiki's **5-star** hotels, prices for deluxe accommodations, with all the trimmings, run about $100-$150 per night. But a huge inventory of rooms go for half that amount and less. If you don't mind being one block from the beach, you can easily find nice hotels for $30-$40. You can even find these prices in hotels on the beach, though most tend to be a bit older and heavily booked by tour agencies. You, too, can get a room in these, but expect the staffs to be only perfunctorily friendly, and the hotels to be a bit worn around the edges. Waikiki's side streets also hold many apartment-hotels that are, in effect, condos. In these you get the benefit of a full kitchen for under $50. Stays of a week or more bring further discounts.

The vast majority of Oahu's rooms are in Waikiki, where even the hotel owners wish to slow down growth.

Central Honolulu has few acceptable places to stay except for some no-frills hotels in and around Chinatown. Bad sections of Hotel Street have dives frequented by winos and prostitutes, not worth the hassle for the few dollars saved. Some upscale hotels around Ala Moana put you near the beach, but away from the heavy activity of Waikiki. The real deal for budget travelers is the city's 3 YMCAs (coed at some), and in the island's only youth hostel. Students can also find rooms, especially during summer break, at the U. of Hawaii campus. For those passing through, 3 **overnight-style** hotels are near the airport.

The remainder of the island, outside Waikiki, was mostly ignored as far as resort development was concerned. In the interior towns, and along the south and most of the windward coasts, you'll be hard pressed to find a room because there simply aren't any. Even today, only a handful of hotels are found on the leeward coast, mostly around **Makaha**. The area has experienced some recent development with a few condos and some full resorts going up, but it remains mostly undeveloped. **Windward Oahu** does have established resorts especially at Turtle Bay, Laie, and Punaluu, but most of the lodging there is in rentable beach houses, and tiny, basic inns.

To round things off, there is a network of **bed and breakfast** homes, YM/WCAs, YHs, Elderhostels, and summer sessions complete with room and board at the U. of Hawaii (see "Honolulu Accommodations" for details). Oahu also offers plenty of spots to pitch a tent at both state and county campgrounds.

CAMPING AND HIKING

Few people equate visiting Oahu with camping. The two seem mutually exclusive, especially when you focus on the mystique of Waikiki, and the dominance of a major city like Honolulu. But between state, county, and private campgrounds, and even a military reserve or two, you have about 20 spots to choose from all over the island. Camping on Oahu, however, is a little different than camping on the Neighbor Islands, which are simply more amenable to camping. In an island state, they're considered *the woods, the sticks, the backcountry,* and camping seems more acceptable there.

Although totally legal, and done by both visitors and residents, Oahu's camping problems are widely divergent, with social and financial implications. When the politically powerful tourist industry thinks of visitors, it imagines people sitting by a hotel pool, drinking *mai tais,* and dutifully spending money! Campers just won't cooperate in parting with their quota of dollars, so there's not much impetus to cater to their wants and needs. Moreover, Honolulu is an international city that attracts both the best and worst kinds of people. The tourist industry, supported by the civil authorities, has a mortal dread that low-lifers, loafers, and bums will ensconce themselves on Oahu's beaches. This would be disastrous for Oahu's image! Mainland cities, not so dependent upon tourism, can obviously be more tolerant of their citizens who have fallen through the social net. So in Oahu they keep a close eye on the campgrounds, enforcing the rules, controlling the situation. The campgrounds are patrolled, adding a measure of strictness along with a measure of security. Even decent people can't bend the rules and slide by a little, where they normally might on the Neighbor Islands.

An odd inherent social situation adds to the problem. Not too long ago, the local people either lived on the beach or used them extensively, oftentimes for their livelihood. Many, especially fishermen and their families, would set up semi-permanent camps for a good part of the year. You can see the remnants of this practice at some of the more remote and ethnically claimed campgrounds. As Oahu, much more than the Neighbor Islands, felt the pressures of growing tourism, beachfront property became astronomically expensive. Local people had to relinquish what they thought of as *their* beaches. The state and county, in an effort to keep some beaches public and therefore undeveloped, created **beach parks**. This insured that all could use the beaches forever, but it also meant that their access would be governed and regulated. Local people, just like visitors, must follow the rules and apply for camping permits limited by the number of days that you can spend in any one spot. Out went the semi-permanent camp and with it, for the local people, the idea of *our* beach. Now, you have the same rights to camp in a spot that

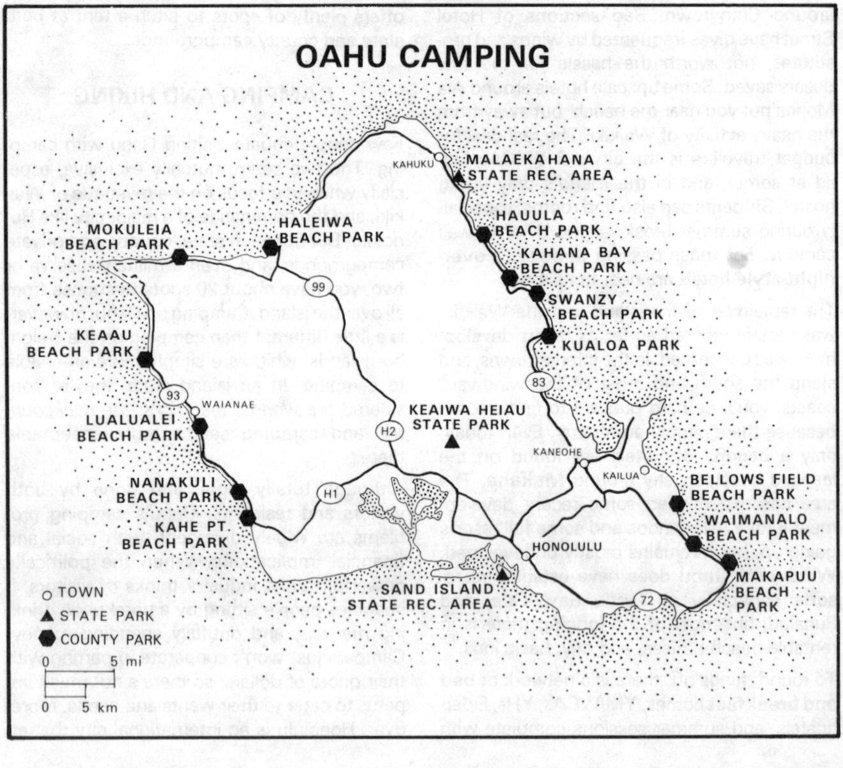

local boys smiling for the camera

may have been used, or even owned, in past generations, by the family of the dark-skinned people next to you. They feel dispossessed, infringed upon, and bitter. And you, especially if you have white skin, can be the focus of this bitterness. This situation, although psychologically understandable, can be a monumental drag. Of course, not all island people have this attitude, and chances are very good that nothing negative will happen. But you must be aware of underlying motivations, so that you can read the vibes of the people around your camp spot.

If all of these "problems" haven't made you want to pull up your tent stakes and head into a more congenial sunset, you can have a great and inexpensive time camping on Oahu. All of this is just the social climate that you *may* have to face, but most likely, nothing unpleasant will happen, and you'll come home tanned, relaxed, and singing the praises of the great outdoors on Hawaii's capital island.

State Parks

Oahu boasts 23 state parks and recreation areas. The majority offer a beach for day use, walks, picnicking, toilets, showers, and pavilions. A few of these, including some very important *heiau,* along with **Washington Place,** the state capitol, **Iolani Palace, the Royal Mausolem,** and **Diamond Head** are designated as state monuments. Three state parks offer tent camping: **Sand Island State Park,** just a few minutes from downtown Honolulu; **Keaiwa State Park,** in the interior on the heights above Aiea; and **Malaekahana State Park,** a mile north of Laie on the windward coast.

Oahu state parks close their gates and parking lots at night. Those *not* offering camping are open from 7:00 a.m. to 8:00 p.m., from May 1 to September 30, closing during the remainder of the year at 6:30 p.m. To camp at the 3 designated parks, you must acquire a permit (free) from Dept. of Forestry, Division of State Parks, 1151 Punchbowl St., Honolulu 96813, tel. 548-7455. Office hours are 8:00 a.m. to 4:15 p.m. Oahu campsite permit reservations can be made no earlier than the fifth Wed. before the first day of camping, but *must* be made at least one week in advance by writing a letter including your name, address, phone number, number of persons in your party, type of permit requested, and duration of your stay. The permits can be picked up on arrival with proof of identification. On Oahu campsites are at a premium and people line up at 8:00 a.m. on the first floor breezeway on the Beretania Street side of the issuing office, just outside the double glass doors, where they are given a number on a first-come first-served basis. After this they go to the third floor where the office is located. **Note!** Camping is allowed *only* from 8:00 a.m. Fri. to 8:00 a.m. Wed., with the other 2 days shut down, supposedly for regrowth. Camping is allowed for only 5 consecutive days in any one month, and don't forget a parking permit for your vehicle, which must remain within the locked park gates at night. *Aloooohaaa!*

County Parks

The city and county of Honolulu has opened 13 (changes periodically) of its 65 beach parks around the island to tent camping, and most allow trailers and RVs. These are the parks at which you're more likely to encounter hassles. A free permit is required, and camping is allowed for one week from Fri. at 8:00 a.m. until the following Wed. at 8:00 a.m., at which time your campsite must be vacated (no camping Wed. and Thurs. evenings). These campsites are also at a premium, but you can write for reservations and pick up your permits on arrival with proper identification. For information and reservations write or visit City and County of Honolulu, Dept. of Parks and Recreation, 650 S. King St., Honolulu, HI 96813, tel. 523-4525. Permits are also available from the satellite city halls around the island. **Note** that all of the beach parks are closed during designated months (they differ from park to park) throughout the year. This is supposedly for cleaning, but really it's to reduce the possibility of squatters moving in. Make sure, if you're reserving far in advance, that the park will be open when you arrive! Don't count on the Parks and Recreation Department informing you!

Camping Gear And Rentals

If you've come without camping gear and wish to purchase some try: **Big 88,** 330 Sand Island Access Road, tel. 845-1688; **The Bike Shop,** 1149 S. King St., tel. 531-7071; for rentals, **Omar the Tentman,** 1336 Dillingham Blvd., tel. 841-1057; and to rent an RV, **Beach Boy Campers,** 1720 Ala Moana, Suite B2-C, Honolulu, HI 96815, tel. 955-6381.

HIKING

The best way to leave the crowds of tourists behind and become intimate with the beauty of Oahu is to hike it. Although the Neighbor Islands receive fewer visitors, a higher percentage of people hike them than Oahu. Don't get the impression that you'll have the island to yourself, but you will be amazed at how open and lovely this crowded island can be. Some cultural and social hikes can be taken without leaving the city, like a stroll through Waikiki and a historical walking tour of downtown Honolulu and Chinatown. But others—some mere jaunts, others quite strenuous—are well worth the time and effort. Remember too that much of Oahu is privately owned, and you must have permission to cross this land, or you may be open to prosecution. Usually private property is marked by signs. Another source that might stomp your hiking plans with their jungle boots is the military. A full 25% of Oahu belongs to Uncle Sam, and he isn't always thrilled when you decide to play in his back yard. Some of the finest walks (like to the summit of Mt. Kaala) require crossing military lands, much of which has been altered by very unfriendly looking installations. Always check and obey any posted signs to avert trouble. The following listings are by no means all-inclusive, but should help you to choose a trail that seems interesting and is within your ability level.

Diamond Head

The most recognized symbol of Hawaii, this is the first place you should head for a strikingly beautiful panorama of Waikiki and greater Honolulu. Called *Leahi* by the Hawaiians, it was named Diamond Head after a group of wild-eyed English sailors espied what they thought to be diamonds glistening in the rocks. Hawaii had fulfilled so many other dreams, why not a mountain of diamonds?! Unfortunately, the glimmer was caused by worthless calcite crystals. No fortune was made, but the name stuck. See p. 263.

To get there, follow Kalakaua Avenue south from Waikiki until it leads onto Diamond Head Road, then quickly a sign points you to Diamond Head Crater. Pass through a tunnel and into the heavily militarized section in the center of the crater; the trail starts here. Although the hike is moderate, you should bring along water, flashlight (a must), and binoculars if you have them. Run by the Division of State Parks, the park is open daily from 6:00 a.m. to 6:00 p.m. A sign at the beginning describes the rigors you'll encounter, and informs that the trail is 7/10ths of a mile long and was built to the 760-foot summit of Leahi Point in 1908 to serve as a U.S. Coast Artillery Observation Station. It was heavily fortified during WW II, and part of the fun is exploring the old gun emplacements and tunnels built to link and service them.

Though only 10 min. from Waikiki, already wildflowers and chirping birds create a peaceful setting. When you come to a series of cement and stone steps, walk to a flat area to the left to find an old winch that hauled the heavy building materials to the top. Here's a wide panorama of the sea, and Koko Head, and notice too that atop every little hillock is an old gun emplacement. Next comes a short, but dark (flashlight!) tunnel and immediately a series of 99 steps. You can avoid the steps by taking the trail to the L, but the footing is slippery and there are no guard rails. Following the steps is a spiral staircase that leads down into a large gun emplacement, through which you walk and come to another tunnel. If you haven't brought a flashlight, give your eyes a few minutes to adjust; there's enough light to make it. Once on top, another stairway and a ladder take you to the very summit.

Judd Trail
This is an excellent trail to experience Oahu's "jungle" while visiting the historic and picturesque **Nuuanu Pali.** From Honolulu take H-1 and turn onto Rt. 61, the Pali Highway. Turn R onto the Old Pali Highway, then right again onto Nuuanu Pali Drive. Follow it for just under a mile to Reservoir No. 2 spillway. The trail begins on the ocean side of the spillway and leads through fragrant eucalyptus and a dense stand of picture-perfect Norfolk pines. It continues through the forest reserve and makes a loop back to the starting point. En route you pass **Jackass Ginger Pool.** In the immediate area are "mud slides," where you can take a ride on a makeshift toboggan of *pili* grass, *ti* leaves, or a piece of plastic, if you've brought one. This activity is rough on your clothes, and even rougher on your body. The wet conditions after a rain are perfect. Afterward, a dip in Jackass Pool cleans the mud and refreshes at the same time. Continue down the trail to observe wild ginger, guava, and *kukui,* but don't take any confusing side trails. If you get lost head back to the stream and follow it until it intersects the main trail.

Tantalus And Makiki Valley Trails
Great sightseeing and hiking can be combined when you climb the road atop Tantalus. A range of trails in this area offer magnificent views. A few roads lead up Tantalus, but a good one heads past Punchbowl along Puowaina Drive, just keep going until it turns into Tantalus Drive. The road switchbacks past some incredible homes and views until it reaches the 2,013-foot summit, where it changes its name to Round Top Drive, then heads down the other side.

The best place to start is at the top of Tantalus

The top of Diamond Head still looks like a military observation point, which it once was.

at the **Manoa Cliff Trailhead,** where a number of intersecting trails gives you a selection of adventure. Once on Round Top Drive, pass a brick wall with the name Kalaiopua Road imbedded in the stonework, and continue until you pass Forest Ridge Way, right after which is a large turn-out on both sides of the road near telephone pole no. 56. To the right is the beginning of ½-mile-long **Moleka Trail** which offers some excellent views and an opportunity to experience the trails in this area without an all-day commitment. The trails are excellently maintained, often by the local Sierra Club. Your greatest hazard here is mud, but in a moment you're in a lovely stand of bamboo, and in 10 minutes the foliage parts onto a lovely panorama of Makiki Valley and Honolulu in the background. These views are captivating, but remember to have "small eyes"—check out the varied colored mosses and fungi, and don't forget the flowers and fruit growing around you. A branch trail to the left leads to Round Top Drive, and if you continue the trail spits into 3: to the right is the **Makiki Valley Trail** that cuts across the valley starting at a Boy Scout Camp on Round Top Drive and ending atop Tantalus; **Ualakaa Trail** branches left and goes for another ½ mile connecting the Makiki Valley Trail with Puu Ualakaa State Park; straight ahead is the **Makiki Branch A Trail** which descends for ½ mile ending at the Division of Forestry Baseyard at the bottom of the valley.

On the mountainside of the Manoa Cliffs Trailhead is the **Connector Trail.** This pragmatic-sounding trail does indeed connect the lower trails with **Manoa Cliffs Trail,** skirting around the backside of Tantalus and intersecting the **Puu Ohia Trail,** which leads to the highest point on Tantalus and the expected magnificent view.

Maunawili Falls Trail

Maunawili Falls is on the other side of Nuuanu Pali, near Maunawili Town. This trail offers adventure into Oahu's jungle, with a rewarding pool and falls at the end. At the third red light as you head down the windward side of the Pali Highway, make a right onto Auloa Road. In a few hundred yards, take the left fork onto Maunawili Road and follow it toward the mountains through a residential area. Turn right onto Aloha Oe Drive, follow it to the end, and make a right on Maleko Road. Take this to the end of the cul-de-sac. To the right is a wooden fence and walkway. A sign says "Private," so don't trespass; instead go under the fence and start up what looks like a jeep trail, but soon becomes a walking path. In 400 yards, at 3 telephone poles, the trail splits into 3 branches. Go straight ahead downhill until you intersect a trail that leads right along the creek. This trail is very muddy, but worth it. Follow it for about 15 minutes until you come to Maunawili Falls—deep enough to dive in. You can also see an upper falls. Above them is an open field perfect for an overnight camp. To the left a path leads past a small banana plantation, along an irrigation ditch cut into the mountainside, paralleled by a wooden walkway. Very few people venture into this safe but fascinating area.

Sacred Falls

On coastal Rt. 83, between Hauula and Punaluu, an HVB Warrior points you to Sacred Falls. Make sure to stop at the **Sacred Falls Bazaar,** across the street from the locked fence that crosses the cane road and begins your hike. Note that you *cannot* drive to the falls. An old commercial venture put out this misinformation, which persists to this day. The walk is a hardy stroll, so you'll need jogging shoes, not thongs. The Sacred Falls Bazaar offers free advice, maps to the falls, and $.05 coffee. All are worth it! The area becomes a narrow canyon, and the sun sets early; don't start out past 3:00 p.m., especially if you want a dip in the stream. The trail was roughed up by Hurricane Iwa, and a sign along it says "Danger. Do not go past this point." Ignore it! The walking is a little more difficult but safe. The area's Hawaiian name was *Kaliuwaa* ("Canoe Leak") and although the original name isn't as romantic as the anglicized version, the entire area was indeed considered sacred. En route, you pass into a very narrow valley where the gods might show disfavor by dropping rocks onto your head. Notice many stones wrapped with a *ti* leaf. This is an appeasement to the gods, so they're not tempted to brain you. Go ahead, wrap a rock; no one will see you! You hear the falls dropping to the valley floor. Above you the walls are 1,600 feet high, but the falls drop only

After a hike into the interior, refresh yourself with a dip in the pool of Maunawiliu Falls.

90 feet or so. The pool below is ample for a swim, but the water is chilly and often murky. A number of beautiful picnic spots are on the large flat rocks.

North Oahu Treks

Some of the hiking in and around northwest Oahu is quite difficult. However, you should take a hike out to **Kaena Point.** You have 2 choices: you can park your car at the end of the road past Dillingham Airfield on the north coast and hike in; or you can park your car at the end of the road past Makua on the Waianae Coast and hike in. Both are about the same distance, and both are hardy but not difficult. The attraction of Kaena Point is huge surf, sometimes 30 feet high. The trail is only 2 miles, from each end, and few people come here except some local fishermen.

Peacock Flat is a good family-style trail that offers primitive camping. Follow Rt. 93 toward Dillingham Airfield and just before getting there turn left onto a dirt road leading toward the Kawaihapi Reservoir. If you want to camp, you need permits from the Division of Forestry and a waiver from the Mokuleia Ranch, tel. 637-4241, which you can get at their office, located at the end of a dirt road just before the one leading to Kawaihapi Reservoir. They also provide instructions and a key to get through 2 locked gates before reaching the trailhead, if you decide to go in from that end. Heading through the Mokuleia Forest Reserve, you can camp anywhere along the trail, or at an established but primitive campground in Peacock Flats. This area is heavily used by hunters, mostly after wild pig.

Dupont Trail takes you to the summit of Mt. Kaala, highest point and by far the most difficult hike on the island. The last mile is downright dangerous, and has you hanging on cliff edges, with the bottom 2,000 feet below! This is not for the average hiker. Follow Rt. 930 to Waialua, make a left at Waialua High School onto a cane road, and follow it to the second gate, about 1½ miles. Park there. You need a hiking permit from the Division of Forestry and a waiver from the Waialua Sugar Company. Atop Kaala, although the views are magnificent, you'll also find a mushroom field of FAA satellite stations.

Hiking Groups And Information

The following organizations can provide information on wildlife, conservation and organized hiking trips. **Hawaiian Trail and Mountain Club,** Box 2238, Honolulu 96804, meets behind Iolani Palace on Saturdays at 10:00 a.m., and Sundays at 8:00 a.m. Their hikes are announced in the *Honolulu Star Bulletin's* "Pulse of Paradise" column. **Hawaii Audubon Society** can be reached at Box 22832, Honolulu 96822. **Sierra Club,** 1212 University Ave., Honolulu 96826, tel. 946-8494, can provide you with a packet describing Hawaii's trails, charted by island, along with their physical characteristics and information on attaining maps and permits. The packet costs $3, postage paid. Write the Division of Forestry, 1151 Punchbowl St., Room 325, Honolulu, HI 96813, tel. 548-2861, and ask for a copy of their *Island of Oahu Recreation Map.* It gives good information on hiking, camping, and hunting with a description of most trails.

SPORTS

If it can be ridden, sailed, glided, flown, bounced, smashed with a racquet, struck with a club, bat, or foot, or hooked with the right bait, you'll find it on Oahu. And lots of it! The pursuit of fun is serious business here, and you can find anything, sportswise, that you ever dreamed of doing.

Snorkel And Scuba

Oahu has particularly generous underwater vistas open to anyone donning a mask and fins. Plenty of spots provide thrills for the beginning snorkeler or diver, while others are only for the experienced diver. Particular spots are listed under "Beaches and Parks" in the travel sections, but some well-known favorites are Hanauma Bay, Black Point off Diamond Head, the waters around Rabbit Island, and some sunken ships and planes just off the Waianae Coast. The following are outfits where you can rent equipment and/or take excursions or certification lessons. Do yourself a favor and wash all the sand off rented equipment. Most shops irritatingly penalize you $1 if you don't. All want a deposit, usually $30, that they put on a credit card slip and tear up when you return. Underwater camera rentals are now normal at most shops, and go for around $10-$12 including film (24 shots), but not developing. Happy diving!

360° Hawaii in the King's Village Mall, Waikiki, 2nd floor, tel. 926-1747, is a surf and sportswear shop that rents snorkeling equipment at moderate prices, with a discount for couples. They let you pick up equipment the night before at no extra charge so you can get an early start and your money's worth. **Surf and Sea,** tel. 637-9887, is a complete dive shop on the North Shore in Haleiwa where you can rent surfboards, boogie boards, sailboards, and just about anything for water sports. They're located along the highway, just past the Union 76 gas station, on the ohter side of the bridge. Here, you can rent anything else you may need.

The following full-service dive shops charge around $40 for an introductory dive, $40 for a one-tank boat dive, and around $150 for a 3-day certification course. Dive shops with a good reputation include: **Waikiki Diving,** 420 Nahua Ave., Waikiki, tel. 922-7178; **Blue Water Snorkel,** tel. 926-4485; **Steve's Diving Adventures,** 1860 Ala Moana Blvd., tel. 947-8900; **South Sea Aquatics,** 1050 Ala Moana Blvd; tel. 538-3854; **Hawaiian Divers,** 2344 Kam Hwy., tel. 845-6644.

Times change but the sea and surfing remain constant at Waikiki. (Fritz Kraft, c. 1930)

Hanauma Bay is a wonderful place to begin snorkeling, but it's very crowded. A number of outfits sponsor snorkel excursions to this underwater park. This is one of those times where you might consider going with a tour, and not on your own—it's cheap, and you don't have to worry about parking. A tour shouldn't cost any more than $8, and sometimes as little as $5 for a half day, including hotel pick-up and return, all snorkeling equipment, a beach mat, fish food, corrective lenses, vests, sometimes a complimentary soft drink, and free use of an underwater camera. Naturally, you're stuffed on a bus, and a normal tour lasts about 3 hours. If you go early in the morning, usually around 7:00 a.m., the bay will be much less crowded, and you can even save a few more dollars. The free tourist literature often has coupons that reduce these prices further! Hanauma Bay snorkeling tours include: **Pacific Interlude,** tel. 848-0949; **Hawaii Snorkeling,** tel. 944-2846; **Budget Snorkel,** tel. 947-2447; **Seashore Snorkeling,** tel. 395-8947.

Surfing

A local Waikiki beachboy by the name of Duke Kahanamoku won a treasure box full of gold medals for swimming at the Olympic games of 1912, and thereafter became a celebrity who toured the Mainland and introduced surfing to the modern world. Duke is the father of modern surfing, and Waikiki is its birthplace. All the Hawaiian Islands have incredibly good surfing conditions, but Oahu is best. Conditions here are perfect for rank beginners up to the best in the world. Waikiki's surf is predictable, and just right to start on, while the **Banzai Pipeline** and Waimea Bay on the North Shore have some of the most formidable surfing conditions on Earth. Makaha Beach in Waianae is perhaps the best all-around surfing beach, frequented by living legends in this most graceful sport. If there is such a thing as "the perfect wave," Oahu's waters are a good place to look for it. Summertime brings rather flat action all around the island, but the winter months are a totally different story, with monster waves on the North Shore, and heavy surf, at times even in the relative calm of Waikiki. *Never* surf without asking about local conditions, and remember that "a fool and his surfboard, and maybe his life, are soon parted." See p. 224 for local and international surfing competitions in Oahu.

Pick a board, any board, at Waikiki.

Lessons? A number of enterprises in Waikiki offer beach services. Often these concessions are affiliated with hotels, and almost all hotel activities desks can arrange surfing lessons for you. An instructor and board go for about $10-$12 per hour. A board alone is half the price, but as in skiing, a few good lessons to start you off are well worth the time and money. Some reputable **surfing lessons** along Waikiki are provided by: Outrigger Hotel, 2335 Kalakaua Ave. tel. 923-0711; Hilton Hawaiian Village, 2005 Kalia Rd., tel. 949-4321; Halekulani Hotel, 2199 Kalia Rd., tel. 923-2311; Big Al Surfing School, 2210 Kalia Rd., tel. 923-4375; and check near the huge rack of surfboards along Kalakaua Ave., just near Kuhio Beach at the Waikiki Beach Center, where you'll find a number of beachboy enterprises at competitive rates. Fort DeRussy Beach Services, tel. 941-7004, is another good one, and in Haleiwa on the North Shore, try Surf and Sea, tel. 637-9887.

Other Water Sports

The fastest growing water sport, both in Hawaii and around the world, is **sailboarding**. Kailua Bay has perfect conditions for this sport, and you can go there any day to see sailboarders skimming the waves with their multihued sails displayed like proud peacocks. Sailboard rental, lessons, and transportation cost about $40 per day. Some established companies include: **Kailua Sailboard Co.**, tel. 262-2555; **Aloha Windsurfing**, tel. 926-1185, out of Waikiki; and **Northshore Windsurfing**, tel. 637-9887.

Those into **jet skiing** might try **Offshore Sports Hawaii**, tel. 395-3434, at the Koko Marina Shopping Center, near Hanauma Bay. If you like waterskiing, **Suyderhoud's Water Ski Center**, tel. 395-3777, also at the Koko Marina Shopping center, can provide all your equipment, rentals, and lessons.

Which way to the beach?

Hang Gliding And Parasailing

For a once-in-a-lifetime treat try **Aloha Parasail**, tel. 521-2446. Strapped into a harness complete with lifejacket, you're towed aloft to glide effortlessly over the water. Aloha Parasail has free hotel pickup.

For those with a very adventurous spirit and a lot of guts, **Tradewinds Hang Gliding**, tel. 396-8557, provides quality instruction in the guaranteed thrill of hang gliding. Beginning lessons on easy slopes $40, advanced with instructor $75. Happy landings!

Horseback Riding

A different and delightful way to see Oahu is from the back of a horse. A few outfits operating trail rides on different parts of the island include: **Gunstock's Ranch**, tel. 488-1593, offering rides over the ranch grounds on the North Shore; **Kualoa Ranch**, tel. 531-8531, by reservation only, on north windward Oahu; **Turtle Bay Hilton**, tel. 293-8693, on the North Shore, non-guests welcome; **Koko Crater Stables**, tel. 395-2682, with rides into Koko Head crater.

Golf

With 24 private, public, and military golf courses scattered around such a relatively small island, it's a wonder that it doesn't rain golf balls. At present 15 links are open to the public, ranging from modest 9-holers to world-class courses, whose tournaments attract the biggest names in golfing today. Prices range from a donation-like $2 to $40 or more. Legendary courses like the super-exclusive **Waialae Country Club** charge upwards of $20,000 membership fees, and have a reputation for such magnificently smooth greens that some of the snobbier members would rather stroke them than the mink upholstery in their Rolls-Royces. An added attraction of playing Oahu's courses is that you get to walk around on some of the most spectacular and manicured pieces of real estate on the island. Some afford sweeping views of the coast like the **Hawaii Kai Championship Course,** while others like the **Pali Golf Course** have a lovely mountain backdrop, or, like Waikiki's **Ala Wai Golf Course,** are set virtually in the center of all the downtown action.

The **Hawaiian Open Invitational Golf Tournament** held in late January or February at the Waialale Country Club brings the world's best golfers. Prize money is close to $1 million, and all 3 major TV networks cover the event. This is usually the only opportunity the average person gets to set foot on this course. Military personnel, or those with military privileges, are welcome to golf at a number of courses operated by all 4 branches of the service. Calling the respective bases provides all necessary information. Those that can't find their way to the links on their own might enjoy the services of **Alii Golf**, tel. 735-0060, or **Kato's Golf Tours,** tel. 947-3010; both take you to a number of island courses and provide carts, green fees, clubs, shoes, and RT transportation as part of their services. For the rest, the following chart should help you tee off.

GOLF COURSES OF OAHU

Course	Par	Yards	Fees Weekday	Weekend	Cart
Kahuku Golf Course ★ ■ P.O. Box 143, Kahuku, HI 96731 tel. 293-5842	35	2699	$1.50	$2.00	
Turtle Bay Hilton and Country Club P.O. Box 187, Kahuku, HI 96731 tel. 293-8811	72	6366	$17.50		$9.50
Bay View Golf Center 45-285 Kaneohe Bay Dr. Kaneohe, HI 96744 tel. 247-0451	54	2231	$5.00	$6.50	$1.00
Pali Golf Course 45-050 Kamehameha Hwy. Kaneohe, HI 96744 tel. 261-9784	72	6493	$3.00	$6.00	$10.40
Olomana Golf Links 41-1801 Kalanianaole Hwy. Waimanalo, HI 96795 tel. 259-7926	72	6449	$8.50	$12.00	$6.00
Hawaii Kai Championshop Golf Course 8902 Kalanianaole Hwy. Honolulu, HI 96825 tel. 395-2358	72	6350	$25.00	$28.00	Incl.
Hawaii Kai Executive Golf Course 8902 Kalanianaole Hwy. Honolulu, HI 96825 tel. 395-2358	55	2433	$7.75	$9.25	$10.00
Waialae Country Club ■ ● 4997 Kahala Ave. Honolulu, HI 96816 tel. 732-1457	72	6906	$20.00		$6.00
Ala Wai Golf Course 404 Kapahulu Ave. HI 96815 tel. 732-7741	71	6111	$8.00	$12.00	$10.40
Moanalua Golf Club ★ 1250 Ala Aolani St. Honolulu HI 96819 tel. 839-2411	36	3042	$7.00	$10.00	$9.00
Pearl Country Club 98-535 Kanonohi St. Aiea, HI 96701 tel. 487-2460	71	6491	$13.00	$18.00	$8.00
Hawaii County Club Kunia Rd. Kunia, HI 96759 tel. 621-5654	71	5664	$7.00	$7.00	$7.00
Sheraton Makaha Resort and Country Club P.O. Box 896 Makaha Valley Rd. Waianae, HI 96792 tel. 695-9544	72	6400	$40.00		$9.50
Makaha Valley Country Club 84-627 Makaha Valley Rd. Waianae, HI 96792 tel. 695-9578	71	6251	$8.00	$13.00	$8.00

N.B. ★ *= 9 hole course* ■ *= no club rentals* ● *= guests only*

TENNIS COURTS OF OAHU

COUNTY COURTS

Under the jurisdiction of the Dept. of Parks & Recreation, 3908 Paki Ave., Honolulu, HI 96815. Tel. 923-7927. Courts listed are in Waikiki and main towns only. There are approximately 30 additional courts around the island.

Location	Name of Court	No. of Courts	Lighted
Aiea	Aiea Recreation Center	2	Yes
Ewa	Ewa Beach Community Park	4	Yes
Kahala	Kahala Recreation Center	2	No
Kailua	Kailua Recreation Center	8	Yes
Kaimuki	Kaimuki Recreation Center	2	Yes
Kalakaua	Kalakaua Recreation Center	4	Yes
Kaneohe	Kaneohe District Park	6	No
Keehi	Keehi Lagoon Courts	12	No
Koko Head	Koko Head District Park	6	Yes
Maunawili	Maunawili Park	2	Yes
Pearl City	Pearl City Recreation Center	2	Yes
Sunset Beach	Sunset Beach Neighborhood Park	2	Yes
Wahiawa	Wahiawa Recreation Center	4	Yes
Waialua	Waialua Recreation Center	4	Yes
Waianae	Waianae District Park	8	Yes
Waikiki	Ala Moana Park	10	Yes
Waikiki	Diamond Head Tennis Center	7	No
Waikiki	Kapiolani Tennis Courts	4	Yes
Waimanalo	Waimanalo District Park	4	No
Waipahu	Waipahu Recreation Center	4	Yes

HOTEL AND PRIVATE COURTS THAT ARE OPEN TO THE PUBLIC

Honolulu	Hawaiian Regent Hotel (fee)	1	No
Honolulu	Ilikai Hotel, The Westin (fee)	7	Yes
Honolulu	King Street Courts (fee)	4	Yes
Honolulu	Waikiki Malia Hotel (fee for non-guests)	1	No
Kailua	Windward Tennis Club (fee)	5	Yes
Waianae	Makaha Resort (fee)	4	Yes

Tennis

Grease up the old elbow because over 168 county-maintained tennis courts are on Oahu. Also, plenty of hotel and private courts are open to the public for a fee, though a few hotels limit play to guests only. You can get a complete list of the county-maintained courts by writing a letter of inquiry and enclosing a SASE to the Dept. of Parks and Recreation, Tennis Division, 3908 Paki Ave., Honolulu, HI 96815, tel. 923-7927. The preceding chart is a partial list of what's available.

Deep Sea Fishing

Oahu's offshore waters are alive with game fish. Among these underwater fighters are marlin, *ahi, ono, mahi mahi,* and an occasional deepwater snapper. The deep-sea boats generally troll the Penguin Banks of the island, and along the generally calm waters of the Waianae Coast, from Barber's to Kaena Point. Rates depend on the size of the boat, but an average 6-passenger boat on a private basis costs about $400. Most anglers opt to share the boat and split costs with others in the party. Expect to spend about $80 for a full day (7:00 a.m. to 4:00 p.m.) and $60 for a half day. All bait and tackle are provided, but you must bring your own lunch. The vast majority of Oahu's fleet moors in **Kewalo Basin,** in Honolulu Harbor along Ala Moana Boulevard next to Fishermen's Wharf. The boat harbor is a sight in itself, and if you're contemplating a fishing trip, it's best to head down there the day before and have a yarn with the captains and returning fishermen. This way you can get a feel for a charter to suit you best. Charter organizations include: **Island Charters,** tel. 536-1555; **Happy Time Charters,** tel. 329-9530; **Sport Fishing Hawaii,** tel. 536-6577, with the largest fleet of all. Many private boats operating out of Kewalo Basin include: *Tina Rei,* tel. 536-5018; *Alii Kai,* tel. 521-3969; *Kahuna Kai,* tel. 524-8142.

A few boats operate out of **Pokai Bay,** in Waianae on the northern leeward coast. One of the best is the *Kamalii Kai Too,* operated by Capt. Jim Hilton, tel. 696-7264. A few boats are even berthed in Haleiwa on the North Shore. One with an excellent reputation is the *Haole Queen,* tel. 637-5189, skippered by Lester Walls. Another good boat is the *Stacy-K,* with Capt. Bill Mattox, tel. 637-7060.

Thrownetting came to Hawaii with Oriental plantation workers and has become a favorite method of fishing.

Freshwater Fishing

The state of Hawaii maintains 2 public freshwater fishing areas on the island. The **Wahiawa Public Fishing Area** is 300 acres of fishable waters in and around the town of Wahiawa. It's basically an irrigation reservoir used to hold water for cane fields. Species regularly caught here are large and smallmouth bass, sunfish, channel catfish, *tucunare,* oscar, carp, snakehead, and Chinese catfish. The other area is the **Nuuanu Reservoir no. 4,** a 25-acre restricted watershed above Honolulu in the Koolau Mountains. It's open for fishing only 3 times per year in May, August, and November. Fish caught here are *tilapia* and Chinese catfish. See p. 178-179 for full information, or write Division of Aquatic Resouces, Dept. of Land and Natural Resources, 1151 Punchbowl St., Honolulu, HI 96813.

Hunting

Who would think that you can find any **wild game** on Oahu, not counting the 2-legged variety. Mostly in the island's tough interior mountains are feral pigs and goats, 2 species of pheasants and doves, Erkel's francolin, and Japanese quail. You can hunt on 14 areas with anything from spears to high-powered rifles. At this time no guide services are available on the island. See p. 179-180 for information on licenses and regulations, or write Division of Forestry and Wildlife, 1151 Punchbowl St., Honolulu, HI 96813, tel. 548-2861.

Spectator Sports

Oahu is home to a number of major sporting events throughout the year. Many are "invitationals" that bring the cream of the crop from both collegiate and professional levels (see p. 106-113). Here are the major sports happenings on the island.

Football is big in Hawaii. The University of Hawaii's Rainbows play during the normal collegiate season at Aloha Stadium near Pearl Harbor. In early January, the **Hula Bowl** brings together 2 all-star teams from the nation's collegiate ranks. You can hear the pads crack in February, when the NFL sends its best players to the **Pro Bowl**.

Basketball is also big on Oahu. The University of Hawaii's Rainbow Warriors play at the **Neal S. Blaisdell Center**, in Honolulu at 777 Ward Street. Mid-April sees some of the nation's best collegiate hoopballers make up for teams to compete in the **Aloha Basketball Classic**.

You can watch the Islanders of the Pacific Coast League play **baseball** during the regular season at Aloha Stadium. Baseball goes back well over 100 years in Hawaii, and the Islanders receive extraordinary fan support.

Watersport festivals include surfing events, usually from November through February. The best-known are: the **Hawaiian Pro Surfing Championships; the Duke Kahanamoku Classic; Buffalo's Big Board Classic**; and the **Haleiwa Sea Spree**, featuring many ancient Hawaiian sports. You can watch some of the Pacific's most magnificent yachts sail into the **Ala Wai Yacht Basin** in mid-July, completing their run from Los Angeles in the annual **Trans Pacific Yacht Race**.

PRACTICAL INFORMATION

Emergency And Health

Police, fire, and ambulance can be summoned from anywhere on Oahu by calling **911**. Reach the **Coast Guard** for search and rescue at tel. 536-4336 and the **Life Guard Service** at tel. 922-3888.

Full-service hospitals include: **Queen's Hospital**, 1301 Punchbowl St., Honolulu, tel. 538-9011; **Kaiser Foundation**, 1697 Ala Moana Blvd., Honolulu, tel. 949-5811.

Medical services and clinics include: **Doctors Emergency and Medical Services**, 1860 Ala Moana Blvd., tel. 943-1111, for emergencies and "house calls" to your hotel, 24 hours a day; **Medi-Mart**, Waikiki, Royal Hawaiian Shopping Center, Bldg. A, Room 401, tel. 922-2335, 9:00 a.m. to 6:00 p.m.; **Waikiki Health Center**, 277 Ohua Ave., tel. 922-4787, for low-cost care including pregnancy and confidential VD testing, open 9:00 a.m to 8:00 p.m. Mon. to Thurs., until 4:30 p.m. Fri., until 2:00 p.m. Saturday. For dental referral call **Dentist Information Bureau** at tel. 536-2135, 24-hour service. You can get a free **blood pressure** check at the fire station in Waikiki, corner of Paki and Kapahulu streets, daily 9:00 a.m. to 5:00 p.m.

Pharmacies around the island include: **Outrigger Pharmacy**, in Waikiki Outrigger Hotel, 2335 Kalakaua Ave, tel. 923-2529; **Longs Drugs**, in Honolulu at the Ala Moana Shopping Ctr., tel. 941-4433, and at the Kaneohe Shopping Center, tel. 235-4511; **Pay 'n Save** at 86-120 Farrington Hwy., Waianae, tel. 696-6387.

For **alternative health care** try: **Accupuncture Clinic**, Waikiki Medical Bldg., 305 Royal Hawaiian Ave. Rm. 208, tel. 923-6939, open Mon. to Fri. 9:00 a.m. to 4:00 p.m.; **Honolulu School of Massage**, 1750 Kalakaua Ave., tel. 942-8552, open 10:00 a.m. to 6:00 p.m., with some later hours; **Colon Therapy of Hawaii**, 122 Oneawa St. Kailua, tel. 261-4511, detoxification and massage administered by Alcyone.

Chiropractic care: Chiropractic Referral Service, 700 Bishop St., tel. 521-5784. Free information and referral to qualified chiropractors; **Chiropractic Dial-a-Tape**, taped messages for what ails you by calling tel. 737-1111; on the leeward side **Dr. Tom Smith**, 1222 Oneawa St., Kailua, tel. 261-4511, limited hours.

Visitor Information

The **Hawaii Visitors Bureau** main office is at 2270 Kalakaua Ave., Honolulu, HI 96815, tel. 923-1811. They also operate a number of information kiosks at the airport. The **Japanese Chamber of Commerce**, with special information on things Japanese is at tel. 949-5531; the **Chinese Chamber of Commerce**, offering information and tours on Chinatown, is at tel. 533-3181. **State Foundation on Culture and Arts,** 335 Merchant St. Rm 202, tel. 548-4657, dispenses information on what's happening culturally on Oahu. For general information, or if you have a hassle, try **Office of Information and Complaints,** tel. 523-4385, or 523-4381.

Reading Material

Besides a number of special-interest Chinese, Japanese, Korean, Filipino, and military newspapers, 2 major dailies are published on Oahu. The *Honolulu Advertiser,* tel. 525-8000, is the morning paper, and the *Honolulu Star Bulletin,* tel. 525-8000, is the evening paper. They combine to make a Sunday paper. A money-saving paper is the *Pennysaver,* tel. 521-9886, featuring classified ads on just about anything. Call for distribution points.

Don't miss out on the **free tourist literature** available at all major hotels, shopping malls, the airport, and stands along Waikiki's streets. They all contain up-to-the-minute information on what's happening, and a treasure trove of free or reduced-price coupons for various attractions and services. Always featured are events, shopping tips, dining and entertainment, and sightseeing. The main ones are: *This Week Oahu,* the best and most complete; *On the Go, Hawaii,* general information about the island attractions; *Waikiki, On the Go,* focusing mostly on Waikiki; *Spotlight Hawaii,* with good sections on dining and sightseeing. Two free tabloids, *Waikiki Beach Press* and *Island News,* offer entertainment calendars and feature stories of general interest to visitors. *Oahu Drive Guide,* handed out by all the major car rental agencies, has some excellent tips and orientation maps. Especially useful to get you started from the airport. For **bookstores,** see p. 200.

Post Offices And Libraries

Many small post offices are found in various towns around the island. The main P.O. in downtown Honolulu is at 3600 Aolele St., tel. 422-0770; in Waikiki at 330 Saratoga Rd., tel. 941-1062; in Kailua at 335 Hahani, tel. 262-7205; in Waianae at 86-015 Farrington Hwy., tel. 696-40323; in Haleiwa at 66-437 Kam Hwy., tel. 637-5755; in Wahiawa at 115 Lehua, tel. 621-8496.

Oahu's **libraries** include: Hawaii State Library, in Honolulu at 478 S. King St., tel. 548-4775; Kailua Library, 239 Kuulei Rd., tel. 261-4611; Library for the Blind and Physically Handicapped, 402 Kapahulu Ave., tel. 732-7767; Waikiki branch next door, at 400 Kapahulu, tel. 732-2777.

Weather And Surf Conditions

For a weather report call 836-0234; for surfing conditions, tel. 836-1952; for Hawaiian waters report, tel. 836-3921.

Helpful Numbers

Arizona Memorial, tel. 922-1626; **babysitting services,** tel. 923-8337, in Waikiki at 922-5575; **Bishop Museum,** tel. 922-1626; **Council of Churches,** tel. 521-2666; **Dept. of Agriculture,** plants, produce, regulations, etc., tel. 836-1415; **directory assistance,** tel. 1-411; Honolulu Harbor, daily ship arrival recording, tel. 537-9260; **Honolulu International Airport,** tel. 836-1411/6431; **Time,** tel. 983-3211; **Whale watch,** tel. 922-1626.

HONOLULU

Honolulu is *the* most exotic city in America. It's not any one attribute that makes this so, it's a combination of things. Honolulu's like an ancient Hawaiian goddess who can change her form at will. At one moment you see a black-eyed beauty, swaying provocatively to a deep and basic rhythm, and in the next a high-tech scion of the computer age sitting straight-backed behind a polished desk. The city is the terminus of "manifest destiny," the end of America's relentless westward drive, until no more horizons were left. Other Mainland cities are undoubtedly more historic, cultural, and perhaps, to some, more beautiful than Honolulu, but none come close to having all of these features in the same overwhelming combination. The city's face, though blemished by high-rises and pocked by heavy industry, is eternally lovely. The Koolau Mountains form the background tapestry from which the city emerges; the surf gently foams along Waikiki; the sun hisses fire-red as it drops into the sea; and Diamond Head beckons with a promise of tropical romance.

In the center of the city, skyscrapers rise as silent, unshakable witnesses to Honolulu's economic strength. In glass and steel offices, businessmen wearing conservative three-piece uniforms are clones of any found on Wall Street. Below, a fantasia of people live and work. In nooks and crannies are an amazing array of arts, shops, and cuisines. In a flash of festival the streets become China, Japan, Portugal, New England, old Hawaii, or the Philippines.

New England churches, royal palaces, bandstands, tall-masted ships, and coronation platforms illustrate Honolulu's history. And what a history! You can visit places where in a mere twinkle of time past, red-plumed warriors were driven to their death over an impossibly steep *pali,* where the skies were alive with screaming Zeros strafing and bombing the only American city threatened by a foreign power since the War of 1812. In hallowed grounds throughout the city lie the bodies of fallen warriors. Some are in a mangled steel sepulcher below the waves, others from 3 wars in a natural bowl of bereavement and silence. And a nearby royal mausoleum holds the remains of those that were "old Hawaii."

Honolulu is the pumping heart of Hawaii. The state government and university are here. So are botanical parks, a fine aquarium and zoo, a floating maritime museum and the world's foremost museum on Polynesia. Art flourishes like flowers, as do professional and amateur entertainment, extravaganzas, and local and world-class sporting events. But the city isn't all good clean fun. The seedier side includes "girlie" shows, raucous G.I. bars, street drugs, and street people. But, somehow this blending and collision of East and West, this hodgepodge of emotionally charged history, this American city superimposed on a unique Pacific setting works well as Honolulu, the "Sheltered Harbor" of man and his dreams.

SIGHTS

The best way to see Honolulu is to start from the middle and fan out on foot for the inner city. You can *do* downtown in one day, but the sights of greater Honolulu require a few days to see them all. It's a matter of opinion where the center of downtown Honolulu actually is, but the King Kamehameha Statue in front of Aliiolani Hale is about as central as you can get, and a perfect landmark from which to start. If you're staying in Waikiki, leave your rental car in the hotel garage and take TheBus (no. 2) for downtown sightseeing. If you can't bear to leave your car behind, head for Aloha Tower. The traffic is not as congested, and a large parking lot close by is open 24 hours, at $.30 per hour, with a 4-hour maximum on the meter. For various sights outside the downtown area, your rental car is fine. A shuttle to the Bishop Museum from Waikiki is free, and some shuttles running out to the Arizona Memorial are more expensive than TheBus ($.60), but so convenient that they're worth the extra few coins.

DOWNTOWN HONOLULU

The **Statue of King Kamehameha** is at the junction of King and Mililani streets. Running off at an angle is **Merchant Street,** the oldest thoroughfare in Honolulu, and you might say "the beginning of the road to modernity." The statue is much more symbolic of Kamehameha's strength as a ruler and unifier of the Hawaiian Islands than as a replica of the man himself. Of the few drawings of Kamehameha that have been preserved, none is necessarily a good likeness. Kamehameha was a magnificent leader and statesman, but by all accounts not very good looking. This statue is one of three. The original, lost at sea near the Falkland Islands en route from Paris where it was bronzed, was later recovered, but not before insurance money was used to cast this second one that stands in Honolulu. The original is in the town of Kapaau, in the Kohala District of the Big Island, not far from where Kamehameha was born (see p. 649), but although they supposedly came from the same mold, they somehow seem quite different. The third stands in Washington, D.C., dedicated when Hawaii became a state. The Honolulu statue was dedicated in 1883, as part of King David Kalakaua's coronation ceremony. Its black and gold colors are striking, but it is most magnificent on June 11, King Kamehameha Day, when 18-foot *lei* are draped around the neck and the outstretched arms.

Behind Kamehameha stands **Aliiolani Hale,** now the State Judiciary Building. This handsome structure, designed by an Australian architect and begun in 1872, was originally commissioned by Kamehameha V as a palace, but

was redesigned as a general court building. It looks much more grand than Iolani Palace across the way. Kamehameha V died before it was finished, and it was officially dedicated by King Kalakaua in 1874. Less than 20 years later, on January 17, 1893, at this "hall of justice," the first proclamation by the Members of the Committee of Safety was read, stating that the sovereign nation of Hawaii was no more, and that the islands would be ruled by a Provisional Government.

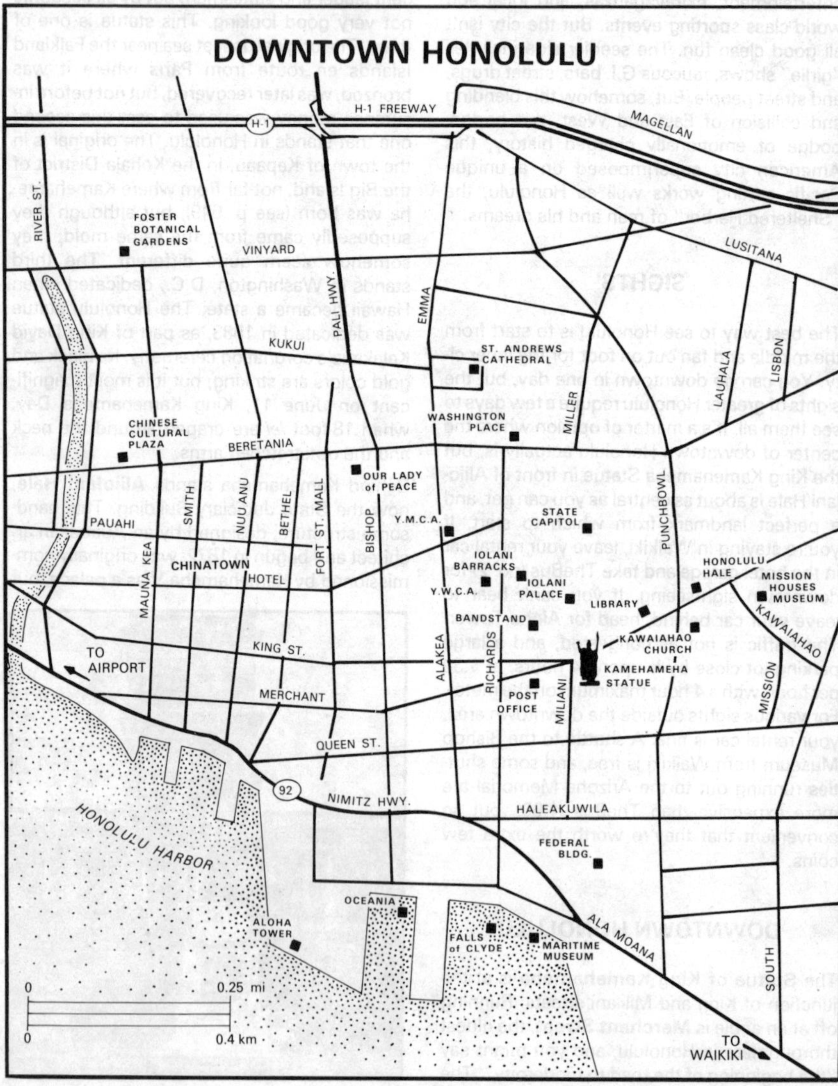

Iolani Palace, the only royal residence in America

Iolani Palace

As you enter the park-like palace grounds, notice the Emblem of Hawaii in the center of the large iron gates. They're often draped with simple *lei* of fragrant *maile.* The quiet grounds are a favorite strolling and relaxing place for many government workers, especially in the shade of a huge banyan, purportedly planted by Kalakaua's wife, Kapiolani. The building, with its glass and iron-work imported from San Francisco, and its Corinthian columns, is the only royal palace in America. Iolani ("Royal Hawk") Palace, begun in 1879 under orders of King Kalakaua, was completed in December 1882 for a cost of $350,000. It was the first electrified building in Honolulu, and had a direct phone line to the Royal Boat House. Non-Hawaiian island residents of the day thought it a frivolous waste of money, but here poignant scenes and profound changes rocked the Hawaiian islands. After 9 years as king, Kalakaua built a **Coronation Stand** that temporarily sat in front of the palace, (now off to the left). In a belated ceremony, Kalakaua raised a crown to his head and placed one on his queen, Kapiolani. During the ceremony, 8,000 Hawaiians cheered, while Honolulu's foreign, tax-paying businessmen boycotted. On August 12, 1898, after only 2 Hawaiian monarchs, Kalakaua and Liliuokalani (his sister), had resided in the palace, the American flag was raised up the flagpole following a successful coup that marked Hawaii's official recognition by the U.S. as a territory. During this ceremony, royal Hawaiian subjects wept bitter tears, while the businessmen of Honolulu cheered wildly.

Kalakaua, later in his rule, was forced to sign a new constitution that greatly reduced his own power to little more than figurehead status. He traveled to San Francisco in 1891, where he died. His body was returned to Honolulu and lay in state in the palace. His sister, Liliuokalani, succeeded him; attempted to change this constitution and gain the old power of Hawaii's sovereigns, the businessmen revolted and the monarchy fell. Iolani Palace then became the main executive building for the Provisional Government, with the House of Representatives meeting in the throne room and the Senate in the dining room. It served in this capacity until 1968. Iolani Palace is open to **guided tours only,** Wed to Sat. 9:00 a.m. to 2:15 p.m.; one hour; $4 adults, $1 children, with no children under 5 admitted. They're popular so make reservations at least a day in advance. Tickets are sold at a window at the Barracks, open Tues. to Sat. 8:30 a.m. to 2:15 p.m. For information and reservations tel. 536-6185.

Palace Grounds

Kalakaua, known as the "Merry Monarch," was credited with saving the *hula.* He also hired Henri Burger, first Royal Hawaiian Bandmaster, and together they wrote *Hawaii Pono,*

Concerts are still given at Kalakaua's royal bandstand.

the state anthem. Many concerts were given from the Coronation Stand, which became known as the **Royal Bandstand.** Behind it is **Iolani Barracks** (Hale Koa), built in 1870 to house the **Royal Household Guards.** When the monarchy of Hawaii fell to Provisional Government forces in 1893, only *one* of these soldiers was wounded in a pathetic show of strength. The Barracks were moved to the present site from nearby land on which the State Capitol was erected. To the right behind the palace are the **State Archives.** This modern building, dating from 1953, holds records, documents, and vintage photos. A treasure trove to scholars, and those tracing their genealogy, and is worth a visit by the general public to view the old photos on display. Free, open Mon. to Fri. 7:45 a.m. to 4:30 p.m. Next door is the **Hawaii State Library,** housing the main branch of this statewide system. As in all Hawaii state libraries, you are entitled to a card on your first visit, and are then eligible to take out books. The central courtyard is a favorite lunch spot for many of the government workers. Some of the original money to build the library was put up by Andrew Carnegie. For information call tel. 548-4775.

Government Buildings

Liliuokalani was deposed and placed under house arrest in the palace for 9 months. Later, after much intrigue that included a visit to Washington, D.C., to plead her case and an aborted counter-revolution, she sadly accepted her fate and moved to nearby **Washington Place.** This solid-looking structure fronts Beretania Street and was originally the home of sea captain John Dominis. It was inherited by his son John Owen Dominis, who married a lovely young Hawaiian aristocrat, Lydia Kapaakea, who became Queen Liliuokalani. She lived in her husband's home, proud but powerless, until her death in 1917. Washington Place is now the official residence of the governor of Hawaii.

To the left of Washington Place is **St. Andrew's Cathedral.** Built in 1867 as an Anglican church, many of its stones and ornaments were shipped from England; Hawaii's monarchs worshipped here, and the church is still very much in use. To the right is the **War Memorial.** Erected in 1974, it replaced an older memorial to the people who perished in WW II. A courtyard and benches are provided for quiet meditation.

Directly in front is the magnificent **Hawaii State Capitol,** built in 1969 for $25 million. The building itself is a metaphor for Hawaii: the pillars surrounding it are palms, the reflecting pool is the sea, and the cone-shaped rooms of the legislature represent the volcanoes of Hawaii. It's lined with rich *koa* from the Big Island, and is further graced with woven hangings and murals, with 2 gigantic, four-ton replicas of the State Seal hanging at both entrances. The inner courtyard has a 600,000-tile mosaic, "Aquarius," rendered by island artist Tadashi Sato, and on one side is a poignant sculpture of **Father Damien of the Lepers.** The state legislature is in session January to March, and opens with dancing, music, and festivities at 10:00 a.m. on the third Wed. in January, public invited. Peek inside, then take the elevator to the fifth floor for outstanding views of the city.

MISSION HOUSES MUSEUM

This living museum, on King Street across from Kawaiahao Church (oldest in Honolulu), is a complex including 2 main houses, a printing house annex, a library and a fine, inexpensive gift shop. It's operated by the **Hawaiian Mission Children's Society** (or Cousin's Society), whose members serve as guides and hosts. Many are direct descendants, or spouses of descendants, of the Congregationalist missionaries who built these structures. Tours are conducted daily 9:00 a.m. to 4:00 p.m., guided tours of the Frame House 9:30 a.m. to 3:00 p.m.; modest admission, tel. 531-0481.

Construction

If you think that precut modular housing is a new concept, think again. The first structure that you enter is the **Frame House**, the oldest wooden structure in Hawaii. Precut in Boston, it came along with the first missionary packet in 1819. Since the interior frame was left behind and didn't arrive until Christmas Day, 1820, the missionary families lived in thatched huts until it was erected. Finally the Chamberlain family occupied it in 1821. Many missionary families used it over the years, with as much as 4 households occupying this small structure at the same time. This is where the Christianizing of Hawaii truly began.

The missionaries, being New Englanders, first dug a cellar. The Hawaiians were very suspicious of the strange hole, convinced that the missionaries planned to store guns and arms in this "fort." Though assured to the contrary, King Liholiho, anxious to save face and prove his omnipotence, had a cellar dug near his home twice as deep and large. This satisfied everyone. Notice the different styles, sizes, and colors of bricks used in the structures. Most of the ships of the day carried brick as ballast. After unloading cargo, the captains either donated or sold the bricks to the missionaries, who incorporated them into the structures. A common local material was coral stone: pulverized coral was burned with lime to make a rudimentary cement, which was then used to bind cut-coral blocks. The pit that was used for this purpose is still discernible on the grounds.

Kitchen

The natives were intrigued with the missionaries, whom they called "long necks" because of their high collars. The missionaries, on the other hand, were a little more wary of their "charges." The low fence around the complex was symbolic as well as utilitarian. The missionaries were obsessed with keeping their children away from Hawaiian children, who at first ran around naked and played many games

left to right: Frame House, Printing House, Chamberlain House (courtesy Mission Houses Museum)

with overt sexual overtones. Almost every evening a small cadre of Hawaiians would assemble to peer into the kitchen to watch the women cook, which they found exceedingly strange because their *kapu* said that *men* did the cooking. In the kitchen, actually an attached cook house, the wood-burning stove kept breaking down. More often than not, the women used the fireplace with its built-in oven. About once a week, they fired up the oven to make traditional New England staples like bread, pies, cakes, and puddings. The missionaries were dependent on the Hawaiians to bring them fresh water. Notice a large porous stone through which they would filter the water to remove dirt, mud, and sometimes brackishness.

The Hawaiians were even more amazed when the entire family sat down to dinner, a tremendous deviation from their beliefs that separated men and women when eating. When the missionaries assembled to dine or meet at the "long table," the Hawaiians silently stood at the open door to watch the evening soap opera. The unnerved missionaries eventually closed the door and cut 2 windows into the wall, which they could leave opened but draped. The long table took on further significance. The one you see is a replica. When different missionaries left the islands, they, like people today, wanted a souvenir. For some odd reason, they elected to saw a bit off the long table. As years went by, the table got shorter and shorter until it was useless.

Residents

The house was actually a duplex. Although many families lived in it, 2 of the best known were the Binghams and the Judds. Much of the existing furniture was theirs. Judd, a member of the third missionary company, assumed the duties of physician to all the missionaries and islanders. He often prescribed alcohol of different sorts to the missionary families for a wide variety of ailments; many records remain of these prescriptions, but not one record of complaints from his patients. The Binghams and Judds got along very well, and entertained each other and visitors, most often in the Judds' parlor because they were a little better off. The women would often congregate here to do their sewing, which was in great demand, especially by members of the royal household. Until the missionary women taught island girls to sew, providing clothing for Hawaii's royalty was a tiresome and time-consuming obligation. The missionaries were self-sufficient, and had the unbounded energy of youth, as the average age was only 25. The husbands often built furniture for their families. Rev. Bingham, a good craftsman, was pressed by Queen Kaahumanu to build her a rocking chair after she became enamored of one made for Mrs. Bingham. The queen weighed almost 400 pounds, so building her a suitable chair was no slim feat! Still, the queen could only use it in her later years when she'd lost a considerable amount of weight. After she died, the Bingham's asked for it to be returned, and it sits in their section of the house. Compare Bingham's chair to another in the Judds' bedroom, jury-rigged by a young missionary husband from a captain's chair. An understatement, found later in his diary, confirmed that he was not a carpenter.

When you enter the Judds' bedroom, note how small it is, and consider that 2 adults and 5 children slept here. As soon as the children were old enough, they were sent back to the Mainland for schooling, no doubt to relieve some of the congestion. Also notice that the windows were fixed, in the New England style, and imagine how *close* it must have been in these rooms. The Binghams' bedroom is also small, and not as well furnished. Bingham's shaving kit remains, and is inscribed with "The Sandwich Isles." In the bedroom of Mary Ward, a missionary woman who never married, notice that the roof was raised to accommodate her canopy bed.

Another famous family that lived in the complex were the Cooks. When the missionary board withdrew its support, the Cooks petitioned them to buy the duplex, which was granted. Shortly thereafter, Mr. Cook, who had been a teacher, formed a partnership with one Mr. Castle, and from that time forward became Castle and Cook, one of Hawaii's oldest and most powerful corporations. The largest building in the compound is **The Chamberlain**

House. This barn-like structure was completed in 1831, and used as a warehouse and living quarters for Levi Chamberlain's family. Goods were stored in most of the structure, while the family occupied 3 modest rooms.

Printing House

The missionaries decided almost immediately that the best way to convert the natives was to speak to them in their own language, and to create a written Hawaiian language which they would teach in school. To this end, they created the **Hawaiian alphabet** consisting of 12 letters, including the 5 vowels and 7 consonants. In addition, to disseminate the doctrines of Christianity, they needed books, and therefore a printing press. On the grounds still stands the **Printing House,** built in 1841 but first used as annex bedrooms by the Hall family. The original printing house, built in 1823, no longer exists. In the Printing House is a replica of the Ramage press brought from New England, first operated by Elijah Lewis. He returned to the Mainland when he was 24, and soon died of TB, but not before he had earned the distinction of being the first printer west of the Rockies. Here were printed biblical tracts, text books, or anything that the king or passing captains were willing to pay to have printed. Although it took 8 hours of hard work to set up one page to be printed, it is estimated that in the 20 years the press operated under the missionaries, over 7 million pages were produced.

Gift Shop

While on the grounds make sure to visit the **bookstore and gift shop.** It's small, but has an excellent collection of Hawaiiana, and some very inexpensive but quality items, such as *tapa* bookmarks for only $.25, and an outstanding collection of Niihau shellwork, considered the finest in Hawaii. Between the bookstore and the research library are restrooms. Also, consider a **Walking Tour of Honolulu,** offered by the museum, that guides you through downtown Honolulu for 2 hours, hitting all the historic sights with an extremely knowledgeable narration by one of the museum's guides (see p. 208). For further information, write Hawaiian Mission Children's Society, 553 S. King St., Honolulu, HI 96813, tel. 531-0481.

KAWAIAHAO CHURCH

This church, so instrumental in Hawaii's history, is the most enduring symbol of the original missionary work in the islands. A sign welcomes you and bids the blessing, "Grace and peace to you from God our Father." The church was constructed from 1836 until 1842 according to plans drawn up by Hiram Bingham, its minister. Before this, at least 4 grass shacks of increasing size stood here. One was destroyed by a sailor who was reprimanded by Rev. Bingham for attending services while drunk; the old sea dog returned the next day and burned the church to the ground. Kawaiahao ("Water of Hao") Church is constructed from over 14,000 coral blocks quarried from offshore reefs. In 1843, following Restoration Day, when the British returned the Hawaiian Islands to sovereignty after a brief period of imperialism by a renegade captain, King Kamehameha III here uttered the profound words in a thanksgiving ceremony that were destined to become Hawaii's motto, *"Ua mau ke ea o ka aina i ka pono,"* "The life of the land is preserved in righteousness."

Other noteworthy ceremonies held at the church were the marriage of King Liholiho and his wife Queen Emma, who bore the last child born to a Hawaiian monarch. Unfortunately, little Prince Albert died at the age of four. On June 19, 1856, Lunalilo, the first king elected to the throne, took his oath of office in the church. A bachelor who died childless, he always felt scorned by living members of the Kamehameha clan, and refusing to be buried with them at the Royal Mausoleum in Nuuanu Valley, he is buried in a tomb in the church's cemetery. Buried along with him is his father Charles Kanaina, and nearby lies the grave of his mother Miriam Kekauluohi. In the graveyard lies Henri Burger, and many members of the Parker, Green, Brown, and Cook families, early missionaries to the islands. Liliuokalani's body lay in state in the church before it was taken to the Royal Mausoleum. A jubilation service was held in the church when Hawaii became a state in 1959. Kawaiahao holds beautiful Christmas services with a strong Polynesian and Hawaiian flavor. Hidden away in a corner of the grounds is an unobtrusive adobe building, remains of a schoolhouse built in 1835 to educate Hawaiian children.

HAWAII MARITIME CENTER

The development of this center is a wonderful concept whose time has finally come. It's amazing that a state and former nation, whose discovery and very birth is so intimately tied to the exploration, navigation, and exploitation of the sea, has never had a center dedicated exclusively to these profoundly important aspects of its heritage. Now the Hawaii Maritime Center, at Pier 7, Honolulu Harbor, Honolulu, HI 96813, tel. 523-5511, is exactly that...but, it's not quite finished yet, and it needs your support as a visitor. The Center now consists of 3 attractions: Aloha Tower, and its 9th floor maritime museum; the classic, and last remaining, fully rigged, 4-masted *Falls of Clyde* floating museum; and the reproduction of a Hawaiian sailing canoe, *The Hokulea,* that recently sailed back in time using ancient navigational methods to retrace the steps of Hawaii's Polynesian explorers. Future plans call for a proposed Kalakaua Boat House to be built upon the pier. It will have a 3-storied lobby for exhibitions of canoes of Oceania, and a wrap-around *lanai.* Inside will be sales offices, restrooms, gift shop, and theater. If you drive, there's excellent parking just near Pier 7; TheBus no. 8 from Waikiki deposits you right there.

Aloha Tower

When this endearing and enduring tourist cliche was built in 1926 for $160,000, the 184-foot, 10-story tower was the tallest structure on Oahu. As such, this landmark, with clocks embedded in all 4 walls, and emblazoned with the greeting and departing word, *Aloha,* became the symbol of Hawaii. Before the days of air transport, ocean liners would pull into the pier to disembark passengers at the foot of the tower, and on these "Steamer Days," festive well-wishers from throughout the city would gather to greet and *lei* the arriving passengers. The Royal Hawaiian Band would even turn out to welcome the guests ashore.

When you take the escalator up from the parking area, notice the huge U.S. customs rooms that at one time processed droves of passengers. Today, the crowds are gone and the tower is quiet. Only a few harbormasters on the top floor oversee the comings and goings of cargo ships. When you enter the tower a sign claims that you can only get to the observation area on the top floor by elevator. You can walk up to the 9th floor if you want, but to get to the very top does necessitate taking the elevator, which has the dubious distinction of being one of the slowest elevators in Hawaii. The Maritime Musuem occupies the 9th floor with a small display of maritime artifacts and a gift shop, open 9:00 a.m. to 4:00 p.m. Future plans call for the entire tower to be taken over to house such worthwhile projects as a film library featuring sounds of the sea, and a general library on all aspects of maritime Hawaii. Once atop the tower, you get the most remarkable view of the harbor and the city. A highrise planned for just next door will surely ruin the view, but many people with good sense, and luckily with some clout, are fighting this project. A remarkable feature of the vista is the reflections of the city and the harbor in

the Falls of Clyde

many of the steel and reflective glass high-rises. It's as if a huge mural were painted on them. Before descending, check out the photos of the vintage ships along the walls of a stainless steel canopy covering the walkway. The tower is open free of charge, daily from 8:00 a.m. to 9:00 p.m.

The *Falls Of Clyde*

This is the last fully rigged, 4-masted ship afloat on any of the world's oceans. She was saved from being scrapped in 1963 by a Seattle bank that was attempting to recoup some money on a bad debt. The people of Hawaii learned of her fate and spontaneously raised money to have the ship towed back to Honolulu Harbor. The *Falls of Clyde* was always a worker, never a pleasure craft. It served the Matson Steamship Company as a cargo and passenger liner from 1898 until 1920. Built in Glasgow, Scotland, in 1878, she was converted in 1906 to a sail-driven tanker; a motor aboard was used mainly to move the rigging around. After 1920, she was dismantled, towed to Alaska and became little more than a floating oil depot for fishing boats. Since 1968, the *Falls of Clyde* has been a floating museum, sailing the imaginations of children and grownups to times past, and in this capacity has perhaps performed her greatest duty. Open daily from 9:30 a.m. to 4:00 p.m., allow at least one hour for an entire tour, adults $3, children to 12 $1, under 6 free.

The *Hokule'a*

The newest and perhaps most dynamic feature of the Center is the ***Hokule'a*** ("Star of Gladness"). This authentic recreation of a traditional double-hulled sailing canoe captured the attention of the world when in 1976 it made a 6,000-mile roundtrip voyage to Tahiti. Piloted by Mau Piailug, a Caroline Islander, only ancient navigational techniques guided it successfully on its voyage. This attempt to relive these ancient voyages as closely as possible included eating traditional provisions only—*poi,* coconuts, dried fish, and bananas. Toward the end of the voyage some canned food had to be broken out! Modern materials such as plywood and fiberglass were used, but by consulting many petroglyphs and old drawings of these original craft, the design and lines were kept as authentic as possible. The sails, made from a heavy cotton, were the distinctive crab-claw type. In trial runs to work out the kinks and choose the crew, she almost sank in the treacherous channel between Oahu and Kauai and had to be towed in by the Coast Guard. But the *Hokule'a* performed admirably during the actual voyage. The experiment was a resounding technical success, but it was marred by bad feelings between members of the crew who argued and drew racial boundary lines. Both Hawaiian and white crew members found it impossible to work as a team, thereby mocking the canoe's name, "Star of Gladness." The tension was compounded by the close quarters of more than a dozen men living on an open deck only 9 feet wide by 40 feet long. The remarkable navigator Piailug refused to return to Hawaii with the craft and instead sailed back to his native island. The *Hokule'a,* sponsored by the Polynesian Sailing Society, will make Pier 7 its home berth when not at sea. This double-hulled canoe, a replica of the ones that Captain Cook found so remarkable, should fascinate you too.

Nearby Attractions

Two other attractions in the area are not part of the Hawaii Maritime Museum: in fact they're the antithesis of what this fine museum stands for. One is a monstrosity of a dinner boat called the ***Rella Mae,*** an old flat-bottomed ferry, whose 4 masts were added for effect. If ever the sails were unfurled, it'd roll around like a drunken tub-of-lard on roller skates. Also berthed close by is the **Oceania Floating Restaurant.** This barge, towed all the way from Hong Kong to Honolulu Harbor in 1972, is billed as the world's largest floating restaurant. It would be described as "modern Oriental rococo." Unlike the *Rella Mae,* the structure is just bizarre enough to make it interesting. Businesses seem to come and go here, but you'll always find a Chinese restaurant and a cocktail lounge in which to relax before continuing your journey.

CHINATOWN

Chinatown has seen its ups and downs in the last 130 years, ever since Chinese laborers were lured from Kwangtung Province to work as contract laborers on the pineapple and sugar plantations. They didn't need a fortune cookie to tell them that there was no future in plantation work, so within a decade of their arrival they had established themselves as merchants, mostly in small retail businesses and restaurants. Chinatown is roughly a triangle of downtown Honolulu bordered by Nuuanu Street on the east, N. Beretania Street on the north, and S. King Street forming the hypotenuse. Twice this area has been flattened by fire, once in 1886 and again in 1900. The 1900 fire was deliberately set to burn out rats that had brought bubonic plague to the city. The fire got out of control and burned down virtually the whole district. Some contended that the fire was allowed to engulf the district in order to decimate the growing economic strength of the Chinese. Chinatown reached its heyday in

The pagoda roof marks a Chinese cemetery.

the 1930s when it thrived with tourists coming and going from the main port at the foot of Nuuanu Street. Today, Chinatown is a mixed bag of upbeat modernization, and rundown sleazy storefronts. Although still strongly Chinese, there are Japanese, Laotians, Vietnamese, and even an Irish pub, O'Toole's, on Nuuanu Street.

Look for the pagoda roof of **Wo Fat's** on the corner of Hotel and Maunakea streets. This is the oldest *chop suey* house in Honolulu, started in 1886 by Mr. Wo Fat, a baker. It's a good landmark for starting your tour. Just down the street the **Hop Hing Market** sells all manner of Oriental goods. Across, on King Street, are 2 practitioners, **Fook Sau Tong's** for Chinese herbs, and **Suen Hang Yee** for acupuncture. Down Smith Street is **Kam Mau Co.**, whose shelves are stacked with every conceivable and inconceivable Oriental food. This is a great place to sample authentic *crack seed.* If your tummy revolts, or if you need a quick tonic head next door to **Lai An Tong's** herb shop where some ground snakeskin, mashed antelope antler, or powdered monkey brain might be just what the doctor ordered. Wonderful pastry shops are here and there, and almost every restaurant is cheap, and if not superlative at least very good.

Shopping

For shopping head to the **Cultural Plaza**, on the corner of Mauna Kea and Beretania streets, but it has been struggling lately and shops come and go with regularity. Nearby you'll find the **People's Open Market**, a cooperative of open-air stalls selling just about everything that Chinatown has to offer at competitive prices. Follow your nose to the pungent odors of fresh fish at **Oahu's Fish Market** on King Street, where ocean delectables can be had for reasonable prices. Then if you want to clear your nose visit the **Kuan Yin Temple**, where Buddha is always praised with some sweet smelling incense. For peace and quiet, or to check out some old-timers playing checkers or dominoes, cross the river and enter **Aala Triangle Park**. Chinatown is relatively safe, especially during the daytime, but at night, particularly along infamous Hotel Street, you have to be careful. When the sun sinks, the neon goes, and the area fires up. Transvestites and hookers slide down the street, shaking their wares and letting you know that they're open for business. Purchasing might leave you with a few souvenirs that you'd never care to *share* with the folks back home.

Tour

You can easily do Chinatown on your own, but for a different slant and some extremely knowledgeable guides try the **Chinese Chamber of Commerce Tour**, tel. 533-3181, that's been operating as a community service for almost 30 years. They'll guide you around Chinatown for only $3, with an optional $4 lunch at Wo Fat's. Or, try the **Hawaiian Heritage Center Tour** from 1026 Nuuanu Ave., tel. 521-2749, every Mon., Wed., and Fri. at 9:30 a.m., for $4, and a lunch at Wo Fat's for $3.50. An excellent source of general information is the **Hawaii Chinese History Center**, 111 N. King St., Honolulu, HI 96817.

PALI HIGHWAY

Cutting across Oahu from Honolulu to Kailua on the windward coast is Rt. 61, better known as the Pali Highway. Before getting to the famous Nuuanu Pali Lookout at the very crest of the Koolau Mountains, you can spend a full and enjoyable day sightseeing. Stop en route at Punchbowl's National Memorial Cemetery, followed by an optional side trip to the summit of Tantalus for a breathtaking view of the city (see p. 215). You can also visit the **Royal Mausoleum** in the vicinity. Take the H-1 Freeway to Vineyard Blvd. (exit 22), cross the Pali Hwy. to Nuuanu St. and follow it up to the mausoleum. If you continue up Nuuanu St., it intersects the Pali Hwy. in a minute or two, but you'll have passed the Punchbowl turn off. This small chapel, built in 1865 by Kamehameha IV, holds the bodies of most of the royal family who died after 1825. Their bodies were interred elsewhere, but were moved here. The mausoleum at one time held 18 royal bodies, but became overcrowded, so they were moved again to little crypts scattered around the grounds. Few tourists visit this serene place open weekdays from 8:00 a.m to 4:00 p.m., tel. 536-7602.

About 2 miles past the Punchbowl turn off, heading up the Pali Hwy. (exit 21-B off H-1), an

the Nuuanu Pali

HVB Warrior points you to the **Walker Home** across from Nuuanu Congregational Church. It's famous for its gardens, and at one time visitors were welcome to come and tour them for a fee. It's hard to tell if this is still happening. The gates are open and no signs tell you to keep out, but an unsmiling housekeeper backed by a steely-eyed German shepherd make you want to wave from your car and keep rolling. Next comes Queen Emma's Summer Palace, (see following) and the Daijingu Temple, a Baptist college, and a Catholic church. It seems as though these sects were vying to get farther up the hill to be just a little closer to heaven. A sign, past Queen Emma's Palace, points you off to **Nuuanu Pali Drive.** Take it! This few-minutes' jog off the Pali Hwy. (which it rejoins) takes you through some wonderful scenery. Make sure to bear right as soon as you pull off and not up the Old Pali Hwy., which has no outlet. Immediately the road is canopied with trees, and in less than half a mile is a bubbling little waterfall and a pool. The homes in here are grand, and the entire area gives a park-like effect. One of the nicest little roads that you can take while looking around, this side trip wastes no time at all.

Queen Emma's Summer Palace

This summer home is more the simple hideaway of a well-to-do family than a grand palace. The interior has only 2 bedrooms, no facilities for guests, and about 3,000 square feet. The exterior has a strong New England flavor, and indeed was prefabricated in Boston. The simple square home, surrounded by a *lanai,* was built from 1847 to 1850, by John Young II, Queen Emma's uncle. When he died, she inherited the property, and spent many relaxing days here, away from the heat of Honolulu, with her husband King Kamehameha IV. Emma used the home little after 1872, and following her death in 1885, it fell into disrepair.

Rescued from demolition by the Daughters of Hawaii in 1913, it was refurbished, and has operated as a museum since 1915. The Palace, at 2913 Pali Hwy., tel. 595-3167, is open daily 9:00 a.m. to 4:00 p.m., admission $3, children under 12 $.50. Although it's just off the Pali Highway, the one and only sign comes up quickly, and many visitors pass it by. If you pass the entranceway to the Oahu Country Club just across the road, you've gone too far.

As you enter, notice the tall *kahili,* symbols of noble rank in the entranceway, along with *lauhala* mats on the floor, which at one time were an unsurpassed speciality of Hawaii. Today, they must be imported from Fiji or Samoa. The walls are hung with paintings of many of Hawaii's kings and queens, and in every room are distinctive Hawaiian artifacts, such as magnificent feather capes, fans, and *tapa* hangings. The furnishings have a very strong British influence. The Hawaiian nobility of the time were enamored with the British. King Kamehameha

IV traveled to England when he was 15 years old; he met Queen Victoria, and the 2 become good friends. Emma and Kamehameha IV had the last child born to an Hawaiian king and queen on May 20, 1858. Named Prince Albert after Queen Victoria's consort, he was much loved, but died when he was only 4 years old on August 27, 1862. His father followed him to the grave in little more than a year; after that, Hawaii elected her kings. Prince Albert's canoe-shaped cradle is here, made in Germany by Wilhelm Fisher from 4 different kinds of Hawaiian wood. His tiny shirts, pants, and boots are still laid out, and there's a lock of his hair, and one from Queen Emma. In every room there is royal memorabilia. The royal bedroom displays a queen-sized bed covered with an exquisite pink and purple *tapa* bedspread There's vintage Victorian furniture, and even a piano built in London by Collard and Collard. A royal cabinet made in Berlin holds porcelains, plates, and cups. After Queen Emma died, it stood in Charles R. Bishop's drawing room, and was later returned. The grounds are beautifully manicured, and the house is surrounded by shrubbery and trees, many of which date from when the royal couple lived here. Restrooms are around back.

Shinto priest at Dai Jingu

Walk around back past the basketball court and keep to the right. Soon you'll see a modest little white building. Look for a rather thick and distinctive rope hanging across the entranceway. This is the Shinto temple **Dai Jingu.** It's not nearly as spectacular as the giant trees in this area, but it is authentic and worth a quick look.

Nuuanu Pali Lookout

This is one of those extra benefit places where you get a magnificent view without any effort at all. Merely drive up the Pali Hwy. to the well-marked turnout, and park. Rip-offs happen, so take all valuables. Before you, if the weather is accommodating, an unimpeded view of windward Oahu lies at your feet. Nuuanu Pali ("Cool Heights") lives up to its name; the winds here are chilly, extremely strong, and funnel right through the lookout. You definitely need a jacket or windbreaker. On a particularly windy day just after a good rainfall, various waterfalls tumbling off the *pali* will actually be blown uphill! A number of roads, punched over and through the *pali* over the years, are engineering marvels. The famous "carriage road" built in 1898 by John Wilson, a Honolulu boy, for only $37,500, using 200 laborers and plenty of dynamite, was truly amazing. Droves of people come here, many in huge buses, and they all go to the railing to have a peek. Even so, by walking down the old road built in 1932 that goes off to the right, you actually get private and better views. You'll find the tallest point in the area, a huge needle-like rock. The wind is quieter here.

Nuuanu Pali figures prominently in Hawaii's legend history. It's said, not without academic skepticism, that Kamehameha the Great pursued the last remaining defenders of Oahu to these cliffs in one of the final battles fought to consolidate his power over all of the islands in 1795. If you use your imagination, you can easily feel the utter despair and courage of these vanquished warriors as they were driven ever closer to the edge. Mercy was not shown nor expected. Some jumped to their deaths rather than surrender, while others fought until they were pushed over. The number of casualties varies considerably, from a few hundred to a few thousand, while some believe the battle never happened at all. Compounding the controversy are stories of the warriors' families, who searched the cliffs below for years, and supposedly found bones of their kinsmen, that they buried. The Pali Lookout is romantic at night, with the lights of Kailua and Kaneohe in the distance, but the best nighttime view is from Tantalus Drive, when all of Honolulu lies at your feet.

PUNCHBOWL, NATIONAL CEMETERY OF THE PACIFIC

One sure sign that you have entered a place of honor is by the hushed and quiet nature that everyone adopts without having to be told. That's the way it is the moment that you enter this shrine. The Hawaiian name, *Puowaina* ("Hill of Sacrifice"), couldn't have been more prophetic. Punchbowl is the almost perfectly round crater of an extinct volcano that holds the bodies of almost 25,000 men and women who fell fighting for the United States, from the Spanish-American War to Vietnam. At one time, Punchbowl was a bastion of heavy cannon and artillery trained on Honolulu Harbor to defend it from hostile naval forces. In 1943 Hawaii bequeathed it to the federal government as a memorial; it was dedicated in 1949, when the remains of an unknown serviceman killed during the attack of Pearl Harbor was the first interred.

As you enter the main gate, a flagpole with the Stars and Stripes unfurled is framed in the center of a long sweeping lawn. A roadway lined with monkeypods adds three-dimensional depth to the impressionistic scene, as it leads to the steps of a marble, altar-like monument in the distance. The eye has a continuous sweep of the field, as there are no elevated tombstones, just simple marble slabs lying flat on the ground. The field is dotted with trees including 8 banyans, a special tree and symbolic number for the many Buddhists buried here. Brightening the scene are plumeria trees, and rainbow shower trees, often planted in Hawaiian graveyards because they produce flowers year round as perennial offerings from the living to the dead when they can't personally attend the grave. All are equal here; the famous like Ernie Pyle, the stalwart who earned the Congressional Medal of Honor, and the unknown who died alone and unheralded on muddy battlefields in God-forsaken jungles. To the right, just after you enter is the office, open Mon. to Fri. 9:00 a.m. to 5:00 p.m. with brochures, and restrooms. Tour buses, taxis, and limousines are lined up here. Don't leave valuables in your car.

The Monument

Like a pilgrim, you climb the steps to the monument, where on both sides marble slabs seem to whisper the names of the 20,000-plus servicemen, all MIAs whose bodies were never found but whose spirits are honored here. The first slabs on the right are for the victims of Vietnam, on the left are those from WW II, and you can see that time is already weathering the marble. They lie together, as they fought and died...men, boys, lieutenants, captains, private soldiers, infantrymen, sailors...from everywhere in America. "In proud memory...this memorial has been erected by the United States of America." At the monument itself, built in 1966, is a chapel and in the middle is a statue of a woman, a woman of peace, a heroic woman of liberty. Around her on the walls are etched maps and battles of the Pacific War whose names still evoke passion: Pearl Harbor, Wake, Coral Sea, Midway, Iwo Jima, the Gilbert Islands, Okinawa. Many of the visitors are Japanese. Many of Hawaii's war dead are also

Japanese. Four decades ago we battled each other with hatred and malice. Today, on bright afternoons we come together with saddened hearts to pay reverence to the dead.

To get to Punchbowl take the H-1 Freeway to Rt. 61, the Pali Highway, and exit at 21-B. Immediately get to the right, where a sign points you to Punchbowl. You'll make some fancy zig-zags through a residential area, but it's well marked and you'll come to Puowaina Street that leads you to the main gate. Make sure to notice landmarks going in, because as odd as it sounds, no signs lead you back out and it's easy to get lost.

UNIVERSITY OF HAWAII

You don't have to be a student to head for the University of Hawaii, Manoa Campus. For one, it houses the **East-West Center**, where nations from Asia and the Pacific present fascinating displays of their homelands. Also, Manoa Valley itself is one of the loveliest residential areas on Oahu. To get to the main campus follow the H-1 Freeway to exit 24B, (University Ave.). Don't make the mistake of exiting at the University's Makai Campus. Follow University Avenue to the second red light, Dole Avenue and make a right onto campus. Stop immediately at one of the parking lots and get a parking map! Parking restrictions are strictly enforced, and this map not only helps to get you around, but saves you many hassles from fines, or having your car towed away. Parking is $.50 an hour, even for visitors, so think about taking TheBus which services this area quite well.

Student Center

Make this your first stop. As you mount the steps, notice the idealized mural of old Hawaii: smiling faces of contented natives all doing interesting things. Inside is the **Information Center**, which dispenses info not only about the campus, but also what's happening socially and culturally around town. They even have lists of cheap restaurants, discos, and student hangouts. Next door are typewriters available to non-students at $2 per day. The food in the cafeteria is institutional, but cheap, and has a Hawaiian twist. If you're visiting on Monday, sorority girls set up a barbecue in front of the Student Center from 11:00 a.m. to 1:00 p.m. and serve you half a chicken with all the trimmings, $4. The **University Bookstore** is excellent, open Mon. to Fri. 8:15 a.m. to 4:15 p.m., Sat., 8:15-11:45 a.m. The **University Art Gallery** is on the 3rd floor, and is worth a look. Free! The exhibits change regularly. Next to the gallery is a lounge filled with overstuffed chairs and big pillows, where you can kick back and even take a quick snooze.

ornate roof of the Center for Korean Studies

East-West Center

Follow Dole Ave. to East-West Rd. and make a left. Free tours, Mon. to Fri. at 1:30 p.m., originate from Bachman Hall at the corner of University and Dole avenues. For more info contact the East-West Center, 1777 East-West Rd., Honolulu, HI 96848, tel. 944-7111. The center's 21 acres were dedicated in 1960 by the U.S. Congress to promote better relations between the countries of Asia and the Pacific with the U.S. Many nations, as well as private companies and individuals, fund this institution of cooperative study and research. John Burn's Hall dispenses information on what's happening in its main lobby, along with self-guiding maps. Thomas Jefferson Hall, fronted by Chinese lions, has a serene and relaxing Japanese garden behind, complete with a little rivulet and a teahouse, named *Jakuan,* "Cottage of Tranquility." The murals inside are excellent, and it also contains a large reading room with relaxing couches. The impressive Thai Pavilion was a gift from the king of Thailand, where it was built and sent to Hawaii to be reconstructed. This 23-ton, solid teak *sala* is a common sight in Thailand. The Center for Korean Studies is also outstanding. A joint venture of Korean and Hawaiian architects, its inspiration was taken from the classic lines of Kyongbok Palace in Seoul. Most of the buildings are adorned with fine artworks: *tapa* hangings, murals, calligraphy, paintings, and sculpture. The entire center is tranquil, and along with the John F. Kennedy Theater of Performing Arts just across the road, is indeed fulfilling its dedication as a place of sharing and learning, culture and art.

BISHOP MUSEUM

This group of stalwart stone buildings holds the greatest collection of historical relics and scholarly works on Hawaii and Polynesian in the world. Referring to itself as a "museum to instruct and delight," in one afternoon walking through its halls, you can educate yourself about Hawaii's history and people, and enrich your trip to the islands ten-fold. Officially named **Bernice Pauahi Bishop Museum,** its founding was directly connected to the last 3 royal women of the Kamehameha Dynasty. Princess Bernice married Charles Reed Bishop, a New Englander who became a citizen of the then independent monarchy in the 1840s. The princess was a wealthy woman in her own right, with lands and an extensive collection of "things Hawaiian." Her cousin, Princess Ruta Keelikolani, died in 1883, and bequeathed Princess Bernice all of her lands and Hawaiian artifacts. Together, this meant that Princess Bernice owned about 12% of all Hawaii! Princess Bernice died less than 2 years later, and left all of her land holdings to the **Bernice Pauahi Bishop Estate,** which founded and supported the Kamehameha Schools, dedicated to the education of Hawaiian children. Though this organization is often confused with the Bishop Museum, they are totally separate. The school shared the same grounds with the museum, but none of the funds from this organization were, or are, used for the museum. When Princess Bernice died, she left her personal property, with all of its priceless Hawaiian artifacts, to her husband, Charles. Then, when Queen Emma, her other cousin, died the following year, she too desired Charles Bishop to combine her Hawaiian artifacts with the already formidable collection and establish a Hawaiian museum. True to the wishes of these

main building of the Bishop Museum

women, he began construction of the museum's main building in 1888, and within a few years the museum was opened. In 1894, after 50 years in Hawaii, Bishop moved to San Francisco where he died in 1915. He is still regarded as one of Hawaii's most generous philanthropists. In 1961, a science wing and planetarium were added, and 2 dormitory buildings are still used from when the Kamehameha School for Boys occupied the same site.

Getting There

To get there, take exit 20A off the H-1 Freeway, which puts you on Rt. 63, the Likelike Highway. Immediately get into the far right lane. In only a few hundred yards, turn onto Bernice Street where you'll find the entrance. TheBus no. 2 (School-Middle St.) runs from Waikiki to Kapalama Street, from which you walk 2 blocks. The museum runs special red double-decker shuttle buses from Waikiki, departing from the Hilton Hawaiian Village, Sheraton, and from King's Alley. These buses also operate special tours of Honolulu, with a stop at the Mission Houses Museum, including a **heritage theater** and **planetarium** show at the museum. The price is right for this excellent tour; for details, prices, and information tel. 922-1770 or 926-2557.

Admission

The museum, located at 1525 Bernice St., Honolulu, HI 96819, tel. 847-3511, is open Mon. through Sat. from 9:00 a.m. to 5:00 p.m., and on the 1st Sun. of the month. Admission is $4.75 adults, $2.50 children 6-17, younger free, but some exhibits and the planetarium are closed to children under six. It's sometimes best to visit on weekends because many weekdays bring teachers and young students, who have more enthusiasm for running around than checking out the exhibits. Food, beverages, smoking, and flash photography are all strictly prohibited in the museum. The natural light in the museum is dim, so if you're into photography you'll need super-fast film (400 ASA performs only marginally). Before leaving the grounds make sure to visit **Atherton Halau** where a *hula* is performed Mon. through Sat. at 10:15 a.m. and 2:00 p.m. Throughout the

An Easter Island-like stone image rises from the grounds of the Bishop Museum.

week, the hall offers demonstrations in various Hawaiian crafts like *lei*-making, featherwork, and quilting. The **planetarium** opens up its skies daily at 11:00 a.m. and 3:15 p.m. There are special nighttime shows and family discount days offered, tel. 847-3511 for details. The snack shop has reasonable prices, and **Shop Pacifica**, the museum bookstore and boutique, has a fine selection of materials on Hawaii, and some authentic and inexpensive souvenirs.

Exhibits

It's easy to become overwhelmed at the museum, so just take it slowly. The number of exhibits is staggering: over 100,000 artifacts, almost 20 million(!) specimens of insects, shells, fish, birds, and mammals, plus an extensive research library, photograph collection, and fine series of maps. The main gallery is highlighted by the rich tones of *koa,* the showpiece being a magnificent staircase. First catch the slide show in the **Kahili Room**. Then get a map at the front desk that lists all of the Halls, along with a description of what theme is found in each, and a suggested route to follow. The following are just a potpourri of the highlights that you'll discover.

To the right of the main entranceway is a fascinating exhibit of the old Hawaiian gods. Most are just called "wooden image" and date from the early 19th century. Among them are: Kamehameha's war-god, Ku; the tallest Hawaiian sculpture ever found, from Kauai; and image of a god from a temple of human sacrifice; and lesser gods, personal *amakua* that controlled the lives of Hawaiians from birth until death. You wouldn't want to meet any of them in a dark alley! Outside, in what's called the **Hawaiian Court**, are implements used by the Hawaiians in everyday life, as well as a botanical collection of plants that have all been identified. The first floor of the main hall is perhaps the most interesting because it deals with old Hawaii. Here are magnificent examples of *kahili,* feathered capes, plumed helmets...all the insignia and regalia of the *ali'i.* A commoner sits in a grass shack, a replica of what Capt. Cook might have seen. Don't look up! Over your head is a 55-foot sperm whale hanging from the ceiling. It weighed over 44,000 pounds alive. You'll learn about the *ukelele,* and how vaudevillians spread its music around the world. *Hula*-skirted damsels from the 1870s peer provocatively from old photos, bare-breasted and with plenty of "cheese cake." Tourists bought these photos even then, although the grass skirts they're wearing were never a part of old Hawaii, but were brought by Gilbert Islanders. See authentic *hula* instruments like a "lover's whistle," a flute played through the nose, and a musical bow, the only stringed pre-European Hawaiian instrument.

Don't miss the *koa* wood collection. This accomplished art form produced medicine bowls, and handsome calabashes, some just simple home bowls, and others reputed to be the earthly home of the wind goddess, and had to be refitted for display in Christianized Iolani Palace. A model *heiau* tells of the old religion, and the many strange *kapu* that governed every aspect of life. Clubs used to bash in the brains of *kapu*-breakers are next to benevolent little stone gods, the size and shape of footballs, that protected humble fishermen from the sea. As you ascend to the upper floors, time becomes increasingly closer to the present. The missionaries, whalers, merchants, laborers, and Westernized monarchs have arrived. Yankee whalers from New Bedford, New London, Nantucket, and Sag Harbor appear determined and grim-faced as they scour the seas, harpoons at the ready. Great blubber pots, harpoons, and figureheads are preserved from this perilous and unglamorous life. Bibles, thrones, the regalia of power and of the new god are all here.

PEARL HARBOR: USS *ARIZONA* MEMORIAL

Even as you approach the pier from which you board a launch to take you to the USS *Arizona,* you know that you're at a shrine. Very few spots in America carry such undeniable emotion so easily passed from one generation to another: here, Valley Forge, Gettysburg, not many more. On that beautiful, cloudless morning of December 7, 1941, at one minute before 8 o'clock, the United States not only entered

USS Arizona *in the throes of death*

the war, but lost its innocence forevermore. The first battle of WW II for the U.S. actually took place about 90 minutes before Pearl Harbor's bombing when the USS *Ward* sank an unidentified submarine sliding into Honolulu. In Pearl Harbor, dredged about 40 years earlier to allow superships to enter, the heavyweight champions of America's Pacific fleet were lined up flanking the near side of Ford's Island. The naive deployment of this "Battleship Row" prompted a Japanese admiral to remark that never, even in times of maximum world peace, could he dream that the military might of a nation would have its unprotected chin stuck so far out, just begging for a right cross to the jaw. When it came, it was a roundhouse right, whistling through the air, and what a doozy! Well before the smoke could clear and the last explosion stopped rumbling through the mountains, 3,581 Americans were dead or wounded, 6 mighty ships had sunk into the ooze of Pearl, 12 others stumbled around battered and punch drunk, and 347 war planes were useless heaps of scrap. The Japanese fighters had hardly broken a sweat, and when their fleet, located 200 miles north of Oahu, steamed away, the "east wind" had indeed "rained." But it was only the first squall of the American hurricane that would follow.

Getting There

There are a few options on how to visit Pearl Harbor and the USS *Arizona* Memorial. If you're driving, the entrance is along Rt. 99, the Kamehameha Highway, about a mile south of Aloha Stadium; well-marked signs direct you to the parking area. You can also take TheBus, nos. 50, 51, and 52 from Ala Moana Center, or no. 20 Airport, from Waikiki, and be dropped off within a minute's walk of the entrance. Depending upon stops and traffic, this can take well over an hour. **Arizona Memorial Shuttle Bus,** a private operation from Waikiki, takes about 20 min. and will pick you up at your hotel, tel. 947-5015, about $2.50 OW, reservations necessary. Returning, no reservation is necessary, just buy a ticket from Gloria, the lady selling them under the green umbrella in the parking lot. The **Arizona Memorial Visitor Center** is a joint venture of the U.S. Park Service and the Navy, and is free! The Park Service runs the theater and museum, and the

Pearl Harbor survivor Louis Grabinski dedicates weekends as an unofficial host aboard the memorial, relating history firsthand to the multitude of visitors.

Navy operates the shuttle boats that take you out to the memorial shrine. The complex is open daily except Mondays from 8:00 a.m. to 3:00 p.m. when you can visit the museum and the theater, and take the shuttle boats out to the memorial. If the weather is stormy, or waves rough, they won't sail so call tel. 422-0561 or 422-2771. As many as 3,000 people visit per day, and your best time to avoid delays is before 9:30 a.m. Also, a number of boats operate out of Kewalo Basin doing **Pearl Harbor Cruises.** Costing about $10 for an extensive tour of Pearl Harbor, they are not allowed to drop passengers off on the Memorial itself.

Bookstore And Theater

As you enter, you're handed a numbered ticket. Until its called, you can visit the bookstore/gift shop and museum. The bookstore specializes in volumes on WW II and Hawaiiana. The museum is primarily a pictorial history, with a strong emphasis on the involvement of Hawaii's Japanese citizens during the war. There are instructions of behavior to "all persons of Japanese ancestry" when bigotry and fear prevailed early in the war, as well as documentation of the 442 Batallion, made up of Japanese soldiers and their heroic exploits in Europe, especially their rescue of Texas' "lost batallion." Preserved newspapers of the day proclaim the "Day of Infamy" in bold headlines. When your number is called you proceed to the comfortable theater where a 20-min. film includes actual footage of the attack. The film is historically factual, devoid of an overabundance of "flag waving and mom's apple pie." After the film you board the launch: no bare feet, no bikinis or bathing suits, but shorts and shirts are fine. Twenty years ago men and women wore suits and dresses as if going to church!

The Memorial

The launch, a large vessel handled and piloted with professional deft usually by women Naval personnel, heads for an alabaster memorial 184 feet long, and straddling the ship that still lies on the bottom. Some view it as a tombstone; others see it as a symbolic ship, bent by struggle in the middle, but raised at the ends pointing to glory. The USS *Arizona* became the focus of the memorial because her casualties were so severe. When she exploded, the blast was so violent that it lifted entire ships moored nearby clear out of the water. Less than 9 minutes later, with infernos raging and huge hunks of steel whizzing through the air, the *Arizona* was gone. Her crew went with her; nearly 1,100 men were sucked down to the bottom, and only 289 somehow managed to struggle to the surface. To the left and right are a series of black and white moorings with the names of the ships tied to them on the day of the attack. The deck of the memorial can hold about 200 people; a small museum holds the ship's bell, and a chapel-like area displays a marble tablet with the names of the dead. Into a hole in the center of the memorial, flowers and memorial wreaths are dropped on special occasions. Part of the superstructure of the ship still rises above the waves, but is slowly being corroded away by wind and sea water. The flag, waving overhead, is attached to a pole anchored to the deck of the sunken ship. Sometimes, on weekends, survivors from the attack are aboard to give firsthand descriptions of what happened that day. Many visitors are Japanese nationals, who often stop and offer their apologies to these Pearl Harbor survivors, distinguished by special military-style hats. The Navy ordered that any survivor wishing to be buried with his crew members had that right. In 1982 a diver took a stainless steel container of the ashes of one of the survivors to be laid to rest with his buddies.

MUSEUMS, GALLERIES, AND GARDENS

Military Museums

The **USS *Bowfin,*** a WW II submarine moored within walking distance of the Arizona Memorial Center, has been turned into a self-guiding museum. It's open from 9:30 a.m. to 4:30 p.m., admission $3 adults, $1 children ages 6-12. In the little compound leading to the sub is a snack bar with some tables, a few artillery pieces, and a torpedo or two. As you enter, you're handed a telephone-like receiver; a recorded transmitted message explains about different areas on the sub. The deck is made from teak wood, and the deck guns could go fore or aft depending on the skipper's preference. You'll also notice two anchors; one, under a fresh coat of paint is pink, salvaged from the sub used in the film *Operation Petticoat.* As you descend, you feel as if you are integrated with a machine, a part of its gears and workings. In these cramped quarters of brass and stainless steel lived 90 to 100 men, all volunteers. Fresh water was in short supply, and the only man allowed to shower was the cook. Officers were given a dipper of water to shave, but all the other men grew beards. Absolutely no place to be alone. The men slept on tiny stacked shelves, and only the officers could control their light switches. The only man to have a miniscule private room was the captain. Topside, twin 16-cylinder diesels created unbelievable noise and heat. A vent in the passageway to the engine room sucked air with such strength that if you passed under it, you'd be flattened to your knees. When the sub ran on batteries under water, the quiet became maddening. The main bunk room, not much bigger than an average bed room slept 36 men. Another 30 or so ran the ship, while another 30 lounged. There was no night and day just shifts. Coffee was constantly available, as well as fresh fruit, and the best mess in all the services. Subs of the day had the best radar and electronics available. Aboard were 24 high-powered torpedos, and ammo for the topside gun. Submariners, chosen for their intelligence and psychological ability to take it knew that a hit from the enemy meant certain

USS Bowfin, *WW II submarine*

death. The USS *Bowfin* is fascinating and definitely worth a visit.

The Navy holds an **open house** on one of its ships berthed at Pearl Harbor on the first Saturday of each month. For information tel. 474-8139. You must enter through the main Nimitz Gate, and then follow the signs to the ship which are usually at the Bravo or Mike piers. On your way to the docking area you stop at the Family Services area where you can pick up some snacks or ice cream at a Baskin-Robbins concession. The sailors conducting the tour are polite and knowledgeable, and the tour is free. Those never in the service can always spot the officers—the guys with the white shoes. Take TheBus to the Nimitz Gate, or if you've visited the Arizona Memorial, a convenient shuttle connects for only $.50.

The **Pacific Submarine Museum** is also reached through the Nimitz Gate. It's free but you need a pass from the gate. It's open Wed. through Sun. 9:30 a.m. to 5:00 p.m., tel. 471-0632.

If you are fascinated by the military and its history, visit the **U.S. Army Museum** at Fort DeRussy, at the corner of Kalia and Saratoga roads. Plenty of displays and historical artifacts, free guided tour, open Tues. through Sun., 10:00 a.m. to 4:30 p.m., tel. 543-2687.

Honolulu Academy Of Arts

This museum has a brilliant collection of modern art, strongly emphasizing Asian artwork. James Michener's outstanding collection of Japanese *ukiyoe* is here, mainly because an unfriendly New York cop hassled him on his way to donate it, while a Honolulu officer was the epitome of *aloha.* Magnificent Korean ceramics, Chinese furniture, Japanese prints, along with Western masterworks from the Greeks to Picasso make the Academy one of the most *rounded* art museums in America. The entire complex surrounds lovely gardens; at the Garden Cafe Restaurant you can enjoy a civilized lunch amidst art and culture. Free tours are conducted at 11:00 a.m. Tues., Wed., Fri., Sat., and at 2:00 p.m. on Thurs. and Sunday. The Academy of Arts is at 900 S. Beretania St. (TheBus no. 2), opposite Thomas Square, tel. 538-1006.

Tennent Art Foundation

At 201-203 Prospect Street, on the *ewa* slope of Punchbowl, it's open Tues. through Sat. 10:00 a.m. to noon, and Sun. 2:00-4:00 p.m., tel. 531-1987. Free. There is a library and the walls hold the paintings of Madge Tennent, one of Hawaii's foremost artists, as well as many other contemporary works. It's beautiful and quiet just to visit.

Foster Botanical Gardens

Fifteen acres of exotic trees, many have been growing in this manicured garden for over 100 years. At one time the private estate of Dr. Hillebrand, physician to the royal court, he brought many of the seedlings from Asia. Two dozen of these trees enjoy lifetime protection by the state. At 180 N. Vineyard St., tel. 531-1939, open daily 9:00 a.m. to 4:00 p.m., free, self-guiding brochures. Guided tours Mon., Tues., and Wed. at 1:30 p.m.; many nature hikes on Oahu and the Neighbor Islands are sponsored by the gardens.

Manoa Road

Leading past the University of Hawaii into Manoa Valley, is a lovely residential area. En route you pass **Punahou School,** one of the oldest and most prestigious high schools in Hawaii. Built in 1841 from lava rock, children of the missionary families or wealthy San Franciscans attended, getting the best possible education west of the Rockies. Manoa Rd. turns into Oahu Avenue. **Waioli Tea Room,** 3016 Oahu Ave., owned and operated by the Salvation Army, is a small park; their snack bar features fresh-baked pastries and serves lunch daily from 11:00 a.m. to 2:00 p.m. Also featured here is the **Little Grass Shack** transported from Waikiki that Robert Louis Stevenson supposedly lived in. Visit the chapel with its distinctive stained-glass windows. Waioli Tea Room is open daily except Sun. from 8:00 a.m. to 3:30 p.m. Reservations, tel. 988-2131.

Paradise Park

These 13 acres of lush tropical plants explode in the 160 inches of annual rainfall that cascades into this farthest section of Manoa Valley. Magnificent blooms compete with the wild plumage of 50 species of exotic birds. You first walk into a giant birdcage laced with paths. The birds perform circus acts at scheduled intervals; some could easily win a spot with Barnum and Bailey for their tricks. This is purely *make-believe Hawaii,* good for a few hours of family fun. The Chuck Machado Luau is held here on Sun. evenings, and Henri Hawaii's Restaurant, on the premises, has good food at not too inflated prices at 3737 Manoa Rd., tel. 988-6686. Admission is $7.95 adults, $5.95 children, open daily 9:30 a.m. to 5:30 p.m., allow 2-3 hours to see the entire park. Drive or take TheBus, no. 8-Paradise Park, from Ala Moana Center. Also, a special tour bus from Waikiki is available.

Moanalua Gardens

Those private gardens of the Damon Estate, at 1352 Pineapple Pl., tel. 839-5334, were given to the original owner by Princess Bernice Bishop in 1884. Just off the Moanalua Freeway, and open to the public, these gardens are not heavily touristed, a welcome respite from the hustle and bustle of the city. Some magnificent old trees include a Buddha tree from Ceylon, and a monkeypod called "the most beautifully shaped tree" in the world by *Ripley's Believe It or Not.* The Moanalua Foundation also sponsors walks deep into Moanalua Valley for viewing the foliage of "natural Hawaii." The free guided walks begin at 9:00 a.m. usually on weekends; make arrangements by calling tel. 839-5334.

Keaiwa Heiau State Park

In the cool heights above Aiea Town, these ancient grounds have a soothing effect the minute you enter. After exiting H-1, take Aiea Heights Road to the park entrance. Overnight tent camping is allowed here, with exceptionally large sites (permit needed, see page 213); for the few other visitors, the gates open at 7:00 a.m. and close at 6:30 p.m. As you enter the well-maintained park (a caretaker lives on the premises), tall pines to the left give a feeling

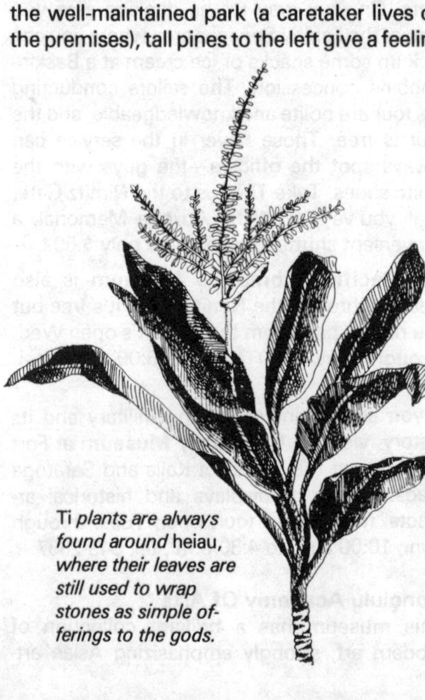

Ti *plants are always found around* heiau*, where their leaves are still used to wrap stones as simple offerings to the gods.*

of alpine coolness. Below, Pearl Harbor lies open, like the shell of a great oyster.

Keaiwa Heiau was a healing temple, surrounded by gardens of medicinal herbs tended by Hawaii's excellent healers, the *kahuna lapaau.* From the gardens, roots, twigs, leaves, and barks were ground into potions and mixed liberally with prayers and love. These potions were amazingly successful in healing Hawaiians before the white man brought his diseases. Walking onto the stone floor of the *heiau,* it's somehow warmer and the winds seem quieter. Toward the center are numerous offerings, simple stones wrapped with a *ti* leaf. Some are old, while others are quite fresh. Follow the park road to the **Aiea Loop Trail,** which heads back 4.5 miles (loop) onto one of the ridges descending from the Koolaus. Pass through a forest of tall eucalyptus trees, viewing canyons to the left and right. Notice, too, the softness of the "spongy bark" trees growing where the path begins. Allow 3 hours for the loop.

HONOLULU BEACHES AND PARKS

The beaches and parks listed here are found in and around Honolulu's city limits. World famous Waikiki has its own entire section (see p. 267). The good thing about having Waikiki so close is that it lures most bathers away from other city beaches, which makes them less congested. The following begins at Blaisdell Park, on the north shore of Pearl Harbor's East Loch, and runs east to Fort DeRussy Beach Park, just a few hundred yards from where the string of Waikiki's beaches begin.

Blaisdell Beach Park

This area's waters, which can all be considered **Pearl Harbor Park,** are too polluted for swimming. It's sad to think that at the turn of the century it was clear and clean enough to support oysters. Pearl Harbor took its name from *Waimomi,* "Water of Pearls," which were indeed harvested from the oysters and a certain species of clam growing here. Today, sewage and uncountable oil spills have done their devastation. Recently, oysters from the Mainland's East Coast have been introduced, and are being harvested from the mud flats. Supposedly, they're fit to eat. Facilities include a pay phone, tables, and restrooms. Access is off Rt.99 just past Aloha Stadium, and before you enter Pearl City.

Keehi Lagoon Beach Park is also polluted, but some people do swim here. The park is at the northern tip of Keehi Lagoon, at 465 Lagoon Drive, just past the **Pacific War Memorial** on Rt. 92, (the Nimitz Highway). Here are restrooms, picnic facilities, a pay phone, and local people use the area for pole fishing and crabbing.

Sand Island State Recreation Area

As you enter this 140-acre park by way of the Sand Island Access Road, clearly marked off the Nimitz Highway, you pass through some ugly real estate—scrap yards, petro-chemical tanks, and other such beauties. Don't get discouraged, keep going! Once you cross the metal bridge, a favorite fishing spot for local people, and then pass the entrance to the U.S. Coast Guard Base, you enter the actual park, 14 acres landscaped with picnic, and playground facilities. Follow the road into the park; pass 2 observation towers that have been built in the middle of a grassy field from where you get an impressive view of Honolulu, and Diamond Head making a remarkable counter-point. The park is excellently maintained, with pavilions, cold water showers, walkways, and restrooms. For day use, the park closes at 6:30 p.m. The camping area is usually empty (state permit required, see p. 213). The sites are out in the open, but a few trees provide some shade.

Unfortunately, you're under one of the main glide-paths for Honolulu International Airport. Many local people come to fish, and the surfing is good, but the beaches for snorkeling and swimming are fair at best. Some of the beach area is horrible, piled with broken stone, rubble, and pieces of coral. However, if you follow the road past the tower and park in the next lot, turn right and follow the shore up to a sandy beach. The currents or wave action aren't dangerous, but remember that this part of the harbor receives more than its share of pollutants. For delicious and inexpensive plate lunches, make sure to stop at Penny's just next door to Dirty Dan's Topless Go-Go Bar on your way down the access road (see p. 254 and p. 257).

Kakaako (Point Panic) Beach Park

This small facility was carved out of a piece of land donated by the University of Hawaii's Biomedical Research Center. Next to Kewalo Basin Harbor, follow Ahuii Street, off Ala Moana Boulevard. You'll come to some landscaped grounds, with a cold water shower and a path leading to the bathing area. Kewalo Basin, developed in the '20s to hold Honolulu's tuna fleet, is home to many charter boats. This area is poor for swimming, known for sharks, but great for bodysurfing. Unfortunately, novices will quickly find out why it's called Point Panic. A long seawall with a sharp drop-off runs the entire length of the area. The wave action is perfect for riding, but all wash against the wall. Beginners stay out!

Ala Moana Park

Ala Moana ("Path to the Sea") Beach Park is by far Honolulu's best. Most visitors congregate just around the bend at Waikiki, but residents head for Ala Moana, the place to soak up the local color. During the week, this beautifully curving white-sand beach has plenty of elbow room. Weekends bring families that come for every water sport Oahu offers. The swimming is great, with manageable wave action, plenty of lifeguards, and even good snorkeling along the reef. Board riders have their favorite spots, and bodysurfing is excellent. The huge area has a number of restrooms, food concessions, tennis courts, softball fields, a bowling green, and parking for 500 cars. Many Oahu outrigger canoe clubs practice in this area, especially in the evening; it's great to come and watch them glide along. A huge banyan grove provides shade and strolling if you don't fancy the beach, or you can bring a kite to play aloft with the trade winds. Ala Moana Park stretches along Ala Moana Avenue, between the Ala Wai and Kewalo Basin Boat Harbors. It's across from the Ala Moana Shopping Center, so you can rush right over if your credit cards start melting from the sun.

Aina Moana Recreation Area

Aina Moana ("Land from the Sea") used to be called Magic Island because it was reclaimed land. It is actually the point of land stretching out from the eastern edge of Ala Moana, and although it has a different name, will appear to be part of Ala Moana. All the beach activities are great here, too.

Kahanamoku Beach

The stretch of sand in front of the Hilton Hawaiian Village is named after Hawaii's most famous waterman, Duke Kahanamoku. The man-made beach and lagoon were completed in 1956. A system of pumps pushes water into the lagoon to keep it fresh. The swimming is great, and plenty of concessions offer surfboards, beach equipment, and catamaran cruises.

local women's canoe club practicing along Ala Moana Park

Fort DeRussy Beach
This is the last beach before reaching the Waikiki beaches proper. You pass through rights-of-way of Fort DeRussy military area where you'll find restrooms, picnic facilities, volleyball courts, and food and beverage concessions. Lifeguard service is provided by military personnel—no duty is too rough for our fighting men and women! A controversy has raged for years between the military and developers who covet this valuable piece of land. The government has owned it since the turn of the century, and has developed what once was wasteland into the last stretch of non-cement, non-highrise piece of real estate left along Waikiki. Since the public has access to the beach, and since Congress voted a few years back that the lands can not be sold, it'll remain under the jurisdiction of the military. **Battery Randolph,** on the military grounds, is open to the public as a military museum.

ACCOMMODATIONS

The vast majority of Oahu's hotels are strung along the boulevards of Waikiki. Most are neatly clustered, bounded by the Ala Wai Canal, and run eastward to Diamond Head. These hotels will be discussed in the Waikiki section. The remainder of greater Honolulu has few hotels, but what do exist are some of Oahu's cheapest. Most are clean, no-frills establishments, with a few others at the airport, or just off the beaten track.

Oahu's YM/WCAs And YH
Oahu has a number of YM/WCAs from which to choose, and the only YH in the state. They vary as far as private room and bath are concerned, facilities offered, and prices. Expect to pay about $15 s with a shared bath, and about $25 d with a private bath.

The **YMCA Central Branch** (men only) at 401 Atkinson Dr., Honolulu, 96814, tel 941-3344 is the most centrally located and closest to Waikiki. You can call ahead, but there are no reservations, no curfew, no visitors after 10:00 p.m.; it has an outside pool, singles, doubles, and private baths. This Y is located just across from the eastern end of Ala Moana Park, only a 10-minute walk to Waikiki.

YMCA Nuuanu (men only), 1441 Pali Hwy., Honolulu 96813, tel. 536-3556, just near the intersection of S. Vineyard Blvd., is a few minutes walk from downtown Honolulu. You'll find a modern, sterile facility, reservations accepted, a pool, shared and single rooms, and private or communal showers.

Armed Services YMCA, open to military or civilian, both men and women accepted at 250 S. Hotel St., Honolulu, tel. 524-5600. No reservations, but a pool, single and double rooms, plenty of sporting facilities, and child care!

YMCA Atherton Branch, 1810 University Ave., Honolulu, tel. 946-0253. Near U. of Hawaii, men and women students are given preferential treatment. Dormitory style, no recreational facilities, cheapest in town, but there's a 3-night minimum, and a one-time membership fee.

YWCA Fernhurst, 1566 Wilder Ave., Honolulu 96822, tel. 941-2231, just off Manoa Rd., across from the historical Punahou School. Singles and doubles with shared bath, women only. Weekly rates. Breakfast and dinner included (except Sunday) for low price. Doors closed 11:00 p.m., but night guard will admit later. Limited reservations depending on availability with deposit. Women can stay for up to one year, and many women from around the world add an international flavor.

The only American Youth Hostel in Hawaii is the **Honolulu International Youth Hostel** (Hale Aloha), 2323 A Seaview Ave., Honolulu, HI 96822, tel. 946-0591, located near the University of Hawaii. This YH is always busy, but will take reservations. AYH members with identity cards are given priority, but nonmembers are accepted on a space-available day-by-day basis. For information and reservations write to the manager, and include SASE and $5.25 (night's lodging) deposit. For information and membership cards write American Youth Hostels, 1332 I St., N.W., Suite 895, Washington, D.C. 20005.

Elderhostel, 100 Boylston St., Suite 200, Boston, MA 02116, offers non-credit courses at Hawaii Loa College, Oahu. For people 60 years and older. Fees begin at $175 and include course, room and board.

University Of Hawaii

Two 6-week summer sessions beginning late May and in early July are offered to bona fide students of accredited universities at the University of Hawaii at Manoa, Oahu. Reasonable rates in residence halls (mandatory meals), and in apartments on campus; special courses with emphasis on Polynesian and Asian culture and languages, including China and Japan. Unbeatably priced tours and outings to points throughout the islands for students and the general public at the Summer Session Activities Office. For information, catalog, and enrollment, write Summer Session Office, University of Hawaii, 2500 Dole St., Krauss Hall 101, Honolulu, HI 96822, tel. 944-1014 or 949-0771.

Moderate/Expensive Hotels

The **Kobayashi Hotel** at 250 N. Beretania St., Honolulu, HI 96817, tel. 536-2377, is in Chinatown, and an old standby as an inexpensive but clean hotel. It's away from all the Waikiki action, and the spartan, linoleumed rooms rent for under $25. Plenty of travelers pass through here, and the hotel's restaurant serves authentic Japanese food with moderate prices.

The **Nakamura Hotel** is a little bit more *uptown* both price and location wise. It's at 1140 S. King St., Honolulu, HI 96814, tel. 537-1951. The rooms are well appointed, carpeted, and have large bathrooms. Some a/c rooms face busy King Street, the *mauka* side rooms are quieter, with plenty of breezes to keep you cool. Often, you can find a room at this meticulously clean hotel when others are booked out, only because it's out of the mainstream.

The **Pagoda Hotel,** 1525 Rycroft St., Honolulu, HI 96814, tel. 800-367-6060, on Oahu 941-6611, behind Ala Moana Park between Kapiolani Blvd. and S. King Street. Because this hotel is away from the "action," you get very good value for your money. Rooms with kitchenettes start at about $50, with 2-bedroom suites at around $90. All rooms have TV, a/c; parking, swimming pool, and well-known Pagoda Restaurant.

The **Ala Moana Americana,** 410 Atkinson Dr., Honolulu, HI 96814, tel. 800-228-3278, on Oahu 955-4811, is another hotel where you're just off the Waikiki strip. It's located just behind Ala Moana Park between Ala Moana and Kapiolani boulevards, with a walking ramp connecting it directly with the Ala Moana Shopping Center. Rooms start at $70 and go up to around $250 for a 2-bedroom suite (6 people). There's a/c, TV, swimming pools, an all-night coffee shop, and the Summit Supper Club on the top of this 36-story hotel.

FOOD

The restaurants mentioned below are outside of the Waikiki area, although many are close, even in walking distance. Others are located near Ala Moana, Chinatown, downtown, and the less touristed areas of greater Honolulu. Some are first-class restaurants, others, among the best, are just roadside stands where you can get a satisfying plate lunch. The restaurants are listed according to price range and location, with differing cuisines mixed in each range. Besides the sun and surf, it's the amazing arrays of food found on Oahu that makes it extraordinary.

Inexpensive: Ala Moana

The following are all located at the **Ala Moana Shopping Center. China House,** open daily for lunch and dinner, tel. 949-6622. This enormous dining hall offers the usual selection of Chinese dishes, but is famous for its *dim sum* (11:00 a.m. to 2:00 p.m.); you pick and choose bite-sized morsels from carts.

La Cocina, open daily for lunch and dinner, tel. 949-9233. Serving Mexican food for under $5 with complimentary chips and salsa. Dining facilities and take-out service. Less spicy offerings to suit American tastes.

Michel's Baguette, 1st floor ocean side. Open weekdays from 7:00 a.m. to 9:00 p.m., Sat. till 5:30 p.m., Sun. 8:00 a.m. to 5:00 p.m., tel. 946-6888. They specialize in french bread, pastries, and croissants baked on the premises. A good selection of tasty soups, salads, and sandwiches. A change from the ordinary burger.

For a cup of exotic coffee or a light lunch (soup and salad) try **Upstart Crow and Company** Bookstore and Coffeehouse, in Ala Moana and Ward Warehouse Centers. You can work off lunch by browsing through some heavy tomes.

Patti's Chinese Kitchen, 1st floor facing the sea, tel. 946-5002, has all the ambience you'd expect from a cafeteria-style Chinese fast-food joint, plus lines about a block long. But don't let either discourage you. The lines move incredibly quickly, and you won't get gourmet food, but it's tasty, plentiful, and cheap. The Princess-Queen Special is steamed rice, fried rice, or noodles, a *chow mein* plus 2 entrees like sweet and sour pork, or a chicken dish—for around $3. The Queen is the same, but add an entree—under $4. You can even have 4 entrees which fill 2 large paper plates. The princesses who eat this much food aren't tiny-waisted damsels waiting for a rescuing prince—they can flatten anyone who hassles them on their own.

Around Town

The **University of Hawaii,** Manoa Campus, hosts a number of restaurants, ranging from an inexpensive cafeteria to international cuisine at the East-West Center. Inexpensive to moderate, the restaurants include: **Moana Gardens,** salad and snacks; **Campus Center Dining Room,** for full meals; and the **International Garden,** at Jefferson Hall in the East-West Center.

The Honolulu Academy of Arts', 900 S. Beretania, **Garden Cafe Restaurant** serves lunches daily in elegant surroundings. For information and reservations, tel. 531-8865.

King's Bakery and Coffee Shop is a favorite of local people, at 1936 S. King St. and Pumehana, tel. 941-5211 (one of 3 locations). They're open 24 hours, and get very busy around 6:00 p.m. when they allow only groups of 2 or more to sit in the few booths; the rest eat at the counter. The menu is American/Hawaiian/Oriental. Full meals are around $5. Not great, but good and wholesome. The bakery has 7-grain bread, whole wheat, but mostly white fluffy stuff with tons of powdered sugar. However, they do offer *tofuti,* a soft ice cream-like dessert made from healthful *tofu.* Their other locations are at the Kaimuki Shopping Center, and Eaton Square. Across the street from King's Bakery are 2 inexpensive eateries, **McCully Chop Suey,** and **Yoshi's Sushi Yakiniku Restaurant.**

Down to Earth Natural Foods, open Mon. to Sat., 10:00 a.m. to 8:30 p.m., Sun. 10:00 a.m. to 6:00 p.m. at 2525 S. King St., tel. 947-7678, is a kind of "museum of health food stores" serving filling, nutritious health-food dishes for very reasonable prices. Sandwiches, like a whopping avocado, tofu, and cheese are under $3. Daily full-meal specials, like vegie stroganoff, eggplant parmigiana, and lasagna are around $4, including salad. There are plenty of items on the menu that will fill you up for under $2. Healthwise, you can't go wrong! Just up the street at 2471 S. King, across from the Star Garden Market, is the tiny **Saimin Bowl** restaurant. Their name says it all, and you can have a huge steaming bowl of soup for a few dollars.

Sekiya's Restaurant and Deli at 2746 Kaimuki Ave., tel. 732-1656, looks like a set from a 1940s tough-guy movie. The food is well prepared and the strictly local clientele will be amazed that you even know about the place. For a quick *bento* or *sushi* to go, try **Matsuri Sushi,** tel. 949-1111, at the corner of Kapiolani Blvd. and McCully. This quick stop is perfect to pick up lunch for a tour on your way out of the Waikiki area.

Suehiro's at 1824 S. King, open daily for lunch and dinner, with take-out service, tel. 949-4584, gets the nod from local Japanese people. The menu here is authentic, the decor strictly Americana, and the food well prepared and moderately priced.

People's Cafe, 1300 Pali Hwy., open Mon. to Sat. 10:00 a.m. to 7:30 p.m., tel. 536-5789. Two going on 3 generations of the same Japanese family have been serving the full range of excellent and inexpensive Hawaiian food at this down-home restaurant. It's not fancy, but the food is good, and the surroundings clean.

Coco's Coffee House at the corner of Kalakaua and Kapiolani is an American standard that's open all night. It's like a million others in the U.S. where you can order a hot roast beef sandwich for a few bucks, or just sip a coffee into the wee hours, staying out of the weather.

M's Coffee Tavern is a favorite with downtown office workers for great lunches, excellent coffee, and cocktails, at 124 Queen St., tel. 531-5739.

Two inexpensive yet authentic restaurants next door to each other at 1679 Kapiolani Blvd., the **Kintoki** Japanese Restaurant, tel. 949-8835, and the **Sukyung** Korean Restaurant. This semi-seedy area has plenty of "girlie bars," but the food is good and authentic, with most items priced below $5.

Penny's Plate Lunches, on the Sand Island Access Road next to Dirty Dan's Topless Go-Go Joint, is one of the cheapest and most authentic Hawaiian plate lunch stands you can find. The most expensive lunch stew *(lau lau)*, pork and butterfish wrapped in a *ti* leaf, costs around $3.50. You can also try baseball-sized *manapua* for around $.60. Penny's is out of the way, but definitely worth a stop.

You can't get much cheaper than free, and that's what the **International Society for Krishna Consciousness** offers every Sun. at 5:30 p.m. for its vegetarian smorgasbord. Their 2-acre compound is just off the Pali Hwy. at 51 Coelho Way, tel. 595-4913. Of course there's a few chants for dessert. *Hare Krishna!*

Fast Foods

Fast-food fanciers and fanatics have nothing to fear on Oahu. There's enough of them to feed an army, mainly because there is an Army, plus a Navy and Marine Corps of young men and women on the island, not to mention the army of tourists. If you're after pizza, burgers, shakes, and fries, choose from 36 **McDonald's**, 13 or so **Jacks-in-the-Box**, 24 **Pizza Huts**, 10 or so **Zippy's**, 6 **Wendy's**, a few **Farrell's** and good old **Dairy Queens**.

MODERATE: UNDER $15

Shiruhachi at 1901 Kapiolani Blvd., tel. 947-4680, is a completely authentic Japanese *sushi* bar operated by Hiroshi Suzuki. As a matter of fact, until recently 90% of the clientele were Japanese, either visiting businessmen or locals in the know, and the menu was only in Japanese. However, everyone is more than welcome. With a beer, you get free *otsumami* (nibbles) with a wide selection of *sushi* and other finger foods like *yakitori* at about $2 for 2 skewers. A separate section of the restaurant turns into a cocktail lounge, somewhat like an *akachochin*, a neighborhood Japanese bar where people go to relax. There's taped music and a dance floor. If you're into authentic Japanese, this is a great one.

Auntie Pasto's at 1099 S. Beretania and the corner of Pensacola, tel. 523-8855, is open daily for lunch, dinner, and late nights. The vibe is upbeat pizza parlor, where you can even bring your own wine. Most of the Italian menu is around $6; the specialty is a fish stew loaded with morsels for about $9. Their large salad with garlic bread is cheap, and enough for 2. No reservations necessary, quiet, comfortable.

Willows is at 901 Hausten, just behind Kapiolani Blvd. on the N side of the Ala Wai Canal, tel. 946-4808. Like a tiny tropical oasis surrounded by the cement of the city, there's a willow-shaped pool, bubbling with uncountable carp. Once inside, the garden opens up, and there are even strolling musicians singing Hawaiian standards. Local people love it, a definite tip-off. The food is Hawaiian/Oriental/American. And the dessert pies are great!

The Old Spaghetti Factory, in the Ward Warehouse Shopping Center, tel. 531-1513, serves up large plates of pasta and other Italian dishes for reasonable prices. If you're Italian you'll of course prefer *mama's* cooking, but this isn't bad for moderately priced Italian-style fast foods.

TGI Fridays is a raucous singles' bar known for some delectable morsels such as stuffed potatoes, quiches, and the like. It's across the street from the Blaisdel Center at 950 Ward Ave., open daily 11:00 a.m. to 2:00 p.m., tel. 523-5841. Plenty of swingers and college students keep the joint jumpin'.

Wo Fat's at 115 N. Hotel St., tel. 533-6393, has had a little experience satisfying customers—oldest eatery in Chinatown, it's been at the same location for over 80 years, and open for business for 100! Besides serving delicious food from a menu with hundreds of Cantonese dishes, the building itself is monumentally ornate. You're entertained just checking out the decor of lanterns, dragons, gilt work, and screens. Most dishes are reasonably priced and start at around $5. This restaurant is highly respected by the people of Chinatown, and is part of the Chinatown Tour offered by the Chamber of Commerce.

Pagoda Floating Restaurant, at 1525 Rycroft, open daily from 7:00 a.m. to 9:30 p.m., tel. 941-6611. The Pagoda is attached to the Pagoda Hotel. The restaurant has 2 levels: an informal dining room on the 1st floor, and a more elegant room on the second. Besides a large menu of Oriental and American standards, they feature a salad bar, and excellent views of the harbor.

EXPENSIVE: OVER $15

John Dominis is where local people go to have an exceptional night out. It's at 43 Ahui St., tel. 523-0955, at the end of a long row of warehouses overlooking Kewalo Basin. The fish couldn't be fresher with large ponds of lobsters and crabs swimming around. The catch of the day is always a good choice, and the *cioppino* (fish stew) is marvelous.

Won Kee Seafood Restaurant, 100 N. Beretania, is a splurge joint where you get delicious seafood. Free parking on Mauna Kea Street. This is the place for Honolulu's in-the-know crowd. Tasteful and elegant surroundings.

Fishermen's Wharf Restaurant, Ala Moana Blvd. at Kewalo Basin, tel. 538-3808. Serves lunch and dinner, reservations necessary. Tough parking, but free with validation in local lots. The restaurant has 2 sections: upstairs is the **Captain's Bridge,** and downstairs is the **Seafood Grotto.** The greatest thing about this restaurant is its location, right on Fishermen's Wharf with plenty of bobbing boats at anchor and local color just outside the windows. The waitresses wear cutesie-pie sailor suits, the waiters striped jerseys. The service is adequate but not special, mostly due to the number of people served—always packed! For a renowned fish restaurant too many offerings are plain old deep-fried. For example, the shrimp stuffed with cheese and crab meat is merely breaded and popped in the fryer. Good, but not special. The cheapest item on the menu is spaghetti, not linguini, with canned clam sauce. Two can dine for around $30, to say you've been there, but you'll hardly hurry back.

The **Chart House** at 1765 Ala Moana Blvd. near Ala Wai Yacht Harbor, open daily 4:00 p.m. (Sun. 5:00 p.m.) till 2:00 a.m., tel. 941-6660. They offer a happy hour until 7:00 p.m., *pu pu* until midnight, and nightly entertainment. Shellfish specialties start at $15, with chicken and beef dishes a few dollars cheaper.

India House, 2632 S. King St., open daily for lunch and dinner, tel. 955-7552. Extraordinary Indian dishes prepared by chef Ram Arora. A wide selection of curries, vegetarian dishes, special *naan* bread, *kabobs,* and fish *tikka.* Specialty desserts of home-made ice cream and toppings.

Windows of Hawaii sits atop the Ala Moana Bldg. at 1441 Kapiolana Blvd., American and Continental. Great views from this revolving

the Pagoda Floating Restaurant

restaurant. Lunch (sandwiches) for under $8, and complete dinners from $15. Extremely popular for sunset. Reservations, tel. 941-9138. Champagne brunch, Sat. and Sun. 10:00 a.m. to 2:00 p.m.

Keo's Thai Restaurant, 625 Kapahulu, open nightly from 5:30-11:00 p.m., tel. 737-8240, has become an institution. It serves great Thai food at expensive prices. They pride themselves on the freshest ingredients, spices tuned up or down to suit the customer, and Keo's recipes taught to each chef personally. There's always a line, with a few benches in the parking lot for waiting customers, but no reservations are taken. The 8-page menu offers most of Thailand's delectables, and vegetarians are also catered to. You can save money and still have the same quality food at **Mekong II,** 1726 S. King, lunch and dinner, tel. 941-6184. Owned by Keo's, it's not as fancy.

Nuuanu Onsen, 87 Laimi Rd., (right off the Pali Hwy., just before Queen Emma's Summer Palace), tel. 538-9184, is one of Honolulu's best-kept secrets. This authentic Japanese tea house serves a gourmet fixed menu. You leave your cares along with your shoes at the entrance, and are escorted by a *kimono*-clad waitress to your lacquered table, where you sit on *tatami* mats and enjoy the serenity of the garden framed by the *shoji* screens. The hostess plays *geisha*-like tea house games if you like. Here you enjoy the experience as much as the meal.

Luau

To have fun at a *luau,* you have to get into the swing of things. Basically a huge banquet, you eat and drink until you're contentedly uncomfortable, somewhat like Thanksgiving on the beach. Entertainment is provided by local performers in what is invariably called a "Polynesian Review." This includes the tourist's *hula,* the fast version with swaying hips and dramatic lighting, a few wandering troubadors singing Hawaiian standards, and someone swinging swords or flaming torches. All the Hawaiian standards like *poi, haupia, lomi* salmon, *laulau,* and *kalua* pig are usually served. If these don't suit your appetite, various Oriental dishes, plus chicken, fish, and roast beef do. If you leave a *luau* hungry, it's your own fault! They range in price from $20-$30 per person. The price oftentimes includes admission to the theme parks at which many are now presented. The least expensive, most authentic, and best *luau* are often put on by local churches or community groups. They are not on a regular basis, so make sure to peruse the free tourist literature where they advertise. The following *luau* are institutions and have been operating for years. If you ask a local person "Which is the best?" you won't get 2 to agree. It's literally a matter of taste. **Chuck Machado's** is every Tues., Fri., and Sun. at 7:00 p.m., tel. 836-0249, at the Waikiki Outrigger Hotel. Great show that you can enjoy just by strolling on the nearby beach. **Paradise Park Luau,** Mon., Wed., and Thurs., a full day beginning at 2:00 p.m. with free transportation and admission to the park, tel. 944-8833. **Germaine's Luau,** often claimed by local people to be *the best,* held at Ewa Beach, tel. 946-3111. **Paradise Cove Luau** boasts a private beach with a shuttle bus departing Waikiki at 4:00 p.m. and returning by 10:00 p.m., tel. 945-3571. The **Great Hawaiian Luau** is held at Makapuu Point, tel. 926-8843.

HONOLULU ENTERTAINMENT

Dancing, Disco, And Lounge Acts

Rumors, in the Ala Moana American Hotel, 410 Atkinson St., tel. 955-4811, is an established disco that cranks up around 9:00 p.m. and features the newest in dance and rock videos. Also, the restaurant atop the building, Windows of Hawaii, supplements your evening meal with a lounge act.

Tony Roma's, 98-150 Kaonohi St. in the Westridge Mall, Aiea Town, tel. 487-9911, offers a lounge act Sun. to Fri., and daily happy hour from 4:30 to 8:30 p.m. and a special *pu pu* menu.

TGI Fridays, 950 Ward Ave., tel. 523-5841, is a lively night spot. Good food, large portions, reasonable prices, and music.

Peco's River Cafe, at 99-016 Kamehameha Hwy., tel. 487-7980, has country music featuring Nick Masters and the Mustangs.

Freebies

At **Centerstage,** Ala Moana Center, various

shows are presented—mostly music (rock, gospel, jazz, Hawaiian) and *hula*. Performances usually start at noon. The **Young People's Hula Show**, every Sun. at 9:30 a.m., is fast becoming an institution. Here, *hula* is being kept alive, with many first-time performers interpreting the ancient movements that they study in their *halau*.

The **Royal Hawaiian Band**, founded over 100 years ago, performs Fri. at noon on the Iolani Palace Bandstand.

Hilo Hattie, 700 Nimitz Highway, the largest manufacturer of alohawear in the state, conducts free tours of the factory complete with hotel pick-up. Up to 80,000 garments are on display in the showroom. It's hard to resist spending: prices and craftsmanship are good, and designs are the most contemporary. Open daily 8:30 a.m. to 5:00 p.m., tel. 537-2926.

The giant pineapple watertower off Iwilei Road guides you to the **Dole Pineapple Factory** (now a subsidiary of Castle and Cook). Here, millions of Hawaii's fruit are canned, juiced, and sliced for shipment around the world. Free samples are available. Least activity is during the winter months, but something fascinating is always going on. In the summertime, at the height of the harvest, this factory can process over 3 million cans of fruit per day! No reservations needed for small groups. Contact the Dole Company at 650 Iwilei Rd., tel. 536-3411, open 9:00 a.m. to 3:00 p.m., small admission.

Girlie Bars And Strip Joints

You'll have no excuse if your maiden Aunt Matilda or local chapter of Friendly Feminists ever catches you going into one of these joints, sonny boy! There's not even a hint of a redeeming social value here, and the only reason they're listed is to let you know where *not to go* if you're offended by raunchy sex shows. Many of these "lounges," as they're called, are strung along the 1600 and 1700 blocks of Kapiolani Blvd., and in the little alleys running off it. Mostly, tough-looking Oriental men own or operate them, and they open and shut quicker than a streetwalker's heart. Inside are 2 types of women: the dancers and the "lap sitters," and there's definitely a pecking order in these hen houses. (For a full description see p. 145.) Most patrons are local men or GI types, with only a smattering of tourists. Personal safety is usually not a problem, but a fool and his money are soon parted in these bars. Here are some *without* the bad reputations that frequently go with this type of clip joint. **Misty II Lounge**, operated by a Vietnamese guy named Dean has been there 5 years, an eternity in this business; Dean immediately fires any girl with bad vibes. This club is at 1661 Kapiolani Blvd., tel. 944-1745. Just behind it in the little alleyway are the **Orchid, Musume,** and **Winners Club**—all about the same. Two clubs considered to be good ones by their patrons are **Butterfly Lounge,** 903 Keamoku, tel. 947-3012, and the **Stop Lite Lounge,** at 1718 Kapiolani, tel. 941-5838.

Chinatown's **Hotel Street** has hookers, both male and female, walking the heels off their shoes. They cruise during the day, but the area really comes alive at night. Mostly, these people are down-and-outers who can't make it against the stiff competition along the main areas of Waikiki. The clientele is usually servicemen and hard-core locals. A few clubs in this area offer strippers. Always be prepared for fights and bad vibes in any of these joints. A few that tourists have entered and survived include the **Zig Zag, My Way,** and **Hubba Hubba Lounge.**

Dirty Dan's, 205 Sand Island Access Rd., tel. 841-9063, is an old-fashioned topless go-go bar, the same as the famous one in San Diego. It's frequented mostly by GIs and can get pretty rowdy, especially late on weekends. The place is clean and prides itself on giving you a fair shake. It's not at all like the grab joints listed above. The women here are young and beautiful and *not* allowed to fraternize with the clientele. You can look, but you *cannot* touch. This helps to keep away the sleaze element. Draft and bottled beer are reasonably priced.

SHOPPING

If you don't watch the time, you'll spend half your vacation moving from one fascinating store to the next. Luckily, in greater Honolulu the majority of shopping is clustered in malls, with specialty shops scattered around the city, especially in the nooks and crannies of Chinatown. For a general overview of what the island has for sale, along with listings for bookstores, flea markets, sundries, and art shops, see p. 198.

Ala Moana Shopping Center

This is the largest shopping center in the state, and if you're the type that wants to get all of your souvenir hunting and special shopping done in one shot, this is the place. It's on Ala Moana Blvd., just across from the Ala Moana Beach Park, open weekdays from 9:30 a.m. to 9:00 p.m., Sat. 9:30 a.m. to 5:30 p.m., Sun. 10:00 a.m. to 5:00 p.m., tel. 946-2811. There's plenty of competition to keep prices down, and more than enough of an array and price range to suit any taste and budget. About 100 stores include all of Hawaii's major department stores like **Sears, Penney's** and **Liberty House**. You'll not only find big-name department stores, but utilitarian shops like shoemakers, eateries, banks, and boutiques featuring everything from flowers to swim fins. It's also a great place to see a cross-section of Hawaiian society. Another pleasantry is a free *hula* show every Sunday at 9:30 a.m. on the **Centerstage** (see p. 256). The **Hawaii Visitors Bureau** maintains an information kiosk just near Centerstage. The following is a mere sampling of what you'll find.

A good one-stop store with plenty of souvenir-quality items at affordable prices is good old **Woolworth's.** They have all of the same sundries as Mainland stores, but plenty of Hawaiian and Oriental baubles fill the shelves.

House of Music sells records and tapes. This is a good store to bring back those island sounds that'll immediately conjure up images of Hawaii whenever they're played. Ground floor, tel. 949-1051.

At **China Silk House,** street level, tel. 946-6248, you'll find the finest silk apparel, along with cloisonne, jade, and carvings. Distinctive gifts.

The Honolulu Book Shop, tel. 941-2274, has the largest selection of books in the state, especially their Hawaiiana section. Books make inexpensive, easy-to-transport, and long-lasting mementos of your trip to Hawaii. Ground level near Centerstage.

Francis Camera Shop, tel. 946-2879, is a well-stocked camera store with a fine selection of merchandise sure to please the most avid camera buff. If you need something out of the ordinary for your camera bag, this is a good place to come. The staff is friendly and will spend time giving you advice. However, the best place to buy film is at **Sears** (no credit cards). **Woolworth's,** and **Long's Drugs** also have good prices, but for cheap and fast developing try **Fromex Photo,** tel. 955-4797, street level, ocean side.

The Crackseed Center, tel. 949-7200, offers the best array of crackseed, (spiced nuts, seeds, and fruits) that have been treats for island children for years. There's also dried and spiced scallops at $68 per pound, and cuttlefish at $2.50 per pound—such a deal! Prices are inflated here, but their selection can't be beat, and you can educate yourself about these same products in smaller stores around the island. Crackseed is not to everyone's liking, but it does make a unique souvenir.

High Performance Kites, tel. 947-7097, features kites made on Molokai and Kauai. The tradewinds make kite-flying a fun-filled pastime. This store offers free lessons at Sandy Beach.

Shirokaya is a Japanese-owned department store between Penney's and Liberty House on the mountain side of the complex. They have a fascinating assortment of gadgetry, nicknacks, handy items and nifty stuff that Nippon is so famous for. It's fun just to look around, and the prices are reasonable. Japanese products are also available at **Iida's,** a local store dating back to the turn of the century, featuring garden ornaments and flower arrangement sets, tel. 946-0888.

Specialty shops in the center include: **Prides of New Zealand**, sheepskin products; **Hawaiian Island Creations, Products of Hawaii**, and **Irene's**, all selling a wide assortment of island-made goods and souvenirs, from cheap to exquisite; **India Imports**, many unique items from the sub-continent, and eelskin products; **Tahiti Imports** with bikinis, *muu muu*, and a wide selection of handicrafts from throughout Polynesia; **Eki Cyclery** for the bike enthusiast; and **Honolulu Sporting Goods** for recreational items of all sorts.

The Ward Warehouse
Located just a few blocks west of Ala Moana Center, at 1050 Ala Moana Blvd., open weekdays 10:00 a.m. to 9:00 p.m., Sat. 10:00 a.m. to 5:00 p.m., Sun. 11:00 a.m. to 4:00 p.m., tel. 531-6411. This modern 2-story complex lives up to its name as a warehouse, with a motif from bygone days when stout wooden beams were used instead of steel. The wide array of shops here includes some inexpensive restaurants, but the emphasis is on arts and crafts, with no less than 10 shops specializing in this field. It's a great place for a stroll, especially to kill time if you intend to dine at one of the famous seafood restaurants in the area, or if you're after a quality souvenir.

In the complex you'll find: **Arts of Okinawa**, and **Artist Guild**, among others; **Upstart Crow Bookstore and Coffeeshop**, for reading materials and a fine lunch; **Birkenstock Footprints**, with their wonderfully comfortable ugly-ducklings; **Imports International**, selling everything from blouses to wicker furniture; and **Thongs and Things** selling all kinds of thongs, even spiked golfing thongs.

Ward Center
Across the street from the Ward Warehouse this relatively new shopping center is gaining a reputation for some exclusive shops. Open weekdays 10:00 a.m. to 9:00 p.m., Sat. 10:00 a.m. to 5:00 p.m., Sun. 11:00 a.m. to 4:00 p.m., tel. 531-6411. In this center you'll mainly find a few gourmet snack shops, a bookstore, and apparel shops.

Bargains And Discounts
For discounts and bargains, try: **Crazy Shirts Factory Outlet**, at 99-969 Iwaena St. Aiea, tel. 487-9919, or 470 N. Nimitz Hwy., Honolulu, tel. 521-0855, seconds and discontinued styles, with a minimum savings of 50%; **Swimsuit Warehouse**, 870 Kapahulu Ave., Honolulu, tel. 735-0040, has women's swimsuits under $20, plus shorts and tops; **The Muumuu Factory**, 1526 Makaloa St., offers great sales—get there early and bring your helmet and shoulder pads to fight off the crowds; **Goodwill Thrift Shop**, at 83 N. King, tel. 521-3105, displays the same bargains as on the Mainland, but with a wide assortment of alohawear; **Nearly New Thrift Shop**, 1144 Koko Head Ave., tel. 732-3272, has consignment sales of quality merchandise; **Symphony Thrift Shop**, 1923 Pensacola, tel. 524-7157, is a consignment shop for used clothing in excellent condition, and usually name brands; **The Discount Store**, 188 S. Hotel St., tel 537-4469, boasts excellent prices on tape recorders, tapes, batteries, and electrical equipment.

Miscellaneous
Everyone, sooner or later, needs a good hardware store. You can't beat the selection at **Kilgo's**, 180 Sand Island Rd., tel. 845-3266. They have it all.

For **sporting goods**, try: **Big 88**, 330 Sand Island Rd., tel. 845-1688, many military items; **Amar Sporting Goods**, 1139 Bethel St., tel. 536-0404, sporting goods, sports wear, and a full range of accessories and equipment.

"It is the meeting place of East and West. The very new rubs shoulders with the immeasurably old. And if you have not found the romance you expected you have come upon something singularly intriguing."
—W. Somerset Maugham

WAIKIKI

Waikiki ("Spouting Water") is like a fresh young starlet from the sticks who went to Hollywood to make it big, and did, though maybe too fast for her own good. Everyone always knew that she had a double-dip of talent and heart, but the fast-lane has its heartaches, and she's been banged around a little by life. Even though her figure's fuller, her makeup's a little askew, and her high heels are worn down, she has plenty of *chutzpah* left, and when the curtain parts and the lights come up, she'll play her heart out for her audience.

Waikiki is a classic study of contradictions. Above all, it is a result of basic American entrepreneurism taken to the nth degree. Along the main strip, high-powered businessmen cut multimillion-dollar deals, but on the sidewalks it's a carnival midway with hucksters, handbillers, and street people selling everything decent and indecent under the tropical sun. To get a true feeling for Waikiki, you must put this amazing strip of land into perspective. The area covers only 7/10 of a square mile, which, at a good pace, you can walk in 15 minutes. On any given day, about 110,000 people crowd its beaches, and boulevards, making it one of the most densely populated areas on Earth. Sixty thousand of these people are tourists; 30,000 are workers who commute from various towns of Oahu and cater to the tourists, and the remaining 20,000 actually call Waikiki home. The turnover is about 80,000 new tourists per week, and the pace never slackens. To the head shakers, these facts condemn Waikiki as a mega-growth area gone wild. To others, these same figures make Waikiki an energized, fun-filled place to be, where "if you don't have a good time, it's your own fault." For the naive or the out-of-touch looking for "grass-shack paradise," the closest they'll come to it in Waikiki is painted on a souvenir ashtray. Those drawn to a smorgasbord of activities, who are adept at choosing the best and ignoring the rest, can't go wrong! People and the action are as constant in Waikiki as the ever-rolling surf.

History

The written record of this swampy area began in the late 1790s. The white man, along with his historians, cartographers, artists, and gunpowder were already an undeniable presence in the islands. Kalanikupule, ranking chief of

Oahu, hijacked the *Jackall,* a small ship commanded by Capt. Brown, with which he intended to spearhead an attack against Kamehameha I. The chief held the *Jackall* for a while, but the sailors regained control just off Diamond Head and sent the Hawaiians swimming for land. The ship then hastened to Kamehameha to report the treachery, and returned with his armada of double-hulled canoes, which beached along Waikiki. The great king then defeated Kalanikupule at the famous battle of Nuuanu Pali, and secured control of the island. Thereafter Waikiki, pinpointed by Diamond Head, became a well-known landmark.

Waikiki's interior was low-lying swampland, long known to be good for fishponds, taro rice, and bananas, but hardly for living. The beach, however, was always blessed with sunshine and perfect waves, especially for surfing, a sport heartily loved by the Hawaiians. The royalty of Hawaii, following Kamehameha, made Honolulu their capital, and kept beach houses at Waikiki. They invited many visiting luminaries to visit them at their private beach. All were impressed. In the 1880s, King Kalakaua was famous for his beach house hospitality. One of his favorite guests was Robert Louis Stevenson, who spent many months here writing one of his novels. By the turn of the 20th C. Waikiki had become a highly exclusive vacation spot. In 1901 the Moana Hotel was built, but immediately a protest was heard because it interfered with the view of Diamond Head. In 1906, Lucius Pinkham, then director of Hawaii's Board of Health, called the mosquito-infested area "dangerous and unsanitary," and proposed to drain the swamp with a canal so that "the whole place can be transformed into a place of unique beauty." By the early 1920s, the Ala Wai Canal was built, its dredgings used to reclaim land, and Waikiki was demarcated. By the end of the 1920s, the Royal Hawaiian Hotel, built on the site previously occupied by the royal beach house, was receiving very wealthy guests who arrived by ocean liner, loaded down with steamer trunks. They ensconced themselves at Waikiki, often staying for the duration of the season.

For about 40 years, Waikiki remained the enchanted domain of Hollywood stars, dignitaries, and millionaires. But for the brief and extraordinary days of WW II, which saw Waikiki barricaded and barb-wired, GIs—regular guys from the Mainland—were given a taste of this "reserved paradise" while on R&R. They brought home tantalizing tales of wonderful Waikiki, whetting the appetite of middle America. Beginning just before statehood and continuing through the '60s to the mid '70s, hotels and condos popped up like fertilized weeds, and tourism exploded with the advent of the jumbo jet. Discounted package tours began to haul in droves of economy-class tourists. Businesses catering to the tastes of penny-pinchers and first-timers elbowed their way into every nook and cranny. For the first time Waikiki began to be described as tacky and vulgar. For the old-timers, Waikiki was in decline. The upscale and repeat visitors started to snub Waikiki, heading for hidden resorts on the Neighbor Islands. But Waikiki had spirit and soul, and never gave in. In the last few years, its declining hotels started a campaign to regain their illustrious images. Millions upon millions of dollars have poured into renovations and remodelings. Luxury hotels renting exclusive and expensive rooms have reappeared, and are doing a booming business. Non-Americans, especially Japanese, still flock for dream vacations, mostly staying at Waikiki hotels, 25% of which are owned by Japanese firms.

Waikiki Today

The Neighbor Islands are pulling more and more tourists away, and depending on point of view, this is either boon or bust for Waikiki. Direct flights to Maui and the Big Island allow more tourists than ever to bypass Oahu but still a whopping 80% of the people visiting the islands spend at least one night in a Waikiki hotel, which offer the lowest room rates in Hawaii. The sublime and the gaudy are neighbors in Waikiki. Exclusive shops are often flanked by buskers selling plastic *hula* dolls. Burgers and beer mingle their pedestrian odors with those of Parisian cuisine. Though Waikiki in many ways is unique, it can also come off as *Anytown, U.S.A.* But most importantly it somehow works, and works well. You may not find "paradise" on Waikiki's streets, but you will find a willing "dancing partner," and if you pay the fiddler, she'll keep the beat

SIGHTS

To see Waikiki's attractions, you have to do little more than perch on a bench or loll on a beach towel. Its boulevards and beaches are world-class for people watching. Some of its strollers and sunbathers are *visions,* while others are real *sights.* And if you keep your ears open, it's not hard to hear every American accent and a dozen foreign languages. Some actual sights are intermingled with the hotels, boutiques, bars, and restaurants. Sometimes, too, these very buildings *are* the sights. Unbelievably, you can even find plenty of quiet spots—in the gardens of Kapiolani Park, and at churches, temples, tea rooms, and ancient Hawaiian special places sitting unnoticed amidst the grandiose structures of the 20th century. Also, both the Honolulu Zoo and Waikiki Aquarium are well worth a visit.

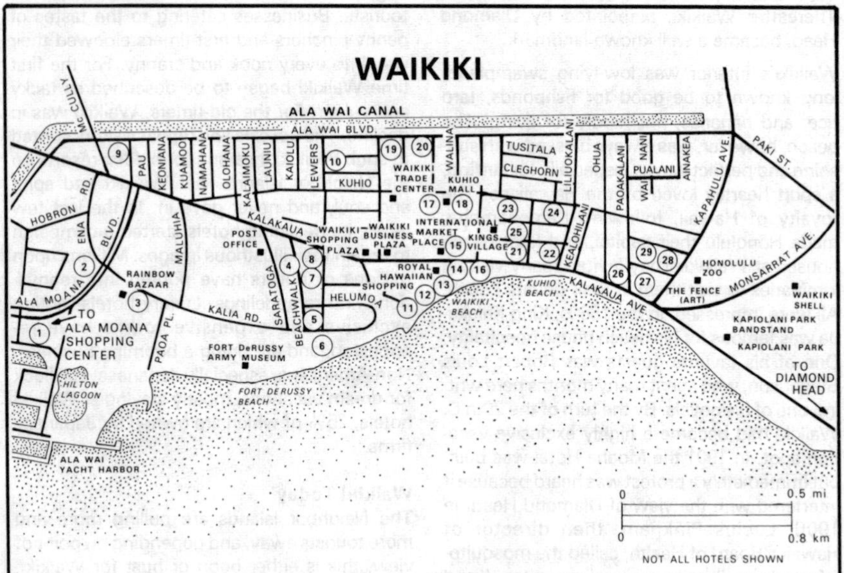

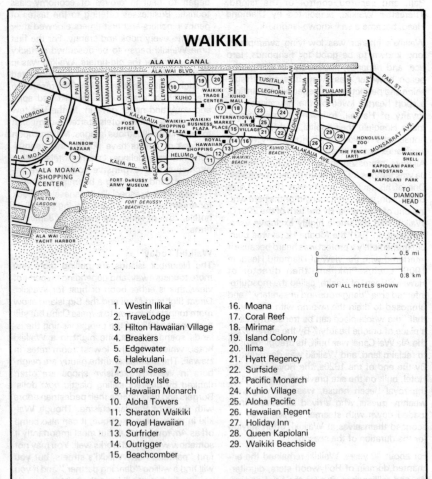

1. Westin Ilikai
2. TraveLodge
3. Hilton Hawaiian Village
4. Breakers
5. Edgewater
6. Halekulani
7. Coral Seas
8. Holiday Isle
9. Hawaiian Monarch
10. Aloha Towers
11. Sheraton Waikiki
12. Royal Hawaiian
13. Surfrider
14. Outrigger
15. Beachcomber
16. Moana
17. Coral Reef
18. Mirimar
19. Island Colony
20. Ilima
21. Hyatt Regency
22. Surfside
23. Pacific Monarch
24. Kuhio Village
25. Aloha Pacific
26. Hawaiian Regent
27. Holiday Inn
28. Queen Kapiolani
29. Waikiki Beachside

Diamond Head, the everlasting signature of Waikiki (Fritz Craft)

Diamond Head

If you're not sandwiched in a man-made canyon of skyscrapers, you can look eastward from anywhere in Waikiki and see Diamond Head. Diamond Head *says* Waikiki. Western sailors have used it as a landmark since the earliest days of contact, and the Hawaiians undoubtedly before that. Ships' artists etched and sketched its motif long before the names of the new-found lands of Hawaii, Waikiki, and Oahu were standardized, and appeared on charts as *Owyhee, Whytete,* and *Woohoo.* The Hawaiian name was *Leahi,* ("Brow of the Ahi"); legend says it was named by Hi'iaka, Madame Pele's younger sister, because she saw a resemblance in its silhouette to this yellowfin tuna. The name "Diamond Head" comes from a band of sailors who found calcite crystals on its slopes and thought they'd discovered diamonds. Kamehameha I immediately made the mountain *kapu* until his adviser John Young informed him that what the seamen found, later known as "Pele's tears," except as souvenirs were worthless. Diamond Head was considered a power spot by the Hawaiians. Previously, Kamehameha had worshipped at a *heiau* located on the western slopes, offering human sacrifice to his bloodthirsty war-god, Ku. Geologically, the 760-foot monolith is about 350,000 years old, formed in one enormous explosion when sea water came into contact with lava bubbling out of a fissure. No new volcanic activity has been suspected in the last 200,000 years. The huge rock is now Hawaii's state monument and a **National Natural Landmark.** Its crater serves as a Hawaii National Guard depot; various hiking trails to the summit bypass installations left over from WW II (see p. 214). Getting there takes only 15 minutes from Waikiki, either by TheBus no. 57, or by car along Diamond Head Road. The southeast *(makai)* face has some of the most exclusive and expensive real estate in the islands. The **Kahala Hilton Hotel** here is regarded by many to be one of the premier hotels in the world, and nearby is the super-snobbish **Waialae Country Club**. Many private estates—homes of multimillionaires, Hollywood stars, and high-powered multinational executives—cling to the cliffside, fronting ribbons of beach open to the public by narrow rights-of-way that oftentimes are hemmed in by the walls of the estates.

Kapiolani Park

In the shadow of Diamond Head is Kapiolani

Park, a quiet 140-acre oasis of greenery, just a coconut's roll away from the gray cement and flashing lights of Waikiki. It has proved to be one of the best gifts ever received by the people of Honolulu, ever since King Kalakaua donated this section of crown lands to them in 1877, requesting it be named after his wife, Queen Kapiolani. In times past it was the site of horse and car races, polo matches, and Hawaii's unique *pa'u* riders, fashionable ladies in long flowing skirts riding horses decked out with *lei*. The park was even the site of Camp McKinley, the U.S. Army HQ in the islands from 1898 to 1907.

It remains a wonderful place for people to relax and exercise away from the hustle of Waikiki. The park is a mecca for jogging and aerobics, with many groups and classes meeting here throughout the day. It also serves as the starting point for the yearly **Honolulu Marathon,** one of the most prestigious races in the world. The beach part of the park, called Sans Souci, is very popular with local people and those wishing to escape the crowds, just a few beach blanket-lengths away (see p. 267-268). Its **Waikiki Shell,** an open-air amphitheater, hosts visiting musical groups, especially during Aloha Week. The Honolulu Symphony is a regular here, providing free concerts especially on summer evenings. Nearby, the **Kapiolani Bandstand** hosts the Royal Hawaiian Band on Sunday afternoons. Also, under the shade of the trees toward Waikiki Beach plenty of street entertainers, including clowns, acrobats, and jugglers, congregate daily to work out their routines to the beat of conga drums and other improvised music supplied by wandering musicians. Families and large groups come here to picnic, barbecue, and play softball. The park grounds are also home to the free **Kodak Hula Show** (see p. 276), Elks Club, prestigious Outrigger Canoe Club founded at the turn of the century, Waikiki Aquarium, and 45-acre Honolulu Zoo.

impromptu performance at Kapiolani Park

Waikiki Aquarium

The first Waikiki Aquarium was built in 1910, its entranceway framed by a *torii* gate. Today's aquarium was built and stocked in 1954, and a plan is now underway to rebuild and refurbish it with a new entranceway, "touch tanks," and an opening directly to the sea. The aquarium, located at 2777 Kalakaua Ave. (TheBus no. 2), tel. 923-9741, is open daily 9:00 a.m. to 5:00 p.m., small donation for adults, children under 16 and seniors free. A self-guiding book describing the marinelife is available for $1, and an audio tour ("magic wand" device) in English and Japanese is $.50.

Although over 300 species of Hawaiian and South Pacific fish, flora, and mammals live in its sparkling waters, the aquarium is much more than just a big fish tank. The floor plan contains 4 galleries of differing themes, and a seal tank. A wonderful teaching exhibit is **Hawaiians By the Sea,** a pictorial on how the Hawaiians built fishponds, made salt, hooks and nets, and used the sea as a food provider. The **South Seas Marine Life** exhibit shows fish found in waters from Polynesia to Australia. The tanks hold sharks, turtles, eels, rays, clams, a seahorse, and colorful coral displays. Another exhibit, **Micronesia Reef Builders,** is perhaps the most amazing of all. It contains live coral that seem more like extraterrestrial

Children and birds flock to the Honolulu Zoo.

flowers than specimens from our own seas. Some are long strands of spaghetti with bulbous ends like lima beans, others are mutated roses, or tortured camellias, all moving, floating, and waving their iridescent purples, golds, and greens in a watery bouquet. When you hear a coach's whistle blow, the seals are about to perform their antics. You can watch these natural hams from the side of the tank, or take a walkway below where plexiglass allows you to see them from underwater.

The aquarium contains a bookshop with a tremendous assortment of titles on fish, birds, reptiles, amphibians, and the flora of Hawaii. Restrooms are behind the bookshop area as you face the main gate. The aquarium sponsors an adopt-a-fish program called *Hanai I Ka I'a:* $2,000 for a harbor seal to $15 for a teardrop butterfly fish. The University of Hawaii offers seminars and field trips through the aquarium, everything from guided reef walks to mini-courses in marine biology. Information is available at the aquarium. Just near the aquarium is the **Waikiki Natatorium,** a saltwater swimming pool built in 1927 as a WW I memorial, allowed to decay over the years until it was closed in 1980. Plans constantly afoot in the House of Representatives call for a restoration.

Honolulu Zoo

The trumpeting of elephants and chatter of monkeys emanates from the jungle across the street at the Honolulu Zoo, 151 Kapahulu Ave., tel. 923-7723, open daily 8:30 a.m. to 4:30 p.m., with special shows in summer at 6:00 p.m., admission $1, yearly pass $3. As you walk along or ride the tram, you find the expected animals from around the world: monkeys, giraffes, lions, big cats, a hippo, even a grizzly bear. The Honolulu Zoo has the *only* reptiles in Hawaii—3 snakes in the Reptile House. Many islanders love this exhibit, because snakes in Hawaii are so exotic! But the zoo is much more than just a collection of animals. It is an up-close escapade through the jungle of Hawaii, with plants, trees, flowers, and vines all named and described. Moreover, the zoo houses Hawaii's indigenous birdlife, which is fast disappearing from the wild: Hawaiian gallinules, coots, hawks, owls, and the *nene,* the state bird, which is doing well in captivity, with breeding pairs being sent to other zoos around the world. The zoo is also famous for its Manchurian cranes, extremely rare birds from Japan, and for successfully mating the Galapagos turtle. A **petting zoo** of barnyard animals is great for kids. A concession stand serves typical junk food and soft drinks.

Free Sights And Curiosities

On the beach near the Surfrider Hotel are the ***kahuna*** **stones,** a lasting remnant of old Hawaii. The Hawaiians believed these stones were imbued with *mana* by 4 priests from Tahiti: Kinohi, Kahaloa, Kapuni, and Kapaemahu. They came to visit this Polynesian outpost in ancient times and left these for the people who have held them in reverence ever since.

The **Urusenke Teahouse** is an authentic teahouse donated to Hawaii by the Urusenke Foundation of Kyoto. It is located at 245 Saratoga Road, which lies along the Waikiki side of Fort DeRussy. Every Wed. and Fri. from 10:00 a.m. to 12:00 p.m., teamaster Yoshibuma Ogawa performs the ancient and aesthetic art of *chanoyu* (tea ceremony). The public is invited (free) to partake of the frothy *matcha*, a grass-green tea made from the delicate tips of 400-year-old bushes. To find delight and sanctuary in this centuries-old ritual among the clatter and noise of Waikiki offers a tiny glimpse into the often puzzling duality of the Japanese soul.

As you walk along Kalakaua Avenue, directly across from Waikiki Beach proper is **St. Augustine Catholic Church**. This modernistic building squashed between high-rises is worth a quick look. The interior, serene with the diffused light of stained glass, looks like a series of A-frames.

Believe it or not, you should pass through the McDonald's at the Royal Hawaiian Shopping Center, to see a permanent collection of Hawaiian art on display. Among the exhibits are carvings, paintings, macrame, and featherwork. Many of the works are by Rocky Kaiouliokahihikoloehu Jensen, a famous island artist.

Even if you're not a guest at the following hotels, you should at least drop by their lobbies for a quick look. Dramatically different, they serve almost as a visual record of Waikiki's changing history. **Moana Hotel**, the oldest, dating from 1901, is a permanent reminder of simpler times when its illustrious clientele would dance the night away at an open-air nightclub suspended over the sea. The Moana houses the Banyan Court Room, named after the enormous banyan tree just outside. From here, "Hawaii Calls" beamed Hawaiian music to the Mainland by shortwave for 40 years beginning in 1935. In its heyday, the show was carried by over 700 stations. The hotel's architecture is a classic example of the now quaint "colonial style." Across the street are the giant, modernistic, twin towers of the **Hyatt Regency**. The lobby, like most Hyatts, is wonderful with a huge waterfall, and a jungle of plants, all stepped down the series of floors, making an effect like the "hanging gardens of Babylon." The **Royal Hawaiian Hotel**, built in 1927 on the site of the old Royal Beach House, once had fresh pineapple juice running in its fountains. Now surrounded by towering hotels, it's like a guppy in a sea of whales. However, it does stand out with its Spanish-Moorish style, painted in distinctive pink. In the old days, only celebrities and luminaries came to stay—who else could afford $3 per day? Although it's younger than the Moana, many consider it the *grande dame* of Hawaiian ho-

prayers amidst the pleasures of Waikiki at St. Augustine Church

tels. But since it now must accommodate everyone (even conventioneers!), many think that the old *dame's* gone senile. The entranceway is elegantly old-fashioned, with rounded archways, over-stuffed couches, and lowboys. You pass through the lobby on a shocking cerise and green rug. All the rooms are appointed in this trademark pink, with matching towels, sheets, and pillow cases. When you visit the Royal Hawaiian, the most elegant lobby is not where you check in. Turn right and follow the long hallway toward the sea. This becomes an open breezeway, with arches and columns in grand style. You'll come to a small circular area in the hotel. Here is the heart, with Diamond Head framed in the distance.

WAIKIKI BEACHES AND PARKS

In the 6 miles of shoreline from Gray's Beach fronting the Halekulani Hotel in central Waikiki to Wailupe Beach Park in Maunalua Bay just east of the Kahala Hilton are at least 17 choice spots for enjoying surf activities. Most of the central Waikiki beaches are so close to each other that you can hardly tell where one ends and another begins. All of these are generally gentle, but as you head east the beaches get farther apart and have their own personalities. Sometimes they're rough customers. As always, never take *moana* for granted especially during periods of high surf. To get information on beaches and their conditions, call Honolulu Water Safety, tel. 922-3888; handicapped people can get information on specialized beach facilities and parks by calling, tel. 523-4182. Now that you've finally arrived at a Waikiki beach, the one thing left to do is kick back and *R-E-L-A-X.*

Waikiki Beach stretches for 2 miles, broken into separate areas. A multitude of concession stands offer everything from shave ice to canoe rides. It's not news that this beach is crowded. Sometimes when looking at the rows of glistening bodies, it appears that if one person wants to tan his other side, everybody else has to roll over with him. Anyone looking for seclusion here is just being silly. Take heart—a big part of the fun is the other people.

Gray's Beach

This westernmost section's name comes from Gray's-By-The-Sea, a small inn once located here. The narrow white-sand beach lies in front of the Halekulani Hotel that replaced it. Take Lewers Street off Kalakaua Avenue and park along Kalia Road; a right-of-way is between the Reef and Halekulani Hotels. The sea is generally mild here and the swimming is always good, with shallow waters and a sandy bottom. Offshore is a good break called **No. 3's,** a favorite with surfers.

Next door is **Royal-Moana Beach** lying between Waikiki's oldest man-made landmarks, the Moana and Royal Hawaiian hotels. Access is unlimited off Kalakaua Avenue. The inshore waters here are gentle and the bottom is sandy and generally free from coral. Offshore are 3 popular surfing areas, **Popular's, Queen's, and Canoes.** Many novices have learned to surf here because of the predictability of the waves, but with so many rookies in the water, and beach activities going on all around, you have to remain alert for runaway boards and speeding canoes.

Waikiki Beach Center And Prince Kuhio Beach Center

When people say "Waikiki Beach," this is the section to which they're referring. Both beaches front Kalakaua Avenue, and a long sand retaining wall called **Slippery Wall** fronts both beaches, creating a semi-enclosed saltwater pool. Here, you'll find surfing, canoeing, snorkeling, and safe year-round swimming along the gently sloping, sandy-bottomed shoreline. There are comfort stations, concession stands, and lifeguards. Be careful of the rough coral bottom at the Diamond Head end of Kuhio Beach. Covered with a coating of oil-slick seaweed, Slippery Wall definitely lives up to its name. Though local youngsters play on the wall, the footing is poor and many knees have been scraped and heads cracked after spills from this ill-advised play. The surf on the seaward side of the wall churns up the bottom and creates deep holes that come up unexpectedly, along with an occasional rip current.

Kapiolani Beach Park

This is the only park along Waikiki with facilities for barbecueing and picnicking. Although it's only a short stroll down the beach from Waikiki, it gets much less use. This is where local families and those in the know come to get away from the crowds. In the park and along the beach are restrooms, volleyball courts, picnic tables, lifeguard towers, a bath house, and concession stand. Activities include surfing, fishing, snorkeling, and year-round safe swimming. Just be careful of the rocky bottom that pops up unexpectedly here and there. Kapiolani Park incorporates **Sans Souci Beach** at the eastern end. This beach in front of the Colony Surf and Kamaina hotels has unlimited access. Changing facilities are found at the deteriorating **Honolulu Natatorium,** a saltwater pool built in the '20s. Many families with small children come to Sans Souci because it is so gentle.

The Natatorium is in a sad state. Battles rage on whether it should be refurbished or torn down. Unless something has been done by the time you arrive, it's better to avoid its murky waters. Be careful of the rocky areas and dangerous drop-offs along the channel, especially in front of the Natatorium. **Kapiolani Park Center** is the beach closest to Waikiki. The swimming is good here, with the best part at the Waikiki end. The beach is at its widest, and the bottom is gently sloping sand. The area called **The Wall** has been designated as a special body-surfing area. Supposedly, board riders are restricted from this area, but if the surf is good they're guaranteed to break the rules. Experts can handle it, but novices, especially with runaway boards, are a hazard.

Around Diamond Head

Kaluahole Beach is located at the Waikiki side of Diamond Head. The water conditions are safe all year around, but the beach is small and lies along a seawall. Once a large beach, it was paved over for building purposes. It has one public right-of-way, poorly marked and sandwiched between private homes. It's almost at the end at 3837 Kalakaua Avenue. The surfing in this area is generally good, and the breaks are known as "Tongg's," named after a local family that lived along this shore.

Diamond Head Beach Park is an unlimited access area along Beach Road (marked). It covers almost 2 acres of undeveloped shoreline. Unfortunately, the beach is very narrow and surrounded by unfriendly rock and coral. The waters, however, are quite protected and generally safe, except in periods of high surf. This area is good for fishing and finding quiet moments.

Kuilei Cliffs Beach Park lies below Diamond Head Road, with access available from 3 lookout areas along the road. You must walk down the cliff trails to the beaches below. Here are plenty of secluded pockets of sand for sunbathing, but poor swimming. The surf is generally rough, and the area is always frequented by surfers. Offshore is hazardous with submerged rocks, but this makes it excellent for diving and snorkeling—for experts only! Currents can be fierce, and you can be dashed against the rocks. Whales can sometimes be spotted passing this point, and to add to the mystique, the area is considered a breeding ground for sharks. Most visitors just peer down at the surfers from Diamond Head Road, or choose a spot of beach for peace and quiet.

Farther east is **Kaalawai Beach.** The swimming is good here and generally safe because of a protecting reef. Many locals come to this area to fish, and it is good for body-surfing and snorkeling. The waters outside the reef are excellent for surfing, and produce some of the biggest waves on this side of the island. Access is by public right-of-way, marked off Kulumanu Place, a small side road running off Kahala Avenue, or by walking along the shoreline from Kuilei Beach.

Kahala Beach lying along Kahala Avenue can be reached by a number of marked rights-of-way located between the high fences of estates in the area. The swimming is not particularly good, but there are plenty of pockets of sand and protected areas where you can swim and snorkel. Local people come to fish, and the surfing is good beyond the reef. The Kahala Hilton is located along this beach at the eastern end. The public can use "their" beach by walking from Kahala Beach. The swimming here is always safe and good because the hotel has dredged the area to make it deeper. Concession stands and lifeguards are provided by the hotel.

Wailupe Beach Park lies on the Waikiki side of Wailupe Peninsula in Maunalua Bay, and will be the last beach covered under Waikiki. This beach park, clearly marked off the Kalanianaʻole Highway, provides restrooms and picnic facilities. The swimming is safe, but the bottom can have either oozy mud or sharp coral in spots. Be careful of the boat channel surrounding the area because the deep drop-off is very abrupt.

ACCOMMODATIONS

Waikiki is loaded with places to stay: 170 properties holding 34,000 rooms jammed into one square mile. And, they come in all categories of hotels and condos, from deluxe to dingy. Your problem won't be finding a place to stay, but choosing from the enormous selection. During *peak season,* (Christmas to Easter and again in summer) you'd better have reservations, or you could easily be left out in the *warm.* The good news is that, room for room, Waikiki is the cheapest place to stay in the state. Hotels along the beach tend to be slightly more expensive than their counterparts on a side street or back lane. The beach-front hotels have the surf at the doorstep, but those a block away have a little more peace and quiet. The following listings are not exhaustive. They couldn't be! Here is just the best from all categories which you can use as a barometer to measure what's available.

Inexpensive

Honolulu's YM/WCAs and youth hostel are near, but not technically in Waikiki. They are the cheapest places to stay, and you'll find a complete list under "Honolulu Accommodations," p. 251.

Coral Surf Apartment Hotel, 2584 Lemon Road, Honolulu, HI 96815, tel. 923-2295, offers studios and one- and 2-bedroom fully furnished apartments. They rent by the day, week, or month. Rates are subject to change but expect to pay: $30 p/d, $200 p/w, and $700 p/m for a studio; $60 p/d, $350 p/w, $1,100 p/m, for 2 bedrooms; one bedroom about 15% cheaper. No TV (rentals available), no phone service, once-weekly maid service, parking for a fee, reservations recommended. The manager lives at the hotel in Rm. 202.

Aloha Pacific Hotel, 2424 Koa St., Honolulu, HI 96815, tel. 922-1211, is directly behind the Hyatt Regency, and not at all fancy but clean. Rates are on a monthly basis only, from $350 to $500. Rooms are furnished with kitchen, bath, a/c, color TV, telephone, and private *lanai.* No maid service, one set of towels provided, parking extra. First-come first-served basis, no reservations, usually full during peak season.

Waikiki Beachside Apartment Hotel, 2556 Lemon Rd., Honolulu, HI 96815, tel. 923-9566, is owned and operated by Mr. and Mrs. Wong who keep a close eye on who they admit and run a very decent and clean hotel. They rent weekly and monthly only, charging from $250 to $1,000, off-season cheaper. Fully furnished units have full kitchens and baths with twin beds and a convertible sofa. Up to 3 people no extra charge. Laundry facilities but no maid service. Reservations reluctantly accepted (they like to see you first). Parking extra.

Waikiki Terrace Hotel, 339 Royal Hawaiian Ave., Honolulu, HI 96815, tel. 923-3253, operated by Shirley Anderson. The facility is rundown, but clean with full kitchenette, bath, laundry facilities, weekly maid service, some with a/c, and parking available. The hotel has an Asian feel with central courtyard and covered porch. Rates from $22 to $30, $5 extra person. Bedrooms have twin beds, and a rollaway provided for extra guests.

Coral Seas Hotel, 250 Lewers St., Honolulu, HI 96815, tel. 923-3881, is an old standby for budget travelers, designed that way by Mr. Pat Kelly, an octagenarian who lives down the street and wanted to provide a good cheap place for people to stay in Waikiki. This is the epitome of the economy tourist hotel and houses Perry's Smorgasbord. It's one of the Outrigger Hotels, and seems to get all the hand-me-downs from the others in the chain. There's a restaurant, cocktail lounge, TV, pool, and parking. Rates are an economical $28 s, $32 d, $10 extra person, and just a few dollars more for a kitchenette. Not to everyone's taste, but with plenty of action and the beach only a few steps away.

The **Edgewater Hotel,** 2168 Kalia Rd., tel. 922-6424, is another budget standby in the palpitating heart of Waikiki. Rates begin at a reasonable $30 s, to $80 for a suite, $10 extra person. Facilities include swimming pool, restaurant (Trattoria-Italian and good), parking, TV, and maid service. Kitchenettes slightly extra.

The **Royal Grove Hotel,** 151 Uluniu Ave., tel. 923-7691, run by the Fong family, gives you a lot for your money. You can't miss its paint-sale pink exterior, but inside it's much more tasteful. The older and cheaper wing is about $25 per room, the newer upgraded wing is around $30. Most are studios and one-bedroom apartments with full facilities.

Moderate

The **Queen Kapiolani Hotel,** 150 Kapahulu Ave., Honolulu, HI 96815, tel. 800-367-5004, on Oahu tel. 922-1941. With its off-the-strip location and magnificent views of Diamond Head, this is perhaps the best, and definitely the quietest, hotel for the money in Waikiki. You're only seconds from the beach; the hotel provides a spacious lobby, parking, restaurant, TV, a/c, shops, and a swimming pool. Rates begin at $55 standard, to $75 for a superior; a few rooms have kitchenettes. Excellent choice for the money, for reservations write directly or to Hawaiian Pacific Resorts, 1150 S. King St., Honolulu, HI 96814. tel. 531-5235.

Queen Kapiolani Hotel

The **Breakers Hotel,** 250 Beach Walk, Honolulu, HI 96815, tel. 800-426-0494, on Oahu 923-3181, is a family-style hotel. Only minutes from the beach, somehow it keeps the hustle and bustle far away. Every room has a kitchenette and overlooks the shaded courtyard of coconut and banana trees. Facilities include a/c, TV, pool, and parking. Studios begin at $65, one bedroom at $90, all fully furnished.

Outrigger Hotels have 6 locations in and around Waikiki offering more than 2,500 rooms. Most of the hotels are along Kuhio Ave., with the Outrigger Waikiki right on the beach. Although they're not luxurious, they do offer good accommodations and all have pools, restaurants, parking, a/c, TV, and parking. Rates vary slightly from hotel to hotel: some have kitchen facilities and cost $50 d to $300 for a suite, $10-15 extra person. For information call 800-367-5170, in Canada 800-826-6786, or write to central reservations, 2335 Kalakaua Ave., Honolulu, HI 96815.

Ilima Hotel, 445 Nohonai St., Honolulu, HI 96815, tel. 800-421-8767, on Oahu tel. 923-1877, fronts the Ala Wai Canal overlooking the Ala Wai Golf Course. This condo-style hotel is a few blocks from the beach—quiet atmosphere and budget rates. They have just completed a $1.5 million renovation, featuring waveless waterbeds in their deluxe suites. Studio units begin at a reasonable $35 s, $8 extra person, and one bedroom $65, 2 bedroom $75. All units have full kitchens, a/c, TV, along with a pool, parking, and maid service. Good value.

Miramar Hotel, 2345 Kuhio Ave., Honolulu, HI 96815, tel. 800-367-2303, on Oahu tel. 922-2077, is in the heart of Waikiki. The hotel, refurbished and renamed in the last few years, offers generous-sized rooms, with *lanai,* pool, restaurant, a/c, TV, and parking. Rates range from $60 s to $70 d, $10 extra person.

Waikiki Shores Apartments, 2161 Kalia Rd., Honolulu, HI 96815, tel. 800-367-2353, on Oahu, tel. 926-4733, has studios, and one-, and 2-bedroom apartments, minimum stay 3 nights. No children under 12, weekly maid service, parking. All units have full kitchens; studios $60, $160 for a 2-bedroom.

Holiday Inn Waikiki Beach, 2570 Kalakaua Ave., Honolulu, HI 96815, tel. 800-465-4329, on Oahu tel. 922-2511. No surprises at a good old Holiday Inn offering a/c, TV, pool, parking, restaurants, and maid service. Standard rooms begin at around $75, $100 for deluxe, and $1,000 for the penthouse. Extra person $15. The Holiday Inn is at a good location just near Kapiolani Park and away from the heavy bustle.

Expensive

The **Moana Hotel,** 2365 Kalakaua Ave., Honolulu, HI 96815, tel. 800-325-3535, on Oahu tel. 922-3111, is the oldest hotel in Waikiki. Now operated by Sheraton Inns, it's been upgraded, but the old feeling of class is intact. The Moana, right on the beach, is the most reasonably priced of the expensive hotels. Rooms in the old wing overlook Banyan Court, scene of a nightly Polynesian Revue. Depending on your outlook, this gives you either a free seat for the spectacle below or unwanted noise. The hotel has a/c (new wing only), TV, restaurants, and nearby parking. Rooms are $60 s, $120 for a superior room. Still an excellent hotel with old-fashioned service.

The **Royal Hawaiian Hotel,** 2255 Kalakaua Ave., Honolulu, HI 96815, tel. 800-325-3535, on Oahu tel. 923-7311, is second oldest, and it too provides an ongoing experience in turn-of-the-century charm. The hotel offers a/c, TV, restaurants, lounges, and a pool. A basic bedroom starts at around $110 s, with suites ranging from $180 to over $1,200. The Moana and Royal Hawaiian are worth a visit even if you don't stay there.

Hyatt Regency, 2424 Kalakaua Ave., Honolulu, HI 96815, tel. 800-228-9005, on Oahu tel. 922-9292, is magnificent. If the frenetic pace gets to be too much, just head for the peaceful lobby with pine trees and cascading waterfall. The hotel offers a/c, TV, lounges, shops, restaurants, swimming pool, and parking. Basic rooms start at around $100 d, $15 extra person, and go to $1,000 for a suite. An excellent choice for an expensive hotel.

The **Hilton Hawaiian Village,** 2005 Kalia Rd., Honolulu, HI 96815, tel. 949-4321, is at the far western end of Waikiki, just below Fort DeRussy. This large complex offers over 2,500 rooms, shopping, restaurants, bars, the Don Ho Polynesian Extravaganza, 5 pools scattered over the manicured grounds, enormous lobbies with immense sculptures, and an evening catamaran sail on the hotel's private boat. Room rates begin at $90 d for a standard, $140 d for a deluxe, and go to $1,200 for a suite. Extra person $15. The Hilton is a self-contained resort.

the Royal Hawaiian Hotel, a quiet corner of classic charm

Luxury

Waikiki is home to 2 of the finest hotels in the world. The **Halekulani Hotel,** in mid-Waikiki at 2199 Kalia Rd., Honolulu, HI 96815, tel. 800-367-2343, on Oahu tel. 923-2311, was an experiment in impeccable taste that paid off. A few years ago the hotel was built with the belief that Waikiki could still attract the luxury-class visitor. Since opening, the hotel, recognized as a member of the **Leading Hotels of the World,** has been constantly filled. It's a hotel that takes care of the smallest details like cloth hand towels, even in the lobby restrooms. When you arrive you are escorted to your room where you register. Soon, a bellman appears bearing a silver tray nestling a fine china plate on an embroidered linen cloth which holds an array of Godiva Chocolates, compliments of the house. Each room, done in 7 shades of white, has 3 telephones, a bathroom as large as many hotel rooms, bath towels the size of parlor rugs, and a private *lanai.* Each night a little white box tied with silver string is placed on your pillow, and inside is a gift from the management. Prices begin at around $175 d, and go to around $500, $35 extra person. If you want to splurge on one night of luxury, the Halekulani is unforgettable.

Long considered one of the finest hotels in the world is the **Kahala Hilton,** 5000 Kahala Ave., Honolulu, HI 96816, tel. 1-800-367-2525, on Oahu tel. 734-2211, technically not in Waikiki, but a few minutes' drive east. The hotel was built 20 years ago and is proud that most of its key workers have been there from the first days. A large number of guests return yearly, and have formed friendships with the workers. Located away from Waikiki and surrounded by the exclusive Waialae Country Club (not even hotel guests are welcome unless they are members), the hotel gives a true sense of peace and seclusion. It has an excellent formal restaurant, The Maile, a private beach, swimming pools, all water-sport gear available, a saltwater pond holding 3 porpoises, and a lovely breezy lobby. The rooms, large with sweeping ocean and mountain views, rent for $150-$350 d, $450-$1,150 for a suite. The Kahala obviously isn't for everyone, but there's no doubt that you definitely get all that you pay for.

FOOD

The streets of Waikiki are an international potluck, with over a dozen cuisines spreading their tables. Because of the culinary competition, you can choose restaurants in the same way that you peruse a buffet table, for both quantity and quality. Within a few hundred yards are all-you-can-gorge buffets, *luau,* dinner shows, fast foods, ice cream, and jacket-and-tie restaurants. The free tourist literature runs coupons, and placards advertise specials for breakfast, lunch, and dinner. Bars and lounges often give free *pupu* and finger foods that can easily make a light supper. As with everything in Waikiki, its restaurants are a close-quartered combination of the best and the worst, but with only a little effort it's easy to find great food, great atmosphere, and mouth-watering satisfaction.

Pedicabbies have the hottest tips on where to play and eat in Waikiki.

Inexpensive

Ferdinand's in the Coral Reef Hotel, 2299 Kuhio Ave., tel. 923-5581, is a no-nonsense place running specials and discount tickets. Basically its an American standard restaurant with a Hawaiian flavor. An attempt is made at entertainment, a Don Ho clone singing in the background. The food is decent but not memorable; with discounts 2 can eat for around $12.

Lam's Chinese Restaurant, 124 Kapahulu, tel. 922-6005, is a basic Chinese restaurant that offers specials. Breakfast is a bargain with hotcakes, eggs, sausage, and coffee for around $2.50. The atmosphere is quiet since it's around the corner from most of the action. A belly-filler only.

Perry's Smorgy at the Outrigger Hotel, 2335 Kalakaua Ave., tel. 926-9872, and at the Coral Seas Hotel, 250 Lewers St., tel. 923-3881, is the epitome of the budget travelers' "line 'em up, fill 'em up, and head 'em out" kind of restaurant. There is no question that you'll waddle away stuffed, but forget about any kind of memorable dining experience. When you arrive, don't be put off by the long lines. They move! First, you run a gauntlet of salads, breads, and potatoes, in the hopes that you'll fill your plate. Try to restrain yourself. Next comes the meat, fish, and chicken. The guys serving up the roast beef are masters of a whole lot of movement and very little action. The carving knife whips around in the air, but does very little damage to the joint of beef. A paper-thin slice is finally cut off and put on your plate with aplomb. The carver then looks at you as if you were Oliver Twist asking for more. Added pressure comes from the long line of tourists behind, who act as if they have just escaped from a Nazi labor camp. An extra bonus is that on Tues., Fri., and Sun. nights the Outrigger Hotel puts on a *luau* complete with entertainment on the beach below the restaurant. So if you arrive around 7:00 p.m. and can manage a window table, you get a terrific seat for some free entertainment.

Peking Garden, 307 Royal Hawaiian Ave., tel. 922-3401, is a hole-in-the-wall eatery just behind the Waikiki Medical Center heading *mauka.* They serve Chinese-American food basically in the form of filling plate lunches for around $3.50. A good choice is the Peking fried chicken.

Shorebird Beach Broiler is on the beach behind the Reef Hotel at 2169 Kalia Rd., tel. 922-2887. Here you'll find a limited but adequate menu of cook-your-own selections for well under $10 (discount tickets save you more). Open from 5:00 p.m. Walk through the lobby to the beach for a remarkable sunset while dining. Included is a good fresh salad bar of vegetables and fruits. Beverages are included, but you pay extra for bread. Nightly there's disco dancing from 9:00 p.m. to 2:00 a.m. Good value and a pleasing setting.

Waikiki Malia Hotel Restaurant, 2211 Kuhio Ave., tel. 923-7621. Open 24 hours, specials for around $7.95; crisp salad bar and a huge well-done baked potato with dinner. Beverages not included. Good value.

It's Greek To Me, at the Royal Hawaiian Shopping Center, 2201 Kalakaua Ave., tel. 922-2733. A combination sandwich bar and restaurant serving traditional Greek food such as *falafel, moussaka,* and *souvlaki.* Fatso sandwiches are about $6.50, while the dinners are generally under $10.

Inexpensive: Kapahulu Avenue

Once **Kapahulu Avenue** crosses Ala Wai Boulevard, it passes excellent inexpensive to moderately priced restaurants, strung one after the other. The first is **Rainbow Drive In,** at the corner of Kanaaina Avenue. It's strictly local, with a kids' hang-out feel, but the plate lunches are hearty and well done for under $4. Another of the same, **K C Drive In** just up the road a few blocks at 1029 Kapahulu, specializes in waffle-dogs, shakes, and even has car hops. Both are excellent stops to pick up plate lunches on your way out of Waikiki heading for the H-1 Freeway.

The first sit-down restaurant on this strip is **Irifune** Japanese Restaurant, at 563 Kapahulu, tel. 737-1141, directly across from **Zippy's,** a fast-food joint. Irifune serves authentic, well-prepared Japanese standards in its small dining room. Most meals begin at $6, with a nightly special for around $8. You're also given a card that is punched every time you eat there; after 20 meals, you get one free.

The next is **Ono Hawaiian Foods,** an institution in *down home* Hawaiian cooking. This is the kind of place that a taxi driver sends you to when you ask for the real thing. It's clean, basic, with the decor being photos of local performers hung on the wall. If you want to try *lomi* salmon, *poi,* or *kalua* pig, this is *da kine place, brah!* Prices are cheap. Open Mon. to Sat. 10:30 a.m. to 7:30 p.m., 726 Kapahulu, tel. 737-2275.

On the next block is the absolutely scrumptious **Rama Thai Restaurant,** at 847 Kapahulu, open daily for lunch, and dinner from 5:30-10:00 p.m., tel.735-2789. Parking's tough around here in the evenings, so try the First Interstate Bank lot nearby. The restaurant is basic, but the food is superlative. Almost half of the menu is vegetarian. All items are *a la carte,* so it's not that cheap; a complete meal costs around $10. The fish-ball soup is out of this world, with plenty for two. The *tofu* in coconut milk is also a great choice. It's across the streeet from the **Love's Bakery Thrift Store.**

To round out the multi-cultural cuisines of Kapahulu Avenue, try **Plaza Manila,** at 750 Palani Ave., and Kapahulu. Open daily except Mon., from 11:00 a.m. to 10:00 p.m., tel. 734-0400. Traditional Filipino dishes with many American and Hawaiian standards.

Fast Foods And Snacks
There are enough formica-tabled, orange-colored, golden-arched, belly-up-to-the-window places selling perfected, injected, and inspected ground cow, chicken, and fish to feed an army...and a navy, and marine corps too. Those needing a pre-fab meal can choose from the royal **Burger King** and **Dairy Queen, Jack-in-his-Box, Ronnie McDonald, Pizza Hut-2-3-4, Wendy's,** and dippy **Zippy's Drive-In.** Addicts find your own pushers!

Farrels Restaurant at the International Market Place and the Royal Hawaiian Center serves ice cream and a good selection of sandwiches and soups for decent prices. Along Kalakaua Avenue are **Baskin Robbins,** and **Haagen Dazs.** For cheap Italian try the **Noodle Shop** in the Waikiki Sand Villa Hotel, tel. 922-4744.

Moderate
Peacock Dining Room, Queen Kapiolani Hotel, 150 Kapahulu, tel. 922-1941. One of the best buffets in Waikiki. Different nights feature different cuisine; don't miss Japanese night. Excellent value.

A number of Italian restaurants here are moderately priced. The most expensive and nicest is **Matteo's Italian Restaurant** in the Marine Surf Hotel, 364 Seaside, tel. 922-5511. They're open from 6:00 p.m. to 2:00 a.m. and have a dress code of no shorts, T-shirts, tank tops, or thongs. Their complete dinners range from chicken a la Wanda (baked in sauce with melted mozzarella for $11.95, to shrimp scampi for around $20. Pasta dishes start at $5.50 for a basic plate of spaghetti. **Trattoria** in the Edgewater Hotel, 2168 Kalia Rd., tel. 923-8415, serves savory dishes from northern Italy. Particularly good are the veal plates with an appropriate bottle of Italian wine. Another good Italian restaurant is **Rudy's** in the Outrigger Surf Hotel, 2280 Kuhio Ave., tel. 923-5949. Italian-owned, they feature tasty minestrone, cannelloni, and fettucini. Good prices.

Benihana of Tokyo at the Hilton Rainbow Bazaar, 2005 Kalia Rd., tel. 955-5955, is a medium-priced Japanese restaurant for those who are jittery about the food and prices. Meals are designed to fit *gaijin* taste, and cooks flash their knives and spatulas at your table—as much a floor show as a dining experience. Good, basic Japanese food, *teppan*-style.

Rascals on Kuhio at the Kuhio Mall, 2301 Kuhio Ave., tel. 922-5566, is open for dinner only, and doubles as a nightclub with late-night suppers served until 3:00 a.m. and dancing until 4:00 a.m. Varied menu of seafood, featuring Cajun-style shrimp soup.

Ezogiku, 2083 and 2310 Kuhio Ave., tel. 941-1646 and 922-3461. Open for 3 meals, featuring basic Japanese, but specializing in inexpensive hearty bowls of *ramen.*

Popo's Margarita Cantina, International Market Place, tel. 923-8373, and **Compadres Mexican Bar and Grill,** Outrigger Prince Hotel, 2500 Kuhio Ave., tel. 924-4007, offer tacos, enchiladas, chips and salsa, done in a reasonably good Mexican style with good value on the combination plates.

Mandarin Palace, the Miramar Hotel, 2345 Kuhio Ave., tel. 926-1110, for lunch and dinner. Highly rated for its Oriental cuisine in a full-blown Chinese atmosphere.

Seafood Emporium, Royal Hawaiian Shopping Center, 2201 Kalakaua Ave., tel. 922-5477. Moderately priced for seafood, with one of the island's largest selections of domestic and imported fish. A good choice for a reasonable lunch or dinner.

The Great Wok of China, Royal Hawaiian Center, 2201 Kalakaua Ave., tel. 922-5373. Decent food, it's fun to eat here as chefs prepare food at your table in, you guessed it, woks. A good assortment of meat, seafood, and vegetable dishes, guaranteed not to be the steam-table variety.

Spat's, Hyatt Regency, 2424 Kalakaua, tel. 922-9292, is a fun restaurant doubling as a disco, featuring passable Italian cuisine, with decent veal dishes and pasta.

Expensive
If you ask a *kamaaina* where to go, after a telltale smirk he'll probably say **Canlis.** This elegant, times-past restaurant is at 2100 Kalakaua Ave., tel. 923-2324. On the upper level, jackets are required; the lower is more casual. It's one of those places that gives better service if you are a known patron. The understated Polynesian atmosphere is slightly better than

the cooking, but expect well-prepared seafood, beef, and poultry. Vermouth on beef dishes and mint in the salads are trademarks. Daily for dinner, lunch weekdays only, reservations of course.

Colony Steak House at the Hyatt Regency, 2424 Kalakaua, tel. 922-9292. As the name implies, excellent cuts of steak that you personally choose, as well as fish and a truly superb salad bar. **Bagwell's,** also in the Hyatt Regency, tel. 922-9292, is a superb French restaurant with an imaginative menu and great wine list. The chef is Yves Menoret, formerly of Alexis in San Francisco. The prices are richer than French pastry.

Restaurant Suntory, Royal Hawaiian Shopping Center, tel. 922-5511, is a very handsome restaurant with different rooms specializing in particular styles like *shabu shabu, teppanyaki,* and *sushi.* The prices used to be worse, but they're still very expensive.

Golden Dragon, Hilton Hawaiian Village, 2005 Kalia Rd., tel. 949-4321, is a local favorite for Cantonese cuisine, serving old standbys like lemon chicken and smoked duck.

Surf Room in the Royal Hawaiian Hotel, 2259 Kalakaua Ave., tel. 923-7311. The menu is solid but uninspired. However, the setting couldn't be lovelier, and the huge buffet is staggering.

Nick's Fishmarket, Waikiki Gateway Hotel, 2070 Kalakaua Ave., tel. 955-6333. Owned by Nick Nickolaus, this restaurant was long renowned as Waikiki's best. Nick has moved on to other enterprises; the menu is still good, super expensive, but not great.

Hy's Steak House, 2440 Kuhio Ave., tel. 922-5555, is one of those rare restaurants that is not only absolutely beautiful, but serves great food as well. Decorated like a Victorian sitting room, its menu offers things other than steaks and chops, but these are the specialties and worth the stiff-upper-lipped price.

ENTERTAINMENT

Waikiki swings, beats, bumps, grinds, sways, laughs, and "gets down." If Waikiki has to bear being called a carnival town, it might as well strut its stuff. Dancing (disco and ballroom), happy hours, cocktail shows, cruises, lounge acts, Polynesian extravaganzas, and the street scene provide an endless choice of entertainment. Small-name Hawaiian trios, soloists, piano men, and sultry singers featured in innumerable bars and restaurants woo you in and keep you coming back. Big-name island entertainers and visiting international stars play the big rooms. Free entertainment includes

The show has been playing to tourists since 1937. Watch the birdie!

hula shows, *ukelele* music, street musicians, jugglers, artists, and street walkers. For a good time, nowhere in Hawaii matches Waikiki.

Bars, Happy Hours, And Lounge Acts

Plaza Lounge, tel. 922-6885, in the Waikiki Shopping Plaza, presents Mel Cabang, a fat, bald, and funny-as-hell Filipino singer-comedian. He plays with the audience, like Don Rickles, but he's so *gestalt* that you can't believe it. His risque repartee, fine guitar-playing, and surprisingly good voice don't quite seem to fit his face. Tuesday to Sat. from 9:00 p.m., no cover, $2 per drink.

Brother Noland is a local talent who appears around town, but most often performs at the lounge in the Waikiki Sheraton, tel. 922-4422. He's the cutting edge for ethnic Hawaiian groups playing hot reggae, originals, and plenty of Stevie Wonder, solo, or with a group, and shouldn't be missed.

Steve and Theresa are excellent Hawaiian musicians. Their sound is a melodious mixture of traditional and contemporary. Accomplished musicians with beautiful voices, they often appear at **La Mex** in the Royal Hawaiian Shopping Center, tel. 923-2906.

In the Park Shore Hotel, 2586 Kalakaua Ave., The bar is a quiet, relaxing place to have a drink. A talented pianist and organist, Andre Branch, plays nightly. Free.

The **Rose and Crown Pub** in King's Village has a pianist playing sing-along favorites. The crowd is collegiate, intent on swilling beer and partying. Noisy, raucous, and fun.

The Grapevine, corner of Prince Edward and Uluniu streets, presents low-key live music. Artists change, but expect a guitarist playing soulful Hawaiian music.

In the International Market Place, the **Cock's Roost Steak House** offers free entertainment, with no minimum or cover. Nearby, the **Crow's Nest** features local and visiting entertainers. If Blue Kangaroo, a hilarious comedy act, is playing, don't miss them.

The Brothers Cazimero have an excellent and well-deserved reputation as one of Hawaii's finest duos, singing a lovely blend of Hawaiian and contemporary music. You can usually catch them at the Royal Hawaiian Hotel's Monarch Room. Dinner and cocktail shows are from 7:00 p.m. Tues. to Sat. Alohawear is fine, tel. 923-7311.

The **Jazz Cellar,** 205 Lewers St., features mostly live rock and roll and some jazz. The place jumps till 4:00 a.m. and has plenty of special nights like Thirsty Tuesdays and Ladies Night. Put on your dancin' shoes, casual attire, tel. 923-9952.

Trappers in the Hyatt Regency is an intimate jazz nightclub, with overstuffed chairs and cozy booths; continuous jazz from 5:30 p.m.

Baron's Studio, Waikiki Plaza Hotel, tel. 946-0277, is home to jazz vocalist Azure McCall. Open nightly, quiet drinks, fine background tunes.

The **Polynesian Pub,** 2490 Kalakaua, tel. 923-3683, offers happy hour nightly and contemporary Hawaiian music. Right priced drinks, no cover.

The Garden Bar, Hilton Hawaiian Village, tel. 949-4321, features John Norris and the New Orleans Jazz Band on Sun. from 2:00 to 6:00 p.m.

Free Entertainment

Check the newpapers and free tourist literature for times to the following events.

The **Royal Hawaiian Band** plays free concerts on Sun. afternoons at the bandstand in Kapiolani Park, oftentimes with singers and *hula* dancers. Also in the park, free concerts are periodically given by a variety of local and visiting musicians at the Waikiki Shell.

The **Kodak Hula Show** is free, though it's a hassle to get in. The show is held on Tues., Thurs., and Fri. at 10:00 a.m. in Kapiolani Park. Extremely popular, people start lining up at 8:00 a.m.; be there by 9:00 if you want a seat. You sit on bleachers with 3,000 people, while Hawaiian *tutu* bedecked in *muumuu, lei,* and smiles play *ukelele* and sing for the *ti*-leaf-skirted dancers. You can buy film and even rent a camera, as befits the show's sponsor, the Eastman Kodak Company—snap away with abandon. The performance dates back to 1937, and some of the original dancers, now in their 80s, still participate. At the finale, the dancers line up on stage with red-lettered placards that spells out H-A-W-A-I-I, so you can

the distinctive mural at The Wave

take your own photo of the most famous Hawaiian postcard. Then the audience is invited down for a free *hula* lesson. People that are too hip hate it, *kamaainas* shy away from it, but if you're a good sport, you'll walk away like everyone else, with a big smile on your face.

A potpourri of contemporary entertainment is also found in Kapiolani Park on weekends. Just across from the zoo, musicians, jugglers, clowns, unicyclists, and acrobats put on a free, impromptu circus. Some of the best are B.J. Patches, Twinkles, and Jingles from a local troupe called Clown Alley.

The *ukelele* tree in front of the Reef Hotel, 2169 Kalia Rd., has heard the lovely melodies of Hawaii for 50 years. Every Sun. at 8:00 p.m., local musicians, and sometimes well-known guests, come to play and be heard.

The **Royal Hawaiian Shopping Center** provides free entertainment throughout the week: quilting, *lauhala* weaving, pineapple cutting, and free *hula* lessons every Friday at 10:00 a.m. with Aunti Maiki Aiu Lake.

Aunty Bella's Leis, 2200 Kalakaua Ave., gives free *lei*-making classes Mon., Wed., and Fri. at 10:30 a.m. The flowers are free and you keep the *lei* that you string.

Discos, Dancing And Nightclubs

Ballroom dancers will enjoy **Tea Dancing at the Royal** in the Monarch Room of the Royal Hawaiian Hotel, featuring the 14-piece Del Courtney Orchestra, Mon. from 5:30 to 8:30 p.m. The **Maile Lounge** at the Kahala Hilton, tel. 734-2211, offers live music for ballroom dancing nightly.

The Wave is a rock 'n roll and new wave hot spot, with live music nightly, 1877 Kalakaua Ave., tel. 941-0424.

The following are disco nightclubs in and around Waikiki. Most have videos, a theme, a dress code of alohawear and shoes, no sandals, and start hopping around 9:00 p.m. with the energy cut off around 4:00 a.m.

The Infinity at the Sheraton Waikiki presents golden oldies and contemporary live music nightly from 8:00 p.m. Good dance floor.

The **Blue Water Cafe,** 2350 Kuhio Ave., once the home of live music, now has disco and videos. Distinguished by it's copper and brass appointment, including full copper doors to the restrooms, pillars are covered in copper, and the ceiling looks like closely fit barrel staves. Waitresses are particularly good looking.

Spats in the Hyatt Regency, tel. 922-9292, is an Italian restaurant that turns into a disco around 9:00 p.m. The decor is 1920s art deco. Classy, well known, and swinging.

Red Lion Dance Palace, 240 Lewers St., tel. 922-1027, offers high-tech video and disco and a pool bar. Beachwear ok, from 2:00 p.m. to 4:00 a.m.

The **3-D Ballroom,** 2260 Kuhio, is a crummy little joint 2 floors up with super-loud music for teenyboppers and punkers.

The Point After, 2552 Kalakaua Ave., tel. 922-6611. Fatso sofas in this football-theme night spot. A local favorite with a dress code.

Masquerade and **Phaze,** next door to each other at the corner of McCully and Kalakaua avenues, feature a heavy sound system and wild light shows. Cutting-edge videos, great dance floors, and wild tunes till 4:00 a.m.

Cilly's, 1909 Ala Wai Blvd., tel. 942-2942, **Annabelle's** at the Westin Ilikai, 1777 Ala Moana Blvd., tel. 949-3811, and **Steel Wings,** also at the Westin Ilikai, are well-known discos where you can't help having a good time. All have reputations as swinging night spots.

Dinner Shows And Polynesian Extravaganzas

Free tickets to these extravaganzas are handed out by condo time-share outfits stationed in booths along the main drags. For attending their sales presentations, usually 90 minutes, you can get tickets to the Don Ho show, among others—but they might be the toughest freebies you've ever earned. The presentation is a pressure cooker. The sales people are pros, who try every imaginable technique to get you to sign. If you're really interested in time sharing, the deals aren't too bad, but if you're there only for the tickets, what a waste of time!

The **Don Ho Show** at the Hilton Hawaiian Village has been attracting huge crowds for years, leaving some thrilled, appalling others. There are some truly dazzling costumes and plenty of glitzy Hawaiian acts, complete with music and dance. Don Ho, a talented vocalist and veteran performer, is either totally relaxed in his role, or dulled by its repetition. Some consider his sexual humor in bad taste, but it's no different from what you hear in most nightclubs. After all, the show isn't a prayer meeting. Don Ho plays with the audience, especially the older folks, making pointed jokes about Mainlanders. Of course everyone roars with laughter—blame it on the potent *mai tais.* There are 2 shows Sun. through Fri.: the dinner show from 6:30 to 8:30 p.m. about $70 per couple, and the cocktail show from 8:00 p.m. about $35 per couple, includes one drink. For details and reservations, tel. 949-4321.

Al Harrington, billed as "The South Pacific Man," has also been attracting crowds for years at the Polynesian Palace in the Reef Towers Hotel on Lewers St., tel. 923-9861. Another wonderfully costumed Polynesian extravaganza takes you on a musical tour through the South Pacific. Personable Harrington takes time to make everyone feel comfortable, and though he too has been doing the show for years, he manages to keep sparkle in his performance. Two dinner shows and 2 cocktail shows nightly except Saturdays. The buffet dinner is reputed to be exceptional. Prices are about $70 per couple for the dinner show, half that for the cocktail shows.

The Kahala Hilton, tel. 734-2211, presents **An Evening With Danny Kaleikini.** This extraordinary island entertainer has been captivating audiences here for almost 20 years. This show has class; it doesn't draw the large budget-oriented crowds. Two shows nightly except Sun., dinner show at 7:00 p.m., cocktail show at 9:00 p.m.

Tavana's Polynesian Spectacular in the Long House of the Hilton Hawaiian Village, tel. 923-0211, combines Polynesian music, song and dance, dramatic effects, and costumes. Two shows nightly: dinner seating at 5:30 and 8:30 p.m., cocktails at 6:30 and 9:00 p.m.

Dick Jensen, The Hula Hut, 286 Beachwalk, tel. 923-3838, is a dinner show with an all-you-can-eat buffet. Seating at 8:00 p.m., $30 per person, cocktail show 8:45 p.m., $18 per person, one cocktail included.

SHOPPING

The biggest problem concerning shopping in Waikiki is to keep yourself from burning out over the endless array of shops and boutiques. Everywhere you look, someone has something for sale, and with the preponderance of street stalls lining the boulevards, much of the merchandise comes out to greet you. The same rule applies to shopping as it does to everything in Waikiki—class next door to junk. Those traveling to the Neighbor Islands should seriously consider a shopping spree in Waikiki, which has the largest selection and most competitive prices in the islands. A great feature about shopping Waikiki is that most shops are only a minute or two from the beach. This enables your sale hound companion to hunt while you relax. There's no telling how much money your partner can save you! "Ingrate! This bathing suit could have cost $50, but I got it for $25. See, you saved $25 while you were lying here like a beached whale." Everyone concerned should easily be mollified. Charge!

The Fence

The best place to find an authentic island-made souvenir at a reasonable price is at **The Fence,** located along the fence of the Honolulu Zoo fronting Kapiolani Park. The new offical name is **Artists of Oahu/Sunday Exhibit.** Some of the island's best artists congregate here to display and sell their works on Wed. and weekends from 10:00 a.m. to 4:00 p.m. Individual tists are only allowed to display one day a week. The Fence was the good idea of Honolulu's current mayor, Frank Fasi, who decided that Oahu's rich resource of artists shouldn't go untapped. There are plenty of excellent artists whose works are sure to catch your fancy. Here are some of the best. **John Costello,** who does colorful island-inspired paintings in pointilism, many of which have a fantastic, dreamlike quality. **Mary Ann Abel,** whose pen and inks of things Hawaiian, especially children's faces, are inspired. **Daniel Wang,** one of the few practicing deaf artists in the U.S. specializes in a remarkable palm painting technique done on rice paper with Chinese inks and watercolors. **Bob Reeves** works with island woods and specializes in *koa* frames. **Caridad Sumile** does beautiful paintings and portraits in watercolors and acrylics. **Marge Claus** has a colorful *batik* style. **Patrick Doell** has a very realistic, almost picture-postcard style. **Maggie Kobayashi** incorporates the female form with nautical suggestions and loves doing mermaids. **"June of Art," Hoegler-Reda** piles on layers of paint to achieve a 3-dimensional quality. **Leonard Wood** loves animals and renders them in quiet pastels. **Cathy Thompson** does dreamy, impressionistic lily ponds. **Joe Hunt** loves the "joy of life" and renders lively paintings of color and movement. **Edna Loo** does whimsical vignettes of children in Hawaiian settings. **Dianne Jeanine** paints soft flowing watercolors of flowers, sunsets and seascapes. **Francine McGee** uses layers of glazing with modern translucent colors to achieve "old master-like" seascapes. **Theresia Brinsen** is noted for the brilliance of the knife-technique in land-seascapes. **Peggy Pai Laughlin** does *batik* and oil on silk and free-stitch embroidery.

Gifts And Souvenirs

Fine Japanese art can be seen and purchased at 2 outstanding shops in Waikiki's Eaton Square, **Gallery Mikado,** and **Gara Kuta-Do.**

ABC Stores scattered throughout Waikiki

Caridad Sumile displays her art at The Fence.

were founded by a local man, Sid Kosasa, who learned the retail business from his father. This "everything store" sells groceries, sundries, and souvenirs. Prices are good especially on specials like lotions and beach mats. Very convenient.

You can purchase colorful, dramatic **Hawaiian calendars** drawn by Herb Kane, a well-known local artist, at all of the Burger King outlets. Fine mementos, they sell for under $3.

Those who just couldn't return home without a deep Hawaiian tan can be helped by visiting **Waikiki Aloe.** They specialize in skin care products, lotions, and tanning supplies. In the Royal Hawaiian Shopping Center, and Kuhio Mall.

The Waikiki Business Plaza, 2270 Kalakaua Ave., houses a number of jewelry stores. In one stop you can get a pretty good idea of prices and availability. Look for jewelry boxes laden with jade, gold, turquoise, pearls, coral, *puka* shells, and eel, snake, and leather goods.

Military Shop of Hawaii has an entire wall dedicated to military patches, along with clothes, memorabilia, and collectibles. At 1921 Kalakaua Ave., tel. 942-3414.

Those with good taste but a limited budget should check out **Hawaiian Wear Unlimited,** liquidators of alohawear from most of Hawaii's big manufacturers. Located at the Royal Hawaiian Shopping Center, daily 9:00 a.m. to 10:00 p.m. Also **Robin Claire** "resale boutique" sells used designer clothing. At 1901 Kapiolani Plaza, tel. 941-8666.

Kite Fantasy, 2863 Kalakaua Ave., is sure to have an aerial toy to tickle your fancy. Of plenty of beaches around the island to fly a kite, Kapiolani Park in Waikiki is one of the best, with free kite lessons, and a daily display at 11:00 a.m. and 2:00 p.m.

For a full range of **photo supplies** at bargain prices try: **Woolworth's,** 2224 Kalakaua Ave.; **Fox Photo** in the International Market Place and the Waikikian and Reef Towers hotels; and **Photo Stores** here and there along Kalakaua, Kuhio, Kalia, and Lewers streets. Handbillers often give money-saving coupons to a variety of photo stores.

Waikiki Shopping Centers

The largest credit card oasis is the **Royal Hawaiian Shopping Center.** This massive complex is 3 stories of non-stop shopping, running for 3 blocks in front of the Sheraton and Royal Hawaiian hotels. It's open daily 9:00 a.m. to 10:00 p.m., til 9:00 p.m. on Sun., tel. 922-0588. This complex provides an excellent mixture of small intimate shops and larger department stores. It's a good place to do some comparative browsing before making your purchases.

Where the Royal Hawaiian Shopping Plaza ends, the **Waikiki Shopping Plaza** begins, but on the other side of the street. Here, you'll find multi-level shopping. The mall's centerpiece is a 5-story waterfall, an impressive sculpture of water and plexiglass. Another feature of this mall is *Waikiki Calls,* a free *hula* show. The plaza is open daily 9:00 a.m. to 11:00 p.m., tel. 923-1191.

The **International Market Place** is an open-air shopping bazaar that feels like Asia. Its natural canopy is a huge banyan, and the entire complex is across from the Moana Hotel at 2330 Kalakaua Ave., open daily from 9:00 a.m. until the vendors get tired at night, tel. 923-9871. Among some fine merchandise and a treasure or two is great junk! If you're after souvenirs like bamboo products, shell work, hats, mats, lotions, alohawear, and carvings, you can't do better than the International Market Place. The worst thing is that everything starts to look the same, the best is that the vendors will bargain. Make offers. Directly behind the marketplace is the relatively new **Kuhio Mall,** at 2301 Kuhio Avenue. Basically the same theme with open-air shops: gifts, fashions, food, and handmade artifacts. Enjoy the free Polynesian Show nightly at 7:00 and 8:00 p.m.

The **Hyatt Regency Shopping Center,** also called the **Atrium Shops,** is located on the first 3 floors of the Hyatt Regency Hotel, 2424 Kalakaua Ave., tel. 922-5522, open daily 9:00 a.m. to 11:00 p.m. The 70 or so shops here are mighty classy: if you're after exclusive fashions or a quality memento, this is the place. There's a Continental-style sidewalk cafe, backed by a cascading indoor waterfall. Often free enter-

The souvenirs come to you in Waikiki.

tainment and fashion shows are put on by the various shops.

Smaller Malls

King's Village, at 131 Kaiulani Ave., just next to the Hyatt Regency, takes its theme from last century, where boardwalks pass 19th century look-a-like shops, complete with a changing of the guard ceremony, nightly at 6:15 p.m. This attractive complex offers free entertainment, and attracts some of the best local street artists who usually set up their stands at night. The **Waikiki Trade Center** is on the corner of Seaside and Kuhio avenues with some of Waikiki's most elegant shops, featuring sophisticated fashions, exquisite artworks, and fine dining. The **Rainbow Bazaar** is a unique mall located at the Hilton Hawaiian Hotel, 2005 Kalia Road. Fun just to walk around, shops feature 3 main themes: Imperial Japan, Hong Kong Alley, and South Pacific Court.

Street Artists/Vendors

You don't have to try to find something to buy in Waikiki—in fact, if you're not careful, the merchandise will come after you! This takes place in the form of street vendors that have been gaining a lot of attention lately. Some view them as a colorful addition to the beach scene, others as a nuisance. These carnival-type salespeople set up their mobile booths mainly along Kalakaua Avenue, with some on Kuhio Avenue and the side streets in between. In dealing with them you can have a positive experience if you remember 2 things: they have some pretty nifty junk, and you get what you pay for.

Also, street artists set up their palettes along busy thoroughfares, and especially at the entrances to small shopping malls. Most draw caricatures of patrons in a few minutes for a few dollars—fun souvenirs. An outstanding street artist is Mai Long, a Vietnamese man who sets up in King's Alley and does superb profiles or full face all in color for less than $10.

And new stars burn into the
ancient skies,
Over the murmurous soft
Hawaiian sea.
—*Waikiki*, Rupert Brooke

Hanauma Bay

SOUTHEAST OAHU
KOKO HEAD TO WAIMANALO

It's amazing how quickly you can leave the frenzy of Waikiki behind. Once you round the bend past Diamond Head and continue traveling east toward Koko Head, the pace slackens measurably...almost by the yard. A minute ago you were in traffic, now you're cruising. It's not that this area is undeveloped; other parts of the island are much more laid-back, but none so close to the action of the city. In the 12 miles you travel from Honolulu to Waimanalo, you pass the natural phenomenon of Koko Crater, a reliable blow hole, the most aquatically active underwater park in the islands, and a string of beaches, each with a different personality. Man has made his presence felt, too. The area has some of the most exclusive homes on the island, as well as Hawaii Kai, a less exclusive project developed by the visionary businessman Henry Kaiser, who 20 years ago created this harbinger of things to come. There's Sea Life Park offering a day's outing of fun for the family, plus shopping centers, the mostly Hawaiian town of Waimanalo, and Bellows Air Force Base, unused by the military and now one of the finest camping beaches on the island. Besides camping, little accommodations are found out here, and few restaurants. This lack of development preserves the area as scenic and recreational, prized attributes that should be taken advantage of before this sunny sandbox gets paved over.

SIGHTS, BEACHES, AND PARKS

The drive out this way accounts for half of the 360 degrees of what is called **The Circle Route.** Start by heading over the Pali Highway down to Kailua, hitting the sights on the way, or come this way first along Diamond Head Road to Rt. 72 as you make the loop back to the city. The only consideration is what part of the day you'd rather stop at the southeast beaches for a dip. For the most part, the sights of this area *are* the beaches, so both are combined in this one section. The following listings assume that you follow Rt. 72 from Waikiki to Waimanalo.

Maunalua Bay

Maunalua ("Two Mountain") Bay is a 4-mile stretch of sun and surf between Diamond Head and Koko Head, with a beach park about every half mile. The first is **Kawaikui Beach Park.** No lifeguard, but the conditions are safe year round, and the bottom is shallow, muddy, and overgrown with seaweed. In times past, islanders came to the confluence of a nearby spring to harvest special *limu* growing only where fresh water meets the ocean. You'll find unlimited access, parking stalls, picnic facilities, and restrooms. Few people use the park, and it's ideal for sunning, but for frolicking in the water, give it a miss.

In quick succession come **Niu and Paiko beaches,** lying along residential areas. Although there is public access, few people take advantage of them because the swimming, with a coral and mud bottom, is less than ideal. Some residents have built a pier at Niu Beach past the mud flats, but it's restricted to their private use. Paiko Lagoon is a state bird sanctuary; binoculars will help with sightings of a variety of coastal birds.

The residential area in the hills behind **Maunalua Bay Beach Park** is Hawaii Kai, built by Henry Kaiser, the aluminum magnate. The controversial development was often denigrated as "suburban blight." Many felt it was the beginning of Oahu's ruination. The park fronts Kuapa Pond, at one time a huge fish pond, later dredged by Kaiser who used the material to build the park which he donated to the city in 1960. Now, most of the land has been reclaimed except for Koko Marina, whose boat launch constitutes the primary use of the park. You'll find a large sandy parking area where **Paradise Jet Skis** rents (look for a tent) their self-powered skis, pricy at $40 per hour, tel. 235-1612. Except for the boat launch (only one on this side of the island), the area is of little recreational use because of the mud or coral bottom. However, swimming is possible and safe, but be careful of the sudden drops created by the dredged boat channels. Two undeveloped parks are located at the end of Poipu Drive, **Kokee and Koko Kai Parks.** The currents and beach conditions make both unsuitable for swimming, but they're popular with surfers. Few others come here, but the views of the bay are lovely with glimpses of Molokai floating on the horizon to the south.

Hanauma Bay State Underwater Park

One of the premier beach parks in Hawaii is located in the sea-eroded crater of an extinct volcano just below Koko Head. People flock here to snorkel, scuba, picnic, and swim. During the day, the parking lot at the top of the hill overlooking the crescent bay below looks like a used car lot, jammed with Japanese imports, vans, and tour buses. A shuttle bus ($.50) runs up and down the hill. If you wan't to avoid the crowds come in the early morning or after 4:00 p.m. when the sun dips behind the crater, and tourists and buses leave on cue. There's still plenty of daylight, plan your trip accordingly.

The reef protects the bay and sends a maze of coral fingers right up to the shoreline. A large sandy break in the reef, **Keyhole,** is a choice spot for entering the water and for swimming. The entire bay is alive with tropical fish. Many have become so accustomed to snorkelers that they've lost their fear entirely, and willingly accept food from your fingers—some so rudely you had better be careful of getting your fingers nibbled. The county provides life guards, restrooms, showers, picnic facilities, pavilion, and food concession. Before you enter the water, do yourself a favor and read the large bulletin board near the pavilion that describes conditions. It divides the bay into 3 areas ranging from beginner to expert, and warns of sections to avoid. Be especially careful of **Witches Brew,** a turbulent area on the right at the mouth of the bay that can wash you into the **Molokai Express,** a notoriously dangerous rip current. Follow a path along the left-hand sea cliff to **Toilet Bowl,** a natural pool that rises and falls with the tides. If the conditions are right, you can sit in it to float up and down in a phenomenon very similar to a flushing toilet.

You can not rent snorkel gear at the park. If you haven't rented from a dive shop in Waikiki where the prices are cheapest, try the Aloha Dive Shop, tel. 395-5922, in the nearby Koko Marina Shopping Center. (See p. 219 for more info, along with excursions to Hanuama Bay.)

For a sweeping view, hike to the summit of **Koko Head,** not to be confused with Koko Crater, another good hike but farther east on Rt. 72. To start your trek, look for a paved road closed off to vehicles by a white metal fence, on the right before the road to the parking lot. A 15-minute hike takes you to the 642-foot summit of Koko ("Blood") Head. This was the last place that young, wandering Madame Pele attempted to dig herself a fiery nest on Oahu; as usual, she was flooded out by her jealous sister. From the summit you get an unobstructed view of Molokai 20 miles across the Kaiwi Channel, the bowl of Hanauma Bay at your feet, and a sweeping panorama of Diamond Head and the Koolau Mountains. Below are 2 small extinct craters, Nono'ula and Ihi'ihilauakea.

Koko Crater
Koko Crater's official name is *Kohelepelepe* ("Fringed vagina"). Legend says that Pele's sister, Kapo, had a magical flying vagina that she could send anywhere. Kamapua'a, the pig god, was intent on raping Pele, when Kapo came to her aid. She dispatched her vagina to entice Kamapua'a, and he followed it to Koko Head where it made the crater, and then flew away. Kamapua'a was unsuccessful when taking a flying leap at this elusive vagina. You can either hike or drive to the crater. To begin the hike, look for the road to the "Hawaii Job Corps Training Center" across from Hanauma Bay. Follow the road down past a rifle range and park at the job training building. Behind is an overgrown tramway track. The remaining ties provide a rough but adequate stairway to the top. At the 1,208-foot summit is an abandoned powerhouse and tramway station. The wood is rotted and the floors are weak! The crater itself lies 1,000-feet below. An easier but less exciting route is to follow Rt. 72 for 2 miles to Wawamalu Beach near the Hawaii Kai Golf Course, and then take a left on Kealahou Street, which leads into the crater. En route you pass **Koko Crater Stables**, tel. 395-2628, which offers guided trail rides into the crater. On the floor of Koko Crater is a botanical garden that, due to the highly unique conditions, specializes in succulents.

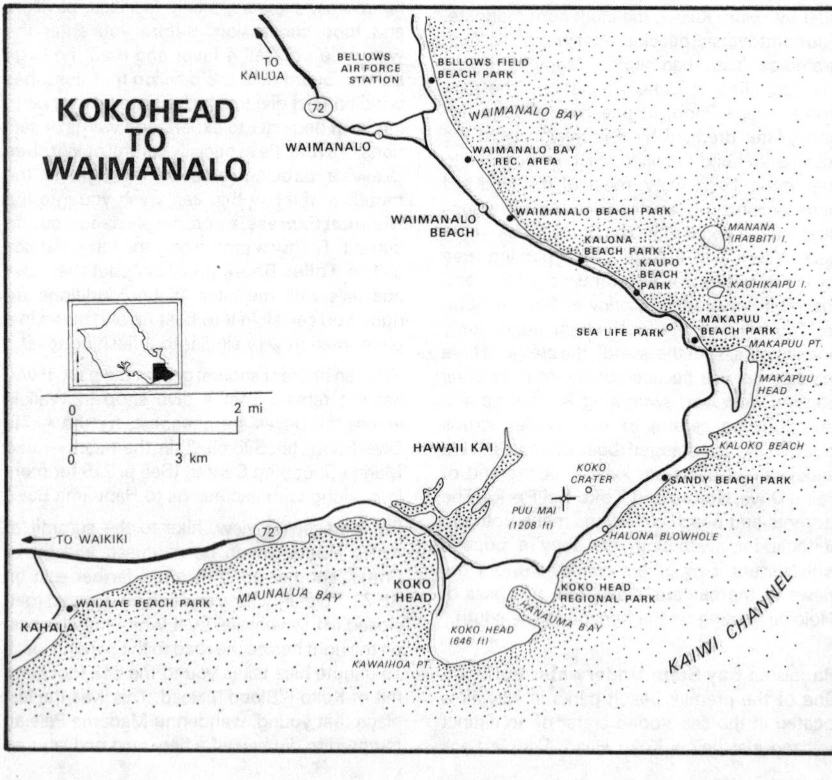

the Japanese Casting Club

Halona Cove

As you round a bend on Rt. 72 you come to the natural lookout of Halona Cove which means "The Peering Place," an excellent vantage point to see whales in season. Just before Halona, a sign will point you to the **Honolulu Japanese Casting Club**, with a stone wall and a monument. The monument at one time was *O Jisan,* the Japanese god of protection, destroyed by overzealous patriots during WW II. The monument was erected after the war, and *O Jisan* was carved into it. Below is a secluded little beach that's perfect for sunbathing. The only way to it is to scramble down the cliff. Swim only on calm days, or the wave action can pull you out to sea and then suck you into the chamber of the famous **Halona Blowhole** just around the bend. There's a turn-out at the blowhole for parking. The blowhole is a lava tube at the perfect height for the waves to be driven into it. The water compresses, and the pressure sends a spume into the air. Be extremely cautious around the blowhole. Those unfortunate enough to fall in face almost certain death.

Sandy Beach Park

Sandy Beach is one of the best bodysurfing beaches on Oahu, and the most rugged of them all. More necks and backs are broken on this beach than on all the other Oahu beaches combined. But because of the east-breaking waves, and bottom, the swells are absolutely perfect for bodysurfing. The lifeguards use a **flag system** to inform you about conditions. The **red flag** means "stay out." When checking out Sandy Beach, don't be fooled by bodysurfers who make it appear easy. These are experts, intimately familiar with the area, and even they are injured at times. Local people refer to the beach as "Scene Beach" because this is where young people come to strut their stuff. This is where the boys are because this is where the girls are. There are restrooms, a large parking area, and 2 lifeguard towers. Rip-offs have happened, so don't leave valuables in your car. *Kau kau* wagons park in the area selling a variety of refreshments.

As the road skirts the coastline, it passes a string of beaches which look inviting, but are extremely dangerous because there is no protecting reef. The best known is **Wawamalu** where people come to sunbathe only. Across the road is **Hawaii Kai Golf Course**, tel. 395-2356. You have a choice of 2 courses: the *Championship,* offering a full round of golf with beautiful views, challenging holes, and excellent greens; or the *Executive,* a shorter par-3 course for those with limited time. This is an excellent public course, but the green fees are high.

The lifeguards do a great job at Sandy Beach.

Makapuu Beach Park
This beach park is below Makapuu ("Bulging Eye") Point, a projection of land marking Oahu's easternmost point, and a favorite launching pad for hang gliding. Makapuu is *the* most famous bodysurfing beach in the entire state, but it can be extremely rugged; more people are rescued here than at any beach on Oahu (except Sandy Beach). In winter the conditions are hazardous, with much of the beach eroded away leaving exposed rocks. With no interfering reef, the surf can reach 12 feet, perfect conditions for bodysurfing, if you're an expert. Board riding is prohibited. In summer, the sandy beach reappears, and the wave action is much gentler, allowing recreational swimming. There are restrooms, lifeguard towers with a flag warning system, and picnic facilities.

Offshore is **Manana** ("Rabbit") **Island**. Curiously, it does resemble a rabbit, but it's so named because rabbits actually live on it. They were released there in the 1880s by a local rancher who wanted to raise them but was aware that if they ever got loose on Oahu they could ruin much of the crop lands. During the impotent counterrevolution of 1894 designed to reinstate the Hawaiian monarchy, Manana Island was a cache for arms and ammunition buried on its windward side. Nearby is tiny Kaohikaipu ("Turtle") Island that, along with Manana, is reserved as a seabird sanctuary.

Sea Life Park
This is a cluster of landlocked tanks holding an amazing display of marine animals that live freely in the ocean just a few hundred yards away. Admission is $7, children ages 7-12 $5, tel. 259-7933, open daily 9:30 a.m. to 4:30 p.m. The park hosts a variety of shows by trained seals, whales, dolphins, and the Ocean Science Theater. In its tanks: the *Hawaiian Reef Tank,* a 300,000-gallon fish bowl, you can see the fish being hand fed, and *Whaler's Cove* where the park's whales perform acrobatics and other tricks. Outside the entrance turnstile is a shopping complex, and The Galley Restaurant. Also, the **Pacific Whaling Museum** is here and free to the public. It houses one of the largest collections of whaling artifacts and memorabilia in the Pacific.

Kaupo Beach Park
This is the first park that you come to along the southeast coast that is safe for swimming. It is between Sealife Park and Waimanalo. The park is undeveloped and with no lifeguards, so you must exercise caution. The shore is lined with protective reef or rocks, and the swimming is best beyond the reef. Close to shore, the jutting rocks discourage most swimmers. Surfers frequent Kaupo, especially beginners, lured by the ideal yet gentle wave action.

Kaiona Beach Park
Just before you enter the ethnically Hawaiian town of Waimanalo, you pass **Kaiona Beach Park,** which you can spot because of the semipermanent tents pitched there. Local people are very fond of the area, and use it extensively. Look inland to view some remarkable cliffs and mountains that tumble to the sea. The area was at one time called *Pahonu,* "Turtle Fence," because a local chief who loved turtle meat erected a large enclosure in the sea into which any turtle that was caught by local fishermen had to be deposited. Parts of the pond fence can still be seen. Facilities include restrooms, showers, and a picnic area. Swimming is safe year round, and tent and trailer camping is allowed with a county permit.

Waimanalo
This small rural town was at one time the center of a thriving sugar plantation owned by the *hapa* Hawaiian nobleman, John Cummins, who was responsible for introducing rabbits to Manana Island. It has fallen on hard times ever since the plantation closed in the late 1940s, and now produces much of Honolulu's bananas, papayas, and anthuriums from small plots and farms. The town sits in the center of Waimanalo Bay which is the longest (3½ miles) stretch of sand beach on Oahu. To many people, especially those from Oahu, it is also the best. Few but adequate travelers' services are in town (see following). The **Olomana Golf Course,** tel. 259-7926, is a 6,000-yard, relatively easy, par-71 course, inexpensive and close to town.

Waimanalo County Beach Park, on the northern end of town, provides camping with a

Bellows Beach Park offers some of the most inviting camping on Oahu.

county permit. The beach is well protected and the swimming is safe year round. Snorkeling is good, and there are picnic tables, restrooms, and recreational facilities including a ball park and basketball courts.

Just outside of town is **Waimanalo Bay State Recreation Area,** which remains largely undeveloped. It is good for picnicking, but the swimming can sometimes be rough. The area, surrounded by a dense ironwood grove, is called "Sherwood Forest," due to many rip-offs by thieves who fancy themselves as Robin Hood, plundering the rich and keeping the loot for themselves. Guess who the rich guys are?

Bellows Beach County Park
A one-time active Air Force base is now one of Oahu's finest beach parks, and there's camping too! As you enter a sign warns that, "This military installation is open to the public only on the following days: weekends—12:00 noon Friday to 6:00 a.m. Monday; federal and state holidays—6:00 a.m. to 6:00 a.m. the following day. Camping is authorized in this park by permit from the City and County of Honolulu, Parks and Recreation Board, only." They mean it! The water is safe for swimming year round, but lifeguards are on duty only during the above stated hours. Bodysurfing and board surfing are also excellent in the park, but snorkeling is mediocre. Surfboards are not allowed in the area between the 2 lifeguard towers. After entering the main gates, follow the road for about 2 miles to the beach area. You'll find picnic tables, restrooms, and cold water showers. The combination of shade trees and adjacent beach make a perfect camping area. The park is marked by 2 freshwater streams, Waimanalo and Puha, at either end.

SERVICES

Except for the excellent camping, you're limited when it comes to accommodations in this area. **Hawaiian Family Inns,** a small cooperative of private homes in and around Hawaii Kai, provides European-style bed and breakfast. Each home differs slightly, but most have a private entrance, bath, yard and beach privileges, and some kitchen facilities. Daily rates are a reasonable $35, less during off season, with weekly and monthly discounts available. The 3 homes involved can be reached by calling tel. 395-3710, 395-4130, or 395-8153.

The first place to pick up supplies as you head east on Rt. 72 is at the **Times Super Market** in the Niu Valley Shopping Center located about halfway between Diamond Head and Koko Head. The store is open until 11:00 p.m., and they have some of the best food prices on the island.

The **Koko Marina Shopping Center** in Hawaii Kai just before Hanauma Bay is much larger with many more shops. For photo supplies and sundries, try Thrifty Drugs, Ben Franklin's, Clic Photo, and Surfside Camera. There are 2 banks, a satellite city hall for camping permits (tel. 395-4481), the Aloha Dive Shop and Suyderhoud's for snorkel and water sports equipment, and a service station. Foodland Supermarket provides most supplies for picnics and camping, and you can dine at Chuck's Steak House, McDonald's, Magoo's Pizza, or Baskin Robbins Ice Cream.

For a tasty and inexpensive lunch try any of a number of *kau kau* wagons around Sandy Beach. **Waimanalo Village** provides basics at Mel's Market where you can pick up almost all camping supplies, 7-11 Convenience Store, and **Bueno Nalo**, a Mexican cafe serving good if not memorable Mexican food for decent prices.

Pine Grove Village is an open air bazaar where local people come to sell handmade products and produce. The majority of items are authentic and priced well below similar products found in Honolulu. Participants and times vary, but a group is usually selling daily until 6:00 p.m. Some excellent buys include local fruits and vegetables, *lei,* shell work, hand-dipped candles, bikinis, jewelry, and leather goods. Price haggling is the norm, and when the sellers stop smiling, that's about the right price.

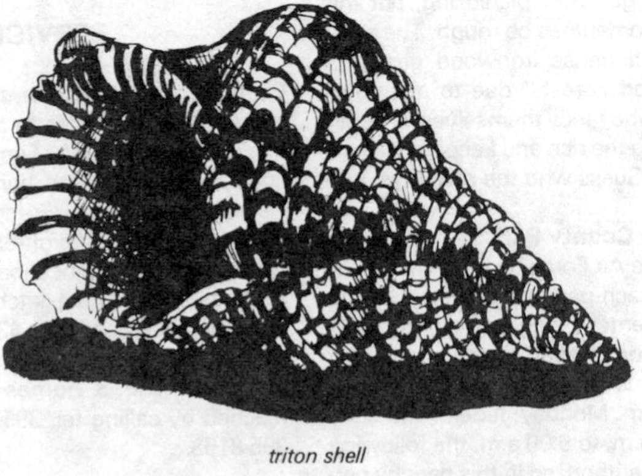

triton shell

Byodo-in Temple

WINDWARD OAHU

Oahu's windward coast never has to turn a shoulder into a harsh and biting wind. The *trades* do blow, mightily at times, but always tropical warm, perfumed with flowers, balmy and bright. Honolulu is just 12 miles over the hump of the *pali,* but a world apart. When *kamaaina* families talk of going to "the cottage in the country," they're most likely referring to the windward coast. In the southern parts, the suburban towns of **Kailua,** and **Kaneohe** are modern in every way with the lion's share of the services on this side. Kailua has Oahu's best windsurfing beach, and a nearby *heiau,* preserved and unvisited, while Kaneohe sits in a huge bay dotted with islands and reef. The coastal **Kamehameha Highway** (Rt. 83) turns inland to the base of the *pali,* passing the **Valley of the Temples,** resplendent with universal houses of worship. At **Kahaluu** starts a string of beaches running north, offering the full range of Oahu's coastal outdoor experience. You can meander side roads into the mountains near the Hawaiian villages of **Waiahole** and **Waiakane,** where the normal way of life is ramshackle cottages on small subsistence farms.

The coast bulges at **Kaawa,** where the **Crouching Lion,** a natural stone formation, seems ready to pounce on the ever-present tour buses that disturb its repose. **Punaluu** is famous for **Pat's,** the only resort in the immediate area, and for **Sacred Falls Park,** a short hike to a peak at Oahu's beautiful and natural heart (if it isn't muddy). Suddenly, you're in manicured **Laie** where Hawaii's Mormon community has built a university, a temple perfect in its symmetry, and the **Polynesian Cultural Center,** a sanitized replica of life in the South Seas, Disney style. The northern tip at **Kahuku,** site of one of Oahu's oldest sugar mills, is where the **North Shore** begins. Kahuku Point houses 2 refuges, one for wildlife, and the other for Oahu's only nudist camp, both protecting endangered species from mankind's prying eyes.

SIGHTS

It makes little difference in which direction you travel the windward coast, but the following sights will be listed from south to north from Kailua to Kahuku. The slight advantage in

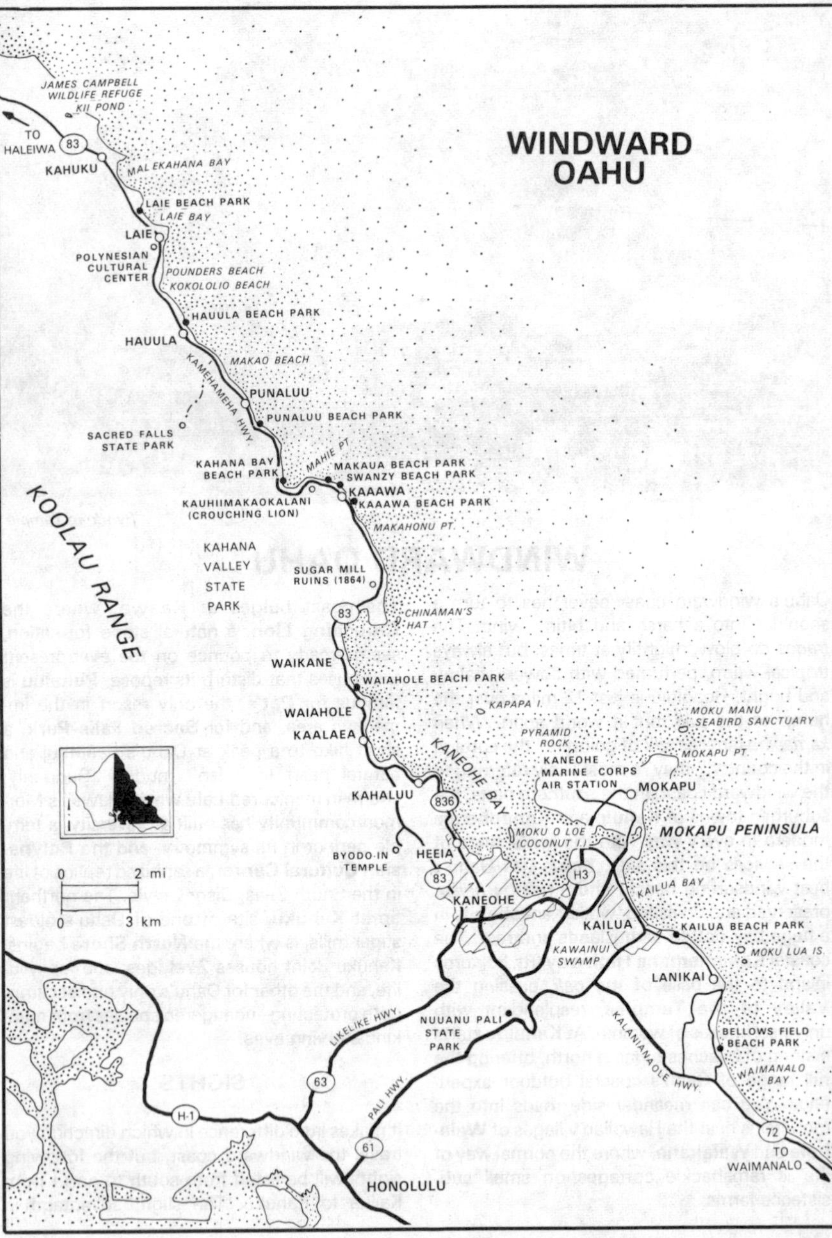
WINDWARD OAHU
JAMES CAMPBELL WILDLIFE REFUGE
KII POND
TO HALEIWA
83
KAHUKU
MALEKAHANA BAY
LAIE BEACH PARK
LAIE BAY
LAIE
POLYNESIAN CULTURAL CENTER
POUNDERS BEACH
KOKOLOLIO BEACH
HAUULA BEACH PARK
HAUULA
KAMEHAMEHA HWY
MAKAO BEACH
PUNALUU
PUNALUU BEACH PARK
SACRED FALLS STATE PARK
KAHANA BAY BEACH PARK
MAHIE PT.
MAKAUA BEACH PARK
SWANZY BEACH PARK
KAAAWA
KAAAWA BEACH PARK
KAUHIIMAKAOKALANI (CROUCHING LION)
MAKAHONU PT.
KOOLAU RANGE
KAHANA VALLEY STATE PARK
SUGAR MILL RUINS (1864)
CHINAMAN'S HAT
WAIKANE
WAIAHOLE BEACH PARK
WAIAHOLE
KAALAEA
KAPAPA I.
MOKU MANU SEABIRD SANCTUARY
PYRAMID ROCK
MOKAPU PT.
KANEOHE BAY
KANEOHE MARINE CORPS AIR STATION
KAHALUU
MOKAPU
836
MOKAPU PENINSULA
MOKU O LOE (COCONUT I.)
BYODO-IN TEMPLE
HEEIA
H3
KAILUA BAY
0 2 mi
0 3 km
KANEOHE
KAILUA
KAILUA BEACH PARK
KAWAINUI SWAMP
MOKU LUA IS.
LANIKAI
NUUANU PALI STATE PARK
KALANIANAOLE HWY.
BELLOWS FIELD BEACH PARK
LIKELIKE HWY.
WAIMANALO BAY
63
PALI HWY.
H-1
72
TO WAIMANALO
61
HONOLULU

traveling this direction is that your car is in the right-hand lane, which is better for coastal views.

Kailua

The easiest way into Kailua ("Two Seas") is over the Koolaus on Rt. 61, the Pali Highway. As soon as you pass through a long tunnel just after Nuuanu Pali Lookout (see p. 239) and your eyes adjust to the shocking brilliance of sunshine, look to your right to see Mt. Olomana. Its 1,643-foot peak is believed to be the volcanic origin of Oahu, the first land to emerge from the seas. Below lies Kailua and the Kawainui Marsh, perhaps the oldest inhabited area on this side of the island. Kamehameha I, after conquering Oahu in 1795, gave all this land to his chiefs that had fought for him. The area became a favorite of the ruling *ali'i* until the fall of the monarchy at the turn of this century. Kailua has approximately 45,000 people, technically making it the state's largest windward city. It's developed with shopping centers, a hospital, and the *best* windsurfing beach in the state (see below) Four golf courses surround the town, and a **satellite city hall** dispenses camping permits.

A good touring loop is to continue straight on Rt. 61 until it comes to the coast. Turn on Kalaheo Road which takes you along the coast to Kailua Beach Park. In the waters offshore will be a spectacle of windsurfers, with their sails puffed out like the proud chests of multicolored birds. To the left of the beach is **Mokapuu** ("Sacred Area") **Island,** home of the Kaneohe Marine Corps Base. Notice the rock that separates the island creates a large natural archway navigable by sizable boats. Most of the little islands in the bay are bird sanctuaries. The farthest, **Moku Manu,** is home to terns and man-o-wars, birds famous for leading fishermen to schools of fish. Up on the coastal bluffs is a gray house with a flat roof, the residence of a local woman called the *Birdlady of Kailua.* The woman has a reputation for taking care of any sick or injured birds that people bring to her. The entire home is carved from rock, including the chairs and table. Every once in a while, tours are offered to the home for a few dollars. They're irregular, so check the local papers, and you may be lucky enough to be there at just the right time.

the Birdlady's perch

Aalapapa Drive gains the heights from the beach and takes you through an area of beautiful homes until you come to **Lanikai Beach.** At one time, trees came down to the shoreline, but it has steadily eroded away. The Navy attempted to start a retaining reef by dumping bargeloads of white bath tile just offshore. Their efforts were not successful, but many homes in town now have sparkling new white-tiled bathrooms! As Aalapapa Drive loops back to town, it changes names to Mokulua; a pull-off here affords an expansive panorama of the bay below. Daytime, it's enjoyable, but in the evening local kids come here to hang out and drink beer.

Ulupoa Heiau was dedicated to the Ulu line of *ali'i* who were responsible for setting up *heiau* dedicated to the sacred birth of chiefs. Oftentimes, the umbilical cord was cut just as a drum was sounded, then the cord *(piko)* was placed in a shallow rock depression at a *heiau.* This temple was supposedly built by the legendary *menehune.* The stone craftsmanship is remarkable—measuring 140 feet wide and 30 feet high. Atop the temple is a pathway that you can follow. Notice small stones wrapped in *ti* leaves placed as offerings. To get there, as you approach Kailua on Rt. 61 look for a red light and a 7-11 store. Turn left onto Uluoa Street, following it to Manu Aloha Street, where you turn right. Follow it to the end and park in the YMCA lot. A small lane leads across Rt. 61 to **Maunawili Falls** (see p. 216).

Kaneohe And Vicinity

The bedroom community of Kaneohe ("Kane's Bamboo") lies along Kaneohe Bay, protected by a huge barrier reef. Within the town is **Hoomaluhia Regional Park,** so large that guided hikes are offered on a daily basis. Offshore is Moku o' Loe, commonly called **Coconut Island.** It became famous as the opening shot in the TV show "Gilligan's Island." In ancient times it was *kapu* and during WW II served as an R&R camp for B-29 crews. Many of the crews felt the island had bad vibes, and reported having a streak of bad luck. Recently Frank Fasi, Honolulu's mayor, suggested that Hawaii's gate-crashing guest, Ferdinand Marcos, should lease Coconut Island. The Philippine dictator has a penchant for islands—perhaps he and Imelda would prefer Alcatraz. In the northern section of town is **He'eia Pier,** launching area for the *Coral Queen,* tel. 247-0375, a glass-bottomed boat that sails throughout the bay. A popular attraction, so make reservations. Unfortunately, in recent years, due to the development of the area, the once crystal-clear bay is becoming murky with silt, but the visibility is still good enough for a fun outing.

Kahekilii Highway

Where Rt. 83 intersects the Likelike Highway on the southern outskirts of Kaneohe, it branches north and changes its name from the Kamehameha Highway to the **Kahekilii Highway** until it hits the coast at Kaalaea. This 4-mile traverse passes 2 exceptionally beautiful valleys: Haiku Valley, and the Valley of the Temples. Neither should be missed.

Haiku Gardens ("Abrupt Break") is a lovely section of commercial area that includes a restaurant (see below) and some quiet condominiums. After you pass a community college, Haiku Road is past 2 red lights. Turn left here and proceed for about ½ mile until you see the entrance. The gardens date from the mid-1800s, when Hawaiian *ali'i* deeded 16 acres to an English engineer named Baskerville. He developed the area, creating a series of spring-fed lily ponds, a number of estate homes, and by planting flowers, fruits, and ornamental trees. Later a restaurant was built, now owned by the Ing family, and the grounds became famous for their beauty, often used for outdoor weddings and special gatherings. You're welcome to walk through the gardens. Proceed from the restaurant down a grassy area to a pond, where perhaps you'll attract an impromptu entourage of ducks, chickens and guinea fowl that squawk along looking for handouts. Amidst the lush foliage is a grass shack used for weddings. A path leads around a larger pond

the lush gardens at the Haiku Restaurant

whose benches and small pavilions are perfect for contemplation. The path leads under a huge banyan, while a nearby bamboo grove serenades with sonorous music if the wind is blowing.

Valley Of The Temples

The concept of this universal faith cemetery is as beautiful as the sculpted *pali* that serves as its backdrop. A rainy day makes it better. The *pali* explodes with rainbowed waterfalls, and the greens turn a richer emerald, sparkling with dew drops. Don't miss the Valley of the Temples Memorial Park, 47-200 Kahekili Hwy., tel. 239-8811. High on a hill sits a Christian chapel, an A-frame topped by a cross. The views can be lovely from up here, but unfortunately the large windows of the chapel perfectly frame some nondescript tract housing, and a Pay n' Save supermarket below. Great planning!

The crown jewel of the valley is **Byodo-In Temple** ("Temple of Equality"), a superbly appointed replica of the 900-year-old Byodo-In of Uji, Japan (depicted on the 10 *yen* coin). The temple dates from June 7, 1968, 100 years to the day when Japanese immigrants first arrived in Hawaii. It was erected through the combined efforts of an American engineering firm headed by Ronald Kawahara in accordance with a plan designed by Kiichi Sano, a famed Kyoto landscape artist. A 3-ton brass bell, which you're invited to strike after making an offering, creates the right vibrations for meditation, and symbolically spreads the word of Amida Buddha. Remove your shoes before entering the temple. The walls hold distinctive emblems of different Buddhist sects. Upstairs wings are roped off, with no entry permitted. Stand on the gravel path opposite the main temple. You'll see a grating with a circle cut in the middle. Stick your face in to see the perfectly framed contemplative visage of Buddha. Cross a half-moon bridge to the left of the temple and follow the path to a small gazebo. Here a rock, perfectly and artistically placed, separates a stream in two, sending the water to the left and right. The pagoda at the top of the path is called the Meditation House. Go to this superbly manicured area to get a sweeping view of the grounds. In front of the Meditation House is a curious tree; pick up one of the fallen leaves, and feel the natural velvet on the backside.

Charlie and the Birdman

The grounds are alive with sparrows and peacocks, and from time to time you'll hear a curious-sounding "yip, yip, yip," and clapping hands. Follow it to discover a remarkable man, Hisayoshi Hirada, the *Birdman of Byodo-In.* Mr. Hirada translates his first name into "long live a good man," and he, well into his 70s, is living proof. Mr. Hirada began training the birds and carp of Byodo-In after his retirement. He would come daily to feed the fish, clapping his hands while he did so. Soon the Pavlovian response took over. Simultaneously, a small and courageous bird, which Hirada *san* calls Charlie, began taking crumbs from his fingers. Now, he simply claps and "yips" to be surrounded by birds and a roiling bubble of fish in the pond at his feet. A small gift shop selling souvenirs, cards, and some refreshments is to the right of the temple. If you wish to photograph the complex, it's best to come before noon, when the sun is at your back as you frame the red and white temple against the deep green of the *pali.*

Waiahole To Punaluu

If you want to fall in love with rural, old-time Oahu, go to the northern reaches of Kaneohe Bay around **Waihole** and **Waikane**, a Hawaiian grassroots area that has so far eluded development. Alongside the road are many more fruit stands than in other parts of Oahu. For a glimpse of *what's happening* look for the Waiahole Elementary School, and turn left up Waiahole Valley Road. The road wheedles its way into the valley, becoming narrower until it turns into a dirt track. Left and right in homey, ramshackle houses lives down-home Hawaii, complete with taro patches in the back yards. Another road of the same type is about ½ mile up Rt. 83 just before you enter Waikane. If you're staying in Waikiki, compare this area with Kuhio Avenue only 45 minutes away!

Chinaman's Hat

Route 83 passes a string of beaches, most with camping. Offshore from Kualoa County Park is Mokoli'i ("Small Reptile") Island, commonly called **Chinaman's Hat** due to its obvious resemblance to an Oriental *chapeau.* If the tides are right, you can walk out to it (sneakers advised because of the coral) where you and a few nesting birds have it to yourself. The road passes through what was once sugarcane country. Most of the businesses failed last century, but you will see the ruins of the Judd Sugar Works a mile or so before reaching Kaawa. The dilapidated mill stands although it was closed more than a century ago. Entering is not advised!

As you come around the bend of Mahie Point, staring down at you is a very popular stone formation, the **Crouching Lion.** Undoubtedly a tour bus or two will be sitting in the lot of the Crouching Lion Inn. As with all anatomical rock formations, it helps to have an imagination. Anyway, the inn is much more interesting than the lion. Built by George Larsen in 1928 from rough-hewn lumber from the Pacific Northwest, the huge stones were excavated from the site itself. The inn went public in 1951 and has been serving tourists ever since (for menu and prices see below).

Punaluu

When islanders say **Punaluu** ("Coral Diving") they usually combine it into the phrase "Pat's of Punaluu" because of the famous resort that's been delighting local people and visitors for years. It's a favorite place to come for a drive in the "country." Punaluu is a long and narrow ribbon of land between the sea and the *pali.* Its built-up area is about a mile or so long, but only a hundred yards wide. It has gas, supplies, camping, and some of the cheapest accommodations anywhere on Oahu (see below). The **Punaluu Art Gallery,** operated by Dorothy Zoler, offers distinctive island art. On the northern outskirts, the sign pointing to **Sacred Falls** is easily pinpointed because of the Sacred Falls Bazaar just across the road (for hiking information see p. 216).

Laie

The "saints" came marching into Laie ("Leaf of the *Ie* Vine") and set about making a perfect Mormon village in paradise. What's more, they succeeded! The town itself is squeaky clean, with well-kept homes and manicured lawns that hint of suburban Midwest America. Dedicated to education, they built a branch of **Brigham Young University** (BYU) that attracts students from all over Polynesia, many of whom work in the nearby Polynesian Cultural Center. The students vow to live a clean life, free of drugs and alcohol, and not to grow beards. God doesn't like beards! In the foyer of the main entrance look for a huge mural depicting Laie's flag-raising ceremony in 1921 which symbolically established the colony. The road leading to and from the university campus is maze-like but easily negotiable.

The first view of the **Mormon Temple,** built in 1919, is very impressive. Square, with simple architectural lines, this house of worship sits pure white against the *pali,* and is further dramatized by a reflecting pool and fountains spewing fine mists. This tranquil, shrine-like church is open daily from 9:00 a.m. to 9:00 p.m., when a slide show telling the history of the Laie colony is presented, along with a guided tour of the grounds. "Smoking is pro-

woodworker at the Polynesian Cultural Center (photo, Bob Cowan)

hibited, and shirts (no halter tops) must be worn to enter." The temple attracts more visitors than any other Mormon site outside of the main temple in Salt Lake City.

The real showcase is the **Polynesian Cultural Center.** PCC, as it's called by islanders, began as an experiment in 1963. Smart businessmen said it would never thrive way out in Laie, and tourists didn't come to Hawaii for *culture* anyway. The PCC now rates as one of Oahu's top tourist attractions, luring about one million visitors annually. Miracles do happen! PCC is a non-profit organization, with proceeds going to the Laie BYU, and to maintaining the center itself. Covering 42 acres, the primary attractions are 7 model villages including examples from Hawaii, Samoa, the Marquesas, Fiji, New Zealand, Tonga, and Tahiti. Guides lead you through the villages either on a walking tour, by shuttle tram, or by canoe over artesian-fed waterways. The villages are primarily staffed with people from the representative island homelands. Remember that most are Mormons, whose dogma colors the attitudes and selected presentations of the staffers. Still, all are genuinely interested in dispensing cultural knowledge about their traditional island ways and beliefs, and almost all are characters that engage in lighthearted bantering with their willing audience. The undeniable family spirit and pride at PCC makes you feel welcome, while providing a clean and wholesome experience, with plenty of attention to detail. The morning begins with **Fiafia Festival**, a *lei* greeting that orients you to the center. Next comes **Music Polynesia**, a historical evolution of island music presented by singers, musicians, and dancers. A brass band plays throughout the day, and the **Pageant of Canoes** begins at 3:00 p.m. The largest extravaganza occurs during an evening dinner show called **This is Polynesia.** Beginning at 7:30 p.m., the center's amphitheater hosts about 3,000 spectators for this show of music, dance, and historical drama. The costumes and lighting are dramatic and inspired; it's hard to believe that the performers are not professionals. PCC is open daily except Sunday from 10:00 a.m. General admission to the center only is $15 adult, $7.50 children under 11, under 5 free. There are also a variety of other packages available including an all-day pass, with dinner buffet and evening show for around $50, children $40. For more information contact PCC at tel. 293-3333. TheBus no. 52 leaves from Ala Moana to the center and takes about 2 hours. The North Shore Shuttle, tel. 946-8987, leaves from the Waikiki Moana Hotel and charges $4 round trip. Most island hotels can arrange a package tour to PCC.

BEACHES

Over a dozen beaches line the 24 miles of the windward coast from Kailua to Kahuku. The majority offer a wide range of water sports and camping. A few offshore islands, refuges for Hawaiian waterbirds, can be visited and explored. You can walk to these islands during low tide, and even camp there. The following beaches are listed from south to north.

Kailua Beaches

Along the shoreline of an exclusive residential area, just south of Kailua sits **Lanikai Beach.** Three clearly marked rights-of-way run off Mokulua Drive, the main thoroughfare. No facilities but good snorkeling and swimming year round, with generally mild surf and a long, gently sloping, sandy beach. The beach runs south for almost a mile, broken by a series of sea walls designed to hold back erosion. Many small craft use the sandy-bottomed shore to launch and land. Popular with local people, but not visited much by tourists.

Kailua Beach Park is the main beach in the area. In the last few years, it has become the sailboarding capital of Hawaii. Local people complain that at one time the beach was great for family outings, with safe conditions and fine facilities. Now, the wind has attracted a daily flotilla of sailborders, kayak racers, and jet skiers. The congested and contested waters are dangerous for the average swimmer. Many sailborders are beginners, so if you're a swimmer, be careful of being run over. The conditions are similar to out-of-control skiers found on the slopes of many mountains. The park boasts a pavilion, picnic facilities, restrooms, showers, lifeguards, boat ramp, and food concession. The surf is gentle year round, and the swimming safe. Children should be careful of the sudden drop-offs in the channels formed by the Kaelepulu Canal as it enters the sea in the middle of the beach park. Good surfing and diving are found around Popoi'a Island just offshore. Follow Rt. 61 through Kailua until it meets the coast, and then turn right on S. Kalaheo St. following it to the beach park.

Kalama Beach is reached by making a right onto N. Kalaheo. This beach has no facilities and is inferior to Kailua Beach Park, but the swimming is good, and sections of the beach have been made off limits to any surf-riding vehicles.

Kaneohe Beaches

Kaneohe Bay offers **Kaneohe Beach Park, He'eia State Park,** and **Laenani Beach Park,** all accessible off Rt. 836 as it heads northward along the coast. All are better for the views of Kaneohe Bay than for beach activities. With restrooms and a few picnic tables, the water is safe year round, but it's murky and lined with mud flats and coral heads. The same condi-

Kailua Beach, the sailboarding capital of Oahu

tions hold true for **Waiahole Beach Park** about 4 miles north, but this area is much less developed, quieter, and good for beachcombing.

Kualoa County Regional Park

With the *pali* in the background, **Chinaman's Hat Island** offshore, and a glistening white strand shaded by swaying palms, Kualoa is one of the finest beach parks on windward Oahu. One of the most sacred areas on Oahu, the *ali'i* brought their children here to be reared and educated, and the area is designated in the National Register of Historic Places. It has a full range of facilities and services including lifeguards, restrooms, and picnic tables. The park is open daily from 7:00 a.m. to 7:00 p.m., with overnight camping allowed with a county permit (mandatory). The swimming is safe year round along the shoreline dotted with pockets of sand and coral. The snorkeling and fishing are good, but the real treat is walking the 500 yards to Chinaman's Hat at low tide. You need appropriate footgear (old sneakers are fine) because of the sharp coral heads. The island is one of the few around offshore Oahu that is not an official bird sanctuary, although many shorebirds do use the island and should not be molested. Because of its exposure to winds, Kualoa is sometimes chilly. Although the park is popular, it is not well marked. It lies along Rt. 83, and if you're heading north, look for a red sign to the Kualoa Ranch. Just past it is an HVB warrior pointing to the park and Chinaman's Hat. Heading south the entrance is just past the HVB warrior pointing to the Kualoa Sugar Mill ruins.

Ka'a'awa And Kahana Bay

Three beach parks in as many miles lie between Ka'a'awa Point and Kahana Bay. The first heading north is **Ka'a'awa Beach Park**, a popular camping beach (county permits) with restrooms, lifeguards, and picnic facilities. An offshore reef running the entire length of the park makes swimming safe year round. A dangerous rip is at the south end of the park at the break in the reef.

Swanzy County Park, 2 minutes north, also has camping with a county permit. The sand and rubble beach lies below a long retaining wall, often underwater during high tide. The swimming is safe year round, but is not favorable because of the poor quality of the beach. Swanzy is one of the best squidding and snorkeling beaches on the windward coast. A break in the offshore reef creates a dangerous rip, and should be avoided.

Kahana Bay County Park is a full-service park with lifeguards, picnic facilities, restrooms, the area's only boat launch, and camping (county permit). Swimming is good year round, although the waters can be cloudy at times, and a gentle shorebreak makes the area ideal for bodysurfing and beginner board riders. This entire beach area is traditionally excellent for *akule* fishing with large schools visiting the offshore waters at certain times of year. It once supported a large Hawaiian fishing village; remnants of fishponds can still be seen.

Punaluu To Hauula

Right along the highway is **Punaluu County Beach Park.** It's always crowded with campers, many of whom live along the coast semi-permanently, moving from one beach park to the next every 30 days, or when they're rousted by authorities. Many camps look pretty run down, but there are usually no real hassles. Punaluu provides shopping, and the beach park has restrooms, cooking facilities, camping by permit, but no lifeguards. The swimming is safe year round inside the protecting reef.

Hauula County Beach Park is an improved beach park with lifeguards, picnic facilities, restrooms, pavilion, volleyball court, and camping (permit). Safe swimming year round inside the coral reef, with good snorkeling, and surfing usually best in the winter months. Rip currents are present at both ends of the beach at breaks in the reef, and deep holes in a brackish pond are formed where Maakua Stream enters the sea. Across the road are the ruins of the historic Lanakila Church (1853), partially dismantled at the turn of the century to build a smaller church near Punaluu.

Laie To Kahuku

At the southern end of Laie is **Pounder's Beach,** so named by students of BYU because of the pounding surf. The park area is privately owned, open to the public, with no facilities. This beach experiences heavy surf and dangerous conditions in the winter months, but its excellent shoreline break is perfect for bodysurfing. The remains of an old pier at which interisland steamers once stopped is still in evidence.

Laie County Park is an unimproved beach park with no facilities, but a one-mile stretch of beach. The shoreline waters are safe for swimming inside the reef, but wintertime produces heavy and potentially dangerous surf. Good snorkeling, fishing, and throw netting by local fishermen, access is by following the stream from the bridge near the Laie Shopping Mall.

Kakela Beach is a privately owned facility where camping is allowed. You must secure a permit in Laie from Zion Securities, 55-510 Kamehameha Hwy., Laie, HI 96762, tel. 293-9201. Check in with the caretaker before using the beach. Good swimming and bodysurfing, the area is improved with restrooms and a picnic area.

Malekahana State Recreation Area

This is the premier camping beach along the north section of the windward coast. Separated from the highway by a large stand of shade trees, it offers showers, restrooms, picnic facilities, and camping (state permit). The park is open to non-campers daily from 7:00 a.m. to 6:30 p.m. Offshore is Moku'auia better known as **Goat Island.** You can reach this seabird sanctuary by wading across the reef during low tide. You'll find a beautiful crescent white-sand beach, and absolute peace and quiet. The swimming inside the reef is good, and it's amazing how little used this area is for such a beautiful spot.

ACCOMMODATIONS

Accommodation listings run from south to north. There aren't many choices, but enough to give you a range. For good **camping** refer to the previous section.

Kailua And Kaneohe

The **Kailua Beachfront Vacation Homes** offer 2 completely furnished and ready-to-move-into rental homes. Minimum stay of 5 days, the one-bedroom homes rents for $80-95 p/d, up to 4 persons, and the 3-bedroom home rents for $160-190 p/d up to 6 persons. The units provide parking, TV, and maid service on request. For information and reservations write Kailua Beachfront Vacation Homes, 133 Kailuana Pl., Kailua, HI 96734, tel. 261-3484.

Pacific Hawaii Bed and Breakfast lists private homes in and around Kailua. Rates and homes differ dramatically, but all are guaranteed to be comfortable and accommodating. For information and location, write Pacific Hawaii Bed and Breakfast, 19 Kai Nanai Pl., Kailua, HI 96734, tel. 262-6026.

The **Bayview Apartment Hotel** has fully furnished one- and 2-bedroom units at $40 s, $50-55 d, up to 3 people, $5 additional person. There's parking, TV, swimming pool, no in-room phones, and a 3-day minimum stay. For reservations and information write Bayview Apartment Hotel, 44-707 Puamohala St., Kaneohe, HI 96744, tel. 247-3635.

The **Windward Marine Resort** in Kaneohe has fully furnished apartments. It calls itself "a small rural resort," and although not far from city lights, it's definitely off the beaten track—literally on the edge of Kaneohe Bay, so close that it boasts fishing from the *lanai* of some apartments. All units have living rooms, color TV, phones, and daily maid service. The resort also offers motorboats, kayaks, sailboards, and small sailboats through its sister organization, North Bay Boat Club. Daily rates are $45-80 one bedroom, $60-90 2-bedroom, $120 3-bedroom, 10% discount on long stays, package deal with Thrifty car rental. For information write Windward Marine Resort, 47-039 Lihikai Dr., Kaneohe, HI 96744, tel. 800-367-8047 ext. 239, Canada 800-423-8733 ext. 239, on Oahu 239-5711.

Punaluu

Two institutions at Punaluu are sure to please. Each is in a different economic and social category, but because they're off the beaten track, both offer great value. **Pat's at Punaluu** is more famous as a restaurant than as condominium apartments, but you'll be pleased with both. Daily rates are $42-54 cottage, $50-58 one bedroom, $60-75 2-bedroom, $82-100 3-bedroom, same rate up to 4 persons, extra person $10. At Pat's are a magnificent beach, parking, TV, a fine restaurant, swimming pool, and weekly maid service. They offer a "room 'n wheels" package, and discounts on long stays. For information write Pat's at Punaluu Condo, 53-567 Kamehameha Hwy., Hauula, HI 96717, tel. 293-8111.

Margaret, proprietor of Countryside Cabins

The **Countryside Cabins** are a wonderful, inexpensive, and definitely funky place to stay. They're owned and operated by a sparkling older woman, Margaret Naai. The entrance is hard to spot, but it's located *mauka* about halfway between Pat's of Punaluu and the Texas Paniolo Cafe. Look for the small white sign that says "Cabins." You're greeted by a large black dog named Smokey. He's a big baby so don't worry. Margaret comes out with a rolled-up newspaper to fend Smokey off because he jumps on her: Smokey weighs 98 pounds, she only 96. Completely furnished studios are $20 daily, $140 weekly, $350 monthly. Unfurnished rooms are $12 s, $14 d, $84 weekly, $200 monthly. Margaret will reserve a room for you if you send a $10 deposit. She's a peach, but she's getting on in years, so it would be best to send a SASE envelope with your deposit and not count on her to remember. For information and reservations, write Countryside Cabins, 53-224 Kamehameha Hwy., Hauula HI 96717, tel. 237-8169.

Laie

The **Laniloa Lodge Hotel** is just outside the Polynesian Cultural Center. They rent studios (no kitchen) for $43 s, $47 d, extra person $4, All rooms have a/c, TV, and there's parking, a pool, and a restaurant that closes early on Sundays. For information write Laniloa Lodge Hotel, 55-109 Laniloa St., Laie, HI 96762, tel. 293-9282.

North Shore Naturalist Park

If you like cavorting naked on the beach and tempting the sun to burn very delicate parts of your body, you'll love the North Shore Naturalist Park. The very private park has restrooms, showers, a snack bar, recreation center, and camping. It costs about $25 per day, $50 per week, which entitles you to camp. Cabins are also available, at around $25 per day, with use of a communal kitchen. The swimming and snorkeling are fair. The exact location is confidential, but 3 red stripes on a telephone pole along the highway are a landmark. Information is sent to you by writing North Shore Naturalist Park, Box K, Laie, HI 96762, tel. 521-4235.

FOOD

Kailua And Vicinity

For a quick snack at a juice bar try **Vim and Vigor,** a small island chain with a half dozen stores. This one's at the corner of Kailua Rd. and Hahani St., tel. 262-9911. Besides normal health food items including Hain products, they serve sandwiches for under $3, and a variety of exotic smoothies for $1.50. Bread choices are whole grain, 9-grain, and pita. Open Mon. through Sat., 9:00 a.m. to 5:00 p.m., Sun. 10:00 a.m. to 4:00 p.m.

If you've got a taste for Japanese or Korean food but not much money to spend, go to the **Bar-B-Q-East** in the Kailua Shopping Center on Kailua Road. For about $4 you get a complete Japanese or Korean dinner. If you want to save even more, at the other end of the shopping plaza is Bar-B-Q-East II, a take-out version of the same restaurant offering main dishes for $1, plus $.50 for *two-scoop-rice.* Avoid their *saimin* (instant cup variety), and don't order a fish sandwich—too greasy.

If you're interested in two distinctly different types of food you can try the **Kailua Health Food Store,** 124 Oneawa St., tel. 261-0353, just across the street from **Taco Bell.** The health food store's juice bar sells smoothies and sandwiches, like King Neptune salad, or vegetarian chili for under $3. Open daily 9:00 a.m. to 5:30 p.m. Next door is **Ching Lee Chop Suey,** a down-home, inexpensive Chinese restaurant where you can have a complete meal for under $5.

Uluniu Street has 3 inexpensive places to eat, one after the other. After making a left from Kuulei Road (Rt. 61) onto Oneawa, a main thoroughfare, turn right onto Uluniu just at the large Kailua Furniture. First is an excellent and authentic hole-in-the-wall Japanese restaurant, **Kailua Okazuya.** They specialize in *donburi,* a bowl of rice smothered with various savories. Try their *o yakodon buri,* chicken and egg with vegetables over rice for under $3. They serve plate lunches and a *sushi* special that can't be beat which includes fresh fish, shrimp, abalone, and octopus for only $4! **Earth Seed Natural Foods,** 354 Uluniu St., tel. 261-9141, operates the Little Kitchen, a full-service restaurant around back, specializing in gourmet vegetarian food at decent prices. They're only open Wed. to Sun. from 5:00 to 9:00 p.m. Almost next door is **The Chinese Garden,** a sit-down and take-out restaurant specializing in *chop suey.*

Jule's Italian Restaurant, 345 Hahani St., next door to the easily spotted Holiday Mart, serves good, reasonably priced Italian food at their counter. They're open Sun. to Thur. 10:00 a.m. to 9:30 p.m., Fri. to Sat. 10:00 a.m. to 11:00 p.m. Choose from a variety of pasta dishes for around $5, *fettuccini alfredo* $7, pizza from $9. Not great food, but appetizing.

For a fine Italian meal try **Florence's,** 20 Kainehe St., tel. 261-1987. Florence has cooked up a few pots of spaghetti over the past 30 years that have kept locals and tourist lucky enough to find this restaurant coming back for more. You receive a full dinner including minestrone, salad, bread, beverage, a side of macaroni, and the entree of the day for $9. Not only inexpensive but *delicioso!* Open for lunch too, with savory meatball sandwiches a great choice.

L'Auberge, 117 Hekili St., tel. 262-4835, is *so Francais*—open for dinner only, Wed. to Sunday. If you're in town then, don't miss it. Owned and operated by the Baltzer family, the small dining room is known for *crepes* stuffed with delicious morsels like crab or mushrooms and garnished with a rich sauce. The fresh fish is excellent, and they sometimes serve Maui rabbit. Fine dining!

Haiku Gardens Restaurant

The Haiku Gardens Restaurant, true to its name, sits surrounded by a fragrant garden in a lovely, secluded valley. (For directions and a full description of the grounds, see p. 292). Open daily except Mondays for lunch from 11:30 a.m., dinner from 5:30 p.m., Sunday brunch from 10:30 a.m., tel. 247-6671. Choose from a daily buffet featuring prime rib for $10.95, children $7.95, or full meals such as mandarin spare ribs $7.95, *mahi mahi* $8.50, or strip steak $13.95. The Sunday champagne brunch is only $8.95 and a favorite of island residents.

Fruit Stands

Follow the Kahekilii Hwy. to Rt. 83 past Waiahole and Waikane, where you'll find some of the best roadside fruit stands on Oahu. One little stand just near the Waiahole Elementary School is manned on non-school days by 2 young sisters, Zalia and Kahea. Their smiles alone are worth a stop. Just up Rt. 83 is another stand that features *drinking coconuts.* Do yourself a favor and have one. Sip the juice and when it's done, eat the custard-like contents. A real island treat, nutritious and delicious.

The Crouching Lion Inn

There was a time when *everyone* passing through Kaaawa stopped at the Crouching Lion Inn. Now *everyone* has become *too many* ever since the tour buses started packing in here for lunch. The Inn, along Rt. 83 in Kaaawa, tel. 237-8511, is beautiful enough to stop at just to have a look, but if you want a reasonably quiet meal, avoid lunchtime and come in the evening. Dinners are pricy and include *mahi mahi* $10, fisherman's catch $20, rack of lamb $17, or Hawaiian chopped steak $10. If you're not hungry and just wish to enjoy the rustic Inn, the cocktail lounge has imported beers for under $2.

Across from Swanzy Beach Park look for **Ha-**

Zalia and Kahea tend their fruit stand.

na's Kitchen. It's a local spot featuring plate lunches for under $4. Great for a lunch or picnic.

Punaluu

Another institution along the windward coast, **Pat's of Punaluu** has an extraordinary view of the coast. The dining room itself is adequate, but not elegant, and serves full breakfasts for $5, lunches including BBQ beef, or *mahi mahi* for around $6, and a lunch buffet priced at $8. The dinner menu runs from $10 for teriyaki chicken to $16 for rack of lamb. Pat's offers terrific specials. Early-bird diners are rewarded with a choice of beef, fish, chicken, or spaghetti, with all the trimmings for only $7. No trip to Pat's is complete without sampling the fresh tarts famous since 1945—your choice of banana, pineapple, or coconut ladled into a fresh oven tart and mounded with whipped cream. Happy Hour from 4:00-7:00 p.m. is special too. Drinks are $1.50, free *pu pu.* Pat's is also famous for *mai tais,* made fresh ($5), and so laced with booze that if you intend on driving, only have one!

What tropical island would be complete without a cowboy cafe serving rattlesnake chili? **Texas Paniolo Cafe** along the highway in Punaluu, tel. 237-8521, is just that, with a foot-stompin' dance floor, country music, and just the right touch of cowboy class. You'll dine on BBQ beef, ribs, chicken, and an assortment of Mexican food all priced around $7.95. A whopping 12-ounce steak is $16, and the rattlesnake chili at $5 *is* authentic. Try their deep-fried bananas with wild honey for dessert.

Laniloa Lodge

Just outside the gates of the Polynesian Cultural Center in Laie, their restaurant features breakfast specials for under $2, and complete dinners with soup, salad, vegies, and Kona coffee for only $6.95. They're open every day from breakfast until 8:00 p.m., except Sunday when the restaurant closes at 2:00 p.m. The food is wholesome but ordinary at the Laniloa Lodge, tel. 293-5888.

The Haaula Shopping Center is home to **Lotus Inn Chop Suey,** tel. 293-5412. You'll get a tasty and filling meal daily from 11:00 a.m. to 9:00 p.m. for under $6. A full menu of Cantonese-style food includes ginger chicken, shrimp, and beef. Happy hour runs from 3:00-7:00 p.m., when well drinks cost $1.25 and are accompanied by free *pu pu.*

SHOPPING AND SERVICES

Kailua has 2 shopping centers, Kailua Shopping Center and Aikahi Park, where you can pick up most essentials. There's also a **Cornet Store** along Kailua Avenue for sundries, lotions, and notions. Thursday mornings bring a

farmer's market into town, and you'll find just about anything at **Holiday Mart** on Hahani Road. Campers can reach the **satellite city hall** for information and permits by calling tel. 261-8575. Medical aid is available from **Castle Medical Center**, tel. 261-0841. A local **chiropractor** is Dr. Tom Smith at 122 Oneawa St., who uses applied kinesiology, and works in conjunction with Alcyone, a colonics therapist, who specializes in detoxification programs and massage, located next door, tel. 261-4511. The **Kailua Sailboard Company**, 19 Hoolai St., tel. 262-2555, rents and sells sailbords for use at Kailua Beach Park. Lessons are available.

Children are the clients at **Keiki Rainbow Tours** in Kaneohe at tel. 235-4206. State licensed, their all-day tours complete with hikes, lunch, and admission to various activities cost about $40. Hotel pick-up is provided. For information write Keiki Rainbow Tours, Box 462, Kaneohe, HI 96744.

The **Hygienic Store** along Rt. 83 just past the Valley of Temples sells groceries and supplies. It's flanked by stalls selling fruits and shellwork at competitive prices.

If you're into horses, try a trail ride with **Island Horseback Tours** in Kaaawa, tel. 946-8765. Ride every day but Sunday with a free hotel pick-up, BBQ on Wed. sunset rides.

In Punaluu visit the **Sacred Falls Bazaar** for a 5-cent cup of coffee, gifts, supplies, and information on the hike to the falls including a free map. Nearby is Dorothy Zoler's **Punaluu Gallery**, tel. 237-8325, featuring island artists.

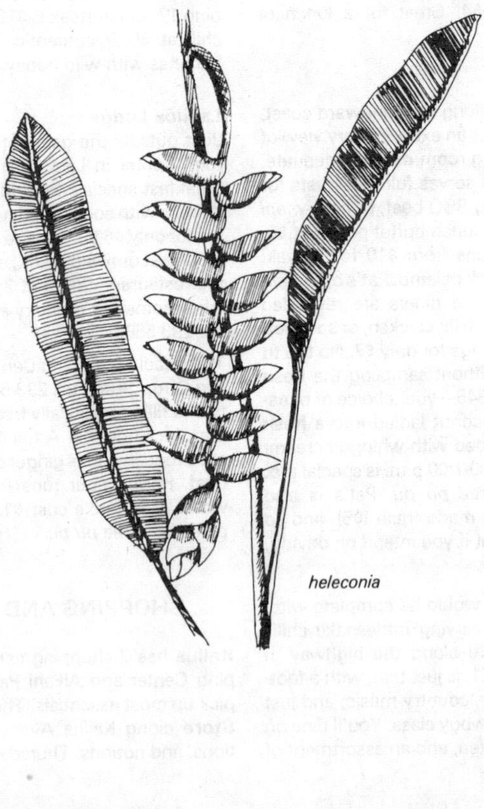

heleconia

Kukaniloko, *royal birthing stones*

CENTRAL OAHU

For most uninformed visitors, Central Oahu is a colorful blur as they speed past in their rental cars en route to the North Shore. Slow down, there are things to see! For island residents, the suburban towns of Aiea, Pearl City, Mililani, and Wahiawa are home. Both routes heading north from Honolulu meet in **Wahiawa**, the island's most central town. The roads cross just near the entrance to **Schofield Barracks**, a warm-up target for Japanese Zeros as they flew on their devastating bombing run over Pearl Harbor. Wahiawa was of extreme cultural and spiritual importance to the early Hawaiians. In town are **healing stones**, whose mystic vibrations were said to cure the maladies of sufferers. In a field not far from town are the ***Kukaniloko,*** the royal birthing stones, where the ruling *ali'i* labored to give birth to the future noblemen of the islands. While in town you can familiarize yourself with Oahu's flora by visiting the **Wahiawa Botanical Garden,** or take a quick look at a serene Japanese temple.

As you gain the heights of the **Leilehua Plateau,** sandwiched between the Waianae and Koolau ranges, a wide expanse of green is planted in cane and pineapple. Just like on supermarket shelves, Del Monte's **Pineapple Variety Garden** competes with Dole's **Pineapple Pavilion,** a minute up the road. Step outside your car door to educate yourself on how these bromeliads are grown, and tantalize your taste buds with a quick nibble. As a traveler's way station, Central Oahu blends services, amenities, and just enough historical sites to warrant stretching your legs, but not enough to bog you down for the day.

SIGHTS

Wahiawa is like a military jeep: basic, ugly, but indispensable. This is a soldiers' town, with servicemen from Schofield Barracks, or nearby Wheeler AFB shuffling along the streets. Most are young, short-haired, short-tempered, and dressed in fatigues. Everywhere you look are cheap bars, burger joints, run-down discos perfumed with sweat and spilled beer, and used furniture stores. Route 99 turns into Rt. 80 which goes through Wahiawa, crossing California Avenue, the main drag, then rejoining Rt. 99 near the Del Monte Pineapple Garden.

Wahiawa has seemingly little to recommend it, and maybe because of its ugliness, when you do find beauty it shines even brighter.

Wahiawa Botanic Gardens

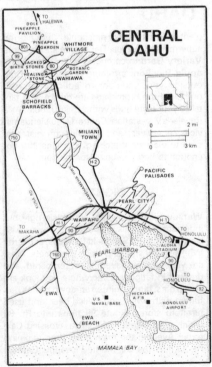

In the midst of town is an oasis of beauty, 27 acres of developed woodlands featuring exotic trees, ferns, and flowers gathered from round the world. Located at 1396 California Ave., they're open daily except Christmas and New Years, from 9:00 a.m. to 4:00 p.m., admission *free.* The parking lot is marked by an HVB warrior; walk through the main entranceway, and take a pamphlet from the box for a self-guiding tour. When it rains, the cement walkways are treacherously slippery, especially if you're wearing thongs. The nicer paths have been left natural, but they can be muddy. Inside the grounds are trees from the Philippines, Australia, Africa, and a magnificent multihued Mindanao gum from New Guinea. Your senses will be bombarded with fragrant camphor trees from China and Japan, and the rich aroma of cinnamon. Everywhere are natural bouquets of flowering trees, entangled by vines and highlighted by rich green ferns. Most specimens have been growing for a minimum of 40 years, so they're well established.

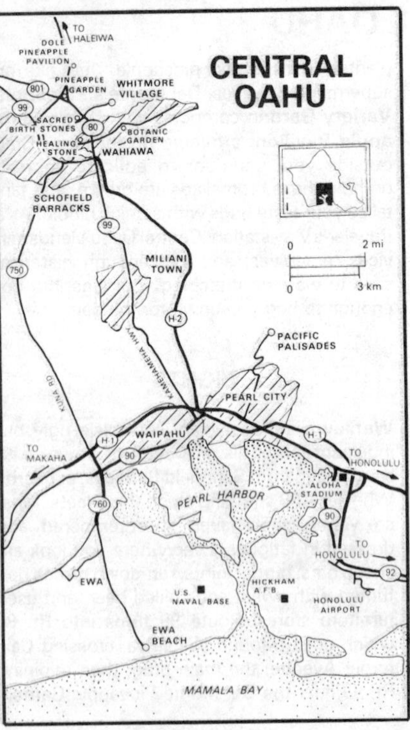

The Healing Stones

Belief in the healing powers of these stones has been attracting visitors since ancient times, and still do. When traveling down Ohai Street (Rt. 80) take a left on California Avenue, and follow it to Kaalalo Place. To glimpse the religion of Hawaii in microcosm, in a few blocks you pass the Riusenji Soto Buddhist Mission, followed by the healing stones, next door to Olive United Methodist Church. If you've never experienced a Buddhist temple, make sure to visit the grounds of **Riusenji Soto Mission.** Usually no one is around, and even if the front doors are locked you can peer in at an extremely ornate altar graced by Buddha, highlighted in black lacquer and gold. On the grounds look for a stone *jizo,* patron of travelers and children. In Japan he often wears a red woven hat and bib, but here he has on a straw hat and *muu muu.*

An HVB warrior marks the stones, just past the Kaalala Elementary School, across the street from a beautiful eucalyptus grove. A humble cinder-block building houses the stones. Built in 1947, when you swing open the iron gate it strikes a deep mournful note, as if it were an instrument designed to announce your presence and departure. Inside the building, 3 stones sit atop rudimentary pedestals. Little scratches mark the stones, and an offertory box is filled with items like oranges, bread, a gin bottle, coins, and candy kisses. A few votive candles flicker before a statue of the Blessed Virgin.

Kukaniloko, The Royal Birthing Stones

Follow Rt. 80 through town for about a mile. At the corner of Whitmore Avenue is a red light: right takes you to Whitmore Village and left puts you on a dirt track that leads to another eucalyptus grove marking the birthing stones. About 40 large boulders are in the middle of a field with a mountain backdrop. One stone looks like the next, but on closer inspection you see that each has a personality. The royal wives would come here, assisted by both men and

humble chapel of the Healing Stones

women of the ruling *ali'i,* to give birth to their exalted offspring. The baby's umbilical cord, a sacred talisman, would be hidden in the cracks and crevices of the stones. Near the largest palm tree is a special stone that appears to be fluted all the way around, with a dip in the middle. It, along with other stones nearby, seem perfectly fitted to accept the torso of a woman in a reclining position. Notice that small fires have been lit in the hollows of these stones, and that they are discolored with soot and ashes.

Schofield Barracks

Stay on Rt. 99, skirt Wahiawa to the west and go past the entrance to Schofield Barracks. The town's image isn't helped when you're confronted by the Nani Kai Apartments just outside the gates to Schofield. They set the tone, sitting there, painted day-glo orange, purple, yellow, and green...a prizewinner of garish bad taste. Schofield Barracks dates from the turn of the century, named after Gen. John Schofield, an early proponent of the strategic importance of Pearl Harbor. A sign tells you that it is still the "Home of the Infantry, Tropic Lightning." If you enter here through the McComb Gate, you can visit the **Tropic Lightning Museum** with memorabilia going back to the War of 1812. There are planes from WW II, Chinese rifles from Korea, and deadly *pungi* traps from Vietnam. The museum has lost many of its exhibits in recent years. They've been taken to the Army museum in Waikiki. But the base is still interesting to visit and remains one of the prettiest military installations in the world. With permission, you can proceed to the Kolekole Pass from where you get a sweeping view of inland and coastal Oahu.

Pineapples

A few minutes past the entrance to Schofield Barracks, Rt. 803 bears left to Waialua, while Rt. 99 goes straight ahead and begins passing rows of pineapple. At the intersection of Rt. 80 is **Del Monte Variety Garden.** You're free to wander about and read the descriptions of the history of pineapple production in Hawaii, and of the genetic progress of the fruit made famous by the islands. This exhibit is much more educational and honest than the **Dole Pineapple Pavilion** just up the road, the one with all the tour buses lined up outside. You too can enter and pay $1.50 for a sad little paper plate half filled with pineapple chunks. Or how about $.60 for a glass of canned pineapple juice from a dispenser that you'd find in any fast-food store. Unless the pineapple harvest has been abundant, you can't even buy a fresh fruit, and when you can, they're no cheaper or fresher than those in any grocery store. The Dole Pineapple Pavilion is firmly entrenched along the tourist route, but as a positive public relations scheme it is a blunder!

FOOD AND SHOPPING

Food

Kemoo Farm at 1718 Wilikina Dr., tel. 621-8481, just past the entrance to Schofield Barracks, has been a *kamaaina* favorite since 1935. The restaurant has a soothing bucolic feeling, perched on the banks of man-made Wahiawa Reservoir. Servings are family style with homemade bread, fresh trout, and rich gravies dolloped over roast beef or duck. Sunday and Wed. feature a brunch complete with island entertainment. Reservations are necessary for these days, and advisable for the remainder of the week. Dinner and drinks for 2 runs about $35.

Dot's Restaurant, off California Ave. at 130 Mango St., tel. 622-4115, is a homey restaurant specializing in American-Japanese food that gives a good square meal for your money. The interior is a mixture of Hawaiian/Oriental in dark brown tones. Lunch specials include butterfish, teriyaki chicken, pork, or beef plates all for around $3.50. *Miso* soup is $2, and simple Japanese dishes go for about $3. The most expensive item on the menu is steak and lobster for $12. Dot's is nothing to write home about, but you definitely won't go hungry.

If you're into fast foods, no problem. The streets are lined with **Jack in the Box,** elbowing **Ronald McDonald,** who's trying to outflash the old **Burger King.**

Shopping

The streets of Wahiawa are lined with stores that cater to residents, not tourists. This means that the prices are right, and if you need supplies or necessities, this would be a good place to stock up. On the corner of California and Oahi streets is a **Coronet Store,** an old-fashioned five and dime, where you can buy anything from sun-tan lotion to a crock pot. The **Big Way Supermarket** is at the corner of California and Kilani avenues.

THE NORTH SHORE

This shallow bowl of coastline stretches from Kaena Point in the west to Turtle Bay in the east. **Mount Kaala,** verdant backdrop to the area, rises 4,020 feet from the Waianae Range, making it the highest peak on Oahu. The entire stretch is a day-tripper's paradise with plenty of sights to keep you entertained. But the North Shore is synonymous with one word: **surfing.** Thunderous winter waves, often measuring 25 feet (from the rear!), rumble along the North Shore's world-famous surfing beaches lined up one after the other—**Waimea Bay, Ehukai, Sunset, Banzai Pipeline.** They attract highly accomplished athletes who come to compete in prestigious international surfing competitions. In summertime *moana* loses her ferocity and lies down, becoming gentle and safe for anyone.

Haleiwa, at the junction of the Farrington Highway (Rt. 930) heading west along the coast and the Kamehameha Highway (Rt. 83) heading east, is fast becoming the central town along the North Shore. The main street is lined with restaurants, boutiques, art galleries, small shopping malls, and sports equipment stores. **Waialua,** just west, is a sugar town with a few quiet condos for relaxation. Farther west is **Dillingham Airfield,** where you can arrange to fly above it all in a small plane, or soar silently in a glider. The road ends for vehicles not far from here, and then your feet have to take you to Kaena Point, where *the* largest waves pound the coast. Heading east, you'll pass a famous *heiau* where human flesh mollified the gods. Then come the great surfing beaches and their incredible waves. Here and there are tidepools rich with discovery, a monument to a real local hero, and **Waimea Falls Park,** the premier tourist attraction of the North Shore.

BEACHES AND SIGHTS

The main attractions of the North Shore are its beaches. Interspersed among them are a few sights definitely worth your time and effort. The listings below run from west to east. The most traveled route to the North Shore is from Honolulu along the H-2 freeway, and then directly to the coast along Rt. 99, or Rt. 803. At Weed Circle or Thompson Corner, where these routes reach the coast, turn left along the Farrington Highway following it to road's end just before Kaena Point, or right along the Kamehameha Highway (Rt. 83) that heads around the coast all the way to Kailua.

Be aware that ***all*** North Shore beaches experience very heavy surf conditions with dangerous currents from October through April. The waters, at this time of year, are not for the average swimmer. Please heed all warnings. In summertime, leap in!

The Farrington Highway

The first town is **Waialua** ("Two Waters"). Take Waialua Beach Road just off the Weed Traffic Circle coming north on Rt. 99, or follow the signs off the Farrington Highway. At the turn of the century, Waialua, lying at the terminus of a sugar-train railway, was a fashionable beach community complete with hotels and vacation homes. Today, it's hardly ever visited. The sugar mill, an outrageously ugly mechanical monster, is still operating and is central to the town. Quiet Waialua, with its main street divided by trees running down the middle, *is* rural Oahu. There's a general store for supplies, post office, and snacks at the **Sugar Bar**, a restaurant in the old Bank of Hawaii building. If you're returning to Haleiwa take Haleiwa Road, a back way through residential areas. Look for Paalaa Road on the right and take it past a small Buddhist temple that holds an *o bon* festival honoring the dead, traditionally observed in July.

Mokuleia Beach Park is the main public access park along the highway. It provides picnic facilities, restrooms, lifeguards, playground area, and camping (county permit). In summertime, swimming is possible along a few sandy stretches protected by a broken offshore reef.

Across the road is **Dillingham Airfield,** small but modern, with restrooms near the hangars and a new parking area. Most days, especially weekends, a few local people sell refreshments from their cars or trucks. The main reason for stopping is to take a small plane or glider ride. **Glider Rides,** tel. 677-3404, take you on a 20-to 30-minute flight for $32 s, $45 double. They fly 7 days a week starting at about 10:00 a.m. on a first-come first-served basis. They suggest you bring a camera, and arrive before 5:00 p.m. to get the best winds. There's always a pilot with you to make sure that your glider ride is a *return* trip. **Surf Air Tours,** tel. 637-7003, flies Cessna 172s or 206s for a half hour along the North Shore for $30 per person, or on a longer *circle island tour* for $50 per person. Both are worthwhile, but the glider ride is more exceptional.

In quick succession after Dillingham Airfield come undeveloped **Kealia Beach,** safe during

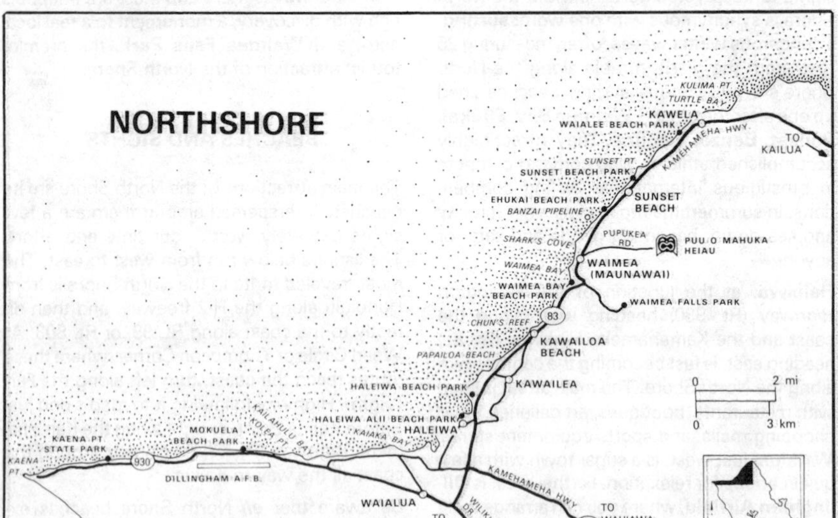

typical rural Buddhist temple, outskirts of Haleiwa

calm periods, and **Mokuleia Army Beach**, improved and open to the public. Local people have erected semi-permanent tents in this area, and guard it as if it were their own. **Camp Harold Erdman** is next, one of the best-known camps on Oahu. This YMCA facility is named after Harold Erdman, a famous Hawaiian polo player killed in the '30s. The facility is used as a summer camp for children, throughout the year for special functions, and as a general retreat area by various organizations. Access is limited to official use.

Kaena Point lies about 2½ miles down the dirt track after the pavement gives out. Count on 3 hours for a return hike and remember to bring water. The Point can also be reached from road's end above Mahuka on the Waianae (leeward) side of the island. Kaena has *the* largest waves in Hawaii on any given day. In wintertime these giants can reach above 40 feet, and their power, even when viewed safely from the high ground, is truly amazing. Surfers have actually plotted ways of riding these waves, which include being dropped by helicopter with scuba tanks. Reportedly, one surfer named Ace Cool has already done it. For the rest of us mortals..."who wants to have that much fun anyway!" Kaena Point is the site of numerous *heiau.* Due to its exposed position, it, like similar sites around the islands, was a jumping-off point for the "souls of the dead." The spirits were believed to wander here after death, and once all worldly commitments were fulfilled, they made their "leap" from earth to heaven. Hopefully, the daredevil surfers will not revive this tradition!

Haleiwa

Haleiwa ("Home of the Frigate Birds") has become the premier town of the region, mainly because it straddles the main road. Here's the majority of shopping, dining, and services along the North Shore. **Haleiwa Ali'i Beach Park** is on the western shores of Waialua Bay, which fronts the town. This beach park is improved with restrooms, lifeguard tower, and small boat launch. Lifeguards man the tower throughout the summer, on weekends in winter. The shoreline is rocks and coral with pockets of sand, and although portions can be good for swimming, the park is primarily noted for surfing, in a break simply called "Haleiwa." Head eastward and cross the **Anahulu River Bridge.** Park for a moment and walk back over the bridge. Look upstream to see homes with tropical character perched on the bank with a bevy of boats tied below. The scene is reminiscent of times gone by.

A much better park is **Haleiwa Beach Park,** clearly marked off the highway on the eastern side of Waialua Bay. Here you'll find pavilions, picnic facilities, lifeguards, restrooms, showers, food concessions, and camping (county permit). The area is good for fishing, surfing, and most importantly, for swimming year round! It's about the only safe place for the average person to swim along the entire North Shore during winter.

Kawailoa Beach is the general name given to the area stretching all the way from Haleiwa Beach Park to Waimea Bay. A string of beaches, **Papailoa, Laniakea,** and **Chun's Reef,** are just off the road. Cars park where the access is good. None of these beaches is suitable for the recreational swimmer. All are surfing beaches, with the most popular being Chun's Reef.

Waimea Bay

The 2-lane highway along the North Shore is pounded by traffic; be especially careful around Waimea Bay. The highway sweeps around till you see the steeple of **St. Peter and Paul Mission** with the bay below. The steeple is actually the remnants of an old rock-crushing plant on the site. **Waimea Bay Beach Park** has the largest rideable waves in the world. This is the heart of surfers' paradise. The park is improved with a lifeguard tower, restrooms, and a picnic area. During a big winter swell, the bay is lined with spectators watching the surfers ride the monumental waves. In summertime, the bay is calm as a lake. People inexperienced with the sea should not even walk along the shorebreak in winter. Unexpected waves come up farther than expected, and a murderous rip lurks only a few feet from shore. The area is rife with tales of heroic rescue attempts, many ending in fatalities. A plaque commemorates Eddie Aikau, a local lifeguard credited with making thousands of rescues. In 1978, the *Hokulea,* the Polynesian Sailing Society's double-hulled canoe, capsized in rough seas about 20 miles offshore. Eddie was aboard, and launched his surfboard to swim for help. He never made it, but his selfless courage lives on.

Look for the well-marked entrance to **Waimea Falls Park** mountainside from the bay. You can drive for quite a way into the lush valley before coming to the actual park entrance. As you enter, a local man sells Hawaiian coconut-frond hats. These are the authentic article, and priced right at around $6. The park is primarily a botanical garden with a fascinating display of flowers and plants, all labeled for your edification. There's entertainment such as *hula,* and you can try your hand at some traditional Hawaiian games. The highlight is professional diving from the 55-foot rock walls into the pool below Waimea Falls. Nature paths, great for carefree roaming, lead into the valley. Admission is $7.50 adults, $5.25 juniors, and $1.25 children, open daily 10:00 a.m. to 5:30 p.m., tel. 638-8511. The **Proud Peacock** serves dinner until 9:00 p.m. Monthly (check the free tourist literature), on Fri. nights closest to the full moon beginning at 8:30 p.m., the park offers a free guided moon-viewing tour.

A perfect place to experience marinelife is the large tidepool next to **Pupukea Beach Park,**

view of the North Shore from Puu O Mahuka Heiau

the first one north of Waimea Bay, across the street from the Shell gas station. A long retaining wall out to sea forms a large and protected pool at low tide. Wear footgear and check out the pools with a mask. Don't be surprised to find large sea bass. A sign warns against spearing fish, but the local people do it all the time. Be careful not to step on sea urchins, and stay away from the pool during rough winter swells when it can be treacherous. The beach park has restrooms, picnic facilities, and fair swimming in sandy pockets between coral and rock, but only in summertime. County camping with a permit *was* allowed in this beach park, and may be available again. The middle section of the park is called **Shark's Cove,** though no more sharks are here than anywhere else. The area is terrific for snorkeling and scuba in season. Look to the mountains, to see **The Mansion** (see below), and next to it the white sculpture of the **World Unity Monument.** If you had to pick a spot from which to view the North Shore sunset, Pupukea Beach Park is hard to beat!

Puu O Mahuka Heiau

Do yourself a favor and drive up the mountain road leading to the *heiau* even if you don't want to visit it. The vast and sweeping views of the coast below are incredible. About one mile past Waimea Bay the highway passes a Foodland on the right. Turn here up Pupukea Road and follow the signs. Ignore the warning at the beginning of the access road; it's well maintained. Puu O Mahuka Heiau is large, covering perhaps 5 acres. Designated as a State Historical Site, its floorplan is huge steps, with one area leading to another just below. The *heiau* was the site of human sacrifice. People still come to pray as is evidenced by many stones wrapped in *ti* leaves placed on small stone piles lying about the grounds. In the upper section is a raised mound surrounded by stone in what appears to be a central altar area. The *heiau's* stonework shows a high degree of craftsmanship throughout, but especially in the pathways. The lower section of the *heiau* appears to be much older, and is not as well maintained.

Drive past the *heiau* access road for a moment and make a left onto Alapio Road. This takes you through an expensive residential area called **Sunset Hills,** and past a home locally called **The Mansion**— look for the English-style boxwood hedge surrounding it. The home was purported to be Elvis Presley's island hide-a-way. Almost next door are the grounds of the **Nichiren Buddhist Temple,** resplendent with manicured lawns and gardens. This area is a tremendous vantage point from which to view Fourth of July fireworks that light up Waimea Bay far below.

The Great Surfing Beaches

Sunset Beach runs for 2 miles, the longest wide sand beach on Oahu. Winter surf erodes the beach, with coral and lava fingers exposed at the shoreline, but in summertime you can expect an uninterrupted beach usually 200-300 feet wide. The entire stretch is technically Sunset Beach, but each world-famous surfing spot warrants its own name though they're not clearly marked and are tough to find...exactly. Mainly, look for cars with surfboard racks parked along the road. The beaches are not well maintained either. They're often trashed, and the restrooms, even at Waimea Bay, are atrocious. The answer is politics and money. Efforts all go into Waikiki where the tourists are. Who cares about a bunch of crazy surfers on the North Shore? They're just a free curiosity for the tourists' enjoyment!

The **Banzai Pipeline** is probably the best-known surfing beach in the world. It dates from *Surf Safari,* an early surfer film made in the 1950s, when it was dubbed "Banzai" by Bruce Brown, maker of the film. The famous tube-like effect comes from a shallow reef just offshore which forces the waves to rise dramatically and quickly. This forces the crest forward to create **The Pipeline.** A lifeguard tower near the south end of the beach is all for improvements that you'll find . Parking is along the roadway. Look for Sunset Beach Elementary School on the left, and the Pipeline is across the road. You can park in the school's lot on non-school days.

Ehukai Beach Park is the next area north. It has a lifeguard tower and restroom, and provides one of the best vantage points from which to watch the surfing action on the Pipeline and Pupukea, the area to the right.

Don't expect much when you come to **Sunset Beach Park** itself. Except for a lifeguard tower, there is nothing. This beach is the site of yearly international surfing competitions. Almost as famous as the surfing break is the **Sunset Rip,** a notorious current offshore that grabs people every year. Summertime is generally safe, but never take *moana* for granted.

ACCOMMODATIONS

Places to stay are quite limited along the North Shore. The best deals are renting beach homes or rooms directly from the owners, but this is a hit-and-miss proposition, with no agency handling the details. You have to check the local papers. The homes vary greatly in amenities. Some are palaces, others basic rooms or shacks, perfect for surfers or those who consider lodging as secondary. Check the bulletin boards outside the **Surf and Sea** Dive Shop in Haleiwa and Foodland supermarket.

The **Turtle Bay Hilton** is a first-class resort on Turtle Bay, the northern extremity of the North Shore, Box 187, 57-091 Kamehameha Hwy., Kahuku, HI 96731, tel. 293-8811. Once a Hyatt Hotel, it was built as a self-contained destination resort. It's surrounded by sea and surf on Kuilima Point, which offers protected swimming year round. The hotel is complete with a golf course, tennis courts, pool, full water activities, horseback riding, shopping, and the fanciest dining on the North Shore. Fully a/c, all rooms have color TV, and most boast a *lanai.* Rates based on double occupancy begin at $100-130 for a studio, extra person $15, $175 cottage, $225-750 for a suite. Room rates are high, but you get much more than what you would pay for a mainstream similar hotel. The Hilton family plan allows children free when they stay in a room with their parents.

The Turtle Bay Hilton has an unobstructed view of the sunrise.

Ke Iki Hale is a small condo complex operated by Alice Tracy, 59-579 Ke Iki Rd., tel. 638-8229. Pass the Foodland Supermarket heading north, and look for a school sign. Turn left here to the beach to find the condo. The property has 200 feet of private beach with a sandy bottom that goes out about 300 feet (half that in winter). The condo is quiet with a home-away-from-home atmosphere. Rates are: one bedroom beachfront, $75 p/d, $500 p/w, $1,800 p/m; 2 bedroom beachfront $95 p/d, $575 p/w, $2,100 p/m. Units on the grounds with no beachfront are about 25% less.

The **Mokuleia Beach Colony,** 68-615 Farrington Hwy., Waialua, HI 96791, tel. 637-9311, provides condominiums in a secluded area along the beach. Each unit is fully furnished, and all have a *lanai.* The condo has tennis courts, pool, and is next door to a polo field. Minimum stay is one week and rates begin at $350 for a poolside cottage to $450 for those along the beach, off-season rates available.

FOOD

Inexpensive

Celestial Natural Foods, in the Haleiwa Shopping Plaza, tel. 637-6729, sells natural and health foods, and vegetarian meals at the snack bar. Smoothies are $2.50; most sandwiches and a variety of salads are under $3.50.

Cafe Haleiwa, a hole-in-the-wall eatery on your left just as you enter town, serves one of the best breakfasts on Oahu. Their "dawn patrol" from 6:00-7:00 a.m. includes eggs and whole-wheat pancakes for $1.50. Specials of the house are whole wheat banana pancakes, French toast, spinach and mushroom quiche, and steaming hot Kona coffee. One of the partners, Jim Sears, is called "the wizard of eggs" and has built up a local following. The cafe attracts many surfers, so it's a great place to find out about conditions.

You can tell by the tour buses parked outside that **Matsumoto's** is a very famous store on the North Shore. What are all those people after? Shave ice. This is one of the best places on Oahu to try this island treat. Not only do the tourists come here, but local families often take a "Sunday drive" just to get Matsumoto's shave ice. Try the Hawaiian Delight, a mound of ice smothered with banana, pineapple, and mango syrup.

For delicious and rich island-flavor ice cream, stop at the take-out window of **Kaala Art and Rainbow Island Tees** just across the street from McDonald's.

Seven-Eleven is on the North Shore just as you enter town. Historic Haleiwa Theater was torn down so that the world could have another convenience store. Almost next door is **Pizza Hut**. Besides pizza, their salad bar isn't bad.

Moderate/Expensive

Steamer's in the Haleiwa Shopping Plaza, tel. 637-5071, is a clean and modern restaurant serving seafood, beef, and chicken. There's plenty of brass, paneled walls, and low lighting. Lunches are especially good with a wide choice of omelets from $5, including one made from crab, shrimp, and mushrooms; all come with blueberry or French muffins. Whet your appetite with *sushi,* steamed clams, or have full fish dinners starting at $10. Dining daily 11:00 a.m. to 11:00 p.m., bar until 2:00 a.m.

The Proud Peacock, Waimea Falls Park, tel. 638-8531, is open daily for lunch and dinner. It's fun to dine here even if you don't enter the park. From the dining room, you can look into some of the nicest gardens while feeding crumbs to the peacocks. The beautiful mahogany bar was made in Scotland almost 200 years ago. You can have a light soup and salad, but their seafood *pupu* platter is hard to beat. Roast pork and roast beef are well-prepared favorites here.

Jameson's By the Sea, 62-540 Kamehameha Hwy., tel. 637-4336, is open daily for lunch, dinner, and cocktails. It's at the north end of Haleiwa overlooking the sea; its outdoor deck is perfect for a romantic sunset dinner. Appetizers include a salmon plate for $6, escargot $5, fresh oysters $7. Desserts, chowder, and salad are $2.50 each. Main dishes like *mahi mahi,* stuffed shrimp, shrimp curry with mango chutney, and sesame chicken range from $10 to $16. The bar is quiet at night and serves a variety of imported beers (try *South Pacific* imported from New Guinea) for $2.75, and a full range of domestic brews for $1.85. The dining room closes at 10:00 p.m. and the bar an hour later.

The **Sea View Inn,** 66-011 Kamehameha Hwy., Haleiwa, tel. 637-4165, is a green cinder-block building on the left before you cross the Anahulu River bridge. A basic menu of fish, beef, and chicken for reasonable prices, and good down-home cooking.

Class

The most expensive and varied dining on the North Shore is at the **Turtle Bay Hilton.** The Garden Terrace features an extensive breakfast, lunch, and dinner buffet. The Cove is open for dinner only and specializes in seafood with a choice of 2 fresh catches of the day.

SHOPPING AND SERVICES

Kaala Art and Rainbow Island Tees as you enter Haleiwa (across from McDonald's), is a perfect place to stop. Browse for authentic island-made art, and the 2 brothers running the place, John and Jim Costello, are knowledgeable long-time residents of the North Shore who don't mind dispensing directions and information. The shop specializes in original art T-shirts, and paintings by John Costello. John often uses pointilism to capture the spirit of the islands in minute detail. Two of the best local artists displayed are Mango and Caridad Sumile. There's a fine postcard selection, candles, hand-chosen souvenirs from throughout Asia and the Pacific, and a smidgen of touristy junk.

Past Matsumoto's Store look for the **Fetig Art Gallery,** tel. 637-4933. Most of the work is by Beverly Fetig who has been painting the islands for a quarter century. For the last few years, she's been painting European scenes, which occupy a room by themselves. The gallery is the oldest on the North Shore, and most of the artists are well known. Prices for original works start at $45 and go up to around $4,000. Only a few prints, by well-known artists and numbered, start at around $175. Even if you can't afford paintings from the Fetig Gallery, it's a good place to see the state of the arts on the North Shore.

The **Haleiwa Shopping Center** provides all the necessities in one-stop shopping: boutiques, pharmacy, photo store, and general food and merchandise. It's in the center of Haleiwa, tel. 622-5179.

For food and picnic supplies try the **Haleiwa IGA,** tel. 637-5004, or **Foodland,** along the highway past Waimea Bay, tel. 638-8081.

For a full range of surfing, snorkeling, and diving equipment try **Surf and Sea** near the Union 76 gas station in Haleiwa. They've got boogie boards, masks and fins, tanks, weights, surfboards, and sailboards. They can even arange flights from Dillingham Airfield.

The best source of general information for the North Shore is to peruse the bulletin boards outside of Surf and Sea, and Foodland.

"...but a diversion, the most common is upon the water...the men lay themselves flat upon an oval piece of plank...they wait the time for the greatest swell that sets on shore, and altogether push forward with their arms to keep on its top, it sends them in with a most astonishing velocity..."

—James King, c. 1779

Makaha Valley...improved?

THE LEEWARD COAST

WAIANAE

The Waianae Coast ("Mullet Waters"), the leeward face of Oahu, is separated physically from the rest of the island by the Waianae Range. Spiritually, culturally, and economically, the separation is even more profound. This area is Oahu's last stand for ethnic Hawaiians, and that phenomenal cultural blending of people called locals. The idea of "us against them" permeates the consciousness of the area. Guidebooks, government pamphlets, and word of mouth warn tourists against going to Waianae because "the natives are restless." If you follow this poor advice, you not only miss the last of undeveloped coastal Oahu, but the absolute pleasure of meeting people who will treat you with genuine *aloha.* Along the coast are magnificent beaches long known for their surf, new condos and developments nestled in secure valleys, and prime golfing, and inland, roads that'll take you to the roof of Oahu. Waianae is the home of small farms, run-down shacks, and families that hold *luau* on festive occasions, where the food and entertainment are the real article. Anyone lucky enough to be invited into this quickly disappearing world will be blessed with one of the last remaining authentic cultural experiences in Hawaii.

The possibility of hassles shouldn't be minimized, as they do happen, but every aggressor needs a victim. The biggest problem is thievery, of the sneak-thief variety. You're marked as a tourist because of your new rental car. If you leave valuables in it, or lying unattended on the beach, they have a good chance of disappearing. But who does silly things like this *anywhere* in America? You won't be accosted, or held up at gunpoint, but if you bother a bunch of local guys drinking beer, you're asking for trouble. Moreover, the toughness of Waianae is self-perpetuating, and frankly the locals *like* the hard reputation. A few years back a feature writer reported that when he visited Waianae some toughs threw rocks at him. No one ever reported this before, but after a big stink was made about it, more and more people had rocks thrown at them when they visited here. In recent years *pakalolo* has had a tremendous effect on the area. Local guys began growing and smoking it. This brought some money back into the depressed region, and it changed the outlook of some of the residents. They felt a camaraderie with other counterculture people, many of whom happened to be *haoles.* They could relax and not feel so threatened with pursuing an often elusive materialistic path. Many became more content with their laid-back life-

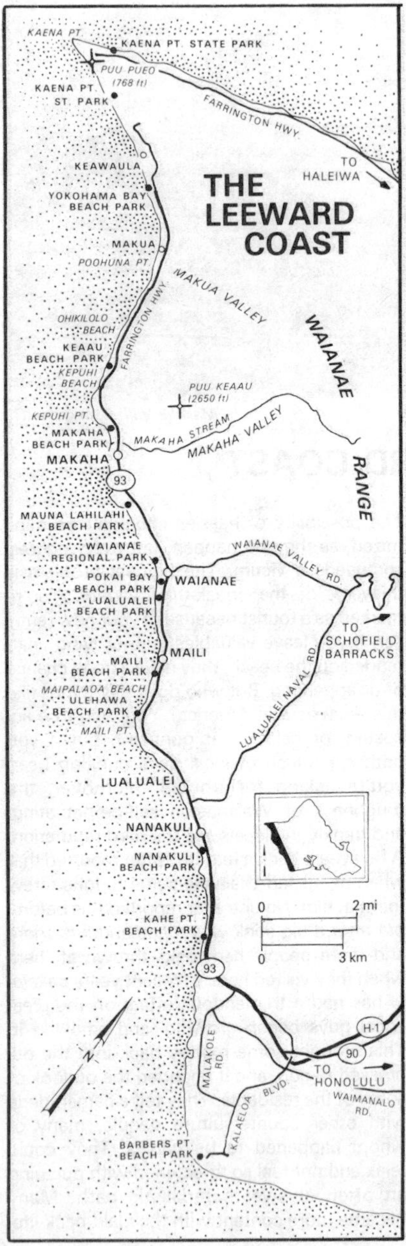

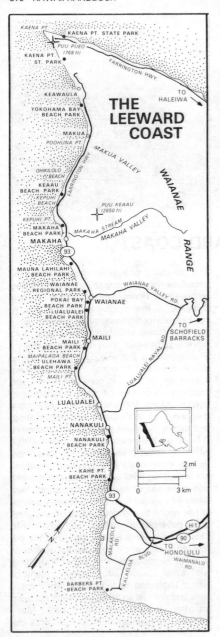

style, and genuinely less interested with the materialistic trip all the way around.

In truth, *we* shouldn't be warned about *them,* but vice versa. The people of Waianae are the ones being infringed upon, and it is they who, in the final analysis, will be hassled, ripped off, and ultimately dispossessed. Recent articles by Oahu's *Development Conference* strongly state that future development will center on the island's northwestern shore...the Waianae Coast! A few rocks are poor weapons against developmental progress which is defined by the big boys with the big dreams and the big bucks to back them up.

BEACHES AND SIGHTS

The Waianae Coast is very accessible. One road takes you there. Simply follow the H-1 freeway until it joins the Farrington Hwy. (Rt. 93). It runs north, opening up the entire coast. A handful of side roads lead into the interior, and that's about it!

Note: Many of the beach parks along this coast offer **camping,** but their status periodically changes to **no camping** without notice. Many of the other campers are local people in semi-permanent structures; the reason that the status changes quickly is to prevent them from squatting. Also, remember that this is the leeward coast with plenty of sunshine. Many of the beach parks do not have shade trees, so be prepared. June is the prettiest month because all the flowers are in bloom, but one of the worst for sunburn. The parks listed below run from south to north.

Heading North

The first beach is **Barbers Point Beach Park,** at the end of Kalaeloa Boulevard. Turn down it where H-1 and the Farrington Hwy. join. The Point was named after Capt. Henry Barber, who was shipwrecked here in 1795. Few people, even island residents, visit this beach park. It's in an industrial area and the shoreline is rocky. One pocket of white-sand beach is open to the public, though it fronts a private residence. The swimming is safe only in summer, and you'll find picnic facilities, restrooms, and camping (county permit).

Wainae's people still have the aloha *spirit.*

Kahe and **Hawaiian Electric Beach Parks** are just where the Farrington Hwy. curves north along the coast. They're the first 2 *real* Waianae beaches, and they're symbolic. You come around the bend to be treated to an absolutely pristine view of the coast with the rolling sea, white-sand beach, cove, and the most hideous power plant you've ever seen. Kahe Beach Park offers restrooms, pavilion, and picnic facilities. The beach is poor except for a section just east of the improved park. Swimming is dangerous except for calm summer days. The Hawaiian Electric Beach Park, across from the power plant, is known as "Tracks" to island surfers because of the railroad tracks that run along the shore here. Facilities include picnic tables, pavilion, restrooms, showers, and parking along the highway. The white-sand beach is wide, and the swimming generally safe. The mild waves are perfect for learning how to surf. If you keep your eyes trained out to sea, the area is beautiful. Don't look inland!

Nanakuli Beach Park is on the southern outskirts of Nanakuli ("Pretend To Be Deaf") Town. If you get to the red light you've gone a little too far. The beach park is community oriented with recreational buildings, basketball courts, baseball diamond, and kiddies' play area. Camping has been permitted with a county permit. Lifeguards work on a daily basis, and the swimming is generally safe except for periods of high winter surf. The northern end of the beach, called Kalanianaole, is generally calmer than the southern end. They're divided by a housing project, but connected by a walkway. The southern section is fronted by a cliff with a small cove below. During periods of calm surf, the waters are crystal clear and perfect for snorkeling.

Ulehawa Beach Park, just north of Nanakuli, offers restrooms, picnic facilities, lifeguards, and sometimes camping. The best swimming is in a sandy pocket near the lifeguard tower. Surf conditions make for good bodysurfing. Most of the park, along a rocky cliff, is undeveloped. Here you'll find unlimited fishing spots. Ahead is a giant outcropping, Maili Point. A shallow lagoon is generally safe for swimming year round. As always, it's best to check with the local people on the beach.

Maili Beach Park is at the southern end of Maili ("Many Small Stones") Town. It lies between 2 streams coming down from the mountains. Facilities include restrooms, picnic facilities, lifeguard tower, and camping, sometimes. The best swimming is in front of the lifeguard tower. The beach is broken into 3 by a housing development. In wintertime the beach disappears, but it returns wide and sandy for the summer. Most of the park is undeveloped.

Lualualei Beach Park has restrooms, camping sometimes, and picnic facilities. The entire park is largely undeveloped and lies along low cliffs and raised coral reef. Swimming is almost impossible. It's primarily good for fishing and looking.

Pokai Beach Park is one of the nicest along the Waianae Coast, located just south of Waianae Town. It provides restrooms, camping sometimes, lifeguards, and boat ramp, which brings plenty of small craft into the area. Don't be surprised to see a replica of a double-hulled canoe often used for publicity purposes. It last appeared in a beer commercial. The park is clean, well maintained, reasonably secure, and family oriented. There's surfing, diving, and safe swimming year round. If you're heading for one beach along Waianae, this is a top choice.

To get a look at a small working harbor or to hire a fishing boat, visit **Waianae Boat Harbor** as you head north from town. Huge installed stones form an impressive man-made harbor, with everything from luxury yachts to aluminum fishing boats. To head inland take **Waia-**

nae Valley Road. You quickly gain the heights of the Waianae Range, and eventually come to a sentry box with a soldier inside. From here Kolekole Road is closed to the public, but if you stop and identify yourself, you'll be given permission to go to **Kolekole Pass.** The awesome view is well worth the trip.

Makaha Beach Park is famous for surfing. Competitions have been held here since the Makaha International Surfing Competition began in 1952. In recent years, a local lifeguard named Richard "Buffalo" Keaulana, known to all who've come here, has begun the Annual Buffalo Big Board Riding Championship. Another famous surfer employed as a lifeguard is Rell Sun. She was one of the first women to gain fame in what is decidedly a male-dominated sport. Both are from the immediate area, and you couldn't find 2 nicer people to talk to anywhere on the island. Paul Strauch Jr., inventor of "hang five," comes to Makaha whenever he has a chance. If you're walking the beach and see a guy surrounded by ocean charts, that's Larry Goddard, a professional surf forecaster. The swimming can be dangerous during high surf, but excellent on calm days. Winter brings some of the biggest surf in Hawaii.

The meaning of Makaha doesn't help its image. It translates as "Fierce," relating to a bunch of bandits who lived in the surrounding hills and terrorized the region. They would wait for small bands of people walking the road, then swoop down and relieve them of their earthly goods. If you follow Makaha Valley Road inland, you pass condos and high-rises clinging to the arid walls of this leeward valley. Surrounded by an artificial oasis of green, this developed resort area provides golfing, and all the amenities of a destination resort. Stop in at the Sheraton Makaha to ask permission to visit the ***Kaneaki Heiau,*** a 17th C. temple restored by the resort under the direction of the Bishop Museum. This temple was dedicated to Lono, the benevolent god of harvest and fertility. The grass and thatched huts used as prayer and meditation chambers, along with a spirit tower, have all been replicated.

Keaau Beach Park has restrooms, picnic facilities, and camping (county permit). The improved part of the park has no beach and is fronted by coral and lava, frequented mostly by fishermen and campers. The sandy unimproved section is not good for swimming, but it does attract a few surfers, and is good for snorkeling and scuba but only during calm periods.

Yokohama Bay is the end of the line. The pavement ends here, and if you're headed for **Kaena Point** (see p. 217) you'll have to walk.

Waianae Boat Harbor

Buffalo, Rell, Larry, and Paul

You could bounce along in a car, but you'd beat it to death. Yokohama Bay is a long stretch of sandy beach that is mostly unimproved. A bath house is here, and the area was named because of the multitude of Japanese fishermen who came to this lonely site. It's still great for fishing! The swimming is hazardous because of the strong wave action and rough bottom. Mostly the area is used by surfers and local people, including youngsters who dive off the large lava rocks. This is inadvisable for people unfamiliar with the area. Many camp here unofficially.

ACCOMMODATIONS

Except for camping, there are no inexpensive places to stay along the Waianae Coast. Some local people let rooms for a good rate, but there is no way to find this out in advance. Your best bet is to check out the **bulletin board** at the Food Giant Supermarket in Waianae. Accommodations range from moderate to expensive, with Makaha Valley being the most developed resort area of Oahu outside of Waikiki. Except for the Sheraton Makaha Resort, all are condos and require a minimum 7 days.

The **Maili Cove** rents one-bedroom apartments for $350-450 per week. They have a swimming pool, parking, TV, along with a few hotel units. Located at 87-561 Farrington Hwy., Waianae, HI 96792, tel. 696-4447.

The **Makaha Beach Cabanas** are in Makaha along the beach just past the high school. All units have *lanai* overlooking the water. They're not fancy, but are spotlessly clean and serviceable. All units are fully furnished with complete kitchens; from $350 per week. Contact the Makaha Beach Cabanas, 84-965 Farrington Hwy., tel. 696-7227.

The **Makaha Shores** are privately owned units that overlook a beautiful white-sand beach and provide great viewing of the surfers challenging the waves below. All units are fully furnished with weekly rates of $290 studio, $400 one-bedroom, and $500 2-bedroom. Contact the condo at 84-265 Farrington Hwy., Makaha 96792, tel. 696-7121.

The least expensive accommodations are at the **Makaha Surfside**. The beach is rocky near the condo, but it makes up for this with 2 pools and a sauna. All units are individually owned and fully furnished. Weekly rates begin at $175 studio to $245-315 one bedroom. For information write Makaha Surfside, 85-175 Farrington Hwy., Makaha 96792, tel. 969-2105.

typical camping beach, Leeward Coast

Makaha Valley Towers rise dramatically from Makaha Valley, but they don't fit in. They're either a testament to man's achievement or ignorance, depending on your point of view. In keeping with the idea of security, you drive up to a gate manned by 2 officers. You're stopped, asked your business, and sent unsmilingly on your way. The condo provides fully furnished units, a/c, TV, and pool. Weekly rates are $350 studio, $400-500 one-bedroom. If you're staying in this ill-fitting high-rise, at least try to get a top floor where you can take advantage of the remarkable view. For rates and information: Makaha Valley Towers, 84-740 Kili Dr., Makaha 96792, tel. 695-9055.

The **Sheraton Makaha Resort** is famous for its hideaway golf course, among the top 5 on Oahu. The 6,400-foot par-72 course is relatively flat and costs $15 guest, $40 non-guest, plus $10 for a mandatory cart. The Sheraton has done an exemplary job with the units, some of the nicest on the island. This is a true destination resort with a complete list of activities including horseback riding, tennis, 2 swimming pools, and a full complement of hotel-sponsored beach and water activities (although the ocean is a few miles away). Rooms begin at $80 d to $250 for a suite. For information and reservations, write Sheraton Makaha Resort, Box 896, Waianae, HI 96792, tel. 800-325-3535, on Oahu 695-9511.

FOOD AND SERVICES

For anyone with an urge to eat a 2-scoop plate lunch, no problem. Little drive-in lunch counters are found in almost every Waianae town. Each serves hearty island food such as teriyaki chicken, pork, or *mahi mahi* for under $4. A good one is the **Nanakuli Drive-In** in the middle of town. **Makaha Drive-In** is more of the same. Another popular spot is **Red Baron Pizza** in the Waianae Shopping Center, tel. 696-2396.

You also see plenty of fruit sellers parked along the road. Their produce couldn't be fresher, and stopping provides you not only with the perfect complement to a picnic lunch, but with a good chance to meet some local people.

Have no fear if you're addicted to fast foods. Some major franchises have decided that your trip to leeward Oahu wouldn't be complete without something processed in a styrofoam box. **Burger King** is in the Waianae Shopping Mall; nearby, **McDonald's** golden arches rise alongside the highway.

The **Fogcutter** is a semi-casual place offering steaks and seafood, 84-111 Orange St., Makaha, tel. 695-9404. Prices are reasonable and the food is good.

The **Rusty Harpoon** is between Waianae and

Maili overlooking the sea. It's probably the best food for the money restaurant along the coast. In keeping with the name the airy interior is rustically nautical, complete with hurricane lamps and of course a few harpoons. The menu is chicken, fish, and beef, but the best deals are the Hawaiian plates. Lunch prices are excellent at around $5, but expect double that for the dinner menu.

The **Sheraton Makaha** has a number of restaurants ranging from sandwich bars to elegant dining. The Kaala Room features an impressive menu of fresh fish, steaks, and Continental cuisine. Get a table with a long sweeping view of the valley, wonderful at sunset. Daily for dinner, tel. 695-9511. The hotel's Pikakae Cafe serves breakfast, lunch, and dinner with an assortment of sandwiches and international dishes.

You can take care of most of your shopping needs at the **Waianae Mall Shopping Center:** Big Way Supermarket, tel. 696-4271, Pay 'n Save Drug Store, tel. 696-6387, and a few clothing and shoe stores.

The **Food Giant** grocery store in Waianae has a good selection of Oriental and Hawaiian food. To know what's happening along the Waianae Coast check out the bulletin board in front. The **Waianae Hawaiian Cultural and Art Center** offers workshops in *lei*-making, *lau hala* weaving, *hula,* and the Hawaiian language. They welcome people either to observe or participate in their programs. For times and schedules contact the **State Foundation of Culture and Arts,** tel. 548-4145.

Pokai Pottery on Pokai St., Waianae, is owned and operated by Bunkie Eakutis. His studio is attached to his home where he makes ceramics sold around the island through the Artists' Guild.

Screw pine (pandanus) fronds are used to create a wide array of lau hala *weavings.*

green turtle

THE NORTHWESTERN ISLANDS

Like tiny gems of a broken necklace, the **Northwestern Hawaiian Islands** spill across the vast Pacific. Popularly called the **Leewards,** most were discovered last century, oftentimes by hapless ships that ground to a sickening halt on their treacherous, half-submerged reefs. Their captains left their names: Lisianski, Kure, French Frigates, Hermes, and Pearl. Even today, craft equipped with the most modern navigational devices must be wary in these waters. They remain among the loneliest outposts on the face of the Earth.

Land And Climate

The Leewards are the oldest islands of the Hawaiian chain, believed to have emerged from the sea at least 6 million years ago; some estimates say 25 million years! Slowly they floated northward past the sub-oceanic hot spot as the other islands were built. Measured from **Nihoa Island,** about 100 miles off the northern tip of Kauai, they stretch for just under 1,100 miles to **Kure Atoll,** last of the **Midway Islands.** There are 13 islets, shoals, and half-submerged reefs in the chain. Most have been eroded flat by the sea and wind, but a few tough volcanic cores endure. Together they make up a land mass of approximately 3,400 acres, the largest being the Midways at 1,280 acres, and the smallest the **Gardner Pinnacles** at just over 2½ acres. The climate is similar to that of the main islands with a slightly larger variance. Temperatures sometimes dip as low as 50 degrees and climb as high as 90 degrees.

Administration And History

Politically, the Leewards are administered by the City and County of Honolulu, except for the Midway Islands, which are under federal jurisdiction. None is permanently inhabited, except for some lonely military and wildlife field stations on Midway, Kure, and the French Frigate Shoals. All are part of the **Hawaiian Islands National Wildlife Refuge,** established at the turn of the century by Theodore Roosevelt. In pre-contact times, some of the islands supported a Tahitian culture markedly different from the one that emerged on the main Hawaiian Islands. Necker Island, for example, was the only island in the entire Hawaiian archipelago on which the inhabitants carved stone figures with a complete head and torso. On many of the others, remnants of *heiau* and agricultural terracing attribute to their use. Over the years, Hawaiians as well as Westerners have exploited the islands for feathers, fertilizer, seals, and fish.

The islands are closely monitored by the U.S. Fish and Wildlife Agency. Permission to land on them is granted only under special circumstances. Studies are underway to determine if the waters around the islands can support some commercial fishing, while leaving a plentiful supply of food for the unique wildlife of these lonely islands.

Wildlife

Millions of seabirds of various species have found permanent sanctuary on the Leewards, using them as giant floating nests and rookeries. Today the populations are stable and growing, but it hasn't always been so. On Laysan, at the turn of the century, egg hunters came to gather uncountable albatross eggs, selling the albumen to companies making photographic paper. They brought their families along, and their children's pets, which included rabbits. The rabbits escaped and multiplied wildly. In no time they invaded the territories of the **Laysan honeycreeper, rail,** and **millerbird,** rendering them extinct. Laysan has recovered and is refuge to over 6 million birds

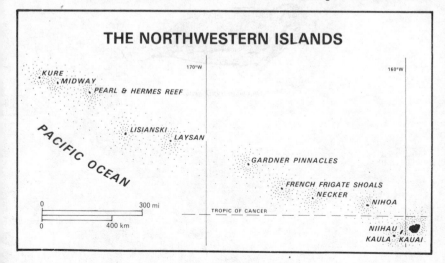

unique figurine of Necker Island

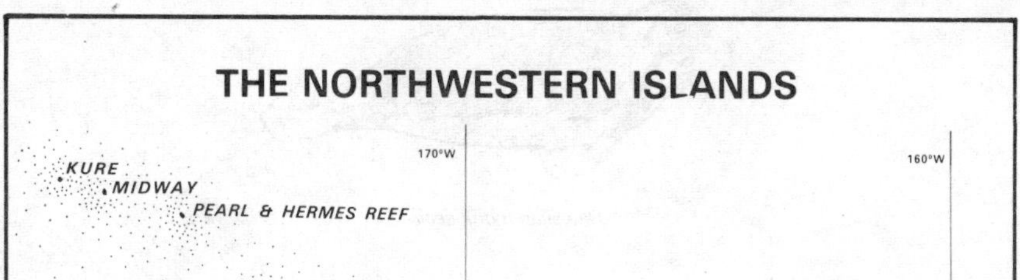

including the rare and indigenous **Laysan teal,** and **finch.** An amazing bird using the rookeries is the **frigate bird.** The male can blow up its chest in a mating ritual like a giant red heart-shaped balloon. Also known as **man-o-war birds,** they oftentimes pirate the catches of other birds, devour chicks, and even cannibalize their own offspring. Some of the most prolific birds of the Leewards are terns, both the delicate all-white **fairy tern,** and its darker relative the **sooty tern.** Other distinctive species include a variety of boobies, and the **Laysan albatross,** which has a wingspan of 10-12 feet, the world's largest.

Besides birds, the islands are home to the **Hawaiian monk seal,** one of only 2 species of indigenous Hawaiian mammals. These beautiful and sleek animals were hunted to near extinction for their skins. Man encroached on their territory more and more, until now they are protected as an endangered species. About 1,000 individuals still cling to existence on various islands.

The **green turtle** is another species that has found a haven here. They were hunted to near extinction for their meat and leather, and of the few colonies around the world, the largest in the U.S. is on the French Frigate Shoals.

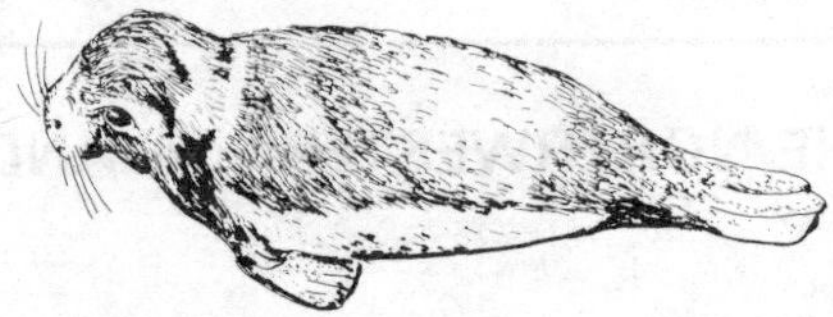

Hawaiian monk seal

MAUI

INTRODUCTION

The *Kumulipo,* the ancient genealogical chant of the Hawaiians, sings of the demi-god Maui, a half-human mythological sorcerer known and revered throughout Polynesia. Maui was a prankster on a grand scale who used guile and humor to create some of the most amazing feats of "derring do" ever recorded. A Polynesian combination of Paul Bunyan and Hercules, Maui's adventures were known as "strifes." He served mankind by fishing up the islands of Hawaii from the ocean floor, securing fire from a tricky mud hen, lifting the sky so humans could walk upright, and slowing down the sun god by lassooing his genitals with a braided rope of his sister's pubic hair. Maui accomplished this last feat on the summit of the great mountain Haleakala ("House of the Sun"), thus securing more time in the day to fish and to dry *tapa*. Maui met his just but untimely end between the legs of the great goddess, Hina. This final prank, in which he attempted to crawl into the sleeping goddess' vagina, left his feet and legs dangling out, causing uproarious laughter among his comrades, a band of warrrior birds. The noise awakened Hina, who saw no humor in the situation. She unceremoniously squeezed Maui to death. The island of Maui is the only island in Hawaii and throughout Polynesia named after a god. With such a legacy the island couldn't help but become known as *"Maui no ka oi,"* "Maui is the best!"

OVERVIEW

In a land of superlatives, it's quite a claim to call your island *the* best, but Maui has a lot to back it up. Maui has more miles of swimmable beach than any of the other islands. Haleakala,

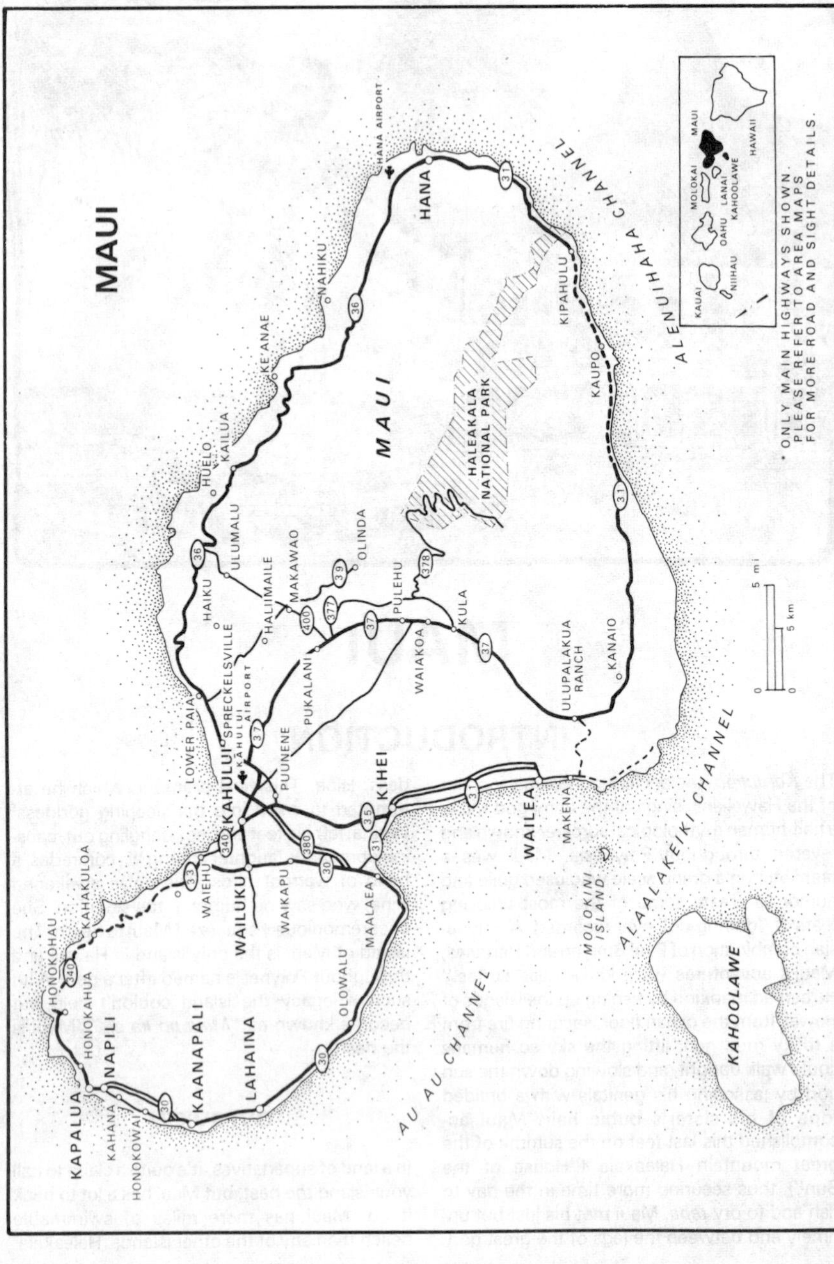
MAUI
MAUI
HALEAKALA NATIONAL PARK
HANA
HANA AIRPORT
NAHIKU
KE'ANAE
KAILUA
HUELO
ULUMALU
HAIKU
LOWER PAIA
SPRECKELSVILLE
KAHULUI
KAHULUI AIRPORT
HALIMAILE
MAKAWAO
OLINDA
PUKALANI
PULEHU
WAIAKOA
KULA
PUUNENE
KIHEI
WAILEA
MAKENA
ULUPALAKUA RANCH
KANAIO
KAUPO
KIPAHULU
WAILUKU
WAIKAPU
WAIEHU
KAHAKULOA
HONOKOHAU
HONOKAHUA
NAPILI
KAPALUA
HONOKOWAI
KAHANA
KAANAPALI
LAHAINA
OLOWALU
MAALAEA
MOLOKINI ISLAND
KAHOOLAWE
AU AU CHANNEL
ALAALAKEIKI CHANNEL
ALENUIHAHA CHANNEL
30
31
33
35
36
37
39
340
377
378
380
400
0
5 mi
5 km
KAUAI
NIIHAU
OAHU
MOLOKAI
LANAI
MAUI
KAHOOLAWE
HAWAII
• ONLY MAIN HIGHWAYS SHOWN.
PLEASE REFER TO AREA MAPS
FOR MORE ROAD AND SIGHT DETAILS.

the massive mountain that *is* East Maui, is the largest dormant volcano in the world. Its hardened lava that rises over 30,000 feet from the sea floor makes it one of the heaviest concentrated masses on the face of the earth. Legitimate claims are made that Maui grows the best onions and potatoes, but the boast of the best *pakololo* may only be a pipe dream, since all islands have great soil, weather, and many enterprising gardeners. Some even claim that Maui gets more sunshine than the other islands, but that's hard to prove.

Maui's Body

If you look at the silhouette of Maui on a map, it looks like the head and torso of a man bent at the waist and contemplating the uninhabited island of Kahoolawe. The "head" is West Maui. The profile is that of a wizened old man whose wrinkled brow and cheeks are the **West Maui Mountains.** The highest peak here is **Puu Kukui,** at 5,778 feet, located just about where the ear would be. If you go to the top of the head, you'll be at Kapalua, a resort community recently carved from pineapple fields. Fleming Beach begins a string of beaches that continues down over the face, stopping at the neck, and picking up again on the chest which is southeast Maui. Kaanapali is the forehead; this massive beach continues almost uninterrupted for four miles. In comparison, this area alone would take in all of Waikiki, from Diamond Head to Ala Moana. Sugarcane fields fringe the mountain side of the road, while condos are strung along the shore. The resorts here are cheek to jowl, but the best are tastefully done with views and access to the beach.

Lahaina would be located at the Hindu "third eye." This town is where it's "happening" on Maui, with concentrations of crafts, museums, historical sites, restaurants, and night spots. Lahaina has always been somewhat of a playground, used in times past by royal Hawaiian *ali'i* and then by Yankee whalers. The "goodtimes" mystique still lingers. At the tip of the nose is Olowalu, where a lunatic Yankee trader, Simon Metcalf, decided to slaughter hundreds of curious Hawaiians paddling toward his ship just to show them he was boss. From Olowalu you can see four islands: Molokai, Lanai, Kahoolawe, and a faint hint of Hawaii far to the south. The back of Maui's head is an adventurer's paradise, complete with a tourist-eliminating rugged road posted with overexaggerated "Proceed No Farther" signs. Back here are tremendous coastal views, bird sanctuaries, *heiau,* and Kahakuloa, a tiny fishing village reported to be a favorite stomping ground of great Maui himself.

The Isthmus

A low flat isthmus planted primarily in sugarcane is the neck that connects the "head" of West Maui to the "torso" of East Maui, which is Haleakala. The Adam's apple is the little port of Maalaea, which has a good assortment of pleasure and fishing boats, and provides an up-close look at a working port not nearly as frenetic as Lahaina. The nape of the neck is made up of the twin cities of Wailuku, the county seat, and Kahului, where visitors arrive at Maui's airport. These towns are where the "people" live. Some say the isthmus, dramatically separating east and west, is the reason Maui is called "The Valley Isle." Head into Iao Valley from Wailuku, where the West Maui Mountains have been worn into incredible peaked monolithic spires. This stunning valley area played a key role in Kamehameha's unification of the Hawaiian Islands, and geologically seems to be a more fitting reason for Maui's nickname.

East Maui/Haleakala

Once you cross the isthmus you're on the immensity of Haleakala. This mountain is a true microcosm and makes up the entire bulging, muscled torso. Its geology encompasses alpine, desert, jungle, pastureland, and wasteland. The temperature, determined by altitude, ranges from sub-freezing to sub-tropical. If you head east along the spine, you'll find world-class sailboarding beaches, artist villages, last-picture-show towns, and a few remaining family farms planted in taro. Rt. 360, the only coastal road, rocks and rolls you over its more than 600 documented curves, and shows you more waterfalls and pristine pools than you can count. After crossing more than 50 bridges, you come to Hana. Here, the "dream" Hawaii that people seek still lives. Farther along is Oheo Stream and its pools, erroneously known as "The Seven Sacred Pools." However, there is no mistaking the amazing energy vibrations in the area. Close by is where Charles Lindbergh is buried, and many celebrities have chosen the surrounding hillsides as their special retreats and hideaways.

On Haleakala's broad chest are macho cowboy towns complete with Wild West rodeos contrasting with the gentle but riotous colors of carnation and protea farms. Polipoli State Park is here, a thick forest canopy with more varieties of imported trees than anywhere in Oceania. A weird cosmic joke places Kihei just about where the armpit would be. Kihei is a mega-growth condo area ridiculed as an example of what developers shouldn't be allowed to do. Oddly enough, Wailea, just down the road, exemplifies a reasonable and aesthetic planned community and is highly touted as a "model" development area. Just at the belly button, close to the *kundalini,* is Makena, long renowned as Maui's "alternative beach." It's the island's last "free" beach with no restrictions, no park rangers, no amenities, and sometimes, no bathing suits.

Finally, when you pilgrimage to the summit of Haleakala, it'll be as if you've left the planet. It's another world: beautiful, mystical, raw, inspired, and freezing cold. When you're alone on the crater rim with the world below garlanded by the brilliance of sunrise or sunset, you'll know that you have come at last to great Maui's heart.

THE LAND

Maui is the second largest and youngest of the main Hawaiian Islands, next to Hawaii. It is made up of two volcanoes: the **West Maui Mountains** and **Haleakala.** The West Maui Mountains are geologically much older than Haleakala, but the two were joined by subsequent lava flows that formed a connecting low, flat isthmus. **Puu Kukui** at 5,778 feet is the the lord of a mountain domain whose old, weathered face has been scarred by an inthered face has been scarred by an inhospitable series of deep crags, valleys, and gorges. Haleakala, in comparison, is an adolescent with smooth, rounded features. This precocious kid looms 10,023 feet above sea level, and is four times larger than West Maui. Its incredible mass, as it rises over 30,000 feet from the ocean floor, is one of the densest on Earth. Its gravitational pull is staggering and it was considered a primary power spot in old Hawaii. The two parts of Maui combine to form 728.8 square miles of land with 120 linear miles of coastline. At its widest, Maui is 25 miles from north to south, and 40 miles east to west. The coastline has the largest number of swimmable beaches in Hawaii, and the interior is a miniature continent with almost every conceivable geological feature evident.

Climate

Maui has similar weather to the rest of the Hawaiian Islands, though some aficionados claim that it gets more sunshine than the rest. The weather on Maui depends more on where you are than on what season it is. The average yearly daytime temperature hovers around 80 degrees F and is moderated by the tradewinds. Nights are just a few degrees cooler. Since Haleakala is a main feature on Maui, you

Haleakala crater

AVERAGE MAXIMUM/MINIMUM TEMPERATURE AND RAINFALL

Island	Town		Jan.	Mar.	May	June	Sept.	Nov.
Maui	Lahaina	high	80	81	82	83	84	82
		low	62	63	68	68	70	65
		rain	3	1	0	0	0	1
	Hana	high	79	79	80	80	81	80
		low	60	60	62	63	65	61
		rain	9	7	2	3	5	7
	Kahului	high	80	80	84	86	87	83
		low	64	64	67	69	70	68
		rain	4	3	1	0	0	2

should remember that altitude drastically affects the weather. Expect an average drop of 3 degrees for every 1,000 feet of elevation. The lowest temperature ever recorded in Hawaii was atop Haleakala in 1961 when the mercury dropped well below freezing to a low of 11 degrees.

Precipitation

Rain on Maui is as much a factor as it is in all of Hawaii. On any day, somewhere on Maui it's raining, while other areas experience drought. A dramatic example of this phenomenon is to compare Lahaina with Mount Puu Kukui, both on West Maui and separated by only seven miles. Lahaina, which translates as "Merciless Sun," is hot, arid, and gets 17 inches of rainfall annually, while Puu Kukui can receive close to 40 *feet* of rain! This rivals Mt. Waialeale on Kauai as the wettest spot on earth. The windward (wet) side of Maui, outlined by the Hana Road, is the perfect natural hothouse. Here, valleys sweetened with blossoms house idyllic waterfalls and pools that visitors treasure when they happen upon them. On the leeward (dry) side are Maui's best beaches: Kapalua, Kaanapali, Kihei, Wailea, and Makena. They all sit in Haleakala's "rain shadow." If it happens to be raining at one, just move a few miles down the road to the next. Anyway, the rains are mostly gentle and the brooding sky, especially at sundown, is even more spectacular than normal.

FLORA AND FAUNA

Maui's indigenous and endemic plants, trees, and flowers are both fascinating and beautiful. Unfortunately, they, like everything else that was native, are quickly disappearing. The majority of flora found interesting by visitors was either introduced by the original Polynesians or later by white settlers. Maui is blessed with state parks, gardens, undisturbed rainforests, private reserves, and commercial nurseries. Combined they offer brilliant and dazzling colors to the landscape.

Silversword

Maui's official flower is a tiny pink rose called a *lokelani.* Its unofficial symbol, however, is the silversword. The Hawaiian name for silversword is *ahinahina* which translates as "gray gray," and the English name derives from a silverfish, whose color it's said to resemble. The silversword is from a remarkable plant family that claims 28 members, with five in the specific silversword species. It's kin to the common sunflower, and botanists say the entire family evolved from a single ancestral species. The members of the silversword family can all hypothetically interbreed and produce remarkable hybrids. Some plants are shrubs, while others are climbing vines, and some even become trees. They grow any-

silversword in bloom

where from desert conditions to steamy jungles. On Maui, the silversword is only found on Haleakala, above the 6,000-foot level, and is especially prolific in the crater. Each plant lives from five to 20 years and ends its life by sprouting a gorgeous stalk of hundreds of purplish-red flowers. It then withers from a majestic six-foot plant to a flat gray skeleton. An endangered species, silverswords are totally protected. They protect themselves, too, from radiation and lack of moisture by growing fuzzy hairs all over their swordlike stalks. You can see them along the Haleakala Park Road at **Kalamaku Overlook,** or by hiking along **Silversword Loop** on the floor of the crater.

Protea

These exotic flowers are from Australia and South Africa. Because they come in almost limitless shapes, sizes, and colors, they captivate everyone who sees them. They are primitive, almost otherworldly in appearance, and they exude a life force more like an animal than a flower. The slopes of leeward Haleakala between 2,000 and 4,000 feet is heaven to protea—the growing conditions could not be more perfect. Here are found the hardiest, highest-quality protea in the world. The days are warm, the nights are cool and the well-drained volcanic soil has the exact combination of minerals that protea thrive on. Haleakala's crater even helps by creating a natural air flow which produces cloud cover, filters the sun, and protects the flowers. Protea make excellent gifts that can be shipped anywhere. As fresh-cut flowers they are gorgeous, but they have the extra benefit of drying superbly. Just hang them in a dark, dry, well-ventilated area and they do the rest. You can see protea, along with other botanical specialties, at the following: **Kula Botanical Garden** (see below), **Upcountry Protea Farm** on Upper Kimo Drive one mile off Haleakala Hwy. (Rt. 377), **Hawaii Protea Co-op,** next to Kula Lodge on Crater Rd., and **Protea Gardens of Maui,** on Hapapa Road off Rt. 377 not far from Kula Lodge.

Carnations

If protea aren't enough to dazzle you, how about fields of carnations? Most Mainlanders think of carnations stuck in a groom's lapel, or perhaps have seen a table dedicated to them in a hothouse, but fields full of carnations! The Kula area produces carnations that grow outside nonchalantly, in rows, like cabbages. They fill the air with an unmistakable perfume, and they are without doubt a joy to behold. You can see family and commercial plots throughout the upper Kula area.

Botanical Gardens, Parks, And State Forests

Those interested in the flora of Maui would find a visit to any of the following both educational and entertaining. In the Kula area visit: **Kula Botanical Gardens,** clearly marked along Rt. 377 (Haleakala Hwy.) a mile from where Rt. 377 joins Rt. 37 at the south end, tel. 878-1715. Three acres of plants and trees including *koa* are in their natural settings. Open daily 9:00 a.m. to 4:00 p.m., $2.50, self-guided tour. **University of Hawaii Experimental Station** is north of the south junction of Rt. 377 and Rt. 37 on Copp Road. Open Mon. to Fri. 7:30 a.m. to 3:30 p.m., closed for lunch, free. Twenty acres of constantly changing plants that are quite beautiful even though the grounds are uninspired, scientific, rectangular plots.

Polipoli Springs State Recreation Area is the finest upcountry camping and trekking area on Maui. At south end of Rt. 377, turn onto Waipoli Road for 10 miles of bad road. Overnight camping is recommended. A wealth of flora and fauna includes native and introduced birds, magnificent stands of redwoods, conifers, ash, cypress, sugi, cedar, and various pine. The area is known for delicious methley plums that ripen in early June. For more info contact Division of State Parks in Wailuku, tel. 244-4354.

Keanae Arboretum, about 15 miles west of Hana on the Hana Hwy. (Rt. 360), is always open, no fee. Native, introduced and exotic plants, including Hawaiian food plants, are in a natural setting with walkways, identifying markers, tropical trees, and mosquitoes. Educational, a must. **Helani Gardens,** one mile west of Hana, open daily 10:00 a.m. to 3:30 p.m., adults $2.00. These 60 acres of flowerbeds and winding jeep trails are the lifetime project of Howard Cooper, lovingly tended, exotic jungle, terrific!

Maui Zoo and Botanical Garden in Wailuku is easily accessible. Get a basic introduction to flora at this tiny zoo, good for tots, and mildly interesting. In central Maui try **Kepaniwai Park,** on Rt. 32 leading to Iao Needle. This tropical setting displays formalized gardens from different nations. Daily, no fee. Finally, for an extremely civilized treat visit the formal gardens of the **Hyatt Regency Hotel** in Kaanapali, open to the public. The architecture and grounds are impeccable.

Maui's Endangered Birds

Maui suffers the same fate as the other islands. Its native birds are disappearing. Maui is the last home of the crested honeycreeper *(akohe'kohe)*. It lives only on the windward slope of Haleakala from 4,500 to 6,500 feet. It once live on Molokai, but no longer. It's rather a large bird, averaging over seven inches long, and predominantly black. Its throat and breast are tipped with gray feathers, while it's neck and underbelly are a bright orange. A distinctive fluff of feathers forms a crown. It primarily eats *ohia* flowers and it's believed that the crown feathers gather pollen and help to propagate the *ohia.* The parrotbill is another endangered bird found only on the slopes of Haleakala above 5,000 feet. It has an olive-green back and a yellow body. Its most distinctive feature is its parrot-like bill which it uses to crack branches and pry out larvae.

The nene, the state bird, lives only on Haleakala and on the slopes of Mauna Loa and Mauna Kea on the Big Island.

Two waterbirds found on Maui are the Hawaiian stilt *(aeo)* and the Hawaiian coot *(alae ke'oke'o).* The stilt is about 16 inches tall and lives on Maui at Kanaha and Kealia ponds. Primarily black with a white belly, its sticklike legs are pink. The adults will pretend to be hurt, putting on an excellent performance of the "broken wing" routine, in order to lure predators away from their nests. The Hawaiian coot is a web-footed water bird that resembles a duck. It's found on all the main islands but mostly on Maui and Kauai. Mostly a dull gray, it has a white bill and tail feathers. It builds a large floating nest and vigorously defends its young. The dark-rumped petrel is slightly different from other primarily marine birds. This petrel is found around the Visitor's Center at Haleakala Crater about one hour after dusk from May through October. The *amakihi* and the *iiwi* are endemic birds that aren't endangered at the moment. The *amakihi* is one of the most common native birds. It's a yellowish-green bird that frequents the high branches of *ohia, koa,* and sandalwood looking for insects, nectar, or fruit. It's less specialized than most other Hawaiian birds, the main reason for its continued existence. The *iiwi* is a bright red bird with a salmon-colored, hooked bill. It's found only on Maui, Hawaii, and Kauai in the forests above 2,000 feet. It, too, feeds on a variety of insects and flowers. The *iiwi* is known for its harsh voice that sounds like a squeaking hinge, but is also capable of a melodious song.

Other indigenous birds found on Maui are the wedge-tailed shearwater, white-tailed tropicbird, black noddy, American plover, and a large variety of escaped exotic birds.

The Humpbacks Of Maui

Humpbacks get their name from their style of exposing their dorsal fin when they dive, which gives them a humped appearance. About 7,000-8,000 humpback whales are alive today, down from an estimated 100,000 at the turn of the century. The remaining whales are divided into three separate global populations: North Atlantic, North Pacific, and South Pacific groups. About 500 North Pacific humpbacks migrate from coastal Alaska starting in November. They reach their peak in February, congregating mostly in the waters off Maui, with a smaller group heading for the waters off Kona on Hawaii. An adult humpback is 45 feet long and weighs in at a svelte 40 tons (80,000 pounds). They come to Hawaii mainly to give birth to a single 2,000-pound, relatively blubberless calf. They nurse their calf for about one year and become impregnated again the next. While in Hawaiian waters humpbacks generally don't eat. They wait until returning to Alaska where they gorge themselves on krill. It's estimated that they can live off their blubber without peril for six months. They have an enormous mouth stretching a third the length of their bodies which is filled with over 600 rows of baleen, a prickly, fingernail-like substance. Humpbacks have been known to blow air under water to create giant bubblenets that help to corral krill. They rush in with mouth agape and dine on their catch.

Humpback's Song

All whales are fascinating, but the humpbacks have a special ability to sing unlike any others. They create their melodies by grunting, shrieking, and moaning. No one knows exactly what the songs represent, but it's clear they're a definite form of communication. The singers appear to be "escort males" that tag along with, and seem to guard, a mother and her calf. The songs are exact renditions that last 20 minutes or more and are repeated over and over again for hours. Amazingly, all the whales know and sing the same song, and the song changes from year to year. The notes are so forceful that they can be heard above and below the water for miles. Some of the deep base notes will even carry underwater for 100 miles! Scientists devote careers to recording and listening to the humpbacks' songs. As yet they're unexplained, but anyone who hears their eerie tones knows that he is privy to a wonderful secret and that the songs are somehow a key to understanding the consciousness of the great humpback.

Whale Watching

If you're on Maui from late Nov. to early May, you have an excellent chance of spotting a humpback. You can often see a whale from a vantage point on land but this is nowhere near as thrilling as seeing them close-up from a boat. Either way, binoculars are a must. Telephoto and zoom lenses are also useful and you might even get a nifty photo in the bargain. But don't waste your film unless you have a fairly high-powered zoom: fixed-lens cameras give pictures with a lot of ocean and a tiny black speck. If you're lucky enough to see a whale "breach" (jump clear of the water), keep watching—they often repeat this a number of times. If a whale dives and lifts its fluke high in the air, expect it to be down for quite a while (15 minutes) and not to come up in the same spot. Other times they'll dive shallow, then bob up and down quite often. From shore you're likely to see whales anywhere along Maui's south coast. If you're staying at any of the hotels or condos along Kaanapali or Kihei and have an ocean view, you can spot them from your *lanai* or window. A good vantage spot is Papawai Point along Rt. 30 and up the road

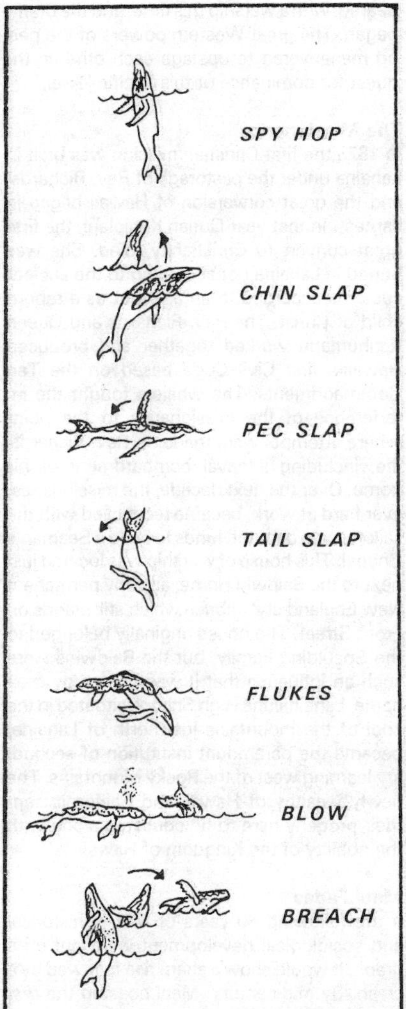

heading west just before the tunnel. Maalaea Bay is another favorite nursing ground for mothers and their calves; you also get to see a small working harbor up close. An excellent viewpoint is Makena Beach on the spit of land separating Little and Big Beaches (local names). If you time your arrival near sunset, even if you don't see a whale, you'll have a mind-boggling light show. For general information, see p. 14; for Maui whale-watching cruises, see p. 346.

HISTORY

The *Kumulipo* tells that Maui was the second island child of Wakea and Papa. Before the coming of the white man and his written record, it's clear that the island was a powerful kingdom. Wars raged throughout the land and kings ruled not only Maui, but the neighboring islands of Lanai and Kahoolawe. By the 16th C., a royal road called the *Alaloa* encircled the island and signified unity. Today, on West Maui, the road is entirely obliterated; only a few portions remain on East Maui. When the white men began to arrive in the late 1700s, Maui became their focal point. Missionaries, whalers and the new Hawaiian kings of the Kamehameha line all made Lahaina their seat of power. For about 50 years, until the mid-19th C., Maui blossomed. Missionaries built the first permanent stone structures in the islands. An exemplary New England-style school at Lahianaluna attracted students even from California cities. Here, too, a famous printing press brought not only revenue but refinement, through the written word. The sugar industry began in secluded Hana and fortunes were made; a new social order under the "Plantation System" began. But by the turn of this century, the "glory years" were over. The whaling industry faded away and Oahu took over as the central power spot. Maui slipped into obscurity. It was revived in the 1960s when tourists rediscovered what others had known: Maui is a beauty among beauties.

Maui's Great Kings

Internal turmoil raged in Hawaii just before discovery by Capt. Cook in 1778. Shortly after contact, the great Kamehameha would rise and consolidate all the islands under one rule, but in the 1770s a king named Kahekili ruled Maui. (Some contend that Kahekili was Kamehameha's father!) The Hana district, however, was ruled by Kalaniopuu of Hawaii. He was the same king who caused the turmoil on the day that Capt. Cook was killed at Kealakekua. Hana was the birthplace of Queen Kaahumanu, Kamehameha's favorite wife. She was the most instrumental *ali'i* in bringing Hawaii into the new age initiated by foreign discovery. In 1776, Kalaniopuu invaded Maui, but his forces were annihilated by Kahekili's warriors at Sand Hill near Wailuku, which means "Bloody Waters." On November 26, 1778, Capt. Cook spotted Maui, but bypassed it because he could find no suitable anchorage. It wasn't until May 28, 1786, that a French expedition led by Commander La Perouse came ashore near Lahaina after finding safe anchorage at what became known as La Perouse Bay. Maui soon became a regular port of call. In 1790 Kamehameha finally defeated Kahekili's forces at Iao Needle and brought Maui under his domain. The great warrior Kahekili was absent from the battle, where Kamehameha used a cannon from the *Fair American,* a small ship seized a few years before. Davis and Young, two marooned seamen, provided the technical advice for these horrible but effective new weapons.

Maui's Rise

The beginning of the 19th C. brought amazing changes to Hawaii and many of these came through Maui—especially the port of Lahaina. In 1793, Captain Vancouver visited Lahaina and confirmed La Perouse's report that it was a fine anchorage. In 1802 Kamehameha stopped with his enormous "Pelelu Fleet" of war canoes on his way to conquer Oahu. He lingered for over a year collecting taxes and building his "Brick Palace" at Lahaina. The bricks were poorly made, but this marked the first Western-style structure in the islands. He also built a fabulous straw house for his daughter Princess Nahienaena that was so well constructed it was later used as the residence of the U.S. Consul. In 1819 the first whaler, *The Bellina,* stopped at Lahaina and marked the ascendancy of Hawaii as the capital of the whaling industry that lasted until the majority of the whaling fleet was lost in the Arctic in 1871. During its heyday, over 500 ships visited Lahaina in one year. Also in 1819, the year of his death, Kamehameha built an Observation Tower in Lahaina so that he could watch for returning ships, many of which held his precious cargo. In that prophetic year the French reappeared, with a warship this time, and the drama began. The great Western powers of the period maneuvered to upstage each other in the quest for dominance of this Pacific jewel.

The Missionaries

In 1823 the first Christian mission was built in Lahaina under the pastorage of Rev. Richards, and the great conversion of Hawaii began in earnest. In that year Queen Kapiolani, the first great convert to Christianity, died. She was buried in Lahaina not according to the ancient customs accorded to an *ali'i,* but as a reborn child of Christ. The Rev. Richards and Queen Kaahumanu worked together and produced Hawaii's first Civil Code based on the Ten Commandments. The whalers fought the interference of the missionaries to the point where attempts were made on Rev. Richards' life, including a naval bombardment of his home. Over the next decade, the missionaries, ever hard at work, became reconciled with the sailors, who donated funds to build a Seaman's Chapel. This house of worship was located just next to the Baldwin Home, an early permanent New England-style house which still stands on Front Street. The house originally belonged to the Spaulding Family, but the Baldwins were such an influence that it was known by their name. Lahainaluna High School, situated in the cool of the mountains just north of Lahaina, became the paramount institution of secondary learning west of the Rocky Mountains. The newly wealthy of Hawaii and California sent their progeny here to be educated along with the nobility of the Kingdom of Hawaii.

Maui Fades

If the following 30 years of Maui's historical and sociological development were put on a graph, it would show a sharp rise followed by a crash. By mid-century, Maui boasted the *first* Constitution, Catholic Mass, Temperance Union, Royal Palace, and steamship service. A census was taken and a prison built to house reveling seamen. Kamehameha III moved the capital to Honolulu and the 1850s brought a smallpox epidemic, the destruction of Wainee Church by a "ghost wind," and the death of David Malo, a classic historian of pre-contact Hawaii. By the late 1860s, the whaling industry

Distinctive New England architecture distinguishes the Baldwin Home, still standing on Front Street in Lahaina.

was dead, but sugar would rise to take its place. The first successful sugar plantation was started by George Wilfong in 1849 along the Hana coast, and the first great sugar mill was started by James Campbell in 1861. The 1870s saw the planting of Lahaina's famous Banyan Tree by Sheriff W.O. Smith, and the first telephone and telegraph cable linking Paia with Haiku.

The 20th Century
When the Pioneer Hotel was built in 1901, Lahaina was still important. Claus Spreckels, "King Sugar" himself, had large holdings on Maui and along with his own sugar town, Spreckelsville, built the Haiku Ditch in 1878. This 30-mile ditch brought 50 million gallons of water a day from Haiku to Puunene so that the "green gold" could flourish. Sugar and Maui became one. Then, because of sugar, Lahaina lost its dominance and Paia became *the* town on Maui during the 1930s, where it housed plantation workers in camps according to nationality. Maui slid more and more into obscurity. A few luminaries brought some passing fame: Tandy MacKenzie, for example, born in Hana in 1892, was a gifted operatic star whose career lasted until 1954. In the 1960s, Maui, as well as all of Hawaii, became accesssible to the average tourist. It was previously discovered by men like Sam Pryor, retired vice-president of Pan Am Airlines, who made his home in Hana and invited Charles Lindbergh to visit, who lived and finally died in this idyllic spot. In the mid '60s, the Lahaina Restoration Foundation was begun. It dedicated itself to the preservation of Old Lahaina, and to other historical sites on the island. It now attempts to preserve the flavor of what once was, while looking to future growth. Today, Maui is once again in ascendancy, and is the second most visited island in Hawaii, after Oahu.

GOVERNMENT

The boundaries of Maui County are a bit oddball, but historically oddball. Maui County encompasses Maui Island, as well as Lanai, Molokai, and the uninhabited island of Kahoolawe. The apparent geographical oddity is an arc on East Maui, from Makawao past Hana and along the south coast almost to Kihei, which is a "shared" political area, aligned with the Kohala District of the Big Island since Polynesian times. These two districts were joined with each other, so it's just a traditional carry-over. The real strangeness occurs in Maui's 5th Senatorial District and its counterpart, the 10th Representative District. These two political areas include West Maui and the islands of Lanai and Molokai. West Maui, with Kaanapali, Lahaina, and Kapalua, is one of the most developed and financially sound areas in all of Hawaii. It's a favorite area with tourists, and is the darling of developers. On the other hand,

Lanai has a tiny population that is totally dependent on a one-company "pineapple economy." Molokai has the largest per capita concentration of native Hawaiians, a "busted economy" with a tremendous share of its population on welfare, and a grassroots movement determined to preserve the historical integrity of the island and the dignity of the people. You'd have to be a political magician to fairly represent all of the constituents in these widely differing districts.

Maui's Representatives
Hawaii's state legislature is comprised of 76 members, with the House of Representatives having 51 elected seats, and the State Senate 25. Members serve for 2- and 4-year terms respectively. All officials come from 76 separate electorates based on population. Maui is represented by three State Senators, all of whom are currently Democrats, and five State Representatives, four of whom are Democrats, with one Republican.

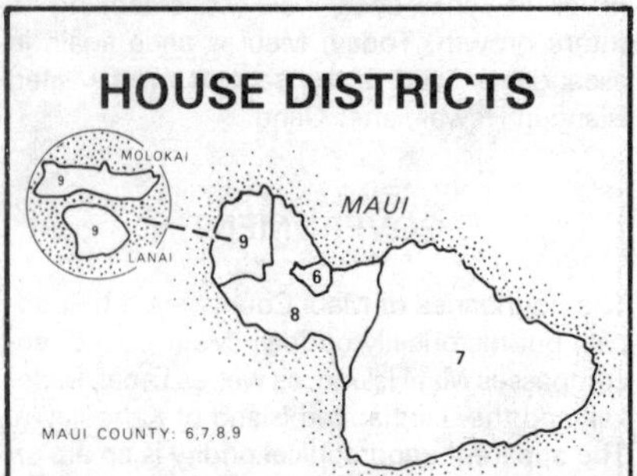

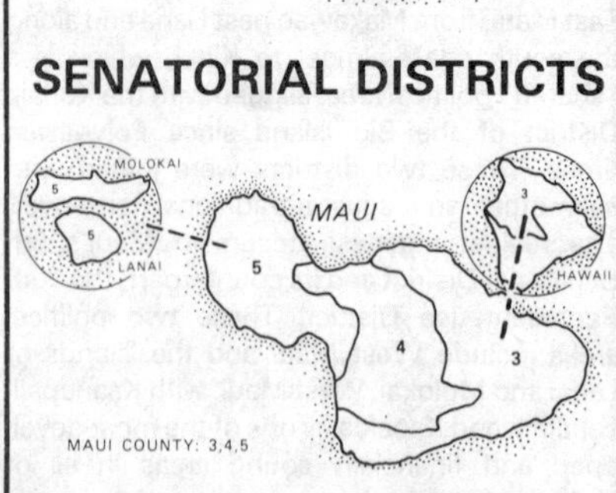

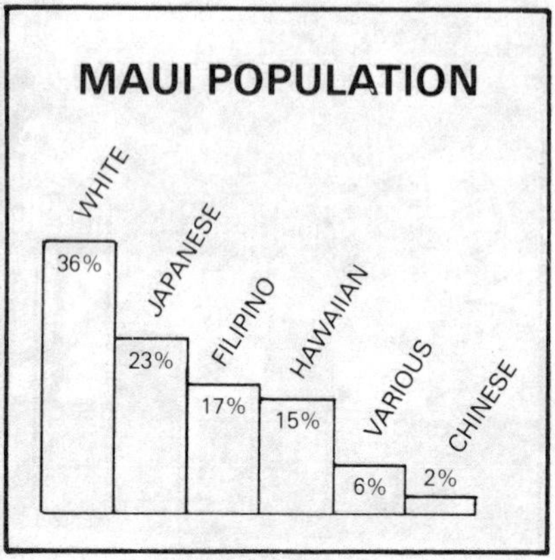

ECONOMY

Maui's economy is a mirror image of the state's economy: it's based on tourism, agriculture, and government expenditures. The primary growth is in tourism, with Maui being the second most frequently chosen Hawaiian destination after Oahu. Over 12,000 rooms are available on Maui in all categories, and they're filled 70 percent of the time. On average, Maui attracts close to a million tourists per year, and on any given day 15,000 visitors enjoy the island. The building trades are still booming, and the majority of the rooms are in Kihei-Wailea, but the Kaanapali area is catching up fast.

Agriculturally, Maui generates revenue through cattle, sugar, pineapples, *pakololo,* and flowers. Cattle grazing occurs on the western and southern slopes of Haleakala, where 20,000 acres are owned by the Ulupala Kua Ranch, and over 32,000 acres by the Haleakala Ranch. The upper slopes of Haleakala around Kula are a gardener's dream. Delicious onions, potatoes, and all sorts of garden vegetables are grown, but are secondary to large plots of gorgeous flowers, mainly carnations and the amazing protea. Sugar is still a very important Maui crop. The largest acreage is in the central isthmus area which is virtually all owned by the Alexander and Baldwin Company. Large sugar tracts along Kaanapali and the far west coast are owned by Amfac and Maui Land and Pineapple. Those lodging in Kaanapali will become vividly aware of the sugar fields when they're burned off just prior to harvesting. Pineapples are grown in the central east between Paia and Makawao where Alexander and Baldwin own most of the land and on the far west coast north of Napili where Maui Land and Pineapple control most of the holdings. Renegade entrepreneurs grow patches of *pakalolo* wherever they can find a spot that has the right vibes and is away from the prying eyes of the authorities. Deep in the West Maui Mountains and along the Hana Coast are favorite areas.

Government expenditures in Maui County are just over $35 millon per year. Only a small military presence on Maui amounts to a tiny Army installation near Kahului, and the Navy owning the target island of Kahoolawe. With tourists finding Maui more and more desirable every year, and with agriculture firmly entrenched, Maui's economic future is bright.

Tourism-related Problems

Two prime examples of the best and the worst development can be found on Maui's south shore at Kihei and Wailea, which are less than 5 miles apart. In the late '60s Kihei experienced a development-inspired "feeding frenzy" that made the real sharks off its shore seem about as dangerous as Winnie the Pooh. Condos were slapped up as fast as cement can dry, their architecture resembling a stack of shoeboxes. Coastline renowned for its beauty was overburdened, and the view was wiped out in the process. Anyone who had the bucks built, and now parts of Kihei look like a high-rise, low-income, federally-funded housing project. You can bet that those who made a killing building here don't live here. Conversely, just down the road is Wailea, a model of what development could (and should) be. The architecture is tasteful, low rise, non-obtrusive and done with people and the preservation of the scenery in mind. It's obviously more exclusive, but access points to the beaches are open to everyone, and the view is still there for all to enjoy. It points the way for the development of the future.

GETTING THERE

Maui, the Hawaiian destination second only to Oahu, attracts over a million visitors per year. A range of direct flights from the Mainland are offered by United Airlines, with limited flights offered by Hawaiian, Western, and American airlines. All other airlines servicing Hawaii, both domestic and foreign, land at Honolulu International Airport and then offer connecting flights on "inter-island carriers"; in most cases they're part of the original ticket price with no extra charge. Different airlines have "interline" agreements with different Hawaiian carriers so check with your travel agent. All major and most smaller inter-island carriers service Maui from throughout Hawaii with over 100 flights per day in and out of Kahului Airport.

Maui's Airports

Again there are three commercial airports on Maui, but the vast majority of travelers will only be concerned with **Kahului Airport**, which 99 percent of the flights in and out of Maui use. Kahului Airport is only minutes from Kahului town, on the northcentral coast of Maui. A full-service facility with most amenities, it has car rental agencies, information booths, lockers, and limited public and private transportation. Major roads lead from Kahului Airport to all primary destinations on Maui.

Hawaiian Airlines opened **Kapalua-West Maui Airport** in early 1987. This brand-new facility is conveniently located between Kaanapali and the Kapalua resort areas, on the *mauka* side of the Honoapiilani Hwy. at Mahinahina. Besides Hawaiian Air, which will operate 29 daily flights connecting West Maui with the rest of Hawaii, seven other commuter airlines have contracted to use the facility. The new facility opens West Maui to its first ever service to all the Hawaiin islands, the South Pacific, and the Mainland's west coast.

The other airport is at Hana on the northeast coast. **Hana Airport** is an isolated strip just west of Hana with no amenities, facilities, or transportation. People flying into Hana Airport generally plan to vacation in Hana for an extended period and have made prior arrangements for being picked up. Since the demise of Royal Hawaiian Airlines, Princeville Airlines has been servicing this route.

Non-stop Mainland Flights

Until recently, United Airlines was the only carrier that offered non-stop flights from the Mainland to Maui, but now there are three competitors. **United,** tel. 800-652-1211, flies daily non-stop to Maui from Chicago, Portland, Seattle, San Francisco, and Los Angeles. Denver passengers fly via San Francisco. **Hawaiian Airlines,** tel. 800-367-5320, operates its second Saturday flight from San Francisco to Kahului; **American Airlines,** tel. 800-252-0421, and **Western Airlines,** tel. 800-227-6105, both fly daily to Maui from Los Angeles.

Hawaiian Air's Dash Transit

Inter-island Carriers

Hawaiian Air offers more flights to Maui than any other inter-island carrier. The majority of flights are to and from Honolulu with an average flight time of 30 minutes. Hawaiian Air offers flights conveniently scheduled "on the hour" commencing from Honolulu at 6:00 a.m., until 8:00 p.m., with 23 additional flights intermingled throughout the day. Return flights from Maui to Honolulu begin 45 minutes after the hour. Hawaiian Air flights to and from Kauai (about 35 minutes flying time) begin at 7:00 a.m. and go until 7:00 p.m. with the same "on the hour" concept, augmented by an additional 10 flights. Three flights go to/from Hilo daily, two in the morning and one in mid-afternoon. Kona, on the Big Island, is serviced with five daily flights. Flights from Maui begin at 7:30 a.m. with the last at 4:39 p.m.; from Kona at 9:50 a.m. with the last at 7:32 p.m. There are two flights from Molokai at 10:15 a.m and 2:35 p.m. both on Dash 7s. Six flights from Maui to Molokai begin at 7:00 a.m. with the last at 3:11 p.m. One flight to Lanai goes at 4:25 p.m., and two flights from Lanai at 7:10 a.m. and 6:00 p.m. Aircraft flown are either DC-9 jets, or Dash 7 turbo-props. Hawaiian Airlines' **transpacific** schedule features four weekly flights between Honolulu and points in the South Pacific. Flights depart for Pago Pago, American Samoa, every Tues., Thurs., Fri., and Sun.; Tues. and Fri. flights continue to Apia, Western Samoa, with Thurs. and Sun. flights to Tonga. Return flights are Wed., Fri., Sat., and Mon. Hawaiian Air tel. 800-367-5320; on Maui tel. 244-9111.

Aloha Airlines' all-jet fleet of 737s flies from Honolulu to Maui over 20 times per day beginning at 6:10 a.m. with the last flight at 7:50 p.m.; to Honolulu at 6:58 a.m., last at 8:35 p.m. Multiple flights throughout the day from Kauai begin at 6:59 a.m. until 7:05 p.m.; to Kauai at 6:58 a.m. and throughout the day until 7:05 p.m. From Hilo, two flights in mid-morning and the last at 5:10 p.m.; to Hilo four flights interspersed from 9:30 a.m. until 4:20 p.m. From Kona at 9:50 a.m. and two in the afternoon with the last at 3:15 p.m.; to Kona five flights from 8:45 a.m. until 4:05 p.m. Aloha Airlines tel. 800-367-5250; on Maui, 877-2025.

Mid Pacific offers flights to and from Maui on its fleet of turbo-prop YS11s. Their more than 30 daily departures from Maui to Honolulu begin at 7:15 a.m. and go throughout the day until 8:55 p.m.; from Honolulu starting at 6:15 a.m. until 7:55 p.m. The carrier has begun a Midnight Maui Express daily-service from Honolulu at 12:15 a.m. More than a dozen flights are offered to and from Kauai beginning at 7:10 a.m., with the last flight at 6:05 p.m. Three flights fly to and from Kona at mid-morning, and early and late afternoon, with 2 flights to/from Hilo at mid morning and late afternoon. Mid Pacific, tel. 800-367-7010; on Maui 242-4906.

Fares for these three major airlines are always very competitive, with each offering special service or amenities to sweeten the deal. Mid Pacific instigated a one-price fare on all flights to all destinations every day of the week. The other two airlines quickly followed suit and that's the state of the fare prices in Hawaii until the marketing departments of any of these airlines comes up with a better idea.

Commuter Airlines

Princeville Airways headquartered in Princeville, Kauai, has begun flights to Kahului and Hana, along with flights to Molokai. These flights continue service on the routes that would have been terminated by the unfortunate closing of Royal Hawaiian Airlines, one of the oldest of Hawaii's commuter companies. For rates and information contact Princeville Airways at 800-367-7090.

Air Molokai is a great way to fly between Molokai and Maui. Their fares are the cheapest, and they fly three times per day with the earliest flight from Molokai at 7:45 a.m. and the last at 5:10 p.m. Contact Air Molokai at tel. 800-352-3616, or in Hawaii at 536-6611.

Reeves Air has regularly scheduled flights between Honolulu, Maui, and Molokai on a daily basis as well as charter service to get you there when you want to go. Their prices are higher, but it's like hiring your own private air taxi. Call Reeves Air at Oahu 833-9555; Maui, 871-4624.

Maui Airlines, one of the newest airlines in Hawaii, got off the ground in 1985. At first they offered flights throughout Hawaii, but now they fly only to/from the Micronesian islands of Guam, Saipan, Rota, and Tinian on 17-passenger Twin Otter aircraft. Their regularly scheduled flights are more expensive than the established commuter lines, while their air tours are about average. Call Maui Airlines at tel. 800-367-2920; Maui, 871-6201.

Whenever you fly any of the commuter airlines, try to get as many stops as possible. Because they fly so low, it's like getting a free flightseeing tour. As always the costs are a bit more than the larger airlines, but it's more fun.

GETTING AROUND

If it's your intention to *see* Maui when you visit, and not just to lie on the beach in front of your hotel, the only efficient way is to rent a car. Limited public transportation, a few free shuttles, taxis, and the good old thumb are available, but all these are flawed in one way or another. Other unique and fun-filled ways to tour the island include renting a bike or moped, or hopping on a helicopter, but these conveyances are highly specialized and are more in the realm of sports than touring.

Public Transportation

The **Grayline Airporter,** tel. 877-5507, will pick you up at or deliver you to Kahului Airport. It services all the popular destinations such as Lahaina/Kaanapali and Kihei/Wailea. At about $7 OW it's a slightly expensive but a no-hassle way to deal with arrival and departure, but out of the question for "every-day" transportation. The Maui Transit System operates **The Blue Shoreline Bus,** tel. 661-3827, which is adequate in the limited area that it services. It runs primarily along the southwest coast between Lahaina and Kaanapali with connections to Napili and Kapalua. These runs are made every 15 minutes during business hours from 8:00 a.m. until 5:00 p.m., then every 30 minutes until 10:00 p.m. The Blue Shoreline Bus stops at all the Kaanapali resorts except for the Whaler; this westbound run is $1.50 no matter how far you go. Three runs a day go from Lahaina eastward to Wailea, with stops at Maalaea and Kihei en route, $1.50-3.50, depending on the distance traveled.

Limited shuttles operate in the major resort areas. The **Kaanapali Jitney,** which runs up and down the Kaanapali Beach area from 9:00 a.m. to 9:00 p.m., costs $2 for an all-day pass. The **Kapalua Shuttle** services all of the hotels and condos in Kapalua from 7:00 a.m. to 11:00 p.m. on an "on call" basis. Your hotel desk will make arrangements for you. The **Wailea Resorts Shuttle** is free and stops at all Wailea Beach hotels and condos from 6:30 a.m. until 10:30 p.m.

The Lahaina Jitney is free and will take you to most tourist attractions around town.

Taxis

About 10 taxi companies on Maui more or less operate in a fixed area. Most, besides providing normal taxi service, also run tours all over the island. Taxis are expensive. For example, a ride from Kahului Airport to Kaanapali is $30 for about six people (about half this much to Kihei). Try Mita Taxi, at the airport, 871-4622; Kahului Taxi at 242-6404; Red and White Cabs in Lahaina at 661-3684; Lahaina Taxi, 661-4147; Wailea Taxi, 879-1059; Kihei Taxi, 879-3000.

Hitchhiking

The old tried-and-true method of hitchhiking—with thumb out, facing traffic, a smile on your interesting face—is "out" on Maui! It's illegal, and if a policeman sees you, you'll be hassled, if not outright arrested. You've got to play the *game.* Simply stand on the side of the road facing traffic with a smile on your interesting face, but put away the old thumb. In other words, you can't actively solicit a ride. People know what you're doing; just stand there. You can get around quite well by thumb, if you're not on a schedule. The success rate of getting a ride to the number of cars that go by isn't that great, but you will get picked up. Locals and the average tourist with family will generally pass you by. Recent residents and single tourists will most often pick you up, and 90 percent of the time these will be white males. Hitching short hops along the resort beaches is easy. People can tell by the way you're dressed that you're not going far and will give you a lift. Catching longer rides to Hana or up to Haleakala can be done, but it'll be tougher because the driver will know that you'll be with them for the duration of the ride. Women, under no circumstances, should hitch alone.

Bicycles

Bicycle enthusiasts should be thrilled with Maui, but the few flaws might flatten your spirits as well as your tires. The countryside is great, the weather is perfect, but the roads are heavily trafficked and the most interesting ones are narrow and have bad shoulders. Peddling to Hana will give you an up-close personal experience, but for bicycle safety this road is one of the worst. Haleakala is stupendous, but with a rise of more than 10,000 feet in less than 40 miles it is considered one of the most grueling rides in the world. A paved bike path runs from Lahaina to Kaanapali that's tame enough for everyone and you can even arrange a bicycle tour of Lahaina. In short, cycling on Maui as your primary means of transportation is not for the neophyte; because of safety considerations and the tough rides, only experienced riders should consider it.

For bike rentals, try: **Aloha Funway Rentals** in Lahaina at 661-8702; **Go Go Bikes Hawaii** in Kaanapali, 661-3063; **A & B Rentals** in

Honokowai, 669-0027; **South Seas Rental** in Lahaina, 661-8655; **Cruiser Bob's** in Lahaina, 667-7717. Bikes rent for about $12 for a 24-hour period, and you can generally get a 3-speed, 10-speed, or a tandem. For bicycle sales, parts, and repairs **The Cycle and Sports Shop** is well equipped and generous in their information about touring. They're at 2 locations: Maui Mall in Kahului, 877-5848, and in Lahaina, 661-4191.

Bicycle Tours

An adventure on Maui that's quickly becoming famous is riding a specially equipped bike from the summit of Mt. Haleakala for 40 miles to the bottom. A pioneer in this field is **Cruiser Bob's,** located at the Lahaina TraveLodge (special room/bike packages available), 667-7717. A van picks you up, takes you to the summit, providing instructions along the way, and then you're fed a great breakfast. You start your downhill coast, then break for a gourmet lunch. It's as fantastic and fun filled as it sounds, but it costs around $80 and for that price good 'ole Bobby Boy has no trouble "cruising" to the bank! The main competition comes from **Bicycle Tours of Maui** at 879-3374, and **Coast to the Coast** at Captain Nemo's in Lahaina, tel. 661-4644. Essentially you get the same experience for about the same amount of money. For downhilling you have to be a good rider; those under 16 require parental release. These outfits offer tamer tours of Lahaina and the beach resorts with admissions into historical sites and museums included. There's no gripe with the Haleakala experience; it's guaranteed thrills, but the price is a bummer!

RENTAL CARS

Maui has over 30 car rental agencies that can put you behind the wheel of anything from a Mercedes convertible to a used station wagon with chipped paint and torn upholstery. Some national companies, inter-island firms, good local companies, and a few fly-by-nights rent clunkers. More than a dozen companies are clustered in little booths at the Kahului Airport, a few at Kaanapali, and none at Hana Airport, but your Hana hotel can arrange a car for you. The rest are scattered around the island with a heavy concentration on Dairy Rd. near Kahului airport. Those without an airport booth either have a courtesy phone or a number to call; they'll pick you up. Stiff competition tends to keep the prices more or less reasonable. Good deals are offered during off-season, with price wars flaring at anytime and making for real savings, but these unfortunately can't be predicted. Even with all these companies, it's best to book ahead. You might not save money, but you can save yourself headaches.

Tips

The best cars to rent on Maui happen to be the cheapest: sub-compacts with standard shift. (If you can drive a standard!) Maui's main highways are broad and well paved, just like major roads on the Mainland, but the backroads, where all the fun is, are narrow twisty affairs. You'll appreciate the downshifting ability of standard transmissions on curves and steep inclines. If you get a big fatso luxury car, it'll be great for "puttin' on the ritz" at the resort areas, but you'll feel like a hippopotamus in the backcountry. If you've got that much money to burn, rent two cars! Try to get a car with cloth seats. Vinyl is too sticky, but sitting on your towel will help. You won't need a/c unless you plan on being in Lahaina a lot. The mile markers on back roads are great for pinpointing sites and beaches, and the lower number on these signs is the highway number, so you can always make sure that you're on the right road. The car rental agencies prohibit travel past Seven Sacred Pools on the other side of Hana, or around the top of the head of Maui. These roads are indeed rugged, but passable; the locals do it all the time. The car companies will

National Car Rental features GM cars.

warn you that your insurance "might" not cover you on these roads. They're really protecting their cars from being banged around. Traveling these roads is not recommended... for the faint-hearted. Be careful, drive slowly, and have fun!

Nationally Known Companies

The following are major firms that have booths at Kahului Airport. **National Car Rental** is one of the best of the nationally known firms. They have GMs, Nissans, Toyotas, Datsuns, vans, jeeps, and station wagons. National offers excellent weekly rates especially on standard sub-compacts. All major credit cards are accepted. On Maui, call 877-5347. **Avis** is also located in Kaanapali. They feature late-model GM cars as well as most imports and convertibles. Call Avis at 871-7575 or in Kaanapali at 661-4588. **Budget** offers competitive rates on a variety of late-model cars. At Kahului call 871-8811, in Kaanapali 661-4660. **Hertz,** perhaps the best known company, offers a wide variety of vehicles with some special weekly rates. Hertz has locations at Kaanapali and Wailea. Call 661-3195 and request the location nearest you. **Dollar** rents all kinds of cars, as well as jeeps and convertibles. At Kahului, call 877-6526; Kaanapali, 661-3037. **Alamo** has good weekly rates. Call 800-327-9633. For **Holiday,** call 877-2464.

Island Companies

The following companies are based in Hawaii and either have a booth at the airport or pick-up service through courtesy phones. **Tropical Rent a Car** has a good reputation for service and prices. Also located at Kaanapali and Kihei, call 877-0002, or 661-0061. **Toms** has a good variety including luxury cars and convertibles. Use marked courtesy phones at the airport or call 871-7721. **El Cheapo** lives up to its name and rents decent vehicles. Use courtesy phones or call 877-5851. **Word of Mouth** has late-model cars with cheaper rates on the older ones. Use a courtesy phone or call 877-2436. **Rent a Wreck** has decent rates on late model cars and cheaper rates on older cars, call 877-5600. **Luxury Sports Car Rental** is good for stepping out in Corvettes, Porsches, or Mercedes. Expensive; call 661-5646. **24 Karat Cars** has convertibles and luxury cars. Located in Kaanapali at 667-6289. **Roberts** has a good reputation, 877-5038. Others include: **Trans Maui,** 877-5222; **AAA,** 871-4610; **Andres,** 877-5378; **Convertibles Hawaii,** 877-0031; **Klunkers,** variable rates at 877-3197.

4-wheel Drive

Though much more expensive than cars, some people might feel safer in them for completely circling Maui. Also unlike cars, the rental companies offering 4WDs put no restrictions on driving past the Sacred Pools or around the head. 4WDs can be had from **El Cheapo,** 877-5851; **Maui Rent a Jeep,** 877-6626; **Maui Sailing Center,** 877-3065; **Hertz,** 877-5167. Variable rates from company to company depend on availability and length of rental.

Camper Rentals

If you want an alternative to staying in hotels or condos, consider a camper. You can rent a camper for an overnight trip to Hana. The convenience offsets the extra cost, and might even save money over staying in a hotel. Unlike cars, campers carry a price per mile charge (about 6 cents). Since most campers sleep at least four people and provide all necessary gear, you might try splitting costs. **Beach Boy Campers** has a good reputation, renting economical Toyota and Nissan models, call, 879-5322. Or try **Holo Holo Campers** at 877-5265.

Motorcycles And Mopeds

Just for running around town or to the beach mopeds are great, but for real open-road exploring you'll need a cycle. Hourly rates average $5, and expect to pay about $25 for the day or up to $125 for the week. For motorcycles try **Aloha Funway Rentals** in Lahaina, 661-8702. They offer sizes from 185 to 1,000cc.

For mopeds: **Go Go Bikes** at the Kaanapali Transportation Center, call 661-3063 or 669-6669; **A & B Mopeds** at the Honokawai General Store, call 669-0027. Motorcycles and mopeds are rented by the hour, day, or week.

SIGHTSEEING TOURS

Tours are offered that will literally let you cover Maui from head to foot; you can walk it, drive it, sail around it, fly over it, or see it from below the water. Almost every major hotel has a tour desk from which you can book. Plenty of booking agencies are along Lahaina's wharf: on Front St. in Lahaina try **Tom Durkwood's Information Booth,** the only free-standing sidewalk booth in Lahaina, or **Visitor Info & Ticket Center** in the Wharf Shopping Complex, 661-5151. Call **Aloha Activity Center** in Kaanapali and Lahaina, 667-9564; in Kihei a good general purpose activities booth is **Activities Unlimited,** just across the street from Kalama Beach Park on Kihei Rd., 879-3688. **Ocean Activities Center** in Kihei, tel. 879-4485, can also book you into a wide variety of activities. Others are found in Wailea, Kahului, and Napili.

Land Tours

It's easy to book tours to Maui's famous areas such as Lahaina, Hana, Kula, Iao Valley, and Haleakela. Normally they're run on either half- or full-day schedules (Hana is always a full day) and range anywhere from $17 to $50 with hotel pick-up included. Big bus tours are run by **Grayline,** tel. 877-5507, and **Roberts,** tel. 877-5038. These tours are quite antiseptic as you sit behind tinted glass in an a/c bus. You get more personalized tours in the smaller vans, such as **Holo Holo Tours,** tel. 661-4858. Among other destinations they'll take you to Hana with a Continental breakfast for $50. **Personalized Small Group Tours,** tel. 871-9551, goes to Hana for $40, or to Haleakela for $30. **No Kai Oi Tours** hits all the high spots and has competitive prices, tel. 871-9008. **Trans Hawaii Maui** specializes in all-day trips to Hana for $40, bring your own lunch, tel. 877-7308. **Maui Special Tours** shows you the sights with an old Maui hand, Jack Groenewout. His personalized tours are enhanced by a storehouse of information about Maui, tel. 879-9944.

The Sugar Cane Train

The old steam engine puffs along from Lahaina to Kaanapali, a 25-min. ride each way, and costs $4.25 OW and $6.50 RT adults, $2 OW and $3.25 RT children to age 12. A free bus shuttles between Lahaina Station and the waterfront to accommodate the most popular tour on Maui. The train runs throughout the day from 9:35 a.m. to 4:10 p.m. It's very popular so book in advance. All rides are narrated and there may even be a singing conductor. All kinds of tours are offered as well: some feature lunch, a tour of Lahaina with admission into the Baldwin House and the *Carthiginian,* and even a cruise on a glass-bottom boat. They're tame, touristy, and fun. The price is right: the deluxe tour including RT train ride, lunch, Lahaina tour, and an all-day Kaanapali Jitney pass for $15. Call the Lahaina Kaanapali and Pacific Railroad at tel. 661-0089

Air Tours

Maui is a spectacular sight from the air. Two small airlines and a handful of helicopter companies swoop you around the island. These joy rides are literally the highlight of many people's experience on Maui, but they are expensive. The excursions vary, but expect to spend at least $100 for a basic half-hour tour. The most spectacular ones take you into Haleakala crater, or perhaps to the remote West Maui mountains where inaccessible gorges lie at your feet. Other tours are civilized; expect a champagne brunch after you visit Hana. Still others take you to nearby Lanai or Molokai to view some of the world's most spectacular sea cliffs and remote beaches. Know, however, that many hikers and trekkers have a beef with the air tours: after they've spent hours, or maybe days, hiking into remote valleys in search of peace and quiet, out of the sky comes the mechanical whir of a chopper.

The two airlines operating out of Kahului Airport are **Paragon Air** at 244-3356, and **Central Pacific Airlines** at 242-7894. The helicopter companies include: **Papillon Helicopters,** flying from Pineapple Hill in Kapalua, call 669-4884; **Kenai Helicopter**, which leaves from Kaanapali at 661-4427; **Awesome Maui Helicopter** at 661-8889; **Maui Helicopter Adventures**, located at the Intercontinental Hotel in Wailea, at 879-1601. All tours are narrated over specially designed earphones, and all helicopter companies will make special arrangements to drop off and pick up campers in remote areas.

Ken Schmitt

Hiking Tour

This special Maui tour is a one-man show operated by an extraordinary man. It's called **Hike Maui**, and as its name implies, it offers walking tours to Maui's best scenic areas accompanied by Ken Schmitt, a professional nature guide. Ken has dedicated years to hiking Maui and has accumulated an unbelievable amount of knowledge about this awesome island. He's proficient in Maui archaeology, botany, geology, anthropology, zoology, history, oceanography, and ancient Hawaiian cosmology. Moreover, he is a man of dynamic and gracious spirit who has tuned in to the soul of Maui. He hikes every day and is superbly fit, but will tailor his hikes for anyone, though good physical conditioning is essential. Ken's hikes are actually workshops in Maui's natural history. As you walk along, Ken imparts his knowledge but he never seems to intrude on the beauty of the site itself.

His hikes require a minimum of two people and a maximum of six. He offers RT transportation from your hotel, gourmet breakfasts, lunches, and snacks with an emphasis on natural health foods. All special equipment, including snorkel gear and camping gear for overnighters, are provided. His hikes take in sights from Hana to West Maui and to the summit of Haleakala, and range from the moderate to the hardy ability level. Half-day hikes last about 5 hours and all-day hikes go for at least 12 hours. The rates vary from $45 (about half for children) to $85. Overnighters are on a sliding scale, by number of people and number of days, but start at $190. A day with Ken Schmitt is a classic outdoor experience. Don't miss it! Ken has an office at the Passport Ocean Safari Shop, Kealia Beach Center, 101 N. Kihei Rd., Kihei, tel. 879-5270. Mailing address is **Hike Maui**, Box 10506, Lahaina, Maui, HI 96761.

OCEAN TOURS

You haven't really seen Maui unless you've seen it from the sea. Tour boats operating out of Maui's harbors take you fishing, whale watching, dining, diving, and snorkeling. You can find boats that offer all of these, or just sail you around for pure pleasure. Many take day-trips to "The Pineapple Island" Lanai, or to Molokai with a visit to Kalaupapa Leper Colony included. Many visit Molokini, a submerged volcano with only half the crater rim above water, that has been designated as a Marine Life Conservation District. The vast majority of Maui's pleasure boats are berthed in Lahaina Harbor and most have a booth right there on the wharf where you can sign up. Other boats come out of Maalaea with a few companies based in Kihei. If you're interested in snorkeling, scuba, fishing, sailing, water or jet skiing, parasailing, sailboarding, or being captain on your own sail boat, see "Sports" below.

The Boats

The following are general tour boats that offer a variety of cruises. The ***Lin Wa*** is a glass-bottom boat that's a facsimile of a Chinese junk. One of the tamest and least expensive tours out of Lahaina Harbor, it departs six times a day from slip #3 and charges $9.50 adults and $4.50 children. It gives you a tour just off Maui's shore and even goes for a whale watch in season. It's little more than a sea-going carnival ride. Call the *Lin Wa,* 661-3392, and remember that it's very popular. The ***Coral Sea*** (tel. 661-8600) is more of the same only it's a bit larger and offers a snorkel/picnic tour. For $39 (children half price) it provides equipment, lunch, and an open bar. It's in slip #1 Lahaina Harbor.

the Lin Wa

Trilogy Excursions, tel. 661-4713, is operated by the Coon Family. They run two trimarans: the 50-foot *Trilogy* and the 40-foot *Kailana,* which carries up to 35 passengers to Lanai. For $85 you get breakfast, then fish and snorkel on your way to Lanai. Once there you anchor in Manele Bay and after a tour of the island you come back to an excellent barbecue. An all-day affair, it provides a sampling of Maui's ocean activities.

Windjammer Cruises, tel. 667-6834, offers similar trips to Lanai aboard their 65-foot, three-masted schooner. They pack in over 100 passengers and on weekends feature a lunch at the Hotel Lanai in place of the barbecue. **Seabird Cruises,** tel. 661-3643, takes day-trips to Lanai or Molokai for $59. Over 100 passengers fit aboard their two 65-foot catamarans, *Aikane II* and *Ono Mana.* They also run the 65-foot *Viajero* that carries 35 passengers. They feature a Kalaupapa Tour on Molokai. Seabird Cruises also offers a sunset cocktail sail for $22 and a snorkel-and-dinner sail for $32. **Unicorn Tours,** tel. 879-6333, takes 50 passengers on *Unicorn I* to Lanai or Molokai on half-day excursions or to both on full-day trips. Prices are $36 to Lanai, $56 to Molokai, and $80 for both. Food and island tours are included. **Captain Nemo's Emporium,** tel. 661-5555, located on Front Street, sails *Seasmoke,* a 58-foot catamaran (built for James Arness and reported to be the fastest "cat" on the island) to Lanai on a snorkel and diving run. They leave at 8:00 a.m. and return at 2:00 p.m. and serve breakfast and lunch for $65.

These companies also have dinner sails, cocktail sails, and whale watches for much cheaper prices, but they tend to pack them in so tight that they're known derisively as "cattle boats." Don't expect the personal attention you'd receive on smaller boats. However, all the boats going to Molokai or Lanai will take passengers for the OW trip. You won't participate in the snorkeling or the food, but the prices (negotiable) are considerably cheaper. This extra service is offered only if there's room. Talk to the individual captains.

Sunset Cruises

These romantic cruises are very popular and are available from many boats. They last for about two hours and cost $20-30 for the basic cruise. If cocktails or dinner is added the price goes up. **Alihilani Yacht Charters,** tel. 661-3047, sails out of Lahaina at sunset on its teak and mahogany 40-foot yacht for $25. They also trip to Lanai for $52 and take you snorkeling for $40. **Kaulana Cruises,** tel. 667-2518, offers a dinner sail for $32 and a cocktail sail for $20 (children half price) on its 70-foot catamaran. They also sail a picnic/snorkel to Lanai. **Scotch**

Mist, tel. 661-0386, has two racing yachts, *Scotch Mist I* and *II.* They are the oldest sailing charters on Maui (1970) and claim to be the fastest sailboats in the harbor: boasting the lightest boat, the biggest sail, and the best crew. They'll cruise, snorkel (varying prices), or take their 19 passengers on a sunset sail complete with champagne for $33 or $25, depending on which boat.

Out of Kihei you might try the **Maui Sailing Center,** tel. 879-5935, which takes six passengers on its Cal 27 for a full-day snorkel/sail to Molokini departing from Maalaea harbor. From Wailea's Ulua Beach you can board the 65-foot *Wailea Kai* catamaran along with 90 others for a picnic/snorkel outing to Molokini. They also offer a popular dinner sail. Contact **Ocean Activities Center**, tel. 879-4485. From Kaanapali the **Sea Sails** makes an evening dinner sail from its anchorage at the Sheraton Beach. Contact **Sea Sport Activities Center** at 667-2759.

Whale Watching

Anyone on Maui from November to April gets the added treat of watching humpback whales as they frolic in their feeding grounds just off Lahaina, one of the world's major wintering areas for the humpback. Almost every boat in the harbor runs a special whale watch during this time of year. A highly educational whale watch is sponsored by the **Pacific Whale Foundation,** located in Kihei at Azeka Plaza, tel. 879-6530. A non-profit organization dedicated to the study and preservation of the whale, their extremely popular three-hour whale watch takes place only on Sundays aboard *Aikane II,* operated by **Seabird Cruises**, tel. 661-3643.

If you're at all interested in whales, visit **Greenpeace** at 628 Front St., Lahaina, tel. 667-2059. Here, Doug Duncan, the office manager, is full of enthusiasm and information about whales. Greenpeace has an educational video on whales, and can book you on a wide variety of whale watching cruises. It costs no more to book through **Greenpeace** and part of your ticket price becomes a tax-deductible donation to the **"Save The Whales"** campaign. Since Lahaina Harbor is an attraction in itself, just go there and stroll along to hand-pick your own boat. Many times the whale watch is combined with a snorkel and picnic sail so prices vary accordingly. Two of the cheapest are aboard the *Lin Wa* and the *Coral Sea.* Others include the *Mareva,* tel. 661-4522, berthed in slip #63. This 38-foot sloop will take you out for a half-day whale watch for $30. *The Kamehameha* is a 15-foot catamaran for snorkeling or whale watching at $17. This "cat" is in slip #67, tel. 661-4522.

If Lahaina is too frenetic for your tastes, head for Kihei where you can get a boat out of Maalaea. Try booking through **The Dive Shop,** tel. 879-5172. They might book you on the *Maui Diamond,* skippered by Capt. Dave Ventura, berthed in Maalaea Harbor; you couldn't make a better choice of sporting boat. Book through the Dive Shop or through Capt. Dave directly, tel. 879-9119, For further information on whales, see p. 332-333.

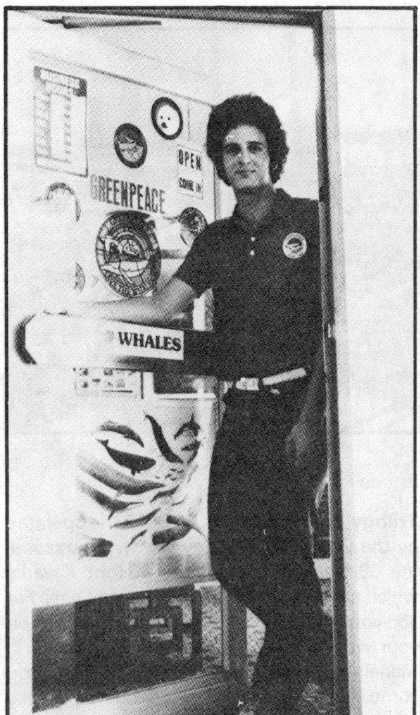

Doug Duncan of Greenpeace

ACCOMMODATIONS

With over 12,000 rooms available, and more being built every day, Maui is second only to Oahu in the number of visitors it can accommodate. There's a tremendous concentration of condos on Maui, plenty of hotels, and a growing number of bed and breakfast inns. Camping is limited to a handful of parks, but what it lacks in number it easily makes up for in quality.

Tips

Maui has an **off-season**, like all of Hawaii, which runs from after Easter to just before Christmas, with the fall months being particularly beautiful. During this period you can save 25% or more on accommodations. If you'll be staying for over a week, get a condo with cooking facilities or a room with at least a refrigerator; you can save a bundle on food costs. You'll pay more for an ocean view, but along Maui's entire south shore from Kapalua to Wailea, you'll have a cheaper and cooler room if you're mountainside, away from the sun.

Your Choices

Over 80 hotels and condos have sprouted on West Maui from Kapalua to Lahaina. The most expensive are in **Kaanapali** and include the Hyatt Regency, Marriott, Maui Surf and Sheraton, strung along some of Maui's best beaches. The older condos just west in Honokawai are cheaper, with a mixture of expensive and moderate as you head toward Kapalua. **Lahaina** itself offers only a handful of places to stay: condos at both ends of town, and the famous non-luxury Pioneer Inn. Most people find the pace a little too hectic, but you couldn't get more in the middle of *it* if you tried. **Maalaea Bay,** between Lahaina and Kihei, has over 20 quiet condos and a few hotels. Prices are reasonable, the beaches are fair, and you're in striking distance of the action in either direction.

Kihei is "condo row," with over 50 of them along the six miles of Kihei Ave., plus a few hotels. This is where you'll find top-notch beaches and the best deals on Maui. **Wailea** just up the road is expensive, but the hotels here are world class and the secluded beaches are gorgeous. **Kahului** often takes the rap for being an unattractive place to stay on Maui. It isn't all that bad. You're smack in the middle of striking out to the best of Maui's sights, and the airport is minutes away for people staying only a short time. Prices are cheaper and Kanaha Beach is a sleeper, with great sand, surf, and few visitors. **Hana** is an experience in itself. You can camp, rent a cabin, or stay at an exclusive hotel. Always reserve in advance and consider splitting your stay on Maui, spending your last few nights in Hana. You can really soak up this wonderful area, and you won't have to worry about rushing back along the Hana Highway. Bed and breakfast inns are available on Maui (see p. 153-154).

CAMPING

A major aspect of the "Maui experience" is found in the simple beauty of nature and the outdoors. Visitors come to Maui to luxuriate at resorts and dine in fine restaurants, but everyone heads for the sand and surf, and most are captivated by the lush mountainous interior. What better way to savor this natural beauty than by hiking slowly through it or pitching a tent in the middle of it? Maui offers a full range of hiking and camping, and what's more, most of it is easily accessible and free. Camping facilities are located near many choice beaches and amid the most scenic areas of the island. They range in amenities from full housekeeping cabins to primitive "hike in" sites. Some restrictions to hiking apply because much of the land is privately owned, so you may need advance permission to hike. But plenty of public access trails along the coast and deep into the interior would fill the itineraries of even the most intrepid trekkers. If you enjoy the great outdoors on the Mainland, you'll be thrilled by these "mini-continents," where in one day you can go from the frosty summits of alpine wonderlands, down into baking cactus-covered deserts, and emerge through jungle foliage onto a sun-soaked subtropical shore.

Note

Descriptions of individual state parks, county beach parks, and Haleakala National Park, along with directions on how to get there, are given under "Sights" in the respective travel chapters.

Haleakala National Park

Camping at Haleakala National Park is free. Permits are not needed to camp at Hosmer Grove, just a short drive from Park Headquarters, or at Oheo Stream Campground (formerly Seven Sacred Pools) near Kipahulu, along the coastal road 10 miles south of Hana. Camping is on a first-come, first-served basis, and there's an official three-day stay limit, but it's a loose count, especially at Oheo which is almost always empty. The case is much different at the campsites located inside Haleakala crater proper. On the floor of the crater are two primitive tenting campsites, one at Paliku on the east side and the other at Holua on the north rim. For these you'll need a wilderness permit available from Park Headquarters. Because of ecological considerations, only 25 campers per night can stay at each site, and a three-night, four-day maximum stay is strictly enforced, with tenting allowed at any one site for only two nights. However, because of the strenuous hike involved, campsites are open most of the time. You must be totally self-sufficient, and equipped for cold weather camping to be comfortable at these two sites.

Also, Paliku, Holua, and another site at Kapalaoa on the south rim offer cabins. Fully self-contained with stoves, water, and nearby pit toilets, they can handle a maximum of 12 campers each. Cots are provided, but you must have your own warm bedding. The same maximum-stay limits apply as in the campgrounds. Staying at these cabins is at a premium—they're popular with visitors and residents alike. They're geared toward the group with rates at $2 per person, but there is a $6 minimum for a single. To have a chance at getting a cabin you must make reservations, so write well in advance for complete information to: Haleakala National Park, Box 537, Makawao, HI 96768, tel. 572-9306. For general information write: National Park Service, 300 Ala Moana Blvd., Honolulu, HI 96850, tel. 546-7584.

State Parks

Ten state parks on Maui are managed by the Department of Land and Natural Resources, through their Division of State Parks. These

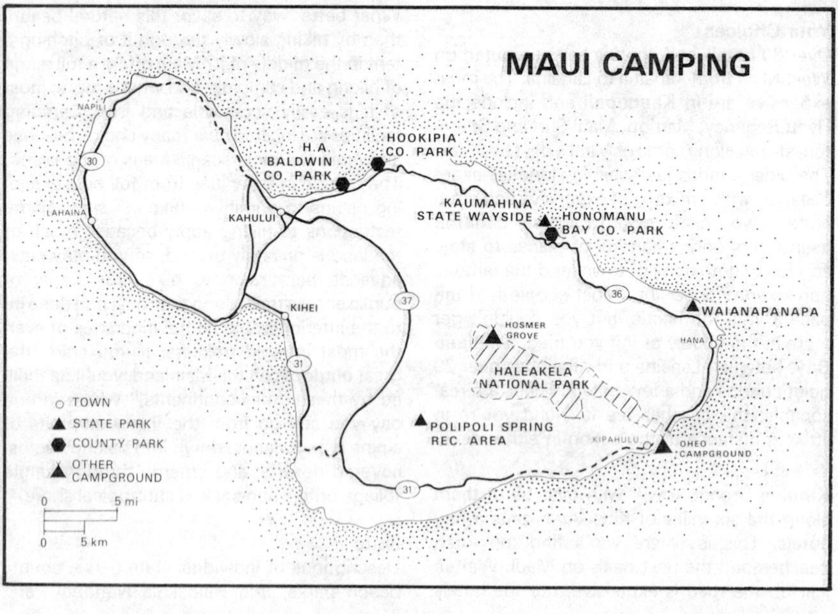

facilities include everything from historical sites to wildland parks accessible only by trail. Some are only for viewing, some are restricted to day use, and three of them have overnight camping. Poli Poli and Wainapanapa offer free tenting, or self-contained cabins are available on a sliding fee; reservations highly necessary. At the other, Kaumahina, tent camping is free. Permits are required at all, and RVs are technically not allowed. For general park rules, see p. 166-167.

Housekeeping cabins are available as indicated in "accommodations" listings. As with camping, permits are required with the same five-day maximum stay. Reservations are absolutely necessary, especially at Wainapanapa, and a 50 percent deposit at time of confirmation is required. A three-day cancellation requirement is necessary for refunds, and payment is to be made in cash, money order, certified check, or personal check; the latter must be received 30 days before arrival so that cashing procedures are possible. The balance is due on date of arrival. Cabins are on a sliding scale of $10 single, $14 double, and about $5 for each person thereafter. These are completely furnished down to the utensils, with heaters for cold weather, and private baths.

Permits can be reserved two months in advance by writing a letter including your name, address, phone number, number of persons in your party, type of permit requested, and duration of your stay. They can be picked up on arrival with proof of identification. Office hours are 8:00 a.m. to 4:15 p.m., Mon. to Friday. Usually, tent camping permits are no problem to secure on the day you arrive, but reserving insures you a space and alleviates anxiety. The permits are available from the Maui (Molokai also) Division of State Parks, 54 High St., Wailuku, 96793, tel. 244-4354; or write Box 1049 Wailuku, HI 96793.

County Parks

Fifteen county parks are scattered primarily along Maui's coastline, and because of their locations, are generally referred to as **beach parks**. Most are for day use only, where visitors fish, swim, snorkel, surf, picnic, and sunbathe, but three have overnight camping. The rules governing use of these parks are just about the same as those for state parks. The main difference is that along with a use permit, county beach parks charge a fee for overnight use. Again, the differences between individual parks are too numerous to mention, but the majority have a central pavilion for cooking, restrooms and cold water showers, individual fire pits, and picnic tables, with electricity usually only at the central pavilion. RVs are allowed to park in appropriate spaces.

Fees And Permits

The fees are quite reasonable at $1 per night per person, children $.50. One safety point to consider is that beach parks are open to the general public and most are used with regularity. This means that quite a few people pass through, and your chances of encountering a hassle or running into a rip-off are slightly higher in beach parks. To get a permit and pay your fees for use of a county beach park, either write in advance, or visit the following issuing office, open 9:00 a.m. to 5:00 p.m., Mon. through Friday. County Parks Department, War Memorial Gym, Baldwin High School, Rm. 102, Route 32, Wailuku, HI 96793, tel. 244-5514.

HIKING

The hiking on Maui is excellent, most times you have the trails to yourself, and the wide possibility of hikes range from a family saunter to a strenuous trek. The trails are mostly on public lands with some crossing private property. With the latter, the more established routes cause no problem, but for others you'll need special permission.

Haleakala Hikes

The most spectacular hikes on Maui are through Haleakala Crater's 30 miles of trail. **Halemauu Trail** is 10 miles long, beginning three miles up the mountain from Park Headquarters. It quickly winds down a switchback descending 1,400 feet to the crater floor. It passes Holua Cabin and goes six more miles to Paliku Cabin, offering expansive views of Koolau Gap along the way. A spur leads to Sliding Sands Trail with a short walk to the Visitors Center. This trail passes Silversword Loop and the Bottomless Pit, two attractions in the crater. **Sliding Sands Trail** might be considered the main trail, beginning from the Visitor Center at the summit and leading 10 miles over the crater floor to Paliku Cabin. It passes Kapaloa cabin en route and offers the best walk through the crater, with up-close views of cinder cones, lava flows, and unique vegetation. **Kaupo Gap Trail** begins at Paliku Cabin and descends rapidly through the Kaupo Gap, depositing you in the semi-ghost town of Kaupo. Below 4,000 feet the lava is rough and the vegetation thick. You pass through the private lands of the Kaupo Ranch along well-marked trails. Without a "pick up" arranged at the end, this is a tough one because the hitching is scanty.

West Maui Mountains

West Maui Trails

The most frequented trails on West Maui are at Iao Needle. From the parking area you can follow the **Tableland Trail** for two miles, giving you beautiful panoramas of Iao Valley as you steadily climb to the tableland above, or descend to the valley floor and follow Iao Stream to a series of small but secluded swimming holes. **Waihee Ridge Trail** is a three-mile trek leading up the windward slopes of the West Maui Mountains. Follow Rt. 34 around the backside to Maluhia Rd. and turn up it to the Boy Scout Camp. From here the trail rises swiftly to 2,560 feet. The views of Waihee Gorge are spectacular. **Kahakuloa Valley Trail** begins from this tiny forgotten fishing village on Maui's backside along Rt. 34. Start from the schoolhouse passing burial caves and old terraced agricultural sites. Fruit trees line the way to trails ending two miles above the town.

Kula And Upcountry Trails

Most of these trails form a network through and around Poli Poli State Park. **Redwood Trail,** 1.7 miles, passes through a magnificent stand of redwoods, past the ranger station, and down to an old CCC camp where there's a rough old shelter. **Tie Trail,** one-half mile, joins Redwood Trail with **Plum Trail,** so named because of its numerous plum trees, which bear during the summer. **Skyline Trail,** 6.5 miles, starts atop Haleakala at 9,750 feet, passing through the southwest rift and eventually joining the **Haleakala Ridge Trail,** 1.6 miles, at the 6,500-foot level, then descends through a series of switchbacks. You can join with the Plum Trail or continue to the shelter at the end. Both the Skyline and Ridge trails offer superb vistas. Others throughout the area include: **Poli Poli,** .6 miles, passing through the famous forests of the area; **Boundary Trail,** 4 miles, leading from the Kula Forest Reserve to the ranger's cabin, passing numerous gulches still bearing native trees and shrubs; **Waiohuli Trail** descends the mountain to join Boundary Trail and overlooks Keokea and Kihei with a shelter at the end; **Waiakoa Trail,** 7 miles, begins at the Kula Forest Reserve Access Road. It ascends Haleakala to the 7,800-foot level and then descends through a series of switchbacks. It covers rugged territory and passes a natural cave shelter. It eventually meets up with **Waiakoa Loop Trail,** 3 miles. All of these trails offer intimate views of native, introduced forests, and breathtaking views of the Maui coastline far below.

Coastal Trails

Along Maui's southernmost tip the **King's Highway Coastal Trail,** 5.5 miles, leads from

La Perouse Bay through the rugged and desolate lava flow of 1790, the time of Maui's last volcanic eruption. Kihei Rd. leading to the trail gets extremely rugged past La Perouse and should not be attempted by car, but is easy on foot. It leads over smooth stepping stones that were at one time trudged by royal tax collectors. The trail heads inland and passes many ancient Hawaiian stone walls and stone foundation building sites. Spur trails lead down to the sea, including a view of Cape Hanamanioa and its Coast Guard lighthouse. The trail eventually ends at private land. **Hana Wainapanapa Coastal Trail,** 3 miles, is at the opposite side of East Maui. You start from Wainapanapa State Park or from a gravel road near Hana Bay and again you follow the flat, laid stones of the "King's Highway." The trail is well maintained but fairly rugged due to lava and cinders. You pass natural arches, a string of *heiau,* blowholes and caves. The vegetation is lush and long fingers of black lava stretch out into cobalt blue waters.

Guides And Books

Those who would rather not hike alone, or who desire a full and rewarding educational experience, should consider tramping with Ken Schmitt's **Hike Maui** (see p. 344). For a well-written and detailed hiking guide, complete with maps, check out *Hiking Maui* by Robert Smith, published by Wilderness Press, 2440 Bancroft Way, Berkeley, CA 94704.

FOOD

If you love to eat, you'll love Maui. Besides great fish, there's fresh beef from Maui's ranches and fresh vegetables from the highlands. The cuisines offered are as cosmopolitan as the people: Polynesian, Hawaiian, Italian, French, Continental, Mexican, and Oriental.

Restaurants

Four five-star restaurants on Maui are: **The Planatation Veranda** at the Kapalua Bay Hotel, **The Swan Court** at the Hyatt Regency, **La Perouse** at the Maui Intercontinental Wailea, and **Raffles** at Stouffer's Wailea Resort. You won't be able to afford these every day, but for that one-time blow out, take your choice.

Great "early-bird specials" are offered at the **Moana Terrace** at Kaanapali's Marriott, the two **Island Fish Houses** in Kahului and Kihei, and at **Leilani's** in the Whalers Village. Also, **Kihei Prime Rib House** offers some dandy specials.

For more moderate fare, try these no-atmosphere restaurants that'll fill you up with good food for "at home" prices: **Ma Chan's** in the Kaahumanu Shopping Center; **Hat's Restaurant** in the Maui Mall and in Paia (especially the $2 breakfast); **Kitada's** in Makawao for the best bowl of *saimin* on the island. For great sandwiches try: **Philadelphia Lou's** in Kahului and Kihei; and the snack bars at all of the island's health food stores, especially **Paradise Fruit Co.** in Kihei.

Great Mexican vegetarian food at **Polli's Restaurant** in Kihei and Makawao, and both **La Famiglia's** in Kaanapali and Kihei have a great happy hour, complete with free chips and salsa. **Longhi's** in Lahaina is well established as a gourmet cosmopolitan/Italian restaurant, and **Mama's Fish House** in Paia receives the highest compliment of being a favorite with the locals. **Piero's** in Paia serves good Italian food and has "open mike" evenings with the best of island color. **Robaire's** is an expensive but authentic French restaurant in Kihei; the breakfast at the Maui Surf's **Eight Bells Restaurant** can't be beat. **Erik's Seafood Grotto** in Kahana is good value, and **Leilani's** and the **Rusty Harpoon** are up-and-comers in the Whaler's Village. The *luau* at the **Maui Lu Hotel** in Kihei is a classic, and the **Maui Beach Hotel** in Kahului has a decent buffet.

Markets

If you're shopping for general food supplies and are not interested in gourmet or specialty items including organic foods, you'll save money by shopping at the big-name supermarkets, located in Lahaina, Kahului, and Kihei, often in malls. Smaller towns have general stores which are adequate, but a bit more expensive. You can also find convenience items at commissaries in many condos and hotels, but these should be used only for snack foods or when absolutely necessary, because the prices are just too high.

The greatest number of supermarkets is found in Kahului. They're all conveniently located along Rt. 32 (Kaahumanu Ave.) in three malls, one right after the other. **Foodland,** open 7 days 8:30 a.m. to 10:00 p.m., is in the **Kaahumanu Shopping Center.** Just down the road in the **Kahului Shopping Center** is the ethnic **Ah Fooks** (open 7 days, 8:00 a.m. to 7:00 p.m., closes early Sat. and Sun.), specializing in Japanese, Chinese, and Hawaiian foods. Farther along in the **Maui Mall** is **Star Market**, open 7 days, 8:30 a.m. to 9:00 p.m., 7:00 p.m. Sunday. Just behind the Maui Mall on E. Kamehameha Ave. is a **Safeway.** Wailuku doesn't have shopping malls, but if you're taking an excursion around the top of West Maui, make a "last chance" stop at **T.K. Supermarket** at the end of N. Market Street in the Happy Valley area. They're open 7 days, but close early on Sunday afternoons.

In Kihei you've got a choice of three markets, all strung along S. Kihei Road, the main drag. **Foodland** in the Kihei Town Center, or **Star Market** just down the road, offer standard shopping. The most interesting is **Azeka's Market** in Azeka Plaza. This market is an institution, and is very famous for its specially prepared (uncooked) ribs, perfect for a barbecue. In Wailea you'll find **Wailea Pantry** in the Wailea Shopping Village, open 7 days, 8:00 a.m. to 7:00 p.m., but it's an exclusive area and the prices will make you sob.

In Lahaina you can shop at **Foodland** in Lahaina Square, just off Rt. 30. More interesting is **Nagasako's** in the Lahaina Shopping Center, just off Front Street. They've got all you need, plus a huge selection of Chinese and Japanese items. Nagasako's is open 7 days, 8:00 a.m to 8:00 p.m., 9:00 p.m. Fri. and 5:00 p.m. Saturday. Just west of Lahaina in Honokawai, you'll find the **Honokawai Superette**. Although a few sundry stores are in various hotels in Kaanapali, this is the only real place to shop. It's open 7 days, 8:00 a.m. to 9:00 p.m. In Napili, pick up supplies at **Napili Village Store,** a bit expensive, but well stocked and convenient. In Olowalu, east of Lahaina, you can pick up some limited items at the **Olowalu General Store.**

In Hana you have the legendary **Hasegawa's General Store**. They have just about everything, and are geared toward standard American selections. Hasegawa's is open 7 days, 7:30 a.m. to 6:00 p.m., and 9:00 a.m. to 3:30 p.m. Sunday. Also in Hana is the **Hana Store**, which actually has a better selection of health foods and imported beers. Open 7 days, 7:30 a.m. to 6:00 p.m.

Another store where you might pick up supplies is **Komoda's** in **Makawao**. They're famous throughout Hawaii for their cream buns, which are sold out by 8:00 a.m. At **Pukalani Superette** in Pukalani, open 7 days, you can pick up supplies and food-to-go including *sushi.* In Paia try **Nagata's** or **Paia General Store** on the main drag. In Kaupakulua you have **Hanzawa's**, a "last chance" store on the back road (Rt. 365) from Hana to Haleakala.

Health Food

Those into organic foods, fresh vegetables, natural vitamins, and take-out snack bars have it made on Maui. At many fine health food stores you can have most of your needs met. Try the **Down to Earth,** in Wailuku; it's an excellent health food store complete with vitamins, bulk foods, and a snack bar. This Krishna-oriented market, on the corner of Central and Vineyard, is open 7 days, 8:00 a.m. to 6:00 p.m., 5:00 p.m. Sat., 4:00 p.m. Sun. **Lahaina Natural Foods** is at the far end of Front Street, towards Kaanapali. Open 7 days, they're a full-service health food store, featuring baked goods and Herbalife vitamins. **Paradise Fruit Company** on S. Kihei Road is terrific. It's not strictly a health food store, but does have plenty of wholesome items. Their food bar is the best. They're open 24 hours, everyday. You can't go wrong! **Tradewinds Natural Foods** in Paia is a full-service health food market. They're open 7 days, 7:00 a.m. to 8:00 p.m.; shorter Sun. hours. You can pick up whatever you need for your trip to Hana. **Maui Natural Foods** in the Maui Mall in Kahului is open 7 days and has a fair selection of fresh foods with a big emphasis on vitamins. **The Silversword Bakery** and the little store right there have a limited but terrific selection of baked goods and natural foods. Many items are on consignment from local kitchens. They're at the Silversword Inn in Kula.

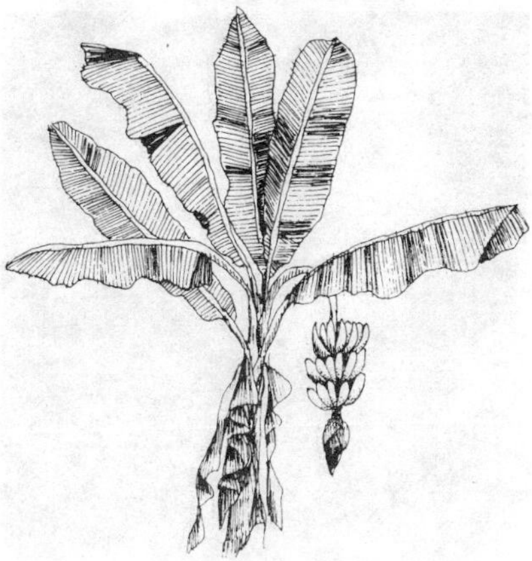

common banana

Fresh Fruit And Fish
What's Maui without its fruits, both from the vine and from the sea? For fresh fish try the Fish Market at **Maalaea Harbor**. They get their fish right from the boats, but they do have a retail counter. In Kihei along S. Kihei Road (just west of Azeka Place), some enterprising fishermen set up a roadside stand whenever they have a good day. Look for their coolers propping up a sign. **Lahaina Fishery** in the Lahaina Shopping Center has a wide selection and reasonable prices. For fresh fruits and vegetables try **The Farmers' Market**. Gardeners bring their fresh Kula vegetables to makeshift roadside markets on Mon. in Lahaina at Front and Baker Streets; on Wed. in Napili close to the Napili Kai, and Fri. in Kihei along Kihei Road. Signboards mark the spot. All along the road to Hana are little fruit stands tucked away. Many times no one is in attendance and the very reasonably priced fruit is paid for on the honor system.

Shopping
This section will provide general information for shopping on Maui for general merchandise, books, arts and crafts, and specialty items. Specific shops are listed in the "Sights" section of this chapter. This should be enough to get your pockets twitching and your credit cards smoldering! Happy bargain hunting!

Shopping Malls
Those who enjoy one-stop shopping will be happy with the choices in Maui's various malls. You'll find regularly known department stores as well as small shops featuring island-made goods. The following are Maui's main shopping malls.

Along Kaahumanu Ave., you'll find **Kaahumanu Mall**, the largest on the island. Here's everything from **Sears** and **Liberty House** to **Sew Special**, a tiny store featuring island fabrics. You can eat at numerous restaurants, buy ice cream cones, and browse for reading material in the **Book Cache**. Here too is **Village Cinema**, and **Idini's Deli** with a fine selection of wine and spirits. Down the road is **Maui Mall**, featuring photo centers, **M J S Music** with a huge selection of island favorites, and the **Cycle and Sport Shop** for your outdoor needs. Sandwiched between these two modern facilities is **Kahului Shopping Center**. It's definitely "down home" with old-timers sitting around outside. The shops here aren't fancy, but they are authentic and you can make some off-beat purchases by strolling through.

Lahaina has the best shopping on Maui in various little shops strung out along Front Street (see "Shopping" in the Lahaina section). The following are the local malls: **The Wharf** on Front Street has a multitude of eating establishments, as well as stores and boutiques in its multi-level shopping facility. Some of the more interesting stores include **The Royal Art Gallery**, **Ecology House**, and the **Woodpecker**, all featuring distinctive artworks and novelty items. When you need a break, get a coffee at **Upstart Crow Bookstore**, great selections and a top-notch snack bar. **Lahaina Market Place**, tucked away on Front Street, features established shops along with open-air stalls. **Lahaina Shopping Center** between Rt. 30 and Front Street has various shops, but check out Cliff McQueen at the **Wizard of Aah's** where you can eat an organic frozen yogurt while talking sports in this combo yogurt-tennis shop. **Whalers' Village** is a Kaanapali mall which features a decent open-air, self-guided museum as you walk around. There are various eateries, bottle shops, **The Book Cache** and a cinema. It's a great place to stroll, buy, and learn a few things about Maui's past. The **Sheraton** and **Marriot Hotel** both have shopping, but the best is at the **Hyatt Regency**. You'll need a suitcase stuffed with money to buy anything, but it's a blast just walking around the grounds and checking out the big-ticket items.

Azeka Place is just along Kihei Road. There's food shopping, a **Liberty House, Mediterranean House,** a dive shop, and activities center along with others. **Wailea Shopping Village** has a wide assortment of boutiques in this exclusive mall just near the Intercontinental and Stouffer's Resorts.

Specialty Items

Some truly nifty and distinctive stores are wedged in among Maui's run-of-the-mill shopping centers, but for real treasures you'll find the solitary little shop the best. Lahaina's Front St. has the greatest concentration of top-notch boutiques, but others are dotted here and there around the island. The following is only a sampling of the best; many more are listed in the individual chapters.

Along Hana Road, the **Maui Crafts Guild** is an exemplary crafts shop that displays the best in local island art. All artists must be selected by active members before their works can be displayed. All materials used must be natural, with an emphasis on those found only in Hawaii. The Guild grew from a great idea originated by **Touchstone Ceramics,** which is still located around back. A wide variety of handcrafted items, open 7 days, 10:00 a.m. to 5:30 p.m. It's located on Rt. 36, on the left as you enter Paia from the west heading toward Hana. **The Shell Stop!** is located near mile marker 18 along the Hana Highway. It's in an agricultural area—the taro patches of Wailuanui, to be exact—so no signs are allowed along the highway. The Shell Stop! is owned by Anna Kapuana. Here, three Hawaiian families gather *opihi,* whose flesh they send to Oahu, but whose shells they fashion into distinctive jewelry. All shells used are from Hawaii, no imports from the S. Pacific and Philippines. Check "Hana Highway" for exact directions.

Makawao is known for rodeos and cowboys; you'll find both, and some good shopping, too! Along Makawao Avenue check

Lovely handmade opihi *jewelry is found at the Shell Stop! in Wailua.*

out: Dana, Peter, or Lyn at **Upcountry Downunder,** importers of top-quality New Zealand woolens, crafts, and fleece products. Just down the street is **Makawao Leather and Gift Shop** where you can buy custom-made, tooled leather products. Across the street is **Outdoor Sports,** basically outdoor outfitters with a western flair. If you've ever wanted to visit a general store from out of a cowboy movie, this is the place. If new purchases don't excite you, see Peter at **Grandma's Attic.** Browse through *Life* Magazines from the '40s, or spin a few records on the old Victrola.

Near Kahului visit the **Pink and Black Coral Factory**. Local craftsmen make distinctive coral jewelry from the amazing corals found under Maui's seas. Divers lose their lives yearly while harvesting these fantastic corals. **Maui Swap Meet** at Maui County Fairgrounds, in Kahului off Puunene Avenue (Hwy. 35); open every Sat. 8:00 a.m to 1:00 p.m. Admission $.50. Great junk! In Wailuku, check out two odd little shops on Market Street: **Maui Wholesale Gold** and **Treasure Imports,** adjacent to each other. They deal in eelskin artifacts from belts to briefcases.

You can't beat Lahaina's Front Street for shopping, with great little shops lined shoulder to shoulder. The following are some good ones: **High as a Kite** sells kites and other delights. **Vagabond** for backpacks, daypacks, beach bags, and T-shirts. **Lahaina Scrimshaw Factory,** touristy but still terrific; great scrimshaw from $.50 baubles to works of fine art. **Jade and Jewels** offers rubies, emeralds, sapphires, ivory sculptures, and brass work from India; great stuff, but costly. **Waterfront Gallery and Gifts,** has lovely jewelry with ocean and Hawaiian motifs, and great models of tall-masted ships that'll thrill kids of all ages. **Tropical Boutique** sells *batik* apparel from Indonesia. **Silks of Lahaina,** on the far end of Front St. heading east, sells top-quality designer silks for women. **Skin Deep Tattooing** if you want to be your own indelible souvenir from Maui. On Lahainaluna Street, they specialize in Polynesian and "new age" primal tattoos.

SPORTS AND RECREATION

Maui won't let you down when you want to go outside and play. More than just a giant sandbox for big kids, its beaches and surf are warm and inviting, and there are all sorts of water sports from scuba diving to parasailing. You can fish, hunt, camp, or indulge yourself in golf or tennis to your heart's content. The hiking is marvelous and the horseback riding along beaches and on Haleakala is some of the most exciting in the world. The information offered in this chapter is merely an overview to let you know what's available. Specific areas are covered in the travel sections. Have fun!

Since your island is blessed with 150 miles of coastline, over 32 of which is wonderful beach, your biggest problem is choosing which one you'll grace with your presence. The following should help you choose just where you'd like to romp about.

Southwest Maui Beaches

The most and best beaches for swimming and sunbathing are on the south coast of West Maui, strung along 18 glorious miles from Kapalua to Olowalu. For an all-purpose beach you can't beat **Kapalua Beach** (Fleming Beach) on Maui's western tip. It has everything: safe surf (except in winter), great swimming, snorkeling, and bodysurfing in a first-class, family-oriented area. Then comes the Kaanapali beaches along Rt. 30, bordered by the hotels and condos. All are open to the public and "rights of way" pass just along hotel grounds. **Black Rock** at the Sheraton is the best for snorkeling. Just east and west of Lahaina are **Lahaina Beach,** convenient but not private; **Launiupoko and Puamana Waysides** with only fair swimming, but great views and grassy beaches. **Olowalu** has very good swimming beaches just across from the General Store, and **Papalaua Wayside** offers seclusion on a narrow beach fringed by *kiawe* trees that surround tiny patches of white sand.

Kihei And Wailea Beaches

The 10 miles stretching from the west end of Kihei to Wailea are dotted with beaches that range from poor to excellent. **Kihei Beach** extends for miles from Maalaea to Kihei. Excellent for walking and enjoying the view, but little else. **Kamaole Beach Parks I, II and III** are at the east end of Kihei. Top-notch beaches, they have it all—swimming, snorkeling, and safety. **Keawakapu** is more of the same. Then comes the great little beaches of Wailea that get more secluded as you head east: Mokapu, Ulua, Wailea, and Polo. All are surrounded by the picture-perfect hotels of Wailea and all have public access. Makena Beach, down an unpaved road east from Wailea, is very special. It's one of the island's best beaches. At one time, alternative people made Makena a haven and it still attracts free-sprited souls. There's nude bathing here in secluded coves, unofficial camping, and freedom. It gets the highest compliment when locals, and those staying at hotels and condos around Maui, come here to enjoy themselves.

Wailuku And Kahului

Poor ugly ducklings! There are shallow, unattractive beaches in both towns and no one spends any time there. However, **Kanaha Beach** between Kahului and the airport isn't bad at all. **Baldwin Beach Park** has the reputation of hostile locals protecting their turf, but the beach is good and you won't be hassled if you "live and let live." **Hookipa Beach** just west of Paia isn't good for the average swimmer but it is the "sailboarding capital" of Hawaii, and you should visit here just to see the exciting, colorful spectacle of people skipping over the ocean with bright sails.

Hana Beaches

Everything about Hana is heavenly, including its beaches. There's **Red Sand Beach,** almost too pretty to be real. **Wainapanapa** is surrounded by the state park and good for swimming and snorkeling, even providing a legendary cave whose waters turn blood red. **Hana Bay** is well protected and safe for swimming. Farther along at **Oheo Stream** (Seven Sacred Pools) you'll find the paradise you've been searching for—gorgeous freshwater pools at the base of wispy waterfalls and fronted by a tremendous sea of pounding surf only a few yards away.

Freshwater Swimming

The best place for swimming is in various stream pools on the road to Hana. One of the very best is **Twin Falls,** up a short trail from Hoolawa Bridge. **Helio's Grave** (marked) is another good swimming spot between Hana and Oheo Stream, which are excellent themselves, especially the upper pools. Also, you can take a refreshing dip at Iao Valley stream when you visit Iao Needle.

SNORKELING AND SCUBA

Maui is as beautiful from under the waves as it is above. There is world-class snorkeling and diving at many coral reefs and beds surrounding the island. You'll find the best, coincidentally, just where the best beaches are: mainly from Kihei to Makena, up around Napili Bay and especially from Olowalu to Lahaina. Backside Maui is great (but mostly for experts), and for a total thrill, try diving Molokini, the submerged volcano, just peeking above the waves and designated Marine Life Conservation district.

Great Underwater Spots

These are some of the best on Maui, but there are plenty more (see "Sights" in individual sections). Use the same caution when scuba diving or snorkeling as when swimming. Be mindful of currents. It's generally safer to enter the water in the center of a bay than at the sides where rips are more likely to occur. The following sites are suitable for beginners to intermediates: on Maui's western tip **Honolua Bay,** a Marine Life Conservation District; nearby **Mokuleia Bay,** known as "Slaughterhouse," but gentle; in Kaanapali you'll enjoy **Black Rock** at the Sheraton Hotel; at **Olowalu,** very gentle with plenty to see; also try **Kamaole Parks II and III** in Kihei and Ulua, and Polo and Wailea beaches in Wailea. Under no circumstances should you miss taking a boat out to Molokini. It's worth every penny!

For **scuba divers,** there are underwater caves at **Nahuna Point** ("Five Graves") between Wailea and Makena, great diving at Molokini, magnificent caves out at the **Lanai Cathedrals** and a sunken Navy sub, the USS *Bluegill,* to explore. Advanced divers *only* should attempt the backside of West Maui, the Seven Sacred Pools and beyond Pu'uiki Island in Hana Bay.

Equipment

Sometimes condos and hotels have snorkeling equipment free for their guests, but if you have to rent it, don't do it from a hotel or condo, but go to a dive shop where it's much cheaper. Expect to spend $7 a day for mask, fins, and snorkel. Scuba divers can rent gear for about $30 from most shops. In Lahaina rent from: **American Dive Maui,** 628 Front, tel. 661-4885; **Central Pacific Divers,** 780 Front, tel. 661-8718; **Hawaii Reef Divers,** 129 Lahainaluna, tel. 667-7647; **Scuba Schools,** 1000 Limahana, tel. 661-8036. In Kihei: an excellent all-around shop is **The Dive Shop,** 1975 S. Kihei Rd., tel. 879-5172; **Maui Dive Shop,** Azeka Pl., tel. 879-3388; **Maui Sailing Center,** at the Kealia Beach Center, tel. 879-6260. You might also consider renting an underwater camera. Expect to spend $12-15, including film.

Scuba Certification

A number of Maui companies take you from your first dive to PADI, NAUI, or NASDS certification. Prices range from $40 for a quickie refresher dive up to around $200 for a 4- to 5-day certification course. Courses or arrangements can be made with any of the dive shops listed above.

Snorkel And Scuba Excursions
Many boats will take you out snorkeling or diving. Prices range from $30 (half day, 4 hours) to $60 (full day, 8 hours), check "Getting Around/Ocean Tours" for many of the boats that do it all, from deep-sea fishing to moonlight cruises. All of the "activities centers" can arrange these excursions for no extra charge, check "Getting Around/Sightseeing Tours" for names and numbers. For an excellent scuba/snorkel excursion, try **The Dive Shop** in Kihei at tel. 879-5172, where you might be lucky enough to go with Capt. Dave Ventura on the *Maui Diamond.* **Snorkeling Hawaii** in downtown Lahaina, tel. 661-8156, has reasonable rates ($16, half day) including equipment, instruction, and hotel pickup. **Sea Safari Travel**, 2770 Highland Ave., Manhattan Beach, CA 90266, even offers a seven-night package for scuba divers to Maui.

World-class Instructor
With a name like **Chuck Thorne,** what else can you expect but a world-class athlete of some kind?! Well, Chuck is a diver who lives on Maui. He's written *The Divers' Guide to Maui,* the definitive book on all the best dive/snorkel spots on Maui. Chuck has a one-man operation, so unfortunately, he must limit his leadership and instruction to advanced divers only. People have been known to cancel flights home to dive with Chuck, and he receives the highest accolades from other watermen. You can buy his book at many outlets or write: Maui Dive Guide, P.O. Box 1461, Kahului, HI 96732. You can contact Chuck through **The Dive Shop,** tel. 879-5172, or at 879-7068.

MORE WATER SPORTS

For great **bodysurfing** try: Ulua, Wailea, Polo or Makena Beaches, the north end of Kamaole Beach Park I in Kihei, Napili Bay, and Baldwin Park. For **surfing** try: Lower Paia Park, Napili Bay, Baldwin Park, Maalaea, and Hookipa Beach. For surfing lessons: **Nancy Emerson,** Maui's surfing champion in Lahaina at tel. 244-3728, $40 private, $25 group.

Sailboarding
This is one of the world's newest sports, and unlike surfing which tends to be male-dominated, women, too, are excellent at surfboarding. Hookipa Beach, just east of Paia, is the "sailboarding capital of the world," and the **O'Neill International Championship** is held here every year in March and April. To rent boards and to take instructions, try: **Maui Sailing Center** at Kealia Beach Center, N. Kihei Rd., tel. 879-5935. You can rent here for $15 an hour or $60 a day. Lessons are extra; **Sail-**

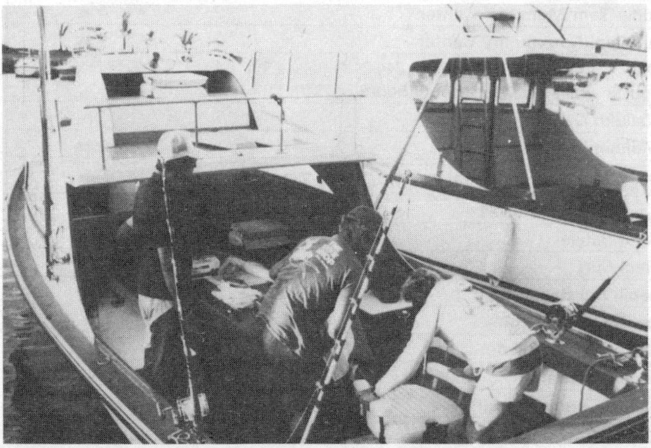

the Maui Diamond *preparing to go after the big ones*

boards Maui, 247 Kaahumanu Ave., Kahului, tel. 877-6882. $25 half day, $35 full. Remember—start with a big board and a small sail! Take lessons to save time and energy.

Jet Skis

To try this exciting sport, contact: **Kaanapali Jet Ski**, at Whaler's Village, tel. 667-7851; **Jamin Jet Skis**, in Kihei, tel. 242-4339.

Parasailing

To rise above it all call **Lahaina Para Sail**, 628 Front St., tel. 661-4887.

Waterskiing

Again, the **Maui Sailing Center**, or **Rainbow Custom Water Sports**, where you can also arrange just about anything dealing with water, at tel. 661-3980.

Sailing

The most popular day sails are from Maui to Molokai or Lanai (fully discussed in "Getting Around/Ocean Tours"). Your basic half-day snorkel and swim sail will be $35. For serious sailors, some top-notch boats in Lahaina Harbor are open for lengthy charters. Try: **Alihilani Yacht Charters**, at Lahaina Harbor; **Mareva**, tel. 667-7013; **Scotch Mist**, tel. 661-0368.

Deep-sea Fishing

The waters around Maui are extremely bountiful. Deep-sea fishing on a **share basis** is approximately $50 half day (4 hours) and $80 full

TENNIS COURTS OF MAUI

COUNTY COURTS

Under jurisdiction of the Dept. of Parks & Recreation, 200 High St., Wailuku, Maui Hi 96793. Phone: 244-7750.

Courts listed are in or near visitor areas. There are 3 additional locations around the island.

* Courts on state land, under state jurisdiction.

Name & Location of Courts		No. of Courts	Lighted
Hana	**Hana Ball Park**	2	Yes
Kahului	**Kahului Community Center**	2	Yes
Kihei	**Kalama Park**	2	Yes
Kihei	***Fronting Maui Pacific Shores**	2	No
Lahaina	**Lahaina Civic Center**	2	Yes
Lahaina	**Malu-ulu-olele Park**	4	Yes
Makawao	**Eddie Tam Memorial Center**	2	Yes
Pukalani	**Pukalani Community Center**	2	Yes
Wailuku	**Maui Community College**/Ph. 244-9181 **Courts available after school hours**	4	No
Wailuku	**Wailuku Community Center**	7	Yes
Wailuku	**Wailuku War Memorial**	4	Yes
HOTEL & PRIVATE COURTS—OPEN TO PUBLIC			
Lahaina	**Maui Marriott Resort**	5	No
Kihei	**Maui Sunset**	2	No
Kaanapali	**Maui Surf**	3	No
Napili Bay	**Napili Kai Beach Club**	2	No
Kaanapali	**Royal Lahaina Hotel**	11	6
Kaanapali	**Sheraton Maui Hotel**	3	Yes
Kapalua	**Tennis Garden**	10	No
Wailea	**Wailea Tennis Center**	14	3

day. On a **private basis,** expect $250 half day, $400 full day. Some of the best boats include: ***Maui Diamond,*** tel. 879-9119; ***Reel Hooker,*** tel. 572-0202; ***Blue Max,*** a real beauty, tel. 244-3259 or 878-6585; in Lahaina you can't go wrong with the ***Judy Ann,*** tel. 667-6672; **Aerial Sportfishing,** tel. 667-9089.

HORSEBACK RIDING

Those who love sightseeing from the back of a horse are in for a big treat on Maui. Stables dot the island, so you have a choice of terrain for your trail ride: a slow canter along the beaches of West Maui, a breathtaking ride through Haleakala Crater, or a backwoods ride out at the Seven Sacred Pools. Unfortunately, none of this comes cheap. In comparison, a bale of alfalfa, which goes for under $5 on the Mainland, fetches $18-22 on Maui. If you plan to do some serious riding, it's advisable to bring jeans (jogging suit bottoms will do) and a pair of boots, or at least jogging shoes.

GOLF COURSES OF MAUI

Course	Par	Yards	Fees Weekday	Fees Weekend	Cart
Makena Golf Course 161 Makena Dr., Makena HI 96779 tel. 879-3344	72	6262	$18.00		$10.00
Wailea Golf Club—Blue Course 161 Wailea Ike Place, Wailea, HI 96713 tel. 879-2966	72	6327	$30.00		$10.00
—Orange Course (Wailea Golf Club)	72	6405	$30.00		$10.00
Royal Kaanapali Beach Golf Course—South Course Kaanapali Beach, Lahaina, HI 96761 tel. 661-3691	72	6250	$30.00		$12.00
—North Course (Royal Kaanapali Golf Course)	72	6305	$30.00		$12.00
Kapalua Golf Club—Village Course 300 Kapalua Dr., Lahaina, HI 96761 tel. 669-8044	71	6194	$40.00		$10.00
—Bay Course (Kapalua Golf Club)	72	6180	$40.00		$10.00
Walehu Municipal Golf Course P.O. Box 507, Walehu, HI 96753 tel. 244-5433	36	6367	$10.00	$15.00	$10.00
Maui Country Club ★ ● 48 Nonohe Pl., Paia, HI 96779 tel. 877-0616	72	3148	$18.00		$6.00
Pukalani Country Club 55 Pukalani St., Pukalani, HI 96788 tel. 572-1314	72	6570	$7.00		$8.00

★ = *9 hole course* ■ = *no club rental* ● = *guests only*

Rick, the top hand at the Rainbow Ranch

The Rainbow Ranch
One of the best stables on Maui is run by Rick, a Canadian cowboy, who arrived here about 10 years ago. You'll have your choice of rides: beginners ride daily at 9:00 a.m., $15, gentle horses; beach ride (very popular) daily, 4:00 p.m., $40, experienced riders; beach and mountain, through pineapple fields, extended ride, experienced riders, $55; picnic rides, b.y.o., 10:30 a.m. to 2:00 p.m., $40; BBQ, 10:30 a.m. to 2:00 p.m., great food, $55. The Rainbow Ranch is also starting a mini rodeo, and Rick has a few pair of rubber boots that he'll lend for free to those lacking proper footwear. No dress code, but no thongs please. **Rainbow Ranch,** P.O. Box 712, Lahaina 96761, tel. 669-4991, the ranch is located at mile marker 29 along Rt. 30 towards Kapalua.

Oheo Riding Stables
These stables, out near the Seven Pools (Hana), are the best riding bargain on the island. Greg, the local-born owner, will take you up to the pools and waterfalls of Kipahulu Valley for $10 per hour (average ride, two hours). He knows the best spots, and his sure-footed horses are specially mountain trained. Just past the Oheo Gulch Campground, tel. 248-7722.

Moomuku Stables
Recently opened, these stables provide unique beach rides and overnight camping at La Perouse Bay. Just past Polo Beach in Wailea on the road to Makena. You can't go wrong with these local cowpokes who have an old-fashioned love and respect for the land, tel. 879-0244.

Haleakala And Environs
A few upcountry companies offer trail rides through the crater or over the mountain. Wear *warm* clothes! Here are some of the best: **Haleakala Outfitters & Guides** offers an all day-ride (9:30 a.m. to 3:30 p.m.) featuring a journey across the face of Haleakala Crater $125. Full-day trip includes picnic lunch. Write c/o Maui Island Tours, P.O. Box 247, Kahului 96732, tel. 877-5581. **Charley's Trailride and Pack Trips** takes you overnight camping in Haleakala, arranging for cabins and supplying all meals. Run by Charles Aki, c/o Kaupo Store, Hana 96713, tel. 248-8209. **Pony Express Tours** offers rides through Halekala with very experienced guides, who give a full narration of the area. Lunch provided. Full day $110, partial $75. Write Pony Express P.O. Box 507, Makawao 96768, tel. 667-2202. **Thompson Riding Stables** guides you over the slopes of Haleakala on one of Maui's oldest cattle ranches. Write Thompson Stables, Thompson Rd., Kula 96790, tel. 878-1910.

Adventures On Horseback
Offers a three-day, two-night horseback camping trip. Everything provided, $1500 for two. Also, waterfall rides from Hana $85, tel. 242-7445.

Kau Lio Stables
Just near Lahaina, they offer two-hour rides leaving at 8:30 and 11:30 a.m. and at 2:30 p.m., $33 including snack. They're located on private land, so they'll pick you up in Kaanapali. Write P.O. Box 16056, Kaanapali Beach, 96761, tel. 667-7869.

MAUI INFORMATION

Emergency
To summon the police, fire department, or ambulance to any part of Maui, dial 911. This help number is available throughout the island. **Helpline,** the island's crisis center, is 244-7407. **Maui Memorial Hospital,** Kaahumanu Ave., Kahului, tel. 244-9056. **Pharmacies:** Kahului, 877-0041; Kihei, 879-1951; Lahaina, 661-3119; Pukalani, 572-8244.

Information
The State operates a **Visitors' Kiosk** at Kahului Airport. Open seven days, 6:00 a.m. to 9:00 p.m., tel. 877-6413, plenty of practical brochures. **Hawaii Visitors Bureau,** 26 N. Puunene Ave., Kahului, tel. 877-7822. Open Mon. to Fri. 8:00 a.m. to 4:30 p.m. **Chamber of Commerce,** Kahului Shopping Center, tel. 877-0425; **Consumer Complaints,** tel. 244-7756. **Time,** 242-0212.

Reading Material
For bookstores try: **The Book Cache** in Kahului at the Kaahumanu Mall, tel. 877-6836, and in Kaanapali at the Whalers Village, tel. 661-3259; **Waldenbooks,** Maui Mall, Kahului, tel. 877-0181; **Upstart Crow,** at The Wharf, Front St., Lahaina, tel. 667-9544. **Libraries,** main branch at 251 High St., Wailuku, tel. 244-3945, other branches in Kahului, Lahaina, Makawao, and Hana. Hodge-podge of hours during the week, usually closed Fri. or Saturday.
Free tourist literature is well done and loaded with tips, discounts, maps, happenings, etc. Found everywhere, in hotels, restaurants, and street stands. They include: ***This Week Maui,*** every Friday; ***Guide to Maui*** on Thursdays; ***Maui Beach Press,*** newspaper format and in-depth articles, every Friday; ***Maui Gold,*** one for each season; ***Drive Guide,*** excellent maps and tips, given out free by all car rental agencies, bi-monthly; ***The Bulletin,*** a TV guide with feature articles and local events; ***Maui News,*** local newspaper, 25 cents, Mon. to Friday.

Parks And Recreation
State Parks in Wailuku, tel. 244-4345; County Parks in Wailuku, tel. 244-5514; Haleakala Natl. Park H.Q., tel. 527-7749.

Weather And Whales
For all Maui weather, tel. 877-5111; for recreational areas, tel. 877-5124; for Haleakala, tel. 572-7749; for marine weather, tel. 877-3477; for whale sighting and reports in season, tel. 661-8527.

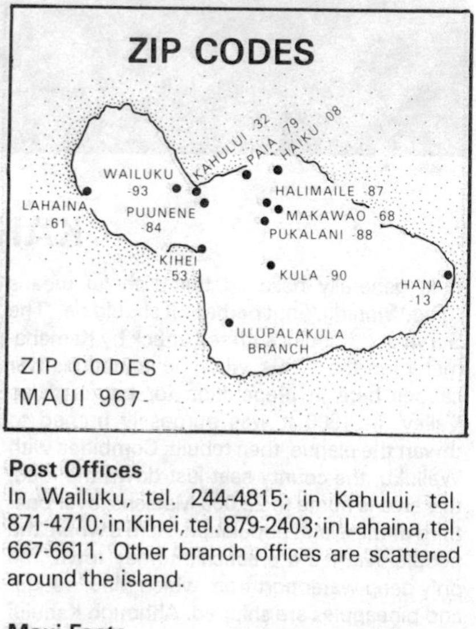

Post Offices
In Wailuku, tel. 244-4815; in Kahului, tel. 871-4710; in Kihei, tel. 879-2403; in Lahaina, tel. 667-6611. Other branch offices are scattered around the island.

Maui Facts
Maui is the second youngest and second largest Hawaiian island after Hawaii. Its nickname is The Valley Island. Its color is pink and its flower is the *lokelani,* a small rose.

KAHULUI

It is generally believed that Kahului means "The Winning," but perhaps it should be "The Survivor." Kahului suffered attack by Kamehameha I in the 1790s, when he landed his war canoes here in preparation for battle at Iao Valley. In 1900 it was purposely burned to thwart the plague, then rebuilt. Combined with Wailuku, the county seat just down the road, this area is home to 22,000 Mauians, over one-third of the island population. Here's where the people live. It's a practical, homey town, the only deep-water port from which Maui's sugar and pineapples are shipped. Although Kahului was an established sugar town by 1880, it's really only grown up in the last 20 years. In the 1960s, Hawaiian Commercial and Sugar Co. began building low-cost housing for its workers which became a model development for the whole of the U.S. Most people land at the airport, blast through for Lahaina or Kihei, and never give Kahului a second look. It's in no way a resort community, but it has the best general purpose shopping on the island, a few noteworthy sites, and a convenient location to the airport.

SIGHTS

Kanaha Pond Wildlife Sanctuary

This one-time royal fishpond is 1½ miles northwest of the airport at the junction of SR Rt. 36 and 37. It's on the migratory route of various ducks and Canadian geese, but most importantly it is home to the endangered Hawaiian stilt *(ae'o),* and the Hawaiian coot *('alae ke'oke'o).* The stilt is a 16-inch-tall, slender bird with a black back, white belly and stick-like pink legs. The coot is a gray-black duck-like bird, which builds large floating nests. An observation shelter is maintained along Rt. 396 (just off Rt. 36). Kanaha Pond is always open and free of charge. Bring binoculars.

Maui Community College

Just across the street from the Kaahumanu Shopping Center on Rt. 32, this is a good place to check out the many bulletin boards for various activities, items for sale and cheaper long-term housing. The **Student Center** is conspicuous as you drive in, and is a good place to get most information. The library is adequate. For those interested in a hot shower, go to the gymnasium and act like you belong. Try not to bring your backpacks, but lockers are available.

Maui Zoo And Botanical Gardens
These grounds are more aptly described as a children's park. Plenty of young families enjoy themselves in this fenced-in area. The zoo houses various colorful birds such as cockatoos, peacocks and macaws, as well as monkeys, baboons, and a giant tortoise that looks like a slow-moving boulder. The chickens, ducks, and swans are run-of-the-mill, but the ostriches, over 7 feet tall, are excellent specimens. With pygmy goats and plenty of sheep, the atmosphere is like a kiddies' petting zoo. It's open daily 9:00 a.m. to 4:00 p.m., free. Turn at the red light onto Kanaloa Avenue off Rt. 32 about midway between Kahului and Wailuku. At this turn is also **Wailuku War Memorial.** Here, too, is a gymnasium and free hot showers.

H. C. & S. Sugar Mill
Tours are given at the mill every Tues. and Thurs. during harvest. Follow Puunene Road (Rt. 350) off Kaahumanu Avenue to Puunene Town, and look for the mill on your left.

Kanaha Beach Park
This is the only beach worth visiting in the area. Good for a swim and a picnic. Follow Rt. 36 towards the airport. Turn left on Keolani Place and left again on Kaa Street.

ACCOMMODATIONS

Kahului features motels instead of hotels since most people are short-term visitors, heading to or from the airport. These accommodations are all bunched together across from the Kahului Shopping Center on the harbor side of Kaahumanu Avenue (Rt. 32). The best are the **Maui Beach Hotel,** tel. 877-0051, and just across a parking lot, its sister hotel, **The Maui Palms,** tel. 877-0071. Both are owned by Hawaiian Pacific Resorts, an excellent hotel group. The Maui Beach has a pool on the second floor, and its daily buffet is good value. The central courtyard, tastefully landscaped, is off the main foyer, which has a Polynesian flavor. The Red Dragon Room provides the only disco (weekends mostly) on this part of the island. For reservations, call (800) 367-5004; inter-island (800) 272-5275. The 2 other hotels, within 100 yards, are the **Maui Hukilau,** tel. 877-3311 and **Maui Seaside,** tel. 877-3311. Both are part of the Sand and Seaside Hotels, an island-owned chain. For reservations, call (800) 367-7000. Except for the Maui Palms, which is about $10 cheaper, all of the above hotels are in the same price range and begin at $50 single.

FOOD

The Kahului area has some elegant dining spots as well as an assortment of inexpensive yet good eating establishments. Here are some of the best.

Inexpensive
Ma Chan's is a terrific little "no atmosphere" restaurant in the Kaahumanu Shopping Center (Kaahumanu Ave.) offers Hawaiian, American, and Asian food—breakfast, lunch, or dinner. Order the specials, such as the shrimp dinner, and for under $4 you get soup, salad, grilled

a Matson Liner in Kahului's active port

shrimp, rice, and garnish. No credit cards, friendly island waitresses, and good quality; tel. 877-7818.

Hats is located in the Maui Mall (Kaahumanu Ave.), tel. 877-6475 (also in Paia). This little no-frills restaurant serves up excellent platters from a variety of cuisines for under $4. Open daily 8:00 a.m. to 9:00 p.m. Especially good breakfast for only $2 including eggs, home fries, breakfast meats, juice, and coffee.

At counter seating in the back of **Toda Drugs**, locals go to enjoy daily specials of Hawaiian and other ethnic foods. Better than you'd think! Daily special under $4. In the Kahului Mall, open daily 8:30 a.m. to 4:00 p.m., tel. 877-4550.

Back-easterners will love **Philadelphia Lou's**, an authentic hoagie (submarine) sandwich shop. A little expensive at $5 per sandwich, but those babies are loaded and really man-sized. Two people could feed off one. In the Kahului Mall on the Lono Avenue side. Open weekdays 7:00 am. to 11:00 p.m., weekends until 2:00 a.m., Sun. til 11:00 p.m., tel. 871-8626. Free ice for coolers with picnic purchase.

Others worth trying include **Shirley's** and **Dairy Queen**, next door to each other across Lono Avenue from Philadelphia Lou's. Both serve good and inexpensive plate lunches and sandwiches, and Shirley's is open early mornings. **Aloha Restaurant** on Puunene Avenue near the Kahului Mall is open daily serving

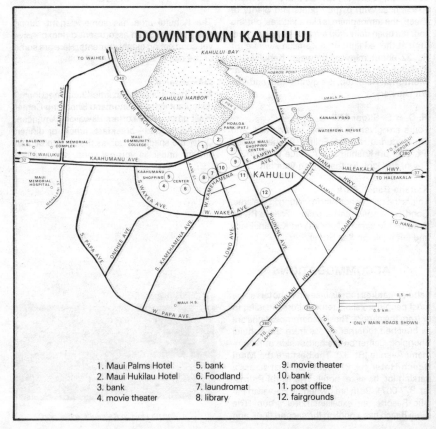

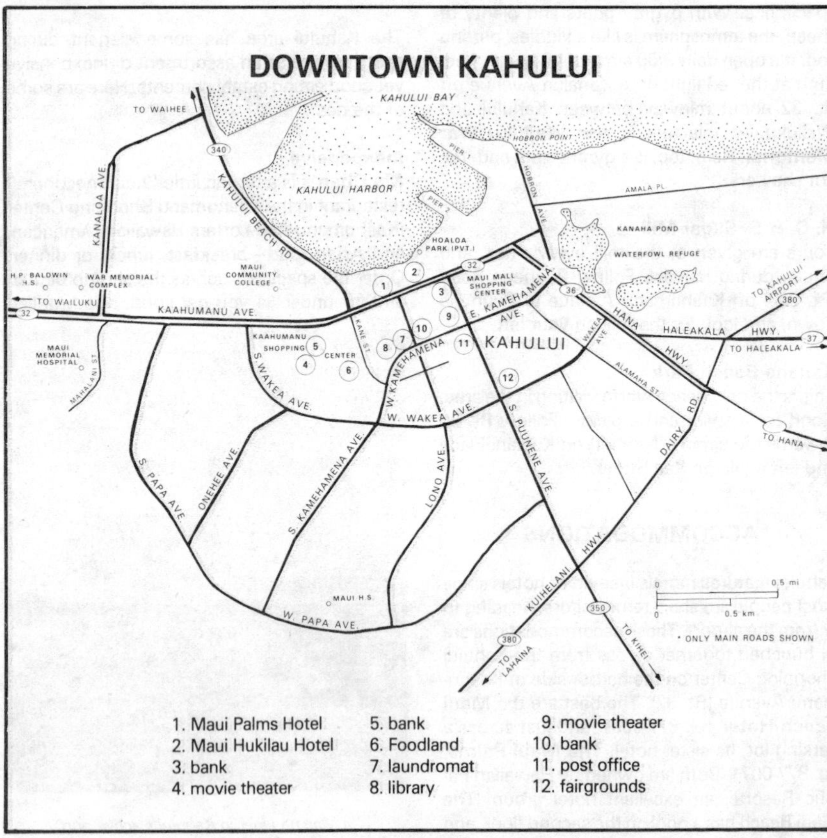

Hawaiian food at cheap prices. Tel. 877-6318.

Finally, for those who need their weekly fix of something fried and wrapped in styrofoam, Kahului's main streets are dotted with McDonald's (Puunene Ave.), Pizza Hut (Kamehameha Ave.), Burger King (Kaahumanu Ave.), and Kentucky Fried Chicken (Wakea St.).

Moderate

The **Maui Beach Hotel** serves good food in the second floor dining room. You can fill up here at their lunch buffet from 11:30 a.m to 2:00 p.m., $6.50 ($5.50 salad bar only), or come for dinner from 5:30 to 8:30 p.m. (except Mon.) for their "Ten Course Chinese Dinner," offered for a very reasonable $9.95 ($5.25 children under 11). Prime rib and seafood dinners are also served. Breakfast (from 7:00 a.m.) features fresh-baked goods from $5.75. For reservations, tel. 877-0051.

Maui Palms Hotel specializes in an authentic "Japanese Imperial Buffet Dinner," every day except Sun. from 5:30 to 8:30 p.m. $9.95. On Sundays an exemplary Hawaiian buffet is offered (same time, price). All-you-can-eat salad bar daily for lunch 11:00 a.m to 1:00 p.m., $6. Excellent sampling of these two island cuisines, tel. 877-0071.

At **Ming Yuen,** for under $7 you can dine on sumptuous Chinese treats such as oysters with ginger and scallions. The hot and sour soup ($4.50) is almost a meal in itself. Inexpensive lunch from 11:00 a.m to 2:00 p.m., dinner 5:00 to 9:00 p.m. Behind the Maui Mall at 162 Alamaha St., off E. Kamehameha Avenue. Cantonese and Szechuan specialties. Reservations suggested, tel. 871-7787.

Vi's Restaurant is at the Maui Hukilau Hotel. Breakfast from 7:00 to 9:45 a.m., dinner 6:00 to 8:45 p.m. Over 20 dinners under $6. Breakfast "special" is adequate but not special, tel. 877-3311.

In the Kaahumanau Mall try: **Guacamole's,** a Mexican restaurant with a cozy atmosphere featuring wall tapestries. A bit costly for Mexican starting at $6; **Apple Annie's** is good for their daily lunch and dinner specials under $4, but overpriced on other items on menu. **The Pizza Factory** down the road in the Maui Mall is owned by Apple Annie's and serves up decent pizza, but not at bargain prices. Little Annie might have a worm in her apples! **Olga's Wayang** in the Kaahumanu Mall serves vegetarian and Indonesian food, tel. 871-4605. **Barrio Fiesta Restaurant** in the Maui Mall specializes in Filipino delicacies opens at 7:00 a.m., tel. 871-7938.

Expensive

The Chart House, on Kahului Bay at 500 N. Puunene Ave. (also in Lahaina), is a steak and seafood house that's not really expensive. This is a favorite with businessmen and travelers in transit to or from the airport. The quality is good and the atmosphere is soothing. Open for dinner daily 5:30 to 10:00 p.m., tel. 877-2476.

Island Fish House is the only really elegant restaurant in Kahului. In the Kahului Building at 333 Lono Ave, they specialize in serving island fish prepared 7 different ways. Open for lunch with slightly cheaper prices. Expect to spend $15 and up per person for dinner, tel. 877-7225.

Liquor

Maui Wine and Liquor at 333 Dairy Rd. (out near the airport) is an excellent liquor store. They have an enormous wine selection, over 80 different types of imported beer, and even delivery service, tel. 871-7006. **Idini's** in the Kaahumanu Mall has a good selection of wine and beer and a top-notch deli offering picnic packages, tel. 877-3978. For a quick stop at a basic bottle shop try **Party Pantry** on Dairy Rd. or at the Maui Beach Hotel.

ENTERTAINMENT

Red Dragon Disco at the Maui Beach Hotel is the only disco and dance spot on this side of

Maui Beach Hotel

the island. Open Fri. and Sat. from 10:00 p.m. to 2:00 a.m. Reasonable dress code and cover charge.

Pizza Factory in the Maui Mall offers live music on Tues. and Wed. evenings. This large warehouse-looking building has fair acoustics, and is also the home of "Rudolph, the Red-Nosed Moose."

Maui Palms Hotel hosts the "Sakuras" every weekend. They specialize in "oldies," and their large repertoire includes "top 40," country, and even Hawaiian and Japanese ballads. Good for listening and dancing!

Village Cinema, tel. 877-6622, is at the Kaahumanu Mall, and **The Maui Theater**, tel. 877-3560, is at the Kahului Mall. In addition, legitimate theater is offered by the **Maui Community Theater**, tel. 877-6712, at the Kahului Fairgrounds. Major productions occur 4 times a year.

SERVICES AND INFORMATION

Shopping

Because of the 3 malls right in a row along Kaahumanu Avenue, Kahului has the best all-around shopping on the island. Here you can find absolutely everything you might need (see "Shopping" in the Introduction). Don't miss the **flea market** at the fairgrounds on Puunene Street every Saturday. You can also shop almost the minute you arrive or just before you leave at 3 touristy but good shops along Airport Road. At the **Little Airport Shopping Center** at the first stop sign from the airport is **Factory Tees and Things** and **Airport Flower and Fruit.** Almost next door is the **Pink and Black Coral Factory.** When Airport Road turns into Dairy Road you'll find **Floral Hawaii.** Both floral and fruit shops can provide you with produce that's pre-inspected and admissible to the Mainland. They also have a large *lei* selection which can be packed to go. The T-shirt stores offer original Maui designs and custom shirts, and The Coral Factory makes distinctive Maui jewelry on the premises.

Services

There are 2 **Banks of Hawaii**, tel. 871-8220, on Puunene Street. **Bank of Maui**, tel. 871-6284, is at Kahului Mall. **City Bank**, tel. 871-7761, is at Kaaahumanu Mall. And find **First Hawaiian Bank**, tel. 877-2311, at 20 W. Kaahumanu Avenue.

Post Offices: The Kahului P.O. is on Puunene Ave. (Rt. 350) just across the street from the Fairgrounds; tel. 871-4710.

The library, at 90 School St., has irregular hours. tel. 877-5048.

Laundromats: The Washhouse is open daily 5:00 a.m. to 10:00 p.m. at 74 Lono Ave., tel. 877-6435. Clean and has a moneychanger. **W & F Washerette** features video games to while away the time, 125 S. Wakea, tel. 877-0353.

tree snail

WAILUKU

Often, historical towns maintain a certain aura long after their time of importance has passed. Wailuku is one of these. Today Maui's county seat, you feel that it also used to be important. Wailuku earned its name, which means "Bloody Waters," from a ferocious battle fought by Kamehameha I against Maui warriors just up the road in Iao Valley. The slaughter was so intense that over 4 miles of the local stream literally ran red with blood. Last century the missionaries settled in Wailuku, and their architectural influences, such as a white-steepled church and the courthouse at the top of the main street, give an impression of a New England town.

Wailuku is a pretty town, especially in the back streets. Built on the rolling foothills of the West Maui Mountains, this adds some character—unlike the often flat layout of many other Hawaiian towns. You can "do" Wailuku in only an hour, though most people don't even give it this much time. They just pass through on their way to Iao Needle, where everyone goes, or to Happy Valley and on to Kahakuloa, around the backside, where the car companies hope that no one goes. You *can* see Wailuku's sights from the window of your car, but don't shortchange yourself this way. Definitely visit the **Bailey House,** now called **Hale Hoikeike,** and while you're out, walk the grounds of **Kaahumanu Church**. Market Street, just off Main, has a clutch of intriguing shops that you can peek into while you're at it.

SIGHTS

Kaahumanu Church

It's fitting that Maui's oldest existing stone church is named after the resolute but loving Queen Kaahumanu. This rock-willed woman is the "Saint Peter" of Hawaii, upon whom Christianity in the islands was built. She was *the* most important early convert, often attending services in Kahului's humble grass hut chapel. In 1832 an adobe church was built on the same spot and named in her honor. Rain and time washed it away, to be replaced by the island's first stone structure in 1837. In 1876 the church was reduced to about half its original size, and what remained is the white-and-green structure we know today. Oddly enough, the steeple was repaired in 1984 by the Skyline Engineers who hail from Massachusetts, the same place from which the missionaries came 150 years earlier! You can see the church sitting there on High Street (Rt. 30), but it's usually closed during the week. Sunday services are at 9 a.m., when the Hawaiian congregation sings the Lord's praise in their native language. An excellent cultural and religious event to attend!

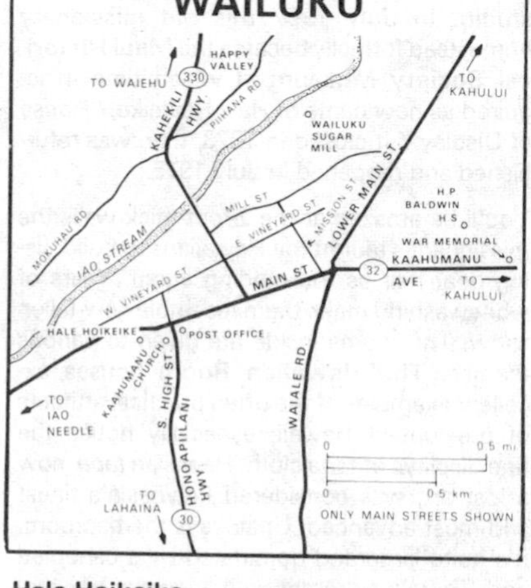

Hale Hoikeike

This is the old **Bailey House,** built from 1833-1850, with various rooms added throughout the years. In the 1840s it housed the "Wailuku Female Seminary," of which Edward Bailey was principal until it closed in 1849. Bailey then went on to manage the Wailuku Sugar Company. More importantly for posterity, he became a prolific painter of various landscapes around the island. Most of his

whitewash and stone interior of Hale Hoikeike

paintings record the period from 1866 through 1896. These paintings are now displayed in the "annex," known as the Bailey Gallery. This one-time seminary dining room was his actual studio. In July 1957 this old missionary homestead formally became the **Maui Historical Society Museum** at which time it acquired its new name of Hale Hoikeike, "House of Display." It closed in 1973, then was refurbished and reopened in July 1975.

You'll be amazed at the 2-foot-thick walls the missionaries taught the Hawaiians to build, using goat hair as the binding agent. Years of whitewashing make them resemble new-fallen snow. The rooms inside are given to various themes. **The Hawaiian Room** houses excellent examples of the often practical artifacts of pre-contact Hawaii; especially notice the fine displays of *tapa* cloth. Hawaiian *tapa,* now a lost art, was considered Polynesia's finest and most advanced. Upstairs is the bedroom. It's quite large and dominated by a canopied bed. There's a dresser with a jewelry box and fine lace gloves. Also, notice the display of Hawaiian *papales* (hats). Traders brought them, and the intrigued Hawaiians soon rendered their own versions in a wide variety of local materials. Peek beind the wooden gate in the rear of the bedroom: swords, dolls, walking canes, toys, and muskets—now only a jumble, one day they'll be a display. Upstairs at the front of the house is the old office. Here you'll find roll-top desks, ledgers, and excellent examples of old-time wicker furniture, prototypes of examples you still see today. Downstairs you'll discover the sitting room and kitchen, heart of the house: the "feelings" are strongest here. There are excellent examples of Hawaiian adzes, old silverware, and plenty of photos. The lintel over the doorway is as stout as the spirits of the people who once lived here. The stonework on the floor is well laid and the fireplace is totally homey.

Go outside! The *lanai* runs across the entire front and down the side. Around back is the canoe shed, housing accurate replicas of Hawaiian-sewn sennit outrigger canoes, as well as Duke Kahanamoku's redwood surfboard. On the grounds you'll also see exhibits of sugarcane, sugar pots, *kunane* boards, and various Hawaiian artifacts. Hale Hoikeike is open daily 9:00 a.m. to 3:30 p.m., on Main Street (Hwy. 32) on your left, just as you begin heading for Iao Valley. Admission is well worth $2 (students $.50). Usually self-guided, tour guides available free if arrangements are made in advance. The bookstore/gift shop has a terrific selection of souvenirs and Hawaiiana at better-than-average prices.

Kepaniwai Park

As you head up Rt. 32 to Iao Valley, you're in for a real treat. Two miles after leaving Wailuku, you come across Kepaniwai Park and

Heritage Gardens. Here the architect, Richard C. Tongg, envisioned and created a park dedicated to all of Hawaii's people. See the Portuguese villa and garden complete with an outdoor oven, a thatch-roofed Hawaiian grass shack, a New England "salt box," a Chinese pagoda, a Japanese tea house with authentic garden, and a bamboo house, the little "sugar shack" that songs and dreams are made of. Admission is free and there are pavilions with picnic tables. This now-tranquil spot is where the Maui warriors fell to the invincible Kamehameha and his merciless patron war-god, Ku. *Kepaniwai* means "damming of the waters"—literally with corpses. Kepaniwai is now a monument to man's higher nature: harmony and beauty.

John F. Kennedy Profile

Up the road toward Iao Valley you come to a scenic area long known as *Pali Ele'ele,* or Black Gorge. This stream-eroded amphitheater canyon has attracted attention for centuries.

Japanese pagoda at Kepaniwai

Amazingly, after President Kennedy was assassinated, people noticed his likeness portrayed by a series of large boulders; mention of a profile had never been noted or recorded there before. A pipe stuck in the ground serves as a rudimentary telescope. Squint through it and there he is, with eyes closed in deep repose. The likeness is uncanny, and easily seen, unlike most of these formations where you have to stretch your imagination to the breaking point.

Iao Valley State Park

This valley has been a sacred spot and a place of pilgrimage since ancient times. Before Westerners arrived, the people of Maui, who came here to pay homage to the "Eternal Creator," named this valley *Iao,* "Supreme Light." In the center of this velvety green valley is a pillar of stone rising over 1,200 feet (actual height above sea level is 2,250 feet), that was at one time a natural altar. Now commonly called "The Needle," it's a tough basaltic core that remained after water swirled away the weaker stone surrounding it. Iao Valley is actually the remnant of the volcanic caldera of the West Maui Mountains, whose grooved walls have been smoothed and enlarged by the restlessness of mountain streams. Robert Louis Stevenson had to stretch poetic license to create a word for Iao when he called it "viridescent."

The road here ends in a parking lot, where signs point you to a myriad of paths that crisscross the valley. The paths are tame and well maintained, some even paved, with plenty of vantage points for photographers. If you take the lower path to the river below, you'll find a good-sized and popular swimming hole; but remember, these are the West Maui Mountains, and it can rain at any time! You can escape the crowds even in this heavily touristed area by following the path toward "The Needle" until you come to the pavilion at the top. As you head back, take the paved path that bears to the right. It soon becomes dirt, skirting the river and the tourists magically disappear. Here are a number of pint-sized pools where you can take a refreshing dip. Iao is for day use only. On your way back to Wailuku you might take a 5-minute side excursion up to Wailuku Heights. Look for the road on your right. There's little here

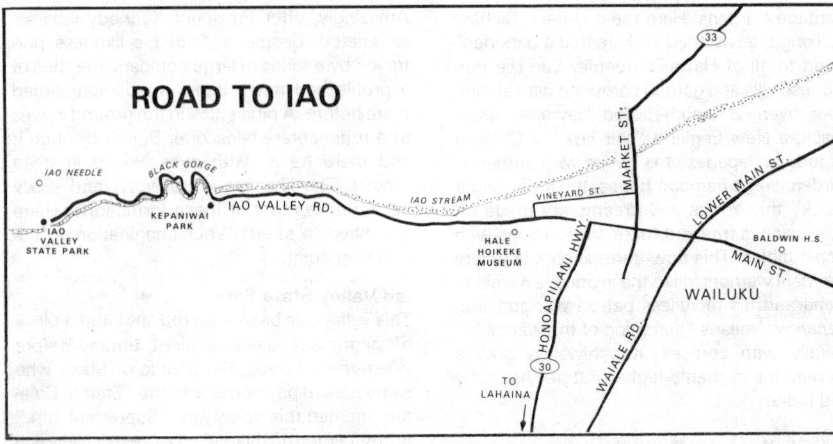

besides a housing development, but the view of the bay below is tops!

Hawaii Tropical Plantation

This new attraction is somewhat out of the ordinary. The Hawaii Tropical Plantation presents a model of a working plantation which you tour by small train. Most interesting is an up-close look at Maui's agricultural abundance. The train takes you through fields of cane, banana, mango, papaya, pineapple, and macadamia nuts; flowers here and there add exotic color. The plantation is in Waikapu, a small village along Rt. 30 between Lahaina and Wailuku. Open daily 8:00 a.m. to 5:00 p.m., restaurant and shopping; tel. 244-7643.

PRACTICALITIES

Accommodations

Visitors to Wailuku mostly stay elsewhere on Maui because there really isn't any place to lodge in town except for one very specialized and very humble hotel. The **Happy Valley Inn** is at 310 N. Market St., Wailuku 96793, tel. 244-4786 (in Happy Valley across from Yori's Restaurant), and costs $16 s, $22 d, ($96 to $132 weekly). Until very recently, it was a "flop house" for locals who were down on their luck. Now, it's an upbeat, clean hotel that is a *mecca* for avid sailboarders, cyclists, and students. The owner, an American named Keenan, is a top-notch sailboarder himself, and provides all the info you'll need on equipment, conditions, and the best beaches in the area. The Happy Valley Inn is basic accommodation (nonsmokers only!) and if you care more about wind and surf conditions, and not what your bedroom looks like, it's the place for you.

Food

The establishments listed below are all in the bargain or reasonable range. The decor in most is basic and homey, with the emphasis placed on the food.

Hale Lava is a little cafe/lodge serving Japanese and American food. For under $4, you can get a full meal. Located at 740 Lower Main (Rt. 340, Kahului Beach Rd.), tel. 244-0871. Opens at 6:00 a.m., closed Monday.

A favorite with locals, **Archie's Place** serves full meals for $4. Specialty is Japanese. Located at 1440 Lower Main (Kahului Beach Rd.), tel. 244-9401. Open daily 10:30 a.m. to 2:00 p.m., 5:00 to 8:00 p.m., closed Sunday.

Paradise Cafe offers vegetarian and Mexican food. Breakfast special might be vegie-cheese omelette with hash browns for $3.75. Located at 16 Market St., tel. 244-5747.

Sang Thai is a small restaurant painted black and white at 123 N. Market, tel. 244-3817. Excellent Thai food with an emphasis on vegetarian cuisine. Open Mon. to Sat. 11:00 a.m. to 3:00 p.m., 5:00 to 10:00 p.m.

Almost next door to Sang Thai at 133 N. Market is **Fujiya's,** tel. 244-0216, offering a full range of Japanese food and *sushi*. Open 11:00 a.m. to 5:00 p.m. The *miso* soup and *tempura* are inexpensive and quite good.

Yori's is more than a restaurant, it's an experience. It's at 309 N. Market in a little red building that says Happy Valley Tavern on the roof. It specializes in Hawaiian food and *luau.* The specialty is squid in coconut milk. Inside, festooning the walls from floor to ceiling, are photos of patrons and friends. You can eat for $5. Open 11:00 a.m. to 9:30 p.m., closed Mon., tel. 244-3121. Just across the street is **Kameta's Sushi** if you're in the mood for these delectables.

Down To Earth sells natural and health foods and has an excellent snack bar—basically a little window around back with a few tables available. $2.75 for a tofu burger with cheese and mock bacon. Really filling! Located at 1910 Vineyard, tel. 242-6821. Open daily 8:00 a.m. to 6:00 p.m., till 5:00 Sat., till 4:00 Sunday.

The best place to people watch and whet your whistle in Wailuku is at **Vineyard Tavern,** 2171 Vineyard, tel. 244-9597.

And, for a different taste treat, try the *mochi* made fresh daily at Wailuku's **Shishido Bakery.**

Shopping

Most shopping in this area is done in Kahului at the 3 big malls. But for an interesting diversion (all shops on Market Street) try: **Maui Wholesale Gold,** selling gold, jewelry and eel-skin items; **Treasure Imports,** selling just about the same type of articles; **Fantasea** for designer women's apparel; **Junktique,** a discovery shop which sells junk, Maui style; **Maui Fishing Supply,** with all you need to land the big ones.

Services

Bank of Hawaii, 2105 Main, tel. 871-8200; First Interstate, 2005 Main, tel. 244-3951. The post office is at High St., tel. 244-4815.

The library is at 251 High St., tel. 244-3945, closed Saturday. For laundry, Happy Valley Wash-o-matic, 300 block of N. Market.

For conventional health care, go to Maui Memorial Hospital, Rt. 32, tel. 244-9056; for alternative health care try the New Life Health Center at 90 Central Ave., tel. 244-9313. Here are a group of naturopaths, chiropractors, and massage therapists. Dr. Jonathan Loube, N.D., is one of the naturopaths who charges a donation, based on what you can pay.

Camping permits at county parks are available at War Memorial Gym, Room 102, Baldwin High School, Rt. 32, tel. 244-5514. Cost $1 adult, $.50 children, per person, per night. Get state park permits at State Building, High St., tel. 244-4354 (see p. 348-349).

Iao Needle

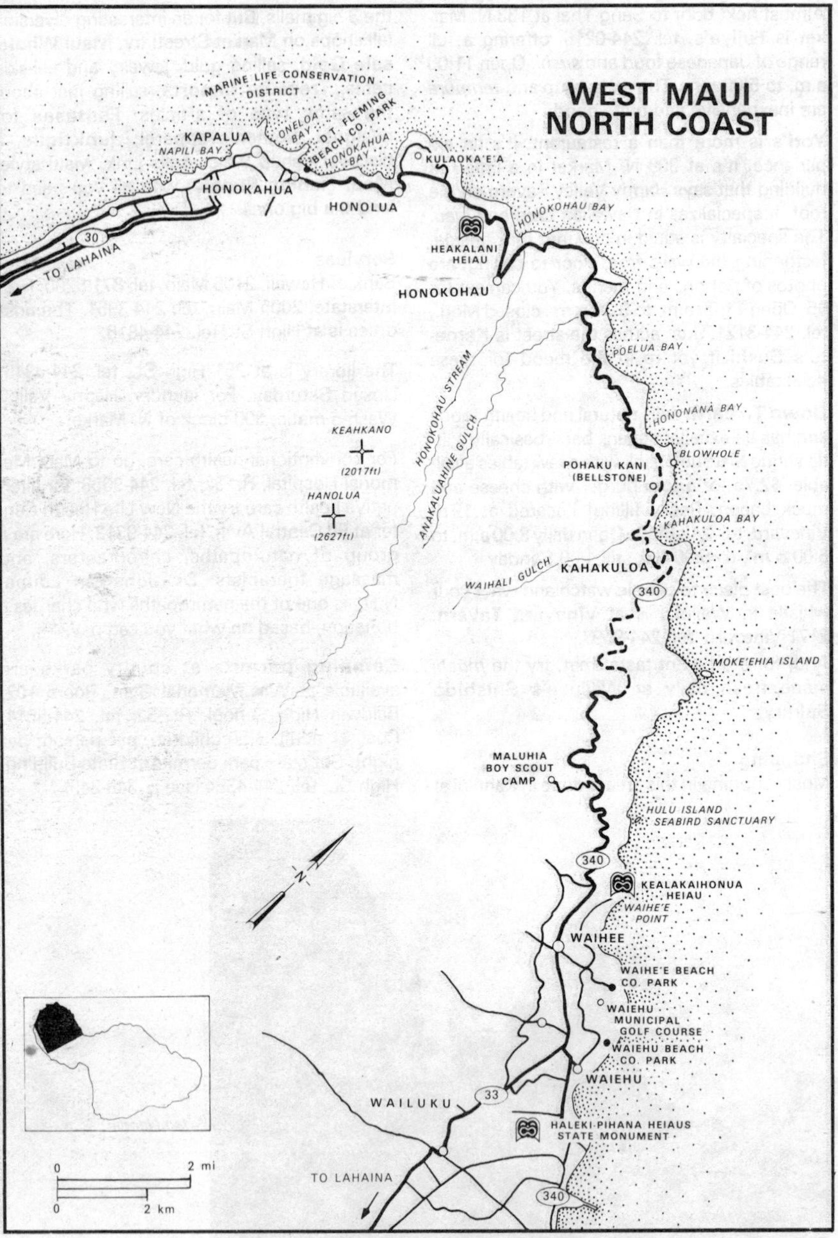
WEST MAUI
NORTH COAST
MARINE LIFE CONSERVATION DISTRICT
ONELOA BAY
D.T. FLEMING BEACH CO PARK
HONOKAHUA BAY
KAPALUA
NAPILI BAY
HONOKAHUA
HONOLUA
KULAOKA'E'A
HONOKOHAU BAY
HEAKALANI HEIAU
30
TO LAHAINA
HONOKOHAU
POELUA BAY
HONOKOHAU STREAM
ANAKALUAHINE GULCH
HONONANA BAY
KEAHKANO
(2017ft)
HANOLUA
(2627ft)
BLOWHOLE
POHAKU KANI
(BELLSTONE)
KAHAKULOA BAY
WAIHALI GULCH
KAHAKULOA
340
MOKE'EHIA ISLAND
MALUHIA
BOY SCOUT
CAMP
HULU ISLAND
SEABIRD SANCTUARY
N
KEALAKAIHONUA
HEIAU
WAIHE'E
POINT
WAIHEE
WAIHE'E BEACH
CO. PARK
WAIEHU
MUNICIPAL
GOLF COURSE
WAIEHU BEACH
CO. PARK
WAIEHU
WAILUKU
33
HALEKI-PIHANA HEIAUS
STATE MONUMENT
0
2 mi
0
2 km
TO LAHAINA

The *pali* from the Haiku Restaurant (O), JDB

1

2

1. Byodo-In Temple (O), JDB;
2. Rural church (M), Bob Cowan

1

2

3

1. John Costello, artist, (JDB);
2. Island woman, Bob Cowan;
3. Filipino and fighting cock (Mo), JDB

1

2

3

4

1. The gods of Puuhonua O Honaunau (H), JDB; **2.** The Hana Coast (M), JDB;
3. Anahulu Stream (O), JDB; **4.** Kepaniwai Park (M), JDB

1 

2 

1. Kaumana Cave (H), JDB;
2. Devastation Trail (H), JDB

1

2

3

1. Richardson's Beach (H), JDB;
2. Road to MacKenzie Park (H), JDB;
3. Pololu Valley meets the sea (H), JDB

1

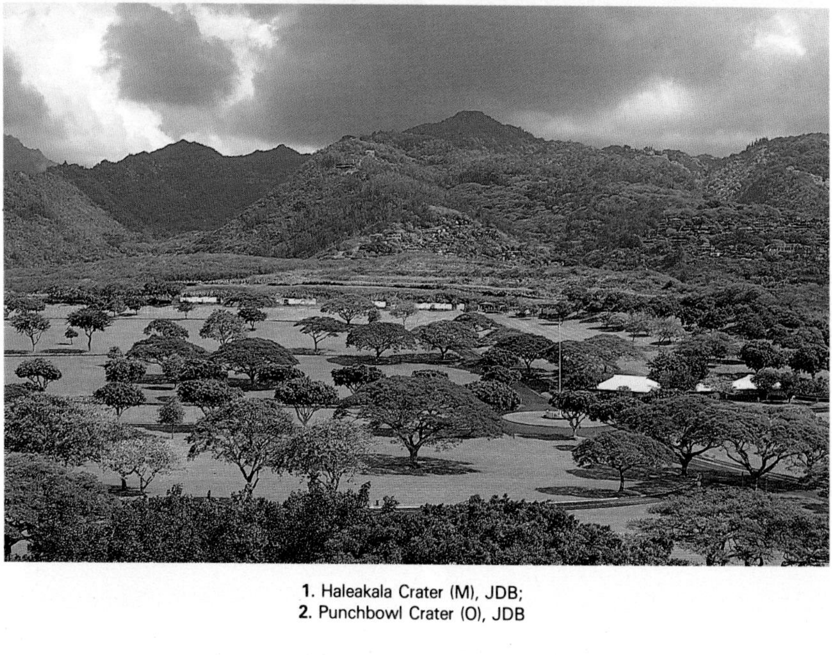
2

1. Haleakala Crater (M), JDB;
2. Punchbowl Crater (O), JDB

1

2

3

4

1. Hula at Haena Heiau (K), JDB; **2.** Suisan Fish Market (H), JDB;
3. Double-hulled canoe at Hanalei (K), JDB; **4.** Filipino gardener, Gary Quiring

1

2

3

1. Waimea Canyon (K), JDB;
2. Hana Road waterfalls (M), JDB;
3. Waipio Valley (H), JDB

1

2

1. Island children (K), JDB;
2. Traditional artist, Bob Cowan

1

2

3

1. Awaawapuhi Trail (K), JDB;
2. Puna Coast (H), JDB;
3. Poipu sunset (K), JDB

1

2

1. Honolulu from Aloha Tower (O), JDB;
2. Paniolo country (H), JDB

KAHAKULOA—WEST MAUI'S BACKSIDE

To get around to the backside of West Maui you can head northeast from Kaanapali, but the majority of those few who defy the car companies and brave the bad road strike out northwest from Wailuku. Before you start this rugged 18-mile stretch, make sure you have adequate gas, water and food. It'll take you a full 3 hours to go from Wailuku to Kapalua. Start heading north on Market Street, down toward the area of Wailuku called **Happy Valley** (good restaurants—see "Food," above). At the end of Market Street (Rt. 330) you'll find **T.K. Supermarket,** your best place to buy supplies (open 7 days). At mile 2, Rt. 330 turns into Rt. 340, which you'll follow toward Kahakuloa Bay and all the way around. In a few minutes, just when you come to the bridge over Iao Stream, will be Kuhio Place on your left. Turn here to **Halekii and Pihana Heiau.** Although uninspiring, this area is historical and totally unvisited.

Back on Rt. 340 you come shortly to **Waihee** (Slippery Water). There's a little store here, but even if it's open it's probably understocked. On the right, a sign points you to **Waiehu Golf Course.** Mostly local people golf here, and the fees during the week are $10 ($15 weekends). The fairways, strung along the sea, are beautiful to play. **Dani's** is an adequate little reastaurant at the golf course. Also here are 2 county beach parks: **Waiehu** and **Waihe'e.** They're secluded and frequented mostly by local people. Although for day use only, they'd probably be OK for an unofficial overnight stay. For Waiehu go left just before the golf course parking lot along the fence; for Waihe'e go left instead of right at the intersection leading to the golf course.

At mile 7 the pavement begins to deteriorate. The road hugs the coastline and gains elevation quickly; the undisturbed valleys are resplendent. At mile 11, just past the Boy Scout Camp, you'll see a metal gate and 2 enormous carved *tiki*. No explanation, just sitting there. You next enter the fishing village of **Kahakuloa** ("Tall Hill") with its dozen weatherworn houses and tiny white church. Here the road is at its absolute roughest and narrowest! The valley is very steep-sided and beautiful. Supposedly, great Maui himself loved this area. Two miles past Kahakuloa, you come to *Pohaku Kani,* the bell stone. It's about 6 feet tall and the same in diameter. Graffiti despoils it. Here the seascapes are tremendous. The surf pounds along the coast below and sends spumes skyward, roaring through a natural blow hole. The road once again becomes wide and well paved and you're soon at **Fleming Beach Park.** Civilization comes again too quickly.

LAHAINA

Lahaina ("Merciless Sun") is and always has been the premier town on Maui. It's the most energized town on the island as well, and you can feel it from the first moment you walk down Front Street. Maui's famed warrior-king Kahekili lived here and ruled until Kamehameha, with the help of new-found cannon power, subdued his son in Iao Valley at the turn at the 19th century. When Kamehameha I consolidated the Island Kingdom, he chose Lahaina as his seat of power. It served as such until Kamehameha III moved to Honolulu in the 1840s. Lahaina is where the modern world of the West and the old world of Hawaii collided, for better or worse. The *ali'i* of Hawaii loved to be entertained here; the **royal surf spot**, mentioned numerous times as an area of revelry in old missionary diaries, is just south of the Small Boat Harbor. Kamehameha I built in Lahaina the islands' first Western structure in 1801, known as the **Brick Palace;** a small ruin still remains. Queens Keopuolani and Kaahumanu, the 2 most powerful wives of the great Kamehameha's harem of over 20, were local Maui women who remained after their husband's death and helped to usher in the new order.

The whalers came preying for "sperms and humpbacks" in 1819 and set old Lahaina Town a-reelin'. Island girls, naked and willing, swam out to meet the ships, trading their favors for baubles from the modern world. Grog shops flourished, and drunken sailors with their brown-skinned doxies owned the debauched town. The missionaries, invited by Queen Keopuolani, came praying for souls in 1823. Led by the Reverend Stuart and Richards, they tried to harpoon moral chaos. In short order, there was a curfew, a *kapu* placed on the ships by wise but ineffectual old Governor Hoapili, a jail and a fort to discourage the strong-armed tactics of unruly captains. The pagan Hawaiians transformed like willing children to the new order, but the Christian sailors damned the meddling missionaries. They even whistled a few cannonballs into the Lahaina homestead of Rev. Richards, hoping to send him speedily to his eternal reward. Time, a new breed of sailor, and the slow death of the whaling industry eased the tension.

Meanwhile, the missionaries built the first school and printing press west of the Rockies at **Lahainaluna**, in the mountains just above the town, along with downtown's **Wainee Church**, the first stone church on the island. Lahaina's glory days slipped by and it became a sleepy "sugar town" dominated by the Pioneer Sugar Mill that has operated since the 1860s. In 1901, the **Pioneer Inn** was built to accommodate inter-island ferry passengers, but no one *came* to Lahaina. In the 1960s, AMFAC had a brilliant idea. They turned Kaanapali, a magnificent stretch of beach just west, into one of the most beautifully planned and executed resorts in the world. The Pioneer Sugar Mill had long used the area as a refuse heap, but now the ugly duckling became a swan, and Lahaina flushed with new life. With superb farsightedness, the **Lahaina Restoration Foundation** was begun in those years and almost the entire town was made a **National Historical Landmark**. Lahaina, subdued but never tamed, throbs with its special energy once again.

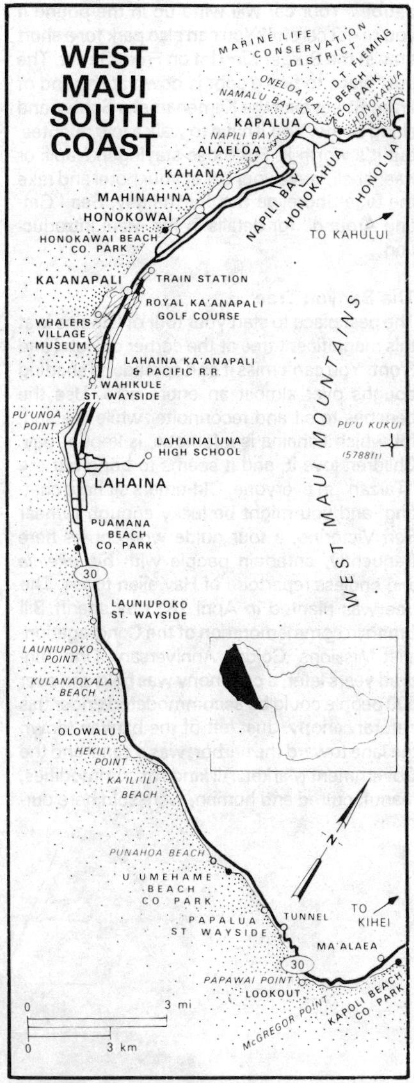

SIGHTS

In short, strolling aroung Lahaina is the best of both worlds. It's busy, but it's bite-sized. It's engrossing enough, but you can "see" it in half a day. The main attractions are mainly downtown within a few blocks of each other. Lahaina technically stretches, long and narrow, along the coast for about 4 miles, but you'll only be interested in the central core, a mere mile or so. All along Front Street, the main drag, and the side streets running off it are innumerable shops, restaurants, and hideaways where you can browse, recoup your energy, or just wistfully watch the sun set. Go slow and savor, and you'll feel the dynamism of Lahaina past and present all around you. Enjoy!

Parking

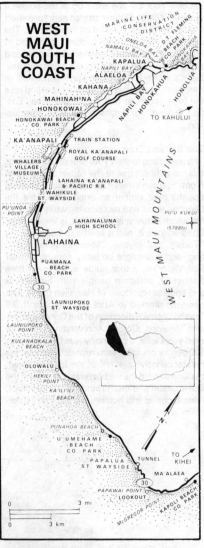

Traffic congestion is a problem that needs to be addressed. Stay away from town from 4:30 to 5:30 p.m. when traffic is heaviest. There're only 2 traffic lights in town, one block apart, and they're not synchronized! The other thing to know to make your visit carefree is where to stash your car. The parking lot on the corner of Wainee and Dickenson streets charges only $1.50 all day. There's another large lot on Prison Street, just up from Front, and 2 smallish lots along Luakini Street. The Lahaina Shopping Center has 3-hour parking. Most of the meters in town are a mere one hour, and the most efficient people on Maui are the "meter patrol!" Your car will wind up in the pound if you're not careful! You can also park for a short time in the Burger King lot on Front Street. The best place to find a spot is down at the end of Front Street past the Kamehameha School and along Shaw. You'll have to walk a few minutes, but it's worth it. For those staying in Napili or Kaanapali, leave your car at your hotel and take the Blue Shoreline Bus for the day. See "Getting Around" for details in the Maui Introduction.

The Banyan Tree

The best place to start your tour of Lahaina is at this magnificent tree at the corner of Hotel and Front. You can't miss it as it spreads its shading boughs over almost an entire acre. Use the benches to sit and reconnoiter while the sun, for which Lahaina is infamous, is kept at bay. Children love it, and it seems to bring out the "Tarzan" in everyone. Old-timers sit here chatting, and you might be lucky enough to hear Ben Victorino, a tour guide who comes here frequently, entertain people with his *ukelele* and endless repertoire of Hawaiian tunes. The tree was planted in April 1873 by sheriff Bill Smith in commemoration of the Congregationalist Missions' Golden Anniversary. One hundred years later, a ceremony was held and over 500 people could be accommodated under this natural canopy. Just left of the banyan, down the lane toward the harbor, was a canal and the Government Market. All kinds of commodities, manufactured and human, were sold here during the whaling days, and it was given the apt name of "Rotten Row."

The Courthouse

Behind the banyan on Wharf Street is the Courthouse. Built in the 1850s from coral blocks recycled from Kamehameha III's ill-fated palace, Hale Piula ("House of Iron"), it also served as the police station, complete with a jail in the basement. Today, the jail is home to the **Lahaina Art Foundation,** where paintings and artifacts are kept behind bars, waiting for patrons to liberate them. Adjacent is **The Fort,** built in the 1830s to show the sailors that they couldn't run amok in Lahaina. It was more for show than for force, though. When it was torn down, the blocks were hauled over to Prison Street to build the real jail, **Hale Pa'ahao.** A corner battlement of the fort was restored, but that's it, because restoring the entire structure means mutilating the banyan.

The *Carthaginian II*

The masts and square rigging of this replica of the enterprising freighters that braved the Pacific tower over Lahaina Harbor. You'll be drawn to it...go! It's the only truly square-rigged ship left afloat on the seas. It replaced the *Carthaginian I* when that ship went aground in 1972 while being hauled to Honolulu for repairs. The Lahaina Restoration Foundation found this steel-hulled ship in Denmark; built in Germany in 1920 as a 2-masted schoon-

the Carthaginian II, *a floating whale museum*

er, it tramped around the Baltic under converted diesel power. The society shipped it 12,000 miles to Lahaina where it underwent extensive conversion until it became the beautiful replica that you see today. The sails are yet to be made for lack of funds.

The *Carthaginian* is a floating museum dedicated to whaling and to whales. Richard Widmark, the actor, narrates a superb film documenting the life of humpbacks. Belowdecks is the museum containing artifacts and implements from the whaling days. There's even a whaling boat which was found intact in Alaska in the 1970s. The light belowdecks is subdued, and while you sit in the little "captains' chairs" the humpbacks chant their peaceful hymns in the background. Flip Nicklin's sensitive photos adorn the bulkheads. It's open daily 9:30 a.m. to 4:30 p.m., but arrive by 3:45 to see all the exhibits and videos. Admission $2.

Small Boat Harbor

Walking along the harbor stimulates the imagination and the senses. The boats waiting at anchor sway in confused syncopation. Hawser ropes groan and there's a feeling of anticipation and adventure in the air. Here you can board for all kinds of seagoing excursions. In the days of whaling there was no harbor. The boats tied up one to the other in the "roads," at times forming an impromptu floating bridge. The whalers came ashore in their chase boats; with the winds always up, departure could be made at a moment's notice. The activity here is still totally dominated by the sea.

Pioneer Inn

This vintage inn, situated at the corner of Hotel and Wharf streets, is just exactly where it belongs. Stand on its verandah with the "honky tonk" piano playing in the open bar behind you and gaze at the *Carthaginian.* Presto...it's magic time! You'll see. It was even a favorite spot for actors like Errol Flynn and later Spencer Tracy when he was in Lahaina filming *Devil at Four O'Clock.* The green and white Inn was only built in 1901 to accommodate interisland ferry passengers, but its style seems much older. If ironwork had been used on the verandah, you'd say it was New Orleans. A new wing was built behind it in 1965 and the two form a courtyard. Make sure to read the

This "old salt" welcomes you to the Pioneer Inn.

hilarious rules governing behavior that are posted in the main lobby. The Inn is still functional. The rooms in the old wing are colorfully seedy—spotlessly clean, but with character and atmosphere. The wooden stairway, painted red, leads upstairs to an uneven hallway lined with a thread-bare carpet. The interior smells like the sea. There's no luxury here, but you might consider one night just for the experience. (See "Accommodations," below, for details). Downstairs the **Snug Harbor Restaurant** serves dinners, and you can't find a better place to watch life go by with a beautiful sunset backdrop than in the **Old Whaler's Grog Shop**.

The Brick Palace

This rude structure was commissioned by Kamehameha I in 1801 and slapped together by 2 forgotten Australian ex-convicts. It was the first Western structure in Hawaii, but unfor-

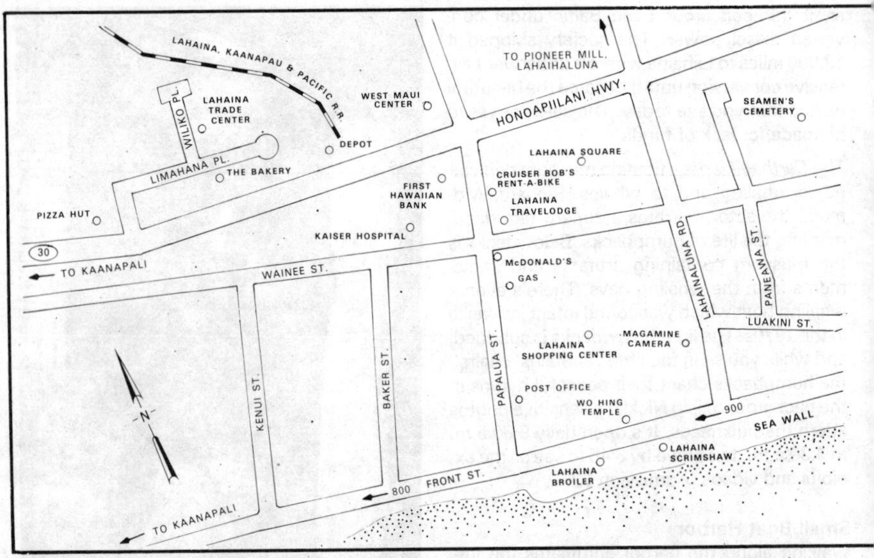

tunately the substandard materials have disintegrated, for the most part. Kamehameha never lived in it, but it was occupied and used as a storehouse until the 1850s. Now, only an archaeological excavation, covered in plexiglass, remains of this site. Just to the right of the Brick Palace, as you face the harbor, is **Hauola Stone,** marked by an HVB Warrior. Formed like a chair, it was believed by the Hawaiians to have curative powers if you sat on it and let the ocean bathe you. Best view at low tide.

Baldwin Home

One of the best attractions in Lahaina is the Baldwin Home on the corner of Front and Dickenson. It was occupied by the Doctor/Reverend Dwight Baldwin, his wife Charlotte, and their 8 children. He was a trained teacher, as well as the first doctor/dentist in Hawaii. The building served as a dispensary, meeting room, and boarding home for anyone in need from the 1830s to 1868. The 2-foot-thick walls are of cut lava, and the mortar was of crushed coral, over which plaster was applied. As you enter, notice how low the doorway is, and that the doors inside are "Christian doors"—with a cross forming the upper panels and with an open Bible at the bottom. The Steinway piano that dominates the entrance was built in 1859. In the bedroom to the right, along with all of the period furniture, is a wooden commode, a prototype of the portable toilet. Also notice the lack of closets; all items were kept in chests. Upstairs was a large dormitory where guests slept.

The doctor's fees are posted and are hilarious. Payment was by "size" of sickness: very big $50, diagnosis $3, refusal to pay $10! The Rev. Baldwin was 41 when he arrived in Hawaii from New England and his wife was 25. She was supposedly sickly (8 children!) and he had heart trouble, so they moved to Honolulu in 1868 to receive better health care. The home became a community center housing the library and meeting rooms. Today, the Baldwin Home is a showcase museum of the Lahaina Restoration Foundation. It's open daily 9:30 a.m. to 5:00 p.m., admission $2, kids free if accompanied by a parent.

Master's Reading Room

Originally a missionaries' store room, the Master's Reading Room was converted to an Officers' Club in 1834. Located next door to the Baldwin Home, these 2 venerable buildings

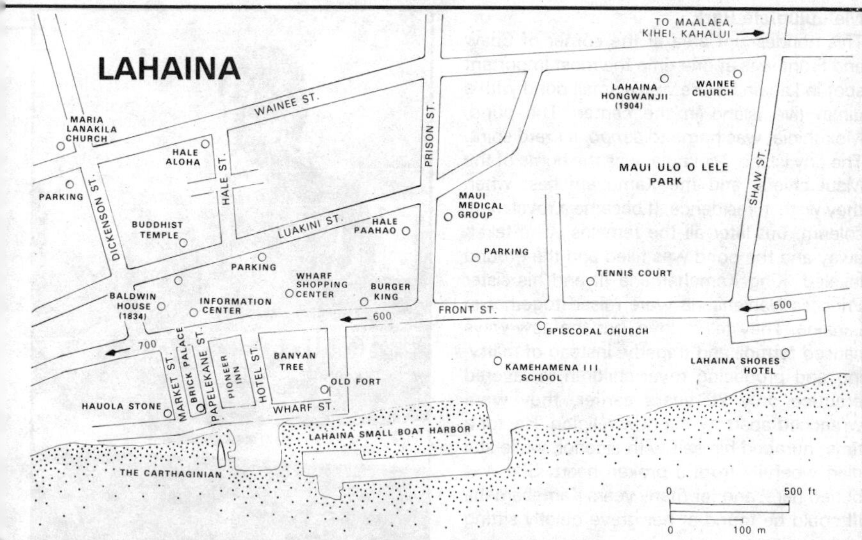

constitute the oldest Western structures on Maui, and fittingly, this uniquely constructed coral stone building is home to the Lahaina Restoration Foundation. The building is not really open to the public, but you can visit to pick up maps, brochures, and information about Lahaina.

The **Lahaina Restoration Foundation**, begun in 1962, is headed by Jim Luckey, an historian in his own right who knows a great deal about Lahaina and the whaling era. The main purpose of the Foundation is to preserve the flavor and authenticity of Lahaina without stifling progress—especially tourism. The Foundation is privately funded and has managed to purchase many of the important historical sites in Lahaina. They own the 2 buildings mentioned, the restored Wo Hing Temple, the land under the U.S. Seamen's Hospital, and the plantation house next door, which they'll own outright in 18 years. The 42 people on the board of directors come from all socio-economic backgrounds. You don't get on the board by how much money you give, but by how much effort and time you are willing to invest in the Foundation; the members are extremely dedicated. Merchants approach the Foundation with new ideas for business and ask how they can best comply with the building codes. The townspeople know that their future is best served if they preserve the feeling of old Lahaina rather than rush headlong into frenzied growth. The historic village of Williamsburg, Virginia, is often cited as Lahaina's model, except that Lahaina wishes to remain a "real" living, working town.

Hale Pa'ahao

This is Lahaina's old prison, located mid-block on Prison Street, and literally means "stuck-in-irons house." It was constructed by prisoners in the 1850s from blocks of stone salvaged from the old defunct Fort. It had a catwalk for an armed guard, and cells complete with shackles for hardened criminals, but most were drunks who yahooed around town on the Sabbath, wildly spurring their horses. The guardhouse and cells were rebuilt in 1959, and the structure is maintained by the Restoration Foundation. The cells, curiously, are made of wood, which shows the inmates weren't that interested in busting out. It's open Mon. to Fri. 9:00 a.m. to 3:00 p.m. Admission free.

Maluuluolele Park

This nondescript area at the corner of Shaw and Front was at one time the most important spot in Lahaina. Here was a small pond with a diminutive island in the center. The pond, Mokuhinia, was home to a *moo,* a lizard spirit. The tiny island, Mokuula, was the home of the Maui chiefs, and the Kamehamehas, when they were in residence. It became a royal mausoleum, but later all the remains were taken away and the pond was filled and the ground leveled. King Kamehameha III and his sister Princess Nahienaena were raised together in Lahaina. They fell in love, but the new ways caused turmoil and tragedy. Instead of marrying and producing royal children, a favored practice only 20 years earlier, they were wrenched apart by the new religion. He, for a time, numbed himself with alcohol, while she died woefully from a broken heart. She was buried here, and for many years Kamehameha III could be found at her grave quietly sitting and meditating.

Wainee Church And Cemetery

The church itself is not impressive, but its history is. This is the spot where the first Christian services were held in 1823. A church was built here in 1832 which could hold 3,000 people, but it was razed by a freak hurricane in 1858. Rebuilt, it survived until 1894, when it was deliberately burned by an angry mob, upset with the abolition of the monarchy in Hawaii and its annexation by the U.S. Another church was built, but it, too, was hit not only by a hurricane but by fire as well. The present structure was built in 1953. In the cemetery is a large part of Maui's history: buried here are Hawaiian royalty. Lying near each other are Queen Keopuolani, her star-crossed daughter, Princess Nahienaena, and old Governor Hoapili, their Royal Tomb marked by two large headstones surrounded by a wrought iron fence. Other graves hold missionaries such as William Richards, and many infants and children.

Churches And Temples

You may wish to stop for a moment at Lahaina's churches and temples dotted around town. They are reminders of the mixture of faiths and peoples that populated this village

The Buddha of the Jodo Mission is a facsimile of the Daibutsu *(Great Buddha) of Kamakura, Japan.*

and added their particular style of energy. **The Episcopal Cemetery** on Wainee Street shows the English influence in the islands. Many of the royal family, including King Kalakaua, became Anglicans, and this cemetery holds the remains of many early Maui families, and of Walter Murray Gibson, the notorious settler, politician, and firebrand of the 1880s. Just behind is **Hale Aloha,** "House of Love," a small structure built by Maui residents in thanksgiving for being saved from a terrible smallpox epidemic that ravaged Oahu but bypassed Maui in 1858. The structure was restored in 1974. Also on Wainee is **Maria Lanakila Church,** the site of the first Roman Catholic Mass in Lahaina, celebrated in 1841. The present structure dates from 1928. Next to the church's cemetery is the **Seamen's Cemetery** where many infirm from the ships that came to Lahaina were buried. Most stones were obliterated by time and only a few remain. Herman Melville came here to pay his last respects to a cousin buried in this yard. **Hongwanji Temple** is also on Wainee, between Prison and Shaw. It's a Buddhist temple with the largest congregation in Lahaina and dates from 1910, with the structure being raised in 1927.

The **Wo Hing Temple** is on Front Street, and is the Lahaina Restoration Foundation's newest reconstruction. It was opened to the public in 1984, and shows the Chinese influence in Lahaina. It's open 9:00 a.m. to 9:00 p.m., small admission. **Holy Innocents Episcopal Church**, built in 1927, is also on Front Street, near Kamehameha III school. Known for its "Hawaiian Madonna," its altar is resplendent with fruits, plants and birds of the islands. The **Lahaina Jodo Mission** is at the opposite end of Front Street, near Mala Wharf on Ala Moana Street. Here the giant bronze Buddha, the largest outside of Asia, was dedicated in 1968 in commemoration of the centennial of the Japanese arrival. The grounds are impeccable and serenely quiet. You may stroll around, but the buildings are closed to the public. If you climb the steps to peek into the temple, kindly remove your shoes.

U.S. Seamen's Hospital

This notorious hospital was reconstructed by the Lahaina Restoration Foundation in 1982. Here is where sick seamen were cared for under the auspices of the U.S. State Department. Allegations during the late 1850s claimed that the care here extended past the grave! Unscrupulous medicos supposedly charged the U.S. government for care of seamen who had long since died. Located at Front and Baker, heading toward Kaanapali, near the Jodo Mission.

Lahainaluna

Head up the mountain behind Lahaina on Lahainaluna Road for approximately 2 miles. On your left you'll pass the **Pioneer Sugar Mill**, in operation since 1860. Once at Lahainaluna ("Above Lahaina") you'll find the oldest school west of the Rockies, opened by the Congregationalist Missionaries in 1831. Children from all over the islands, and many from California, came here to school, if their parents could afford to send them away to boarding school. Today, the school is West Maui's public high school, but many children still come here to board. The first students were not only given a top-notch academic education, but a practical one as well. They not only built the school buildings, many were also apprentices in the famous **Hale Pa'i** (Printing House) that turned out Hawaii's first newspaper and made Lahaina famous as a printing center.

One look at Hale Pa'i and you think of New England. It's a white stucco building with blue trim and a wood-shake roof. It was restored in 1982 and is open Mon. to Sat. 9:00 a.m. to 4:00 p.m., admission $2. (If you visit the Baldwin

Hale Pai, the oldest printing house west of the Rocky Mountains.

Home, admission to Hale Pa'i is included.) If you visit the campus when school is in session, you may go to Hale Pa'i, but if you want to walk around, please sign in at the vice-principal's office. Lahainaluna H.S. is still dedicated to the preservation of Hawaiian culture. Every year, in April, they celebrate the anniversary of one of their most famous students, David Malo. Considered Hawaii's first scholar, he authored the definitive *Hawaiian Antiquities.* His final wish was to be buried "high above the tide of foreign invasion" and his grave is close to the giant "L" atop Mount Ball, behind Lahainaluna. On the way back down to Lahaina, you get a wide, impressive panorama of the port and the sea.

Heading East

Five miles east of Lahaina along the coastal road (Rt. 30) is the little village of Olowalu. Today, little more than a general store and a French restaurant are here. This was the place of the Olowalu Massacre perpetrated by Capt. Metcalfe. Its results were far-reaching, greatly influencing Hawaiian history. Two seamen, Young and Davis, were connected with this incident, and with their help Kamehameha I subdued all of Hawaii. Behind the store are petroglyphs. Follow the dirt track behind the store for about one-half mile; make sure you pass a water tower within the first few hundred yards because there are 3 similar roads here. You'll come to the remains of a wooden stairway going up a hill. There once was an HVB Warrior here, but he might be gone. Claw your way up the hill to the petroglyphs, which are believed to be 300 years old. If you continue east on Rt. 30, you'll pass **Papawai** and **McGregor Point**, both noted for their vistas and as excellent locations to spot migrating whales in season. The road sign merely says "Scenic Lookout."

BEACHES

The best beaches around Lahaina are just west of town in Kaanapali, or just east toward Olowalu. A couple of adequate places to spread your towel are right in Lahaina, but they're not quite on a par with the beaches just a few miles away.

Maluulu O Lele Park

"The Breadfruit Shelter of Lele" is in town and basically parallels Front Street. It's crowded at times and there's plenty of "wash up" on this beach. It's cleaner and quieter at the east end down by Lahaina Shores, a one-time favorite with the *ali'i.* There are restrooms, the swimming is fair, and the snorkeling acceptable past the reef. **Lahaina Beach** is at the west end of town near Mala Wharf. Follow Front to Puunoa Place and turn down to the beach. This is a good place for families with tots because the water is clear, safe, and shallow.

Puamana Beach County Park

About 2 miles before you enter Lahaina from the east along Rt. 30, you'll see signs for this beach park. A narrow strip between the road and the sea, the swimming and snorkeling are only fair. The setting, however, is quite nice with picnic tables shaded by ironwood trees. The views are terrific and this is a great spot to eat your plate lunch only minutes from town.

a quiet beach east of Lahaina

Launiupoko State Park a mile farther east, has restrooms and showers, but no beach. This is more of a pit stop than anything else.

Wahikuli State Park
Along Rt. 30 between Lahaina and Kaanapali. It's a favorite with local people and excellent for a picnic and swim. Restrooms and tennis courts are just across the street. The park is very clean and well maintained.

ACCOMMODATIONS

Lodging in Lahaina is limited, surprisingly inexpensive, and an experience...of sorts. Most visitors head for Kaanapali, because Lahaina tends to be hot and hot to trot, especially at night. But you can find good bargains here, and if you want to be in the thick of the "action," you're in the right spot.

Pioneer Inn
The oldest hotel on Maui still accommodating guests. At 658 Wharf St., Lahaina, HI 96764, tel. 661-3636. Absolutely no luxury whatsoever, but a double scoop of atmosphere. Here's the place to come if you want to save money, and be the star of your own movie with the Pioneer Inn as the stage set. Enter the tiny lobby full of memorabilia, follow the creaking stairway up to a wooden hallway painted green on green. This is the old wing. Screen doors cover inner doors to clean but basic rooms which open out onto the building-long *lanai* overlooking the harbor, and have ceiling fans. $18/$21, shared bath, private bath (showers) a few dollars extra. Music and the sounds of life from the bar below late in the evening at no extra charge. The "new wing," basic modern, circa 1966, is attached. Starting at $36, it's no bargain. It offers a private *lanai,* bath, a/c, and overlooks the central courtyard. Pool. The old section is fun; the new section is only adequate.

Lahainaluna Hotel
You can't really have a town without a "down-at-the-heels" hotel, and this is Lahaina's. It is, however, clean and safe. What better place for an adventurous traveler to stay than a hotel that cuts costs by suggesting you bring your

the Pioneer Inn

own beach towel, and offers no maid service for stays less than 3 days? $30 for preferred rooms with a/c, TV (b&w), private shower, and view of mountains or harbor, $27.50 with no view. There are even unadvertised rooms "in the back" that go for cheaper, usually for residents or for a long-term stay. The Lahainaluna Hotel is at 127 Lahainaluna Rd., Lahaina, HI 96761, tel. 661-0577. There are only 18 rooms and they do sell out.

Maui Islander
Located a few blocks away from the hubbub, at 660 Wainee St., Lahaina 96761, tel. 667-9766, 800-367-5226. A very adequate hotel offering rooms with kitchenettes, studios, and suites up to 3 bedrooms for 7 guests or more. All a/c with TV, pool and tennis courts. Homey atmosphere with daily planned activities. Basic hotel rooms start at $70, studios $85, $6 extra per person.

Lahaina Shores
This 6-story condo was built before the Lahaina building code limited the height of new construction. Located at the east end of town, at 475 Front St., Lahaina 96761, tel. 661-4835, 800-367-2972. The tallest structure in town, it's become a landmark for incoming craft. It offers a swimming pool and spa and is located on the only beach in town. From a distance, the southern mansion facade is striking: up close, though, it becomes painted cement blocks and false colonnades. The rooms, however, are a

good value for the money. The basic contains a full bathroom, powder room, large color TV, and equipped kitchen. They're all light and airy, and the backside views of the harbor or frontside of the mountains are the best in town. Studios begin at $85, suites $112, $9 for additional guests.

Lahaina Roads
This condo/apartment is at the far west end of town at 1403 Front St., Lahaina 96761, tel. 661-3166. There is a 3-night minimum stay with a one-week minimum during peak season. All units have fully equipped kitchens, a/c, TV, and maid service on request. One-bedroom units start at $65 to $85 (high season), $7 additional guests. No credit cards honored. Discounts are offered for more than one-week stays.

Puamana
One-bedroom units (fully equipped) begin at $75. Special car rental rates are offered. This condo is located one mile southeast of town. Write Box 515, Lahaina 96767, tel. 667-2551, 800-367-5630. Check in at Manager's Office in Lahaina at 910 Honoapiilani, no. 11.

FOOD

Lahaina's menu of restaurants is gigantic; all palates and pocketbooks can easily be satisfied: there's fast food, sandwiches, *sushi,* happy hours, and elegant cosmopolitan restaurants. Because Lahaina is a dynamic tourist spot, restaurants and eateries come and go with regularity. The following is not an exhaustive list of Lahaina's food spots—it couldn't be. But there is plenty listed here to feed everyone at breakfast, lunch, and dinner. Bon appetit!

Inexpensive
Lahaina Natural Foods at 1295 Front Street, west end almost out of town toward Kaanapali. Open 7 days, 8:00 a.m to 8:00 p.m., Sun 6:00 p.m., tel. 667-2251. They have an excellent deli and feature fresh-baked goods. Take out picnic lunches and tables on the premises at the Waterfront Cafe. Great sandwiches and you can't beat the smoothies for 99 cents.

If you're looking for atmosphere, drive on by **Naokee's, Too.** Also at Lahaina's west end at 1307 Front St., tel. 667-7513. They feature "regular" island food like chicken, pork, and beef, with rice, macaroni salad, and corn. Plate lunches $4, specialty one-pound steak $6.95. Basic but good.

Expresso Cafe at 693 Front, tel. 661-4710, is the kind of place that locals keep secret. Its motto is "yours, mine and auras." It's a tiny little place where you can have an excellent coffee, or a sandwich on whole wheat or pita bread. Good pastries. More for a snack, a quick breakfast or to people-watch.

Their name almost says it all at **The Fish Fry** in the Lahaina Shopping Center, tel. 667-9243, but they also have filling plate lunches for under $4, sandwiches for under $2, and a wide range of omelettes for under $3. Limited seating, good value. Open daily.

A tiny "no name" ***sushi* bar** and plate lunch place is on Prison Street just after you turn toward the mountains off Front Street. Look for it across the street from the "bus parking" lot. Very reasonable prices.

Your sweet tooth will begin to sing the moment you walk into **The Bakery** at 911 Limahana, near the "Sugar Cane Train Depot" off Honoapiilani Road (Hwy. 30) as you head toward Kaanapali. You can't beat their stuffed croissants for under $1, or their sandwiches for under $2! Coffee is a mere 40 cents, and their pastries, breads and pasta are goooood! Open daily 7:00 a.m. to 5:00 p.m., until noon on Sun., tel. 667-9062. The **Cafe Allegro**, next door, has decent and inexpensive Italian-style food, and pizza.

Togo's at the Lahaina Shores Village, 505 Front., tel. 667-6917. Open Sun. to Thurs. 9:30 a.m. to midnight, Fri. and Sat. closes earlier, is your basic good old sub shop selling "stubbies, regulars, and giants" from $3-15.

Fast Food
Fanatics can get their fix at: **Burger King,** Front St., near the Banyan Tree; **McDonald's,** at the Lahaina Shopping Center; **Skipper's,** for deep-fried seafood at The Wharf Shopping Center; **Kentucky Fried Chicken** at the Lahaina Shopping Center; **Pizza Hut** at 127 Hinau Street.

Local combos regularly perform in many of Lahaina's pubs and restaurants.

Moderate

Hamburger Mary's is at the southeast end of town at 608 Front St., tel. 667-6989. This is a Maui branch of the same restaurant in San Francisco. Walk along the gravelled walkway to the entrance and beer garden around back. Soup and salad for $7 will definitely fill you up. Tremendous sandwiches up to $6.75. Famous, enormous (2 people?) hamburgers for $5.50. The best deal is breakfast, served all day, with an assortment of omelettes for under $3. Popular with gay people of both sexes, literally and figuratively. Open daily 7:00 a.m. to 11:00 p.m.

The **Harbor Front Restaurant** on the second floor at The Wharf Shopping Center on Front Street, tel. 667-8212, has a logo that reads "established a long time ago." Lunch up to $6, $5 sandwiches, $15 dinners. A display case at the entrance holds the fresh catch-of-the-day. The interior is surprisingly well-done with many hanging plants in distinctive planters, high-backed wicker chairs, with white tables and bright orange table settings.

Blackbeard's is also at The Wharf, tel. 667-9535. Lunch from 11:00 a.m. to 4:00 p.m., dinner from 5:00 to 10:00. They have an excellent happy hour and feature live music nightly. Good selection of imported beers. Try the Hawaiian fruit boat for $3.95, or buy a submarine at $.50 an inch.

Tortilla Flats is on the lower level of The Wharf Shopping Center, tel. 667-9581. Daily 11:30 a.m. to 10:00 p.m. Mexican food at very reasonable prices, and huge margaritas! Unfortunately, it varies in the quality of cooking depending on the day's chef, according to workers at The Wharf who are in the know.

Greenthumb's overlooks the harbor at 839 Front, tel. 667-6126. Daily 10 a.m. to 10 p.m. Plenty of salads to choose from and vegetarians are not forgotten. You can fill up for under $6. These guys are new and are trying hard (and succeeding) to build a good reputation. For a light meal, you can't go wrong. Take out, too.

The Oceanhouse is at 831 Front St., tel. 661-3359. Daily lunch 11:00 a.m. to 2:30 p.m., dinner 5:00 p.m. to 10:00 p.m. Happy hour with free munchies and beer 85 cents, well drinks $1. Known for its extensive salad bar. Lunch is available for under $5. Dinner begins at $8. There's an "early bird special" with a good discount from 5:00 to 6:00 p.m. Nice atmosphere and terrific sunset view.

Find **Moose McGuillicuddy's** on the upper level of **Mariner's Alley** at 844 Front St., tel. 667-7758. Daily 7:30 a.m. until the wee hours. They have a large-screen TV, overstuffed chairs and a great view overlooking Front Street. Plenty of specials including an "early bird " breakfast for only $1.99, a "beggar's banquet" for $2.29. Mid-day and evening happy hours offer truly inexpensive drinks, featuring margaritas in 11 flavors and highballs for 90 cents. Every night features a different event: Monday, dance; Tuesday, tequila; Wednesday, live music, etc. The big Moose is OK.

Marco's Italian Restaurant is also at Mariner's Alley just downstairs from Moose, tel. 661-8877. Daily breakfast 9:00 to 11:00 a.m., dinner from 5:00 p.m. The breakfasts tend to be Continental with coffee and pastry. Dinners are well priced at less than $10. Calzone is only $6, lasagna $8.50. Good Italian salads for $4.50.

Lahaina Broiler is at the west end of town in the 800 block of Front Street, under the enormous monkeypod tree, tel. 661-3111. You can't get closer to the sea than this almost open-air restaurant. Great sunsets, better-than-average island cooking for a good price.

The Keg, changed from the well-known **Blue Max,** is at 730 Front St., tel. 661-3137. Comfortable decor of old couches, coffee tables, etc. Like old aunty's parlor. Also a terrific view of "the roads." Happy hour, and good lunch specials. At night it becomes a disco/restaurant. At one time any celebrity passing through, such as Elton John, stopped in for a drink and a jam.

The **Whale's Tail** is next door to The Wharf Shopping Plaza, second level at 666 Front St., tel. 661-3676. Daily lunch 11:30 a.m. to 2:30 p.m., dinner from 5:00 p.m. They usually offer a musician playing guitar, or sometimes an entire band. Teriyaki and Oriental steak for $7.95, seafood entrees from $10. Children's menu.

Harpooner's Lanai is in the Pionner Inn, tel. 661-3636. Daily breakfast from 7:00 a.m., lunch from 11:30 a.m. Basic but good foods including pancakes and Portuguese bean soup. Most dishes and sandwiches under $5. Also, **South Seas** on the harbor side of the Pioneer Inn. Seafood and cook-your-own, all for under $10. Children's menu. Daily dinner only, tel. 661-3636.

Ma's Dimsum is in the Lahaina Square, tel. 667-9378. Daily except Sun., from 11:00 a.m. to 5:00 p.m. Chinese take out featuring a wide variety of *dimsum.* All kinds of plate lunches available for picnicking.

Fujiyama is also at Lahaina Square, tel. 667-6207. Open Mon. to Fri. 11:00 a.m. to 1:30 p.m. and from 5:00 to 9:00 p.m. *Teppenyaki* dinners at your table for $15. A full *sushi* bar. Most Japanese favorites like *tempura* and *sukiyaki.*

Organ Grinder, 811 Front St., tel. 661-4593, is a family-run business giving you your money's worth. Terrific sandwiches that'll fill you up. Open for breakfast, too.

Kimo's, 845 Front St., tel. 661-4811, has great harbor and sunset views on the lower level. Popular, but no reservations taken. They offer seafood from $8 and are known for their "catch-of-the-day," usually the best offering on the menu. The downstairs bar has top-notch well drinks featuring brand name liquor. A limited menu for children.

Bettino's, 505 Front, Lahaina Shores Village, tel. 661-8810, is open daily from 7:00 a.m. Off the beaten track and a favorite with locals. Italian offerings like fettucine from $6.95. Also, steaks and seafood. Renowned for their enormous salads. Worth the trip, and when others are overcrowded you can usually find a good table here. The **Whaler's Pub** just next door has good drinks and an exemplary view. Friendly atmosphere and no trouble finding a great table.

Blackie's Bar is on Rt. 30 about one-half mile out of town toward Kaanapali. Look for the orange roof. Daily 10:00 a.m. to 10:00 p.m., tel. 667-7979. An institution, sort of, selling Mexican food and burgers! Known for jazz on Sun., Mon., and Fri. evenings from 5:00 to 8:00 p.m.

The **Chart House** at the far west end of Lahaina at 1450 Front St., tel. 661-0937, serves daily dinner 5:00 to 9:30 p.m. No reservations, and a wait is common. They have another, less crowded restaurant in Kahului. Good selection of seafood and beef. Reasonably priced with a decent salad bar.

Expensive

When you feel like putting a major dent in your budget, and satisfying your desire for some gourmet food, you should be pleased with one of the following:

Alex's Hole-in-the-Wall, down an alleyway at 834 Front, will put a little hole in your wallet. The food is Italian with delights like veal parmigiana for $17.95, and chicken cacciatore for $12.95. The pasta is locally made and fresh. Open daily except Sun., from 6:00 to 10:00 p.m., tel. 661-3197.

Longhi's, 888 Front St., tel. 667-2288, serves daily from 7:30 a.m. to 10:00 p.m. Longhi owns the joint and he's a character. He feels that his place has "healing vibes" and that man's basic food is air. He's got an old dog, Freddy, who might still be alive (you can't tell by looking at him). If you don't like eating where a dog eats, then hit the road. The waiters come around and recite the menu to you. Pay attention. Prawns amaretto and shrimp Longhi are a good choice. Save room for the fabulous desserts that circulate on a tray, and from which you may choose. There's always a line, no reservations, and it's hard not to have a fine meal. Breakfast is terrific, too.

Gerard's, at the Lahaina Market Place, corner of Lahainaluna Road, tel. 661-8939, is open daily for lunch and dinner, Sunday dinner only. Menu changes daily. Oh so French! The owner is the chef, so care goes into the food.

La Bretagne, at the east end town at 562 C Front St., is in a vintage historical house, tel. 661-8966, daily dinner only. Reservations. French? But of course, mon cherie! $20 and up. Elegant dining with exemplary desserts.

Chez Paul, 5 miles east of Lahaina in Olowalu, is secluded, French (what else!), romantic, and very popular. The wine list is tops, the desserts fantastic and the food, magnifique! Prices start at $20. On Rt. 30, tel. 661-3843. Daily from 5:30 p.m. Credit cards? For sure—no one carries that much cash!

ENTERTAINMENT

Lahaina is one of those places where the real entertainment is the town itself. The best thing to do here is to stroll along Front Street and people-watch. As you walk along, it feels like a block party with the action going on all around you. Some people duck into one of the many establishments along the south side of Front Street for a breather, a drink, or just to watch the sunset. It's all free, enjoyable, and safe.

Night Spots

All of the evening entertainment in Lahaina is in restaurants and lounges (see "Food" for details). The following should provide you with a few laughs: jazz at **Blackie's** every Fri. and Sat. evening; jam sessions and popular combos at the **Whale's Tale** and **Blackbeard's** nightly; disco at **Moose McGuillicuddy's** nightly; jam sessions at **The Keg,** formerly the Blue Max. Many of the other restaurants and lounges offer live performances on any given night.

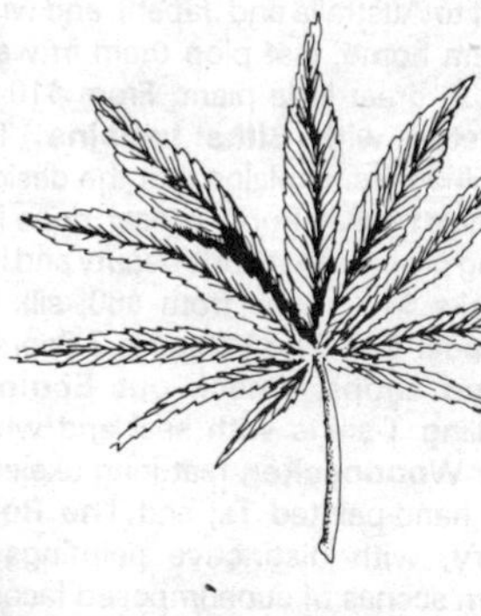

Drugs

Like everywhere in Hawaii, the main street drug is *pakalolo*. If you're "looking," cruise Front Street, especially around the sea wall, and make friendly eye contact with the local guys. Listen for that distinctive "joint sucking" sound or for a whispered, "Buds?" It's usually vacuum-packed in Seal-a-Meal plastic bags, but if the guy won't let you smell it, or better yet taste it, try again. Usually all deals are straight, although inflated, business transactions.

Hookers

Lahaina had more than its share last century, and thankfully they haven't had a great resurgence, like Waikiki. In the words of one longtime resident, "There's no prostitution in Lahaina. People come as couples. For single people, there's so much free stuff around that the pros would go hungry."

SHOPPING

Once learned, everybody loves to do the "Lahaina Stroll." It's easy. Just act cool, nonchalant, and give it your best strut as you walk the gauntlet of Front Street's exclusive shops and exotic boutiques. The fun is just in being here. If you begin in the evening, go to the east end of town and park down by Prison Street; much easier to find a spot and you walk westward catching the sunset. On Prison, check out **Dan's Exotic Greenhouse,** specializing in birds and *fukobonsai.* These miniatures were originated by David Fukomoto. They're mailable (except to Australia and Japan), and when you get them home, just plop them in water and presto...a great little plant. From $10-20. On Front start with **Silks Lahaina.** The manager, Jill Jones, explains that the designs are all originals by Gay Pope, a local, done in a unique dying process that adds beauty and longevity. Slacks $100, tops from $60, silk accessories under $20. **The Wharf** is 3 floors of eateries and shops. Check out **Ecology House,** selling T-shirts with seal and whale motifs; **The Woodpecker,** featuring ukeleles, flutes, and hand-painted Ts; and **The Royal Art Gallery,** with distinctive paintings of island dream scenes of superimposed faces in the clouds. Make sure to visit the **Lahaina Art Foundation** in the old jail basement of the Court House. **Greenpeace** is a "must stop" especially during whale season. Profits on items sold here go to ecological causes. **The Scentuous Shop** will make you swoon with its assortment of heady perfumes and oils that make great gifts. Don't miss the **Lahaina Scrimshaw Factory.** The staff here is not only knowledgeable on this old art, but also willing to chat. Pieces in all price ranges. **Jade and Jewels** is a treasure chest laden with rubies, emeralds, and carvings from India and China. **Whale of a Shirt** sells Ts for under $10, **Apparels by Pauline** are reasonably priced, and Alexia features natural clothing with supernatural price tags. Check out the aerotechnics at **High as a Kite,** the assortment of shoes at **Peg Leg's,** and the outdoor gear and good prices at **Vagabond.**

For artwork, try **Lahaina Gallery** on Lahainaluna, **Village Gallery** on Front, and **Nagamine Camera** for your photo needs. **Lahaina Shopping Center** has a clutch of practical shops along with Cliff McQueen's **Wizard of Ahs,** where you can eat organic yogurt in a tennis pro shop. **Skin Deep Tattooing** on Lahai-

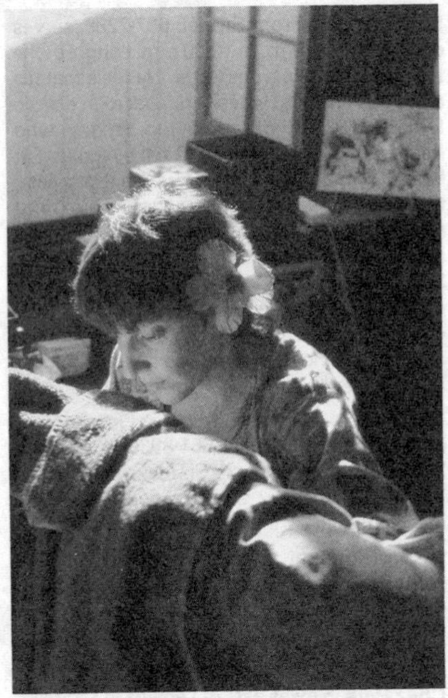

artist at Skin Deep Tattoo Parlor

naluna offers you a permanent memento, features "new-age primal, tribal tattooing," with female artists for shy ladies. The **Waterfront Gallery and Gifts** will tickle big kids with their fine ships, models, and imported sheepskins. Across from **Lahaina One Hour Photo** you find tucked away **Tropical Boutique** with batiks from Java, and **Pacific Visions** where cut glass and etched crystals will dazzle your senses.

SERVICES AND INFORMATION

Emergency: For fire, police, or ambulance, dial 911 throughout the Lahaina area. **Banks:** In Lahaina during normal banking hours try: **Bank of Hawaii** in the Lahaina Shopping Center, tel. 661-8781; **First Interstate** at 135 Papalaua St., tel. 667-9714; **First Hawaiian** Papalaua St., tel. 661-3655.

Post Office
The post office is in the Lahaina Shopping Center off Papalaua Street, tel. 667-6611; **Mail Home Maui** is a post office contract station located at The Wharf Shopping Plaza, 658 Front St., tel. 667-6620. They're open 7 days from 10:00 a.m. to 5:00 p.m. Along with the normal stamps, etc., they specialize in sending packages home. They've got mailing boxes, tape and packaging materials. They also sell souvenir packs of coffee, nuts, candies, and teas which might serve as a last-minute purchase, but are expensive.

Laundromat
Try **Maui Dry Cleaning,** Lahaina Shopping Center, tel. 667-2659.

Medical Treatment
A concentration of all types of specialists is found at **Lahaina Medical Group,** located at Lahaiana Square, tel. 667-2534. Alternatively, the **Lahaina Health Center,** at the west end of town at 1287 Front St., tel. 667-6268, offers acupuncture, chiropractic, therapeutic massage, and podiatry. Most practitioners charge approximately $30 for their services. Pharmacies in Lahaina include: **Craft's** at the Lahaina Shopping Center, tel. 661-3119, and **Valley Isle** at 130 Prison, tel. 661-4747.

Information
The following groups and organizations should prove helpful: **Lahaina Restoration Foundation,** Box 338, Lahaina, Maui, HI 96761, tel. 661-3262, or in the "Master's Reading Room" along Front Street. They are a storehouse of information about historical Maui, and make sure to pick up their brochure, "Lahaina, A Walking Tour of Historic and Cultural Sites"; **Library** at 680 Wharf St., tel. 661-0566; open Mon. through Thursday. Stop in at **Upstart Crow and Co.** in the upper level of The Wharf Mall along Front Street. They have an excellent book selection as well as a gourmet coffee and sandwich shop if you get tired browsing. The **Kelsey Gallery** at 129 Lahainaluna Rd. also deals in a limited supply of books; also see "Information" in the main Introduction for newspapers, radio stations, and general information sources.

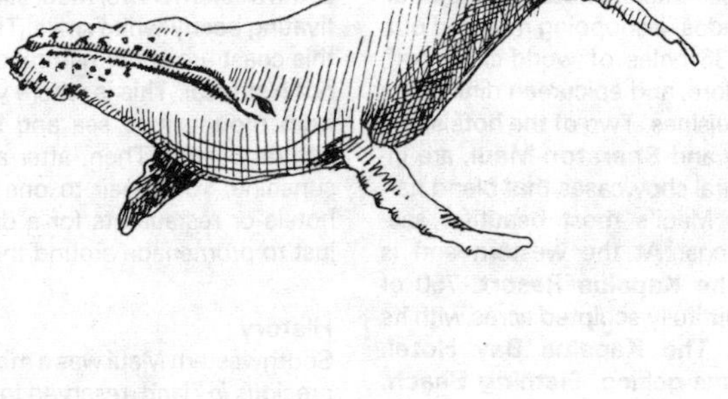

KAANAPALI

Five lush valleys, nourished by streams from the West Maui Mountains, stretch luxuriously for 10 miles from Kaanapali west to Kapalua. All along the connecting **Honoapiilani Highway** (Rt. 30), the dazzle and glimmer of beaches is offset by black volcanic rock. Two sensitively planned and beautifully executed resorts are at each end of this drive. Kaanapali Resort is 500 acres of fun and relaxation at the east end. It houses 6 luxury hotels, 6 beautifully appointed condos, a shopping mall and outdoor museum, 36 holes of world-class golf, tennis courts galore, and epicurean dining in a chef's salad of cuisines. Two of the hotels, the **Hyatt Regency** and **Sheraton-Maui**, are inspired architectural showcases that blend harmoniously with Maui's most beautiful seashore surroundings. At the western end is another gem, **The Kapalua Resort**, 750 of Maui's most beautifully sculpted acres with its own showcase, **The Kapalua Bay Hotel**. Here, too, is prime golfing, **Fleming Beach**, perhaps the best on the island, exclusive shopping, horseback riding, and tennis aplenty.

Kaanapali, with its 4 miles of glorious beach, is Maui's westernmost point. In general, it begins where Lahaina ends, and continues west along Rt. 30 until a mile or so before the village of Honokawai. Adjacent at the west end are the villages of Honokawai and Kahana that service the condos tucked away here and there along the coast and mountainsides. Both are practical stops where you can buy food, gas, and all necessary supplies to keep your vacation rolling. The accommodations are not as grand, but the beaches and vistas are. Along this entire southwestern shore, Maui flashes its most captivating pearly-white smile. The sights all along this coast are either natural or man-made, but not historical. This is where you come to gaze from mountain to sea and bathe yourself in natural beauty. Then, after a day of surf and sunshine, you repair to one of the gorgeous hotels or restaurants for a drink or dining, or just to promenade around the grounds.

History

Southwestern Maui was a mixture of scrub and precious *lo'i* land, reserved for taro, the highest life-sustaining plant given by the gods. The farms stretched to Kapalua, skirting the numerous bays all along the way. The area was important enough for a "royal highway" to be built by chief Piilani, and it still bears his name.

Westerners used the lands surrounding Kaanapali to grow sugarcane, and **The Lahaina, Kaanapali and Pacific Railroad**, known today as the "Sugarcane Train," chugged to Kaanapali Beach to unburden itself onto barges that carried the cane to waiting ships. Kaanapali, until the 1960s, was a blemished beauty where the Pioneer Sugar Mill dumped its rubbish. Then AMFAC, one of the "Big Five," decided to put the land to better use. In creating Hawaii's first planned resort, they outdid themselves. Robert Trent Jones was hired to mold the golf course along this spectacular coast, while the Hyatt Regency and its grounds became an architectural marvel. The Sheraton-Maui was built atop, and integrated with, Puu Kekaa ("Black Rock"). This area is a wave-eroded cinder cone, and the Sheraton architects used its sea cliffs as part of the walls of the resort. Here, on a deep underwater shelf, daring divers descend to harvest Maui's famous black coral trees. The Hawaiians believed that Puu Kekaa was a very holy place where the spirits of the dead left this earth and migrated into the spirit world. Kahekili, Maui's most famous 18th C. chief, often came here to leap into the sea below. This old-time daredevil was fond of the heart-stopping activity, and made famous "Kahekili's Leap," an even more treacherous seacliff on nearby Lanai. Today, the Sheraton puts on a sunset show where this "leap" is re-enacted.

Unfortunately, developers picked up on AMFAC's great idea and built condos up the road starting in Honokawai. Interested in profit, not beauty, they earned that area the dubious title of "condo ghetto." Fortunately, the Maui Land and Pineapple Co. owned the land surrounding the idyllic Kapalua Bay, and Colin Cameron, one of the heirs to this holding, had visions of developing 750 acres of the plantation's 20,000 into the extraordinary **Kapalua Bay Resort**. He teamed up with Rockresort Management, headed by Laurence Rockefeller, and the complex was opened in 1979.

Transportation
The **Blue Shoreline Bus** runs all along the southwest coast from Kapalua to Lahaina and points east. Kaanapali is serviced by the **Kaanapali Jitney**. The Sugarcane Train offers a day of fun for the entire family. For details see

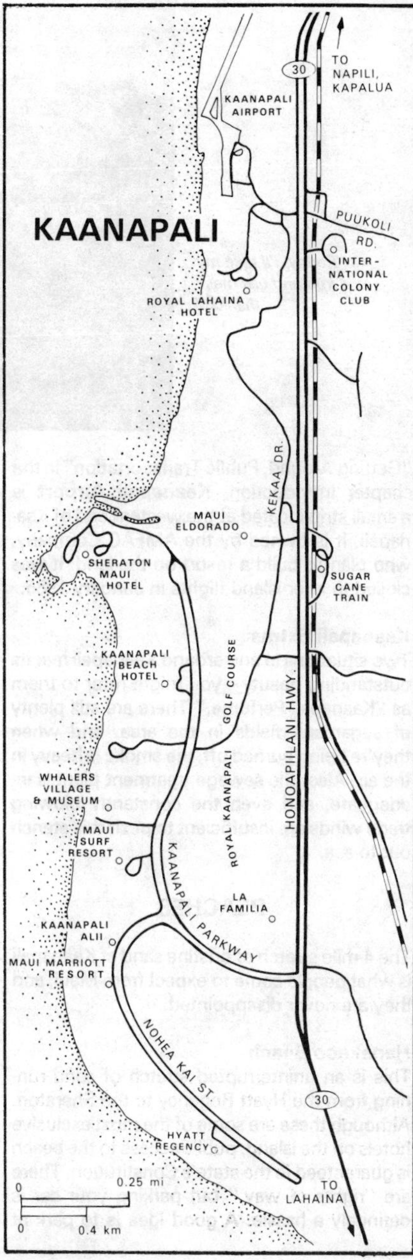

"Caddy, I'll take my 4-iron and gas mask thanks."

"Getting Around, Public Transportation" in the chapter Introduction. **Kaanapali Airport** is a small strip located at the western end of Kaanapali. It is owned by the AMFAC Company, who plan to build a resort on the land. It was closed to inter-island flights in January 1986.

Kaanapali Extras

Two situations in and around Kaanapali mar its outstanding beauty—you might refer to them as "Kaanapali Perfume." There are still plenty of sugarcane fields in the area, and when they're being burned off, the smoke is heavy in the air. Also, the sewage treatment plant is inadequate, and even the constantly blowing trade winds are insufficient to push this stench out to sea.

BEACHES

The 4-mile stretch of pristine sand at Kaanapali is what people come to expect from Maui, and they are never disappointed.

Hanakaoo Beach

This is an uninterrupted stretch of sand running from the Hyatt Regency to the Sheraton. Although these are some of the most exclusive hotels on the island, public access to the beach is guaranteed in the state's Constitution. There are "rights of way," but parking your car is definitely a hassle. A good idea is to park at **Wahikuli State Park** and walk westward along the beach. You can park (10 cars) in the Hyatt's lower lot and enter along a right of way. There's access between the Hyatt and the Marriott (no parking) and between the Marriott and the Kaanapali Alii, which also has limited parking. There is parking near the Sheraton (11 cars) and at the Whaler's Shopping Center, but you must pass through the gauntlet of shops.

Black Rock

One of the most easily accessible and visually engaging snorkeling spots on Maui is located at the Sheraton's Black Rock. "No Parking" signs are everywhere, but you can find a spot. Follow the main road past the Sheraton until it climbs the hill around back. You'll take your chances parking in the lot just near the "Discovery Room" sign, because parking tickets are given here sporadically. Turn around instead and head back down the hill. Park on the right, where you'll see many cars. The sign says "No Parking," but usually you aren't ticketed here. Walk back up the hill and through the hotel grounds until you come to a white metal fence. Follow the fence down toward the sea. You'll come to a spur of rock jutting out and that's it. The entire area is like an underwater marine park. Enter at the beach area and snorkel west around the rock, staying close to the cinder cone. There are schools of reef fish, rays, and even a lonely turtle.

Sports
For a full listing of the sporting facilities and possibilities in the Kaanapali area, contact the Aloha Activity Center in the Whalers Village, tel. 661-3815. **Golf** at the Royal Kaanapali North/South costs $27 plus $11 for a mandatory cart. Both courses are a par 72, tel. 661-3691. For **tennis,** the most famous is the Royal Lahaina Tennis Ranch with 11 courts, tennis clinics, and tournaments. The Sheraton has 3 courts, the Hyatt 5, the Whaler 3 courts, one each at the Kaanapali Royal and Kaanapali Plantation and three at the Maui Surf. For **water sports,** catamarans are available twice a day from Kaanapali Beach. Contact any major hotel activities desk in the resort area, or **Kaanapali Jet Ski** at the Whalers Village, tel. 667-7851.

ACCOMMODATIONS

The Kaanapali Resort offers accommodations ranging from "moderate deluxe" to "luxury." There are no budget accommodations here, but just west toward Honokawai are plenty of reasonably priced condos. As usual, they're more of a bargain the longer you stay, especially if you can share costs with a few people by renting a larger unit. And as always, you'll save money on food costs. The following should give you an idea of what's available.

Hyatt Regency
Located at Kaanapali's eastern extremity, at 200 Nohea Kai Drive, Lahaina 96761. Reservations are made at 800-228-9000, or on Maui at 667-7474. The least expensive room in this truly luxury hotel is $175 a day; they go as high as $1,500 for the Presidential Suite. Of course, like many Hyatts, you don't have to stay there to appreciate its beauty. If you visit, expensive valet parking is only in front of the hotel. Around back is a lot, but most spaces are numbered by the room with only a few for visitors. During the day, if a numbered one is empty, you can take your chances.

The moment you enter the main lobby the magic begins. A multi-tiered architectural extravaganza opens to the sky, birds fly freely, and magnificent potted plants and full-sized palm trees create the atmosphere of a modern Polynesian palace. Nooks and crannies abound where you can lounge in kingly wicker thrones. The walls are adorned with first-class artworks and tapestries, while glass showcases hold priceless ceramics. Peacocks strut their regal stuff amid impeccable Japanese gardens, and ducks and swans are floating alabaster on a symmetry of landscaped ponds. Around the swimming pool, guests luxuriate on huge pink hotel towels. The pool's architecture is inspired by the islands: grottoes, caves, waterfalls, and a huge slide are all built in. A swinging wood bridge connects the sections, and you can have an island drink at a sunken poolside bar. There's an exclusive 5-star restaurant, a disco for human peacocking, and the "Elephant Walk," a covey of specialty shops and boutiques. The hotel offers half-hour scuba lessons in the pool for $10, beach dives for $49, and a 4-day certification course including all rental equipment and dives for $350.

Sheraton-Maui
These 505 rooms are built around Kaanapali's most conspicuous natural phenomenon, Black Rock. For reservations, tel. 800-325-3535, or on Maui 661-0031. The prices are not as astronomical as the Hyatt's, with a basic room at $140, up to $350 for an oceanside suite. The snorkeling around Black Rock is best in the area. There are 2 pools, and the view from the upper-level **Berkentine Bar** is worth the price of a drink. A catamaran is available to guests, and you can rent snorkeling equipment at a poolside kiosk, but the prices are triple what you pay at a dive shop.

the Sheraton Maui

Royal Lahaina

This massive 514-room complex is the most extensive in Kaanapali, as well as being one of the first. The **Maui Kaanapali** is completely enveloped by it. Reservations can be made at 800-227-4700, in California at 800-622-0838, on Maui at tel. 661-3611. Prices for standard rooms start at $105, cottages go for $150-250, and suites are up to $950. There are no less than 7 restaurants and 6 swimming pools on the well-maintained grounds. It's also home to the **Royal Lahaina Tennis Ranch,** boasting 10 courts and a stadium.

Other Hotels

For Kaanapali, the following hotels might be considered a bargain. The **Kaanapali Beach** offers standard rooms from $105, has a distinctive whale-shaped pool and tennis privileges at the Royal Lahaina, tel. 800-227-4700, on Maui tel. 661-0011. **The Maui Marriott Resort** is actually a luxury hotel. Standard studios begin at $170 and go up to $1,200 for a suite. However, they offer a 50% reduction coupon from April 15 to December 15, found in the free tourist magazines. You cannot make reservations through a travel agent, or the 800-228-9290 number to use it. You must call the hotel at 808-667-1200 to redeem the coupon on a space-available basis.

Condos

Generally much less expensive than the hotels, most begin at $70 per night. They all offer full kitchens, some maid service, swimming pools, and often convenience stores and laundry facilities. There are usually off-season rates, and discounts for longer stays. Combinations of the above are too numerous to mention, so it's best to ask all pertinent questions when booking. Not all accept credit cards, and a deposit is the norm when making reservations. The following should give you an idea of what to expect. **International Colony Club** on the *mauka* side of Rt. 30, tel. 661-4070 offers individual cottages at $90, $10 extra person, 4-day minimum. **The Whaler** at the Whaler's Village, tel. 800-267-2936, on Maui tel. 661-4861, is in the heart of things, and offers swimming pools and great beach frontage. From $135 to $350. Lobby, sauna, market, and tennis courts.

Others in Kaanapali proper include **Maui Eldorado,** tel. 800-421-0680, on Maui tel. 661-0021, surrounded by the golf course, from $65. **Kaanapali Plantation,** tel. 661-4446, from $85 with a $10 discount for 14 days or longer. Maid service and most amenities. **Kaanapali Royal,** a golfer's dream right on the course, tel. 800-367-7040, on Maui tel. 523-7785, from $110 with substantial low-season and long-term discounts. **Hale Kaanapali** at Kaanapali's far west end near the airport, tel. 661-3611.

FOOD

Every hotel in Kaanapali has at least one restaurant, with numerous others scattered throughout the area. Some of the most expensive and exquisite restaurants on Maui are found in these hotels, but surprisingly, at others you can dine very reasonably, even cheaply.

La Familia

This is a reasonably priced Mexican restaurant. Their happy hour, from 4:30 to 6:00 p.m., offers excellent margaritas for 99 cents, along with free chips and salsa. The most expensive item on the menu is $12, with the majority of meals under $7. They also offer a $2 coupon on dinner checks over $10. Their staff is gracious and friendly. They are located at 2290 Kaanapali Parkway (the first sign pointing to Kaanapali from Lahaina), tel. 667-7902.

Apple Annie's

Also on Kaanapali Parkway. You can get a variety of sandwiches, omelettes and light meals for around $6. Their offerings are well-prepared and wholesome, but overpriced for what you get; tel. 661-3160.

Royal Lahaina Resort

You have no less than 3 establishments from which to choose. A *luau* is prepared nightly in the Luau Gardens, and the biggest problem of the Polynesian Review is standing up after eating mountains of traditional food. Adults $31, children under 12 $17, reservations tel. 661-3611.

Moby Dick's is a seafood restaurant open for dinner only, tel. 661-3611. Entrees are reasonably priced for around $12, but you pay for all the extras like soup and salad which can push your bill to $20 or more. Royal Ocean Terrace is open daily for breakfast, lunch, and dinner, offering a breakfast buffet and better-than-average salad bar. Sunday brunch from 9:00 a.m. until 2:00 p.m. is a winner, tel. 661-3611.

Eight Bells Restaurant
In the Maui Surf Hotel, tel. 661-4411. Open for breakfast and dinner, but call to check for specific hours, which vary. Their dinners are acceptable for around $12, but their $6.95 breakfast buffet is legendary. Arrive the last hour and eat your fill, which should easily suffice until dinner.

Swan Court
You don't come here to eat, you come here to dine, peasant! Anyone who has been enraptured by those old movies where couples regally glide down a central staircase to make their grand entrance will have his fantasies come true. Although expensive, you get your money's worth with attention to detail; prosciutto is served with papaya, ginger butter with the fresh catch-of-the-day, and pineapple chutney with the oysters. The wine list is a connoisseur's delight. The Swan Court offers a sumptuous breakfast/brunch buffet daily from 6:30 a.m. It's $10.50 per person, and worth the price for the view alone. Save this one for a very special evening. Located in the Hyatt Regency, daily breakfast and dinner, tel. 667-7474.

Spats II is also at the Hyatt, tel. 667-7474, dinner only. They specialize in Italian food with the average entree around $16. At night this becomes a disco, and fancy duds are in order. **Lahaina Provision Co.**, tel. 667-7474, could only survive with a name like that because it's at the Hyatt. Regular broiled fare, but you get a bowl of ice cream, and are free to go hog-wild with chocolate toppings at their famous chocoholic bar. Guaranteed to make you repent all your sins!

Discovery Room
At the Sheraton, tel. 661-0031. Daily for breakfast and dinner. Basic American food like baked chicken, well prepared with all the trimmings, for $20. Entertainment is offered at dinner and at the 9:30 p.m. cocktail show. A *luau* is offered Tues., Thurs., and Sun. from 5:30 p.m., adults $30, children $18. Features Chief Faa, the fire knife dancer. Reservations tel. 667-9564.

Lokelani
At the Maui Marriott, tel. 667-1200, dinner only, from 6:00 p.m. Full dinners such as sauteed catch-of-the-day with all trimmings from $14.

Enjoy exclusive dining and shopping at the Hyatt.

Also, **Nikko's Japanese Steak House,** tel. 667-1200, dinner from 6:00 p.m. No cheap imports here. Prices are high, but the Japanese chef works right at your table slicing meats and vegetables quicker than you can say "samurai." An expensive but fun meal.

Peacock Restaurant
Located at 2550 Kehaa Drive, tel. 667-6847. Daily lunch and dinner. This elegant restaurant was at one time the Kaanapali golf course clubhouse. As its name implies, it's a bit fancy with ritzy Oriental decor. Dinners cost about $20, and the house specialty is an uncommon dish, Maui rabbit. Their pork in mango sauce is exotic, and so is the *poisson cru* appetizer.

Kapa Room
At the Maui Surf Hotel, tel. 661-4411. A *luau* for the unusually low price of $21.50, every night except Tuesday. Maui's early history is the theme for stories and dance.

Kaanapali Beach Hotel Restaurant
The hotel might be fancy but the restaurant is down to earth. Good old cafeteria-style American food. Dinner specials only $5. Daily breakfast, lunch, and dinner, tel. 661-0011.

Whaler's Village
This shopping mall has a half dozen or so dining establishments. You can find everything from pizza and frozen yogurt to lobster tail. Prices range from bargain to moderate. An up-and-comer is **Leilani's.** Their selections go from surf to turf. They offer famous Azeka ribs for $10.95, a *sushi* bar, and a daily dinner special from 5:00 to 6:30 p.m. for $8.50. This includes entree, and soup or salad. Call 661-4495. **El Crab Catcher** is a well-established restaurant featuring seafood, with a variety of crab dishes, steaks, and chops. They have a sunken bar and swimming pool with the beach only a stride or two away. Desserts are special here from $10. Popular, so reserve at tel. 661-4423.

The **Rusty Harpoon,** previously a "do-it-yourself" broiler, has remodeled and changed its image. They offer a completely new menu and pleasing atmosphere. Piano music at night and popular with younger set. Lunch from 11:00 a.m. to 3:30 p.m., dinner from 6:00 to 9:30 p.m. No one will mutiny over the seafood, chicken, and beef offered at the **HMS Bounty** for around $10, Children's portions cheaper. Daily for breakfast, lunch, and dinner with an "early bird special" from 5:00-6:30 p.m. Popular, no reservations, tel. 661-0946. **Yami Yogurt** sells wholesome, well-made sandwiches for $3 and under. Salads, too, and yogurt, of course. No seating, but plenty of spots outside, tel. 661-8843. **Ricco's Deli** makes hefty sandwiches for under $4. Their mini-pizzas make a good inexpensive lunch, tel. 669-6811.

ENTERTAINMENT

If you're out for a night of fun and frivolity, Kaanapali will keep you hopping. The dinner shows accompanying the *luau* at the Hyatt Regency and Maui Surf feature pure island entertainment. The Maui Surf's "Here's Hawaii" is a sensitive, funny, and well-done musical production with a cast of only five. The songs tell the story of Maui's history, led by Audrey Meyers and Jeffrey Apaka. "Drums of the Pacific" is a musical extravaganza that you would expect from the Hyatt. There are torch-lit processions, and excitingly choreographed production numbers, with all the *hula*-skirted *wahines* and *malo*-clad *kanes* that you could imagine. Flames add drama to the settings and the grand finale is a fire dance. At both shows you're dined and entertained by mid-evening.

Those with dancing feet can boogie the night away at the Hyatt's **Spats II.** There is a dress code and plenty of room for those "big dippers" on this very large dance floor. Practice your waltzes for the outdoor **Pavilion Courtyard** at the Hyatt. The **Banana Moon** at the Marriott offers the best of both worlds—dance music and quiet, candle-lit corners for romance. Most hotels, restaurants, and lounges offer some sort of music. Often it's a local combo singing Hawaiian favorites, or a piano-man tinking away in the background. The only movie theater in Kaanapali is the **Village Cinema,** tel. 661-0922, in the Whaler's Village.

SHOPPING

There are 3 places to shop in Kaanapali: at the **Whaler's Village Mall**, which is affordable, at the **Maui Marriott** for some distinctive purchases, and at the **Hyatt Regency** where most people get the jitters even window shopping.

Whaler's Village Shopping Mall And Museum

This unique outdoor mall doubles as quite a passable museum, with showcases filled with items, mostly from the whaling days, accompanied by informative descriptions. You can easily find anything here that you might need. Some of the shops are: **Book Cache,** featuring fine books with an entire section dedicated to Hawaiiana, tel. 661-3259. **Superwhale Children's Boutique,** tel. 661-0260, all beach wear and alohawear for the *keiki.* **Lahaina Scrimshaw Factory,** tel. 661-4034, for fine examples of scrimshaw and other art objects from affordable to expensive. **Liberty House,** tel. 661-4451, for usual department store items. **Ka Honu Gift Gallery,** tel. 661-0137, for a large selection of arts and crafts inspired by the islands. There are many other shops tucked away here and there. They come and go with regularity.

The Hyatt Regency Mall

Off the main lobby and surrounding the gardens are a number of exclusive shops. They're high-priced, but their offerings are first class. Call 667-7421 and ask for the store of your choice. **Elephant Walk** specializes in primitive art such as tribal African masks and carved wooden statues. **Gold Point's** name says it all with baubles, trinkets, bracelets, and rings all in gold. **Sandal Tree** has footwear for men and women with the emphasis on sandals. **Mark Christopher** is a series of shops selling jewelry, glassware, fabrics, and beach wear.

Maui Marriott

The main store here is a **Liberty House,** tel. 667-6142, with the emphasis on clothing. **Hawaii I.D.** is an upbeat dive shop with masks, fins, boards and the rest; **Friendship Store's** art objects, clothing, silks, and goods are all from the Republic of China. There are also women's stores and jewelry shops.

SERVICES AND INFORMATION

Banks

Most larger hotels can help with some banking needs, especially with the purchasing or cashing of TCs; **Bank of Hawaii** has a branch at 2580 Kekaa Drive, tel. 667-6251.

Medical

Dr. Ben Azman maintains an office at the Whaler's Village, tel. 667-9721, or after hours tel. 244-3728.

Camera Needs

Shops are: **Makai Camera** in the Whaler's Village; **Hawaiian Vision** and **Sandy's Camera** in the Royal Lahaina complex; **Island Camera** in the Sheraton.

Laundromat

The **Washerette Clinic** in the Sheraton.

Information

For a complete source of information on all aspects of the Kaanapali area contact Kaanapali Beach Operators Association, Box 616, Kaanapali, Maui, HI 96761, tel. 661-3271.

HONOKOWAI AND KAHANA

You head for Honokowai and Kahana if you want to enjoy Maui's west coast and not spend a bundle of money. They're not quite as pretty as Kaanapali or Kapalua, but proportionate to the money you'll save, you come out ahead. To get there, travel along the **Honoapiilani Hwy.**, take **Lower Honoapiilani Hwy.** through Honokowai and continue on it to Kahana.

BEACHES

Honokowai Beach Park is right in Honokowai Town just across from the Superette. Here you have a large lawn with palm trees and picnic tables, but a small beach. The water is shallow, and tame—good for tots. The swimming is not as nice as Kaanapali, but take a dip after shopping. Snorkeling is fair, and you can get through a break in the reef at the west end. **Kahana Beach** is near the Kahana Beach Resort; park across the street. Nothing spectacular, but the protected small beach is good for tots. Great view of Molokai and never crowded.

ACCOMMODATIONS

At last count there were well over 3 dozen condos and apartment complexes in the 3 miles encompassing Honokowai and Kahana. There are plenty of private homes out here as well, which give you a good cross-section of Hawaiian society. A multimillion-dollar spread may occupy a beach, while out in the bay is a local fisherman with his beat-up old boat trying to make a few bucks for the day. Many of the condos built out here were controversial. Locals refused to work on some because they were on holy ground, and a few actually experienced bad luck jinxes as they were being built. The smarter owners called in *kahuna* to bless the ground and the disturbances ceased.

Honokowai Palms

At 3666 Lower Honoapiilani Hwy., Lahaina 96761, (near Honokawai), tel. 669-6130. This condo is an old standby for budget travelers. You can get a one-bedroom unit for $50 during high season, $40 during low. There are weekly and monthly discounts, $6 for an extra person in a room, $100 deposit required, no credit cards, 3-night minimum, and maid service extra. With a pool, this condo is clean and adequate.

Hale Ono Loa

At 3823 Lower Honoapiilani Hwy., Lahaina 96761, tel. 800-367-2927, or on Maui 669-6362. A bit more upbeat. From $52 for a double, with prices rising as you ascend floors, up to $85 for 2 bedrooms. Three-day minimum, complete kitchens, partial maid service, pool.

Makani Sands

3765 Lower Honoapiilani Hwy., Lahaina 96761, tel. 669-8223. From $70 for a single, $6 additional persons. Swimming pool, 3-day minimum, maid service every 4 days.

Mahana

110 Kaanapili Shore Pl., Lahaina 96761, tel. 800-472-8449 in California, others 800-854-8843, Canada collect 714-497-4253, on Maui tel. 661-8751. A nicer place on the beach toward Kaanapali. Studio $60 up to $125 for a suite. Pool, tennis, shop, maid service on request, full kitchens, 5-night minimum.

Valley Isle

4327 Honoapiilani Hwy. (Kahana), Lahaina 96761, tel. 800-854-8843, in California 800-472-8449, on Maui 669-5511. from $60, restaurant, cocktails, pool, shop, maid service on request, 5-night minimum.

Kaanapali Shores

100 Kaanapali Shores Pl., Lahaina 96761, tel. 800-367-5124, on Maui tel. 667-2211. An uptown condo toward Kaanapali from $110. Restaurant, lounge, shop, pool, tennis courts.

Noelani

At 4095 Lower Honoapiilani Hwy., Lahaina 96761, tel. 800-367-6030, on Maui tel.

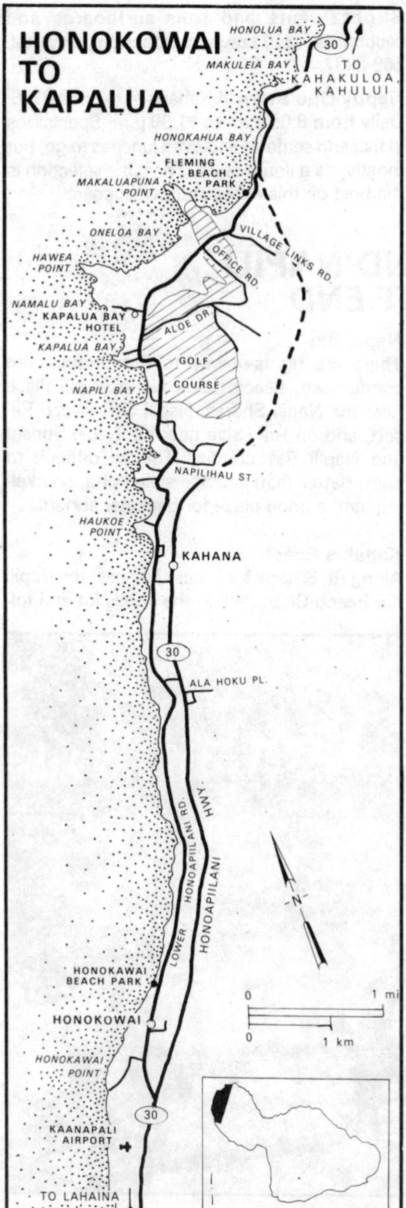

669-8374. Studios from $65. Two pools, BBQ area, fully equipped kitchens, and color TVs.

FOOD AND ENTERTAINMENT

Ricco's
At the **Happy Opu Store** in Kahana, tel. 669-6811. Good old-time deli featuring fresh-baked pizza. Large sandwiches for $3 and lunches to go.

Dollies
4310 Honoapiilani Hwy. (Kahana), tel. 667-2623. From breakfast to late evening. Sandwiches, pizza, food to go. Deliveries to condos! Good food and fair prices, like turkey or roast beef with Swiss and jack for $4.65.

Erik's Seafood Grotto
4242 Lower Honoapiilani Hwy., second floor of Kahana Villa, tel. 669-4806. Daily for dinner 5:30 to 10:00 p.m. Very good fish selection. "Sunset Special" from 5:30 to 6:30 p.m., $8.95, menu changes daily. Dinners include chowder, bread basket, and potato or rice. Most dinners $12-13 with a good selection of appetizers.

Kahana Keyes
At Kahana Beach, tel. 669-8071. Known for their salad bar and fresh fish. Daily lunch 10:00 a.m. to 2:30 p.m., dinner 5:00 to 10:00 p.m. "Early Bird Special" from 5:00 to 7:00 p.m., $8.95. "Nightly Special," Dungeness crab and prime rib, all you can eat for $14.95. Live music nightly from 7:30 p.m.

The Kahana Keyes Restaurant is the only show in town around here, and luckily it ain't bad! Nightly from 7:30 local bands perform. All types of music are offered, from rock to Hawaiian, and the large dance floor is hardly ever crowded.

SHOPPING

Honokowai Superette
The only real place west of Lahaina to shop for groceries and sundries. Located on Lower Honoapiilani Hwy. in Honokawai, tel. 669-6208. Daily from 8:00 a.m. to 9:00 p.m. The prices are

just about right at this supermarket. Condo convenience stores in the area are good in a pinch but charge way too much. Stock up here; it's worth the drive.

Honokowai Store is not really a store at all. It rents all manner of surf equipment, masks and snorkels, and even mopeds, tel. 669-6013 in Honokawai.

Skootz rents and sells surfboards and sailboards. 4310 Lower Honoapiilani Hwy., tel. 669-0937.

Happy Opu Store in Kahana at tel. 669-6776. Daily from 8:00 a.m. to 11:00 p.m. Specializes in fish and seafood and even lunches to go, but mostly it's a liquor store. The wine selection is the best on this entire southwest coast.

KAPALUA AND NAPILI THE WEST END

Kapalua sits like a crown atop Maui's head. One of the newest areas on Maui to be developed, it's been nicely done. Out here is the **Kapalua Bay Resort**, golfing, horseback riding, terrific beaches, and even a helicopter ride.

BEACHES

Some of the very best beaches that Maui has to offer are clustered in this area. The following listing proceeds from south to north.

Napili Bay

There are rights-of-way to this perfect, but condo-lined, beach. Look along Napili Place near the Napili Shores, Napili Surf Beach Resort, and on Hui Drive near the Napili Sunset and Napili Bay condos. They're difficult to spot. Better than average swimming, snorkeling, and a good place for beginner surfers.

Kapalua Beach

Along Rt. 30 look for access just past the Napili Kai Beach Club. Park in the public lot and fol-

horseback riding on Fleming Beach

low the path through the tunnel to the beach. Another beautiful crescent beach that's popular, though usually not overcrowded. The well-formed reef here has plenty of fish for snorkeling. Also, restrooms, showers, and beach concessions.

D.T. Fleming Beach

One of Maui's best. Clearly marked along Rt. 30. Parking, showers, and BBQ grills. Excellent swimming except in winter when there's a pounding surf. Fair snorkeling and good surfing.

Oneloa Beach

A short mile past Fleming's. A small sandy beach down a steep path. Those who brave it can camp without a hassle from the officials.

Mokuleia Beach

Also known as "Slaughterhouse." You can spot it because the R.V. Deli, a lunch wagon, is usually parked here. About 200-300 yards after mile marker 32. This beach has great bodysurfing, but terribly dangerous currents in the winter when the surf is rough. Be careful. Follow the trail to the left for the beach. The path straight ahead takes you to a rocky lava flow. The entire area is a marinelife conservation district and the underwater life is fabulous.

Honolua Bay

Just past Mokuleia Bay heading north, look for a dirt road, then park. Some can try the road, but it's very rugged. Good for swimming, snorkeling, and especially surfing. Many people stay the night without much problem.

Sports

The following are offered in the Kapalua area: **Kapalua Bay Golf Club,** par 71, $35 green fees and a mandatory $10 cart; **Kapalua Bay Club Villa,** par 73, $35 fees and a $10 cart. **Tennis** is found at the Napili Kai Beach Club, $4 guests, $6 visitors; Kapalua Bay Hotel **Tennis Garden,** free to guests, $4 others, dress code, tel. 669-5677. **Horseback riding** at the Rainbow Ranch, see "Sports" in the main "Introduction" for details.

ACCOMMODATIONS

Napili, just south of Kapalua Bay, sports a string of condos and a hotel or two. Almost all front the beach, which is hardly ever crowded. The premier resort, however, is the **Kapalua Bay Hotel and Villas.** This, like other grand hotels, is more than a place to stay, it's an experience. The main lobby is partially open and accented with an enormous skylight. Plants trail from the ceiling. Below is a tropical terrace and restaurant and all colors are soothing and subdued. Although relaxing, it's the kind of a place where if you don't wear an evening gown to go to the bathroom, you feel underdressed. The least expensive room in the hotel itself is one with a garden view at $120 off-season. The villas with a mountain view are $100 off-season. All climb rapidly to the $200-300 range. You can have the "American Plan," consisting of breakfast and dinner, for an extra $40. You must make a 3-nights' deposit, refundable only with 14-days' notice. There are 5 restaurants in the complex and magnificent golfing at the Kapalua Villa Club.

Kapalua Bay Hotel and Villas

Napili Kai Beach Club

At 5900 Honoapiilani Rd., Lahaina 96761, tel. 800-367-5030, on Maui tel. 669-6271. Expensive at $100 per studio, but you do have a kitchenette. The beach is a crescent moon here with gentle wave action. There are 5 pools, putting greens, tennis courts, and the Kapalua Bay Golf Course just a 9-iron away. All rooms have Japanese touches complete with *shoji* screens. There's dancing and entertainment at their famous Restaurant of the Maui Moon.

Maui's backside is rugged yet scenic north of Kapalua.

Napili Bay

At 33 Hui Drive, Lahaina 96761, tel. 800-421-0680, on Maui 669-6044. For this neck of the woods, it's reasonably priced from $65 for a studio off ocean to $80 for a studio by the sea, up to 4 people. All have queen-sized beds, *lanai,* full kitchens, maid service, and laundromat. Three-day minimum.

Napili Surf Beach Resort

50 Napili Pl., Napili 96761, tel. 669-8002. Studios from $60. Long-term stay discount. Deposit of $150 required. Two pools, fantastic beach, maid service, full kitchens and laundry. They also operate the **Napili Puamala,** adjacent, which is a bit cheaper.

FOOD

R.V. Deli

This is a lunch wagon that parks almost every day at Mokuleia Bay (Slaughterhouse). Dogs, burgers, fries, and the like, plus yarns by Peter L. Dyck, proprietor.

Kapalua Bay Resort Restaurants

There's a complete menu of restaurants, so you can choose from sandwich shops to elegant dining. **Market Cafe** is found in the "Shops" area tel. 669-4888. Foods from around the world including wines, meats, cheeses, and pastries. All kinds of gourmet items, with delicious but expensive sandwiches, from $5. The **Resort Dining Room,** tel. 669-5656, known for its full breakfasts and lunch buffets at $14.50. The atmosphere is pure island with open-air dining. Dress up! **Bay Club,** at the resort entrance, tel. 669-8008, daily lunch 11:30 a.m. to 2:00 p.m., dinner 5:30 to 9:30 p.m. On a promontory overlooking the beach and Molokai in the distance. The pool is right here. Dress code. Expect to spend $20 for a superbly prepared entree. **Plantation Veranda** offers daily dinner only, with varying hours, tel. 669-5656. Atmosphere highlighted by natural woods, flowers everywhere, and original paintings by Pegge Hopper. Extensive wine list and magnificent entrees by Chef James Makinson. Formal dining.

Napili Shores Resort

Two restaurants are located at this resort, 5315 Honoapiilani Hwy., about one mile before Kapalua Town. **Orient Express,** tel. 669-8077, is open daily except Mon., dinner only from 5:00 to 10:00 p.m. Thai and Chinese food with a flair for spices. Duck salad and stuffed chicken wings are a specialty. "Early Bird Specials" before 7:00 p.m., take out and reasonably priced under $8. **Monaco,** tel. 669-8077. has dinner from 6:00 p.m. until midnight. French and Italian cuisine. Veal, pasta, and velvet chairs. Delisioso!

Restaurant Of The Maui Moon
At the Napili Kai Beach Club, 5900 Honoapiilani Rd., Lahaina 96761, on Maui tel. 669-6271. Daily for breakfast, lunch, and dinner. Breakfast buffet $7, lunch $5, dinner $15. Hawaiian and Oriental dishes, with an extensive salad bar for $10. There is Hawaiian music nightly and a wonderful show put on by children who have studied their heritage under the guidance of the Napili Kai Foundation.

SHOPPING

Kapalua Resort And Shops
There is a cluster of exclusive shops at the resort. **Andrade,** tel. 669-5266, fine apparel for men and women, an island tradition for 60 years; **Auntie Nani's Children's Boutique,** tel. 669-5282, for clothes and distinctive quilts. Many items have the Kapalua "butterfly logo"; **Kapalua Shop,** tel. 669-4172—if you want to show off that you've at least been to the Kapalua Resort, all items of clothing sport the logo. **Mandalay Imports,** tel. 669-6170, has a potpourri of silks and cottons from the East, especially Thailand. **La Perle,** tel. 669-8466, for pearls, diamonds, and jewels; **Trouvalle,** tel. 669-5522, sports an amazing collection of offbeat artifacts from throughout Asia; **T. Fujii,** tel. 669-4759, has Japanese treasures in bronze, lacquer, silk, and woodblock prints.

Napili Village Store
At Napili Bay, tel. 669-6773. A well-stocked little store and a known landmark. Good for last-minute items, and fairly good prices for where it is. You can pick up picnic items and sandwiches. There's a surf shop next door. **Napili Shores Condo Store** is mainly a convenience store for last-minute items.

banyan tree

Maalaea Harbor

KIHEI AND VICINITY

Kihei ("Shoulder Cloak") takes it on the chin whenever anti-development groups need an example to wag their finger at. For the last 2 decades, building along both sides of Kihei Road, which runs the length of town, has continued unabated. Since there was no central planning for the development, mostly high-rise condos and a few hotels were built wherever they could be squeezed in: some are lovely; some are crass. There's hardly a spot left where you can get an unobstructed view of the beach as you drive along. That's the "slam" in a nutshell. The good news is Kihei has so much to recommend it, that if you refrain from becoming fixated on this one regrettable feature, you'll thoroughly enjoy yourself, and save money, too.

The developers went "hyper" here because it's perfect as a tourist area. The weather can be counted on to be the best on all of Maui. Haleakala, looming just behind the town, catches rainclouds before they drench Kihei. Days of blue skies and sunshine are taken for granted. On the other side of the condos and hotels are gorgeous beaches, every one open to the public. Once on the beachside, the condos don't matter anymore. The views out to sea are unobstructed vistas of Lanai, Kahoolawe, Molokini, and West Maui, which gives the illusion of being a separate island. The buildings are even a buffer to the traffic noise! Many islanders make Kihei their home, so there is a feeling of real community here. It's quieter than Lahaina, with fewer restaurants and not as much action, but for sun and surf activities, this place has it all.

Sights

The 6-mile stretch bordered by beach and mountain that makes up Kihei has always been an important landing spot on Maui. Hawaiian war canoes moored here many times during countless skirmishes over the years; later, Western navigators such as George Vancouver found this stretch of beach to be a congenial anchorage. A totem pole across from the **Maui Lu Hotel** marks the spot where Vancouver landed. During WW II, when a Japanese invasion was feared, Kihei was considered a likely spot for an amphibious attack. Overgrown pill-boxes and rusting tank traps are still found along the beaches. Many look like cement porcupines with iron quills. Kihei is a natural site with mountain and ocean vistas.

It's great for beachcombing down toward Maalaea, but try to get there by morning because the afternoon wind is notorious for creating minor sand storms.

BEACHES

Maalaea Beach

Three miles of windswept sand, partially backed by Kealia Pond and bird sanctuary. Many points of access between Maalaea and Kihei along Rt. 31. The strong winds make it undesirable for sunning and bathing, but it's a windsurfer's dream. Also the hard-packed sand is a natural track for joggers, who are profuse in the morning and afternoon. The beachcombing and strolling are quiet and productive.

Mai Poina Oe Iau Beach Park

On Kihei's western fringe, fronting Maui Lu Hotel. Limited paved parking, or just along the road. Showers, tables, restrooms. Long and narrow white-sand beach, good safe swimming, but still plagued by strong winds by early afternoon. Windsurfer's delight.

Kaonouluulu Beach Park

Parking, picnic tables, showers, BBQs. Very safe swimming and lesser winds. Small beach but not overcrowded.

Kalama Beach

About the middle of town. More for looking and outings than beach activities. Large lawn ending in a breakwater with little beach in summer and none in winter. Thirty-six acres of pavilions, tables, BBQ pits, volleyball, basketball, tennis courts, baseball diamond, and soccer field. Great views of Molokai and Haleakala.

Kamaole I, II, And III

These beach parks are at the south end of town near Kihei Town Center. All 3 have beautiful white sand, picnic tables, and all the amenities. Shopping and dining are nearby. I and II have lifeguards. The swimming and bodysurfing are good. III has a kiddies' playground. Snorkeling is good for beginners on the reef between II and III. Much coral and colorful reef fish.

ACCOMMODATIONS

The emphasis in Kihei is on condos. With keen competition among them, you can save some money while having a more "homey" vacation. Close to 100 condos, plus a smattering of vacation apartments, cottages, and even a few hotel resorts, are all strung along Kihei Road. As always, you pay more for ocean views. Don't shy away from accommodations on the *mauka* side of Kihei Road. You have total access to the beach, some superior views of Haleakala, and usually pay less money.

Hotels

The Kihei area offers 2 hotels that are reasonably priced and well appointed. **Maui Lu Resort,** 575 S. Kihei Rd., Kihei, HI 96753, tel. 800-367-5244 Mainland, tel. 808-879-5808 Canada collect, tel. 800-592-3351 Hawaii, 879-5881 Maui. This hotel attempts to preserve the old Hawaii with its Aloha Department and its emphasis on *ohana.* An abundance of activities here includes *hula* lessons, a first-class *luau,* tennis, a Maui-shaped pool, and tiny private beaches strung along its 30 acres. Rooms from $65, $10 extra person, include refrigerators and hot drink unit. These are mostly in the new wing toward the mountains, which is also quieter. Cottages start at $85 and are separate units with full kitchens.

Surf and Sand Hotel, at 2980 S. Kihei Rd., Kihei, HI 96753, tel. 800-367-2958, on Maui 879-7744. This is a very affordable and well-maintained hotel just before you get to Wailea at the south end of town. It's owned and operated by Bob Zuern, who lives at the hotel, so you get personalized attention. Garden units from $35 or suites to 4 people $78-118. Ocean units $45-55. Kitchenettes available—add $10. It fronts a sand beach, provides Polynesian entertainment and offers "room and car" specials. There's also a jacuzzi. You can't go wrong!

Condominiums

Lihi Kai, 2121 Ili'ili Rd., Kihei 96753, tel. 879-2335. These cottages and apartments are such a bargain they're often booked out by returning guests. They're not plush, there's no

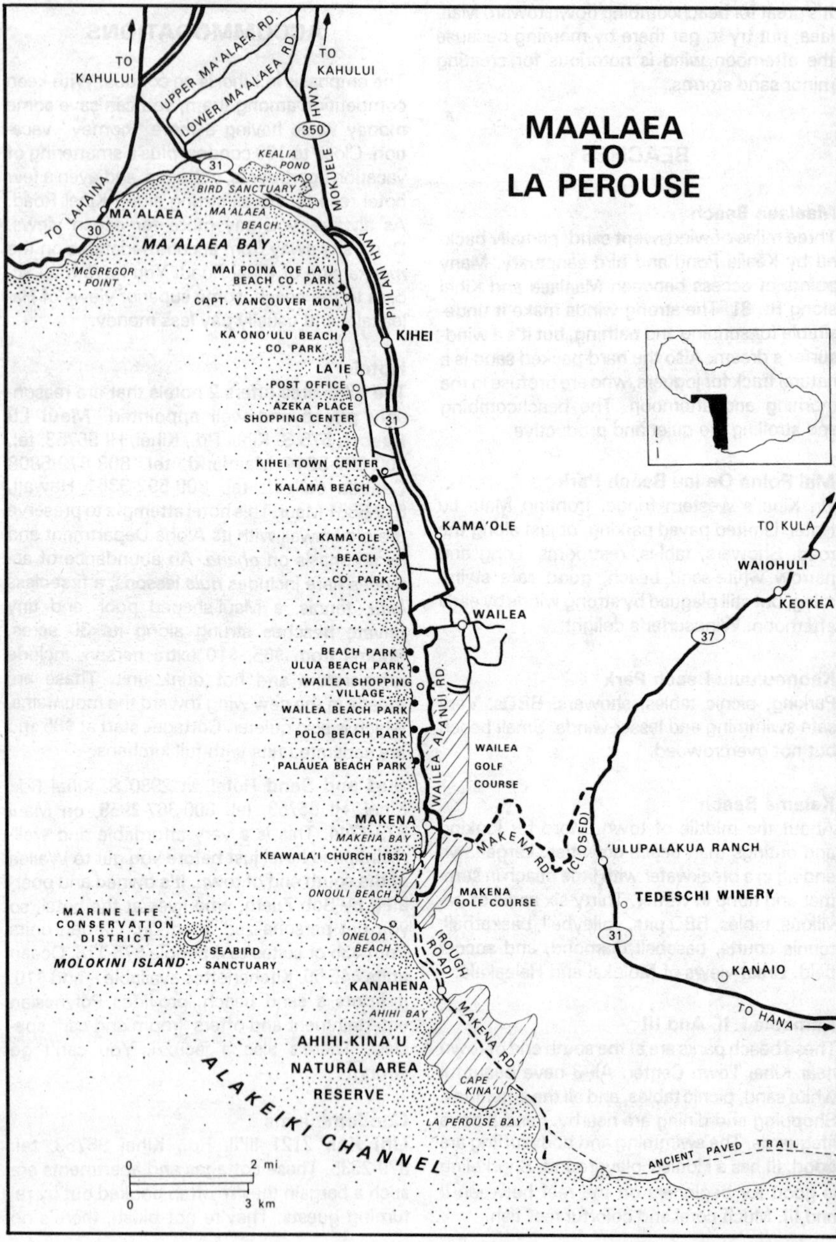
MAALAEA TO LA PEROUSE
TO KAHULUI
UPPER MA'ALAEA RD.
LOWER MA'ALAEA RD.
TO KAHULUI
350
HWY
MOKUELE
31
KEALIA POND
BIRD SANCTUARY
TO LAHAINA
MA'ALAEA
MA'ALAEA BEACH
30
MA'ALAEA BAY
McGREGOR POINT
PIILANI HWY
MAI POINA 'OE LA'U BEACH CO. PARK
CAPT. VANCOUVER MON.
KA'ONO'ULU BEACH CO. PARK
KIHEI
LA'IE
POST OFFICE
AZEKA PLACE SHOPPING CENTER
31
KIHEI TOWN CENTER
KALAMA BEACH
KAMA'OLE
KAMA'OLE BEACH CO. PARK
WAILEA
BEACH PARK
ULUA BEACH PARK
WAILEA SHOPPING VILLAGE
WAILEA BEACH PARK
POLO BEACH PARK
PALAUEA BEACH PARK
WAILEA ALANUI RD.
WAILEA GOLF COURSE
TO KULA
WAIOHULI
KEOKEA
37
MAKENA
MAKENA BAY
KEAWALA'I CHURCH (1832)
MAKENA RD.
(CLOSED)
'ULUPALAKUA RANCH
ONOULI BEACH
MAKENA GOLF COURSE
TEDESCHI WINERY
31
MARINE LIFE CONSERVATION DISTRICT
MOLOKINI ISLAND
SEABIRD SANCTUARY
ONELOA BEACH
(ROUGH ROAD)
KANAHENA
KANAIO
TO HANA
AHIHI BAY
MAKENA RD.
AHIHI-KINA'U NATURAL AREA RESERVE
CAPE KINA'U
LA PEROUSE BAY
ALAKEIKI CHANNEL
ANCIENT PAVED TRAIL
0
2 mi
0
3 km

pool, but they're homey and clean, with little touches like banana trees growing on the property. $35 daily, $175 weekly, $465 monthly, deposit required, self-service laundromat, and you pay the maid. Write Jeanette M. DiMeo, owner/manager, at the above address well in advance.

Nona Lani Cottages, 455 S. Kihei Rd., Kihei 96753, tel. 879-2497. Owned and operated by Dave and Nona Kong. Clean and neat units on the *mauka* side of Kihei Road. All units have full kitchen, queen beds and day beds with full baths. Laundry facilities, public phones, and BBQs on premises. High season $65 double, small discount for longer stays, $10 additional person. Low season $46, 3-night minimum.

Sunseeker Resort, 551 S. Kihei Rd., tel. 879-1261, write Box 276, Kihei 96753. Studio with kitchenette $29, one bedroom $39, 2 bedroom $50, $6 additional person. Special rates off season and long term. Deposit required. Not bad at all.

Nani Kai Hale, 73 N. Kihei Rd., Kihei 96753, tel. 800-367-6032, on Maui tel. 879-9120. Very affordable at $29 bedroom with bath, $42 studio with kitchenette, 2 bedroom, 2 bath $80. Substantial savings during off season. Seven-day minimum, monthly rates, children under 5 free. Good beach, sheltered parking, pool, laundry facilities, private *lanai,* and BBQs on premises. Good views.

Menehune Shores, 760 S. Kihei Rd., Kihei 96753, tel. 879-5828. Write Kihei Kona Rentals, Box 556, Kihei 96753. This huge condo is on the beach overlooking an ancient fishpond. All units have an ocean view. The building is highlighted with Hawaiian petroglyphs. $70 one bedroom, $90 2 bedroom, $100 3 bedroom, 5 day minimum. No credit cards. Low-season savings of 30%. Full kitchens with dishwasher, washer and dryer, and disposals. Each unit is individually owned, so furnishings vary, but the majority are well furnished. A lot for the money.

Maui Sunset, 1032 S. Kihei Rd., Kihei 96753, tel. 800-331-8076, in Hawaii tel. 800-922-3311. Contact manager Ron Stapes on Maui at 879-1971. Two large buildings containing over 200 units. Some are on a time-share basis, and usually have nicer furnishings. Same rate year round based on double occupancy at $62 one bedroom, $84 2 bath 2 bedroom, $116 3 bath and bedroom. Full kitchens. Pitch and putt golf green, pool, kiddie pool, beach front, and rooftop "whale" observation deck. Quality tennis courts.

Hale Kai O Kihei, 1310 Uluniu Rd., Kihei 96753, tel. 879-2757. Weekly rate based on double from $305-425 (high season) for one bedroom, $440-555 (high season) for 2 bedroom up to 4 people, additional person $7.50. No children under 6. Pool, parking, maid service on request.

Kauhale Makai, 930 S. Kihei Rd., write Maui Beachfront Rentals, from $45 studio, $55 one bedroom, $75 2 bedroom, $7.50 additional person. Swimming pool, kiddie pool, BBQs, putting green, sauna, 4-day minimum.

Kamaole Sands

Kamaole Sands, at 2695 S. Kihei Rd., Kihei 96753, tel. 879-0666, reservations tel. 800-367-6046. All apartments come completely furnished with full baths and kitchen. Prices are: $90-140 one bedroom, $120-160, 2 bedroom, $165-200 3 bedroom; 15% disount off season, and rental car package available. The Kamaole Sands is a full-service resort offering much more than just a place to stay. The Sandpiper Grill serves inexpensive breakfast and lunch, cafeteria style, sit-down dinners featuring succulent Maui ribs for $7.95, and theme night cuisines for under $10. The condo's tennis pro improves your game with clinics at the 4

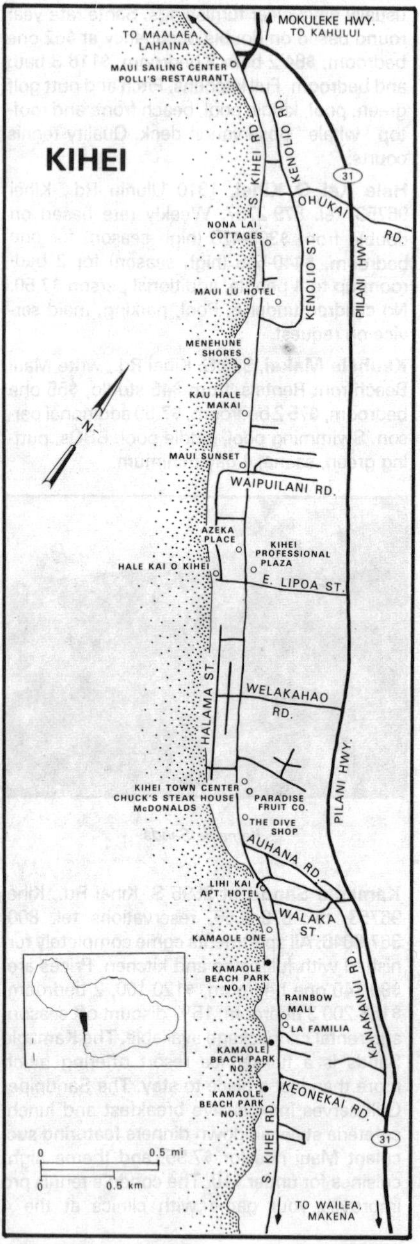

courts, ranging from *stroke of the day* to *children's tennis.* Guests are entertained and enriched with a stunning variety of social activities, arts and crafts, and educational exhibits. These include: a slide show presenting "What to see and do on Maui"; free *hula* show (complimentary *mai tai*) performed by the Kihei School of Hawaiian arts every Tues. evening; *lei*-making on Tues. and Fri. at 1:00 p.m., and Hawaiian quilting on Sat., 11:30 a.m.; a marine biologist introduces the flora and fauna of Maui in a slide show on Wed., at 7:30 p.m.; Hawaiian ladies come to sell their traditional arts and crafts on Thurs.; children are entertained Fri. mornings 11:00-12:00 with *Keiki Hawaiian Stories,* $5, by a *tutu* who sings and plays guitar; you can taste tropical fruits at poolside on Sat. at 2:00 p.m., or take a free snorkel and scuba lesson daily; Sun. brings *hula* lessons from 4:00-5:00 p.m.; and, if you have any energy left, try Tues., Thurs., and Sat. exercise class $5, from 8:30 a.m. For a full and memorable experience stay at the Kamaole Sands!

Maui Hill, 2881 S. Kihei Rd., tel. 800-879-6321. Contact Oihana Management, 2145 Wells, Wailuku, HI 96793, tel. 800-367-5234, on Maui tel. 800-879-7751. Upbeat condo with a Spanish motif and plenty of space. Near Wailea. Rates, one bedroom from $105, 2 bedroom from $115, 3 bedroom from $130. Deluxe furnishings, pool, tennis courts, maid service.

FOOD

Inexpensive

Azeka's Snacks, Azeka Pl., S. Kihei Road. Open daily except Sun., 9:30 a.m. to 4:00 p.m. Basically take-out, featuring 90-cent hamburgers and a variety of plate lunches for $3.50. Popular with locals and terrific for picnics. Also try **Philadelphia Lou's** in the shopping plaza. Open daily 7:00 a.m. to 11:00 p.m. and until midnight on weekends. Breakfast, lunch, and limited dinner menu, but the real specialty are foot-and-a-half hoagies. These babies are loaded in the Back East tradition and, for $7.50, they can fill 2 people easily. A scoop of all-natural Maui ice cream is $1. Kids hang out here and play videos, so it's noisy. Best to take out.

International House of Pancakes is toward

the rear of Azeka Place. Open daily 6:00 a.m. to midnight, Fri. and Sat. until 2:00 a.m. Same American standards as on the Mainland with most sandwiches and plate lunches under $5, dinners under $7 and breakfasts anytime around $4. Not exotic, but basic and filling. **Apple Annie's Sailmaker,** also at Azeka Place, tel. 879-4446. Daily from breakfast to late, late evening. Normal selection of Apple Annie sandwiches, entrees, and salads. A touch expensive for what you get. Nightly entertainment in the loft.

Paradise Fruit Co., 1913 S. Kihei Rd., across from McDonald's. Daily 24 hours, tel. 879-1723. This is a fruit stand and vegetable market that has a top-notch snack bar offering hearty, healthy sandwiches (under $3.50), vegetarian dishes, and a good selection of large, filling salads. Try the pita melt for $3.50, and any of the smoothies. A few tables out back, worth a stop!

Moderate

Polli's Mexican Restaurant, 101 S. Kihei Rd., tel. 879-5275. Daily 11:00 a.m. to midnight. Polli's has a well-deserved reputation for good food at fair prices. Their first all-natural vegetarian Mexican restaurant is in Makawao, and this new branch opened in the last year. The decor is classical Mexican with white stucco and tiled floors. There's an outdoor deck area with a great sunset view. Main dishes are under $7, with a la carte tostadas for $3.50 and soup for $1.50. Imported beers $2.50. No lard is used and all oils are cold pressed. Meticulously clean, large portions, and friendly atmosphere.

La Famiglia, at Kai Nani Village Plaza, 2511 S. Kihei Rd., tel. 879-8824. Across from Kamaloe Park no. 2. Mexican food from $4 with organic ingredients, when possible. Good-looking, pleasant waitresses. Happy hour (4:00 to 6:00 p.m.) features huge frosty margaritas, the kind that give you a headache if you drink too fast, for 99 cents, with free chips and salsa. Dishes are well prepared with large portions. Upstairs is **Kihei Prime Rib House** open from 5:00 p.m., tel. 879-1954. A touch expensive with most entrees from $12.95, but this includes a well-stocked salad bar. Scrumptious appetizers like *sashimi* and lobster casserole for around $5, coupled with a baked potato with the works for $1.50, make a meal. Salad bar only $7.95. "Early bird" specials under $10 from 5:00 to 6:00 p.m. Children's menu. Walls are adorned with carvings by Bruce Turnbull and paintings by Sigrid, two well-known artists.

Expensive

Maui Lu Hotel, 575 S. Kihei Rd., tel. 879-5858. On Mon., Wed., and Fri., a *luau* and a Polynesian review are held in the hotel's Luau Garden, including limitless cocktails and a sumptuous buffet with all the specials—including *imu* pork, *poi,* and a huge assortment of salads, entrees, and side dishes. $28, tax and gratuity included. Also, the **Aloha Mele Luncheon** is a tradition at the hotel. Again a laden buffet with cocktails from 11:00 a.m. to 1:30 p.m., Thurs. only. $12.50 includes the luncheon, entertainment, tax, and tip.

Robaire's, 61 S. Kihei Rd., tel. 879-2707. Tuesday to Sat. 6:00 to 10:00 p.m. Fine dining in this intimate French restaurant. The cooking is done by Robaire and his brother Jacques. The decor isn't fancy, but the food is delicious. Specialties are veal Napoleon and rack of lamb. The fresh fish is also excellent. Seafood from $15, chicken cordon bleu $12.50. French and California wine list. Excellent selections.

Waterfront Restaurant, at the Milowai Condo in Maalaea Harbor, tel. 244-9028. Daily from 5:30 to 10 p.m. Whole baked fish in oyster sauce for 2 $16.50. Lobster and crab, from $18. Scampi, $14.50. Great sunsets. Tropical drinks.

Buzz's Wharf, at Maalaea Harbor, tel. 244-5426. Daily, dinner only. Seafood and fresh fish are the specialties. Most dishes under $12. Waterfront atmosphere. Great sunsets and views from the second story overlooking the harbor.

Chuck's Steak House, Kihei Town Center, tel. 879-4488. Lunch, Mon. to Fri. 11:30 a.m. to 2:30 p.m., dinner nightly from 5:30 p.m. No reservations necessary, but call to see how busy it is. Emphasis on steaks and ribs mostly under $12. Children's menu under $8. Daily specials and "early birds" sometimes. Dirt pie and sandwiches under $4. Salad bar a la carte, $6.95. Standard American, with an island twist.

SHOPPING

Azeka Place Shopping Center, along S. Kihei Rd., in about the center of town. Here you'll find all the practicals: bank (Bank of Hawaii, tel. 879-5844), post office (1254 S. Kihei Rd.), and gas station. **Azeka's Market** is well-stocked, and its meat department features famous Azeka ribs for BBQs. There's also a great community bulletin board listing apartments, yard sales, and all odds and ends. In the Plaza are **Ben Franklin, Mediterranean House** selling swimwear, and a small **Liberty House.** There's also **Kihei Natural Foods,** a hardware store, and a florist. This is where the "people" do their one-stop shopping.

sailboards at Kealia Beach

Kihei Town Center

A small shopping center just south of Azeka offers a **Foodland, Kihei Drug Mart,** a bank, art gallery, McDonald's, and a few clothing stores.

Food

At Azeka's Market, **Paradise Food Company,** 1913 Kihei Rd., **Foodland** at Kihei Town Center, and **Star Market** at 1310 S. Kihei Road.

Sporting Goods And Rentals

You'll find all you need at **Maui Sailing Center,** 145 N. Kihei Rd., in Sugar Beach Resort, or at 101 N. Kihei Rd., at Kealia Beach Center. Daily 8:00 a.m. to 5:00 p.m. They offer rental cars, windsurfing equipment and lessons, beach equipment, sailboats, snorkeling sets, bicycles, jet skis, ski boats and drivers, and tours. **The Dive Shop,** 1975 S. Kihei Rd., tel. 879-5172. Owned and operated by Linda Kowalsky, this is your one-stop dive shop, and more. Tours, excursions, snorkel and scuba equipment, bicycles, and mopeds. **Maui Dive Shop** in Azeka Place has a full range of equipment and rentals.

ENTERTAINMENT

Kihei isn't exactly a hot spot when it comes to evening entertainment. There is the **Polynesian Review** at the Maui Lu *luau*. The **Surf and Sand Hotel** offers Polynesian entertainment nightly, and there's a disco at **Apple Annie Sailmaker** from 9:00 p.m. to 2:00 a.m. Wed. to Sat., cover charge. Many of the restaurants offer entertainment on a hit and miss basis, usually one artist with a guitar, a small dinner combo, or some Hawaiian music. These are usually listed in the free tourist brochures.

WAILEA AND BEYOND

Wailea ("Waters of Lea") isn't for the hoi polloi. It's a deluxe resort area custom-tailored to fit the egos of the upper class like a Bijan original. This section of southeastern Maui was barren and bleak until Alexander and Baldwin Co. decided to landscape it into an emerald 1,450-acre oasis of golf courses and world-class hotels. Every street light, palm tree, and potted plant is a deliberate accessory to the decor so that the overall feeling is soothing, pleasant, and in good taste. To dispel any notions of snootiness, the 5 sparkling beaches that front the resorts were left open to the public and even improved with better access, parking areas, showers, and picnic tables; a gracious gesture even if state law does require open access! You know when you leave Kihei and enter Wailea. The green, quiet and wide tree-lined avenues give the impression of an upper-class residential area. Wailea is where you come when you're "putting on the ritz," and with the prices you'll encounter it would be helpful if you *owned* the Ritz. At both the **Intercontinental Hotel** and **Stouffer's Resort** you'll find 5-star dining, and exclusive shopping at the Wailea Shopping Center. Both hotels are first-rate architecturally and the grounds are exquisite. They're definitely worth a stroll, but remember your Gucci shoes.

Onward And Backward

If you turn your back to the sea and look toward Haleakala, you'll see its cool, green forests and peak wreathed in mysterious clouds. You'll want to run right over, but you can't get there from here! Outrageous as it may sound, you have to double back 18 miles to Kahului and then head down Rt. 37 for another 20 miles just to get to the exact same spot on Rt. 37 that you can easily see. On the map there's a neat little road called **Makena Road** that connects the Wailea/Makena area with Upcountry in a mere 2-mile stretch, but it's closed! An ongoing fight over who's responsible for its maintenance keeps it that way. Once this appalling situation is rectified, you'll be able easily to travel to the **Tedeschi Winery**, and continue on the "wrong way" to Hana, or go left to Kula and Upcountry. For now, however, happy motoring!

BEACHES

If you're not fortunate enough to be staying in Wailea, the best reason for coming here are its beaches. These little beauties are crescent moons of white sand that usually end in lava outcroppings on both ends. This makes for sheltered swimmable waters and good snorkeling and scuba. Many of the hotel guests in Wailea seem to hang around the hotel pools, maybe peacocking or just trying to get their money's worth, so the beaches are surprisingly uncrowded. The following beaches are listed from west to east, toward Makena.

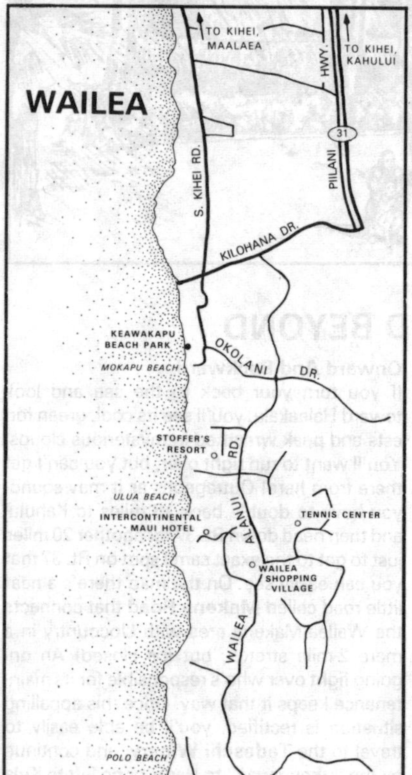

Keawakapu

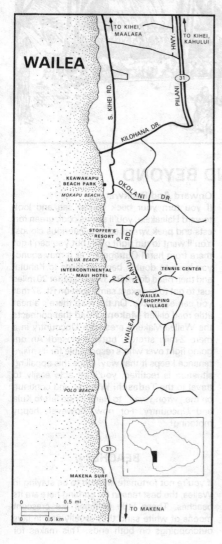

The first Wailea beach, almost a buffer between Kihei and Wailea, is just past the Mana Kai Resort. Turn left onto Kamala Place, or proceed straight on S. Kihei Road until it dead ends. Plenty of parking at both accesses. No amenities. Lovely white-sand beach with sandy bottom. Good swimming and fair snorkeling. A beginner's dive spot offshore where an underwater junkyard forming an artificial reef holds a few hundred cars.

Mokapu And Ulua

These 2 beaches are shoulder to shoulder, separated only by a rock outcropping. Turn right off Wailea Alanui Drive at the first turn past the Westin Wailea Hotel. Clearly marked. Parking area and showers. Resort beaches, especially cared for. Beautiful white sand, perfect for swimming. Good snorkeling at the rock outcropping separating these 2 beaches. Or swim out to the first reef just in front of the rocks for excellent snorkeling.

Wailea Beach

Travel one-half mile past the Wailea Town Center and turn right onto a clearly marked access road. Good parking, with showers and toilets. Beach and surf equipment rental. A short but wide beach of pure white sand. Good swimming and bodysurfing, but snorkeling only fair.

Polo Beach

Follow Wailea Alanui Drive toward Makena until it starts getting rugged. Turn right at the clearly marked sign near Polo Beach Condo. Paved parking, showers and toilets. Good for swimming and sunbathing with few tourists. Excellent snorkeling in front of the rocks separating Polo from Wailea Beach. Tremendous amount of fish, and one of the easiest spots to get to.

ACCOMMODATIONS

Stouffer's Wailea Resort

This is a superbly appointed resort. When you drive to the main lobby, you're actually on the fifth floor, with the ones below terraced down the mountainside to the white-sand beach. The lobby has huge oak and brass doors, and original artworks adorn the walls, including an intricate tapestry made of natural fibers. There are 5 restaurants, a luxurious pool area, and a beach in the area and grounds that would make Tarzan and Jane envious. Room rates are $215-350 with suites to $1,000. Family Plan, with children under 18 free in their parents' room, and a modified American Plan. Stouffer's even offers a 50% discount coupon for certain rooms between April and December 15. You can only stay 4 days, however. Such a deal! Write 3550 Wailea Alanui Dr., Wailea, HI 96753, tel. 800-385-5000, tel. 879-4900 on Maui.

Stouffer's Wailea Beach Hotel

Makena Surf

This spacious oceanfront condo is 2 miles past Wailea proper near Polo Beach at 96 Makena Rd., Kihei, HI 96753. Contact Village Resorts Inc., tel. 800-367-7052, or the condo directly at tel. 800-367-2963, tel. 879-4555 on Maui. Rates based on double occupancy are one-bedroom from $175 4 persons maximum, 2-bedroom from $250 up to 6 people, 3-bedroom from $350 up to 8, $20 additional person. The rooms are cheaper on upper floors, and rates are for high season with low season about 20% cheaper. Amenities include a/c, color TV, full kitchen, *lanai,* whirlpool bath in each unit, 2 swimming pools, 4 tennis courts, 2-night minimum, deposit necessary.

Maui Intercontinental Hotel

This hotel is a class act. Even the Wrong Way signs on the premises say "*Please,* Do Not Enter." The rooms are lavish with folding screens, original artwork, deep carpets and coordinated bedspreads, full baths, 2 *lanai,* refrigerators, and magnificent views no matter which way you're oriented. Rates are based on double occupancy and run $95-135. Suites are available from $135-525. About a 20% reduction from April 1 through December 23. The Family Plan includes no charge for children under 18 in their parents' room; and during off-peak season they get their own adjoining room free. The American Plan is $44 per day, modified at $35. The hotel offers room and car packages, golfer's and tennis specials, and honeymoon packages. There are 3 lovely pools, 4 restaurants, and the beach. For information write Box 779, Kihei-Wailea, HI 96753, tel. 800-367-2960 Mainland, tel. 800-537-5589 from Honolulu, tel. 879-1922 on Maui. This is living!

Independent from the hotel, but using its facilities, the **Waves of Wailea** presents Hawaii's first fitness vacation package. The program includes room, gourmet health-conscious meals, classes, equipment, and seminars. Rates begin around $1,700 which will trim down your wallet at least. For information, tel. 800-367-8047.

Polo Beach Club

20 Makena Rd., Wailea 96753, tel. 879-8847. Near Polo Beach toward Makena. Condo apartments fully furnished. From $130, 6 people maximum. Low-season discounts. Pool, jacuzzi, and seclusion.

Wailea Luxury Condos

3750 Wailea Alanui, Wailea, HI 96753, tel. 800-367-5246 Mainland, tel. 879-1595 collect from Hawaii or Canada. This complex is made up of 3 separate villages: **Ekolu,** from $110, near the golf course; **Ekahi,** the least expensive, from $70 near the tennis courts; **Elua,** the most expensive, from $115 near the sea. All units are plush. $10 additional people, monthly discounts, 4-night minimum.

FOOD

Raffles' Restaurant

At Stouffer's Wailea Beach Resort, tel. 879-4900, reservations a must. Dinner daily from 6:30 to 10:30 p.m. Sunday brunch from

9:00 a.m. to 2:00 p.m., a prize winner! Semi dress-up, with tasteful alohawear OK. Inspired by the famed Raffles of Singapore, this restaurant lives up to the tradition. *Sashimi,* oysters Rockefeller, crab cocktail, and fresh Hawaiian prawns are appetizers, from $6.50. Vichysoisse or onion soup from $3.50. Salads galore, including mushrooms, spinach, Manoa lettuce, and filet mignon for $5.50. Roast rack of lamb, $22, *opakapaka* in sorrel sauce. Wines from the best vineyards around the world. Magnificent desserts. The Sunday brunch for $19.50 is worth every penny. Omelettes made to order, chops, steaks, fish, champagne, eggs benedict, breakfast meats. All first class, all servings constantly replenished. **Palm Court** is also at the hotel, through the lobby and look over the rail. Open nightly from 6:00 p.m. Buffet for a fixed $15.50, and every night has a theme: Monday Oriental, Tuesday Italian, Thursday French. Plenty of salads and soup from the kettle for $4.50. A definite bargain for the amount and quality of the food. **Maui Onion** down by the pool will make your eyes tear. $6 for a hamburger, $2.75 for Maui onion rings. Even at Stouffer's, too much!

La Perouse Restaurant

At Maui Intercontinental Hotel, tel. 879-1922. Dinner nightly from 5:30 p.m., reservations a must. This elegant restaurant is gaining an international reputation. The surroundings themselves of rich *koa* wood and an immense ironwork gate at the entry set the theme. A dress code requires collared shirts, but most people dress up. No shorts. The Callallo Crabmeat soup is a must. The bouillabaisse is out of this world. Breadfruit vichysoisse is unique. Wines from the private cellar start at $20, but the house wine by the glass is an affordable $2.50. The best selections are the seafood, but the chicken and lamb are also superb. Save room for dessert offered on a pastry cart laden with exotic choices. This is no place for will power. Enjoy one of the best meals ever, and don't worry about the second mortgage tonight. **Kiawe Broiler** offers more moderately priced dinners at the hotel. Daily lunch from 11:00 to 4:00 p.m., dinner 6:00 to 10:00 p.m, basically *kiawe,* broiled chops and steaks from $13, salad bar a deal at $7.25. Informal setting with high-backed rattan decor. **Lanai Terrace** at the hotel, tel. 879-1922, offers Sunday brunch from 9:00 a.m to 2:00 p.m. All you can eat of first-quality buffet breakfast and lunch foods that are well prepared and beautifully presented. $15.50, and worth every pound...penny! ***Luau*** every Sun. and Thurs. evening, old Hawaii lives again from 6:00 p.m. Lavish buffet and *imu* ceremony. $24.50 adults, $12.50 children under 10 years. Also try the **Inu Inu Lounge** for *sushi,* **Makani's Coffee Shop** for reasonably priced American standard, and the **Wet Spot** by the pool if you want to get soaked for a $6 sandwich.

Golf Ball Soup

The following restaurants are located at the golf links in the area. **Wailea Steak House,** 100 Wailea Ike Dr., on the 15th fairway of Wailea Blue Golf Club, tel. 879-2875. Daily for dinner from 5:30 p.m. Reasonably priced for this neck of the woods with steaks from $12 and chicken from $10. A decent salad bar for $8. Quiet with good sunset views. **Fairway,** at Wailea Golf Course Club House, tel. 879-4060. Breakfast, lunch, and dinner. Reasonably priced, filling breakfasts, good lunches, and a wide selection of dinners, from $13. **Makena Golf Course Restaurant,** tel. 879-1154. Daily from 9:30 a.m. Nothing special, but well-prepared sandwiches, burgers, and fries. Convenient as the last stop to Makena.

SHOPPING AND SERVICES

The only shopping in this area is **Wailea Shopping Center,** just east past the Intercontinental Hotel off Wailea Alanui Drive. It has the usual collection of boutiques and shops. **Superwhale** offers alohawear for children; **Ocean Activities Center** is as its name implies; **Party Pantry,** tel. 879-3044, for food items and liquor; **Golden Reef** selling distinctive island coral jewelry including gold, black, and pink coral.

Golf

You have 3 choices of golf courses in Wailea, all open to the public. **Wailea Golf Course** has two 18 holers—The Orange Course and The

Blue Course. Both are a par 72 and charge $40 for green fees and mandatory cart. Half price to Wailea Hotel guests and residents. **Makena Golf Course** is past Wailea toward Makena, tel. 879-3344, par 72. More reasonably priced at $26, including cart.

Tennis

Many condos have their own courts; check individually for general public use. Usually no problem. **Wailea Tennis Center**, tel. 879-1958, has 14 courts, with 3 lighted and 3 grass, open daily 7:00 a.m. until 9:00 p.m. Per hour rates: $10 single, $12 double (high season); nights $12 single, $17 double (high season); grass courts, $18 single, $24 double.

Transportation

The **Maui Transit System**, tel. 661-3827, runs 3 buses daily between Lahaina and Wailea. You pay by the distance traveled. **Wailea Shuttle** is a complimentary jitney constantly making trips up and down Wailea Alanui Drive, stopping at all major hotels and condos. It operates 6:30 a.m. to 10:30 p.m. With a little walking, this is a great way to hop from one beach to the next.

MAKENA TO LA PEROUSE

Just a skip down the road eastward is Makena Beach, but it's a world away from Wailea. Once the paved roads of Wailea give way to dirt, you know you're in Makena country. This was a hippie enclave during the '60s and early '70s, and the free-wheeling spirit of the times still permeates the area. For one, "Little Makena" is a nude beach, but so what? You can skinny-dip in Connecticut. This fact gets too much attention. What's really important is that Makena is *the last* pristine coastal area of Maui that hasn't succumbed to development...yet. As you head down the dirt road you'll notice Hawaii's unofficial bird, the building crane, arching its mechanical neck and lifting girders into place. The Japanese firm of Seibu Hawaii is building the Seibu Prince Hotel, and more will surely follow. There's unofficial camping at Makena, with plenty of beach people who live here semi-permanently. There's nothing in the way of amenities past Wailea, so make sure to stock up on all supplies (for water see "Keawalai Church," below). The police come in and sweep the area now and again, but mostly it's mellow. They do arrest the nudists on Little Makena, but this is more to make the point that Makena "ain't free no more." Rip-offs can be a problem, so lock your car, hide your camera, and don't leave anything of value in your tent. Be careful of the *kiawe* thorns when you park; they'll puncture a tire like a nail.

Makena is magnificent for bodysurfing and swimming. Whales frequent the area and come quite close to shore during the season. Turtles waddled on Makena early in this century, where they came to lay their eggs in the warm sand. Too many people gathered the eggs and the turtles scrambled away forever. The sunsets from **Red Hill**, the cinder cone separating Makena from Little Makena, are among the best on Maui going down between Lanai, Kahoolawe, and West Maui. The silhouettes of pastel and gleaming colors are awe-inspiring. Oranges, russets, and every shade of purple reflect off the clouds that are caught here. Makena attracts all kinds: gawkers, burnouts, adventurers, tourists, and free spirits. It won't last long, so go and have a look now!

Keawalai Church

About two-thirds of the way from Polo Beach to Makena, you'll pass this Congregational church, established in 1832. It was restored in 1952 and services are held every Sunday at 11:00 a.m. Many of the hymns and part of the sermon are still delivered in Hawaiian. There is a public telephone in front of the church, and drinking water. Enter the grounds and go behind the garage-type building to the left of the church itself, where you'll find a sink and a water tap.

Small Beaches

You'll pass by these beaches as you head toward Makena. There's usually few people and no amenities. **Palauea** and **Poolenalena** are about three-quarters of a mile past Polo. Good swimming and white, sloping sands. **Nahuna Point** ("Five Graves") is just over a mile past Polo. An old graveyard marks the entrance. Not good for swimming but great for scuba because of deep underwater caves. Snorkelers can enjoy this area, too. **Papipi** is along the road a mile and a half past Polo. Parking in lot. Small sand beach. Too close to road. **Oneuli** ("Black Sand Beach") is past Polo, not quite 3 miles. Turn down a rutted dirt road for a third of a mile. Not good for swimming. Good diving. Unofficial camping.

Makena Beach

Bounce along for 3 miles past Polo Beach. Look for a wide dirt road that 2 cars can pass on. Turn right and follow the rutted road for a few hundred yards. This is **Oneloa Beach**, generally called **Makena Big Beach.** You can go left or right to find parking. Left is where most people camp. Right leads you to **Puu Olai** (Red Hill), a 360-foot cinder cone. When you cross it you'll be on **Little Makena,** a favorite nude beach. Both beaches are excellent for swimming (beware currents in winter), bodysurfing, and superb snorkeling in front of Red Hill.

Ahihi-Kinau Natural Reserve

Look for the sign 4 miles past Polo Beach. Here you'll find a narrow beach and the remnants of a stone wall. It's an underwater reserve, so the scuba and snorkeling are first-rate. The best way to proceed is along the reef toward the left. Beware not to step on the many spiny urchins in the shallow waters. If you do, vinegar or urine will help with the stinging. The jutting thumb of lava to your left is **Cape Kinau.** This was Maui's last lava flow, occurring in 1790.

La Perouse Bay

Just shy of six miles from Polo Beach. After Ahihi-Kinau the road is rugged and cut along the lava flow. Named after the French navigator La Perouse, first Westerner to land on

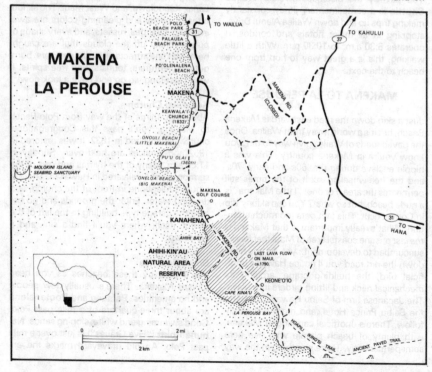

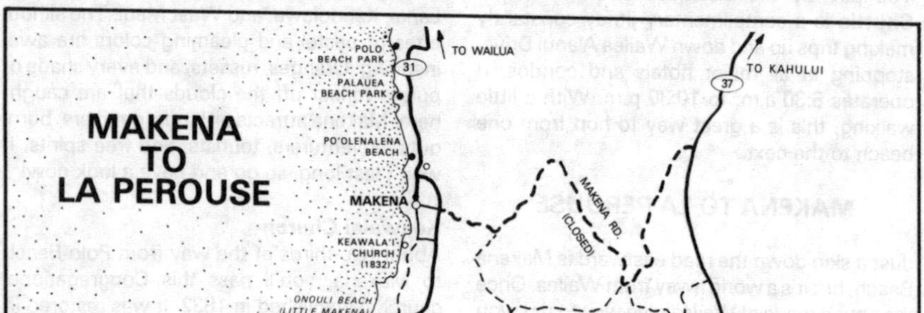

Jungle John, pickup truck entrepreneur

Maui, in May 1786. Good for snorkelers and divers but beware the urchins on entry. If you walk left you'll come across a string of pocket-sized beaches. The currents can be tricky along here. Past the bay are remnants of the *Hoapili* ("King's") Trail.

PRACTICALITIES

Accommodations

They've arrived! In August 1986, the Tokyo-based Prince Hotels opened the 300-room, 6-story **Maui Prince Hotel** along a private beach in Makena. The complex, tastefully done, is surrounded by landscaped gardens, complete with ponds, bridges, and a small stream. In keeping with the "destination resort" concept, the hotel offers 2 pools, tennis courts, 4 restaurants, a catamaran, and 18 holes of golf (still being completed). Rates from $200 for a room to $350-700 for a suite. For information write 5400 Makena Alanui Rd., Kihei, HI 96753, tel. 800-321-6284, on Maui tel. 874-1111.

Services

Except for the phones back at Makena Golf Club and the water at Keawalai Church you won't find any amenities. There is, however, an "alternative" entrepreneur who calls himself Jungle John. If you remember the TV show, "Green Acres," he's a Mr. Hainey-type, who just happens to have everything you need. He parks his green pickup at Big Beach (if the police haven't rousted him by now). He's a born salesman, but with a heart of gold. He's got sandwiches, cold drinks, and a smattering of beach and surf gear. Under extenuating circumstances, he'll look after your gear.

UPCOUNTRY

Upcountry is much more than a geographical area to the people who live there: it's a way of life, a frame of mind. You can see Upcountry from anywhere on Maui by lifting your gaze to the slopes of Haleakala. There are no actual boundaries, but this area is usually considered to run from Makawao in the north all the way around to Kahikinui Ranch in the south, and from below the cloud cover up to about the 3,000-foot level. It encircles Haleakala like a large green floral bib patterned by pasture lands and festooned with wild and cultivated flowers. In this rich soil and cool to moderate temperatures, cattle ranching and truck farming thrive. Up here, *paniolo* ride herd on the range of the enormous 20,000-acre **Haleakala Ranch**, spread mostly around Makawao, and the even larger 30,000 acres of the **Ulupalakua Ranch** which *is* the hills above Wailea. **Pukalani**, the largest town, is a way station for gas and supplies. **Makawao** is a real cowboy town with saddleries, rodeos, and hitching posts. It's also sophisticated, with some exclusive shops and fine dining.

Kula is Maui's flower basket. This area is one enormous garden producing brilliant blooms and hearty vegetables. **Poli Poli State Park** is a forgotten wonderland of tall forests, a homogenized stand of trees from around the world. **Tedeschi Winery** in the south adds a classy touch to Upcountry; you can taste wine in an historic jailhouse. There are plenty of commercial greenhouses and flower farms to visit all over Upcountry, but the best is a free Sunday drive along the mountain roads and farm lanes, just soaking in the scenery. The purple mists of mountain jacaranda and the heady fragrance of eucalyptus encircling a mountain pasture manicured by herds of cattle is a portrait of the soul of Upcountry.

MAKAWAO

Makawao is proud of itself; it's not *like* a cowboy town, it *is* a cowboy town. Depending on the translation that you consult, it means, "Eye of the Dawn," or "Forest Beginning." Both are appropriate. Surrounding lowland fields of cane and pineapples give way to upland pastures rimmed with tall forests, as Haleakala's morning sun shoots lasers of light through the town. Makawao was settled late last century by Portuguese immmigrants who started raising cattle on the upland slopes. It loped along as a *paniolo* town until WW II, when it received an infusion of life from a nearby military base in Kokomo. After the war it settled back down and became a sleepy village again, where as many horses were tethered on the main street as cars were parked. The majority of its false-front, one-story buildings are a half-century old, but their prototype is strictly "Dodge City, 1850." During the 1950s and '60s, Makawao started to decline into a bunch of worn-out old buildings. It earned a reputation for drinking, fighting, and cavorting cowboys, and for a period was derisively called "Macho-wao."

In the 1970s it began to revive. It had plenty to be proud of and a good history to fall back on. Makawao is *the* last real *paniolo* town on Maui and, with Kamuela on the Big Island, is one of the last two in the entire state. At the Oskie Rice Arena, it hosts the largest and most successful rodeo in Hawaii. Its Fourth of July parade is a marvel of homespun humor, *aloha,* and an old-fashioned good time. Many people ride their horses to town, leaving them to graze in a public corral. They do business at stores operated by the same families for 50 years. Though much of the dry goods are country-oriented, a new breed of merchant has come to town. You can buy a sack of feed, a rifle, designer jeans, and an imported silk blouse all on one street. At its eateries you can have lobster, vegetarian Mexican, or a steamy bowl of *saimin,* reputed to be the best on Maui.

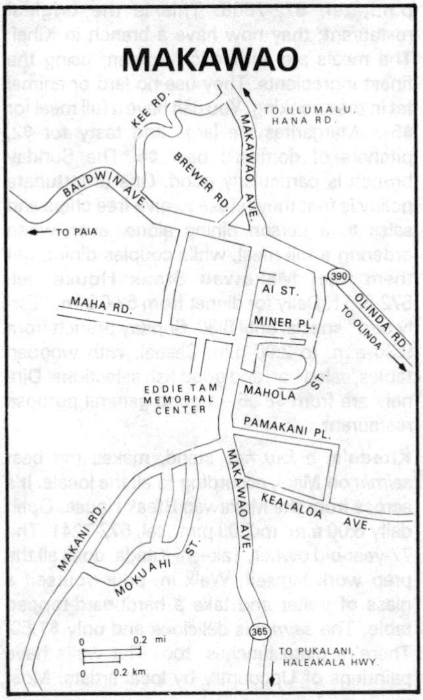

Everyone, old-timers and newcomers alike, agrees that Makawao must be preserved, and they work together. They know that tourism is a financial lifeline, but shudder at the thought of Makawao becoming an Upcountry Lahaina. It shouldn't. It's far enough off the track to keep the average tourist away, but easy enough and definitely interesting enough to make a side trip there absolutely worthwhile.

Getting There

The main artery to Makawao is through Paia as you travel Rt. 360, (Hana Road). In Paia Town turn right onto Baldwin Avenue at the corner marked by the gaily painted "Ice Creams and Dreams" shop. From here it's about 6 miles to Makawao.

Sights

En route on Baldwin Avenue, you pass the **sugar mill,** a real-life Carl Sandburg poem. It's a green monster trimmed in bare light bulbs at night, dripping with sounds of turning gears, cranes, and linkbelts, all surrounded by packed, rutted, oil-stained soil. Farther along Baldwin Avenue sits **Holy Rosary Church,** and its sculpture of Father Damien of the Lepers. The rendering of Damien is idealized, but the leper, who resembles a Calcutta beggar, has a face that conveys helplessness, but at the same time faith and hope. It's worth a few minutes' stop. Coming next is **Makawao Union Church,** and it's a beauty. Like a Tudor mansion made completely of stone with lovely stained-glass windows, the entrance is framed by 2 tall and stately royal palms.

The backway reaches Makawao by branching off Rt. 36 through Ulumalu and Kokomo. Just

False-front stores line Makawao Avenue.

where Rt. 36 turns into Rt. 360, there's a road to the right. This is Kapakilui Rd., or Rt. 365 (some maps show it as Rt. 400). Take it through back-country Maui, where horses graze around neat little houses. Haleakala looms on the horizon; guavas, mangoes, and bananas grow wild. At the first Y, bear left to Kaupakulua. Pass a large junkyard and continue to Kokomo. There's a general store here. Notice the mixture of old and new houses—Maui's past and future in microcosm. Here, the neat little banana plantation on the outskirts of the diminutive town says it all. Pass St. Joseph's Church and you've arrived through Makawao's back door. This is an excellent off-track route to take on your way to or from Hana. You can also come over Rt. 365 through Pukalani, incorporating Makawao into your Haleakala trip.

Nearby Attractions

Take Olinda Road out of town. All along it custom houses have been built. Look for **Pookela Church,** a coral block structure built in 1843. In 4 miles you pass **Rainbow Acres,** tel. 572-8020. Open Fri. and Sat. 10:00 a.m. to 4:00 p.m., they specialize in succulents. At the top of Olinda turn left onto Piiholo Road, which loops back down. Along it is **Aloha o ka Aina,** a nursery specialing in ferns. Open Wed. and Sun. 10:00 a.m. to 4:00 p.m. You'll also pass **Olinda Nursery,** offering general house plants. Open Fri. and Sat. 10:00 a.m. to 4:00 p.m.

Food

All the following establishments are on Makawao or Baldwin avenues. An excellent place to eat is **Polli's Mexican Restaurant** (vegetarian). Open daily 11:30 a.m. to 10:30 p.m., tel. 572-7808. This is the original restaurant; they now have a branch in Kihei. The meals are authentic Mexican, using the finest ingredients. They use no lard or animal fat in their cooking. You can have a full meal for $5-6. Margaritas are large and tasty for $2, pitchers of domestic beer $5. The Sunday brunch is particularly good. One unfortunate policy is that they refuse to give free chips and salsa to a person dining alone, even when ordering a full meal, while couples dining get them free! **Makawao Steak House,** tel. 572-8711. Daily for dinner from 5:00 p.m. "Early bird" special until 6:30. Sunday brunch from 9:30 a.m. to 2:00 p.m. Casual, with wooden tables, salad bar, and good fish selections. Dinners are from $8.95—a good general purpose restaurant.

Kitada's, a *kau kau* stand, makes the best *saimin* on Maui, according to all the locals. It's across from the Makawao Steak House. Open daily 6:00 a.m. to 2:00 p.m., tel. 572-7241. The 77-year-old owner, Takeshi Kitada, does all the prep work himself. Walk in, pour yourself a glass of water and take a hardboard-topped table. The *saimin* is delicious and only $1.50. There're plate lunches, too. The walls have paintings of Upcountry by local artists. Most show more heart than talent. Bus your own table while Kitada-san calculates your bill on an abacus. His birthday, May 26, has become a town event.

Komoda's is a corner general store that has been in business for over 50 years. They sell everything, but their bakery is renowned far and wide. They open at 6:30 a.m. with people already lined up outside to buy their cream buns and homemade cookies—all gone by 9:00. **Mountainside Liquor and Deli**, tel. 572-0204, can provide all the fixings for a lunch, or a full range of liquid refreshments. **Rodeo General Store** has a selection of fish and gourmet foods. **Whole Food Co.** is a health food store that can supply basic needs.

Shopping

Some unique and fascinating shops here can provide you with distinctive purchases. **Upcountry Down Under**, tel. 572-7103, specializes in imported New Zealand woolens, crafts, and skins. They also carry stuffed animals, rugby jerseys, sweaters, and backpacks. Lyn Lone runs the shop along with Dana and Peter Marshal. **Collections Boutique**, open daily til 9:00 p.m., import items from throughout Asia: *batik* from Bali, clothes from India, jewelry and handicrafts from various countries. Operated by Pam Winans. **Grandma's Attic** is a discovery shop operated by Pris and Moe Moler. Everything in here is nifty: old Victrolas, vintage *Life* Magazines, furniture, jewelry. It has the feeling of a museum and is worth a stop.

Outdoor Sports, tel. 572-8736, is a gem of a general store and an attraction in itself. The owner, Gary Moore, is a relative newcomer who helped restore the integrity of Makawao and became a town historian in his own right. He carries guns, ammo, boots, saddles, big barrels full of hardware, even wood-burning stoves. He sells gifts and camping equipment, which is also for rent. Wander around inside just for the fun of it. **Makawao Leather** specializes in hand-carved leatherwork—everything from chaps to head bands. **Hui Noeau** ("Club of Skills") is a local organization that features traditional and modern arts. Their member artisans produce everything from ceramics to *lau hala* (weaving). They are housed at Kaluanui, a mansion built in 1917 by the Baldwin family. They sponsor an annual Christmas Fair featuring their creations.

Events

Makawao has a tremendous rodeo season every year. Most meets are sponsored by the Maui Roping Club. They start in the spring and culminate in a massive rodeo on July 4th, with over $22,000 in prize money. These events attract the best cowboys from around the state. The organization of the event is headed by a long-time resident, Brendan Balthazar, who welcomes everyone to participate with only one rule, "Have fun, but maintain safety."

KULA

Kula could easily provide all of the ingredients for a full-course meal fit for a king. Its bounty is staggering: vegetables to make a splendid chef's salad, beef for the entree, flowers to brighten the spirits, and wine to set the mood. Up here, soil, sun, and moisture create a garden symphony. Sweet Maui onions, cabbages, potatoes, grapes, apples, pineapples, lettuce, and artichokes grow with abandon. Herefords and black angus graze in knee-deep fields of sweet green grass. Flowers are everywhere: beds of proteas, camellias, carnations, roses, hydrangeas, and blooming peach and tangerine dot the countryside like daubs from van Gogh's brush. As you gain the heights along Kula's lanes, you look back on West Maui with a perfect view of the isthmus. You'll also enjoy wide-open spaces and rolling green hills fringed with trees like a lion's mane. Above, the sky changes from brooding gray to blazing blue, then back again. Kula is a different Maui—quiet and serene.

Getting There

The fastest way is the same as if going to Haleakala Crater. Take Rt. 37 through Pukalani, turn onto Rt. 377, and when you see Kimo Road on your left and right, you're in Kula country. If you have the time take the following scenic route. Back in Kahului start on Rt. 36 (Hana Hwy.), but as soon as you cross Dairy Road look for a sign on your left pointing to Pulehu-Omaopio Road. Take it! You'll wade through acres of sugarcane, and in 6 miles these 2 roads

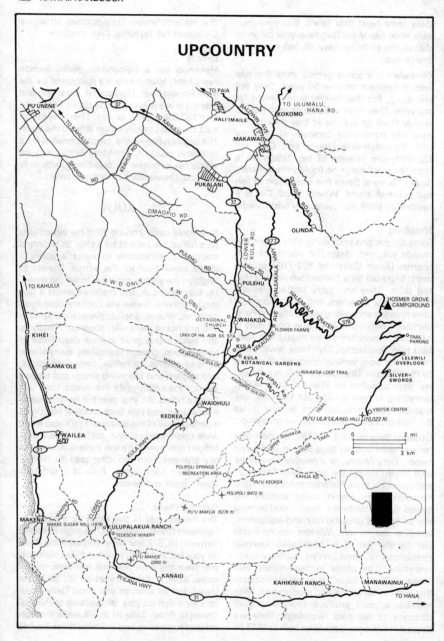

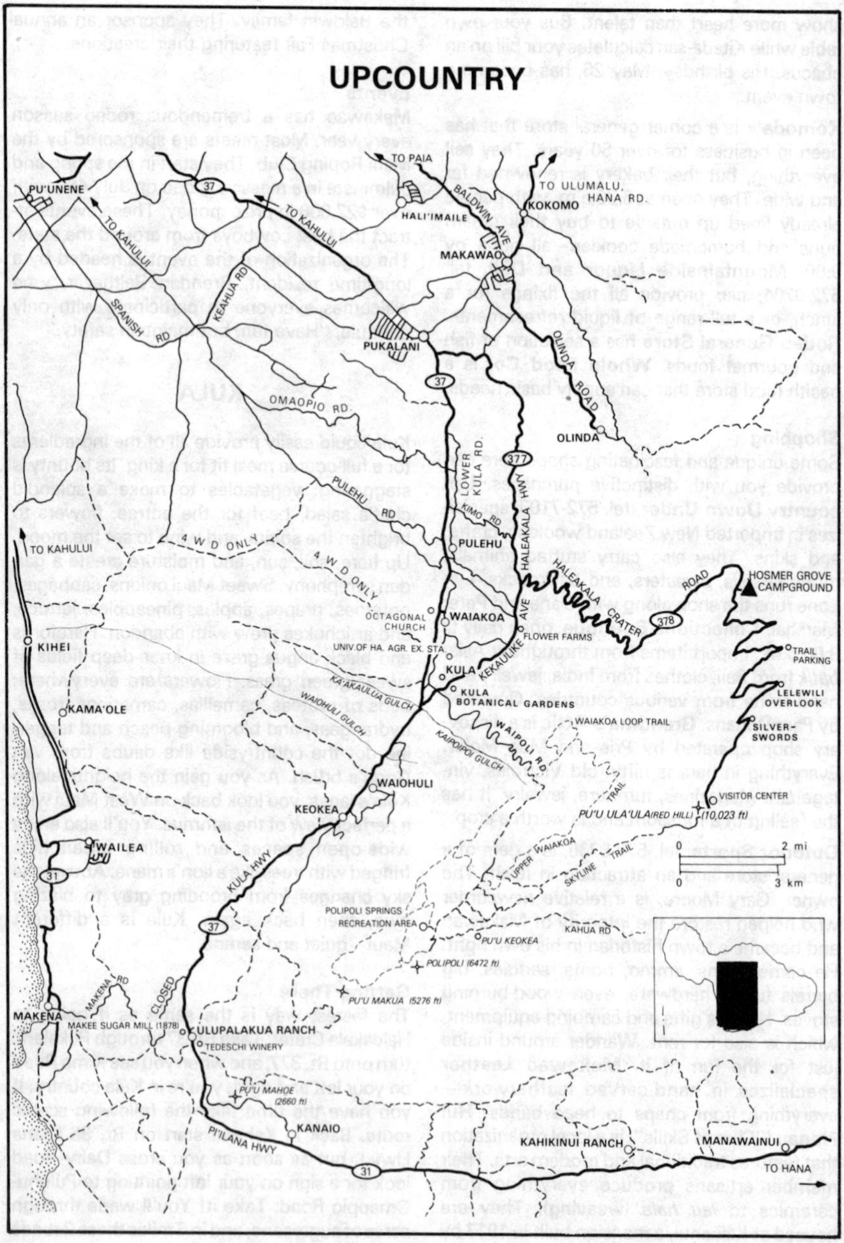
UPCOUNTRY
TO PAIA
PU'UNENE
37
TO KAHULUI
HALI'IMAILE
TO ULUMALU, HANA RD.
KOKOMO
BALDWIN AVE
TO KAHULUI
MAKAWAO
KEAHUA RD
SPANISH RD
PUKALANI
OLINDA ROAD
37
OMAOPIO RD.
OLINDA
LOWER KULA RD.
377
PULEHU RD
TO KAHULUI
W. D. ONLY
W. D. ONLY
KIMO RD
PULEHU
HALEAKALA HWY
HALEAKALA CRATER ROAD
HOSMER GROVE CAMPGROUND
OCTAGONAL CHURCH
WAIAKOA
378
UNIV. OF HA. AGR. EX. STA.
FLOWER FARMS
KEKAULIKE AVE
TRAIL PARKING
KIHEI
KULA
KAKAULUA GULCH
KULA BOTANICAL GARDENS
LELEWILI OVERLOOK
WAIOHULI GULCH
KAMA'OLE
WAIAKOA LOOP TRAIL
KAIPOIPOI GULCH
WAIPOLI RD
SILVER SWORDS
TRAIL
WAIOHULI
KEOKEA
VISITOR CENTER
PU'U ULA'ULA (RED HILL) (10,023 ft)
UPPER WAIAKOA
SKYLINE TRAIL
0 2 mi
0 3 km
WAILEA
31
KULA HWY
POLIPOLI SPRINGS RECREATION AREA
37
KAHUA RD
PU'U KEOKEA
POLIPOLI (6472 ft)
MAKENA RD
CLOSED
PU'U MAKUA (5276 ft)
MAKENA
MAKEE SUGAR MILL (1878)
ULUPALAKUA RANCH
TEDESCHI WINERY
PU'U MAHOE (2660 ft)
KANAIO
PI'ILANA HWY
KAHIKINUI RANCH
MANAWAINUI
31
TO HANA

will split. You can take either, but Omaopio to the left is better because, at the top, it deposits you in the middle of things to see. Once the roads forks, you pass some excellent examples of flower and truck farms. You'll also go by the cooperative **Vacuum Cooling Plant** where many farmers store their produce. Then Omaopio Road will come again to Rt. 37 (Kula Hwy.). Don't take it yet. Cross and continue until Omaopio dead ends, in a few hundred yards. Turn right onto Lower Kula Road and watch for Kimo (Lower) Drive on your left, and take it straight uphill. This brings you through some absolutely beautiful countryside and in a few miles crosses Rt. 377, where a right will take you to Haleakala Crater Road.

Pukalani

This way station town is uninteresting but a good place to get gas and supplies. There's a shopping mall where you can pick up just about anything you'll need. **Bullock's** restaurant just past the mall serves a wide assortment of good value sandwiches. The moonburger is a tradition, but a full breakfast here for under $3 will give you all the energy you'll need for the day ahead. They also have plate lunches and some island-flavored shakes. **Cross Roads Restaurant** in the mall is open daily for lunch and dinner: basically American standard from sandwiches to full meals.

Kula Lodge

The Kula Lodge is on Rt. 377 just past Kimo Drive and just before Haleakala Crater Road. RR 1, Box 475, Kula HI 96790, tel. 878-1535. Lodging here is in $80-95 chalets. All have fireplaces with wood provided, and all have excellent views of lower Maui. The lobby and main dining areas are impressively rustic. The walls are covered with high-quality photos of Maui: windsurfers, silverswords, sunsets, cowboys, and horses. The main dining room has a giant bay window with a superlative view. Breakfast is served daily from 7:00 a.m., lunch from 11:30 a.m. to 2:30 p.m., dinner from 5:00 p.m. Entertainment in the evenings.

Hawaii Protea Cooperative

Next door to the Kula Lodge, open Mon. through Fri. 9:00 a.m. to 4:30 p.m., tel. 878-6273. Don't miss seeing these amazing flowers. (For a full description see "Flora" in the main Introduction). Here you can purchase a wide range of protea that can be shipped back home. Live or dried, these flowers are fantastic. They start at $20, but are well worth the price. The sales people are friendly and informative, and it's educational just to visit.

protea

Upper Kimo Road

If you want to be intoxicated by some of the finest examples of Upcountry flower and vegetable farms, come up here. First, head back down Rt. 377 past the Kula Lodge and turn on **Upper Kimo Road** on your right. At the very end is **Upcountry Protea Farm**, daily 8:00 a.m. to 4:30 p.m. Box 485F, Kula, HI 96790, tel. 878-6015. They have over 50 varieties of protea and other flowers. You can walk the grounds or visit the gift shop where they offer gift packs and mail order.

Silversword Inn
Proceed past the Kula Lodge on Rt. 377 toward Haleakala to the Silversword Inn, tel. 878-1232. This congenial inn offers chalet-type accommodations at $40 for 4 people. All have an excellent view, but units 3 and 5 have extraordinary sunset exposure. The restaurant is open for breakfast, lunch, and dinner, and the huge circular fireplace is cozy against the Upcountry chill. On the grounds is the **Silversword Bakery**, tel. 878-2179. When open, they offer custom baking using organic ingredients and no preservatives or colorings. Also on the grounds is the unique **Silversword Store**. Just about everything offered is handmade or home-cooked, as well as aromatic bags of **Grandma's Maui Coffee.** This wild coffee is prepared by a 92-year-old *tu tu* after being hand-picked by her grandson. There're jellies and jams from the ladies at the local church and handicrafts all under $10. There's fresh-squeezed orange and guava juice, fresh-baked *malasadas,* and even Coca-Cola in the little 6-ounce bottles!

A field of cacti adds that cowboy feel to Upcountry.

Kula Botanical Gardens
Follow Rt. 377 south and look for the Gardens on your left just before the road meets again with Rt. 37. The gardens are open daily from 9:00 a.m. to 4:00 p.m. Admission is $2.50, under 12 for 50 cents, tel. 878-1715. Here are 3 acres of identified plants on a self-guided tour. There are streams and ponds on the property, and plants include native *koa* and *kukui,* as well as many introduced species. The gardens are educational and will give names to many flowers and plants that you've observed around the island. It makes for a relaxing afternoon, with picnic tables provided.

Poli Poli State Park
If you want quietude and mountain walks, come here, because few others do. Just past the botanical garden look for the park sign on your left leading up Waipoli Road. This 10-mile stretch is only partially paved, and the second half can be very rutted and muddy. As always, it's worth it. Poli Poli is an established forest of imported trees from around the world: eucalyptus, redwoods, cypress, and sugi pines. You can hike the **Redwood Trail** to a shelter at the end. Camping permits are required and are available from the Division of State Parks, Box 1049, Wailuku, HI 96793, tel. 244-4354. The cabin here is a spacious 3-bedroom affair with bunks for up to 10 people. It starts at $10 single and goes up about $5 per person. It's rustic, but all camping and cooking essentials are provided, including a wood-burning stove. If you want to get away from it all, this is your spot.

Others
The University of Hawaii maintains an experimental station of 20 acres of flowers that they change with the seasons. Located on Copp Road off Rt. 37. Open Mon. to Fri. 7:30 a.m. to 3:30 p.m. A self-guided tour map is available at the office, which is closed during lunch hour. **Holy Ghost Church** on Lower Kula Road, just past Kula Town, is an octagonal building raised in 1897 for the many Portuguese who worked the farms and ranches of Upcountry. There's a gas station in Kula Town.

Tedeschi Winery
Continue south on Rt. 37 through the town of Keokea, where you'll find gas, 2 general stores, and an excellent park for a picnic. Past Keokea you'll know you're in ranch country. The road narrows and herds of cattle graze in pastures that seem like manicured gardens highlighting *panini* (prickly pear) cactus. You'll pass Ulupalakua Ranch and then come to the Tedeschi Winery **tasting room** on the left. Open for tasting daily 9:00 a.m. to 5:00 p.m., tel. 878-6058. Here, Emil Tedeschi and his partner Pardee Erdman, who also owns the 30,000-acre Ulupalakua Ranch, offer samples of their wines. This is the only winery in all of Hawaii. When he moved here in 1963 from California and noticed climatic similarities to the Napa Valley, Erdman knew that this country could grow decent wine grapes. Tedeschi comes from California, where his family has a small winery near Calistoga. The partners have worked on making their dream of Maui wine a reality since 1973.

It takes time and patience to grow grapes and turn out a vintage wine. While they wait for their Carnelian grapes to mature and be made into a sparkling wine, they ferment pineapple juice, which they call Maui Blanc. If you're expecting this to be a sickeningly sweet syrup, forget it. Maui Blanc is surprisingly dry and palatable. There's even an occasional pineapple sparkling wine called Maui Brut. Both are available in restaurants and stores around the island. 1984 saw the first scheduled release of the winery's Carnelian champagne. You can taste the wines at the 100-year-old tasting room, which is a plaster and coral building. It served as the jailhouse of the old Rose Ranch owned by James Makee a Maui pioneer sugarcane planter.

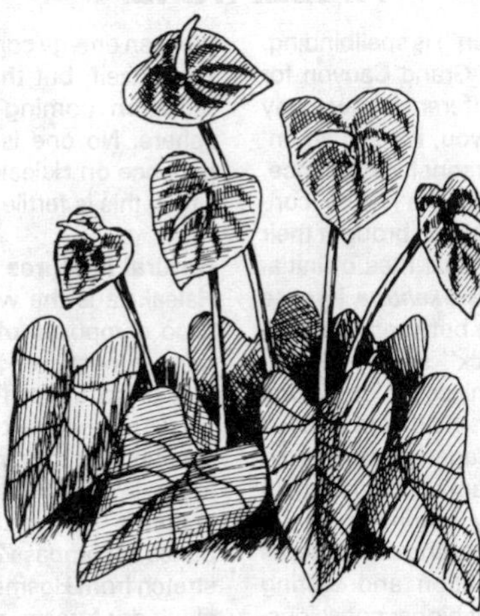

anthurium

HALEAKALA

Haleakala ("House of the Sun") is spellbinding. Like seeing Niagara or the Grand Canyon for the first time, it makes no difference how many people have come before you, it's still an undiminished, powerful, personal experience. The mountain is a power spot, a natural conductor of cosmic energy. *Kahuna* brought their novitiates here to perform final rites of initiation. During the heyday of the *kahuna,* intense power struggles took place between the healing practitioners and "black" sorcerers atop the mountain. The "Bottomless Pit," a natural feature on the crater floor, held tremendous significance for both. Average Hawaiians did not live on Haleakala, but came now and again to quarry tool-stones. Only *kahuna* and their apprentices lived here for any length of time, as a sort of spiritual preparation and testing grounds. Today, students of higher consciousness from around the world are attracted to this natural empire because of the rarefied energy. They claim that it accelerates personal growth, and compare it to remote mountain and desert areas in the Holy Lands. Even the U.S. Air Force has a facility here, and their research indicates Haleakala as *the* strongest natural power point in America. Not only is there an energy configuration coming from the Earth itself, but there is also a high focus of radiation coming from outside the atmosphere. No one is guaranteed a spiritual experience on Haleakala, but if you're at all sensitive, this is fertile ground.

Natural Features

Haleakala is the world's largest dormant volcano composed of amazingly dense volcanic rock, almost like poured cement. Its 20,000 feet or so under the sea make it one of the tallest mountains on Earth. Perhaps this mass accounts for the strange power of Haleakala as it sits like a mighty magnetic pyramid in the center of the North Pacific. The park's boundaries encompass 27,284 variable acres, which stretch from Hosmer Grove to Kipahulu, and include dry forests, rainforests, desert, and subtropical beaches. The most impressive feature is the crater itself. It's 3,000 feet deep, 7½ miles long, 2½ miles wide, accounting for 19 square miles, with a circumference of 21 miles. A mini mountain range of 9 cinder cones marches across the crater floor. They look deceptively tiny from the observation area, but the smallest is 600 feet, and the tallest, Puu O

Maui, is 1,000 feet high. Haleakala was designated as a national park in 1961. Before that it was part of the Big Island's Volcanoes Park. The entire park is a nature preserve dedicated to Hawaii's quickly vanishing indigenous plants and animals. Only Volcanoes and Haleakala are home to the ***nene,*** the Hawaiian wild goose, and the **silversword,** a fantastically adapted plant. (For full descriptions, see "Fauna and Flora" in the main "Introduction.")

The Experience

If you're after *the* experience, you must see the sunrise or sunset. Both are magnificent, but both perform their stupendous light show with astonishing speed. Also, the weather must be cooperative. Misty, damp clouds can surround the crater, blocking out the sun, and then pour into the basin, obscuring even it from view. The *Maui News* prints the hours of sunrise and sunset on a daily basis that vary with the season, so make sure to check. The park provides an accurate daily weather recording at tel. 877-5124. For more specific information, you can call the Ranger Station at 572-7749. Plan on taking a minimum of 1½ hours to arrive from Kahului, and to be safe, arrive at least 30 minutes before, because even one minute is critical. The sun, as it rises or sets, infuses the clouds with streaks, puffs, and bursts of dazzling pastels, at the same time backlighting and edging the crater in glorious golds and reds. Prepare for an emotional crescendo that will brim your eyes with tears at the majesty of it all. Engulfed by this magnificence, no one can remain unmoved.

Crater Facts

Haleakala was formed primarily from *pahoehoe* lava. This lava is the hottest natural substance on earth, and flows like swift fiery rivers. Because of its high viscosity, it forms classic shield volcanoes. Plenty of *a'a'* is also found in the mountain's composition. This rock comes out partially solidified and filled with gasses. It breaks apart and forms clinkers. You'll be hiking over both, but be especially careful on *a'a',* because its jagged edges will cut you as quickly as coral. The crater is primarily formed from erosion, and not from caving in on itself. The erosion on Hawaii is quite accelerated due to carbonic acid buildup, a by-product of the quick decomposition of abundant plant life. The rock breaks down into smaller particles of soil which is then washed off the mountain by rain, or blown off by wind. Natural drainage patterns form, and canyons begin to develop and slowly eat their way to the center. The 2 largest are **Keanae Valley** in the north and **Kaupo Gap** in the south. These canyons, over time, moved their heads past each other to the center of the mountain where they took several thousand feet off the summit, and formed a huge amphitheater-like crater.

Some stones that you encounter while hiking will be very light in weight. They once held water and gasses that evaporated. If you knock two together, they'll sound like crystal. Also, be observant for **Maui diamonds**. They're garnet stones, a type of pyroxene, or crystal. The cinder cones in the crater are fascinating. They're volcanic vents with a high iron content and may form electromagnetic lines from the Earth's center. It's not recommended to climb

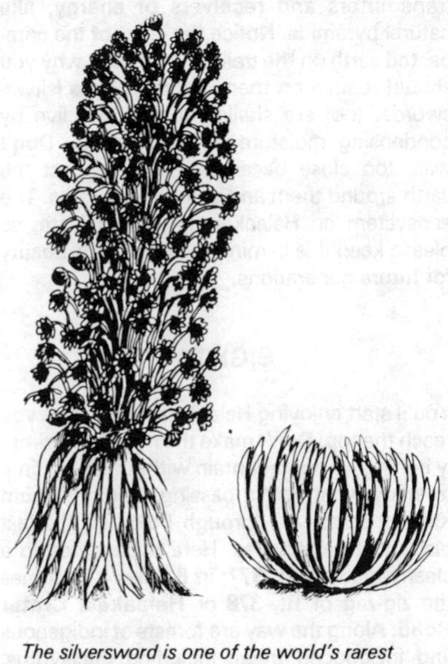

The silversword is one of the world's rarest plants. Don't walk too close when observing or you could destroy the roots.

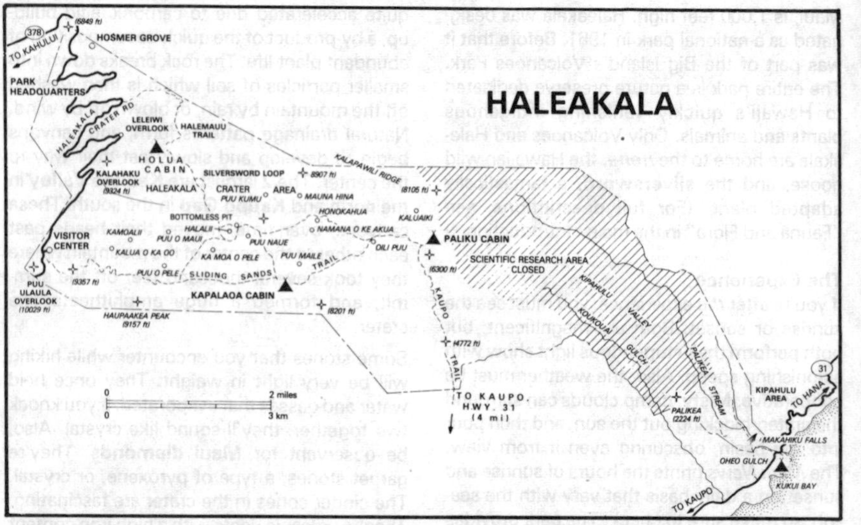

them, but many people have, even spending the night within. On top, they're like funnels, transmitters and receivers of energy, like natural pyramids. Notice the color of the compacted earth on the trails. It's obvious why you should remain on them. All the plants (silverswords, too) are shallow-rooted and live by condensing moisture on their leaves. Don't walk too close because you'll compact the earth around them and damage the roots. The ecosystem on Haleakala is very delicate, so please keep this in mind to preserve its beauty for future generations.

SIGHTS

You'll start enjoying Haleakala long before you reach the top. Don't make the mistake of simply bolting up the mountain without taking time to enjoy what you're passing. Route 37 from Kahului takes you through Pukalani, the last place to buy supplies. Here it branches to a clearly marked Rt. 377; in 6 miles it becomes the zig-zag of Rt. 378 or **Haleakala Crater Road.** Along the way are forests of indigenous and introduced trees, including eucalyptus, beautifully flowering jacaranda and stands of cactus. The vistas change rapidly from one vantage point to the next. Sometimes it's the green rolling hills of Ireland, and then instantly it's the tall, yellow grass of the plains. This is also cattle country, and don't be surprised to see all breeds, from Holsteins to Brahmas.

Headquarters

The first stopping point on the Crater Road is **Hosmer Grove Campground** (see below) on your left. Proceed past here a few minutes and you'll arrive at **Park Headquarters.** Campers can get their permits here and others will be happy to stop for all manner of brochures and information concerning the park. There are some silverswords outside and a cage for *nene* around back. After you pass Park HQ, there's trail parking on your left (see "Hikes," below). Following are 2 overlooks, **Leleiwi** and **Kalahaku.** Both offer tremendous views and different perspectives on the crater. They shouldn't be missed—especially Kalahaku where there are silverswords and the remnants of a traveler's lodge from the days when an expedition to Haleakala took 2 days.

Visitor's Center

At road's end is the Visitor's Center, approximately 10 miles up the mountain from HQ. It's open from 8:30 a.m. to 4:00 p.m. and contains a clear and concise display featuring the geology of Haleakala. Maps are available, and the ranger talks, given every hour on the hour, are particularly informative (especially those by Ranger Jitsume Kunioke,) delving into geology and the legends surrounding the great mountain.

Walks

One of the outside paths leads to **Pakaoao** ("White Hill"). An easy quarter-mile hike will take you to the summit, and along the way you'll pass stone shelters and sleeping platforms from the days when Hawaiians came here to quarry the special tool-stone. It's a type of whitish slate that easily flakes and is so hard that when you strike two pieces together it rings almost like iron. Next comes **Puu'ulaula** ("Red Hill"), the highest point on Maui at 10,023 feet. Atop is a glass-encased observation area (open 24 hours). This is where many people come to view the sunrise and sunset. From here, if the day is crystal clear, you can see all of the main Hawaiian islands except Kauai. The space colony on the crater floor below is **Science City.** This research facility is manned by the University of Hawaii and the Department of Defense. It is not open to the public.

Hikes

There are 3 trails in Haleakala Crater: Halemauu, Sliding Sands, and Kaupo. **Halemauu Trail** starts at the 8,000-foot level along the road about 4 miles past HQ. It descends quickly to the 6,600-foot level on the crater floor. En route you'll pass Holua Cabin, Silversword Loop, the Bottomless Pit (a mere 65 feet deep), and then a portion of Sliding Sands Trail, and back to the Visitor's Center. You shouldn't have any trouble hitching back to your car from here.

Sliding Sands begins at the summit of Haleakala near the Visitor's Center. This is the main crater trail and gives you the best overall hike. It joins the Kaupo Trail at Paliku Cabin; alternatively, at Kapaloa Cabin you can turn left to the Bottomless Pit and exit via Halemauu Trial. This last choice is one of the best, but you'll have to hitch back to your car at the Visitor's Center, which shouldn't be left for the dwindling late-evening traffic going up the mountain.

The **Kaupo Trail** is long and tough. It follows the Kaupo Gap to the park boundary at 3,800 feet. It then crosses private land, which is no problem, and deposits you in the semi-ghost town of Kaupo. This is the rugged part of the Hana loop that is forbidden by the rental car companies. You'll have to hitch west just to get to the scant traffic of Rt. 31, or 9 miles east to Oheo Gulch and its campground, and from there back along the Hana Road.

Along your walks, expect to see wild goats. These are often eradicated by park rangers, because they are considered an introduced pest. For those inclined, crater walks are conducted by the rangers during the summer months. These vary in length and difficulty so check at the ranger station. There are also horseback tours of the crater (see "Sports" in the main "Introduction"). Hikers should also consider a day with the professional guide, Ken Schmitt. His in-depth knowledge and commentary will make your trip not only more fulfilling, but enjoyably informative, as well. (See "Getting Around" in the main "Introduction.")

PRACTICALITIES

Making "Do"

If you've come to Hawaii for sun and surf, and you aren't prepared for alpine temperatures, you can still enjoy Haleakala. For a day trip, wear your jogging suit or a sweater, if you've brought one. Make sure to wear socks, and even bring an extra pair as make-shift mittens. Use your *dry* beach towel to wrap around inside your sweater as extra insulation, and even consider taking your hotel blanket, which you can use Indian-fashion. Make rain gear from a large plastic garbage bag. Cut holes for head and arms and this is also a good windbreaker. Take your beach hat, too. Don't worry about looking ridiculous in this get-up—you will! But you'll also keep warm! Remember that for every thousand feet you climb, the temperature drops 3 degrees, so the summit is about 30 degrees (F) cooler than at sea level. As the sun reaches its zenith, if there are no rain clouds, the crater floor will go from about 50 to 80 degrees. It can flip-flop from blazing hot to dismal and rainy a number of times in the same day. The nights will drop below freezing, with the coldest recorded temperature a bone-chilling 14 degrees. Dawn and dusk are notorious for being bitter. Because of the altitude, be aware that the oxygen level will drop, and those with any imparing conditions should take precautions. The sun is ultra strong atop the mountain and even those with deep tans are subject to burning. Noses are particularly susceptible.

Trekkers

Any serious hikers or campers must have sturdy shoes, good warm clothes, rain gear, canteens, down bag, and a serviceable tent. Hats and sunglasses are needed. Compasses are useless because of the high magnetism in the rock, but binoculars are particularly rewarding. No cook fires are allowed in the crater, so you'll need a stove. Don't burn any dead wood—the soil needs all the decomposing nutrients it can get. Drinking water is available at all of the cabins within the crater. This environment is particularly delicate. Stay on the established trails so that you don't cause undue erosion. Leave rocks and especially plants alone. Don't walk too close to silverswords or any other plants because you'll compact the soil. Leave your pets at home; ground-nesting birds here are easily disturbed. If Nature "calls," dig a very shallow hole, off the trail, and cover your toilet paper and all with the dirt. Urinating on it will hasten the decomposition process.

Camping

Admission to the park is free, and unless you'll be staying in a cabin, camping is also free, but you must obtain a camping permit from Park HQ. The **Hosmer Grove** campground is at the 6,800-foot level, just before Park HQ. The free camping here is limited to 25 people, but there's generally room for all. There's water, pit toilets, grills, and a pavilion. It was named after Ralph Hosmer who tried to save the watershed by planting fast-growing foreign trees like cedars, pines, and junipers. He succeeded, but this destroyed any chance of the native Hawaiian trees making a comeback.

Oheo Campground is a primitive camping area over at the Seven Pools. It's part of the park, but unless you're an intrepid hiker and descend all the way down the Kaupo Trail, you'll come to it via Hana (see "Hana and Beyond"). There are campsites in the crater at **Holua, Paliku,** and **Kapalaoa.** All 3 offer cabins, and tent camping is allowed at the first 2. Camping at any of these is extremely popular, and reservations for the cabins must be made months in advance. A lottery of the applicants chosen for sites keeps it fair for all. Environmental impact studies limit the number of campers to 25 per area per day. Camping is limited to a total of 3 days, with no more than 2 at each spot. For complete details write: Haleakala National Park, Box 369, Makawao, HI 96768, tel. 572-7749. Also, see the camping chart in the main "Introduction."

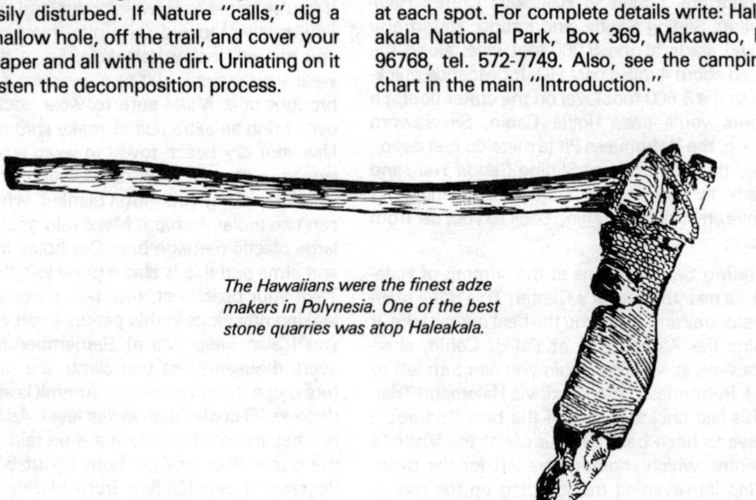

The Hawaiians were the finest adze makers in Polynesia. One of the best stone quarries was atop Haleakala.

THE HANA ROAD

On the long and winding road to Hana's door, most people's daydreams of "paradise" come true. A trip to Maui without a visit to Hana is like ordering a sundae without a cherry on top. The 50 miles that it takes to get there from Kahului are some of the most remarkable in the world. The Hana Road (Rt. 36) starts out innocently enough, passing **Paia Town.** The inspiration for Paia's gaily painted storefronts looks like it came from a jar of jelly beans. Next come some north shore surfing beaches where windsurfers fly, doing amazing aquabatics. Soon there are a string of "rooster towns," so named because that's about all that seems to be stirring. Then Rt. 36 becomes Rt. 360 and at the 3-mile marker, the *real* Hana Road begins.

The semi-official count tallies over 600 rollicking turns and more than 50 one-lane bridges, inducing everyone to slow down and soak up the sights of this glorious road. It's like passing through a tunnel cut from trees. The ocean winks with azure blue through sudden openings on your left. To the right, streams, waterfalls, and pools sit wreathed with jungle and wildflowers. Coconuts, guavas, mangoes, and bananas grow everywhere on the mountainside. Fruit stands pop up regularly as you creep along. Then comes **Keanae** with its arboretum, and taro farms indicate that many ethnic Hawaiians still live along the road. There are places to camp, picnic, and swim, both in the ocean and in freshwater streams.

Then you reach **Hana** itself, a remarkable town. The great queen Kaahumanu was born here, and many celebrities live in the surrounding hills seeking peace and solitude. Past Hana, the road becomes even more rugged and besieged by jungle. It opens up again around **Oheo Stream** (or Seven Pools). Here waterfalls cascade over stupendous cataracts forming a series of pools until they reach the sea. Beyond is a rental car's no-man's land, where the passable road toughens and Haleakala shows its barren volcanic face scarred by lava flows.

LOWER PAIA

Paia ("Noisy") was a bustling sugar town that took a nap. When it awoke, it had a set of whiskers and its vitality had flown away. At the turn of the century, many groups of ethnic field workers lived here, segregated in housing clusters called "camps" that stretched up Baldwin Avenue. Paia was the main gateway for sugar on East Maui, and even a railroad functioned here until 20 years ago. During the 1930s, its population, at over 10,000, was the largest on the island. Then fortunes shifted toward Kahului, and Paia lost its dynamism, until recently. The townsfolk have pumped new life into its old muscles. The old shops catering to the practical needs of a "plantation town" were replaced. The storefronts were painted and spruced up. A new breed of merchant with their eye on passing tourists has taken over. Now Paia (Lower) focuses on boutiques, crafts, and artwork. Since you've got to pass through on your way to Hana, it serves as a great place not only to top off your gas tank, but also to stop for a bite and a browse. The prices are good for just about everything, and it boasts one of the island's best fish restaurants and art shops. Paia, under its heavy makeup, is still a vintage example of what it always was—a homey, serviceable, working town.

Sights

A mile or so before you enter Paia on the left is **Rinzai Buddhist Temple**. The grounds are pleasant and worth a look. **Mantokuji Buddhist Temple** in Paia heralds the sun's rising and setting by ringing its huge gong 18 times at dawn and dusk.

Baldwin County Park is on your left about 7 miles past Kahului on Rt. 36; this spacious park is good for swimming, shell collecting, and a decent winter surf. There's tent and trailer camping (county permit required) and full amenities. Unfortunately, Baldwin has a bad reputation. It's one of those places that locals have staked out with the attitude of "us against them." Hassles and robberies have been known to occur. Be nice, calm, and respectful. For the timid, to be on the safe side, be gone.

Hookipa Beach Park is about 10 minutes past Paia. There's a high, grassy sand dune

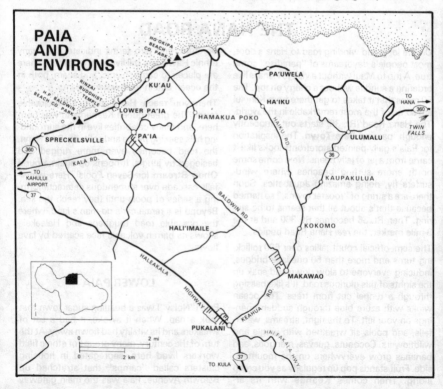

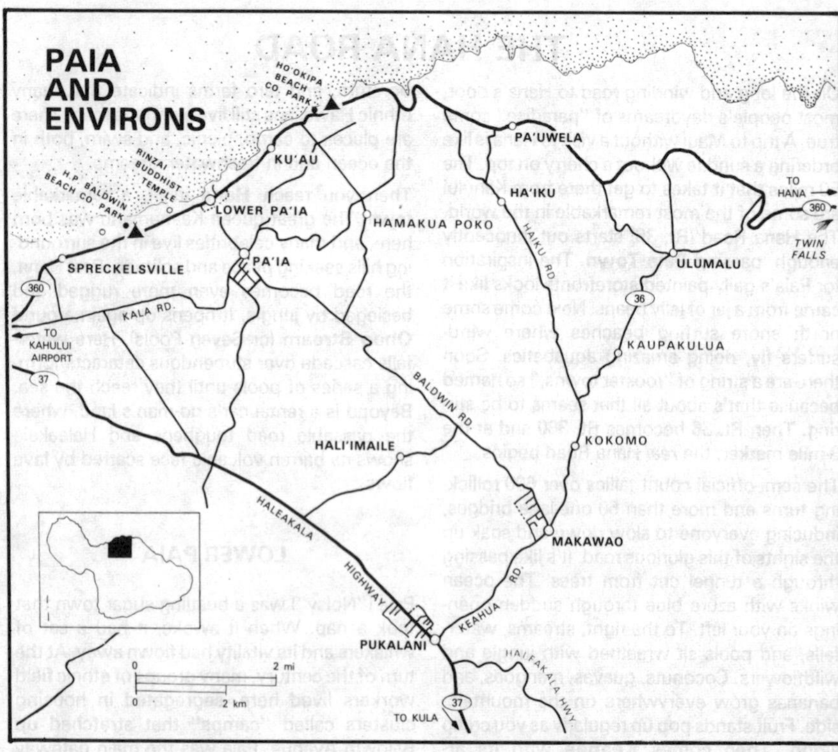

Fill up here before heading down the Hana Road.

along the road and the park is down below, where you'll enjoy full amenities and camping with a county permit. Swimming is advisable only on calm days. Wicked currents. Primarily a surfing beach that is now regarded as one of the best sailboarding areas in Hawaii, this is home to the "O'Neill International Windsurfing Championship," held yearly during early spring. The world's best sailboarders come here, trying to win the $10,000 prize. A colorful spectacle. Bring binoculars.

Food

Hat's Restaurant is at the corner of Baldwin Ave., as you enter town. Daily breakfast, lunch, and dinner, tel. 579-8045. A semi-sidewalk cafe popular with locals. Owned and operated by Joe Pavao, a lifelong island resident of Portuguese descent. You can't beat their $2 breakfast special. Nothing fancy, but good food, cheap prices, and clean.

Dillon's, Hana Rd., Paia, tel. 579-9113. Daily breakfast, lunch, and dinner. From the outside you'd expect Marshall Dillon and Kitty to come sashaying through the swinging doors, but inside it's Polynesian with a sort of German beer garden out back. The food is well prepared and the portions large. Mostly steaks, chops, and fish with a Hawaiian twist. Moderate to expensive.

Piero's Garden Cafe, Hana Rd., Paia, tel. 579-9730. Daily breakfast, lunch, and dinner. Piero's is an Italian cafe where you can eat for under $6. They offer a breakfast special of poached eggs and mozzarella cheese for $2.25. Gourmet coffee. Funky surroundings with entertainment nightly. This includes an "open mike" on Thursdays and jazz on Sundays.

Mama's Fish House, just past Paia on the left, but look hard for the turn-off near the blinking yellow light. Turn left at the ship's flagpole and follow "angel fish" sign down to Kuau Cove. Daily dinner only, reservations recommended, tel. 579-9672. Mama's has the best reputation possible—it gets thumbs up from local people. The fish is fresh daily, with some broiled over *kiawe.* Vegetables come from local gardens and the herbs are Mama's own. Special Hawaiian touches with every meal. Expensive, but worth it. Make reservations for the evening's return trip from Hana.

Quickies all in and around town: **Tradewinds Natural Foods,** a well-stocked health food store with a snack bar. Daily 7:00 a.m. to 8:00 p.m., Sun. 9:00 a.m. to 6:00 p.m. Early opening makes this a good place to stock up with healthy foods for the Hana Road. **Charlie P. Woofers,** a saloon with pool tables, selling food and beer. **Picnics** on Baldwin Ave., sandwiches and burgers for under $4. **Ice Cream and Dreams,** frosty yummies at the corner of Baldwin Avenue.

Shopping

Maui Crafts Guild is on the left just before entering Paia, at 43 Hana Rd., Box 609, Paia, HI

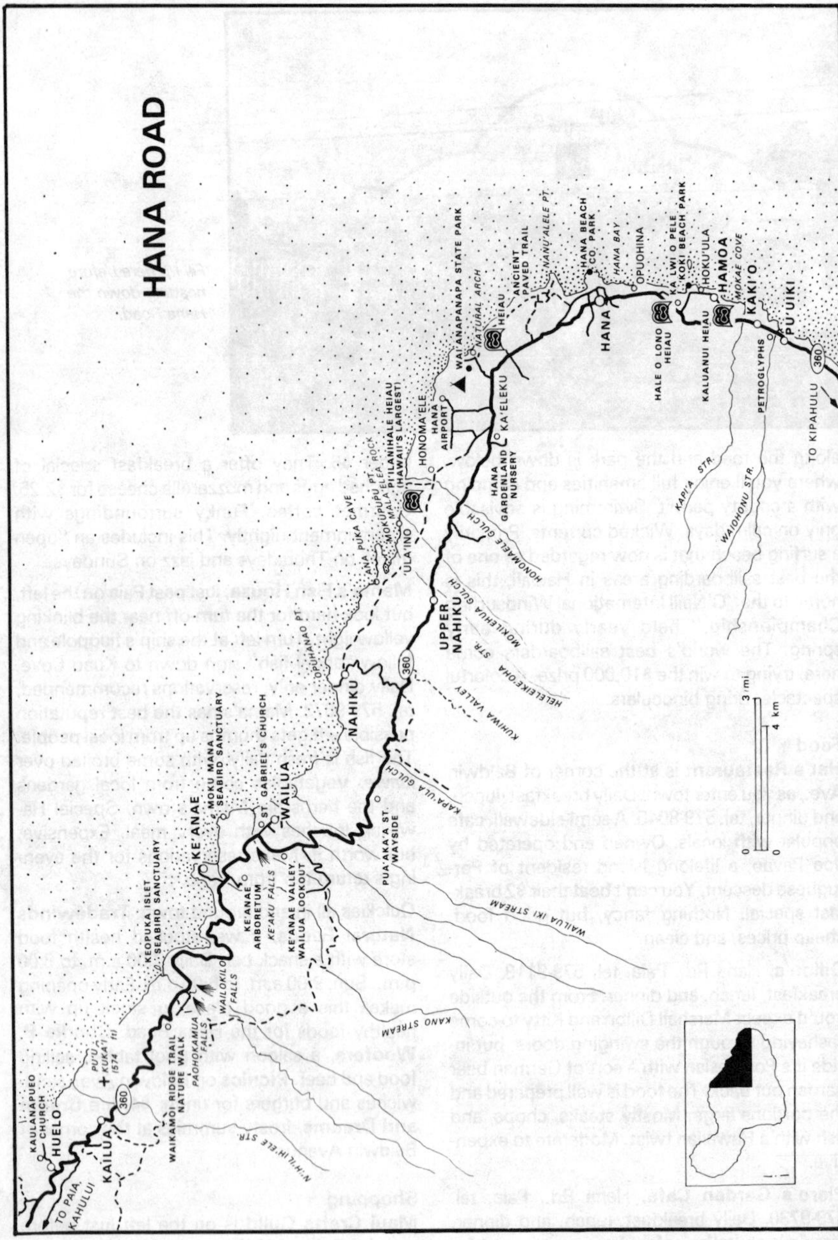
HANA ROAD
WAI'ANAPANAPA STATE PARK
NATURAL ARCH
ANCIENT PAVED TRAIL
NANU'ALELE PT.
HANA BEACH CO. PARK
HANA BAY
OPUOHINA
KA LWI O PELE
KOKI BEACH PARK
HOKU'ULA
HAMOA
MOKAE COVE
KAKI'O
PU'UIKI
HANA
HALE O LONO HEIAU
KALUANUI HEIAU
PETROGLYPHS
360
TO KIPAHULU
KAPI'A STR.
WAIOHONU STR.
HEIAU
KA'ELEKU
HANA AIRPORT
HONOMA'ELE
PI'ILANIHALE HEIAU (HAWAII'S LARGEST)
MALA 'ELEA ROCK
MOKUPUPU PT.
'ANA PUKA CAVE
'ULA'INO
HANA GARDENLAND NURSERY
HONOMAELE GULCH
MOKULEHUA GULCH
HELELEIKE'OHA STR.
UPPER NAHIKU
KUHIWA VALLEY
OPIHIKAO PT.
NAHIKU
ST. GABRIEL'S CHURCH
WAILUA
MOKU MANA SEABIRD SANCTUARY
KE'ANAE
KEOPUKA ISLET SEABIRD SANCTUARY
KE'ANAE ARBORETUM
KE'AKU FALLS
KE'ANAE VALLEY WAILUA LOOKOUT
PUA'AKA'A ST. WAYSIDE
KAPA'ULA GULCH
WAILUA IKI STREAM
KANO STREAM
WAILOKILO FALLS
PAOHOKAMUA FALLS
WAIKAMOI RIDGE TRAIL NATURE WALK
PU'U KUKA'I (574 ft)
KAULANAPUEO CHURCH
HUELO
KAILUA
TO PAIA, KAHULUI
3 mi
4 km

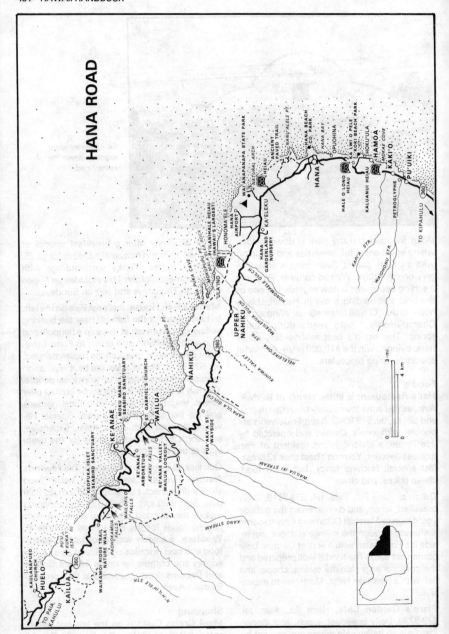

54 BRIDGES OF HANA, MAUI, HAWAII

1 O'o-pu-ola	life maturing	28 Pu-a-pa-pe	baptismal
2 Ma-ka-na-le	bright vision	29 Ka-ha-wai-ha-pa-pa	extensive valley
3 Ka-ai-ea	breathtaking view	30 Ke-a-a-iki	burning star (sirius)
4 Wai-a-ka-mo'i	waters of the king	31 Wai-oni (Akahi)	first ruffled waters
5 Pu-oho-ka-moa	sudden awakening	32 Wai-oni (Elua)	second ruffled waters
6 Hai-pue-na	glowing hearts	33 Lani-ke-le	heavenly mist
7 Ko-le'a	windborne joy	34 He-lele-i-ke-oha	extending greetings
8 Hono-manu	bird valley	35 Ula-i-no	intense sorrow
9 Nu'a-'ai-lua	large abundance	36 Moku-lehua	solemn feast
10 Pi-na-ao	kind hearted	37 'O-i-lo-wai	first sprouting
11 Pa-lauhulu	leaf sheltered	38 Hono-ma-'e-le	land of deep love
12 Wai-o-ka-milo	whirling waters	39 Ka-wai-pa-pa	the forbidden waters
13 Wai-kani	sounding waters	40 Ko-holo-po	night traveling
14 Wai-lua-nui	increasing waters	41 Ka-ha-wai-'oka-pi-a	frugal valley
15 Wai-lua-iki	diminishing waters	42 Wai-o-honu	water of the turtle
16 Ko-pi-li-ula	sacred ceremony	43 Papa'a-hawa-hawa	stronghold
17 Pu'a-aka-a	open laughter	44 Ala-ala-'ula	reawakening
18 Wai-o-hu-e	deceptive waters	45 Wa-i-ka-ko'i	time of demand
19 Wai-o-hu-e-'lua	second deceptive water	45 Pa-'ihi	place of majesty
20 Pa-akea	spacious enclosure	47 Wai-lua	water spirits
21 Ka-pa-'ula	to hold sacred	48 Wa-'i-lua	scattered spirits
22 Hana-wi (Akahi)	first whistling wind	49 Pu'u-ha-o-a	burning hill
23 Hana-wi (Elua)	second whistling wind	50 Pae-hala	pandanus clusters
24 Ma-ka-pi-pi	desire for blessings	51 Maha-lawa	place of rest
25 Ku-hiwa	precious love	52 Hana-lawe	proud deduction
26 Ku-pu-koi	claiming tribute	53 Pua-a-lu-'u	prayer blossoms
27 Ka-ha-la-o-wa-ka	lightning flash	54 O'he'o	enduring pride

Interpretations Inez MacPhee Ashdown

Inez MacPhee Ashdown's translations of the Hana Road bridges; layout by artist Sam Eason, a longtime Hana resident.

96779, tel. 579-9693. Open daily from 10:00 a.m. to 5:30 p.m. The Crafts Guild is one of the best art outlets in Hawaii. It's owned and operated by the artists themselves, all of whom must pass a thorough "jurying" by present members. All artists must be islanders, and they must use natural materials found in Hawaii to create their work. Items are tastefully displayed and it's an experience just to look. You'll find a wide variety of artwork and crafts including pottery, furniture, beadwork, woodcarving, bamboo work, stained glass, *batik,* and jewelry. Different artists man the shop on different days, but phone numbers are available if you want to see more of something you like. Prices on smaller items are reasonable, and this is an excellent place to make that one "big" purchase. Around the rear of the premises is **Touchstone Gallery,** which offers excellent and unique pottery.

Other stores are along the main street. **Paia Art Center** is a good idea that hasn't really started rolling yet. It's a collection of artists whose organization seems lacking, and the offerings, though good, are meager. **Paper Weights** has women's fashions and T-shirts. **Antiques and Uniques,** the name says it all. **Bounty Music,** music store with a good selection of instruments and a great storefront. **Mad Hatter** is a terrific little store loaded with hats. Their motto, "If you've got the head, I've got the hat." Cheaper than the Lahaina branch.

THE ROAD BEGINS

The road to Hana holds many spectacles and surprises, but one of the best is the road itself...it's a marvel! The road was hacked out from the coastline in 1927, every inch by hand using pick and shovel. An ancient Hawaiian Trail followed the same route for part of the way, but mostly people moved up and down this coastline by boat. What makes the scenery so special is that the road snakes along Maui's windward side. There's abundant vegetation and countless streams flowing from Haleakala, carving gorgeous valleys. There are a few scattered villages with a house or two that you hardly notice, and the beaches, although few, are empty. Mostly, however, it's the "feeling" that you get along this road. Nature is close and accessible, and it's so incredibly "south sea island" that it almost seems artificial. But it isn't.

Driving Tips

You've got 30 miles of turns ahead when Rt. 36 (mile marker 22) becomes Rt. 360 (mile marker 0) and the fun begins. The Hana Road has the reputation of being "bad road," but this isn't true. It's narrow, with plenty of hairpin turns, but it's well banked, has clearly marked bridges, and there's always maintenance going on (which can slow you up). Years back, it was a harrowing experience. When mudslides blocked the road, drivers were known to swap their cars with those on the opposite side and carry on to where they were going. The road's reputation sets people up to expect an ordeal, so they make it one, and unfortunately, drive accordingly. Sometimes it seems as though tourists demand the road to be rugged, so that they can tell the folks back home that they, too, "survived the road to Hana." This popular slogan appears on T-shirts, copyrighted and sold by Hasegawa's famous store in Hana, and perpetuates this belief. You'll have no problem, and you'll see much more if you just take it easy.

Your speed will often drop below 10 miles per hour, and will rarely exceed 25. Standard shift cars are better for the turns. Cloudbursts occur at anytime so be ready for slick roads. A heavy fall of fruit from roadside mango trees can also coat the road with slippery slime. Look as far up the road as possible and don't allow yourself to be mesmerized by the 10 feet in front of your hood. If your tire dips off a rough shoulder, don't risk losing control by jerking the wheels back on immediately. Ride it for a while and either stop or wait for an even shoulder to come back on. Local people trying to make time will often ride your rear bumper, but generally they won't honk. Pull over and let them by when possible.

From Kahului to Hana, it'll take 3 hours, not counting some recommended stops. The greatest traffic flow is from 10:00 a.m. to noon; returning "car trains" start by 3:00 p.m. and are heaviest around 5:00 p.m. Many white-knuckled drivers head for Hana as if it were a prized goal, without stopping along the way. This is ridiculous. The best sights are *before* and *after* Hana; the town itself is hardly worth the effort. Expect to spend a long day exploring the Hana Road. To go all the way to Oheo

Twin Falls

Stream and take in some sights, you'll have to leave your hotel at sunup and won't get back until sundown. If your budget can afford it, think of staying the night in Hana (reservations definitely) and return the next day. This is a particularly good alternative if you have an afternoon departing flight from Kahului Airport. Also, most tourists seem terrified of driving the road at night. Actually it's easier. There is far less traffic, road reflectors mark the center and sides like a runway, and you're warned of oncoming cars by their headlights. Those in the know make much better time after dark!

Twin Falls

This is one of the first places to stop and enjoy. Park just before Hoolawa Bridge, coming up after mile marker 2 on Rt. 360. Go under the white gate in the center of the parking area and follow the jeep trail. Stay on the trail for about 15 minutes, ignoring the little cattle trails left and right. Plenty of guavas along here are free for the picking. Once you've reached the top of the hill, bear left toward the creek. The first pool is fed by the 2 waterfalls that give the area its name. Walk farther up the creek for better pools and more privacy. The next large pool has a rope to swing from, and some people go skinny-dipping along here.

Huelo
This is a quiet "rooster town" famous for **Kaulanapueo Church** built in 1853. The structure is made from coral and is reminiscent of New England architecture. It's still used, and a peek through the door will reveal a stark interior with straight-backed benches and a platform. Few bother to stop, so it's quiet, and offers good panorama of the village and sea below. At the turnoff to Huelo between mile markers 3 and 4, there's a **public telephone,** in case of emergency. The next tiny town is Kailua; the multicolored trees in this area are rainbow eucalyptus. Plenty of mountain apple trees are along this stretch.

Waikamoi Ridge
This nature walk is a good place to stretch your legs and learn about native and introduced trees and vegetation. The turnout is clearly marked along the highway. The trail leads through tall stands of identified trees. For those never before exposed to a bamboo forest, it's most interesting when the wind rustles the trees so that they knock together like natural percussion instruments. Picnic tables are available at the start and end of the trail. Back on the road at the next bridge is excellent drinking water. There's a stone barrel with a pipe coming out, and local people come to fill jugs with what they call "living water."

Beach Parks
Less than 2 miles past Waikamoi Ridge will be **Kaumahina State Wayside** along the road, and **Honomanu County Park,** down at Honomanu Bay. Permits are required to camp. There are no amenities at Honomanu, but Kaumahina has them all. Camping here is in a rainforest with splendid views out to sea overlooking the rugged coastline and the black-sand beach of Honomanu Bay. Puohokamoa Falls are just a short walk away. Honomanu is not good for swimming because of strong currents, but is good for surfing.

Keanae
Clearly marked on the left will be **Keanae Arboretum.** A hike through this facility will exemplify Hawaiian plantlife in microcosm. There are 3 sections: native forest, introduced forest, and traditional Hawaiian plants and foodstuffs. You can picnic and swim along Piinaau Stream. Hardier hikers can continue for another mile through typical (identified) rainforest. **Camp Kaenae YMCA** is just after the arboretum. It looks exactly as its name implies, set in a gorgeous natural pasture. There are various bunkhouses for men and women. Arrival time between 4:00 and 6:00 p.m., $5. For more information call the camp at 248-8355.

The first bridge past the camp offers a good and easily accessible swimming hole. **Kaenae Peninsula** is a thumb-like appendage of land formed by a lava flow. A great lookout there is poorly marked. Look for a telephone pole with a *tsunami* loudspeaker atop and pull off just there. Below you'll see neat little farms, mostly raising taro. Most people living on the peninsula are native Hawaiians. They still make *poi* the old-fashioned way: listen for the distinctive thud of *poi*-pounding in the background.

the Keanae Peninsula

Though *kapu* signs abound, the majority of people are friendly. A public road circles the peninsula, but fences across it give it a private vibration. If you visit, realize that this is one of the last patches of ground owned by Hawaiians and tended in the old way. Be respectful, please.

Some of Maui's best fruit prices are at little stands along the Hana Road.

Fruit Stands

Past Kaenae between mile markers 17 and 18 is a roadside stand where you can buy hot dogs, shave ice, and some fruit. Notice the picture-perfect, idyllic watercress farm on your left. Past mile marker 18 on the right is a fruit stand operated by a fellow named Joseph. He not only has coconuts and papayas, but also little-tasted exotic fruits like mountain apples, star fruit, pineapple, and strawberry guavas, and Tahitian lemons. An authentic fruit stand worth a stop. Another one, operated by a Hawaiian woman, is only 50 yards on the left. If you have a hankering for fruit, this is the spot.

Wailua

At mile marker 18, you come to **Wailua.** Turn left here on Wailua Road, following signs for **Coral Miracle Church**. Here, too, you'll find the **Miracle of Fatima Shrine,** so named because a freak storm in the 1860s washed up enough coral onto Wailua Beach so that the church could be constructed by the Hawaiian congregation. Across from the shrine is **The Shell Stop!,** open daily 9:00 a.m. to 5:00 p.m. This distinctive shop is owned and operated by Anna Kapuana from her 2-story home. Three local families collect *opihi* (limpets) from the nearby bay, and dive for shells on the surrounding reef. The *opihi* are a favorite Hawaiian delicacy, and gallon containers sent to Oahu bring good profits, but Anna and family have learned to fashion the purplish shells into elegant jewelry. A variety of shell work and *objets d'art* are offered. All items are made from authentic Hawaiian shells; none are imported from the Philippines or Tahiti which is the case in most jewelry and shell shops. Anna is a storehouse of information which she's willing to share, often inviting her customers to relax on her *lanai.* For an original piece of jewelry and a distinctive island memento, visit The Shell Stop!

Puaa Kaa State Wayside

This lovely spot is about 14 miles before Hana. There's no camping, but there are picnic tables, grills, and restrooms. Nearby are are Kopiliula and Waikani Falls. A stream provides some smaller falls and pools suitable for swimming.

Nahiku

The village, reached by a 3-mile road, has the dubious distinction of being one of the wettest spots along the Hana Road. At the turn of the century it was the site of the Nahiku Rubber Co., the only commercial rubber plantation in the U.S. Many rubber trees still line the road, although the venture collapsed in 1912 because the rubber was poor due to the overabundance of rainfall. The village lost its vitality and only a few homes remain. Some local people augment their incomes by growing *pakalolo* in the rainforest of this area.

Hana Airport

At mile marker 28, just before you reach the airport, there is an excellent **fruit stand** operated by a newly arrived Vietnamese family. They sell drinking coconuts for $1.50, guava juice for 50 cents, and home-made coconut candy. Next, pass **Hana Gardenland Nursery,** where you're free to browse and picnic. They have fresh-cut flowers daily, and the prices are some of the best on Maui. Past the Gardenland is a road leading left. This rough track will take you to Ulaino and **Piilanihale Heiau,** Hawaii's largest, with massive walls that rise over 50 feet. It's on private land, but accessible. In less than a mile past here, a sign will point left to **Hana Airport,** where Princeville Airlines operates flights servicing Hana.

Waianapanapa State Park

Only 3 miles outside Hana, this state park offers not only tent camping, but cabins sleeping up to 6 on a sliding scale, at $10 single up to $30 for 6. The cabins offer hot water, a full kitchen, electricity, and bedding. A deposit is required. They're very popular so book far in advance by writing Division of State Parks (see "Camping," in the main "Introduction.") Even for those not camping, Waianapanapa is a "must stop." Pass the office to the beach park and its black-sand beach. The swimming is dangerous during heavy surf because the bottom drops off quickly, but on calm days it's mellow. The snorkeling is excellent. Just offshore is a clearly visible natural stone bridge. Write Box 1049, Wailuku HI 96753, tel. 244-4354.

A well-marked trail leads to **Waianapanapa Caves.** The tunnel-like trail passes through a thicket of vines and *hao,* a bush used by the Hawaiians to mark an area as *kapu.* The caves are like huge smooth tubs formed from lava. The water trapped inside is crystal clear. These caves mark the site of a Hawaiian legend, in which a lovely princess named Popoalaea fled from her cruel husband, Kakae. He found her hiding here and killed her. During certain times of the year millions of tiny red shrimp invade the caves, turning the waters red, which the Hawaiians say are a reminder of the poor slain princess. Along the coastline here are remnants of the ancient Hawaiian **paved trail** that you can follow for a short distance.

Helani Gardens

Your last stop before Hana town, clearly marked on the right, these gardens are a labor of love begun 30 years ago and opened to the public in 1975. Howard Cooper, founder and long-time Hana resident, still tends them. The gardens are open daily 9:00 a.m to 3:00 p.m., adults $2, children $1, seniors $1.50, picnic tables and restrooms. Mr. Cooper's philosophy on life graces a bulletin board just before you cross the 6 bridges to heaven. In brief he says, "Dont hurry, don't worry, don't forget to smell the flowers." It's a self-guided tour with something for everyone. The "lower gardens" are 5 acres formally manicured, but the 65 acres of "upper garden" are much more wild and open to anyone wishing to stroll around. The lower gardens have flowering trees and shrubs, vines, fruit trees and flowers and potted plants everywhere. People see many of these plants in nurseries around the country, and may even have grown some varieties at home, but these specimens are huge. There are baobab trees, ginger plants, carp ponds, even papyrus. The fruit trees alone could supply a supermarket. The upper gardens are actually a nursery where plants from around the world are raised. Some of the most popular are heleconia and ginger, and orchids galore. In one giant tree,

Howard Cooper and grandson

Mr. Cooper's grandchildren have built a tree house, complete with picture windows, electricity, and plumbing! The entire operation is family run, with Howard himself conducting some tours and his grandson, Matthew, running the admission office. In Mr. Cooper's own words, "Helani Garden is where heaven touches the earth." Be one of the saved!

HANA AND VICINITY

Hana is about as pretty a town as you'll find anywhere in Hawaii, but if you're expecting anything stupendous you'll be sadly disappointed. For most it will only be a quick stopover at a store or beach en route to Oheo Stream: the townsfolk refer to these people as a "rent-a-car tourists." The lucky who stay in Hana, or those not worried about time, will find plenty to explore throughout the area. The town is built on rolling hills that descend to Hana Bay with much of the surrounding lands given to pasture, while trim cottages wearing flower corsages line the town's little lanes. Before the white man arrived, Hana was a stronghold that was conquered and reconquered by the kings of Maui and those of the north coast of the Big Island. The most strategic and historically laden spot is Kauiki Hill, the remnant of a cinder cone that dominates Hana Bay. This area is steeped in Hawaiian legend, and old stories relate that it was the demi-god Maui's favorite spot. It's said that he transformed his daughter's lover into Kauiki Hill and turned her into the gentle rains that bathe it to this day.

Changing History

Hana was already a plantation town in the mid-1800s when a hard-boiled sea captain named George Wilfong started producing sugar on his 60 acres. Over the years the laborers came from the standard mixture of Hawaiian, Japanese, Chinese, Portuguese, Filipino, and even Puerto Rican stock. The *luna* were Scottish, German, or American. All have combined to become the people of Hana. Sugar production faded out by the 1940s and Hana began to die, its population dipping below 500. Just then, San Francisco industrialist Paul Fagan purchased 14,000 acres of what was to become the **Hana Ranch.** Realizing that sugar was *pau,* he replanted his lands in *pangola* range grass and imported Hereford cattle from another holding on Molokai. Their white faces staring back at you as you drive past are now a standard part of Hana's scenery. Fagan loved Hana and felt an obligation to and affection for its people. He decided to retire here, and with enough money to materialze just about anything, he decided that Hana could best survive through limited tourism. He built the **Hotel Hana Maui** which catered to millionaires, mostly his friends, and began operation in 1946. Fagan owned a baseball team, the San Francisco Seals, and brought them to Hana in 1946 for spring training. This was a brilliant publicity move because sportswriters came along; becoming enchanted with Hana, they gave it a great deal of copy and were probably the first to publicize the phrase "Heavenly Hana." It wasn't long before tourists began arriving.

Unfortunately, the greatest heartbreak in modern Hana history occurred at just about the same time, on April 1, 1946. An earthquake in Alaska's Aleutian Islands sent huge tidal waves that raked the Hana coast. These destroyed hundreds of homes, wiping out entire villages, and most tragically swept away many people in their watery arms of death. Hana recovered, but never forgot. Life went on, and the menfolk began working as *paniolo* on Fagan's spread, and during round up would drive the cattle through town and down to Hana Bay where they were forced to swim to waiting barges. Other entire families went to work at the resort, and so Hana lived again. It's this legacy of quietude and old-fashioned *aloha* that attracted people to Hana over the years. Everyone knows that Hana's future lies in its uniqueness and remoteness, and no one wants it to change. The people as well as the tourists know what they have here. What really makes Hana "heavenly" is similar to what's preached in Sunday school: everyone wants to go there, but not everyone makes it.

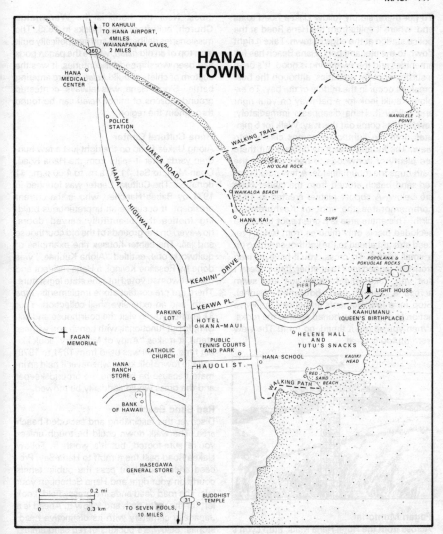

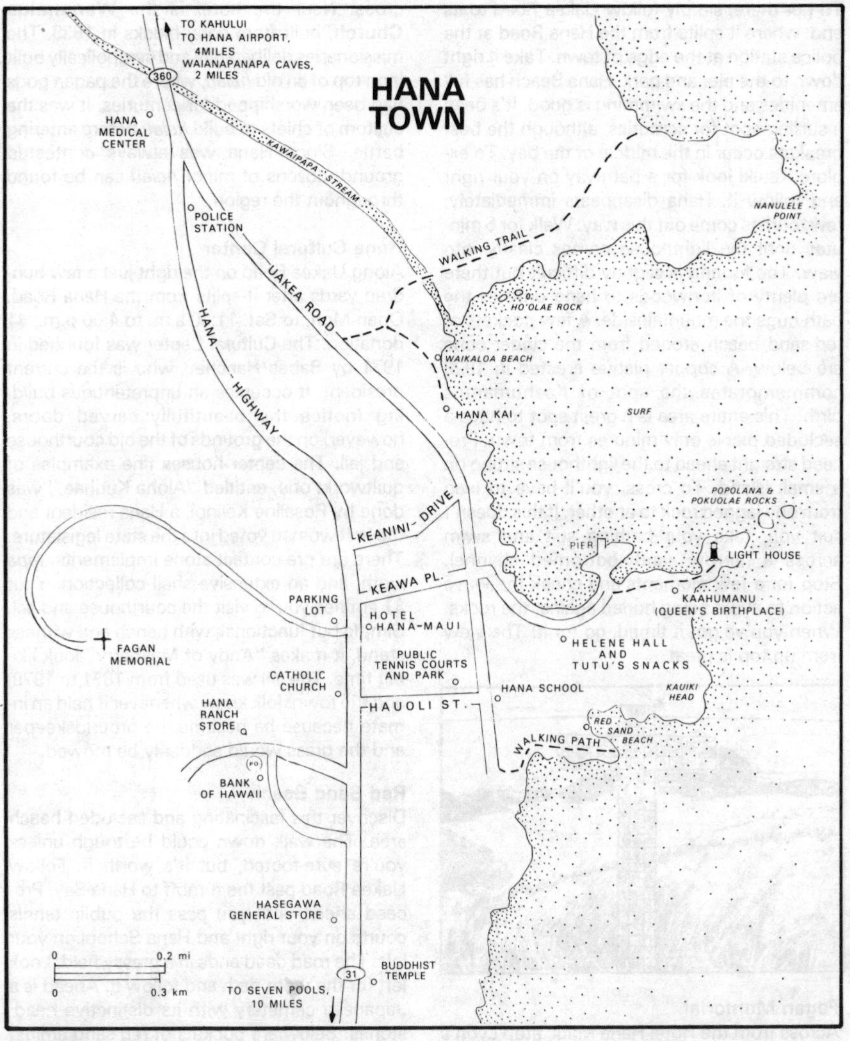

Hana Bay

Dominating the bay is the red-faced Kauiki Hill. Fierce battles raged here, especially between Maui chief Kahekili and Kalaniopuu of Hawaii, just before the islands were united under Kamehameha. Kalaniopuu held the natural fortress until Kahekili forced a capitulation by cutting off the water supply. It's believed that Kamehameha himself boarded Capt. James Cook's ship after a lookout spotted it from this hill. More importantly, Queen Kaahumanu, Kamehameha's favorite and the Hawaiian *ali'i* most responsible for ending the old *kapu* system and leading Hawaii into the "new age," was born in a cave here in 1768. Until very recent times fish spotters sat atop the hill looking for telltale signs of large schools of fish.

To get there, simply follow Uakea Road to its end, where it splits from the Hana Road at the police station at the edge of town. Take it right down to the pier and park. Hana Beach has full amenities and the swimming is good. It's been a surfing spot for centuries, although the best breakers occur in the middle of the bay. To explore Kauiki look for a pathway on your right and follow it. Hana disappears immediately; few tourists come out this way. Walk for 5 minutes until the lighthouse comes clearly into view. The footing is slightly difficult but there are plenty of ironwoods to hang onto as the path hugs the mountainside. A few pockets of red-sand beach eroded from the cinder cone are below. A copper plaque erected in 1928 commemorates the spot of Kaahumanu's birth. This entire area is a great spot to have a secluded picnic only minutes from town. Proceed straight ahead to the lighthouse sitting on a small island. To cross, you'll have to leap from one jagged rock to another. If this doesn't suit you, take your bathing suit and swim across a narrow sandy-bottomed channel. Stop for a few moments and check the wave action to avoid being hurled against the rocks. When you've got it timed, go for it! The view from up top is great.

Fagan Memorial

Across from the Hotel Hana Maui, atop Lyon's hill, is a lavastone cross erected to the memory of Paul I. Fagan, who died in 1960. The land is privately owned, but it's OK to go up there if the gate is open. If not, inquire at the hotel. From atop the hill you get the most panoramic view of the entire Hana area. After a rain, magic mushrooms have been known to pop up in the "cow pies" in the pasture surrounding the cross. Near the hotel is the **Wananalua Church,** built from coral blocks in 1838. The missionaries deliberately and symbolically built it on top of an old *heiau,* where the pagan gods had been worshipped for centuries. It was the custom of chiefs to build *heiau* before entering battle. Since Hana was always contested ground, dozens of minor *heiau* can be found throughout the region.

Hana Cultural Center

Along Uakea Road on the right just a few hundred yards after it splits from the Hana Road. Open Mon. to Sat. 11:00 a.m. to 4:00 p.m., $1 donation. The Cultural Center was founded in 1971 by Babes Hanchett who is the current president. It occupies an unpretentious building (notice the beautifully carved doors, however) on the grounds of the old courthouse and jail. The center houses fine examples of quiltwork: one, entitled "Aloha Kuuhae," was done by Rosaline Kelinoi, a Hana resident and the first woman voted into the state legislature. There are pre-contact stone implements, *tapa* cloth, and an extensive shell collection. Your $1 entitles you to visit the courthouse and jail. Simple but functional, with bench and witness stand, it makes "Andy of Mayberry" look like big time. The jail was used from 1871 to 1978, and the townsfolk knew whenever it held an inmate because he became the groundskeeper and the grass would suddenly be mowed.

Red Sand Beach

Discover this fascinating and secluded beach area. The walk down could be tough unless you're sure-footed, but it's worth it. Follow Uakea Road past the turnoff to Hana Bay. Proceed ahead until you pass the public tennis courts on your right and Hana School on your left. The road dead ends in a grassy field. Look left for the worn path and follow it. Ahead is a Japanese cemetery with its distinctive headstones. Below are pockets of red sand amidst fingers of black lava being washed by sky-blue water. There are many tide pools here. Keep walking until you are obviously in the hollowed-out amphitheater of the red cinder cone. Pat the walls to feel how crumbly they are—realize the red "sand" is eroded cinder. The water in the cove is fantastically blue against the redness.

the Hotel Hana-Maui, the epitome of elegant tranquility

Across the mouth of the bay are little pillars of stone, like castle parapets from a fairy kingdom, that keep the water safe for swimming. This is a favorite fishing spot for local people and the snorkeling is good, too. The beach is best in the morning before 11:00; afterwards it can get hot if there's no wind. The coarse red sand massages your feet, and there's a natural jacuzzi area in foamy pools of water along the shore. A man by the name of Les Eade is infatuated with the area and has become the unofficial caretaker. If a cinder boulder rolls down he'll break it up to preserve the beach area. He's planted coconut palms on the beach and he generally keeps it clean. He's also known for giving children large balloons. Learn from him: use the beach, but preserve its beauty.

Koki Beach Park

The beach park is a mile or so out of town heading toward the Seven Pools. Look for the first road to your left with a sign directing you to Hamoa Village/Beach. Koki is only a few hundred yards on the left. The riptides are fierce in here so don't swim unless it's absolutely calm. The winds can whip along here, too, while at Hamoa Beach, less than a mile away, it can be dead calm. Koki is excellent for beachcombing and for a one-night's unofficial bivouac.

A very special person named Smitty lived in a cave on the north side of the beach. Hike left to the end of the beach and you'll find a rope ladder leading up to his platform. A distinguished older man, he "dropped out" a few years back and came here to live a simple monk's existence. He kept the beach clean and saved a number of people from the riptide. He was a long-distance runner who would tack up a a "thought for the day" on Hana's public bulletin board. People loved him and he loved them in return. In 1984 the roof of his cave collapsed and he was killed. When his body was recovered, he was in a kneeling position. At his funeral, all felt a loss, but there was no sadness because all were sure that Smitty had gone home.

Hamoa Beach

Follow Hamoa Road a few minutes past Koki Beach until you see the sign for Hamoa. Between Hamoa and Koki are the remnants of an extensive Hawaiian fishpond, part of which is still discernible. This entire area is an eroding cinder cone known as **Kaiwi o Pele** ("the bones of Pele"). This is the spot where the swinish pig-god, Kama pua'a, ravished her. Pele also fought a bitter battle with her sister here, who dashed her on the rocks, giving them their anatomical name. Out to sea is the diminutive Alau Island, a remnant left over by Maui after he fished up the Hawaiian islands. You can tell that Hamoa is no ordinary beach the minute you start walking down the paved, torch-lined walkway. This is the semi-private beach of the Hotel Hana Maui. But don't be intimidated, because no one can own the beach in Hawaii. Hamoa is terrific for swimming and bodysurfing. The hotel guests are shuttled here by a bus that arrives at 10:00 a.m. and departs by 4:00 p.m. That means that you have this lovely beach to yourself before and after these times. There is a pavilion that the hotel uses for its Fri. night *luau,* as well as restrooms and showers.

ACCOMMODATIONS

Hotel Hana Maui

The hotel is the legacy of Paul Fagan, and operates as close to a family-run hotel as you can get. It's only had 4 managers in the last 40 years, and many of the personnel have either been there that long, or the jobs have passed to their children. The hotel gets as much as 80% repeat customers, who feel like they're visiting old friends. In 1985 the hotel was sold to the Rosewood Corporation of Dallas, Texas, which has had enough sense to leave well enough alone. Rates start at $263 single, $335 double, up to $475. This, however, includes 3 meals under the full American plan. There is a pool, tennis courts, superb horseback riding, outdoor camp-outs, *hula* lessons, golfing, and a famous *luau.* The entire scene isn't stiff or fancy, but it is first class! Write Hotel Hana Maui, Hana, HI 96713, tel. 800-367-5224, tel. 248-8211 on Maui. Tel. 800-252-0211 in California, tel. 800-421-0000 outside California.

Heavenly Hana Inn

The second most famous Hana hotel, it resembles a Japanese *ryokan* (inn). Walk through the formal garden and remove your shoes on entering the open-beamed main dining hall. The 4 suites seem like little apartments broken up into sections by *shoji* screens. Rates are from $50 single/double to $68 for 4. The present owner is Alfreda Worst, who purchased it from a Japanese family about 16 years ago. The inn is homey and delightful. Write Box 146, Hana 96713, tel. 248-8442.

Aloha Cottages

Box 205, Hana, HI 96713, tel. 248-8420. Owned and operated by Zenzo and Fusae Nakamura, and the best bargain in town. The cottages are meticulously clean, well built, and well appointed. For $42 double, $6 additional person, you get 2 bedrooms, a full kitchen, living room, deck, and outdoor grills. Mrs. Nakamura is very friendly and provides daily maid service. The fruit trees on the property provide free fruit to guests.

Hana Kai

These resort apartments are at Box 38, Hana, 96713, tel. 248-8435. All are well maintained and a lot for the money. Studios from $50, deluxe one bedroom from $60. All have private *lanai* with exemplary views of Hana Bay. Maid service, laundry facilities, and BBQs.

Hana Bay Vacation Rentals

Stan and Suzanne Collins offer 10 private cottages in and around Hana for rent on a daily and long-term (discounted) basis. They start at $55 and go up to $185. Their rentals include everything from a rustic cabin to a beachfront 3-bedroom home with banana and breadfruit trees in your own front yard. This small company has an excellent reputation for quality and service. Write Box 318, Hana, HI 96713, tel. 248-7727.

Others

You might try **Purdy's Cottages,** a one-time ranch with a few cottages for rent, starting at $36, tel. 248-8391.

FOOD AND SHOPPING

As far as dining out goes, there's little to choose from in Hana. The **Hotel Hana Maui** offers breakfast, lunch, and dinner buffets. Prices vary according to your choice of options, but expect to spend $5 for breakfast, $10 for lunch, and $31 for dinner. There's also a self-serve coffee shop. **Tu Tu's Snack Shop** is at the community center building at Hana Bay; window service with tables available. Full breakfast, $4, plate lunches, and *saimin.* This building was donated by Mrs. Fagan to the community.

Hasegawa's General Store

Along the Hana Road heading south out of town. Open weekdays 7:30 a.m. to 6:00 p.m.,

Sun. 9:00 a.m. to 3:30 p.m., tel. 248-8231. In the ranks of "general stores," Hasegawa's would be commander-in-chief. It's been in the family for 75 years and is currently run by Harry Hasegawa. While your tank is being filled, you can buy anything from a cane knife to a computer disk. There are rows of food items, dry goods, and a hardware and parts store out back. There's cold beer, film, blue jeans, and picnic supplies, and somehow it all crams in there. Everybody goes to Hasegawa's, and it's a treat just to browse and people-watch.

Waiku Originals
Along the Hana Road on the right about one mile before entering town. Everything in the shop is handmade in Hana. Prints, cards, wall hangings, and original T-shirts. Owned and operated by Bill and Anita. Not heavily stocked, but some good choices.

Hana Store
Take the Hana Road into town. Make the first right past St. Mary's Church and go up to the top of the hill. Open Mon. to Sat. 7:30 a.m. to 6:30 p.m., Sun. 8:00 a.m. to 6:30 p.m., tel. 248-8261. It's a general store with the emphasis on foodstuffs. Not as well stocked as Hasegawa's, they do carry a better supply of imported beers, and food items geared toward vegetarians.

SERVICES AND INFORMATION

Hana Medical Center
Along the Hana Road, clearly marked on the right just as you enter town, tel. 248-8294. Open weekdays 8:00 a.m. to 5:00 p.m. No doctors on Thurs. or Sunday.

Police Station
At the Y between Hana and Uakea roads, just as you enter town. Emergency dial 911.

Services
Bank of Hawaii, tel. 248-8015, open Mon. to Thurs. 3:00 to 4:30 p.m., Fri. 3:00 to 6:00 p.m.; The **P.O.** is open weekdays 8:00 a.m. to 4:30 p.m. Both are next door to Hana Store (see above). **Library** is at Hana School open Mon. to Fri. 8:00 a.m. to 5:00 p.m.

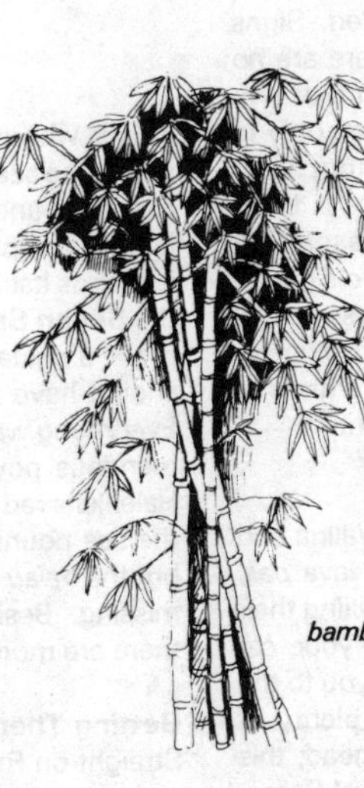

bamboo

BEYOND HANA

Now you're getting into adventure. The first sign is that the road gets steadily worse after Hana. It begins to narrow, then the twists and turns begin again, and it's pot-holed. Signs warn, "Caution: Pig Crossing." There are no phones, no gas, and only a fruit stand or two with one store that can be counted on only to be closed. The faint-hearted should turn back, but those with gumption are in for a treat. There're roadside waterfalls, cascading streams filling a series of pools, a hero's grave, and some forgotten towns. If you persevere all the way, you pop out at the Tedeschi Winery, where you can reward yourself with a glass of bubbly before returning to civilization.

Wailua Falls

About 7 miles after leaving Hana, Wailua and Kanahualui Falls tumble over steep lava *pali,* filling the air with a watery mist and filling their pools below. They're just outside your car door, and a 5-minute effort will take you to the mossy grotto at the base. There's plenty of room to park. If not for Oheo up ahead, this would be a great picnic spot, but wait! Sometimes roadside artists park here. In a few minutes you pass a little shrine cut into the mountain. This is the **Virgin By The Roadside.** It's usually draped with fresh *lei.*

OHEO GULCH

This is where the enormous **Kipahulu Valley** meets the sea. Palikea Stream starts way up on Haleakala and steps its way through the valley, leaving footprints of waterfalls and pools until it spends itself in the sea. The area was named the **Seven Sacred Pools** by white men. They made a mistake, but an honest one. The area should have been held sacred, but it wasn't. Everything was right here. You can feel the tremendous power of nature: bubbling waters, Haleakala red and regal in the background, and the sea pounding away. Hawaiians lived here but the *heiau* that you would surely expect are missing. Besides that there aren't 7 pools, there are more like 24!

Getting There

Straight on Rt. 31 10 miles out of Hana, you'll come to a large cement arch bridge (excellent view) and then a sign that says "Camping." Park here in the large grassy lot where you'll also find clean, well-built out houses for your convenience.

Warnings And Tips

Before doing any exploring, try to talk to one of the rangers, Eddie Pu and Perry Bednorse, generally found around the parking area. They know a tremendous amount of natural history concerning the area and can inform you about the few dangers in the area, such as the flash flooding that occurs in the pools. Ranger Pu has received a "Presidential Citation" for risking his life on 5 occasions to pluck drowning people from the quickly rising streams. For those intending to hike or camp, bring your own water; as yet no potable water is available. Don't be put off by the parking area, which looks like a used-car lot for Japanese imports. Ninety-nine percent are gone by sundown. The vast majority of the people go to the easily accessible "lower pools." The best is a stiff hike up the mountain to the "upper pools," a bamboo forest and a fantastic waterfall.

The Lower Pools

Head along the clearly marked path from the parking area to the flat, grass-covered peninsula. The winds are heavy here as they enter the mouth of the valley from the sea. A series of pools to choose from are off to your left. It's amazing to lie in the last one and look out to the sea crunching the shore just a few yards away. Move upstream for the best swimming in the largest of the lower pools. Be careful, because you'll have to do some fairly difficult rock climbing. The best route is along the righthand side as you face up the valley. Once you're satiated, head back up to the road along the path on the left-hand side. This will take you up to the bridge that you crossed when arriving, one of the best vantage points to look up and down this amazing valley.

The Upper Pools

Very few people head for the upper pools. However, those who do will be delighted. The trail is called **Waimoku Falls Trail**. Cross the road at the parking lot and go through the gate into a pasture, remembering to close it after you. A sign will tell you that Makahiku Falls is a half-mile uphill and Waimoku Falls are 2 miles distant. The toughest part is at the beginning as you huff-puff your way straight uphill. The trail leads to a fenced overlook from where you can see clearly the lace-like Makahiku Falls. Behing you, a few paces and to the left, will be a water-worn, trench-like path. Follow it to the very lip of the falls and a gorgeous little pool. You can swim safely to the very edge of the falls. The current is gentle here, and if you stay to the right you can peer over the edge and remain safe behind encircling boulders. Be extremely conscious of the water rising, and get out immediately if it does!

After refreshing yourself, continue your hike as the path heads through a grassy area. Oddly enough you come to an actual turnstile. Here you'll cross the creek where there's a wading pool, and then zig-zag up the opposite bank. After some enormous mango trees, you start going through a high jungle area. Suddenly you're in an extremely dense bamboo forest. The trail is well cut as you pass through the green darkness of this stand. If the wind is

Officer Eddie Pu

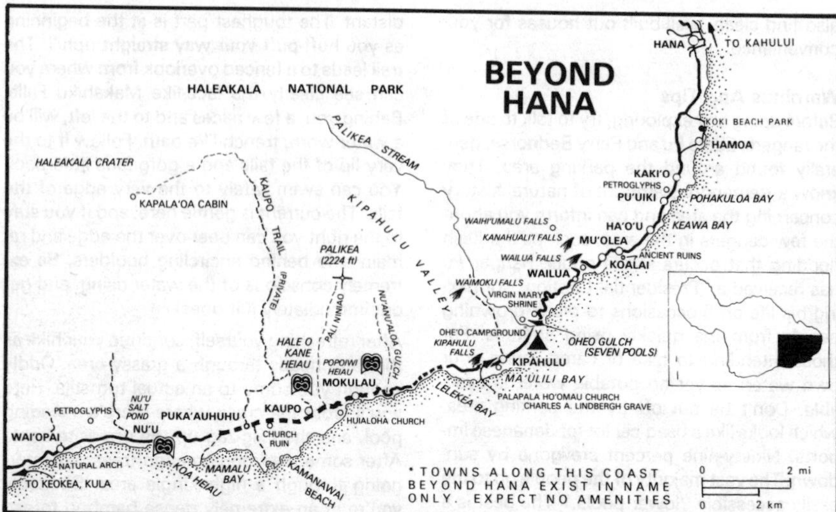

blowing, the bamboo will sing a mournful song for you. Emerge into more mangoes and thimbleberries and there's the creek again. Turn left and follow the creek, without crossing yet, and the trail gets distinct again. There's a wooden walkway, and then, eureka!...Waimoku Falls. It cascades over the *pali,* and is so high that you have to strain your neck back as far as it will go. It's more than a falls, it's silver filigree. You can stand in the shallow pool below surrounded by a sheer rock amphitheater. The sunlight dances in this area and tiny rainbows appear and disappear. There is a ranger-led hike to the falls on Saturdays. Horseback rides are also available from the nearby Oheo Riding Stables, tel. 248-7722.

Camping

This is part of Haleakala National Park. It's free to camp for a 3-day limit (no one counts too closely) and no permit is necessary. The campgrounds are primitive and always empty. From the parking lot follow the sign that says "Food Tent" and proceed straight ahead on the dirt track. Bear right to a large grassy area overlooking the sea, where signs warn not to disturb an archaeological area. Notice how spongy the grass seems to be here. You'll see a very strange palm tree that bends and twists up and down from the ground like a serpent. Move to the trees just behind it to escape the wind.

BEYOND OHEO

Route 31 beyond Oheo is genuinely rugged and makes the car companies cry. It can be done, however, with even the tourist vans making it part of their regular route. In 1½ miles you come to **Palapala Hoomau Church** (St. Paul's) and its tiny cemetery where Charles Lindbergh is buried. People, especially those who are old enough to remember the "Lone Eagle's" historical flight, are drawn here like pilgrims. The public is not really encouraged to visit, but the human tide cannot be stopped. If you go, please follow all of the directions posted. Up ahead a sign will read "Samuel F. Pryor, Kipahulu Ranch." Mr. Pryor was a vice-president of Pan Am and a close chum of Lindbergh. It was he who encouraged Lindbergh to spend his last years in Hana. Sam Pryor raises gibbons and lives quietly with his wife. Kipahulu Ranch has seen other amazing men. Last century a Japanese *samurai* named Sentaro Ishii lived here. He was enormous, especially for a Japanese of that day, over 6 feet tall. He came in search of work, and at the age of 61 married Kehele, a local girl. He lived in Kipahulu until he died at the age of 102.

Past Sam Pryor's place is B.B. Smith's fruit stand (which isn't always open) and another follows shortly. The road really begins to get rugged. The vistas open up at the beginning of the Kaupo Gap just when you pass **Huialoha Church**, built in 1859. Then the village of **Kaupo** and the Kaupo Store. The sign reads "This store is usually open Mon. to Fri., around 7:30 to 4:30. Don't be surprised if it's not open yet. It soon will be unless otherwise posted. Closed Saturday and Sunday and when necessary." Only a few families live in Kaupo, old ones and new ones trying to live independently.

Kaupo Store

The last of a chain of stores that stretched all the way from Keanae and were owned by the Soon Family. Nick Soon was kind of a modern-day wizard. He lived in Kaupo, and among his exploits he assembled a car and truck brought piecemeal on a barge, built the first electric generator in the area, and even made a model airplane from scratch that flew. He was the son of an indentured Chinese laborer. After Kaupo you'll be in the heart of the Kaupo Gap. Enjoy it because in a few minutes the pavement will pick up again and you'll be back in the civilized world.

the Kaupo Gap

KAHOOLAWE

The island of Kahoolawe is clearly visible from many points along Maui's south shore, especially when it's lit up like a firecracker during heavy bombardment by the U.S. Navy. Kahoolawe is a target island, uninhabited except for a band of wild goats that refuse to be killed off. Kahoolawe was a sacred island born to Wakea and Papa, the 2 great mythical progenitors of Hawaii. The birth went bad and almost killed Papa, and it hasn't been any easier for her ill-omened child ever since. Kahoolawe became synonymous with Kanaloa, the man-god. Kanaloa was especially revered by the *kahuna ana ana,* the "black sorcerers" of old Hawaii. Kanaloa, much like Lucifer, was driven from heaven by Kane, the god of light. Kanaloa held dominion over all poisonous things and ruled in the land of the dead from his power spot here on Kahoolawe. There are scores of archaeological sites and remnants of *heiau* all over the bomb-cratered face of Kahoolawe. A long, bitter feud has raged between the U.S. Navy that wishes to keep the island as a bombing range, and Protect Kahoolawe Ohana, a Hawaiian native-rights organization that wants the sacred island returned to the people.

The Land
Kahoolawe is 11 miles long and 6 miles wide, with 29 miles of coastline. The tallest hill is **Lua Makika** in the northeast section at 1,477 feet. There are no natural lakes or ponds on the island, but it does get some rain and there is a stream running through Ahupu Gulch.

MODERN HISTORY

It's perfectly clear that small families of Hawaiians have lived on Kahoolawe for countless generations and that religious rites were carried out by many visiting *kahuna* over the centuries, but mostly Kahoolawe was left alone. In 1917 Angus MacPhee, a cattleman, leased Kahoolawe from the Territorial Government for $200 per year. The lease would run until 1954 with a renewal option, if by 1921 MacPhee could show reasonable progress in taming the island. Harry Baldwin bought into the **Kahoolawe Ranch** in 1922, and with his money and MacPhee's know-how, Kahoolawe turned a neat profit. The island then supported indigenous vegetation such as *ohia,* mountain apple, and even Hawaiian cotton and tobacco. MacPhee planted eucalyptus and range grass from Australia, which caught on well and stopped much of the erosion. Gardens were planted around the homestead and the soil proved to be clean and fertile. Within a few years Kahoolawe Ranch cattle were being shipped regularly to markets on Maui.

The Navy Arrives

In 1939, with the threat of war on the horizon, MacPhee and Baldwin, stimulated by patriotism, offered a small tip of Kahoolawe's southern shore to the U.S. Army as an artillery range. One day after the attack on Pearl Harbor, the U.S. Navy seized all of Kahoolawe to further "the war effort" and evicted MacPhee, immediately disenfranchising the Kahoolawe Ranch. Kahoolawe has since become the most bombarded piece of real estate on the face of the Earth. During WW II the Navy praised Kahoolawe as being *the* most important factor in winning the Pacific War, and it has held Kahoolawe to the present day.

The Book On Kahoolawe

Inez MacPhee Ashdown lived on the island with her father and was a driving force in establishing the homestead. She has written a book, *Recollections of Kahoolawe,* available

The "Save Kahoolawe Ohana" resolutely builds a long house, pitting prayers and chants against naval artillery.

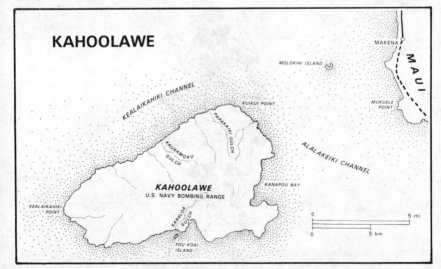

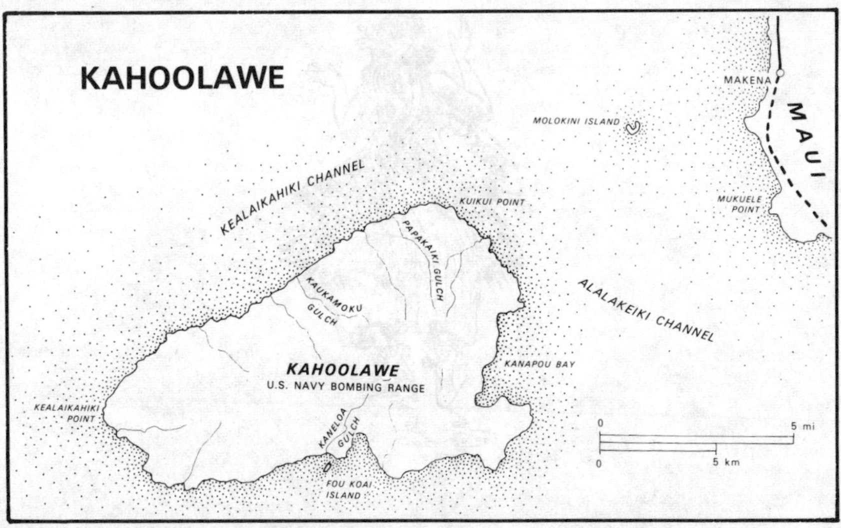

from Topgallant Publishing Co., Honolulu. This book chronicles the events from 1917 until the military takeover, and is rife with myths, legends, and historical facts about Kahoolawe. Mrs. Ashdown is in her late eighties, going blind and in failing health but her mind remains brilliant. She resides on Maui.

The Problem

Hawaii has the dubious distinction of being the most militarized state in the Union. All 5 services are represented, and it's the headquarters of CINCPAC (Commander in Chief, Pacific) which controls 70% of the Earth's surface, from California to Africa's east coast, and to both poles. Kahoolawe is the epitome of this military dominance with every inch of its 73 square miles owned by the federal government. The Protect Kahoolawe Ohana is opposed to this dominance and wants the Navy to return the island to native Hawaiian control. The Navy says that Kahoolawe is still very important to national security and that it is a barren and lifeless island, anyway.

The *Ohana*

The Protect Kahoolawe Ohana is an extended group, favoring traditional values based on *aloha aina* (love of the land) which is the primary binding force for all Hawaiians. They want the bombing and desecration of Kahoolawe to stop. They maintain that the island should return to Hawaiian Lands inventory with the *kahu* (stewardship) in the hands of native Hawaiians. The point driven home by the Ohana is that the military has totally ignored and belittled native Hawaiian values, which are now beginning to be asserted. They maintain that Kahoolawe is not a barren wasteland, but a vibrant part of their history and religion. Indeed, Kahoolawe was placed on the National Register of Historic Sites, but instead of being preserved, which is normal for this prestigious distinction, it is the only historic site that is actively destroyed. The Ohana has gained legal access to the island for 10 days per month, for 10 months of the year. They have built a *halau* (long house) and use the time on Kahoolawe to dedicate themselves to religious, cultural, and social pursuits. The Ohana look to Kahoolawe as their *pu'uhonua* (refuge), where they gain strength and knowledge from each other and the *aina.* The question is basic: is Kahoolawe's future that of target island or sacred island?

LANAI

INTRODUCTION

Lanai, in the long dark past of Hawaiian legend-history, was a sad and desolate place inhabited by man-eating spirits and fiendish bloodcurdling ghouls. It was redeemed by spoiled but tough Prince Kaululaau, exiled there by his kingly father, Kakaalaneo of Maui. Kaululaau proved to be not only brave, but wily too, and he cleared Lanai of its spirits through trickery, and opened the way for human habitation. Lanai was, for many generations, a burial ground for the *ali'i* and therefore filled with sacred *mana* and *kapu* to commoners. Later, reports of its inhospitable shores filled the logs of old sailing vessels. In foul weather, captains navigated desperately to avoid its infamously treacherous waters, whose melancholy white-caps still outline "Shipwreck Beach" and give credence to its name.

Lanai Today

The vast majority of people visiting the Hawaiian Islands view Lanai from Lahaina on West Maui, but never actually set foot upon this lovely quiet island. For two centuries, first hunters, and then lovers of the humpback whale, have come to peer across the waters of the Auau Channel, better known as the "Lahaina Roads," in search of these magnificent giants. Lanai in Hawaiian means "Hump," and it's as if nature built its own island-shrine to the whale in the exact spot where they are most plentiful. Lanai is a victim of its own reputation. Nicknamed the "Pineapple Island," most visitors are informed by even long-time residents that Lanai is a dull place covered in one large pineapple plantation. It's true that Lanai has the largest pineapple plantation in the world, 16,000 cultivated acres, which account for about 90% of U.S. production. But the island has 74,000 acres that remain untouched and perfect for exceptional outdoor experiences. Besides, the pineapple fields are themselves interesting endless rows of the porcupine plants, sliced and organized by a labyrinth of roads, contoured and planted by improbable looking machines, and tended by mostly Filipino workers in wide-brimmed hats and goggles.

Around And About

The people of Lanai live in one of the most fortuitously chosen spots for a working village in the world: Lanai City. All but about 2 dozen of the island's 2,600 permanent residents make their home here. Nestled near the ridge of mountains in the northeast corner of the Palawai Basin, Lanai City is sheltered, cooled, and characterized by a mature and extensive grove of Norfolk pines planted in the early 1900s by the practical New Zealand naturalist, George Munro. This evergreen canopy creates a parklike atmosphere about town, while reaching tall green fingers to the clouds. A mountainous spine tickles drizzle from the water-bloated bellies of passing clouds for the thirsty, red, sunburned plains of Lanai below. The trees, like the bristled hair of an annoyed cat, line the **Munro Trail** as it climbs Lanaihale, highest spot on the island (3,370 feet). The Munro Trail's magnificent panoramas encompass sweeping views of no less than 5 of the 8 major islands as it snakes along the mountain ridge, narrowing at times to less than 30 yards across. Here are limitless paths for trekking and four-wheel driving. Maunalei Gulch, a vast precipitous valley, visible from "The Trail," was the site of a last-ditch effort of Lanai warriors to repel an invasion by the warrior king of the Big Island at the turn of the 18th century. Now its craggy arms provide refuge to mouflon sheep as they execute death-defying leaps from one rocky ripple to the next. On the valley floors roam axis deer, and on the northwest grasslands are the remnants of an experimental herd of pronghorn antelope brought from Montana in 1959. After saturating yourself with glories of Lanai from the heights, descend and follow a well-paved road from Lanai City to the southern tip of the island. Here, **Manele** and

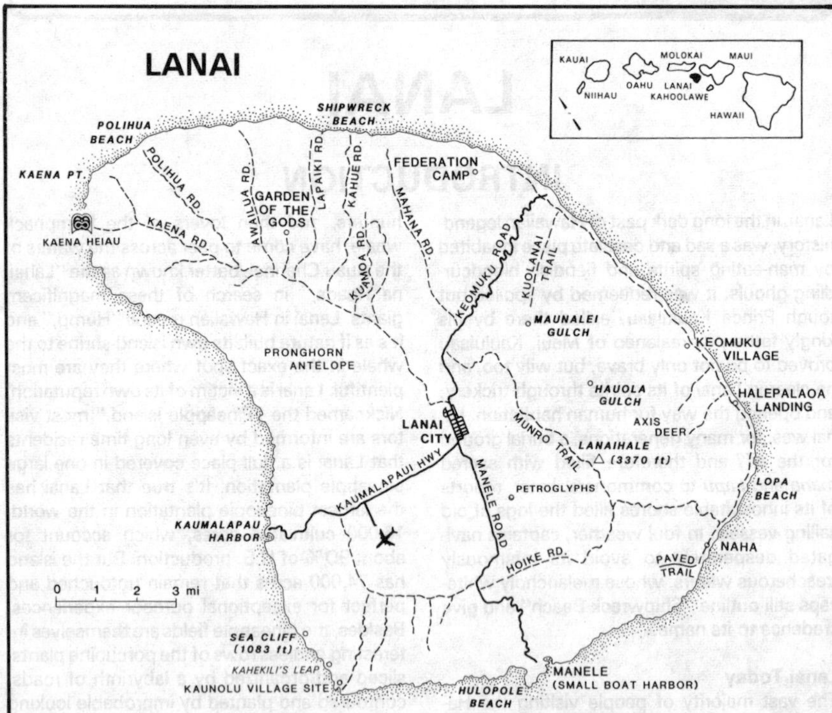

Lanaihale bristling with Norfolk pines

Hulopoe bays sit side by side. Manele is a favorite spot of small sailing craft that have braved the channel from Lahaina. Manele, a virtually untouched Underwater Marine Park, is regarded as one of the premier snorkeling spots in the entire island chain. Hulopoe Bay, just next door, is as salubrious a spot as you can hope to find. It offers camping and all that's expected of a warm, sandy, palm-lined beach.

Adventure

You can hike or 4WD to Kaunolu Bay, one of the best-preserved ancient Hawaiian village sites. Kamehameha the Great came to this ruggedly masculine shore to fish and frolic his summers away with his favorite cronies. Here, a retainer named Kahekili leaped from a sea cliff to the ice-blue waters below, and challenged all other warriors to prove their loyalty to Kamehameha by following his example and hurling themselves off what today is known as **Kahekili's Leap.**

You can quickly span a century by heading for the southeast corner of Lanai and its 3 abandoned villages of Lopa, Naha, and Keomuku. Here legends abound. *Kahuna* curses still guard a grove of coconut trees which are purported to refuse to let you down if you climb for their nuts without offering the proper prayers. Here are also the remnants of a sugar train believed to have caused its cane enterprise to fail because the rocks of a nearby *heiau* were disturbed and used in its track bed. An enchanting abandoned Hawaiian church in Keomuku insists on being photographed.

You can head north along the east shore to **Shipwreck Beach,** where the rusting hulk of a liberty ship, along with timbers and planks from the great wooden square-riggers of days gone by, lie along the beach, attesting to the authenticity of its name. Shipwreck Beach is a shore stroller's paradise, a real beachcomber's boutique. Also along here are some thought-provoking petroglyphs. Other petroglyphs are found on a hillside overlooking the "pine" fields of the Palawai Basin.

If you hunger for a totally private beach, head north for the Polihua Trail. En route, just to keep you from being bored, you'll pass through a fantastic area of ancient cataclysm aptly called The **Garden of The Gods.** This raw baked area of monolithic rocks and tortured earth turns incredible shades of purple, red, magenta, and yellow as the sun plays upon it from different angles. You have a junction of trails here. You can bear left to lonely **Kaena Iki Point** where you'll find Lanai's largest *heiau,* a brooding setting full of weird power vibrations. If you're hot and dusty and aching for a dip, continue due north to trail's end where the desolation of the Garden suddenly gives way to the gleaming brightness of virtually unvisited Polihua Beach.

After these daily excursions, return to the

green serenity of Lanai City and the relaxing **Lanai Lodge,** the only hotel in town. Even if you're only spending a few days, you'll be made to feel like you're staying with old friends. You won't have to worry about bringing your dancing shoes to Lanai, but if you've had enough hustle and bustle and yearn to stroll in quietude, sit by a crackling fire, and look up at a crystal-clear sky, head for Lanai. Your jangled nerves and ruffled spirit will be glad you did.

THE LAND

The sunburned face of Lanai seems parched but relaxed as it rises in a gentle, steady arc from sea level. When viewed from the air it looks like an irregularly shaped kidney bean. The 6th largest of the 8 main islands, Lanai is roughly 140 square miles, measuring 18 miles north to south and 13 miles east to west at its longest points. A classic single-shield volcano, at one time Lanai was probably connected to Maui and Molokai as a single huge island. Marine fossils found at the 1,000-foot mark and even higher in the mountains indicate its slow rise from the sea. Its rounded features appear more benign than the violent creases of its closest island neighbors; this characteristic earned it the unflattering Hawaiian translation of "Hump." More lyrical scholars, however, have refuted this translation, and claim the real meaning has been lost to the ages, but Lanai does looks like a hump when viewed from a distance at sea. It's topography is simple. A ridge of rugged mountains runs north to south along the eastern half of the island and their entire length is traversed by the Munro Trail. The highest peak is Lanaihale (3,370 feet). This area is creased by precipitous gulches: the two deepest are Mauanalei and Hauola at more than 2,000 feet. The topography tapers off steadily as it reaches the sea to the east. A variety of beaches stretch from the white sands of Polihua in the north, along the salt-and-pepper sands of Naha on the east, and end with the beautiful rainbow arches of Manele and Hulopoe in the south. Palawai, Lanai's central basin, is completely cultivated in manicured, whorling fields of pineapple. Early this century, Palawai was covered in cactus. The west coast has phenomenal sea cliffs accessible only by boat. Some of the most majestic are the Kaholo Pali which run south from Kaumalapu Harbor, reaching their most amazing ruggedness at Kaunolu Bay. At many spots along this area the sea lies more than 1,500 feet below. Starting at Lanai City in the center, a half hour of driving in any direction presents a choice of this varied and fascinating geography.

Climate

The daily temperatures are quite balmy, especially at sea level, but it can get blisteringly hot in the basins and on the leeward side, so be sure to carry plenty of water when hiking or 4WDing. Lanai City gets refreshingly cool in the evenings and early mornings, but a light jacket or sweater is plenty, although thin-blooded residents bundle up.

Water

Lying in the rain shadow of the West Maui Mountains, even its windward side receives only 40 inches of rainfall a year. The central basins and leeward shores taper off to a scant 12 inches, not bad for pineapples and sun wor-

AVERAGE MAXIMUM/MINIMUM TEMPERATURE AND RAINFALL

Island	Town		Jan.	Mar.	May	June	Sept.	Nov.
Lanai	Lanai City	high	70	71	75	80	80	72
		low	60	60	62	65	65	62
		rain	3	3	2	0	2	4

N.B. Rainfall in inches; temperature in F°

shippers. Lanai has always been short of water. Its scruffy vegetation and red-baked earth are responsible for its inhospitable reputation. There are no real rivers; the few year-round streams are found only in the gulches of the windward mountains. Most ventures at colonizing Lanai, both in ancient and modern times, were kept to a minimum because of this water shortage. The famous Norfolk pines of Lanai City, along with other introduced greenery, greatly helped the barrenness of the landscape and provided a watershed. The rust-red earth remains unchanged, and if you get it onto your clothes, it'll remain there as a permanent souvenir.

FLORA AND FAUNA

Most of Lanai's flora and fauna have been introduced. In fact, the Norfolk pine and the regal mouflon sheep were a man-made attempt to improve the natural, often barren habitat. These species have adapted so well that they now symbolize Lanai, along with, of course, the ubiquitous pineapple. Besides the mouflon, Lanai boasts pronghorn antelope, axis deer, and a few feral goats. A wide variety of introduced game birds include the Rio Grande turkey, ring-necked pheasant, and an assortment of quail, francolins, and doves. Like the other Hawaiian Islands, Lanai, unfortunately, is home to native birds that are headed for extinction. Along the Munro Trail and on the windward coast you pass through forests made up of Norfolk and Cook Island pines, tall eucalyptus stands, shaggy ironwoods, native *koa,* and silver oaks. Everywhere, dazzling colors and fragrances are provided by Lanai's flowers.

Flowers

Although Lanai's official flower is the *kaunaoa,* it's not really a flower, but an airplant that grows wild. It's easily found along the beach at Keomuku. It grows in conjunction with *pohuehue,* a pinkish-red, perennial seashore morning glory. Native to Hawaii, the *pohuehue* grows in large numbers along Lanai's seashore. It's easy to spot, and when you see a yellow-orange vinelike airplant growing with it, you've found Lanai's *kaunaoa,* which is traditionally fashioned into *lei.* The medicinal *ilima,* used to

Norfolk pine

help asthma sufferers, is found in large numbers in Lanai's open fields. Its flat, open, yellow flower is about one inch in diameter and grows on a waist-high shrub. Two other flowers considered by some to be pests are the purple *koali* morning glory, and the miniature red and yellow flowering lantana known for its unpleasant odor. Both are abundant on the trail to the Garden of the Gods.

Norfolk Pine

These pines were discovered by Capt. Cook and named after Norfolk Island on which they were found in the South Pacific. Imported in great numbers by George Munro, they adapted well to Lanai and helped considerably to attract moisture and provide a firm watershed. Exquisitely ornamental, they can also be grown in containers. Their perfect cone shape makes them a natural Christmas tree, used as such in Hawaii; some are even shipped to the Mainland for this purpose.

Endemic Birds

The list of native birds still found on Lanai gets smaller every year, and those still on the list are rarely seen. The *amakahi* is about 5 inches long with yellowish-green plumage. The males deliver a high-sounding tweet and a trilling call. Vegetarians, these birds live mostly on grasses and lichens, building their nests in the uppermost branches of tall trees. Some people believe that the *amakahi* is already extinct on Lanai. The *uau* or Hawaiian petrel is a large bird with a 36-inch wingspan. Its head and back are shades of black with a white underbelly. This "fisherbird" lives on squid and crustaceans that it regurgitates to its chicks. Unfortunately, the Hawaiian petrel nests on the ground, sometimes laying its eggs under rocks or in burrows, which makes it an easy prey for predators. Its call is reported to sound like a small yapping dog. The *apapane* is abundant on the other main islands, but dwindling rapidly on Lanai. It's a chubby red-bodied fellow about 5 inches long with a black bill, legs, wingtips, and tail feathers. It's quick, flitty, and has a wide variety of calls and songs from beautiful warbles to mechanical buzzes. Its feathers were sought after by Hawaiians to produce distinctive ornate featherwork.

Axis Deer

This shy and beautiful creature came to Lanai via Molokai where the first specimens arrived in 1868 as a gift from the Hawaiian consul in Hong Kong. Its native home is the parkland forests of India and Sri Lanka. The coats of most axis deer are golden tan with rows of round lifetime spots, along with a black stripe down the back and a white belly. They stand 3-4 feet at the shoulder, with bucks weighing an average 160 pounds and does about 110. The bucks have an exquisite set of symmetrical antlers that always form a perfect 3 points. The antlers can stand 30 inches high and more than 20 inches across, making them coveted trophies. Does are antlerless and give birth to one fawn, usually from Nov. to Feb., but Hawaii's congenial weather makes for good fawn survival anytime of year. Axis deer on Lanai can be spotted anywhere from the lowland *kiawe* forest to the higher rainforests along the Munro Trail. Careful and proper hunting management should keep the population stable for many generations. The meat from axis deer is reported to have a unique flavor, different from Mainland venison—one of the finest tasting of all wild game.

pronghorn antelope

Mouflon Sheep

Another name for these wild mountain sheep is Mediterranean or European bighorn. One of only 6 species of wild sheep in the world, mouflon are native to the islands of Sardinia and Corsica whose climates are quite similar to Hawaii's. They have been introduced throughout Europe, Africa, and North America. Although genetically similar to domestic sheep, they are much more shy, lack a woolly coat, and only infrequently give birth to twins. Both rams and ewes are a similar tannish brown, with a snow-white rump which is all that most people get to see as these always-alert creatures quickly and expertly head for cover. Rams weigh about 125 pounds (ewes a bit less) and produce a spectacular set of recurved horns. They need little water to survive, going for long periods only on the moisture in green plants. On Lanai they are found along the northwest coast in the grasslands and in the dry *kiawe* forest.

Pronghorn Antelope

Not a true antelope, this animal is a native to the western states of North America. Both males and females produce short black antlers that curve inward at the tip. Males average 125 pounds (females about 90). Pronghorns are a reddish tan with two distinct white bands across the neck and a black patch under the ear. They can also flare the hair on their rump to produce a white flag when alarmed. In 1959, 38 pronghorn were brought to Lanai in an attempt to introduce another big game animal. Lanai's upper grasslands seemed perfectly suited to the pronghorn, closely resembling the animal's natural habitat in Montana, and hopes ran high for survival. At first the herd increased, but then the numbers began to slowly and irreversibly dwindle. Experts felt that the animals were confused by the nearby salt water and those that drank it quickly died. Also, the new grasses of Lanai caused digestion problems. Poaching added even more problems to the troubled pronghorns. It's tough to spot the few individuals that remain, but with good field glasses and perseverance you might catch some browsing on *haole koa* in the north-central grasslands of Lanai. The fact that even a few pronghorn remain decades after introduction gives some hope that these noble animals can still make a permanent home for themselves in Hawaii.

HISTORY

Kakaalaneo peered across the mist-shrouded channel between West Maui and Lanai, and couldn't believe his eyes. Night after night, the campfire of his son Kaululaau burned, sending its faint but miraculous signal. The boy was still alive! Kaululaau had been given every advantage of his noble birth. But still the prince had proved to be unmanageable. King Kakaalaneo had even ordered all children born on the same day as his son to be sent to Lahaina where they would grow up as his son's friends and playmates. Spoiled rotten, young Kaululaau had terrorized Lahaina with his pranks and one day went too far: he destroyed a new planting of breadfruit. Even the chief's son could not trample the social order and endanger the livelihood of the people. So finally the old *kahuna* had to step in. Their justice was hard and swift. Kaululaau must be banished to the terrible island of Lanai, where the man-eating spirits dwelled. There he would meet his fate, and no one expected him to live. But weeks had passed and Kalulaau's nightly fires burned. Could it be some ghoulish trick? Kakaalaneo sent a canoe to investigate. It returned with incredible news. The boy was fine! All the spirits were banished! Kaululaau had cleansed the island of its evil fiends and opened it up for the people to come and settle.

Oral History

In fact, it's recorded in the Hawaiian oral genealogical tradition that a young Kaululaau did open Lanai to significant numbers of inhabitants in approximately A.D. 1400. Lanai passed through the next few hundred years as a satellite of Maui, accepting the larger island's social, religious, and political dictates. During this period, Lanai supported about 3,000 people who lived by growing taro and fishing. Most inhabited the eastern shore facing Maui, but old homesites show that the population became established well enough to homestead the entire island. Lanai was caught up in the Hawaiian wars that raged in the last two decades of the 1700s, and was ravaged and pillaged in 1778 by the warriors of Kalaniopuu, aging king of the Big Island. These hard times marked a decline in Lanai's population; accounts by Western sea captains who passed even a few years later noted that the island looked desolate, with no large villages evident. Lanai began to recover and saw a small boost in population when Kamehameha the Great established his summer residence at Kaunolu on the southern shore. This kept Lanai vibrant for a few years at the turn of the 19th century, but it began to fade soon thereafter. The decline continued until only a handful of Hawaiians remained by the 20th century. The old order ended completely when one of the last traditional *kanaka,* named Ohua, hid the traditional fish god, Hunihi, and died shortly thereafter in his grass hut in the year 1900.

Early Foreign Influences

No one knows his name, but all historians agree that a Chinaman tried his luck at raising sugarcane on Lanai in 1802. He brought boiling pots and rollers to Naha on the east coast, but after a few years of hard luck gave up and moved on. About 100 years later a large commercial sugar enterprise was attempted in the same area. This time the sugar company even built a narrow-gauge railroad to carry the cane. A story goes that after disrupting a local *heiau* to make ballast for the rail line, the water in the area, never in great abundance to begin with, went brackish. Again sugar was foiled.

In 1854 a small band of Mormon elders tried to colonize Lanai by starting a "City of Joseph" at Palawai Basin. This began the career of one of Hawaii's strangest, most unfathomable, yet charismatic early leaders. Walter Murray Gibson came to Palawai to start an idyllic settlement for the Latter-Day Saints. He energetically set to work improving the land with funds from Utah and hard work of the other Mormon settlers. The only fly in Gibson's grand ointment occurred when the Mormon Church discovered that the acres of Palawai were not registered to the church at all but to Walter Murray Gibson himself! He was excommunicated and the bilked settlers relocated. Gibson went on to have one of the strangest political careers in Hawaiian history, including championing native rights, and having unbelievable influence at the royal Hawaiian court. His land at Palawai passed on to his daughter who became possessed by the one evil spirit Kaululaau failed to eradicate; she tried to raise sugarcane, but was fated, like the rest, to fail.

A few attempts at cattle raising proved uneconomical, and Lanai languished. The last big attempt at cattle raising produced The Ranch, part of whose lands make up the Cavendish Golf Course in Lanai City. This enterprise did have one bright note. A New Zealander named George Munro was hired as the manager. He imported all manner of seeds and cuttings in his attempt to foliate the island and create a watershed. The Ranch failed, but Munro's legacy of Norfolk pines stands as a proud testament to this amateur horticulturalist.

The Coming Of Pineapples

The purchase of Lanai in 1922 was one of the niftiest real estate deals in modern history. James D. Dole, the most enterprising of the pineapple pioneers, bought the island—lock, stock, and barrel—from the Baldwins, an old missionary family, for $1.1 million. That comes to only $12 per acre, though many of those acres were fairly scruffy not to mention Lanai's bad economical track record. Dole had come

This ungainly looking vehicle works the fields gently plucking pineapples.

from Boston at the turn of the century to figure out how to can pineapple profitably. Dole did such a remarkable job of marketing the "golden fruit" on the Mainland that in a few short years, Midwestern Americans who'd never even heard of pineapples before were buying cans of it regularly from the shelves of country grocery stores. In 1922, Jim Dole needed more land for his expanding pineapple fields, and the arid basin of Palawai seemed perfect. Lanai Plantation was an oligarchy during the early years with the plantation manager as king. One of the most famous of these characters was H. Broomfield Brown who ran Lanai Plantation in the '30s. He kept watch over the fields from his house through a telescope. If anyone loafed, he'd ride out into the fields to confront the offender. Mr. Brown personally "eyeballed" every new visitor to Lanai: all prostitutes, gamblers, and deadbeats were turned back at the pier. An anti-litter freak, he'd even reprimand anyone who trashed the streets of Lanai City. During the labor strikes of the 1960s, workers' grievances were voiced and Lanai began to function as a more normal enterprise. With pineapple well established on the world market, Lanai finally had a firm economic base. From a few thousand fruits in the early days, the flow today can reach a million fruits per day during the height of the season. They're shipped from man-made port at Kaumalaupau specially built to accommodate Lanai's "pines."

ECONOMY

Pineapples! Lanai's 16,000 acres of them make up the largest single pineapple plantation in the world, producing 90% of the U.S. yearly total. The entire island is owned by Castle and Cooke and operated by its subsidary, The Dole Co., whose name has become synonymous with pineapples. A handful of tiny hereditary plots are still held by Hawaiian families and oddly enough, nearly half the working families own their homes, purchased from Dole. In one way or another, everyone on Lanai owes his livelihood to pineapples, from the worker who twists his ankle in a "pine" field to the technician at the community hospital who X-rays it. Workers come and go all day long from equipment depots in Lanai City. Most field hands are Filipinos, some very recent arrivals to the U.S. Unskilled workers start at minimum wage. A union member who's worked for Dole for a few years can make a decent living. Japanese and *haoles* hold most of the foreman and middle management jobs, although Dole is an equal opportunity employer.

Competition And Technology

Today foreign production, especially in the Philippines, has greatly increased and gives the Hawaiian pineapple industry some competitive headaches—though Dole feels its claim to fame is secure. They're after a premium-pack pineapple, according to Jim Parker, the plantation manager, who states, "Nobody gets more money for their pineapple than Dole does, because nobody ever matches Dole for quality." Pineapple cultivation is as tough as any other business and all competitors are after the very best technology. Dole is a leader in technology, and though they've been cutting down on the number of acres under cultivation, they have at the same time increased yield through intensified methods such as irrigation, which they pioneered. Other methods have been receiving negative publicity lately. A recent furor involved a chemical called heptaclore used to kill ants on pineapples. All the pineapple producers use heptaclore, and though believed to be a carcinogen, it carries a federal label of approval. If guidelines are followed, it's considered safe, and according to testing, no heptaclore is found in the actual fruit itself. But in this case, pineapple stalks and leaves were chopped and sold to dairy farmers as feed. The milk produced had intolerable amounts of heptaclore. Health food stores on Oahu refused to sell milk outright and the dairies involved recalled their milk until it was once again considered safe. Dole was not the company involved, but all the producers felt the heat from consumers. Still, the port at Kaumalapau is very busy sending off the fruits of Lanai's labor. There is work on Lanai for any islander that wants it, and almost all do. The standard of living is working class: decent, hopeful, and proud.

THE PEOPLE

Lanai is characterized by the incredible mix of racial strains so common in Hawaii—Filipino, Japanese, Hawaiian, Chinese, and Caucasian. It is unique, however, in that 50-60% of its people are Filipino. The Filipinos, many recent immigrants, were solicited by Castle and Cooke to work as laborers on the pineapple plantation. Mostly 18- to 25-year-old men, the majority speaks Ilocano and may have come to join relatives already on Lanai. Most arrive on their own; they learn English and from Lanai they spread out. As workers they're perfect: industrious and quiet. At night you wonder where they all are. Due to the tremendous shortage of eligible women, most workers stay home or fish or have a beer in the back yard with buddies. And on Sundays, there is the illegal (officially non-existent) cock fight. For high living, everyone heads for Maui or Oahu. The next largest racial groups are Japanese (18%) and white (12%). The Japanese started as the field workers before the Filipinos, but now along with the whites are Lanai's professionals and middle management. The races coexist, but there are still unseen social strata. There's even a small Chinese population (one percent) who fulfill their traditional role as shopkeepers. A good 10% of Lanaians are Hawaiians. Finally, almost 10% fall into the "mixed" category, with many of these Filipino-Hawaiian.

Juan Torquesa cruising the city park

Community

Lanai has a strong sense of community and uniqueness that keeps the people close. For example, during a bitter, 3-month strike in 1964, the entire community rallied and all suffered equally: laborers, shopkeepers, and management. All who remember say that it brought out the best in the island tradition of *aloha.* If you really want to meet Lanaians, just sit in the park in the center of Lanai City for an hour or two. You'll notice a lot of old-timers, who seem to be very healthy. You could even strike up a conversation with some of the following men who are an excellent core sample of social and historical Lanai. There's Manuel Paval, a retired Dole supervisor, who knows a great deal about the construction of the commercial wharf and how they built things in the old days. Choyu Yara came to the islands as a young man. Despite little formal education he worked his way to Dole's top management, and is well versed in the agricultural history of the island. Juan Torquesa, a Filipino you might see driving by in his jeep full of nets and fish, was instrumental in building the off roads in Lanai. Mostly alone on his bulldozer, he blazed trails which he still uses himself as he tends his nets. Shiro Hokama was one of the founding organizers of the labor movement in Lanai; Molokai Oshiro worked his way up from laborer to businessman, and as a young athlete was a weightlifiting friend of Harold Sakata, another Lanai boy, who gained notoriety as "Odd Job," the hat-throwing human butcher block in the James Bond thriller, *Goldfinger.* There's Jim Parker, Dole's plantation manager, urbane, frank and a no-nonsense type who will make the time to talk to you and is acutely aware of Dole's social obligations on Lanai. Lastly, you might really be lucky and run into Lloyd Cockett, a living history book. His great grandfather, Joseph Keliihananui, was the last of the independent Hawaiian farmers of Palawai. Raised in Keomoku, Lloyd still knows the old ways. As a young horseman, he carried seedlings for Munro and helped him plant the famous Norfolk pines. Lloyd spent his life as a worker on Lanai, but he is a natural anthropologist. He was a main source of information while serving as a guide to Lanai's remote Hawaiian ruins for the Bishop Museum's famed Dr. Emory.

Lorrie, Reggie, and Howard, second and third generation of Lanai's plantation workers

Other Faces

It should strike you that the above list is made up only of men. That in itself is a social comment about Lanai. Where are the women? They're in the traditional roles at home, nurturing and trying to add the pleasantries of life. Some are field workers too. You might notice no famous crafts of Lanai and no artists working commercially. This is not to say there is no art on Lanai, but the visitor rarely sees it. One reason that Lanai produces so little commercial art is it's a workers' island with virtually no unemployment, so everyone is busy making a living. Old-timers are known to make superb fishing poles, nets, and even their own horseshoes. The island ladies are excellent seamstresses and with the rising interest in *hula,* make lovely *lei* from the beautiful *kunaoa,* Lanai's flower. If you turn your attention to the young people of Lanai, you'll see the statewide problem of babies having babies. Teenage pregnancy is rampant, and teenage parents are common. Young guys customize their 4WDs although there's no place to go, and Taka's Snack Shop is now exclusively given over to video games. If as a young person you wish to remain on Lanai, then in almost every case your future will be tied to Dole. If you have other aspirations, "it's goodbai to Lanai." These islanders are some of the most easygoing and relaxed people you'll encounter in Hawaii, but with the electronic age extending its long arms of communication, even here they're not nearly as "backwater" as you might think.

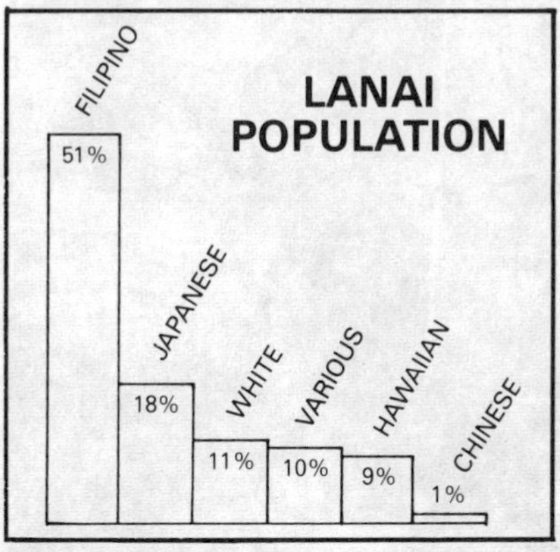

GETTING THERE

By Air

Hawaiian Air flies comfortable DC9s and turboprop Dash Transits to Lanai. They have one flight on Friday and Sunday from Kauai, Oahu, Molokai, Maui, and Hawaii, with another flight on Monday from Oahu only. Flights originating on the Big Island and Kauai are on DC9s; those from Honolulu, Molokai, and Maui are on Dash Transits. If you get the "jitters" on small aircraft and want the security and comfort of a larger plane, fly Hawaiian Air. Air Molokai operates 8-passenger Cessna 402s, and two vintage 30-passenger DC3s. Air Molokai offers 3 one-hour flights daily from Honolulu to Lanai via Molokai. They depart at 8:00 and 10:30 a.m. and 5:00 p.m. One flight daily leaves from Maui at 12:35 p.m. Air Molokai's prices are about 10% cheaper than Hawaiian Air (see p. 124, and p. 127).

Lanai Airport is a dusty little strip out in the pineapple fields about 4 miles southwest of Lanai City. The one-room terminal offers *no* shops, car rental booths, lockers, public transportation, or even access to a toilet, unless there's a scheduled flight. A bulletin board near the door has all the practical information and phone numbers you'll need.

By Boat
One other possibility for getting to Lanai is going by pleasure boat from Maui. Many Lanai and Maui residents travel by this route and even receive special *kamaaina* rates. These are basically tour boats specializing in snorkeling, dinner cruising, whale watching, and the like, but they're also willing to drop you off and pick you up at a later date. It's an enjoyable and actually inexpensive way of going. You'll have to make your own arrangements with the boat captains, mostly berthed at Lahaina Harbor. This alternative is particularly attractive to campers as they anchor on Lanai at Manele Bay, just a 5-minute walk from the campsites at Hulopoe. There are no fixed rates for this service, but *kamaainas* pay about $20. Expect to pay more but use this as a point of reference. Some companies to try are: Trilogy, tel. 661-4743; Sea Bird, tel. 661-3643; and Windjammer, tel. 661-8384, all at Lahaina Harbor. Remember that in effect, you're going standby, but there is generally room for one more.

GETTING AROUND

Public Transportation
No public transportation operates on Lanai, but Oshiro's Service Station (see below) will pick you up at the airport; if you're renting a vehicle from them, they'll charge $5 RT; if not it's $6.20 OW. Lanai City Service will pick you up at the airport if you're renting from them, and charge $4 if you drop off their vehicle at the airport when you're leaving. The Hotel Lanai, tel. 565-7211, might pick you up if you're intending to stay there, but you must arrange this in advance and the word is that they've been getting hassled recently for providing this service.

Car Rental
Oshiro Service and U-Drive, Box 516, Lanai City, HI 96763, tel. 565-6952, rents modern Japanese compacts for $25-35 p/d, plus gas. Oshiro's has one or two real clunkers out back that they let go cheaper. These beauties, held together primarily by rust and chicken wire, go for $18 a day (open to negotiation). Oshiro's re-

Maybe you can hitch a ride with a pleasure boat from Lahaina to Manele Bay.

quires a deposit to hold reservations. **Lanai City Service**, Lanai City, HI 96763, tel. 565-6780, is now a subsidiary of Trilogy Excursions and rents Toyotas for $24-28 p/d, pickups $40 p/d, vans $75 p/d (insurance compulsory).

4WD Rental

With only 22 miles of paved road on Lanai and rental cars firmly restricted to these, there is no real reason to rent one. The *real* adventure spots of Lanai require a 4WD vehicle. Oshiro's rents jeeps for $65-75 p/d, and Lanai City Service rents various 4WDs for $55-75 p/d. Although this might seem expensive, if you plan your day's outing wisely you get a whole lot of excitement for your money. Mind-boggling spots on Lanai are reachable only on foot or by 4WD. Unfortunately, even the inveterate hiker will have a tough time because the best trailheads are quite a distance from town, and you'll spend as much time getting to them as hiking the actual trails.

Many people who have little or no experience driving 4WDs are under the slap-happy belief that they are unstoppable. Oh, that it were true! They do indeed get stuck, and it's usually miserable getting them unstuck. Glenn Oshiro will give you up-to-the-minute info on the road conditions. Oshiro's also provides a good off-road map. They tend to be a bit conservative on where they advise you to take "their" vehicles, but they also live on the island and are accustomed to driving off-road which balances out their conservative estimates. Also, remember road conditions change rapidly: a hard rain on the Munro Trail can change it from a flower-lined path to a nasty quagmire, or wind might lay a tree across a beach road. Keep your eye on the weather and if in doubt, don't push your luck. If you get stuck, you'll not only ruin your outing and have to hike back to town, but you'll also be charged for a service call which can be astronomical, especially if it's deemed to be due to your negligence. Most of your off-road driving will be in *compound*—4WD, first gear, low range.

Hitchhiking

Like everywhere else in Hawaii, hitching is technically illegal, but the islanders are friendly and are quite good about giving you a lift. Lanai, however, is a worker's island and the traffic is really skimpy during the day. You can only reasonably expect to get a ride from Lanai City to the airport or to Manele Bay since both are on paved roads and frequented by normal island traffic. There is a very slim chance of picking up a ride out through the "pine" fields toward the Garden of the Gods or Kaunolu, for example, so definitely don't count on it.

ACCOMMODATIONS

Hotel Lanai

Being the only hotel on the island, you'd think the lack of competition would make it arrogant, indifferent, and expensive. Instead, it is a delight. The hotel has gone through very few cosmetic changes since it was built in 1923 as a guest lodge primarily for visiting executives of Dole Pineapple which still owns it. Its architecture is simple Hawaiiana, and its setting among the tall pines fronted by a large lawn is refreshingly rustic. With a corrugated iron roof and 2 wings connected by a long enclosed veranda, it looks like the main building at a Boy Scout Camp. But don't be fooled. The hotel is managed by Byrd Gleason for Ocean Activities of Maui, which leases it from Castle and Cooke. The 10 remodeled rooms may not be plush, but they are cozy as can be. All have been painted in lively colors, and are clean with private baths, but no phones or TVs. Room rates are $51 s, $58 d, and $65 triple. The hotel has the only bar in town on its enclosed veranda where guests and at times a few islanders have a quiet beer and twilight chat before retiring at the ungodly hour of 9 o'clock. The main dining room (and only real restaurant on Lanai) is large, and lined with hunting trophies. So if you're lured by the quiet simplicity of Lanai and wish to avail yourself of one of the last family-style inns of Hawaii, write for reservations to Byrd Gleason, Hotel Lanai, Lanai City, HI 96763, tel. 565-7211, or Ocean Activities Center, 3750 Wailea Alanui D-2, Wailea, HI 96753, tel. 800-624-8849. With 10 rooms, reservations are a must.

Lanai Realty

Lanai's first house rental agency recently opened for business. All houses are completely

the Hotel Lanai

furnished including linens, kitchen utensils, washer/dryer, and TV. They rent 3-bedroom homes for $75-80 p/d, $450-500 p/w, $1500-1600 p/m, up to 6 people; 4-bedroom, $125 p/d (more on weekends), $800 p/w, $2700 p/m (8 people). Check-in 2:00 p.m., check-out 11:00 a.m., 50% deposit required, no credit cards, checks OK, 2-day minimum. Write Kathy Oshiro, Lanai Realty, Box 67, Lanai City, HI 96763, tel. 565-6597 or 565-6960.

Lanai Vacation Cottages

This small complex of 3 hunters' cottages is run by the Koele Company, land managers for Castle and Cooke on Lanai. The cottages are usually rented in conjunction with a hunting trip complete with guide service, but it isn't mandatory. Located on 9th St. just behind the Hotel Lanai, the main house has 4 bedrooms (sleeping capacity 14), 2 bathrooms, fully furnished kitchen, sitting room, dining room, and utility room with iron and board, but no washer and dryer. The cost is a flat $125 a day regardless of the number of guests (up to 14). The 2 other cottages are designated as "front" and "rear." The front cottage has 2 bedrooms with 4 twin beds; the back cottage provides one bedroom with 2 twin beds. Although the front cottage sleeps more, the price for these are the same, $70. All 3 are provided with linens, blankets, and towels. A one-night deposit is required to hold a reservation, refundable as long as cancellation is received 2 weeks in advance. For reservations contact: Koele Company, Box L, Lanai City, Lanai, HI 96763, tel. 565-6661. The Koele Co. is easily located in the large Dole Co. offices just across Lanai Ave. from the park in downtown Lanai City.

Lanai Bucks Hunting Lodge

This lodge is an anomaly even to long-time island residents, many of whom claim they've never heard of it. It seems impossible on such a small island, but when contacted by mail the lodge does answer. Word is that Bucks Lodge provides small, unadorned, barrack-type rooms with kitchen privileges for $25. If interested write to: Gwendolyn Kaniho, Lanai Bucks Hunting Lodge, Box 879, Lanai City, Lanai, HI 96763. No phone number available.

Camping

The only official camping permitted to nonresidents is located at Manele Bay, administered by the Koele Company. Reservations for one of the 6 official campsites here are a must, although unbelievably there's usually a good chance of getting a space. Koele Co. officials state that they try to accommodate any "overflow" unreserved visitors, but don't count on it. Since Lanai is by and large privately owned by Castle and Cooke Inc., the parent company of Koele, you really have no recourse but to play by their rules. It seems they want to hold visitors to a minimum and keep strict tabs on the ones that do arrive. Nonetheless, the campsites at Manele Bay are great. Lining the idyllic beach, they're far enough apart to afford some privacy. The showers are designed so that the pipes, just below the surface, are solar heated. This means a good hot shower during daylight and early evening. Campsite use is limited to 7 nights. The fee includes a one-time $5 registration and $4.50 pp. For reservations write to the Koele Co., Box L, Lanai City, Lanai, HI 96763, tel. 565-6661. Permits, if not mailed in advance, are picked up at the Koele office. If visiting on the spur of the moment from a neighboring island, it's advisable to call ahead. Camping gear can be rented from Lanai City Service (see p. 465).

Note

While hiking or 4WDing the back roads of Lanai, especially along Naha, Shipwreck, and Polihua Beach, a multitude of picture-perfect camping spots will present themselves, but they can be used only by Lanai residents, although there's little supervision. A one-night bivouac would probably go undetected. No other island allows unofficial camping and unless it can be statistically shown that potential visitors are being turned away, it seems unlikely that the Koele Co. will change its policies. If you're one of the unlucky ones who have been turned down, write your letter of protest to parent company Castle and Cooke, 965 N. Nimitz Hwy., Honolulu, HI 96817, tel. 548-6611.

SPORTS AND RECREATION

No question that Lanai's *forte* is its natural unspoiled setting and great outdoors. You can really get away from it all on Lanai. Traffic jams, neon lights, blaring discos, shopping boutiques, and all that jazz just don't exist here. The action is swimming, hiking, snorkeling, fishing, and some hunting. Two tennis courts and a nifty golf course set among the island's Norfolk pines round off the activities. Lanai is the place to revitalize your spirits—you want to get up with the birds, greet the sun, stretch, and soak up the good life.

Tennis And Golf

You can play tennis at 2 lighted courts at the Lanai School. They have rubberized surfaces called "royal duck" and are fairly well maintained—definitely OK for a fun game. Golfers will be delighted to follow their balls around Cavendish Golf Course on the outskirts of Lanai City. This 9-hole, 3100-yard, par-36 course is set among Norfolk pines. It's free to islanders; guests are requested to pay $5 on the honor system. Just drop your money in the box provided. Come on, pay up! It's definitely worth it!

Snorkeling And Scuba

Lanai, especially around Manele Bay, has some

GOLF AND TENNIS LANAI

Course	Par	Yards	Fees Weekday	Fees Weekend	Cart
Cavendish Golf Course ★ ■ Koele Company, P.O. Box L, Lanai City, HI 96763 tel. 565-9993	36	3071	$5.00		—

N.B. ★ *= 9 hole course* ■ *= no club rentals*

This tennis court is open to the public, call ahead to check availability.

Location	Name of Court	No. of Courts	Lighted
Near Lanai School	Lanai City	2	Yes

of the best snorkeling and scuba in Hawaii. If you don't have your own equipment, try renting it from the tour boats that come over from Maui. The *Trilogy* operated by the Coon family often does this. Their van is parked at Manele Bay, and if someone is around he might rent you some. Lanai City Service, a subsidiary of Trilogy, rents snorkeling equipment and underwater cameras. Your other choice is to buy it from Pine Isle or Richards Market, but their prices are quite high. If you're the adventurous sort, you can dive for spiny lobsters off Shipwreck or Polihua, but make absolutely sure to check the surf conditions as it can be super treacherous. It would be best to go with a local.

Hotel Lanai operates the 22-foot *Lanai'i Kai.* This dive boat departs daily after breakfast, and returns for lunch. They specialize in snorkel, scuba, and night dives.

Hunting

The first cliche you hear about Lanai is that it's one big pineapple plantation. The second is that it's a hunter's paradise. Both are true. The big game action is provided by mouflon sheep and axis deer. Also spotted are the protected yet failing population of pronghorn antelope which, thankfully, can only be shot with a camera. Various days are open for the hunting of game birds which include: ring-neck and green pheasant; Gambel, Japanese, and California quail; wild turkey; and a variety of doves, francolins, and partridge. Hunting of mouflon sheep and axis deer is open to the public only in the northwest of the island which is leased to the state of Hawaii by the Koele Company. Brochures entailing all necessary information can be obtained free of charge by writing to Dept. of Land and Natural Resources, 1151 Punchbowl Street, Honolulu, HI 96813. The Lanai regional office is at 338 8th St., Lanai City, HI 96763. Licenses are required ($7.50 resident, $15.00 non-resident) and can be purchased by mail from Dept. of Land and National Resources or picked up in person at their office on Lanai.

mouflon sheep

Public archery hunting of mouflon sheep is restricted to the first and second Sundays of August and rifle season occurs on the third and fourth Sundays, but hunters are restricted by public drawing. Axis deer regular season (rifle, shotgun, and bows) opens on the 9 consecutive Sundays up to and including the last Sunday in April, also restricted by public drawing. Archery season for axis deer is the two Sundays preceding the regular season. Bag limits are one mouflon ram and one deer. Axis deer is hunted year-round on the private game reserves of the Koele Co., although the best trophy season is May through November. The rates are $180 per day for a hunting permit. Guide service is not officially mandatory, but you must prove that you have hunted Lanai before and are intimately knowledgeable about its terrain, hunting areas, and procedures. If not, you must acquire the services of either Kazu Ohara or Gary Onuma, two excellent rangers on Lanai. Guide service is $150 a day and an additional $50 per hunter/per party. This service includes all necessities from airport pick-up to shipping the trophy. A box lunch and all ground transport to and from the hunt are also provided. For full details write to Chief Ranger, Koele Co., Box L, Lanai City, HI 96763, tel. 565-6661.

Fishing

No commercial or charter fishing boats operate out of Lanai, but that's not to say there are no fish. On the contrary, one of the island's greatest pastimes is this relaxing sport. Any day in

checking out the pools along rugged Shipwreck Beach looking for a likely spot to "thrownet"

Lanai City Park, you'll find plenty of old-timers to ask where the fish are biting. If you have the right approach and use the right smile, they just might tell you. Generally, the best fishing and easiest access on the island is at Shipwreck Beach running north toward Polihua. Near the lighthouse ruins is good for *papio* and *ulua,* the latter running to 50 pounds. Many of the local fishermen use throw nets to catch the smaller fish such as *manini,* preferred especially by Lanai's elders. Throw netting takes skill usually learned from childhood, but don't be afraid to try even if you throw what the locals call a "banana" or one that looks like Maui (a little head and a big body). They might snicker, but if you laugh too, you'll make a friend.

Mostly you'll fish with rod and reel using frozen squid or crab, available at Lanai's general stores. Bring a net bag or suitable container. This is the best beachcombing on the island and it's also excellent diving for spiny lobster. There is good shore fishing (especially for *awa)* and easy accessibility at Kaumalaupu Harbor, from where the pineapples are shipped. It's best to go after 5:00 p.m. when wharf activity has slowed down. There is also superb offshore fishing at Kaunolu, Kamehameha's favorite angling spot on the south shore. You can catch *aku* and *kawakawa,* but to be really successful you'll need a boat. Finally, Manele Hulopoe Marine Life Conservation Park has limited fishing, but as the name implies, it's a conservation district so be sure to follow the rules prominently posted at Manele Bay.

PRACTICALITIES

Lanai City is the only place on the island where you can dine, shop and take care of business.

Restaurants

By far the best restaurant in town is at the **Hotel Lanai.** The sumptuous meals that come out of this kitchen are less than $10 and include homemade pies and fresh fish and vegetables whenever possible. Budgeters can order a large stuffed potato, salad, soup of the day, and drink for under $7. Restaurant hours are breakfast 7:00 a.m. to 9:30 a.m., lunch 11:00 a.m. to 1:00 p.m., dinner 6:00 p.m. to 8:00 p.m. But if you're looking for a breakfast or snack with a true island flavor, try one of the following.

Dahang's Bakery has recently remodeled and can even be called chic for Lanai. Their tasty pastries are sold out by early morning, and the breakfasts of eggs, bacon, potatoes, and the like cost about $3.50. They also have good plate lunches for about the same price. Open every day but Wed. from 6:00 a.m. to 2:00 p.m., breakfast is served until 10:00 a.m., no lunch on Sunday. Just up the road is an authentic workers' restaurant and sundries store called **S.T. Property.** No one should visit Lanai without at least stopping in here for morning coffee. It's totally run-down, but it's a pure cultural experience. Arrive before 7:00 a.m.

when the company whistle calls most of the workers to the fields. All you have to do is look around at the faces of the people to see the spirit of Lanai.

Food And Shopping

The food situation on Lanai is discouraging. Everything has to be brought in by barge. There's very little fresh produce, hardly any fresh fish, even chicken is at a premium which seems impossible given the huge Filipino population. People surely eat differently at home, but in the two tiny restaurants (Dahang's and S.T. Property) open to the traveler the fare is restricted to the "two scoop rice and teri beef" variety, with fried noodles and spam as the *piece de resistance.* Salad to most islanders is a potato-macaroni combination sure to stick to your ribs and anything else on the way. Vegetables are usually a tablespoon of grated cabbage and soy sauce. The 2 grocery stores in town are fairly well stocked with basics, but anyone into health foods or vegetarianism should carry supplies and use the markets for staples only. The markets are almost next door to each other: **Pine Isle Market,** run by Kerry Honda, and **Richards Shopping Center,** both open Mon. to Sat. 8:00 a.m. to 12 noon and 1:30 p.m. to 5:30 p.m. They supply all your basic camping, fishing, and general merchandise needs.

Money

Try full-service **First Hawaiian Bank** in Lanai City for all your banking needs. All major businesses accept TCs. The *only* credit cards accepted on Lanai are MasterCard and Visa. None of the others, including venerable American Express, is accepted.

Post Office

The Lanai P.O., tel. 565-6517, is across the street from the Dole offices on Lanai Avenue. Open daily from 8:00 a.m. to 4:30 p.m., it's full service, but they do not sell boxes or padded mailers to send home beachcombing treasures. You can get packaging materials at the two stores in town.

Useful Phone Numbers

Oshiro Service Station, tel. 565-6952; Lanai City Service, tel. 565-6780; Hotel Lanai, tel. 565-7211; Koele Co. (camping and hiking info), tel. 565-6661; Dept. of Land and Natural Resources, tel. 565-6688; Lanai Airport, tel. 565-6757; Lanai Community Library, tel. 565-6996; police, tel. 565-6525.

LANAI CITY

Lanai City (pop. 2,600) would be more aptly described and sound more appealing if it were called Lanai Village. A utilitarian town, it was built in the 1920s by Dole Pineapple. The architecture, field-worker plain, has definitely gained "character" in the last 60 years. It's an excellent spot for a town, sitting at 1,600 feet in the shadow of Lanaihale, the island's tallest mountain. George Munro's Norfolk pines have matured, and now give the entire town a green, shaded, parklike atmosphere. It's cool and breezy—a great place to launch off from in the morning and a welcome spot to return to at night. Most visitors head out of town to the more spectacular sights and never take the chance to explore the back streets.

Houses

As you'd expect, most houses are square boxes with corrugated roofs, but each has its own personality. Painted every color of the rainbow, they'd be garish in any other place, but here they break the monotony and seem to work. The people of Lanai make their living from the land and can work wonders with it. Around many homes are colorful flower beds, green gardens bursting with vegetables, fruit trees, and flowering shrubs. When you look down the half-dirt, broken-pavement roads at a line of these houses, you can't help feeling that a certain nobility exists here. The houses are mud-spattered where the rain splashes red earth against them, but inside you know they're sparkling clean. Even some modern suburban homes sprawl on the south end of town. Most of these belong to Lanai's miniature middle-class and would fit unnoticed in any up-and-coming neighborhood on the Mainland.

Downtown

If you sit on the steps of Hotel Lanai and peer across its huge front yard, you can scrutinize the heart of downtown Lanai City. Off to your right are the offices of the Dole Co. sitting squat and solid. In front of them, forming a type of town square, is Dole Park where old-timers come to sit and young mothers bring their kids for some fresh air. No one in Lanai City rushes to do anything. Look around and you'll discover a real fountain of youth: many octagenarians with a spring in their step. Years of hard work without being hyper or anxious is why they say they're still around. The park is surrounded by commercial Lanai. There's no-

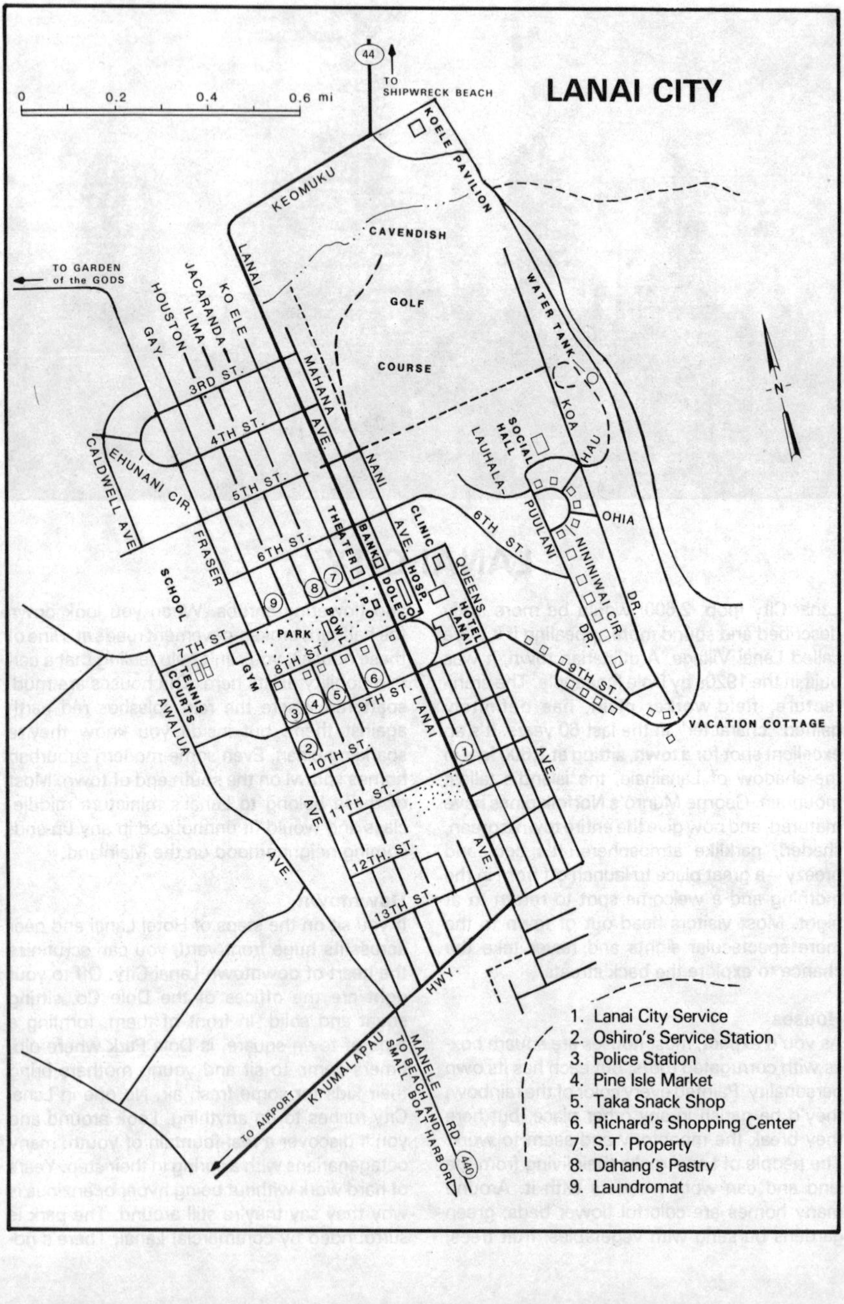
LANAI CITY
0
0.2
0.4
0.6 mi
44
TO SHIPWRECK BEACH
TO GARDEN of the GODS
KOELE
PAVILION
KEOMUKU
CAVENDISH
GOLF
COURSE
WATER TANK
LANAI
KO ELE
ILIMA
JACARANDA
HOUSTON
GAY
3RD ST.
4TH ST.
5TH ST.
6TH ST.
7TH ST.
8TH ST.
9TH ST.
10TH ST.
11TH ST.
12TH ST.
13TH ST.
MAHANA AVE.
NANI AVE.
CALDWELL AVE
EHUNANI CIR.
FRASER
SCHOOL
THEATER
BANK
CLINIC
HOSP.
DOLE CO.
P.O.
BOWL
PARK
GYM
TENNIS COURTS
AWALUA
AVE.
LANAI
HOTEL LANAI
QUEENS
AVE.
SOCIAL HALL
LAUHALA
KOA
HAU
OHIA
PUULANI
AVE
NININIWAI CIR
DR.
DR.
6TH ST.
9TH ST.
VACATION COTTAGE
N
HWY
KAUMALAPAU
TO AIRPORT
MANELE RD.
TO BEACH AND SMALL BOAT HARBOR
440
1. Lanai City Service
2. Oshiro's Service Station
3. Police Station
4. Pine Isle Market
5. Taka Snack Shop
6. Richard's Shopping Center
7. S.T. Property
8. Dahang's Pastry
9. Laundromat

where to *go* except over to the school yard to play some tennis or to Cavendish Golf course for a round of nine holes. Lanai City had a movie theater, but it screened its last picture show a while back. You can plop yourself at Dahang's Pastry Shop or S.T. Properties for coffee, or stay in the park if you're in the mood to strike up a conversation—it won't take long. Go over to Taka's Snack Shop. Anywhere else, this building would seem abandoned—inside are a few video games and maybe a bag of potato chips to buy if they're not all gone.

Meander down Lanai Ave. past a complex of agricultural buildings and shops. Heavy equipment leaks grease in their rutted dirt lots, where Lanai shows its raw plantation muscle. Just down the street is a complex of log buildings with shake-shingled roofs. These rustic barracks are for the summer help that come to pick the pineapples—often Mormon kids from Utah out to make some money and see a bit of the world. They're known to be clean-living and quiet, and it's ironic that Lanai was once a failed Mormon colony. Do yourself a favor—get out of your rental car and walk around town for at least 30 minutes. You'll experience one of the most unique villages in America.

MUNRO TRAIL

The highlight of visiting Lanai is climbing the Munro Trail to its highest point, Lanaihale (3,370 feet), locally called **The Hale**. As soon as you set foot on Lanai the silhouette of this razor-back ridge with its bristling coat of Norfolk pines demands your attention. Set off for The Hale and you're soon engulfed in its cool stands of pines, eucalyptus, and ironwoods, all colored with ferns and wildflowers. George Munro, a New Zealander hired as the manager of the Lanai Ranch a short time before Jim Dole's arrival, is responsible. With a pouch full of seeds and clippings from his native New Zealand, he trudged all over Lanai planting, in an attempt to foliate the island and create a permanent watershed. Driven by that basic and primordial human desire to see things grow, he climbed The Hale time and again to renew and nurture his leafy progeny. Now, all benefit from his labors.

Getting There

There are 2 ways to go to The Hale, by foot or 4WD. Some local people go on horseback, but horses aren't generally for hire. Head out of town on Rt. 44 toward Shipwreck Beach. Make sure to start before 8:00 a.m.; cloud cover is common by early afternoon. After less than 2 miles, still on the Lanai City side of the mountains, take the first major gravel road to the right. In about mile the road comes to a Y—go left. You immediately start climbing and pass through a forested area past a series of gulches (see below). Continue and the road forks; again bear left. Always stay on the more obviously

a precipitous gulch along the Monroe Trail

traveled road. The side roads look muddy and overgrown and it's obvious which is the main one. Robert Frost would be disappointed.

The Trail

As you climb, you pass a profusion of gulches, great red wounds cut into Lanai's windward side. First comes **Mauanalei Gulch** ("Mountain Lei"), deep and brooding from where Lanai draws its water through a series of tunnels bored through the mountains. It's flanked by **Koolanai Trail**, a rugged and dangerous footpath leading all the way to the coast. Next is **Hookio Gulch**, a battleground where Lanai's warriors were vanquished in 1778 by Kalaniopuu and his ferocious fighters from the Big Island. All that remains are a few room-sized notches cut into the walls where the warriors slept and piled stones to be hurled at the invaders. After Hookio Gulch, a trail bears left bringing you to the gaping mouth of **Hauola Gulch**, over 2,000 feet deep. Keep your eyes peeled for axis deer that seem to defy gravity and manage to cling and forage along the most unlikely and precipitous cliffs. Be very careful of your footing—even skilled Lanai hunters have fallen to their deaths in this area.

The jeep trail narrows on the ridge to little more than 100 feet across. On one side are the wild gulches, on the other the bucolic green, whorling fingerprints of the pineapple fields. Along the trail you can munch strawberries, common guavas, and as many thimbleberries as you can handle. At the crest of The Hale, let your eyes pan the horizon to see all the main islands of Hawaii (except for Kauai). Rising from the height-caused mirage of a still sea is the hazy specter of Oahu to the north, with Molokai and Maui clearly visible just 10 miles distant. Haleakala, Maui's magical mountain, has a dominant presence viewed from The Hale. Sweep right to see Kahoolawe, bleak and barren, its body shattered by the bombs of the U.S. Navy, a victim of their controversial war games. Eighty miles south of Kahoolawe is the Big Island, its mammoth peaks, Mauna Loa and Mauna Kea, looming like ethereal islands floating in the clouds.

Just past the final lookout a sign for **Awehi Trail** leads left to Naha on the beach. It's extremely rough and you'll definitely need a 4WD in compound low to get down. Most people continue straight ahead and join up with Hoike Road that flattens out and takes you through the pineapple fields until it joins with Rt. 44 just south of Lanai City. If you have time for only one outing on Lanai or funds budgeted for only one day of 4WD rental, make sure to treat yourself to the unforgettable Munro Trail.

HEADING SOUTH

Joseph Kaliihananui was the last of the free Hawaiian farmers to work the land of Lanai. His great-grandson, Lloyd Cockett, still lives in Lanai City. Joseph made his home in the arid but fertile Palawai Basin that was later bought by Jim Dole and turned into the heart of the pineapple plantation. Just south of Lanai City on Rt. 440 (Manele Rd.), the Palawai Basin is the crater of the extinct single volcano of which Lanai is formed. Joseph farmed sweet potatoes, which he traded for fish. He gathered his water in barrels from the dew that formed on his roof and from a cone-trickling spring. His lands supported a few cattle among its now-extinct heavy stands of cactus. Here too Walter Murray Gibson attempted to begin a Mormon colony which he later aborted, supposedly because of his outrage over the idea of polygamy. Nothing noteworthy remains of this colony, but high on a hillside overlooking Palawai are the Luahiwa Petroglyphs, considered to be some of the best-preserved rock hieroglyphics in Hawaii.

the gentle crescent of Hulupoe Beach

Luahiwa Petroglyphs

The route through the maze of pineapple roads that lead to the petroglyphs is tough to follow, but the best recipe for success is being pointed in the right direction and adding a large dollop of perseverance. Heading south on Manele Rd., look to your left for the back side of a triangular yield sign at Hoike Rd., the main pineapple road. Hoike Rd. was once paved but has now disintegrated into gravel. After turning left onto Hoike, head straight toward a large water tank on the hill. You pass 2 round-bottomed irrigation ditches, easily spotted as they're always green with grass due to the water they carry. At the second ditch turn left and follow the road, keeping the ditch on your right. Proceed until you come to a silver water pipe about 12 inches in diameter. Follow this pipe as it runs along a hedgerow until you reach the third power pole. At the "No Trespassing" sign, bear left.

Follow this overgrown trail up the hill to the boulders on which appear the petroglyphs. The boulders are brownish-black and covered in lichens. Their natural arrangement resembles an oversized Japanese rock garden. Dotted on the hillside are sisal plants that look like bouquets of giant green swords. As you climb to the rocks be very careful of your footing—the ground is crumbly and the vegetation slippery. The boulders cover a 3-acre area; most of the petroglyphs are found on the south faces of the rocks. Some are hieroglyphics of symbolic circles, others are picture stories complete with canoes gliding under unfurled sails. Dogs snarl with their jaws agape, while enigmatic triangular stick-men try to tell their stories from the past. Equestrians gallop, showing that these stone picture-books were done even after the coming of the white man. The Luahiwa Petroglyphs are a very special spot where the ancient Hawaiians still sing their tales across the gulf of time.

Hulupoe And Manele Bays

Proceed south on Rt. 440 to Lanai's most salubrious spots, the twin bays of Manele and Hulopoe. At the crest of the hill, just past the milepost, you can look down on the white, inviting sands of Hulopoe to the right, and the rockier, small boat harbor of Manele on the left. The island straight ahead is Kahoolawe, and on very clear days you might be able to glimpse the peaks of Hawaii's Mauna Loa and Mauna Kea. Manele Bay is a picture-perfect anchorage where a dozen or so small boats and yachts are tied up on any given day. Tour boats from Maui also tie up here, but according to local sailors the tourists don't seem to come on the weekends. Manele and Hulopoe are a Marine Life Conservation District with the rules for fishing and diving prominently displayed on a large bulletin board at the entrance to Manele. Because of this, the area is superb for snorkeling. Rent gear in town at Lanai City Service to be safe, or try to beg some from the tour boats.

Hulopoe Bay offers very gentle waves and soothing, crystal-clear water. The beach is a beautiful expanse of white sand fringed by palms with a mingling of large boulders that really set it off. This is Lanai's offical camping area with 6 sites available. All are well spaced, each with a picnic table and fire pit. A series of shower stalls made of brown plywood provides just enough privacy, allowing your head and legs to protrude. The water is surprisingly warm—the pipes feeding the showers are laid close to the surface so that the water is solar heated. After refreshing yourself you can fish from the rock promontories on both sides of the bay. It's difficult to find a more wholesome and gentle spot anywhere in Hawaii.

Kaumalapau Harbor

A side trip to Kaumalapau Harbor is worth it. This man-made facility ships more than a million pineapples a day during peak harvest, the only one of its kind in the world. Besides, you've probably already rented a vehicle and you might as well cover these few paved miles from Lanai City on Rt. 44 just to have a quick look. En route you pass Lanai's odiferous garbage dump which is a real eyesore. Hold your nose and try not to notice. The harbor facility itself is no-nonsense commercial, but the coastline is reasonably spectacular, with a glimpse of the island's dramatic sea cliffs. Also, this area has super-easy access to some decent fishing, right off the pier area.

KAUNOLU: KAMEHAMEHA'S GET AWAY

An the southwestern tip of Lanai is Kaunolu Bay. At one time, this vibrant fishing village surrounded *Halulu Heiau,* a sacred refuge where the downtrodden were protected by the temple priests with intervention from the benevolent gods. Kamehameha the Great would escape Lahaina's blistering summers and come to these very fertile fishing waters with his loyal warriors. Some proved their valor to their great chief by diving from Kahikili's Leap, a man-made opening in the rocks 60 feet above the sea. The remains of over 80 house sites and a smattering of petroglyphs dot the area. The last inhabitant was Ohua, elder brother of Joseph Kaliihananui, who lived in a grass hut just east of Kaunolu in Mamaki Bay. Ohua was entrusted by Kamehameha V to hide the *heiau's* fish god, Kuniki; old accounts by the area's natives say that he died because of mishandling this stone god. The natural power still emanating is obvious, and you can't help feeling the energy that drew the Hawaiians to this sacred spot.

Getting There

Proceed south on Manele Rd. from Lanai City through Palawai Basin until it makes a hard bend to the left. Here, a sign points you to Manele Bay. Do not go left to Manele, but proceed straight and stay on the once-paved pineapple road. At a dip by a huge silver water pipe, go straight through the pineapple fields until another obvious dip at 2 orange pipes (like fire hydrants) on the left and right. Turn left here onto a rather small road—pineapples on your left and tall grass along the irrigation ditch on your right. Follow the road left to a weather-worn sign that actually says "Kaunolu Road." This dirt track starts off innocently enough as it begins its plunge toward the sea. Only 2 miles long, the local folks consider it the roughest road on the island. It *is* a bone-cruncher, but if you take it super slow, you should have no real problem. Plot your progress against the lighthouse on the coast. This area is excellent for spotting axis deer. The deer are nourished by *haole koa,* a green bush with a brown seed pod that you see growing along the road. This natural feed also supports cattle, but is not good for horses, causing the hair on their tails to fall out.

Kaunolu

The village site lies at the end of a long dry gulch which terminates at a rocky beach, suitable in times past as a canoe anchorage. This entire area is a mecca for archaeologists and anthropologists. The most famous was the eminent Dr. Kenneth Emory of the Bishop Museum; he filed an extensive research report on the area. At its terminus, the road splits left and right. Go right to reach a large *kiawe* tree with a rudimentary picnic table under it. Just in front of you is a large pile of nondescript rocks purported to be the ruined foundation of Kamehameha's house. Unbelievably, this sacred area has been trashed out by disrespectful and ignorant picnickers. Hurricane Iwa also had a hand in changing the face of Kaunolu, as its tremendous force hit this area head on and even drove large boulders from the sea onto the land. As you look around, the ones that have a whitish appearance were washed up on the shore by the fury of Iwa.

The villagers of Kaunolu lived mostly on the east bank and had to keep an ever-watchful eye on nature because the bone-dry gulch could suddenly be engulfed by flash floods. In the center of the gulch, about 100 yards inland, was *Paao,* the area's freshwater well. *Paao* was *kapu* to menstruating women, and it was believed that if the *kapu* was broken, the well would dry up. It served the village for centuries. It's totally obliterated now; in 1895 a Mr. Hayselden tried to erect a windmill over it, destroying the native caulking and causing the well to turn brackish—another example of Lanai's precious water being tampered with by outsiders, causing disastrous results.

The Sites

Climb down the east bank and cross the rocky beach. The first well-laid wall close to the beach on the west bank is the remains of a canoe shed. Proceed inland and climb the rocky bank to the remains of *Halulu Heiau.* Just below in the undergrowth is where the well was located. The *heiau* site has a commanding view of the area, best described by the words of Dr. Emory himself: "The point on which it is located is surrounded on three sides by cliffs and on the north rises the magnificent cliff of Palikaholo, terminating in Kahilikalani crag, a thousand feet above the sea. The ocean swell entering Kolokolo Cave causes a rumbling like thunder, as if under the *heiau.* From every point in the village the *heiau* dominates the landscape." As you climb the west bank, notice that the mortarless walls are laid up for over 30 feet. If you have a keen eye you'll notice a perfectly square firepit right in the center of the *heiau.*

This area still has treasures that have never been catalogued. For example, you might chance upon a Hawaiian lamp, as big and perfectly round as a basketball, with an orange-sized hole in the middle where *kukui* nut was

Archaeological treasures like this stone bell still lie undisturbed at Kaunolu Village site.

burned. Old records indicate that Kuniki, the temple idol itself, is still lying here face down no more than a few hundred yards away. Lloyd Cockett, whose great uncle was Ohua, ill-fated keeper of the fish god, has made many trips to this area, even guiding Dr. Emory's expeditions. He knows of treasures like a stone bell that when struck with another stone rings as clear as one of metal. If you happen to discover an artifact do not remove it under any circumstance. Follow Lloyd's advice, "I wouldn't take the rock because we Hawaiians don't steal from the land. Special rocks you don't touch."

Kahikili's Leap

Once you've explored the *heiau,* you'll be drawn toward the sea cliff. **Kaneapua Rock,** a giant tower-like chunk, sits perhaps 100 feet offshore. Below in the tide pool are basin-like carvings in the rock-salt evaporation pools, the bottoms still showing some white residue. Follow the cliff face along the natural wall obstructing your view to the south. You'll see a break in the wall about 15 feet wide with a very flat rock platform. From here **Shark Island,** which closely resembles a shark fin, is perfectly framed. This opening is **Kahikili's Leap,** named after a Lanai chief, not the famous chief

Lloyd Cockett at Kahekili's Leap with Shark Island framed in the background

of Maui. Here, Kamehameha's warriors proved their courage by executing death-defying leaps into only 12 feet of water, and clearing a 15-foot protruding rock shelf. Scholars also believe that Kamehameha punished his warriors for petty offenses by sentencing them to make the jump. Kahikili's Leap is a perfect background for a photo. Below, the sea surges in unreal aquamarine colors. Off to the right is Kolokolo Cave above which is another, even more daring leap at 90 feet. Evidence suggests that Kolokolo is linked to Kaunolu Gulch by a lava tube that has been sealed and lost. On the beach below Kahikili's Leap the vacationing chiefs played *konane,* and many stone boards can still be found from this game of Hawaiian checkers.

Petroglyphs

To find them, walk directly inland from Kaneapua Rock, using it as your point of reference. On a large pile of rocks are stick figures, mostly with a bird-head motif. Some heads even look like a mason's hammer. This entire area has a masculine feeling to it. There aren't the usual swaying palms and gentle sandy beaches. With the stones and rugged sea cliffs, you get the feeling that a warrior king would enjoy this spot. Throughout the area is *pili* grass used by the Hawaiians to thatch their homes. Children would pick one blade and hold it in their fingers while reciting *"E pili e, e pili e, au hea kuu hale."* The *pili* grass would then spin around in their fingers and point in the direction of home. Pick some *pili* and try it yourself before leaving this wondrous, powerful area.

THE EAST COAST

SHIPWRECK BEACH

Heading over the mountains from Lanai City to Shipwreck Beach offers you a rewarding scenario: an intriguing destination point with fantastic scenery and splendid panoramas on the way. Head north from Lanai City on Rt. 440 (Keomuku Rd.). In less that 10 minutes you crest the mountains, and if you're lucky the sky will be clear and you'll be able to see the phenomenon that guided ancient navigators to land: the halo of dark brooding clouds over Maui and Molokai, a sure sign of landfall. Shorten your gaze and look at the terrain in the immediate vicinity. Here are the famous precipitous gulches of Lanai. The wounded earth bleeds red while offering patches of swaying grass and wildflowers. It looks like the canyons of Arizona have been dragged to the rim of the sea. As you wiggle your way down Keomuku Rd., look left to see the rusting hull of a WW II Liberty Ship sitting on the shallow reef almost completely out of the water. For most, this derelict is the destination point on Shipwreck Beach.

The Beach

As you continue down the road, little piles of stones, usually 3, sit atop a boulder. Although most are from modern times, these are called *ahu,* a traditional Hawaiian offering to insure good fortune while traveling. If you have the right feeling in your heart and you're moved to erect your own *ahu,* it's OK, but under no circumstances disturb the ones already there. Farther down, the lush grasses of the mountain slope disappear, and the scrub bush takes over. The pavement ends and the dirt road forks left (north) to Shipwreck Beach, or straight ahead (south) toward the abandoned town of Naha. If you turn left you'll be on an adequate sandy road, flanked on both sides by thorny, tire-puncturing *kiawe* trees. In less than a mile is a large open area to your right. If you're into unofficial camping, this isn't a bad spot for a one-night bivouac—the trees here provide privacy and an excellent windbreak against the constant strong ocean breezes. About 2 miles down the road is Federation Camp, actually a tiny village of unpretentious beach shacks built by Lanai's workers as "get-aways" and fishing cabins. Charming in their humbleness and simplicity, they're made mostly from recycled timbers and boards that have washed ashore. Some have been worked on quite diligently and skillfully and are actual little homes, but somehow the rougher ones are more attractive. You can drive past the cabins for a few hundred yards, but to be on the safe side, park just past them and begin your walk.

ahu, *a traveler's wish for happy trails*

Petroglyphs

At the very end of the road is a cabin that a local comedian has named the "Lanai Hilton." Just off to your left *(mauka)* are the ruins of a lighthouse. Look for a cement slab where two grafitti artists of bygone days carved their names: John Kupau and Kam Chee, Nov. 28, 1929. Behind the lighthouse ruins an arrow points you to "The Bird Man of Lanai Petroglyphs." Of all the petroglyphs on Lanai these are the easiest to find; trail-marking rocks have been painted white by Lanai's Boy Scouts. Follow them to a large rock that has the admonition "Do Not Deface." Climb down the path with a keen eye—the rock carvings are small, most only about 10 inches tall. Little childlike stick figures, they have an intriguing birdhead whose symbolic meaning has been lost.

Hiking Trail

The trail along the beach goes for 8 long hot miles to Polihua Beach. This trip leads through the Garden of the Gods and should be done separately, but at least walk as far as the Liberty Ship, about a mile from the cabins. The area has some of the best beachcombing in Hawaii; no telling what you might find. The most sought-after treasures are glass floats used by Japanese fishermen that have bobbed for thousands of miles across the Pacific. You might even see a modern ship washed onto the reef, like the Canadian yacht that went aground in the spring of 1984. Navigational equipment has improved, but Shipwreck Beach can *still* be a nightmare to any captain caught in its turbulent whitecaps and long ragged coral fingers. This area is particularly good for lobsters and shore fishing. And you can swim in shallow sandy-bottom pools to refresh yourself as you hike.

Try to time your return car trip over the mountain for sundown. The tortuous terrain, stark in black and white shadows, is awe-inspiring. The larger rocks are giant sentinels: it's easy to feel the power and attraction they held for the ancient Hawaiians. As you climb the road on the windward side with its barren and beaten terrain, the feelings of mystery and mystique attributed to spiritual Lanai are obvious. You come over the top and suddenly the valley—manicured, rolling, soft and verdant with pineapples and the few lights of Lanai City beckoning.

KEOMUKU AND NAHA

Until the turn of this century, most of Lanai's inhabitants lived in the villages of the now-deserted east coast. Before the coming of Westerners, 2,000 or so Hawaiians lived along these shores fishing and raising taro. It was as if they wanted to keep Maui in sight so that they didn't feel so isolated. Numerous *heiau* from this period still mark the ancient sites. The first white men also tried to make a go of Lanai along this stretch. The Mauanalei Sugar Co. tried to raise sugarcane on the flat plains of Naha but failed and pulled up stakes in 1901—the last time that this entire coastline was populated to any extent. Today, the ancient *heiau* and a decaying church in Keomuku are the last vestiges of habitation, holding out against the ever-encroaching jungle. You can follow a jeep trail along this coast and get a fleeting glimpse of times past.

The whistling wind is now the choir at the abandoned Hawaiian Church in Keomuku Village.

Japanese Cemetery at Halepaloa Landing

Getting There
Approach Keomuku and Naha from one of two directions. The most straightforward is from north to south. Follow Rt. 440 (Keomuku Road) from Lanai City until it turns to dirt and branches right (south) at the coast. This road meanders for about 15 miles all the way to Naha. Though the road is partial gravel and packed sand and not that rugged, you definitely need a 4WD. It's paralleled by a much smoother road that runs along the beach, but it can only be used at low tide. Many small roads connect the two, so you can hop back and forth between them every 200-300 yards. Consider 2 tips: first, if you take the beach road you can make good time and have a smooth ride, but could sail past most of the sights since you won't know when to hop back on the inland road; second, be careful of the *kiawe* trees—the tough, inch-thick thorns can puncture tires as easily as nails. The other alternative is to take Awehi Trail, a rugged jeep track about halfway between Lopa and Naha. This trail leads up the mountain to the Munro Trail, but because of its ruggedness it's best to take it down from The Hale instead of up. A good long day of rattling in a jeep would take you along the Munro Trail, down Awehi Trail, then north along the coast back to Rt. 44. If you came south along the coast from Rt. 44, it'd be better to retrace your steps instead of heading up Awehi. When you think you've suffered enough and have been bounced into submission by your jeep, remember that many of these trails were carved out by Jaun Torqueza. He trail-blazed alone on his bulldozer, unsupervised, and without benefit of survey. Now well into his 70s, he can be found in Dole Park in Lanai City, except when he's out here fishing.

Keomuku Village
There isn't much to see in Keomuku ("Stretch of White") Village other than an abandoned Hawaiian church. Though this was the site of the Mauanalei Sugar Co., almost all the decaying buildings were razed in the early 1970s. A few hundred yards north and south of the town site are examples of some original fish ponds. They're tough to see (overgrown with mangrove), but a close observation gives you an idea of how extensive they once were. The **Hawaiian church** is definitely worth a stop—it almost pleads to be photographed. From outside you can see how frail it is, so if you go in tread lightly—both walls of the church are caving in and the floor is humped in the middle. The altar area, a podium with a little bench, remains. A banner on the fading blue-green walls reads "*Ualanaano lehova Kalanakila Malmalama,* October 4, 1903." Only the soft wind sounds where once strong voices sang vibrant hymns of praise.

A few hundred yards south of the church is a walking trail. Follow it inland to ***Kahea Heiau*** and a smattering of petroglyphs. This is the *heiau* disturbed by the sugarcane train; its desecration was believed to have caused the

cursed coconuts of Naha

sweet water of Keomuku to turn brackish. Lloyd Cockett, (see p. 462), another of Lanai's living cultural assets, was raised here. He helped the famous anthropologist Dr. Emory gather facts about Lanai, as well as George Munro plant Lanai's evergreens. When he was a lad, the people of Keomuku learned to survive on the brackish water and kept a special jug of fresh water for visitors.

Heading South

Farther south a Japanese cemetery and monument were erected for the deceased workers who built **Halepaloa Landing,** from where the cane was shipped. Today, only rotting timbers and stonework remain, but the pier is an excellent vantage point for viewing Maui, and a good spot to fish. The next landmark is a semi-used get-away called "Whale's Tale." A boat sits in the front yard. This is a great place to find a coconut and have a free roadside refreshment. Also, a very fruitful *kamani* nut tree sits right at the entrance. The nut looks like an oversized bean. Place your knife in the center and drive it down. The *kamani,* which tastes like a roasted almond, is 99% husk and one percent nut.

The road continues past **Lopa,** ending at **Naha.** You pass a few coconut groves on the way. Legend says that one of these was cursed by a *kahuna*—if you climb a tree to get a coconut you will not be able to come down. Luckily, most tourists have already been cursed by "midrift bulge" and can't climb the tree in the first place. When you get to Naha check out the remnants of the paved Hawaiian walking trail before slowly heading back from this decaying historical area.

THE GARDEN OF THE GODS AND POLIHUA

The most ruggedly beautiful, barren, and inhospitable section of Lanai is out at the north end. After passing through a confusing maze of pineapple fields, you come to the appropriately named Garden of the Gods. Waiting is a fantasia of otherwordly landscapes—barren red earth, convulsed ancient lava flows, tortured pinnacles of stone, psychedelic striations of vibrating colors, especially moving at sunrise and sunset. Little-traveled trails lead to Kaena Point, a wasteland dominated by sea cliffs where adulterous Hawaiian wives were sent into exile for a short time in 1837. Close by is Lanai's largest *heiau,* dubbed Kaenaiki, so isolated and forgotten that its real name and function were lost even to Hawaiian natives by the middle of the 19th century. After a blistering, sun-baked, 4WD drubbing, you emerge at the coast on Polihau, a totally secluded, pure-white beach where sea turtles once came to bury their eggs in the natural incubator of its soft warm sands.

Getting There

Lanai doesn't hand over its treasures easily, but they're worth pursuing. To get to the Garden of the Gods you have to tangle with the pineapple roads. Head north out of Lanai City on Fraser Avenue. At the fields, it turns to dirt and splits in 4 directions. Two roads bear right, one goes left, and the main road (which you follow) goes straight ahead. This road proceeds north and then bears left, heading west. Stay on it and ignore all minor pineapple roads. In less than 10 minutes you come to a major crossroad. Turn right heading north again, keeping the ridge of Lanai's mountains on your right. This road gets smaller, then comes to a point where it splits in 4 again! Two roads bear left, one bears right, and the one you want goes straight ahead, more or less. Follow it, and in 5 minutes if you pass through an area that is very thick with spindly pine trees on both sides of the road, you know you're heading in the right direction. The road opens up in spots; watch for fields of

the Garden of the Gods

wildflowers. Shortly, a marker points you off to the right on Lapaiki Road. This is a bit out of the way, but if followed you'll get a good view of the Garden, and eventually wind up at Shipwreck Beach. It's better, however, to proceed straight ahead to another marker pointing you down Awailua Trail to the right and Polihua straight ahead. Follow Polihua Trail, and soon you finally come to the Garden and another marker for Kaena Rd., which leads to magnificent sea cliffs and Kaenaiki Heiau.

Hiking

Anyone wishing to hike this area should drive to the end of the pineapple fields. It's at least half the distance and the scenery is quite ordinary. Make sure to bring plenty of water and a windbreaker because the heavy winds blow almost continuously. Sturdy shoes and a sun hat are also needed. There is no official camping at Polihua Beach, but again anyone doing so overnight probably wouldn't meet with any hassles. Those with super-keen eyes might even pick out one of the scarce pronghorn antelope that live in the fringe of surrounding grasslands.

The Garden Of The Gods

There, like a shocking assault on your senses, is the bleak, red, burnt earth, devoid of vegetation, heralding the beginning of the Garden. The flowers here are made of rock, the shrubs are the twisted crusts of lava, and trees are baked minarets of stone. The colors are subtle shades of orange, purple, and sulfurous yellow. The jeep trail has been sucked down by erosion and the Garden surrounds you. Stop many times to climb a likely outcropping and get a sweeping view. The wind rakes these badlands and the silence penetrates to your soul. Although eons have passed, you can feel the cataclysmic violence that created this haunting and delicate beauty.

Polihua Beach

Abruptly the road becomes smooth and flat. Straight ahead, like a mirage too bright for your eyes, an arch is cut into the green jungle, framing white sand and moving blue ocean. Once you arrive, as you face the beach, to the right it's flat, expansive, and the sands are white, but the winds are heavy; if you hiked 8 miles, you'd reach Shipwreck Beach. More interesting is to the left, which has a series of lonely little coves. The sand is brown and coarse and large black lava boulders are marbled with purplish-gray rock embedded in long, faulted seams. Polihua is not just a destination point where you come for a quick look. It takes so much effort coming and going that you should plan on having a picnic and a relaxing afternoon before heading back through the Garden of the Gods and its perfectly scheduled sunset light show.

MOLOKAI

INTRODUCTION

Molokai is a sanctuary, a human time capsule where the pendulum swings inexorably forward, but more slowly than in the rest of Hawaii. It has always been so. In ancient times, Molokai was known as *Pule-oo,* "Powerful Prayer," where its supreme chiefs protected their small underpopulated refuge, not through legions of warriors but through the chants of their *kahuna.* This powerful, ancient mysticism, handed down directly from the goddess Pahulu, was known and respected throughout the archipelago. Its *mana* was the oldest and strongest in Hawaii, and its practitioners were venerated by nobility and commoners alike—they had the ability to "pray you to death." The entire island was a haven, a refuge for the vanquished and *kapu* breakers of all the islands. It's still so today, beckoning to determined escapees from the rat race!

Ironically, the blazing lights of super-modern Honolulu can easily be seen from western Molokai, while Molokai as viewed from Oahu is fleeting and ephemeral, appearing and disappearing on the horizon. The island is home to the largest number of Hawaiians. In effect it is a tribal homeland: over 2,500 of the island's 6,000 inhabitants have more than 50% Hawaiian blood and, except for Niihau, it's the only island where they are the majority. The 1920s Hawaiian Homes Act allowed *kuleana* of 40 acres to anyone with more than 50% Hawaiian ancestry. *Kuleana* owners form the grass-roots organizations that fight for Hawaiian rights and battle the colossal forces of rabid developers who have threatened Molokai for decades.

AN OVERVIEW

Kaunakakai And West

Kaunakakai, the island's main town, is like a Hollywood sound stage where Jesse James or Wyatt Earp would feel right at home. The town is flat, treeless, and 3 blocks long. Ala Malama, its main shopping street, is lined with false-front stores; pickup trucks are parked in front where horses and buggies ought to be. To the west are the prairie-like plains of Molokai. The northern section of the island contains **Pala'au State Park** where a campsite is always easily found, and **Phallic Rock**, a natural shrine where island women came to pray for fertility. Most of the west end is owned by the mammoth 70,000-acre **Molokai Ranch.** Part of its lands supports 6,000 head of cattle, **Wildlife Safari Park**, and herds of axis deer imported from India in 1867.

The 40-acre *kuleana* are here, as well as abandoned Dole and Del Monte pineapple fields. The once thriving pineapple company towns of **Maunaloa** and **Kualapuu** are now semi-ghost towns since the pineapple companies pulled up stakes in the last few years. Maunaloa is trying to hold on as an embryonic artist colony, and the Kualapuu area attracts its one-time Filipino workers mostly on weekends where they come to unofficially test their best cocks in the pit.

On the western shore is the Sheraton Molokai Hotel and a handful of condos perched above the island's best beaches. Here, 7,000 acres sold by the Molokai Ranch to the Louisiana Exploration Development Company is slated for development. This area, rich with the finest archaeological sites on the island, is a hot-bed of contention between developers and preservationists. The Sheraton, however, is often pointed to as a well-planned development, a kind of model compromise between the factions. Its first-rate architecture, in low Polynesian style, blends well with the surroundings and is not a high-rise blight on the horizon.

The East Coastal Road

Highway 450 is a magnificent coastal road running east from Kaunakakai to Halawa Valley. A slow drive along this writhing country thoroughfare rewards you with easily accessible beach parks, glimpses of fish ponds, *heiau,* wildlife sanctuaries, and small one-room churches strung along the road like rosary beads. Almost every mile has a historical marker pointing to such spots as the **Smith and Bronte Landing Site**, where 2 pioneers of trans-Pacific flight ignominiously alighted in a mangrove swamp, and **Paikalani Taro Patch**, the only one from which Kamehameha V would eat *poi*.

On Molokai's eastern tip is **Halawa Valley,** a real gem accessible by car. This pristine gorge has a just-right walk to a series of invigorating waterfalls and their pools, and a beach park where the valley meets the sea. The majority of the population of Halawa moved out in 1946 when a 30-foot *tsunami* washed their homes away and mangled their *taro* fields, leaving a thick salty residue. Today only a handful of mostly alternative lifestylers live in the valley among the overgrown stone walls that once marked the boundaries of manicured and prosperous family gardens. Just south on the grounds of Puu o Hoku Ranch is **Kalanikaula,** the sacred *kukui* grove of Lanikaula, Molokai's most powerful *kahuna* of the classic period. This grove was planted at his death and became the most sacred spot on Molokai. Today the trees are dying.

The Windward Coast

Kalaupapa leper colony, a lonely peninsula of land completely separated from the world by a hostile pounding surf and a precipitous 1,500-foot *pali,* is a modern story of human dignity. Kalaupapa was a howling charnel house where the unfortunate victims of leprosy were banished to die. Here humanity reached its lowest ebb of hopelessness, violence, and depravity—until one tiny flicker of light arrived—Joseph deVeuster, a Belgian priest known throughout Hawaii as Father Damien, came in 1873. In the greatest example of pure *aloha* yet established on Hawaii, he became his brothers' keeper. Tours of Kalaupapa operated by well-informed former patients are enlightening and educational.

East of Kalaupapa along the windward (northeast) coast is a series of amazingly steep and isolated valleys. The inhabitants moved out at

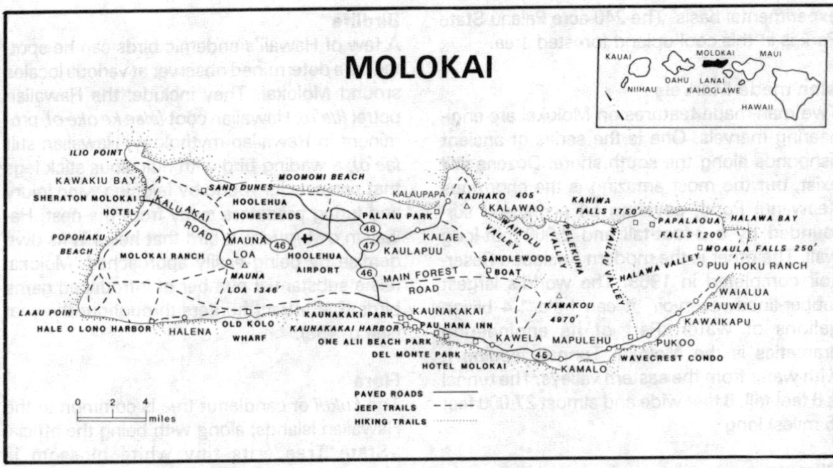

the beginning of this century except tor one pioneering family that returned a few years ago to carve out a home. Well beyond the farthest reaches of the last road, this emerald-green primeval world awaits. The *pali* here mark the tallest sea cliffs in the world, and diving head-first is **Kahiwa Falls** ("Sacred One"), the highest in Hawaii at 1,750 feet. You get here only by helicopter excursion, boat in the calmer summer months, or by foot over dangerous and unkempt mountain trails. For now, Molokai remains a sanctuary, reminiscent of the Hawaii of simpler times. Around it the storm of modernity rages, but still the "Friendly Island" awaits those willing to venture off the beaten track.

THE LAND

Molokai is the fifth largest Hawaiian island. Its western tip, at Ilio Point, is a mere 22 miles from Oahu's eastern tip, Makapuu Point. Resembling a jogging shoe, Molokai is about 38 miles from heel to toe and 10 miles from laces to sole, totaling 165,760 acres, with just over 88 miles of coastline. Most of the arable land on the island is owned by the 70,000-acre Molokai Ranch primarily on the western end, and the 14,000-acre Puu o Hoku Ranch on the eastern end. Molokai was formed by 3 distinct shield volcanoes. Two linked together to form Molokai proper, and a later eruption formed the flat Kalaupapa Peninsula.

Physical Features

Although Molokai is rather small, it has a great deal of geographical diversity. Western Molokai is dry with rolling hills, natural pastures, and a maximum elevation of only 1,381 feet. The eastern sector of the island has heavy rainfall, the tallest sea cliffs in the world, and craggy narrow valleys perpetually covered in a velvet cloak of green mosses. Viewed from the sea it looks like a 2,000-foot vertical wall from surf to clouds, with tortuously deep chasms along the coastline. Mount Kamakou is the highest peak on Molokai at 4,970 feet. The south-central area is relatively swampy, while the west and especially northwest coasts around Moomomi have rolling sand dunes. Papohaku Beach, just below the Sheraton on western Molokai, is one of the most massive white-sand beaches in Hawaii. A controversy was raised when it was discovered that huge amounts of sand were dredged from this area and hauled to Oahu; the Molokai Ranch was pressured and the dredgings ceased. The newly formed and very political Office of Hawaiian Affairs (OHA) became involved, and a court case on behalf of native Hawaiian rights is pending. A hefty section of land in the north-central area is a state forest where new species of trees are planted on an experimental basis. The 240-acre Palaau State Park is in this cool upland forested area.

Man-made Marvels

Two man-made features on Molokai are engineering marvels. One is the series of ancient fishponds along the south shore. Dozens still exist, but the most amazing is the enormous Keawanui Pond, covering 54 acres and surrounded by a 3-foot-tall and 2,000-foot-long wall. The other is the modern Kualapuu Reservoir completed in 1969. The world's largest rubber-lined reservoir, it can hold 1.4 billion gallons of water. Part of its engineering dramatics is the Molokai Tunnel, feeding it with water from the eastern valleys. The tunnel is 8 feet tall, 8 feet wide and almost 27,000 feet (5 miles) long.

Climate

The average island temperature is 75-85 F, (24 C). The yearly average rainfall is 30 inches; the east receives a much greater percentage than the west.

FLORA AND FAUNA

The land animals on Molokai were brought by man. The island is unique in that it offers **Molokai Ranch Wildlife Safari** on the grounds of Molokai Ranch in the western sector, with more than 400 animals mostly imported from the savannahs of Africa (see p. 522). And who knows? Perhaps in a few hundred years after some specimens have escaped there might be such a thing as a "Molokai giraffe" that looks like any other giraffe except that the markings resemble flowers.

Birdlife

A few of Hawaii's endemic birds can be spotted by a determined observer at various locales around Molokai. They include: the Hawaiian petrel *(ua'u);* Hawaiian coot *(alae ke oke o),* prominent in Hawaiian mythology; Hawaiian stilt *(ae'o),* a wading bird with ridiculous stick legs that protects its young by feigning wing injury and luring predators away from the nest; Hawaiian owl *(pueo),* a bird that helps in its own demise by being easily approached. Molokai has a substantial number of introduced game birds that attract hunters throughout the year (see p. 498).

Flora

The *kukui* or candlenut tree is common to the Hawaiian islands; along with being the official "State Tree," its tiny white blossom is Molokai's flower. The *kukui,* introduced centuries ago by the early Polynesians, grows on lower mountain slopes and can easily be distinguished by its pale green leaves.

HISTORY

The oral chant *"Molokai nui a Hina..."* ("Great Molokai, child of Hina") refers to Molokai as the island-child of the goddess Hina and the god Wakea, male progenitor of all the islands; Papa, Wakea's first wife, left him in anger as a result of this unfaithfulness. Hina's cave, just east of Kaluaaha on the southeast coast, can still be visited and has been revered as a sacred spot for countless centuries. Another ancient spot, Halawa Valley, on the eastern tip of Molokai, is considered one of the oldest settlements in Hawaii. As research continues, settlement

AVERAGE MAXIMUM/MINIMUM TEMPERATURE AND RAINFALL

Island	Town		Jan.	Mar.	May	June	Sept.	Nov.
Molokai	Kaunakakai	high	79	79	81	82	82	80
		low	61	63	68	70	68	63
		rain	4	3	0	0	0	2

N.B. Rainfall in inches; temperature in F°

dates are pushed further back, but for now scholars agree that early wayfarers from the Marquesas Islands settled Halawa in the mid-7th century.

Molokai, from earliest times, was revered and feared as a center for mysticism and sorcery. **Ili'ili' opae Heiau** was renowned for its powerful priests whose incantations were mingled with the screams of human sacrifice. Commoners avoided Ili'ili'opae, and even powerful *kahuna* could not escape its terrible power. One, Kamalo, lost his sons as sacrifices at the *heiau* for their desecration of the temple drum. Kamalo sought revenge by invoking the help of his personal god, the terrible shark deity, Kauhuhu. After the proper prayers and offerings, Kauhuhu sent a flash flood to wipe out Mapulehu Valley where Ili'ili'opae was located. All perished except for Kamalo and his family who were protected by a sacred fence around their home.

This tradition of mysticism reached its apex with the famous Lanikaula, "prophet of Molokai." During the 16th C., Lanikaula lived near Halawa Valley and practiced his arts, handed down by the goddess Pahulu, who even predated Pele. Pahulu was the goddess responsible for the "old ocean highway," which passed between Molokai and Lanai and led to *Kahiki,* lost homeland of all the islanders. Lanikaula practiced his sorcery in the utmost secrecy and even buried his excrement on an offshore island so that a rival *kahuna* could not find and burn it, which would surely cause his death. Hawaiian oral history does not say why Kawelo, a sorcerer from Lanai and a friend of Lanikauala, came to spy on Lanikaula and observed him hiding his excrement. Kawelo burned it in the sacred fires, and Lanikaula knew that his end was near. Lanikaula ordered his sons to bury him in a hidden grave so that his enemies could not find his bones and use their *mana* to control his spirit. To further hide his remains, he had a *kukui* grove planted over his body. **Kalanikaula** ("Sacred Grove of Lanikaula") is still visible today, though most of the trees appear to be dying (see p. 509).

Western Contacts

Captain James Cook first spotted Molokai on November 26, 1778, but because it looked bleak and uninhabited he decided to bypass it. It wasn't until 8 years later that Capt. George Dixon sighted and decided to land on Molokai. Very little was recorded in his ship's log about this first encounter, and Molokai slipped from the attention of the Western world until Protestant missionaries arrived at Kaluaaha in 1832 and reported the native population at approximately 6,000.

In 1790 Kamehameha the Great came from the Big Island as a suitor seeking the hand of Keopuolani, a chieftess of Molokai. Within 5 years he returned again, but this time there was no merrymaking: he came as a conquering emperor on his thrust westward to Oahu. His warring canoes landed at Pakuhiwa Battleground, a bay just a few miles east of Kauanakakai; it's said that warriors lined the shores for more than 4 miles. The grossly outnumbered warriors of Molokai fought desperately, but even the incantations of their *kahuna* were no match for Kamehameha and his warriors. Inflamed with recent victory and infused with the power of their horrible war-god Ku, ("with the bloody mouth dripping with maggots"), they slaughtered the Molokai warriors and threw their broken bodies into a sea so filled with sharks that their feeding frenzy made the waters appear to boil. Thus subdued, Molokai slipped into obscurity once again as its people turned to a quiet life of farming and fishing.

Molokai Ranch

Molokai remained almost unchanged until the 1850s. The Great Mahele of 1848 provided for private ownership of land, and giant tracts were formed into the Molokai Ranch. About 1850, German immigrant Rudolph Meyer came to Molokai and married a high chieftess named Dorcas Kalama Waha. Together they had 11 children, with whose aid he turned the vast lands of the Molokai Ranch into productive pastureland. A man of indomitable spirit, Meyer held public office on Molokai as well as becoming the island's unofficial patriarch. He managed Molokai Ranch for the original owner, Kamehameha V, and remained manager until his death in 1898, by which time the ranch was owned by the Bishop Estate. In 1875, Charles Bishop had bought half of the 70,000 acres of Molokai Ranch and his wife Bernice, a Kamehameha decendant, inherited the remainder. In 1898, the Molokai Ranch was sold

Hawaiian Homes Lands of northcentral Molokai

to businessmen in Honolulu for $251,000. This consortium formed the American Sugar Co., but after a few plantings the available water on Molokai turned brackish and once again Molokai Ranch was sold. Charles Cooke bought controlling interest from the other businessmen in 1908, and Molokai Ranch remains in the Cooke family to this day.

Changing Times

Very little happened for a decade after Charles Cooke bought the Molokai Ranch from his partners. Molokai did become famous for its honey production, supplying a huge amount to the world up until WW I. During the 1920s, political and economic forces greatly changed Molokai. In 1921, Congress passed the Hawaiian Homes Act, which set aside 43,000 acres on the island for people who had at least 50% Hawaiian blood. By this time, all agriculturally productive land in Hawaii was already claimed. The land given to the Hawaiians was very poor and lacked adequate water. Many Hawaiians had long since left the land, being raised in towns and cities. Now out of touch with the simple life of the taro patch, they found it very difficult to readjust. To prevent the Hawaiians from selling their claims and losing the land forever, the Hawaiian Homes Act provided that the land be leased to them for 99 years. Making a go of these 40-acre parcels *(kuleana)* was so difficult that successful homesteaders were called "Molokai Miracles."

In 1923 Libby Corporation leased land from Molokai Ranch at Kaluakoi and went into pineapple production; Del Monte followed suit in 1927 at Kualapuu. Both built company towns and imported Japanese and Filipino field laborers, swelling Molokai's population and stabilizing the economy. Many of the native Hawaiians sub-leased their tracts to the pineapple growers, and the Hawaiian Homes Act seemed to backfire. Instead of the homesteaders working their own farms, they were given monthly checks and lured into a life of complacency. Those who grew little more than family plots became, in effect, permanent tenants on their own property. Much more importantly, they lost the psychological advantage of controlling their own future and regaining their pride as envisioned in the Hawaiian Homes Act.

Modern Times

For the next 50 years life was quiet. The pineapples grew, providing security. Another large ranch, **Puu O Hoku** ("Hill of Stars") was formed on the eastern tip of the island. It was originally owned by Paul Fagan, the amazing San Francisco entrepreneur who also developed Hana, Maui. In 1955, Fagan sold Puu O Hoku to George Murphy, a Canadian industrialist, for a meager $300,000, about 5% of its present worth. The ranch, under Murphy, became famous for beautiful white Charolias cattle, a breed originating in France.

In the late 1960s "things" started quietly happening on Molokai. The Molokai Ranch sold about 7,000 acres to the Kaluakoi Corp., which they controlled along with the Louisiana Land and Exploration Company. In 1969 the long-awaited Molokai reservoir was completed at Kualapuu; finally west Molokai had plenty of water. Shortly after Molokai's water problem appeared to be finally under control, Dole Corp. bought out Libby in 1972, lost millions in the next few years, and shut down its pineapple production at Maunaloa in 1975. By 1977 the 7,000 acres sold to the Kaluakoi Corp. was developed, and the Molokai Sheraton opened along with lowrise condominiums and homesites selling for a minimum of $150,000. Lo and behold, sleepy old Molokai with the tiny Hawaiian Homes farms was now prime real estate and worth a fortune. To complicate the picture even further, Del Monte shut down its operations in 1982, throwing more people out of work. Today Molokai is in a period of flux. There is great tension between developers, who are viewed as "carpetbaggers" interested only in a fast buck, and those who consider themselves the last remnants of a lost race holding on desperately to what little they have left.

ECONOMY

If it weren't for a pitifully bad economy, Molokai would have no economy at all. At one time the workers on the pineapple plantations had good steady incomes and the high hopes of the working class. Now with all the jobs gone, Molokai has been transformed from an island with virtually no unemployment to a hard-luck community where a whopping 80-90% of the people are on welfare. Inexplicably, Molokai also has the highest utility rates in Hawaii. Some say this is due to the fact that the utility company built a modern biomass plant, and didn't have enough biomass to keep it operating—the people were stuck with the fuel tab. The present situation is even more ludicrous when you consider that politically Molokai is part of Maui County. It is lumped together with Kaanapali on Maui's southern coast, one of Hawaii's most posh and wealthy areas, where the vast majority of people are recent arrivals from the Mainland. This amounts to almost no political-economic voice for grassroots Molokai.

Agriculture

The word that is now bandied about is "diversified" agriculture. What this means is not pinning all hope to one crop like the ill-fated pineapple, but planting a potpourri of crops. Attempts at diversification are evident as you travel around Molokai. Fields of corn and wheat are just west of Kaunakakai; many small farmers are trying truck farming by raising a variety of garden vegetables that they hope to sell to the massive hotel food industry in Honolulu. The problem is not in production, but transportation. Molokai raises excellent crops, but little established transport exists for the perishable vegetables. A barge service, running on a loose twice-weekly schedule, is their only link to the market. No storage facilities on

Small private enterprise like gathering coconuts helps bolster Molokai's flagging economy.

Molokai make it tough to compete in the hotel food business which requires the freshest vegetables. Unfortunately, vegetables don't wait well for late barges.

Development

A debate rages between those in favor of tourist development, which they say will save Molokai, and grass-roots organizations championed by OHA (Office of Hawaiian Affairs), which insists unchecked tourism development will despoil Molokai and give no real benefit to the people. A main character is the Kaluakoi Corp., which wants to build condos and sell lots for $500,000 each. They claim that this, coupled with a few more resorts, will bring in jobs. The people know that they will be relegated to service jobs (maids and waiters), while all the management jobs go to outsiders. Most islanders feel that only rich people from the Mainland can afford million-dollar condos, and that eventually they will become disenfranchised on their own island. Claims are that outsiders have no feeling for the *aina* (land), and will destroy important cultural sites whenever growth dictates. A few years back the Kaluakoi Corp. hired an "independent" research team to investigate Kawakiu Bay, known to be an ancient adz quarry. After weeks of study, this Maui-based research team reported that Kawakiu was of "minor importance." Hawaii's academic sector went wild. The Society of Hawaiian Archaeology dispatched their own team under Dr. Patrick Kirch who stated that Kawakiu was one of the richest archaeological areas in Hawaii. In one day they discoverd 6 sites missed by the "independent" research team, and stated that a rank amateur could find artifacts by merely scraping away some of the surface.

Reasonable voices call for moderation. Both sides agree Molokai must grow, but the growth must be controlled, and the people of Molokai must be represented and included as beneficiaries. Some local residents, such as Aka Hodgins, manager of Molokai Ranch, is for tourism but slow growth; Jeff Thai, president of Destination Molokai, is for tourism but against mass building; Phil Boyden, a V.P. of Kaluakoi Corp., says they have reduced their original plans to build 33,000 units down to 23,000 with a *de facto* population growth of 8,000; Walter Ritte, an original member of Hui Aloha who battled the Molokai Ranch for beach access to Kawakiu and is now an elected member of OHA, is against tourism growth directed from the outside, but in favor of limited tourism directed by the people. The last word is by Sophie Duvachelle, a realtor on Molokai for the last 45 years. She says that though everyone loves the peace and quiet on Molokai, many unfairly say "let me in, but don't let anyone else in."

THE PEOPLE

Molokai is obviously experiencing a class struggle. The social problems hinge on the economy—the collapse of pineapple cultivation and the move toward tourism. The average income on Molokai is quite low and the people are not consumer oriented. Tourism, especially "get-away condos," brings in the financially affluent. This creates friction; the "have-nots" don't know their situation until the "haves" come in and remind them. Today, most people hunt a little, fish, and have small gardens. Some are small-time *pakalolo* growers who get over the hard spots by making a few dollars from some backyard plants. There is no organized crime on Molokai. The worst you might run into is a group of local kids drinking on a weekend in one of their favorite spots. It's a territorial thing. If you come into

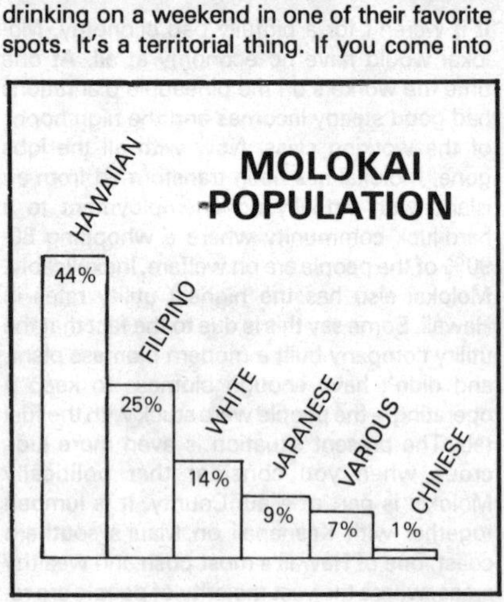

their vicinity they might feel their turf is being invaded, and you could be in for some hassles. All this could add up to a bitter situation except that the true nature of most of the people is to be helpful and friendly. Just be sensitive to smiles and frowns and give people their space.

Ethnic Identity
An underground link exists between Molokai and other Hawaiian communities such as Wainae on Oahu. Molokai is unusual in that it is still Hawaiian in population and influence, with continuing culturally based outlooks which remain unacceptable to Western views. Ethnic Hawaiians are again becoming proud of their culture and heritage, as well as politically aware and sophisticated, and are just now entering the political arena. Few are lawyers, doctors, politicians, or executives. With ethnic identity returning, there is beginning to be a majority backlash against it. Among non-Hawaiian residents, it's put down, or unacknowledged as a real occurrence. Social problems on Molokai relate directly to teenage boredom and hostility in the schools, fueled by a heavy drinking scene. A disproportionate rate of teen pregnancy is a direct by-product. Teachers unofficially admit that they prefer a student who has smoked *pakalolo* to one who's been drinking. It mellows them out. The traditional educational approach is failing. *Ho'opono'opono* is a fascinating family problem-solving technique still very much employed on Molokai. The process is like "peeling the onion" where a mediator, usually a respected *kapuna,* tries to get to the heart of a problem. Similar to group therapy, it's a closed family ordeal, never open to outsiders, and lasts until all emotions are out in the open and all concerned feel "clean."

GETTING THERE

The major airline servicing Molokai, and the only one providing jet service, is **Hawaiian Air**. Regularly scheduled flights throughout the day and early evening arrive from all the major islands. Depending on the flight the planes are either DC9s or 4-engine turbo-prop Dash's. Five of 7 flights originating in Honolulu are direct and take about 20 minutes in the air. Also, two 18-minute direct flights come from Maui. Flights originating on Kauai stop at Honolulu; those from Kona and Hilo on the Big Island stop en route at Maui. If you're after comfort with reasonably competitive prices, Hawaiian Air is your best bet.

Commuter Airlines
Molokai's own airlines, **Air Molokai-Tropic Airlines,** is a real gem. They connect Molokai with Honolulu, Maui, and Lanai with their fleet of Cessna 402s. Their recently decommissioned WW II DC3 had flown over 5,000,000 miles, and worn out more than 30 pairs of engines. Air Molokai has a varied schedule throughout the day between Molokai and Honolulu, with a few flights to and from Maui and Lanai. Round-trip weekday rates are just about unbeatable at $30 Honolulu-Molokai; $60 Maui-Molokai; $40 Lanai-Molokai; add $5 on weekends. On Molokai, tel. 567-6102; Honolulu, 536-6611; other islands, 800-352-3616, Mainland 800-262-6055.

Molokai's own Air Molokai

Polynesian Air is another small airline that's a treat. They fly the classic Beachcraft 18, the same flown on the old TV program, "Sky King." This model is the most manufactured and best-known small cargo-passenger plane in the world. Although Polynesian Air flies to other islands, their flea-hop from Kalaupapa to Hoolehua topside can't be beat at $15. Regularly scheduled flights might be delayed for such emergencies as dropping off 2 fighting cocks on Lanai, or waiting for Molokai's famous bread to come out of the ovens so it can be delivered. Don't be surprised if your pilot takes out a couple of seats to lighten the load, or invites you to sit co-pilot. These pilots are real pros who know island aviation extremely well. On Molokai, tel. 567-6647.

Others

Reeves Aviation offers 24-hour charter service, as well as regularly scheduled flights between Oahu, Maui, and Molokai; Oahu, tel. 833-9555; Maui, 871-4624; Molokai, 553-3803. **Paradise Air** flies daily from Oahu to Molokai on their 5-seater Piper Aztecs, in Honolulu tel. 833-7197. You can tour Kalaupapa and then take a 5-minute hop topside to Hoolehua (see "Kalaupapa" p. 514).

GETTING AROUND

Public Transportation

No public transportation services Molokai. Only one limited shuttle goes between Hoolehua Airport and the Sheraton Hotel complex on the west end. Operated by Rare Adventures Ltd., they run a van every hour on the hour from 8:00 a.m. to 5:00 p.m. Fare is a stiff $6 OW for the 10-mile ride, tel. 552-2622.

Rental Cars

Molokai offers a limited choice of car rental agencies—make reservations to avoid being disappointed. All rental car companies on Molokai are uptight about their cars being used on dirt roads (there are plenty), and strongly warn against it. No jeeps are available on Molokai at this time, but it's always in the air that one of the car companies will make them available sometime in the future.

Molokai Island U Drive, Hoolehua airport tel. 567-6156/6046 from 7 a.m. to 5:30 p.m., is a local firm with a good reputation. It offers a range of cars from standard-shift compacts to automatic station wagons. Their best deal is a standard compact for around $25 p/d, $130 weekly, unlimited mileage, insurance extra. Molokai Island U Drive honors all major credit cards, but has a company policy of not readily renting to campers or hunters. **Tropical Rent A Car** also has a booth at the airport and a range of vehicles with competitive prices, tel. 567-6118. **Avis** offers a free shuttle to their cars which are kept in Kaunakakai. They have higher rates than the other companies and offer no weekly discounts. 553-3866.

Hitchhiking

The old thumb gives fair to good results on Molokai. Most islanders say they prefer to pick up hitchers who are making an effort by walking along, instead of lounging by the side of the road. It shows that you don't have a car, but do have some pride. Getting a ride to or from Kaunakakai and the airport is usually easy.

Guided Tours

A few limited tours are offered on Molokai, but they only hit the highlights. If you rent a car, you can get to them just as easily on your own. **Gray Line Hawaii** offers half- and full-day tour in vans or buses. Call their desk at the Sheraton, tel. 567-6177. **Roberts Hawaii**, tel. 552-2988, offers similar tours, but must be booked 48 hours in advance. These appeal more to day-trippers from Honolulu.

The exception to the above might be **4x4 Mountain Adventures**, which specializes in off-road and outback Molokai. They offer full-day trips for $50, half-day $30, including a barbeque lunch. 4x4 also offers overnight ($80) and weekly (up to $350) campouts with all food and equipment provided. Reduced rates for children and special rates for groups. Write, 4X4 Adventures, Box 335, Kaunakakai, HI 96748, tel. 553-5936. **Halawa Valley Trail Rides** offers personal and group tours to their incredible valley (see p. 497). Excellent tours of Kalaupapa, including a unique mule ride down to the peninsula, are offered (see p. 517).

Helicopter Flights

An amazing way to see Molokai is by helicopter. This method is admittedly expensive, but dollar for dollar it is "the" most exciting way of touring, and can get you places that no other means can. A handful of companies operate mostly from Maui that include overflights of Molokai. One of the best is **Papillion Helicopters,** on Maui tel. 669-4884. Flights start at $160 and often include champagne and a picnic lunch. Though they'll put a big hole in your budget, most agree they are among the most memorable experiences of their trip.

SHOPPING

Arts And Crafts

Molokai only has a handful of shops where you can buy locally produced crafts and Hawaiiana. Maunaloa, the once thriving plantation town, is now holding on as a semi artist colony. Its location on the west end, not too far from the Molokai Sheraton and surrounding condos, gives it some hope for the future. In Maunaloa look for **Fay's One,** an unpretentious shop selling uncommon island handicrafts, windchimes, cotton clothing, and general Hawaiiana at affordable prices. Owned and operated by Fay Huff, open Tues. to Sat. 9:30 a.m. to 1:30 p.m., or by appointment, tel. 552-2486. Also try **Big Wind Kite Factory,** owned by Jonathan Sosher, an escapee from L.A. Jon sells reasonably priced silk and paper kites that look great sailing overhead on Molokai's excellent winds or as a hanging on your wall. Free lessons with the purchase of a kite. Open most days, tel. 552-2364. A few more shops in Maunaloa worth a look include: **Plantation Gallery,** which features deerhorn jewelry and scrimshaw; **Dolly Hale,** which sells island dolls made of *kukui* nuts, shells, palm leaves, etc.; **Molokai Mountain Jewelry,** featuring custom-made jewelry; and **Materials and Things,** that carry Molokai "red dirt" T-shirts. In Kauankakai you can try **Ocean Spray,** operated by Ted and Deena Kanemitsu. They sell sundries, ceramics, T-shirts, postcards, and a variety of souvenirs. On Ala Malama Street is **Port of Call,** with the best selection of Hawaiiana books on the island. A well-stocked though small shop is **Jo's of Molokai Gift Shop,** located at the Hotel Molokai. They have a good selection of souvenir items and beachwear. Jo's husband, Bob, gained notoriety a few years back as the taped voice on "Mission: Impossible," which self-destructed after giving the particulars of the episode's mission.

SPORTS AND RECREATION

Since Molokai is a great place to get away from it all, you would expect an outdoor extravaganza. In fact, Molokai is a "good news, bad news" island when it comes to sports, especially in the water. Molokai has few excellent beaches with the 2 best, Halawa and Papohoku, on opposite sides of the island; **Papohoku Beach** on the west end is treacherous during the winter months. Surfers, windsurfers, and Hobie Cat enthusiasts will be disappointed with Molokai except at a few locales at the right time of year, while bathers, sun worshippers, and families will love the small secluded beaches with gentle waves located around the island.

Molokai has a small population and plenty of undeveloped "outback" land. This *should* add up to great trekking and camping, but the land is mostly privately owned and the tough trails are poorly maintained. However, permission is usually granted to trek across private land, and those bold enough to venture into the outback will virtually have it to themselves. Day-hiking trails and lightly used camping areas with good facilities are no problem. Molokai has tame, family-oriented beach parks along its southern shores, superb hunting and fishing, an excellent golf course, and fine tennis courts. Couple this with clean air, no city hustle or noise, and a deliciously casual atmosphere, and you wind up with the epitome of relaxation.

Eastern Beaches

The beaches of Molokai have their own temperament, ranging from moody and rebellious to sweet and docile. Heading east from Kaunakakai along Rt. 450 takes you past a string of beaches that varies from poor to excellent. Much of this underbelly of Molokai is fringed by a protective coral reef that keeps the water flat, shallow, and at some spots murky. This area was ideal for fish ponds but leaves a lot to be desired as far as beaches are concerned. The farther east you go, the better the beaches become. The first one you come to is **One Ali'i Park,** about 4 miles east of Kaunakakai. Here you'll find a picnic area, campsites, good fishing, and family-class swimming where the kids can frolic with no danger from the sea. Next you pass **Kakahaia Beach Park,** and **Kumimi Beach,** one of a series of lovely sandy crescents where the swimming is fine. Just before you reach Puko'o Town, a small dirt road on your right goes to a hidden beach perfect for a secluded swim (see p. 509).

Halawa Bay, on Molokai's far east end, is the best all-around beach on the island. It's swimmable year round, but be extra careful during the winter months. The bay protects the beach for a good distance; beyond its reach the breakers are excellent for surfing. The snorkeling and fishing are good to very good.

West End Beaches

The people of Molokai favor the beaches on the northwest section of the island. **Mo'omomi Beach** is one of the best and features good swimming, fair surfing, and pleasurable snorkeling along its sandy, rocky bottom. You have to drive over a dirt road to get there. Although the car rental agencies are against it, the only problem is the dust. From Mo'omomi you can walk west along the beach and find your own secluded spot.

Very few visitors go south from Maunaloa Town, but it is possible and rewarding for those seeking a totally secluded area. As you enter Maunaloa Town a dirt track goes off to your left. Follow it through the Molokai Ranch gate (make sure to close it behind you). Follow the rugged but passable track down to the coast, the ghost town of Halena, and **Hale O Lono Harbor,** start of the Aloha Week Outrigger Canoe Race. A tough jeep track also proceeds east to collapsing **Kolo Wharf** and very secluded areas. The swimming is only fair because of murky water but the fantasy of a deserted island is pervasive.

Papohaku and **Kepuhi** beaches just below the Molokai Sheraton are excellent, renowned for their vast expanses of sand. Unfortunately, they're treacherous in the winter with giant swells and heavy rips which make them a favorite for surfers. Anyone not accustomed to strong sea conditions should limit themselves to sunning and wading only to the ankles. Dur-

Halawa Beach

ing the rest of the year this area is great for swimming, becoming like a lake in the summer months. North of Kepuhi Bay is an ideal beach named **Kawakiu.** Although it's less than a mile up the coast, it's more than 15 miles away by road. You have to branch off Rt. 46 and follow it north well before it forks towards the Sheraton. A sign reading "Right of Way to Beach" points you down a 7-mile dirt track. This area is well established as an archaeological site and access to the beach was a hard-fought controversy between the people of Molokai and the Molokai Ranch. Good swimming depending upon tide conditions, and free camping on weekends.

Snorkeling And Scuba

Some charter fishing boats arrange scuba and snorkeling excursions, but scuba and snorkeling on Molokai is just offshore and you don't need a boat to get to it. **Molokai Fish and Dive** in Kauanakakai, tel. 553-5926, is a full-service dive and snorkel shop. They have very good rental rates, can give you directions to the best spots, and arrange excursions. Beginners will feel safe at One Ali'i Park where the sea conditions are mild, though the snorkeling is mediocre. The best underwater area is the string of beaches heading east past mile marker 18 on Rt. 45. You'll wind up at Halawa Bay which is tops. Moo'momi Beach on the northwest shore is very good, and Kawakiu Beach out on the west end is good around the rocks, but stay away during winter.

Surfing

The best surfing is out on the east end past mile marker 20. Pohakuloa Point has excellent breaks, which continue eastward to Halawa Bay. Moo'momi Beach has decent breaks; Kawakiu's huge waves are suitable only for experts during the winter months. Surfboards are available in Kauanakakai from Molokai Fish and Dive, as well as Ocean Spray, both on Ala Malama Street.

Horesback Riding

Halawa Valley Trail Rides offer unique guided or unsupervised (experienced riders only) riding through this lush, pristine gorge. Your tour takes you to otherwise unseen sites in Halawa Valley and culminates with a lunch break and refreshing swim at 250-foot Moaula Falls. Your guide is Junior Rollins, legendary long-term resident of Halawa whose commentary on the sites, legends, and history of the valley is priceless. Cost is $25 with guide, $20 without. Call their answering service at tel. 558-8163, 24 hours in advance due to the remoteness. Wear jeans and shoes if possible. **H&S Stables** near the Sheraton offers 2-hour trail rides along the beaches and hills of the west end. Price is $20, tel. 552-2555, or inquire at Sheraton Tour Desk.

Fishing

The Penguin Banks of Molokai are some of the most fertile waters in Hawaii. Private boats as well as the commercial fishing fleet out of Oahu come here to try their luck. Trolling produces excellent game fish such as marlin, *mahi mahi, ahi,* a favorite with *sashimi* lovers, and *ono,* with its reputation of being the best-tasting fish in Hawaii. Bottom fishing, usually with live bait, yields *onaga* and *uku,* a gray snapper favored by local people. Molokai's shoreline, especially along the south and west, offers great bait casting for *ulua* and *ama ama. Ulua* is an excellent eating fish, and with a variance in weight from 15 to 110 pounds, can be a real whopper to catch from shore. Squidding, *limu* gathering, and torch fishing are all quite popular and productive along the south shore especially around the old fish pond sites. These remnants of Hawaii's one-time vibrant aquaculture still produce mullet, the *ali'i's* favorite, an occasional Samoan crab, the less desirable introduced *tilapia,* and the better-left-alone barracuda.

Fishing Boats

Molokai Ranch operates the 48-foot *Noio,* equipped to handle marlin, tuna, shark, or any of the big fighters. Contact **Noio Fishing and Trading Co.,** Box 696, Kaunakakai 96748, tel. 553-5115. The *Welakaho* is a 24-footer specializing in deep-sea fishing, snorkeling, and excursions. Write George Peabody, Box 179, Kaunakakai 96748, tel. 558-8253. *The Alele II* is a twin-diesel, 35-foot, fully equipped fishing boat. It also offers whale-watching tours and sightseeing cruises to Molokai's north shore. Contact Chris Lightfoot at Box 121, Kaunakakai 96748, tel. 558-8910. The **Molokai Fish and Dive Co.** arranges deep-sea charters as well as excursions and shoreline sailing. Contact them at Box 576, Ala Malama St., Kaunakakai 96748, tel. 553-5926.

Hunting

The best hunting on Molokai is on the private lands of the 44,000-acre Molokai Ranch, open to hunting year-round. However, the enormous fees charged by the Ranch have effectively stopped hunting on their lands to all but the very determined or very wealthy. A permit to hunt game animals (axis deer, barbary sheep, Indian black buck) costs $350 per day with an additional $650 preparation fee if you bag a trophy animal. The Molokai Ranch also offers year-round bird hunting for a mere one-time yearly fee of $200. For info contact **Molokai Ranch,** tel. 553-5115.

Public hunting lands on Molokai are open to anyone with a valid state hunting license. Wild goats and pigs can be hunted in various hunting units year round on weekends and state holidays. Bag limits are 2 animals per day. Axis deer hunting is limited to licenses drawn on a state public lottery with a one buck bag limit per season which extends for 9 consecutive weekends up to and including the last Sun. in April. Hunting game birds (ring-necked pheasants, various quail, wild turkey, partridge, and francolins) is open on public lands from the first Sat. in November to the third Sun. in January. A special dove season opens in January. For

axis deer

full info contact the Division of Forestry and Wildlife, Puu Kapeelua Ave., Hoo'lehua, Molokai, HI 96729, tel. 553-5415.

The oldest arrival still extant in the wild is the *pua'a* (pig). Molokai's pigs live in the upper wetland forests of the northeast, but they can actually thrive anywhere. Hunters say the meat from pigs that have lived in the lower dry forest is superior to those that acquire the muddy taste of ferns from the wetter upland areas. Pigs on Molokai are hunted mostly with the use of dogs who pin them by the ears and snout while the hunter approaches on foot and skewers them with a long knife.

A pair of **goats** originally left by Capt. Cook on the island of Niihau spread to all the islands, and were very well adapted to life on Molokai. Originally from the arid Mediterranean, goats could live well without any surface water, a condition quite prevalent over most of Molokai. They're found primarily in the mountainous area of the northeast.

The last free-roaming arrival to Molokai were **axis deer.** Molokai's deer came from the upper reaches of the Ganges River, sent to Kamehameha V by Dr. William Hillebrand while on a botanical trip to India in 1867. Kamehameha V sent some of the first specimens to Molokai where they prospered. Today they are found mostly on western Molokai, though some travel the south coast to the east.

Golf

Molokai's 2 courses are as different as custom-made and rental clubs. The **Kaluakoi Golf Course,** tel. 552-2739, is a picture-perfect beauty that would challenge any top pro. Laid out by master links designer Ted Robinson, it's located out at the Sheraton Molokai. The 6,618-yard, par-72 course winds through an absolutely beautiful setting including 5 holes strung right along the beach. Green fees are $26 including a mandatory electric cart. There's a complete pro shop, driving range, and practice greens. Guests at the Sheraton receive reduced rates. The PGA head pro is Marty Keiter, the director Ben Neeley.

Molokai's other golf course is the homey **Ironwood Hills Golf Club**. This rarely used but well-maintained fun course is 9 holes, 2,790

MOLOKAI: GOLF AND TENNIS

Course	Par	Yards	Fees Weekday	Fees Weekend	Cart
Ironwood Hills Golf ★ ■ Course Del Monte, Molokai, HI 96757 tel. 567-6121	35	6218	$5.00		—
Kaluakoi Golf Course P.O. Box 26, Mounalo, HI 96770 tel. 552-2739	72	6218	$26.00		$10.00

N.B. ★ *= 9 hole course* ■ *= no club rentals* ● *= guests only*

These tennis courts are open to the public, call ahead to check availability

Location	Name of Court	No. of Courts	Lighted
Kepuhi Beach	Sheraton Molokai	4	Yes
Kualapuu	Del Monte	7	No
Molokai High	Hoolehua	2	Yes
Star Route	Wavecrest	2	Yes

yards, par 35, run by the Del Monte Corp. in Kualapuu. Green fees are an affordable $5 that you pay at Del Monte offices. The course is close to town and you'll get directions by calling Del Monte at tel. 567-6121.

Tennis

The best courts are at the **Sheraton**: 4 lighted Lakloyd courts. They offer a free tennis clinic run by pro Mike Miura every Fri. at 4:00 p.m., tel. 552-2555 ext. 548 to reserve. Two courts are available at the **Ke Nani Kai Condos** out near the Sheraton which are free to guests. Two courts at the **Wavecrest Condo** east of Kaunakakai on Rt.45 are also free to guests. Public courts are available at Molokai High School and at the Community Center in Kaunakakai.

CAMPING AND HIKING

The best camping on Molokai is at **Palaau State Park** off Rt. 470, in the cool mountains overlooking Kalaupapa Peninsula. It's also the site of Molokai's famous Phallic Rock. Here you'll find pavilions, grills, picnic tables, and fresh water. What you won't find is crowds; in fact, most likely you'll have the entire area to yourself. The camping here is free, but you need a permit good for 7 days from the Dept. of Land and Natural Resouces in Kaunakakai, tel. 567-6083. Camping is permitted free of charge at **Waikolu Lookout** in the Molokai Forest Reserve, but you'll have to follow a tough dirt road (Main Forest Road) for 10 miles to get to it. A free permit must be obtained from the Division of Forestry in Hoolehua, tel. 553-5019.

Seaside camping is allowed at **One Ali'i Park** just east of Kaunakakai, and at **Kakahaia** farther east. These parks have full facilities but due to their beach location and easy access just off Rt. 450 are often crowded, noisy, and bustling. Also, you are a target here for any rip-off artists. A county permit ($1 p/d) is required and available from County Parks and Recreation in Kaunakakai, tel. 553-5141. The Hawaiian Homelands Dept in Hoolehua, tel. 567-6104, offers camping at **Kioea Park**, one mile west of Kaunakakai. The permit to this historical coconut grove is $5 p/d. One of the most amazing royal coconut groves in Hawaii, it's a treat to visit, but camping here, though quiet, can be a hassle. Make sure to pitch your tent away from any coconut-laden trees if possible, and vacate the premises if the winds come up.

Free camping is allowed at any of the Molokai Ranch camp spots along the southwest section of Molokai on the beach east and west from the ghost town of Halena. You can also camp free at **Moo'momi Beach** on the island's northwest shore on a grassy plot where the pavilion used to be. You can't officially camp at Halawa Bay Beach Park but if you continue along the north side of the bay you'll come to a well-used but unofficial campground fringed by ironwoods and recognizable by old fire pits. This area does attract down-and-outers so don't leave your gear unattended.

Trekking

Molokai should be a hiker's paradise and there are exciting, well-maintained, easily accessible trails, but others cross private land, skirt guarded *pakololo* patches, are poorly maintained, and tough to follow. This section provides a general overview of the trekking possibilities available on Molokai. Full info is given in the respective "Sights" sections.

One of the most exciting hassle-free trails descends the *pali* to the **Kalaupapa Peninsula.** You follow the well-maintained mule trail down, and except for some "road apples" left by the mules, it's a totally enjoyable experience suitable for an in-shape family. You *must* have a reservation with one of the 2 guide companies to tour the former leper colony (see p. 516). Another excellent trail is at Halawa Valley which follows **Halawa Stream** to cascading Moaula Falls where you can take a refreshing dip if the famous *moo,* a mythical lizard said to live in the pool, is in the right mood. This trail is strenuous enough to be worthwhile and thrilling enough to be memorable.

Molokai Forest Reserve, which you can reach by driving about 10 miles over the rugged Main Forest Road (passable by 2WD only in the dry season) has fine hiking. At road's end you'll find the Sandlewood Measuring Pit. The hale and hearty who push on will find themselves overlooking Waikolu and Pelekunu, 2 fabulous and enchanted valleys of the north coast.

The most formidable trail on Molokai is the one that completely crosses the island from south to north and leads into **Wailau Valley.** It starts innocently enough at Iliiliopae Heiau about 15 miles east of Kaunakakai, but as you gain elevation it gets increasingly tougher to follow. After you've trekked all day, the trail comes to an abrupt halt over Wailau. From here you have to pick your way down an unmarked, slippery and treacherous 3,000-foot *pali*. Don't attempt this trail alone. It's best to go with the Sierra Club, which organizes a yearly hike, or with a local person who knows the terrain. Halawa Valley is one of the last untouched valleys of bygone days. Here are bananas, papayas, and guavas left over from the last major inhabitants that left early in this century. The local people that summer here, and the one family that lives here year round, are generous and friendly, but also very aware and rightfully protective of the last of old Hawaii in which they live. If you hike into Wailau Valley remember that in effect you are a guest. Be courteous and respectful and you'll come away with a unique and meaningful island experience.

MOLOKAI: INFORMATION PLEASE

Telephone numbers of service agencies that you might find useful: Ambulance 553-5911; Police, 553-5355; Hospital, 553-5331; County Parks and Recreation, 553-5141; Dept. of Land and Natural Resouces, 567-6083; Division of Forestry, 553-5019; Fire Department, 553-5401; Hawaiian Homelands, 567-6104; Library, 553-5483; Office of Hawaiian Affairs (OHA), 553-3611; Pharmacy, 553-5790; Post Office, 553-5845.

Kapuaiwa Coconut Grove

KAUNAKAKAI

No matter where you're headed on the island you have to pass through Kaunakakai ("Beach Landing"), the tiny port town that is Molokai's hub. An hour spent walking the 3 blocks of Ala Malama Street, the main drag, gives you a good feeling for what's happening. As you walk along you might hear a mechanical whir and bump in the background...Molokai's generating plant almost in the middle of town! If you need to do any banking, mailing, or shopping for staples, Kaunakakai's the place. Hikers, campers and even day trippers should get all they need here since shops, both east and west, are few and far between, and understocked. Evenings are quiet with no bars or night spots in town, but a cup of coffee or a lunch at either the Hop Inn or the Mid-Nite Inn should yield some small talk and camaraderie.

SIGHTS

Head toward the lagoon and you'll see Kaunakakai's pineapple wharf stretching out into the shallow harbor for over a half mile. Townsfolk like to drive their cars onto it, but it's much better to walk out. The fishing from the wharf isn't great but it's handy and you never can tell. If you decide to stroll out here look for the remains of Lot Kamehameha's summer house near the canoe shed on the shore.

Kapuaiwa Coconut Grove

A 3-minute drive or a 10-minute walk west brings you to this royal coconut grove planted in the 1860s for Kamehameha V (Lot Kamehameha) or Kapuaiwa to his friends. These symbolically provided the king with food for the duration of his life. The grove has diminished from the 1,000 trees originally planted, but more than enough remain to give a sense of grandeur to the spot. Royal coconut palms are some of the tallest of the species, and besides providing nuts, they served as natural beacons pinpointing the spot inhabited by royalty. Now the grove has a park-like atmosphere and mostly you'll have it to yourself. Pay heed to the signs warning of falling coconuts. An aerial bombardment of hefty 5-pounders will rudely customize the hood of your rental car. Definitely do not walk around under the palms if the wind is up. Just next to the grove is Kiowea Park where camping is permitted for $5 p/d through the Hawaiian Homelands Department (see p. 499).

KAUNAKAKAI

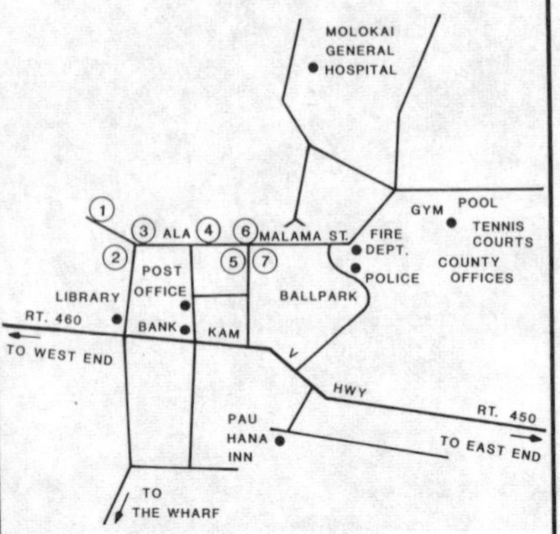

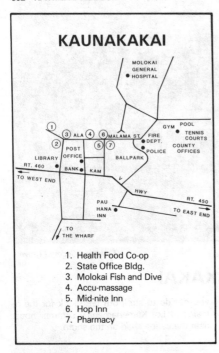

1. Health Food Co-op
2. State Office Bldg.
3. Molokai Fish and Dive
4. Accu-massage
5. Mid-nite Inn
6. Hop Inn
7. Pharmacy

Church Row

Sin has no chance against this formidable defensive line of churches standing altar to altar along the road across from Kapuaiwa Coconut Grove. A grant from Hawaiian Homelands provides that a church can be built on this stretch of land to any congregation that includes a minimum number of Hawaiian-blooded parishioners. The churches are basically one-room affairs that wait quietly until Sunday morning when worshippers come from all over the island. Let there be no doubt, old Satan would find no customers around here as all spiritual loopholes are covered by one denomination or another. Visitors are always welcome, so come to join in. Be wary of this stretch of road—all services seem to let out at the same time on Sunday morning, causing a miniscule traffic jam.

Classic Fishponds

Molokai is known for its fish ponds, which were a unique and highly advanced form of aquaculture prevalent from at least the early 13th century. Molokai, because of an abundance of shallow, flat waters along its southeastern shore, was able to support a network of these ponds numbering over 5 dozen during their heyday. Built and tended by the commoners for the royal *ali'i,* they provided succulent fish that could easily be rounded up at anytime for a meal or impromptu feast. The ponds were formed in a likely spot by erecting a wall of stone or coral. It was necessary to chose an area that had just the right tides to keep the water in the ponds circulating, but not so strong as to destroy the encircling walls. Openings were left in the wall for this purpose. **Kalokoeli Pond** is about 2 miles east of Kaunakaki along Rt. 450. Easily seen from the road, it's an excellent example of the classic fishpond. You can proceed a few more minutes east until you come to a large coconut grove just a half mile before One Ali'i Beach Park. Stop here for a sweeping view of **Ali'i Fishpond,** another fine example.

ACCOMMODATIONS

Kaunakakai has only 4 places to stay, and besides camping, the only other place to lodge on the entire island is way out on the west end at the exclusive Sheraton Molokai or the 2 condos that surround it. Head for Kaunakakai and its limited but adequate accommodations if you want to save money. The choices are all along the *makai* side of Rt. 450 as you head east from town.

Pau Hana Inn

For years the Pau Hana ("Work's Done") Inn had the reputation for being *the* budget place to stay on Molokai. Now all that's left is the reputation, although it's still cheap. The main reason for the demise of this otherwise character-laden hotel is the total lack of friendly spirit displayed by the staff. The owners live on Oahu, and the Pau Hana shows the lack of that special caring touch. It's the type of place where you feel as if you're interrupting the front desk clerk from reading her favorite movie magazine. All the character of the Pau Hana could still be brought out if someone had the inclination. Special touches still remain like windows of the dining room left open so that birds can fly in to peck crumbs off the floor. A fireplace is lit in the morning to take the chill off the place; hanging over it is a noble stag with wide perfect antlers and tearful eyes. Outside, in the courtyard bar, a magnificent Bengalese banyan provides the perfect setting to sit back and relax. The waitresses, mostly a phantasm of transvestites, are the only friendly people around the place who go out of their way to make you feel welcome and comfortable. The Pau Hana Bar is a favorite with local people. Friday and Saturday nights can get rough. Usually tourists are left alone, but there are plenty of drunken domestic arguments, and if you're in the wrong place at the wrong time the local color that you might get is a black eye. It's clear that the Pau Hana Inn needs some love and care, quickly. Rates are: Long House, a barracks-type building, clean with linoleum floors $20-25 s/d (try to get a room on the seaside end away from the swimming pool pump that runs all night); Cottage Unit, a separate little bungalow from $27 to $35 s depending on view; Deluxe, $35-42 or Deluxe Kitchenette (3-day minimum) $39-49. For reservations write Pau Hana Inn, Box 860, Kaunakakai, Molokai, HI 96748, tel. 553-5342 or 800-367-8047.

Molokai Shores

This is a relatively new condo with full kitchens, large living rooms and separate bedrooms, a few minutes east of the Pau Hana. The white walls contrasting with the dark brown floors are hung with tasteful prints. Plenty of lounge furniture is provided along with a table for outside dining and barbecues. The upper floor of the 3-story buildings offers an open beam ceiling including a full loft. Some units have an extra bedroom built into the loft. The grounds are very well kept, quiet, and restful. The swimming pool fronts the gentle but unswimmable beach, and nearby is a classic fishpond. The only drawback with the Molokai Shores is that the architecture resembles a housing project. It's pragmatic and neat, but not beautiful. Rates are $68 s/d, one-bedroom deluxe; $70 loft, 3rd floor; $90 2-bedroom deluxe, 2 baths; $8 for each additional person. For information write Hawaiian Islands Resorts, Box 212, Honolulu, HI 96810, tel. 531-7595, or, Molokai Shores, Star Route, Kaunakakai, Molokai, HI 96748, tel. 553-5945 or 800-367-7042.

Hotel Molokai

The hotel was built in 1966 by an architect (Mr. Roberts) enamored with the south seas, who wanted to give his hotel a Polynesian village atmosphere. He succeeded. The buildings are 2-story, semi A-frames with sway-backed roofs covered with split wood shingles. Outside staircases lead to the large, airy studios that feature a *lanai* with swing. No cooking facilities, but a refrigerator in every room is handy. Although the Hotel Molokai is a semi-condo, there is full maid service, a friendly staff, great dining, nightly entertainment, a well-appointed gift shop, and swimming pool. The rates, s/d, vary from $42-52 for a studio, $62-72 for a deluxe ocean front, add $8 for each additional person. For information write Hotel Molokai, Box 546, Kaunakakai, HI 96748, tel. 553-5347 or 800-367-8047, on Oahu tel. 531-4004.

Honey Girl, Nalani, and host Butch Dudoit of the Hotel Molokai

Wavecrest Resort Condominium

Depending on your point of view the Wavecrest is either a secluded hideaway, or stuck out in the sticks away from all the action. It's east of Kaunakakai on Rt. 450 just at mile marker 13. You'll find *no* hustle, bustle, anxiety, nightlife, restaurants, or shopping except for a tiny general store that sells the basics for not too much of a mark-up. The Wavecrest sits on 5 well-tended acres fronting a lovely-to-look-at lagoon which isn't good for swimming. Enjoy a putting green and lighted tennis courts free to guests (fee for non-guests). Even if you feel that you're too far from town, remember nothing is going on there anyway. Another attraction is that local fishermen put in just next to the Wavecrest and sell their fish for unbeatable prices. Guests can barbecue on gas grills provided. Rates, s/d, minimum 3 nights, are $51-61 one bedroom; $61-71 2-bedroom up to 4 people. Monthly rates are attractive at $600 to $900 for one- and 2-bedroom units respectively. For information write Wavecrest Resort, Star Route, Kaunakakai, HI 96748, tel. 558-8101 or 800-367-2980.

FOOD AND ENTERTAINMENT

Like the hotel scene, Molokai has only a handful of places to eat, but among these are veritable institutions that if missed make your trip to Molokai incomplete. The following are all located on Kaunakakai's main street. Just ask anyone where they are.

Inexpensive

The 45-year-old **Mid-Nite Inn**, tel. 553-5302, started as a *saimin* stand by Mrs. Kikukawa, the present owner's mother. People would come here to slurp noodles while waiting for the midnight inter-island steamer to take them to Honolulu. The steamers are gone but the restaurant remains. The Mid-Nite is clean, smells delicious, and looks dingy, which is relative because all of Kaunakakai looks run down. Large, with naugahyde atmosphere, it's open for breakfast 6:00-10:30 a.m., lunch 10:30 a.m. to 1:30 p.m., dinner 5:30-9:00 p.m., closed Sunday. Breakfasts start at $2, while $2.75 gets a cheese omelette, and all include hot coffee, tea or cocoa. $1.75 buys a mahi-burger, $1 a hamburger, and $1.25 for tuna salad, white bread only! Daily specials, like breaded shrimp, cost under $5, and the menu features pork tofu, veal cutlets, beef stew, and flank steak for around $5. No credit cards accepted, but smiles and small talk from travelers are greatly appreciated.

The **Kanemitsu Bakery** has been in business for almost 70 years, and is still run by the same family! The bakery is renowned for its *Molokai breads,* boasting cheese and onion among its best. Small inter-island airlines even hold up their planes to get their shipment from the bakery. It's open in the morning for breakfast and serves coffee. Mrs. Kanemitsu's cookies are scrumptious, and anyone contemplating a picnic or a day hike should load up.

The **Hop-Inn**, tel. 553-5465, is a Chinese restaurant across from the Mid-Nite Inn where you can fill up for $5. The menu is large, but

Local families come to socialize at the Mid-Nite Inn.

don't let that fool you. Next to many listings is a penciled-in "out," especially the fish dishes. The funky building at one time housed the Kaunakakai Hotel. The Hop-Inn sells some bad local art strung around the place hanging by clothes pins. Some are so dusty that you can't make them out. It's better that way. A few curios toward the back are mildly interesting while you wait for your *chop suey*.

Rabang's Filipino Restaurant looks like a great find, being little more than a hole in the wall, but the place is never open, and locals say the food was mediocre to awful on any given day. A peek through the greasy window reveals an inexpensive ethnic menu thumbtacked to the wall. Another tattered sign reads, "Rooms for rent tel. 553-3769," but they're probably no better than the food.

Hotel Restaurants

The **Pau Hana Inn** offers a full menu with most dinners being under $10. Start with breakfast for under $3.50, or carbo-load with 4 huge slices of island French toast for only $2. Enjoy nightly entertainment, usually a soloist singing island songs, with a combo performing weekends. Relax at the Pau Hana Bar, with its famous banyan tree atmosphere, with an early evening cocktail. On the weekends, the crowds get rowdy, and there is an annoying cover charge, even for hotel guests who only want a quiet drink.

The Hotel Molokai has an exemplary salad bar including *soup du jour* and non-sprayed local vegetables. Combined with an entree, such as fresh *mahi mahi* (grilled, not deep-fried), it can't be beat for around $10. Host, Butch Dudoit, goes out of his way to make you feel welcome, and island music is provided by the talented Kimo Paleka. If Kimo looks familiar you might have seen him at the airport handling bags for Hawaiian Air. With a pair of strong arms by day and gentle guitar fingerings at night, Kimo typifies the Hawaiian man of today.

Grocery Stores And Shopping

For those into natural health food the **Molokai Buyers Co-op** is at the end of Ala Malama Street near the 76 gas station, and is excellent. They're open Mon. to Fri. 9:00 a.m. to 6:00 p.m., Sat. 9:00 a.m. to 1:00 p.m., tel. 553-3377. The fruits and vegetables with a green sticker on the price list are organically grown. They also have huge sandwiches for $2.50, along with fresh juice and smoothies. The jam-packed shelves hold rennetless cheese, fresh yogurt, Haagen-Dazs ice cream, no vitamins, but a good selection of herbs, oils, and spices. If you can't find what you need ask Molly, the general manager.

For general shopping the **Friendly Market,** combined with **Takes Variety Store** down the street, sell just about everything. For that special evening try **Molokai Wines and Spirits** that has a small but good selection of vintage wines as well as gourmet treats.

The **Wavecrest Condo Store** is at the entrance of the Wavecrest, 13 miles east of Kaunakakai. They have a small selection of staples and a good selection of booze and wine. More importantly local fishermen put in at the Wavecrest beach—it's your best chance to get fresh fish at a very reasonable price.

Just before mile marker 16 (3 miles east of Wavecrest) you'll see a little fallen-down shack on the *mauka* side of the road called the **Neighborhood Store.** This is positively the last place to buy anything if you're headed out to the east end. The stock is meager, the prices are high, but it's worth a stop for the laid-back flavor even if you only buy a soft drink.

Services And Information

The following phone numbers may be of use in Kaunakakai: Bank of Hawaii, 553-3273; Fire Department, 553-5401; Maui Community College, 553-5518; Molokai Clinic, 553-5353; Molokai Drug Store, 553-5790; Molokai Hospital 553-5331. The Friendly Market has a community bulletin board outside. It might list cars for sale, Hawaiian genealogies, or fund-raising *sushi* sales. Have a look!

EAST TO HALAWA VALLEY

The east end of Molokai, from Kaunakakai to Halawa Valley, was at one time the most densely populated area of the island. At almost every mile post is an historical site or point of interest, many dating from pre-contact times. A string of tiny churches attests to the coming of the missionaries in the mid-1800s, and a crash-landing site was an inauspicious harbinger of the deluge of Mainlanders bound for Hawaii in this century. This entire stretch of Rt. 450 is almost entirely undeveloped, and the classical sites such as *heiau,* listening stones, and old battlegrounds are difficult to find, although just a stone's throw from the road. The local people like it this way as most would rather see the south shore of Molokai remain unchanged. A determined traveler might locate the sites, but unless you have local help, it will mean hours tramping around in marshes or on hillsides with no guarantee of satisfaction. Some sites such as *Iliilope Heiau* are on private land and require permission to visit. It's as if the spirits of the ancient *kahuna* protect this area.

SIGHTS

It's a toss-up whether the best part about heading out to the east end is the road itself or the reward of Halawa Valley at the end. Only 30 miles long, it takes 90 minutes to drive. The road slips and slides around corners, bends around huge boulders, and dips down here and there into coves and inlets. The cliff face and protruding stones have been painted white so that you can avoid an accident, especially at night. Sometimes the ocean and road are so close that spray splatters your windshield. Suddenly you'll round a bend to see an idyllic house surrounded by palm trees with a gaily painted boat gently rocking in a protected miniature cove. Behind is a valley or verdant hills with colors so vibrant they shimmer. You negotiate a hairpin curve and there's Lanai and Maui, black on the horizon, contrasted against the waves as they come crashing in foamy white and blue. Down the road chugs a pickup

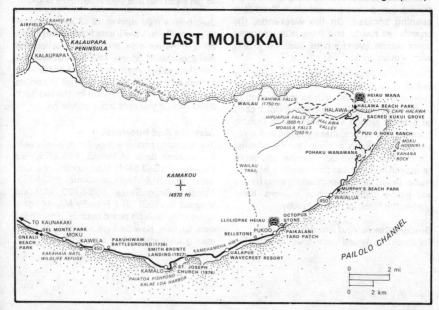

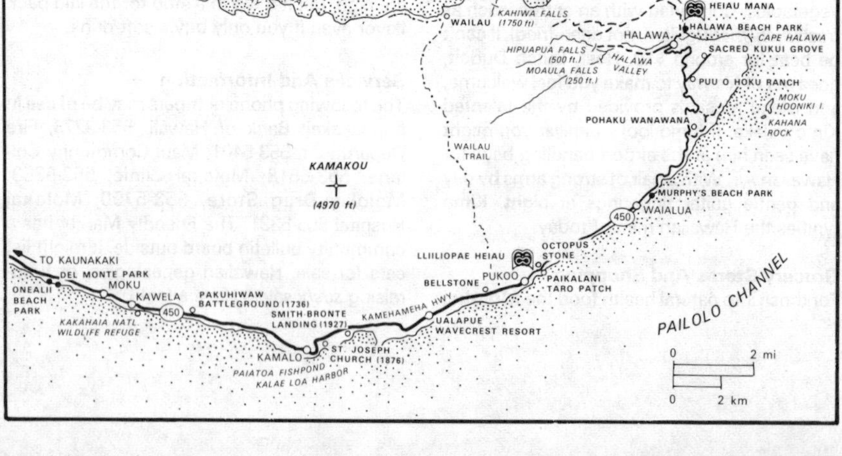

picturesque coconut grove and fishpond typical of east Molokai

truck full of local people. They wave you a "hang loose" as their sincere smiles light up your already glorious day. Out in one of the innumerable bays are snorkelers, while beyond the reef surfers glide in exhilarating solitude.

The local people think of the road as "their road." Why not? They use it as a sidewalk, playground, and extension of their back yards. Dogs snooze on it, while the rumps of grazing stock are only inches away from your fender. The speed limit is 35, but go slower and enjoy it more. The mile markers stop at mile 17, then 4 miles farther you come to the best part. Here, the well-tended 2-lane highway with the yellow stripe plays out. The road gets old and bumpy, but the scenery gets much more spectacular. It's about 9 miles from where the bumpy part begins until you reach the overlook at Halawa Valley. Have a full tank of gas, plenty of drinking water, a picnic lunch, and your sense of wonder.

Oneali'i Beach Park

Five minutes past the Hotel Molokai brings you to a stand of perhaps 80 coconut palms. Here is a little-used, unnamed beach park with an excellent view of one of the string of fishponds that are famous in this area. **Oneali'i Beach Park,** only a few minutes farther along, is open for camping. It is too close to the road, not well shaded, and a bit overused to be comfortable. The swimming here is only fair for those who like a challenging surf, but excellent for families with little children who want calm waters. Clean restrooms and showers are available and the grounds are generally in good shape. Those not camping here would find it pleasant enough for a day excursion, but it is nothing compared with what is farther east along the road.

About 2 minutes past Oneali'i, Makanui Road leads up the hillside on the *mauka* side of the road. A 2-minute ride up this road exposes the beginnings of a development. Only the roads and street lights are in place at this time, but the condos won't be far behind. As you gain the heights (one of the only roads that allows you to do so) you'll have an excellent view of the coastline with a panorama of the fishponds below and Lanai and Maui out to sea. Just beyond this road is another just like it leading into a future sub-division with a similar overview.

Kawela

The Kawela area was a scene of tragedy and triumph in Molokai's history. Here was Pakuhiwa, the battleground where Kamehameha I totally vanquished the warriors of Molokai on his way to conquering Oahu. In nearby Kawela Gulch was *Pu'u kaua,* the fortress that Kamehameha overran. The fortress oddly doubled as a *pu'u honua,* a temple of refuge, where the defeated could find sanctuary. Once the battle had been joined, and the outcome inevitable, the vanquished could find peace and solace in the very area that they had so recently defended.

Today the area offers refuge as **Kakahai'a Beach Park and National Wildlife Sanctuary.** The beach park is not used heavily: it too is close to the road. The fish pond here is still used though, and it's not uncommon to see people in it gathering *limu*. This is also an excellent area for coconut trees, with many nuts lying on the ground for the taking. Kakahai'a, designated a National Wildlife Sanctuary, is an area where birdwatchers can still be captivated by the sight of rare endemic birds.

Kamalo To Pukoo

This 6-mile stretch is loaded with historical sites. Kamalo is one of Molokai's natural harbors used for centuries before most of the island commerce moved to Kaunakakai. **Kamalo Wharf** (turn left down the dirt road at mile marker 10) still takes large sailboats from throughout the islands. It's a great place to meet local fishermen and inquire about crewing on island-cruising boats. A daily boat for Maui will give you a lift for $10.

Saint Joseph Church, next in line, was built in 1876 by Father Damien. It's small, no more than 16 by 30 feet, and very basic. Inside is a small wooden altar adorned with flowers held in a canning jar. A picture of Father Damien and one of St. Joseph adorn the walls. Outside is a black metal sculpture of Damien.

One mile or so past St. Joseph's, an HVB marker points out the **Smith and Bronte Landing Site.** These 2 aviators safely crash-landed their plane here on July 14, 1927, completing the first trans-Pacific civilian flight, in just over 25 hours. All you can see is a mangrove swamp, but it's not hard to imagine the relief of the men as they set foot even on soggy land after crossing the Pacific. They started a trend that would bring over 4,000,000 people a year to the islands. The Wavecrest Condo is nearby at mile marker 13, and if you're not staying there, it's your next to last chance to pick up supplies, water, or food before proceeding east.

Before Pukoo are 2 noteworthy sites. **Kalua'aha Church** looks like a fortress with its tiny slit windows, 3-foot-thick plastered walls and buttresses. It was the first Christian church on Molokai built by the Protestant missionaries, Rev. and Mrs. Hitchcock, in 1844. Used for worship until the 1940s, it has since fallen into disuse. The roof is caving in, but the parishioners have repair plans. Then comes ***Ili'ili'opae Heiau,*** one of Hawaii's most famous human sacrifice temples, and a university of sorcery, as it were, where *kahuna* from other islands were tutored. All of the wooden structures on the 267-foot stone platform have long since disappeared. Legend holds that all of the stone was carried across the island from Wailau Valley and perfectly fitted in one night of amazing work. Legend also holds that the sorcerers of Ili'ili'opae once sacrificed 9 sons of a local fisherman. Outraged, he appealed to a powerful shark god for justice. The god sent a flash flood to wipe out the evil sorcerers, washing them into the sea where the shark god waited to devour them. The trailhead for Wailau Valley begins at Ili'ili'opae, but since the temple is now on private land it is necessary to receive permission to visit it. The easiest way to go about this is to stop at the "activities desk" of any of the island hotels or condos. They have the right telephone numbers and procedures.

St. Joseph's Church

Our Lady of Sorrows Church, another built by Father Damien in 1874 and rebuilt by the parishioners in 1966, is next. Inside are beautiful pen-and-ink drawings of the Stations of the Cross imported from Holland. Just past Our Lady of Sorrows an HVB marker points to **bell stones,** but they're almost impossible to locate. Before you get to Pukoo is the **Neighborhood Store** near mile marker 16. Look for a house high on the hill with a multicolored stone wall surrounding it. The Neighborhood Store is the little shack at the foot of the driveway. This is your last chance to pick up supplies. Just past Pukoo another HVB warrior shows the way to **octopus stone,** a large stone painted white next to the road. It is believed that this is the remainder of a cave inhabited by a mythical octopus, and that the stone still has magical powers.

One hundred yards past the Neighborhood Store a sign says "Public Access to Beach." Follow it until the road bears left and proceed for another 200 yards. Here are 2 perfect miniature rainbow beaches. They're excellent for swimming with good wave action and a gently tapering sandy bottom. Across the cove is the Manae Canoe Club on private land. This area is great if you want to get away from it all.

On To Halawa Valley

Past Pukoo, the road gets very spectacular. Many blow-your-horn turns pop up as you weedle around the cliff face following the natural roll of the coastline. Coming in rapid succession are incredibly beautiful bays, and tiny one-blanket beaches, where solitude and sunbathing are perfect. Be careful of surf conditions! Some of the fruitful valleys behind them are still cultivated for *taro,* and traditional community life beckons young people from throughout the islands to come and learn the old ways. Offshore is the crescent of **Moku Ho'oniki Island,** and Kanaha Rock in front. The road swerves inland, climbing the hills to the 14,000 acres of **Puu O Hoku** ("Hill of Stars") Ranch. People often mistake one of the ranch buildings along the road as a store. It's a print shop, but the people inside can direct you to an overlook where you can see the famous and sacred *kukui* grove where Lanikaula, one of the most powerful sorcerers of Molokai, is buried. The different-looking cattle grazing these hilly pastures are French Charolais, imported by Puu O Hoku and now flourishing on these choice pasture lands. The road comes to a hairpin turn where it feels like you'll be airborne. Before you is the magnificent chasm of Halawa Valley with its famous waterfalls sparkling against the green of the valley's jungle walls. Hundreds of feet below frothy, aquamarine breakers roll into the bay.

Halawa Valley And Bay

This choice valley rich in soil and watered by Halawa Stream is believed to be the first permanent settlement on Molokai, dating to the

The Neighborhood Store provides the basics.

Halawa Valley

early 7th century. Your first glimpse is from the road's overlook from which you get a spectacular panorama across the half-mile valley to Lamaloa Head forming its north wall, and eastward, deep into its 4-mile cleft, where lies Moaula Falls. Many people are so overwhelmed when they gaze from the overlook into Halawa that they don't really look around. Turn to your right and walk only 15 yards directly away from Halawa. This view gives a totally different perspective of a deep V valley and the pounding surf of its rugged beach—so different from the gently arching haven of Halawa Bay. For centuries Halawa's farmers carved geometric terraces for *taro* fields until a tidal wave of gigantic proportions inundated the valley in 1946, and left a plant-killing deposit of salt. Most people pulled out and left their homes and gardens to be reclaimed by the jungle.

Follow the paved road into the valley until you see a house that was obviously a church at one time. Starting here, horseshoes tacked onto the trees direct you to **Halawa Valley Trail Rides** on the far side of the bay. Even if you're not into riding horses follow the signs to the best beach access in the valley. Cross Halawa Stream and follow the road as far as you can. Here you have a choice of bathing in the cool freshwater stream or in the surf of the protected bay. Don't go out past the mouth of the bay because the currents can be treacherous. This area is great for snorkeling and fishing, as well as having one of the only good surfing beaches on Molokai.

Halawa Bay is a beach park, but it's not well maintained. There are toilet facilities and a few dilapidated picnic tables, but no official overnight camping, and the water is not potable. You can bivouac for a night on Puu O Hoku Ranch land at the far north end of Halawa Bay under a canopy of ironwood trees, but be aware that this area attracts rip-offs and it's not safe to leave your gear unattended.

A long-term resident of Halawa, expert on the legends, myths, and history of the region, is Junior Rollins. He lives in the formidable stone house at the very end of the road on the far side of Halawa Bay. He feels that his house is lucky and secure because it's one of the only dwellings that survived the *tsunami* of 1946. He and his partner Megan run Halawa Valley Trail Rides (see p. 497). If you're not inclined to walk to Moaula Falls you couldn't make a better choice than to go on a trail ride with Junior or Megan: you'll not only have a great time on horseback exploring the valley, but be entertained with stories and vignettes of the way life used to be in the valley. Living just next door to Junior is an island fisherman named Glenn and his wife Cathy. Glenn is an expert seaman and knowledgeable about the waters on this side of Molokai. He is willing to take people to Wailau Valley for $30 OW. The only problem is no phone, so you'll have to catch him at home or leave a note where he can contact you. Things are less efficient at Halawa Bay, and that's the beauty of it.

Moaula Falls

One of *the* best walks on Molokai is to the famous 250-foot Moaula ("Red Chicken") Falls. Depending on recent rainfall it can be very difficult to get there, and although Moaula Falls is quite famous, the trail to it is very poorly maintained. Valley residents claim that a full 50% of the people headed for Moaula never get there. They start out wrong! After parking at the turn-out at the bottom of the road, follow the dirt road past the little church and the group of houses for about 10 minutes (½ mile) until it turns into a foot path. Pass a few houses heading toward Halawa Stream, keeping the stone wall on your left. This is where most people go wrong. You must cross the stream to the right-hand bank! If you stay on the left bank, you'll get into thick underbrush and miss the falls completely. *Sometimes* an arrow points across the stream, but it comes and goes at the whim of vandals.

Halawa Stream can be a trickle or torrent, depending upon recent rains. If the stream's hard to cross, Moaula will be spectacular. A minute after crossing, the trail continues under a thick canopy of giant mango trees. The luscious fruits are ripe from early spring to early fall. The trail goes up a rise until it forks at a trail paralleling the stream. Take the left fork and follow the water pipe until it crosses the stream once again. This entire area shows the remains of countless *taro* patches and homesites. Groves of *kemani* trees mark the sites where *ali'i* were buried, their tall trunks at one time used by Hawaiian fishermen and later by sailors as a landmark. Start listening for the falls and let your ears guide you.

Legend recalls that a female lizard, a *moo,* lives in the gorgeous pool at the bottom of the falls. Sometimes she craves a body and will drag a swimmer down to her watery lair. The only way to determine her mood is to place a *ti* leaf (abundant in the area) in the pool. If it floats you're safe, but if it sinks the lady lizard wants company—permanently! Minor gods live in the rocks above Moaula Falls pool who want to get into the act too. They'll drop tiny rocks on your head unless you make an offering (a penny under a *ti* leaf will do).

After you've crossed Moaula Stream and are heading the last 100 yards or so to the falls, a branch trail leads to the right up the cliff where it divides again in about 150 yards. If you take the left fork you come to another pool at the bottom of **Upper Moaula Falls,** but you have to scale the almost vertical cliff face aided only by a wire cable attached to the rock wall. The right fork leads you into heavy brush, but if you persevere for 500 yards or so you come to the cascading brilliance of 500-foot **Hipuapua Falls** and its smaller but totally refreshing swimming hole.

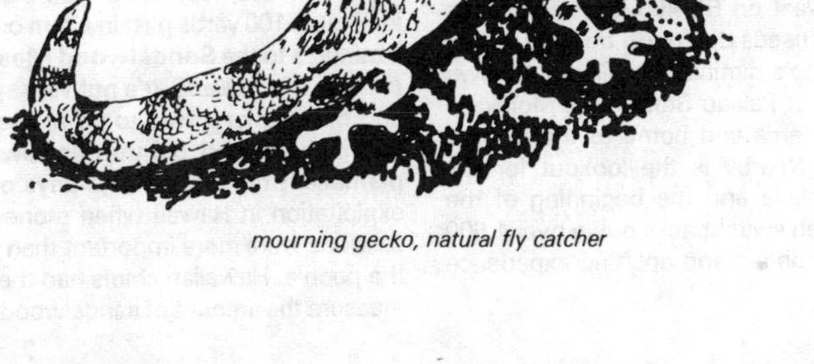

mourning gecko, natural fly catcher

CENTRAL MOLOKAI AND KALAUPAPA

As you head west from Kaunakakai on Rt. 460 toward Molokai Airport you pass fields planted in various crops. These are Molokai's attempt at diversified agriculture since the demise of pineapple a few years ago. Iowa-like corn fields make it obvious that the experiment is working well and has a chance, if the large corporations and the state government get behind it. The cultivated fields give way to hundreds of acres filled with skeletons of dead trees. It's as if some eerie specter stalked the land and devoured their spirits. Farther along, the **Main Forest Road** intersects, posted for 4WD vehicles but navigable in a standard car during dry weather. This track leads to the Sandalwood Measuring Pit, a depression in the ground, which is a permanent reminder of the furious and foolhardy trading of last century. Here too along little-used trails are spectacular views of the lost valleys of Molokai's inaccessible northeast shore. West on Rt. 460, another branch road, Rt. 470, heads due north through Kualapuu, Del Monte's diminishing pineapple town to road's end at Palaau State Park, Molokai's best camping area and home to the famous Phallic Rock. Nearby is the lookout for Kalaupapa Peninsula and the beginning of the mule trail which switchbacks down over 1,600 feet to the humbling and uplifting experience of Kalaupapa.

Main Forest Road

After mile marker 3, west on Rt. 460 from Kaunakakai, is a bridge (just past the Seventh Day Adventist Church) with a white fence on both sides. There, heading into the mountains, is a red dirt road called Main Forest or Maunahui Road. Your car rental agency will tell you that this road is impassable except in a 4WD, and they're right—if it's raining! Follow the rutted road up into the hills and you'll soon be in a deep forest of *ohia,* pine, eucalyptus, and giant ferns thriving since they were planted early this century. The cool, pleasant air mixes pleasantly with rich earthy smells of the forest. In just under 6 miles a sign says "Main Forest Road." If you miss this sign look for a Boy Scout Camp (also under 6 miles) that'll let you know that you're on the right road. Ignore many small roads branching off.

After 10 miles, look for a road sign "Kamiloloa," park 100 yards past in a turn out and walk 5 minutes to the **Sandalwood Measuring Pit** *(Lua Na Moku Iliahi).* It's not very spectacular, and this is a long way to go to see a shallow hole in the ground, but the Sandalwood Pit is a permanent reminder of the days of mindless exploitation in Hawaii when money and possessions were more important than the land or the people. Hawaiian chiefs had the pit dug to measure the amount of sandalwood necessary to fill the hold of a ship. They traded the aromatic wood to Yankee captains for baubles, whiskey, guns, manufactured goods, and tools. The traders carried the wood to China where they made huge profits. The trading was so lucrative that the men of entire villages were forced into the hills to collect it, even to the point where the *taro* fields were neglected and famine gnawed at the door. It only took a few years to denude the mountains of their copious stands of sandalwood, even more incredible when you consider that all the work was done by hand and all the wood was carried to the waiting ships on the coast using the *makaainana* as beasts of burden.

Travel past the Sandalwood Pit for about one mile and you'll come to **Waikolu Overlook** ("Three Waters"). From here you can peer down into this pristine valley 3,700 feet below. If rains have been recent, hundreds of waterfalls spread their lace as they fall to the green jungle. The water here seeps into the ground, which soaks it up like a huge dripping sponge. A water tunnel, bored into the valley, collects the water and conducts it for more than 5 miles until it reaches the 1.4 billion gallon Kualapu'u Reservoir. Only drive to this area on a clear day, because the rain will not only get you stuck in mud, but also obscure your view with heavy cloud cover.

Hiking trails through this area are poorly marked, poorly maintained, and strenuous—great qualifications for those who crave solitude and adventure. Up-to-the-minute information and maps are available from Dept. of Land and Natural Resources in Kaunakakai, tel. 567-6618. **Hanalilolilo Trail** begins not far from Waikolu Lookout and tramps through high mountain forests of *ohia* until it comes to a breathtaking view of **Pelekunu Valley** ("Foul Smelling, No Sunshine"). Don't let the name fool you. Hawaiians lived happily and well in this remote, north shore valley for centuries. Time, aided by wind and rain, has turned the 4,000-foot sea cliffs of Pelekunu into the tallest in the world. Today, Pelekunu is more remote and isolated than ever. No permanent residents, islanders come sporadically to camp, and only in the summer when the waters are calm enough to land.

East from this area is the 2,774-acre **Kamakou Preserve**, established by the Nature Conservancy of Hawaii in 1982. It seeks to preserve this unique forest area, home to 5 species of endangered Hawaiian birds, 2 of which are endemic only to Molokai. There are 250 species of Hawaiian plants and ferns, 219 of which grow nowhere else in the world. Even a few clusters of sandalwoods tenaciously try to make a comeback. The land was donated by the Molokai Ranch, but they kept control of the water rights. Two officials of the ranch are on the Conservancy board which causes some people to look suspiciously at their motives. The Kamakou Preserve manager is Ed Misaki. Most trails have been mapped and hunting is encouraged througout the area.

Palaau State Park

Proceed west from Kaunakakai on Rt. 460 for 4 miles until it intersects Rt. 470 heading north to Kualapuu and Palaau State Park. As you pass Del Monte Headquarters in Kualapuu look left

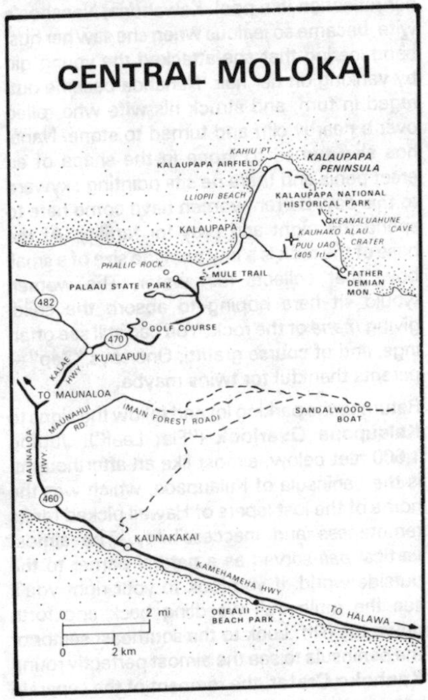

to see the world's largest rubber lined reservoir. The town itself is withering, and has no amenities or stores. A few minutes past Kualapuu are the stables for Molokai Mule Rides which take you down to Kalaupapa. Even if you're not planning a mule ride (see below), make sure to stop and check out the beauty of the countryside surrounding the mule stables. Follow the road until it ends at a parking lot for Palaau State Park.

In the lot, 2 signs direct you to the Phallic Rock and to the Kalaupapa Overlook (which is not the beginning of the trail down to the peninsula). Palaau State Park is the best camping on Molokai although it's quite a distance from the beach (see p. 499). Follow the signs from the parking lot for about 200 yards to **Phallic Rock** ("Kauleomamahoa"). Nanahoa, the male fertility god inhabiting the anatomical rock, has been performing like a champ and hasn't had a "headache" in centuries. Legend says that Nanahoa lived nearby and one day sat to admire a beautiful young girl who was looking at her reflection in a pool. Kawahuna, Nanahoa's wife, became so jealous when she saw her husband leering that she attacked the young girl by yanking on her hair. Nanahoa became outraged in turn, and struck his wife who rolled over a nearby cliff and turned to stone. Nanahoa also turned to stone in the shape of an erect penis and there he sits pointing skyward to this day. Barren women have come here to spend the night and pray for fertility. At the base of the rock is a tiny pool the size of a small bowl that collects rain water. The women would sit here hoping to absorb the child-giving *mana* of the rock. You can still see offerings, and of course grafitti. One says "Zap"—parents thankful for twins maybe.

Return to the parking lot and follow the signs to **Kalaupapa Overlook** ("Flat Leaf"). Jutting 1,600 feet below, almost like an afterthought, is the peninsula of Kalaupapa, which was the home of the lost lepers of Hawaii picked for its remoteness and inaccessibility. The almost vertical *pali* served as a natural barrier to the outside world. If you look to your right you'll see the mule trail weedling back and forth down the cliff. Look to the southeast sector of the peninsula to see the almost perfectly round **Kauhako Crater**, the remnant of the separate volcano that formed Kalaupapa.

THE KALAUPAPA EXPERIENCE

No one knew how the dreaded disease came to the Hawaiian Islands, but they did know that if you were contaminated by it your life would be misery. Leprosy has caused fear in the hearts of man since biblical times, and last century King Kamehameha V and his advisers were no exception. All they knew was that lepers had to be isolated. Kalawao Cove, on the southeast shore of Kalaupapa Peninsula, was regarded as *the* most isolated spot in the entire kingdom. So it was to Kalawao that the lepers of Hawaii were sent to die. Through crude diagnostic testings, anyone who had a suspicious skin discoloration, ulcer, or even bad sunburn was rounded up and sent to Kalawao. The islanders soon learned that once sent, there was no return. So the afflicted hid. Bounty hunters roamed the countryside. Babies, toddlers, teenagers, wives, grandfathers—none were immune to the bounty hunters. They hounded, captured, and sometimes killed anyone that had any sort of skin ailment. The captives were ripped from their villages and loaded on a ship. No one would come near the suspected lepers on board and they sat open to the elements in a cage. They were allowed only one small tin box of possessions. As the ship anchored in the always choppy bay at Kalawao, the cage was opened and the victims were tossed overboard. Their contaminated cage followed along with a few sealed barrels of food and clothing that had been collected by merciful Christians. Those too weak or sick or young drowned. The unlucky made it to shore. The crew waited nervously with loaded muskets in case any of the howling, walking nightmares on shore attempted in their delirium to board the ship.

Hell On Earth

Waiting for the newcomers were the forsaken. Abandoned by king, country, family, friends, and apparently the Lord himself, they became animals—beasts of prey. Young girls with hardly a blemish were raped by reeking deformed men in rags. Old men were bludgeoned, their tin boxes ripped from their hands. Children and babies cried and begged for food, turning instinctually to the demented women who had lost all motherly feelings. Finally too weak even to whimper they died of starvation. Those victims that could made rude dwellings of sticks and stones, while others lived in caves or on the beach open to the elements. Finally, the conscience of the kingdom was stirred in 1866: the old dumping ground of Kalawao was abandoned and the lepers were exiled to the more hospitable Kalaupapa Peninsula, just a few hundred yards to the west.

The Move To Kalaupapa

The people of the sleepy village of Kalaupapa couldn't believe their eyes when they saw the ravaged ones. But these lepers now sent to Kalaupapa were treated more mercifully. Missionary groups and *kokua* ("helpers") provided food and rudimentary clothing. An end was put to the lawlessness and depravity. Still, the lepers were kept separate. For the most part they lived outdoors or in very rude huts. They never could come in direct contact with the *kokua.* If they met a healthy person walking along a path, they had to grovel at the side. Most fell to the ground, hiding their faces and attempting to crawl like beaten dogs under a bush. Many *kokua* horrified by Kalaupapa left on the next available boat. With no medical attention, death was still the only release from Kalaupapa.

Father Damien just weeks before his death from Hansen's Disease

Light In Hell

It was by accident or miracle that **Joseph Damien de Veuster,** a Catholic priest, came from Belgium to Hawaii. His brother, also a priest, was supposed to come but he became ill and Father Damien came in his place. Damien spent a few years in Hawaii, building churches and learning the language and ways of the people, before he came to Kalaupapa in 1873. What he saw touched his heart. He was different from the rest, having come with a sense of mission to help the lepers and determined to bring them hope and dignity. The other missionaries saw Kalaupapa as a place not to live, but to die. Damien saw the lepers as children of God, who had the right to live and be comforted. When they hid under a bush at his approach, he picked them up and stood them on their feet. He carried water all day long to the sick and dying. He bathed their wounds and built them shelters with his own 2 hands. When clothes or food or materials ran short, he walked topside and begged for more. Other church groups were against him and the government gave him little aid, but he persevered. Damien scraped together some lumber and fashioned a flume pipe to carry water to his people who were still dying mainly from pneumonia and tuberculosis brought on by neglect. Damien worked alone, long days until he dropped exhausted at night.

Father Damien built **St. Philomena** church and invited the lepers inside. Those grossly afflicted could not control their mouths, so spittle would drip to the floor. They were ashamed to soil the church, so Damien cut squares in the floor through which they could spit onto the ground. Slowly a light began to shine in the hearts of the lepers and the authorities began to take notice. Conditions began to improve, but there were those that resented Damien. Robert Louis Stevenson visited the settlement, and after meeting Damien wrote an open letter that ended "...he is my father." Damien contracted leprosy, but by the time he died in 1889 at the age 49, he knew his people would be cared for. In 1936, Damien's native Belgium asked that his remains be returned. He was exhumed and his remains sent home, but a memorial still stands where he was entered at Kalaupapa.

The Light Grows Brighter

Mother Mary Ann Cope, a Franciscan nun from Syracuse, N.Y., arrived in 1888 to carry on the work. In addition, many missionary groups sent volunteers to help at the colony. Thereafter the people of Kalaupapa were treated with dignity and given a sense of hope. In 1873, the same year that Damien arrived at Kalaupapa, Norwegian physician Gerhard Hansen isolated the bacteria that causes leprosy, and shortly thereafter the official name of the malady became Hansen's Disease. By the turn of this century, adequate medical care and good living conditions were provided to the patients at Kalaupapa. Still, many died, mostly from complications such as TB or pneumonia. Families could not visit members confined to Kalaupapa unless they were near death, and any children born to the patients who were now starting to marry were whisked away at birth and adopted, or given to family members on the outside. Even until the 1940s people were still sent to Kalaupapa because of skin ailments that were never really diagnosed as leprosy. Many of these indeed did show signs of the disease, but there is always the haunting thought that they contracted it after arrival at the colony. Jimmy, one of the guides for Damien Tours, was one of these. He had some white spots as a child that his Hawaiian grandmother would treat with herbs. As soon as she stopped applying the herbs, the spots would return. A public health nurse at school saw the spots, and Jimmy was sent to Kalaupapa. At the time he was given only 10 years to live. In the mid 1940s sulfone drugs were found to arrest most cases of Hansen's Disease, and the prognosis for a normal life improved. By the 1960s further breakthroughs made Hansen's Disease non-contagious, and the patients at Kalaupapa were free to leave and return to their homes. No new patients were admitted, but most already living in the only home they'd ever known opted to stay. The community of patient residents is less than 100 today, and the average age is about 60. Kalaupapa will be turned into a national park soon, but the residents are assured a lifetime occupancy.

Getting There

It shouldn't be a matter of *if* you go to Kalaupapa, but *how* you go. You have choices. You can fly, ride a mule, walk, or walk and fly. No matter how you go you **can not** walk around Kalaupapa unescorted. You must take an official tour and children under 16 are not allowed. If you're going by mule or air, arrangements are made for you by the companies, but if you're walking you have to call ahead to one of the following who will make arrangements to meet you at the entrance to the community. Contact **Damien Tours,** tel. 567-6171, or **Ike's Scenic Tours,** tel. 567-6437. Both tour companies charge $15 for a fascinating, 4-hour tour conducted by one of the patients. Definitely worth the money, the insight you get from the patient-tour guide is priceless and unique. No food or beverages,

the simple interior of St. Philomena's Church

except water, are available to visitors, so make sure to bring your own.

Molokai Mule Rides, tel. 526-0888, rents mules to take you down the 1,600-foot *pali* for $50 including the tour of Kalaupapa. The mules are sure-footed, well-trained animals which expertly negotiate 26 hairpin switchbacks on the trail to the bottom. Restrictions say riders must weigh under 225 pounds, and be in generally good physical condition. The stables are clearly marked on Rt. 470.

If you're walking to Kalaupapa, follow the mule trail down, cut by Manuel Farinha in 1886. Go past the stables and look for a road to the right. At the trailhead is a small metal building with an odd sign that reads "Advance Technology Center Hawaii USA." The mules leave by 9:00 a.m., so make sure you go ahead of them! The trail is well maintained and only mildly strenuous. It could be muddy in spots but you'll notice gravel all the way down that is carried by the bagful, and deposited daily by the mules. While on the subject, be careful of *other* mule deposits as you walk along. It takes just about an hour and a half to make the descent. Once down wait at the beginning of the paved road near the Lion's International sign. Your tour guide will pick you up there.

You can fly in and out, or out only which is a good alternative and relatively cheap. Air Molokai, tel. 536-6611 or 800-352-3616, offers RT for $25 or $15 OW. Polynesian Air, tel. 567-6697, which is a delight, offers RT for $25 or $12 OW. More expensive flights are offered from the other islands by Reeves Air from Honolulu, tel.553-3803. Hawaiian Air, tel. 553-5321, Oahu 537-5100, or 800-367-5320, has a package for $135 which includes RT from Honolulu, the mule ride, lunch, and the Kalaupapa tour. Papillon Helicopters, tel. 669-4884, flies into Kalauapapa from Maui. If you decide to fly notice the breakers at the end of the runway sending spray 90 feet into the air. The pilots time their take-off to miss the spray!

Jimmy (center) makes guests feel at home as they break for lunch in his lovely flower garden.

Moomomi Beach Road

MOLOKAI'S WEST END

Long before contact with the Europeans, the west end of Molokai was famous throughout the Hawaiian Islands. The culture centered around Maunaloa, the ancient volcanic mountain that formed the land. On its slopes the goddess Laka learned the *hula* from her sister and spread its joyous undulations to all the other islands. Not far from the birthplace of the *hula* is Kaluakoi, one of the two most important adze quarries in old Hawaii. Without these stone tools, no canoes, bowls, or everyday items could have been fashioned. Voyagers came from every major island to trade for this perfect stone of Kaluakoi. With all this coming and going, the always small population of Molokai needed godly protection. Not far away at Kalaipahoa, the "poison wood" sorcery gods of Molokai lived in a grove that supposedly sprouted to maturity in one night. With talismans made from this magical grove, Molokai kept invading warriors at bay for centuries.

Most of the island's arable land is out here. The thrust west began with the founding of the Molokai Ranch, whose 70,000 acres make up 50% of the good farmland on the island. The ranch was owned last century by Kamehameha V, and after his death was sold to private interests who began the successful raising of Santa Gertrudis cattle imported from the famous Texas King Ranch. The ranch still employs *paniolo,* with the life of riding the range and rodeo still strong.

The Northwest

The northwest section of Molokai, centered around **Hoolehua,** is where the Hawaiian Homes parcels are located. The entire area has a feeling of heartland America, and if you ignore the coastline in the background you could easily imagine yourself in the rolling hills of Missouri. Don't expect a town at Hoolehua. All that's there is a little post office and a building or two.

The real destination is **Moomomi Beach** ("Jewelled Reptile"). Follow Rt. 460 until it branches north at Rt. 480 a mile east of the airport. Follow Rt. 480 until it turns left onto Farrington Highway in Hoolehua, and past for about 4 miles until it turns into a red dirt road. Go for about 5 minutes, bearing right at the main intersection until you come to an area where a foundation remains of a burned bath house. Below you is Moomomi. This area is a favorite with local people who come here to swim, fish, and surf. The swells are good only in winter, but the beach becomes rocky at this time of year. The tides bring the sand in by April and the swimming until November is good. Moomomi Beach goes back in Hawaiian legend. Besides the mythical lizards that inhabited this area, a great shark god was born here. The mother was a woman that became impregnated by the gods. Her husband was angry that her child would be from the spirit world so he directed her to come and sit on a large rock down by the beach. She went into labor and began to cry. A tear, holding a tiny fish, rolled down her cheek and fell into the sea. He became a powerful shark god and the rock upon which his mother sat is the large black one just to the right of the beach.

If you feel adventurous you can head west along the beach. Every 10 minutes or so you come to a tiny beach that you have entirely to yourself. Being so isolated, be extremely careful of surf conditions. About 2 miles west of Moomomi is **Keonelele,** a miniature desert of sand dunes. The wind whips through this region and carries the sand to the southwest shore. Geologists haunt this area trying to piece together Molokai's geological history. The Hawaiians used Keonelele as a burial site, and strange footprints found in the soft sandstone supposedly foretold the coming of white men. Today, Keonelele is totally deserted; although small, it gives the impression of a vast wasteland. Camping (no permit necessary) is allowed on the grassy area overlooking Moomomi Beach, but since a fire claimed the bath house, there are no showers or toilets. Water is available from a tap near the old foundation. You will be personally safe camping here, but if you leave gear unattended it could walk off.

Kawakiu Beach

This secluded and pristine beach on the far northwestern corner of Molokai was an item of controversy between the developers of the Kaluakoi Corporation and the grass-roots activists of Molokai. For years access to the beach was restricted, and the Kaluakoi Corp. planned to develop the area. It was known that the area was very important during pre-contact times, and rich in unexplored archaeological sites. The Kaluakoi Corp. hired a supposed "team" of experts that studied the site for months, and finally claimed that the area had no significant

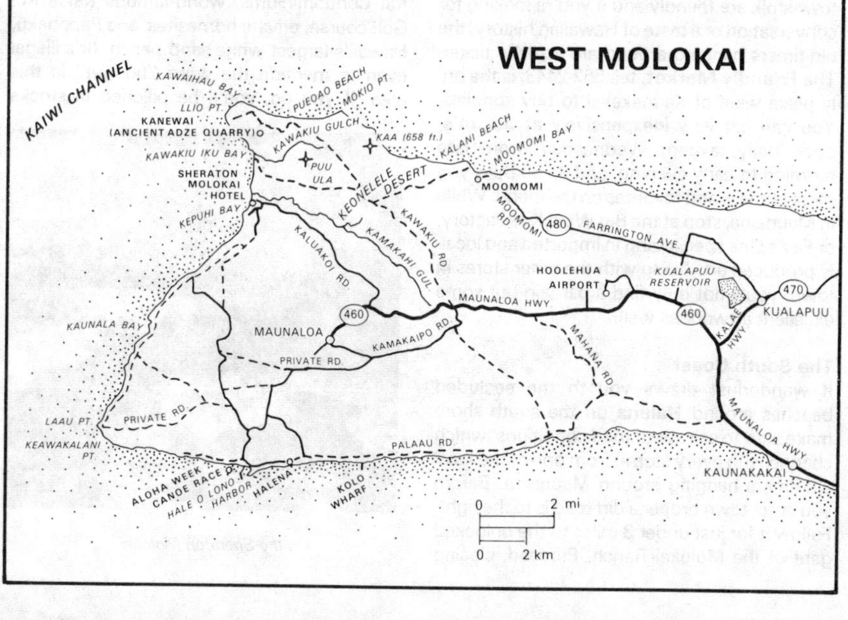

archaeological importance. Their findings were hooted at by local people and by scholars from various institutions that knew better. This controversy resulted in the Kawakiu Beach being open to the public with plans of turning it into a beach park along with the preservation of the archaeological sites. The swimming here is excellent with the sandy bottom tapering off slowly. Camping is permitted in the large grove of trees from Fri. to Sun. with permission from the Molokai Ranch. To get there, keep your eyes peeled as you follow Rt. 460 past the airport for about 4 miles, and spot a small sign on the right that says "Right of way to beach." The 7 miles of dirt road from here are dusty and not well maintained, but passable at most times. Just before you reach Kawakiu the road branches—go right to the beach.

Maunaloa Town

Most people heading east-west between Kaunakakai and the Molokai Sheraton never make it into Maunaloa Town. That's because Rt. 460 splits just east of Maunaloa, and Kaluakoi Road heads north toward the Sheraton and away from the town. With the pineapple gone and few visitors coming, the town is dying. The townsfolk are friendly and if you're looking for conversation or a taste of Hawaiian history, the old-timers hanging around are just the ticket. The **Friendly Market**, tel. 552-2443, is the only place west of Kaunakakai to buy supplies. You can eat very inexpensively at **Jo Jo's**, open daily, except Wednesday, from late morning to early evening, and $3.50 buys you most of the island favorites on the menu. While in Maunaloa, stop at the Big Wind Kite Factory, or Fay's One specializing in imported and locally produced art. Along with the other stores in town, you'll not only find a bargain but some excellent artwork as well.

The South Coast

If wanderlust draws you to the secluded beaches around **Halena** on the south shore make sure to ask about road conditions (which change with every storm) from one of the local old-timers hanging around Maunaloa. Before you enter town proper a dirt road is to the right. Follow it for just under 3 miles to the unlocked gate of the Molokai Ranch. Proceed, closing the gate behind you, and bounce and rattle down the road for just under 2 miles. At the fork, go right and then almost immediately left. Follow the road to the end and then walk a few hundred yards to Halena. You'll have the entire area and shoreline to yourself. There's no official camping here, but no one will bother you. Obviously bring all the food and water you'll require. If you go west from Halena, you'll come to **Hale o Lono** in about one mile, the launch point for the annual outrigger canoe race to Oahu. There's an old harbor area from which sand from Papohaku Beach was shipped to Oahu for building purposes. If you go east, back at the fork to Halena, you'll come to the dilapidated **Kolo Wharf** (2 miles) from which Molokai once shipped its pineapples. The road is even more remote and rougher, so getting stuck will mean a long hike out and an astronomical towing charge. It's best to walk from Halena along the coast.

The Kaluakoi Resort And West End

This entire west end of Molokai is designated as the Kaluakoi Resort, owned by the Louisiana Land and Exploration Company. The complex includes the Sheraton Molokai Hotel, Ke Nai Kai Condominiums, world-famous Kalua Koi Golf course, private homesites, and Papohaku, Hawaii's largest white-sand beach. (It's illegal even to mention the word "budget" in this area. If you do, you'll be pilloried in stocks

the Sheraton Molokai

Papohaku Beach fronting the Sheraton looks across the Kaiwi Channel to the bright lights of Honolulu.

made from melted credit cards and lashed with a Gucci whip!)

Accommodations And Restaurants

The **Sheraton Molokai** is a showcase hotel and the destination point for most of the people coming to Molokai. The low-rise buildings are made primarily of wood. The architecture is superb and blends harmoniously with the surrounding countryside. The grounds are impeccable and all the trees and shrubbery are labelled to provide a miniature botanical tour. All rooms have color TVs, refrigerators, and those on the second floor have open-beam construction. Most rooms have at least a partial ocean view and because of the constant cool breezes, no air conditioning is provided or necessary. There are ceiling fans, however. Actually, for a first-class hotel the rates aren't bad. The least expensive room is $90-125 d, and includes green fees at the Kalua Koi Golf Course. The rates go up to $175 for an Ocean Cottage Suite, but many hotels on the other islands get a lot more for a lot less. Lighted tennis courts are free to guests (free clinics Tues., Fri., Sat.) as well as bicycles for rent. A small Liberty House provides limited shopping along with a sundries store selling snacks, magazines, and liquor. Also, notice the hotel's only swimming pool. It's tiled with black tiles. People think that it's to hold the heat, but actually it was a whim of one of the owners, whose wife's favorite color is black. For information write Sheraton Molokai Hotel, Box 1977, Maunaloa, HI 96770, tel. 552-2555 or 800-325-3535

The Sheraton's **Ohia Lodge**, is the best restaurant on the island. They serve a complete seafood dinner for about $16.00, rack of lamb $17, spaghetti calamari $8.50. Soups and salads are quite reasonable under $5, but the best value is the buffet served every Fri. and Sat. for $15.95. The other hotel restaurant is the less pretentious **Paniolo Broiler.** The motif is cowboy, complete with corral, cactus, branding irons, and saddles. The best value is the salad bar for $9.95, but steaks, chops, and lamb for around $17 are the specialties. A poolside snack bar is handy but expensive.

Ke Nani Kai Condos are *mauka* of the road leading to the Sheraton and they charge from $65-$85 for one of their fully furnished studios; 2 bedrooms from $85-$105. The complex is new so all studios are in excellent condition. Write Ke Nani Kai, Box 126, Molokai, HI 96770, tel. 552-2761 or 800-367-7040.

Paniolo Hale is another condo complex nearby. Studios start at $75 d, $95 one bedroom, $115 2 bedroom. Two-bedroom units have hot tubs and enclosed *lanai.* Guests of the Paniolo Hale can use the Sheraton's tennis courts for a small fee. Write Paniolo Hale, Box 146, Molokai, HI 96770, tel. 552-3731 or 800-367-2984.

Excursions And Attractions

The **Molokai Ranch Wildlife Park** is a one-square-mile preserve on the ranch lands, open to the public, which houses over 400 grazing animals from Africa and India. Among the exotic occupants are giraffe, kudu, ibyx, antelope, and ostrich that have lost their fear of man and can be seen from very close quarters. The environment and grazing of west Molokai is almost identical to the animals' home in East Africa; because of this and the exemplary care afforded by the caretaker, Pilipo Solotario, the Wildlife Park has one of the best reputations in the world. Tours depart from the Sheraton, Mon. through Sat. approximately every 2 hours beginning at 8:00 a.m. with the last at 4:30 p.m. The tour costs $12 for adults and $6 for children under 12. For information call 552-2555 or 552-2376.

Papohaku Beach, the best attraction in the area, doesn't have a price tag. Papohaku Beach is the giant expanse of white sand in front of and running south from the Sheraton. The sands here are so expansive that they were dredged and taken to Oahu in the 1950s. During the winter months a great deal of sand is stripped away and large lava boulders and outcroppings are exposed. Every spring and summer the tides carry the sand back and deposit it on the enormous beach.

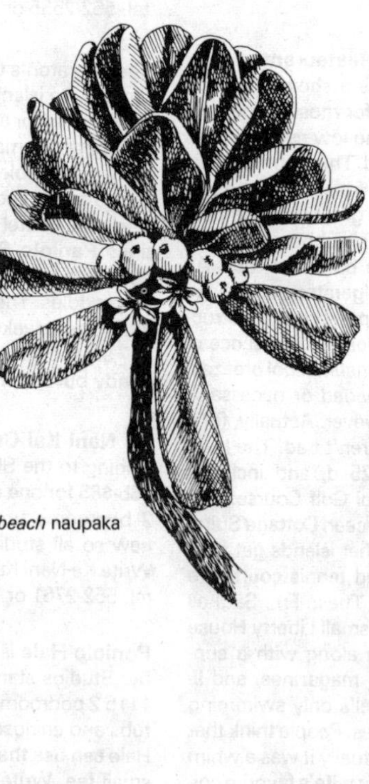

beach naupaka

John Webber, c. 1779
(Hawaii State Archives)

HAWAII

INTRODUCTION

The island of Hawaii is grand in so many ways. Nicknamed "The Orchid Island" and "The Volcano Island," both are excellent choices: it produces more of these delicate blooms than anywhere else on earth; and Pele, the fire goddess, makes her mythological home here, where she regularly sends rivers of lava from the world's largest and most active volcanoes. But Hawaii has only one real nickname to the people who live there, "the Big Island." Big isn't necessarily better, but when you combine it with beautiful, uncrowded, traditional, and inexpensive, it's hard to beat. The Big Island was first to be inhabited by the Polynesian settlers, yet it's geologically the youngest of the Hawaiian Islands at barely a million years old. Like all the islands in the Hawaiian chain, it's a mini-continent, whose geographical demarcations are made much more apparent because of its size. There are parched deserts, steaming fissures, jet-black sand beaches, raw semi-cooled lava flows, snow-covered mountains, entire forests encased in hardened stone, and lush valleys where countless waterfalls break through the rock faces of 1,000-foot-tall chasms. There are small working villages that time has passed by, the state's most tropical city, and an entire arid coast stretching over 90 miles where the sun is guaranteed to shine. You'll find some of the islands' least expensive accommodations, as well as 4 of the world's most exclusive resorts. Historically, the Big Island is loaded with religious upheavals, the births and deaths of great men, vintage missionary homes and churches, reconstructed *heiau,* and even a royal palace. Here is the country's largest privately owned ranch where cowboy life is the norm, America's only coffee plantations, and enclaves of the counter-culture where alternative people are still trying to keep the faith of the '60s. Sportsmen love it here, too. The Big Island is a mecca for tri-athletes, and offers snow skiing in season, plenty of camping and hiking, and the best marlin waters in all the oceans of the world. There are direct flights to the Big Island, where the fascination of perhaps not "old" Hawaii, but definitely "simple" Hawaii, still lingers.

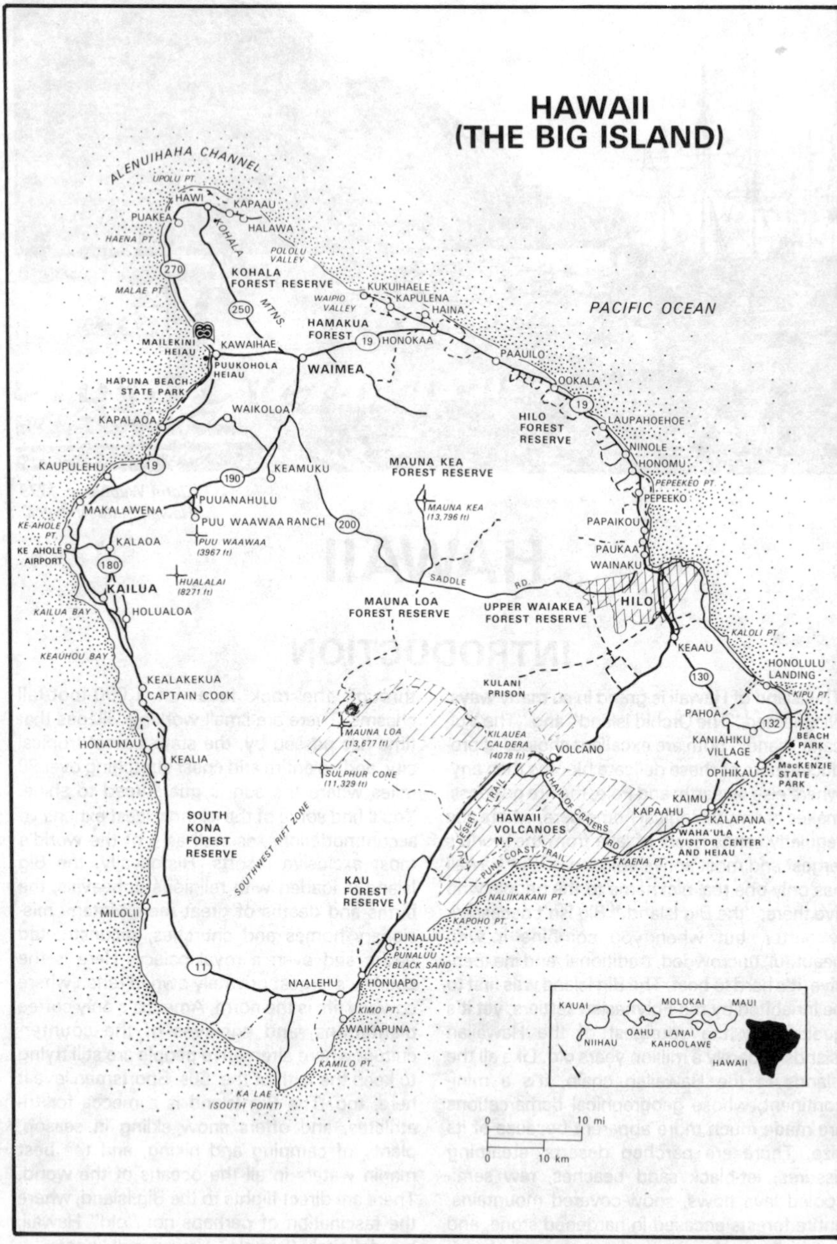
HAWAII
(THE BIG ISLAND)
ALENUIHAHA CHANNEL
UPOLU PT.
HAWI
KAPAAU
PUAKEA
HALAWA
HAENA PT.
KOHALA
POLOLU VALLEY
270
KOHALA FOREST RESERVE
MALAE PT.
KUKUIHAELE
WAIPIO VALLEY
KAPULENA
HAINA
PACIFIC OCEAN
250
MTNS.
HAMAKUA FOREST
MAILEKINI HEIAU
KAWAIHAE
19
HONOKAA
PUUKOHOLA HEIAU
WAIMEA
PAAUILO
HAPUNA BEACH STATE PARK
OOKALA
WAIKOLOA
19
KAPALAOA
HILO FOREST RESERVE
LAUPAHOEHOE
NINOLE
KAUPULEHU
19
KEAMUKU
MAUNA KEA FOREST RESERVE
HONOMU
190
PEPEEKEO PT.
MAKALAWENA
PUUANAHULU
PEPEEKO
MAUNA KEA (13,796 ft)
KE-AHOLE PT.
PUU WAAWAA RANCH
200
PAPAIKOU
KE AHOLE AIRPORT
KALAOA
PUU WAAWAA (3967 ft)
PAUKAA
180
WAINAKU
HUALALAI (8271 ft)
SADDLE RD.
KAILUA
HILO
KAILUA BAY
HOLUALOA
MAUNA LOA FOREST RESERVE
UPPER WAIAKEA FOREST RESERVE
KALOLI PT.
KEAUHOU BAY
KEAAU
HONOLULU LANDING
KEALAKEKUA
KULANI PRISON
130
CAPTAIN COOK
KIPU PT.
PAHOA
132
MAUNA LOA (13,677 ft)
KILAUEA CALDERA (4078 ft)
HONAUNAU
BEACH PARK
KANIAHIKU VILLAGE
KEALIA
VOLCANO
MacKENZIE STATE PARK
SULPHUR CONE (11,329 ft)
OPIHIKAU
CHAIN OF CRATERS RD.
KAU DESERT TRAIL
KAIMU
SOUTH KONA FOREST RESERVE
HAWAII VOLCANOES N.P.
KAPAAHU
KALAPANA
SOUTHWEST RIFT ZONE
WAHA'ULA VISITOR CENTER AND HEIAU
PUNA COAST TRAIL
KAENA PT.
KAU FOREST RESERVE
NALIIKAKANI PT.
MILOLII
KAPOHO PT.
PUNALUU
PUNALUU BLACK SAND
11
NAALEHU
HONUAPO
KIMO PT.
KAUAI
MOLOKAI
MAUI
WAIKAPUNA
NIIHAU
OAHU
LANAI
KAHOOLAWE
HAWAII
KAMILO PT.
KA LAE (SOUTH POINT)
0
10 mi
0
10 km

OVERVIEW

Hilo on the east coast and Kailua-Kona on the west are the 2 ports of entry to the Big Island. At opposite ends of the island as well as the cultural spectrum, a friendly rivalry exists between the two. It doesn't matter at which one you arrive, because a trip to the Big Island without visiting both is unthinkable. Better yet, split your stay and use each as a base while you tour. Hawaii is the only island big enough that you can't drive around it comfortably in one day, nor should you even try. Split into 6 districts, each is interesting enough to spend at least one day exploring.

Hilo And Vicinity

Hilo is the oldest port of entry, the most tropical town in Hawaii, and the only major city built on a windward coast. Hilo is one tremendous greenhouse where exotic flowers and tropical plants are a normal part of the landscape, and entire city blocks canopied by adjoining banyans are taken for granted. The town, which hosts the yearly Merry Monarch Festival, boasts an early-morning fish market, Japanese gardens, the Lyman House Museum, and a profusion of natural phenomena including Rainbow Falls and Boiling Pots. Plenty of rooms in Hilo are generally easily available, and its variety of restaurants will titillate anyone's taste buds. Both go easy on the pocketbook while maintaining high standards.

Saddle Road begins just outside of Hilo. It slices directly across the island through a most astonishing high valley or "saddle" separating the mountains of Mauna Loa and Mauna Kea. A passable road, the bane of car rental companies, heads 13,796 feet straight to the top of Mauna Kea, where a series of astronomical observatories, like giant mushrooms, peer into the heavens through the clearest air on Earth.

Northeast

Hamakua refers to the entire northeast coast where streams, wind, and pounding surf have chiselled the lava into towering cliffs and precipitous valleys known locally by the unromantic name of "gulches." All the flat lands here are awash in a green sea of sugarcane. A spur road from the forgotten town of Honomu leads to Akaka Falls, whose waters tumble over a 442-foot cliff, making them the highest sheer drop of water in Hawaii. North along the coastal road is Honokaa, a one-street town of stores, restaurants, and craft shops. The main road bears left here to the cowboy town of Waimea, but a smaller road inches farther north. It dead ends at the top of Waipio Valley, cradled by cliffs on 3 sides with its mouth wide open to the sea. The valley is reachable only by foot, 4WD vehicle, or on horseback. On its verdant floor a handful of families live simply by raising taro, a few head of cattle, and some horses. Waipio was a burial ground of Hawaiian *ali'i,* where *kahuna* traditionally came to commune with spirits. The enchantment of this "power spot" remains.

Southeast

Puna lies south of Hilo and makes up the majority of the southeast coast. Here are the greatest lava fields that have spewed from Kilauea, the heart of Volcanoes National Park. An ancient flow embraced a forest in its fiery grasp, entombing trees that stand like sentinels which are seen today in Lava Tree State Monument. Cape Kumukahi, a pointed lava flow that reached the ocean in 1868, is officially the easternmost point in Hawaii. Just below is a string of beaches featuring ebony-black sand. Past the small village of Kapaahu, the road skirts the coast before heading inland along Chain of Craters Road to Volcanoes National Park. En route, it passes Wahaula Visitor Center and Heiau, where human sacrifice was introduced to the islands. Chain of Craters Road continues upward through a forbidding, yet vibrant, wasteland of old lava flows until it comes to the Visitors Center atop Kilauea, where this living volcano fumes and throbs. From here miles of hiking trails crisscross the park and lead to the very top of Mauna Loa. You can view the natural phenomena of steaming fissures, boiling mud, Devastation Trail, and the Thurston Lava Tube, large enough to accommodate a subway train. Here, too, you can lodge or dine at Volcano House, a venerable inn carved into the rim of the crater.

Kau, the southern tip of the island, is primarily a desert. On well-marked trails leading left and right from the main road you'll discover ancient petroglyphs, and an eerie set of footprints, the remnants of an ill-fated band of warriors smothered under the moist ash of a volcanic eruption, whose demise marked the ascendancy of Kamehameha the Great. Here are some lovely beaches and state parks you'll have virtually to yourself. A tiny road leads to Ka Lae ("South Point"), the most southerly piece of ground in the United States.

Kona

Kona, the west coast, is in every way the opposite of Hilo. It's dry, sunny, and brilliant, with large expanses of old barren lava flows. When watered the rich soil blossoms, as in South Kona, renowned for its diminutive coffee plantations. The town of Captain Cook, named after the intrepid Pacific explorer, lies just above the very beach where he was slain because of a terrible case of miscommunication 2 centuries ago. Ironically, nearby is the restored *Puuhonua o Honaunau Heiau*, where mercy and forgiveness were rendered to any *kapu*-breaker or vanquished warrior who made it into the confines of this safe refuge. Kailua, a nice town without a center, is nonetheless the center of Kona, with Keahole airport just north of town. The town itself boasts an array of art and designer shops; world-class triathletes come here to train, and charter boats depart in search of marlin. Within Kailua is Mokuaikuaa Church, a legacy of the very first packet of missionaries to arrive in the islands, and Hulihee Palace, a vacation home of the Kamehameha line of kings.

Northward, the Kona District offers a string of beaches. Just outside Kailua is a nude beach, one of a very few in Hawaii, and farther up the coast is Hapuna Beach, best on the island. In 1965, Lawrence Rockefeller opened the Mauna Kea Resort here. For the last 2 decades, this resort along with its sculptured coast-hugging golf course, has been considered one of the finest in the world. Just south is the Kona Village Resort, whose guests arrive at a private airstrip and spend $300 per night for a "simple" grass shack on the beach. Its serenity is broken only by the soothing music of the surf, and the not-so-melodious singing of "Kona nightingales," a pampered herd of wild donkeys that frequent this area.

North

Kohala is primarily the peninsular thumb on the northern extremity of the island, although it does dip south along the coast and eastward into rolling hills. At its base is Waimea (Kamuela), center of the enormous Parker Ranch. Here in the cool mountains, cattle graze in chest-high grass and *paniolo,* astride their sturdy mounts, ride herd in time-honored tradition. Hunters range the slopes of Mauna Kea in search of wild goat and boar, and the Fourth of July is shattered by the wild whoops of cowboys at the world-class Parker Ranch Rodeo. Along the coast are beach parks, empty except for an occasional local family picnic. There are a series of *heiau,* and on the northernmost tip a broad plain, overlooking a sweeping panorama, marks the birthplace of Kamehameha the Great. The main town up here is Hawi, holding on after the sugar companies pulled out a few years ago. Down the road is Kapaau, where Kamehameha's statue resides in fulfillment of a *kahuna* prophecy. Along this little traveled road, a handful of artists offer their crafts in little shops. At road's end is the overlook of Pololu Valley, where a steep descent takes you to secluded beaches and camping in an area once frequented by some of the most powerful sorcerers in the land.

THE LAND

Science and the oral history of the *Kumulipo* differ sharply on the age of the Big Island. The scientists say that Hawaii is the youngest of the islands, being a little over one million years old; the chanters claim that it was the first "island-child" of Wakea and Papa. It is, irrefutably, closest to the "hot spot" on the Pacific floor, evidenced by Kilauea's frequent erruptions and by **Loihi Seamount,** located 30 miles off the southeast coast, which is even now steadily growing about 3,000 feet below the waves. The geology, geography, and location of the Hawaiian Islands, and their ongoing drifting and building in the middle of the Pacific, make them among the most unique pieces of real estate on Earth; and the Big Island is the *most* unique of them all.

Size

The Big Island dwarfs all the others at 4,038 square miles and growing. This makes up about 63% of the state's total land mass, allowing all the others to fit inside of it 2 times over. With 266 miles of coastline, the island stretches about 95 miles from north to south and 80 miles from east to west. Cape Kumukahi is the easternmost point in the state, and Ka Lea ("South Point") is the most southern point in the country.

The Mountains

The tremendous volcanic peak of **Mauna Kea** ("White Mountain"), located in north-central Hawaii, has been extinct for over 4,000 years. Its seasonal snowcap earns Mauna Kea its name and reputation as a good skiing area in winter. Over 18,000 feet of mountain below the surface rises straight up from the ocean floor—making Mauna Kea actually 31,796 feet tall, a substantial 2,768 feet taller than Mt. Everest. Some consider it the tallest mountain in the world, but at 13,796 feet above sea level, there is no doubt that it is the tallest peak in the Pacific. Almost on top, at 13,020 feet, is **Lake Waiau,** the highest lake in the state and third highest in the U.S. Mauna Kea was obviously a sacred mountain to the Hawaiians, and its white dome was a welcome beacon to seafarers. On its slope is the largest adze quarry in Polynesia, whose first-class basalt was fashioned into prized tools. The atmosphere atop the mountain, as it sits in mid-Pacific so far from any pollutants, is the most rarefied and cleanest on Earth. Its clarity makes it a natural for astronomical observatories, and the complex of telescopes on its summit is internationally manned, providing data to scientists around the world.

Even though **Mauna Loa** ("Long Mountain") is at a respectable 13,677 feet, its height isn't its claim to fame. This active volcano is 60 miles long by 30 wide, equaling 10,000 cubic miles of iron-hard lava, making it the densest and most massive mountain on Earth. In 1950 a tremendous lava flow belched from its summit reaching an astonishing rate of 6,750,000 cubic yards per hour. Seven lava rivers flowed for 23 days emitting over 600 million cubic yards that covered 35 square miles. If the lava were asphalt, there would have been enough to build a 256,000-mile 2-lane highway, or one capable of circling the Earth 10 times. There were no injuries but the villages of Kaapuna and Honokua were partially destroyed along with the Magoo Ranch. The **Kohala Mountains** to the northwest are the oldest. This section looks more like the other Hawaiian islands with deep gorges and valleys along the coast, and a green forested interior.

Kilauea, whose pragmatic name means "The Spewing," is the world's most active volcano. In the last hundred years, it has erupted on the average once every 11 months. The Hawaiians believed that the old goddess Madame Pele inhabited every volcano in the Hawaiian chain, and her home is now Halemaumau Crater in Kilauea Caldera. Kilauea is the most scientifically watched volcano in the world, with a permanent observatory built right into the crater rim. When it erupts, the flows are so predictable that observers run toward the mountain, not away from it! The flows, however, can burst out from fissures far from the center of the crater in areas that don't seem

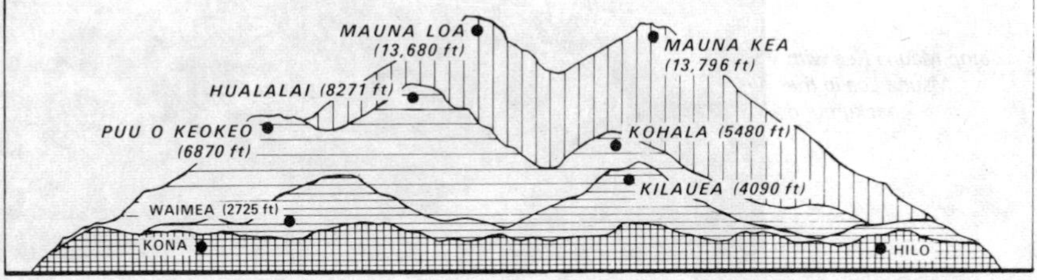

"active." Mostly, this happens occurs in the Puna District. In 1959, Kilauea Iki Crater came to life after 91 years, and although the flow wasn't as massive as others, it did send blazing fountains of lava 1,900 feet into the air. Kilauea has been very active within the last few years, with eruptions occurring at least once a month, and expected to continue. Most activity has been from a yet unnamed vent below Pu'uo. You might be lucky enough to see this phenomenon while visiting.

Tsunami

Hilo has been struck with the worst tidal waves in modern history. A giant wave smashed the islands on April 1, 1946, and swept away 159 people and over 1,300 homes; Hilo sustained most of these losses. Again, on May 23, 1960, Hilo took the brunt of a wave that rumbled through the business district killing 61 people. There is an elaborate warning system throughout the island with warning procedures and Inundation Maps listed in the front of the telephone directory.

Beaches

The Big Island takes the rap for having poor beaches—this isn't true! They are certainly few and far between, but they are spectacular. Hawaii is big and young, so distances are greater than on other islands, and the wave action hasn't had enough time to grind the new lava into sand. The Kona and Kohala coast beaches, along with a few nooks and crannies around Hilo, are gorgeous. Puna's beaches are incredible black sand, and the southern part of the island has a string of hidden beaches enjoyed only by those intrepid enough to get to them.

CLIMATE

The average temperature around the island varies between 72 and 78 degrees. Summers raise the temperature to the mid-80s and winters cool off to the low 70s. Both Kona and Hilo seem to maintain a year-round average of about 80 degrees. As usual, it's cooler in the higher elevations, and Waimea (Kamuela) sees most days in the mid 60s to low 70s, while Volcanoes maintains a steady 60 degrees. Atop Mauna Kea, the temperature rarely climbs above 50 degrees or dips below 30, while the summit of Mauna Loa is about 10 degrees warmer.

Rainfall

The big difference, weatherwise, is not temperature, but precipitation. Hawaii has some of the wettest and driest coastal (tourist) areas in the islands. The line separating wet from dry can be dramatic. Waimea, for example, has an actual dry and wet side of town, as if a boundary line split the town in two! Houses on the dry side are at a premium. Kona and Hilo are opposites. The Kona Coast is almost guaran-

atop Mauna Kea with Mauna Loa in the background

AVERAGE MAXIMUM/MINIMUM TEMPERATURE AND RAINFALL

Island	Town		Jan.	Mar.	May	June	Sept.	Nov.
Hawaii	Hilo	high	79	79	80	82	82	80
		low	62	62	61	70	70	65
		rain	11	15	7	10	10	15
	Kona	high	80	81	81	82	82	81
		low	62	64	65	68	68	63
		rain	4	3	2	0	2	1

N.B. Rainfall in inches; temperature in F°

teed to be sunny and bright, receiving as little as 15 inches of rainfall per year. Both Kona and the Kau Desert to the south are in the rain shadow of Mauna Loa, and most rainclouds coming from east to west are pierced by its summit before they ever reach Kona. Hilo is wet, with predictable afternoon and evening showers—they make the entire town blossom. Though this reputation keeps many tourists away, given its predictability and the ability to avoid the rain, it shouldn't. Hilo does get as much as 150 inches of rainfall per year, with a record of 153.93 inches set in 1971. It holds the dubious honor for the most rainfall recorded by the National Weather Service to fall in a town in a 24-hour period; a drenching 22.3 inches in February 1979.

FLORA AND FAUNA

The indigenous plants and birds of the Big Island have suffered the same fate as those of the other Hawaiian Islands; they're among the most endangered species on Earth and disappearing at an alarming rate. There are some sanctuaries on the Big Island where native species still live, but they must be vigorously protected. Do your bit to save them; enjoy but do not disturb.

BIRDS

You'll spot birds all over the Big Island from the coastal areas to the high mountain slopes. Some are found on other islands as well, but the ones listed below are found only or mainly on the Big Island. Every bird listed is either threatened or endangered.

Hawaii's Own

The **Hawaiian goose** *(nene)* is the state bird, found on the scrubland slopes of Hulalai and Mauna Loa. They have been introduced to Haleakala on Maui, but some experts claim that they lived naturally only on Hawaii. They were almost extinct by 1957, when a program to raise them in captivity began at Pohakuloa along the Saddle Road, and at the Wildfowl Trust in England. They've made a comeback, but their future is still precarious.

The **Hawaiian crow,** or *alala,* is reduced to less than 200 birds who live on the slopes of Hualalai and Mauna Loa, above the 3,000-foot level. They look like a common raven, but they have a more melodious voice and sometimes dull brown feathers. They breed in early spring and the greenish-blue, black-flecked eggs hatch from April to June. They are extremely nervous while nesting and any disturbance will cause them to abandon their young.

The **akiapola'au** is a 5-inch yellow bird hardly bigger than its name. It lives mainly on the eastern slopes in *ohia* and *koa* forests above 3,500 feet. It has a long curved upper bill for probing and a smaller lower bill that it uses woodpecker fashion. Listen for the distinctive rapping sound to spot this melodious singer.

i'o

The **Hawaiian hawk** *('io)* lives on the slopes of Mauna Loa and Mauna Kea below 9,000 feet. They travel from here to other parts of the island and can often be seen kiting in the skies over Volcanoes National Park. These birds symbolized the *ali'i*. They, like Mainland species, hunt small rodents and other birds. Reduced habitat and predation have caused their numbers to dwindle.

Marine Birds

Two coastal birds that breed on the high slopes of Hawai's volcanoes and feed on the coast are: the **Hawaiian petrel** *('ua'u),* and the **Newell shearwater** *('a'o).* The *'ua'u* lives on the barren high slopes and craters where it nests in burrows or under stones. Breeding season lasts from mid March to mid October. Only one chick is born and nurtured on regurgitated squid and fish. They suffer heavily from predation. The *'a'o* lives more in the forested slopes of the interior. They breed from April to November, and spend their days at sea and nights inland. Feral cats and dogs reduce their numbers considerably.

Forest Birds

The following birds are found in the upland forests of the Big Island. The ***elepaio*** is found on other islands but is also spotted in Volcanoes Park. This long-tailed (often held upright), 5-inch brown bird (the *amakua* of canoe builders) can be coaxed to come within touching distance of the observer. The **Hawaiian thrush** *(oma'o)* is a fairly common bird found above 3,000 feet in the windward forests of Hawaii. This 8-inch gray bird is a good singer, often seen perching with distinctive drooping wings and a shivering body. The ***akepa*** is a 4- to 5-inch bird. The male is a brilliant orange to red, the female a drab green and yellow. They're found mainly on Hulalai and in windward forests. The 6-inch bright yellow ***palila*** is found only on Hawaii in the forests of Mauna Kea above 6,000 feet. They depend exclusively upon *mamane* trees for survival, eating its pods, buds, and flowers. *Mamane* seedlings are destroyed by feral sheep. As goes the *mamane,* so goes the *palila.*

oma'o

MAMMALS

Hawaii had only 2 indigenous land mammals, the monk seal and the hoary bat. The latter is found only on Hawaii in any great numbers. The remainder of the Big Island's mammals are transplants. But like anything else, including people, that have been in the islands long enough, they take on characteristics that make them "local."

Hawaii's Animals

The following are animals found primarily on the Big Island. The **Hawaiian hoary bat** *(ope 'ape'a)* is cousin to Mainland bats, strong fliers that made it to Hawaii eons ago where they developed their own species. Their tails have a whitish coloration, therefore their name. They are found on Maui and Kauai, but mostly on the Big Island where they have been spotted even on the upper slopes of Mauna Loa and Mauna Kea. They have a 13-inch wingspan, and unlike other bats, are solitary creatures, roosting in trees. They give birth to twins in early summer, and can often be spotted over Hilo and Kealakekua bays just around sundown.

Feral dogs *(ilio)* are found on all the islands, but especially on the slopes of Mauna Kea, where packs chase feral sheep. Poisoned and shot by local ranchers, their numbers are diminishing. Black dogs, thought to be more tender, are still eaten in some Hawaiian and Filipino communities.

Feral sheep are escaped descendants of animals first brought to the islands by Capt. Vancouver in the 1790s, and later from merinos raised for their exceptional wooly fleece. They exist only on the Big Island, on the upper slopes of Mauna Loa, Mauna Kea, and Hualala; by the 1930s, their numbers topped 40,000 head. The fleece is a buff brown, and their 2-foot-wide recurved horns are often sought as hunting trophies. They are responsible for the overgrazing of young *mamane* trees, necessary to the endangered bird, *palila*. In 1979, a law was passed to exterminate or remove the sheep from Mauna Kea, so that the native *palila* could survive.

Mouflon sheep were introduced to Lanai and Hawaii to cut down on overgrazing and serve as trophy animals. These Mediterranean sheep can interbreed with the feral sheep and produce a hybrid. They live on the upper slopes of Mauna Loa and Mauna Kea. Unfortunately, their introduction has not been a success. No evidence concludes that the smaller family groups of mouflon cause less damage than the herding feral sheep, and hunters reportedly don't like the meat as much as feral mutton.

Feral donkeys, better known as "Kona nightingales," came to Hawaii as beasts of burden. Domesticated ones are found on all islands, but a few wild herds still roam the Big Island, all along the Kona coast, especially near the exclusive Kona Village Resort at Kaupulehue.

Feral cattle were introduced by Captain Vancouver, who gave a few domesticated head to Kamehameha; immediately a *kapu* against killing them went into effect for 10 years. The lush grasses of Hawaii were perfect, and they bred like wildfire. By the early 1800s they were out of control, and were hunted and exterminated. Finally, Mexican cowboys were brought to Hawaii to teach the local men how to be range hands. From this legacy sprang the Hawaiian *paniolo*.

Humpback whales migrate to Hawaiian waters yearly, arriving in late December and departing by mid March (see p. 14-18). The best places to view them in the waters off the Big Island are along the South Kona coast, especially at Kealakekua Bay and Ka Lea ("South Point"), with many sightings off the Puna coast around Isaac Hale Beach Park.

BILLFISH

Although these magnificent game fish occur in various South Sea and Hawaiian waters, catching them is easiest in the clear, smooth waters off the Kona Coast. Billfish are commonly called swordfish, sailfish, marlin, and *a'u*. Their distinctive feature is the long, spear-like or swordlike snout, and prominent dorsal fin. The three main billfishes caught are the blue, striped, and black marlin. Of these the **blue marlin** is the leading game fish in Kona waters. The blue has tipped the scales at well over 1,000 pounds, but the average fish goes 300 to 400. When alive this fish is a striking cobalt blue, but death brings on a color change to slate blue. They feed on skipjack tuna; throughout the summer, fishing boats look for schools of tuna as a tip off to blues in the area. The **black marlin** is the largest and most coveted catch for blue-water anglers. This solitary fish is infrequently found in the banks off Kona. Granddaddies can weigh 1,800 pounds, but the average is a mere 200. The **striped marlin** is the most common commercial billfish, a highly prized food served in finer restaurants, or sliced into *sashimi.* Their coloration is a remarkable royal blue, and spectacular leaps when caught give them a great reputation as fighters. Smaller than the other marlin, a 100-pounder is a very good catch. For more information see "Sports" in this chapter.

HISTORY

The Big Island plays a significant role in Hawaii's history. A long list of "firsts" have occurred here. Historians generally believe (backed up by the oral tradition) that the Big Island was first to be settled by the Polynesians. The dates now used are from A.D. 600 to 700. Hawaii is geographically the closest island to Polynesia; Mauna Loa and especially Mauna Kea, with its white summit, present an easily spotted landmark. Psychologically, the Polynesian wayfarers would have been very attracted to Hawaii as a lost homeland. Compared to Tahiti and most other South Sea islands (except for Fiji), it's huge. It *looked* like the "promised land." Some may wonder why the Polynesians chose to live atop an obviously active volcano, and not bypass it for a more congenial island. The volcanism of the Big Island is comparatively gentle, and the lava flows follow predictable routes and rarely turn killer. The animistic Hawaiians would've been drawn to live where the godly forces of nature were so apparent. The *mana* would be exceptionally strong, and therefore the *ali'i* would be great. Human sacrifice was introduced to Hawaii at Wahaula Heiau in the Puna District in the 13th C., and from there *luakini* (human sacrifice temples) spread throughout the islands.

The Great One

The greatest native son of Hawaii, Kamehameha, was born under mysterious circumstances in the Kohala District, probably in 1753. He was royal born to Keoua Kupuapaikalaninui, the chief of Kohala, and Kekuiapoiwa, a chieftess from Kona. Accounts vary, but one claims that before his birth, a *kahuna* prophesized that this child would grow to be a "killer of chiefs." Because of this, the local chiefs conspired to murder the infant. When Kekuiapoiwa's time came, she secretly went to the royal birthing stones near Mookini Heiau and delivered Kamehameha. She entrusted her baby to a man servant, and instructed him to hide the child. He headed for the rugged and remote coast around Kapaau. Here Kamehameha was raised in the mountains, mostly by men. Always alone, he earned the nickname "the lonely one."

Regardless of the circumstances surrounding his birth, Kamehameha did become a renowned warrior and a loyal retainer to his uncle, Kalaniopuu, the *Moi* of Hawaii. With Kalaniopuu, he boarded Capt. Cook's ship and sailed from Maui to Hawaii, and speculation has it that he was with his uncle when Cook was killed at Kealakekua Bay. Before Kalaniopuu died, he called a council at Waipio Valley and there named his weak and ineffectual son Kiwalao king. He also made Kamehameha the keeper of the feathered family war-god, Kukailimoku, or Ku The Land Snatcher. Kiwalao and his half-brother Keoua engaged in a civil war

The gods remain ready at Pu'uhonua o Honaunau.

over land rights. Kamehameha, aided by disgruntled chiefs from Kona, waged war on both, and at Mokuohai, Kiwalao was killed. Kamehameha went on to fight on Maui. By this time he had acquired a small ship, the *Fair American,* and with the help of cannon manned by 2 white sailors, Davis and Young, he defeated the Maui warriors at Iao Valley. If he could defeat Keoua at home, he would be king of all Hawaii.

The Gods Speak

A great oracle from Kauai announced that war would end on Hawaii only after a great *heiau* was built at Puukohala, dedicated by the corpse of a great chief. Kamehameha instantly set about building this *heiau,* and through cunning, wisdom, and true belief placed the conquest of Hawaii in the hands of the gods. Meanwhile, a great fleet of war canoes belonging to Kahekili of Maui attacked Kamehameha's forces at Waimanu, near Waipio. Aided again by the *Fair American* and Davis and Young, Kamehameha won a decisive battle and subdued Kahekili once and for all. Keoua seized this opportunity to ravage Kamehameha's lands all the way from Waipio to Hilo. He sent his armies south through Kau, but when the middle legions were passing the foot of Kilauea, it erupted and suffocated them with poisonous gas and a heavy deposit of ash. Footprints, encased in the cement-like ash, still mark their last steps. Kamehameha and Keoua both took this as a direct sign from the gods. Kamehameha returned to Puukohala and finished the *heiau.* Upon completion he summoned Keoua, who came by canoe with a small band of warriors resplendent in feather helmet and cape. He knew the fate that awaited him, and when he stepped ashore he was slaughtered by Keeaumoku. Keoua's body was laid on the altar, and at that moment the islands of Hawaii were united under one supreme ruler, Kamehameha, The Lonely One. He ruled until his death in 1819, and his passing marked the beginning of the end for old Hawaii.

Great Changes

The great navigator and explorer, Captain Cook, was killed at Kealakekua Bay on February 14, 1779. Kalaniopuu was still alive at the time and Kamehameha was only a minor chief,

kapu *sticks*

although Cook had previously written about him in the ship's log when he came aboard off Maui. During Kamehameha's reign ships from America, England, and various European countries came to trade. Americans monopolized the lucrative sandalwood business with China, and New England whalers discovered the rich whaling waters. The Englishman, Captain Vancouver, became a trusted adviser of Kamehameha, and told him about the white man's form of worship, while introducing plants and animals such as oranges, grapes, cows, goats, and sheep. He even interceded for Kamehameha with his headstrong queen, Kaahumanu, and coaxed her out from her hiding place under a rock, when she sought refuge at Puuhonua o Honaunau. When Kamehameha died in 1819, Hawaii was ripe for change. His 2 great queens, Kaahumanu and Keopuolani, realized that the old ways were coming to an end. They encouraged Liholiho (Kamehameha II) to end the *kapu* system. Men and women were forbidden to eat together, and those that violated this main *kapu* were immediately killed to placate the gods who would surely intercede with grave destruction. Keopuolani defied this belief when she sat down with Kauikeaouli, the 7-year-old brother of Liholiho. The gods remained quiet. Encouraged, Liholiho called for a great *luau* at Kailua, and openly sat down to eat with his chiefs and chieftesses. Symbolically, the impotent gods were toppled with every bite, and *heiau* and idols were razed throughout the land. Into this spiritual vortex sailed the **Brig Thaddeus** on April 4, 1820. They had set sail from Boston on October 23, 1819, lured to the Big Island by Henry Opukahaia, a local boy born at Napoopoo in 1792. Coming ashore at Kailua, the first missionary packet convinced Liholiho to give them a one-year trial period. Hawaii changed forever in those brief months. By 1824 the new faith had such a foothold that Chieftess Kapiolani climbed to the firepit atop Kilauea and defied Pele. This was even more striking than the previous breaking of the food *kapu* because the strength of Pele could actually be seen. Kapiolani ate forbidden *ohelo* berries and cried out "Jehovah is my God." Over the next decades the governing of Hawaii slipped away from the Big Island and moved to the new port cities of Lahaina and later Honolulu. In 1847, the Parker Ranch began with a 2-acre grant given to John Parker. He coupled this with 360 acres given to his *ali'i* wife Kipikane by the land division known as the Great Mahele.

GOVERNMENT

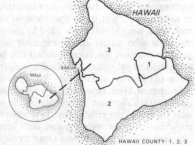

The county of Hawaii is almost entirely Democratic with a token Republican state senator or representative here and there. Of the 25 State Senatorial Districts, Hawaii County is represented by 3. The First District is the whole southern part of the island, from Puna to Kailua; its representative is one of the few Republicans holding office on the island. The Second District is mainly Hilo, and the Third District takes in the whole northern section, and is a shared district with East Maui. The combination of these 2 areas has been traditional, even from old Hawaiian times.

Of 51 seats in the State House of Representatives, Hawaii County has 4. The Fourth District is again shared with East Maui and takes in most of South Kohala. At this time, all representatives are Democrats, except for a Republican representing Kailua-Kona, Fifth District.

PEOPLE

With 93,000 people, the Big Island has the second largest island population in Hawaii, just under 10% of the state's total. However, it has the smallest population density of the main islands, with only 23 people per square mile. Hilo has the largest population with 36,000 residents, followed by Kailua with barely 5,000, and Captain Cook with 2,000 or so. The ethnic breakdown of the 93,000 people is as follows: 34% white, 27% Japanese, 19% Hawaiian, 14% Filipino, 2% Chinese, 4% other.

ECONOMY

The Big Island's economy is the most agriculturally based county in the state. Over 6,000 farm hands, horticultural workers and *paniolo*

SENATORIAL DISTRICTS

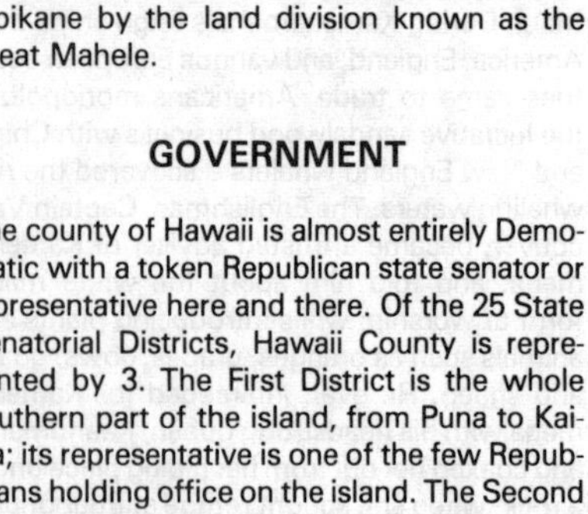

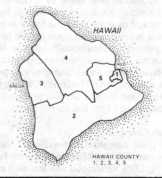

HOUSE DISTRICTS

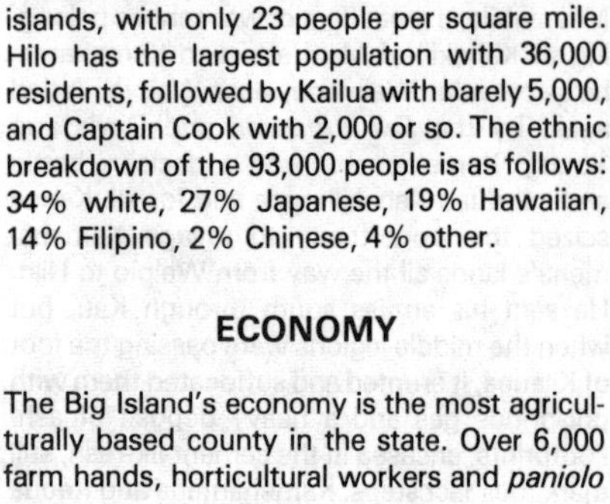

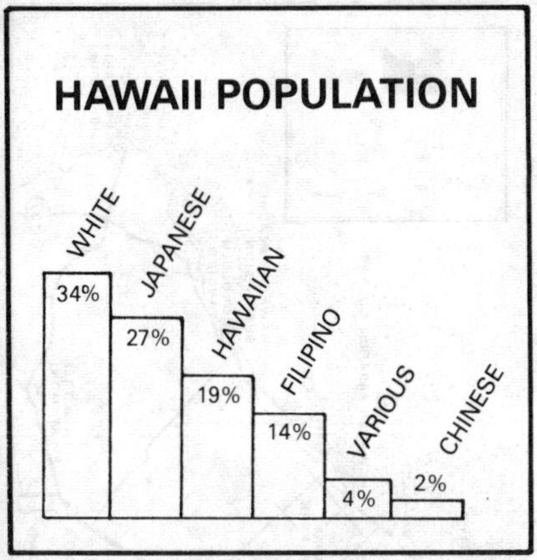

work the land, producing over half of the state's vegetables and melons, and over 75% of the fruit, leading all other islands especially in papayas. The Big Island also produces 33 million pounds of macadamia nuts, all the state's production, except for a small farm here and there on the other islands. The Big Island is also awash in color and fragrance as 300 or more horticultural farms produce the largest number of orchids and anthuriums in the state.

Sugar

Hawaii is the state's largest sugar grower with over 90,000 acres in cane. These produce 4 million tons of refined sugar, 40% of the state's output. The majority of sugar land is along the Hamakua Coast, long been known for its abundant water supply. At one time, the cane was even transported to the mills by water flumes. Another large pocket of cane fields is in the southern part of the island, mostly in Puna.

Coffee

The Kona District is a splendid area for raising coffee; it gives the beans a beautiful tan. Lying in Mauna Loa's rain shadow, it gets dewy mornings, followed by sunshine, and an afternoon cloud shadow. This coffee has long been accepted as gourmet quality, and is sold in the better restaurants throughout Hawaii, and in fine coffee shops around the world. It's a dark full-bodied coffee with a rich aroma. Approximately 650 small farms produce nearly $4 million dollars a year in coffee revenue. Few however make it a full-time business.

Cattle

Hawaii's cattle ranches produce over 18 million pounds of beef per year, 65% of the state's total. More than 360 independant ranches are on the island, but they are dwarfed both in size and production by the massive Parker Ranch, which alone is three-quarters the size of Oahu.

Military

There are just under 200 Army personnel on the island, with about the same number of dependants. Most of these people are attached to the enormous Pohakuloa Military Reserve in the center of the island. There are also a few minor installations around Hilo and at Kilauea.

Tourism

Over 3,000 island residents are directly employed by the hotel industry, and many more indirectly serve the tourists. The slightly more than 7,000 hotel rooms have the greatest concentration in Kona. They have the lowest occupancy rate in the state, which rarely rises above 60%. Of the major islands, Hawaii receives the fewest tourists annually, only about 7,000 on any given day.

GETTING THERE

Almost all travelers to the Big Island arrive by air. A few lucky ones come by private yacht, and in season the cruise ship SS *Constitution* docks in Hilo on Sunday mornings, then sails around the island to Kailua. For the rest, the island's 2 major airports are at Hilo and Kailua-Kona, with a few secondary strips here and there. Almost every flight to the Big island has a stopover, mostly at Honolulu, but these are efficient, at no extra cost. The following should help you plan your arrival.

The Airports

The largest and only international airport on Hawaii is **General Lyman Field,** tel. 935-0809, which services Hilo and the eastern half of the island. It's a modern facility with full amenities and its runways can handle all jumbo jets. The

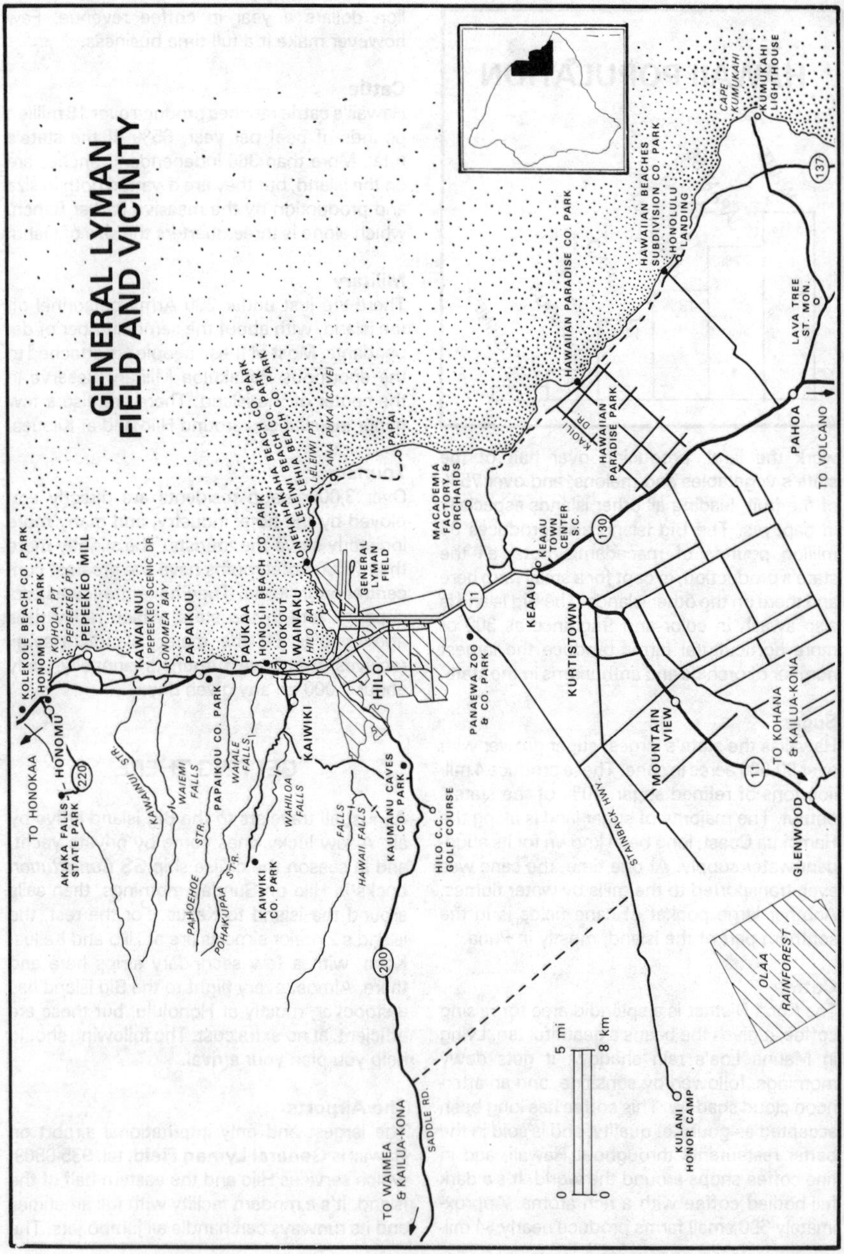

GENERAL LYMAN FIELD AND VICINITY
TO HONOKAA
HONOMU
KOLEKOLE BEACH CO. PARK
HONOMU CO. PARK
KOHOLA PT.
PEPEEKEO PT.
PEPEEKEO MILL
AKAKA FALLS STATE PARK
220
KAWAINUI STR.
KAWAI NUI
PEPEEKEO SCENIC DR.
ONOMEA BAY
WAIEMI FALLS
PAPAIKOU
PAHOEHOE STR.
PAPAIKOU CO. PARK
WAIALE FALLS
POHAKUPAA STR.
PAUKAA
HONOLII BEACH CO. PARK
KAIWIKI CO. PARK
LOOKOUT
WAINAKU
WAHILOA FALLS
KAIWIKI
HILO BAY
ONEKAHAKAHA BEACH CO. PARK
LELEIWI BEACH CO. PARK
LEHIA BEACH CO. PARK
LELEIWI PT.
ANA PUKA (CAVE)
PAPAI
GENERAL LYMAN FIELD
HILO
HAWAII FALLS
FALLS
KAUMANU CAVES CO. PARK
200
HILO C.C. GOLF COURSE
SADDLE RD.
TO WAIMEA & KAILUA-KONA
11
PANAEWA ZOO & CO. PARK
MACADEMIA FACTORY & ORCHARDS
KEAAU
KEAAU TOWN CENTER S.C.
130
KURTISTOWN
STAINBACK HWY.
MOUNTAIN VIEW
KULANI HONOR CAMP
5 mi
8 km
OLAA RAINFOREST
TO KOHANA & KAILUA-KONA
GLENWOOD
HAWAIIAN PARADISE PARK
HAWAIIAN PARADISE CO. PARK
HAWAIIAN BEACHES SUBDIVISION CO. PARK
HONOLULU LANDING
PAHOA
TO VOLCANO
LAVA TREE ST. MON.
137
CAPE KUMUKAHI
KUMUKAHI LIGHTHOUSE

2-story terminal has an information center, restaurant, a number of vendors including *lei* shops, and lockers. Most major car rental agencies have a booth outside the terminal; a taxi for the 3-mile ride to town costs about $4.50. This airport features 20 acres of landscaped flowers and an assortment of fountains and waterfalls supplied by rainwater collected on the terminal's roof. **Keahole Airport,** tel. 329-2484, is 9 miles north of Kailua and handles the air traffic for Kona. The terminal is a series of open-sided Polynesian-style buildings. Here too are lockers, food, visitor information, various vendors, and most car rental agencies. The Gray Line limousine can take you to Kailua for under $10, while a private cab to your hotel is $15 more. **Waimea-Kohala Airport,** tel. 885-4520, is just outside Waimea (Kamuela). There are few amenities and no public transportation to town. **Upolu Airport,** tel. 889-9958, is a lonely strip on the extreme northern tip of the island, with no facilities whatsoever. Both are serviced only on request by small charter airlines.

Nonstop Flights

Only 2 nonstop flights go to Hawaii from the Mainland. Both are on United Airlines, and land at Keahole Airport serving Kailua-Kona. The Los Angeles flight departs daily at 12:05 p.m. and arrives in Kailua at 3:38 p.m. The San Francisco flight departs daily at 8:40 a.m. and arrives at 11:53 a.m. In the past during peak season, United has run a flight to General Lyman Field in Hilo, but it's an on-and-off affair depending on the number of travelers. It's also interesting to note that General Lyman Field is an international airport, and most island flights landed there in the past. Now, with the Kona Coast gaining popularity, the flights have shifted to that side of the island.

Stopover Flights

All the major carriers have arrangements for getting you to the Big Island. American carriers such as Western, Continental, and American, along with foreign carriers like Canadian Pacific, Qantas, and Japan Airlines land at Honolulu. There they have an inter-line agreement with island carriers including Hawaiian Air, Aloha, or Mid-Pacific, which then take you to the Big Island. This does involve a plane change, but your baggage can be booked straight through. Hawaiian Air has expanded to Mainland flights from San Francisco and Los Angeles, with connecting flights in Honolulu to Kona. They offer the added convenience of dealing with one airline, although you may change planes in Honolulu.

Inter-island Carriers

Getting to the Big Island from the other islands is easy and convenient. **Hawaiian Air** offers the most flights. From Honolulu to Kona, 15 flights are spread throughout the day from 6:00 a.m. to 6:40 p.m. The same scheduling applies to Hilo, except that there are slightly fewer flights, the last departing Honolulu at 7:10 p.m. Hawaiian Air also offers daily flights from Kauai, Molokai, Lanai, and Maui to both Hilo and Kona. Most are aboard DC9 jet aircraft, with some on the 4-prop Dash Transits. **Aloha Airlines** has the second largest number of flights to Hawaii from the other islands. Their 10 daily Honolulu-Kona runs start at 6:00 a.m. with the last at 6:50 p.m.; Hilo flights go throughout the day from 6:00 a.m. to 7:20 p.m. They also fly from Kauai and Maui. **Mid Pacific** flies from Honolulu, Maui and Kauai to Hilo and Kona. They offer about half the number of flights as the other 2 carriers, but they too are conveniently dispersed throughout the daylight hours.

GETTING AROUND

The first thing to remember when traveling on the Big Island is that it *is* big, over 4 times larger than Rhode Island. A complete range of vehicles is available for getting around, everything from helicopters to mopeds. Hawaii, like Oahu, has good public transportation. Choose the conveyance that fits your style, and you should have no trouble touring the Big Island.

Public Transportation

The county of Hawaii maintains the Mass Transportation System (MTS), known throughout the island as the **Hele-on Bus**. For information, schedules and fares contact the MTS at 25 Aupuni St., Hilo 96720, tel. 961-6722 or 935-8241. The main bus terminal is in downtown Hilo at Mooheau Park, just at the corner of Kamehameha Avenue and Mamo Street. It's only a ticket window (schedules available) in an open pavilion with a few benches. Like bus terminals everywhere, it has a local franchise of derelicts and down-and-outters, but they leave you alone. What the Hele-on Bus lacks in class, it more than makes up for in *color* and affordability. the Hele-on operates Mon. through Sat. from approximately 6:00 a.m. to 6:00 p.m. depending on the run. It goes just about everywhere on the island—sooner or later. If you're in a hurry definitely forget about taking it, but if you want to meet the people of Hawaii, there's no better way. The base fare is $.50, which increases whenever you go into another zone. You can also be charged an extra $1 for a large backpack or suitcase. Don't worry about that—the Hele-on is one of the best bargains in the country. The routes are far too numerous to mention, but one goes from Kealia, south of Captain Cook, through Kailua all the way to Hilo on the east coast via Waimea, Honokaa, and Honomu. This sojurn covers 110 miles in just over 4 hours and costs $4.50, the most expensive fare in the system. You can take the southern route through Kau passing through Naalehu, Volcanoes, and on to Hilo. This trip takes just over 2 hours and costs $3.

The county also maintains the **Banyan Shuttle** in Hilo. This bus does 5 runs Mon. through Fri. from 9:00 a.m. to 2:55 p.m. The Shuttle costs $.50, but you can buy a $2 pass for one-day unlimited use. The Shuttle runs from the Hukilau Hotel at the end of Banyan Drive to the Mooheau Bus Terminal in downtown Hilo. En route it stops at the better hotels, Puainako Town Center, Hilo, and Kaikoo Malls, Lyman Museum, and Rainbow Falls, where you're allowed 10 minutes for a look.

Kailua-Kona also has shuttle service. The **Alii Shuttle** cruises Alii Drive 6 times daily, 9:30 a.m. to 6:00 p.m., from the post office in Kailua south to the Kona Surf Hotel for a fixed fare of $.50. The **London Bus** is a double-decker imported from England. It travels from the World Square Shopping Center in downtown Kailua along Alii Drive, and terminates at the Kona Surf Hotel in Keauhou. The London Bus runs from 9:00 a.m. to 9:30 p.m., free!

Hitchhiking

The old thumb works on the Big Island about as well as anywhere else. Some people hitchhike rather than take the Hele-on Bus not so much as to save money, but to save time! A good idea is to check the bus schedule (and routes), and set out about 30 minutes before the scheduled departure. If you don't have good luck, just wait for the bus to come along and hail it down. It'll stop.

Taxis

General Lyman Field in Hilo and Keahole Airport north of Kailua always have taxis waiting for fares. From Hilo's airport to downtown costs about $7, and from Keahole to most hotels along Alii Drive in Kailua is $15. Obviously, taxi is no way to get around if you're trying to save money. Most taxi companies, both in Kona and Hilo, run sightseeing services for a fixed price. In **Kona** try: Kona Airport Taxi, tel. 329-7779; Paradise Taxi, tel. 329-1234; Marina Taxi, tel. 329-2481. In **Hilo** try: Hilo Harry's, tel. 935-7091; Bob's Taxi, tel. 935-5247; BIA Taxi, tel. 935-8303.

Car Rental Tips

The Big Island has rental agencies from national to local firms. Renting a car is the best way to tour the island, but keep these few special tips in mind. Most car companies charge you a fee if you rent the car in Hilo and drop it off in Kona, and vice versa. This is usually less than $15, so check. The agencies are prejudiced against the Saddle Road and the spur road leading to South Point, both of which offer some of the *most* spectacular scenery on the island. Their prejudice is unfounded because both roads are paved, generally well maintained, and no problem if you take your time. They'll claim the insurance will not cover you if you have a mishap on these roads. A good automobile policy at home will cover you in a rental car, but definitely check this before you take off. It's even possible, but not recommended, to drive to the top of Mauna Kea, if there is no snow. Plenty of signs to the summit say "4WD Only," but you can make it if you have the guts. Don't even hint of these intentions to the car rental agencies, or they won't rent you a car.

No way whatsoever should you attempt to drive down to Waipio Valley in a car! The grade is unbelievably steep, and only a 4WD compound first gear can make it. Simply, you have a good chance of being killed if you try it in a car.

Gas stations are farther apart than on the other islands, and sometimes they close very early. As a rule, fill up whenever the gauge reads half full. Both General Lyman Field and Keahole Airport have a gauntlet of car rental booths and courtesy phones outside the terminal.

National Companies

The following are national firms represented at both airports. Kona numbers begin with "3," Hilo with "9." One of the best is **National Car Rental,** featuring GM cars, tel. 329-1674 or 935-0891. **Hertz,** tel. 329-3566 or 935-2896; **Dollar,** tel. 329-2744 or 961-6059; **Avis,** tel. 329-1745 or 935-1290; **Budget,** tel. 329-3581 or 935-9678; **American International,** tel. 329-2926 or 935-1108.

Local Companies

The following companies have a booth or courtesy phone at the airport. Sometimes, if business is slow, they'll deal on their prices. **Wiki Wiki,** tel. 329-1752 or 935-6861; **Gray Line,** tel. 329-3161 or 935-1654; **Robert's,** tel. 329-1688 or 935-2858; **Tropical,** tel. 329-2347 or 935-3385; **Phillip's,** tel. 329-1730 or 935-1936; **Marquez,** tel. 329-3411 or 935-2115; **Liberato's,** tel. 329-3035 or 935-8089.

4WD Rentals

To get off the beaten track try: **Hilo Motors,** in Hilo only at tel. 961-1225, for jeeps; **Wiki Wiki,** tel. 329-1752 or 935-5201, for Toyota Land Cruisers, available in Hilo only; **Hawaiian Rent a Jeep,** in Kona only at tel. 329-5077. Most 4WDs rent for approximately $45 per day including mileage.

Camper/RV Rentals

Seventeen county, state, and national parks make Hawaii the best island for camping. An excellent outfit is **Travel Camp,** 1266 Kamehameha Ave., Hilo, HI 96720, tel. 935-7406. The owner, Mr. Gordon Morse, can put you into anything from a compact cabover that sleeps 2, through various sizes of motor homes up to a 24-foot fully contained deluxe model that sleeps 6. Price varies according to size, but the cheapest is $47 p/d, and the most expensive with stereo, TV, and a/c is $94, plus $.20 per mile (all units). A $50 deposit is required with higher rates for rentals less than 4 days. Book well in advance. **Beach Boy Campers** are at General Lyman Field, tel. 961-2022. Write to 1720 Ala Moana Blvd., Suite B-2, Honolulu, HI 96815, for information and reservations. They offer everything from mini cabovers to 24-foot motor homes. Prices and requirements are comparable with Travel Camp.

Bicycles

With all the triathletes coming to Hawaii, and all the fabulous little-trafficked roads, you'd think Hawaii would be great for a biker! It is, but only if you bring your own. If you intend on renting a bike, your choices are meager. Try the following: **Pacific United Rental,** at 1080 Kilauea Ave., Hilo, tel. 935-2974, rentals limited to the Hilo area; **Bicycle Warehouse,** 74-5539 Kaiwi Bay 5, Kailua-Kona, tel. 329-9424; **Island Cycle Rentals,** at Jack's Diving Locker at the Kona Inn Plaza, tel. 329-7585. Also try the Tobacconist Shop, downstairs from Buzz's Steak House in the Kailua Bay Inn Shopping Plaza in downtown Kailua. They have sturdy one-speed town bikes for $2.50 p/h, or $9 p/d. Not good for heavy-duty touring but great for getting around town.

Sightseeing Tours
For a guided tour, or to see the Big Island from the air or sea, try one of the following. **Kona Coast Activities,** at the Kona Inn Shopping Village in downtown Kailua, tel. 329-2971, is a general-purpose activity center that can book you on just about anything from sightseeing to sport fishing. Sightseeing tours are operated by **Grayline,** tel. 329-9337 or 935-2835 and **Akamai Tours,** tel. 329-7324. Their small window vans are available for anything from a half-hour tour of Kona for $14 to an all-day circle-island tour for $38.

Waipio Valley Shuttle

4WD tours include: **Hawaii Natural History Tours,** tel. 966-7044, whose professional guides take you on coastal, volcanic, or botanical tours; **Paradise Valley,** tel. 329-9282, will take you off-road to just about anywhere you want to go; **Waipio Valley Shuttle,** tel. 775-7121, for a 2-hour tour down to Waipio Valley for $15 (see p. 574).

Air tours are a great way to see the Big Island, but they are expensive. Expect to spend a minimum of $100-$175. Kilauea Volcano erupting is like winning the lottery for these small companies: they then charge whatever the market will bear. Try one of the following: **All Island Air Service** helicopter or Cessna flights from Keahole Airport, tel. 325-7635, free hotel/condo pick-up; **Anuenue Aviation** at General Lyman Field, tel. 961-5591 for narrated flights in Cessnas; **Big Island Air,** offers small plane flights from Keahole Airport, 2-person minimum, tel. 329-3459; **Kenai Helicopters** fly from the Kona Surf Hotel, tel. 322-9321; **Hilo Bay Air** for helicopter rides, tel. 969-1545. Plenty of others swarm from the other islands when the volcano is displaying.

ACCOMMODATIONS

Finding suitable accommodations on Hawaii is never a problem. The 7,000-plus rooms available have the lowest annual occupancy rate of any in the islands at only 65%. Except for the height of the high seasons and during the Merry Monarch Festival in Hilo, you can count on finding a room at a bargain. Many places offer kitchenettes and long-term discounts as a matter of course. The highest concentrations of rooms are strung along Alii Drive in Kailua-Kona—over 4,500 in condos, apartment hotels, and standard hotels. Hilo has almost 2,000 rooms, and many of its hotels are "gone condo" where you can get some great deals. The rest are scattered around the island in small villages from Naalehu in the south to Hawi in the north, where you can almost count on being the only off-island guest. You can comfortably stay in the cowboy town of Waimea, or perch above Kilauea Crater at one of the oldest hotel sites in the islands. There are bed and breakfasts, and the camping is superb, with a campsite almost guaranteed at anytime.

The Range
The Big Island has a tremendous range of accommodations. Three of the world's greatest luxury resorts are within minutes of each other on the Kohala coast: The Mauna Kea Beach Hotel, Mauana Lani, and Kona Village Resort. The Mauna Kea, built by Lawrence Rockefeller,

has everything the name implies. The other two are just as superb with hideaway "grass shacks," exquisite art collections as an integral part of the grounds, world-ranked golf courses, and perfect crescent beachs.

Most won't stay at these, but Kona has fine hotels like the King Kamehameha and Kona Hilton in downtown Kailua. Just south towards Keahou are a string of reasonably priced yet luxury hotels like the Kona Lagoon. Interspersed among the big hotels are little places with homey atmospheres and great rates. Hilo offers the best accommodation bargains. Luxury hotels such as the Hilo Hawaiian and Naniloa Surf are priced like mid-range hotels on the other islands. There are also semi-fleabags in town that pass the basic cleanliness test, and go for as little as $12 per day along with gems like the Dolphin Bay Hotel that gives you so much for your money it's embarrassing. And for a real treat, head to Volcanoes National Park and stay at Volcano House where raw nature has thrilled kings, queens, and luminaries like the humorist Mark Twain for over a century.

If you want to get away from everybody else, no problem, and you don't have to be rich to do it. Pass-through towns like Captain Cook and Waimea have accommodations at very reasonable prices. You can have a self-growth retreat in Puna at Kalani Honua Culture Center, or you can stay in Honokaa, or down in Tom Araki's Hotel in Waipio Valley for $8 per night. If that isn't cheap enough, how about staying at a defunct century-old girl's boarding school in Kapaau for a whopping $3.64 per night?

B&Bs

The Big Island has 2 companies representing B&B homes. The average price is from $20 to $60. For full information write: **Bed and Breakfast Hawaii,** Box 449, Kapaa, HI 96746, tel.822-7771, Oahu tel. 536-8421, **Pacific Hawaii B&B,** 19 Kainani Pl., Kailua, HI 96734.

CAMPING

The Big Island has the best camping in the state with more facilities and less competition for campsites than on the other islands. Over 3 dozen parks fringe the coastline and sit deep in the interior; almost half offer camping. The others boast a combination of rugged hikes, easy strolls, self-guided nature walks, swimming, historical sites, and natural phenomena. The ones with campgrounds are state, county, and nationally operated, ranging from remote walk-in sites to housekeeping cabins. All, except for the National Park, require inexpensive camping permits, and although there is usually no problem obtaining sites, always write for reservations well in advance allowing a minimum of one month for letters to go back and forth.

General Information

Most campgrounds have pavilions, fireplaces, toilets (sometimes pit), running water, but usually no individual electrical hookups. Pavilions often have electric lights, but sometimes campers appropriate the bulbs, so it's wise to carry your own. Drinking water is available, but at times brackish water is used for flushing toilets and for showers, so read all signs regarding water. Backcountry shelters have catchment water, but never hike without an adequate supply of your own. Cooking fires are allowed in established firepits, but no wood is provided. Charcoal is a good idea. When camping in the mountains, be prepared for cold and rainy weather. Women, especially, should never hike or camp alone, and all should exercise precaution against theft, though it's not as prevalent as on the other islands. Camping equipment is available from: **Pacific United Rent All,** 1080 Kilauea Ave., Hilo, tel. 935-2974; **Kona Rent All,** 74-5602 Alapaa St., Kailua-Kona, tel. 329-1644.

County Parks

The county-maintained parks are open to the public for day use, and permits are only required for camping (tents or RVs). For information write: Dept. of Parks and Recreation, County of Hawaii, Hilo, HI 96720, tel. 961-8311. The main office is located behind the Kaikoo Mall at 25 Aupuni Street. You can pick up your permits here, but only during business hours Mon. to Friday. If you'll be arriving after hours or on a weekend, have the permits mailed to you. Branch offices are at Hale Halawai in

Kailua-Kona, tel. 329-1989, and at Captain Cook, tel. 323-3046. Fees are $1 per adult, per day; children 13 to 17, $.50; youngsters free. Pavilions for exclusive use are $5 p/d with kitchen, $2 without.

State Parks

Day use of state parks is free, with no permit required, but you will need one for tent camping and for cabins. If you want a cabin, at least one week's notice is required regardless of availability. You can pick up your permit if you arrive during normal business hours, but again it saves time if you do it all by mail. Write: Dept. of Land and Natural Resources, Div., of State Parks, Box 936, Hilo, HI 96720, tel. 961-7200. The main office is at 75 Aupuni Street. Cabins or A-frames are offered at: Mauna Kea's Pohakuloa Camp, tel. 935-7237; Hapuna, tel. 882-7995; Kalopa, tel. 775-7114; and Niaulani

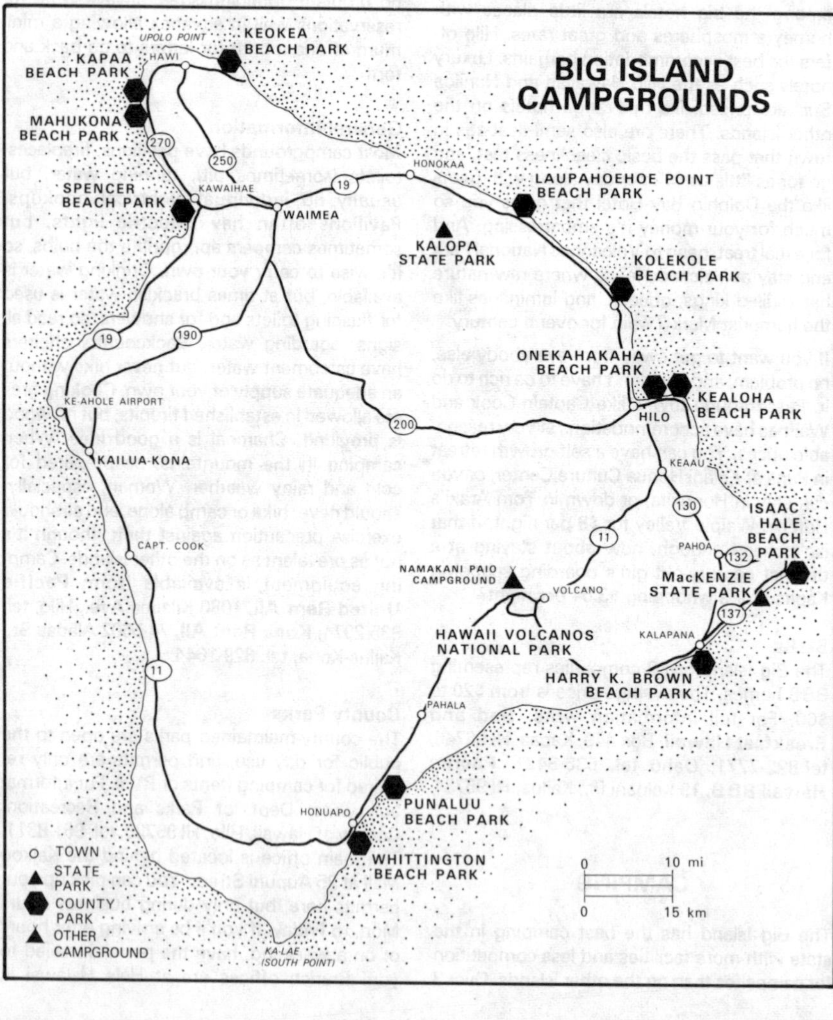

Cabin at Kilauea State Park. Fees and regulations vary slightly so specify exactly which facility you require, for how long, and for how many people when writing for permit. For example, the A-frames at Hapuna are a flat $7 per night with a 4-person maximum; Niaulani Cabin is on a sliding scale from $10 for one person, to $30 for 6 people.

National Parks
Both day use and overnight camping at Volcanoes National Park is free and no permits are required. The drive-in campgrounds throughout the park can be reserved, but usually operate on a first-come first-served basis. Your stay is limited to 7 days per campground per year. A-frame cabins are provided at Namakani Paio Campgrounds, and arrangements are made through Volcano House, Hawaii Volcanoes National Park, HI 96718, tel. 967-7321. There are walk-in trail cabins and shelters throughout the park; they are free, you can't reserve them and you should expect to share them with other hikers. Coleman stoves and lanterns are provided, but you provide the fuel. Basic bedding and cooking utensils are also there for your convenience. Shelters, in the park along the coast, are 3-sided open affairs that only offer a covering against the elements. For information on camping and hiking in the park, write Hawaii Volcanoes National Park, HI 96718.

Hiking Tips
Hiking on the Big Island is stupendous. There's something for everyone from civilized walks to the breathtaking Akaka Falls to huff-puff treks to the summit of Mauna Loa. The largest number of trails, and the most outstanding according to many, are laced across Volcanoes Park. After all, this is the world's most active volcano. You can hike across the crater floor, spurred on by the knowledge that it can shake to life at any moment. Or dip down off the mountain and amble the lonely trails in the Kau desert, or along remnants of the King's Coastal Trail in Puna. The most important thing to do, before heading out in Volcanoes, is to stop at the Ranger HQ and inquire about trail conditions. Make absolutely sure to register, giving the rangers your hiking itinerary. In the event of an eruption, they will be able to locate you and send a helicopter if necessary. Follow this advice, your life may depend upon it! Everyone can enjoy vistas on Devastation Trail, Sulfur Bank, or at the Thurston Lava Tube without any danger whatsoever. In the north you'll find Waipio, Waimanu, and Pololu valleys. All offer secluded hiking and camping, where you can play Robinson Crusoe on your own beach and gather a variety of island fruits from once cultivated trees gone wild.

SPORTS AND RECREATION

You'll have no problem having fun on the Big Island. Everybody goes outside to play. You can drive golf balls over lagoons, smack tennis balls at over 50 private and public courts, ski, snorkel, windsurf, gallop a horse, bag a wild turkey, or latch on to a marlin that'll tail-walk across a windowpane sea. Choose your sport and have a ball.

Deep-sea Fishing
The fishing around the Big Island ranges from excellent to outstanding! It's legendary for marlin fishing, but there are other fish in the sea. A large fleet of charter boats with skilled captains and tested crews is ready, willing, and competent to take you out. Most fishing occurs on the Kona side from early spring to late fall. August is the optimum month. Rough seas keep most boats in during December and January; many venture out by February. You can hire a boat for a private or share charter, staying out for a full day or half day. Boats vary, but 6 anglers is about average. Approximate rates are: private, full day $325-$350, half day $250-$300; share, full day $65-$110, half day $60-$75. Full days are 8 hours, half days 4, with three-quarter days available too! No licenses are required and all gear is provided. Bring your own lunch, beverages, and camera. To charter a boat contact the individual captains directly, check at your hotel activities desk, or book through one of the following: **Kona Activities Center**, Box 1035, Kailua-Kona, HI 96740, tel. 329-3171; **Kona Coast Activities**, Box 5397, Kailua-Kona, HI 96740, tel. 329-2971; **Kona Charter Skippers Assoc.**, Box 806, Kailua-Kona, HI 96740, tel. 329-3600; **Mauna Kea Beach Hotel**, Travel Desk, Box 218, Kamuela, HI 96743, tel. 882-7222.

Most boats are berthed at Honokohau Harbor off Rt. 19, about midway between downtown Kailua and Keahole Airport. Big fish are weighed in at Kailua Pier, in front of the Hotel King Kamehameha. An excellent publication listing boats and general information concerning deep-sea fishing is *Hawaii Fishing Charter Guide.* This tabloid is available free at newsstands, hotel/condo lobbies, etc. For subscription rates write to Box P, Kailua-Kona, HI 96745.

Coastal And Freshwater Fishing

You don't have to hire a boat to catch fish! The coastline is productive too. *Ulua* are caught all along the coast south of Hilo, and at South Point and Kealekekua Point. *Papio* and *hahalalu* are caught in bays all around the island, while *manini* and *ama'ama* hit from Kawaihai to Puako. Hilo Bay is easily accessible to anyone, and the fishing is very exciting especially at the mouth of the Wailuku River.

Freshwater fishing is limited to the **Waiakea Public Fishing Area**, a state-operated facility in downtown Hilo. This 26-acre pond offers a variety of saltwater and brackish fish. A license is required. You can pick them up at sporting goods stores or at the Division of Conservation and Resources Enforcement Office, 75 Aupuni St., Hilo, HI 96720, tel. 961-7291.

Water Sports

Those in the know consider the **deep diving** along the steep drop-offs of Hawaii's geologically young coastline some of the best in the state. This means that only advanced divers should attempt deep-water dives, but beginners and snorkelers will have many visual thrills inside the protected bays and coves. (See "Beaches" in the travel sections.) Snorkel and scuba rental gear as well as escorted dives and lessons are available from: **Nautilus Dive Center**, 382 Kamehameha Ave., Hilo, tel. 935-6939—their free dive map is quite informative; **Gold Coast Divers** in the Hotel King Kamehameha, Kailua, tel. 329-1328; and **Sea Camp Hawaii** in Kailua, tel. 329-3388. The Beach Shack operated by Joel Petersen in front of the Hotel King Kamehameha is the starting point for the Kona triathlon and has good prices on snorkel rentals as well as kayaks and Hobie Cats. Larger hotels often have snorkel equipment for guests, and if it isn't free, it always costs more than if you rented it from a dive shop. Scuba and snorkel cruises are booked through the various activity centers previously mentioned under "deep-sea fishing," and at your hotel travel-desk.

The **surfing** off the Big Island is uninspiring compared to that off the other islands. The reefs are treacherous and the surf is lazy. Some surfers bob around off the north section of Hilo Bay, and sometimes in Kealakekua and Waiulua bays on the Kona side. Puna also attracts a few off Isaac Hale and Kaimu beaches. However, the winds are great for sailboarding. Rentals (roof racks provided) and lessons are available from Jerry Classen of **West Hawaii Sailboards,** tel. 329-3669 or 885-7744.

Skiing
Bored with sun and surf? Strap the "boards" to your feet and hit the slopes of Mauna Kea. There are no lifts so you'll need a 4WD to get to the top, and someone willing to pick you up again at the bottom. You can rent 4WDs from the car rental agencies already mentioned, but if that seems like too much hassle just contact **Ski Guides Hawaii**, Box 2020, Kamuela, HI 96743, tel. 885-4188 or 889-6747. Here you can rent skis and they'll provide the "lifts" to the top. You can expect snow from December to May, but you can't always count on it.

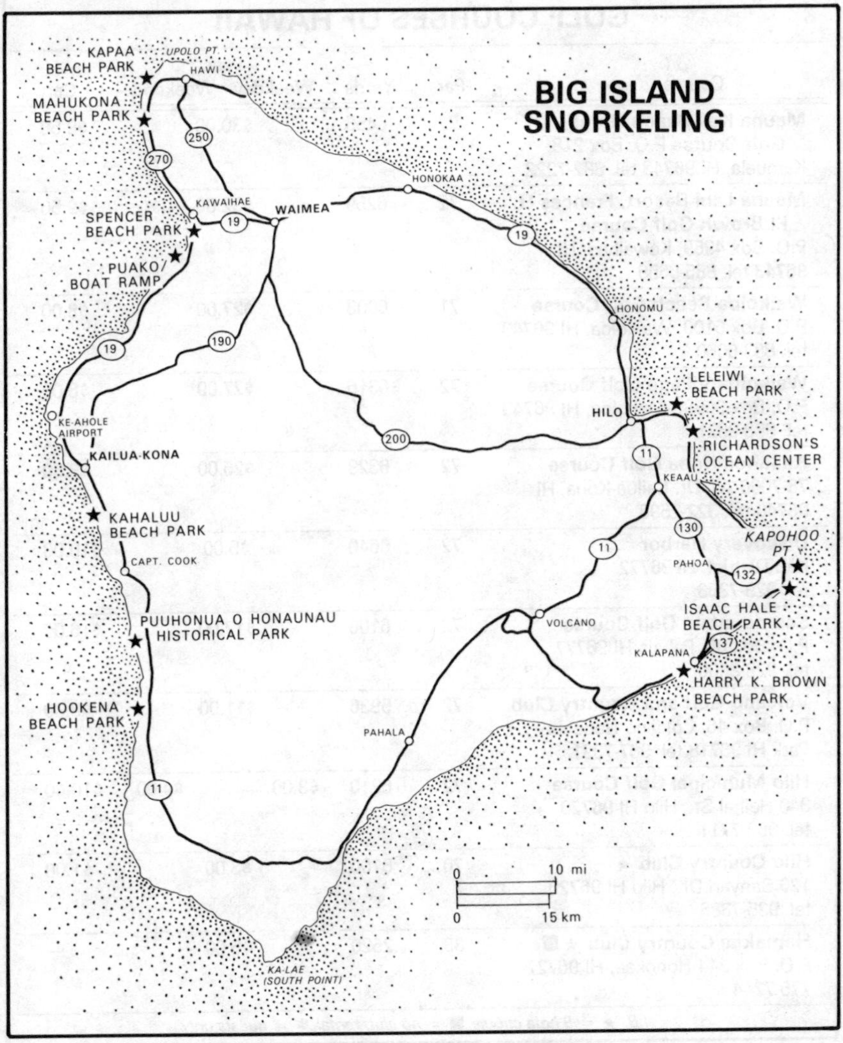

Golfing

The Big Island is a long way to go just to golf, but plenty of people come here for that reason alone. Robert Trent Jones Sr. and Jr. have both built exceptional courses here. Dad built the Mauna Kea Beach Hotel course, while the kid built his at the Waikoloa Beach Resort. Both links are in south Kohala, with another spectacular course at the nearby Mauna Lani. If these are too rich for your blood at $40 or so,

GOLF COURSES OF HAWAII

Course	Par	Yards	Fees		Cart
			Weekday	Weekend	
Mauna Kea Beach Hotel Golf Course P.O. Box 218, Kamuela, HI 96743 tel. 882-7222	72	6455	$30.00		$9.50
Mauna Lani Resort, Frances H. I'I Brown Golf Course P.O. Box 4959, Kawaihae, HI 96743 tel. 885-6655	72	6259	$32.00		$9.50
Waikoloa Beach Golf Course P.O. Box 5100, Waikoloa, HI 96743 tel. 883-6060	71	6003	$27.00		$8.00
Waikoloa Village Golf Course P.O. Box 3068, Waikoloa, HI 96743 tel. 883-9621	72	6316	$27.00		$8.00
Keauhou-Kona Golf Course 78-7000 Alii Dr. Kailua-Kona, HI 96740 tel. 322-2595	72	6329	$25.00		$9.50
Discovery Harbor Kau District, HI 96772 tel. 929-7353	72	6640	$5.00		$10.00
Seamountain Golf Course P.O. Box 85, Pahala HI 96777 tel. 928-8000	72	6106	$17.00		$16.00
Volcano Golf and Country Club P.O. Box 46, Colcano National Park HI 96718 tel. 967-7331	72	5936	$11.00		$8.00
Hilo Municipal Golf Course 340 Haihai St., Hilo HI 96720 tel. 959-7711	72	6210	$3.00	$4.00	$10.40
Hilo Country Club ★ 120 Banyan Dr., Hilo HI 96720 tel. 935-7388	70	6100	$3.00		$1.00
Hamakua Country Club ★ ■ P.O. Box 344 Honokaa, HI 96727 775-7244	33	2520	$5.00		—

N.B. ★ = 9 hole course ■ = no club rental ● = guests only

you can hit 9 holes in Hilo for about $5. How about golfing at Volcano Golf Course, where, if you miss a short putt, you can blame it on an earthquake.

Tennis
Many tennis courts dot Hawaii, and plenty of them are free. County courts are under the control of the Dept. of Parks and Recreation who maintain a combination of lighted and unlit courts in Hilo, Kona, and Waimea. Some private and hotel courts are open to the public for a fee, while others restrict play to guests only.

Hunting
Huge unpopulated expanses of grasslands, forests, and scrubby mountainsides are very good for hunting. The Big Island's game includes feral pig, sheep, and goats, plus a variety of pheasant, quail, dove, and wild turkey. Mauna Kea Beach Hotel guests can hunt on the Parker Ranch, while the **McCandless Ranch** near Captain Cook supplies guides for its 30,000 acres. For information contact Steve Arrington, Box 63 G, Captain Cook, HI 96704, tel. 328-2349/2389. Public game lands are all over the island where a license is required to take

TENNIS COURTS OF HAWAII

COUNTY COURTS

Under jurisdiciton of the Dept. of Parks & Recreation,
25 Aupuni St. Hilo, HI 96720. Tel. 961-8311.
Courts listed are in the Hilo, Waimea, and Kailua-Kona areas.
There are 9 additional locations around the island.

Location	Name of Court	No. of Courts	Lighted
Hilo	Hoolulu Park	8	Yes
Hilo	Lincoln Park	4	Yes
Hilo	Mohouli Park	2	No
Hilo	University of Hawaii—Hilo College	2	No
Kona	Kailua Park	4	Yes
Kona	Kailua Playground	1	Yes
Kona	Keauhou Park	1	No
Waimea	Waimea Park	2	Yes

HOTEL & PRIVATE COURTS THAT ARE OPEN TO THE PUBLIC

Hilo	Sheraton-Walakea Village Hotel (fee)	2	No
Kailua-Kona	Hotel King Kamehameha (fee)	2	Yes
Kailua-Kona	Kona Hilton Beach & Tennis Resort (fee)	4	Yes
Kailua-Kona	Kona Lagoon (fee for non-guests)	2	Yes
Kamuela	Waimea Park	2	Yes
Keauhou-Kona	Keauhou Beach Hotel (fee)	6	Yes
Keauhou-Kona	Kona Surf Hotel Racket Club (fee)	7	Yes
Pahala	Seamountain Tennis Center (fee)	4	No
Waikoloa	Waikoloa Village (fee)	2	Yes

Judy Ellis, lady wrangler

birds and game. For full information, write Division of Forestry and Wildlife, 1643 Kilauea Ave., Box 4849, Hilo, HI 96720, tel. 961-7221.

Horseback Riding

A classic way to see an island known for its cattle and cowboys is from the back of a horse. The best trail rides are offerd by **Ironwood Outfitters,** Box 832, Kamuela, HI 96743, tel. 885-4941. These stables, run by a lady wrangler Judy Ellis, are located along Rt. 250 between Kamuela and Hawi near mile marker 11. Judy's a farm girl from Iowa who's spent all her life around horses. She came to the Big Island in the early '70s and made her living breaking rough stock. Now she offers a variety of trail rides over the spectacular 30,000 acres of the Kahua Ranch. Her well-adapted "mountain horses" cost $18 p/h and the most popular ride is a 3-hour "mountain ride" for $40. Judy tailors rides to suit just about any situation. Her rides are popular, so book in advance.

Waipio Valley Ranch offers the most unique rides on Hawaii. It's a new outfit operated by Sherri Hannum and Wayne Teves. Since Sherri and Wayne live down in phoneless Waipio, you must contact them 24 hours in advance by calling their answering service at Waipio Woodworks (topside in Kukuihaele) at tel. 775-0958. It's well worth the extra effort. The partners have lived in Waipio for 10 years and know its history, geology, and legends intimately. They offer pick up service from Kukuihaele for their half-day ($55) and full-day ($100) rides. They treat their guests like family, offering tasty local treats and a refreshing dip either off Waipio's Black Sand Beach or at the myth-shrouded Nanaue Falls. If you have time, don't miss this adventure. (For more information see p. 574).

Tamer but enjoyable rides are offered by the **Mauna Kea Beach Hotel** (non-guests too!), tel. 882-7222. They have an arrangement with the Parker Ranch which will supply a *paniolo* to guide you over the quarter-million acres of open range on the slopes of Mauna Kea. The stables are at Parker Ranch HQ in Waimea. Rates are $16 p/h. The **Waikoloa Countryside Stables,** Box 3068, Waikoloa Village, HI 96743, tel. 883-9335, have 10,000 acres to gallop over. They offer a variety of rides with the basic cost at $14 p/h. A specialty is a sunset 2-hour ride at $25.

INFORMATION AND SERVICES

Emergency

Police phone numbers vary by community so check the inside front cover of the telephone directory for a complete list. **Ambulance and fire** all island, tel. 961-6022. **Hospitals:** Kealakekua, tel. 322-9311; Hilo, tel. 961-4211; Honokaa, tel. 775-7211; Kohala, tel. 889-6211;

Kau, tel. 928-8331. **Drug stores:** Long's Drugs, 555 Kilauea Ave., Hilo, tel. 935-3357; Kona Coast Drugs, Kailua, tel. 329-8886; Village Pharmacy, Waimea, tel. 885-4418.

Information

The best information is dispensed by the **Hawaii Visitors Bureau,** 180 Kinoole St., Suite 104, Hilo, tel. 935-5271; 755-719W, Alii Dr., Marlin Plaza, Kailua, tel. 329-1782; also at the Wailoa Center just near the State Building in Hilo at tel. 961-7360. The State Visitor Information centers at the airports, Hilo tel. 935-1018, and Kona tel. 329-3423, are good sources of information available on arrival. **Chamber of Commerce,** 180 Kinoole St., Hilo, tel. 935-7178.

Alternative Health Care

The Big Island is blessed with some of the finest natural healers and practitioners in the state. For a holistic healing experience of body, mind, and soul, the following are highly recommended. **School of Hawaiian Lomi Lomi,** Box 221, Captain Cook, HI 96704, tel. 323-2416 or 328-2472. Here, Margaret Machado, assisted by her husband Daniel, provides the finest *lomi lomi* and traditional Hawaiian herbal cures in the islands. Both are renowned *kapuna* who dispense a heavy dose of love and concern with every remedy prescribed.

The **Kona School of Massage,** tel. 322-0048, offers state-certified massage courses and mini-courses for the beginner or experienced therapist. A full range of massage, anatomy, and physiology are part of the coursework preparing the student for a Hawaii State License. Courses last for 100 hours and cost approximately $500.

Acupuncture and Herbs is the domain of Angela Longo. This remarkable woman is not only a superbly trained, licensed practitioner of traditional Chinese medicine and acupuncture, but she covers all bases by holding a Ph.D. in biochemistry from U.C. Berkeley. For a totally holistic health experience contact Angela at her Kona office, tel. 322-2114, or at her Waimea/Kamuela office, tel. 885-7886.

To revitalize those aching muscles and to put a spring in your step the following massage practitioners have magic in their hands: **Kiauhou Massage and Spa** by the two Nancys, Sturdvin and Kahalewai, at the Kiauhou Beach Hotel, tel. 322-3441, room 227. Open Tues., Thurs., and Sat. 10:00 a.m. to 5:00 p.m., and Mon., Wed., and Fri. 5:00 p.m. to 8:00 p.m. **Massage by Nasisu**, tel. 322-0048, for a relaxing and therapeutic massage. To get that just right chiropractic adjustment try **Rodgers Chiropractic Arts** with Howard Rodgers, D.C., in the WOW Building, Kailua, tel. 329-2271, or **Kohala Chiropractic** with Dr. Bob Abdy, Hawi, tel. 889-5858, Kamuela, tel. 885-6847.

Reading Material

Make sure to pick up copies of the following free literature. Besides maps and general information, they often include money-saving coupons. Available at most hotels/condos and at all tourist areas, published weekly, they include: *Guide to Hawaii*, *Big Island Beach Press*;

Ms. Angela Longo

This Week Big Island. Harry Lyons' *Kona Coast* is a monthly tabloid offering topical island editorials, restaurant critiques, humorous anecdotes and jokes, and an advertisers' bulletin board. Island newspapers include: *Hawaii-Tribune Herald,* a Hilo publication, and *West Hawaii Today* published in Kona. **Libraries** are located in towns and schools all over the island. The main branch is at 300 Waianuenue Ave., Hilo, tel. 935-5407. They provide all information regarding libraries; in Kailua-Kona at 75-140 Hualalai Rd., tel. 329-2196. Please refer to the "Shopping" chapter for bookstores.

Weather Information
Receive 24-hour recorded information regarding volcanic activity by calling 967-7977; weather information, tel. 961-5582; Coast Guard, tide conditions, tel. 935-6370.

Post Office
Branch post offices are found in most major towns. The following are the main ones: Hilo, tel. 935-2821; Kailua, tel. 329-2927; Captain Cook, tel. 323-3663; Waimea/Kamuela, tel. 885-4026.

Island Facts
Hawaii has 3 fitting nicknames: the Big Island, the Volcano Island, and the Orchid Island. It's the youngest, most southerly, and largest (4,038 square miles) island in the Hawaiian chain. Its color is red, and the island *lei* is fashioned from the *lehua,* an *ohia* blossom.

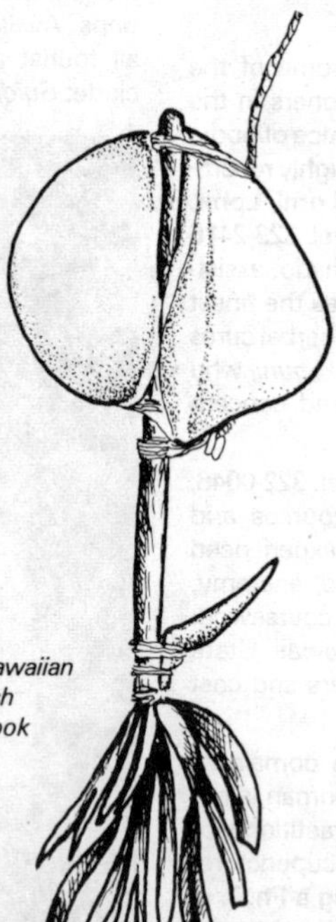

Hawaiian fish hook

HILO

Hilo is a blind date. Everyone tells you what a beautiful personality she has, but...But?...it rains: 133 inches a year. Mostly the rains come in winter, and are limited to predictable afternoon showers, but they do scare some tourists away, keeping Hilo reasonably priced and low keyed. In spite of, and because of, the rain, Hilo is gorgeous. It's one of the oldest permanently settled towns in Hawaii, and the largest on the windward coast of the islands. Hilo's weather makes it a natural greenhouse. Twenty acres of exotic orchids and flowers line the runways at the airport! Botanical gardens and flower farms surround Hilo like a giant *lei,* and shoulder-to-shoulder banyans canopy entire city blocks. To counterpoint this tropical explosion, Mauna Kea's winter snows backdrop the town. The crescent of Hilo Bay blazes gold at sunrise, while a sculpted lagoon, Oriental pagodas, rock gardens, and even a tiny island connected by footbridge line its shores. Downtown's waterfront has the perfect false-front buildings that always need a paint job. They lean on each other like "old salts" that've had one too many. Don't make the mistake of underestimating Hilo, or counting it out because of its rainy reputation. For most, the blind date with this exotic beauty turns into a fun-filled love affair.

SIGHTS

Hilo is the eastern hub of the island. Choose a direction, and an hour's driving puts you in a time-lost valley, deep into *paniolo* country, sitting on the blackness of a recent lava flow, or surveying the steaming fumaroles of Volcanoes Park. In and around town are museums, riverbank fishing, cultural centers, plenty of gardens, waterfalls, a pot-holed riverbed, and lava caves. Hilo's beaches are small, rocky, and hard to find—perfect for keeping crowds away. Hilo is bite-sized, but you'll need a rental car or the Banyan Shuttle to visit most of the sights around town.

Lyman Mission House And Museum

At 276 Haili St., Hilo 96720, tel. 835-5021. Open daily except Sun. 9:00 a.m. to 4:00 p.m. Admission $2.50 adults, $1.25 children (6 to 18 years). This admission allows you into both the original Lyman House and the Museum, the large new building just next door.

This well-preserved New England-style frame house was the homestead of the Lymans, a Congregationalist missionary family. It's the

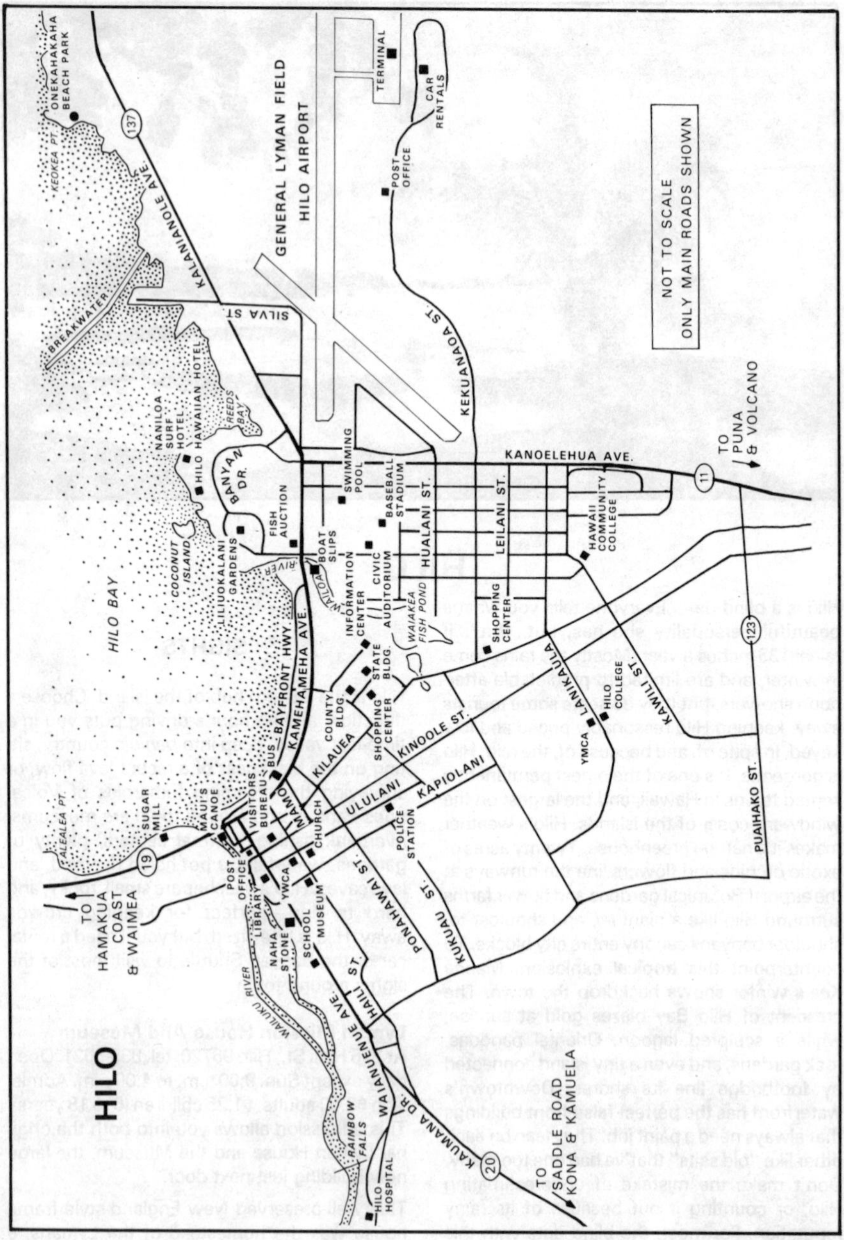
HILO
NOT TO SCALE
ONLY MAIN ROADS SHOWN
ONEKAHAKAHA BEACH PARK
KEOKEA PT.
137
KALANIANAOLE AVE.
GENERAL LYMAN FIELD
HILO AIRPORT
TERMINAL
CAR RENTALS
POST OFFICE
BREAKWATER
SILVA ST.
KEKUANAOA ST.
NANILOA SURF HOTEL
HILO HAWAIIAN HOTEL
REEDS BAY
BANYAN DR.
SWIMMING POOL
BASEBALL STADIUM
KANOELEHUA AVE.
TO PUNA & VOLCANO
11
HAWAII COMMUNITY COLLEGE
LEILANI ST.
HUALANI ST.
FISH AUCTION
LILIUOKALANI GARDENS
COCONUT ISLAND
HILO BAY
BOAT SLIPS
CIVIC AUDITORIUM
INFORMATION CENTER
WAILOA RIVER
WAIAKEA FISH POND
SHOPPING CENTER
STATE BLDG.
COUNTY BLDG.
SHOPPING CENTER
BAYFRONT HWY.
KAMEHAMEHA AVE.
BUS
KILAUEA
MAMO
KINOOLE ST.
LANIKAULA
KAWILI ST.
123
YMCA
HILO COLLEGE
PUAIHAKO ST.
ULULANI
KAPIOLANI
PONAHAWAI ST.
KUKUAU ST.
POLICE STATION
CHURCH
MUSEUM
YMCA
SCHOOL
NAHA STONE
LIBRARY
POST OFFICE
VISITORS BUREAU
MAUI'S CANOE
SUGAR MILL
ALEALEA PT.
19
TO HAMAKUA COAST & WAIMEA
HAILI ST.
WAIANUENUE AVE.
WAILUKU RIVER
RAINBOW FALLS
HILO HOSPITAL
KAUMANA DR.
20
TO SADDLE ROAD KONA & KAMUELA

oldest frame building on Hawaii, built by David and Sarah Lyman in 1839. In 1856, a second story was added, which provided more room and a perfect view of the harbor. In 1926, Haili Street was extended past the home, and at that time the Wilcox and Lyman families had the house turned parallel to the street so that it would front the entrance. It was opened as a museum in 1932. The furniture is authentic "Sandwich Isles" circa 1850, the best pieces fashioned from *ohia.* Much of it has come from other missionary homes although many pieces belonged to the original occupants.

The floors, mantles, and doors are deep, luxurious *koa.* The main door is a "Christian Door," built by the Hilo Boys Boarding School. The top panels form a cross and the bottom depicts an open Bible. Many of the artifacts on the deep windowsills are tacked down because of earthquakes. One room was used as a schoolroom/dayroom where Mrs. Lyman taught arithmetic, map-making, and proper manners. The dining room holds an original family rocking chair and table that would be set with "blue willow" china seen in a nearby hutch. Some of the most interesting exhibits are small personal items like a music box that still plays, and a collection of New England autumn leaves that Mrs. Lyman had sent over to show her children what that season was like. Upstairs are bedrooms occupied by the parents and the 8 children (6 boys). Their portraits hang in a row. Emma, youngest of the eight, kept a diary and faithfully recorded eruptions, earthquakes, and *tsunami*. Scientists still refer it for some of the earliest recorded data on these natural disturbances. The master bedroom has a large *koa* bed with pineapples carved into the bedposts, handmade by a sea captain who lived in Hilo. The bedroom mirror is an original, in which many Hawaiians received their first surprised look at themselves. Connected to the master bedroom is the nursery that holds a cradle used by all 8 children. It's obvious that the Lymans did not live luxuriously, but they were comfortable in their new island home.

Next door to the Lyman House, in a modern 2-story building, is the museum. As you enter, you are greeted by a bust of King David Kalakaua, the Merry Monarch, who reigned from 1874 until 1891. The first floor is designated as the **Island Heritage Gallery.** On entering is a replica of a Hawaiian grass house complete with thatched roof and floor mats. Nearby are Hawaiian tools: hammers of clinkstone, chisels of basalt, and state-of-the-art "stone age" polishing stones with varying textures used to rub bowls and canoes to a smooth finish. Hawaiian fiberwork, the best in Polynesia, is next. As well as coconut and pandanus, the Hawaiians used the pliable air root of the *ie'ie.* The material, dyed brown or black, was woven into intricate designs. There are fish hooks, stone lamps, mortars and pestles, *lomi lomi* sticks, even a display on *kahunas,* with a fine text on the *kapu* system. Pre-contact displays give way to *kimono* from Japan, a Chinese herbal medicine display, and a nook dedicated to Filipino heritage. Saying good-bye is a bust of Mark Twain, carved into a piece of the very monkeypod tree that he planted in Waiohinu in 1866.

Upstairs is the **Earth Heritage Gallery.** The mineral and rock collection here is rated one of the top ten in the entire country, and by far the best in Polynesia. Marvel at thunder eggs, agates, jaspers, India blue mezolite, aquamarine lazerite from Afghanistan, and hunks of weirdly shaped lava. These displays are the lifelong collection of the great-grandson of the original Rev. Lyman. Anything coming from the earth can be exhibited here: shells named and categorized from around the world, petrified wood, cases of glass paperweights, crystals, Chinese artifacts, and Japanese screens. Scientific works from Kilauea and Mauna Kea are explained, and an entire section is dedicated to the vanishing flora and fauna of Hawaii. The museum is an educational delight.

Walking Tour

After leaving the Lyman Museum, it's a short walk over to Hilo's library, 300 Waianuenue Ave. Sitting at the entrance are 2 large stones. The larger is called **Naha Stone,** known for its ability to detect any offspring of the ruling Naha clan. The test was simple: place a baby on it, if it remained silent, it was Naha, if it cried, it wasn't. It is believed that this 7,000-pound monolith was brought from Kauai by canoe and placed near Pinao Temple in the imme-

Rainbow Falls

diate vicinity of what is now Wailuku Drive and Keawe Street. Kamehameha the Great supposedly fulfilled a prophecy of "moving a mountain" by budging this stone. The smaller stone is thought to be an entrance pillar of the Pinao Temple. Just behind the library is the Wailuku River. Pick any of its bridges to give you a panoramic view down to the sea. Often, local fishermen try their luck from the grassy banks. The massive boulder sitting in the mouth of the river is known as Maui's Canoe.

Natural Sites

A few miles out of town, heading west on Waianuenue Avenue, are 2 natural spectacles definitely worth a look. Just past Hilo High School a sign directs you to Wailuku River State Park. Here is **Rainbow Falls**, a most spectacular yet easily visited sight. You'll look over a circular pool in the river below that's almost 100 feet in diameter, and cascading into it is a lovely waterfall. The falls deserve their name because as they hit the water below their mists throw flocks of rainbows into the air. Underneath the falls is a huge cavern. Most people are content to look from the vantage point near the parking lot, but if you walk to the left a stone stairway leads to a private viewing area directly over the falls. Here the river, strewn with volcanic boulders, pours over the edge. Follow the path for a minute or so along the bank to come to a gigantic banyan tree and a different vantage point.

Follow Waianuenue Street for 2 more miles past Hilo Hospital to the heights above above town. A sign to turn right onto Pee Pee Falls Street points to the **Boiling Pots**. Usually no one is here. At the parking lot is an emergency phone and toilets. Follow the path past "No Swimming" signs to an overlook. Indented into the riverbed below are a series of irregularly shaped holes that look like a peg-legged giant left his "peg print" in the hot lava. Seven or 8 are like naturally bubbling jacuzzis. Turn your head upriver to see Pee Pee Falls, a gorgeous 5-spouted waterfall. You'll have this area to yourself, and it's great for a quiet picnic lunch.

Around Banyan Drive

If your Hilo hotel isn't situated along Banyan Drive, go there. This bucolic road skirts the edge of the Waiakea Peninsula, sticking out into Hilo Bay. Lining the drive is an almost uninterrupted series of banyans that seem like a giant hedgerow, while the fairways and greens of the Banyan Golf Course take up the center of the tiny peninsula. Park your car at one end and take a 15-minute stroll through this park-like atmosphere; the banyans have been named for well-known American luminaries. Boutiques and a variety of restaurants sit coolly under the trees.

Liliuokalani Gardens are formal Japanese-style gardens located along the west end of Banyan Drive. Meditatively quiet, they offer a beautiful view of the bay. **Coconut Island** just offshore is connected by a footbridge leading from the gardens. Along the footpaths are pagodas designed for relaxing, *torii* gates, stone lanterns, and half-moon bridges spanning a series of ponds and streams. Few people visit, and if it weren't for the striking fingers of black lava and coconut trees, you could easily be in Japan.

Suisan Fish Market is at the corner of Banyan Drive and Lihiwai Street which crosses Kamehameha Avenue. This fish auction draws island fishermen of every nationality. The auctioneer's staccato is pure pidgin. Restaurateurs, housewives, and a smattering of tourists gather by 7:30 a.m. to eyeball the catch of the day. Boats tie up and fishermen talk quietly about the prices. Next door a small snack shop sells sandwiches and piping hot coffee. Grab a cup and walk over to the gardens through a nearby entrance—you'll have them to yourself.

Cross Lihiwai Street heading south. **Waiakea Pond,** a brackish lagoon where people often fish, is on your right. To the left is **Hoolulu County Park, Civic Center Auditorium,** and a city nursery brimming with orchids. The **Culture Center Nihon** is here, at 123 Lihiwai Street, which displays artworks and cultural exhibits from Japan. The center is also a restaurant and *sushi* bar, with a special room set aside for the "tea ceremony." (For more details see "Food" below.)

On the opposite side of Waiakea Fish Pond (drive down Kamehameha Avenue and make a left onto Pauahi Street since no bridges cross), you'll find **Wailoa Information Center** dispensing all manner of brochures and pamphlets on Hilo's and the Big Island's activities. The walls of this 10-sided building are used to display works of local artists and cultural/historic exhibits, changed on a monthly basis. Across the parking lot in a grassy area is the **Tsunami Memorial,** dedicated to those who lost their lives in the devastating tidal waves that raked the island. Volcanic stone, inlaid with blue and green tile, has been laid to form a circular wall that undulates and peaks like a wave. It's worth a look.

Hilo's Gardens

Hilo's greatest asset is its flowers. Its biggest cash crops are orchids and anthuriums. Flowers grow everywhere, but to see them in a more formalized way visit one of the following nurseries in and around town. **Hilo Tropical Gardens,** (formerly Kong's Floraleigh), 1477 Kalanianaole Ave., Hilo, HI 96720, tel. 935-4957, is open daily 9:00 a.m. to 5:00 p.m. Go on a free self-guided tour through the gardens where all plants have been labeled. Everything's here: plumeria, lipstick trees, anthuriums, orchids, birds of paradise, even pineapples, coconuts, and papayas. You can purchase all manner of dried and fresh-cut flowers, seeds, packaged plants, seedlings, and corsages. A boutique offers handmade

Liliuokalani Gardens

Hawaiian products. The "no-pressure" sales people are courteous and friendly. Shipping purchases is no problem.

Heading toward Volcanoes Park 3-4 miles from town on Rt. 11 takes you by a variety of nurseries offering free tours. Most grow orchids and anthuriums among other exotic plants. For a visual treat visit: **Hirose Nurseries,** 2212 Kanoelehua Ave., tel. 959-4561; **Nani Mau Gardens** at 421 Makalika St. (left off Rt. 11,) tel. 959-9442; **Kualoa Farms** at the corner of Mamaki (off Rt. 11) and Kealakai streets, tel. 959-4565, daily 8:00 a.m. to 4:00 p.m. A guided tour takes you over some of the 62 acres planted in anthuriums, *ti* plants, torch gingers, and macadamia and papaya orchards.

BEACHES

If you define a beach as a long open expanse of white sand covered by a thousand sunbathers and their beach umbrellas, then Hilo doesn't have any. If a beach, to you, can be a smaller, more intimate affair where a good but not gigantic number of tourists and families can spend the day on pockets of sand between fingers of black lava, then Hilo has plenty. Hilo's best beaches all lie to the east of the city along Kalanianaole Avenue. Not all are clearly marked, but are easily spotted by cars parked along the road or in makeshift parking lots. Kalanianaole Avenue runs 6 miles from downtown Hilo to where it dead ends at Lelei Point.

Hilo Bayfront Park is a thousand yards of black sand that narrows considerably as it runs west from the Wailoa River toward downtown. At one time it went all the way to the Wailuku River and was renowned throughout the islands for its beauty, but commercialism of the harbor has ruined it. By the 1960s, so much sewage and industrial waste had been pumped into the bay that it was considered a public menace, and then the great *tsunami* came. Reclamation projects created the Wailoa River State Recreation Area at the east end, and shorefront land became a buffer zone against future inundation. Few swimmers come to the beach because the water is cloudy and chilly, but the sharks don't seem to mind! The bay is terrific for fishing and picknicking, and the sails of small craft and windsurfers can always be seen. It's a perfect spot for canoe races, and many local teams come to train. Notice the judging towers and canoe sheds. Toward the west end, near the mouth of the Wailuku River, surfers catch long rides during the winter months, entertaining spectators.

Coconut Island Park is reached by footbridge from a spit of land just outside of Liliuokalani Gardens. It was at one time a *pu'uhonua* ("place of refuge") that lay across from a human sacrificial *heiau* on the peninsula side. Coconut Island has restrooms, pavilion, and picnic tables shaded by tall coconut trees and ironwoods. A favorite picnic spot for decades, there's a diving tower and a sheltered natural

canoe sheds at Hilo Bayfront Park

Richardson's Beach

pool area for children. The only decent place to swim in Hilo Bay, it also offers the best panorama of the city, bay, and Mauna Kea beyond.

Reeds Bay Beach Park is on the east side of the Waiakea Peninsula at the end of Banyan Drive. It too is technically part of Hilo Bay, and offers good swimming, though the water is notoriously cold because of a constantly flowing freshwater spring. Most people just picnic here, and fishermen frequent the area.

Keaukaha Beach, located on Puhi Bay, is the first in a series of beaches as you head east on Kalanianaole Avenue. Look for Baker Avenue, and pull off left into a parking area just near an old pavilion. Not an official beach park, it is a favorite spot with local people who swim at "Cold Water Pond," a spring-fed inlet at the head of the bay. A sewage treatment plant fronts the western side of Puhi Bay. Much nicer areas await just up Kalanianaole Avenue.

Onekahakaha Beach Park has it all: safe swimming, white-sand beach, lifeguards, all amenities, and camping. Turn left onto Machida Lane and park in the lot of Hilo's favorite "family" beach. Swim in the large sandy-bottom pool protected by the breakwater. Outside the breakwater the currents can be fierce and drownings have been recorded. Walk east along the shore to find an undeveloped area of the park with many small tidal pools. Beware of sea urchins.

James Kealoha Park is next; people swim, snorkel, and fish, and during winter months it's a favorite surf spot. A large grassy area is shaded by trees and a picnic pavilion. Just offshore is Mahikea Island, also known as Scout Island because local boy scouts often camp here. This entire area was known for its fishponds, and inland, just across Kalanianaole Avenue, is Loko'aka Pond, a commercial operation providing the best mullet on the island.

Leleiwi Beach Park lies along a lovely residential area carved into the rugged coastline. Part of the park is dedicated to the Richardson Ocean Center, and the entire area is locally called **Richardson's Beach.** Look for Uwau Street, just past the Mauna Loa Shores Condo, and park along the road here. Spot a fancy house surrounded by tall coconut trees and follow the pathway through the grove. Use a shower that's coming out of the retaining wall surrounding the house. Keep walking until you come to a sea wall. A tiny cove and black-sand beach is the first in a series. This is a terrific area for snorkeling with plenty of marine life. Walk east to a natural lava breakwater. Behind it pools are filled and flushed by the surging tide. The water breaks over the top of the lava and rushes into the pools, making a natural jacuzzi. This is one of the most picturesque swimming areas on the island. At Leleiwi Beach Park proper (3 pavilions), the shore is open to the ocean and there are strong currents. It's best to head directly to Richardson's.

Lehia Park is the end of the road. When the pavement stops follow the dirt track until you come to a large grassy field shaded by a variety of trees. This unofficial camping area has no amenities whatsoever. A series of pools like those at Richardson's are small, sandy-bottomed, and safe. Outside of the natural lava breakwater is treacherous. Wintertime often sends tides surging inland here, making Lehia unusable. This area is about as far away as you can get and still be within a few minutes of downtown Hilo.

ACCOMMODATIONS

Accommodations in Hilo are hardly ever booked out, and they're reasonably priced. Sounds great, but many hotels have "gone condo" to survive, while others have simply shut their doors, so there aren't as many as there once were. During the Merry Monarch Festival (late April), the entire town is booked solid! The best hotels are clustered along Banyan Drive, with a few gems tucked away on the city streets.

Banyan Drive Hotels

The following hotels all lie along Banyan Drive. They range from moderate to deluxe. All are serviced by the Banyan Shuttle (see p. 538).

Hilo Hawaiian Hotel, 71 Banyan Dr., Hilo, HI 96720, tel. 935-9361 or 800-367-5004. This classy hotel's prices start at $42-45; all rooms have a/c, phone, and TV, plus pool. The Hilo Hawaiian occupies the most beautiful grounds of any hotel in Hilo. From the vantage of the hotel's colonnaded veranda, you overlook formal gardens, Coconut Island, and Hilo Bay. The hotel buffet, especially seafood on Tues. and Fri., is absolutely out of this world (see below). Built like a huge arc, its architecture has been slammed in the past, but it blends well with its surroundings and expresses the theme set by Hilo Bay, that of a long sweeping crescent. As a deluxe hotel, the Hilo Hawaiian is great.

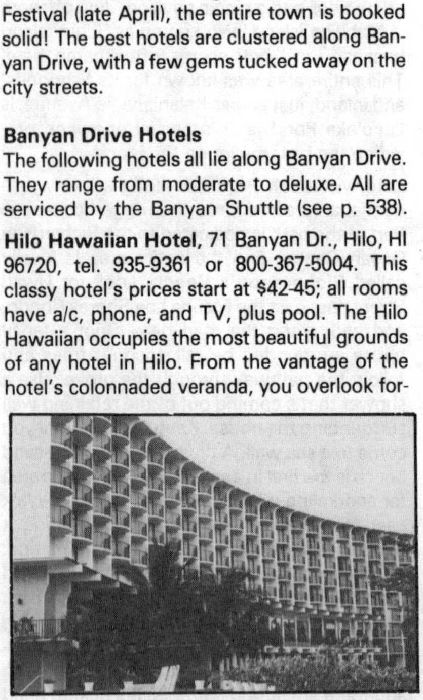

Hilo Hawaiian Hotel

Naniloa Surf Hotel, 93 Banyan Dr., Hilo, HI 96720, tel. 935-0831, or 800-367-5360. This massive 386-room hotel offers deluxe accommodation starting at $50. They offer a/c, TV, hotel pool, parking, and tennis. The pool setting, just above the lava, is the nicest in Hilo. HQ of the Merry Monarch Festival, the original hotel dates back over 60 years, and has built up a fine reputation for value and service.

Hilo Bay Hotel, is sandwiched between the above deluxe hotels at 87 Banyan Dr., Hilo, HI 96720, tel. 935-0861 or 800-442-5841. Rooms here begin at $32 double, with the most expensive under $50. The Hilo Bay offers good value, but it's a bit of "mutton dressed as lamb." The building is yellow stucco, with wood-shingled *lanai* running around the outside. There is parking, pool, and all rooms are clean, have TV, a/c, and phones. Uncle Billy's Polynesian Marketplace is part of the complex.

You can't miss the orange and black **Hilo Hikilau Hotel,** 126 Banyan Drive, tel. 935-0821 or 800-367-7000. This is the budget hotel on Banyan Drive. It's island-owned by the Kimi family, and like the others in this small chain, it's clean, well kept, and has Polynesian-inspired decor. Room prices vary according to the amount of business happening at the time, and can dip as low as $20 s but expect to pay about $30. The grounds are laid out around a central courtyard and the pool is secluded away from the street. This family-style hotel has a motel atmosphere, where the friendly staff go out of their way to make you feel welcome.

The following hotels are found along Hilo's downtown streets. Some are in quiet residential areas, while others are along busy thoroughfares. They are moderately to inexpensively priced.

Dolphin Bay Hotel is a sparkling little gem—simply the best hotel bargain in Hilo one of those places where you get more than what you pay for. It sits on a side street in the Pu'ueo section of town at the north end of Hilo Bay: 333 Iliahi St., Hilo 96720, tel. 935-1466. John Alexander is the owner/manager. The hotel was built by his father who spent years in Japan, and you'll be happy to discover this influence when you sink deep into the *ofuro*-type tubs in every room. The 18 units all have full modern kitchens, a $19 single studio apartment, to a 2-bedroom, fully furnished unit for $48. Deluxe units upstairs have open-beam ceilings and a *lanai,* and with 3 spacious rooms feel like an apartment. No TV, swimming pool, or a/c, but there are fans and excellent cross ventilation. The grounds and housekeeping are immaculate, and bananas, papayas, and other exotic fruits are found in hanging baskets free for guests. Weekly and monthly rates range from $156/$510 d for a studio to $300/$880 d for a 2-bedroom deluxe. Make reservations, because everyone who has found the Dolphin Bay comes back again and again.

The **Lanikai** (formerly Hotel Palm Terrace) is just down the street from the Dolphin Bay at 100 Puueo St., tel. 935-5556. Oftentimes no one is in the lobby to register you, but the resident manager is around somewhere. This hotel is a bit run-down, but you can't beat the $14 s, and $17 d, or the $65 to $100 weeklies. For this you'll get a small, adequately furnished room that may have a refrigerator and hot plate.

Hilo Hotel is downtown at 142 Kinoole St., Hilo 96720, tel. 961-3733. This small old hotel, with one section dating from 1888, may appeal to your sense of adventure and nostalgia. That's about all it'll appeal to, as it sits along a busy street under the spreading boughs of a huge rubber tree. However, it does pass the 2 basic tests: friendliness and cleanliness. The basic rooms in both old and new wings are under $20. Old wing rooms have phones; new wing rooms are quieter and have a/c. A big front porch holds rocking chairs, and complimentary coffee is served at the pool every morning. The Hilo Hotel is home to the Fuji Restaurant, one of the best in Hilo.

The **Iolani Hotel**, 193 Kinoole St., Hilo 96720, tel. 961-9863, and the **Kamaaina Hotel** at 110 Haili St., tel. 961-9860, are your basic flea-bag dives. You can get a room at both for about $65 a week if you can ever find anyone to check you in.

FOOD

Inexpensive Dining

Mun Cheong Lau is a cheap Chinese joint in downtown Hilo at 126 Keawe St., tel. 935-3040. If you want to eat with the "people," this is the spot, and it's open until 2:00 a.m. Soups on the front of the menu are $2.80, those on the back are $1.50, and there's very little difference except the price; the bowls are generous. Entrees like crispy chicken in oyster sauce for under $5 are delicious at any price.

Ting Hao Mandarin Kitchen is a family affair run by Alice Chang and her sister. At the moment they are located at the Lanikai Hotel at 100 Puueo St., tel. 935-9697, but they plan to move out to the new Puainako Town Center Mall, just south of town on Rt. 11. Open week-

days 11:00 a.m. to 8:30 p.m., weekends 5:00-8:30 p.m. Wherever they are, seek them out for a mouth-watering, home-cooked meal. The 2 most expensive items on the menu are Seafood Treasure for $6, and half a tea-smoked duck for $7; all others are under $5. Service is slow due to individual order cooking, and those in the know pick up a handout menu and call to place their orders 30 minutes before arriving.

Dick's Coffee House in the Hilo Shopping Center, tel. 935-2769, is American standard with a Hawaiian twist. Open daily 7:00 a.m. to 10:00 p.m., Sun. 7:00 to 10:30 a.m. This place could be Smalltown, U.S.A., with the walls covered in pennants except that the waitresses wear outrageously colorful Hawaiian-style uniforms. Excellent prices for decent food such as full meals with soup, salad, dessert, and coffee for $4.50.

Hukilau Restaurant at the Hukilau Hotel, 136 Banyan Way, is open daily 7:00 a.m. to 9:00 p.m. Along with passable breakfasts and dinners, the Hukilau Restaurant unfortunately offers an all-you-can-eat daily lunch special for $2.45 that's popular with senior citizens. "How can I go wrong," you ask? Everything is mercilessly deep fried with enough grease to plug the Alaska pipeline, and the rest is out of a can.

Tomi Zushi hole-in-the-wall Japanese restaurant is a favorite with local people. It's at 68 Mamo St., tel. 961-6100. More of the same is Jimmy's at 362 Kinoole, tel. 935-5571, where you can fill up for under $4.

Moderately Priced

J.D's Banyan Broiler is next door to the Neolani Hotel at 111 Banyan Drive, tel. 961-5802. You save money here by being your own chef. Sirloin steak is $10.75, lobster $17.50, and the catch-of-the-day $8.50. All trimmings are included. The atmosphere is very casual in this airy Polynesian-style restaurant.

Uncle Billy's at the Hilo Bay Hotel along Banyan Dr., tel. 935-0861, is open for breakfast featuring a $1.99 "aloha special" from 6:30 to 9:00 a.m., dinner from 5:00 to 8:30 p.m. Enjoy the free nightly *hula* show from 6:30 to 7:30 p.m. The interior is neo-Polynesian with a Model T Ford as part of the decor. Basically a fish and steak restaurant serving up shrimp scampi for $9.95, steaks at $11, and catch-of-the-day from $7.75—good, fun place to dine.

Ken's Pancake House is one of a chain but you can have a good meal for a good price (cocktails too). Open 24 hours, it's conveniently located on the way to the airport at 1730 Kamehameha Ave., tel. 935-8711.

Nihon Culture Center, 123 Lihiwai St., tel. 969-1133 (reservations required), presents authentic Japanese meals and an excellent *sushi* bar, and combination dinners along with cultural and artistic displays. Open daily for breakfast, lunch, and dinner until 9:00 p.m., *sushi* bar until 10:00 p.m.

Reuben's Mexican Restaurant will enliven your palate with its zesty dishes. The food is well prepared and the atmosphere is homey. Beer, wine, and margaritas are available. Open daily 10:00 a.m. to 11:00 p.m., Sun. 4:00 to 9:00 p.m., 336 Kamehameha Ave., tel. 961-2552. Ole'!

Rosey's Boathouse is a cosy restaurant with a friendly atmosphere at 761 Piilani St., tel. 935-2112 (reservations suggested). Dinner is served from 5:30 to 10:00 p.m. The buffet and salad bar are well worth the money, and entrees for around $10 include steak and seafood. Enjoy local entertainment in the cocktail lounge nightly.

Expensive Restaurants

Queen's Court Restaurant at the Hilo Hawaiian Hotel on Banyan Drive, tel. 935-9361, offers a nightly buffet that is *the* best on Hawaii. Connoisseurs usually don't consider buffets to be gourmet quality, but the Queen's Court proves them wrong. Each night has a different food theme but the Tues. and Fri. evening "Seafood Buffet" would give the finest restaurants anywhere a run for their money. The dining room is grand with large archways and windows overlooking Hilo Bay. A massive table is laden with fresh island vegetables and 15 different salads. Next, on seafood night, comes clams steamed and on the half shell, oysters, shrimp, crab, *sushi,* and *sashimi.* Then the chefs take over. Resplendent in white uniforms and chef's hats they stand ready to saute or broil your choice of fish, which always includes best cuts like swordfish or *ono.* Beverages include white, rose, and rich red wines, plus fresh-squeezed guava and orange juice. The dessert table entices with fresh fruits and imported cheeses, and dares you to save room for cream pies, fresh-baked cookies and eclairs. The price is an unbelievable $14.95. Sunday morning Champagne Brunch is more of the same quality at $10.75. Make reservations especially on seafood night, because the Hilo Hawaiian attracts many Hilo residents who love great food.

Sandalwood Room is the main restaurant of the Naniloa Surf Hotel on Banyan Drive, tel. 935-0831. Here, in an elegant room overlooking the bay and lined with aromatic sandalwood, you can feast on a selection of recipes from around the world. Zesty curries, rich French sauces, chops done in wine, and Polynesian-inspired dishes are offered on this full and expensive menu.

Fuji Restaurant, as its name implies, is a fine Japanese restaurant at the Hilo Hotel, 142 Kinoole St., tel. 961-3733. Specialties are *teppenyaki* (beef cut thinly and cooked right at your table), or *uminoko* (seafood cooked at your table). *Tempura* and various *teishoku* (full meals) are part of the menu, and most dinners cost about $17.

KK Tei Restaurant, 1550 Kamehameha Ave., tel. 961-3791, is a favored restaurant of many local people. The centerpiece is a *bonsai* garden complete with pagodas and arched moon bridges. Cook your own beef, chicken, or fish at your tableside *hibachi* and dip them into an array of savory sauces, or the chefs will prepare your selection from their full menu of Japanese dishes. Entrees cost about $10 in this unique Oriental setting. This restaurant, for those in the know, achieves gourmet status.

Fast Foods And Snacks

People interested in health food will be more than happy with the snack bars at both of Hilo's health food stores: **Hilo Natural Foods,** 306 Kilauea Ave., tel. 935-7002, and **Abundant Life,** 90 Kamehameha Ave., tel. 935-7411 (see p. 562-563). OK! For those that must, **McDonald's** is at 88 Kanoelehua Ave. and 177 Ululani Street. **Wendy's** is at 438 Kilauea Ave., and **Pizza Hut,** which actually has a decent salad bar, is at 326 Kilauea Avenue. On Banyan Drive just outside of the Naniloa Surf Hotel, get delicious scoops of ice cream featuring island flavors like macadamia nut, at the **Ice Cream Factory,** and nearby is the **Banyan Snack Shop** which dispenses whopping plate sandwiches like a *loco moko*—2 scoops of rice and a hamburger covered in a fried egg and gravy—for only $1.75. The breakfast specials here are very cheap too.

ENTERTAINMENT

Hilo doesn't have a lot of nightlife, but it's not a morgue either. You can dance, disco, or listen to a quiet piano at a few lounges and hotels around town. **Note:** Since most of these

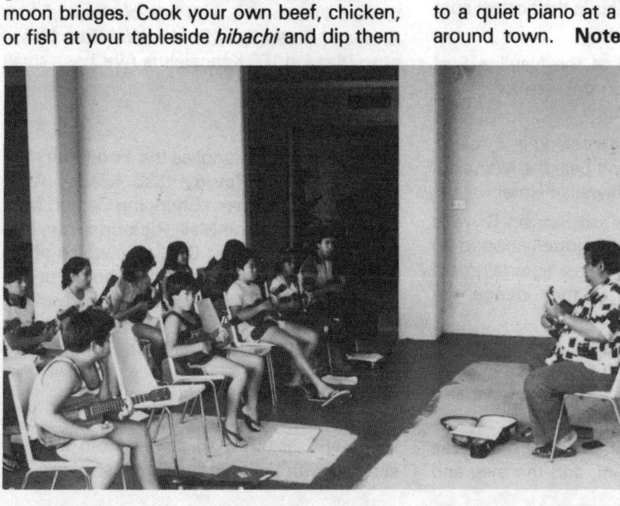

local ukelele *class practicing for the Merry Monarch Festival*

entertainment spots are also restaurants, their addresses and phone numbers can be found above in "Food."

Music

Rosy's Boathouse has a quiet lounge where you'll find a large selection of imported beers. The emphasis is on socializing and talking. The room is small and there's no place to dance, but they do feature entertainment almost every night. Usually it's a mellow combo, but even if it's rock and roll, the volume is kept unobtrusive. Kivin Kalauli, a local guitarist with an excellent voice, sings at Rosy's on Tues. and at J.D's Banyan Broiler on Wednesdays. He's accompanied by a fine bass guitarist named Adam Kay. Don't miss them.

J.D's Banyan Broiler along Banyan Drive transforms from a restaurant into a night-spot at about 10:00 p.m. The music cranks up and it's usually rock 'n' roll. There's no dance floor, but don't let that hold you back if you really have "dancin' feet." It's a younger crowd with plenty of enthusiasm, and keeps rolling until about 2:00 a.m.

Apple Annie's, a restaurant/lounge at 100 Kanoelehua Ave., tel. 961-5884, is part of an island chain. They serve sandwiches and pizza in the downstairs restaurant, and upstairs in the loft a full dance band wails away at night. Mostly younger people come here to tear up the sizable dance floor. This is the hottest spot in town.

The **Polynesian Room** at the Naniloa Surf Hotel becomes a disco on the weekends and stays open until 3:00 a.m.

If you're looking for quiet listening in a "piano bar" atmosphere, you can't beat the **Menehune Lounge** at the Hilo Hawaiian Hotel.

The **Hilo Lagoon Hotel** on Banyan Drive is now a condo that hasn't gotten around to changing its name. They have entertainment on Mon., Wed., and Fri. at their lounge, the Windjammer Cabin.

Uncle Billy's at the Hilo Bay Hotel has 2 dinner *hula* shows nightly at 6:30 and 7:30 p.m.

Others

City Tavern on Mamo Street is as classless as its name. It's a tough joint, and the men and women (you can't always tell which is which) who hang out there will be happy to bust your nose. Some of the clientele make their money by selling *pakalolo*. If you're inclined to buy, make your score and hit the road.

To catch a flick try the **Waiakea Theaters** I, II and III at the Waiakea Mall on Kanoelehua Ave., tel. 935-9747; downtown, the **Palace Theater** is on Haili Street. You'll enjoy great listening on **KIPA Rainbow Radio.** This AM station at 620 on your dial plays an excellent selection of contemporary music with few commercial interruptions. It sounds the way FM used to be. K-BIG FM 98 is worth listening too, and KAOI FM 95 from Maui puts out some really good tunes.

SHOPPING

Hilo has the best general-purpose shopping on the island. Stock up on film and food before you do any touring or camping. The main shopping center is the **Kaiko'o Mall** at 777 Kilauea Ave. which includes a J.C. Penney's, Ben Franklin's, Mall Foods, The Book Gallery, and Long's Drugs. The **Hilo Shopping Center** is about one-half mile south on Kilauea Avenue at the corner of Kekuanoa Street. This smaller mall has only a handful of local shops. **Puainako Town Center** is Hilo's newest mall located at 2100 Kanoelehua Ave. (Rt. 11 south toward Volcanoes), with lots of shops, Foodland, and Serendipity Books. **Waiakea Shopping Plaza** at 100 Kanoelehua Ave. has a small clutch of stores.

Food Markets

For groceries and supplies try: **Food Fair,** 194 Kilauea Ave.; **Safeway,** 333 Kilauea Ave.; **Foodland** at Puainako Shopping Center; **Mall Foods** in the Kaikoo Mall; **Pick and Pay,** Hilo Shopping Center; and **Da Store** which offers groceries and sundries, open 24 hours, at 776 Kilauea Ave. For a real treat visit the early morning (over by 8:00 a.m.) **Suisan Fish Auction** at 85 Lihiwai Street. A retail fresh fish market is next door (see p. 555).

Health Food Stores

Hilo has 2 health food stores. Both are well stocked with bulk foods, vitamins, juices, and

Suisan Fish Auction is perfect for bargains and local color.

have a snack bar and informative bulletin boards with listings from *tai chi* to aura balancing. **Abundant Life Natural Foods** is in downtown Hilo at 90 Kamehameha Hwy. at the corner of Waianuinui Street. Open daily 8:30 a.m. to 6:00 p.m., Sun. 10:00 a.m. to 3:00 p.m., tel. 935-7411. **Hilo Natural Foods** is at 306 Kilauea Ave., just next door to Pizza Hut. Open Mon. to Fri. 8:30 a.m. to 6:30 p.m., Sat 9:00 a.m. to 5:00 p.m., tel. 935-7002.

Bookstores

Hilo has 3 excellent bookstores. **Basically Books** downtown at 169 Keawe St., tel. 961-0144, is a print shop-plus with a good selection of Hawaiiana and an unbeatable selection of maps. You can get anywhere you want to go with their nautical charts, road maps, and topographical maps, including sectionals for serious hikers and trekkers. Their collection covers most of the Pacific. The **Book Gallery** is a full-selection bookstore featuring Hawaiiana, hardcover, and paperbacks. They're at the Kaikoo Mall, open daily, tel. 935-2447. At **Serendipity Bookstore**, you too might stumble over some interesting discoveries, as the name implies. Look for this complete bookstore at the Puainako Town Center. Open daily, tel. 959-5841. **Bookfinders of Hawaii** at 150 Haili St., tel. 961-5055, specializes in hard-to-find and out-of-print books. If you want it, they'll get it.

Gifts And Crafts

If you're looking for that special island memento or souvenirs to bring home to family and friends, Uncle Billy covers all the bases and along with everything else offers the **Polynesian Market Place** adjacent to the Hilo Bay Hotel. Open daily 8:00 a.m. to 9:00 p.m., it sells a lot of good junk, liquor, resortwear, and fancy food items. **Hilo Hattie** has a store in front of the Hilo Hawaiian Hotel on Banyan Drive, but for a huge selection of alohawear, visit their outlet at 933 Kanoelehua St. (Rt. 11). This fashion factory has all you need in island clothing. Open daily 8:30 a.m. to 5:00 p.m., free tour and hotel pick-up. **Kamaaina Crafts**, 1477 Kalanianaole Ave., tel. 935-4957, sells handmade crafts from the Big Island. They have an excellent and varied selection of *lau hala* weavings, carvings, macrame, and flowers. **Hawaiian Handcrafts** at 760 Kilauea Ave., tel. 935-5587, specializes in woodcarvings. Here, Dan DeLuz uses exotic woods to turn out bowls, boxes, and vases, and sells shells from around the Pacific.

Halemanu Crafts is a delightful shop 4 miles south of town on Rt. 11. When heading for Volcanoes, look for an HVB Warrior (sometimes he's stolen) that points to "Lauhala Weaving" to your right. Follow the signs along Halemanu Drive until it dead ends. It's worth it. Mostly senior citizens from the Hilo area display their fine *lau hala* weavings here. A great purchase is a woven hat for $18. It's flexible, airy, and will last for years. On the grounds you'll notice pandanus trees, or screw pines with their long leaves; these are the *lau hala* that are woven and sold in the shop. The woman operating the shop shows you around and gives you some background on the weaving process. They're open daily 8:30 a.m. to 4:30 p.m. with few crowds and plenty of time to spend on you.

SERVICES AND INFORMATION

Emergency

When in need call: **Police** 935-3311; **Fire-Ambulance** tel. 961-6022; **Hilo Hospital** at 1190 Waianuenue St., tel. 961-4211.

Information

The following will be helpful: **Hawaii Visitors Bureau,** 180 Kinoole St., tel. 935-5271; **Chamber of Commerce,** 180 Kinoole St., tel. 935-7178; **Hilo Public Library,** 300 Waianuenue St., tel. 935-5407; **University of Hawaii** in Hilo at 1400 Kapiolani St., tel. 961-9311.

Banks

For your money needs try the following: **City Bank** at the Kaikoo Mall, tel. 935-6844; **First Interstate** at 100 Waianuenue Ave., tel. 935-2826; **Central Pacific,** 525 Kilauea Ave., tel. 935-5251; **First Hawaiian,** 1205 Kilauea Ave., tel. 969-2211.

Laundromats

Self-service laundries are: **Kaikoo Coin Laundry,** Kaikoo Mall, tel. 961-6490, daily 6:00 a.m. to 9:00 p.m.; **Mitchell Wash-O-Matic** at Hilo Shopping Center, tel. 935-1970, daily 6:00 a.m. to 10:00 p.m.

Mauna Kea Observatory

THE SADDLE ROAD

Slicing west across the Hilo District with a northward list is Rt. 200, the Saddle Road. Everyone with a sense of adventure loves this bold cut across the Big Island along a high valley separating the 2 great mountains, Mauna Loa and Mauna Kea. Along it you pass explorable caves, a *nene* sanctuary, camping areas, and a spur road leading to the very top of Mauna Kea. Besides, it's a great time-saver for anyone traveling between Hilo and Kona. Keep your eyes peeled for convoys of tanks and armored personnel carriers as they sometimes sally forth from Pohakuloa Military Camp.

Getting There

The car rental companies cringe when you mention the Saddle Road. Some even intimidate you by saying that their insurance won't cover you on this road. They're terrified you'll rattle their cars to death. For the most part these fears are totally groundless. For a few miles the Saddle Road is corrugated because of heavy use by the military, but, by and large, it's a good road, no worse than many others around the island. If you bypass it, you'll miss some of the best scenery on the Big Island. From Hilo, follow Waianuenue Avenue west past Rainbow Falls. Saddle Road (Rt. 200) splits left within a mile or 2 and is clearly marked. If you follow it across the island, you'll intersect Rt. 190 on which you can turn north to Waimea, or south to Kona.

SIGHTS

Kaumana Caves

In 1881 Mauna Loa's tremendous eruption created a huge flow of lava. The lava became rivers that crusted over forming a tube through which molten lava continued to flow. Once the eruption ceased, the lava inside siphoned out leaving the tube that we now call Kaumana Caves. The caves are only 5 miles out of Hilo along Rt. 200, clearly marked next to the road. Oddly enough, they are posted as a fallout shelter. Follow a staircase down into a gray hole draped with green ferns and brightened by wildflowers. You can walk about 50 yards into the cave before you'll need a flashlight. It's a thrill to turn around and look at the entranceway with blazing sunlight shooting through the ferns and wildflowers. The floor of the cave is cemented over for easy walking.

Kaumana Caves

Another cave visible across the way is undeveloped and more rugged to explore.

Two miles past Kaumana Caves is **Hilo Municipal Golf Course,** a 5,991-yard, par-72 course where you can golf for under $5.

Mauna Kea

The lava along both sides of the road is old as you approach Mauna Kea ("White Mountain"). The lowlands are covered with grass, ferns, small trees, and mossy rocks. Twenty-seven miles out of Hilo, a clearly marked road to your right leads to the summit of the 13,796 foot Mauna Kea. A sign warns you this road is rough, unpaved, and narrow, with no water, food, fuel, restrooms, or shelters. Moreover, you can expect winds, rain, fog, hail, snow, and altitude sickness. Intrigued? Proceed, it's not as bad as it sounds. A 4WD vehicle is advised, and if there's snow it's impossible without one, but a car can make it. Four miles up and you pass **Hale Pohaku** ("House of Stone") which looks like a ski resort; many of the scientists from the observatory atop the mountain live here. A sign says you need a permit from the Dept. of Land and Natural Resources (in Hilo) and a 4WD vehicle to proceed. Actually, the road is graded, banked, and well maintained. As you climb, you pass through the clouds to a barren world, devoid of all vegetation. The earth is red and rolling in a series of volcanic cones. You get an incredible vista of Mauna Loa peeking through the clouds and what seems like the entire island lying at your feet. Lake Waiau, which unbelievably translates as "Swim Water," is almost at the top at 13,020 feet, making it the third highest lake in the U.S. If the vistas aren't enough, bring a kite along

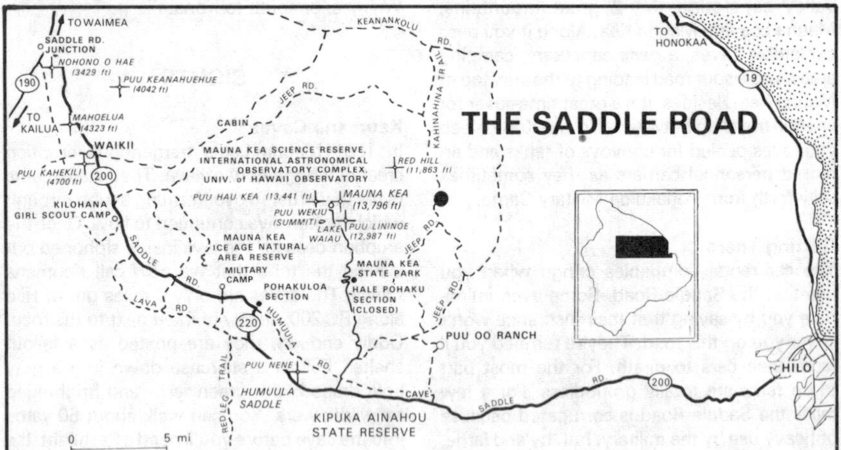

the road to Mauna Kea

and watch it soar in the winds of the Earth's upper atmosphere.

Atop the mountain is a mushroom grove of astronomical observatories. The crystal-clear air and lack of dust and light pollution rank the **Mauna Kea Observatory Complex** as *the* best in the world. At close to 14,000 feet, it is above almost 40% of the Earth's atmosphere. Those who work up here must come down every 4 days because the thin air seems to make them forgetful and susceptible to making minor calculation errors. Scientists from around the world book months in advance for a look through the telescopes. Here, the Keck Foundation from Los Angeles is planning to build the world's largest telescope, measuring over 30 feet across. Visitors are welcome to tour the complex and to have a look through the telescopes on special weekends from May through September. Reservations are a must, and arrangements are made by calling the Mauna Kea Support Services in Hilo at tel. 935-3371. You must provide your own transportation to the summit.

Mauna Kea State Park

This area, known as Pohakuloa ("Long Stone"), is 5 miles west from the Mauna Kea Observatory Road (33 miles from Hilo). The altitude is 6,500 feet and the land begins to change into rolling grasslands for which this *paniolo* country is famous. Here you'll find a cluster of 7 cabins that can be rented (arrange in advance) from the Dept. of Land and Natural Resources, Division of State Parks, 75 Aupuni St., Hilo, HI 96720, tel. 961-7200. The cabins are completely furnished with cooking facilities and hot showers. You'll need warm clothing, but the days and nights are unusually clear and dry with very little rain. The park is within the Pohakuloa Game Management Area, so expect hunting and shooting in season. A few minutes west is the Pohakuloa Military Camp, whose manuevers can sometimes disturb the peace in this high mountain area. Follow the Saddle Road about 20 miles west to intersect Rt. 190 on which you can turn right (north) to Waimea in 7 miles, or left (south) to Kailua in 33 miles.

Waipio Valley

HAMAKUA COAST

Inland the Hamakua Coast is awash in a green rolling sea of sugarcane, while along the shore cobalt waves foam into razor-sharp valleys where cold mountain streams meet the sea at lonely pebbled beaches. For 50 miles, from Hilo to Waipio along the Belt Road (Rt. 19), the Big Island has grown its cane for 100 years or more. Water is needed for sugar, a ton to produce a pound, and this coast has plenty. Huge flumes once carried the cut cane to the mills. Last century so many Scots worked the plantations hereabouts that Hamakua was called the "Scotch Coast." Now most residents are a mixture of Scottish, Japanese, Filipino, and Portuguese ancestry. Side roads dip off Rt. 19 into one-family valleys where a modest weatherbeaten home of a plantation worker sits surrounded by garden plots on tiny hand-hewn terraces. These valleys, as they march up the coast, are unromantically referred to as "gulches." From the Belt Road's many bridges, you can trace silvery-ribboned streams that mark the valley floors as they open to the sea. Each is jungle-lush with wildflowers and fruit trees transforming the steep sides to emerald green velvet.

SIGHTS

The ride alone, as you head north on the Belt Road, is gorgeous enough to be considered a sight. But there's more! You can pull off the road into sleepy one-horse towns where dogs are safe sleeping in the middle of the road. You can visit a plantation store in Honomu on your way to Akaka Falls, or take a cautious dip at one of the seaside beach parks. If you want solitude, you can go inland to a forest reserve and miles of trails. The largest town on the coast is Honokaa, with supplies, handmade mementos, and a macadamia nut factory. You can veer west to Waimea from Honokaa, but don't. Take the spur road, Rt. 240, to Waipio Valley, known as the "Valley of Kings," one of the most beautiful in all of Hawaii.

Honomu

During its heyday Honomu ("Silent Bay") was a bustling center of the sugar industry boasting saloons, a hotel/bordello, and a church or two for repentance. Now, Honomu is only a stop as you head somewhere else. It's 10 miles north of

Hilo and a mile or so inland on Rt. 220 which leads to Akaka Falls. In town is the **Honomu Plantation Store.** Proprietors Tom and Jan Unger open it daily from 7:30 a.m. to 9:00 p.m., tel. 963-6203. A display of old photographs shows life in a plantation town at the turn of the century. Inside are groceries, gifts, T-shirts, handcrafts, and a snack bar. Enjoy free samples of sugarcane and raw macadamia nuts too.

Down the road on the left is a string of false-front buildings. **Sandwich Island Subs** occupies one that was once the local pool hall. Inside, Lee and Garry Godin, 2 escapees from Canada's cold, will make you a giant, 2-fisted submarine sandwich that can fill 2 for under $4. Lee and Garry also feature free sugarcane, and delicious scoops of island ice cream. It's a good stop if you plan to picnic at Akaka Falls.

Akaka Falls

Follow Rt. 220 from Honomu past dense sugarcane fields for 3½ miles to the parking lot of Akaka Falls. From here, walk counterclockwise along a paved "circle route" that takes you through everybody's idea of a pristine Hawaiian valley. For 40 minutes you're surrounded by heliconia, gingers, orchids, ferns, and bamboo groves as you cross bubbling streams on wooden footbridges. Many varieties of plants that would be in window pots anywhere else are giants here, almost like trees. An overlook views Kahuna Falls as it spills into a lush green valley below. The trail becomes an enchanted tunnel through hanging orchids and bougainvillea. In a few moments you arrive at Akaka Falls. The mountain cooperates with the perfect setting, a semi-circle for the falls to tumble 420 feet in one sheer drop. After heavy rains expect a mad torrent of power; during dry periods marvel at liquid-silver thread forming mist and rainbows. The area, maintained by the Division of State Parks, is one of the most easily accessible forays into Hawaii's beautiful interior.

Akaka Falls

Kolekole Beach Park

Look for the first tall bridge (100 feet high) a few minutes past Honomu, where a sign points to a small road that snakes its way down the valley to the park below. Amenities include showers, restrooms, grills, electricity, picnic tables, and a camping area (county permit). Kolekole is very popular with local people who use its 5 pavilions for all manner of special occasions, usually on weekends. A black-sand beach fronts an extremely treacherous ocean. The entire valley was inundated with over 30 feet of water during the great 1946 *tsunami*. The stream running through Kolekole comes from Akaka Falls, 4 miles inland. It forms a pool complete with waterfall that is safe for swimming but quite cold.

Laupahoehoe Point

This wave-lashed peninsula is a finger of smooth *pahoehoe* lava that juts into the bay. Located about halfway between Honomu and Honokaa, at one time the valley supported farmers and fishermen who specialized in catching turtles. Laupahoehoe was the best boat-landing along the coast, and for years canoes and later schooners would stop here. A plaque commemorates the tragic loss of 20 schoolchildren and their teacher who were taken by the great *tsunami* of 1946. Afterwards, the village was moved to the high ground overlooking the point. Laupahoehoe

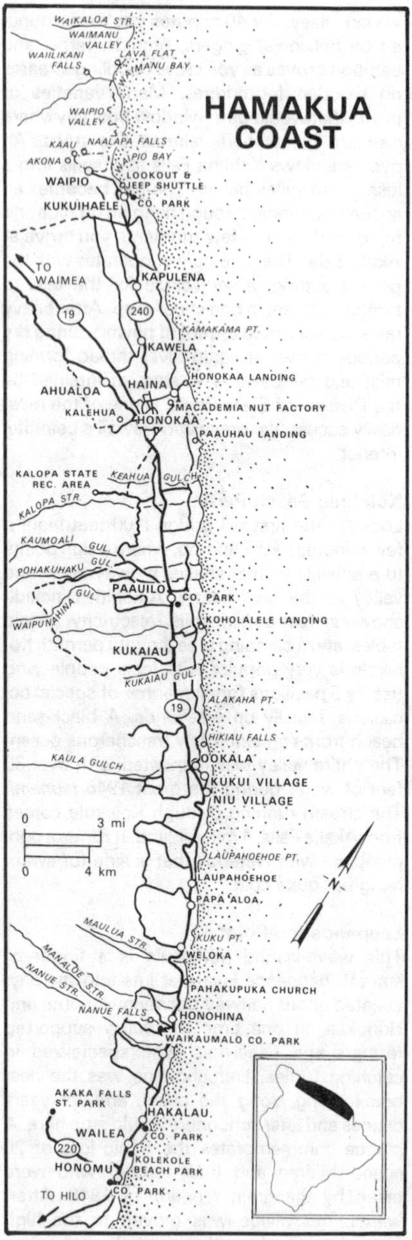

Beach Park now occupies the low peninsula: picnic tables, showers, electricity, and a county camping area. The sea is too rough to swim, but many fishermen still come here, along with some daring surfers. Laupahoehoe makes a beautiful rest stop along the Belt Road.

Ten miles inland from Laupahoehoe Point along a very rugged jeep trail is **David Douglas Historical Monument.** This marks the spot where the naturalist, after whom the Douglas fir is named, lost his life under mysterious circumstances. Douglas, on a fact-gathering expedition on the rugged slopes of Mauna Kea, never returned. His body was found at the bottom of a deep pit that was used, at the time, to catch feral cattle. Douglas had spent the previous night at a cabin occupied by an Australian who had been a convict. Many suspected that the Austalian had murdered Douglas in a robbery attempt and thrown his body into the pit as an alibi. No hard evidence of murder could be found, and the death was officially termed accidental.

HONOKAA

With a population of nearly 2,000, Honokaa ("Crumbling Bay") is the major town on the Hamakua Coast. Here you can continue on Rt. 19 to Waimea, or take Rt. 240 through Honokaa and north to Waipio, which you should not miss. First, however, stroll the main street of Honokaa, where a number of shops specialize in locally produced handicrafts. It's also the best place to stock up on supplies or gasoline. The surrounding area is the center of the macadamia nut industry.

Kalopa State Park

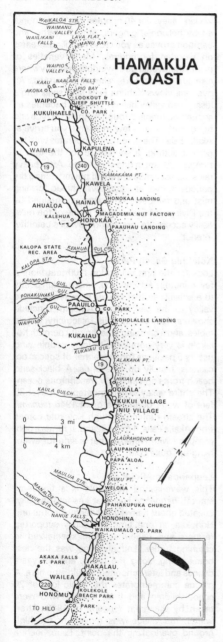

This spacious natural area is 12 miles north of Laupahoehoe (2 miles south of Honokaa), and 2 miles inland on a well-marked secondary road. Little used by tourists, it's a great place to get away from it all. Hiking is terrific throughout the park on a series of nature trails where much of the flora has been identified. All trails are well marked and vary widely in difficulty. The park provides an excellent opportunity to explore some of the lush gulches of the Hamakua Coast, as well as tent camping (state permit) and furnished cabins that can house up to 8 people (see p. 542-543).

Hawaiian Holiday Macadamia Nut Factory
This factory is on a side road that leads from the middle of town down a steep hill toward the sea. A self-guided tour explains how John MacAdams discovered the delicious qualities of these nuts, and how they were named after him. The macadamia nut industry was started in Honokaa, when W.H. Purvis, a British agriculturalist who had been working in Australia, brought the first trees to Honokaa in 1881, one of which is still bearing! Then in 1924, W. Pierre Naquin, then manager of the Honokaa Sugar Co., started the first commercial nut farm in the area. You can buy a large variety of macadamia items from butters to candies. A delicious and nutritious munchy is a 5-oz. vacuum-packed can of nuts for $2.09.

Practicalities
Centrally located along Rt. 24 is the **Hotel Honokaa Club.** Contact Henry Morita, Manager, Box 185, Honokaa, tel. 775-0533. What it lacks in elegance it makes up for in cleanliness and friendliness. The hotel, mostly used by local people, is old and appears run-down. Upstairs rooms (view and TV) are $12.48 s, $18.72 d. The more spartan downstairs rooms go for $8.82 s, $12.98 d. The Hotel dining room serves the best meals in town. Breakfasts are served daily from 6:30 to 11:00 a.m., lunch from 11:00 a.m. to 2:00 p.m., and dinner nightly from 5:30 to 8:00 p.m. The cooking is homestyle with a different dinner special daily, such as a seafood platter for $5.75, *mahi mahi* special $6, lobster and steak $13.25. Specials include rice, potatoes, salad, and coffee. Weekends rock with **live entertainment** and dancing.

Along the main street the **Tourist Cocktail Lounge** has live music on Sat. from 8:30 p.m. until after midnight. To save money, get a filling plate lunch at the local **Dairy Queen.** Pick up supplies and even a few health food items at **T. Kaneshiro Store** and **K.K. Market** in town.

If you're looking for souvenirs and handcrafts try a shop owned by Mr. R. Hirata that merely says **Shirtmaker,** just before the turnoff to the macadamia nut factory. Along the main street is a junkbox of discovery shops sporting names like **Bargain Shack, Cottage Treasures,** and **Waimio Sandbox. All sell bric-a-brac and local handmade items. Kamaaina Woods** is a quality shop where local craftsmen make bowls and various art objects using exotic woods. Honokaa, away from the more heavily touristed areas, has some excellent bargains.

KUKUIHAELE

For all of you loking for the "light at the end of the tunnel," Kukuihaele ("Traveling Light") is it. On the main road, **Last Chance** grocery and gas station stocks basic supplies, a small assortment of handicrafts and gift items. **Waipio Woodworks,** owned and operated by Joe Mathieu and his 4 sons, tel. 775-0958, is one of the best art shops on the island (north end of town). Joe is a master woodworker who thinks nothing of letting the first turning of a wooden

Joe Mathieu, woodworker

bowl age 3 years before it's given the finishing touches. Ask Joe to show you around—all the work is done in the rear of the shop. The main tool is a lathe that Joe built himself from a 4-speed truck transmission held firm by over a ton of cement. The wood used comes from the nearby forests: *koa,* mango, guava, and monkeypod. The turnings and shavings all go into the garden as mulch and compost. Joe's art shop showcases some of the best island artists (you must be local to have your work displayed), but the prices are not cheap. Edwin Caton, a well known artist, sells his paintings here ($175 to $600). A large *koa* bowl can be $300, with salad bowls going for $30. Katherine Merrill displays her pottery, among stained glass, lithographs, and batiks. Items in Waipio Woodworks transcend souvenir status, and fall into the category of "works of art."

Accommodations

Enjoy the privacy of **Hamakua Hideaway,** Box 5104, Kukuihaele, HI 96727, tel. 775-7425. A B&B only 15 minutes walk from Waipio Overlook, they offer the home, s/d, for $40 daily, with reduced weekly and monthly rates available.

WAIPIO VALLEY

Waipio is the way the Lord would have liked to fashion the Garden of Eden, if he hadn't been on such a tight schedule. You can read about this incredible valley, but you really can't believe it until you see it for yourself. Route 24 ends a minute outside of Kukuihaele at an overlook, and 1,000 feet below is Waipio ("Arching Water"). The valley is a mile across where it fronts the sea at a series of high sand dunes. It's vibrantly green, always watered by Waipio Stream and lesser ones that sprout as waterfalls from the *pali* at the rear of the valley. The green is made even more striking offset by a wide band of black-sand beach. The far side of the valley ends abruptly at a steep *pali* that is higher than the one on which you're standing. A 6-mile trail leads over it to Waimanu Valley, smaller, more remote, and more luxuriant.

Travelers have long extolled the amazing abundance of Waipio. From the overlook you can make out the overgrown outlines of garden terraces, *taro* patches, and fishponds in what was Hawaii's largest cultivated valley. Every foodstuff known to the Hawaiians flourished here; even Waipio pigs were said to be bigger than anywhere else. In times of famine, the produce from Waipio could sustain the populace of the entire island (estimated at 100,000 people). On the valley floor and alongside the streams you'll still find avocado, banana, coconuts, passionfruit, mountain apples, guava, breadfruit, tapioca, lemons, limes, coffee, grapefruit, and pumpkins. The old fishponds and streams are alive with prawns, wild pigs roam the interior, and there are abundant fish in the sea. The lovingly tended order, most homes, and the lifestyle were washed away in the *tsunami* of 1946. Now Waipio is unkempt, a wild jungle of mutated abundance. The valley is a neglected maiden with a dirty face and disheveled, windblown hair. Only love and nurturing can refresh her lingering beauty.

Legend And Oral History

Waipio is a mystical place. Inhabited for over 1,000 years, it figures prominently in old Hawaiian lore. In the primordial past, Wakea, progenitor of all the islands favored the valley, and oral tradition holds that the great gods Kane and Kanaloa dallied in Waipio intoxicating themselves on *awa.* One oral chant relates that the demi-god Maui, that wild prankster, met his untimely end here by trying to steal baked bananas from these two drunken heavyweights. Lono, god of the *makahiki,* came to Waipio in search of a bride. He found Kaikilani, a beautiful maiden who lived in a breadfruit tree near **Hiilawe Waterfall,** which tumbles 1,300 feet to the valley below and is Hawaii's highest free-falling falls.

Nenewe, a shark-man, lived near a pool at the bottom of another waterfall on the west side of Waipio. The pool was connected to the sea by an underwater tunnel. All went well for Nenewe until his grandfather disobeyed a warning never to feed the boy meat. Once Nenewe tasted meat he began eating Waipio residents after first warning them about sharks as they passed his sea-connected pool on their way to fish. His constant warnings roused suspicions. Finally, a cape he always wore was ripped from his shoulders, and there on his back was a shark's mouth! He dove into his pool and left Waipio to hunt the waters of the other islands.

Pupualenalena, a *kupua* (nature spirit), takes the form of a yellow dog who can change his size from tiny to huge. He was sent by the chiefs of Waipio to steal a conch shell that was constantly blown by mischievous water sprites, just to irritate the people. The shell was inherited by Kamehameha and is now in the Bishop Museum. Another dog-spirit lives in a rock embedded in the hillside halfway down the road to Waipio. In times of danger, he comes out of his rock to stand in the middle of the road as a warning that bad things are about to happen.

Finally, a secret section of Waipio's beach is called *Lua o milu,* the legendary doorway to the land of the dead. At certain times, it is believed, ghosts of great *ali'i* come back to Earth as "Marchers of the Night," and their strong chants and torch-lit processions fill the darkness in Waipio. Many great kings were buried in Waipio, and it's felt that because of their *mana,* no harm will come to the people that live here. Oddly enough, the horrible *tsunami* of 1946 and a raging flood in 1979 filled the valley with wild torrents of water. In both cases, the devastation to homes and the land was tremendous, but not one life was lost. Everyone who still lives in Waipio will tell you that somehow, they feel protected.

taro patch (Hawaii State Archives)

Recorded History

Great chiefs have dwelt in Waipio. King Umialiloa planted *taro* just like a commoner, and fished with his own hands. He went on to unite the island into one kingdom in the 15th century. Waipio was the traditional lands of Kamehameha the Great, and in many ways was the basis of his earthly and spiritual power. He came here to rest after heavy battles, and offshore was the scene of the first modern naval battle in Hawaii. Here, Kamehameha's war canoes faced those of his nemesis, Keoua. Both had recently acquired cannon bartered from passing sea captains. Kamehameha's artillery was manned by 2 white sailors, Davis and Young, who became trusted advisers. Kamehameha's forces won the engagement in what became known as the "Battle of the Red Mouthed Gun."

When Capt. Cook came to Hawaii, 4,000 natives lived in Waipio; a century later only 600 remained. At the turn of this century many Chinese and Japanese moved to Waipio and began raising rice and *taro.* People moved in and out of the valley by horse and mule and there were schools and a strong community spirit. Waipio was painstakingly tended. The undergrowth was kept trimmed and you could see clearly from the back of the valley all the way to the sea. WW II arrived and many people were lured away from the remoteness of the valley by a changing lifestyle and a desire for modernity. The tidal wave in 1946 swept away most of the homes, and the majority of people pulled up stakes and moved away. For 25 years the valley lay virtually abandoned. The Peace Corps considered it a perfect place to build a compound in which to train volunteers headed for Southeast Asia. This too was abandoned. In the late '60s and early '70s a few "back to nature" hippies started trickling in. Most only played "Tarzan and Jane" and moved on, especially after Waipio served them a "reality sandwich" in the form of the flood of 1979.

Waipio Now

A few gutsy families with a real commitment stayed on and continue to revitalize Waipio. The valley now supports perhaps 50 residents. A handful of elderly Filipino bachelors who worked for the sugar plantation continue to live in Waipio. One old fellow you may encounter is Millatone who is always surrounded by his surrogate family, a pack of a dozen or so dogs. About 50 more people live topside, but come down to Waipio to tend their gardens. On entering the valley, you'll see a lotus-flower pond, and if you're lucky enough to be there in December, it will be in bloom. It's tended by an 80-year-old Chinaman, Mr. Nelson Chun, who wades in chest-deep water harvesting the sausage-linked lotus roots by clipping them with his toes! Margaret Loo comes to harvest

Millatone and friend

wild ferns served at the exclusive banquets at the Mauna Kea Beach Resort. Fannie and Ramuldo Dulduloa tend their *taro* patch, and Seiko Tanashiro is perhaps the most famous *taro* farmer because of his *poi* factory that produces "Ono Ono Waipio Brand Taro."

Getting There

The road leading down to Waipio is outrageously steep and narrow. If you attempt it in a regular car, it'll eat you up and spit out your bones. Over 20 fatalities have occurred since people started driving it, and it has only been paved since the early 1970s. You'll definitely need 4WD, low range, to make it; downhill vehicles yield to those coming up. The **Waipio Valley Shuttle** operated by Les Baker runs 90-minute narrated tours of Waipio. You travel in a Land-Rover nicknamed the "African Queen," while Les fords streams and bumps along through the vegetation telling legends and pointing out historical spots. The trip costs $15, $5 children under 12, and runs daily from 8:00 a.m. to 5:00 p.m. leaving from the overlook at 90-minute intervals. If you decide to hike down or stay overnight, Les will haul you out but he charges from $10 to $25 for this service depending on if he has to make a special trip. This seems pricey especially since an entire tour is only $15! For reservations, a must on weekends, contact Waipio Valley Shuttle at Box 128, Kukuihaele, HI 96727, tel. 775-7121. If you have the energy, the hike down the paved section of the road is only just over one mile, but it's a tough mile coming back up! Expect to take 3 to 4 hours down and back, adding more time to swim or look around. For details see "Camping and Hiking" below.

For a fun-filled experience guaranteed to please, try horseback riding with **Waipio Ranch.** Sherri Hannum, a young mother of 3 that moved to Waipio from Missouri almost 15 years ago, and Wayne Teves, a family man whose Portuguese ancestors settled in Honokaa about 100 years ago, are partners in Waipio Ranch. Both are infatuated with horses and Waipio, which they know like the back of their hand. They mount you on a sure-footed Waipio pony and spend all day telling you legends and stories while leading you to waterfalls, gravesites, *heiau,* and finally a beach ride with

Sherri Hannum and Wayne Teves

a refreshing dip. Technically, you should bring your own lunch, but no one goes hungry in Waipio. Sherri packs a big lunch of homemade Portuguese sweet bread, *shoyu* chicken, and adds specialties like wild fern salad, fried *taro,* topping it off with a selection of fruits gathered fresh from the valley. They extend Waipio hospitality to their guests. Because of the remoteness, you must make arrangements 24 hours in advance by calling Joe Matthieu at tel. 775-0958. Joe owns Waipio Woodworks, topside in Kukuihaele, and takes reservations for the ranch. Wayne will pick you up there in his 4WD and take you down to Waipio. Half-day tours cost $55, and run from 9:00 a.m. to 1:00 p.m. and again from 1:30 p.m. to 5:30 p.m. Full-day tours cost $100 and go from 9:00 a.m. to 5:30 p.m. (minimum of 2 and a maximum of 4 riders required). Sorry, but no children under 12. Go prepared with long pants, shoes, and a swimsuit. A ride with Wayne and Sherri isn't just an adventure, it's an experience with memories that'll last a lifetime.

Camping And Hiking

Hiking down to Waipio and continuing over the *pali* to Waimanu Valley 7 miles away is one of the top 3 treks in Hawaii. You must be fully prepared for camping and in excellent condition to attept this hike. Also, drinking water from the streams and falls is not always good due to irrigation and cattle grazing topside; bring purification tablets or boil it to be safe. To get to Waimanu Valley, a switchback trail leads over the *pali* about 100 yards inland from the beach. The trail ahead is rough, as you go up and down about 14 gulches before reaching Waimanu. At the 9th gulch is a trail shelter. Finally, below is Waimau Valley, half the size of Waipio but more verdant, and even wilder because it has been uninhabited for a longer time. Cross Waimanu Stream in the shallows where it meets the sea. Pick your own beach-front camping spot and relax. For drinking water (remember to treat it) walk along the west side of the *pali* until you find a likely waterfall. For camping in Waipio Valley you must get a permit from the Hamakua Sugar Co., tel. 776-1511. The office is located about 15 minutes from the overlook in Paauilo and you must pick up the permit in person. Camping is allowed in designated areas only on the east side of Waipio Stream. Many hikers and campers have stayed in Waipio overnight without a permit and have had no problem. Remember, however, that most of the land, except for the beach, *is* privately owned.

Waipio Beach, stretching over a mile, is the longest black-sand beach on the island. The surf here can be very dangerous and there are many rip-tides. During the summer, the sands drift to the western side of the valley and in winter they drift back east. If there is strong wave action, swimming is not advised. It is, however, a good place for surfing and fishing.

Accommodations

Waipio has a hotel! Owned and operated by Tom Araki, it was built by his dad to serve as a residence for the officers of a nearby, now defunct, Peace Corps training camp. You'll find 8 basic but clean rooms. Light is provided by kerosene lamp, and you must bring your own food to prepare in a communal kitchen. Tom, at 75, is a treasure-house of information about Waipio, and a "character." He's more interested in tending his *taro* patch, telling stories, and drinking wine, than he is in running a hotel. His philosophy, which has enabled him to get along with everyone from millionaires to hippies, is a simple "live and let live." The Waipio Hotel has become known and it's even fashionable to stay there. For reservations, write Tom Araki, 25 Malama Pl., Hilo, HI 96720, or call Tom down in Waipio Valley at tel. 775-0368.

Waipio Hotel

PUNA

The Puna District was formed from rivers of lava spilling from Mauna Loa and Kilauea again and again over the last million years or so. The molten rivers stopped only when they hit the sea where they fizzled and cooled, forming a chunk of semi-raw land that bulges into the Pacific—marking the state's easternmost point at **Cape Kumukahi.** These titanic lava flows have left phenomenal reminders of their power. **Lava Tree State Monument** was once a rainforest whose giant trees were covered with lava like hot dogs dipped in batter. The encased wood burned, leaving a hollow stone skeleton. You can stroll through this lichen-green rock forest before you head farther east into the brilliant sunshine of the coast. Little-traveled side roads take you past a multitude of orchid, anthurium, and papaya farms, oases of color in a desert of solid black lava. At Cape Kumukahi is a lighthouse, and north is an ancient paved trail passing beaches where no one ever goes.

Southward is a string of popular beaches—some white, some black. You can camp, swim, surf, or just play in the water to your heart's delight. Villages have gas and food, and all along the coast you can visit natural areas where the sea tortured the hot lava into caves, tubes, arches, and even a natural bathtub whose waters are flushed and replenished by the sea. There are historical sites where petroglyphs tell vague stories from the past, and where generations of families placed the umbilical cords of the newborn into man-made holes in the rock. On Puna's south coast are remains of ancient villages, including Kamoamoa where you can camp. The Park **Visitors Center** is just before Chain of Craters Road, which is the eastern gateway to Volcanoes Park. Here, you'll find an archaeological museum, and the restored **Waha'ula Heiau,** where human sacrifice was introduced into Hawaii in the 13th century. The **Hawaiian Belt Road** (Rt. 11) is a corridor cutting through the center of Puna. It goes through the highlands to Volcanoes Park passing well-established villages and scattered housing developments as new as the lava on which they precariously sit. Back in these hills new-wave gardeners grow "Puna butter" *pakalolo,* as wild and raun-

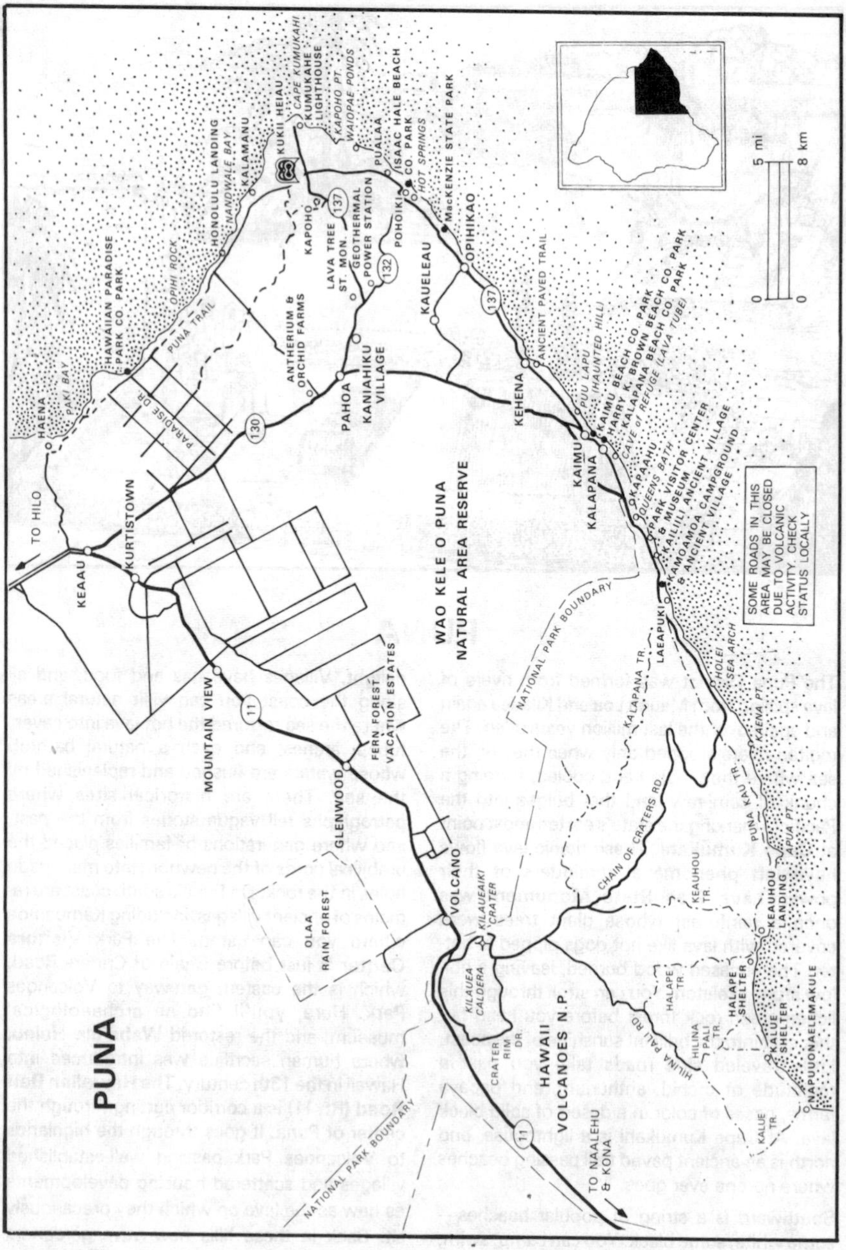
PUNA
TO HILO
KEAAU
KURTISTOWN
HAENA
PAKI BAY
HAWAIIAN PARADISE PARK CO. PARK
PARADISE DR.
PUNA TRAIL
OPIHI ROCK
HONOLULU LANDING
NANAWALE BAY
KALAMANU
KUKII HEIAU
CAPE KUMUKAHI
KUMUKAHE LIGHTHOUSE
KAPOHO PT.
WAIOPAE PONDS
ISAAC HALE BEACH CO. PARK
PUALAA
HOT SPRINGS
MacKENZIE STATE PARK
KAPOHO
LAVA TREE ST. MON.
GEOTHERMAL POWER STATION
POHOIKI
ANTHERIUM & ORCHID FARMS
OPIHIKAO
KAUELEAU
ANCIENT PAVED TRAIL
PAHOA
KANIAHIKU VILLAGE
KEHENA
PUU LAPU (HAUNTED HILL)
KAIMU BEACH CO. PARK
HARRY K. BROWN BEACH CO. PARK
KALAPANA BEACH CO. PARK
CAVE of REFUGE (LAVA TUBE)
KAIMU
KALAPANA
KAPAAHU
QUEENS BATH
PARK VISITOR CENTER & MUSEUM
KAILIILI ANCIENT VILLAGE
KAMOAMOA CAMPGROUND & ANCIENT VILLAGE
SOME ROADS IN THIS AREA MAY BE CLOSED DUE TO VOLCANIC ACTIVITY. CHECK STATUS LOCALLY
WAO KELE O PUNA NATURAL AREA RESERVE
NATIONAL PARK BOUNDARY
KALAPANA TR.
LAEAPUKI
HOLEI SEA ARCH
KAENA PT.
APUA PT.
PUNA KAU TR.
KEAUHOU TR.
KEAUHOU LANDING
HALAPE SHELTER
HALAPE TR.
HILINA PALI TR.
HILINA PALI RD.
KALUE SHELTER
KALUE TR.
NAPUUONAELEMAKULE
CHAIN OF CRATERS RD.
MOUNTAIN VIEW
GLENWOOD
FERN FOREST VACATION ESTATES
VOLCANO
OLAA RAIN FOREST
KILAUEAIKI CRATER
KILAUEA CALDERA
CRATER RIM DR.
HAWAII VOLCANOES N.P.
NATIONAL PARK BOUNDARY
TO NAALEHU & KONA
11
130
132
137
0
5 mi
0
8 km

chy as its name. On the border of Puna and the Kau District to the south is **Volcanoes National Park..** Here the goddess Pele resides at Kilauea Caldera, center of one of the world's most active volcanoes.

HAWAII BELT ROAD—HILO TO VOLCANOES

If you're heading for Volcanoes Park, Rt. 11 (Hawaii Belt Road) splits in Keaau and passes through the high mountain villages of Mountain View, Glenwood, Volcano, and then enters the park. If "making time" is your main consideration, this is the way to go. However, if you want much more exciting scenery and a host of natural and historic sites, head south on Rt. 130 toward Pahoa and the east coast. It takes a full day and then some to see and appreciate Volcanoes Park, so if you're returning to Hilo in the evening, plan on taking the Belt Road back; Rt. 130 shouldn't be traveled at night. The Belt Road, although only 2 lanes, is straight, well surfaced, and scrupulously maintained. In short, if time is on your side, take one day to visit Volcanoes, using the Belt Road for convenience, and another to "Sunday drive" Rt. 130 along the coast.

Keaau

Keaau is the first town south of Hilo (10 miles) on Rt. 11, and although pleasant enough, is little more than a Y in the road. At the junction of Rt. 11 and Rt. 130 is **Keaau Town Center,** a small shopping mall with a handful of variety stores, a laundromat, and a sizable Ben Franklin's, where you can pick up supplies. Across the street and a few hundred yards down Rt. 130 is **Keaau Natural Foods.** (Oddly enough, next door is a store selling Hawaiian game cock supplies!) Keaau Natural Foods has a large stock of organic food items, but no juice or snack bar. However, pre-made sandwiches like *tempeh* burgers with all the trimmings are $2, and plans exist to open a bakery outlet on the premises. Around the corner is **Virna's Fast Food Spot** whose name says it all.

Mountain Villages

Heading south on Rt. 11, at approximately 10-mile intervals, are Mountain View, Glenwood, and Volcano. In **Mountain View** are a snack shop, grocery store, and gas station. Look for a vintage farm house, painted blue, sitting on the left-hand side of the road. This is **Tinny Fisher's Antique Shop,** owned and operated by Charles and Dorothy Wittig. What started as "yard sale treasures" about 10 years ago has turned into a unique curio, antique, and collectibles shop. They specialize in glassware, jewelry, and handmade furniture. There are no facilities in **Glenwood,** but a few minutes down the road you pass **Akatsuka Tropical Orchids and Flower Gardens,** open daily 8:30 a.m. to 5:00 p.m. If tour buses don't overflow the parking lot, stop in for a look at how orchids are grown or to use the clean restrooms. They offer a complimentary orchid to all visitors. Just before entering Volcanoes Park, a sign points to the right down a short side road to **Volcano Village:** gas station, store, and the Ohia Tree Restaurant that along with a full, not too inflated menu, sells absolute necessities like *sushi* and beer. Volcano House, overlooking Kilauea Crater, can't be beat for location, but it is totally swamped by tour buses especially at lunch and dinner time. Drive the 10 minutes to the Ohia Tree if you want to avoid a long wait in line.

ROUTE 130 AND THE SOUTHEAST COAST

The most enjoyable area in the Puna District is the southeast coast, with its beaches, and most of the points of natural and historical interest. If you take Rt. 130 south from Keaau, in about 12 miles you pass **Pahoa.** As in Keaau, Pahoa is primarily a crossroad. You can continue due south on Rt. 130 to the seaside villages of **Kaimu** and **Kalapana** where Rt. 130 joins coastal Rt. 137 feeding into Chain of Craters Road. You might go directly east from Pahoa along Rt. 132. This lovely tree-lined country road takes you past **Lava Tree State Monument** which shouldn't be missed, and then branches northeast intersecting Rt. 137 and terminating at **Cape Kumukahi.** If this seems just *too* far out of the way, head down **Pohoiki Road,** just past Lava Tree. You bypass a controversial geothermal power station, then reach the coast at **Isaac Hale Beach**

Park where Rt. 137 heads directly south to Kalapana passing the best Puna beaches en route. Fortunately for you, this area of Puna is one of those places that no matter which way you decide to go, you really can't go wrong.

Pahoa

You can breeze through this "one-street" town, but you won't regret stopping if even for a few minutes. A raised wooden sidewalk passing false-front shops is fun to walk along to get a feeling of last century. Most of these shops are family-run fruit and vegetable stands supplied by local gardeners. Selections depend upon whether the old pickup truck started and made it to town that day. There's also **Pahoa Cash and Carry,** a regular grocery store, and **Pahoa Natural Groceries,** specializing in organic fruits and juices and as nearly well stocked as the store in Keaau. You can eat cheaply at **Magoo's Pizzeria, Pagoda Chop Suey,** or the local **Dairy Queen** that serves plate lunches. **Luguin's Place** is a reasonably priced Mexican restaurant that offers a combination of tasty platters for under $5. The best place to eat in town is at the **Pahoa Inn,** where the chef serves up a variety of cuisines from veal parmigiana, to Korean teriyaki chicken. Vegetarians will be happy to find **Not Jest Juice,** a shop specializing in fresh tropical juices, homebaked breads, and vegie sandwiches. Operated by Melinda Jackson and Robyn Taylor, open Mon. to Sat. 8:00 a.m. to 4:00 p.m., tel. 965-9407.

Lava Tree State Monument

In 1790, slick, fast-flowing *pahoehoe* lava surged through this *ohia* forest covering the tree trunks from the ground to about the 12-foot level. The moisture inside the trees cooled the lava, forming a hardened shell. At the same time tremors and huge fissures cracked the earth in the area. When the eruption ended, the still-hot lava drained away through the fissures leaving the encased tree trunks standing like sentinels. The floor of the forest is so smooth in some areas that the lava seems like asphalt. Each lava tree has its own personality; some resemble totem poles, and it doesn't take much imagination to see old craggy faces staring back at you. The most spectacular part of the park is just as you enter. Immense trees loom over cavernous cracks *(puka)* in the earth and send their roots, like stilled waterfalls, tumbling down into them. To get there take Rt. 132 east from Pahoa for 3 miles and look for the well-marked entrance on the left. Brochures are available as you enter.

Cape Kumukahi

It's fitting that Kumukahi means "First Beginning" since it is the easternmost point of Hawaii recognized as such by the original Polynesian settlers. Follow Rt. 132 past Lava Tree for about 10 miles until it hits the coast, where a lighthouse sits like an exclamation point. Along the way, get an instant course in volcanology; easily chart the destructive and regenerative forces at work on Hawaii. At the

lava trunks and new growth at Lava Tree State Monument

5-mile marker a HVB Warrior points out the lava flow of 1955. Tiny plants give the lava a greenish cast and shrubs are already eating into it, turning it to soil. An extensive flat basin with papaya orchards grows in the raw lava. The contrast of the black lifeless earth and the vibrant green of the trees is startling. In the center of the flatland rises a cindercone, a caldera of a much older mini-volcano unscathed by the modern flows; it is gorgeous with lush vegetation. An HVB Warrior points out the lava flow of 1960, and you can see at a glance how different it was from the flow of 5 years earlier. When Rt. 132 intersects Rt. 137, go straight ahead down a paved road for 2 miles to the Cape Kumukahi Lighthouse. People in these parts swear that on the fateful night in 1960, when the nearby village of Kapoho was consumed by the lava flow, an old woman (a favorite guise of Madame Pele) came to town begging for food and was turned away by everyone. She next went to the lighthouse asking for help, and was cordially treated by the lighthouse keeper. When the flow was at its strongest, it came within yards of the lighthouse and then miraculously split, completely encircling the structure but leaving it unharmed as it continued out to sea for a considerable distance.

Kalani Honua

Kalani Honua is a combination retreat, culture center, and health spa. They offer a wide variety of activities and services including holistic massage, meditation, yoga, *hula, lei*-making, language classes, computers, woodworking, music of all kinds, and general crafts. You come here to relax and recuperate, especially during the family-oriented summer camp running from early June to late August, or on a daily basis from 10:00 a.m. to 4:00 p.m. The grounds have a commune-type atmosphere, plus swimming pool, hot tub, assembly studios, classrooms, and cedar lodges with kitchen facilities and private rooms. It's the only place along the Puna Coast that offers lodging and vegetarian fare. Rates are $18 s (shared bath), $22 d; group rates are even cheaper. Kalani Honua is a few miles north of Kalapana on Rt. 137. Look for a large "Visitors Welcome" sign. For more information write: Kalani Honua, Box 4500, Kalapana, HI 96778, tel. 935-0127.

Kaimu And Kalapana

These two seaside villages along coastal Rt. 137 are bypassed by Rt.130, so make sure to keep your eye out. The small road connecting these two routes is famous for ***Puu Lapu*** ("Haunted Hill"), a natural curiosity where cars appear to defy gravity by rolling uphill. Kaimu, little more than a wide spot in the road, is famous for Kaimu Beach Park, better known as Black Sand Beach. Kalapana is an actual town with a beach park of its own (see "Beaches and Parks" below). While in town stop at the well-stocked **Kalapana Store and Drive In,** the only place in these parts to pick up supplies. It's operated by a septuagenarian, Walter Yamaguchi, who was featured in *Time* Magazine back in 1977 when a lava flow stopped only a few yards from his home. Yamaguchi-*san* knows about lava flows because he used to live in Kapoho before it became a lava pond in 1960. Along with learning the background of this area by talking to Mr. Yamaguchi, you can pick up some decent sandwiches, including a *mahi* burger for $3. Star of the Sea Catholic Church is a small but famous structure better known as **The Painted Church**. A minute's walk from the store, a cheery sign bids you "Welcome." A brief history of the area asserts that Kalapana was sort of a spiritual magnet for Roman Catholic priests. Old Spanish documents support evidence that a Spanish priest, crossing the Pacific from Mexico, actually landed very near here in 1555! Father Damien, famous priest of the Molokai Leper Colony, established a grass church about 2 miles north and conducted a school when he first arrived in the islands in 1864. The present church dates from 1928 when Father Everest Gielen began its construction. Like an inspired but much less talented Michelangelo, this priest painted the ceiling of the church working mostly at night by oil lamp. Father Everest was transferred to Lanai in 1941, and it wasn't until 1964 when Mr. George Heidler, an artist from Atlanta, Georgia, came to Kalapana and decided to paint the unfinished lower panels in the altar section. The artwork itself can only be described as gaudy but sincere. The colors are wild blues, purples, and oranges. The ceiling is adorned with symbols, portraits of Christ, the angel Gabriel, and scenes from the Nativity. Behind the altar a painted perspective gives the impression that you're looking down a long hallway at an altar that hangs suspended in air. The church is definitely worth a few minutes at least.

Park Visitor Center

The Park and Visitor Center marks the eastern entrance of Hawaii Volcanoes National Park, and here Rt. 130 becomes Chain of Craters Road. The Center sits along the coast (mile marker 27), and Kilauea Crater is 27 miles inland. The highly educational complex includes the restored Waha'ula Heiau and a museum. Numerous coastal trails lead from the Center to remnants of Hawaiian villages in the area. All trails are self guided, with historical and botanical information posted along the way. Most trails take less than an hour to complete. Before exploring Waha'ula Temple, just behind the Center, make sure to enter the museum containing an excellent selection of Hawaiiana, and definitely take the time to watch a short film about the geology of the highly volcanic area. The Center dispenses maps and brochures daily from 9:00 a.m. to 5:00 p.m.

Waha'ula Heiau ("Temple of the Red Mouth") radically changed the rituals and practices of the relatively benign Hawaiian religion by introducing the idea of human sacrifice. The 13th century marked the end of the frequent comings and goings between Hawaii and the "Lands to the South" (Tahiti), and began the isolation which would last 500 years until Capt. Cook arived. Unfortunately, this last influx of Polynesians brought a rash of conquering warriors carrying ferocious gods who lusted for human blood before they would be appeased. Paao, a powerful Tahitian priest, supervised the building of Waha'ula and brought in a new chief, Pili, to strengthen the diminished *mana* of the Hawaiian chiefs due to their commonplace practice of intermarriage with commoners. Waha'ula became the foremost *luakini* (human sacrifice) temple in the island kingdom and held this position until the demise of the old ways in the 1820s. The *heiau* is not at all grandiose, merely an elevated rock platform smoothed over with pebbles. Inside a self-guided tour reveals the nature of the old practices and where and how they were carried out. It's easy for modern people to condemn the old ways, but a sensitive historical account at the *heiau* makes one realize that within the context of Hawaiian beliefs, these practices were not considered barbaric.

Chain Of Craters Road

As you climb from the flatlands, a dramatic change takes place. Heading toward Kilauea, this area seems perpetually overcast and cloudy. Every bend in the road, and they are uncountable, offers a panoramic vista. There are dozens of pulloffs, many of which are named, like Naulu ("Sea Orchards"), where plaques provide geological information about past eruptions and lava flows. Afer you've gained the 3,000-foot level the name of the road is apparent in one crater after another until you reach Crater Rim Drive and begin circling Kilauea Caldera (see "Hawaii Volcanoes National Park" chapter for full coverage). The ride up from the coast takes about one hour as long as you don't take any side trips. One definitely worth the time and effort is Pu'u Loa Petroglyphs.

Where Chain of Craters turns inland from the coast a roadside marker indicates the **Kau Puna Trail**, and just across the road is the **Pu'u Loa Petroglyph Field**. The Kau Puna Trail leads along the coast where you can find shelters at Keauhou and Halape. Rain catchment tanks provide drinking water. All campers must register at the Kilauea Visitors Center.

common motif of stick man surrounded by holes for umbilical cords at Pu'u Loa petroglyph

In 1975 an earthquake rocked the area generating a tidal wave that killed 2 campers. More than 30 others had to be helicoptered to safety. Only registering will alert authorities of your whereabouts in case of a disaster. A number of trails cross in this area and you can take them back up to Chain of Craters Road or continue on a real expedition through the Kau Desert. The Kau Puna Trail requires full trekking and camping gear.

The walk out to **Pu'u Loa Petroglyphs** is delightful, highly educational, and only takes one hour. The trail, although it traverses solid lava, is discernible. The tread of feet over the centuries has discolored the rock. As you walk along there are *ahu,* traditional trail markers that are piles of stone shaped like little Christmas trees. Most of the lava field leading to the petroglyphs is undulating *pahoehoe* and looks like a frozen sea. You can climb bumps of lava, from 8 to 10 feet high to scout the immediate territory. Mountainside, the *pali* is quite visible and you can pick out the most recent lava flows—the blackest and least vegetated. As you approach the site, the lava changes dramatically and looks like long strands of braided rope. The petroglyphs are in an area about the size of a soccer field. A wooden walkway encircles them and insures their protection. A common motif is a circle with a hole in the middle, like a donut. There are men with triangular-shaped heads, and some rocks are entirely covered with designs while others have only a symbolic scratch or two. At the back end of the walkway a sign proclaims that Pu'u Loa meant "Long Hill" which the Hawaiians euphemised into "Long Life." For countless generations, fathers would come here to place pieces of their infants' umbilical cord into small holes as an offering to the gods to grant long life to their children. Concentric circles surrounded by the holes held the umbilical cords. The entire area, an obvious power spot, screams in utter silence, and the still-strong *mana* is easily felt.

BEACHES, PARKS AND CAMPGROUNDS

All of Puna's beaches, parks, and campgrounds lie along coastal Rt. 137 stretching for 20 miles from Pohoiki to Kamoamoa. Surfers, families, transients, even nudists have their favorite beaches along this southeast coast. For the most part, swimming is possible, but be cautious during high tide. There is plenty of sun, snorkeling sites, good fishing, and the campgrounds are almost always available.

Isaac Hale County Beach Park

You can't miss this beach park located on Pohoiki Bay, at the junction of Rt. 137 and Pohoiki Road. Just look for a jumble of boats and trailers parked under the palms. At one time Pohoiki Bay served the Hawaiians as a canoe landing, then later became the site of a commercial wharf for the Puna Sugar Company. It remains the only boat launching area for the entire Puna Coast, used by pleasure boaters and commercial fishermen. Due to this dual role, it's often very crowded. Full amenities include pavilions, restrooms, and showers (county permit). Experienced surfers dodge the rip-current in the center of the bay, and swimming is generally good when the sea is calm. Pohoiki Bay is also one of the best scuba sites on the island. Within walking distance of the salt and pepper beach are hotsprings that bubble into lava sinks surrounded by lush vegetation. They're popular with tourists and residents, and provide a unique and relaxing way to wash away sand and salt.

MacKenzie State Recreation Area

This popular state park was named for Forest Ranger A.J. MacKenzie, highly regarded throughout the Puna district and killed in the area in 1938. The park's 13 acres sit among a cool grove of ironwoods originally planted by MacKenzie. A portion of the old King's Highway, scratched out by prisoners last century as a form of community service, bisects the area. Many people who first arrive on the Big Island hang out at MacKenzie until they can get their start. Consequently, the park receives its share of hard-core types, which has earned it a reputation for rip-offs. Mostly it's safe, but if you're camping, take precautions with your valuables. The entire coastline along MacKenzie is bordered by rugged black lava sea cliffs. Swimming is dangerous, but the fishing is excellent. Be extremely careful when beach-walking, especially out on the fingers of lava; over the years, people have been swept away by freak waves. MacKenzie Park is located along Rt. 137, 2 miles south of Isaac Hale—full amenities and state permits for overnight camping.

Kehena

Kehena is actually 2 pockets of black-sand beach below a low sea cliff. Entrance to the beach is marked only by a scenic pulloff on Rt. 137, about 5 miles south of MacKenzie; usually a half dozen cars are parked there. At one time Kehena was very popular, and a stone staircase led down to the beach. In 1975 a strong earthquake jolted the area, breaking up the stairway and lowering the beach by 3 feet. Access is down a well-worn path, but make sure to wear sneakers because the lava is rough. The ocean here is dangerous, and often pebbles and rocks whisked along by the surf can injure legs. Once down on the beach head north for the smaller patch of sand, because the larger patch is open to the sea and can often be awash in waves. The black sand is hot, but a row of coconut palms provides shade. The inaccessibility of Kehena makes it a favorite "no-hassle" nudist beach with many "full" sunbathers congregating here.

Kaimu County Beach Park

When people refer to **Black Sand Beach** they actually mean Kaimu Beach Park. This is one of the major scenic attractions along the Puna Coast, and most travelers stop here at least long enough for a photo. There are no amenities except for a few picnic tables, but there is Black Sands Beach Drive-In just across the road, where you can pick up sandwiches and soft drinks. The coconut palms run right down to the waters edge whose white foam is in striking contrast to the coal-black sands. An earthquake in 1975 dropped the beach 3 feet, severly diminishing it and bringing the waters in to undermine the shoreline palms. The swimming here is extremely dangerous, and the lifeguard tower is there not to signify safe swimming but to protect unsuspecting tourists. Kaimu was the best surfing spot on the Puna Coast, but the earthquake changed the ocean floor enough to dramatically affect the break. Surfers still congregate here, but those in the know maintain that Kaimu isn't what it used to be. Signs along the beach warn against removing the black sand as souvenirs. Please obey them, as the natural erosion process is already drastically reducing the volume of sand. Kaimu Beach Park is in the tiny village of Kaimu, along Rt. 137 just after it splits from Rt. 130 heading south.

Harry K. Brown Beach Park

Located in the village of Kalapana a mile south of Kaimu is this county beach park which is also famous for its black-sand beach. Harry K. Brown Beach Park is the most popular surfside spot in Puna. It offers some of the only safe swimming in the area as well as full amenities and camping (county permit). In the park proper, across from the beach, are remnants of a local *heiau,* and a collection of important cultural stones from around the district. These were brought here in 1934 in an attempt to protect them from vandalism. At one time, signs

Kaimu Black Sand Beach

told their history, but now one can only guess what the slab-like and round stones were used for. Swimming offshore from the beach is very dangerous because it's unprotected from the open ocean and there are strong rips. A safe protected ocean pond at the southwest end of the beach once served as a canoe landing. Families enjoy this area, but be careful of the hot black sand especially on children's tender feet. You can always spot newcomers to the area. They're the ones walking barefooted who get halfway across the beach and start an impromptu version of the Mexican hat dance! Kalapana is the best surfing in Puna. The choice spot is called "Drainpipes," for expert surfers only. An annual contest attracts the best island surfers to Kalapana.

Kamoamoa Village And Campground
Two miles south of the Park and Visitor Center, about 4 miles south of Kalapana on Rt. 137, is the site of the old Hawaiian village of Kamoamoa and its campground. Look for a sign along the road directing you *makai* to a parking area. The free lightly used campground is more than adequate with large separated camping sites, flush toilets, and shaded picnic grove. A pavilion houses an ingenious cooking stove: a cement culvert rigged as an efficient woodburner. A half-mile trail begins here that takes you through native and exotic lowland forest along the coast to Kamoamoa Village and the remains of a *heiau.* Plaques along the trail give historical, cultural, and botanical facts concerning the area. As you walk along, you come to old burial sites, low round humps about 15 feet in diameter that resemble upside-down bowls. The pathway continues along the coast to a low flat stone that marked the floor of a canoe shed. Following are the remains of a *heiau* and just off the coast a clearly visible natural stone bridge. The path ends at the remains of Kamoamoa Village. Look for a grove of coconut trees, a short variety that're easily picked. Grass houses once sat atop the low stone platforms within the compound area. No camping is allowed in this area, but tenters have been known to make it a one-night bivouac just for the experience.

Devastation Trail

VOLCANOES NATIONAL PARK

Hawaii Volcanoes National Park is an unparalleled experience in geological grandeur. The western end of the park is the summit of stupendous **Mauna Loa,** the most massive mountain on Earth. The park's heart is **Kilauea Caldera,** encircled by 11 miles of **Crater Rim Drive.** Starting out you pass the Park and Visitor Center where you can give yourself a crash course in geology while picking up park maps and information. Nearby is **Volcano House,** Hawaii's oldest hotel, which has hosted a steady stream of adventurers, luminaries, royalty, and heads of state ever since it opened its doors in the 1860s. Amidst all the natural wonders is a golf course—for those who want to boast they've done it all after hitting a sand wedge from a volcanic fissure. Just down the road is one of Hawaii's last remaining indigenous forests, providing the perfect bucolic setting for a bird sanctuary. Mauna Loa Road branches off and quickly deteriorates to a 4WD track, then becomes a foot trail for the hale and hardy trekking to the 13,679-foot summit.

The rim drive continues past steam vents, sulphur springs, and tortured fault lines that always seem on the verge of gaping wide and swallowing. You can peer into the maw of **Halemaumau Crater,** home of the fire goddess, Madame Pele. For those unromantic enough to think that gods and goddesses don't rule the world, **Hawaiian Volcano Observatory** has been monitoring geologic activity since the turn of the century. Nearby is **Devastation Trail,** an elevated boardwalk across a desolate black lava field where gray lifeless trunks of a suffocated forest lean like old gravestones. Within minutes is **Thurston Lava Tube,** a magnificent natural tunnel *leid* by amazingly vibrant fern grottoes at the entrance and exit. The indomitable power of Volcanoes Park is apparent to all who come here. Mark Twain, enchanted by his sojourn through Volcanoes in the 1860s, quipped "the smell of sulphur is strong, but not unpleasant to a sinner." Amen brother! Wherever you stop to gaze, realize that you are standing on a thin skin of cooled lava in an unstable earthquake zone atop one of the world's most active volcanoes.

Geologic History: Science Or Madame Pele

Madame Pele is an irascible old dame. Perhaps it's because she had such a bad childhood. All she ever wanted was a home of her own where she could house her family and entertain her lover, a handsome chief from Kauai. But her sea goddess sister, Namakaokaha'i, flooded her out wherever she went after Pele seduced her husband, and the pig god, Kama pu'a, ravished her for good measure. So Pele finally built her love nest at Halemaumau Crater at the south end of Kilauea Caldera. Being a goddess obviously isn't as heavenly as one would think, and whenever the pressures of life get too much for Pele, she blows her stack. These tempestuous outbursts made Pele one of the most revered gods in the Hawaiian pantheon because her presence and might were so easily felt.

For a thousand years Pele was appeased by offerings of pigs, dogs, sacred *ohelo* berries (her favorite) and now and again an outcast man or two (never women) that would hopefully turn her energy from destruction to more comfortable pursuits. In the early 1820s, the chieftess Kapiolani, an ardent convert to Christianity, officially challenged Pele, toppling her like the other gods of old. Kapiolani climbed down into Pele's crater and ate the sacred *ohelo* berries, flagrantly violating the ageless *kapu*. She then took large stones and defiantly hurled them into the firepit below while bellowing, "Jehovah is my God. It is He, not Pele, that kindled these flames."

Yet today, most residents, regardless of background, have an inexplicable reverence for Pele. The goddess has modernized her tastes, switching from *ohelo* to juniper berries that she prefers in liquid form as shots of gin! The Volcano Post Office receives an average of 3 packages a week containing lava rocks taken by tourists as souvenirs. Pele looks upon these rocks as her children and taking them, to her, is kidnapping. Always the accompanying letters implore the officials to return the rocks because ever since the offender brought them home, his luck has been bad. The officials take the requests very seriously, returning the rocks with the customary peace offering: a shot of gin. Many follow-up "thank you" letters have been written to express relief of the bad luck being lifted. Pele is believed to take human form. She customarily appears before an eruption as a ravishing beauty or a withered old hag, and is often accompanied by a little white dog. She looks to be treated cordially, and it's said that she will stand by the roadside at night hitching a ride. After a brief encounter, she departs and seems to mysteriously evaporate into the ether. Kindness on your part is the key, and if you come across a strange woman at night treat her well—it might not help, but it definitely won't hurt.

Eruptions

The first white man atop Kilauea was the Rev. William Ellis, who scaled it in 1823. Until the 1920s, the floor of the caldera was exactly what people thought a volcano would be, a burning lake of fire. Then the forces of nature changed, and the fiery lava subsided and hardened over. Today, Kilauea is called the only "drive-in" volcano in the world, and in recent years has been one of the most active, erupting about once every 10 months. When it goes off, it is not a nightmare scene of people scrambling away for their lives, but just the opposite; people flock *to* the volcano. Most thrillseekers are in much greater danger of being run over by a hustling tour bus coming to see the fireworks than of ever being entombed in lava. The volcanic action is soul-shakingly powerful, but predictable and almost totally safe. The Hawaiian Volcanic Observatory has been keeping watch since 1911, making Kilauea one of the best understood volcanoes in the world. The vast volcanic field is creased by rift zones, or natural pressure valves. When the underground magma builds up, instead of kaboom!, as in Mt. St. Helens, it bubbles to the surface like a spring and gushes out a river of lava. Naturally, anyone or anything in its path would be burned to a cinder, but scientists routinely walk within a few feet of the still-flowing lava to take readings. The lava establishes a course that it follows much like an impromptu mountain stream caused by heavy rains.

This does not mean that the lava flows are entirely benign, or that anyone should visit the area during an eruption without prior approval by the Park Service. When anything is happening the local radio stations give up-to-the-minute news, and the Park Service provides a recorded message at tel. 967-7977. In 1790 a puff of noxious gases was emitted from Kilauea and descended on the Kau Desert, asphyxiating a rival army of Kamehameha that just happened to be in the area. Eighty people died

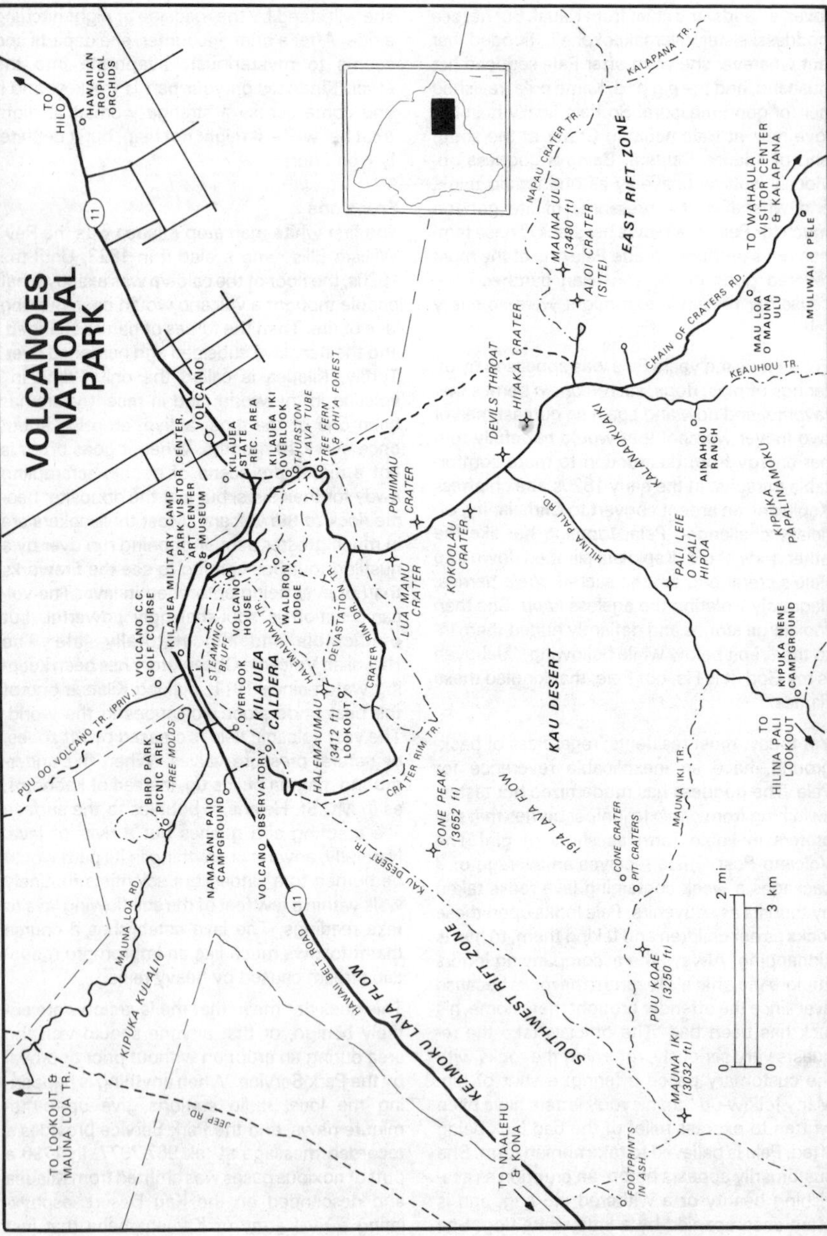
VOLCANOES NATIONAL PARK
TO HILO
HAWAIIAN TROPICAL ORCHIDS
11
VOLCANO
PARK VISITOR CENTER, ART CENTER
MUSEUM
KILAUEA STATE REC. AREA
KILAUEA IKI OVERLOOK
THURSTON LAVA TUBE
TREE FERN & OHI'A FOREST
PUHIMAU CRATER
DEVILS THROAT
HIIKA CRATER
MAUNA ULU (3480 ft)
ALOI CRATER (SITE)
NAPAU CRATER TR.
KALAPANA TR.
EAST RIFT ZONE
TO WAHAULA VISITOR CENTER & KALAPANA
CHAIN OF CRATERS RD.
MAU LOA O MAUNA ULU
MULIWAI O PELE
KEAUHOU TR.
AINAHOU RANCH
HILINA PALI RD.
KALANAOKUIKI
KIPUKA PAPALINAMOKU
PALI LEIE O KALI HIPOA
KIPUKA NENE CAMPGROUND
TO HILINA PALI LOOKOUT
KOKOOLAU CRATER
LUA MANU CRATER
CRATER RIM DR.
DEVASTATION TR.
WALDRON LEDGE
VOLCANO HOUSE
HALEMAUMAU TR.
KILAUEA CALDERA
OVERLOOK
STEAMING BLUFF
HALEMAUMAU LOOKOUT (3412 ft)
CRATER RIM TR.
KAU DESERT
1974 LAVA FLOW
CONE PEAK (3652 ft)
CONE CRATER
PIT CRATERS
MAUNA IKI TR.
PUU KOAE (3250 ft)
MAUNA IKI (3032 ft)
FOOTPRINTS IN ASH
0 2 mi
0 3 km
KAU DESERT TR.
SOUTHWEST RIFT ZONE
KEAMOKU LAVA FLOW
TO NAALEHU & KONA
VOLCANO OBSERVATORY
NAMAKANI PAIO CAMPGROUND
KILAUEA MILITARY CAMP
VOLCANO C.C. GOLF COURSE
TREE MOLDS
BIRD PARK PICNIC AREA
PUU OO VOLCANO TR. (PRIV.)
MAUNA LOA RD.
KIPUKA KULALIO
HAWAII BELT ROAD
JEEP RD.
TO LOOKOUT & MAUNA LOA TR.

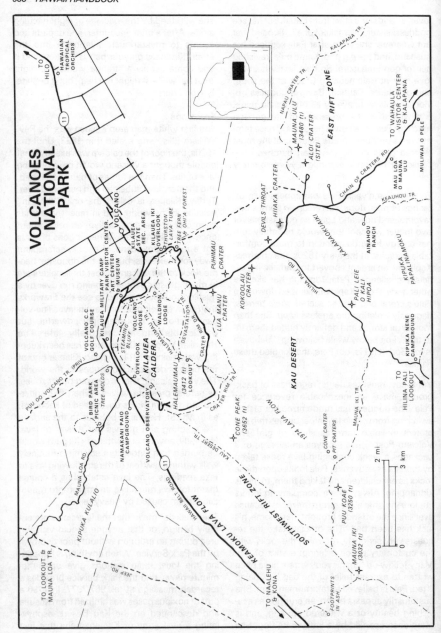

in their tracks. In 1881 a flow of lava spilled toward undeveloped Hilo, and engulfed an area within today's city limits. In 1942, a heavy flow came within 12 miles of the city. Still, this was child's play in comparison with the unbelievable flow of 1950. Luckily, this went down the western rift zone where only scattered homes were in its path. It took no lives as it disgorged well over 600 million cubic yards of magma that covered 35 square miles! The flow continued for 23 days and produced 7 huge torrents of lava that sliced across the Belt Road in 3 different areas. At its height, the flow traveled 6 miles per hour, and put out enough material to pave an 8-lane freeway twice around the world. In 1960, a flow swallowed the town of Kapoho on the east coast. In 1975 Hawaii's strongest earthquake in recorded history caused a *tsunami* to hit the southeast coast killing 2 campers, and sunk almost the entire Puna Coast by 3 feet. There is only one way to treat the power of Hawaii's magnificent volcanoes: not with fear, but with the utmost respect.

Rivers of lava one on top of the other. The darker the lava, the newer the flow.

Mauna Loa, at 13,679 feet, is a mere 117 feet shorter than its neighbor Mauna Kea, which is the tallest peak in the Pacific, and by some accounts, tallest in the world. Measured from its base, 18,000 under the sea, it would top even Mt. Everest. Mauna Loa is the most massive mountain on Earth, displacing 10,000 cubic miles of solid iron-hard lava. This titan weighs more than California's entire Sierra Nevada range! In fact, Mauna Loa ("Long Mountain"), at 60 miles long and 30 wide, occupies the whole southern half of the Big Island, with Volcanoes Park merely a section of its great expanse.

SIGHTS

The sights of Volcanoes National Park are arranged one after another along **Crater Rim Drive.** A side road now and again takes you to places of special interest such as **Tree Molds** or **Bird Park,** 10-minute detours. **Mauna Loa Road** is also off the beaten track but worth a look, along with the **Kau Desert Footprints,** 6 miles south from the Visitors Center on the Hawaiian Belt Road. Most of the sights are the "drive up" variety, but plenty of major and minor trails lead off here and there.

Tips

Expect to spend a long full day atop Kilauea to take in all the sights. Try to arrive by 9:00 a.m. with a picnic lunch to save time and hassles. Kilauea Caldera, at 4,000 feet, is about 10 degrees cooler than the coast. Oftentimes it's overcast and there can be showers. Wear your walking shoes and bring a sweater and/or windbreaker. Binoculars, sunglasses, and a hat will also come in handy. Those with respiratory ailments should note that the fumes from the volcano can cause added problems. Just stay away from areas of steam vents and don't overdo it, and you should be fine. Crater Rim Drive is a circular route; it matters little which way you proceed. Take your choice, but the following sights are listed counterclockwise beginning from Kilauea Visitor Center. Your biggest problem will be timing your arrival at the "drive in" sights to avoid the steady stream of tour buses.

Kilauea Visitor Center

The best place to start is at the Visitor Center Park HQ. The turnoff is clearly marked off Belt Road (Rt. 11). By mid-morning it's jammed so try to be an early bird. The Center is well run by the National Park Service. They offer a free lecture and film about geology and volcanism, with tremendous highlights of past eruptions. It runs every hour on the hour starting at 9:00

a.m. Also, a self-guided natural history museum gives more information about the geology of the area with plenty of exhibits of the flora and fauna. You will greatly enrich your visit if you take a half-hour tour of the museum. Anyone trekking to the backcountry for safety's sake *must* inform the rangers at the Center, especially during times of eruption. Do not be foolhardy! There is no charge for camping (see p. 594) and the rangers can give you up-to-the-minute information on trails, backcountry shelters, and cabins. Trails routinely close due to lava flows, tremors, and rockslides. The rangers cannot help you if they don't know where you are. Many day trails leading into the Caldera from the Rim Road are easy walks that need no special preparation. The backcountry trails can be very challenging, and detailed maps (highly recommended) are sold at the Center along with special-interest geology and natural history publications prepared by the Hawaii Natural History Association. The Visitor Center is open daily 9:00 a.m. to 5:00 p.m., tel. 967-7988 for trail and camping information, or 967-7977 for a recorded message concerning the latest news on any volcanic activity.

Volcano House

Have you ever dreamed of sleeping with a goddess? Well, you can cuddle up with Madame Pele by staying at Volcano House (for details see p. 595). If your plans don't include an overnight stop, go in for a look. Sometimes this is impossible, because not only tour buses from the Big Island disgorge here, but tour groups are flown in from Honolulu. Stopping at the bar provides refreshments and a tremendous view of the crater. Volcano House still has the feel of a country inn, although in reality it's a Sheraton Inn. This particular building dates from the 1940s, but the site has remained the same since a grass hut was perched on the rim of the crater by a sugar planter in 1846. He charged $1 a night. A steady stream of notable visitors has come ever since: almost all of Hawaii's kings and queens dating from the middle of last century, as well as royalty from Europe. Mark Twain was a guest, followed by Franklin Roosevelt, and most recently a contigency of astronauts lodged here and used the crater floor to prepare for walking on the moon. In 1866 a large grass hut replaced the first, and in 1877 a wooden Victorian-style hotel was built. It is now the Volcano Art Center, and has been moved just across the road. The longest owner/operator of Volcano House was Mr. George Lycurgus, who took over management of the hotel in the 1890s. His son, Nick, followed him and managed the hotel until the 1960s.

Art and history buffs should walk across the street to the **Volcano Art Center,** which is the original 1877 Volcano House. You not only get to see some fine arts and crafts ($.25 suggested donation), but you can take a self-guided tour of this mini-museum. In fact, this is Hawaii's oldest hotel.

Fiddlehead ferns are prevalent along trails where the lava has weathered.

CRATER RIM DRIVE

So many intriguing nooks and crannies run along Crater Rim Drive where you can stop for a look, that you'll have to force yourself to be picky if you intend to cover the park in one day. Actually, you can easily walk to **Sulphur**

Banks from Volcano Art Center along a 10-minute trail. If driving, signs along the Rim Drive direct you, and your nose will tell you when you're close. As you approach these fumaroles, the earth surrounding them turns a deep reddish-brown, covered over in yellowish-green sulphur. The rising steam is caused by surface water leaking into the cracks that becomes heated and rises as vapor. Kelauea releases hundreds of tons of sulphur gases every day, with Sulphur Banks being merely an obvious example. This gaseous activity stunts the growth of vegetation, and when atmospheric conditions cause a low ceiling, they sometimes cause the eyes and nose to water. The area is best avoided by those with heart and lung conditions.

Steam Vents comes next, also fumaroles, but without sulphur. The entire field behind the partitioned area is steaming. The feeling is like being in a sauna. There are no strong fumes to contend with here, just the tour buses. **Kilauea Military Camp** follows—not open to the public. The camp serves as an R&R facility for military personnel.

Hawaiian Volcano Observatory

This observatory has been keeping tabs on the volcanic activity in the area since the turn of the century. The actual observatory is filled with delicate seismic equipment and is closed to the public, but a lookout nearby gives you a dentist's view into the mouth of Halemaumau Crater ("House of Ferns"), Pele's home. Steam rises and you can feel the power, but it was an even more phenomenally spectacular view until 1924 when it was a lake of molten lava. The lava has since sunk below the surface, which is now crusted over. Scientists do not predict a recurrence in the near future, but no one knows Pele's mind. This is a major stop for the tour buses, but a 2-minute saunter along the hiking trail gives you the view to yourself. Information plaques in the immediate area tell of the history and volcanology of the park. One points out a spot to observe the perfect shield volcano form of Mauna Loa—most times too cloudy to see. Another reminds you that you're in the middle of the Pacific, an incredible detail you tend to forget when atop these mountains. Here too is Uwekahuna ("Wailing Priest") Bluff, where the *kahuna* made offerings of appeasement to Pele. A Hawaiian prayer commemorates their religious rites.

Moon Walks

A string of interesting stops follows the Observatory. One points out the **Kau Desert**, an inhospitable site of red-earth plains, studded with a few scraggly plants (see p. 593). Next comes the **Southwest Rift**, a series of cracks running from Kilauea's summit to the sea. You can observe at a glance that you are standing directly over a major earthquake fault. Dated lava flows follow in rapid succession until you arrive at **Halemaumau Trail**. The well-maintained trail is only one-quarter mile long and gives an up-close view of the crater. The area is rife with fumaroles and should be avoided by those with respiratory problems. At the end you're treated to a full explanation of Halemaumau. Farther along the road a roped-off area was once an observation point that caved in. You won't take the ground under your feet for granted! Close by is **Keanakakoi**, a quarry from which superior stone was gathered to make tools. It was destroyed by a flow in 1877. If that seems to be in the remote past, realize that you are now on a section of road that was naturally paved over with lava from a "quickie" eruption in 1982!

Most visitors hike along **Devastation Trail**. The half mile it covers is fascinating, one of the most photographed areas in the park. It leads across a field devastated by a tremendous eruption from **Kilauea Iki** ("Little Kilauea") in 1959, when fountains of lava shot 1,900 feet into the air. The area was once an *ohia* forest that was denuded of limbs and leaves, then choked by black pumice and ash. The vegetation has regenerated since then, and the recuperative powers of the flora is part of an ongoing study. The trail begins as a cinder path, then becomes an elevated boardwalk. Notice that many of the trees have sprouted aerial roots trailing down from the branches: this is total adaptation to the situation, as these roots don't normally appear. As you move farther along the trail little tufts of grass and bushes peek out of the pumice, and there are even some wild raspberries. But then the surroundings become totally barren where absolutely nothing grows, and look like the nightmare of a nuclear holocaust.

Thurston Lava Tubes

If the Devastation Trail produced a sense of melancholy, the Thurston Lava Tubes make you feel like Alice walking through the looking glass. Inside is a fairy kingdom. As you approach, the expected billboard gives you the low-down on the geology, and flora and fauna of the area. Take the 5 minutes to educate yourself. The paved trail starts as a steep incline which quickly enters a fern forest. All about you are fern trees, vibrantly green with native birds flitting here and there. As you approach the lava tube, it seems almost manmade, like a perfectly formed tunnel leading into a mine. At the entrance, ferns and moss hang down, and if you stand just inside the entrance looking out, it's as if the very air is tinged with green. If there were such things as elves and gnomes, they would surely live here. The walk through takes about 10 minutes, and the tube rolls and undulates through narrow passages and into large "rooms." At the other end, the fantasy world of ferns and moss reappears.

vintage photo of the Thurston Lava Tubes

Small Detours

Less than one mile past Kilauea Military Camp, a road branches from the Rim Drive, crosses Rt. 11, and links up with Mauna Loa Road. If you're interested in golfing, natural phenomena, or trekking to the summit of Mauna Loa, take it. As an added incentive, a minute down this road leaves 90% of the tourists behind. **Volcano Golf and Country Club** is an 18-hole, 6,119-yard, par-72 course. Green fees are $14, and carts are available; tel. 967-7550. To beat the heavy lunch crowd at Volcano House, try the International Sportsman Restaurant at the course, tel. 967-7331. When the road crosses Rt. 11 turn right, and follow it east for one mile to the entrance of the course.

Tree Molds is an ordinary name for an extraordinary place. Cross Rt. 11 and follow the signs for 5 minutes to a cul-de-sac. At the entrance, a billboard tries hard to dramatically explain what occurred here. In a moment, you realize that you're standing atop a lava flow, and that the scattered potholes are entombed tree trunks. Unlike Lava Tree State Monument, where the magma encased the tree and flowed away, the opposite action happened here. The lava stayed put while the tree trunk burned away, leaving 15- to 18-foot-deep holes.

Bird Sanctuary

Kipuka Puaulu is a sanctuary for birds and nature lovers who want to leave the crowds behind, just under 2 miles down Mauna Loa Road. The first sign for Bird Park takes you to an ideal picnic area; the second, 100 yards beyond, takes you to Kipuka Puaulu Loop Trail. As you enter the trail, a bulletin board describes the birds and plants, some of the last remaining indigenous fauna and flora in Hawaii. Please follow all rules. The trail is self guided, and pamphlets describing the stations along the way are dispensed from a box 50 feet down the trail. The loop is only one mile long, but to really assimilate the area, especially if you plan to do any bird watching, expect to spend an hour minimum. It doesn't take long to realize that you are privileged to see some of the

apapane

world's rarest plants, such as a small nondescript bush, called *aalii.* In the branches of the towering *ohia* trees you might see an *elepaio,* or an *apapane,* two natives. Common finches and Japanese white eyes are imported birds that are here to stay. There's a fine example of a lava tube, and an explanation of how ash from eruptions provided the soil and nutrients for the forest to grow. Orange nasturtiums and blue morning glory, beautiful but deadly, have taken over acres of the hillside, wiping out all the natural vegetation. This is a microcosm of the demise of Hawaii's flora and fauna. When you do come across a native Hawaiian plant, it seems somehow older, almost prehistoric. If a pre-contact Hawaiian could be materialized, even here in this preserve, he would recognize only a few plants and trees. More than 4 times as many plants and animals have become extinct in Hawaii in the last 200 years than on all of the North American continent. As you leave, listen for the melodies coming from the treetops, and hope the day never comes that no birds sing.

Further Afield

Mauna Loa Road continues westward and gains elevation for approximately 10 miles. Just past Kipuka Puaulu a "Caution—Earthquake Damage" sign promises excitement on the road ahead. At the end of the pavement, at 6,662 feet, you find a parking area and lookout. A trail leads from here to the summit of Mauna Loa. (See "Camping and Hiking" following.) It takes 3 to 4 days to hike, under no circumstances by novice hikers or those unprepared for cold alpine conditions. At 6,000 feet altitude is already a concern.

The **Kau Desert Footprints** are 6 miles south along Rt. 11 from the Visitors Center between mile markers 37 and 38, designated as the Kau Desert Trail Head. People going to or from Kailua-Kona can see them en route, and those staying in Hilo should take the time to visit the Footprints. The trek across the small section of desert is fascinating, and the history of the Footprints makes the experience more evocative. The trail is only 1.6 miles RT, and can be hustled along in less than 30 minutes, but allow at least an hour mostly for observation. The predominant foliage is a red bottlebrush that contrasts with the bleak surroundings—the feeling throughout the area is one of foreboding. You pass a wasteland of *a'a'* and *pahoehoe* lava flows to arrive at the Footprints. A metal fence in a sturdy pavilion surrounds the footprints. They look like they're cast in cement. Actually they're formed from pisolites: particles of ash stuck together with moisture,

Kau Desert

which formed mud that hardened like plaster. In 1790 Kamehameha was waging war with Keoua over the control of the Big Island. One of Keoua's warrior parties of approximately 80 people attempted to cross the desert while Kilauea was erupting. Toxic gases descended upon them and the warriors and their families were enveloped and suffocated. They literally died in their tracks, which remain as the Footprints. This unfortunate occurrence was regarded by the Hawaiians as a direct message from the gods proclaiming their support for Kamehameha. Keoua, who could not deny the sacred signs, felt abandoned and shortly thereafter became a human sacrifice at Puukohala Heiau built by Kamehameha to honor his war-god Kukailimoku. For the Kau District see p. 622.

Camgrounds And Cabins

The main campground in Volcanoes is **Namakani Paio,** down a short service road behind Hawaii Volcano Observatory. There is no charge for tent camping and no reservations are required, but you must get a permit (limited to 7 days) from Park HQ. A cooking pavilion has fireplaces but no wood is provided. **Cabins** are available through Volcano House. Each accommodates 4 people and costs $14. A $10 key deposit gives access to the shower and toilet; linens are an optional extra. Check in at Volcano House at 3:00 p.m. and check out by 12:00 p.m. For information and reservations write Volcano House at the above address.

Kipuka Nene is another campground, approximately 10 miles south of Park HQ down Hilina Pali Road. Much fewer people camp here and it too is free. You must get a 7-day permit from HQ, and you'll find a cooking pavilion, fireplaces, but no firewood.

Niaulani Cabin is operated by the Division of State Parks. The cabin is outside the park along Old Volcano Road, about a half mile south of the Village General Store in Volcano Village. The cabin is completely furnished with full kitchen and bathroom facilities. It accommodates up to 6 people, and the rates are on a sliding scale determined by number of people and length of stay: one person for one day is $10, 2 persons is $14, and 6 persons is $30. Reservations and a deposit are required. For full details write Dept. of Land and Natural Resources, Div. of State Parks, Box 936, Hilo, HI 96720, tel. 961-7200. Upon arrival the key is picked up from the Div. of State Parks office at 75 Aupuni St., Hilo, between 7:45 a.m. to 4:30 p.m. Holidays and weekends the key is left at the Hilo Airport Information booth.

HIKING

The slopes of Mauna Loa and Volcanoes Park are a trekker's paradise. You'll find trails that last for days or just an hour or two. Many have shelters, and those trails that require an overnight stay provide cabins. Because of the possibility of an eruption or earthquake, it is *imperative* to check in at Park HQ, where you can also pick up current trail info and maps (see p. 589).

The hike to the summit of **Mauna Loa** (13,679 feet) is the most grueling. The trailhead is at the lookout at the end of the pavement of Mauna Loa Road. Hikers in excellent condition can make the summit (RT) in 3 days, but 4 would be more comfortable. There is a considerable height gain so expect chilly weather even in summer, and snow in winter. Altitude sickness is also a problem. En route you pass through *nene* country, with a good chance to spot these lava-adapted geese. Fences keep out feral goats, so remember to close gates after you. The first cabin is at Red Hill (10,092 feet) and the second is at the summit. They provide stoves, lanterns, and heating devices, but carry your own Coleman fuel. Water is from roof catchment and should be boiled. The summit treats you to a sweeping panorama that includes Haleakala. Mauna Loa's Mokuaweoweo Caldera is over 3 miles long and has vertical walls towering 600 feet. From November to May, if there is snow, steam rises from the caldera. The trail cabin is down inside.

The **Crater Rim Loop Trail** begins at Park HQ and follows the Crater Rim Road, crossing back and forth a number of times. Hiking the entire 11 miles takes a full day, but you can take it in sections as time and energy permit. It's a well-marked and maintained trail, and all you need is warm clothing, water, and determination. For your efforts, you'll get an up-close view of all of the sights outlined along Crater Rim Drive.

Kilauea Iki Trail begins at the Thurston Lava Tube, or at Park HQ via the Byron Ledge Trail. This 5-mile trail generally takes 3 to 4 hours as it passes through the center of Kilauea Iki Caldera. It's easy to link up with the Byron Ledge Trail or with the Halemaumau Trail. You can return north to Park HQ or continue on either of these 2 trails to Halemaumau Parking Area directly south of Park HQ.

Halemaumau Trail provides the best scenery for the effort. It begins at Park HQ and descends into Kilauea Caldera covering 6 miles (5 hours). If possible, arrange to be picked up at Halemaumau Parking area due south of Park HQs.

ACCOMMODATIONS AND FOOD

If you intend to spend the night atop Kilauea, your choices of accommodation are few and simple. Volcano House provides the only hotel, cabins are available at the campgrounds, and there are plenty of tenting sites.

Volcano House is managed by Sheraton Inns. Don't be frightened away by the daytime crowds. They disappear with the sun. Then Volcano House metamorphoses into what it has always been: a quiet country inn. The 37 rooms are comfy but old-fashioned. Who needs a pool or TV when you can look out your window into a volcano caldera? Volcano House charges a reasonable $34 s, $48 d, $10 additional person. Box 53, Hawaii Volcanoes National Park, HI 96718, tel. 967-7321 or 800-325-3535.

Volcano Vacation, Box 608, Kailua-Kuna, HI 96745, tel. 322-3869, offers a fully furnished, 2-bedroom luxury cabin complete with sauna and fireplace for $80 p/d, plus, $1,500 p/m, deposit required.

Food

Volcano House offers a full menu for breakfast, lunch, and dinner. The quality is good and the prices reasonable; however, the lunchtime buffet is overwhelmingly crowded and should be avoided if possible. The **Ohia Tree Restaurant** along Rt. 11 in Volcano Village is open from 7:00 a.m. to 4:00 p.m. It's a casual cafe with not too inflated prices (no credit cards), specializing in soup and sandwiches. You can also buy beer, picnic supplies, and what mountain cafe would be complete without selling *sushi?* If you're golfing, or want to get away from the crowds, have a satisfying meal at **International Sportsman Restaurant Extraordinaire** at Volcano Golf Course. The cuisine is quite good, with a full lunch menu. For those primarily interested in sightseeing, you'll save time and money by bringing your own picnic lunch.

"I have seen Vesuvius since, but it was a mere toy, a child's volcano, a soup kettle compared with this."

—Mark Twain (on Kilauea)

KONA

Kona is long and lean, and takes its suntanned body for granted. This district *is* the west coast of the Big Island and lies in the rain shadows of both Mauna Loa and Mauna Kea. You can come here expecting brilliant sunny days and glorious sunsets, and you won't be disappointed; this reliable sunshine has earned it the nickname of "The Gold Coast." Offshore, the fishing grounds are legendary, especially for marlin that lure game fishermen from around the world. There are actually two Konas, North and South, and both enjoy an upland interior of forests, ranches, and homesteads, while most of the coastline is low, broad, and flat. If you've been fantasizing about swaying palms and tropical jungles dripping with wild orchids, you might be in for "Kona shock," especially if you fly directly into Keahole Airport. Around the airport the land is raw black lava that can appear as forbidding as the tailings from an old mining operation. Don't despair. Just north is one of the premiere resorts in Hawaii, with a gorgeous white beach lined with dancing coconut palms, and throughout Kona the lava has been transformed into beautiful gardens with just a little love and care.

Kailua-Kona is the heart of North Kona, by far the most developed area in the district. Its **Ali'i Drive** is lined with shops, hotels, and condos, but for the most part the shoreline vista remains intact because the majority are low-rise. To show just how fertile lava can be when tended, miles of multi-hued bougainvillea and poinsettias line Ali'i Drive like a *lei* that leads to the flower pot of the **Kona Gardens.** East of town is **Mt. Hualalai** (8,271 feet), where local people still earn a living growing vegetables and *taro* on small truck farms high in the mountain coolness. **South Kona** begins in the town of **Captain Cook.** Southward is a region of diminutive coffee plantations, the only ones in the U.S. The bushes grow to the shoulder of the road and the air is heady with the rich aroma of roasting coffee. Farther south, rough but passable roads branch from the main highway and tumble toward hidden beaches and tiny fishing villages where time just slips away. From north to south Kona is awash in brilliant sunshine, where the rumble of surf and the plaintive cry of seabirds create the music of peace.

SIGHTS

The entire Kona District is both old and historic. This was the land of Lono, god of fertility and patron of the *Makahiki* Festival. It was also the spot where the first missionary packet landed and changed Hawaii forever, and it's been a resort ever since the 19th century. In and around **Kailua** are restored *heiau,* a landmark lava church, and a royal palace where the monarchs of Hawaii came to relax. The coastline is rife with historical sites of lesser *heiau,* petroglyph fields, and curious amusement rides dating from the days of *Makahiki.* Below the town of Captain Cook is **Kealakekua Bay,** the first and main *haole* anchorage in the islands. This bay is overwhelming with historical significance, alternately being a place of life, death, and hope, from where the spirit of Hawaii was changed for all time. Here on the southern coast is a Hawaiian "temple of refuge," restored and made into a National Historical Park. The majority of Kona's sights are strung along Rt. 11. Except for Kailua-Kona, where a walking tour is perfect, you need a rental car to visit the sights; the Big Island's Hele-On Bus is too infrequent to be feasible. The sights listed below are arranged from Kailua heading south.

Mokuaikaua Church

Kailua is one of those towns that would love to contemplate its own navel if it could only find it. It really doesn't have a center, and if you had to pick one, it would have to be the 112-foot steeple of Mokuaikaua ("The trees are felled, now let us eat") Church. This highest structure in town has been a landmark for travelers and seafarers ever since the church was completed in January 1838. The church claims to be the oldest house of Christian worship in Hawaii. The site was given by King Liholiho to the first Congregationalist missionaries who arrived on the brig *Thaddeus* in 1820. The actual construction was undertaken in 1836 by the Hawaiian congregation under the direction of Rev. Asa Thurston. Much thought was given to the orientation of the structure: designed so the prevailing winds blow through the entire length of the church keeping it cool and comfortable. The walls of the church are fashioned from massive rough-hewn lava stone, mortared with plaster made from crushed and burned coral that was bound with *kukui* nut oil. The huge cornerstones are believed to have been salvaged from a *heiau* built in the 15th C. by King Umi. The masonry is crude but effective—still sound after 150 years.

Inside, the church is extremely soothing, expressing a feeling of strength and simplicity. The resolute beams are native *ohia,* pegged together and closely resembling the fine beam work used in barns throughout 19th C. New England. The pews, railings, pulpit, and trim are all fashioned from *koa,* a rich brown lustrous wood that just begs to be stroked.

Mokuaikaua Church

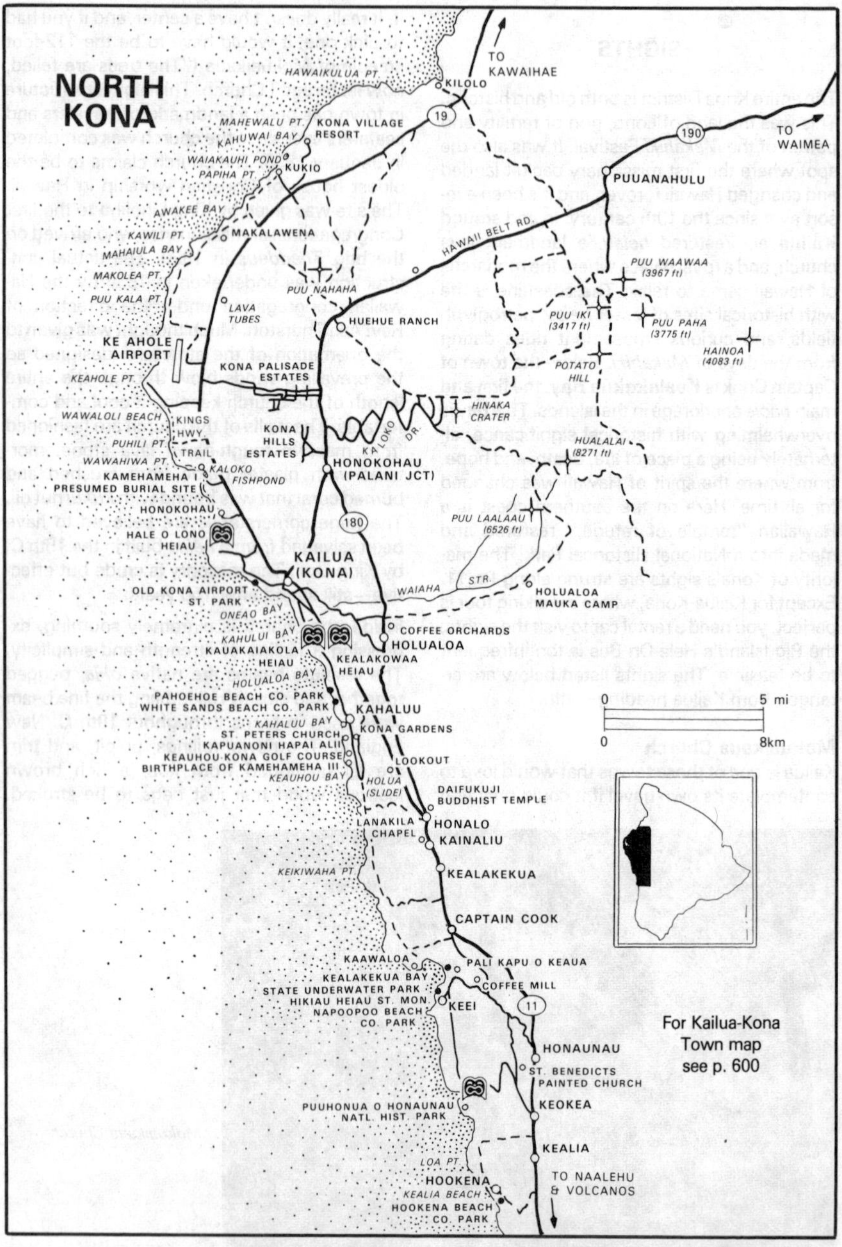
NORTH KONA
TO KAWAIHAE
KILOLO
HAWAIKULUA PT.
19
MAHEWALU PT.
KONA VILLAGE RESORT
KAHUWAI BAY
WAIAKAUHI POND
KUKIO
PAPIHA PT.
AWAKEE BAY
KAWILI PT.
MAKALAWENA
MAHAIULA BAY
MAKOLEA PT.
PUU KALA PT.
PUU NAHAHA
LAVA TUBES
HUEHUE RANCH
KE AHOLE AIRPORT
KONA PALISADE ESTATES
KEAHOLE PT.
WAWALOLI BEACH
KINGS HWY TRAIL
PUHILI PT.
WAWAHIWA PT.
KONA HILLS ESTATES
KALOKO DR.
HONOKOHAU (PALANI JCT)
KALOKO FISHPOND
KAMEHAMEHA I PRESUMED BURIAL SITE
HONOKOHAU
HALE O LONO HEIAU
180
KAILUA (KONA)
OLD KONA AIRPORT ST. PARK
ONEAO BAY
WAIAHA STR.
KAHULUI BAY
KAUAKAIAKOLA HEIAU
COFFEE ORCHARDS
HOLUALOA
KEALAKOWAA HEIAU
HOLUALOA BAY
PAHOEHOE BEACH CO. PARK
WHITE SANDS BEACH CO. PARK
KAHALUU
KAHALUU BAY
KONA GARDENS
ST. PETERS CHURCH
KAPUANONI HAPAI ALII
KEAUHOU-KONA GOLF COURSE
BIRTHPLACE OF KAMEHAMEHA III
KEAUHOU BAY
LOOKOUT
HOLUA (SLIDE)
DAIFUKUJI BUDDHIST TEMPLE
LANAKILA CHAPEL
HONALO
KAINALIU
KEIKIWAHA PT.
KEALAKEKUA
CAPTAIN COOK
KAAWALOA
PALI KAPU O KEAUA
KEALAKEKUA BAY
STATE UNDERWATER PARK
COFFEE MILL
HIKIAU HEIAU ST. MON.
KEEI
11
NAPOOPOO BEACH CO. PARK
HONAUNAU
ST. BENEDICTS PAINTED CHURCH
PUUHONUA O HONAUNAU NATL. HIST. PARK
KEOKEA
KEALIA
LOA PT.
TO NAALEHU & VOLCANOS
HOOKENA
KEALIA BEACH
HOOKENA BEACH CO. PARK
TO WAIMEA
190
PUUANAHULU
HAWAII BELT RD.
PUU WAAWAA (3967 ft)
PUU IKI (3417 ft)
PUU PAHA (3775 ft)
HAINOA (4083 ft)
POTATO HILL
HINAKA CRATER
HUALALAI (8271 ft)
PUU LAALAAU (6526 ft)
HOLUALOA MAUKA CAMP
0
5 mi
0
8km
For Kailua-Kona Town map see p. 600

Although the church is still used as a house of worship, it also has the air of a museum, housing paintings of historical personages instrumental in Hawaii's Christian past. The crowning touch is an excellent model of the brig *Thaddeus,* painstakingly built by the men of the Pacific Fleet Command and presented to the church in 1934. The church is open daily from sunrise to sunset, and volunteer hostesses answer your questions from 10:00 a.m. to noon, and 1:00 p.m. to 3:30 p.m. Mokuaikaua Church is a few hundred yards south of Kailua Pier on the *mauka* side of Ali'i Drive.

Hulihee Palace

Go from the spiritual to the temporal by walking across the street from Mokuaikaua Church and entering Hulihee ("Flight") Palace. This 2-story Victorian structure commissioned by Hawaii's first governor, John Kuakini, also dates from 1838. A favorite summer getaway for all the Hawaiian monarchs that followed, especially King Kalakaua, it was used as such until 1916. At first glance, the outside is unimpressive, but the more you look the more you realize how simple and grand it is. The architectural lines are those of an English country manor, and indeed Great Britain was held in high esteem by the Hawaiian royalty. Inside, the palace is bright and airy. Most of the massive carved furniture is made from *koa.* The most magnificent pieces include a huge formal dining table, 70 inches in diameter, fashioned from one solid *koa* log. Upstairs is a tremendous 4-poster bed that belonged to Queen Kapiolani, and 2 magnificent cabinets that were built by a Chinese convict who was serving a life sentence for smuggling opium. King Kalakaua heard of his talents and commissioned him to build the cabinets. They proved to be so wonderfully crafted that after they were completed the king pardoned the Chinaman. Prince Kuhio, who inherited the palace from his uncle, King Kalakaua, was the first Hawaiian delegate to Congress. He decided to auction off all the furniture and artifacts to raise money, supposedly for the benefit of the Hawaiian people. Providentially, the night before the auction each piece was painstakingly numbered by the royal ladies of the palace, and the name of the person bidding for the piece was dutifully recorded. In the years that followed the **Daughters of Hawaii**, who now operate the palace as a museum, tracked down the owners and convinced many to return the items for display. Most of the pieces are privately owned, and because each is unique, the owners wish no duplicates to be made. It is for this reason, coupled with the fact that flash bulbs can fade the wood, that a strict *no photography* policy is enforced. Delicate and priceless heirlooms include a tiger-claw necklace belonging to Kapiolani, and there's a portrait gallery of Hawaiian monarchs. There are also personal and mundane items, like old report cards showing a 68 in philosophy for King Kalakaua, and lining the stairs a collection of spears reputedly belonging to the great Kamehameha himself. Hulihee Palace, tel. 329-1877, is on the *makai* side of Ali'i Drive, open daily from 9:00 a.m. to 4:00 p.m., last tour at 3:30, and on Sat. from 9:00 a.m. until noon, admission $4. A hostess is usually on duty, such as Auntie Lee Collins who is very knowledgeable in Hawaiiana; if you're lucky, Tuffy, a tour guide who could easily be a stand-up comedian, will escort you through the palace.

Ahuena Heiau

Directly behind the King Kamehameha Hotel, at the north end of "downtown" Kailua, is the restored Ahuena Heiau. Built around Kamakahonu ("Eye of the Turtle") Beach, it's in a very important historical area. Kamehameha I, the great conqueror, came here to spend the last years of his life, settling down to a peaceful existence after so many years of war and strife. The king, like all Hawaiians, reaffirmed his love of the *aina* and tended his own royal *taro* patch on the slopes of Mt. Hualalai. After he died his bones were prepared according to ancient ritual on a stone platform within the temple, then taken to a secret burial place just north of town which is believed to be somewhere near Wawahiwa Point. It was Kamehameha who initiated the first rebuilding of Ahuena Heiau, a temple of peace and prosperity dedicated to Lono, god of fertility. The rituals held here were a far cry from the bloody human sacrifices dedicated to the god of war, Kukailimoku, that were held at Puukohola Heiau, which Kamehameha had built a few leaues north and a few decades earlier. At Ahuena, Kamehameha gathered the sage *kahuna* of the land who held discourse in the Hale Mana (main prayer house) on topics concerning wise government and statesmanship. It was here that Liholiho, Kamehameha's son and heir, was educated, and as a grown man, it was here that Liholiho sat down with the great queens, Kapiolani and Kaahumanu, and broke the ancient *kapu* of eating with women, thereby destroying the old order.

The tallest structure on the grounds of the temple is the *anuu* (oracle tower) where the chief priest, in deep trance, received messages from the gods. Throughout the grounds are superbly carved *kia akua* (temple images) in the distinctive Kona style, considered some of the finest of all Polynesian art forms. The spiritual focus of the *heiau* was to man's higher nature, and the tallest figure, crowned with an image of the golden plover, was that of Koleamoku, a god of healing. Another interesting structure is a small thatched hut of sugarcane leaves, Hale Nana Mahina, which means "house from which to watch the farm land." Kamehameha would come here to meditate while a guard kept watch from a nearby shelter. The commanding view from the doorway affords a sweeping panorama from the sea to the king's plantations on the slopes of Mt. Hualalai. Though the reconstructed temple grounds are impressive, done under the auspices of the Bishop Museum, they are only one-third of the original. The *heiau* is open daily from 9:00 a.m. to 4:00 p.m., and admission is free. You can wander around following a self-guided tour, or the King Kamehameha Hotel, tel. 329-2911, offers free tours of the temple and their own hotel grounds. This includes a walk through the lobby, where various artifacts are displayed, and an extremely informative botanical tour that highlights the medicinal herbs of old Hawaii. The hotel tours are operated at 10:00 a.m. and again at 1:30 p.m. Don't miss this excellent educational opportunity, well worth the time and effort!

While in the area make sure to visit the **Kailua Pier**, across the street from the *heiau*. Fishing boats are in and out all day, with most charters returning around 5:00 p.m. You'll have a chance to see some of the marlin that Kona is noted for, but if you have a sympathetic heart or weak stomach it might not be for you. This area is frantic with energy during the various "Billfish Tournaments" (see "Events") held throughout the year.

Along Ali'i Drive

Ali'i Drive heads south from Kailua, passing the majority of Kona's resorts. Mountainside, a continuous flow of flowers lines the road like a *femme fatale's* seductive boa, while seaside

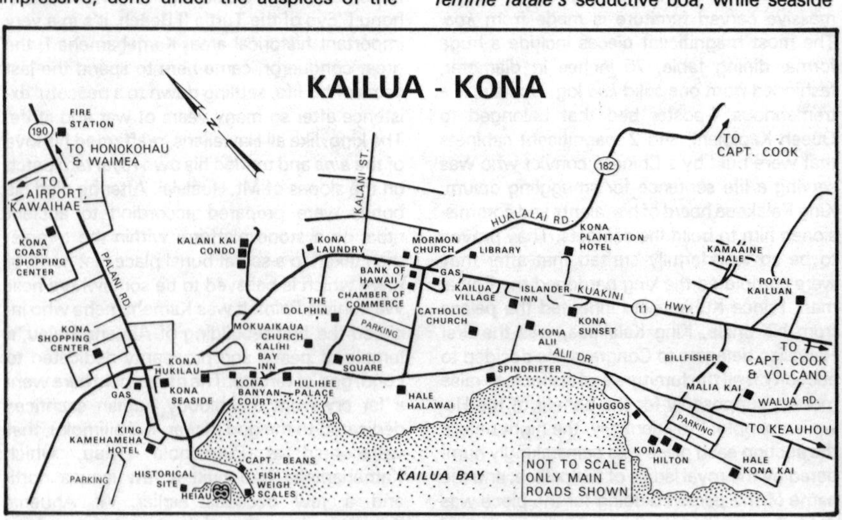

Ahuena Heiau

the coastline slips along, rugged and bright, making Ali'i Drive a soothing sight. If you want to concentrate on the scenery and not the driving, take the free **London Bus** from Kailua-Kona to the parking lot of the Kona Surf Hotel, or the **Ali'i Shuttle** (see p. 538). Both regularly cruise this main drag.

For your first stop, look for signs to Kahaluu Beach Park; pull in and park here. On the rocky northern shore of this bay is St. Peter's Catholic Church. Its diminutive size, capped by a blue tin roof that winks at you from amidst the lava like a bright morning glory in an ebony vase, has earned it the nickname **Little Blue Church.** Built in 1889 on the site of an old partially reclaimed *heiau,* a favorite spot to take a snapshot. Inside is the epitome of simplicity with bare wood walls and a simple crucifix. The only splash of color is a bouquet of fresh flowers on the altar.

Do yourself a favor and visit the grounds of the **Kona Surf Hotel,** which have graciously been open to the public. You're free to stroll around on your own, and non-guests can take a tour on Wed. and Fri. at 9:00 a.m. Here are 14 acres of ponds and gardens that are glorious with the perfumes and blooms of over 30,000 plants, flowers, fruits, and shrubs gathered from throughout Polynesia. To complement the natural setting of the grounds, a profusion of Oriental and Hawaiian artwork has been placed here and there. Inside, the main hallways of the 4 wings are resplendent with over $1,000,000 worth of wall hangings and tapestries.

A short stroll or a minute's drive south brings you to **Keauhou Bay.** Here is a cluster of historical sites. Ask for a free area map available at the Keauhou Bay Hotel. Along the shoreline is a number of partially developed *heiau* sites. You'll also find a *holua,* grass-covered rocks that were slicked with water to form a slide. Hawaiians rode it on wooden sleds especially during the Makahiki Festival.

Across the street is the **Kona Gardens,** 12 acres of beauty planted with flora from throughout the Pacific. They're open daily 9:00 a.m. to 5:00 p.m., tel. 322-2751, and charge a hefty $5 adult, $3 children ages 7 to 12. This includes a video highlighting the flora, fauna, and volcanic activity on the Big Island. Paved walkways lead through the gardens where most plants are identified. The grounds are built around an archaeological site that includes petroglyphs, graves, homesites, and minor *heiau.* If the price was just a touch lower, it would be worth it.

For those itching to buy a souvenir or original artwork, make sure to visit the **Kona Flea Market,** just outside the Kona Gardens, every Sat. from 7:30 a.m. to 2:30 p.m. Vendors come from around the island, and the offerings are always different. Admission is free and it's a good place to browse for that "just right" memento.

HEADING SOUTH

Ali'i Drive eventually turns up the mountainside and joins Rt. 11, which in its central section is called the **Kuakini Highway.** This road quickly passes the towns of **Kainaliu** ("Bail the Bilge"), **Kealakekua,** and **Captain Cook.** You'll have ample opportunity to stop along the way for gas, picnic supplies, or just to browse. These towns have some terrific restaurants, health food stores, and boutiques (see below). If you've come from Kailua-Kona via the Kuakini Highway, you pass through the town of **Honalo,** worth a quick peek into **Dai Fukuji Buddhist Temple** along the road. It's open daily 9:00 a.m. to 4:30 p.m., free. Inside are 2 ornate altars; feel free to take photos but please remember to remove your shoes. Another road, parallel to Rt. 11 but higher up the mountainside, affording a grand view of the countryside, is Rt. 180. If you're traveling to and from Kailua-Kona a number of times it's worth taking this back road. The main interest here is in the town of **Holualoa** ("The Sledding Course"). Here an old coffee mill has been renovated and reopened as the **Kona Art Center,** which houses artworks by local artists and features exhibits and classes.

Royal Kona Coffee Mill And Museum
In the town of Captain Cook, **Napoopoo Road** branches off Rt. 11 and begins a rollercoaster ride down to the sea where it ends at Kealakekua Bay. En route it passes the well-marked Royal Kona Coffee Mill. Along the way you can't help noticing the trim coffee bushes planted along the hillside. Many counterculture types have taken up residence in semi-abandoned "coffee shacks" throughout this hard-pressed economic area, but this cheap, idyllic, and convenience-free life isn't as easy to arrange as it once was. The area is being "rediscovered" and getting more popular. For those just visiting, the tantalizing smell of roasting coffee and the lure of a "free cup" are more than enough stimulus to make you stop. Mark Twain did! The museum is small, of the nontouchable variety with most exhibits behind glass. Mostly they're old b&w prints of the way Kona coffee country used to be. Some heavy machinery is displayed out on the back porch. The most interesting is a homemade husker built from an old automobile. While walking around be careful not to step on a couple of lazy old cats so lethargic they might as well be stuffed. Perhaps a cup of the local "java" in their milk bowl would put a spring in their feline step! Inside, more or less integrated into the museum, is a small gift shop. You can pick up the usual souvenirs, but the real treats are gourmet honeys, jellies, jams, candies, and of course coffee. Buy a pound of Royal Kona Blend for about $4, but for 100% Royal Kona it's around $7. Actually, it's cheaper at other

Kona Theater in downtown Captain Cook

retail outlets and supermarkets around the island, but you can't beat the freshness of getting it right from the source. Refill anyone? The museum is open daily 8:00 a.m. to 4:30 p.m., tel. 328-2511. Mailing address: Mauna Kea Coffee Co., Box 829, Captain Cook, HI 96704.

Kealakekua Bay

Continue down Napoopoo Road through the once-thriving fishing village of Napoopoo ("Holes"), now just a circle on the map with a few houses fronted by neat gardens. At road's end, you arrive at Kealakekua ("Road of the God") Bay. Relax a minute and tune in all your sensors because you're in for a treat. The bay is not only a **Marine Life Conservation District** with a fine beach and top-notch snorkeling (see "Beaches," following), but it drips with history. *Mauka,* just at the parking lot, is the well-preserved **Hikiau Heiau,** dedicated to the god Lono, who had long been prophecied to return from the heavens to this very bay, whose coming would usher in a "new order." Perhaps the soothsaying *kahuna* were a bit vague on the points of the "new order," but it is undeniable that at this spot of initial contact between Europeans and Hawaiians, great changes occurred whose ramifications radically altered the course of Hawaiian history.

The *heiau* is carved into the steep *pali* forming a well-engineered wall. From these heights the temple priests had a panoramic view of the ocean to mark the approach of Lono's "floating island," heralded by tall white *tapa* banners. The platform formed by the *heiau* was meticulously backfilled with smooth small stones; a series of stone footings, once the bases of grass and thatch houses used in the religious rites, is still very much intact.

Captain James Cook, leading his ships *Resolution* and *Discovery* under billowing white sails, entered the bay on the morning of January 17, 1778, during the height of the Makahiki Festival, and the awestruck natives were sure that Lono had returned. Immediately, traditional ways were challenged. An old crewman, William Watman, had just died, and Cook went ashore to perform a Christian burial atop the *heiau.* This was, of course, the first Christian ceremony in the islands, and a plaque at the *heiau* entrance commemorates the event. Another plaque is dedicated to Henry Opukahaia, a young native boy taken to New England where he was educated and converted to Christianity. Through impassioned speeches begging salvation for his pagan countrymen, he convinced the first Congregationalist missionaries to come to the islands in 1820. But long before these events, on the fateful day of February 4, 1778, a few weeks after open-armed welcome, the goodwill camaraderie that had developed between the English voyagers and their island hosts turned sour, due to terrible cultural misunderstandings. The sad result was the death of Capt. Cook. This magnificent man, who had resolutely sailed and explored the greatest sea on Earth, stood helplessly in knee-deep water, unable to swim to rescue-boats sent from his waiting ships. Hawaiians, provoked to a furious frenzy because of unintentioned insult, beat, stabbed, and clubbed the great captain and 4 of his marines to death. (For a full accounting of these events, see p. 27.) A 27-foot, white marble obelisk erected to Cook's memory in 1874 "by some of his fellow countrymen" is at the far northern end of the bay. Here too is a bronze plaque often awash by the waves that marks the exact spot where Cook fell. You can see the marble obelisk from the *heiau,* but actually getting to it is tough. Expert snorkelers have braved the mile swim to the point, but be advised it's through open ocean, and Kealakekua Bay is known for sharks that come in during the evening to feed. A rugged jeep/foot trail leads down the *pali* to the monument, but it's poorly marked and starts way back near the town of Captain Cook almost immediately after Napoopoo Road branches off from Rt. 11. If you opt for this route, you have to backtrack to visit the coffee museum and the *heiau* side of the bay.

Heading For Pu'uhonua O Honaunau

This historical park, the main attraction in the area, shouldn't be missed. Once known as **City of Refuge Park,** in keeping with the emergence of "Hawaiian heritage," the official name is coming more into use. The best way to get there is to bounce along the 4 miles of coastal road from Kealakekua Bay. En route, you pass a smaller, more rugged road to **Keei;**

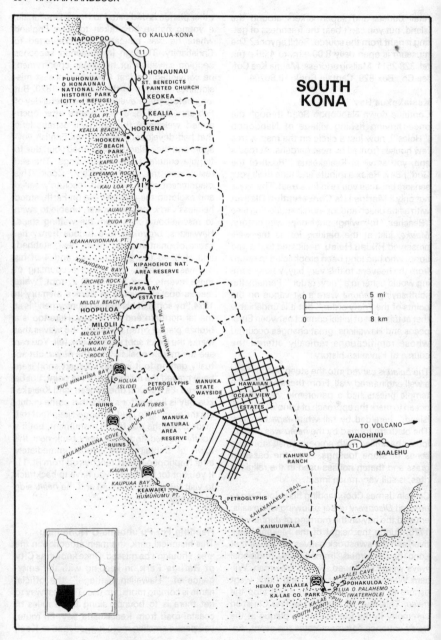

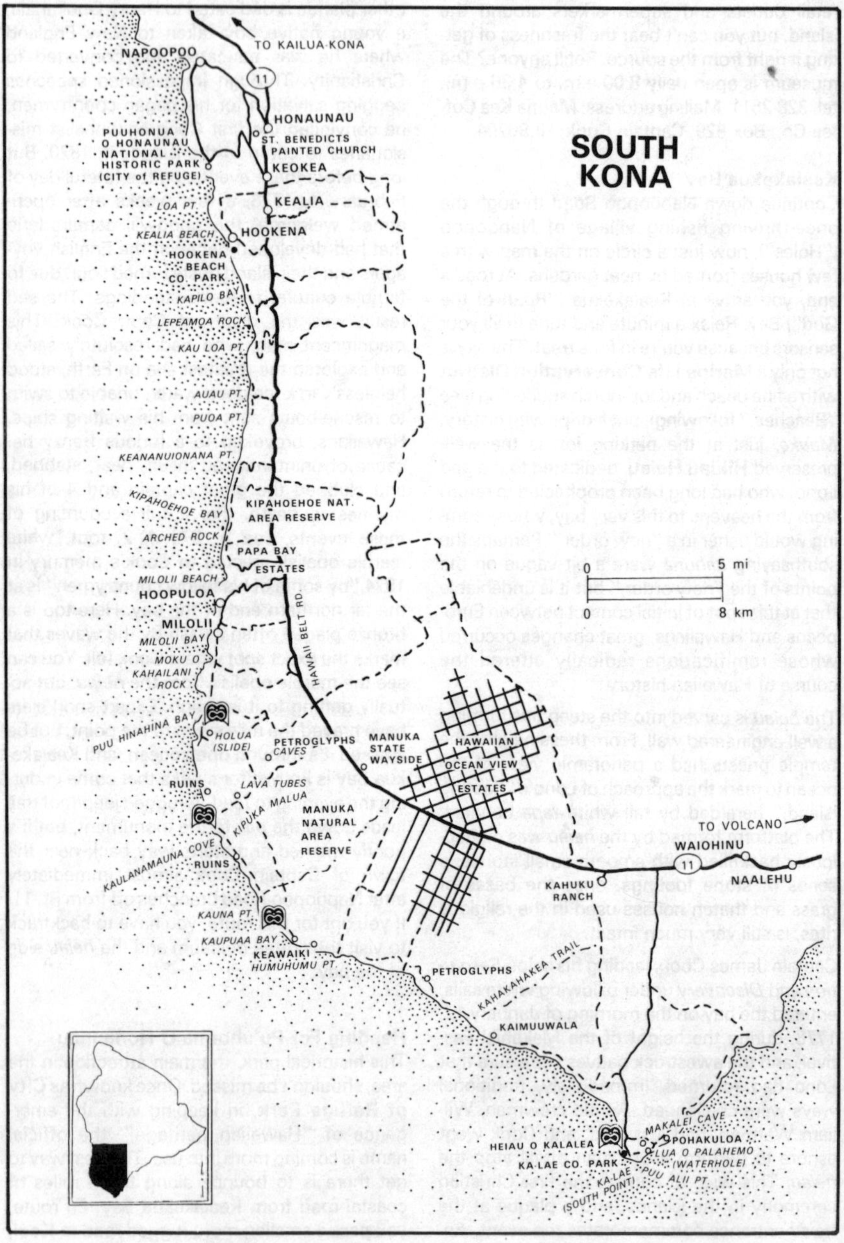
SOUTH
KONA
TO KAILUA-KONA
11
NAPOOPOO
HONAUNAU
ST. BENEDICTS
PAINTED CHURCH
KEOKEA
PUUHONUA
O HONAUNAU
NATIONAL
HISTORIC PARK
(CITY of REFUGE)
LOA PT.
KEALIA
HOOKENA
KEALIA BEACH
HOOKENA
BEACH
CO. PARK
KAPILO BAY
LEPEAMOA ROCK
KAU LOA PT.
AUAU PT.
PUOA PT.
KEANANUIONANA PT.
KIPAHOEHOE BAY
KIPAHOEHOE NAT.
AREA RESERVE
ARCHED ROCK
PAPA BAY
ESTATES
MILOLII BEACH
HOOPULOA
MILOLII
MILOLII BAY
MOKU
KAHAILANI
ROCK
HAWAII BELT RD.
0
5 mi
0
8 km
PUU HINAHINA BAY
HOLUA
(SLIDE)
PETROGLYPHS
CAVES
MANUKA
STATE
WAYSIDE
HAWAIIAN
OCEAN VIEW
ESTATES
LAVA TUBES
RUINS
KIPUKA MALUA
MANUKA
NATURAL
AREA
RESERVE
KAULANAMAUNA COVE
RUINS
TO VOLCANO
WAIOHINU
11
NAALEHU
KAHUKU
RANCH
KAUNA PT.
KAUPUAA BAY
KEAWAIKI
HUMUHUMU PT.
PETROGLYPHS
KAHAKAHAKEA TRAIL
KAIMUUWALA
MAKALEI CAVE
HEIAU O KALALEA
POHAKULOA
LUA O PALAHEMO
(WATERHOLE)
KA-LAE CO. PARK
PUU ALII PT.
KA-LAE
(SOUTH POINT)

this side trip ends at a black-sand canoe launch area, and a cozy white-sand beach that's good for swimming. A channel has been sliced through the coral that leads to an underwater grotto. On the shore are remains of Kamaiko Heiau, where humans were once sacrificed.

The other, more direct way to Pu'uhonua O Honaunau is to take Rt. 160 at Keokea where it branches off Route 11 at mile marker 104. Either going or coming this way, make sure to take a 5-minute side trip off Rt. 160 to **St. Benedict's Painted Church**. This small house of worship is fronted by lattice work, and with its gothic-style belfry looks like a little castle. Inside, a Belgian priest, John Berchman Velghe, took house paint and with a fair measure of talent and religious fervor painted biblical scenes on the walls. His masterpiece is a painted illusion behind the altar that gives the impression of being in the famous Spanish cathedral in Burgos. Fray John was pastor here from 1899 until 1904, when he did these paintings, like others that he had done in small churches throughout Polynesia. Before leaving, visit the cemetery with its petroglyphs and homemade pipe crosses.

Pu'uhonua O Honaunau National Historical Park

The tall royal palms surrounding this compound shimmer like neon against the black lava so prevalent in this part of Kona. Planted for the purpose, these beacons promised safety and salvation to the vanquished, weak, war-tossed, and *kapu* breakers of old Hawaii. If you made it to this "temple of refuge," scurrying frantically before avenging warriors or leaping into the sea to swim the last desperate miles, the attendant *kahuna,* under pain of their own death, had to offer you sanctuary. *Kapu*-breakers were particularly pursued because their misdeeds could anger the always moody gods who might send a lava flow or tidal wave to punish all. Only the *kahuna* could perform the rituals that would bathe you in the sacred *mana,* and thus absolve you from all wrongdoing. This *pu'uhonua* ("temple of refuge") was the largest in all of Hawaii, and be it fact or fancy, you can feel its power to this day.

The temple complex sits on a 20-acre finger of lava bordered by the sea on 3 sides. A massive 1,000-foot mortarless wall, measuring 10 feet high and 17 feet thick, borders the site on the landward side and marks it as a "temple of refuge." Archaeological evidence dates the use of the temple from the mid 16th C., and some scholars argue that it was a well-known sacred spot as much as 200 years earlier. Actually, 3 separate *heiau* are within the enclosure. In the mid 16th C., Keawe, a great chief of Kona and the great-grandfather of Kamehameha, ruled here. After his death, he was entombed in Hale O Keawe Heiau at the end of the great wall, and his *mana* reinfused the temple with cleansing powers. For 250 years the *ali'i* of Kona continued to be buried

the main temple complex of Pu'uhonua O Honaunau

here, making the spot more and more powerful. Even the great Queen Kaahumanu came here seeking sanctuary. As a 16-year-old bride, she refused to submit to the will of her husband Kamehameha, and defied him openly, often wantonly giving herself to lesser chiefs. To escape Kamehameha's rampage, she made for the temple. Kaahumanu chose a large rock to hide under, and she couldn't be found until her pet dog barked and gave her away. Kaahumanu was coaxed out only after a lengthy intercession by Captain George Vancouver, who had become a friend of the king. The last royal personage buried here was a son of Kamehameha who died in 1818. Soon afterwards, the "old religion" of Hawaii was dead and the temple grounds were abandoned but not entirely destroyed. The foundations were left intact for this largest "City of Refuge" in the Hawaiian Islands.

In 1961, the National Park Service opened Pu'uhonua O Honaunau after a complete and faithful restoration was carried out. Careful consultation of old records and vintage sketches from early ships' artists gave the restoration a true sense of authenticity. Local artists used traditional tools and techniques to carve giant *ohia* logs into faithful renditions of the temple gods. They now stand again, protecting the *heiau* from evil. One of the most curious is a god-figure, with his maleness erect, glaring out to sea as if looking for some voluptuous mermaid. All the buildings are painstakingly lashed together in the Hawaiian fashion, but instead of using traditional cordage, which would have added the perfect touch, nylon rope was substituted. Entrance to the park is free. Stop at the Visitors Center where you can pick up a map and brochure for a self-guided tour. Exhibits line a wall, complete with murals done in heroic style. Push a button and the recorded messages give you a brief history of Hawaiian beliefs and the system governing daily life. Educate yourself. The Visitors Center, tel. 328-2326, is open daily 7:30 a.m. to 5:30 p.m., with rangers giving tours from 10:00 a.m. to 3:30 p.m. The beach park section (see below) is open 6:00 a.m. to midnight. The setting of Pu'uhonua O Honaunau couldn't be more idyllic. It's a picture-perfect cove with many paths leading out onto the sea-washed lava flow. Follow the wall toward the northwest to a large flat rock perfect for lying back and watching the sun set.

Idol hands are the devil's workshop.

Hookena

If you want to see how the people of Kona still live, visit **Hookena.** A mile or two south of the Pu'uhonua O Honaunau turnoff, or 20 miles south of Kailua-Koa, take a well-marked spur road *makai* off Rt. 11 and follow it to the sea. The village is in a state of disrepair, but a number of homey cottages and some semi-permanent tents are used mostly on weekends by local fishermen. Hookena also boasts a beach park with showers, picnic tables, but no potable water or camping. For drinking water, a tap is attached to the telephone pole when you begin your descent down the spur road. The black-sand (actually gray) beach is broad, long, probably *the* best in South Kona for both swimming and body surfing. If the sun gets too hot, plenty of palms lining the beach provide not only shade but a picture-perfect setting. Until the road connecting Kona to Hilo was finally finished in the 1930s, Hookena shipped the produce of the surrounding area from its bustling wharf. At one time, Hookena was the

a canoe break at Hookena Beach Park

main port in south Kona and even hosted Robert Louis Stevenson when he passed through the islands in 1889. Part of the wharf still remains, and nearby a fleet of outrigger fishing canoes is pulled up on shore. The surrounding cliffs are honeycombed with burial caves, and if you walk a half mile north, you'll find the crumpled walls and steeple of Maria Lanakila Church, leveled in an earthquake in 1950. The church was another "Painted Church," done by Father John Velghe in the same style as St. Benedict's.

Milolii

This active fishing village is approximately 10 miles south of Pu'uhonua O Honaunau. Again, look for signs to a spur road off Rt. 11 heading *makai.* The road, leading through bleak lava flows, is extremely narrow but worth the detour. Milolii means "Fine Twist," and earned its name from times past when it was famous for producing *'aha,* a sennit made from coconut husk fibers, and *olona,* a twine made from the *olona* plant that was the best for fish nets. The people of Milolii supplement their fishing income by growing ferns and anthuriums on soil that they truck in. This is one of the last villages in Hawaii where traditional fishing is the major source of income, and where old-timers are heard speaking Hawaiian. Fishermen still use small outrigger canoes, now powered by outboards, to catch *opelu,* a type of mackerel that schools in these waters. The method of catching the *opelu* has remained unchanged for centuries. Boats gather and drop packets of chum made primarily from *poi,* sweet potato, or rice. No meat is used so sharks won't be attracted. In the village, a little understocked store is operated by old-timer Eugene Kaupiko, though the whole family pitches in. Mr. Kaupiko has lived in Milolii all his life, and is the unofficial mayor. He's seen a lot in his 78 years. He met actor Jimmy Stewart who bought land nearby, and what he remembers most about meeting Elvis Presley who came here in the 1960s, was looking off his porch and seeing nothing but "girls, girls, girls." Milolii has a **beach park** that is a favorite with local people on the weekends. Technically, it's a county park (permit), but no one checks. Tents are pitched in and around the parking lot, just under the ironwoods at road's end. Notice that a number of

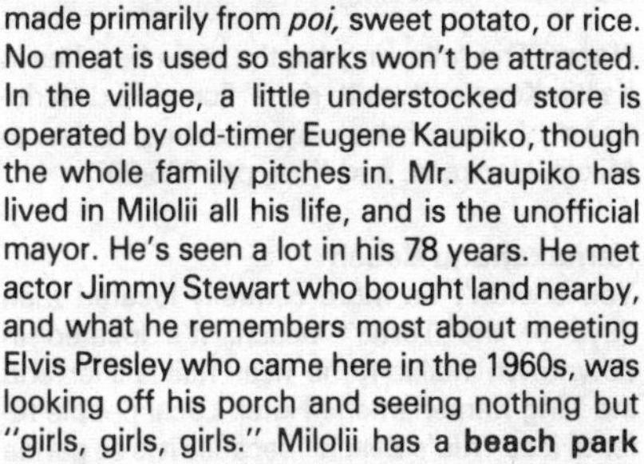

Eugene Kaupiko, unofficial mayor of Milolii

them appear to be semi-permanent. There are pit toilets, a basketball court, but no running water so bring some. Swimming is safe inside the reef and the tidepooling in the area is some of the best on the south coast.

BEACHES AND PARKS

If Kona is short on anything, it is beaches. The ones that it has are adequate and quite striking in their own way, but they tend to be small, few, and far between. Most people expecting a huge expanse of white sands will be disappointed. These beaches do exist on the Big Island's west coast, but they are north of Kailua-Kona in the Kohala District. Kona does, however, have beaches alive with marinelife, providing excellent and safe snorkeling and top-notch tidepooling.

Note: The following are the main beaches in Kailua-Kona and south Kona. For more descriptions of out-of-the-way beaches, refer to Milolii, Hookena, and Keei, pp. 605-607.

Kamakahonu Beach

You couldn't be more centrally located than "Eye of the Turtle" beach. It's located in downtown Kailua-Kona near Kailua Pier and the King Kamehameha Hotel. Local people refer to it as "Kid's Beach" because it is so gentle and perfect for a refreshing dip. Big kids come here to play too, when every year world-class athletes churn the gentle waters into a fury at the start of the Ironman Triathlon. Rent snorkel gear, kayaks, and Hobie Cats for a reasonable price from the **Beach Shack,** located on the beach itself. Restrooms are on the pier.

Old Kona Airport State Recreation Area

In 1970 the old Kona Airport closed and the state of Hawaii turned it into a beach park. To get there simply walk along the shoreline for a few hundred yards north of the King Kamehameha Hotel. If driving, follow Alii Drive to the junction just before the North Kona Shopping Center and turn left on the Kuakini Hwy. Extension. Facilities include showers, restrooms, and picnic area. Parking is unlimited along the old runway. The white-sand beach is sandwiched between water's edge and the runway. You can enter the water at some shallow inlets, but the bottom is often rocky and the waters can be treacherous during high surf. The safest spot is a little sandy cove at the southern end of the beach. Snorkeling is good at the northern end of the beach, and offshore a break makes Old Airport popular with Kona surfers. There is no official camping at the park, but people often do at the north end. A heavy controversy came down when a developer purchased the land adjacent to the north end of the park, then closed it to camping. Local fishermen had camped here for years. Protesting in 1981, they raised a tent village named Kukaiilimoku, which ended when the leaders were arrested for trespassing. It's also disputed that the developer had claimed 8 acres that actually belong to the state. The controversy goes on.

Honokohau Beach

All types of people come to Honokohau Beach including fishermen, surfers, and snorkelers, but primarily it's known as a **nudist beach.** Follow Rt. 19 north from Kailua-Kona for 3 miles and turn left on the marked road leading to the Honokohau Small Boat Harbor. Stay to the right and park almost at the end of the access road in a dirt pulloff. Look for a blue painted rock with a sign that says "Beach." Follow the well-worn path into the vegetation past a garbage pit. Keep walking for a few minutes to the beach. Honokohau is a well-established nudist beach with no hassles. This area was well populated during old Hawaiian days and plenty of archaeological sites are to be explored along the shoreline. The swim-

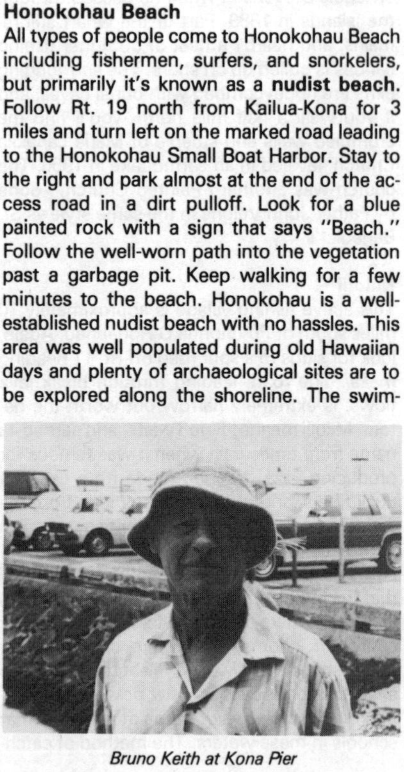

Bruno Keith at Kona Pier

St. Peter's Catholic Church, known as the Little Blue Church, marks the area fronted by Kahaluu Beach Park.

ming is safe but shallow. There are no facilities. People often camp here overnight, but you have to backpack everything in. After a swim, walk to the north end of the beach, where a trail leads inland through thick vegetation. Follow it to the "Queen's Bath," a brackish pond surrounded by rock cairns holding spring-fed sweetwater which is great for rinsing off. On the way out pause at the active small boat harbor. Although there are "shark" signs, snorkelers frequent the bay.

One of the main local proponents of nudism is longtime Kona resident, Dr. Bruno Keith. He approaches nudism almost like a religion: if people were free enough to be naked together, the world would be a better place. After all, *desperados* and the like would have a tough time hiding their guns! Mr. Keith, when not at the beach, is often found around Kailua Pier—a bronzed, spry old gent who favors aloha shirts and a floppy hat. He often carries a brown paper bag full of exotic fruits picked off his property, and gives them away to tourists. His background is amazing, and he's fond of telling stories, especially about nudism. He claims that he's gone "skinny dipping" with both John Kennedy and Lyndon Johnson, among others. He's been a doctor, journalist, and school teacher, all while traveling the world. He landed in Kona about 30 years ago, fell in love, and stayed on. Bruno is a man of good spirit, and although not a native Hawaiian, he definitely knows the meaning of *aloha.*

Alii Drive Beaches

The following beaches are strung one after the other, along Kailua-Kona's Alii Drive. The first is **Pahoehoe Beach Park,** about 3 miles south of town center. It's not very much of a swimming beach with only one small pocket of white sand next to a low sea wall, but it's handy spot to pull off to view the coastline or have a picnic.

White Sands Beach Park (a.k.a **Magic Sands** or **Disappearing Sands,**) is an excellent spot for a dip...if the sand is there. Every year, usually in March and April, the sands are stripped away by heavy seas and currents, exposing rough coral and making the area rugged for the average swimmer. People still come during those months, because it's a good vantage point for observing migrating humpback whales. The sands always come back, though, and when they do it's terrific for all kinds of water sports, including bodysurfing and snorkeling. The annual **Magic Sands Bodysurfing Contest** is held during the winter months. The best board surfing is just north of the beach in a break the locals call "Banyans." White Sands' amenities include picnic pavilions, showers, and restrooms, and is a favorite spot with local people and tourists.

Kahaluu Beach Park on Kahaluu Bay has always been a productive fishing area. Even today, fishermen come to "throw net," and large family parties surround their favorite fish with a huge *hukilau* net, and then all participants share in the bounty. Because of this age-old tradition, the area has not been designated a marine conservation district. Kahuluu became a beach park in 1966. This insured that the people of Kona would always have access to this favorite spot which quickly became surrounded by commercial development. Amenities include picnic tables, showers, restrooms, even a basketball court. The swimming is very good, but the real attraction is snorkeling. The waters are very gentle and Kahaluu is a perfect place for family or beginning snorkelers. However, stay *within* the bay because a powerful and dangerous rip current lurks outside, and more rescues are made on this beach than any other in Kona. The shoreline waters are alive with tropical fish: angelfish, parrotfish, the works. Bring bread or cheese with you, and in a minute you'll be surrounded by a live rainbow of colors. Some fish are even bold enough to nip your fingers. It's very curious that when these semi-tame fish spot a swimmer with a spear gun, they'll completely avoid him. They know the difference! Unfortunately, Kahaluu is often crowded, but it is still much worth a visit.

Napoopoo Beach Park

This beach park is located at Kealakekua Bay (see p. 603 for details). The bay, since long before the arrival of Captain Cook, has been known as a safe anchorage, and draws boats of all descriptions. The area, designated a **Marine Life Conservation District,** lives up to its title by being an excellent scuba and snorkeling site. Organized tours from Kailua-Kona often flood the area with boats and divers, but the ocean expanse is vast and you can generally find your own secluded spot to enjoy the underwater show. The best snorkeling is at the north of the bay near the Captain Cook Monument. If you haven't come on a tour boat the only way over is to hike a rugged jeep trail, or to snorkel over. If you decide on the latter bear in mind you have to cross over a mile of "blue water," and that sharks feed in the bay after sundown! If you've just come for a quick dip or to enjoy the sunset, look for beautiful yellow-tailed tropic birds that frequent the bay. Napoopoo Beach Park has full amenities including showers, picnic tables, and restrooms.

ACCOMMODATIONS

Almost all of Kona's accommodations lie along the 6 miles of Alii Drive from Kailua-Kona to Keauhou. A super-luxury hotel is just north of Kailua-Kona, while most hotels/condos fall in the moderate to expensive range. A few inexpensive hotels are scattered here and there along Alii Drive, and back up in the hills are a "sleeper" or two that are cheap but decent. The following list should provide you with a good cross-section.

Camping Note

It's sad but true: except for the limited beach park in the village of Milolii, 25 miles south of Kailua-Kona, there is *no* official camping in all of the Kona District. Campers wishing to enjoy the Kona Coast must go north to the Kohala District to find a campground. Some unofficial camping does exist in Kona (see "Beaches and Parks" above), but as always this generates certain insecurities. Bivouacking for a night or two in any of the unofficial camp spots should be hassle-free. Good luck!

Expensive

Hotel King Kamehameha is located in downtown Kailua-Kona at 75-5660 Palani Rd., Kailua-Kona, HI 96740, tel. 329-2911 or 800-227-4700. Its spot was a favorite of Hawaiian royalty, and Kamehameha the Great spent the last days of his life here. It's one of the only Kona hotels that has its own beach, adjacent to the restored *Ahuena Heiau.* The walls of the lobby are lined with artifacts of war, and a hotel staff member gives historical and botanical tours of the grounds. Rooms have a/c, TV, and phones, are appointed in shades of blue and rattan, and all feature *lanai* with sweeping panoramas of the bay and Mt. Hualalai. Prices begin at $70 for a standard room, up to $420 for a 3-bedroom suite. The hotel, operated by AMFAC, has a variety of restaurants, cocktail lounges, tennis courts, shops, and a pool.

The **Kona Surf Resort** is located at Keauhou Bay, 6 miles south of Kailua-Kona; its parking lot is the terminus of coach service from the airport and for the free "London Bus." The building, comprised of 4 wings and lined with over $1 million worth of art, are architecturally superb. The impeccable hotel grounds are a magnificent match and open to the public (see p. 601). The hotel features the **S.S. James Makee** Restaurant and nightly entertainment in their Puka and Poi Pounder Rooms. All 535 rooms have a/c, phones, and TVs. Prices begin at $90 s/d up to $850 for a 2-bedroom suite. There are 2 swimming pools, lighted tennis courts, and the Keauhou-Kona Golf course is just next door with special rates and starting times for hotel guests. For information write Kona Surf Resort, 78-128 Ehukai St., Kailua-Kona, HI 96740, tel. 322-3411, 800-367-8011.

The **Kona Hilton Beach and Tennis Resort** has become a Kona landmark. The rooms are spacious and all include a *lanai,* (so protected from view that it easily serves as an outdoor room). The tennis facilities are superb, and an ocean-fed pool is sheltered from the force of the waves by huge black lava boulders. There is evening entertainment in the Mele Mele Bar, and fine food (kosher too) is served in the Hele Mai Dining Room. Rates run from $75 for a standard room to $350 for a suite. For information write Kona Hilton Beach and Tennis Resort, Box 1179, Kailua-Kona, HI 96745, tel. 329-3111 or 800-452-4411.

At the **Royal Sea Cliff Resort** the Hotel Corporation of the Pacific offers first-rate condo apartments. They run from studios at $65-95 per day, to 2-bedroom suites ranging from $110-145, extra person $10. There's free tennis, daily maid service, 2 swimming pools, and cable, color TV. Package deals are available. Contact, Royal Sea Cliff Resort, 75-6040 Alii Dr., Kailua-Kona, HI 96740, tel. 329-8020 or 800-367-5124.

Kona Lagoon Hotel

Moderate Hotels And Condos

Just down the road from the Kona Surf is the **Kona Lagoon Hotel**, operated by Hawaiian Pacific Resorts. Most rooms feature a *lanai* that overlooks a tranquil lagoon, and all have a/c, color TV, and phones. There is a swimming pool, tennis courts and the nearby Kailua-Keauhou Golf Course. Dining and cocktails are provided at the Tonga Room and the Wharf Restaurant, and the Polynesian Long House meeting facility accommodates up to 700 people. Rates begin at a reasonable $58 d, $8 additional person. For information write Kona Lagoon Hotel, 78-6780 Alii Dr., Kailua-Kona, HI 96740, tel. 322-2727 or 800-367-5004.

The **Keauhou Beach Hotel** is built on a historic site that includes the remains of a *heiau* and a reconstruction of King Kamehameha III's summer cottage. The hotel is famous for its bougainvillea that plummets over the 7-story face of the hotel. Kahaluu Beach Park is adjacent, and the entire area is known for fantastic tide pools. The hotel hosts a *luau* every Thurs. and Sunday. Standard rooms begin at $55 and all have a/c, TV, phone, private *lanai,* and small refrigerators. The Keauhou Beach Hotel is at 78-6740 Alii Dr., Kailua-Kona, HI 96745, tel. 322-3441, or call AMFAC Resorts at 800-227-4700.

The **Casa De Emdeko** is a condominium that receives the best possible praise: people that have lodged there once always return. It's a quiet, low-rise condo surrounding a central courtyard. There's a freshwater and a saltwater pool, maid service every 3 days, and a sauna. All units have a/c, full kitchens, and *lanai.* Prices start at $70 d, $8 extra person, for a garden-view apartment with every seventh night free. Contact Casa De Emdeko at 75-6082 Alii Dr., Kailua-Kona, HI 96745, tel. 329-2160, (resident manager), or through the booking agent of Kona Vacation Resort, tel. 329-6488 or 800-367-5168 and ask for Peggy or Sue. Note: the previous resident manager was down on accommodating children; now gone, that policy left with her.

Kona Islander Inn condominium apartments are well appointed for a reasonable price. Conveniently located within walking distance of downtown Kailua-Kona, it's just next door to the Spindrifter Restaurant. The style is "turn-of-the-century plantation," shaded by tall palms. All 100 units have phone, off-road parking, a/c, and TV. For information write Kona Islander Inn, 75-5776 Kuakini Hwy., Kailua-Kona, HI 96740, tel. 329-3181. Also, Smedley Travel, 1321 Whytecliff Rd., Palatine, IL 60067, tel. 312-358-0273.

A few reasonably priced and attractive condominium apartments include: **Kona Mansion,** a quarter mile from downtown, offers one bedroom suites for up to four persons from $45 to $48. There's a swimming pool, parking, TV, and maid service on request, with a minimum stay of five nights. Contact Hawaiian Apartment Leasing, 1240 Cliff Drive, Laguna Beach, CA 92651, tel. 714-497-4253 or 800-854-8843, in California, tel. 800-472-8449. Also available through Clyde M. Crawfoot Realty, see following for address. **Alii Villas,** ocean-side just a half-mile from Kailua-Kona, offers full kitchens, *lanai,* TV, parking, pool, and BBQs. Rates vary from one-bedroom units at $45 daily to $252 weekly for 2 to 3 guests, 2-bedroom (all units waterfront) from $60 daily to $380 weekly for 4 guests. Additional guests extra. There is a 20% monthly discount, and every seventh night is free. **Kona Billfisher** near downtown offers full kitchens, pool, BBQs, limited maid service, and gazebo. One-bedroom units rent from $40 daily for up to 4 persons, 2-bedroom from $60 up to 6 guests. Weekly and monthly rates and discounts. **Kona Plaza** in downtown has a swimming pool, sundecks, plus ramps and elevators for the handicapped. Daily rates are $40 d, $50 up to 4. Weekly, monthly, and off-season rates available. For all of the above, contact Clyde M. Crawfoot Realty, Box 263, Kailua-Kona, HI 96740, tel. 329-0154.

The **Kona Bay Hotel** is a locally owned downtown hotel run by Uncle Billy and his Kona family. Its best feature is the friendly and warm staff. The hotel is a remaining wing of the old Kona Inn, torn down to accommodate the shopping center across the road. The Kona Bay is built around a central courtyard and garden containing Kimo's restaurant, a pool, and bar. Like Uncle Billy's Hilo Bay Hotel, the motif is "cellophane Polynesian," highlighted by some artificial palms. The rooms are a combination of basic and superior with a/c, TV, green carpeting, and with one wall papered and the other bare cinderblock. All rooms have a mini-fridge, and some can be outfitted with a kitchenette. Rates begin at $41 s, to $44 d, add $8 for a kitchenette; car rental package available. The Kona Bay is at 75-5739 Alii Drive, Kailua-Kona, HI 96740, tel. 329-1393 or 800 367-5102.

Inexpensive

For a reasonable and homey hotel try the **Kona Tiki** along Alii Drive. Featuring refrigerators in all rooms (some kitchen units) and complimentary coffee and donuts daily; also free island fruits and fishing poles lying around for guests. The hotel is close to the road so it's a bit noisy in the day but quiets down at night. Rooms are clean, with ceiling fans, but a touch gaudy with green and white paneling. All units face the ocean so everyone gets a view. They're lovely *lanai,* a pool, and a trim little garden of raked sand. Prices are $33 s/d, $5 extra person, and a nominal charge for kitchen facilities. Minimum 3 days, a/c, but no phones in rooms. Contact Kona Tiki Hotel, Box 1567, Kailua-Kona, HI 96745, tel. 329-1425.

Kona White Sands apartment hotel is operated by a character, Ralph E. (for Excellent) Smith and his wife Samantha. It's a 2-story building just across from the famous White (Disappearing) Sands Beach. All units are fully furnished, with electric kitchens, *lanai,* and cross ventilated, with a 2-day minimum; prices are $35-42 s/d, $6 extra person. For information write Kona White Sands Apartments, Box 594, Kailua-Kona, HI 96745, tel. 329-3210.

Kona Magic Sands condominium is next door to Dorian's Restaurant at 77-6452 Alii Dr., Kailua-Kona, HI 96740, tel. 329-9177. The resident manager is Lee Gilbert. Amenities include TV, parking, cocktail lounge, pool, and maid service on request. Rates on studios are from $31 to $55 d, $5 extra person, 4-night minimum. There's a 15% off-season discount and monthly and weekly rates. This condo is acceptable for the money, but nothing special.

Kona Hukilau Hotel is another downtown hotel at 75-5646 Palani Rd., Kailua-Kona HI, 96740, tel. 367-7000 or 800-367-7000. It's part of the island-owned Sands, Seaside, and Hukilau chain. Its sister hotel, the Kona Seaside, is just up the road; they share pools and other facilities. Most rooms have a/c, cross ventilation, *lanai,* but no TV. There's a sun deck and central area with enclosed courtyard and lobby. Prices range from $39 standard to $59 deluxe, double. A car package adds $10 daily.

Cheap

So you came to Kona for the sun, surf, and scenery and couldn't care less about your room so long as it's clean and the people running the hotel are friendly? Well, you can't go wrong with any of the following out-of-the-mainstream hotels. They're all basic, but none are flea-bags.

Manago Hotel in Captain Cook has been in the Manago family for 70 years, and anyone who puts his name on a place and keeps it there that long is doing something right. The old section of the hotel along the road is clean but a little worse for wear. For $13 nightly you get to lounge in well-used furniture, share a bath, and cool off the soles of your feet on the bare linoleum floor. For $18-21 s, $21-24 d, extra person $3, you're accommodated in the new wing where you have a *lanai,* private bath, and can train your eyes to catch the brilliance of the Kona sunset by practicing looking at the orange floor and pink furniture. Psychedelic! The views from the hotel grounds of the Kona Coast are terrific. You can dine in a restaurant in the old section, or just watch TV. For information write, Manago Hotel, Box 145, Captain Cook, Kona, HI 96704, tel. 323-2642.

The **Kona Hotel** is in the mountain village of Holualoa, along Rt. 180, tel. 324-1155. Primarily, the 11 units are always rented to local people who spend the work-week in Kailua-Kona's seaside resorts and then go home on weekends. $10-15 will get you a clean room with a shared bath, but no reservations are taken and your best bet for getting a room is on weekends.

Teshima's Inn, tel. 322-9140, is a small clean family-run hotel in the mountain village of Honalo at the junction of Routes 180 and 11. It's operated by septuagenerians, Mr. and Mrs Harry Teshima, somewhat like a Japanese *minshuku* with all rooms fronting a Japanese garden. The rooms at $12 s, $16 d, are spartan but very clean.

FOOD

Inexpensive

So budget traveler, you've been asking yourself, "where's the best restaurant in town, with the most food at lowest prices, with that down-home atmosphere?" **The Ocean View Inn** is it! The gigantic menu of Chinese, American, Japanese, and Hawaiian food is like a mini directory. Lunch and dinner range from $3 to $7, and a huge breakfast goes for about $3. They're open daily except Mon. from 6:30 a.m. to 2:45 p.m., and from 5:30-9:00 p.m. Located at the north end of Alii Dr., just before the King Kam Hotel, tel. 329-9998.

Stan's Restaurant is an open-air establishment one notch up in both price and atmosphere from the Ocean View Inn, which is just next door. Here you have a cocktail lounge and a stab at atmosphere with some cozy lighting and rattan furniture. Breakfast is pleasing with an assortment of island-inspired hotcakes, no lunch is served, and dinner ranges from $5 to $8, starting at 5:00 p.m., tel. 329-1655.

Sibu is an Indonesian *sate* restaurant serving savory marinated meats and vegetables spiced with zesty sauces and flame grilled. Most dishes, starting at $4, though not large are satisfying, especially served with the seasoned rice. They make a perfect lunch or late-evening snack. Located along Alii Dr., in the Kona Banyan Court Shopping Plaza, open daily except Sun. from noon until 9:00 p.m., tel. 329-1112.

Tom Bombadill's food and drink take their inspiration from Tolkien's Middle Earth, but its location is a lot noisier perched over Alii Drive and overlooking the Hilton's tennis courts. They talk about the view, but your neck will have to stretch like the mozzarella on their pizza to see it. The bar pours domestic beers at $1.65, imports $2.50, pitchers $5.50, and a free "Bud Lite" bumper with every shot. Watch out! The menu includes hamburgers $4, soups $1.75, Mexican pizza appetizers $3.75, and a variety of chicken, fish, and shrimp platters from $5. All of these meals are good, but the real specialty is pizza, from $8 up depending upon size and toppings. Open daily 11:00 a.m. to 10:00 p.m., tel. 329-1292.

Inexpensive Out-Of-Town Eateries

All of the restaurants in this section happen to fall in the inexpensive range. None merits a special trip, but all are worth stopping in if you're hungry when you go by. Actually, some are great, especially for breakfast and brunch. Read on!

Teshima's Restaurant at the junction of Rt. 11 and Rt. 180 in the mountain village of Honalo is just like the small, clean, and homey Teshima Inn. Here, amongst unpretentious surroundings, you can enjoy a full lunch for $5, sandwiches under $2, or dinner including various Japanese dishes for $5-6. If you're interested in a good square meal, you can't go wrong; tel. 322-9140.

The **Aloha Theater Cafe** is part of the lobby of the Aloha Theater in Kainaliu. The enormous breakfasts ($3-6) feature locally grown eggs, and homemade muffins and potatoes. Lunchtime sandwiches ($4-6) are super-stuffed with varied morsels from tofu and avocado to eggplant sesame cheeseburgers. There's also a variety of soups and salads and a few Mexican dishes. This is an excellent place for breakfast or picnic supplies on your way south. Also, check out the bulletin board for local happenings, sales, services, and the like. Open daily from 7:30 a.m. to closing around 8:00 p.m., tel. 322-3383.

It's hard to miss the red and yellow sign for the **Kona Theater Cafe** as it blinks out at you from the pink and purple background of the Kona Theater. Your basic breakfast, lunch, and dinner are served throughout the week, but the real goer is the Sunday all-you-can-eat brunch for $6.50 from 10:00 a.m. to 2:00 p.m. Open Tues. to Sat. 6:00 a.m. to 9:00 p.m., at the Kona Theater along Rt. 11 in downtown Captain Cook, tel. 328-2587.

Check out the unique architecture of the Aloha Theater Cafe in Kainaliu.

dining room of the Spindrifter

The **Manago Hotel** dining room is a favorite with local people who consider the down-home cooking some of the best on the island. The menu is limited, as are the serving times of 7:00-9:00 a.m., 11:00 a.m. to 2:00 p.m., 5:00-7:30 p.m., tel. 323-1642.

Ohana Food Co-op in Kealekekua has a full range of health foods and a snack bar where you can pick up some heavy-duty sandwiches for a few dollars. Also along Rt. 11 in town is the **Canaan Deli.** This full-service deli has an Italian flair. The owner is from New York City, and the "Big Apple's" deli tradition of a lot of food for little money is carried on. You can't go wrong for spaghetti and meatballs for $4.25, eggplant parmagiana or fettucini for $5.75. The pizza is also good and they serve a full assortment of herbal and English teas.

Moderate

The **Spindrifter** is another Kona restaurant with a remarkable seaside setting. The gently rolling surf lapping at the shore is like free dessert. Full breakfasts, 6:30 a.m. to 12:00 p.m. from $4, waffles and pancakes cheaper. Lunch from 11:00 a.m. to 3:00 p.m., dinner from 5:30 p.m. to 10:00 p.m. Sandwiches from $3, salads $5, fresh fish, seafood, and beef from $10, salad bar $5.95. Happy hour daily from 11:00 a.m. to 6:00 p.m. features an assortment of *pu pu.* The Spindrifer is in walking distance from downtown at 75-5776 Alii Dr., tel. 329-1344.

Cousin Kimo's Restaurant, tel. 329-1393, is located in the courtyard of Uncle Billy's downtown Kona Bay Hotel. Following in the semi-plastic Polynesian tradition of Uncle Billy, they serve fair to passable food at reasonable prices: a delicious well-prepared catch-of-the-day, cut of savory beef, or fried-to-death frozen *mahi mahi.* The all-you-can-eat salad bar comes with full meals, and displays crisp island vegetables and fruits right next to items fresh from the can! A stuffed marlin, seemingly too huge and colorful to be real, gazes down at everyone from the wall. Free *hula* shows are part of the bargain every night at 6:30 and 7:30 p.m. Open daily from 6:30 a.m. (breakfast specials $1.99), this restaurant could be an "old reliable" with just a touch more care in the food preparation.

Reuben's Mexican Cafe is tucked away in the downtown Kona Plaza and serves up hefty portions of south-of-the-border fare at good prices. There's a full menu from *chili rellenos* to *huevos rancheros* all between $5 and $7, and the only "slam" against Reuben's is that the dishes are a bit too tame. Reuben's does have the best prices on imported beers—offering Dos Equis, Corona, and Heineken for only $2. Open daily 11:00 a.m. to 11:00 p.m., Sun. 3:00-11:00 p.m., tel. 329-7031.

Jose's Mexican Restaurant is operated by the Martinez family, with about the same menu as Reuben's at comparable prices. The dishes here are a touch more authentic and zesty. Jose's is on Rt. 11, 5 minutes above Kailua-Kona at the Aloha Village Shopping Center. Open daily 11:00 a.m. to 10:00 p.m., Sunday brunch 10:00 a.m. to 9:00 p.m., tel. 329-6391.

Buzz's Steak House is one of an island-owned chain out of Honolulu. They've built their reputation on serving up hefty orders at matching prices for chops, steaks, and Korean-style BBQ ribs. Fresh hot bread and the salad bar are filling and priced reasonably. Most sandwiches $5, dinners from $8. They have reliable quality and are located upstairs in the Kailua Bay Inn Shopping Plaza in downtown Kailua-Kona. The atmosphere in this open and airy perch overlooking the bay is congenial. Open daily for lunch 11:00 a.m. to 3:30 p.m., dinner 5:30-10:00 p.m., tel. 329-1571.

Don Drysdale's Club 53 is owned by the famous Dodger pitcher, and in the good sense of the word can best be described as a saloon. The amiable bar and grill serves reasonably priced beer, drinks, and sandwiches until 1:00 a.m. Sports fans away from home can always catch their favorite events on the bar's TV. Soup and salads from $2.50, a wide variety of *pu pu* from $4, sandwiches from $3 to $5, and the special peanut butter cream pie at $2.35. Drysdale's is one of the most relaxing and casual bars in town. Overlooking the bay at the Kona Inn Shopping Village, open daily 10:00-2:00 a.m. tel, 329-6651.

The Kona Galley is a well-established Kona favorite serving fresh fish and combination platters in its soothing open-air dining room. It also specializes in seafood, and is known for its Saturday night prime rib. Reasonably priced lunch, with the dinner menu more expensive. Open daily 11:00 a.m. to 10:00 p.m., along Alli Dr., just near the pier, tel. 329-3777.

Quinn's seems to be Kona's yuppie bar. The local in-crowd comes here to the patio for sandwiches, vegetarian specialties, seafood, and beef. Daily from lunch until 1:00 a.m. for late-night dining, Sun. until 10:00 p.m. Across from the King Kamehameha Hotel, tel. 329-3822.

Tonga Room, tel. 322-2727, at the Kona Lagoon Hotel serves breakfast, lunch, and dinner in this Polynesian-style longhouse. A "special" is held here every Fri., see *"Luau* and Buffet" following. Also at the Kona Lagoon, **The Wharf,** tel. 322-2727, specializes in a respectable selection of beef and seafood at good prices. Open daily, with reservations for dinner suggested.

Expensive

Dorians Restaurant, tel. 329-3195 is along Alii Drive next to White Sands Beach. It's an elegant restaurant with high-back wicker chairs, crystal everywhere, and white linen table settings. The quality of the food matches the prices. Sit on the veranda next to the sea, $4 minimum order per person—better than inside. The bar serves domestic beer $2, imported beer $2.50, well drinks $2, exotics $4, happy hour daily 3:00-6:00 p.m. The lunch menu is less expensive, offering French onion soup $3, shrimp cocktail $7.50, clams and pasta $8.75, fettucini $10, plus a variety of sandwiches from vegetarian to steak from $4 to $10. One of the only places in town offering oysters on the half shell, $6 half dozen. Dinnner is superb; expect to spend $20 per person. Featured are 48-inch platters, 2-person minimum, such as The Continental with lamb chops, steak, and baby lobster tails; the best is the Chef's Silver Platter. All come with baked potato parmigiana, vegetables, house salad, and freshly baked bread. Open daily, lunch 11:00 a.m. to 2:30 p.m., dinner from 6:00 p.m., Sunday champagne brunch from 10:00 a.m. to 2:00 p.m.

At **Huggo's** Restaurant it's difficult to concentrate on the food because the setting is so spectacular. If you were any closer to the sea, you'd be in it, and of course the sunset is great. Waiters and waitresses are outfitted in aloha-wear and each table features various inlaid maps of the Pacific. The salad bar is exceptional and lunch is reasonable with tasties like tostada, shrimp cocktail, and Reuben sandwiches for under $6. A specialty is the seafood chowder at $2 a cup, $3 a bowl, made with clams and fresh fish and seasoned with sherry, cream, and butter. Chowder and salad is $6.50. Dinner menu includes steak scampi, Kona chicken, and prime rib from $8 to $15. Kona coffee is served and the best day to eat lunch is on Thursday, because Wednesday night's feature is prime rib and any leftover cuts are part of Thursday's buffet. Huggo's swings with live music nightly and is open daily 11:00 a.m. to 2:00 p.m. for lunch, and from 5:30 for dinner. Try Huggo's, tel. 329-1493, on Alii Drive next door to the Kona Hilton.

S.S. James Makee is a fancy Continental restaurant at the Kona Surf Hotel. The nautical decor is commemorative of the restaurant's namesake, an old island steamer. The limited menu includes shrimp Kamehameha, teriyaki steak, various veals, and filet mignon. Fresh fish of the day is always well prepared and a good choice. A major part of the minimum $20 per person dining experience is the atmosphere. Open daily for dinner from 6:00 p.m. by reservation only—of course, matey! Tel. 322-3411.

The Kona Inn Restaurant is a lovely but lonely carry-over from the venerable old Kona Inn. Part of the deal for tearing down the Kona Inn and putting up the sterile Kona Inn Shopping Village was giving the restaurant a prime location. On entering, notice the marlin over the doorway and a huge piece of hung glass through which the sunset sometimes beams. The bar and dining area are richly appointed in native *koa.* The menu doesn't match the decor, offering well-prepared but uninspired chicken, fish, and steak at expensive prices. If you want to enjoy the view, the best thing in this restaurant, try a cocktail and a *sashimi* plate at $5.95, or an omelette, which is filling and rightly priced. Open daily for lunch, and dinner, and Sunday brunch, downtown Kailua-Kona at the Kona Inn Shopping Village, tel. 329-4455.

Adjacent is **Fisherman's Landing** with excellent food, and an even better location being closer to the shore. You walk down a cobblestone pathway to find 5 Hawaiian dining huts separated by ponds and wooden bridges. Entrees by chef Curtis Masuda feature Kona-caught fish delicately broiled over a *kiawe* fire. The lunch menu has a variety of sandwiches, stir-frys, and steaks starting at $5. Dinner is more sumptuous with shrimp scampi, lobster, and Oriental specialties. Open daily, lunch 11:30 a.m. to 2:00 p.m., dinner 5:30-10:00 p.m., tel. 326-2555.

Oui oui monsieur, but of course we have zee Restaurant Francais. It is **La Bourgogne,** with master chef Guy Chatelard. For those who just can't live without escargots, shrimp Provencal, pate, or pheasant, you've been saved. How much $? Plenty, *mon petite!* Located 5 minutes from downtown on Rt. 11 (Kuakini Hwy.) Open Tues. to Fri. 11:30 a.m. to 2:00 p.m., Mon. to Sat. 6-10:00 p.m., tel. 329-6711.

The Pottery is a small privately owned chain out of Honolulu where art and dining become one. The decor in this romantic hideaway is accented by ceramics made on the premises, along with your table setting and even some pots that you can take home. Specialties include steaks, Cornish game hens, prawns, and fresh fish. Expect to spend $15 for an entree. Open daily for dinner. Located a few minutes from town at 75-5995 Kuakini Hwy., tel. 329-2277.

The **Kona Ranch House** is a delightful restaurant with something for everyone. It has 2 rooms: the family-oriented Paniolo Room where hearty appetites are filled family style, and the elegant Plantation Lanai, where both palate and sense of beauty are satiated. This restaurant, highlighted by copper drainpipes, brass ceiling fans, wicker furniture, and lattice work all on a natural wood and brick background, is the epitome of plantation dining. The Kona Ranch House is a classy establishment, where you get more than what you pay for. Prices range from reasonable to expensive, and the menus in the 2 separate rooms reflect this. Open daily from 6:30 a.m. to 10:00 p.m., Sunday brunch, reservations needed for the Plantation Lanai. Located 2 minutes from downtown at the corner of Kuakini Hwy. and Palani Road, tel. 329-7061.

Eclipse Restaurant is one of Kona's newest Continental restaurants. Offerings range from the simple to complex and include oysters Rockefeller, mustard and brandy cream sauce served over pepper steak, seafood, and veal and prawns. The owner/chef prepares a specialty nightly. Dinner only from 5:00-9:00 p.m. At night the chrome deco restaurant transforms into a disco. On Kuakini Hwy., across from Foodland, tel. 329-4686.

Kanazawa-tei is a Japanese restaurant and *sushi* bar that boasts chefs directly from Japan. Specialties include *sukiyaki, teriyaki,* and *tempura.* Daily specials a bargain. At 75-5845 Alii

Dr., across from Kona Hilton. Open daily for lunch and dinner, closed Wed., reservations suggested, tel. 326-1881.

Fast Foods And Snacks

In the Kona Inn Shopping Village try: **Mrs. Barry's Cookies**, homemade yummies including macadamia nut, chocolate chip, and peanut butter. Gift boxed to send home; just follow your nose to the **Coffee Cantata** and drink a cup in the little courtyard; **Kona Kai Farms Coffee House**, featuring a sampler cup of Kona coffee; **Billy Boy's Cafe** for a heaping "plate-lunch special" for around $3.50.

Around town, The **Bartender's Ocean Breeze** serves up 12 oz. mugs of ice-cold beer for $1, and grill-your-own burgers for $2.75. Other snacks available on Alii Dr., near the Kona Hilton tennis courts, tel. 329-7622. **Attila's** at the Kona Marina has icy schooners of beer at "Kona's longest bar." Featuring fish 'n chips, shrimp, chicken, and teriyaki. Open daily, tel. 326-1150. **The Farm Restaurant** at the Kailua Bay Inn Shopping Plaza features a rich and wholesome menu with most items under $5. Breakfast specials include eggs, hash browns, and banana walnut pancakes for only $2.25. Lunch on kettle soups from $1, and sandwiches for around $3.50. **Suzanne's Bake Shop** is just behind this little mall near Hilo Hattie's, and offers a variety of mouthwatering baked goods and snacks. Early birds will love the 5:00 a.m. opening. **The World's Greatest Sandwich Shop** is also just near Hilo Hattie's. They have pastrami, turkey, or honey-baked ham for $3, vegie sandwiches for $2.50, plus tuna salad and the like all served on special buns made on the island. **Paniolo Pizza** at the Kona Coast Shopping Plaza has delicious pizza, plus sandwiches, Mexican food, and limited Italian dinners. They deliver! Call 329-1302. **Pizza Hut** is on Puainako Street, and you'll find **McDonald's** golden arches on Kuakini Highway. On your way to Pu'uhonua O Honaunau (see "Sights") you might consider stopping in at **Barry's Nut Farm** along Rt. 160. They'll give you a free tour of the gardens and nursery, or you can browse for pottery, or buy sandwiches and drinks. Open daily 9:00 a.m. to 5:00 p.m., tel. 328-9930.

***Luau*, Buffets, And Such**

A sumptuous feast is held at the **Kona Village Resort.** It's worth attending this *luau* just to visit and be pampered at this private hotel beach. Adults around $40, children under 12 half price. Held every Friday, by reservation only, tel. 325-5555. The *imu* ceremony is at 6:00 p.m., followed by no host cocktails, the *luau* and Hawaiian entertainment at 8:00 p.m. Also, limited reservations are accepted during the week for lunch, dinner, and special dinners and buffets.

Hotel King Kamehameha has a long-standing *luau* every Sun., Tues., Wed., and Friday. The *imu* ceremony begins at 6:15 p.m., cocktails from 6:00-7:00 p.m., the *luau* begins at 7:00 p.m. and is followed by entertainment. Adults $36, children under 12 $20. Reservations, tel. 329-2911.

Keauhou Beach Hotel offers a *luau* every Sun., Wed., and Friday. *Imu* ceremony at 6:00 p.m., cocktails 6:30-7:30 p.m., followed by the *luau* and entertainment at 7:30 p.m. Adults $30, children under 12 $20. Reservations, tel. 322-3441.

Kona Hilton Beach Resort has a *luau* from time to time, and advertises in the free tourist literature. Particulars available when the *luau* is happening. Adults $25, children 12 to 18 $16, under 12 $12.50, tel. 329-3111.

Kona Lagoon Hotel does a special *"Kamaaina pa'ina"* complete with authentic Hawaiian entertainment and *luau* cuisine. Hosted every Fri. from 11:00 a.m. to 2:00 p.m. in the Tonga Room by George Naope. A terrific time had by all for only $8.75 per person, tel. 322-2727.

Captain Bean's Dinner Cruise departs Kailua Pier daily at 5:00 p.m. and returns at 8:00 p.m. You are entertained while the bar dispenses liberal drinks and the deck groans with all-you-can-eat food. Besides, you get a terrific panorama of the Kona Coast from the sea. You can't help having a good time on this cruise, and if the boat sinks with all that food and booze in your belly, you're a goner...but what a way to go! Minimum age 18 years, $30 includes tax and tip. Reservations suggested, tel. 329-2955.

Kona Chuckwagon Buffet gives you all-you-can-eat, or more precisely all you care to eat. Breakfast $3.50, 7:00-10:00 a.m., lunch $5, 11:00 a.m. to 5:00 p.m., dinner $6.50, 5:00-9:00 p.m. Expect a lot of fried food, heavy on the gravies, instant potatoes, white breads, and canned vegetables. You can go "hog belly" here, so it's hard to complain, but don't expect anything beyond cafeteria food. Open daily, at Casa De Emdeko on Alii Dr., tel. 329-2818.

ENTERTAINMENT

Kona nights come alive mostly in its restaurants and the dining rooms of the big hotels. The most memorable experience for most is free: watching the sunset from Kailua Pier, and taking a leisurely stroll along Alii Drive. All of the *luau* previously mentioned have "Polynesian Revues" of one sort or another, which are generally good, clean, sexy fun, but of course these shows are limited only to the *luau* guests. Those that have "dancin' feet," or wish to spend the evening listening to live music, there's a small but varied selection from which to choose. **Note:** All the hotels and restaurants listed below have been previously mentioned in either the "Accommodations" or "Food" sections, so please refer there for addresses and directions.

Free

Hula shows take place every Tues. and Thurs. at the Kona Inn Shopping Plaza in downtown Kailua. The performance starts at 6:00 p.m. near Billy Boy's Cafe. The **Kona Surf Hotel** puts on a free Polynesian Revue entitled "A Night in Hawaii" in its Nalu Terrace every night except Sunday. The extravaganza begins at 7:45 p.m. and lasts about one hour. It's a fun-filled show, and just being on the fabulous grounds of this hotel at sunset is worth the trip. **Cousin Kimo's Restaurant** at the Kona Bay Hotel presents 2 free dinner shows of *hula* and a medley of Hawaiian tunes nightly at 6:30 and 7:30 p.m. If you're not into dining, you can order a drink and watch the fun.

Around Town

Huggo's Restaurant with its romantic waterfront setting along Alii Drive features live music nightly from 8:30 p.m. until 12:30 a.m. Tuesday through Thurs. the place swings with the cool rhythms of the Doug Johnson Jazz Trio. Weekends bring more jazz, or contemporary E-Z listening with a touch of rock now and again.

The **Kona Lagoon Hotel** takes care of everyone. You can sway to the gentle rhythms of Hawaiian tunes every day at *Le'a Le'a* Time, from 4:30 to 7:30 p.m., or you can boogie the night away at CJ's Disco, in the Wharf Room, from 10:00 p.m. until 2:00 a.m., Thurs. to Saturday.

The **Keauhou Beach Hotel** soothes you with E-Z listening Hawaiian-style nightly at the Sunset Rib Lanai from 9:30 until midnight, or rocks you in Don The Beachcomber's Disco in the transformed main dining room.

The **Kona Surf Resort** is a tough act to follow. Besides its free nightly Polynesian show, it offers Hawaiian tunes by two local groups from 4:00-6:00 p.m. and again from 6:00-7:30 p.m., and if that's not enough, the *pu pu* are free at the earlier show. Still more! In the evening a quiet piano tinkles in the S.S. James Makee Restaurant from 6:00-11:00 p.m., or you can glide around the dance floor in the Puka Bar to live music from 9:00 p.m. until closing. More yet!! From Tues. through Sat., the Poi Pounder Nightclub beats out "top 40" dancin' tunes from 9:00 p.m. until the wee hours.

At the **Kona Hilton** piano bar you can enjoy happy hour from 4:30-6:00 p.m. with free *pu pu* while listening to the mellow piano which begins at 4:30 and goes until closing. The Windjammer Lounge has dancing music nightly, except Mon. from 8:30 p.m. until closing.

In downtown Kailua-Kona you can pick your fun at the **Hotel King Kamehameha.** The Billfish Bar has happy hour from 5:00-7:00 p.m. with nightly entertainment from 5:00-10:00 p.m. You'll hear everything from country to contemporary with Hawaiian tunes thrown in so you won't forget where you are. Weekends bring E-Z listening, contemporary, and Hawaiian music to Moby Dick's in the hotel.

Around town, the **Eclipse Restaurant** becomes a swinging disco from 10:00 p.m. until 1:30 a.m. every night; the **Spindrifter Restaurant** offers a variety of live music throughout the week beginning at 8:30 p.m.; at the **Keauhou-Kona Golf Course Restaurant** you can enjoy live music including local artists and Hawaiian contemporary every evening from 7:00 p.m.; on weekends the **Pottery Steak House** offers piano music for listening and dancing enjoyment; for a quiet beer, sports talk, or just hanging out with the local people try **Quinn's, Drysdale's,** or the **Ocean View Inn** all in downtown Kailua-Kona.

For movies try: the **World Square Theater** in the World Square Shopping Plaza; the **Hualalai Theater** in downtown Kailua-Kona; the **Aloha Theater** in Kainaliu; or, the **Kona Theater** in Captain Cook, which has drawn some heat lately from civic groups for showing "skin flicks" on Thurs. evenings. This latter bit of information is supplied for those who are offended by porno flicks so they'll know where *not to go* on a Thursday evening.

SHOPPING

Kona Malls

The Kailua-Kona area has an abundance of 2 commodities near and dear to a tourist's heart: sunshine and plenty of shopping malls. One of the largest malls in Kailua is the **Kona Inn Shopping Village,** in central Kailua, at 75-5744 Alii Drive. This shopping village boasts more than 40 shops selling fabrics, fashions, art, fruits, gems and jewelry, photo and music needs, food, and even exotic skins. The **World Square** is in central Kailua, and besides a variety of shops selling everything from burgers to bathing suits, it offers public restrooms and a Visitor Information Center. The **Kona Banyan Court,** also in central Kailua, has a dozen shops with a medley of goods and services. You'll also find the **Kailua Bay Inn Plaza** along Alii Drive; the **Akona Kai Mall** across from Kailua Pier; the **Kona Coast Shopping Plaza,** and the **Kona Shopping Center** both along Palani Road. The **Hotel King Kamehameha Mall** features a cluster of specialty shops and a Liberty House. Finally, the **Rawson Plaza,** at 74-5563 Kaiwi St., is just past the Kamehameha Hotel in the industrial area. This practical, no-frills area abounds in "no-name" shops selling everything you'll find in town but at substantial savings.

South Kona Malls

If, god forbid, you haven't found what you need in Kailua, or if you suddenly need a "shopping fix," even more malls are south on Rt. 11. The **Keauhou Shopping Village** is at the corner of Alii Dr. and Kamehameha III Road. Continuing south on Rt. 11 you'll spot the **Kainaliu Village Mall** along the main drag, and if you aren't satisfied yet, the **Kealekekua Ranch Center,** is in Captain Cook, down the road. This 2-story mall offers a nutrition center, fashions, and general supplies.

Food Markets

Kailua-Kona has a **Foodland,** open 24 hours, and **K. Tanaguchi Market,** generally the cheapest, both in the Kona Coast Shopping Center. The **Casa De Emdeko Liquor and Deli** is south of town center at 75-6082 Alii Drive. It's well stocked with liquor and groceries, but at convenience-store prices. Others include the **King Kamehameha Pantry,** tel. 329-9191, selling liquors, groceries and sundries, and the **Keauhou Pantry,** tel. 322-3066, in Keauhou along Alii Dr., selling more of the same.

South of Kailua-Kona both **Foodland** and **Kamigaki Store** are in Kealakekua, and **Sure Save** is in Kealakekua Shopping Center. The

Woody sets up his traveling van art shop just about every day near Huggo's Restaurant. He knows Kona and his paintings show it.

Shimizu Market is south on Rt. 11 in Honaunau. Farther south between mile markers 77 and 78 you'll find the very well-stocked **Ocean View General Store,** tel. 929-9966, which sells groceries, snacks, and gas.

Health Food Stores
The Kona keeps you healthy with **Kona Healthways** in the Kona Coast Shopping Center, tel. 329-2296. Besides a good assortment of health foods, they have cosmetics, books, and dietary supplements; the **Aloha Village Store** is in Kainaliu on the left-hand side of Rt. 11 heading south. They're a full-line natural foods store, open daily 8:00 a.m. to 7:00 p.m., tel. 322-9941; down Rt. 11 in Kealekekua is the **Ohana Food Co-op** housing a full range of health foods and a snack bar.

Mauna Loa Nutrition, tel. 323-3955, Kealakekua Ranch Center, Captain Cook, is a "health store" not a "health food store." Although you can refresh with snacks and drinks, the store stocks herbs, crystals, an extensive collection of body-care products, and the largest and lowest-priced selection of **Birkenstock** footwear in the islands. Owned and operated by 2 urbane and refreshing world travelers, Wayne and Mars Stier, it's well worth stopping, if just to chat. Wayne has authored 3 fine and insightful travel books which Mars distributes through their own company, Meru Publishing.

Bookstores
In Kailua-Kona be sure to venture into the **Middle Earth Bookshop** at 75-5719 Alii Ave., in the Kona Plaza Shopping Arcade, tel. 329-2123. This jam-packed bookstore has shelves laden with fiction, non-fiction, paperbacks, hardbacks, travel books, maps, and Hawaiiana. A great place to browse.

Art And Specialty Shops
Real treasure hunters will love the **Kona Garden's Flea Market** held every Wed. and Sat. 8:00 a.m. to 2:00 p.m. at the Kona Botanical Gardens along Alii Drive, tel. 322-2751.

In the Hotel King Kamehameha the **Tribal Arts Gallery** sells carvings, jewelry, and fabrics from exotic lands throughout the Pacific Basin, while **The Shellery** lives up to its name giving you baubles, bangles, and beads all made from shells.

The Seaside Mall across from the Kamehameha Hotel features the **Butterfly Boutique** selling locally designed and made beachwear and casual wear, and the smaller **Kona Botik** specializing in bikinis.

In the World Square Shopping Center visit the **Showcase Gallery** operated by Jean Hamilton. All the talented offerings of glasswork, beadwork, featherwork, enameling, and shell *lei* come from the islands, mostly from the Big

Island. Across the way the **Coral Isle Art Shop** presents modern versions of traditional Hawaiian carvings. You'll find everything from *tikis* to scrimshaw, with exceptionally good carvings of sharks and whales for a pricy $75 or so. The **Smuggler's Loft** bills itself as a "man's store" and sells a wide variety of nautical items with *objets d'art* mostly in brass, bronze, or ceramics.

At the Kona Inn Shopping Village you can buy eel skin accoutrements at **Exotic Skins,** distinctive island fabrics at **Fare Tahiti Fabrics,** custom jewelry at **Jim Bill's Gemfire,** handpainted one-of-a-kind original clothing at **Noa Noa,** and distinctive Hawaiian black coral jewelry and scrimshaw at **Original Maui Divers.**

Along Alii Drive, on the corner of Hualalai Road, is **Pacific Vibrations** for T-shirts, bikinis, even surfboards. Farther along Alii Drive, near Huggo's Restaurant, check out Robert "Woody" Woodward," a local artist who sets up daily in his van and captures the magic of the Kona Coast on his canvases.

For some practical purchases at wholesale prices check out **Kona Jeans** for shirts, tops, footwear, and jeans, at 74-5576 Kaiwi Street.

SERVICES AND INFORMATION

For **Ambulance and Fire:** tel. 961-6022; **Police** in Kona communities, tel. 323-2645; the **Kona Hospital** in Kealekekua, tel. 322-9311; **Pharmacy,** Kona Coast Drugs in Kailua, tel. 329-8886, or Pay 'N' Save Drugs at tel. 329-3577. For **alternative health care services and massage,** both well established in Kailua-Kona, see p. 549.

An **Information Gazebo** is open daily 7:00 a.m. to 9:00 p.m. along the boardwalk in the Kona Inn Shopping Village. They can handle all your questions from dining to diving. The **Hawaii Visitors Bureau** maintains an office in the Kona Plaza, at 75-5719 Alii Dr., tel. 329-7787. The **library** is at 75-140 Hualalai Rd., tel. 329-2196. The Hele Mai Laundromat is at the North Kona Shopping Center, at the corner of Alii Dr. and Palani Rd., tel. 329-3494. For more "services and info" see p. XXX.

First Interstate Bank, tel. 329-4481, is at 75-5722 Kuakini Hwy.; **First Hawaiian Bank,** Kona office at tel. 329-2461; **Bank of Hawaii** maintains 2 offices in Kailua at tel. 329-7033, Kealekekua at tel. 322-9377. The **post office** is on Palani Rd., tel. 329-1927.

KAU

The **Kau District** is simple and straightforward like the broad open face of a country gentleman. It's not boring, and it does hold pleasant surprises for those willing to look. Formed entirely from the massive slopes of Mauna Loa, it presents some of the most ecologicaly diverse land in the islands. The bulk stretches 50 miles from north to south and almost 40 miles from east to west. Kau tumbles from snowcapped mountain through the cool green canopy of highland forests. Lower it becomes pasturelands of belly-deep grass ending in blistering hot black sands along the coast, encircled by a necklace of foamy-white sea. At the bottom of Kau is **Ka Lae** ("South Point"), the southernmost tip of Hawaii, and the southernmost point in the U.S. Latitudinally it lies 500 miles south of Miami and twice that below Los Angeles. Ka Lae was probably the first landfall made by the Polynesian explorers on the islands. A variety of archaeological remains support this belief. Most people dash through Kau on the Hawaii Belt Road, heading to or from Volcanoes National Park. Its main towns, **Naalehu** and **Pahala,** are little more than "pit stops." The Belt Road follows the old Mamalahoa Trail, where, for centuries, nothing moved faster than a contented man's stroll. Kau's beauties, mostly tucked away down secondary roads, are hardly given a look by most unknowing visitors. If you take the time and get off the beaten track, you'll discover black and green sand beaches, the world's largest macadamia nut farm, wild-west rodeos, and an electricity farm sprouting windmill generators. The upper slopes and broad pasturelands are the domain of hunters, hikers, and *paniolo,* who still ride the range on sure-footed horses. In Kau are sleepy plantation towns that don't even know how quaint they are, and beach parks where you can count on finding a secluded spot to pitch a tent. Time in Kau moves slowly, and *aloha* still forms the basis of day-to-day life.

SIGHTS

The following sights are listed from west to east along Rt. 11, with detours down secondary roads indicated whenever necessary. The majority of Kau's pleasures are accessible by standard rental car, but many secluded coastal spots can be reached only by 4WD. For example, **Kailiki**, just west of Ka Lae, was an important fishing village in times past. A few archaeological remains are found here, and the beach has a green cast due to the lava's high olivine content. Few tourists ever visit; only hardy fishermen come here to angle the coastal waters. Spots of this type abound, especially in Kau's sections. Those willing to abandon their cars at the end of the road and hike in are rewarded with areas unchanged and untouched for generations. The forested slopes above Manuka provide ample habitat for introduced, and now totally successful, colonies of wild pigs, pheasants, and turkeys. Some popular hiking areas are covered in the Volcanoes Park section (see p. 582). Be advised that the entire district is subject to volcanic activity and except where indicated it has no water, food, shelter, or amenities. If hoofing it, or 4WDing isn't your pleasure, consider a stop at **Manuka State Wayside,** 12 miles west of South Point Road just inside the Kau District. This civilized scene has restrooms, pavilions, and trails through manicured gardens surrounded by an arboretum. All plants are identified, and this is an excellent rest or picnic stop.

South Point

The Hawaiians simply called this Ka Lae, "The Point." Some scholars believe Polynesian sailors made landfall here as early as A.D. 150, and that their amazing exploits became navigating legend long before true colonization began. A paved, narrow, but passable road branches off from Rt. 11 approximately 6 miles west of Naalehu, and drops directly south for

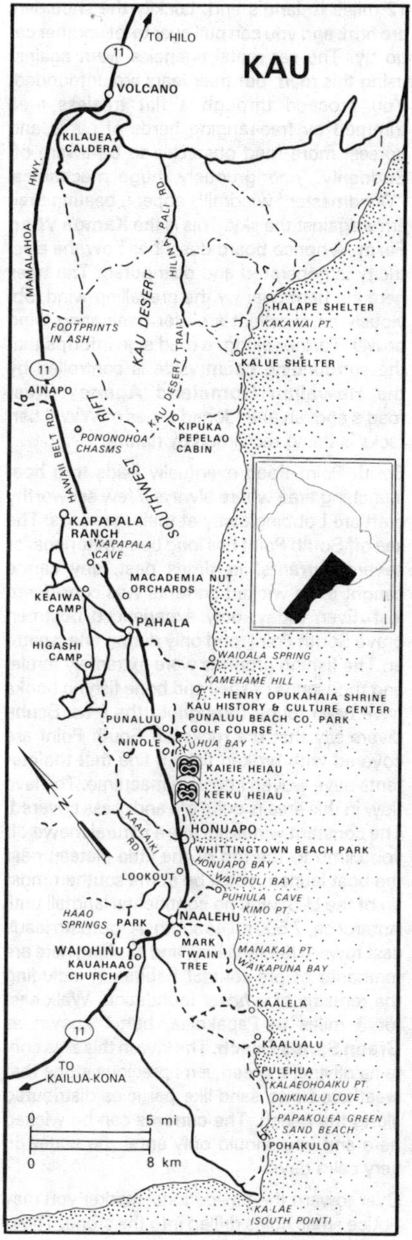

12 miles to land's end. Luckily the shoulders are firm, and you can pull over to let another car go by. The car rental agencies warn against using this road, but their fears are unfounded. You proceed through a flat treeless area trimmed by free-ranging herds of cattle and horses: more road obstacles to be aware of. Suddenly, incongruously, huge mechanical "Windmaster" windmills appear, beating their arms against the sky. This is the **Kamoa Wind Farm.** A notice board describes how the electricity is generated and distributed. The trees here are bent over by the prevailing wind, obviously an excellent area for generating wind power. Farther along, a road sign informs that the surrounding countryside is controlled by the **Hawaiian Homeland Agency.** Near road's end, an abandoned series of WW II barracks is being reclaimed by nature.

South Point Road eventually leads to a boat launching area where always a few seaworthy craft are bobbing away at their moorings. The sea off South Point has long been notorious for severe currents. In times past, any canoe caught in its wicked currents was considered lost. Even today, only experienced boatmen brave South Point, and only during fine weather. The fishing grounds were extremely fertile, and thousands of shell and bone fishing hooks have been found throughout the area. Scuba divers say that the rocks off South Point are covered with broken fishing line that the currents have woven into wild macrame. The lava flow in this area is quite old and grass covered. The constant winds act like a natural mower. If you climb to the top of the little plateau near the boat launch, you'll be at the southernmost tip of the U.S. with no continental landfall until Antarctica, 7,500 miles south. A footpath leads east toward Kaulana Bay, and all along here are remnants of pre-contact habitation including the remains of a *heiau* foundation. Walk east for 3 miles to Papakolea, better known as **Green Sands Beach.** The lava in this area contains olivine, a green semi-precious stone that weathered into sand-like particles distributed along the beach. The currents can be wicked here and you should only enter the water on very calm days.

Over toward the navigational marker you may notice small holes drilled into the stone. These were used by Hawaiian fishermen to secure their canoes by long ropes to land while the current carried them a short way offshore. In this manner, they could fish without being swept away. Today fishermen still use these holes, but instead of manned canoes they use floats or tiny boats to carry their lines out to sea. The *ulua,* tuna, and *ahi* fishing is renowned throughout this area. When the *kona* winds blow out of the South Pacific, South Point takes it on the chin. The weather should always be a consideration when you visit. There is no official camping or facilities of any kind at South Point, but plenty of boat owners bivouac for a night to get an early start in the morning.

Heading East

As you head east toward Naalehu, you pass through the tiny town of **Waiohinu.** Just past the Shirakawa Motel on the *mauka* side of the road is the **Mark Twain Monkeypod Tree.** Unfortunately, Waiohinu's only claim to fame except for its undisturbed peace and quiet blew down in a heavy windstorm in 1957. Part of the original trunk, carved into a bust of Twain, is on display at the Lyman House Museum in Hilo. Now, a few shoots have begun sprouting from the original trunk and in years to come the Monkeypod Tree will be an attraction again.

Next you come to sizable **Naalehu,** complete with markets and even a hardware store. Just east is **Whittington Beach Park,** followed by Ninole, where you'll find **Punaluu Beach Park** which is famous for its black-sand beach. Punaluu was an important port during the sugar boom of the 1880s and even had a railroad. Notice the tall coconut palms in the vicinity, unusual for Kau. Punaluu means "Diving Spring," so named because freshwater springs can be found on the floor of the bay. Native divers once paddled out to sea, then dove with calabashes that they filled with fresh water from the underwater springs. This was the main source of drinking water for the region.

Ninole is also home to the **Seamountain Resort and Golf Course,** built in the early 1970s by a branch of the C. Brewer Company. The string of flat-topped hills in the background are the remains of volcanoes that became dormant about 100,000 years ago. In sharp contrast with them is **Loihi Seamount**, 20 miles offshore and about 3,000 feet below the surface of the sea. This very active submarine volcano is steadily building, and should reach the surface in the next thousand years or so. Near Ninole is **Hokuloa Church**, which houses a memorial to Henry Opukahaia, the Hawaiian most responsible for encouraging the first missionaries to go to Hawaii to save his people from damnation.

Eight miles east is **Pahala**. The Hawaii Belt Road flashes past this town, but if you drive into it, heading for the tall stack of the Kau Sugar Co., you'll find one of the best preserved examples of a classic sugar town in the islands. It was once gospel that sugar would be "king" in these parts forever, but the huge stone stack of the sugarmill puffs no more, while in the background the whir of a modern macadamia nut processing plant breaks the stillness. Another half hour or so of driving from Pahala puts you in Volcanoes National Park. For Kau Desert Footprints see p. 593.

BEACHES, PARKS, AND CAMPING

Between Pahala and Naalehu is **Punaluu Beach Park**, a county park (permit) with full amenities. Punaluu boasts some of the only safe swimming on the south coast. Head for the northeast section of the beach near the boat ramp. Stay close to shore because a prevailing rip current lurks just outside the bay. Just near the beach is **Joe and Pauline's Curio Shop**. If you have time stop in; these people have a reputation for being more interested in offering *aloha* than in selling you a trinket. **Ninole Cove Park**, part of the Seamountain Resort, is in walking distance and open to the public. For day use, you might consider parking near the pro shop. As you walk to the beach from here you pass a freshwater pond, quite cold but good for swimming.

Whittington Beach Park, 3 miles north of Naalehu, is another county park with full amenities and camping. This park is tough to spot from the road because it's not clearly marked. As you're coming down a steep hill from Naalehu you'll see a bridge at the bottom. Turn right and you're there. The park is a bit run down, but never crowded. If you follow the dirt roads to its undeveloped sections you encounter many old ruins from the turn of the century when Honuapo Bay was an important sugar port.

Green Sands Beach is locally known as Mahana, 3 miles east of South Point on a rugged 4WD road. Most of the olivine here is only sand size, but rough seas that inundate the beach and crash against the *pali* sometimes dislodge larger gem-quality stones. Be careful of the footing down to the beach. Use the path on the south face of the *pali*, and enter the water only on very calm days. Expect to find no water or shade. Generally only a few fishermen, hikers, and a nudist or two frequent the area.

PRACTICALITIES

One thing you won't be hassled with in the Kau District is deciding on where to eat or spend the night. The list is short and sweet.

Accommodations

The **Shirakawa Motel**, Box 467, Naalehu, HI 96772, tel. 929-7462, is a small, clean, comfortable hotel where your peace and quiet is guaranteed. Open since 1928, the Japanese family that runs it is as quiet and unobtrusive as *ninja*. Prices are a reasonable $16 s, $19 s with kitchen, $23 d with kitchen, a 10% discount for a one-week stay, and 15% for longer.

Seamountain Resort at Punaluu is a condominium/hotel complex. For information and reservations write Box 70, Pahala, HI 96777, tel. 928-8301. Prices range from a studio at $55 s to a 2-bedroom apartment for $109. These condos offer a restaurant, tennis and golf course, pool, maid service (weekly), and require a 2-day minimum stay.

Food

In **Naalehu** you can gas yourself or your car at the **Luzon Liquor Store**, open Mon. to Sat. 7:00 a.m. to 7:30 p.m., Sun. till 6:00 p.m., closed Tues., tel. 929-7103. For a quick sandwich or a snack try the **Naalehu Coffee Shop**, open daily, tel. 929-7238. They also have a large assortment of souvenirs and tourist junk. To prove you're still in America, the town boasts the **Plantation Stop,** a pizza and hamburger joint that also features chicken to go. Open daily, tel. 929-9280.

The **Naalehu Fruit Stand** is a favorite with locals. Besides fresh fruit and vegetables, you'll find pizza, sandwiches, and souvenirs. Open daily from 9:00 a.m., tel. 929-9009. In **Waiohinu,** just west of Naalehu, you can pick up supplies at **Wong Yuen General Store and Gas Station,** open 8:30 a.m. to 5:00 p.m., sun. to 3:00 p.m., tel. 929-7223.

The only real "dining" in the area is at the **Punaluu Black Sands Restaurant,** daily for breakfast, lunch, and dinner, tel. 928-8344. The menu is varied, from moderate to expensive. The setting couldn't be more lovely as it sits just off the Seamountain Golf Course overlooking the black-sand beach. Unfortunately, all those pesky tourists dieseling by in their tour buses think so, too. The opposite side of the coin is the diminutive **M. Toma Bakery and Restaurant,** that serves up pastries and sandwiches as wholesome as its name. This little husband-and-wife affair is on Pahala's main street, tel. 965-8255. If you intend to explore Volcanoes Park, this is an excellent place to pick up a picnic lunch.

Sports

Besides the great outdoors and the sea, the only organized sporting facility in Kau is at the Seamountain Resort. Here you'll find 4 unlit tennis courts, and a 6,106-yard, 18-hole, par-72 golf course. Green fees are $17, cart $16, and clubs are available for $10.

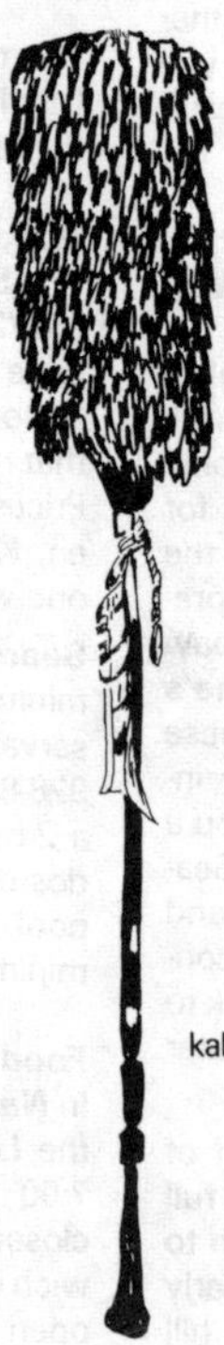

kahili

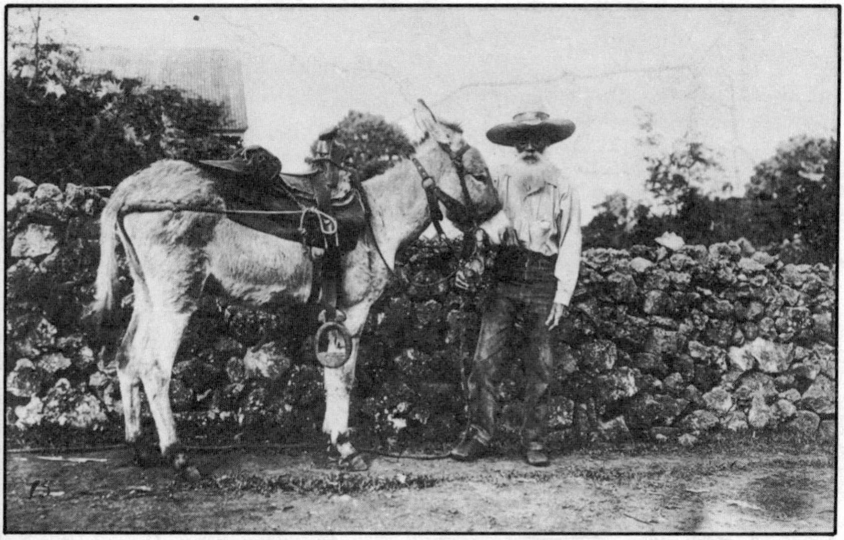

SOUTH KOHALA

The Kohala District is the peninsular thumb in the northwestern portion of the Big Island. At its tip is **Upolo Point**, only 40 miles from Maui across the **Alenuihaha Channel.** Kohala was the first section of the Big Island to rise from beneath the sea. The long-extinct volcanoes of the Kohala Mountains running down its spine have been reduced by time and the elements from lofty ragged peaks to rounded domes of 5,000 feet or so. Kohala is divided into North and South Kohala. **South Kohala** boasts *the* most beautiful swimming beaches on the Big Island, along with good camping and world-class hotels. Inland is **Waimea** (Kamuela), the *paniolo* town and center of the massive Parker Ranch. Founded last century by John Parker, its 200,000 acres on the western slopes of Mauna Kea now make it the largest privately owned ranch in America.

Getting There From Hilo

If you're approaching Kohala from Hilo or the east side of the island, you can take 2 routes. **The Saddle Road** (Rt. 200) comes directly west from Hilo and bypasses Mauna Kea and the Observatory Road. This very scenic road has the alluring distinction of being the least favorite route of the car rental agencies. The Saddle Road intersects Rt. 190 where you can turn north for 6 miles to Waimea, or south for 32 miles to Kailua-Kona (see p. 566). **Route 19,** the main artery connecting Hilo with the west coast, changes its "locally known" name quite often, but it's always posted as Route 19. Directly north from Hilo it hugs the coast along Hamakua where it is called the "Hawaiian Belt Road." When it turns west in Honokaa heading for Waimea it's called the "Mamalahoa Highway." From Waimea directly west to Waikui on the coast Rt. 19 becomes "Kawaihae Road," and when it turns due south along the coast heading for Kailua-Kona the moniker becomes the "Queen Kaahumanu Highway." The routes heading to Kohala from Kailua-Kona are discussed in the following sections. Many are "sights" in and of themselves, with lovely panoramas and leisurely "back-lane" rides.

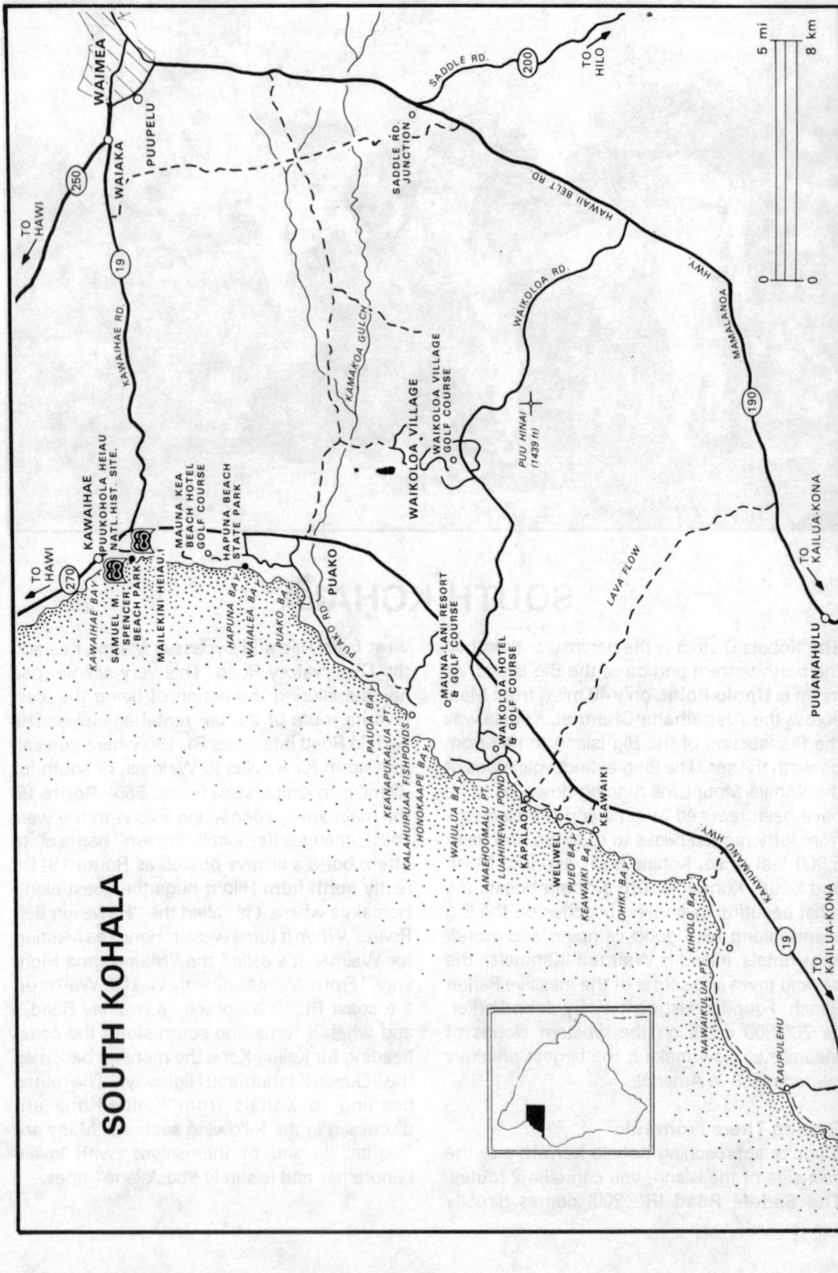
SOUTH KOHALA
WAIMEA
PUUPELU
WAIAKA
250
TO HAWI
19
KAWAIHAE RD.
SADDLE RD.
200
TO HILO
SADDLE RD. JUNCTION
HAWAII BELT RD.
0
5 mi
0
8 km
WAIKOLOA RD.
MAMALANOA HWY.
190
KAMAKOA GULCH
WAIKOLOA VILLAGE
WAIKOLOA VILLAGE GOLF COURSE
PUU HINAI (1439 ft)
KAWAIHAE
PUUKOHOLA HEIAU NATL. HIST. SITE
MAUNA KEA BEACH HOTEL GOLF COURSE
HAPUNA BEACH STATE PARK
TO HAWI
270
KAWAIHAE BAY
SAMUEL M. SPENCER BEACH PARK
MAILEKINI HEIAU
HAPUNA BAY
WAIALEA BAY
PUAKO BAY
PUAKO
PUAKO RD.
PAUOA BAY
KEANAPUKALUA PT.
KALAHUIPUAA FISHPONDS
HONOKAAPE BAY
MAUNA LANI RESORT & GOLF COURSE
WAIKOLOA HOTEL & GOLF COURSE
WAIULUA BAY
ANAEHOOMALU PT.
LUAHINEWAI POND
KAPALAOA
WELIWELI
PUEO BAY
KEAWAIKI BAY
KEAWAIKI
OHIKI BAY
KIHOLO BAY
NAWAIKULUA PT.
KAHUWANU HWY.
19
TO KAILUA-KONA
KAUPULEHU
LAVA FLOW
TO KAILUA-KONA
PUUANAHULU

SOUTH KOHALA: THE COAST

The shoreline of South Kohala, from Anaehoomalu Bay north to Kawaihae Bay, is rich in super-deluxe resorts that are perhaps the finest in the state. This coast's fabulous beaches are known not only for swimming and surf, but for tidepooling and awe-inspiring sunsets as well. Also, the 2 main beaches offer camping and even rental cabins. There are little-disturbed and rarely visited archaeological sites, expressive petroglyph fields well off the beaten track, the educational **Puukohola Heiau**, and even a rodeo. No "towns" are along the coast, in the sense of a laid-out community with a main street and attendant businesses and services. The closest facsimile is Kawaihae, with a small cluster of restaurants, shops, and a gas station. Waikoloa Village also provides some services with exclusive boutique shopping in the resorts.

Route 19, The Queen Kaahumanu Highway

As you begin heading north from Kailua-Kona on coastal Rt. 19 (Queen Kaahumanu Hwy.), you leave civilization behind. There won't be a house or any structures at all, and you'll know why they call it the "Big Island." Perhaps to soften the shock of what's ahead, magnificent bushes loaded with pink and purple flowers line the roadway...for a while. Notice too that friends and lovers have gathered and placed white rocks on the black lava forming pleasant graffiti messages such as "Aloha Mary," and "Love Kevin."

Suddenly you're in the midst of enormous flows of old *a'a* and *pahoehoe* as you pass through a huge and desolate lava desert. At first it appears ugly and uninviting, but the subtle beauty begins to grow. On clear days you can see Maui floating on the horizon, and *mauka* is the formidable presence of Mauna Kea streaked by sunlight filtering through its crown of clouds. Along the roadside, little wisps of grass have broken through the lava. Their color, a shade of pinkish gold, is quite extraordinary, and made more striking juxtaposed against the inky-black lava. Caught by your headlights at night, or especially in the magical light of dusk, the grass wisps come alive, giving the illusion of wild-haired gnomes rising from the earth.

Around mile marker 70, the land softens and changes. The lava is older, carpeted in rich green grass appearing as rolling hills of pastureland. No cows are in evidence, but be aware of "Kona nightingales," wild jack-asses that roam throughout this area, which can be road hazards. Also, these long flat stretches can give you "lead foot." Be careful! The police patrol this strip heavily, using unmarked cars (high-performance Trans Ams and the likes are favorites) looking for unsuspecting tourists that have been "road hypnotized." Kailua-Kona to the Sheraton Royal Waikoloa Hotel at Anaehoomalu is about 30 miles, with another 10 miles to the Mauna Kea Beach Hotel near Kawaihea. If you're day-tripping to the beaches, expect to spend an hour each way.

SIGHTS AND NEARBY COMMUNITIES

The following sights, beaches, and accommodations are listed from south to north. Since most of the accommodations of South Kohala are themselves sights, and lie on the best beaches, make sure to cross-reference the following sections. All, except for Waikoloa Village, lie along coastal Route 19 which is posted with mile markers, so finding the spots where you want to stop is easy.

Waikoloa Road

If you're interested in visiting Waimea (Kamuela) and still seeing the South Kohala coast, you might consider turning right off Rt. 19 between mile markers 74 and 75 onto Waikoloa Road. This is a great deal of territory to cover in one day! This route cuts inland for 13 miles, connecting coastal Rt. 19 with inland Rt. 190 leading to Waimea. About halfway, you pass the planned and quickly growing community of **Waikoloa Village.** The village has a gas station, market, and a few restaurants and shops. This is also the home of **Waikoloa Stables,** tel. 883-9335, that hosts a number of rodeos and wild-west shows (see p.548) along with saddle horses and a variety of trail rides for the visitor. Here too is the **Waikoloa Village Golf Course,** tel. 883-9621, a private course open to the public. You can chase that little white ball for par 72 over 6,316 yards for about $40 including cart

In the village you'll find **Waikoloa Villas** Box 3066, Waikoloa Village Station, Kamuela, HI 96743, tel. 800-367-7042, on Hawaii tel. 883-9588. Rates are one-bedroom $65-80 d, 2-bedroom $85-95 d, 3-bedroom (loft) $105-115 d, $8 extra person, 2-night minimum stay. Amenities include swimming pool, nearby golf, and weekly maid service. All units are fully furnished with complete kitchens. The condo offers a money savings condo/car package.

Puako

This alluring area is located *makai* on a side road off Rt. 19 about 4 miles south of Kawaihae. Hawaiians lived here in times past, but a modern community has been building along the 3 miles of Puako Bay since the 1950s. A thin ribbon of white sand runs the length of the beach that provides fair swimming, good fishing and snorkeling, and terrific tidepooling. Sunsets here are also magnificent and you'll usually have a large stretch of beach to yourself, but remember your flashlight for the walk back because there's no lighting. Near-shore scuba diving is excellent with huge caverns and caves to explore, and a colorful concentration of coral and marinelife. Along Puako Road is **Hokuloa Church,** built by Rev. Lorenzo Lyons in 1859. This musically talented reverend mastered the Hawaiian language and composed lovely ballads such as "Hawaii Aloha," which has become the unofficial anthem of the islands. Follow the road through the village to where it ends at a green gate; this is the beginning of the extensive field of **Puako Petroglyphs.** The entrance is marked by an HVB Warrior; the path leading to the rock carvings takes about 20 minutes each way. (Access and brochures are also available from the nearby Sheraton Hotel's front desk.) These markings are considered some of the finest and oldest in Hawaii, but carvings of horses and cattle signify ongoing art that happened long after Westerners appeared. Circles outlined by a series of small holes belonged to families who placed the umbilical cords of their infants into these indentations to tie them to the *aina* and give them strength for a long and good life. State archaeologists and anthropologists have reported a deterioration of the site due to vandalism, so please look but don't deface and stay on all established paths.

Pu'ukohola Heiau

Don't miss this completely restored Hawaiian temple designated as a National Historical Site located one mile south of Kawaihae where coastal Rt. 19 turns into Rt. 270 heading into North Kohala. This site, covering 77 acres, includes **Mailekini Heiau** and the nearby **John Young** house site. It is administered by the National Park Service, open daily 7:30 a.m. to 4:00

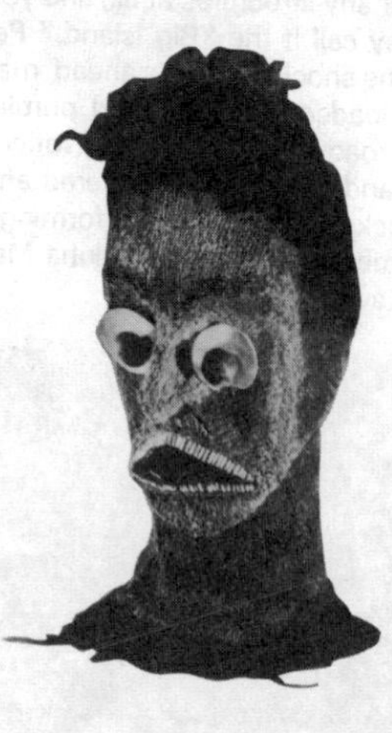

the war god Ku

John Young by ship's artist A. Pellion
(Hawaii State Archives)

p.m., admission free. As you enter, pick up a map highlighting the main points of interest, and it's worthwhile checking out the Visitors Center where Ranger Benjamin Saldua and others provide excellent information. Puukohola ("Whale Hill") received its name either because the hill itself resembles a whale, or because migrating whales pass very close offshore every year. It was designated to become a hill of destiny.

Kamehameha I built this *heiau* in 1790 on the advice of Kapoukahi, a prophet from Kauai who said that Kamehameha would unify all the islands only after he built a temple to his wargod Kukailimoku. Kamehameha complied, building this last of the great Hawaiian *heiau* from mortarless stone that when finished measured 100 by 224 feet. The dedication ceremony of the *heiau* is fascinating history. Kamehameha's last rival was his cousin, Keoua Kuahuula. This warlike chief, through prophecy and advice from his own *kahuna,* realized that it was Kamehameha who would rise to be sovereign of all the islands. Kamehameha invited him to the dedication ceremony, but en route Keoua, in preparation for an inevitable outcome, performed a death purification ceremony by circumcizing his own penis. When his canoes came into view, they were met by a hail of spears and musket balls. Keoua's body was carried to Kukailimoku's altar and Kamehameha was the unopposed sovereign of the Big Island, and within a few years of all of Hawaii. Nearby is the house site of John Young, an English seaman who became a close adviser to Kamehameha, who dubbed him Olohana, "All Hands." Young taught the Hawaiians how to use cannon and musket and fought alongside Kamehameha in many battles. He turned *Mailekini Heiau* into a fort, which was again used over a century later during WW II by the Army as an observation area. Young became a respected Hawaiian chief, and grandfather of Queen Emma. He's one of only two white men buried at the Royal Mausoleum in Nuuanu Valley on Oahu.

Kawaihae Town

The port marks the northern end of the South Kohala coast. Here Rt. 19 turns eastward toward Waimea, or turns into Rt. 270 heading up the coast into North Kohala. Kawaihae Town is basically utilitarian with wharfs and fuel tanks. A service-cluster has a shop or two, and the Harbor Hut, the one and only reasonably priced restaurant in the vicinity (see p. 635).

BEACHES, PARKS, AND CAMPGROUNDS

Anaehoomalu Bay

After becoming transfixed by the monochromed, blackness of Kohala's lava flows for almost 30 miles, a stand-out green of palm trees beckons in the distance. Between mile markers 76 and 77, a well-marked access road heads *makai* to the Royal Waikoloa Hotel and historic **Anaehoomalu Bay.** The bay area, with its freshwater springs, coconut trees, blue lagoon, and white-sand beach is a picture-perfect seaside oasis. Between the large coconut grove and the beach are 2 well-preserved fishponds where mullet was raised *only* for consumption by the royalty that lived nearby, or those happening by in seagoing canoes. Throughout the area along well-marked trails are **petroglyphs,** a segment of the cobblestone **King's High-**

Kauna'oa Beach, the best on the South Kohala Coast

way, and numerous archaeological sites including house sites and some hard-to-find burial caves. The white-sand beach is open to the public with access, parking, picnic tables, and showers at the south end. Although the sand is a bit grainy, the swimming, snorkeling, scuba, and windsurfing are fine. Walking north along the bay brings you to an area of excellent tide pools with waters heavily populated by marinelife. The next beach north is at Puako (see p. 630).

Hapuna Beach State Park

Approximately 12 miles north of Anaehoomalu is the *second* best, but the *most* accessible white-sand beach on the island. (The best, Kaunaoa, is listed next.) **Camping** is offered in 6 A-frame screened shelters that rent for $7 per night and accommodate up to 4. Provided are sleeping platforms (no bedding), electric outlets, cold-water showers, and toilets in separate comfort stations, and a shared range and refrigerator in a central pavilion. Check in at 2:00 p.m., check out 10:00 a.m. Very popular so reserve, deposit required. Receive full information by contacting Division of State Parks, Box 936 (75 Aupuni St. to pick up key on arrival), Hilo, HI 96720, tel. 961-7200. There is unofficial camping south along **Waialea Bay** that you can get to by walking or taking a turnoff at mile marker 69. Hapuna Beach is wide and spacious, almost 700 yards long by 70 wide in summer, with a reduction by heavy surf in winter. A lava finger divides the beach into almost equal halves. During good weather the swimming is excellent, but a controversy rages because there is no lifeguard. During heavy weather, usually in winter, the rips are fierce, and Hapuna has claimed more lives than any other beach park on all of Hawaii! At the north end is a small cove almost forming a pool that is always safe, a favorite with families and children. Many classes in beginning scuba and snorkeling are given in this area, and shore-fishing is good throughout. At the south end good breaks make for tremendous bodysurfing (no boards allowed), and those familiar with the area make spectacular leaps from the sea cliffs.

Kauna'oa Beach

Better known as **Mauna Kea Beach** because of the nearby luxury hotel of the same name, is less than a mile north of Hapuna Beach and is considered to be the best beach on the Big Island. In times past, it was a nesting and mating ground for green sea turtles, and although these activities no longer occur because of human pressure on the habitat, turtles still visit the south end of the beach. Mauna Kea Beach is long and wide, and the sandy bottom makes for excellent swimming. It is more sheltered than Hapuna, but can still be dangerous. Hotel beach boys, always in attendance, are unofficial lifeguards who have saved many unsuspecting tourists. During high surf, the shoreline is a favorite with surfers. All beaches in Hawaii are public, but *access* to this beach was won only by a lawsuit against the

Mauna Kea Beach Hotel in 1973. The ruling forced the hotel to open the beach to the public, which they did in the form of 10 parking spaces, a right of way, and public shower, and toilet facilities. To keep the number of non-guests down, only 10 **parking passes** are handed out each day on a first-come first-served basis. Pick them up at the guard house as you enter the hotel grounds. These entitle you to spend the day on the beach, but on weekends they're gone by 9:30 a.m. You can wait for someone to leave and then get the pass, but that's unreliable. The hotel also issues a pass for a one-hour visit to the hotel grounds (overstaying is a $10 fine). You can use this pass to drop off family, friends, beach paraphernalia, and picnic supplies, then use an easy mile-long **nature trail** connecting Hapuna and Mauna Kea beaches, which is used by the majority of people unable to get a pass. Also, the hotel issues a "Food and Drink" pass that entitles you to stay as long as you wish, if you get it validated at one of the restaurants or snack bars. So as long as you're in there, you might as well use the beach for the price of a soft drink. In time the hotel will catch on, so test the waters before winding up with a fine.

Spencer County Beach Park

Look for the entrance a minute or two past Puukohola Heiau on Rt. 19 just before entering Kawaihae. Trails lead from the beach park up to the *heiau,* so you can combine a day at the beach with a cultural education. The park is named after Samuel Mahuka Spencer, a long time island resident who was born in Waimea, served as county mayor for 20 years, and died in 1960 at Honokaa. The park provides pavilions, restrooms, cold-water showers, electricity, picnic facilities, and even tennis courts. Day use is free, but tent and trailer **camping** is by county permit only, at $1 per day (see p.541). Spencer Beach is protected from wind and heavy wave action by an offshore reef and by breakwaters built around Kawaihae Port. This makes it the safest and best swimming beach along South Kohala's shore and a favorite with local families with small children. The wide shallow reef is home to a wide spectrum of marinelife, making the snorkeling easy and excellent. The shoreline fishing is also excellent.

ACCOMMODATIONS, FOOD, AND SHOPPING

Except for a few community-oriented restaurants in Waikoloa Village, and the reasonably priced Harbor Hut, a roadside restaurant in Kawaihae, all of the food in South Kohala is served in the elegant but expensive restaurants of the luxury hotels. These hotels also provide the **entertainment** along the coast, mostly in the form of quiet musical combos and dinner shows. The **shopping,** too, is in the exclusive boutiques found in the hotel lobbies and mini-malls. The following hotels lie along coastal Rt. 19 and are listed from south to north.

Kona Village Resort

So you want to go "native," and you'r dreaming of a "little grass shack" along a secluded beach? No problem! Just as long as you have about $300 a day to spend, give or take $100. The **Kona Village Resort** is a once-in-a-lifetime dream experience. Located on Kaupulehu Bay, a picture-perfect cove of white sand dotted with coconut palms, the village lies 15 miles north of Kailua-Kona, surrounded by 12,000 open acres promising seclusion. The accommodations, called "beachcomber hales," are individual renditions of thatch-roofed huts found throughout Polynesia. They are simple but luxurious, and in keeping with the idea of getting away from it all have no TVs, radios, or telephones. At one time you had to fly into the hotel's private airstrip, but today you can arrive by car. The resort gives you your money's worth, with tennis, ping pong, *lei* greetings, water sports, and a variety of cocktail parties and *luau.* Guided tours are also offered to the many historic sites in the area. Prices go $197-352 s, $265-395, which includes a full American Plan (3 meals). There is a strict reservations and refund policy, so check. For information, contact Kona Village Resort, Box 1299, Kailua-Kona, HI 96740, tel. 325-5555 or 800-367-5290.

Sheraton Royal Waikoloa Hotel

The Sheraton chain wanted to enter the luxury hotel market with a splash, and in 1981 opened the $70 million, 543 room Sheraton Royal Waikoloa Hotel. They found the perfect spot (off Rt. 19 between mile markers 77 and 78) at Anaehoomalu Bay, and produced a class act. The hotel lobby is a spacious open-air affair, beautifully appointed in *koa* with *objets d'art* tastefully displayed here and there. All rooms are tastefully decorated and provide a/c, color TV, king-size beds, and private lanai. Rates begin at $80-160 s/d for a standard, to $225 for a cabana and $310 for a suite, $15 additional person. The Sheraton offers a special 50% rate reduction from mid-May to mid-September. For reservations write Sheraton Royal Waikoloa, Box 5000, Waikoloa, HI 96743, tel. 885-6789, Mainland, tel. 800-325-3535, Canada tel. 800-268-9330. On the superbly kept grounds are 6 tennis courts, numerous ponds, and a swimming pool. Special features include a small shopping arcade with a dozen or so choice shops, horseback riding, and free shuttle service to Kailua-Kona. There's even a helicopter pad. The focal points, however, are 2 marvelous golf courses designed by Robert Trent Jones Jr. He learned his trade from his dad, whose masterpiece is just up the road at the Mauna Kea Resort.

You have a choice of dining facilities. The **Garden Room** features American cuisine, open daily for breakfast, lunch, and dinner. The atmosphere is relaxed and the prices are affordable for such a hotel. **The Tiare** offers elegant dining in elegant surroundings for elegant prices. The Continental cuisine includes shrimp novelle, rack of lamb, lobster, and roast duckling served to the melodious notes of a jazz trio. Open Wed. to Sun. 6:30-10:00 p.m., tel. 885-6789, reservations recommended. The **Royal Terrace** opens its doors to the sea and provides island or western entertainment with dinner daily from 6:30-10:30 p.m. Featured are seafood, catch-of-the-day, and prime rib. Expensive.

The Westin Mauna Kea

This hotel has set the standard of excellence along Kohala's coast ever since former Hawaii Governor William Quinn interested Lawrence Rockefeller in the lucrative possibilities of building a luxury hideaway for the rich and famous. Beautiful coastal land was leased from the Parker Ranch, and the resort opened in 1965. The Mauna Kea was the only one of its kind for a few years until the other luxury hotels were built along this coast. It's getting a bit older, and getting some stiff competition from the nearby luxury hotels, but class is always class, and it still receives very high accolades as a resort.

The hotel's classic, trend-setting **golf course** by the master, Robert Trent Jones, has been voted among America's 100 greatest courses and as Hawaii's finest. Also, *Tennis Magazine* chose the hotel as among the "50 greatest U.S. tennis resorts." The hotel itself is an 8-story terraced complex of simple, clean-cut design. The

the Westin Mauna Kea, an enclave of class and elegance along the Kohala coast

grounds and lobbies showcase over 1,600 museum-quality art pieces from throughout the Pacific, and over a half million plants add greenery and beauty to the surroundings. The landings and lobbies, open and large enough to hold full-grown palm trees, also display beautiful tapestries, bird cages with their singing captives, and huge copper pots on polished brick floors. The Mauna Kea offers a modified American Plan, European Plan (mid-April-mid-Dec.), the best beach on the island, and its own catamaran for seagoing adventure. The hotel has become such a landmark that tour buses visit its grounds daily. There are million dollar condos on the grounds and guests tend to come back year after year. There's no charge for looking. The beautifully appointed rooms, starting at $198 E.P.d, to $378 A.P.d, are free of TVs, but feature an extra-large *lanai,* and specially made wicker furniture. For full information contact Westin Mauna Kea, Box 218, Kamuela, HI 96743, tel. 882-7222 or 800-227-3000.

Sumptuous dining is presented in the 3-level **Dining Pavilion,** and in the **Batik Room,** where French, Island, Italian, and German delicacies create a international gastronomical symphony. There's also a weekly *luau* in the North Garden.

Mauna Lani Resort And Golf Club
Marvel at this exclusive hotel in the center of the gorgeous **Francis I'i Brown Golf Course,** whose artistically laid-out fairways, greens, and sand traps makes it a modern landscape sculpture. The course is carved from lava with striking ocean views in every direction. It's not a tough course, though it measures 6,813 yards, par 72. Green fees are expensive, with preferred starting times given to hotel guests. Call the Pro Shop at 882-7255. As soon as you turn off Rt. 19, the entrance road, trimmed in purple bougainvillea, begins to set the mood for this $70 million, 350-room hotel that opened in 1983. The emphasis was placed on relaxation and luxury, as each oversized room, the majority with an ocean view, cost an average of $200,000 each, the most ever spent per unit in Hawaii. The hotel has a tennis garden with 10 courts, a lovely beach and lagoon area, a health spa, exclusive shops, and swimming pools. The Mauna Lani's rooms begin at $195. For full information contact Mauna Lani Bay Hotel, Box 4000, Kawaihae HI, 96743, tel. 885-6622 or 800-367-2323, in Hawaii tel. 800-992-7987.

The **Third Floor Restaurant** (actually on the ground floor) is patterned after the gourmet restaurant of the same name in Waikiki, and its imaginative French cuisine is *magnifique,* along with the prices. You can dine from a noteworthy menu at slightly lower prices at the **Bay Terrace.** A superb shop owned by Herman Miller, named **HFM** is just off the main lobby. Mr. Miller has been a collector of Chinese art since the '30s, and displayed here are museum-quality pieces from his personal collection. Mr. Miller also showcases the woodwork of Billy Parks, a former pro football player who has turned his hand to creating exquisite Oriental furniture. All pieces are handmade and connected by traditional intricate joinery.

Puako Beach Apartments
Puako Village has the only reasonably priced accommodations in this diamond-studded neck of the woods. The 38 modern units start from $50 to $120 (4 bedrooms), $5 extra person. All units have a kitchen, laundry facilities, *lanai,* and twice-weekly maid service. There is ample parking, TV, and a swimming pool. Write Puako Beach Apartment, 3 Puako Beach Dr., Kamuela, HI 96743, tel. 882-7711.

Harbor Hut Restaurant
Located in Kawaihae, on the right-hand side of Rt. 270 heading north, this restaurant serves everything from take-out sandwiches for a few dollars to sit-down dinners for not much more. The garden out back, with umbrella-covered tables and the bows of old boats for atmosphere, is a relaxing place to dine especially after a sunny day on the beach. Here you can enjoy the catch of the day or *mahi mahi* for about $5. The service is friendly but slow. The Harbor Hut is open daily 6:30 a.m. to 9:00 p.m., tel. 882-7783.

WAIMEA (KAMUELA)

Boundary-wise, **Waimea** is in South Kohala. Because of its inland topography of high mountain pasture, mostly covering Mauna Kea's western slopes, it could be considered a district in its own right. Also, it has a unique culture inspired by the range-riding *paniolo* of the expansive **Parker Ranch.** This spread, founded early last century by John Palmer Parker, dominates the heart and soul of the region. Waimea revolves around ranch life and livestock. A herd of rodeos and "wild west shows" are scheduled throughout the year. But a visit here isn't one-dimensional. In town are home accommodations and inspired country dining. For fun and relaxation there's a Visitor and Ranch Center, a wonderful museum operated by John Parker's great-great grandaughter and her husband, a litany of historic shrines and churches, and a fresh-air abundance of wide open spaces not so easily found in the islands. The town is split almost directly down the center—the east side is the wet side, and the west is the dry side. Houses on the east side are easy to find and reasonable to rent; houses on the dry side are expensive and usually unavailable. You can literally walk from verdant green fields and tall trees to dry desert in a matter of minutes. This imaginary line also demarcates the local twofold social order: upper-class ranch managers (dry), and working class *paniolo* (wet). However, the air of Waimea, refreshed and cooled by fine mists *(kipuupuu)* combines with only 20 inches of rainfall a year into the best mountain weather in Hawaii. Waimea is equally known as **Kamuela,** the Hawaiianized version of Samuel, after one of John Parker's grandsons. Kamuela is used as the post office address, so as not to confuse Waimea with a town of the same name on the island of Kauai.

Getting There

The main artery connecting Waimea and Kailua-Kona is Rt. 190, also known as the Hawaiian Belt Road. This stretch is locally called the Mamalahoa Highway. From Kailua-Kona, head out Palani Road until it turns into Route 190. As you gain elevation heading into the interior, look left to see the broad and flat coastal lava flows. Seven miles before reaching Waimea, Saddle Road (Rt. 200) intersects from the right, and now the highlands, with grazing cattle amidst fields of cactus, look much more like Marlboro Country than the land of *aloha.* The Saddle Road and Rt. 19, connecting Waimea with Hilo and points east, have been fully described on p. 565. The **Waimea-Kohala Airport,** tel. 885-4520, is along Rt. 190 just a mile or so before entering town. Facilities are a basic restroom and waiting area with a few car rental windows. Unless a flight is scheduled, even these are closed.

Route 250, the back road to Hawi, is a delightful country lane that winds through glorious green grazing lands for almost 20 miles along the leeward side of the Kohala Mountains. It begins in the western outskirts of Waimea and ends in Hawi on the far north coast. One of the most picturesque roads on the island, it's dotted with mood-setting cactus and small "line shacks." Suddenly vistas open to your left, and far below are expansive panoramas of rolling hills tumbling to the sea. At mile marker 8, is **Von Holt Memorial Park,** a scenic overlook perfect for a high mountain picnic. Past here at mile marker 13 is **Ironwood Outfitters,** a horse ranch and riding stable owned and operated by Judy Ellis. Trail rides with Ms. Ellis through this upland *paniolo* country are among the best that you can find on the island (see p. 548).

SIGHTS

Parker Ranch Visitors Center And Museum

This is the first place to stop. It's open daily (except Sundays and most holidays) from 9:30 a.m. until 3:30 p.m., tel. 885-7655, adults $2.25. After spending an hour at the center's 2 museums and taking in the slide presentation, you'll have a good overview of the history of the Parker Ranch, and therefore Waimea. The **John Palmer Parker Museum's** exhibits depict the history and genealogy of the 6 generations of Parkers who have owned the ranch. At the entrance is a photo of the founder, John Parker, a seaman who left Newton, Massachusetts, on a trading vessel in 1809, and landed in Kealakekua, becoming a fast friend of Kamehameha the Great. Parker, then only 19, continued his voyages, returning in 1814 and marrying Kipikane, a chieftess and close relative of Kamehameha. In the interim, domesticated cattle, a present from Capt. Vancouver to Kamehameha, had gone wild due to neglect, and were becoming a dangerous nuisance all over the Big Island. Parker was hired to round up the best and to exterminate the rest of these cattle. While doing so, he chose the finest head for his own herd. In 1847 King Kamehameha III divided the land by what was known as the *Great Mahele,* and John Parker was granted Royal Deed No. 7, for a 2-acre parcel on the northeast slopes of Mauna Kea. His wife, being noble born, was entitled to 640 acres, and with these lands and tough determination, the mighty 225,000-acre Parker Ranch began. It remains the largest privately owned ranch in the U.S., and on its fertile pastures over 50,000 cattle and 1,000 horses are raised.

In the museum old family photos include one of Rev. Elias Bond who presided over a Christian marriage for Parker and his Hawaiian wife in 1820. Preserved also are old Bibles, clothing from the era, and an entire *koa* hut once occupied by woodcutters and range riders. There're fine examples of quilting, stuffed animals, an arsenal of old weapons, and even a vintage printing press. A separate room is dedicated to **Duke Kahanamoku,** the great Hawaiian Olympian and "Father of Modern Surfing." Inside are paddles he used, his bed and dresser, legions of medals, cups, and trophies he won, and even Duke's walking sticks. The 15-minute slide presentation in the comfortable **Thelma Parker Theater** begins whenever enough people have assembled after going through the museums. The slides present a thorough and professional rendition of the Parker Ranch history, along with sensitive glimpses of ranch life of the still very active *paniolo.* The last line of the narration says, "When you can grasp that one of the cowboys here is named Irving Ching, only then can you understand the Parker Ranch."

Imiola Church

Head east on Rt. 19 to "church row," a cluster of New England-style structures on the left, a few minutes past the Parker Ranch Center. Most famous among them is Imiola ("Seeking Life") Church. It was built in 1857 by the Rev.

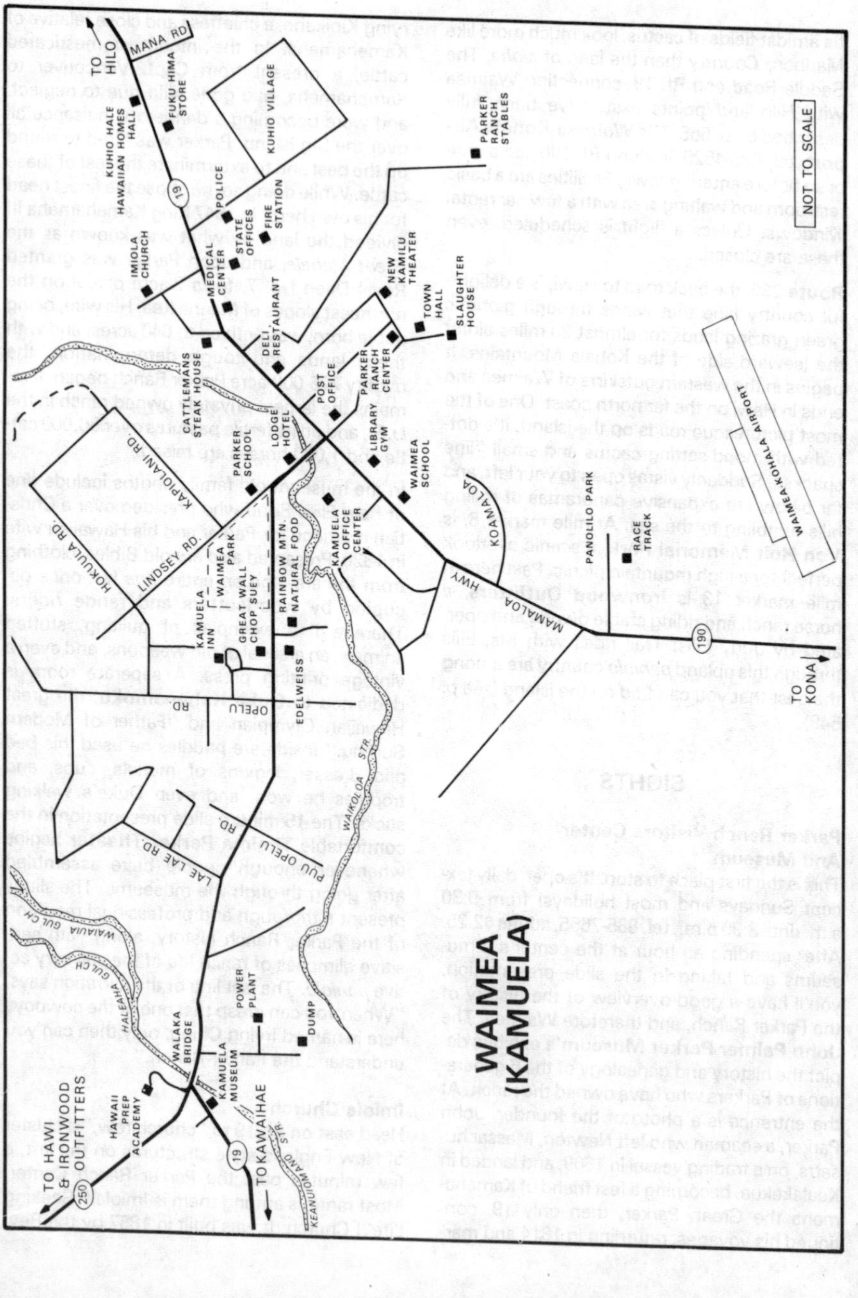
WAIMEA
(KAMUELA)
NOT TO SCALE
TO HILO
MANA RD
KUHIO HALE HAWAIIAN HOMES HALL
FUKU HIMA STORE
KUHIO VILLAGE
PARKER RANCH STABLES
19
POLICE
FIRE STATION
STATE OFFICES
IMIOLA CHURCH
MEDICAL CENTER
NEW KAMILU THEATER
TOWN HALL
SLAUGHTER HOUSE
DELI RESTAURANT
CATTLEMANS STEAK HOUSE
POST OFFICE
PARKER RANCH CENTER
LIBRARY GYM
LODGE HOTEL
KAPIOLANI RD
PARKER SCHOOL
WAIMEA SCHOOL
KOANALOA
WAIMEA-KOHALA AIRPORT
HOKUULA RD
LINDSEY RD
WAIMEA PARK
KAMUELA INN
GREAT WALL CHOP SUEY
RAINBOW MTN. NATURAL FOOD
KAMUELA OFFICE CENTER
PANOLILO PARK
RACE TRACK
MAMALOA HWY
190
TO KONA
EDELWEISS
OPELU RD
LAE LAE RD
PUU OPELU RD
WAIKOLOA STR
WAIAUIA GUL CH
HALEAHA GUL CH
POWER PLANT
DUMP
WALAKA BRIDGE
KAMUELA MUSEUM
HAWAII PREP ACADEMY
TO HAWI & IRONWOOD OUTFITTERS
250
19
TO KAWAIHAE
KEANUIOMANO STR

Lorenzo Lyons, who mastered the Hawaiian language and translated some of the great old Christian hymns into Hawaiian, as well as melodic Hawaiian chants into English. The current minister is a friendly and urbane man, Rev. Bill Hawk, a new arrival, who is assisted by his wife Sandra. The yellow clapboard church with white trim would be at home along any New England village green. When you enter, there is an oddity: the pulpit is at the near side and you walk around it to face the rear of the church. The walls and ceilings are of rich brown *koa,* but the pews, supposedly of the same lustrous wood, have been painted pink! The hymnals contain many of the songs translated by Father Lyons. Outside is a simple monument to Rev. Lyons, along with a number of gravesites of his children. A tour of the church is free, and definitely worth a quick visit.

Kamuela Museum
The Kamuela Museum, largest privately owned museum in Hawaii, is a fantastic labor of love. For the septuagenarian owners, founders, and curators, Albert and Harriet Solomon, it's a vocation that began in 1968 and fulfilled a prophecy of Albert's grandmother who was pure Hawaiian and a renowned *kahuna* from Pololu Valley. When Albert was only 8 years old, his grandmother foretold that he would build "a great longhouse near 3 mountains, and that he would become famous, visited by people from all over the world." This prediction struck him so much that he wrote it down although only 8 years old and kept it throughout his life. When grown, he married Harriet, the great-great granddaughter of John Palmer Parker, and the 2 lived in Honolulu for most of their adult lives, where Albert was a policeman. For 50 years the Solomon's collected, collected, and collected! Also Harriet, being a Parker, inherited many family heirlooms from the Ranch, while other family members gave her items to exhibit. The museum is west of town center on Rt. 19–50 yards after the junction with Rt. 250 heading toward Hawi. An HVB Warrior, facing in the wrong direction, marks the spot. The museum, dedicated to Mary Ann Parker, John Parker's only daughter, is open every day of the year from 8:00 a.m. to 5:00 p.m., tel. 885-4724, admission $2, children under 12, $1.00.

As you enter, the screen door purposefully bangs like a shot to signal Albert and Harriet that another visitor has arrived. Mrs. Solomon directs you through the museum, almost like a stern "schoolmarm" who knows what's best for you, but actually she's a sweetheart who has plenty of time for her guests and is willing to "talk story." Inside it's easy to become overwhelmed as you're confronted with everything from sombreros to a stuffed albatross, moose head, and South American lizard. An extensive weapons collection includes Khyber rifles,

Mrs. Harriet Solomon, curator of the Kamuela Museum

Japanese machine guns, swords, and knives. If you enjoy Hawaiiana, there's *kahili, konane* boards, *poi* pounders, stone sinkers and hooks, wooden surfboards, and heavy stones, like bowling balls, used to test strength. Antiques of every description include Japanese and Hawaiian feathered fans, carved Chinese furniture, an antique brass diving helmet, and even buffalo robes used by the pioneers. And everywhere are old photos commemorating the lives of the Parkers down through the years. Before you leave go into the back room where the view through a huge picture window perfectly frames a pond and a remarkable slice of *paniolo* country.

PRACTICALITIES

Accommodations

As far as staying in Waimea is concerned, you won't be plagued with indecision. Of the 2 hotels in town, both are basic and clean, one inexpensive and the other upscale.

Kamuela Inn is your basic cinderblock, 19-unit motel located down a small cul-de-sac on Rt. 19 just before Opelu Road. Quiet clean rooms with a large bath go for $20 s, $26 d, $35 with kitchenette. If no one is at the office, go to room 8. There is usually no problem finding a vacancy. Write Kamuela Inn, Box 1994, Kamuela, HI 96743, tel. 885-4516.

The Parker Ranch Lodge is located along Linsey Road in "downtown" Waimea, but don't let "downtown" fool you because it's very quiet. The rooms are called junior suites, and all have kitchenettes, vaulted ceilings, and full baths. The suites are well appointed with rich brown carpeting, large writing desks, 2 easy chairs, phones, and TVs. The brown board and batten inn sits off by itself and lives up to being in *paniolo* country by giving the impression of being a gentleman's bunkhouse. Rates are $36 s, $42 d, $7 additional person. For information write Parker Ranch Lodge, Box 458, Kamuela, HI 96743, tel. 885-4100.

Food

One of the cheapest places in Waimea to get good standard American food is at the **Kamuela Drive In Deli.** This no-nonsense eatery, frequented by local people, is next door to the Parker Ranch Center. They get the folks in these parts started at 5:00 a.m. with a hearty breakfast for a few dollars. Plate lunches of teriyaki beef and the like sell for $2.50 to $3.00. If you're into food and not atmosphere, this is the place.

Massayo's is another basic eatery open daily 5:00 a.m. to 3:00 p.m., where you can get hearty breakfasts and plate lunches with an Oriental twist for $2 to $3. It's in the Hayashi Building near the Kamuela Inn. If you've got a hankerin' for pizza, cowpoke, try **Wild Horse Pizza** opposite the fire station. They're open for lunch Mon. to Sat. 11:00 a.m. to 2:00 p.m., for dinner Mon. to Thurs. 5:00-9:00 p.m., Fri. to Sat. 5:00-11:00 p.m., tel. 885-4794. Besides pizzas and full meals they serve quality soups and sandwiches at affordable prices. **Homer's U.S. Meal Service** is on Rt. 19 heading east toward Hilo. This is another spanking clean, down-home place with rather a different variety of items on a self-service menu. Specialties include vegie subs and a "Buffalo Bill," a combination of roast beef, melted cheese, sprouts, and special horseradish sauce. There's homemade honey lemonade, and a gourmet choice of desserts including cheesecakes and cream pies. Easy on the wallet. Open Mon. to Sat. 10:00 a.m. to 4:00 p.m., tel. 885-7411.

The best inexpensive place to eat in Waimea is at **Rainbow Mountain Natural Foods.** However, since this is primarily a natural foods co-op, you'll have to be content eating your lunch sitting on an old orange crate out on the veranda. The hearty menu includes hefty tofu salad subs for $2.75, vegie burgers $3, savory soups including *miso* for $1.25, and pizza, burritos, chapatis, and fresh garden salads all for around $3. Every day a different ethnically inspired full meal is served for $4.50, and there is a juice bar and mouth-watering bakery items. Open daily 9:00 a.m. to 7:00 p.m., kitchen closes at 6:30 p.m., tel. 885-7202.

For mid-range fare try **Great Wall Chop Suey** near the Kamuela Inn. Its appealing selection of standard Chinese dishes costs from $3 to $5. This restaurant is open Tues. to Thurs. 11:00 a.m. to 8:30 p.m., Fri. to Sun. 11:00 a.m. to 9:00 p.m., closed Mon., tel. 885-7252.

a modern paniolo *of the Parker Ranch*

The Edelweiss is Waimea's newest restaurant, and chef Hans-Peter Hager, formerly of the super-exclusive Mauna Kea Beach Hotel serves gourmet food in rustic but elegant surroundings. Inside heavy posts and beams exude that "country feeling," but fine crystal and pure-white tablecloths let you know you're in for some superb dining. The wine cellar is quite extensive with selections of domestic, French, Italian, and German wines. The Continental menu is rich with escargot, filet mignon, weinerschnitzel, and basic German fare such as pork with sauerkraut. Prices are "reasonably expensive," with more affordable lunches like soup, turkey sandwiches, and chicken salad in papaya for under $5. The Edelweiss is open daily except Mon. from 11:30 a.m. to 2:00 p.m. and for dinner from 5:30 p.m., tel. 885-6800. On Rt. 19 across from the Kamuela Inn.

The fanciest place in Waimea is **The Parker Ranch Broiler,** in the Parker Ranch Center. Put on your best duds and sashay into the cushy red velvet saloon, or into the tasteful *koa*-panelled main dining area. The chef, Al Salvador, chooses the best cuts of "Parker Ranch beef," a variety of savory meat dishes from $11. There's also clam chowder for $2.75, steak sandwiches for $7.50, *Paniolo* burgers $3.95, Korean short ribs $4.95, grilled cheese sandwich $2.45, and spinach salad $3.95. Even if you don't dine here, it's worth a trip to the bar just for the atmosphere. Open daily for lunch and dinner, tel. 885-7366; also in the Ranch Center are 2 bakeries and an ice cream shop.

Shopping, Services, And Information

There is shopping in and around town, but the greatest concentration of shops is at the Parker Ranch Center, with over 30 specialty stores. The **Paddock Shop** sells boots, cowboy hats, shirts, skirts, and buckles and bows. There are many handcrafted items made on the premises. Open daily, tel. 885-4977. **Setay,** a unique fine jewelry shop sells china, crystal, silver, and gold, tel. 885-4127. **Upcountry Downunder** features imported woolen goods and toys from New Zealand, tel. 885-4229.

Around town try: **Waimea Design Center** offering Oriental handicrafts and Hawaiian *koa* bowls and furniture, tel. 885-6171, along Rt. 19; **Waimea Sand Box** where you'll find books, handmade baskets, *koa* artifacts, and maps, tel. 885-4737, on Rt. 19; **Suzumi** selling fine women's apparel with imports from around the world, at the Ironwood Center, Rt. 19, tel. 885-6422. **The Warehouse,** a small shopping complex, whose specialty shops sell books, coffees, spices, flowers, and alohawear, tel. 885-7905. **Nikko Natural Fabrics** will dress you in cottons, woolens, and silks, and adorn your walls with batiks and fine fiber arts, tel. 885-7661, in the Kamuela Country Plaza.

For **food shopping** at the Parker Ranch Center there's the **Sure Save Supermarket,** the

Kamuela Meat Market featuring fine cuts of Parker Ranch beef, and **Big Island Natural Foods** selling snacks, sundries, lotions, potions, notions, and coffee. West on Rt. 19 stop at the excellent **Rainbow Mountain Natural Foods**, tel. 885-7202, for a full service natural foods co-op (see p. 640).

There ain't much happening around the old town entertainment-wise, but **free *hula* lessons** are given at the Parker Ranch center on Mon. afternoons. You can soak up local color at the **Ben Franklin's** at the Ranch Center where locals like to congregate. The **bulletin board** at Rainbow Mountain Natural Foods is a storehouse of local information. The **Paniola Press** is a free paper with local feature stories and ads; available around town.

Police can be reached at tel. 885-7334, and **ambulance and fire** is tel. 961-6022. **Physicians** are available at Lucy Henriques Medical Center, tel. 885-7921. A chiropractor in town is Frederick Chard, tel. 885-4440. Angela Longo is a practitioner of **acupuncture** and a Chinese herbalist, tel. 885-7886 (see p. XXX). Richard Leibman is a naturopathic physician, tel. 885-4611. The **Chock Inn Launderette** is west on Rt. 19 at tel. 885-4655.

NORTH KOHALA

North Kohala was the home of Kamehameha the Great. From this fiefdom he launched the conquest of all the islands. The shores and lands of North Kohala are rife with historical significance, and with beach parks where no one but a few local people ever go. Here cattle were introduced to the islands in the 1790s by Capt. Vancouver, an early explorer and friend of Kamehameha. Among North Kohala's cultural treasures are **Lapakahi State Historical Park,** a must stop, that offers "touchable" exhibits where you can become actively involved in Hawaii's traditional past and ***Pu'u Koha Heiau,*** the last great traditional temple built in Hawaii. Northward is the very place of **Kamehameha's birth,** and within walking distance is **Mookini Heiau,** one of the oldest in Hawaii and still actively ministered by the current generation of a long line of *kahuna.* **Hawi** comes next, a sugar town whose economy recently turned sour when the sugar company drastically cut back its local operations. Hawi is making a comeback, along with this entire northern shore, which has seen an influx of small boutique-like businesses and art shops. In **Kapaau** a statue of Kamehameha I peering over the chief's ancestral dominions fulfills an old *kahuna* prophecy. On a nearby side road is historic **Kalahikiola Church,** established in 1855 by Rev. Elias Bond. On the same side road is the old **Bond Homestead,** the most authentic yet virtually unvisited missionary home in all of Hawaii. Financially strapped, but lovingly tended by the remaining members of the Bond family, it's on the National Historical Record, and even rents *the* cheapest rooms on all of the Big Island. The main coastal road ends at **Pololu Valley Lookout,** a premiere *taro* valley of old Hawaii. A walk down the steep *pali* into this valley is a walk into timelessness with civilization disappearing like an ebbing tide.

Getting There

In Kawaihae, at the base of the North Kohala peninsula, Rt. 19 turns east and coastal Rt. 270, known as the Akoni Pule Highway, heads north along the coast. It passes through both of North Kohala's 2 major towns, Hawi and Kapaau, and ends at the *pali* overlooking Pololu Valley. All the historical sites, beach parks, and towns in the following sections are along this route, listed from south to north.

Upolu Airport, tel. 889-9958, is a lonely strip at Upolu Point, the closest spot to Maui. A sign points the way at mile marker 20 along coastal Rt. 270. Here, you'll find only a bench and a public telephone. The strip is serviced only on request by the small propeller planes of charter and commuter airlines.

SIGHTS, BEACHES, AND TOWNS

Lapakahi State Historical Park

This 600-year-old reconstructed Hawaiian fishing village, combined with adjacent **Koai'e Cove Marine Conservation District**, is a stand-out hunk of coastline 12 miles north of Kawaihae. Gates are open daily from 8:00 a.m. to 4:00 p.m., when park guides are in attendance. Sometimes, especially on weekends, they take the day off, and it's OK to park outside the gate and take the self-guided tour, although the knowlegeable anecdotes of the guides make the tour much more educational. As you enter, the small grass shack near some *lahala* trees stocks annotated brochures, and yellow water jugs. As you walk counterclockwise around the numbered stations, you pass canoe sheds, and a fish shrine dedicated to *Ku'ula,* to whom the fishermen always dedicated a portion of their catch. A salt-making area demonstrates how the Hawaiians evaporated sea water by moving it into progressively smaller "pans" carved in the rock. There are numerous homesites along the wood-chip trail. Particularly interesting to children are exhibits of games like *konane* (Hawaiian checkers), and *ulimika,* a form of bowling using stones that the children are encouraged to try. Throughout the area, all trees, flowers, and shrubs are identified, and as an extra treat, migrating whales come close to shore from December through April. Don't leave without finding a shady spot and taking the time to look out to sea. For information write Lapakahi State Park, Box 100, Kapaau, HI 96755, tel. 889-5566.

local school children trying their hand at Hawaiian games

Mahukona And Kapaa Beach Parks

Mahukona County Beach Park is a few minutes north of Lapakahi down a well-marked side road. As you approach, notice a number of abandoned buildings and warehouses left standing from when Mahukona was an important port from which the Kohala Sugar Co. shipped its goods. Still existing is a pier with a hoist used by local fishermen to launch their boats. The harbor is filled with industrial debris which makes for some good underwater exploring, and snorkeling the offshore reef is rewarded with an abundance of sealife. Swimming off the pier is also good, but all water activities are dangerous during winter months and high surf. Picnic facilities include a large pavilion and tables, with a large green tank holding the drinking water. There are also cold-water showers and restrooms, with electricity available in the pavilion. Although numerous signs close to the pavilion say "No Camping," both tent and trailer camping is allowed with a county permit near the parking lot.

Kapaa Beach Park is 5 minutes farther north. Turn *makai* on a side road and cross a cattle grate as you head toward the sea. This park is even less visited than Mahukona. The rocky beach makes water entry difficult. It's primarily for day use and fishing, but there are showers, a restroom and a pavilion. Camping is allowed with a county permit. Neither of these 2 beaches is spectacular, but they are secluded with easy access. If you're interested in a very quiet spot to contemplate a lovely panorama of Maui in the distance, this is it.

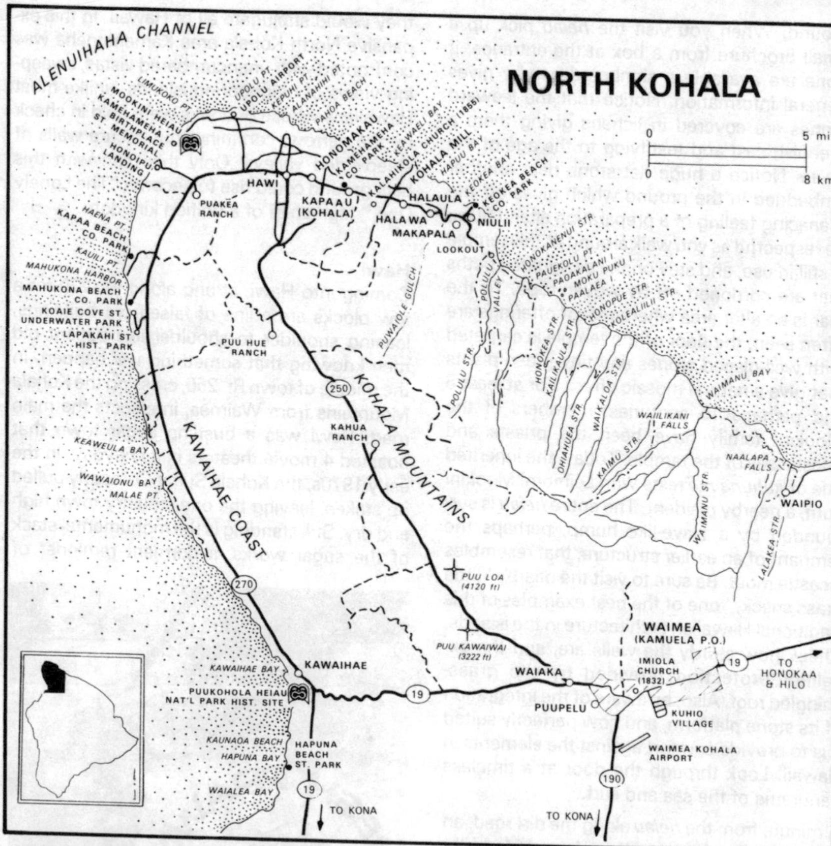

Mookini Luakini Heiau And Kamehameha's Birthplace

At mile marker 20 turn down a one-lane road to Upolu Airport. Follow it past 3 large silos until it reaches the end of the runway. Turn left on an improved dirt road for 2 miles to *Mookini Luakini Heiau.* This entire area is one of the most rugged and isolated on the Big Island, with wide windswept fields, steep sea cliffs, and pounding surf. Only *ali'i* came here to purify themselves and worship, sometimes offering human sacrifices. In 1963, *Mookini Heiau* was the first Hawaiian site to be listed in the National Historical Sites Registry. Legend says that the very first temple at Mookini was built as early as 480 A.D. This incredible date implies that Mookini must have been built immediately upon the arrival of the first Polynesian explorers, who many scholars maintain arrived in large numbers a full 2 centuries later. More believable oral history relates that the still-standing foundation of the temple was built by the Tahitian high-priest Paao, who came with conquering warriors from the south in the 12th C., bringing the powerful *mana* of the fierce war-god Kukailimoku. The oral tale relates that the stones for the temple were fitted in a single night, passed hand to hand by a human chain of 18,000 warriors for a distance of 14 miles from Pololu Valley. They created an irregular rectangle measuring 125 by 250 feet, with 30-foot-high and 15-foot-thick walls all around. When you visit the *heiau* pick up a small brochure from a box at the entrance; if none are available a signboard nearby gives general information. Notice that the leeward stones are covered in lichens giving them a greenish cast and testifying to the age of the *heiau.* Notice a huge flat stone near another embedded in the ground which gives off the menacing feeling of a preparation altar. Please be respectful as you walk around as this temple is still in use, and stay on the designated paths that are cordoned off by woven rope. To the rear is an altar area where recent offerings are often seen; the floor of the temple is carpeted with well-placed stones and tiny green plants that give a natural mosaic effect. For at least 8 and perhaps 15 centuries, members of the Mookini family have been the priests and priestesses of the temple. Today, the inherited title of *kahuna nui* rests with Leimomi Mookini Lum, a nearby resident. The entire *heiau* is surrounded by a wave-like hump, perhaps the remnant of an earlier structure, that resembles a castle moat. Be sure to visit the nearby "little grass shack," one of the best examples of this traditional Hawaiian architecture in the islands. Check how sturdy the walls are, and the excellent protection provided by the grass-shingled roof. Also, be aware of the integration of its stone platform, and how perfectly suited it is to provide comfort against the elements in Hawaii. Look through the door at a timeless panorama of the sea and surf.

A minute from the *heiau* along the dirt road, an HVB Warrior points to Kamehameha's birthplace, **Kamehameha Akahi Aina Hanau**. The entrance to the area is at the backside, away from the sea, with vehicular traffic blocked by a handsome wooden gate. Inside the low stone wall are some large boulders, believed to be the actual "birthing stones" where the high chieftess Kekuiapoiwa, wife of a warrior *ali'i,* gave birth to Kamehameha sometime around 1752. It is fitting that this male child, born as his island prepared a battle fleet to invade Maui, would grow to be the greatest of the Hawaiian Chiefs—a brave, powerful, but lonely man, just like the flat plateau upon which he drew his first breath. In the background, the temple's ritual drums and haunting chants dedicated to Ku were the infant's first lullabies. He would grow to accept Ku as his god, and together they would subjugate all of Hawaii. In this expansive North Kohala area Kamehameha was confronted with unencumbered vistas, sweeping views of neighboring islands, unlike most Hawaiians whose outlooks were held in check by the narrow, confining, but secure walls of steep-sided valleys. Only this man with this background could rise to become "The Lonely One," high-chief of a unified kingdom.

Hawi

Coming into Hawi, strung along Rt. 270 for a few blocks are a line of false-front buildings, leaning shoulder to shoulder like patient old men knowing that something *will* happen. In the middle of town Rt. 250, crossing the Kohala Mountains from Waimea, intersects the main road. Hawi was a bustling sugar town that boasted 4 movie theaters in its heyday. In the early 1970s, the Kohala Sugar Company pulled up stakes, leaving the one-industry town high and dry. Still standing is the monumental stack of the sugar works, a dormant reminder of

Mike Evans, the Prawn Man

what once was. The people of Hawi have always had grit, and instead of moving away they're hanging in, and doing a good job of revitalizing their town. Spirit, elbow grease, and paint are their chief allies. Hanging in are a handful of local shops selling food and household goods, an information center, a hotel (the only functional one in North Kohala), a restaurant or two, pizza parlor, and some remarkable craft shops and boutiques (see below).

The town has been helped by an infusion of new people moving in to develop businesses focused on tourism. One such new-wave pioneer is Mike Evans, the "Prawn Man of Hawi," who with little more than a dream and determination developed **Kona Aquatics,** an aquaculture business that raises prawns. This is the only operation of its kind on Hawaii, and Mike has largely developed the techniques on his own over the past 7 years. In the beginning, Mike had to peddle his produce door to door. Now his supply can't keep up with the demand, and he's only open for a few hours on Thursday afternoons when buyers from the big hotels and ordinary seafood-loving folks line up anxiously to buy his prawns. This is on a first-come first-served basis and they always sell out...real fast. Ask anyone in town to direct you to the road leading down a steep hill towards the sea to the prawn farm. Look for a series of ponds terraced down the hillside and follow the road through the gate. Mike lives on the premises with his young son. Mike says that he has *somehow* become a very, very popular guy, always one of the first invited to parties ranging from family gatherings on the beach to millionaires' banquets... "and ah, Mike, bring some of those prawns along, will ya?"

Kapaau

Kapaau is a sleepy community, the last town for any amenities on Rt. 270 before you reach the end of the line at Pololu Overlook. There's a gas station, grocery store, library, bank, and police station. Most young people have moved away seeking economic opportunity, but the old folks remain, and macadamia nuts are bringing some vitality back into the area. Here too, but on a smaller scale than in Hawi, local artists and some new folks are starting shops and businesses catering to tourists. The main

original Kamehameha statue

attraction in town is **Kamehameha's Statue,** in front of the Kapaau Courthouse. The statue was commissioned by King Kalakaua in 1878, at which time an old *kahuna* said that the statue would feel at home only in the lands of Kamehameha's birth. An American sculptor living in Italy, Thomas Gould, was hired to do the statue, and he used John Baker, a part Hawaiian and close friend of Kalakaua as the model. Gould was paid $10,000 and he produced a remarkable and heroic sculpture that was sent to Paris to be bronzed. It was freighted to Hawaii, but the ship carrying the original statue sank just off Port Stanley in the Falkland Islands, and the 9-ton statue was thought lost forever. With the insurance money, Gould was recommissioned and he produced another statue that arrived in Honolulu in 1883 where it still stands in front of the Judiciary Building. Within a few weeks, however, a British ship arrived in Honolulu, carrying the original statue that had somehow been salvaged and unceremoniously dumped in a Port Stanley junk yard. The English captain bought it there and sold it to King Kalakaua for $850. There was only one place for the statue to be sent: to the then-thriving town of Kapaau in the heart of Kamehameha's ancestral homelands. Every year on the night before Kamehameha Day, the statue is freshly painted with a new coat of house paint, but underneath the bronze remains as lustrous and strong as the great king's will.

Kamehameha County Park, down a marked side road, has a full recreation area including an Olympic pool open to the public, basketball courts and weight rooms in the main building, along with outside tennis courts with night lighting. There is a kiddie area, restrooms, and picnic tables, all free.

Kalahikiola Church

A few minutes east of town an HVB Warrior points to a county lane leading to Kalahikiola Congregational Church. The road is delightfully lined with palm trees, pines, and macadamias like the formal driveway which it once was. Pass the weathering buildings of the **Bond Estate,** and follow the road to the church on the hill. This church was built by Rev. Elias Bond and his wife Ellen, who arrived at Kohala in 1841 and dedicated the church in 1855. Rev. Bond and his parishioners were determined to overcome many formidable obstacles in building Kalahikiloa ("Life from the Sun") Church, so that they could "sit in a dry and decent house in Jehovah's presence." They hauled timber for miles, quarried and carried stone from distant gulches, raised lime from the sea floor, and brought sand by the jarfull all the way from Kawaiahae to mix their mortar. After 2 years of backbreaking work and $8,000, the church finally stood in God's praise, 85 feet long by 45 wide. The attached belltower, oddly out of place, looks like a shoe box standing on end and topped by 4 mean-looking spikes. Note that the doors don't swing but slide—some visitors leave because they think it's locked. Inside the church is dark and cool, and inexplicably the same type of spikes on the belltower flank both sides of the altar. There is also a remarkable *koa* table, and pamphlets ($.25) describe the history of the church.

The Bond Estate

The *most* remarkable and undisturbed missionary estate still extant in Hawaii is the old Bond Homestead and its attendant buildings which include the now defunct Kohala Girls School. The estate is kept up by 10 surviving cousins of the Bond family, and the caretaker is Mr. Lyman Bond, who lives nearby and raises macnuts. The Bond family has applied numerous times to state and federal authorities for financial help, even offering to turn over control of the estate so as to preserve it as a living museum. It's already on the National Historical Register. But, after a feasibility study by the powers-that-be concluded that 200 patrons per day would be necessary to "turn a profit," impossible in North Kohala, these civic-minded historians weren't interested. Now, Mr. Lyman Bond, great grandson of Elias Bond, graciously shows the house to interested visitors free of charge. However, arrangements to tour the estate are made on a one-to-one basis by phoning Mr. Bond at tel. 889-5108 or 882-7873. He endeavours to find a convenient time to both the visitor and himself for a personalized tour that takes at minimum one hour. The Bond Estate *is not* a museum, but private property; consider yourself a guest and act accordingly. Also note that Lyman Bond rents out rooms in the old girls school for the cheapest rates in Hawaii (see below).

When you enter the grounds, the clock turns back 100 years. The first buildings were completed in 1841 by Rev. Isaac Bliss, who preceeded Elias and Ellen Bond. The main buildings, connected in New England farm fashion, have steep pitched roofs designed to keep off the "back east" snows. They worked equally well here to keep rainwater out, as they were originally covered in thatch. All of the original furniture and family possessions are still placed as if they were all just out for the afternoon, although the family has not lived in the house since 1925 when it was occupied by Dr. Benjamin Bond. In the majority of missionary homes and museums in Hawaii, suitable period furniture had to be purchased or replicas made to fill the house, but here it is all original! The homey dining and writing room is dominated by a large table that can take 6 leaves because the Bond's never knew how

Lyman Bond in the sitting room of his family homestead

many there would be for dinner—4 or 60 that might have landed by schooner in the middle of the afternoon. A full set of dishes waits undisturbed in the sideboard. A cozy little parlor has comfortable wicker rocking chairs, and a settee under a photo of Elias Bond himself. The reverend built the settee and most of the furniture in the house. His furniture from New England arrived on a later ship, but being the Sabbath, the reverend refused to have it unloaded. Unfortunately, the ship caught fire and all the Bond's personal possessions were lost. In the kitchen area a refrigerator dating from the '20s looks like a bank vault. It ran on electricity from a generator on the homestead that was frequently used by local plantation owners to recharge their batteries. Off in a side room an old wooden bathtub is as sound as the day it was built. In Rev. Bond's bedroom is a crocheted "primer" dated 1817, made by his sister Eliza who died before he came to Hawaii. He brought it as a memento and it still hangs on the wall. Upstairs are 2 large rooms in disrepair, which contain a treasure trove of antiques. Notice too, the sturdy barn-style architecture of pegs and beams.

The small wing attached to the main house called "The Cottage" was built when Dr. Benjamin Bond was first married. The family ate together in the main house, so it's only a totally Victorian bedroom and sitting room, abounding with photos and antiques. The attached bathroom was once a summer house that was dragged to the present location by a steam tractor, then plumbed. As you look around, you'll feel that everything is here except for the people.

Keokea Beach Park

Two miles past Kapaau toward Pololu you pass a small fruit stand and an access road heading *makai* to secluded Keokea Beach Park. The park, on the side of the hill going down to the sea, is very picturesque and luxuriant. It is a favorite spot of North Kohala residents especially on weekends, but receives little use during the week. The rocky shoreline faces the open ocean so swimming is not advised except during summer calm. There is a pavilion, restrooms, showers, and picnic tables. A county permit is required for tent and trailer camping.

Pololu Valley And Beyond

Finally you come to Pololu Valley Overlook. Off to the right is a small home belonging to Bill Sproat, a man of mixed Hawaiian ancestry and a longtime resident of Pololu. Bill, whose vim and vigor belie his 81 years, was a mule skinner throughout the area for 50 years. He is a treasure house of knowledge and home-spun wisdom, and still speaks fluent Hawaiian. His mother was a Hawaiian lady who became a school teacher down in Pololu, and his dad was an adventurer who came to Hawaii in the 1890s. Bill's grandmother was a *kahuna* who

Bill Sproat

lived in the valley and never converted to Christianity. Most of the folks feared her dark powers, but not Bill who, although a strong Christian, learned much about Hawaii and its ways from his grandmother. If Bill is in his yard, perhaps tending a mule, make sure to stop and talk with him.

It's about 12 miles from Pololu to Waipio Valley, with 5 U-shaped valleys in between, including Honokea and Waimanu, 2 of the largest. From the lookout it takes about 15 minutes to walk down to the floor of Pololu. The trail is well maintained as you pass through a heavy growth of *lauhala,* but it can be slippery when wet. At the bottom is a gate that keeps grazing animals in; make sure to close it after you! The **Kohala Ditch,** a monument to labor-intensive engineering, is to the rear of these valleys. It carried precious water to the sugar plantations. Pololu and the other valleys were all inhabited, and were among the richest wet taro plantations of old Hawaii. Today, abandoned and neglected, introduced vegetation has taken them over. The black-sand beach fronting Pololu is lined with sand dunes, with a small sandbar offshore. The rip current here can be very dangerous, so enter the water only in summer months. The rip fortunately weakens not too far from shore; if caught go with it and ride the waves back in. Many people hike into Pololu for seclusion and back-to-nature camping. Make sure to boil the stream water before drinking. Plenty of wild fruits grow that can augment your food supply, and the shoreline fishing is excellent. The trails leading eastward to the other valleys are in disrepair and should not be attempted unless you are *totally* prepared, and better yet, accompanied by someone who knows the terrain.

PRACTICALITIES

Accommodations

You won't spend a lot of time wondering where you'll be staying in North Kohala. If you don't intend on camping, only one hotel welcomes you, another doesn't, and you can rent an old plantation manager's house, or a very modest room at the Bond estate.

The Old Hawaii Lodging Company in Hawi was long known as Luke's Hotel. It has now been taken over by new managers, John and Karen Gray, who lease the hotel from the Luke family. This young couple hail from Texas, bringing their famous "Texas-sized" hospitality with them. They've traveled extensively throughout Micronesia and the South Pacific, and have now settled down in North Kohala. The hotel has always catered to local working people or island families visiting the area. It is basic, adequate, and clean. Located in central Hawi, it has a quiet little courtyard, restaurant, swimming pool, and TV. Rooms are a very reasonable $17 s, $20 d, $6 additional person, discounts on long stays and for sharing a bathroom. Write Old Hawaii Lodging Company, Box 521, Kapaau, HI 96755, tel. 889-5577.

The Kohala Club Hotel, tel. 889-6793, is an odd-ball little country hotel along Rt. 270 in Kaapau. At one time, it was known as "The British Club," since many of the sugar company foremen who frequented it were British. In the dining room hangs a large painting of Queen Victoria that was supposedly saluted and toasted by her loyal subjects far from home. Now, the hotel is operated by a reclusive Japanese family that seems more surprised than pleased if you turn up looking for a room.

The **Hawaiian Plantation House** (Aha Hui Hale), Box 10, Hawi, HI 96719, tel. 889-5523 was once a plantation manager's house. The white clapboard structure sits on 4 lush acres, letting its 2 bedroom suites for $65 d, $10 extra person, communal kitchen.

Mr. Lyman Bond, tel. 889-5108, caretaker of the Bond Estate (see p. 648), rents very modest rooms in the old **Kohala Girls School** section of the homestead. These buildings are very old, with few conveniences or amenities. Basically, you'll have to take care of yourself with no towels, linens, or housekeeping provided. Mr. Bond *prefers* renting these rooms to school and civic organizations, but he will rent to travelers...if they are the right sort, which translates as clean, quiet, and respectful! Rates are $3.64 per night, with shared bath, kitchen, and refrigerator space.

Food

You can get a good inexpensive meal at **Old Hawaii Lodging Company** hotel restaurant in downtown Hawi. Omelettes with the works are under $3; cheeseburgers are $1.10, soup $.85, and most sandwiches under $1.50; fried chicken and the trimmings are $3.75, hamburger steak $3, and *mahi mahi* $5.75. There is also a cocktail lounge at this no-frills, downhome restaurant.

The **Ohana Pizza & Beer Garden,** tel. 889-5888, also in downtown Hawi, is a new enterprise featuring very good pizza from $4 to $12.75 depending upon size and toppings. This clean, friendly restaurant also offers hefty sandwiches $2.95, pasta dinners $3.95, salads $1.35, and homemade garlic bread $1. You can order wine or a chilled mug of draft Budweiser $.90, or Michelob $1.15. The staff of local people are friendly and hospitable. A great place to pick up a picnic lunch.

Pololu Valley

Mits Drive In, tel. 889-6474, is a small roadside restaurant in Kapaau where you can pick up a fast hamburger, hot dog, soft drink, or snack. Inexpensive.

For **food shopping** try: **Union Market,** tel. 889-6450, along Rt. 270 coming into Kapaau selling not only general merchandise and meats, but also a hefty assortment of grains, nuts, fruits, and locally made pastries and breads; **H. Naito** is a general grocery, dry goods and fishing supplies store in Kapaau, tel. 889-6851; **K. Takata** is a well-stocked grocery store in Hawi, tel. 889-5261; **T. Doi & Sons** a small general store just north of Kawaihae on the right, as you head up to the North Kohala peninsula, also sells sandwiches and drinks to go. For a special treat try **Tropical Dreams,** a locally owned company in Kohala that handmakes gourmet macadamia nut butters. Some of their mouth-watering butters are flavored with Kona coffee, chocolate, and *lehua* honey. They also make a variety of jellies and jams including passionfruit and papaya-coconut. Can't resist? Contact Tropical Dreams for their full brochure at Box 557, Kapaau, HI 96755, tel. 889-5386. Gift package assortments a specialty.

Shop

Diamonds and Rust is a buy-sell-trade discovery shop on the right-hand side of Rt. 270 just before entering Kapaau. It's owned and operated by Donald Rich, tel. 889-5844. Inside you find teddy bears, golf clubs, clothing, books, jewelry, and "artworks." The merchandise changes almost daily, so you'll never know what you'll find. Don Rich is a friendly guy who's willing to chat. Stop in and browse.

Next door is **Gallery One,** owned and operated by artist Gary Ackerman. Besides showcasing his own sensitive, island-inspired paintings, he displays local pottery and carvings. He also has a variety of artwork from throughout the Pacific including pottery from New Zealand, primitive carvings from the Philippines, and handcrafts from New Guinea. Gary either travels himself hand picking these fine pieces, or they're purchased by his wife who is a stewardess. The one-of-a-kind selections here are tasteful and expensive.

Hana Koa is a woodworking shop owned by artist Don Wilkinson, who learned the trade of making fine antique furniture replicas from his father. His work is authentic and excellent. He works primarily in *koa* and focuses on the early 1900 period. He is also a friend of Mr. Phil Hooten, an old-timer in Kohala, who fashions authentic carvings of old Hawaiian artifacts from ivory, turtleshell, and bone. Don, a friendly storehouse of information, lives along Rt. 250 heading in from Waimea, tel. 889-6444.

Another local artist is **David Gomes**, tel. 889-5100, a guitar and ukelele maker. He works in *koa* and other woods and does inlay in shell, abalone, and wood. His beautiful instruments take from 4 to 6 months to complete. His small shop is located about a half mile on the Kapaau side of the junction of Rts. 270 and 250. Next door is a hobby and crafts store.

In Hawi **Dawn's**, tel. 889-5112, sells sport clothes, T-shirts, and alohawear. The **Heritage Tree** is a specialty *hula* supply store in Kapaau across from the Kamehameha statue. If you're looking for a small variety of traditional arts and crafts, this shop is worth a stop.

Services And information

The **Kohala Visitors Center** dispenses maps, information, and *aloha.* It's open daily and located just near the junction of Rts. 270 and 250 in Hawi. Next door is the local **laundromat,** a semi open-aired affair that can be used just about all the time. **Police** can be reached at tel. 889-6225; **Emergency** fire and ambulance at tel. 961-6022.

If you are having any aches and pains see Dr. Robert Abdy at **Kohala Chiropractic Center,** tel. 889-5858. With offices in Hawi and Waimea this Palmer graduate employs a low-force adjustment technique and utilizes the Toftness Radiation Detector in his treatments.

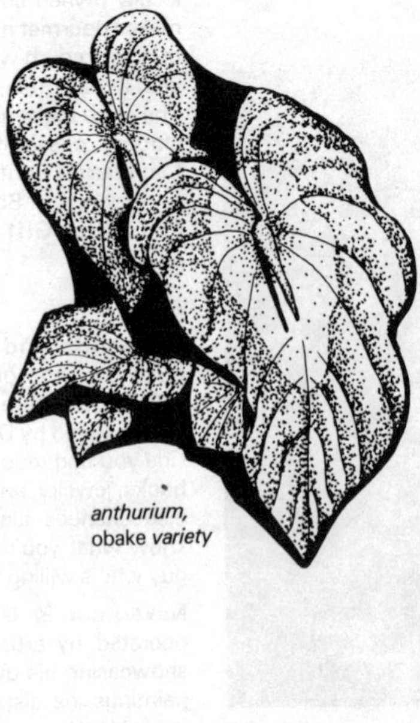

anthurium, obake *variety*

Aloha & Mahalo

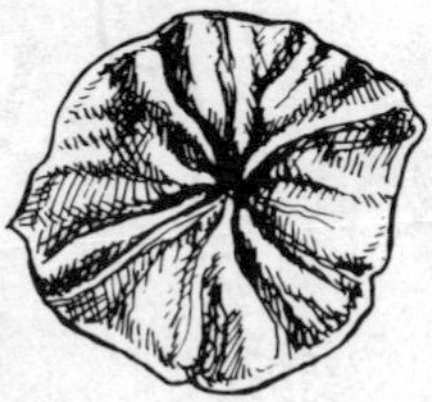

KAUAI

The Garden Island

KAUAI

INTRODUCTION

Kauai is the oldest of the main Hawaiian Islands, and Nature has had ample time to work, sculpting it into a beauty among beauties. Flowers and fruits burst from its fertile soil, but "Kauai, The Garden Island" is much more than greenery and flora, it's the poetry of land itself! Its mountains have become rounded and smooth, and its streams tumbling to the sea have cut deep and wide, giving Kauai the only navigable river in Hawaii. The interior is a dramatic series of mountains, valleys, and primordial swamp. The great gouge of Waimea Canyon, "Grand Canyon of the Pacific," is an enchanting layer of pastels where uncountable rainbows form prismatic necklaces from which waterfalls hang like silvery pendants. The northwest is the seacliffs of Na Pali, mightiest in all of Oceania, looming 4,000 feet above the pounding surf. Perhaps its greatest compliment is that Kauai is where other islanders come to look at the scenery. Only 100 miles (25 minutes) by air from Honolulu, you land just about the time you're finishing your in-flight cocktail. Everything seems quieter here, rural but upbeat, with the main town being just that, a town. The pursuit of carefree relaxation is unavoidable at 5-star hotels where you're treated like a visiting *ali'i,* or camping deep in interior valleys or along secluded beaches where reality *is* the fantasy of paradise.

Kauai is where Hollywood comes when the script calls for "paradise." The island has a dozen major films to its credit, everything from idyllic scenes in *South Pacific* to the lurking horror of Asian villages in *Uncommon Valor. King Kong* tore up this countryside in search of love, and Tattoo spots "de plane, boss" in "Fantasy Island." In *Blue Hawaii,* Elvis' hips mimicked the swaying palms in a famous island grove, while torrid love scenes from "The Thorn Birds" were steamier than the jungle in

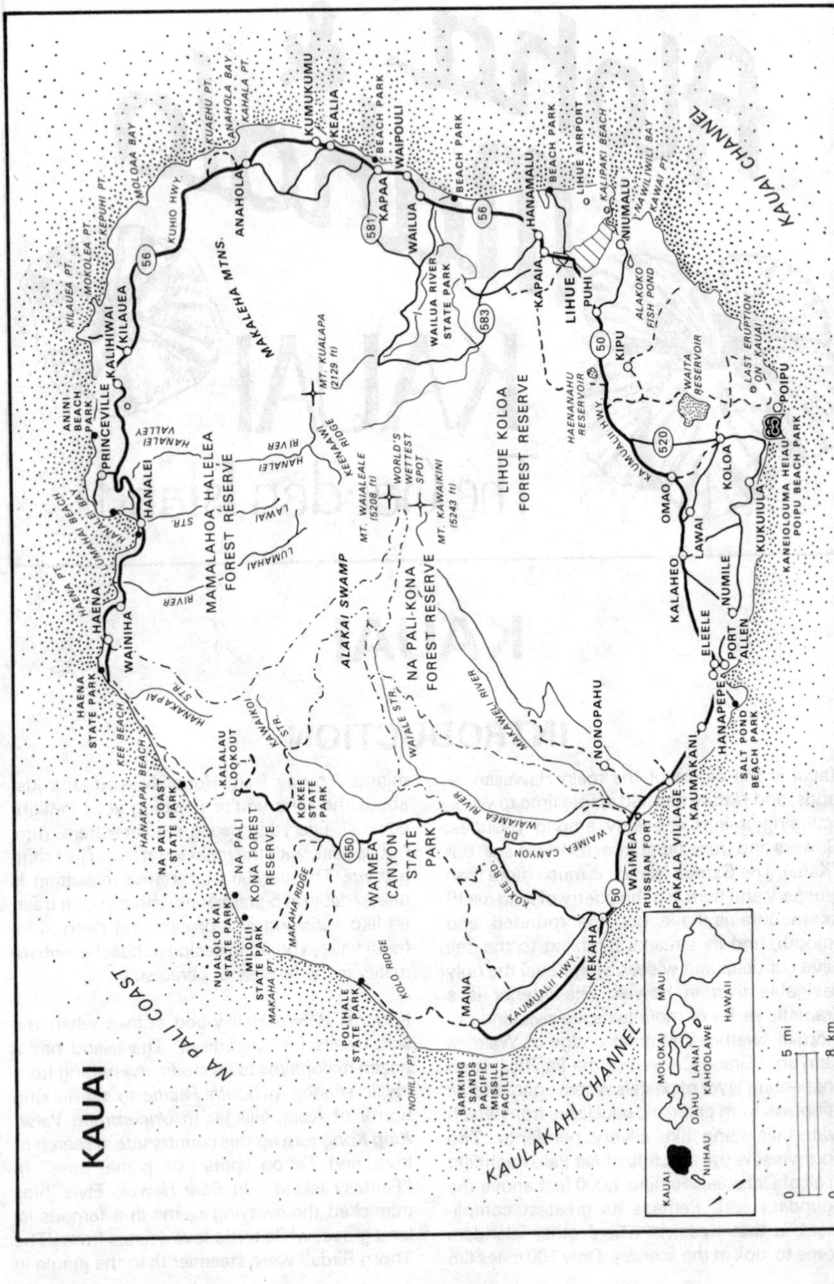
KAUAI
NA PALI COAST
KAULAKAHI CHANNEL
KAUAI CHANNEL
HAENA STATE PARK
HAENA
WAINIHA
HANALEI
PRINCEVILLE
ANINI BEACH PARK
KALIHIWAI
KILAUEA
KILAUEA PT.
MOKOLEA PT.
KEPUHI PT.
MOLOAA BAY
KUAEHU PT.
ANAHOLA BAY
KAHALA PT.
KUHIO HWY
ANAHOLA
KUMUKUMU
KEALIA
BEACH PARK
WAIPOULI
KAPAA
WAILUA
HANAMALU
BEACH PARK
LIHUE AIRPORT
KALIPAKI BEACH
NIUMALU
NAWILIWILI BAY
KAWAI PT.
LIHUE
PUHI
KAPAIA
ALAKOKO FISH POND
KIPU
WAITA RESERVOIR
LAST ERUPTION ON KAUAI
POIPU
KANEIOLOUMA HEIAU
POIPU BEACH PARK
KOLOA
KUKUIULA
OMAO
LAWAI
KALAHEO
NUMILE
ELEELE
PORT ALLEN
HANAPEPE
SALT POND BEACH PARK
KAUMAKANI
PAKALA VILLAGE
WAIMEA
RUSSIAN FORT
KEKAHA
KAUMUALII HWY
MANA
BARKING SANDS PACIFIC MISSILE FACILITY
NOHILI PT.
POLIHALE STATE PARK
MAKAHA PT.
MILOLII STATE PARK
NUALOLO KAI STATE PARK
NA PALI COAST STATE PARK
HANAKAPAI BEACH
KEE BEACH
HANAKAPAI STR.
KALALAU LOOKOUT
NA PALI KONA FOREST RESERVE
KOKEE STATE PARK
WAIMEA CANYON STATE PARK
MAKAHA RIDGE
KOLO RIDGE
KOKEE RD.
WAIMEA CANYON DR.
WAIMEA RIVER
NONOPAHU
MAKAWELI RIVER
WAIALAE STR.
KAWAIKOI STR.
ALAKAI SWAMP
NA PALI-KONA FOREST RESERVE
MT. WAIALEALE (5208 ft)
WORLD'S WETTEST SPOT
MT. KAWAIKINI (5243 ft)
LIHUE KOLOA FOREST RESERVE
MAMALAHOA HALELEA FOREST RESERVE
LUMAHAI RIVER
HANALEI RIVER
HANALEI VALLEY
KEENAWI RIDGE
MT. KUALAPA (2129 ft)
MAKALEHA MTNS.
WAILUA RIVER STATE PARK
HAENANAHU RESERVOIR
HAENA PT.
LUMAHAI BEACH
HANALEI BAY
56
581
583
50
520
550
KAUAI
NIIHAU
OAHU
MOLOKAI
LANAI
KAHOOLAWE
MAUI
HAWAII
0 5 mi
0 8 km

the background. But "The Garden Island" is much more than just another pretty face—the island and its people have integrity. In November 1982, Hurricane Iwa ripped ashore and slapped Kauai around like the moll in a Bogart movie. Her people immediately set about rebuilding hotels and homes, while nature took care of the rest. In no time, her mussed hair was combed and her streaked makeup was daubed into shape. Now, the hurricane damage is mostly a memory and Kauai has emerged a touch more self assured, and as beautiful as ever.

AN OVERVIEW

Kauai is the most regularly shaped of all the major islands, more or less round, like a partially deflated beach ball. The puckered skin around the coast forms bays, beaches, and inlets, while the center is a no-man's land of mountains, canyon, and swamp. Almost everyone arrives at the major airport in **Lihue,** although another small strip in Princeville has limited service by commuter aircraft. Lihue is the county seat and major town with government agencies, full amenities, and a wide array of restaurants and shopping. For many years the town's only full-service resort was the **Westin Kauai,** but the **Hilton** has recently opened a hotel-condo on Kauai Beach Road. Lihue also boasts some of the cheapest accommodations on the island in small family operated hotels; however, most visitors head east for Wailua/Kapaa or west to the fabulous Poipu Beach area. Lihue's **Kauai Museum** is a must stop, where you'll learn the geological and social history of the island, immensely enriching your visit. On the outskirts of town is the oldest **Lutheran Church** in the islands, and the remarkably preserved **Grove Farm Homestead,** a classic Hawaiian plantation that is so intact that all that seems to be missing are the workers. At Nawiliwili Bay you can see firsthand the *menehune's* handiwork at the **Menehune Fish Pond,** still in use. Just east are the 2 suburbs of **Kapaia** and **Hanamaulu.** Here too you'll find shopping and restaurants and the junction of Rt. 53 leading inland along the west bank of the Wailua River and terminating at a breathtaking panorama of **Wailua Falls.**

Heading northeast from Lihue along Rt. 56 takes you to **Wailua** and **Kapaa.** En route, you pass **Wailua Golf Course,** open to the public, beautiful, and cheap. Wailua town is built along the Wailua River, the only navigable stream in Hawaii. At the mouth of the river is a "temple of refuge" and a state park, while upstream are more *heiau,* petroglyphs, the heavily touristed yet beautiful Fern Grotto, royal birth stones, and remarkable overviews of the river below complete with cascading waterfalls. **The Coco Palms Hotel** of Wailua is an island institution set in the heart of the most outstanding coconut grove on Kauai. Its evening torch-lighting ceremony is the best authentic fake-Hawaii on the island, and it's free even to non-guests. Up Rt. 53 toward Kapaa you pass **The Market Place,** an extensive mall that'll satisfy your every shopping need and then some. In the vicinity, a clutch of first-rate yet affordable hotels and condos line the beach. **Kapaa** is a worker's town with more down-home shopping, and good, inexpensive restaurants. Heading north towards Hanalei, you pass **Pohakuloa Point,** an excellent surfer's beach, **Anahola Beach Park,** where the water and camping are fine, and **Moloa'a Bay,** a secluded beach that you can have mostly to yourself.

Before entering **Kilauea,** the first town in Hanalei District, unmarked side roads lead to secret beaches and unofficial camp spots. Kilauea offers a **Slippery Slide,** where a gentle and accommodating waterfall flips you into a large freshwater pond. A small coastal road leads you to **Kilauea Lighthouse,** a beacon of safety for passing ships and for a remarkable array of birds that come to this wild-fowl sanctuary. Nearby is **Crater Hill,** a 568-foot perch from where the mighty expanse of the Pacific lies at your feet. **Princeville** is next, largest planned resort in Hawaii, featuring its own airstrip. Here an entire modern village is built around a superb golf course and the newest exclusive hotel on Kauai.

Down the narrowing lane and over 2 bridges is **Hanalei.** Inland is a terraced valley planted in taro just like the old days. Oceanside is Hanalei Bay, a safe anchorage and haven to seagoing yachts that have made it a port of call ever since Westerners began coming to Hawaii. On the outskirts is **Waioli Mission**, a preserved home and museum dating from 1841. Then come a string of beaches, uncrowded and safe for swimming and snorkeling. You pass through the tiny village of **Wainiha**, with the island's "last resort." In quick succession comes **Haena Beach Park**, the **wet and dry caves**, and the end of the road. Here are beach houses for those who want to get away from it all, a *heiau* dedicated to *hula*, and the location where the beach scenes from "The Thorn Birds" was filmed. From here only your feet and love of adventure take you down the **Kalalau Trail** to back-to-nature camping. You pass along a narrow foot trail down the **Na Pali Coast** skirting emerald valleys cut off from the world by impenetrable 4,000-foot seacliffs, mightiest in the Pacific. All along here are *heiau*, ancient village sites, caves, lava tubes, and the romantic yet true **Valley of the Lost Tribe** waiting at trail's end.

From Lihue west is a different story. Route 50 takes you past the **Kukui Grove Mall** and then through **Puhi**, home of Kauai Community College. As the coastal **Hoary Head Mountains** slip past your window, **Queen Victoria's Profile** squints down at you. **Maluhia Road**, famous for its tunnel-like line of eucalyptus branches off towards **Koloa**, a sugar town now rejuvenated with shops, boutiques, and restaurants. Continuing to the coast is **Poipu Beach**, the best on Kauai with its bevy of beautiful hotels and resorts.

Westward are a string of sugar towns. First is **Kalaheo** where an island philanthropist, Walter McBride, gave the munificent land gift that has become **Kukui O Lono Park**. Here you'll find a picture perfect Japanese garden surrounded by an excellent yet little played golf course. West on Rt. 50 is **Hanapepe**, a good stop for supplies and famous for its restaurants. The road skirts the shore passing **Olokele**, a perfect caricature of a sugar town with its neatly trimmed cottages, and **Pakala**, an excellent surfing beach. Quickly comes **Waimea** where Capt. Cook first came ashore, and on the outskirts is the **Russian Fort**, dating from 1817 when all the world powers were present in Hawaii, jockeying to influence this Pacific gem. In Waimea or farther westward in **Kekaha**, the road branches inland leading along the rim of **Waimea Canyon**. This is what everyone comes to see, and none are disappointed. The wonderfully winding road serves up lookout after lookout and trail after trail. You end up at **Kokee State Park** and the **Kalalau Valley Lookout** where you're king of the mountain, and 4,000 feet below is your vast domain of Na Pali. Past Kekaha is a flat stretch of desert vast enough that the military has installed **Barking Sands Missile Range**. The pavement ends and a good tourist-intimidating "cane road" takes over, leading you to the seclusion of **Polihale State Park** where you can swim, camp, and luxuriate in privacy. If Madame Pele had her choice, she never would have moved.

THE LAND

Kauai was built by one huge volcano that became extinct about 6 million years ago. Mount Waialeale in central Kauai is its eastern rim, and speculation holds that Niihau, 20 miles off the west coast, was at one time connected. The volcanic "hot spot" under Kauai was sealed by the weight of the island; as Kauai drifted northward it burst through again and again building the string of islands from Oahu to Hawaii. The island now lies 100 miles off Oahu, northernmost of the 6 major islands and fourth largest. It is approximately 33 miles wide and 25 miles long at its farthest points, which account for 554 square miles with 90 miles of coastline. A simplified but chronologically accurate account of Kauai's emergence is a version of the Pele myth retold in the *Kumulipo* which depicts the fire goddess as a young, beautiful woman who visits Kauai during a *hula* festival and becomes enraptured with Lohiau, a handsome and mighty chief. She wants him as a husband and determines to dig a fire-pit home where they can reside in contented bliss. Unfortunately, her unrelenting and unforgiving sea-goddess sister pursues her, forcing Pele to abandon Kauai and Lohiau. Thus, she wandered and sparked volcanic eruptions on Oahu, Maui, and finally atop Kilauea Crater on Hawaii where she now resides.

Phenomenal Features Of Kauai

Located almost smack-dab in the middle of the island is **Mt. Kawaikini** (5,243 feet) and adjacent **Mount Waialeale** (5,148 feet), highest points on Kauai. Mt. Waialeale is an unsurpassed "rain magnet" drawing an estimated 480 inches (40 feet) of precipitation per year, and earning itself the dubious distinction of being "the wettest spot on Earth." Don't be intimidated—this rain is amazingly localized with only 20 inches per year falling just 20 miles away. Visitors can now enter this mist-shrouded world aboard helicopters which fly through countless rainbows and hover above a thousand waterfalls. Draining Waialeale is **Alakai Swamp,** a dripping sponge of earth covering about 30 square miles of trackless bog. This patch of mire contains flora and fauna found nowhere else on Earth. For example, *ohia* trees, mighty gaints of the upland forests, grow here as natural *bonsai* that could pass as potted plants. On the western border is **Waimea Canyon** running north to south. Whipping winds, pelting rain and the incessant grinding of streams and rivulets have chiseled the red bedrock to depths of 3,600 feet and expanses 10 miles wide. On the western slopes of Waimea Canyon is the **Na Pali Coast,** a scalloped, undulating vastness of cliffs and valleys forming a bulwark 4,000 feet high.

Other mountains and outcroppings around the island have formed curious natural formations. The **Hoary Head Mountains,** a diminutive range barely 2,000 feet tall south of Lihue, form a profile of Queen Victoria. A ridge just behind Wailua gives the impression of a man in repose and has been dubbed **The Sleeping Giant.** Another small range in the northeast, the **Anahola Mountains** had until recently an odd series of boulders that formed "Hole in the Mountain," mythologically created when a giant hurled his spear through sheer rock. Erosion has collapsed the formation but the tale lives on.

Land Ownership

Of the total usable land area (405,194 acres), 62% is privately owned. Of this, almost 90% is controlled by only half a dozen or so large landholders, mainly Gay & Robinson, AMFAC, Alexander & Baldwin, C. Brewer & Co., and Grove Farm. The remaining 38% is primarily owned by the state which includes a section of Hawaiian Homes lands, and a small portion is owned by the county of Kauai and the federal government. As everywhere in Hawaii, no one owns the beach and public access is guaranteed.

the Na Pali Coast

Channels, Lakes, And Rivers

Kauai is separated from Oahu by the **Kauai Channel.** Reaching an incredible depth of 10,900 feet, and 72 miles wide, it is by far the state's deepest and widest channel. Inland, man-made **Waita Reservoir** north of Koloa is the largest body of fresh water in Hawaii, covering 424 acres with a 3-mile shoreline. The **Waimea River,** running through the floor of the canyon, is the island's longest at just under 20 miles, while the **Hanalei River** emptying into Hanalei Bay moves the greatest amount of water at 150 million gallons per day. But the **Wailua River** has the distinction of being the state's only navigable stream, although passage by boat is restricted to a scant 3 miles. The flatlands around Kekaha were at one time Hawaii's largest body of inland water. They were brackish and drained last century when the Waimea Ditch was built to irrigate the cane fields.

Climate

Kauai's climate will make you happy. Along the coastline the average temperature is 80 degrees in spring and summer, and about 75 during the remainder of the year. The warmest areas are along the south coast from Lihue westward, where the mercury can hit the 90s in mid-summer. To escape the heat any time of year, head for Kokee atop Waimea Canyon, where the weather is always moderate.

In the areas most interesting to visitors, rain is not a problem. The driest section of Kauai is the desert southwest from Polihale to Poipu Beach (5 inches) up to a mere 20 inches around the resorts. Lihue receives about 30 inches; as you head northeast toward Hanalei, rainfall becomes more frequent but is still a manageable 45 inches per year. Cloudbursts in winter are frequent, but short lived.

Thanksgiving was not a very nice time on Kauai back in November 1982. Along with the stuffing and cranberries came an unwelcomed guest who showed no *aloha,* **Hurricane Iwa.** What made this rude 80-mile-per-hour party-crasher so unforgettable was that she was only the fourth storm to come ashore on Hawaii since records have been kept, and the first since the late 1950s. All told, she caused $200 million dollars worth of damage. A few beaches were washed away, perhaps forever, and great destruction was done to beach homes and resorts, especially around Poipu. Trees were twisted from the ground and bushes were flattened, but Kauai is strong and fertile and the damage was superficial and temporary. Like all the islands, Kauai has a very competent warning system in place, and thank God, there was no loss of life. Chances of encountering another hurricane on Kauai in the foreseeable future are very rare indeed.

HISTORY

Kauai is *first* of the islands in many ways. Besides being the oldest main island geologically, it's believed that Kauai was the first island to be populated by Polynesian explorers. This colony was theoretically well established as early as A.D. 200, which predates the populating of the other islands by almost 500 years. Even Madame Pele chose Kauai as her first home and was content here until her sister drove her away. Her fires went out when she moved on, but she, like all visitors, never forgot Kauai.

Mu* And *Menehune

Hawaiian legends give accounts of dwarflike aborigines on Kauai called the *Mu* and the *Menehune.* These 2 hirsute tribes of pixie-like creatures were said to have lived on the island before and after the the arrival of the Polyne-

AVERAGE MAXIMUM/MINIMUM TEMPERATURE AND RAINFALL

Island	Town		Jan.	Mar.	May	June	Sept.	Nov.
Kauai	Hanapepe	high	79	80	81	84	82	80
		low	60	60	61	65	62	61
		rain	5	2	0	0	2	3
	Lihue	high	79	79	79	82	82	80
		low	60	60	65	70	68	65
		rain	5	3	2	2	5	5
	Kilauea	high	79	79	80	82	82	80
		low	62	64	66	68	.69	65
		rain	5	5	3	3	1	5

N.B. Rainfall in inches; temperature in F°

sians. The *Mu* were fond of jokes and games, while the *Menehune* were dedicated workers, stonemasons par excellence, who could build monumental structures in just one night. Many stoneworks around the island that can still be seen are attributed to these hard-working nocturnal creatures, and a wonderfully educational exhibit concerning these pre-contact leprechauns is presented at the Kauai Museum. Legends, supported by anthropological theory, say that some non-Polynesian peoples actually did exist on Kauai. According to oral history, their chief felt that too much interplay and intermarriage was occurring with the Polynesians. He wished his race to remain pure so he ordered them to leave on a "triple-decker floating island," and they haven't been seen since, though if you ask a Kauaian if he or she believes in the *Menehune,* the answer is likely to be, "Of course not! But, they're there anyway." Speculation tells us that they may have been an entirely different race of people, or perhaps the remaining tribes of the first Polynesians. It's possible that they were cut off from the original culture for so long that they developed their own separate culture, and that the food supply was so diminished that their very stature was reduced in comparison to other Polynesians.

Written History

The written history of Hawaii began when Capt. James Cook sailed into Waimea Bay on Kauai's south shore on the afternoon of September 20, 1778, and opened Hawaii to the rest of the world. In the years just preceding Cook's discovery, Hawaii was undergoing a unique change. Kamehameha the Great, a chief of the Big Island, was in the process of conquering the islands and uniting them under his rule. King Kaumualii of Kauai was able to remain independent from Kamehameha's rule by his use of diplomacy, guile, and the large distances separating his island from the others. Finally, after all the other islands had been subjugated, Kaumualii joined Kamehameha through negotiations, not warfare; he retained control of Kauai by being made governor of the island by Kamehameha. After Kamehameha died, his successor, Kamehameha II, forced Kaumualii to go to Oahu where arrangements were made for him to marry the great queen Kaahumanu, the favorite wife of Kamehameha, and the greatest surviving *ali'i* of the land. Kaumualii never returned to his native island.

Hawaii was in a great state of flux during this period. The missionaries were coming, along with adventurers and schemers from throughout Europe. One of the latter was George Scheffer, a Prussian in the service of Czar Nicholas of Russia. He convinced Kaumualii to build a Russian fort in Waimea in 1817, which Kaumualii saw as a means to discourage other Europeans from overrunning his lands. A loose alliance was made between Kaumualii and Scheffer. The adventurer eventually lost the czar's support, and Kaumualii ran him off the island. The remains of **Fort Elizabeth** still stand. Around the same time, George Kaumualii, the king's son who had been sent to Boston to be educated, was accompaning the first missionary packet to the islands. He came with Rev. Sam Whitney, whom Kaumualii invited to stay, and who planted the first sugar on the island and taught the natives to dig wells. **Wailoi Mission House**, just north of Hanalei, dates from 1836 and is still standing and preserved as a museum. Nearby, Hanalei Bay was a commercial harbor for trading and whaling. From here, produce such as oranges were shipped from Na Pali farms to California. In Koloa Town, on the opposite end of the island, a stack from the Koloa Sugar plantation, started in 1835, marks the first succesful sugar refining operation in the islands. Another successful enterprise was **Lihue Plantation**. Founded by a German firm in 1850, it prospered until WW I when anti-German sentiments forced the owners to sell out. In Lihue Town, you can still see the Haleko Shops, a cluster of 4 2-story buildings that show a strong German influence. The **Lihue Lutheran Church** has an ornate altar very similar to ones found in old German churches.

During the 1870s and '80s, leprosy raged throughout the kingdom and strong measures were taken. Those believed to be afflicted were wrenched from their families and sent to the hideous colony of Kalaupapa on Molokai. One famous Kauaian leper, Koolau, born in 1862 in Kekaha, refused to be brought in and took his family to live in the mountain fortress of Na Pali. He fought he authorities for years and killed all those sent to take him in. He was made popular by Jack London in his short story, *Koolau, The Leper.*

When WW II came to Hawaii, Nawiliwili Harbor was shelled on Dec. 31, 1941, but there was little damage. The island remained much the same, quiet and rural until the late '60s when development began in earnest. The first resort destination on the island was the Coco Palms Hotel in Wailua followed by development in Poipu, and another in Princeville. Meanwhile, Hollywood had discovered Kauai, and featured its haunting beauty as a *silent star* in dozens of major films. Today, development goes on, but the island remains quiet, serene, and beautiful.

FLORA AND FAUNA

Kauai exceeds its reputation as "The Garden Island." It has had a much longer time for soil building and rooting of a wide variety of plant life, so it's lusher than the other islands. Lying on a main bird migratory route, lands such as the Hanalei National Wildlife Sanctuary have long since been set aside for their benefit. Impenetrable inland regions surrounding Mt. Waialeale and dominated by the Alakai Swamp have provided a natural sanctuary for Kauai's own bird and plant life. Because of this, Kauai is home to the largest number of indigenous birds still extant in Hawaii, though even here they are tragically endangered. Like the other Hawaiian Islands, a large number of birds, plants, and mammals have been introduced in the past 200 years. Most have either aggressively competed for, or simply destroyed, the habitat of indigenous species. As the newcomers gain dominance, Kauai's own slide inevitably toward oblivion.

Introduced Fauna

One terribly destructive predator of native ground-nesting birds is the **mongoose.** Introduced last century as a cure for a rat infestation, it has only recently made it to Kauai where a vigorous monitoring and extermination process is underway. More acceptable game mammals found in Kauai's forests include feral goats and pigs, although they too have caused destruction by uprooting seedlings and by

the mongoose, an experiment gone bad

overgrazing shrubs and grasses. Game fowl that have successfully acclimatized include francolins, ring-necked pheasants, and an assortment of quail and dove. All are hunted at certain times of year (see p. 679).

One game animal found only on Kauai is the **black-tailed deer.** Kauai's thriving herd of 700 individuals started as a few orphaned fawns from Oregon in 1961. These handsome animals, a species of western mule deer, are at home on the hilly slopes west of Waimea Canyon. Although there is little noticeable change in seasons in Hawaii, bucks and does continue to operate on genetically transmitted biological time clocks. The males shed their antlers during late winter months and the females give birth in spring. Hunting of black-tails is allowed only by public lottery in October.

Common Birds

Kauai is rich in all manner of birds, from migratory marine birds to upland forest dwellers. Many live in areas you can visit, others you can see by taking a short stroll and remaining observant. Some, of course, are rare and very difficult to spot. Some of the most easily spotted island birds frequent almost all areas from the Kekaha Salt Ponds to Kalalau and the upland regions of Kokee, including the blazing red **northern cardinal;** the comedic, brash **common myna;** the operatic **western meadowlark,** introduced in 1930 and found only on Kauai; the ubiquitous **Japanese white-eye;** sudden fluttering flocks of **house finches;** that arctic traveler the **golden**

plover, found along mud flats everywhere; the **cattle egret,** a white 20-inch heron found anywhere from the backs of cattle to the lids of garbage cans. Introduced from Florida in 1960 to control cattle pests, they have so proliferated that they are now considered a pest; the **white-tailed tropic bird,** snow-white elegance with a 3-foot wingspan and a long wispy kite-like tail.

Marine And Water Birds

Among the millions of birds that visit Kauai yearly, some of the most outstanding are its marine and water birds. Many beautiful individuals are seen of **Kilauea Point,** where they often nest on **Mokuae'ae Islet.** The **Laysan albatross** *(moli)* is a far-ranging Pacific flier whose 11-foot wingspan carries it in effortless flight. This bird has little fear of man, and while on the ground is easily approachable. It also nests along Barking Sands. The **wedge-tailed shearwater** *(ua'u kani)* is known as the "moaning bird" because of its doleful sounds. These birds have no fear of predators and often fall prey to feral dogs and cats. Also seen making spectacular dives for squid off Kilauea Point is the **red-footed booby,** a fluffy white bird with a blue bill and a 3-foot wingspan. One of the most amazing is the **great frigatebird,** an awesome specimen with an 8-foot wingspan. Predominantly black, the males have a red throat pouch that they inflate like a balloon. These giants, the kings of the rookery, often steal food from lesser birds. They nest off Kilauea Point, are also seen along Kalalau Trail, and even at Poipu Beach.

Many of Kauai's water birds are most easily found in the marshes and ponds of **Hanalei National Wildlife Sanctuary,** though they have also been spotted on some of the island's reservoirs, especially at **Menehune Fish Pond** and its vicinity. The **Hawaiian stilt** *(ae'o)* is a 1½-foot-tall wading bird with pink stick-like legs. The **Hawaiian coot** *(alae ke'oke' o)* is a gray-black duck-like bird with a white belly and face. The **Hawaiian gallinule** *(alae ula),* an endemic Hawaiian bird often found in Hanalei's taro patches, has a duck-like body with a red face tipped in yellow. It uses its huge chicken-like feet to hop across floating vegetation. The **Hawaiian duck** *(koloa maoli)* looks like a mallard, and because of interbreeding with common ducks, is becoming rarer as a distinctive species.

Indigenous Forest Birds

Kauai's upland forests are still home to many Hawaiian birds; they're dwindling but holding on. You may be lucky enough to spot some of the following. The **Hawaiian owl** *(pueo),* one of the friendliest *amakua* in ancient Hawaii, hunts both by day and night. The ***elepaio*** is an indigenous bird so named because its song sounds like its name. A small brown bird with white rump feathers found around Kokee, it's very friendly and can even be prompted to come to an observer offering food. ***Anianiau*** is a 4-inch yellow-green bird found around Kokee. Its demise is due to a lack of fear of man. The ***nukupu'u,*** extinct on the other islands except for a few on Maui, is found in Kauai's upper forests and bordering the Alakai Swamp. It's a 5-inch bird with a drab green back and a bright yellow chest.

the friendly elepaio

Birds Of The Alakai Swamp

The following scarce birds are some of the last indigenous Hawaiian birds, saved only by the inhospitality of the Alakai Swamp. All are endangered species and under no circumstances should they be disturbed. The last survivors include: the ***o'u,*** a chubby 7-inch bird with a green body, yellow head, and lovely whistle ranging half an octave; relatively common **Hawaiian creeper,** a hand-sized bird with a light

Hunting of Hawaiian birds to pluck their blazing yellow and red feathers used to fashion the magnificent capes of rank worn by the ali'i *started many on the road to extinction long before the white man arrived.*

green back and white belly, which travels in pairs and searches bark for insects; puaiohi, a dark brown 7-inch bird with a white belly that is so rare that its nesting habits are unknown. ***O'o'a'a',*** although its name may resemble the sounds you make getting into a steaming hot tub, is an 8-inch black bird which played a special role in Hawaiian history. Its blazing yellow leg feathers were used to fashion the spectacular capes and helmets of the *ali'i.* Even before the white man came, this bird was ruthlessly pursued by specially trained hunters that captured it and plucked its feathers. The ***akialoa*** is a 7-inch greenish-yellow bird with a long, slender, curved bill.

GOVERNMENT, PEOPLE AND ECONOMY

Kauai County is comprised of the inhabited islands of **Kauai** and **Niihau,** and the uninhabited islands of **Kaula** and **Lehua.** Lihue is the county seat. It's represented by 2 **state senators** elected from the 24th District, a split district including north Kauai and the Waianae Coast of Oahu, and the 25th District which includes all of southern Kauai and Niihau. Kauai has 3 **state congressmen** from the 49th District which is again a split district with north Kauai and the Wainae coast, the 50th District around Lihue, and the 51st District which includes all of southern and western Kauai.

Economy

The economy of Kauai, like that of the entire state, is based on tourism, agriculture, and the military. The strongest-growing factor is **tourism.** Kauai, third most visited island after Oahu and Maui, attracts about 750,000 visitors annually, accounting for 21% of the state's total. Approximately 4,500 hotel and condo units are available, averaging a 70% occupancy rate. At one time, Kauai was the most difficult island on which to build a resort because of a strong grass-roots anti-development faction. Recently, this trend is changing due to the recession that hit everyone after Hurricane Iwa scared off many tourists. Island residents realized how much their livelihood was tied to tourism, and a recent ad campaign depicting tourists as visitors has helped in their acceptance. Also, the resorts being built on Kauai are first rate, and the developers are savvy enough to create "destination areas" instead of more high rise boxes of rooms. Two of the finest hotels in Hawaii include the recently completed **Sheraton Princeville** overlooking Hanalei Bay and the fabulous **Waiohai Resort** of Poipu Beach. Also, Kauai's quality of room compared to price is the state's best.

Agriculture still accounts for a hefty portion of Kauai's income. **Sugar** has taken a recent downward trend from a yearly yield of $85 million in 1980 to about $50 million today. Kauai produces about 6% of the state's diversified agricultural crop with a strong yield in **papaya.** But in 1982, California banned the importation of Kauai's papaya because they were sprayed with EDB. Hanalei Valley and many other smaller areas produce 5 million pounds of taro that is quickly turned into *poi,* and the county produces 2 million pounds of guava, as well as pineapple, beef, and pork for its own use, and a growing aquaculture industry produces prawns.

The **military** influence on Kauai is small but vital. NASA's major tracking facilities in Kokee Park are now being turned over to the Navy and Air Force. At **Barking Sands,** the Navy operates BARSTUR, an underwater tactical range for training in antisubmarine warfare. Also along Barking Sands (a fitting name!) is a **Pacific Missile Range** operated by the Navy, but available to the Air Force, Department of Defense, NASA, and the Department of Energy. Visitors to these facilities are few and far between, and as welcome as door-to-door encyclopedia salesmen.

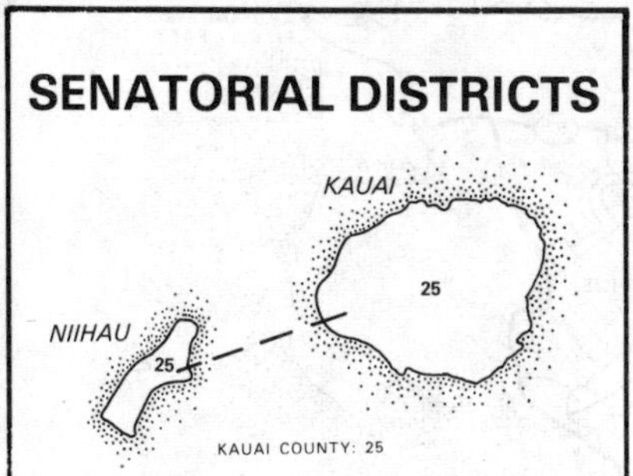

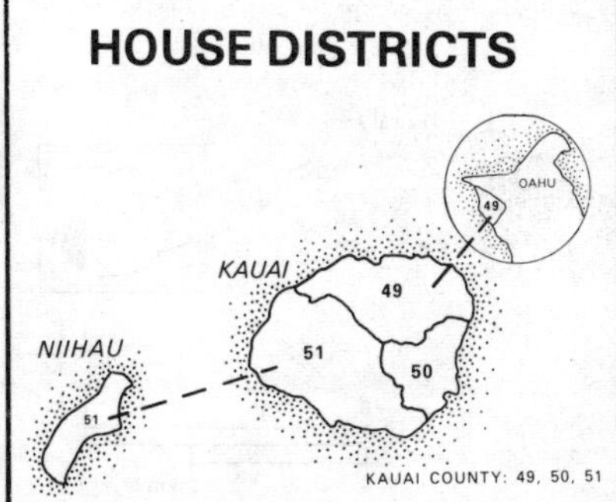

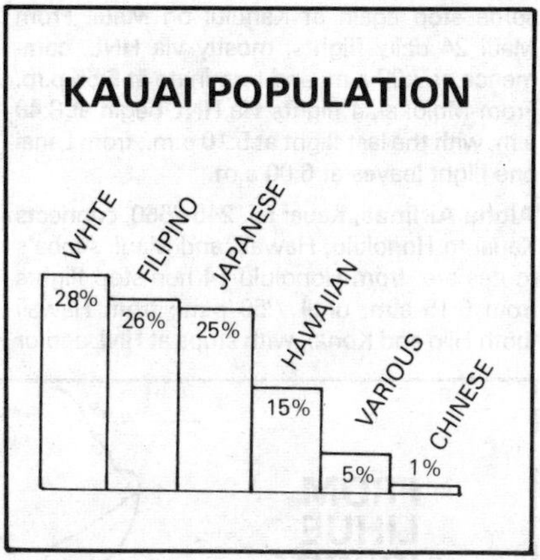

Population
Kauai County's 40,000 people, plus 200 relatively pure-blood Hawaiians living on Niihau, account for only 4% of the state's total population, the least populous county. Also, 325 military personnel and their dependents live on the island (see "Economy" above for more details). The largest town is **Kapaa** with 4,500 people, followed by **Lihue** with 4,000. Ethnically, there is no clear majority on Kauai. The people of Kauai include: 28% **Caucasian;** 25% **Japanese;** 26% **Filipino;** 15% **Hawaiian** including those of mixed blood; 1.3% **Chinese;** and the remaining 5% Koreans, Samoans, and a smattering of blacks and Indians.

GETTING THERE

Kauai's Lihue Airport is connected to all the Hawaiian Islands by direct flight, but no nonstop flights from the Mainland are currently operating. All Mainland and international passengers arrive via Honolulu, from which the 3 major inter-island carriers offer numerous daily flights.

Hawaiian Air, Kauai tel. 245-3671, offers the largest number of daily flights on both their DC-9 jet aircraft, and their 4-prop Dash Transits. From Honolulu, 15 non-stop flights go from 6:10 a.m. to 7:50 p.m. From Hawaii (both Hilo and Kona), 11 flights begin at 7:00 a.m. and end at 6:45 p.m. Most flights stop at HNL, some stop again at Kahului on Maui. From Maui 24 daily flights, mostly via HNL, commence at 7:03 a.m. and terminate at 6:56 p.m. From Molokai, 4 flights via HNL begin at 8:40 a.m. with the last flight at 5:10 p.m.; from Lanai one flight leaves at 6:00 a.m.

Aloha Airlines, Kauai tel. 245-2560, connects Kauai to Honolulu, Hawaii, and Maui. Aloha's routes are: from Honolulu 14 non-stop flights from 6:15 a.m. until 7:50 p.m.; from Hawaii (both Hilo and Kona), with stops at HNL and/or Maui, 7 flights from 6:52 a.m. to 6:25 p.m.; from Maui 16 flights via HNL from 6:58 a.m. to 7:05 p.m.

Mid-Pacific Air, Kauai tel. 245-7775, flies to Kauai from Honolulu, Maui, and Hawaii: from Honolulu 17 non-stop flights from 6:15 a.m. until 7:25 p.m.; from Hawaii, both Hilo and Kona via HNL and/or Maui, 4 flights from 8:15 a.m. to 4:25 p.m.; from Maui via HNL 12 flights from 7:15 a.m. to 6:05 p.m.

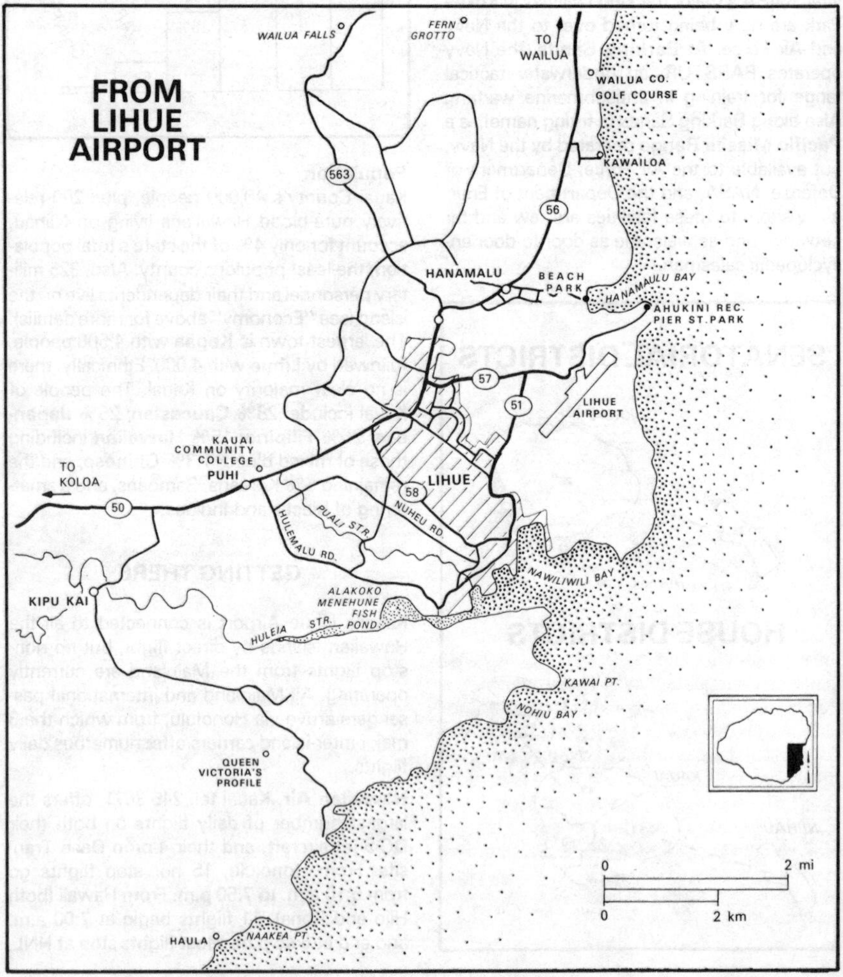

Average flying times to Kauai are 35 minutes from Honolulu, one to 2 hours from the Big Island depending upon stops, and just over one hour from Maui including the stop in Honolulu. Outgoing and incoming flights are dispersed equally throughout the day.

Princeville Airways, tel. 826-3770 Kauai, 800-652-6541 Neighbor Islands, 800-323-3345 Mainland, is a commuter airline operating flights to and from Princeville Airport on Kauai's north shore. Flying comfortable 18-passenger Twin Otter DeHavaland aircraft, they connect the resort community of Princeville with Honolulu and the Big Island: daily from Honolulu, 6 flights begin at 6:30 a.m. until 6:00 p.m., to HNL also 6 flights from 7:30 a.m. to 7:00 p.m.; from Hawaii's landing strip at Waikoloa and the secondary airport of Kamuela, 3 flights daily from 7:40 a.m. with the last at 6:30 p.m.

The Airports

Lihue Airport receives 99% of Kauai's flights. Located less than 2 miles from downtown Lihue, no public transportation is available, so you must either rent a car, hitch (fairly good), or hire a taxi (about $5 to Lihue). The terminal, small but adequate, has a Visitor Information Kiosk, restaurant and cocktail lounge, toilets, and a gift shop. The gift shop sells pre-inspected island fruit that's boxed and ready to transport; tel. 245-6273. All major car rental agencies, and a good number of local firms, maintain booths just outside the main entranceway. Also, outside under the sign that says "Porter Service" are about 10 suitcase-sized **lockers** that rent for $1 per day. **Princeville Airport** is basically a strip servicing Princeville, located along Rt. 56 just east of town. The terminal is a cute little building made inconspicuous by the immense beauty surrounding it, and there is a toilet, telephone, and a Hertz car rental booth.

GETTING AROUND

The most common way to get around Kauai is by rental car. Plenty of agencies keep prices competitive. As always, reserve during peak season, and take your chances to shop around and score a good deal in the off season. Kauai also has very limited bus service, expensive taxis, bicycle, mopeds and scooter rentals, and the good old (legal) thumb.

Car Rental Agencies

Many agencies maintain rental booths or courtesy phones at Lihue Airport. **National Car Rental,** tel. 245-3502, features GM cars and accepts all major credit cards. They rent without a credit card if you leave a $50 p/d deposit, less if you take full insurance coverage. **Budget,** tel. 245-4572, also maintains offices at the Coco Palms and at Poipu Beach, **Hertz,** tel. 245-3356, is competitively priced with many fly/drive deals. They also maintain a booth at Princeville Airport. Others are **Alamo,** tel. 245-8953, with free pickup and delivery at Princeville, tel. 826-7233; **Avis,** tel. 245-3512; and **Dollar,** tel. 245-4708, which also rents camping gear.

Smaller local and island companies with reliable reputations are: **Wiki Wiki Wheels,** tel. 245-6944; **Tropical,** tel. 245-6988, with free prompt pick-up service from Lihue; **Tony's,** tel. 245-2774, booth at the airport, featuring late-model Datsuns, only $12.50 daily, and they rent without a credit card for a $30 p/d deposit; **Watase's,** tel. 245-3251, advertises cheap come-on rates, but be careful there isn't a hidden $.10 per mile charge; **Robert's,** tel. 245-4008, has good cars and reasonable rates and can also supply convertibles and VW buses.

Specialty rental agencies include: **Rent-a-Jeep,** 3137 Kuhio, tel. 245-9622, for 4WDs, convertibles, VW buses, and cheap older cars; **Westside-U-Drive,** tel. 332-8644, at Poipu Beach, for 4WDs, convertibles, and cars; expensive but fun are **mopeds** and **scooters**

available from **South Shore Activities,** tel. 742-6873, at Poipu Beach, and **Fun Wheels,** tel. 245-8576, near the Kauai Surf Hotel in Nawiliwili.

Public Transportation

Public transportation on Kauai is limited to a free shuttle or two, the Aloha Bus servicing only Lihue and Kapaa, and taxis.

Aloha Bus, tel. 822-9532, runs a circuit from the Westin Kauai in Nawiliwili through Lihue and out to Kukui Grove Mall, then along Kuhio Hwy. through Wailua to Kapaa where it turns around at the Market Place Shopping Center. It stops at all the main resorts along the way including the Coco Palms, and you can hail the bus at any convenient point along the road. Bus service is daily (except Sunday and most holidays), from 8:15 a.m. until 4:20 p.m.; it takes about one hour to make the entire loop. A plan is always afoot to extend the service to Poipu and Princeville, and to run for longer hours. Get up-to-the-minute info by calling the above number. Fares are $1 per zone, and there are 2 zones; backpacks and suitcases are $.50 extra unless they're small enough to hold on your lap.

A few shuttle vans operate from the airport to Lihue, Kapaa, and Poipu hotels for between $2 and $5; the on-call **Princeville Jitney** services the Princeville resort area and the Princeville airport.

Taxis are all metered and charge a hefty price for their services. Approximate rates are $5 Lihue, $12 Kapaa, $20 Poipu, and $40 Princeville. Cabs wait outside the airport, or call some local companies: **Akiko's,** tel. 822-3613, in Wailua; **Scotty's,** tel. 245-2271, in Lihue; **Wailua Taxi,** tel. 822-3671, with 24-hour service.

Hitchhiking

Using your thumb to get around is legal on Kauai, but you must stay off the paved portion of the road. For short hops in and around the towns, like from Koloa to Poipu or from the airport to Lihue, thumbing isn't difficult. But getting out to the Kalalau Trail, or to Polihale on the east end, when you're toting a backpack and appear to be going a longer distance, is tough. Many drivers aren't going that far, or they just don't want to take the chance of being stuck with someone for the distance. As on all the islands, your best chances of being picked up is by a visiting or local *haole.* Again, women *should not* hitch alone!

Bicycles

Riding a bike around Kauai is fairly easy, thanks to lack of big hills, except for the Kokee area. Traffic is moderate, especially in the cool of early morning when it's best for making some distance. Roads are generally good, but shoulders aren't wide. Rental shops include: **Bicycles Kauai,** 1379 Kuhio Hwy., Kapaa, tel. 822-3315; **South Shore Activities,** tel. 742-6873, adjacent to the Sheraton at Poipu Beach; and a few old klunkers for guests at the Westin Kauai. Bike shops, including the above, for those who have brought their own velocipedes (about $10 inter-island) include: **Kawamoto's,** tel. 822-4771, in Kapaa specializing in Schwinns, and **Kauai Sports,** tel. 245-8052, at the Kukui Grove Mall. Both are conveniently open Mon. to Sat. 9:00 a.m. to 6:00 p.m., and Sun. 9:00 a.m. to 3:00 p.m., for parts or repairs.

SIGHTSEEING TOURS

Magnificent Kauai is fascinating to explore by land, sea, or air. Looking around on your own is no problem, but some of the most outstanding areas are more expediently seen with a professional guide. For example, to appreciate the terrific Kalalau Valley Trail fully, you need proper gear and a minimum of 3 days. If you don't have that kind of time or energy, take a Zodiac (motorized raft) down the Na Pali Coast, landing at Kalalau. You can return the same day, or disembark, camp, and return on the next boat.

A number of helicopter companies operate their whirlybirds over the inaccessible and beautiful interior. Outdoor purists disparage this mode of transport, saying, "if you can't hike in you shouldn't be there," but that's tunnel vision and not always appropriate. Plenty of day trails through Waimea Canyon reward you with magnificent panoramas, and wild pig hunters are in there all the time, but to go deep into the mist-shrouded interior, especially through the Alakai Swamp, the average traveler "can't get there from here"...it's just too rugged and dangerous! The only reasonable way to see it is by helicopter, and except for the noise, choppers actually have less of an impact on the ecosystem than hiking over it. Fishing charters not only provide the thrill of latching onto a big one, but many troll the fertile waters of Niihau, skirting its inlets and bays, which gives at least a glimpse of the "Forbidden Island."

Van And Bus Tours

On Kauai, the tour companies run vans, but some larger companies also run buses. Less personalized, tours on a full-sized coach are generally cheaper. Wherever a bus can go, so can your rental car, but you can relax and enjoy the scenery without worrying about driving. Also, the drivers are very experienced with the area and know many stories and legends with which they annotate and enrich your trip. Coach tours vary, but the average is a half-day (about $15), or full-day ($25) tour that takes you to Waimea Canyon, and/or Hanalei and the north shore. Often a tour to the Fern Grotto is considered the "highlight"...that should say it all! The larger companies that supplement their vans with buses are: **Grayline Hawaii**, tel. 245-3344; **Robert's Tours**, tel. 245-9558; and **Kauai Island Tours**, 245-4777.

Vans, where the group is small and the service is personalized, are the better way to go. On Kauai, the companies are often husband-and-wife teams, so they really aim to please. An excellent company is **Kauai Mountain Tours**, Box 72, Koloa, HI 96756, tel. 742-9737. They run comfortable and specially equipped 4WD GMC Suburbans, and specialize in Waimea Canyon and Kokee State Park. You get well off-the-beaten track into remote areas tough to find on your own. Their guides, like Anthony native Hawaiians, are excellent. He has a tremendous amount of knowledge on the flora and fauna, and has been known to bring in specimens of very rare plants and flowers so that local artists can sketch them for posterity. However, he won't tell where he found them! Kauai Mountain Tours provide lunches specially prepared by the Green Garden Restaurant. Tours last about 6 hours and begin at 8:00 a.m. Another small but good company is **Niele Tours**, Box 239, Kapaa, HI 96746, tel. 245-8673. They offer full-day around-the-island tours at $35, and half-day tours, to Waimea Canyon $19, or Hanalei $17 in 12-seater vans. No lunch provided. **Chandlers**, Box 3001, Lihue HI 96766, tel. 245-9134, operates around-the-island tours for approximately $20 half day, $40 full day. **Holo Holo Kauai**, tel. 245-9134, offers more of the same at comparable prices and also provides breakfast and lunch.

Papillon Helicopters can take you into the virtually inaccessible interior.

Helicopter Tours

All the helicopter companies on Kauai are safe and reputable, and most fly Bell Jet Ranger equipment. Flying in a chopper is a thrilling experience, like flying in a light plane...with a twist. They take you into all those otherwise inaccessible little nooks and crannies. Routes cover the entire island, but the highlights are flying into Waimea Canyon and the Alakai Swamp, where you see thousands of waterfalls, and even 360-degree rainbows floating in mid-air. Then to top it off, you fly the Na Pali Coast, swooping along its ruffled edge and dipping down for an up-close look at its caves and giant sea cliffs. Earphones are provided to cut the noise of the aircraft and play soul-stirring music as a background to the narration provided by the pilot. The basic "Around the Island" one-hour flight runs about $100, and you can tailor your own flight, which might include a swim at a remote pool along with a champagne lunch, but these are more costly. Discounts of up to 15% for some of the companies are always featured in the ubiquitous free tourist brochures.

The granddaddy of them all is **Jack Harter Helicopters,** Box 306, Lihue, HI 96766, tel. 245-3774. Jack, along with his wife Beverly, literally started the helicopter business on Kauai, and have been flying the island for over 20 years. Jack flies from the heliport at the Westin Kauai, and although he doesn't advertise, is always booked up. He knows countless stories about Kauai and just about everywhere to go on the island. He gives you a full hour and a half in the air, and his logo, "Imitated by all, equalled by none," says it all.

The slickest and best of the new companies is **Papillon Helicopters,** Box 339, Hanalei, HI 96714, tel. 826-6591. They fly from their own heliport at Princeville, just past mile marker 26, with some flights leaving from Lihue Airport, and offer the largest variety of tours. Besides taking you around the island, one tour features a drop-off with gourmet picnic lunch at a secluded hideaway. At their facilities in Princeville, you are treated to a pre-flight video orientation, while hostesses offer munchies, juice, and wine.

Other companies flying out of Lihue Airport with good reputations and competitive prices are: **Mehehune Helicopters,** 3222 Kuhio Hwy. Lihue, HI 96766 tel. 245-7705, discounts offered; **Island Helicopters,** Box 3101, Lihue, tel. 245-8588, owned and piloted by Curt Lofstedt, who also hires Rudy Dela Cruz, a local instructor with the Air National Guard; **South Seas Helicopters,** tel. 245-7781, 15% discount; **Kenai Helicopters,** with flights from Lihue and the Sheraton Kauai at Poipu, tel. 245-8591; and **Will Squyre Helicopters,** tel. 245-8881, a one-man operation with personalized service from a man who loves his work.

Wailua River Cruises

You too can be one of the many floating up the Wailua River on a large canopied motorized barge. The Fern Grotto, where the boat docks, is a natural amphitheater festooned with hanging ferns, one of the most touristed spots in Hawaii. The oldest company is **Smith's Motor Boat Service,** tel. 822-4111, in operation since 1947. The extended Smith Family still operates the business and members serve in every capacity. On the way up river you're entertained with music and legend, and once at the Fern Grotto, where many couples have been married, a small but well-done medley of island songs is performed. Daily cruises depart every half hour from Wailua Marina from 9:00 a.m. till 4:00 p.m. Adults $7, children $4. *Luau* cruises are held every Tues. and Thurs. evening at 6:15 to 9:00 p.m., adults $20, children $12. The food and entertainment are enjoyable and relaxing, but not extra special. **Waialeale Boat Tours,** tel. 822-4908, is the only competition. They're at the marina also, and have a smaller operation with just about the same rates.

Zodiacs, Kayaks, And Canoes

The exact opposite experience from the tame Wailua River trip is an adventurous ride down the Na Pali Coast in a motorized rubber raft, a double-hulled canoe on Hanalei Bay, or a specially built kayak along the coast and up small little-visited rivers.

A **Zodiac** is a very tough motorized rubber raft. It looks like a big, fat, unwieldy inner-tube that bends itself and undulates with the waves like a floating waterbed. These seaworthy craft, powered by twin Mercury 280s and originally designed in France, have 5 separate air chambers for unsinkable safety. They'll take you for a thrilling ride down the Na Pali Coast, stopping along the way to whisk you into caves and caverns. Once at Kalalau Valley, you can swim and snorkel before the return ride; round trip including the stop takes about 5 hours. If you wish, you can stay overnight and be picked up the next day, or hike in or out and ride only one way; this service is $50 OW, $95 RT. They also take ice chests and equipment. You roll with the wind and sea going down the coast and head into it coming back. The wind generally picks up in the afternoon, so for a more comfortable ride, book the morning cruise. All are popular so make reservations. Rates vary with the service, but the ultimate once-in-a-lifetime ride is around $100. Shorter trips vary from $35-65. Bring bathing suit, snorkel gear (rental available), lunch, drinks (cooler provided), camera with plastic bag for protection, sneakers for exploring, and a windbreaker for the return ride. Summer weather permits excursions almost every day, but winter's swells are turbulent and these experienced seamen won't go if it's too rough. Take their word for it! Oldest and best known of the 2 Zodiac com-

The Na Pali Zodiac will whisk you along this rugged coast, dipping into sea caves along the way.

panies is **Na Pali Zodiac,** Box 456, Hanalei, HI 96714, tel. 826-9371. It's owned and operated by "Captain Zodiac," Clancy Greff and his wife Pam. They provide you with all the information you need, and directions to their special take-off spot. They now operate a Maui/Lanai expedition, too. **Na Pali Coast Boat Charter,** Box 71, Hanalei, HI 96714, tel. 826-6044, is owned and operated by Capt. Tom Hegarty. He also knows Na Pali and gives you a great ride. Their cruises are cheaper and provide complimentary snorkel gear, beverages, and light snacks. Daily departures 8:30 a.m. and 2:30 p.m. Make reservations.

For an exceptional, fun-filled experience try a double-hulled canoe sail on Hanalei Bay with **Ancient Hawaiian Adventures,** at the Hanalei Canoe Club, tel. 826-6088. This is the only traditional, double-hulled sailing canoe operating in Hawaii. Your captain, John Koon, who built the boat, and Carlos Andrade, a native Kauaian waterman who's very knowledgeable about the area, take you on a fascinating excursion. You can swim, snorkel (gear provided), then catch the waves of Hanalei. All this for only $25, with the sunset sail only $15. This is a winner, and these 2 men are tops. Don't miss it! Another safe, fun-filled trip is provided by **Kauai Canoe Expeditions,** tel. 245-5122, at the Kauai Canoe Club near Menehune Fish Pond in Nawiliwili, tel. 245-5122. They take you canoeing up the Huleia River, and along the fishpond into a wildfowl refuge. **Kauai River Expeditions,** operated by Bob and Gary Crane from the Westin Kauai, tel. 826-9608, is a little different. They instruct you in the use of *royak,* a combination canoe and kayak that isn't nearly as tippy or tough to manage. Once you master it, they lead you up little-explored waterways on the Kalihi Wai River. Their 3-hour expeditions, complete with a boxed lunch, is a reasonable $26. **Island Adventures** offers a half-day adventure that includes snorkeling, a ride in a double-hulled canoe and/or windsurfing, and a *royak* trip. Their package is a very affordable $39. Contact Island Adventure at Box 3370, Lihue, HI 96766, tel. 245-9662. All of the above are good family-style fun.

ACCOMMODATIONS

Kauai is very lucky when it comes to places to stay, a combination of happenstance and planning. Kauai was not a major Hawaiian destination until the early '70s. By that time, all concerned had wised up to the fact that what you *didn't do* was build endless miles of high-rise hotels and condos that blotted out the sun and ruined the view of the coast. Besides that, a very strong grass-roots movement here insisted on tastefully done low-rise structures that blend into and complement the surrounding natural setting. This concept mandates "destination resorts," the kind of hotels and condos that lure visitors because of superb architecture, artistic appointments, and luxurious grounds. There is room for growth on Kauai, but the message is clear: Kauai is the most beautiful island of them all and the preservation of this delicate beauty benefits everyone. The good luck doesn't stop there. Kauai leads the other islands in offering the best quality rooms for the price.

Hotels And Condos

Approximately 75 properties have a total of 6,000 available rooms, of which 35% are condominium units. Almost all the available rooms on Kauai are split between 4 major destinations: Poipu Beach, Lihue, Wailua/Kapaa, and Princeville/Hanalei. Except for Kokee Lodge overlooking Waimea Canyon, little is available west of Poipu. Specialized and inexpensive accommodations are offered inland from Poipu at Kahili Mountain Park, but these very basic cottages are just a step up from what you'd find at a Boy Scout camp. Long stretches along the coast between the major centers have no lodgings whatsoever. The north shore past Hanalei has one resort, a few condos, and some scattered guest homes, but you won't find any large concentration of rooms.

Poipu, the best general-purpose beach and most popular destination on Kauai, has 4 major hotels and a host of condos. Prices are reasonable, and most of the condos offer long-term discounts. For years **Lihue** had only one luxury hotel, the Kauai Surf (now the Westin Kauai), which overlooks Nawiliwili Bay. Recently another deluxe resort, the Kauai Hilton, has opened its doors. In and around Lihue are also most of Kauai's inexpensive hotels, guest cottages, and one mandatory "flea bag." Small hotels, and especially the guest cottages, are family run. They're moderately priced, very clean, and more than adequate. However, you have to drive to the beach.

Wailua/Kapaa on the east coast has good beaches and a concentration of accommodations, mostly hotels. Here you'll find the Kauai Resort Hotel, which traditionally has brought in most of the big-name entertainment to Kauai. The Coco Palms in Wailua is a classic. Used many times as a Hollywood movie set, that's the vibe. It's terrific nonetheless, and has a very loyal clientele, the sure sign of a quality hotel. The Coconut Plantation is just east of Coco Palms and has an extensive shopping center, 4 large hotels (another Sheraton), and a concentration of condos. Almost all sit right on the beach and offer superior rooms at a standard price.

Princeville is a planned "destination resort." It boasts a commuter airport, shopping center, 1,000 condo units, and the Sheraton Princeville Hotel, a showcase resort overlooking Hanalei Bay. From here to Haena are few accommodations until you get to the Hanalei Colony Resort, literally "the last resort."

Bed And Breakfast

B&Bs are available on Kauai, in fact, a major booking agency, **Bed and Breakfast Hawaii,** is located in Kapaa along the Kuhio Highway. It was on Kauai, while hiking the Na Pali Coast, that Evie Warner and Al Davis were inspired to open the agency. To receive a copy of their directory listing homes on Kauai and all other islands, write Bed and Breakfast Hawaii, Box 449, Kapaa, Hi 96746, tel. 822-7771, on Oahu tel. 536-8421. Evie and Al are the best in the business.

CAMPING

Kauai is very hospitable to campers and hikers. More than a dozen state and county parks offer camping, and a network of trails leads into the interior. Different types of camping suit everyone: you can drive right up to your spot at a convenient beach park, or hike for a day through incredible country to build your campfire in total seclusion. A profusion of "secret beaches" have unofficial camping, and the State Division of Forestry even maintains free campsites along its many trails. Kokee State Park provides affordable self-contained cabins, and RV camping (rental available) is permitted at many of the parks. Hikers can take the Kalalau Trail, perhaps the premiere hiking experience in Hawaii, or go topside to Kokee and follow numerous paths to breathtaking views over the bared-teeth cliffs of Na Pali. Hunting trails follow many of the streams into the interior, or if you don't mind mud and rain, you can pluck your way across the Alakai Swamp. Wherever you go, enjoy but don't destroy, and leave it as beautiful as you found it.

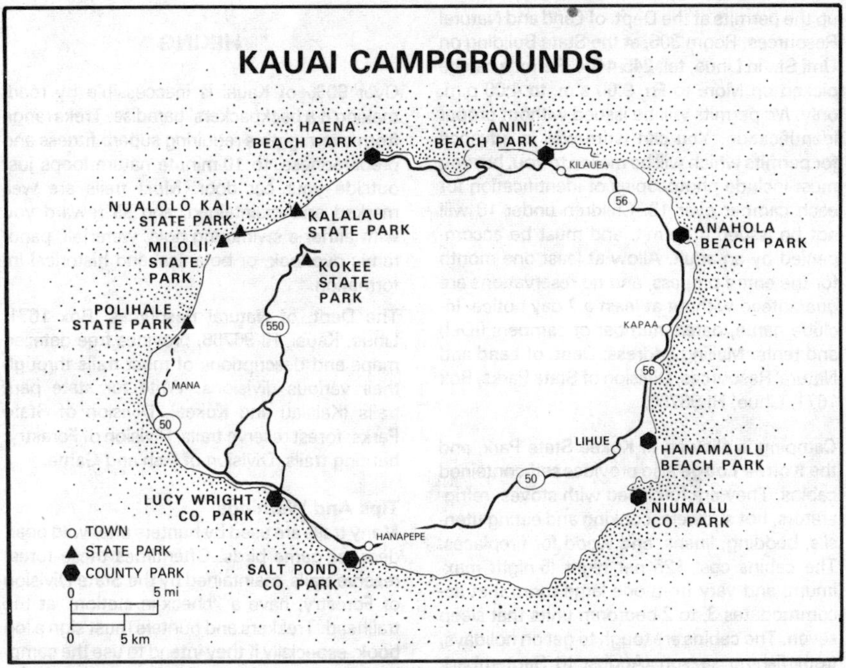

General Information

All the campgrounds, except for the state parks along Na Pali, provide grills, pavilions (some with electricity), picnic tables, cold-water showers, and drinking water. No one can camp "under the stars"; all must have a tent. RV camping is allowed only at certain county and state parks around the island. Campsites are unattended, so be careful with your gear, especially radios, stereos, and cameras. Your tent and sleeping bag are generally OK. Always be prepared for wind and rain, especially along the north shore.

County Parks

A permit is required to camp at all county-maintained parks. The cost is $3 per person p/d, children under 18 free if accompanied by parent or guardian. Permits are issued for 4 nights, with one renewal for a total of 8 nights per campground. The issuing office is at the War Memorial Convention Center Complex off Hardy St. in Lihue. Go behind the Convention Center to a row of 7 small gray buildings and look for the Dept. of Public Works/Parks and Recreation Division at 4193 Hardy St., Lihue, HI 96766, tel. 245-8821. They're open from 9:00 a.m. to 4:30 p.m., Mon. to Friday. At all other times, including weekends and holidays, you can pick up your permit just around the corner at the Kauai Police Dept., Lihue Branch, 3060 Umi St., tel. 245-9711. Write in advance for information and reservations to the Dept. of Public Works, but do not send money! They'll send you an application, and after returning it with the appropriate information, your request will be logged in their reservations book. You'll also receive brochures and maps of the campgrounds. You must pick up and pay for your permit when you arrive at the Parks and Recreation office, or at the police station.

State Parks

A permit is required to camp at all state parks. Permits are free, and camping is restricted to 5 nights within a 30-day period per campground, with a 2- and 3-night maximum at some of the stopovers along the Kalalau Trail. You can pick up the permits at the Dept. of Land and Natural Resources, Room 306, at the State Building on Umi St., in Lihue, tel. 245-4444. Permits can be picked up Mon. to Fri. 9:00 a.m. to 4:00 p.m. only. *No* permits will be issued without proper identification. You can write well in advance for permits which will be mailed to you, but you must include photocopies of identification for each camper over 18. Children under 18 will not be issued a permit, and must be accompanied by an adult. Allow at least one month for the entire process, and no reservations are guaranteed without at least a 7-day notice. Include name, dates, number of campers (IDs!) and tents. Mailing address: Dept. of Land and Natural Resources, Division of State Parks, Box 1671, Lihue, HI 96766.

Camping is allowed at Kokee State Park, and the **Kokee Lodge** also provides self-contained cabins. They are furnished with stoves, refrigerators, hot showers, cooking and eating utensils, bedding, linens, and wood for fireplaces. The cabins cost $25 per night (5-night maximum) and vary from one large room that accommodates 3, to 2-bedroom units that sleep seven. The cabins are tough to get on holidays, trout fishing season (August to September), and during the wild plum harvest in June and July. For reservations write Kokee Lodge, Box 819, Waimea, Kauai, HI 96796, tel. 335-6061. Please include a SASE, number of people, and dates requested. A $25 deposit is required for confirmation of reservation. Write well in advance. Check-in is at noon, check out 10:00 a.m. The lodge is open Mon. to Thurs. 8:30 a.m. to 5:30 p.m., until 10:00 p.m. Fri. and Saturday.

RVs And Rental Equipment

At **Beach Boy Campers,** Box 3208, Lihue, HI 96766, tel. 245-9211, rates vary according to unit, but mini-cabovers for 2 are about $40 per night, with totally self-contained motorhomes at $55-60 per night. Also, a full range of backpacking and camping equipment is rented by **Hanalei Camping and Backpacking,** Ching Young Village, Box 1245, Hanalei, HI 96714, tel. 826-6664. They rent everything from rain gear to tents and sleeping bags daily, overnight, or weekly, and also provide backpack storage.

HIKING

Over 90% of Kauai is inaccessible by road, making it a backpackers' paradise. Treks range from overnighters requiring superb fitness and preparedness, to 10-minute nature loops just outside your car door. Most trails are well marked and maintained, and all reward you with either a swimming hole, waterfall, panoramic overlook, or botanical and historical information.

The Dept. of Natural Resources, Box 1671, Lihue, Kauai, HI 96766, provides free detailed maps and descriptions of most trails through their various divisions. Write for state park trails (Kalalau and Kokee), Division of State Parks; forest reserve trails, Division of Forestry; hunting trails, Division of Fish and Game.

Tips And Warnings

Many trails are used by hunters after wild boar, deer, or game birds. Oftentimes these forest reserve trails, maintained by the State Division of Forestry, have a "check-in station" at the trailhead. Trekkers and hunters must sign a log book, especially if they intend to use the camping areas along the trails. The comments by previous hikers are worth reading for up-to-the-minute information on trail conditions. Many roads leading to the trailheads are marked for 4WD only. Heed the warning, especially during rainy weather when roads are very slick and swollen streams can swallow your rental car. Also remember: going in may be fine, but a sudden storm can leave you stranded. Maps of the trails are usually *only* available in Lihue from the various agencies, not at trailheads. Water is unsafe to drink along the trails, and should only be drunk from catchment barrels, or boiled. Expect wind and rain at anytime along the coast or in the interior. Exercise normal caution when entering the ocean, and never swim during periods of high surf. Make sure to check in at stations and leave your itinerary. A few minutes of filling in forms could save your life.

Kokee Trails

Maps of Kokee Trails are supposed to be available at the ranger's booth in the park. Unfortunately, only one ranger handles all of Kokee, and he never has the luxury of remaining in his box. Chances are you can't get the maps there. Never attempt to climb up or down a *pali*. You *can not* go from Kokee down to the valleys of Na Pali. Every now and again someone attempts it and is killed. The *pali* are impossibly steep and brittle. Your hand-holds and footholds will break from under you. Don't be foolish. If you're going into the Alakai Swamp, remember that all the birds and flora you encounter are unique, most fighting extinction. Also, your clothes will become permanently stained with swamp mud, a wonderful memento of your trip. Before attempting any of the trails, please sign in at Park HQ.

A number of trails lead off **Kokee Drive**, most are marked and well maintained. The first you encounter is **Cliff Trail**, only a few hundred yards long and leading to a spectacular overview of the canyon. Look for feral goats on the canyon ledges. **Canyon Trail** continues off Cliff Trail for 1 ½ miles. It hugs the north rim of the canyon and offers many views. **Halemanu-Kokee Trail** begins off a secondary road, from the old ranger station just before the military installation. It travels just over a mile and is a self-guiding nature trail. With plenty of native plants and trees, it's a favorite area for indigenous birds.

One of the best trails off Kokee Road is the **Kukui Trail**. The well-marked trailhead is between mile markers 8 and 9. The trail starts

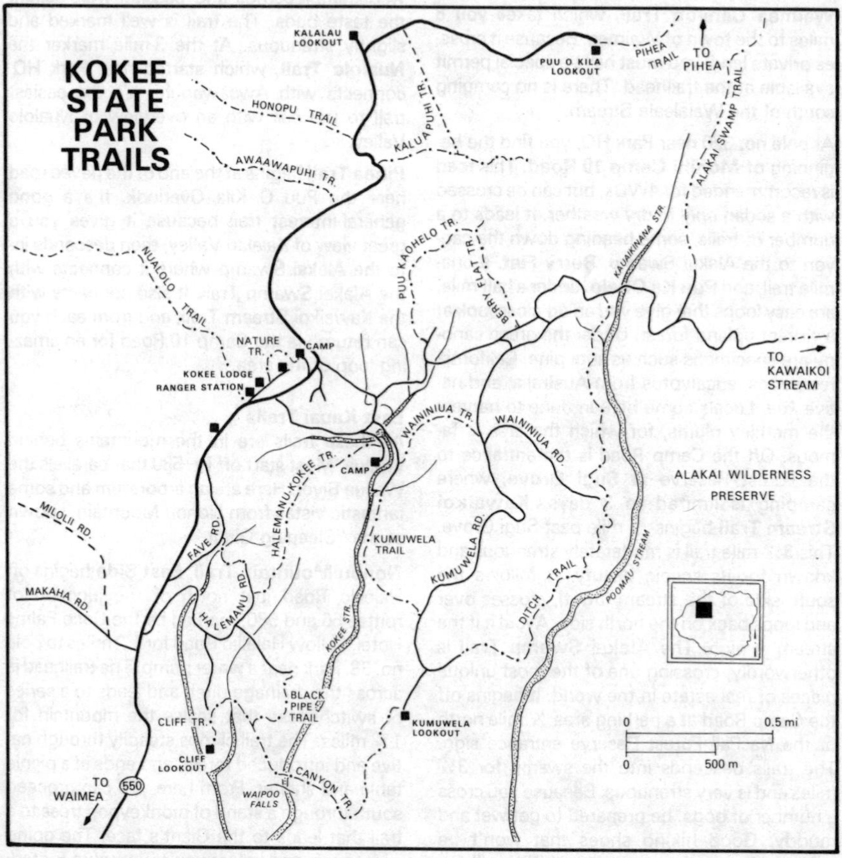

with the **Iliau Nature Loop,** an easy, 10-minute, self-guided trail. Notice the pygmy palms among the many varieties of plants and flowers. The sign-in hut for the Kukui Trail is at the end of the Nature Loop. Read some of the comments before heading down. The trail descends 2,000 feet through a series of switchbacks in 2½ miles. It ends on the floor of the canyon at Wiliwili Camp site. From here the hale and hardy can head up the Waimea River for ½ mile to the beginning of the **Koaie Canyon Trail.** This 3-mile trail takes you along the south side of Koaie Canyon, along which are plenty of pools and campsites. This trail *should not* be attempted during rainy weather because of flash flooding. You can also branch south from the Kukui Trail and link up with the **Waimea Canyon Trail,** which takes you 8 miles to the town of Waimea. Because it crosses private land, you must have a special permit available at the trailhead. There is no camping south of the Waialeale Stream.

At pole no. 320 near Park HQ, you find the beginning of **Mohihi Camp 10 Road.** This road is recommended for 4WDs, but can be crossed with a sedan *only* in dry weather. It leads to a number of trails, some heading down the canyon to the Alakai Swamp. **Berry Flat,** a one-mile trail, and **Puu Ka Ohelo,** under a half mile, are easy loops that give you an up-close look at a vibrant upland forest. Under the green canopy are specimens such as sugi pine, California redwoods, eucalyptus from Australia, and native *koa.* Locals come here in June to harvest the methley plums, for which the area is famous. Off the Camp Road is the entrance to the Forest Reserve at **Sugi Grove,** where camping is limited to 3 days. **Kawaikoi Stream Trail** begins ¾ mile past Sugi Grove. This 3½-mile trail is moderately strenuous and known for its scenic beauty. It follows the south side of the stream (trout), crosses over and loops back on the north side. Avoid it if the stream is high. The **Alakai Swamp Trail** is otherwordly, crossing one of the most unique pieces of real estate in the world. It begins off the Camp Road at a parking area ¼ mile north of the Na Pali Forest Reserve entrance sign. The trails descends into the swamp for 3½ miles and is very strenuous. Because you cross a number of bogs, be prepared to get wet and muddy. Good hiking shoes that won't be sucked off your feet are a must! The trail follows abandoned telephone poles from WW II, and then a series of brown and white (keep an eye out) trail markers. Along the way, if you smell anise, that's the *mokihana* berry, fashioned with *maile* for wedding *lei.* The trail ends at Kilohana, an expansive vista of Wainiha and Hanalei Valley.

One of the most rewarding trails for the time and effort is **Awaawapuhi Trail.** The trailhead is after Park HQ, just past pole no. 152 at the crest of the hill. It's 3 miles long and takes you out onto a thin finger of *pali,* with the sea and an emerald valley 2,500 feet below. The sun dapples the upland forest that still bears the scars of Hurricane Iwa. Everywhere flowers and fiddlehead ferns delight the eyes, while wild thimbleberries and passion fruit delight the taste buds. The trail is well marked and slightly strenuous. At the 3-mile marker the **Nualolo Trail,** which started near Park HQ, connects with Awaawapuhi. It's the easiest trail to the *pali* with an overview of Nualolo Valley.

Pihea Trail begins at the end of the paved road near the Puu O Kila Overlook. It's a good general-interest trail because it gives you a great view of Kalalau Valley, then descends into the Alakai Swamp where it connects with the Alakai Swamp Trail. It also connects with the Kawaikoi Stream Trail, and from each you can return via the Camp 10 Road for an amazing loop of the area.

East Kauai Trails

All these trails are in the mountains behind Wailua. Most start off Rt. 580 that parallels the Wailua River. Here are an arboretum and some fantastic vistas from Nonou Mountain, known as the "Sleeping Giant."

Nonou Mountain Trail, East Side begins off Haleilio Road just north of the junction of routes 56 and 580, marked by the Coco Palms Hotel. Follow Haleilio Road for 1.2 miles to pole no. 38. Park near a water pump. The trailhead is across the drainage ditch and leads to a series of switchbacks that scales the mountain for 1¾ miles. The trail climbs steadily through native and introduced forest, and ends at a picnic table and shelter. From here you can proceed south through a stand of monkeypod trees to a trail that leads to the Giant's face. The going gets tough, and unless you're very sure-footed, stop before the narrow ridge with a 500-foot drop you must cross. The views are extraordinary and you'll have them to yourself.

Nonou Mountain Trail, West Side is found after turning onto Rt. 580 at the Coco Palms. Follow it a few miles to Rt. 581, turn right for just over a mile and park at pole no. 11. Follow the right of way until it joins the trail. This will lead you through a forest of introduced trees planted in the 1930s. The West Trail joins the East Trail at the 1½-mile marker and proceeds to the picnic table and shelter. This trail is slightly shorter and not as arduous. For both, bring water as there is none on the way.

Follow Rt. 580 until you come to the U. of H. Experimental Station. Keep going until the pavement ends and then follow the dirt road for almost a mile. A developed picnic and freshwater swimming area is at Keahua Stream. On the left is a trailhead for **Keahua Arboretum.** The moderate trail is ½ mile through a forest reserve maintained by the Division of Forestry, where marked posts identify the many varieties of plants and trees. The **Kuilau Trail** begins about 200 yards before the entrance to the arboretum, on the right. This trail climbs the ridge for 2½ miles, en route passing a picnic area and shelter. Here are some magnificent views of the mountains; continue to pass through a gorgeous area complete with waterfalls. After you cross a footbridge and climb the ridge, you come to another picnic area. A few minutes down the trail from here and you join the **Moalepe Trail,** which starts off Olohena Road 1½ miles down Rt. 581 after it branches off Route 580. Follow Olohena Road to the end and then take a dirt road for 1½ miles to the turnaround. The last part can be extremely rutted and slick in rainy weather. This trail is a popular horseback-riding trail. It gains the heights and offers some excellent panoramas before joining the Kuilau Trail.

The Kalalau Trail

This is *the* trail on Kauai. The Kalalau is a destination in and of itself, and those who have walked these phenomenal 11 miles never forget it. (See p. 668 for alternative rides in or out of Kalalau.) The trail leads down the Na Pali Coast, as close as you can get to the Hawaiian paradise of old. Getting there is simple: follow Rt. 56 until it ends and then hike. But before you start be aware that the entire area falls under the jurisdiction of the Division of State Parks, and a ranger at Kalalau Valley oversees matters. The trailhead has a box where you sign in, and maps are available. Day-use permits are required beyond Hanakapiai (2 miles in); camping permits are required to stay overnight at Hanakapiai, Hanakoa, and Kalalau. You can camp for 5 nights, but no 2 consecutive nights are allowed either at Hanakapiai and Hanakoa. You need a good waterproof tent, sleeping bag, repellent (fierce mosquitos), first-aid kit, biodegradable soap, food, and toiletries. There are many streams along the trail, but the water can be biologically contaminated and cause horrible stomach distress. Boil it or use purification tablets. Little firewood is available, and you can't cut trees, so take a stove. The trail is well marked by countless centuries of use, so you won't get lost, but it's rutted, root strewn, and muddy. Mileage posts are all along the way. Streams become torrents during rains, but recede quickly. Just wait! Mountain climbing is dangerous because of the crumbly soil, and the swimming along the coast is unpredictable with many rips. Summers, when the wave action returns sand to the beach, is usually fine, but stay out from September to April. At Hanakapiai a grim reminder reads, "This life-saving equipment was donated by the family and friends of Dr. Rulf Fahleson, a strong swimmer, who drowned at Hanakapiai in March 1979." Pay heed! In keeping with the tradition of "Garden of Eden," many people hike the trail *au natural,* and more than just knees have been scraped on the way. Also, private parts unaccustomed to sunburn can make you wish you hadn't. Don't litter; carry out what you carried in.

Many people not intending to go the full route go as far as Hanakapiai. This is a fairly strenuous 2-mile hike, the first mile uphill, the last down, ending at the beach. Camp at spots on either side of the stream along the beach, or in shelters 5 and 10 minutes farther along. You can also camp in the caves at the beach, but only during summer at low tide. Follow the stream to the **Hanakapiai Loop Trail**. This takes you past some magnificent mango trees and crumbling stone-walled enclosures of ancient *taro* patches. After ½ mile the trail turns back to the beach, or you can continue to **Ha-**

nakapiai Falls. Follow the trail to the ¾-mile marker where it crosses the stream. If the stream is tough to cross, turn back. The trail up ahead is narrow and dangerous during periods of high water. If it's low, keep going—the 300-foot falls and surrounding amphitheater are magnificent. You can swim in the pools away from the falls, but not directly under: rocks and trees can come over at any time.

Hanakapiai to **Hanakoa** is 4 miles of serious hiking (2-3 hours) as the trail steadily climbs, not returning to sea level until reaching Kalalau Beach 9 miles away. Switchbacks help with the ascent, and although heavily traversed, the trail can be very bad in spots. Before arriving at Hanakoa, you must go through **Hoolulu** and **Waiahuakua** valleys. Both are lush with native and introduced plants heavily cultivated by native Hawaiians. Still growing but gone wild are coffee, guava, *ti,* and mountain apples. Shortly, Hanakoa comes into view. It's wide and many terraces are still intact from when it was a major food-growing area. You can use the old walls as windbreaks, or you can spend the night in the roofed shelter. Nearby is a Forestry Service trail-crew shack that's open to hikers if the crew isn't using it. Hanakoa is rainy, but it's intermittent and the sun always follows. The swimming is fine in the many stream pools. A ⅓-mile hike just after the 6-mile marker takes you past more terraces good for camping before coming to **Hanakoa Falls.** The terraces are wonderful, but the trail is subject to being washed away, and is treacherous with many steep sections.

Hanakoa to **Kalalau Beach** is under 5 miles and takes about 3 tough hours. Start early in the morning because it's hot, and although you're only traveling 5 miles, it gets noticeably drier as you approach Kalalau. The views along the way are ample reward. The power and spirit of the incomparable *aina* becomes predominant. Around the 7-mile marker you enter lands that until quite recently were part of the Makaweli cattle ranch. The vegetation turns from lush foliage to lantana and sisal, a sign of the aridness of the land. After crossing Pohakuao Valley, you climb the *pali* and on the other side is Kalalau. The lovely valley, 2 miles wide and 3 deep, beckons with its glimmering freshwater pools. It's a beauty among beauties, and was cultivated until the 1920s. Many terraces and house sites remain. Plenty of guava, mango, and Java plum can be found. You can camp on the beach, hot in the daytime. Many people opt for the trees fronting the beach, or in the caves west of the waterfall. You can't camp along the stream, at its mouth, or in the valley. The waterfall has a freshwater pool, where feral goats come in the morning and evening to water.

A *heiau* is atop the little hillock on the west side of the stream. Follow the trail here up-valley for 2 miles to **Big Pool.** Along the way you pass "Smoke Rock," where *pakalolo* growers at one time came to smoke and "talk story." A long-time resident from the days of "flower power" is Bobo. The nymph of Kalalau, she's been there forever. Stories about her are legendary. She raised 2 daughters in Kalalau, often floating down the treacherous coast with her babes on an inner tube or surfboard. Once, she paddled 8 miles in to shore on a surfboard when a yacht she was crewing on foundered. Bobo then walked the Kalalau Trail for help at night, hiked back and floated back out to the yacht. She's as brown as a bean and as free as they come. When she goes to town, she often forgets to take her clothes, and the way she "parties" is even wilder than the way she lives. Bobo probably knows more about Kalalau than anyone alive. You'll know her if you see her! Big Pool is really two pools connected by a natural water slide. Riding it is great for the spirit, but tough on your butt. Enjoy! See map p. 731.

SHOPPING

Kauai has plenty of shopping of all varieties: food stores in every town, boutiques and specialty stores here and there. Health food stores and farmers' markets, 2 extensive shopping malls, even a flea market. The following is the overview; specific stores, with their hours and descriptions, are covered in the travel sections.

Shopping Centers

The **Kukui Grove Center,** tel. 245-7748, is one of the 2 largest malls on Kauai. It's a few minutes west of Lihue along the Kaumuali'i Hwy. (Rt. 50). Lihue has 2 small shopping centers off Rice Street: **Lihue Shopping Center,** tel. 245-3731, with a small clutch of shops, a restaurant or two, a bank, and a supermarket. The

the entrance to The Market Place

Rice Shopping Center, tel. 245-2033, featuring boutiques, variety stores, and a computer store. Just down the road in Nawiliwili is **Menehune Village** across from the Kauai Surf Hotel, featuring souvenirs and alohawear.

The Market Place, tel. 822-3641, Kauai's other extensive shopping mall, is along the Kuhio Hwy. (Rt. 56) in Waipouli between Wailua and Kapaa. The Market Place is even larger than Kukui Grove and offers over 60 shops in a very attractive open-air setting. The **Kapaa Shopping Center**, tel. 822-4971, a mile or 2 farther along Rt. 56, is a small mall. Heading north from Kapaa you come to the **Princeville Center**, tel. 826-6561. This center provides the main shopping for the residents of this planned community. Farther north in Hanalei, find limited shopping at the **Ching Young Shopping Center**, tel. 826-7222.

Specialty Shops And Boutiques

You can't go wrong in the following shops. The **Kauai Museum Shop** on Rice St. in Lihue; **Kapaia Stitchery**, tel. 245-2281, has beautiful handmade quilts, embroideries, and 100% cotton alohawear. **Rehabilitation Unlimited of Kauai**, tel. 822-4975, in Wailua, is where some of Kauai's special citizens create well-crafted items at very reasonable prices. **Remember Kauai**, tel. 822-0161, 4-734 Kuhio Hwy. between Wailua and Kapaa, sells a very wide selection of coral and shell necklaces featuring famous Niihau shell work, bracelets, earrings, buckles, and chains. The **Awapuhi Emporium**, tel. 822-3581, 788 Kuhio Hwy. in Kapaa, is a discovery shop with some terrific old Hawaiiana such as *tapa* cloth, feather *lei*, and *koa* bowls (a good, inexpensive *lei* shop next door sells *lei* and flower jewelry). A co-op of 4 goldsmiths displays their craftsmanship at **Goldsmith Gallery**, tel. 822-9287, in the Waipouli Plaza at 4-901 Kuhio Hwy., Kapaa. The **Only Show In Town**, tel. 822-1442, downtown Kapaa, is a "must stop" curio and antique store where Paul Wroblewski has amassed the largest and most bizarre collection of priceless antiques, bric-a-brac, and junk in all of Hawaii. Dozens of first-rate island artists display their artwork at the **North Shore Gallery**, tel. 828-1684 along Rt. 56 just before Kilauea. Excellent bargains are found at **Spouting Horn Flea Market** near Poipu Beach where buskers set up stalls selling cut-rate merchandise.

Bookstores

The best and most extensive bookstore on Kauai is **Rainbow Books**, tel. 245-3703 at the Kukui Grove Shopping Center in Lihue. Here you'll find a wide selection of Hawaiiana, bestsellers, and guidebooks. **Waldenbooks**, tel. 245-7162, is also in the Kukui Grove. **Paperback Hut**, tel. 822-3216, is a loaded bookshelf of a store located at the Market Place Shopping Center.

Food Stores And Supermarkets

Groceries and picnic supplies can be purchased in almost every town on the island. Many of the markets in the smaller towns also sell a limited selection of dry goods and gifts. The general rule is the smaller the store, the bigger the price. The largest and cheapest stores with the biggest selections are in Lihue and Kapaa. **Big Save Value Centers** sell groceries, produce, and liquors in Hanalei,

Kapaa, Lihue, Koloa, Kalaheo, Eleele, Waimea, and Kekaha. Most stores open weekdays 8:30 a.m. to 9:00 p.m., weekends until 6:00 p.m. **Foodland** operates a large store at the Lihue Shopping Center, at the Waipouli Center, and the Princeville Shopping Center. The Princeville store is the largest and best-stocked market on the north shore. All open weekdays from 8:30 a.m. to 8:00 p.m. with earlier closings on weekends. **Star Supermarket** is a well-stocked store in Kukui Grove Mall.

Smaller markets around the island include: **Yoneji's Market** at 4253 Rice St., Lihue, an overflowing market and dry-goods store where you can soak up the local color; the **Hanamaulu Store** in Hanamaulu, a decent selection; heading north from Kapaa are **Anahola Market** in Anahola, **Grandma's Market** in Kilauea, **Kong Lung** general store in Kilauea which also sells gourmet items and souvenirs, and the "last chance" limited selection **Wainiha Store** in Wainiha; south of Lihue look for **Poipu Market** across the street from Poipu Beach where the selections and prices aren't too bad, the **Hanapepe Food Store** in Hanapepe, **Ishimara's** in Waimea and **Kuramotos's** in Kekaha.

Health Food, Fresh Fish, And Farmers' Markets

If not the best, at least the most down-to-earth health food store on Kauai is **Ambrose's Kapuna Natural Foods,** tel. 822-7112, along the Kuhio Hwy. across from the Foodland Supermarket in Kapaa. Ambrose is a character worth visiting just for the fun of it. He's well stocked with yogurt, juices, nuts, grains, and island fruits. If he's not in the store just give a holler around the back. He's there! **General Nutrition Center,** tel. 245-6657, in the Kukui Grove Center, is a full-service health food store, and home of the **Kauai Juice Club** where Ernie Merriweather handmakes Kauai's freshest and purest juices. Expensive but worth it, also available at stores around Kauai. **Hale O Health,** tel. 245-9053, in the Rice Center in Lihue, is a limited health food store featuring tonics and vitamins. **Hanapepe Food Store,** tel. 335-3225, in Hanapepe, has a reasonable selection of herbs, juices, teas, remedies, and snacks. **Kauai Gardens,** tel. 822-7746, in Kapaa, is a better-than-average store with a wide selection of vitamins, produce, fruits, nuts, and grains. They also feature a restaurant that caters to vegetarians. On the north shore try **Healthy Jones,** tel. 826-6990, Hanalei, where you'll find bulk foods, produce, and a juice and snack bar.

A **farmers' market** is along Rt. 56 in Kapaa—a large selection of island produce at very good prices. Visit a weekly farmers' market in Lihue at the Wilcox School on Hardy Street for a cultural treat. Every Fri. afternoon local gardeners bring their produce to town. The stories and local color are more delicious than the fruit.

An excellent fish store is **Kuhio Fish Market** in Kapaa, open Mon. through Sat. 9:00 a.m. to 8:30 p.m. and Sun. till 6:00 p.m. They have fresh fish daily and often offer specials. Fish can also be purchased at **J & R Seafoods** at 4361 Rice St. in Lihue and at **Nishimura's Market** in Hanapepe.

SPORTS

Kauai is an exciting island for all types of sports enthusiasts, with golfing, tennis, hunting, fresh- and saltwater fishing, and all manner of water sports. You can rent horses, or simply relax on a cruise. The following should start the fun rolling.

Rental Equipment

Snorkel equipment costs $5-8, with many of the hotels providing it gratis to guests. A complete array of equipment can be rented at the following: **South Shore Activities,** tel. 742-6873, in Poipu near the Sheraton; **Pacific Ocean Adventures,** tel. 822-3455, in the Sheraton and Coconut Plantation, Kapaa; **Pedal n' Paddle,** tel. 826-9069, in Hanalei on the north shore.

Fishing Boats, Whale Watches, And Cruises

Some excellent fishing grounds are off Kauai, especially around Niihau, and a few charter boats are for hire. Most are berthed at Nawiliwili Harbor, with some at Hanalei Bay. Some private yachts offer charters, but these come and go with the tides. **Whale-watching cruises** run from January through April. An ex-

Most of Kauai's charter boats are berthed at Nawiliwili Harbor.

cellent charter service is **Lady Ann Charters,** tel. 245-8538, at Nawiliwili. They run 2 boats, the *Lady Ann,* a 32-footer, and the *Island Voyager.* Fishing excursions are halfday $70, three-quarter day $90, fullday $110. Halfday exclusive $300, fullday $500, 6-people maximum on all runs. *Lady Ann* also motors down the Na Pali Coast for $70, swinging into caves for diving and snorkeling. Whale watches (2 hours) are $35. They are also associated with *Tanya,* a 44-foot catamaran for those who wish to see Kauai under sail. **Ocean Ventures,** tel. 245-3011, sails a 25-footer for fishing charters, sunset cruises, or whale watching. **Alana Lynn Too,** tel. 337-1112, has a 33-footer for charter or cruise. **Lucky Lady,** tel. 245-5171, with Capt. John Teixeira, runs a 33-foot twin-diesel craft off Niihau for the big ones, whale watching in season, or bottom fishing "Hawaiian style." **Open Sea Charters,** tel. 822-3661 or 822-4662, operates a 36-footer from the small boat harbor at Port Allen in Eleele. **Captain Sundown,** tel. 826-7395, takes you fishing, sailing, whale watching, or cruising on a catamaran out of Hanalei Bay. A basic 2-hour sail is $25.

Freshwater Fishing And Hunting

Kauai has trout and bass. Rainbow trout were introduced in 1920 and thrive in 13 miles of fishable streams, ditches, and reservoirs in the Kokee Public Fishing Area. The season begins on the first Sat. of August and goes for 16 days. After that you can only fish on Sat., Sun., and holidays in August and September. Large- and smallmouth bass are also popular game fish on Kauai. Introduced in 1908, they're hooked in reservoirs and in the Wailua River and its feeder streams. Bass are in season all year. **Bass Guides of Kauai,** tel. 245-8914, goes freshwater game fishing for $75 halfday $125 fullday. Tourist licenses cost $3.75 and are good for 30 days.

Kauai is the only island with black-tailed deer, hunted mostly in October, and only by public lottery. Because they thrive on island fruits, their meat is sweeter and less gamey than Mainland deer. Feral pigs and goats are also favorite game animals. Birds include pheasant, francolins, quail, and dove. For complete information on hunting and fishing, write Dept. of Land and Natural Resources, Div. of Forestry and Wildlife, Box 1671, Lihue, HI 96766, tel. 245-4444.

Snorkeling And Scuba

The best beaches for snorkeling and scuba are along the northeast coast from Anahola to Kee. The reefs off Poipu, roughed up by Hurricane Iwa, are making a remarkable comeback. **Get Wet Kauai,** tel. 822-4884, runs a fullday snorkel/scuba complete with box lunch for $55, or snorkel only for $25. Hotel pick-up available. **Sea Sage,** tel. 822-3841, gives snorkeling and scuba lessons by Nikolas and Howard, who are very familiar with Kauaian waters, plus spear fishing and underwater photography. **Aquatics Kauai,** tel. 822-9422, are professional divers renting snorkel and scuba equipment, and giving instruction and certification courses. Basic diver course, with individualized instruction $225, halfday snorkel $17.50, among others. **Fathom Five Divers,** tel. 742-6991, Koloa, takes you snorkeling for $20, introductory scuba lesson $55. Their basic certification course is $275. **Kauai Divers,** tel. 742-1580, also in Koloa, goes snorkeling for $20, diving for $50, with a 5-day course at $250. The **Waiohai Hotel** offers an introductory scuba lesson in the hotel pool.

Horseback Riding

Most trail rides go into the interior or along the north shore. You can hire mounts from **Highgates Ranch,** tel. 822-3182, in Wailua Homesteads. **Pooku Stables,** tel. 826-6777, along Rt. 56, Princeville, lead rides into Hanalei Valley for $13, along the beach for $26, and picnicking for $40.

Golf And Tennis

The 5 golf courses on Kauai offer varied and exciting golfing. Kukuiolono Golf Course, a mountain-top course in Kalaheo, is never crowded and worth visiting just to see the gardens: Wailua Golf Course is a public course with reasonable green fees, considered excellent by visitors and residents. Princeville boasts 27 magnificent holes sculpted around Hanalei Bay. The Kauai Surf Hotel Golf Course has been a favorite for years, and guests get a special price. Kiahuna Golf Village is the island's newest course, conveniently located in Poipu.

The following is a list of private and public tennis courts. Most hotel tennis courts are open to

KAUAI'S GOLF COURSES

Course	Par	Yards	Fees Weekday	Fees Weekend	Cart
Kauai Surf Golf & Tennis Club 3500 Rice Street, Lihue, HI 96766 tel. 245-3631	72	6392	$17		$8.00
Wailua Municipal Golf Course P.O. Box 1017, Kapaa, HI 96746 tel. 245-8092	72	6631	$10.00	$11.00	$11.50
Kukuiolono Plantation Golf ★ Course P.O. Box 987, Lihue, HI 96766 tel. 332-9151	36	3173	$5.00		$5.00
Kiahuna Plantation Golf Course Route 1, Box 37, Koloa, HI 96756 tel. 742-9595	70	5669	$30.00		Incl.
Princeville Makai Golf Course Ocean Course ★ P.O. Box 3040, Lihue, HI 96722 tel.826-9666	36	3051	$38.00		$20.00
Lake Course ★ (Princeville Makai Golf Course)	36	3171	$38.00		$20
Woods Course ★ (Princeville Makai Golf Course)	36	3113	$38.00		$20.00

N.B. ★ = *9 hole course*

TENNIS COURTS OF KAUAI

COUNTY COURTS

Under jurisdiction of the Dept. of Parks & Recreation,
P.O. Box 111, Lihue, Kauai, HI 96766. Tel. 245-4751
Courts listed are in Lihue and near the Wailua and Poipu areas.
There are additional locations around the island.

Location	Name of Court/Location	No. of Courts	Lighted
Hanapepe	Next to stadium	2	Yes
Kekaha	Next to park	2	Yes
Kalahea	Kalawai Park	2	Yes
Kapaa	New Park	2	Yes
Koloa	Next to fire station	2	Yes
Lihue	Next to convention hall	2	Yes
Wailua	Wailua Park	4	Yes
Waimea	Next to High School	4	Yes
HOTEL & PRIVATE COURTS THAT ARE OPEN TO THE PUBLIC			
Hanalei	Hanalei Bay Resort	11	Yes
Hanalei	Princeville at Hanalei (fee)	6	No
Kalapaki Beach	Westin Kauai (fee)	10	No
Kapaa	Holiday Inn Kauai Beach (fee)	3	No
Poipu	Poipu Kai Resort (fee for non-guests)	4	No
Poipu Beach	Kiahuna Beach & Tennis Resort (fee)	10	Yes
Poipu Beach	Waiohai & Poipu Beach Hotel (fee)	6	Yes
Wailua Beach	Coco Palms Hotel (fee)	9	Yes

non-guests, usually for a fee. Some such as the **Poipu Kai Resort, Waiohai Hotel,** and **Princeville Condominiums** have fine courts, but charge even guests for their use.

INFORMATION AND SERVICES

Emergency: police, fire, and ambulance tel. 911.

Hospitals include: Wilcox Memorial, 3420 Kuhio Hwy., Lihue, tel. 245-1100; Kauai Veterans, in Waimea at tel. 338-9431; Samuel Mahelona Hospital, in Kapaa at 822-4961.

Physicians at: Kauai Medical Group, 3420 B Kuhio Hwy., tel. 245-1500; a fine pediatrician with 4 young children of his own is Dr. Terry Carolan, at 4491 Rice St., Lihue, tel. 245-8566.

Pharmacies: Kapaa Pharmacy, tel. 822-9818; Long's Drugs, Kukui Grove, tel. 245-7771; Westside Pharmacy, Hanapepe, tel. 335-5342.

Weather

For a recorded message 24 hours, tel. 245-6001.

Information

An information kiosk is operated by the HVB at

Lihue Airport. The main HVB office is at 3016 Umi St., Lihue, tel. 245-3971.

Reading Material

Free tourist literature, such as ***This Week Kauai,*** and ***Kauai Beach Press,*** is available at all hotels and most restaurants around the island. They contain money-saving coupons and up-to-the-minute information on local events. They come out every Monday. ***Kauai Drive Guide*** is available from the car rental agencies and contains tips, coupons, and good maps.

There are 2 island newspapers, ***The Garden Island,*** published 4 times weekly, and the ***Kauai Times,*** appearing once a week.

The central **library** is at 4344 Hardy St., Lihue, tel. 245-3617. Most of the larger towns have their own branch. Check with the main library for times and services. For bookstores, see p. 677.

The central **post office** is at 4441 Rice St., Lihue, tel. 245-4994. Main branches are located at Kapaa, tel. 822-5421, and Waimea, tel. 338-9973.

Laundromats are found at: Waipouli Wash and Dry, Waipouli Town Center, tel. 822-3223; Lihue Washerette, 4444 Rice Street.

Island facts: Kauai's nickname is "The Garden Isle," and is the oldest of the main Hawaiian islands. Its *lei* is made from the *mokihana,* a small native citrus fruit, and its color is purple.

bird of paradise

LIHUE

The twin stacks of the **Lihue Sugar Company** let you know where you are...in a plantation town on one of the world's most gorgeous islands. Lihue ("Open To Chill") began growing cane in the 1840s, and its fields are still among Hawaii's most productive. The town has correspondingly flourished, and boasts all the modern conveniences, complete with chrome and glass shopping centers, libraries, museums, and a hospital. But the feeling is still that of a sugar town. The county seat, Lihue, has 4,000 residents and 2 traffic lights. It isn't the geographical center of the island, Mt. Waialeale has that distinction, but it is halfway along the coastal road that encircles the island, making it a perfect jumping-off point to explore Kauai. It has the island's largest concentration of restaurants, the most varied shopping, a major resort, and right-priced accommodations. If you're going to find any night life at all, except for the lounges at the big resorts, it'll be here. But don't expect much. Good beaches are within a 5-minute drive, and you can be out of town and exploring long before your shave ice begins to melt.

KAUAI MUSEUM

If you really want to enrich your Kauai experience, this is the first place to visit. Spending an hour or two here infuses you with a wealth of information regarding Kauai's social and cultural history. The 2-building complex is at 4428 Rice St. in downtown Lihue, tel. 245-6931, open Mon. to Fri. 9:30 a.m. to 4:30 p.m., admission $3, under 18 free. The main building, dedicated to Albert Spencer Wilcox, son of pioneer missionaries at Hanalei, was dedicated in 1924. It has a Greco-Roman facade, and was the public library until 1970. Its 2 floors house the main gallery, dedicated to ethnic heritage and island art exhibits that are changed on a regular basis. As you enter, the **Museum Shop** is to the right: books, Hawaiiana prints, and a fine selection of detailed U.S. Geological Survey maps of the entire island. Some inexpensive but tasteful purchases include baskets, wooden bowls, and selections of *tapa* (made in Fiji). Native craftspeople are studying Fijian techniques and hope to recreate this lost art. The main room contains an extensive and fascinating exhibit of calabashes, *koa* furniture, quilts, and feather *lei* work. One large calabash belonged to Princess Ruth who gave it to a local child. Its finish, hand rubbed with the original *kukui* nut oil, still shows a fine luster. The rear of the main floor is dedicated to the **Senda Gallery,** with its collection of vintage photos shot by W.J. Senda, a Japanese immigrant from Matsue who arrived in 1906. These black and whites are classics, opening a window onto old Kauai.

Kauai's fascinating natural and cultural history begins to unfold when you walk through the courtyard into the **William Hyde Rice Building.** Notice the large black iron pot used to cook sugarcane. The exhibits are self-explanatory, chronicling Kauai's development over the centuries. The Natural History Tunnel contains windows showing the zones of cultivation on Kauai, along with its beaches and native forests. Following is an extensive collection of Kauai shells, old photos, and displays of classic *muu muu.* The central first floor area has a model of a Hawaiian village with an extensive collection of weapons, and some fine examples of adzes used to hollow conoes; a model of HMS *Resolution* floats at anchor off Waimea. An excerpt from the ship's log records Capt. Cook's thoughts on the day that he discovered Hawaii for the rest of the world.

As you ascend the stairs to the secono floor

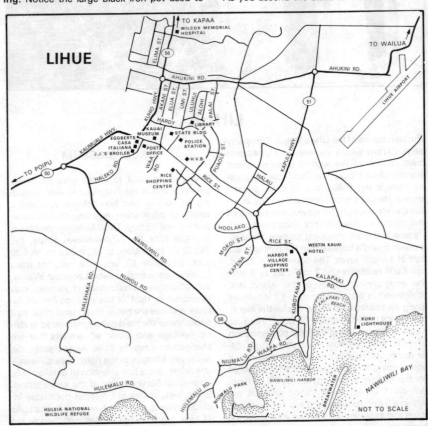

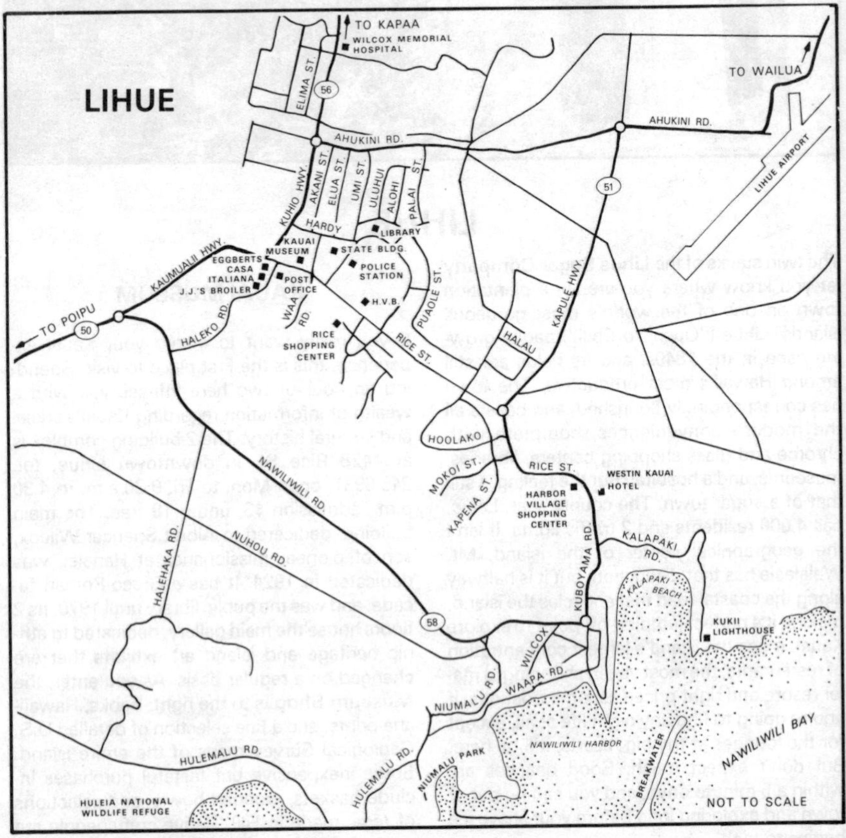

time moves on. Missionaries stare from old photos, their countenances the epitome of piety and zeal. Just looking at them makes you want to repent! Most old photos record the plantation era. Be sure to see the **Spalding Shell Collection,** gathered by Colonel Spalding, an Ohio Civil War veteran who came to Kauai and married the daughter of Capt. James Makee, owner of the Makee Sugar Company. Besides shells from around the world are examples of magnificent *koa* furniture, table settings, children's toys, dolls, and photos of Niihau, about all that the outside world ever sees.

Follow the ramp to the ground floor and notice the resplendent examples of feather capes on the wall. On the main floor, behind a curtain, pushing the button begins a 6-minute film of Kauai taken from a helicopter. This pictorial is a treat for the eyes; soothing Hawaiian chanting in the background sets the mood. Next, the final treat. A thorough, well-done exhibit teaches you about the legendary *menehune* and *mu*— their kings, work habits, beliefs, and why they disappeared from Kauai.

Kauai Museum

GROVE FARM HOMESTEAD

Grove Farm is a plantation started in 1864 by George Wilcox, the son of missionaries who preached at Hanalei. George earned his degree in engineering in Honolulu and returned to Kauai to work for the original owner of the surrounding acreage. The first owner saw no future in the parched land and sold 500 acres to Wilcox for $1,000. Through a system of aqueducts, Wilcox brought water down from the mountains and began one of the most profitable sugar plantations in Hawaii. The homestead was a working plantation until the mid-1930s when George died and operations were moved elsewhere. The remaining family continued to occupy the dwellings and care for the extensive grounds. In 1971, Mabel Wilcox, a neice of the founder, dedicated the family estate to posterity. Well advanced in years but spirited in mind, she created a non-profit organization to preserve Grove Farm Homestead as a museum. We can now reap the benefits by visiting this self-sufficient farm every Mon., Wed., and Thursday. Well-informed guides (such as Charlotte Duval who came to Kauai as a young bride in 1926 and became well acquainted with the Wilcoxes and plantation life) take you on a 2-hour tour of the grounds and various buildings. Admission is $3 adults, $1 children under 12. Tours are by *reservation only!* Call 245-3202 at least 24 hours in advance to make arrangements. The homestead is located off Nawiliwili Road; precise directions are given when you call. Drop-in visitors will be turned away. Groups are limited to 20 people to give full attention to detail and minimize wear and tear on the buildings. Tours begin at 10:00 a.m. and 1:15 p.m. Be prompt please!

Living History

The first thing you notice when entering Grove Farm is the rumble of your tires crossing a narrow-gauge railroad track. The tracks meant sugar, and sugar meant prosperity and change for old Hawaii. The minute that you set foot upon Grove Farm Homestead you can feel this spirit permeating the place. This is no "glass-case" museum. It's a real place with living history, where people experienced the drama of changing Hawaii.

George Wilcox never married. In love once, he was jilted, and that ended that. In 1870 his brother Sam came to live on the homestead. In 1874 Sam married Emma, daughter of missionaries from the Big Island. She had been educated in Dearborn, Michigan, and had recently returned to Hawaii. The couple had 6 children, 3 boys and 3 girls. Two of the boys survived to manhood and managed the farm, but both met with tragic deaths. Of the girls only Henrietta, the oldest, married. The two other sisters, Miss Elsie and Miss Mabel were single all their lives Miss Elsie became very involved in politics, while Mabel went to Johns Hopkins University and earned a degree as a registered nurse. Her parents wouldn't let her leave home until she was 25 years old, when they felt she could cope with the big, bad world. She returned in 1911 and opened a public health office on the grounds.

The Tour

The buildings, furnishings, orchards, and surrounding lands are part of the oldest intact sugar plantation in Hawaii. You meet your guide at the plantation office, which has a safe dating from 1880, when it was customary to pay for everything in cash. On top sits a cannonball that's been there as long as anyone could remember. Perhaps it was placed there by Mr. Pervis, the original bookkeeper. As time went on the safe's combination, which is in letters not numbers, was lost. Recently a safe cracker was hired to open it, and inside was the combination written in a big, bold hand... BALL. You cross the grounds to a simple dwelling and enter the home of the Moriwakis. Mrs. Moriwaki came to Grove Farm as a "picture bride," though she was born in Hawaii and taken back to Japan as a child. She's found in the kitchen near the big house where she's been the cook for almost 50 years. She returns on tour days to explain her role in running the homestead. Her home is meticulously clean and humble, a symbol of Japanese plantation workers' lives on Hawaii. Notice the food safe. There were no ice boxes for most workers in Hawaii and they kept vermin away by placing sardine cans filled with water or kerosene in-

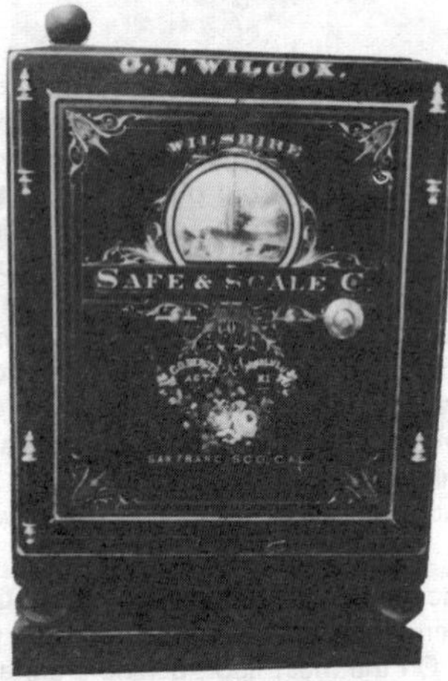

side. A small print of Mt. Fuji and a *geisha* doll in a glass case are simple yet meaningful touches. Together they are a memory of the past and the hope of a brighter future that all plantation workers sought for their children.

As you walk around, notice how lush and fruitful the grounds are—all sorts of trees and plants. At one time the workers were encouraged to have their own gardens. A highlight is a small lattice-work building half submerged in the ground. This is the **fernery,** at one time a status symbol of the good life in Hawaii. There was great competition among the ladies of Victorian Hawaii who were proud of their ferns, and you became an instant friend if you presented a new and unique variety while on a social visit. Behind the Wilcox Home is a small schoolhouse built in 1900. It later became Mabel Wilcox's public health office; now a depository for all sorts of artifacts and memorabilia, it's called the **Trunk Room**. A photo of Mabel shows her in a Red Cross uniform. By all accounts, Mabel was a serious but not humorless woman. Her dry and subtle wit, given away only by her sparkling eyes, is obvious in the photo.

Wilcox Home

Shoes are removed before entering this grand mansion. The Wilcoxes were pleasant people given to quiet philanthropy, but their roots as New England missionaries made them frugal.

The women always wore homemade cotton dresses and in the words of a tour guide, "nothing was ever thrown away by this family." The home is comfortable and smacks of culture, class, and money—in the old-fashioned way. As you enter, you'll be struck with the feeling of space. The archways were fashioned so they get smaller as you look through the house. This shrinking perspective gives an illusion of great length. The walls and staircase are of rich, brown *koa.* Much of the furniture was bought second hand from families returning to the Mainland. This was done not out of a sense of frugality, but simply because it often was the only good furniture available. A piano here belonged to Emma Wilcox; the profusion of artwork includes many original pieces, often done by visitors to the homestead. One long-time visitor, a sickly girl from the East Coast, did some amazing embroidery. Her finest piece on display took 10 years to complete. Portraits of the family include a good one of George Wilcox. Notice a Japanese chest that Miss Mabel won in a drawing while she was in Japan with her sister Elsie and Uncle George in 1907. Notice too the extensive collection of Hawaiiana that the family accumulated over the decades. In the separate kitchen wing, is a stove that is still functional after 100 years of hard use. A porch, so obviously homey during rainstorms, looks out onto a tea house. Everything in the home is of fine quality and in good taste. It's a dwelling of peace and tranquility.

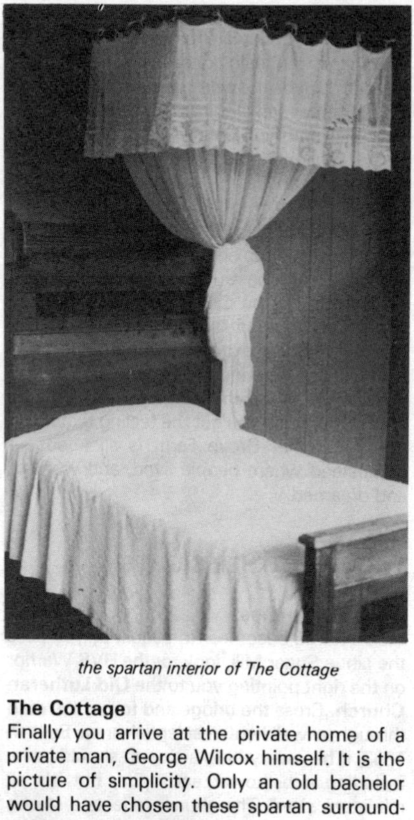

the spartan interior of The Cottage

The Cottage

Finally you arrive at the private home of a private man, George Wilcox himself. It is the picture of simplicity. Only an old bachelor would have chosen these spartan surround-

the rich interior of the Wilcox Home

ings. An inveterate cigar smoker along with his brother Sam, both were forbidden by the ladies to smoke in the main house. Here, he did as he pleased. Maybe the women were right, George died of throat cancer...in 1933 at the age of 94! The first room you enter is his office. George was a small man and a gentleman. Whenever he left the house, he donned a hat. You'll notice a collection of his favorites hanging on pegs in the hall way. One of his few comforts was a redwood tub he'd soak in for hours. This self-made millionaire kept his soap in an old sardine tin, but he did use fine embroidered towels. His bedroom is simple, bright, and airy. The mattress is of extremely comfortable horse hair. Outside his window is a profusion of fruit trees, many of which George planted himself. As the tour ends you get the feeling that these trees are what Grove Farm is all about—a homestead where people lived, and worked, and dreamed.

OTHER SIGHTS

Lihue's Churches

When Rt. 56 becomes Rt. 50 just as you pass the Lihue Sugar Mill, look for the HVB Warrior on the right pointing you to the **Old Lutheran Church.** Cross the bridge and follow the road through a well-kept residential area. Built in 1883, it has everything a church should have, including a belltower and spire, but it's all miniature sized. The church reflects a strong German influence that dominated Lihue and its plantation until WW I. The turn-of-the-century pastor was Hans Isenberg, brother of the plantation founder and husband to Dora Rice from the old *kamaaina* family. Pastor Isenberg was responsible for procuring the Lihue Horse Trough, an ornate marble work imported from Italy in 1909, now on display at the Haleko Shop's botanical gardens in downtown Lihue. The outside of the church is basic "New England," but inside, the ornate altar is reminiscent of baroque Germany. On a nearby hill is **Lihue Union Church** that was mostly attended by the common people. Its Hawaiian cemetery is filled with simple tombstones, and plumeria trees eternally produce blossoms for the departed ones. If you follow the main road past the Lutheran church it dead ends at an enormous cane field. This sea of green runs to the mountains and lets you know just how much sugar still dominates the way of life in Lihue and on Kauai in general.

Around Town

Across the street from Lihue Shopping Center, a stone's throw from the twin stacks of the sugar mill, are 4 solid-looking buildings known as the **Haleko Shops.** Once the homes of German plantation managers before they gave up their holdings during WW I, they're now occupied by restaurants and shops—part of the shopping center across the road. Around them is a botanical garden. Each plant carries a description of its traditional use and which ethnic group brought it to the island. (Look for the Lihue Horse Trough imported by Pastor Isenberg.) While browsing at Lihue Shopping Center, you're treated to a small Japanese garden complete with carp pond, and notice the Kauai Store, a great grandchild of the Lihue Plantation Store, that still sports its logo, a man clutching a spyglass.

Follow Umi Street off Rice to Hardy Street and turn down to the **Kauai Library.** In the entrance is a wall hanging, a batik by Jerome Wallace that is the largest painting of its type in the world.

Follow Rice Street toward Nawiliwili Harbor and it turns into Rt. 51 known as Wa'apa Road. Then come to the junction of Rt. 58 known as Nawiliwili Rd., where you turn right for the **Menehune Gardens.** The gardens are open daily 8:30 a.m. to 4:30 p.m., tel. 245-2660, adults $1.50, children under 12 $.75. The owners, who often serve as the guides, are Mr. and Mrs. Kailikea. They have a deep love and respect for the *aina* and its plants which they are more than happy to share with you. Every plant is labeled and you can go alone, but the experience is enriched by a guide, who'll describe each plant and how it was used. On the grounds is an immense banyan tree that covers more than an acre. After the tour Aunty Sarah and her husband will sing ancient Hawaiian chants for you, and for a brief glimmering moment you'll have a glimpse of old Hawaii. The peace and quiet alone is worth the admission charge.

Take Nawiliwili Road to Niumalu Road and turn left, following it to Hulemalu Road. You pass the predominantly Hawaiian settlement of Niumalu. Along Hulemalu Road is a lookout, below which is **Alakoko Pond** ("Rippling Blood"), commonly known as Menehune Fishpond. You have a sweeping view of Huleia Stream, the harbor, and the Hoary Head Mountains in the background. The 900-foot mullet-raising fishpond is said to be the handiwork of the *menehune.* Legend says that they built this pond for a royal prince and princess. They made only one demand, that no one would watch them in their labor. The indefatigable *menehune* passed the stones needed for the construction from hand to hand in a double line that stretched for 25 miles, and all in one night. The royal prince and princess could not contain their curiosity, and climbed to a nearby ridge to watch the little people. They were spotted by the *menehune,* who stopped building, leaving holes in the wall, and turned the royal pair into twin pillars of stone still seen on the mountainside overlooking the pond.

Wailua Falls

Wailua Falls

Between Hanamaulu and Lihue Rt. 583 branches from Rt. 56 and heads into the interior. As the road lifts up and away from the ocean, you realize that the rolling terrain surrounded by lofty mountain peaks is completely given over to sugarcane. To the left and right are small homes with a usual patch of tropical fruit trees. Route 583 ends at mile marker 3. Far below, Wailua Falls tumbles 80 feet over a severe *pali* into a large round pool. It's said that the *ali'i* would come here to dive from the cliff into the pool as a show of physical prowess; commoners were not considered to be infused with enough *mana* to perform this feat. Many of the trees are unwilling trellises for rampant morning glory. Pest or not, it's still beautiful as its blossoms climb the limbs. A sign at the best spot to take a photo warns, "Danger! Do not go beyond guardrail." A trail down to the falls is particularly tough and steep. If you make it down, you'll have the falls to yourself, but you'll be like a goldfish in a bowl with the tourists, perhaps jealously, peering down at you. See map p. 664.

BEACHES AND PARKS

Lihue has very convenient beaches. You can sun yourself within 10 minutes from anywhere in town, with a choice of beaches on either Nawiliwili or Hanamaulu bays. Few tourists head to Hanamaulu Bay, while Nawiliwili Bay is a classic example of "beauty and the beast." There is hardly a more beautiful harbor than Nawiliwili's, with a stream flowing into it and verdant mountains all around. However, it is a working harbor complete with rusting barges, groaning cranes, and petro-chemical tanks. Private yachts and catamarans bob at anchor with their bright colors reflecting off dappled waters, and as your eye sweeps the lovely panorama it runs into the dull gray wall of a cement works. It's one of those places that separates perspectives: some see the "beauty" while others focus on the "beast."

Kalapaki Beach

This most beautiful beach at Nawiliwili fronts the lavish Kauai Surf Hotel. Just follow Rice Street until it becomes Rt. 51 where you'll soon

The wharf at Nawiliwili Harbor is a favorite local fishing spot.

see the bay and entrance to the hotel on your left. The hotel serves as a type of giant folding screen, blocking out most of the industrial area and leaving the lovely views of the bay. Many people drive into the Westin Kauai and park either at the lot near the entrance or around back near the pool. Access to the beach is open to anyone, but you have a lot less hassle with parking and using the hotel pool and showers if you order a light breakfast or lunch at one of the restaurants. The ice cream at the hotel ice cream parlor is delicious! You can also pass the hotel, pull into the lot at the Kalapaki Beach Broiler, and enter the beach from there. The wave action is gentle at most times with long swells combing the sandy-bottomed beach. Kalapaki is one of the best swimming beaches on the island, fair for snorkeling, and a great place to try either bodysurfing or beginning with a board. Two secluded beaches in this area are generally frequented by local people. Head through the hotel grounds following the road to the golf course clubhouse. From here you'll see a lighthouse on Ninini Point. Keep the lighthouse to your left as you walk across the course to the bay. Below are 2 small crescent beaches. The right one has numerous springs that flow up into the sand. Both are good for swimming and sunbathing. You can also head for **Nawiliwili County Beach Park** by following Rt. 51 past the Kauai Surf until you see the Kaiser Cement Plant; on the left is the beach park. Here are showers, picnic tables, and a pavilion along with some shady palm trees for a picnic. This park is fine for swimming and sunning, but it's much better to walk up to your left and spend the day at Kalapaki Beach.

Niumalu County Beach Park

This county-maintained beach park (permit) is along the Huleia Stream on the west end of Nawiliwili Harbor. Many small fishing and charter boats are berthed nearby and local men use the wharf area to fish and "talk story." There is no swimming and you are surrounded by the industrial area. However, you are very close to Lihue and there are pavilions, showers, toilets, and camping both for tents and RVs. To get there take Rt. 58 past the Menehune Gardens and then left on Niumalu Road, or Mokihana Street off Rt. 51 and follow it along the harbor until you arrive at the beach park.

Ahukini Recreation Pier

As the name implies, this state park is simply a pier from which local people fish. And it's some of the best fishing around. Follow Rt. 57 to Lihue Airport. With the airport to your left keep going until the road ends at a large circular parking lot and fishing pier. The scenery is only fair, so if you're not into fishing give it a miss.

Hanamaulu County Beach Park

This is a wonderful beach, and although it is very accessible and good for swimming, very few tourists come here. There is not only a beach, but to the right is a lagoon area with pools formed by Hanamaulu Stream. Local families frequent this park, particularly loved by children as they can play Tom Sawyer on the banks of the heavily forested stream. There are picnic tables, showers, toilets, a pavilion, and camping (county permit). In Hanamaulu Village, turn *makai* off Rt. 56 onto Hanamaulu Road, take the right fork onto Hehi Road, and follow it to the beach park.

ACCOMMODATIONS

If you like simple choices, you'll appreciate Lihue; only 2 fancy resorts are here, the rest are either family-run hotel/motels or apartment hotels. Prices are also best here because Lihue isn't considered a prime resort town. But you can get *anywhere* on the island in less than an hour. Although it's the county seat, the town is quiet, especially in the evenings, so you won't have to deal with noise, or hustle and bustle.

Inexpensive Hotels, Motels, And Apartments

Motel Lani, owned and operated by Janet Naumu, offers clean, inexpensive rooms at the corner of Rice and Hardy streets. The lobby is actually an extension of Janet's home, where she and her children often watch TV. There are 10 Mexican pink units, 3 of which offer cooking facilities, and although close to the road they're surprisingly quiet. All rooms have a small desk, dresser, bath, fan, refrigerator, and are cross ventilated. No TVs. Janet usually doesn't allow children under 3 years old, especially if they misbehave, but she's reasonable and will make exceptions. A small courtyard with a BBQ is available to guests. Rates (2-night minimum) are $16 s, $22 up to 3 people, $6 additional person, slightly more for only one night, rooms with cooking facilities (hard to get) $20. For reservations write: Motel Lani, Box 1836, Lihue, HI 96766, tel. 245-2965.

Head down Rice Street toward Nawiliwili; at the corner of Wilcox Road is the **Ocean View Motel.** The motel is across from Nawiliwili Beach Park, and just a stroll from Kalapaki Beach. Its owner and manager, Spike Kanja, built the place. From this pink, 3-story building you can scan the harbor, and you'll have an unobstructed view of the cement works! Spike's proud of his carp pond, about all there is to be proud of, although the basic rooms are clean. All rooms have refrigerators and start at (1st and 2nd floors) $17 s, $18 d, (3rd floor) $21 s, $22 d, $6 additional person. For reservations write: Ocean View Motel, 3445 Wilcox Rd., Nawiliwili, HI 96766, tel. 245-6345.

The **Hale Niumalu Motel** is off the main drag near the boat harbor in Niumalu. The 2 buildings were at one time overflow accommodations for a big hotel, but are now independently owned. The rooms are large, well kept but plain. The best feature is a screened *lanai* with a profusion of hanging plants. Prices are terrific at $15 s/d, $5 additional person. They offer weekly and monthly rates too. Across from Niumalu Park at the corner of Niumalu and Hulemalu roads, tel. 245-3316.

The **Hale Lihue** is a quiet, clean, and basic motel (another one painted pink, there must have been a terrific sale!) on Kalena Street, a little side road off Rice. It was owned and operated for many years by a lovely Japanese couple, Mr. and Mrs. Morishige, whose hospitality made it an institution. They retired in 1984 and sold the hotel to a "man from Los Angeles," whose name Mrs. Morishige couldn't remember. She'd been assured, however, that he would keep "everything the same," news that past guests will be happy to hear. Rates are $14.56 s, $16.64 d, for a basic room with ceiling fan, $18.72 s, $23.92 d, for rooms with a/c and a kitchenette on the 1st floor. For reservations write: Hale Lihue Motel, 2931 Kalena St., Lihue, HI 96766, tel. 245-3151.

The **Hale Pumehana Motel** is across the street from the Foodland in the Lihue Shopping Center, at 3083 Akahi Street. The sign welcoming you to the "house of warmth" reads "Hale Pumehana Motel-Liquor." Don't be put off. The place is a touch run-down, but OK, and the sign refers to a small liquor store/deli on the premises. The yellow and brown building has drab little rooms for $18 s or d, $4 extra person. No phones, no TVs, but ceiling fans. Reservations write: Hale Pumehana Box 1828, Lihue, HI 96766, tel. 245-2106.

The **Ahana Motel Apartments** is the *best* deal for the money. At 3115 Akahi St., a half block from the Hale Pumehana Motel on the left, it's in town, but on a side street away from traffic and noise. A window for checking in is on the front porch. The sign says, "if no one answers the doorbell, come and look for me in the yard." Who you're looking for is Rosy, the owner. The sleeping rooms are adequate with fans and b&w TVs, going for $16 s/d, but the real deals are the kitchenettes and apartments. The kitchenettes are large rooms with a full-size stove, sink, and fridge; the apartments give you a bedroom and a kitchen. Both are $22.88 s/d, $4 extra person, and a 2-bedroom apartment is $38. The Ahana is popular and a good sign is that it always gets return guests. For reservations write: Ahana Motel Apartments, Box 892, Lihue, HI 96766, tel. 245-2206.

The **Tip Top Motel,** 3173 Akahi Street, is a combination lounge, restaurant, and bakery popular with local folks. It's a functional 3-story building made of cinder block, and you guessed it...painted pink! The lobby/cafe/bakery is open 6:45 a.m. to 9:00 p.m. The rooms are antiseptic in every way, a plus as your feet stay cool on the bare linoleum floor. Just to add that mixed-society touch, instead of a *Gideon's Bible* in the dresser drawer, you get *The Teachings of Buddha* placed by the Sudaka Society of Honolulu. Rates are $18 s, $24 d, add $4 extra person up to 4. For reservations: Tip Top Motel, Box 1231, Lihue, HI 96766, tel. 245-2333.

If you want to get out of town you can find basic accommodations at the **Elima Hale Hotel,** near the Wilcox Memorial Hospital, on Elima Street between Hanamaulu and Lihue. They offer rooms (some private baths) with TVs, refrigerators, and use of a kitchen. Rates are $16 s, $24 d, with monthly and weekly discounts. For information write: Elima Hale Hotel, 3360 Elima St., Lihue, HI 96766, tel. 245-9950.

Kauai Hilton and Beach Villas

Deluxe Accommodations

The **Kauai Hilton and Beach Villas** is one of Kauai's newest hotel/condos. On 25 landscaped acres overlooking Hanamaulu Beach, it offers 350 hotel rooms, all with mini-refrigerators, and 150 villas with full kitchens. The hotel pool is in 3 sections connected by tiny waterfalls and cascades. Dining amenities include late-night room service, cocktail lounge, **Gilligan's** for dining and dancing, and the **Jacaranda Room** main dining hall. There are 4 tennis courts, saunas, jacuzzis, and watersport equipment. Rates are hotel $110 standard, $125 superior; one-bedroom villa $120, 2-bedroom villa $185 (same rate for up to 4 people), $275-375 suite (off-season discounts on all). For information write: Kauai Hilton, 4331 Kauai Beach Dr., Lihue, HI 96766, tel. 800-445-8667, on Kauai 245-1955.

The **Kauai Surf Hotel** billed itself as "Hawaii's most complete resort," and although others may be newer and fancier, this claim wasn't too far off. And especially now, since it's been purchased by Westin Hotels, refurbished and redubbed the **Westin Kauai**, it should easily live up to this claim once again when it reopens in September, 1987. The core structure is doubly unique: built before the new ordinances took effect, its 11 floors make it the tallest hotel on the island; and it was a prototype for the concept of "destination resort" that provides all the activities a guest might require. There are 500 acres of beautifully landscaped grounds, 5 restaurants, shops galore, 8 championship tennis courts, 2 Jack Nicklaus golf courses, one of Hawaii's loveliest pools, helicopter sightseeing service, horse-drawn carriage rides, and all insulated only minutes from town on Kalapaki, Lihue's finest beach. There were two wings, the newer bright and cheery with *lanai* decorated with hanging plants. However, the older section was a bit drab, and its rooms, though well maintained, were showing their 26 years. All will be face-lifted by Westin and a brand-new luxury 12-story tower, called the Royal Beach Club, will be added, where a room will cost $350. Standard room prices will begin at $180 to $285, with luxury suites to $1,800. All rooms have complimentary coffee-making machines, and most have small refrigerators. The American Plan is also offered at the hotel. For information contact: Westin Resorts, tel. 800-228-3000.

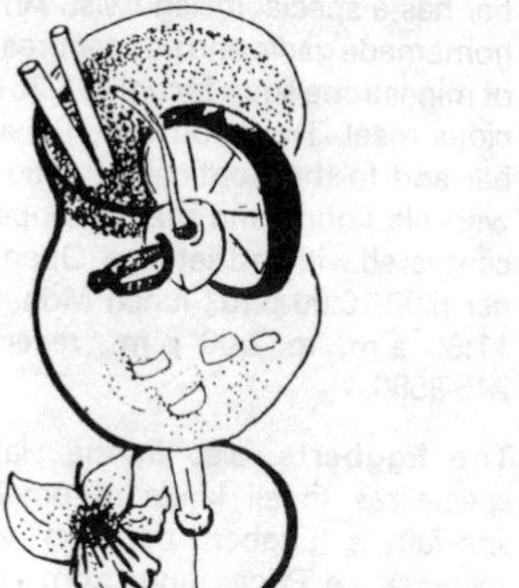

FOOD

Dining in Lihue is a treat. The menu of restaurants in and around town is the most extensive on the island. You can have savory snacks at *saimin* shops or at bargain-priced eateries frequented by local people. You'll find pizza parlors and fast-food chains. Stepping up in class, there are Continental, Italian, and Japanese restaurants, while moderately priced establishments serve up hearty dishes of Mexican, Chinese, and good old American fare. Finally, fancier dining is found in some of the big hotels. The dining in Lihue is good to your palate and to your budget.

Inexpensive

If you ask anyone in Lihue where you can "chow down" for cheap, they'll send you to **Ma's.** It's already an institution. Their building on Halenani Street, behind B.J. Furniture on Rice Street, is a bit run-down but clean. A few tourists find it, but mostly it's local working people. Lunches are good, but the super deals are breakfast and Hawaiian food. The coffee, which is free with breakfast, arrives hot in a large pot about as soon as your seat hits the chair. The menu is posted above the kitchen. You can start the day with a 2-egg special for $1.55, or with "the works" which includes either potatoes, or fried noodles with bacon or sausage and toast for $3. From the Hawaiian menu try *kalua* pork with 2 eggs and rice for $3.10, *poi* and *lomi* salmon for $2.65, Kauai sausage for $3.50, or a pound of *kalua* pork for $5.50. Don't bother the guy that orders this last item! Follow Rice Street until you see Kress Street, make a right and follow it to the corner where you'll find Ma's at 4277 Halenani St., open daily 5:00 a.m. to 1:30 p.m., Sat. and Sun. 12:30 a.m. to 10:00 a.m., tel. 245-3142.

Hamura Saimin is just around the corner from Ma's. People flock to this old counter all day long for giant steaming bowls of *saimin.* But the real show is around 2:00 a.m. when all the bars and discos let loose their revelers. There is no decor, just good food. Your first time, try the Saimin Special which gives you noodles, slivers of meat and fish, vegetables, *won ton,* and eggs, all floating in a golden broth. The small menu is variations on the same theme with nothing over $3. Open daily at 2956 Kress St., tel. 245-3271.

Judy's Saimin is newer than Hamura's, but if it keeps serving good food, it'll be an institution too. Besides *saimin,* Judy offers lunches and dinners mostly with a Japanese twist at reasonable prices. This little shop is on the lower street level of the Lihue Shopping Center, tel. 245-2612.

Genting not only has an odd name for a Chinese restaurant, it has an odd location—it's in the grease bay of an old gas station that's made from lava rock and has a false grass-shack roof fashioned from cement. You walk through a doorway and overhead is a wildly painted chicken and dragon. Inside the set up is cafeteria style, with choices before you in stainless steel hot plates. Doesn't sound appetizing, but the food is surprisingly good and the staff is friendly. A two-item dish with fried rice is only $2.95. Take-out orders too. In the Garden Island Plaza, Rt. 56 (just before entering town), open daily except Sun., 10:00 a.m. to 9:00 p.m., tel. 245-6520.

Tip Top Restaurant/Bakery is the downstairs of the Tip Top Motel. A local favorite with unpretentious but clean surroundings, the food is wholesome but uninspired, just like the service. Breakfast is the best deal for around $2, and the macadamia nut pancakes are delish! Plate lunches are under $4 and dinners under $6. You can choose anything from pork chops to teriyaki chicken, and you'll get soup, salad, rice, and coffee. The *bento* (box lunches), either American style or Oriental are a good deal at $3. Visit the bakery section and let your eyes tell your stomach what to do. The *malasadas* is fresh daily. On Akahi Street between Rice and Rt. 57, open daily 6:45 a.m. to 9:00 p.m., tel. 245-2333.

Dani's is another favorite with local people. It's been around a while and has a good reputation for giving you a hearty meal for a reasonable price. The food is American-Hawaiian-Japanese. Most full meals range from $2.50 to $4 and you have selections like *lomi* salmon, tripe stew, teri beef and chicken, and fried fish. Dani's is at 4201 Rice St. toward Nawiliwili near the fire department. Open Mon. to Sat. 5:00 a.m. to 2:00 p.m., Sun. 5:00 a.m. to 11:00 p.m., tel. 245-4991.

Finally there's the **Pine Tree Inn,** an informal co-op type of beach hangout used by local people, with visitors welcome. A gaily painted pavilion at the far end of the jetty in Nawiliwili Beach Park, you bring your own beer and soft drinks and put them in the cooler to share. At night, cook-outs happen—bring some food for the grill. Mostly the vibe is mellow, but test the waters first. Don't consume more than you bring and you'll have an authentic island good time.

Moderate—In Lihue

The majority of restaurants in and around Lihue charge as little as $5, and average $10. Most of these restaurants advertise specials and discounts in the free tourist literature.

J.J.'s Broiler is one of those can't-go-wrong places. Ask anyone in Lihue where you can get a good steak and they'll send you to this refurbished German plantation house in the Haleko Shops, across from the Lihue Shopping Center. They serve fresh fish and a good salad bar, but the real specialty is Slavonic steak, slices of tenderloin in a rich garlic and wine sauce. Dinner for 2, with drink and salad bar, is around $30. You can also dine on the *lanai.* Make reservations, it's very popular! At 2971 Haleko Rd., Lihue, tel. 245-3841, it's open for lunch Mon. to Fri. 11:00 a.m. to 2:00 p.m., dinner nightly.

Casa Italian is also in the Haleko Shops, just behind easily spotted Eggberts Restaurant. Its husband-wife team, from New York, tries to make each dish special. The menu features manicotti, canelloni, and veal. The hefty salad bar has a special Italian twist. An order of the homemade garlic and pepper bread and a bowl of minestrone soup for only $1.25 makes a delicious meal. The good wine list and espresso bar add to the Continental patio atmosphere with tile floors, and marble-topped tables accentuated with red settings. Open daily for dinner 5:30-10:00 p.m., lunch Mon. through Fri., 11:30 a.m. to 2:00 p.m., reservations, tel. 245-9586.

The Eggberts, also in the Haleko Shops, specializes in all kinds of omelettes. Their specialty is "Eggberts benedict" with a special secret sauce. Prices range from a plain 2-egger for $2.50, up to a vegetarian delight for $4.95, while 3-egg omelettes are slightly more expensive but could easily make a meal for 2. Lunch and dinner feature beef, chicken, and fish from $6 to $12. The service is friendly, the coffee hot and quick, and the atmosphere bright. 4483 Rice St., daily breakfast and lunch 6:00 a.m. to 2:00 p.m., dinner 5:30-9:30 p.m., tel. 245-6325.

Kenny's is across the street at the entrance of the rotunda in Lihue Shopping Center. A definite favorite with the lunch crowd, their mouth-watering sandwiches are around $5. Dinner starts at 5:30 p.m. Entrees include seafood, steaks, and a salad bar. Open for cocktails until 1:00 a.m., closed Sun. tel. 245-6522.

Restaurant Kiibo serves authentic Japanese meals without a big price tag. Many Japanese around town come here to eat. The low stools at the counter are reminiscent of a Japanese *akachochin* or *sushiya.* Savory offerings of *udon, tempura,* teriyaki, and a variety of *teishoku* (specials) all are accompanied by a picture showing you just what you'll get. The service is quick and friendly, most offerings are only $4-5. Restaurant Kiibo is *ichiban!* Located just off Rice Street, at 2991 Umi St., open daily, lunch 11:00 a.m. to 1:30 p.m. (attracts many office workers), dinner 5:30-9:00 p.m., tel. 245-2650.

The **Barbecue Inn** has been in business for 3 decades, and if you want a testimonial, just observe the steady stream of local people, from car mechanics to doctors, heading for this restaurant. The atmosphere is "leatherette and formica," but the service is homey, friendly, and prompt. Japanese and American servings are huge. Over 30 entrees range from a chicken platter to seafood and even prime rib. The Friday teriyaki platter is a good choice. Most meals are complete with soup/salad, banana bread, vegetables, beverage, and dessert for around $6 and up. Breakfast goes for a reasonable $2, with lunch at bargain prices. The homemade pies are amazing for only $.50. Cocktails. No credit cards accepted. 2982 Kress St., open daily 7:30 a.m. to 8:45 p.m. tel. 245-2921.

La Luna Mexican Restaurant is one of those places that should be terrific. They have everything: a comfortable, quiet setting giving a south-of-the-border courtyard feeling, friendly waitresses, entertainment from jazz to Hawaiian, and a varied menu. So why aren't they? The cooking is adequate but not great. Most entrees are under $5, but you pay a lot for what you get. *Salsa* comes free, but chips are an extra $1 even if you order a full meal. La Luna does have steady customers, especially those who come to socialize at night. Many think it's *muy bueno,* but decide for yourself, *amigo.* 4261 Rice St., tel. 245-9173.

The **Club Jetty** overlooks Nawiliwili Harbor. Follow the access road at the beach park to the end, where it sits with a commanding view of the bay. It's especially picturesque on Friday evenings when the USS *Independence,* a cruise ship silhouetted by deck lights, lies at anchor. The restaurant serves an American menu with steaks, seafood, and a salad bar, but their house specialty is extensive Cantonese cuisine. Sweet-and-sour spare ribs in fresh pineapple with a side of fried rice at $5.25 is about average. *Mahi mahi* or chicken dinners cost $8.95, and luscious soups like abalone and vegetable are $4.25. The club has recently changed from a family place with local entertainment to a hot shot disco at night. Loyal customers liked the old beat better! From Wed. to Sat. you can boogie and drink imported beers until 3:00 a.m. Dinner is served daily from 5:00-9:00 p.m., tel. 245-4970. Reservations, especially for a table with a view, are needed.

The **Bull Shed** in Nawiliwili's Menehune Shopping Village has a reputation for serving the best prime rib on Kauai, and usually lives up to it. The salad bar is also praiseworthy, served in a loaded-down canoe, but it's best early on busy nights, before it's hit too hard. They serve lobster, tenderloin fillet, and teriyaki steak or chicken. Open daily for dinner from 5:30 p.m., tel. 245-4551. While in the Menehune Village also check out **Kauai Chop Suey,** a no-frills, reasonably priced Chinese restaurant. Relatively new, it already has a steady clientele. Most dishes are well prepared, under $5. Open Tues. to Sat. 11:00 a.m. to 2:00 p.m. lunch, Tues. to Sun. 4:30-9:00 p.m. dinner, take out for picnics available, tel. 245-8790. If you just want a cool drink and a place to relax try **Papa Joe's.** Although the complex is new, this little bar seems like a neighborhood watering hole with local clientele, pool table, and wooden floors.

Moderate—Around Lihue

Rosita's Mexican restaurant has recently moved from Nawiliwili to Kukui Grove Shopping Center. The new setting is upbeat and tasteful. You sit in semi-enclosed booths for privacy. The margaritas are large and tasty. Enjoy a full range of dinners including combination platters from $5.25. Their loyal clientele comes out from Lihue. Open daily for lunch from 11:30 a.m. to 3:00 p.m., dinner from 5:30-10:00 p.m., tel. 245-8561.

Beef and Pasta is along Rt. 56 in Hanamaulu. Just look for a gigantic 10-ton gear from the old sugar mill marking Old Hanamaulu Town. Inside is dark and intimate with lighting provided by stained-glass chandeliers. Entrees include beef dishes from $7, and pasta and ravioli from $6.50 with a trip to the salad bar. Take out pizza or have a slice with salad for only $1.50. Open daily except Tues. 11:30 a.m. to 2:30 p.m. lunch, 6:00-10:00 p.m. dinner, tel. 245-6832.

Next door is the **Hanamaulu Restaurant & Tea House.** They must be doing something right to have lasted in the same location for 50 years. The decor is basic but the menu, including *sushi, yakiniku,* and a variety of Japanese and Chinese dishes, is varied and priced right. Open daily except Mon. 9:00 a.m. to 1:30 p.m. for lunch, 4:30-9:30 p.m. dinner, tel. 245-2511.

Expensive

If you want both classy dining and a choice of restaurants, head for the **Westin Kauai.** Prices vary from moderate to expensive among the 11 restaurants, and each cuisine is specialized with an emphasis on American, Hawaiian, seafood, or steaks. The atmosphere and prices range from reasonable and casual at the Tempura House, where you can nibble succulent *sushi,* to formal dining with jacket required at the Palace Restaurant at the golf club. There's casual dining with a dinner show at the Boat House Supper Club, or enjoy the view with cocktail at the open air Varanda at the Boat House.

The **Kauai Hilton** offers 2 restaurants: **The Jacaranda Terrace** is known for casual breakfasts, lunches, and dinners, while the **Midori** somehow combines Japanese and French cuisine in what they call "nouvelle style." *Tofu cordon bleu* anyone? Dinner only, tel. 245-1955.

Fast Foods

Yes, the smell of the Colonel's frying chicken overpowers the flower-scented air, and the Golden Arches glimmer in the bright Kauai sun. **Pizza Hut, McDonald's,** and **Kentucky Fried Chicken** are all located along the Kuhio Highway. **Burger King** is in the Kukui Grove Shopping Mall.

ENTERTAINMENT

Lihue is not the entertainment capital of the world, but if you have the itch to step out at night, a few places can scratch it

Club Jetty Restaurant in Nawiliwili transforms from a family restaurant to a throbbing disco/live music dance bar Wed. through Saturday. The flashing lights crank up around 10:00 p.m. There's a cover, but drinks aren't too inflated.

The **Westin Kauai Hotel** has various entertainment in its lounges and restaurants. You can be entertained with a Polynesian extravaganza, listen to the tinkling and strumming of a local combo, waltz and tango in the various supper clubs, or boogie the night away in **Natasha** (dress code), the hotel's disco until 4:00 a.m.

For some quality entertainment, mainly for listening, **La Luna Mexican Restaurant** on Rice Street brings in local talent nightly. The setting is relaxing and the mood mellow. It's great for meeting people and you can even hear yourself talk!

There must be an undeclared *tortilla war* going on because the other destination for conversation and live music is **Rosita's** at Kukui Grove Mall. The surroundings are quite elegant with stained-glass lanterns, murals on white stucco walls, and plenty of plants. The atmosphere is more convivial after a few margaritas which are the house specialty.

The **Kauai Hilton** has dancing and entertainment at **Gilligan's.** The hotel *luau* and "Flames of Fantasy" show are also available and costs adults $36, children $26. To save some money try the cocktail show for $18 adults, $13 for children...at a cocktail show?

Sometimes the Kukui Grove Mall presents free entertainment, usually of a Hawaiian nature. The schedule varies but these shows mainly occur on weekends. Check the free tourist literature to see if anything's going on—they're worth the effort!

SHOPPING

Lihue makes you reach for your wallet, with good cause. A stroll through one of its shopping centers is guaranteed to send you home with more in your luggage than you came with. Kauai's best selections and bargains are found here. It helps that Lihue is a *resort* town second to being a *living* town. Kauaians shop in Lihue; the reasonable prices that local purchasing generates are passed on to you.

Clothing And Apparel

Don't pass up **Hilo Hatties**, at least to educate yourself on products and prices. An institution in alohawear, though their designs may not be one of a kind, their clothing is very serviceable and well made. Specials are always offered in the free tourist literature, along with clearance racks at the store itself. They also have a selection of gifts and souvenirs. Plenty of incentives to get you in include free hotel pick-up from Poipu to Kapaa, a tour of the factory, free refreshments while you look around, and free on-the-spot alterations. Look for them at 3252 Kuhio Hwy., on the east end of town. Open every day from 8:30 a.m. to 5:00 p.m., tel. 245-3404.

Kapaia Stitchery is where you find handmade and distinctive fashions. This shop is along Rt. 56 in Kapaia, a tiny village between Hanamaulu and Lihue. The owner is Julie Yukimura who, along with her grandmother and a number of very experienced island seamstresses, create fashions, quilts, and embroideries that are beautiful, painstakingly made, and right priced. You can choose a garment off the rack or have one tailor-made from the stitchery's wide selection of cotton fabrics. You can't help being pleased with this fine shop!

Rainbow Rags is an outlet store for bargains in factory overruns and samples. Alohawear doesn't change that much and never goes out of style anyway. Some shirts are under $10 and dresses under $15. **Lina's Fashions** features Hawaiian wear, jewelry, quilting, and island-inspired bridal gowns. Both shops are located in the Rice Shopping Center in Lihue. More of the same type of clothing at discount prices is found at **Garment Factory to You** in the Lihue Shopping Center. This store is as practical as its name.

For more practical items try **Sears, LM Jeans** for all shapes and sizes of jeans, and **Foot Locker** for athletic shoes, all at the Kukui Grove Center. Also, you can't go wrong taking a promenade through the tasteful shops located on the ground floor of the Kauai Resort Hotel. You'll find everything from artwork to clothing. Prices tend to be higher, but selections are more distinctive.

Arts, Crafts, And Souvenirs.

If you're after just filling a shopping basket with trinkets and gimjicks for family and friends back home, go to **Woolworths** and **Gem** in Lihue, or **Long's Drugs** in the Kukui Grove. Their bargain counters are loaded with terrific junk for a buck or two. For better-quality souvenirs, along with custom jewelry, try **Linda's Creations** at 4254 Rice Street. This shop, owned and operated by Joe and Linda Vito, is well stocked with items ranging from silk wallets for $2 to lovely vases for over $100. **Kauai Museum Shop** at the Kauai Museum has authentic souvenirs and items Hawaiian with competitive prices. **Mandala's** is a combination head shop and souvenir store on Rt. 56 in the Garden Island Plaza, a small complex across from McDonald's.

Rainbow Books at Kukui Grove has plenty more between its cover than just books. Their selection of reading material and maps is exemplary, but they also feature striking artwork by Hawaiian artists. The rear of the large store is called **Stone's Gallery**; its walls are brightened by serigraphs by Pegge Hopper and lovely pieces by Carol Bennet and James Kay. Ceramics, photos, and prints round out the selections. Also at the mall check out **See You In China**. A square-masted "China trader" would sink if it had this store's large selection in its hold—plenty of *objects d'art* from the Orient along with jewelry, clothing, stationery, and gift items. **Kahana Ki'i Gallery** is found in the Garden Island Plaza on Rt. 56 across from McDonald's: stuffed unicorns, plenty of art by local artists, batiks, ceramics, and Niihau shells. See "Niihau" for a description of Niihau shell work, the finest and most exclusive in Hawaii.

Photo Needs

For a full-line photo store go to **Don's Camera Center,** 4286 Rice St., tel. 245-6581. All you'll need from a wide selection of famous brands, camera repair, and one-day processing. **Thrifty Drug** at the Kukui Grove has inexpensive film and processing. **Foto Fast Kauai** near McDonald's on the Kuhio Hwy. (Rt. 56) develops film in one hour. They do minor repair and rent cameras, tel. 245-7881.

tree fern

the famous lagoon at the Coco Palms

WAILUA

Wailua ("Two Waters") is heralded by the swaying fronds of extra tall royal palms, and whenever you see these, like the *kahili* of old, you know you're entering a special place. The Hawaiian *ali'i* knew a choice piece of real estate when they saw one, and they cultivated this prime area at the mouth of the Wailua River as their own. Through the centuries they built many *heiau* in the area, some where unfortunates were slaughtered to appease the gods, others where the weak and vanquished could find succor and sanctuary. The road leading inland along the Wailua River was called the King's Highway. Commoners were confined to traveling only along this road and could approach the royal settlement by invitation only. The most exalted of the island's *ali'i* traced their proud lineage to Puna, a Tahitian priest, who according to the oral tradition arrived in the earliest migrations, and settled here.

Even before the Polynesians came, the area was purportedly settled by the semi-mythical ***Mu.*** This lost tribe may have been early Polynesians who were isolated for such a long time that they developed different physical characteristics from their original root stock. Or perhaps they were a unique people all together, whom history never recorded. But like another island group, the ***Menehune,*** they were dwarfish creatures who shunned outsiders. Unlike the industrious *Menehune,* who helped the Polynesians, the *Mu* were fierce and brutal savages whose misanthropic characters confined them to solitary caves in the deep interior along the Wailua River where they led unsuspecting victims to their deaths.

Wailua today has a population of over 1,500, but you'd never know it driving past, as most houses are scattered in the hills behind the coast. Though an older resort area, it's not at all overdeveloped. The natural charm is as vibrant as ever. The beaches can be excellent depending upon conditions, and there's shopping, restaurants, and nightlife close at hand. With development increasing both to the east and west, perhaps now, as in days of old, the outstanding beauty of Wailua will beckon once again.

SIGHTS

Wailua is primarily famous because of two attractions, one natural, the other man-made. People flock to these, but in the hills behind the settlement along King's Highway are deserted *heiau,* sacred birthing stones, old cemeteries, and meditative views of the river below.

Fern Grotto

Nature's attraction is the Wailua River itself, Hawaii's only navigable stream that meanders 3 miles inland toward its headwaters atop forbidding Mt. Waialeale. Along this route is the **Fern Grotto,** a tourist institution of glitz, hype, and beauty rolled into one. Two local companies run sightseeing trips (and special *luau* night) to the grotto on large motorized barges. As you head up river, the crew tells legends of

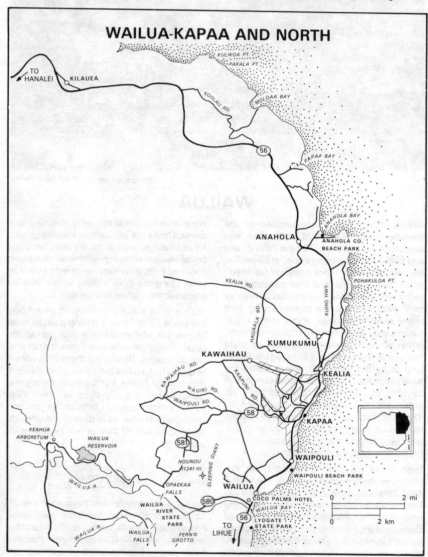

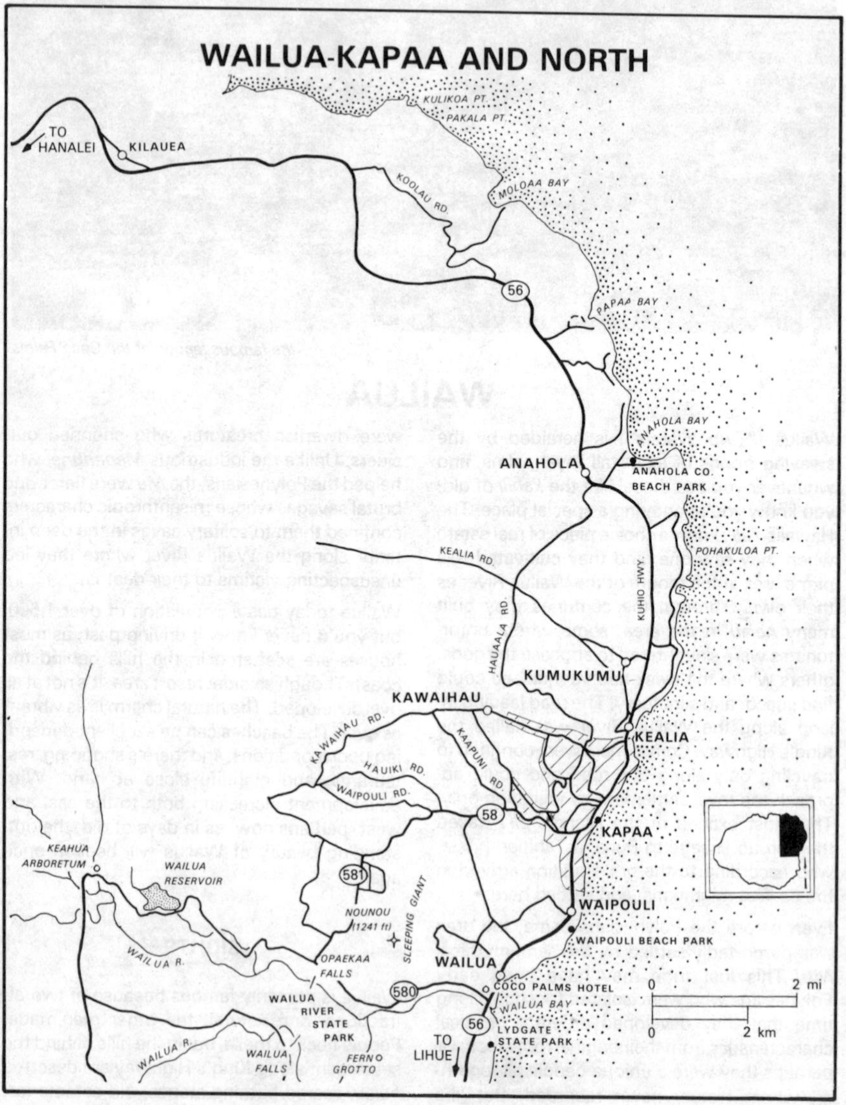

the area and seranades visitors with Hawaiian songs. The grotto itself is a huge rock amphitheater, whose ever-misty walls create the perfect conditions for ferns to grow. And grow they do, wildly and with abandon, filling the cavern with their deep musty smell and penetrating green beauty. Here in the natural cathedral, a duet breaks into the "Hawaiian Wedding Song," where over the years a steady stream of brides and grooms have come to exchange vows. The Fern Grotto trip is an amusement ride, but it's also the only way to get there. It's enjoyable and memorable, but you have to stay in the right frame of mind, otherwise it's too easily put down. (For tours see p. 668.)

The Coco Palms

The Coco Palms Resort is a classic Hawaiian hotel, one of the first tourist destinations built on the island. The Polynesian-inspired buildings are interspersed amidst a monumental coconut grove planted by a German immigrant in the early 1800s. His aspiration was to start a copra plantation, and although it failed, his plantings matured into one of the largest stands of coconut trees in the islands. Nightly, the hostelry's famous "torch-lighting ceremony" takes place under the palm canopy that encircles a royal lagoon, once used to fatten succulent fish for the exclusive use of the *ali'i.* Everyone is welcome to the ceremony, guest or not, and if you're in the area around sundown definitely go. Some may put the performance down as "fake traditional," but it's the *best* "fake traditional" on the island, both dramatic and fun. It was started by Grace Guslander, the congenial hostess famous for her cocktail parties, who recently retired.

The hotel grounds are inspiring, and often when Hollywood needed "paradise" they came here. Parts of past movie sets still remain. Notice the authentic-looking cement palm trees used to blend in the construction of some of the buildings. There's a small zoo, museum, and a chapel built by Columbia Pictures for a Rita Hayworth movie. More than 2,000 marriages have been performed in this chapel ever since, and the list keeps growing. When Tattoo informs Mr. Rourk about "de plane, boss" in the popular TV serial *Fantasy Island,* it is into the Coco Palms grove that he drives the jeep. Elvis came here to film *Blue Hawaii,* and segments of *South Pacific* were shot on the grounds. Frank Sinatra found out who the "chairman of the board" really was when one day he was swept out to sea from a nearby beach. "Old blue eyes" used his velvet voice to scream for help, and was rescued by local men from the fire department using a surfboard. After the rescue, Sinatra discovered that they had no boat; showing the class he's famous for, he bought them a spanking new Criscraft. The hotel bought the beach house known as the "Sinatra House" and rented it out. Sinatra was later upstaged when John Kennedy visited a number of times, and the house was renamed the "President's House." The hotel divested itself of this property recently. As soon as you walk onto the grounds you feel romantic. You can't help it. No one's immune! The Coco Palms is a peaceful garden. Let it surround you.

fancy floral display at the Coco Palms

Paradise Pacifica

A large banner stretched across the entranceway of this 30-acre botanical garden proclaims it a "tropical paradise." Once inside, all plants are labeled; many are ordinary island foliage, others rare and exotic even for the "Garden Island." The entire area is sheltered and well watered, and it's easy to imagine how idyllic life was for the original Hawaiians. Some of the buildings include a *luau* house, and lagoon theater used on the special nights with entertainment. Peacocks and chickens pecking beneath the trees are natural groundskeepers, preventing insects and weeds from overpowering the gardens. The "villages,"—Japanese-, Philippine-, and Polynesian-inspired settlements—are merely plywood facsimiles. However, the grounds themselves are beautifully kept and much more impressive. For those who won't be trekking into the Kauaian backcountry, and especially for those who will, Paradise Pacifica provides an excellent opportunity to familiarize yourself with Kauai's plants, flowers, and trees. For years, mini-trams carried tourists around the grounds; recently the gardens have been in a state of flux. The state leases the site to the highest bidder and this process has just taken place. Rates should be about $5 adults, $2.50 children. For information, tel. 822-4911. To get there follow the road to the end at the Wailua Marina and park in the large lot.

Historical Sites And Heiau

The King's Highway (Rt. 580) running inland from Wailua, and Rt. 56, the main drag, have a number of roadside attractions and historical sites dating from the pre-contact period. Most are just a short stroll away from your car and well worth the easy effort. The mountains behind Wailua form a natural sculpture of a giant in repose, aptly called **The Sleeping Giant**. You have to stretch your imagination just a little to see him, and although not entirely a bore, like most giants, he's better left asleep.

Along Rt. 56 just before the Coco Palms, a tall stand of palms on the east side of the Wailua River, are part of Lydgate State Park, and mark the spot of **Hauola O' Honaunau,** a temple of refuge that welcomed offending *kapu* breakers of all social classes. Here miscreants could atone for their transgressions and have their spiritual slates wiped clean by the temple priests, enabling them to return to society with paying with their lives. Both the refuge and **Hikina Heiau** are marked by a low encircling wall. The area is extremely picturesque as the Wailua River meets the sea. Perhaps it's knowledge about the temple of refuge that creates the atmosphere, but here, as at all of these merciful temple sites, the atmosphere is calm and uplifting, as if some spiritual residue has permeated the centuries. It's a good spot to relax in the cool of the grove and there are picnic tables available.

As Rt. 580 meanders inland, you pass Wailua River State Park. Then immediately look for **Poaiahu Arboretum** and its convenient turnout. The arboretum is merely a stand of trees along the roadside with a few comfortable benches. Across the road is **Holo Holo Ku Heiau,** where the unfortunate ones who didn't make it to the temple of refuge were put to death and offered to the never-satisfied gods. This temple is one of Kauai's most ancient, and the altar itself is the large slab of rock near the southwest corner. As if to represent the universality of the life-death cycle, **Pohaku Hoo Hanau,** the "royal birthing stones," are within an infant's cry away. Royal mothers came here to deliver the future kings and queens of the island. The stones somehow look comfortable to lean against and perhaps their solidity reinforced the courage of the mother. In the vicinity, but tough to find, a small path leads to the **bell stone;** pounded when a royal *wahine* gave birth, its peal could be heard for miles. Behind the *heiau,* a silver guardrail leads up the hill to a small, neatly tended **Japanese Cemetery.** The traditional tombstones chronicling the lives and deaths of those buried here turn green with lichens against the pale blue sky.

Back on Rt. 580 you start weedling your way uphill. You can see how eroded and lush Kauai is from this upland perch. On your left is the lush Wailua Valley watered by the river, and on your right a relatively dry gulch separated by a spit of land perhaps only 200 yards wide. Notice too, the dark green freshwater as it becomes engulfed by the royal blue of the ocean in the distance. As you climb look for a HVB Warrior pointing to **Opaekaa Falls,** way off in

Japanese cemetery just off Rt. 580

the distance. If you follow a pathway from the turn-out to an overlook, below are the remnants of a village with grass shacks falling in on themselves. Take a look around to see how undeveloped Kauai is.

Beaches, Parks, And Recreation

Wailua has few beaches, but they're excellent. **Wailua Municipal Golf Course** skirts the coast fronting a secluded beach, and because of its idyllic setting is perhaps the most beautiful public links in Hawaii. Even if you're not an avid golfer, you can take a lovely stroll over the fairways as they stretch out along the coastline. Green fees are a reasonable $10 weekdays, $11 weekends, with carts and clubs for rent. For info call Kauai Dept. of Public Works, tel. 245-2163. Below the links is a secluded beach. You can drive to it by following the paved road at the western end of the course and continuing until it becomes dirt and branches to the sea. The swimming is good in sheltered coves and the snorkeling is better than average along the reef. Few ever come here, and plenty of nooks and crannies are good for one night's bivouac.

Lydgate Beach Park is a gem. It's clearly marked along Rt. 56 on the west side of the Wailua River, behind the Kauai Resort Hotel complex. Two large lava pools make for great swimming even in high surf. The smaller pool is completely protected and perfect for tots, while the larger is great for swimming and snorkeling. This beach is never overcrowded, and you can find even more seclusion by walking along the coast away from the built-up area. If you head to the river, the brackish water is refreshing, but stay away from where it meets the ocean, creating tricky, wicked currents. The beach across the river fronting the Coco Palms is very treacherous and should only be entered on calm days when lifeguards are in attendance. Lydgate State Park also provides sheltered picnic tables under a cool canopy provided by a thick stand of ironwoods, plus grills, restrooms, and showers, but no camping.

ACCOMMODATIONS

The hotel scene in Wailua is like the beaches, few but good. Your choices are the famous Coco Palms Hotel, the Kauai Resort Hotel with its admirable location fronting Lydgate Park, and the economical Wailua Bay View (don't confuse this one with the Wailua Bayview in Lihue) across from the Coco Palms.

The **Coco Palms Resort** has recently changed hands. Once owned by AMFAC, it now belongs to Park Lane International, a San Francisco-based firm which operates it through Wailua Associates. The new owners have gone to great lengths to keep the friendly and cordial atmosphere that made the hotel memorable to all past visitors. While the 35 acres of grounds are outstanding as ever, AM-

FAC let the physical plant deteriorate. The new owners are spending $7 million refurbishing the hotel: redecorating rooms, and adding a health spa, more tennis courts (clay), coffee shop, and walkway to the beach. When you enter, the unusual lobby is a harmonious blend of Polynesian longhouse and European cathedral. The huge chandeliers hang like birds of paradise spreading subdued red and yellow light; a *koa* staircase leads to the upper levels. The front desk is a series of conga-like drums, and there is always a magnificent floral display of Kauai's most exotic blooms. There are nightly performances of the torch lighting ceremony, Grace Guslander's inspired cocktail parties 3 times a week, tennis courts, 3 swimming pools, and a variety of cocktail lounges and restaurants. The chapel has services every Sunday, and a hotel mini-mall sells gifts and a few necessities. Rooms are in different wings with names like **Top of the Palms, Ali'i Kai** and **Sea Shell.** For a terrific view of the lagoon and the torch-lighting ceremony, request a room in Top of the Palms at no extra cost. Deluxe-size rooms have a refrigerator, and bathroom basins are huge "killer clam shells" for which the Palms has become famous. Even if you are after more modest accommodations for a long-term stay, a night or two at the Coco Palms is definitely worth it. Rates are $85-120 for rooms, $140 King's cottage, $160 Queen's Cottage, suites to $350. For information contact the Coco Palms Resort, Wailua, Kauai, HI 96746, tel. 800-542-2626, on Kauai tel. 822-4921.

The **Kauai Resort Hotel** has a lovely setting above Lydgate Park, with the Hauola Temple of Refuge adjacent to the grounds. Incorporated into the architecture are a series of cascading pools and a *koi* (carp) pond that boils with frenzied color during feeding time. The main lobby is a huge affair with swooping beams in longhouse style. There is a Polynesian review nightly, a *luau,* and the hotel buffet receives the ultimate compliment of the high attendance by local people. The hotel is the best place on Kauai for name entertainment—Mainland performers such as Jesse Colin Young, and Hawaii's own, like the Peter Moon Band. Rooms are well appointed and most have ocean views. Rates are from $55 standard to $80 for a super deluxe, and from $55 to $60 for cabanas which are separate from the main facility with unobstructed views of the beach. For information contact Hawaiian Pacific Resorts, 1150 S. King St., Honolulu, HI 96814, tel. 800-272-5275.

The **Wailua Bay View** Condominiums, across from the Coco Palms Hotel near the Sea Shell Restaurant, are as close to the beach as you can get. They offer parking, restaurants, swimming pool, maid service on request and require a 5-night minimum stay. One-bedroom suites with fully furnished kitchens, baths, and washer and dryer are $95 for up to 4 people. Write for info to Wailua Bay View 320 Papaloa Rd., Kapaa, HI 96746, tel. 822-3651. For reservations contact Hawaiian Apartment Leasing, 1240 Cliff Drive, Laguna Beach, CA 92651, tel. 800-854-8843, in California 800-472-8449.

FOOD

Not to break the pattern, the food scene is akin to Wailua's accommodations and beaches: not a smorgasbord to choose from, but a good range of prices and cuisine.

Inexpensive

Kinipopo Pizza and Stuff serves pizza and submarine sandwiches in its newly opened premises along Rt. 56 past the Coco Palms Hotel on the right as you head for Kapaa. Their hefty pizzas range from a small cheese at $5.45 to a huge pie with the works for $14.95. The subs are $3.85 with cheaper sandwiches available. This restaurant is expanding and may be serving Italian dinners in the near future. If they're anything like their pizza and subs, they ought to be good. Open daily 10:00 a.m. to 10:00 p.m., tel. 822-9222.

The **Wailua Marina Restaurant** overlooking the Wailua River offers inexpensive to moderately priced "local-style" food, and free hotel pick-up in the Wailua area for dinner. If you're going on a Fern Grotto boat trip, you may consider eating here, but the crowds can be overwhelming during the day. Breakfast 8:30-11:00 a.m. is under $3, lunches until 2:00 p.m. offer plates like a small tenderloin, fries, and a tossed green salad for $5, and dinner (5:30-9:00 p.m.) entrees like Korean barbecue ribs or breaded veal cutlets for under $7. The setting is beautiful, and there's never a wait after the last boat upriver. At the Wailua Marina, tel. 822-4311.

Some will be happy, and others sad, to hear that fast foods have arrived in Wailua. Across from the Coco Palms, a **Sizzler Steakhouse** is rising. Soon the aroma of BBQed beef will be wafting on the ocean breeze.

Moderate

The best moderately priced meal in Wailua is the nightly buffet at the **Kahili Room** in the Kauai Resort Hotel. Generally, buffets are ho-hum, but this one's terrific, with as many local people as hotel guests. The menu changes through the week, but the best of the best is the seafood extravaganza every Sun., Tues., and Friday. For $15.95 you get the catch of the day, steamed shrimp, crab, clams, oysters, and *sushi,* plus fried chicken and roast beef along with tables laden with salads and desserts. Monday it's Chinese, Wednesday Japanese ($14.95), and Thursday features the *Kamaaina* Buffet, a lavish spread of island favorites for $14.50. All give you a great chance to sample the wide range of island dishes and are served from 6:00-8:30 p.m. For reservations tel. 245-3931. The Kauai Resort also features a ***luau*** every night except Mon. and Fri., beginning with an *imu* ceremony at 6:00 p.m. Even with plenty of food, *lei* greeting, and Polynesian spectacular, somehow the *luau* isn't quite as good as the buffet, especially since it costs almost double at around $30. The Kauai Resort provides free shuttle service to most area hotels. Reservations are suggested at tel. 245-3931.

The **Sea Shell Restaurant,** part of the Coco Palms Hotel, has long been a favorite with visitors and residents. Well-prepared island fish entrees are from $10 to $20 and include a basic salad bar. A good standby is the catch of the day, but if it's *mahi mahi* you can bet the day's fishing was poor and the *mahi* is frozen. A prawn bucket steamed in beer is inexpensive and makes a light, tasty meal. This restaurant is popular, so make reservations and if possible sit at window tables both for a view and fresh ocean breezes, tel. 822-3632.

A more romantic setting is **A Wok in the Palms** open-air restaurant near the main bar in the Coco Palms. Dinner for 2 with wine is less than $30, and you overlook the lagoon while being serenaded by a classical guitarist. **The Lagoon** is the Coco Palms' main dining room. The menu is average, service friendly, and the setting exceptional—overlooking the lagoon. They're open daily for breakfast, lunch, and dinner. Subdued candlelight and a free dinner show make the room more romantic in the evenings. For reservations at both rooms, tel. 822-4921.

Expensive

The legend of *Kintaro,* a pint-sized boy born to an old couple from inside a peach pit, is slightly less miraculous than this excellent and authentic Japanese restaurant owned and operated by a Korean gentleman, Don Kim. From the outside **Restaurant Kintaro** is nothing special, but inside it transforms to the simple and subtle beauty of Japan. Moreover, the true spirit of Japanese cooking is presented, with the food as pleasing to the eye as to the palate. The *sushi* bar alone, taking up an entire wall, is worth stopping in for. The dinners are expertly and authentically prepared, equaling those served in fine restaurants in Japan. If you have never sampled Japanese food before, Restaurant Kintaro is the best place to start. Those accustomed to the cuisine can choose from favorites like *tempura, sukiyaki,* a variety of *soba,* and the old standby teriyaki. Open daily for dinner only, along Rt. 56 just past the Coco Palms, reservations a must at tel. 822-3341.

SHOPPING

If you're after an authentic island gift made with love, make sure to stop in at the **Kauai Closet Thrift Shop.** The store employs handicapped people who manufacture souvenirs and mementos from coconuts, shells, and palm fronds. They have a wide assortment of bric-a-brac, and items like coconut windchimes, with many items priced under $1. The shop is located at the junction of Rts. 56 and 580 across from the Coco Palms, open weekdays 8:00 a.m. to 4:30 p.m.

The Coco Palms has a shopping arcade on 2 levels, with a florist, photo store, drugs and sundries, jewelry, souvenirs, and ice cream. Hilo Hattie has a small outlet, and there's a tiny Liberty House.

To purchase or rent any water sports equipment, go to **Ocean Odyssey,** owned and operated by Terry Donnelly. Snorkel equipment is $6.50 for 24 hours, boat dives $55, certification courses $250, and even an underwater photography course for $50. They're located diagonally across from the Shell Restaurant along Rt. 56, tel. 822-9680.

Next door to Ocean Odyssey is the **Black Coral Store,** specializing in shells, scrimshaw, and "sunken treasure." You walk through hanging-shell curtains into the store where you'll find a large selection of shells in bins conveniently labeled with the scientific and Hawaiian name—give yourself a mini-course in the shells you'll encounter along the beach. The children will be happy to purchase a "scoop" of various shells for only $.50.

Directly across the street is **Kinipopo General Store.** This small market sells groceries, sundries, and liquors.

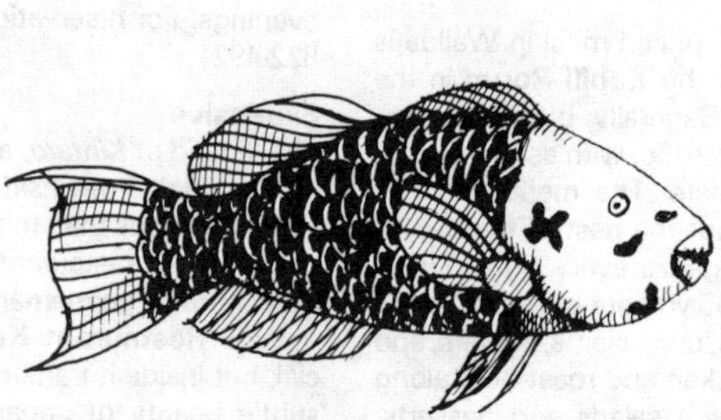

parrot fish

the Anahola Mountains

KAPAA AND VICINITY

Kapaa means "fixed, or crystalized," as in "fixed course." In the old days when the canoes set out to sail to Oahu, they'd always stop first at Kapaa, get their bearings, then make a beeline directly across the channel to Oahu. Yachts still do the same today. Kapaa is a different kind of town, with unusual contrasts. At the south end is **Waipouli** ("Dark Water"), actually a separate municipality along the main drag, though you'd never know it. Clustered here are newish hotel, condos, full-service shopping mall, restaurants, nightlife—a "live-in resort" atmosphere. The heart of Kapaa itself is a worker's settlement, with modest homes, pragmatic shops, some down-home eateries, and a funky hotel. Actually, a few more people live here than in Lihue, and the vibe is a touch more *local.* There are no sights per se. You spend your time checking out the shops, scanning the color-mottled mountains of the interior, and combing the beaches, especially those heading north toward Hanalei. Two minutes upcoast you're in wide open spaces. Cane roads cut from Rt. 56 and rumble along the coast. Small oceanside communities like **Anahola** and **Moloa'a Bay** pop up, their residents split between beach-house vacationers and settled *kamaaina.* What distinguishes Kapaa is its unpretentiousness. This is "everyday paradise," where the visitor is made to feel welcome, and then stands in line with everyone else at the supermarket. Generally the weather is cooperative throughout the area, prices on all commodities and services are good, beaches are fair to spectacular, and the pace unhurried. Kapaa isn't the choicest vacation spot on the island, but you can have a great time here while saving money too.

Beaches And Parks

Central Kapaa beaches begin at **Waipouli Beach Park,** fronting the cluster of hotels just north of the Market Place Shopping Center, and end near the royal coconut grove by the Sheraton Hotel. The town interrupts the beach for a while this side of the Waikaea Canal, and then the beach picks up again as **Kapaa Beach Park** running north for almost a mile until it ends near a community swimming pool. A number of small roads lead from Rt. 56 to the nearby beach. Kapaa Beach Park is just over 15 acres, with pavilion, picnic tables, showers, toilets, and grills. The beach is pretty to look at, but this section of town is run down. The feeling here is that it *belongs* to the locals, although no undue hassles have been reported.

As soon as you cross the Kapaa Stream on the

north end of town you're in the "one-store village" of Kealia. Past mile marker no. 1, look for Ray's Auto Saloon, and turn off onto the cane road. At the junction is **Kealia Beach.** This wide white strand curves along the coast for a half mile. Not a beach park, so no facilities, but during calm weather the swimming is good, and few people are ever here except for some local fishermen.

Continue along the cane road (watch for oncoming trucks!) for just over 2 miles. The ride is much more picturesque than Rt. 56, as you skirt the coastline, heading for **Pohakuloa Point** and a surfing beach that the locals call **Donkey Beach.** Look for a tall stand of ironwoods, a make-shift rutted pull-off, and a wide sandy beach below. A footpath leads down to it. This area is very secluded and good for unofficial camping. Unfortunately, the undertow is severe, especially during rough weather, and only experienced surfers challenge the waves here. You can sunbathe and take dips, but remain in the shallows close to shore. Continue north on the cane road until it intersects Rt. 56 again. Be even more careful of the monolithic cane trucks because a sign here that everyone ignores, points "One Way" in the *other* direction—and who are you to argue, in a subcompact whose only trace of extreme foolhardiness would be a grease spot in the road?

Nearby Villages And Beaches

Route 56 north from Kapaa is a visual treat. Out your window, the coastline glides along forming an ever-changing panorama. Development is virtually non-existent until you get to Kilauea in the Hanalei District. To your left are the **Anahola Mountains,** jagged, pointed, and intriguing. Until recently, you could crane your neck to see **Hole-in-the Mountain,** a natural arrangement of boulders that formed a round *puka.* Legend says it was formed by an angry giant who hurled his spear with such force that he made the hole. But time and storms have taken their toll and the hole has collapsed.

The first village that you come to is **Anahola,** at mile marker no. 14. Here is the **Anahola General Store** selling groceries, souvenirs, vegetables, and liquor. If you'd like to brighten your day or evening with an inexpensive plumeria *lei,* ($2.50 single strand, $4.50

Anahola Village church backdropped by the distinctive Anahola Mountains

doubles) call ahead and order one from Albert Christian in Anahola at tel. 822-5691. Next door to the general store is a small p.o. and **Dwayne's Ono Burger,** a clean, friendly roadside stand where you can get burgers or fish 'n' chips. Prices are a bit stiff at $3.50, but the burgers are large, delicious, and heavy with cheese and trimmings. Tables for a quick lunch are provided, but hold your appetite until you get to the nearby beach. Look to your right for Aliomanu ("Oil of the Shark") Road and follow it for a few minutes to the mouth of the Anahola River as it spills into the bay. Or, take Anahola Road off Rt. 56 before you get to the general store to a long strand of white sand that forms one of the best beaches on the north shore. The south end of the bay is **Anahola Beach Park** with a developed picnic area, shower, grills, restrooms, and camping (county permit). Tall ironwoods provide a natural canopy. The swimming is safe in the protected cove near the beach park, as is a refreshing dip in the freshwater river. As you walk north the waves and rips get tougher. It's not advisable to enter the water, although some experienced board riders do challenge the waves. However, the reef comes close to shore at this end, and wherever you can find a sheltered pocket is good for snorkeling. Local anglers love this spot for near-shore fishing. The entire area is popular with local people, but never overcrowded. This is an excellent place to camp for a few days, or just to stop in for a refreshing plunge, going or coming from Hanalei and the north shore.

The turnoff to Moloa'a ("Matted Roots") Bay is announced by a roadside fruit stand at mile marker no. 17. The fruit stand, an outlet for a nearby papaya farm, has the best prices and most succulent fruit on the island. Turn down Koolau Road, follow it to Moloa'a Road, and take this narrow but paved road to the end. **Moloa'a Bay** is a magnificent but rarely visited beach. The road leading down is a luscious little thoroughfare, cutting over domed hillocks by a series of switchbacks. The jungle canopy is thick and then it opens into a series of glens and pastures. Off to the sides are vacation homes perched on stilts made from telephone poles. A short drive takes you to road's end and a small cluster of dwellings. Park here, and follow the path marked "Right of way to the beach." Here, a stream comes into the bay, providing a great place to wash off the ocean water after a dip. The beach is lovely, bright, and wide, forming a crescent moon. To the N the beach ends in a grassy hillock, and south it's confined by a steep *pali.* Swimming at all north shore beaches is advised only during calm weather, and is best at the south end of the beach. Snorkeling is good, but you'll have to swim the channel out to the base of the *pali* which is unadvisable if the waves are rough. Although a few homes are around, Moloaa is a place of peaceful solitude. Sunsets are lightshows of changing color, and you'll probably be the solitary spectator.

ACCOMMODATIONS

Inexpensive

Hotel Coral Reef is definitely inexpensive and it definitely has character. Toward the north end of Kapaa between the main road and the beach, this humble hotel has a deluxe view of the bay. Although it closely resembles one, the Coral Reef isn't a "flea bag," because it's clean, well tended and attracts decent clientele. The hotel is friendly, homey, and funky. The lobby is small, not conducive to relaxing, adorned only by a fish tank. Outside a few discarded tires sink slowly into the "grounds" as hotel guests keep the mosquitos at bay while cooking dinner over a smokey fire in the homemade BBQ. The rooms in the old wing are clean and cheap at $19. The decor is watermarks streaking the

A freshwater stream meets the sea at Moloa'a Bay.

discolored wallpaper. The new wing is cleaner, brighter, and has an A-plus view of the bay. Large and airy rooms with linoleum floors and refrigerators go for only $26. For reservations, Hotel Coral Reef, 1516 Kuhio Hwy., Kapaa, HI 96746, tel. 822-4481.

Moderate

Part of the Hawaiian-owned Hukilau Hotels, **Kauai Sands** is a better-than-average budget hotel with a convenient location, spacious grounds, accommodating staff, large relaxing lobby, budget restaurant, and pool. The color scheme of the main building is a shocking blue and red. Most rooms front a central courtyard. Deluxe rooms have refrigerators, a/c, and TVs for $49 s, standards have ceiling fans and no TVs or refrigerators for $44 s. The rooms are all clean, and have the bluish-green bedspreads, drapes, and carpets seemingly favored by budget hotels. For reservations, Hukilau Hotels, 2222 Kalakaua Ave., Suite 714, Honolulu, HI 96815, tel. 800-367-7000, on Kauai just before the Market Place, at 420 Papaloa Rd., Wailua, HI 96746, tel. 822-4951.

For a deluxe hotel at moderate prices, you can't go wrong with the **Kauai Beach Boy Hotel,** located along the coastline at the Coconut Plantation. This "Beach Boy," part of the AMFAC chain, is cool and quiet; most rooms surround a central courtyard and pool. All rooms have showers (no tubs), color TV, free in-room movies, and a small fridge. The decor is pleasant "Hawaiian style," with out-of-place orange, purple, and green countertops. Each unit has a powder room, large closet, and full mirror, with superior rooms having their own *lanai* and sliding louvered doors. The hotel is known for a wide variety of activities, plus excellent, inexpensive dining at its Hale Kai Room. The Boogie Palace offers nightly cocktails and dancing. For reservations, AMFAC Resorts, 2255 Kuhio Ave., Box 8520, Honolulu, HI 96815, tel. 800-227-4700, on Kauai Waipouli Beach, Kapaa, HI 96746, tel. 822-3441.

The **Kapaa Shore Condo** is along the main road just north of the Coconut Plantation. These one- and 2-condo units offer a swimming pool, heated jacuzzi, tennis courts, and maid service on request. All units are bright and cheerful, with full kitchen, washers, dryers, and dishwashers. One-bedroom units accommodate up to four for $55, and 2-bedroom units house up to 6 for $75, 5-night minimum stay. For reservations, Hawaiian Apartment Leasing, 1240 Cliff Dr., Laguna Beach, CA 92651, tel. 800-472-8449, on Kauai, 40-900 Kuhio Hwy., Kapaa, HI 96746, tel. 822-3055.

Other reasonably priced condominiums in the area include the **Kapaa Sands,** with tennis courts, pool, and maid service on request. Studios are $48, 2 bedroom $68, full kitchens and bath, 3-night minimum. For reservations, Kapaa Sands, Box 3292, Lihue, HI 96766, tel. 822-4901. The **Islander on the Beach** is a right-priced condominium located in the Coconut Plantation Resort. You get deluxe surroundings at modest prices in studio apartments from $54 to $76. For reservations, Hotel Corp. of the Pacific, 2255 Kuhio Ave., Honolulu, HI 96815, tel. 800-367-5124; on Kauai, 484 Kuhio Hwy., Kapaa, HI 96746, tel. 822-7417. The **Pono Kai Condominium** is a step up in class offering one-bedroom units at $72-$108, and two bedrooms at $99-136. Also available from Hotel Corp. of the Pacific, and on Kauai at 1250 Kuhio Hwy., tel. 822-9831.

Expensive

Amidst a huge grove of swaying palms sits the **Sheraton Coconut Beach Hotel,** a transformed Holiday Inn that's now the fanciest hotel in Kapaa. The palm grove once belonged to the family of the famous swimmer and actor, Buster Crabbe of "Buck Rogers" fame. He and his twin brother, Bud, were born and raised right here, and Buster learned to swim along this very coast. The lobby is alive with trees, flowers, and vines trellised from the balconies. Wicker chairs, a huge "carpet sculpture," and a 40-foot waterfall add comfort and grandeur. The Voyage Room is an indoor-outdoor restaurant, and the hotel *luau* is the best on the island. Make sure to check out the fine photos hanging along the main hall, and the superb replica of a double-hulled sailing canoe. Also, the charts in the Chart Room, that look like those nifty old ragged-edged maps of yore, are the real McCoy. They belong to Mr. Rate Bowman, who displays at the hotel. The Sheraton has just undergone a massive "sprucing-up." The rooms, already beautiful, are even more so with matching decor like rose and lavender carpets, drapes, and bedspreads. Every room has its own refrigerator, small *lanai,* and original artwork. Bathrooms and dressing rooms are spacious. The 4th floor offers enormous, high-ceiling deluxe rooms with private *lanai,* and breathtaking views of the ironwoods and ocean below. The Sheraton is pricy at $85-135, but you do get all that you're pay for. Write Sheraton Coconut Beach Hotel, Coconut Plantation, Kapaa, HI 96746, tel. 800-325-3535, on Kauai 822-3455.

Colony Resorts manages a number of deluxe condos in and around the Coconut Plantation. The **Plantation Hale** is a condominium that also offers daily rates. It's near the Sheraton, but on the other side of the road away from the beach. Each unit is like a small apartment with full kitchen, bath, dining room, eating cubby, and sitting area. Rates for up to 4 people, $70-80, at 484 Kuhio Hwy., tel. 822-4911. A touch more classy is the **Lae Nani,** offering one- and 2-bedroom units on the beach at 410 Papaloa Rd., tel. 822-4938, and the **Lanikai,** offering the same at 390 Papaloa Rd., tel. 822-7456. All reservations from Colony Resorts, 32 Merchant St., Honolulu, HI 96813, tel. 523-0411, or their agent Hawaiian Apartment Leasing, 1240 Cliff Dr., Laguna Beach, CA 92651, tel 800-472-8449.

FOOD

Inexpensive

A low yellow building in downtown Kapaa houses **Chic's Diner.** It's one of those places that you go back to time and again for a good hearty meal, when you don't care much about the surroundings. They serve no-nonsense food including *saimin,* burgers, and sandwiches under $3, and hefty subs for $4.75 ($2.50 for a half). Pizzas range from a one-topping "baby" for $3.75 to a 5-topping "giant" for $19.50. The best value, however are their meals like teribeef for $3.90, and tasty and filling half-chicken plates for $4.75. *Kalbi,* Korean-style ribs, are the most expensive item on the menu for $5.25. Eric, Chic's owner, also serves domestic and imported beers, and wine by the glass. Chic's is open for breakfast, lunch, and dinner, and they also deliver by calling 822-9816.

First be warned that **Waipouli Chop Suey** may have recently moved to Lihue, and if it has, go and find it! It's one of those rare places that when they hand you the bill, it doesn't seem as though you've been charged enough for the fine meal that you've consumed. Their daily specials are full-course meals for under $4, or get a regular Chinese dinner including chicken, shrimp, chop suey, fried and steamed rice, and tea for $5. A seafood combination is $6.75, a 7-course meal for $8 per person, a 9-course for $10 per person, and this includes items like abalone, crab, shrimp, spare ribs, and chicken. Moreover, the owner/chef is friendly and puts that added attention into every plate. You can't go wrong at Waipouli Chop Suey, open daily (great breakfasts, too) from 7:30 a.m. to 9:30 p.m., for the time being at the Waipouli Plaza Building, in the small mall at 4-901 Kuhio Hwy., Kapaa.

The **European Deli** is also in the Waipouli Plaza next door to Zippy's. This connoisseur's delight features a delectable array of cheeses, lunch meats, fresh salads, sweets, and an excellent selection of imported and domestic wines. Their picnic basket costs $13 and feeds two. You keep the basket (check for money-saving coupons in the free tourist literature for this civilized service). Or eat at a few tables in the deli with choices like golden mushroom soup and fresh-baked bread for $1.50, bagel and cream cheese for $1.50, a bear claw and coffee $1.05, and an assortment of luscious sandwiches such as smoked turkey or Black Forest ham for $3.50. Those who love deli munchies will be very happy with the European Deli, open daily 6:00 a.m. to 9:00 p.m., or call ahead to have your "north shore" picnic lunch prepared at tel. 822-7788.

The next little complex down from Waipouli Plaza at 971 Kuhio Hwy. has 2 restaurants where you can get good hearty ethnic meals. The **Aloha Diner,** open daily except Sun. 10:30 a.m. to 10:00 p.m., tel. 822-3851, offers cheaper a la carte selections like *kalua* pig $3.80, chicken long rice $2.75, or squid *luau* for $3. Lunch specials run around $4.50, with full dinners from $6.50. There is no atmosphere, the service is slow and friendly, and most people eating here are residents. Next door is **Shiro's Japanese Restaurant** which serves American standards as well. Breakfast specials are $2.55, omelettes $2.90. On the daily lunch and dinner special, choose items like shrimp *tempura* $5.15, pork *tofu* $3.65, or hamburger steak for $4.10. A money-saving lunch is a huge bowl of *wonton min* and a side of rice for $2.85. And you must have a slice of the home-made pineapple or passionfruit chiffon pie for $1. Shiro's is open daily except Tues. from 6:00 a.m. to 9:00 p.m.

The **Ono Family Restaurant** is a step up from the others mentioned here, but the prices are right. The atmosphere is "functional cozy," with nice touches like carpeted floors, ceiling fans, even a chandelier. Creative breakfasts include Eggs Margo (a take-off on Eggs Benedict) with turkey, tomatoes, and Hollandaise sauce over poached eggs and an English muffin for $4.65, pancakes $1.85, and a variety of omelettes like a "local boy" which combines Portuguese sausage and *kimchi.* Lunch salads are $2.65, the island's best burger is $2.85, or try a fish sandwich for $3.75. For dinner you can't go wrong with a mushroom melt burger for $4.55, and from the broiler and grill try sirloin steak $7.95, BBQ ribs $7.95, teri chicken $6.95, and even a Mexican plate for $4.25 with nachos at $3.65. The daily fish special is always terrific, and depending upon the catch goes for about $12. That's the Ono Family Restaurant in downtown Kapaa, at 4-1292 Kuhio Hwy., open daily from 7:00 a.m., closed Sunday evenings, tel. 822-1710.

Fast Foods

The **Market Place Shopping Center** overflows with fast foods and inexpensive eateries. You can grab a dog or sandwich at **J.J's Doghouse,** or a meal at **J.J.'s Smokehouse,** or try soup and salad at the **Saimin Inn** for $3.50. **Ramona's** will fix you up a Mexican combo plate for around $3, and there are plenty of places to buy snacks, sweets, nuts, and ice cream. **Farrell's** serves breakfasts, sandwiches, and fruit cakes, and nearby is **Don's Deli** with a counter full of savories, and picnic baskets and directions to go.

Grab a taco at **Tropical Taco** in the Kapaa Shopping Center, open daily from 11:00 a.m. except Sun., or stop in 24 hours a day at **Zippy's** fast-food joint sitting prominently on the Kuhio Highway. **McDonald's?** Yes. Look for the arches along the highway. But if you want some *really* down-home cooking try **Cindy's Saimin,** about as big as a closet, just near the Ono Family Restaurant along Kuhio Highway. It's open daily 10:00 a.m. to 2:00 p.m. and then from 6:30-11:00 p.m. Mon. to Thursday. Here *saimin* or *wonton* soup cost as little as $1.25. Cindy has competition just down the block from **Dan's Inn of Kauai,** whose name is bigger than the restaurant. Dan's specializes in large plates of Hawaiian food for well under $5. The hours are a bit strange, open 7:00 a.m. to noon Sun. to Tues., closed Wed., open 7:00 a.m. to noon, then again 4:30-7:30 p.m. Thurs. to Saturday.

Moderate

When you don't want to fool around deciding on where to get a good meal head for the north end of Kapaa and the local favorite **Kountry Kitchen.** Open daily 6:00 a.m. to 9:30 p.m., the tables are usually packed with regulars during peak dining hours. Breakfasts are full meals of hefty omelettes from $2.65 for a plain, to a "hungryman special" for $6.25. Lunches range from $3-5, and full dinners like country ribs, sesame shrimp, and baked ham served with soup, bread, potatoes/rice and vegies are from $6-8. The food is tasty, the service prompt and friendly, and the portions large. The Kountry Kitchen is at 1485 Kuhio Hwy., tel. 822-3511.

Norberto's El Cafe is a family-run Mexican restaurant from *sombrero* to *zapatos.* Then what's it doing on a side street on a Pacific island next to the Kung Fu X-rated Roxy theater? Hey *gringo,* don't look a gift burro in the face! They serve nutritious, delicious, wholesome food, and they cater to vegetarians, as all dishes are prepared without lard or animal fats. Full-course meals of burritos, enchiladas, and tostadas are around $8, children's plates are $5, while a la carte dishes are from $3-4. The best deals are the chef's specials of burrito el cafe, Mexican salad, and chili relleno all for under $5. Beer on tap is $4.50 a pitcher, or if you really want to head south of the border by way of sliding under the table, a pitcher of margaritas is only $4.50. If you have room after stuffing yourself like a *chimichanga* try a delicious chocolate cream pie or homemade rum cake. The cafe is extremely popular with local folks and tables fill as soon as they're empty. Look for Norberto's on Kukui St. off Rt. 56 in downtown Kapaa, tel. 822-3362, daily except Sun. for lunch 11:00 a.m. to 1:30 p.m., dinner 5:30-9:30 p.m.

As soon as you enter the restaurant section of the **Kauai Gardens** you'll know that they love growing things, and you might mistake it for a greenhouse. It's the epitome of a fern bar with plants and flowers everywhere, and they're for sale. What makes it even more attractive is the basic building was little more than a warehouse that love and creativity turned into something beautiful. Wicker chairs, soothing colors, glass-topped tables, and small stained-glass chandeliers make the perfect blend of casual elegance. But that's not all! The food happens to be terrific, too. The front entrance leads to a deli and semi health food store; buy espresso, vitamins, fresh vegies, fruits, health food products, cheeses, lunch meats, lox, and liquor. Deli selections to eat in or out are reasonable, like enormous slabs of lasagna or quiche for $3.95. Lunch is from 11:00 a.m. to 3:00 p.m., 3:00-5:00 p.m. brings table service of light deli fare, and dinner with full service in the Garden Room is from 5:30-10:30 p.m. At that time you can choose from appetizers like *sashimi* or crab-stuffed mushrooms for $5, fresh soups of vegetable, *gazpacho* or cream of watercress for $2.50, sirloin steak $11.75, French wine stew $8.95, *mahi mahi* $9.50, veal stuffed with crab $16.50, stir-fry vegetables $7.75, and fresh fish with macadamia nuts which is the wonderful house specialty. The Kauai Gardens is one of those places that always seems right. You can drop in for a beer and a burger fresh off the beach, or put on your best for a romantic evening of fine dining. The Kauai Gardens at the north end of Kapaa, 4-1639 Kuhio Hwy., tel. 822-7746.

J.J's Boiler Room, tel. 822-4411, is in the Market Place Shopping Center. Like their restaurant in Lihue, you can't go wrong if you're after steak or beef. Open daily for dinner from 5:00 p.m. they offer beef kabobs at $9.95, steak and lobster $16.95, the famous "Slavonic steak" of thin-sliced meat broiled in wine and garlic for $10.85, and salad bar for $6.25. You can save money by visiting **J.J.'s Create-a-Steak** also in the Market Place where you do your own BBQ, tel. 822-1869.

Al and Don's Restaurant, in the Kauai Sands Hotel off Rt. 56, is open daily from 7:00 a.m., tel. 822-4951. The service and food are good but not memorable. However, the view from the spacious booths overlooking the seacoast is magnificent. Prices are reasonable for their 22 dinner and 40 breakfast selections. Perhaps this is the problem: though you don't get the "bum's rush," the place feels like one of those feeding troughs in Waikiki that caters to everyone and pleases no one. You can't complain about breakfast like $2.95 for eggs, toast, hash browns, and coffee. And you won't be disappointed with their "build-your-own-omelette" for $3.25. Dinner includes soup and salad bar with adequate entrees like *ahi* or swordfish for $7.50, top sirloin $7.95, and chicken exotica for $6.95. Their bar serves good drinks for reasonable prices. When you leave Al and Don's, you won't feel like complaining, but you won't rush back either.

Almost Expensive

The following restaurants are "in between," with prices that aren't really expensive, but have just enough class to fall into that category. You won't be out of place dressed in snazzy casual attire.

The menu at the **Bull Shed** starts with beef kabobs for $7.95, prime rib at $12.50, and steak and lobster at $14.95. The wine list is better than average and includes Domaine Chandon champagne for $25. Insiders go for the extensive salad bar at only $5.50, but be warned that the pickings get all jumbled together as the night goes on, and the salad bar peaks out by 7:30. The Bull Shed is open daily for cocktails and dinner from 5:00 p.m. at 796 Kuhio Hwy., down the little lane across from McDonald's, tel. 822-3791.

The **Rib n' Tail** is the same category as the Bull Shed: prime rib for $12.95, chicken valentino $10.95, BBQ ribs $9.95, and an assortment of fish and lobster dinners from $10 to $16. Salad bar with garlic bread is $6.25; they specialize in homemade cheesecake and mud pie. Open daily from 5:00 p.m., happy hour 4:30-6:00 p.m. Mon. to Fri., entertainment Tues. and Sun., in the small complex behind the Shell gas station north of the Kapaa Shopping center, tel. 822-9632.

Uncle Bill prepares the imu *for the Sheraton's* luau.

The **Hale Kai Dining Room** at the Kauai Beach Boy Hotel gives a lot of quality for your money. They serve breakfasts from 6-10:00 a.m. with all the eggs, omelettes, waffles, and crepes around $4-5. Dinner is from 6:00-9:00 p.m. with a la carte ranging from a mushroom burger at $5 to steak and scampi or the fresh fish for $13.95. The buffet has a differing international theme every night. Saturday night's prime rib buffet is famous and popular. Sunday starts with a champagne brunch from 9:30 a.m. to 1:00 p.m. There's easy listening dinner music nightly from 6:30-8:00 p.m. except Tues. and Friday. Casual atmosphere at the Kauai Beach Boy in the Coconut Plantation, tel. 822-3441.

Expensive, *Luau,* And Buffets

The **Voyage Room** at the Sheraton Coconut Beach Hotel is the only real classy restaurant on this part of the island. The room is cheerful, spacious, and trimmed with classical island decor of high-backed rattan furniture. The service is first rate and you're made to feel "waited upon," an always welcomed addition to every meal. The salad bar, exemplary for quality, quantity, and style, is a bargain at under $7 including soup. Entrees of beef, fish, roast duck, rack of lamb, and chicken rochambeau are $12-20. In the Sheraton Hotel, open daily for breakfast, lunch, and dinner, tel. 822-4222.

This Sheraton presents a buffet and a dinner show every Mon. and Thurs. from 6:30-9:30 p.m. in the **Paddle Room.** Entertainment is by local island artists and the price is about $30. The real treat is the hotel *luau* which everyone agrees is best on the island. It's held every night except Mon. and Sat. in a special "long house" under a canopy of stars and palm trees. The *luau* master is Uncle Bill, who learned the art from his grandparents "just the other day in 1922!" His ethnic combination of Hawaiian-Italian gives him instant credibility as a fine cook. He starts the *imu,* with the aid of his grandchildren, every morning at 10:30. He can lay in the hot stones and banana stalks so well that the underground oven maintains a perfect 400 degrees. In one glance he can gauge the weight and fat content of a succulent porker and decide just how long it should be cooked. The water content in the leaves covering the pig steam and roast it at the same time so that the meat falls off the fork. Uncle Bill says about his *luau,* "All that you can't eat in the *imu* are the hot stones." You arrive at 7:00 p.m. to an open bar. The *imu* ceremony is at 7:15, followed by cocktails. At 8:00 the *luau* begins with tables laden with pork, chicken, Oriental beef, salmon, fish, exotic fruits, salads, coconut cake, and *haupia.* Then at 9:00 you recline and watch a Polynesian review of local dancers and musicians. Adults around $30, children $20, reservations suggested, tel. 822-3455.

ENTERTAINMENT

The night scene in Kapaa isn't very extensive, but there is enough to satisfy everyone. In the area you'll usually find one good disco, dinner show, easy-listening music, and Polynesian extravaganza.

The **Vanishing Point** is a disco located upstairs in the main building of the Waipouli Plaza, tel. 822-1610. It's reputed to be *the* hot spot of Kapaa. The basic dress code is slacks, shirt with collar, and shoes. Admission is $1 after 9:00 p.m., $2 on weekends, and a two-drink minimum. If you have the energy, you can dance until 4:00 a.m.

The **Boogie Palace** lives up to its name at the Kauai Beach Boy Hotel. The music is live and the crowd lively every night from 9:00 p.m.

The **Jolly Roger Restaurant** at the Market Place usually books a solo guitarist or small band that plays rock, folk, and contemporary. You can listen or dance nightly from 9:00 p.m. The atmosphere is casual, the talk friendly.

The **Sheraton Hotel** offers a little of everything. You can enjoy free *pu pu* and entertainment at Cook's Landing in the evenings from 4:30-6:30 p.m. The dinner show in the Paddle Room presents a full performance of Hawaiian dance and music. And swing, rock, and Hawaiian music accompany the *luau.*

The **Market Place** shopping center hosts a free Polynesian review every Thurs. through Sat. at 4:00 p.m. The local dancers and musicians put as much effort into their routines as if this were the big time. Be warned that local sneak thieves have rifled cars in the parking lot knowing that their owners are preoccupied watching the show.

SHOPPING

Kapaa teems with shopping opportunities. Lining Kuhio Highway is a major shopping mall, The Market Place, and at least 3 smaller shopping plazas. All your needs are met in a variety of food stores, health stores, drug stores, a farmers' market, fish vendors, and some extraordinary shops and boutiques tucked away here and there. You can easily find photo supplies, sporting equipment, "treasures," and inexpensive *lei* to brighten your day. Like dealing with the sun, enjoy yourself, but don't overdo it.

The Market Place

The name doesn't lie about this cluster of over 60 shops, restaurants, galleries, and movie theaters. Prices are kept down because of the natural competition of so many shops, and each tries to "specialize," which usually means good choices for what strikes your fancy. As you walk around notice the blown-up photos that give you a glimpse into old Hawaii. **Tramp Steamer Trading Company** is a variety store with wooden carvings, alohawear, basketry, and jimjicks aplenty for everyone back home with selections starting from $.50. The **Necklace Gallery** is just that with enough to drop even Mr. T to his knees. The **Paperback Hut** will keep you in used reading material for $.25 to $1.50. **Golden Buddha** uses Buddha as the central theme and sells a variety of items, artifacts, and jewelry including handcrafted *kukui*-nut *lei* for around $13. **Julie's Butterflies** float everywhere on wings of tissue, steel, and stained glass. **Pottery Tree** overflows with everything from junk to fine pieces. Select from stained-glass chandeliers, I Love Hawaii mugs, and some cheap yet nice shell mobiles. **Hilo Hattie** has a shop here, among a drawerful of beachwear and T-shirt stores. **Sandalworks** takes care of your tootsies; **High as a Kite** is great for high fliers that add fun to any beach outing. **Kahn Gallery** features the fine work of Hawaii's artists along with basketry, sculpture, woodcarvings, and superb jewelry. Expensive but once-in-a-lifetime purchases. And if all this gets too tiresome, you can have a delicious coffee at **Kona Kope** or just escape to the dark and cool of one of the 2 cinemas.

The **Kapaa Shopping Center** is much smaller and more pragmatic. Here, you'll find a Big Save Value Center; Clic Photo for inexpensive film and fast developing; Kapaa Bakery for sweets, bread, and goodies; Kapaa Laundry, J & S Sporting Goods; and a restaurant and fast-food shop.

The **Awapuhi Emporium** is a must-stop at 788 Kuhio Hwy. tel. 822-3581, in a tired little building across the street from Foodland. It specializes in handmade Hawaiiana. Inside the dusty glass cases are old maps, feather *lei, tapa* cloth, *koa* bowls, glass floats, and a varied selection of Oriental artworks. Prices are reasonable and the antiques, junk, and art pieces constantly change like the tides.

Next door is a tiny *lei* shop. It's open if Liz, the *lei* lady, puts out her sign that simply says ***Leis,*** which depends on her supply of fresh flowers. If she's open rush in because they won't last long. She'll make you a lovely *lei* for $5, and what she calls "flower jewelry" of necklaces, hair adornments, and brooches for $4. Liz usually opens around 11:00 a.m., till as late as 7:00 p.m.

Remember Kauai 4-734 Kuhio Hwy., tel. 822-0161, just past the Sheraton, specializes in unique Hawaiian jewelry, like necklaces made from shells, beads, wood, and gold. The counters shine with belt buckles, pins, and a large collection of gemstones from around the world. Niihau shell work is available, and fine specimens run up to $1,200. The scrimshaw, done by Kauai artists on fossilized walrus ivory, adds rich texture to everything from knives to paperweights.

Goldsmith Gallery is among the finest shops in all of Hawaii. Four jewelers make all of the individual pieces, most with Hawaiian motifs. Diamonds, gold, and opals from Australia add brilliance (and a hefty price tag) to the artwork. Much of the jewelry is commissioned, and some fine *cloisonne* boxes and a few stained-glass hangings are displayed. In the Waipouli Plaza, tel. 822-9287.

In the center of old Kapaa Town is an antique and curio shop named **The Only Show In Town**, and it's a mind bender. It's owned and operated by Paul Wroblewski, a tall handsome Polish fellow given to wearing white patent leather shoes, and enough jewelry to attract lightning from a clear sky. The shop is magnificent, more like a mad museum than anything else. The walls and showcases are covered with silk top hats, stuffed antelopes, glass balls, Catholic statuary, and a collection of dolls from around the world. There are toys, postcards, clothes, jewelry, instruments of all sorts, and old photos and movie posters. A separate section sells used clothing, like an upscale Salvation Army specializing in inexpensive alohawear. Even if you don't buy, you'll be missing one of Kapaa's main "sights" if you don't stop in here at 1384 Kuhio Hwy., tel. 822-1442.

Hanalei Bay

THE NORTH SHORE

The north shore is a soulful song of wonder, a contented chant of dream-reality, where the "Garden Island" harmonizes gloriously. The refrain is a tinkling melody, rising, falling, and finally reaching a booming crescendo deep in the emerald green of Na Pali. In so many ways this region is a haven: tiny towns and villages that refused to crumble when sugar pulled out; a patchwork quilt of diminutive *kulianas* homesteads of native Hawaiians running deep into luxuriant valleys where ageless stone walls encircle fields of *taro*; a winter sanctuary for migrating birds, and gritty native species desperately holding to life; and, a haven for its myriad visitors, the adventuring, vacationing, life-tossed, or work weary who come to its shores seeking the setting so conducive to finding peace of body and soul.

The north shore is only 30 miles long, but oh, what miles! Along its undulating mountains, one-lane roads, and luminescent bays are land-locked caves still umbilically tied to the sea; historical sites, the remnants of peace or domination once so important and now reduced by time; and living "movie sets," some occupied by villas of stars or dignitaries, enough to bore even the worst name-dropper. Enduring, too, is the history of old Hawaii in this fabled home-land of the *menehune,* overrun by the Polynesians who set up their elaborate kingdoms built on strict social order. The usurpers' *heiau* remain, and from one—swaying, stirring, and spreading throughout the island kingdoms—came the *hula.*

Starting in **Kilauea** you can plunge down a natural "slippery slide," into a freshwater pool, visit an extensive artists' gallery, a one-man French bakery, an "everything" general store, or marvel at the coastline from bold promontories pummelled by the sea. Then there are the north shore beaches, Oriental fans of white sand, some easily visited as official parks, others hidden, the domains of simplicity and free spirits. **Princeville** follows, a convenient but incongruous planned community, vibrant with its own shopping mall, airport, and flexing "condo" muscles. Over the rise is **Hanalei,** more poetic than its lovely name, a tiny town, a yachties' anchorage, good food, spirited, slow, a bay of beauty and enchantment. The cameras once rolled at **Lumahai Beach** its neighbor, and an entire generation shared the dream of paradise when they saw this spot in *South Pacific.* Next in rapid succession are **Wainiha,** and **Haena** with its few amenities, the last available indoor lodging, restaurant, bar, and little of the world's most relaxed lifestyle. The road ends at **Kee Beach,** where adventure begins with the start of the Na Pali Coast Trail. The North Shore remains for most visitors the perfect setting for seeking and maybe actually finding peace, solitude, the dream, yourself.

KILAUEA

There's no saying *exactly* where it begins, but Kilauea is generally considered the gateway to the north shore. The village was built on sugar, which melted away almost 20 years ago. Now the town holds on as a way station to some of the most intriguing scenery along this fabulous coast. Look for mile marker no. 23 and a **76 Gas Station** on your right. A snack shop is nearby. This is where you turn onto **Kolo Road,** following the signs to Kilauea Lighthouse and Bird Sanctuary. The promontory that it occupies, Kilauea Point, is the northernmost tip of the main Hawaiian Islands. Before heading out there, notice the bright, cheery, and well-kept homes as you pass through this community. The home-owners, perhaps short on cash, are nonetheless long on pride, and surround their dwellings with lovingly tended flower gardens. The bungalows, pictures of homey contentment, are ablaze with color.

Sights

As you head down Kolo Road, you pass the post office. Where it intersects Kilauea Road sits **Christ Memorial Church** on the right. Hawaii seems to sprout as many churches as bamboo shoots but this one is special. The shrubbery and flowers immediately catch your eye, their vibrant colors matched by the stained-glass windows imported from England. The present church was built in 1941 from cut lava stone. Inside is a hand-hewn altar, and surrounding the church is a cemetery with some old tombstones for long departed parishioners. Go in, have a look, and perhaps meditate for a moment.

Before turning on Kilauea Road to the lighthouse go straight past Kilauea School and **St. Sylvester's Catholic Church.** This church is octagonal with an odd roof. Inside are murals painted by Jean Charlot, a famous island artist. The church, built by Fr. John Macdonald, was an attempt to reintroduce art as one of the bulwarks of Catholicism. Park in the church lot to begin your 5-minute walk to the **Slippery Slide.** Take the trail on your left through some brush for only 30 feet until it opens onto another-wider trail that looks like it once was a road. You'll hear the river. Turn left, and within 25 yards is a pathway wide enough for a car. Pass it by and almost immediately is a well-established path; follow it toward the roar of the water. The footing can be slippery, but the hardest part down the steep bank has a well-placed tree whose roots provide a crude staircase. The pool below the slide varies in size depending upon recent rains. This factor also governs the slide itself. If the conditions are

The Slippery Slide varies depending upon recent rains.

great frigatebird

right, not too much or too little water, you can cascade down this natural sluice and be unceremoniously deposited into the pool below. Use good judgment as the drop is 10-15 feet, and well-padded posteriors are a decided advantage. An added bonus for your efforts is a profusion of wild fruit trees in the area—bananas and mangos waiting to be plucked.

Head down Kilauea Road past the Kong Lung Store and a dozen or so homes on your left. Keep going until Kilauea Road makes a hard swing to the left. Here, proceed straight ahead up Mihi Road, and you pass a little Japanese cemetery on your right. This road is extremely tipped and banked, but passable! It crosses what appears to be the beginning of a development and turns to red dirt. If it's raining don't go...much too slippery! As you proceed you might wonder why you should make this effort to overlook the ordinary scenery below on the landward side. Atop the hill the spindly aluminum arms of TV antennas make the effort seem even less worthwhile. Just wait! At the road's end, park. You are now atop Mokolea Point's **Crater Hill,** and 560 feet straight down is the Pacific, virtually unobstructed until it hits Asia. The sea cliff is like a giant stack of pancakes, layered and jagged, with the edges eaten by age, and covered with a green syrup of lichen and mosses. The cliff is undercut, and you have the sensation of floating in mid-air. Shorten your gaze and notice the profusion of purple and yellow flowers all along the edge. Near the antennas is a 6-foot square block of cement with an orange dot painted in the middle. Stand here and spin slowly for a wonderful 360-degree panorama. The cliffs are a giant rookery for sea birds. Keep your eyes peeled for the **great frigatebird** kiting on its 8-foot wing span, or the **red-footed booby,** a white bird with black wing tips darting here and there, and always wearing red dancing shoes.

Mokolea Point

If you want a more civilized experience of the same view with perhaps a touch less drama, head down Kilauea Road to the end and park at **Kilauea Lighthouse and Bird Sanctuay**. This facility, built in 1913 and at one time manned by the Coast Guard but now under the jurisdiction of the National Park Service, boasts the largest "clamshell lens" in the world, capable of sending a beacon 90 miles out to sea. The area is alive with permanent and migrating birds. A bulletin board at the entrance gives you a fast lesson in birdlife—worth reading. A leisurely 30-minute walk takes you out onto this amazingly narrow peninsula where you'll learn more about the plant and birdlife in the area. This facility is open Sun. to Fri. 12:00-4:00 p.m. Admission is free.

Kilauea Point and lighthouse

Beaches

The Kilauea area has some fantastic beaches. One is a beach park with full amenities and camping, one is hidden and rarely visited, while others are for fishing or just looking.

Secret Beach lives up to everything that its name implies. Before entering Kilauea look for the North Shore Art Gallery in a large barn-like building on the left. Almost directly across Rt. 56 a rough little dirt road goes up the bank and through some fields. This tiny road is before the nearby crossroad marked by a highway sign. Follow it for about one mile until it turns right at an iron gate. Continue to a parking area and a little homemade sign saying "Beach Trail." Walk along the barbed wire fence and begin down the slope to the beach. You pass through some excellent jungle area before emerging at Secret Beach in less than 15 minutes. If you expect Secret Beach to be small, you're in for a shock. This white-sand strand is huge. Off to the left you can see Kilauea Lighthouse, dazzling white in the sun. Along the beach is a fine stand of trees providing shade and perfect for pitching a tent. A stream coming into the beach when you come down the hill is OK for washing but not drinking. For drinking water head south along the beach and keep your eyes peeled for a freshwater spring coming out of the mountain. What more can you ask for? The camping is terrific and free of hassles.

Kilauea Bay offers great fishing opportunities, unofficial camping, and beautiful scenery. Proceed through Kilauea Town along Kilauea Rd. and pass Kong Lung Store. Take the second dirt road to the right. Follow it down to what the local people call Quarry Beach. Although easy to get to, this wide sandy beach is rarely visited. Characteristic of Kauai, Kilauea Stream runs into the bay. The swimming is good in the stream and along the beach, but only during calm periods. Plenty of places along the stream bank or on the beach are good for camping. Many local fishermen come here to catch a transparent fish called *oio* that they use for bait. It's too bony to fry, but they have figured out an ingenious way to get the meat. They cut off the tail and roll a soda pop bottle over it, squeezing the meat out through the cut. They then mix it with some water, hot pepper, and bread crumbs to make delicious fish balls.

Kalihiwai Beach is just past Kilauea Town off Rt. 56 and down Kalihiwai Road (marked). If you go over the Kalihiwai River you've gone too far, even though another sign says Kalihiwai

Road. This coastal road once went through, but the devastating *tsunami* of 1946 took out the lower bridge and the road is now divided by the river. In less than half a mile you come to an off-the-track white-sand beach lined by ironwoods. The swimming and body surfing are outstanding during the right conditions. The river behind the ironwoods has formed a freshwater pool for rinsing off but there are no amenities whatsoever. People camp among the ironwoods without a problem.

Pass the first Kalihiwai Road, go over the bridge and turn left on the second Kalihiwai Road. Follow this to Anini Road ending at the remarkable **Anini County Beach Park.** The reef here is the longest exposed reef off Kauai; consequently the snorkeling is first rate. It's amazing to snorkel out to the reef in no more than 4 feet of water and then to peer over the edge into waters that seem bottomless. Windsurfers also love this area, and their bright sails can be seen year round. Follow the road to the end where a shallow brackish lagoon and large sandbar make the area good for wading. At the south end of the beach are full amenities with toilets, picnic tables, grills, a pavilion, and camping (county permit).

Shopping

A must-stop is the **North Shore Art Gallery**, operated by Sarah Adams and dedicated exclusively to showcasing island artists. The numbers change, but approximately 60 contributing artists at any given time are displayed in the five big rooms. Many are from Kauai, but plenty are from throughout the state, and they are some of the best. The walls and display cases brim with an exemplary array of styles and subject matter: X-rays of shells have been photographically printed and look like remarkable pen and inks, along with paintings, etchings, shell work, macrame, basketry, pottery, and carvings. You can even buy original postcards for only a $1, and prints for under $5. Every year around mid May, an **art fair** has booths manned by craftspeople willing to give demonstrations in their particular medium. Also, in the big barn out back, which will one day be part of the gallery, dances are held on the weekends ($2). The North Shore Art Gallery, tel. 828-1684, is clearly marked along Rt. 56 just before Kilauea Town.

An institution in this area is **Kong Lung Store** that's been serving the needs of the north shore plantation towns for almost a century. But, don't expect just bulk rice and pipe fittings. On the shelves are also gourmet cheeses, fine wines, and all of the accoutrements necessary for a very civilized picnic. Another section is a clothing boutique selling namebrand beach, casual, and alohawear. Enter an adjoining room to find an art gallery specializing in carvings, pottery, and Niihau shell work. Notice too the old-fashioned rag carpets woven with modern pastel material. Kong Long is located along Kilauea Lighthouse Road, tel. 828-1822, open daily 9:00 a.m. to 5:00 p.m.

Do you find "paradise" incomplete without a slice of mouth-watering French pastry? Well, it's available at **Jacques French Bakery**. Before Kong Lung Store turn right on Oka Street and follow your nose to the large Quonset hut which houses the bakery. Jacques and his staff handmake every loaf using whole wheat, bran, and other all-natural ingredients. You can choose a butter-melting box of croissants, or a rich loaf of honey-bran bread. Munch your treats and wash them down with steaming hot cups of Kona coffee at a few tables. Jacques' bread is available at restaurants around the island and at Big Save stores.

PRINCEVILLE

Princeville is 11,000 acres of planned luxury overlooking Hanalei Bay. Last century the surrounding countryside was a huge ranch, Kauai's oldest, established in 1853 by Englishman R.C. Wyllie. After an official royal vacation to the ranch by Kamehameha IV and Queen Emma in 1860, the name was changed to Princeville in honor of their son, Prince Albert. The young heir unfortunately died within 2 years and his heartbroken father soon followed. Since 1969, Consolidated Gas and Oil of Honolulu has taken these same 11,000 acres and developed them into a prime vacation community dedicated to keeping the humdrum world far away. Everything is provided: shopping, dining, recreational facilities especially golf and tennis, and even its own fire and police force and airport. First-rate condos are scattered around the property and a new multi-tiered Sheraton Hotel perches over the bay. The guests expect to stay put, except for an occasional day trip. Management and clientele are in league to provide and receive satisfaction. And without even trying it's just about guaranteed.

Sights

The sights around Princeville are exactly that, beautiful sweeping vistas of **Hanalei Valley** and the sea, especially at sunset. People come just for the light show and are never disappointed. When you proceed past the Princeville turn-off keep your eyes peeled for a **scenic overlook.** Don't miss it! Drifting into the distance is the pastel living impressionism of Hanalei Valley. Down the center, the liquid silver Hanalei River flows until it meets the sea where the valley broadens into a wide flat fan. Along its banks impossible shades of green vibrate as the valley steps back for almost 9 miles, all cradled in the protective arms of 3,500-foot *pali.* Turned on or off by recent rains, waterfalls tumble over the *pali* like lace curtains billowing in a gentle wind, or with the blasting power of a fire hose. Local wisdom says that "when you can count 17 waterfalls it's time to get out of Hanalei." The valley has always been one of the most accommodating places in all of Hawaii to live, and its abundance was ever-blessed by the old gods. Madame Pele even sent a thunderbolt to split a boulder so that the Hawaiians could run an irrigation ditch through its center to their fields.

In the old days, Hanalei produced *taro,* and deep into the valley the outlines of the ancient fields can still be discerned. Then the white man came and planted coffee which failed, sugar which petered out, or cattle which grazed it away. During these times Hanalei had to *import poi* from Kalalau. Later Chinese plantation laborers moved in. The valley was terraced again, but this time the wet fields were given to rice. This crop proved profitable for many years and was still grown as late as the 1930s. Then, amazingly, the valley began to slowly revert back to *taro* patches. It was designated a **National Wildlife Refuge,** and the native water birds such as the Hawaiian coot, duck, and gallinule (see p. 661) loved it and reclaimed their ancient nesting grounds. Today, the large, green, heart-like leaves of *taro* carpet the valley, and the abundant crop produces about 50% of Hawaii's *poi.* You can go into Hanalei Valley; however, you're not permitted in the designated wildlife areas except for fishing or hiking along the river. Never disturb any nesting birds. Look below to where a bridge crosses the river. Just there, Ohiki Road branches inland. Drive slowly along it to view the simple and quiet homesteads, nesting birds, wildflowers, and terraced fields of this enchanted land.

Golf, Tennis, And Other Activities

Those addicted to striking hard dimpled white balls or fuzzy soft ones have come to the right spot. In Princeville, golf and tennis are the royal

The airport marks the beginning of the planned community of Princeville.

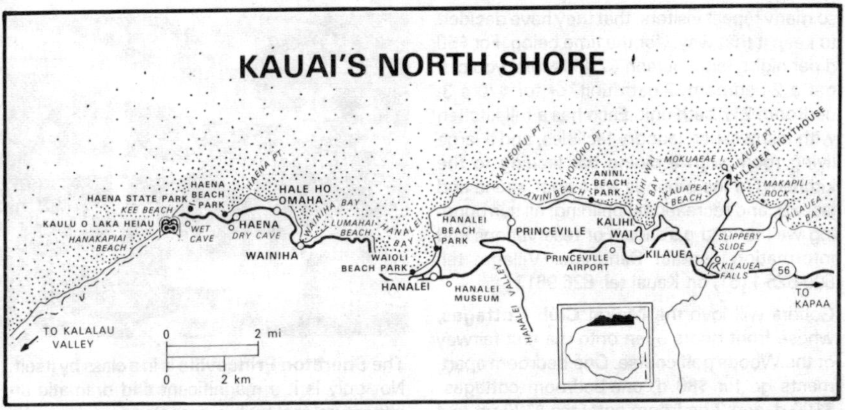

couple. The **Princeville Makai Course** offers 27 holes of magnificent golf designed by Robert Trent Jones Jr. This course, chosen as one of America's top 100 courses, hosted the 26th annual World Cup in 1978. There are 3 9-hole par-36 courses you can use in any combination that radiate from the central Clubhouse. They include the **Woods, Lake,** and **Ocean** courses, the names highlighting their special focus. Open to the public, golf costs approximately $50 per 18-hole round, including golf cart, with guests charged about half that amount. Plenty of package deals to the resort include flights, accommodations, and unlimited golf. For example, for around $150 (double occupancy), you get 2 nights and 3 days in a Makai Club condo and unlimited golf with confirmed tee times. Get information by calling in Hawaii 800-652-6541 or from the Mainland 800-367-7090.

You can charge the net on 22 professional tennis courts, day or night. There are 2 pro shops, lessons of all sorts, and even video playback so that you can burn yourself up a second time while reviewing your mistakes. Court use is $4 per hour with special daily, group, and package rates available. Information on tennis is available by calling the numbers listed under golf.

Two miles before Princeville is the Princeville Airport. **Papillon Helicopters,** tel. 826-6591, operates their magical mystery tours deep into Kauai's interior from here. They are a once-in-a-lifetime unforgettable experience. (For details see p. 167-168.)

If flying isn't your pleasure, how about loping along on horseback? **Pooku Stables,** tel. 826-6777, is located a half mile before the entrance to Princeville. Here you can rent a mount that takes you throughout the area's fascinating countryside. Prices vary from $13 to $40 depending upon the ride.

Accommodations

The condos and hotel rooms in Princeville all fall into the high-moderate to expensive range. The best deals naturally occur off-season (fall), especially if you plan on staying a week or more. Oddly enough, a project like Princeville should make booking one of its many condos an easy matter, but it's sadly lacking on this point. Lack of a centralized organization that handles reservations causes the confusion. Each condo building can have half a dozen booking agents all with different phone numbers and widely differing rates! The units are privately owned and the owners simply choose one agency or another. Some of the price differences are amazing! An effort has been made here to give the least expensive booking agent for the following listings, but this could vary, so be forewarned. If you're going through a travel agent at home, be aware of these discrepancies and insist on the least expensive rates.

The best deal in Princeville is offered by **Sandpiper Village Condominiums**. By chance they stumbled onto a good thing. When they first opened they priced their units low to attract clientele. The response was so good, with so many repeat visitors, that they have decided to keep it that way...for the time being. For $60 d per night, extra person $7, kids free, you can get a 2-bedroom, 2-bath unit, or for $70 a 3-bedroom 2½-bath unit. Each has a full kitchen with dishwasher, laundry facilities, and a large living room with a dining bar leading to the kitchen. On the grounds are a pool, sauna and jacuzzi, and recreational building, all surrounding well-tended gardens. For reservations and information contact Sandpiper Village, tel. 800-525-1161, on Kauai tel. 826-9613.

Golfers will love the **Makai Club Cottages,** whose front doors open onto the first fairway of the Woods golf course. One-bedroom apartments go for $80 d, one-bedroom cottages $100 d, and 2-bedroom cottages $120 up to 4 persons. Each unit has a fully equipped kitchen, and some have added amenities like a deep Japanese *ofuro* (hot tub). There's maid service, pool, and nearby tennis. For information contact Princeville Management Co., Box 3040, Princeville, HI 96722, tel. 800-367-7090, on Kauai tel. 826-6561.

Other condos in the development are expensive, charging a minimum $100 per night. They're out to please and don't skimp on the luxuries. For example, the **Ka Eo Kai** gives you a massive 2,300-square-foot unit with *lanai,* custom kitchen, fireplace, stereo, and big-screen TV. The units accommodate 7 comfortably. **The Cliffs** have a dramatic setting overlooking the sea, and are a bit cheaper. Their one- to 4-bedroom units can be broken into single rooms that help keep prices down. They have a jacuzzi, swimming pool, maid service on request, and 3-night minimum stay. The **Hanalei Bay Resort** and **Hanalei Colony Resort** also offer reasonable accommodations. The Bay has a bit more going for it with tennis courts, 2 swimming pools, and a good restaurant on the premises. Other good units include the **Paniolo, Poa,** and the **Hale Moi.** Each can be booked, but not exclusively, by Hanalei Aloha Rental Management, Box 1109, Hanalei, HI 96714, tel. 800-367-8047, on Kauai tel. 826-9833. They have package deals with National Car Rental. Another good agency managing a number of properties is Hawaiian Apartment Leasing Co., 1240 Cliff Drive, Laguna Beach, CA 92651, tel. 800-854-8843, in California tel. 800-472-8449.

The **Sheraton Princeville** is in a class by itself. Not only is it a magnificent and dramatic architectural feat built in tiers stepping down the point of the peninsula, but it is the only hotel in Princeville. (Local folks who hated to lose one of the premiere views on the north shore say it looks like a prison of tiny concrete squares.) All but 16 of the 300 rooms have either a bay or an ocean view. The lobby offers a "history of Hanalei," complete with antique quilts and missionary furniture. There are restaurants, pool, shops, lounges, and free shuttle service to the nearby links. Single rooms rent for $160-250, while suites go $350-600. For information write Sheraton Princeville Hotel, Box 3069 Princeville, HI 96722, tel. 800-826-4400, on Kauai tel. 826-9644.

Food

The restaurants, mostly located within the condos, are expensive but good. The **Bali Hai** an open-air restaurant in the Hanalei Bay Resort, enjoys an excellent reputation not only for its food, but for its superb atmosphere and prize-winning view of the beach, especially at sunset. Bamboo, batik, and tapestries hung in this bi-level restaurant add an informal elegance. Breakfast and lunch are mainly eggs, omelettes, salads, and sandwiches, with dinner more outstanding and more pricy. The menu includes chicken, fish, and beef dishes with none under $10. Children's platters are slightly less. Open daily, tel. 826-6522.

Beamreach is an intimate restaurant stowed away in the Pali Ke Kua Condominium. Open only for dinner, it's a favorite with yachties which is reflected in its nautical decor. It serves fish, lobster, and chicken, but is especially noted for its beef which is flown in twice weekly from Kansas! Prices are from $10 with children's portions slightly cheaper. Two house specialties, the large salad with croutons and the strawberry daquiri from the bar, are exceptional. Reservations are necessary, tel. 826-9131.

The **Princeville Lanai** is an open-air restaurant right on the fairways. It serves Continental and American fare, with a touch of Oriental. Lunchtime sandwiches are good and reasonably priced, and the Sunday brunch is really decent, tel. 826-6228.

The word is that the restaurants and snack bars in the Sheraton are overpriced for what you get...except for **Nobles.** This is the signature restaurant of the hotel and its decor is reminiscent of Victorian England, a favorite motif of Hawaii's last monarch. The gourmet food is pricey but well prepared and served with great civility.

Princeville isn't immune to fast food. You can order guess what at the **Pizza Burger** in the Princeville Center. Also, its neighbor, **Tortilla Flats,** serves Mexican food, but most complain that it's bland and tasteless.

Entertainment

The **Princeville Lanai Restaurant** hosts live music nightly, ranging from Hawaiian to jazz to contemporary sounds. The **Bali Hai Restaurant** is the setting for *hula* every Thurs. evening performed by the local Halau O Hanalei, and on Sat. evening a *luau* is offered, followed by a Polynesian Review.

Shopping And Services

The shopping in Princeville is clustered in the main buildings as soon as you enter the property. A few stores sell souvenirs and gifts, but since Princeville is a self-contained community, most are practical shops: bank, butcher shop, fast food, and **Foodland** supermarket. The latter is important because it offers the cheapest food prices on the North Shore. Before it was built, the local people would drive to Kapaa to shop; now they come here. One of the last gas stations on the north shore is **Princeville Chevron.** If your gauge is low make sure to tank up if you're driving back down the coast. They're open Mon. to Thurs. 7:00 a.m. to 7:00 p.m., Fri. to Sat. until 8:00 p.m., and Sun. until 6:00 p.m.

HANALEI TOWN

If Puff the Magic Dragon had resided in the sunshine of Hanalei instead of the mists of Hanalee, Little Jackie Paper would still be hangin' around. You know you're entering a magic land the minute you drop down from the heights and cross the Hanalei River. The narrow one-lane bridge is like a gateway to the enchanted coast forcing you to slow down and take stock of where you are. To add to your amazement, as you look "up valley" over a sea of green taro, what else would you expect to to find but a herd of buffalo? (They're imported by a local entrepreneur trying to cross-breed them with beef cattle.) Hanalei ("Lei-Making Town") compacts a lot into a little space. You're in and out of the town in "two blinks," but you'll find a small shopping center, some terrific restaurants, beach and ocean activities, historical sites, and a cultural and art center. You also get 2 superlatives for the price of one: the epitome of a north shore laid-back village, and a truly magnificent bay. In fact, if one was forced to choose the most beautiful bay in all of Hawaii, Hanalei (and Lumahai, the silent star of the movie *South Pacific,* just north of town), would definitely be among the finalists.

Sights

Hanalei Town and Beach are sights in themselves. Don't make this sojourn up the North Coast without getting out to stretch your legs; you'll do yourself a disservice. Overlooking the bay on a tall bluff are the remains of an old Russian fort (1816) from the days when Hawaii was lusted after by many European powers. It's too difficult to find, but knowing it's there adds a little spice. As you enter town look for the Hanalei Trader. Just past is **Hanalei Museum,** on the left, one of Hawaii's funkiest museums. Often closed, and seemingly an addendum to a small stand selling plate lunches and *saimin,* it's great just because it is so unostentatious. Go around back to the little outhouse-like shed holding a few items, rusty and muddy, like an old sink and a mirror. The experience is cultural, like being invited into someone's back

Waioli Mission House

yard. Down the block, on the right next to Na Pali Zodiac, and old building houses the **Hawaiian Trading and Cultural Center**. Don't get *too* excited because this good idea doesn't have its act together yet. They have some authentic Hawaiian crafts, and some awful touristy junk, too. You can buy handmade jewelry and pick through the offerings at Auntie Louise's Hulaland, but the only really worthwhile items are lovely, fresh plumeria *lei* for only $2.95.

Waioli Mission House Museum

As you leave town, look to your left to see **Waioli Hui'ia Church**. If you're in Hanalei on Sun. do yourself a favor and go to the services to be uplifted by a choir of rich voices singing hymns in Hawaiian. They do justice to the meaning of *Waioli,* which is "Healing or Singing Waters." The **Waioli Mission House** is a must-stop whenever you pass through. You know you're in for a treat as soon as you pull into the parking lot completely surrounded by trees, creeping vines, ferns, even papaya. You walk over stepping stones through a formal garden with the jagged mountains framing a classical American homestead. Most mission homes are "New England-style," and this one is too, inside. But outside it's "Southern" because the missionary architect was a Kentuckian, Rev. William P. Alexander, who arrived with his wife Mary Ann in 1834 by double-hulled canoe from Waimea. Although a number of missionary families lived in the home over the next 10 years, in 1846 Abner and Lucy Wilcox arrived, and the home became synonymous with this family. Indeed, it was owned and occupied by the *kamaaina* Wilcox family until very recently. It was George, the son of Abner and Lucy, who founded Grove Homestead over by Lihue. Miss Mabel Wilcox, his niece who died in 1978, and her sister Miss Elsie who was the first woman representative of Hawaii in the '30s, set up a non-profit educational foundation that operates the home.

Your first treat will be meeting Joan, the lovely curator. A "fuss pot" in the best sense of the word, she's like a proper old auntie who gives you the "hairy eyeball" if you muss up the doily on the coffee table. Joan knows an unbelievable amount of history and anecdotes, not only about the mission house, but about the entire area and Hawaiiana in general. The home is great, and she makes it better. The first thing she says, almost apologetically to Mainlanders, is "take off your shoes. It's an old Hawaiian custom and feels good to your feet." You enter the parlor where Lucy Wilcox taught native girls who'd never seen a needle and thread before to sew. Within a few years, their nimble fingers were fashioning *muumuu* to cover their pre-Christian nakedness. In the background an old clock ticks. In 1866 a missionary coming to visit from Boston was given $8 to buy a clock. He bought one and here it is keeping time 120 years later. The picture on it is of the St. Louis

Courthouse. Paintings of the Wilcoxes and their children line the walls. Lucy looks like a happy, sympathetic woman. Abner's books line the shelves. Notice an old copy of *Uncle Tom's Cabin,* and *God Against Slavery.* His preserved letters show that he was a very serious man, not given to humor. He and Lucy didn't want to come to Hawaii at first, but then loved the place. He worried about his sons, and about being poor. He even wrote letters to the king urging that Hawaiian be retained as the first language, with English as a second. He and Lucy returned to New England for a visit in 1869, where both took sick and died.

During the time that this was a mission household, 9 children were born in the main bedroom, 8 of them boys. Behind it is a nursery, the only room that has had a major change; Lucy and Mabel had a closet built and an indoor bathroom installed in 1921. Upstairs is a guest bedroom that the Wilcoxs dubbed the "room of the tattling prophet," because it was invariably occupied by visiting missionaries. Also used by Abner Wilcox as a study, the books in the room are original primers printed on Oahu. The homestead served as a school for selected boys who were trained as teachers. It was also a self-sufficient farm where they raised chickens and cattle. Around the home are artifacts, dishes, and knickknacks from last century. Notice candle molds, a food locker, a charcoal iron, and the old butter churn. Lucy Wilcox churned butter that she shipped to Honolulu in buckets, which brought in some good money. The Reverend, along with his missionary duties, was a doctor, teacher, public official, and veterinarian. From the upstairs window you can still see the same view from last century, Hanalei Bay, beautifully serene and timeless. The Waioli Mission House is open Tues. to Sat. 9:00 a.m. to 3:00 p.m., and is free! There is a bucket for donations; please be generous remembering that many of the missionary homes in Hawaii soak you to take a tour, but not here.

Beaches

Since the days of the migrating Polynesians, **Hanalei Bay** has been known as one of the Pacific's most perfect anchorages. Used as one of Kauai's 3 main ports until very recently, it's still a favorite port of call for world-class yachts. They start arriving in mid May and stay throughout the summer when 40 to 50 magnificent boats bob in the bay, making the most of the easy entrance and sandy bottom. They leave by October, when even this inviting bay becomes rough, with occasional 30-foot waves. When you drive to the bay, the section under the trees near the river is called **Black Pot.** It received this name from an earlier time when the people of Hanalei would greet the yachties with island *aloha* which of course included food. A fire was always going with a large black pot hanging over it, into which everyone contributed and then shared in the

The hearth is the center of Waioli Mission House.

John Koon sailing his double-hulled canoe up the Hanalei River

meal. Across the road and up river a few hundred yards is **Hanalei Canoe Club.** This small local club has produced a number of winning teams in statewide competitions, oftentimes appearing against much larger clubs. You might notice one of their boats, a double-hulled sailing canoe, one of the last still sailing Hawaiian waters. Rides are available (see p. 669). The sweeping crescent bay is gorgeous. Hanalei River empties into it, and all around it's protected by embracing mountains. A long pier is in the center, and 2 reefs front the bay, **Queen** to the left and **King** to the right. The bay provides excellent sailing, surfing, and swimming, mostly in summer. The swimming is good near the river, and at the west end, but rip currents can appear anywhere, even around the pier area, so be careful. The state maintains 3 parks on the bay, all with picnic areas and restrooms. A small truck sells plate lunches near the river; local fishermen often use the bay to launch their boats and are often amenable to selling their catch. Many local people camp here on weekends and holidays.

Lumahai Beach is a *femme fatale,* lovely to look at but treacherous. This hauntingly beautiful beach, meaning "Twist of Fingers," is what dreams are made of: white sand curving perfectly at the bottom of a dark lava cliff with tropical jungle in the background. The rip tides here are fierce even with the reef, and the water should never be entered except in very calm conditions. Look for a vista point at mile marker 33. Cars invariably park here. Make sure to pull completely off the road because this is a popular spot and patrolled by the police who will ticket you. An extensive grove of *hala* trees is just as you set off down a steep and often muddy footpath leading down to the beach. You can also drive to another pull-off just before mile marker 34 at the north end of the beach. This access is much easier and you can walk to the south end if you want seclusion. Up here is a small, swift stream with a sandy bottom, good for a dip.

Food

Hanalei has a number of eating institutions, ranging from excellent restaurants to *kau kau* wagons. The food is great at any time of day, but those in the know time their arrival to coincide with sunset. They watch the free show and then go for a great meal.

The first restaurant you encounter is the **Hanalei Dolphin,** right at the bridge over the Hanalei River as you come down Rt. 56 from Princeville. For years it has enjoyed a reputation as the north shore's premiere seafood restaurant, although meat dishes are also served. The restaurant was damaged by Hurricane Iwa and has since been remodeled, but its menu remains much the same. Don't mull over the menu, however; listen to the waiters instead. They'll tell you what's good tonight—believe them. You can't go wrong starting with the clam chowder. The Hanalei Dolphin is open daily for dinner from 6:00-10:00 p.m. No reservations are taken.

You've got to stop at the **Tahiti Nui,** if just to look around and have a cool drink. The original owner, Louise Marston, was dedicated to creating a friendly, family atmosphere and she succeeded admirably. The restaurant is now run by her daughter and son-in-law, but the tradition carries on. Inside, it's pure Pacific island. The decorations are modern Polynesian longhouse, with blowfish lanterns and stools carved from palm tree trunks. The bar is center of the action. Oldtimers drop in to "talk story" and someone is always willing to sing and play a Hawaiian tune. The mai tais are fabulous. Just sit out on the porch, kick back, and sip away. The weeknight menu is limited and fairly expensive. It includes fresh fish, beef, and chicken, all prepared with an island twist and priced upward of $10. You sit at long tables and eat family style. The Tahiti Nui is famous for its *luau*-style party, Mon., Wed., and Friday. There's singing, dancing, and good cheer all around, a perfect time to mingle with the local people. The bar is open daily from noon to 2:00 a.m. Dinner nightly, tel. 826-6277.

The **Hanalei Shell House** is deliciously funky and reasonably priced. Many local people come here to "talk story" in the evenings, oftentimes providing spontaneous entertainment. It's just down the road from the Tahiti Nui near the Na Pali Zodiac office. They're open for breakfast, lunch, and dinner, with music and drinks going to the wee hours. Breakfast includes omelettes for under $4, lunch is mainly salads and sandwiches with the special priced under $4, and dinner entrees start at $9, tel. 826-9301

Foong Wong specializes in Cantonese cuisine, located upstairs in the new Ching Young Village Shopping Center. Their extensive menu includes dishes like squid $5, crab and black bean $11, chop suey $4.15, fish with oyster sauce $3.75, and many plate lunches for under $5. Unfortunately, Foong Wong's gets its fortune cookies crumbled. The word is that the portions are large, but bland, and the atmosphere is sterile. Open 10:30 a.m. to 2:30 p.m., Tues. to Sun. for lunch, 4:30-9:00 p.m. nightly for dinner, tel. 826-6996.

Hanalei Town has a great collection of fast, inexpensive, and downright delicious places to eat. The problem is which one to choose! **Norberto's El Cafe,** the family-owned restaurant from Kapaa with a vegetarian twist, has a small restaurant and take-out window on your right in the middle of town. Their food is *muy bueno* and you can choose munchies like nachos for $1.75, tacos and burritos for around $4. For a mouth-watering burger with all the trimmings, a plate lunch, or an undisputedly luscious bowl of *saimin,* the latter only in the evening, try the food stand at the **Hanalei Museum** on your left just as you enter town. Competing with Norberto's, this institution known for its great food and cheap prices is a green *kau kau* wagon called the **Tropical Taco** that dispenses lunches from 11:00 a.m. to around 4:00 p.m. through a side window. The van is usually parked next to the Hanalei Trader as you enter town. If you're after health food, visit **Healthy Jones** in the Ching Young Village Shopping Center. They're small, but carry all the necessities for a good healthy lunch or picnic. If the little food monster gets a hold of you and a slab of tofu just won't do, across from Healthy Jones is a no-name plate-lunch joint that also sells mouth-watering homemade pies like coconut cream, passionfruit, pumpkin, and French apple.

Shopping And Services

The **Ching Young Village** in the center of town is a small shopping center. Among its shops are **Big Save Supermarket,** a number of variety and gift stores, and a great backpacking and sports rental store—the **Hanalei Liquor Store** is on the right just as you enter town. Friendly, with a good selection and prices. The **Hanalei Trader** is the 2-story building as you enter town. This is it for gas on the north shore. They also sell a wide assortment of fishing and camping gear. Around the corner from the Tahiti Nui is **Happy Talk,** selling paperback books, music, and Hawaiiana.

Outdoor And Sporting Services

Hanalei is alive with outdoor activities. The following is merely a quick list of what's available. The services provided by the majority of the establishments listed here have been fully described in the Kauai Introduction either under "Sightseeing Tours," "Sports," or "Camping."

Na Pali Zodiac does stupendous rides up the Na Pali coast in a seagoing rubber raft, hiking drop-off service too; tel. 826-9371. **Na Pali Coast Charter,** tel. 826-6044, and **Sea Kauai,** tel. 828-1488, are 2 other Zodiac companies. An extensive range of backpacking and hiking equipment to rent or buy is available from **Hanalei Camping and Backpacking** in the Ching Young Center at tel. 826-6664. **Pedal and Pedal,** also in the center, rents snorkel gear, bikes, boats, sailboats, surfboards, and windsurfers at tel. 826-9069. A variety of sailing and fishing adventures are available from: **Hawaiian Adventures,** tel. 826-6088; **Coastal Charters,** tel. 826-7394; **Blue Water Sailing,** tel. 826-9231; **Kayak Kauai,** tel. 826-9844; **Kilo Sportfishing,** tel. 826-9318; **Lady Ann Cruises,** tel. 245-8538; and **Luana Hawayaks,** tel. 826-9195.

ROAD'S END

Past Hanalei you have 6 miles of pure magic until the road ends at Kee Beach. To thrill you further and make your ride even more enjoyable, you'll find historical sites, natural wonders, a resort, restaurant, grocery store, and the *heiau* where the *hula* was born, overlooking a lovely beach.

Sights, Accommodations, And Services

As you drive along you cross one-lane bridges, and pass little beaches and bays, one after another, invariably with a small stream flowing in. Try not to get jaded peering at "just another North Shore gorgeous beach." Over a small white bridge is the village of **Wainiha,** ("Angry Water"). Here is the **Wainiha Store** where you can pick up supplies. Talk to Mary here if you're looking for a place to stay. People from around the area come to the store and post a flyer if they're renting a room. You can still get a shack on the beach! Attached to the store is a snack shop. They have great island-inspired natural smoothies for $2, a meal in themselves. It's not hard to find a bunch of local guys hanging around, perhaps listening to reggae music, who could brighten your day by selling you some of the local produce!

After the store you cross 2 bridges in a row, and they're dillys! Be careful. Between mile markers 36 and 37 look for a road branching off to **Tunnels Beach.** It's superb for snorkeling and scuba with a host of underwater seacaves off to the left as you face the sea. Both surfing and windsurfing are great, and the swimming is too if the sea is calm. Off to the right and down a bit is a nude beach. Careful not to sunburn delicate parts!

Next up look for signs to the **Hanalei Colony Resort,** literally the "last resort." You can rent very comfortable, spacious, 2-bedroom condos here. The brown board and batten buildings blend into the surroundings. The resort has a jacuzzi and swimming pool, with complimentary snorkel gear. Doubles vary from $70

the gaping maw of Maniniholo ("Dry Cave")

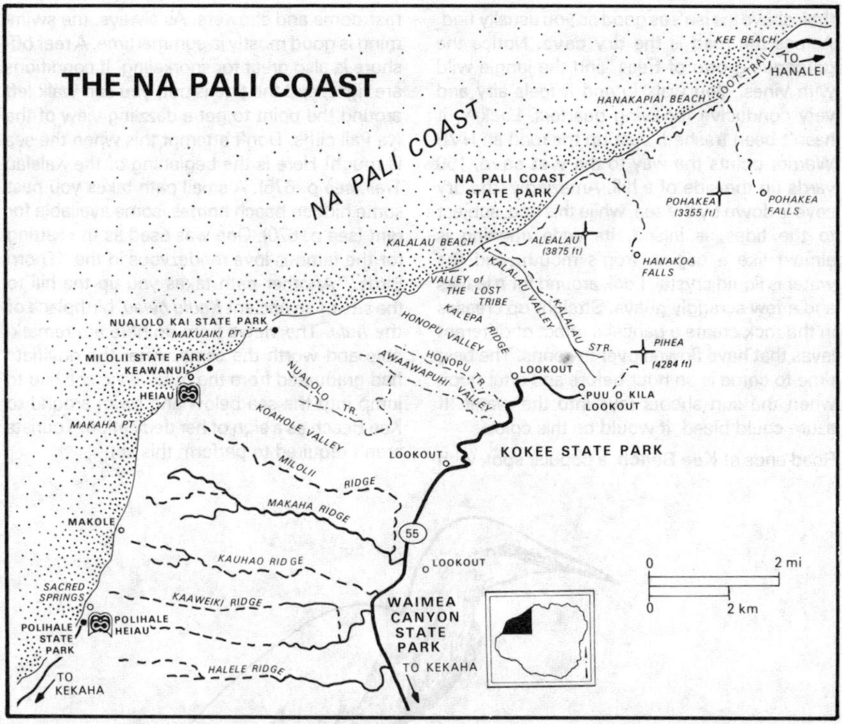

to $115 depending upon the view. Additional persons are $12, and a car rental package is available. For information contact Hanalei Colony Resort, Box 206, Hanalei, HI 96714, tel. 800-421-0767, in California tel. 800-252-0327, on Kauai tel. 826-6235. On the premises is the newly opened **Charo's Restaurant**—yes, *that* Charo! It replaces the old Sandgroper. The lunch and dinner menu features fresh fish and steaks. The drinks are great and the views outstanding. Open daily, lunch 11:30 a.m. to 3:00 p.m., dinner 5:30-10:00 p.m., reservations tel. 826-6422.

Just past Hanalei Resort, near the dot on the map signalling **Haena,** look for the entrance to the **YMCA Camp Naue.** Here, half a dozen buildings are filled with bunks and a separate toilet area and cooking facilities. The camp caters to large groups but is open to single travelers for the staggering sum of $2 per night. The camp has a varied schedule of availability: January to February open, February to May weekends only, June 1 to June 15 open, June 15 to July 15 special camping, August Kauai YMCA members only, September to January open. You can get full information from YMCA HQ at Poipu Beach by writing YMCA of Kauai, Box 1786, Lihue, HI 96766, tel. 742-1182 or 742-1200.

Haena County Beach Park, just before road's end, is a large, flat, field-like area, where you carve out your own camping site. For your convenience the county provides tables, a pavilion, grills, showers, and camping (permit). The swimming is good only when the sea is gentle, and in summertime a reef offshore is great for snorkeling. The cold stream running through the park is always good for a dip. Look for 2 *kau kau* wagons usually parked here. You can get some snacks but they're expensive and their shave ice isn't as good as you usually find. Across the road is the **dry cave.** Notice the gorgeous grotto of trees, and the jungle wild with vines. You walk in and it feels airy and very conducive for living quarters. Luckily, it hasn't been trashed. Just up the road an HVB Warrior points the way to the **wet cave,** 150 yards up the side of a hill. Amazingly, the dry cave is down by the sea, while this one, subject to the tides, is inland. Its wide opening is almost like a gaping frog's mouth, and the water is liquid crystal. Look around for *ti* leaves and a few scraggly guava. Straight up creases in the rock create a pancake effect of different lavas that have flowed over the eons. The best time to come is an hour before and after noon when the sun shoots rays into the water. If azure could bleed, it would be this color.

Road ends at **Kee Beach,** a popular spot, with restrooms and showers. As always, the swimming is good mostly in summertime. A reef offshore is also great for snorkeling. If conditions are right, and the tide is out, you can walk left around the point to get a dazzling view of the Na Pali cliffs. Don't attempt this when the sea is rough! Here is the beginning of the Kalalau Trail (see p. 675). A small path takes you past some hidden beach homes, some available for rent (see p. 670). One was used as the setting for the famous love rendezvous in the "Thorn Birds." Another path takes you up the hill to the site of an ancient *Kaulu heiau,* birthplace of the *hula.* The views from up here are remarkable and worth the climb. After the novitiate had graduated from the *hula heiau,* she had to jump into the sea below and swim around to Kee Beach as a sign of her dedication. Tourists aren't required to perform this act.

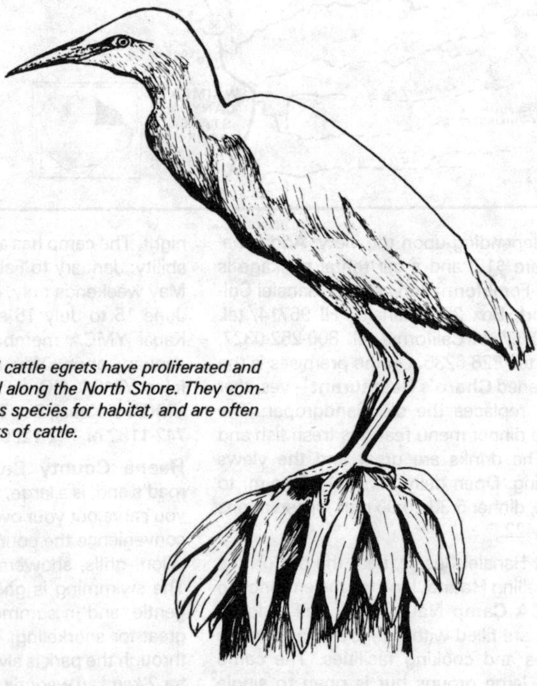

Recently introduced cattle egrets have proliferated and are now common all along the North Shore. They compete with indigenous species for habitat, and are often seen riding the backs of cattle.

SOUTHWEST KAUAI

The sometimes turbulent but forever enduring love affair between non-Polynesian travelers and the Hawaiian Islands began in southwest Kauai when Capt. Cook hove to off Waimea Bay and a long-boat full of wide-eyed sailors made the beach. Immediately, journals filled with glowing descriptions of the loveliness of the newly found island and its people, and the liaison has continued unabated ever since.

The **Kaumuali'i Highway** (the "Royal Oven" road—Rt. 50) steps west from Lihue, with the **Hoary Head Mountains** adding a dash of beauty to the south and Queen Victoria's Profile winking down from the heights. Soon, **Maluhia Road** ("Peaceful") branches to the south through an open *lei* of fragrant eucalyptus trees lining the route. It enters **Koloa,** site of the first sugar mill in the islands, and a still-vibrant tourist town filled with shops, restaurants, and a distinctly island atmosphere. Just south is **Poipu Beach,** Kauai's greatest concentration of condos and luxury hotels, where you can count on the weather to be bright and sunny and the surf to be relaxing and accommodating. Quickly come the towns of **Omao, Lawai,** and **Kalaheo,** way stations on the road west. Hereabouts 3 separate botanical gardens create a living canvas of color in blooms.

After Kalaheo, the road dips south again and passes **Port Allen**, a still-active harbor, then goes on to **Hanapepe,** at the mouth of the Hanapepe River, whose basin has long been known as some of the best *taro* lands in the islands. Tiny "sugar towns" and hidden beaches follow until you enter **Waimea Town,** whose right flank was once dominated by a Russian fort, the last vestige of a dream of island dominance gone sour. Captain Cook landed at Waimea in mid-afternoon of January 20, 1778, and a small monument in town center commemorates the great event. A secondary road leading north from Waimea and another from Kekaha farther west converge inland, then meander along Waimea Canyon, the Pacific's most superlative gorge. **Kekaha,** with its belching sugar stacks, marks the end of civilization, and the hard road gives out just past the **Barking Sands Missile Range**. A "cane road" picks up and carries you to the wide sun drenched beach of **Polihale** ("Protected Breast"), the end of the line, and the southern extremity of the Na Pali Coast.

SIGHTS AND VILLAGES

The **Koloa District** starts just west of the Hoary Head Mountains and ends on the east bank of the Hanapepe River. It mostly incorporates the ancient *ahuapua'a,* a land division shaped like a piece of pie with its pointed end deep in the Alakai Swamp and the broad end along the coast. *Koloa* means "duck," probably named because of the preponderance of ponds throughout the district that attract these water-loving fowl. Its villages are strung along Rt. 50, except for Koloa and Poipu, which lie south of the main road.

The adjoining pie-shaped *ahuapua'a* is the **Waimea District** whose broad end continues from Hanapepe until it terminates about midway up the Na Pali Coast. Waimea means "Red Waters," named after the distinctive color of the Waimea River that bleeds from Mt. Waialeale, cutting its way through Waimea Canyon and depositing the rich red soil at its mouth.

Note: Places to **stay, eat,** and **shop** are listed under the following villages so that you'll know what to expect as you drive along. Since Koloa and Poipu account for the majority of these amenities with too many to mention here, they appear on p. 746-752.

Puhi

This village is technically in Lihue District, but since it's the first settlement you pass heading west, it's included here. Two signs tip you off that you're in Puhi; one for **Kauai Community College** on the left, the other for **Queen Victoria's Profile** on the right. It's beneficial to keep abreast of what's happening at the college by reading the local newspaper and free tourist brochures. Oftentimes, workshops and seminars concerning Hawaiian culture, folk medicine, and various crafts are offered. Mostly, they're open to the general public and free of charge. Queen Victoria's Profile isn't tremendously remarkable, but a definite resemblance to this double-chinned monarch is naturally fashioned from boulders. More importantly look for the **People's Market** across from the college. Here, you can pick up supplies, especially fruit and vegetables, and they offer excellent prices (from $3) for freshly strung plumeria *lei,* an inexpensive way to brighten your day.

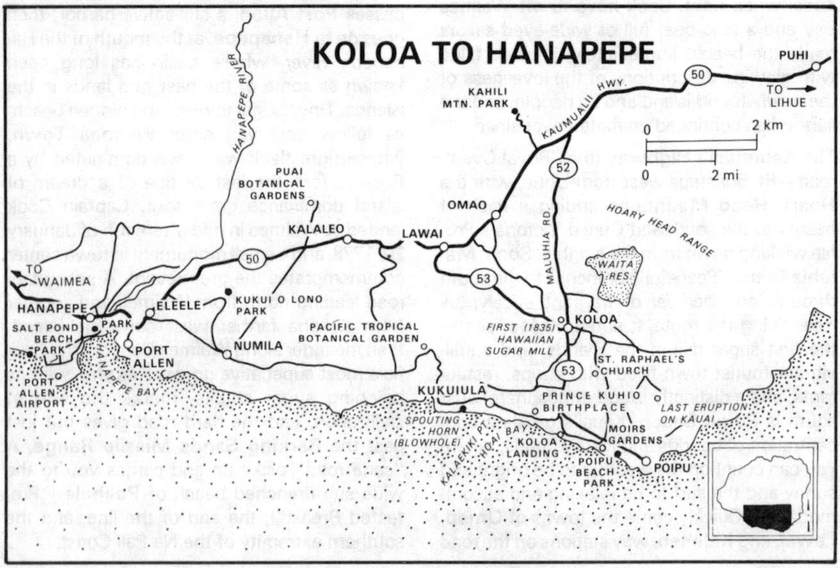

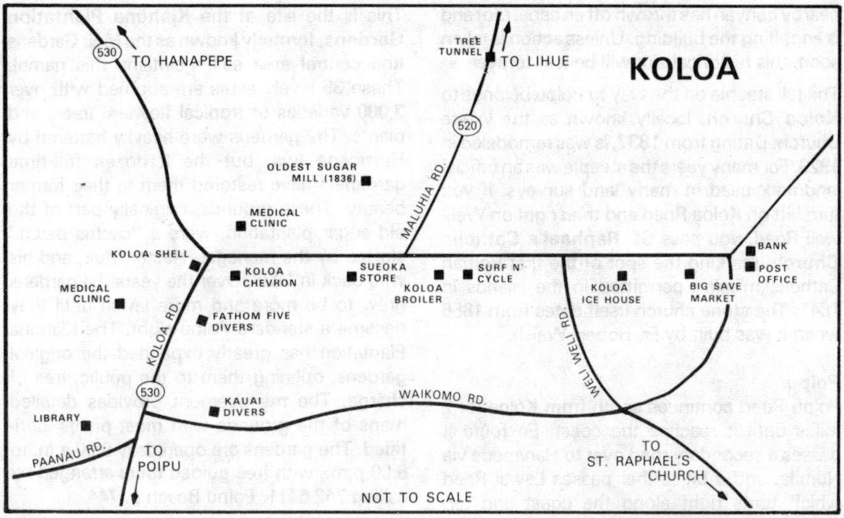

Koloa

Four miles past Puhi, Maluhia Road (Rt. 52) dips south off Rt. 50 and heads for Koloa. But if you continue 3 minutes west on Rt. 50, a sign on the right directs you inland to **Kahili Mountain Park.** Keep this in mind because it's the least-expensive private accommodation available near Poipu (description following). As you head down Maluhia Road, passing through a fragrant tunnel of trees also called **Eucalyptus Avenue.** Brought from Australia, they're now very well established, adding beauty and shade to over a mile of this narrow country lane.

Koloa Town attracts a large number of tourists and packs them into a small area. There are plenty of shops, restaurants, and water sports rentals in town. The traffic is hectic around 5:30 p.m. and parking is always a problem, but you can easily solve it. Just as you are entering town look to your right to see a weathered stone chimney standing alone in a little field. Park here and simply walk into town avoiding the hassles. This unmarked edifice is what's left of the **Koloa Sugar Plantation,** established in 1835, site of the first successful attempt at refining sugar in the islands. Although of major historical significance, the chimney is in a terrible state of disrepair—many broken beer bottles litter the inside. Notice, too, that a

the remains of the Koloa Sugar Plantation

nearby banyan has thrown off an aerial root and is engulfing the building. Unless action is taken soon, this historical site will be lost forever.

The tall steeple on the way to Poipu belongs to **Koloa Church,** locally known as the White Church. Dating from 1837, is was remodeled in 1929. For many years the steeple was an official landmark used in many land surveys. If you turn left on Koloa Road and then right on Weliweli Road, you pass **St. Raphael's Catholic Church,** marking the spot of the first Roman Catholic mission permitted in the islands in 1841. The stone church itself dates from 1856 when it was built by Fr. Robert Walsh.

Poipu

Poipu Road continues south from Koloa for 2 miles until it reaches the coast. En route it passes a secondary road over to Hanapepe via Numila, and a bit farther passes Lawai Road which turns right along the coast and terminates at the Spouting Horn. Poipu Road itself bends left to the beach past a string of condos and hotels, into what might be considered the town, except nothing in particular makes it so. As you pass the mouth of Waikomo Stream, you're at **Koloa Landing,** once the islands' most important port after Lihue and Honolulu. When whaling was king, dozens of anchored ships traded with the natives for provisions. Today nothing remains. Behind Poipu is **Pu'uhi Mount,** site of the last eruption believed to have occurred on Kauai.

Along Poipu Road look for the driveway into the Kiahuna Plantation Resort on the right across from the Kiahuna Shopping Village. This is the site of the **Kiahuna Plantation Gardens,** formerly known as the Muir Gardens (the central area still maintains this name). These 35 lovely acres are adorned with over 3,000 varieties of tropical flowers, trees, and plants. The gardens were heavily battered by Hurricane Iwa, but the 2 dozen full-time gardeners have restored them to their former beauty. These grounds, originally part of the old sugar plantation, were a "cactus patch" started by the manager, Hector Muir, and his wife back in 1938. Over the years the gardens grew to be more and more lavish until they became a standard Poipu sight. The Kiahuna Plantation has greatly expanded the original gardens, opening them to the public, free of charge. The management provides detailed maps of the grounds with most plants identified. The gardens are open daily 9:00 a.m. to 6:00 p.m., with free guided tours arranged by calling 742-6411. Poipu Beach p. 744.

Turn onto Lawai Road to pass the **Birthplace of Prince Kuhio.** Loved and respected, Prince Cupid, a nickname by which he was known, was Hawaii's delegate to Congress from the turn of the century until his death in 1922. He often returned to the shores of his birth whenever his duties permitted. Farther along is **Kukui'ula Bay.** Before Hurricane Iwa pummelled this shoreline, the bay was an attractive beach park where many small boats made anchor. Today you can still launch a boat here, but the surrounding area is still recovering from the storm. Notice a number of homes with their roofs caved in, and the palm trees, denuded of their leaves, standing like plucked feather dusters.

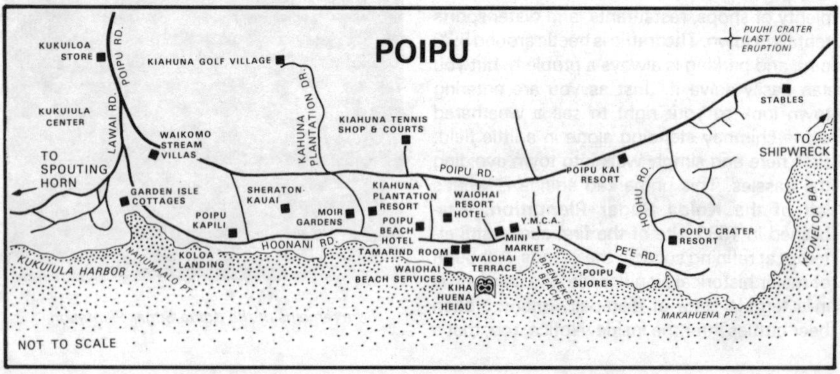

the Spouting Horn in action

In a moment you arrive at the **Spouting Horn.** A large parking area has many stalls marked for tour buses. At the **flea market** here you can pick up trinkets and souvenirs. Don't make the mistake of looking just at the Spouting Horn. Have "big eyes" and look around at the full sweep of this remarkable coastline! The Spouting Horn is a lava tube that extends into the sea with its open mouth on the rocky shore. The wave action causes the spouting phenomenon which can blow spumes quite high depending on surf conditions. In the old days, they say it shot higher, but that the salt spray damaged the nearby cane fields. Supposedly, the plantation owners had the opening made larger so that the spray wouldn't carry as far. Photographers wishing to catch the Spouting Horn in action have an ally. Just before it shoots, a hole behind the spout makes a large belch, and a second later the spume flies. Be ready to click.

Lawai

This village is along Rt. 50 at the junction of Rt. 53 which comes up from Koloa. In times past *ali'i* from throughout the kingdom came here to visit an ancient fishpond in the caldera of an extinct volcano. Legend says that this was the first attempt by Madame Pele to dig herself a fiery home. A hundred yards down Rt. 53 is the **Hawaiian Trading Post.** Their snack bar features delicious scoops of island-flavor ice cream, and they provide some picnic tables in a pleasant grove of mango and banana trees out back. The store sells handcrafted items as well as a large selection of souvenirs, treasures, and tourist junk. Selections include T-shirts, shell work, carvings, and an excellent display of shells that should be featured but are stuck away on a back counter. For $5 or so, you can treat a lot of people back home with purchases from here.

The 186 acres of the **Pacific Tropical Botanical Gardens** constitute the only tropical plant research facility in the country. They're located on Hailima Road off Rt. 53 a mile or so before you reach Lawai. They were chartered by Congress in 1964, and add about 1,000 plants to their collection each year. These gardens are so enchanting that many visitors regard them as one of the real treats of their trip. The gardens are only open to the public on Tues. and Thurs. mornings, and reservations for the limited tour are a must, tel. 332-8131. If you really want a spot, it's best to write well in advance to the Gardens at Box 340, Lawai, Kauai, HI 96765. The tour, led by a knowledgeable horticulturist, often a volunteer from "Helping Hands," lasts for about 2 hours and costs $10. Wear good walking shoes. The staggering variety of tropical plants flourishing here range from common bamboo to romantic orchids. The tour also includes a walk through the adjoining private gardens of John Allerton, a member of the Mainland cattle family which founded the First National Bank of Chicago. This garden dates from last century when Queen Emma made the first plantings here at one of her summer vacation homes. John Allerton, assisting and carrying on the work of his father Robert, scoured the islands of the South Pacific to bring back their living treasures. Oftentimes, old *kamaaina* families would send cuttings of their rarest plants to be included in the collection. For 20 years, father and son helped by a host of gardeners cleared the jungle and planted. Here and there are streams, pools, and statuary that help set the mood.

Kalaheo
This is the first sizable town between Lihue and Hanapepe where you can pick up anything you need to continue west. In town are a gas station, liquor store, and a Big Save Market, all along Route 50. Those in condos or with cooking facilities might even stop in at Medeiro's Farm, just up the hill toward Kukui O Lono Park, for fresh chicken and eggs. If you're interested in a pizza, salad bar, or sandwich to go, stop in at **Brick Oven Pizza**. They offer many varieties including whole wheat crust and vegetarian. The basic pizza is $4.25. Open daily 11:00 a.m. to 11:00 p.m., tel. 332-8561. If you're heading to Waimea or Polihale, call ahead to have it ready for you. You can also wake up your taste buds at **Manana's Mexican Food**. They're reasonably priced and offer the full assortment of Mexican fare. Open daily for dinner except Mon., 5:30-10:00 p.m., tel. 332-9033.

Kukui O Lono Park is a personal gift from Walter D. McBryde. Accept it! It's off-the-beaten track, but definitely worth the trip. Turn left in Kalaheo at the liquor store and mini mart and go up the hill following the road for 5 minutes until you come to Puu Street. Follow it until you see large stone gates and a metal picket fence. Inside the park is a golf course, arboretum, and Japanese-style garden. To get to the clubhouse follow the dirt road to your right for about a half mile; for the gardens and McBryde's memorial turn left. At the clubhouse are a pro shop and snack bar run by a very accommodating man, Mr. Kajitani. He knows a lot about the park and the surrounding area and is willing to chat. A round of golf on the par-70, 154-yard course is only $5; clubs and a pull cart are only $1. This isn't a swanky resort, but it's great fun and the sweeping views of the coast below are striking. The gardens begin with a commemorative plaque to Walter D. McBryde, the well-known plantation owner who donated the land to the people of Kauai in 1919. Behind the plaque formalizing the garden is a "bambi-esque" casting of a deer, a *torii* gate framing a portion of the coast below, some stone lanterns, and perfectly placed in the center of one of the nicest views, a microwave dish! The center of the garden offers peace and tranquility. You cross a small bridge lined with stones placed on their edges, and the whole scene is conducive to zen-like meditation. Enjoy it.

Olu Pua Gardens are the former formal gardens of the Kauai Pineapple Plantation that have been opened to the public. Just outside of Kalaheo look for a large American flag flying on the right. A sign informs that you're on a private drive leading to a "12-acre plantation manager's estate, featuring tropical gardens with the finest collection of flowers and native plants in Hawaii." A bit boastful, but with some merit. As you approach, more signs inform you that admission is $4 for adults, $.50 children, open daily 8:30 a.m. to 5:00 p.m., tel. 332-8182. Since the property is private, the managers want to control the flow of visitors. You pass a

Silhouetted tori *marks Kukui O Lono Park.*

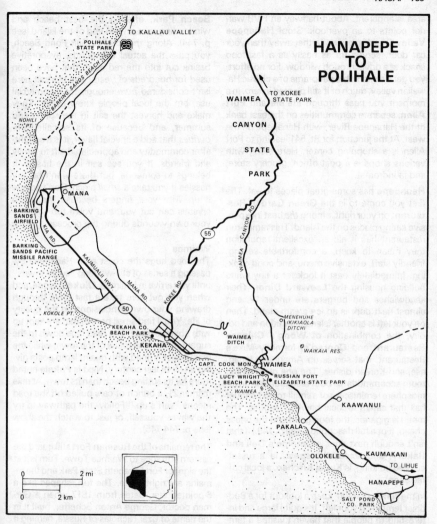

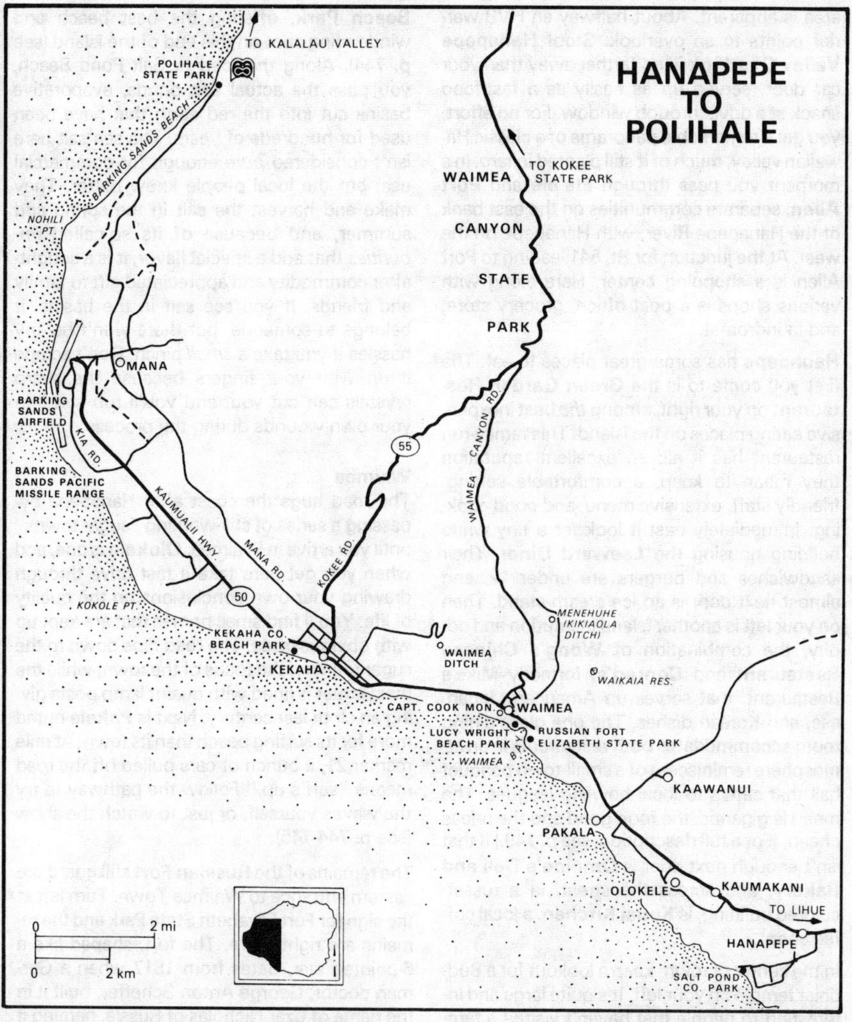

little bamboo gateway leading to a gorgeous house on top of the hill. Sound your horn and an attendant appears. Here too is a small boutique selling beadwork, windchimes, postcards, plants, and books on Hawaiiana. You're given a booklet and a self-guiding map, and are then free to tour the gardens. If you prefer a guided tour, they're given free (tips accepted) at 10:30 a.m. and 2:30 p.m. There are basically 4 gardens: a **kau kau** garden filled with exotic fruit trees; a **sunken garden** alive with eucalyptus, hibiscus, and jasmine; a **palm garden** that lives up to its name; and, a **jungle garden** with tropical exotics like mahogany, vanilla orchids, and heliconia.

Hanapepe

As you roll along from Kalaheo to Hanapepe (''Crushed Bay'') you're surrounded by sugarcane fields, and the traditional economy of the area is apparent. About halfway an HVB warrior points to an overlook. Stop! **Hanapepe Valley Overlook** is no farther away than your car door, served up as easily as a fast-food snack at a drive through window. For no effort, you get a remarkable panorama of a classic Hawaiian valley, much of it still planted in *taro*. In a moment you pass through **Ele'ele** and **Port Allen,** separate communities on the east bank of the Hanapepe River, with Hanapepe on the west. At the junction for Rt. 541 leading to Port Allen is a shopping center. Here along with various shops is a post office, grocery store, and laundromat.

Hanapepe has some great places to eat. The first you come to is the **Green Garden Restaurant** on your right, among *the* best inexpensive eating places on the island. This family-run restaurant has it all: an excellent reputation they mean to keep, a comfortable setting, friendly staff, extensive menu, and good cooking. Immediately past it look for a tiny white building housing the **Leeward Diner.** Their sandwiches and burgers are under $2, and almost next door is an ice cream stand. Then on your left is another island institution and oddity, the combination of **Wong's Chinese Restaurant** and **Conrad's,** formerly Mike's Restaurant, that serves up American, Japanese, and Korean dishes. The one giant dining room accommodates both restaurants in an atmosphere reminiscent of a small-town banquet hall that caters to local bowling leagues. The menu is gigantic, the food good and the prices cheap. (For a full description, see p. 749.) If that isn't enough next door is **Omoide's Deli and Bakery,** and across the street, in a russet-colored building, is **Kauai Kitchen,** a local coffee shop.

In the center of town, keep a lookout for a Buddhist temple on your left. It's quite large and interesting to people that haven't visited a temple before. As you leave town, a small gift shop called **The Station** sits on the right. A friendly young woman sells yarn, crochet material, and Hawaiian-style needlepoint designs. On the western outskirts of town, just past The Station, a sign points *makai* down a side road to the Kauai Humane Society and Hanapepe Refuse Disposal. Take it to a small cemetery where an HVB warrior points to **Salt Pond County Beach Park,** offering the best beach and windsurfing spot on this end of the island (see p. 744). Along the road to Salt Pond Beach, you pass the actual salt ponds, evaporative basins cut into the red earth that have been used for hundreds of years. The sea salt here isn't considered *pure* enough for commercial use, but the local people know better. They make and harvest the salt in the spring and summer, and because of its so-called *impurities* that add a special flavor, it is a sought-after commodity and appreciated gift to family and friends. If you see salt in the basins, it belongs to someone, but there won't be any hassles if you take a *small* pinch. Don't scrape it up with your fingers because the sharp crystals can cut you, and you'll rub salt into your own wounds during the process.

Waimea

The road hugs the coast after Hanapepe bypassing a series of still-working "sugar towns" until you arrive in Waimea. **Olokele** is one, and when you get here take a fast drive through drawing your own conclusions on the quality of life. You'll find small homes that are kept up with obvious pride. The road dips down to the sugar refinery, the focus of the town, while the main street is lined with quaint lamp posts giving an air of last century. Next is **Pakala** noted more for its surfing beach than its town. At mile marker 21, a bunch of cars pulled off the road means "surf's up." Follow the pathway to try the waves yourself, or just to watch the show (see p. 744-745).

The remains of the **Russian Fort** still guard the eastern entrance to Waimea Town. Turn left at the sign for Fort Elizabeth State Park and the remains are right there. The fort, shaped like a 6-pointed star, dates from 1817 when a German doctor, George Anton Scheffer, built it in the name of Czar Nicholas of Russia, naming it after the potentate's daughter. Scheffer, a self-styled adventurer and one-time Moscow policeman, saw great potential in the dominance of Hawaii, and built other forts in Honolulu and along the Waioli River that empties into Hanalei Bay on Kauai's north shore. Due to political maneuverings with other European nations, Czar Nicholas never warmed to Scheffer's enterprises and withdrew official support. For a time, Kauai's King Kaumuali'i continued to fly the Russian flag, perhaps in a subtle attempt to play one foreign power against another. The fort fell into disrepair and was virtually dismantled in 1864 when 38 guns of various sizes were removed. The stout walls, once 30 feet thick, are now mere rubble, humbled by time-encircling nondescript underbrush. However, if you climb onto the ramparts you'll still get a commanding view of Waimea Bay.

Capt. Cook's achievements were surely more deserving than the uninspiring commemorative markers around Waimea. Whether you revere him as a great explorer or denigrate him as an opportunistic despoiler, his achievements in mapping the great Pacific were unparalleled, and changed the course of history. In his memory are **Captain Cook's Landing,** an uninspired marker near Lucy Wright Beach Park, commemorating his "discovery" of the Sandwich Islands at 3:30 p.m. on September 20, 1778, and **Captain Cook's Monument,** on a little island-type median strip in downtown Waimea. If you're fascinated by Kauai's half-legendary little people, you might want to take a look at the **Menehune Ditch,** a stone wall encasing an aqueduct curiously built in a fashion unused and apparently unknown to the Polynesian settlers of Hawaii. The oral tradition states that the ditch was built by the expressed order of Ola, high chief of Waimea, and that he paid his little workers in *opae,* a tiny shrimp that was their staple. On payday, they supposedly sent up such a great cheer that they were heard on Oahu. Today, the work is greatly reduced, with many of the distinctively hand-hewn boulders used in buildings around the island, especially in the Protestant church in Waimea. Some steadfastly maintain that the *menehune* never existed, but a census taken in the 1820s, at the request of capable King Kaumuali'i, officially lists 65 persons living in Wainiha Valley as *menehune!*

Waimea Town itself has little of interest as far as sights go, but it does have some reasonably good restaurants and shopping. Along the main road is **Ishihara's Market** where you'll find all the necessities. Next door is **The Tourist Trap,** run by a friendly woman named Nancy who sells handcrafted items like hand-painted tiles, carvings, mirrors surrounded by shell work, and highly sought-after Niihau shell *lei.* Across the street is **Ben Franklin's,** a variety store that features a lunch counter with, believe it or not, terrific local dishes at very reasonable prices, and next door to that is **Menehune Saimin,** a great little restaurant operated by local ladies, selling steaming bowls of homemade Oriental soups for "can't go wrong" prices. In this area is a Chevron gas station, Mexican food, liquor store, photography supplies, and West Side Sporting Goods.

Waimea, "Grand Canyon of the Pacific"

Waimea Canyon State Park

The "Grand Canyon of the Pacific" is an unforgettable part of your trip, and you shouldn't miss it for any reason. The **Waimea Canyon Road** begins on the outskirts of Waimea, heading inland for 6 miles where it joins **Kokee Road** coming up from Kekaha. Either route is worthwhile, and you can catch both by going in one leg and coming out the other. (Also see p. 672, 673, and 745.) The serpentine route

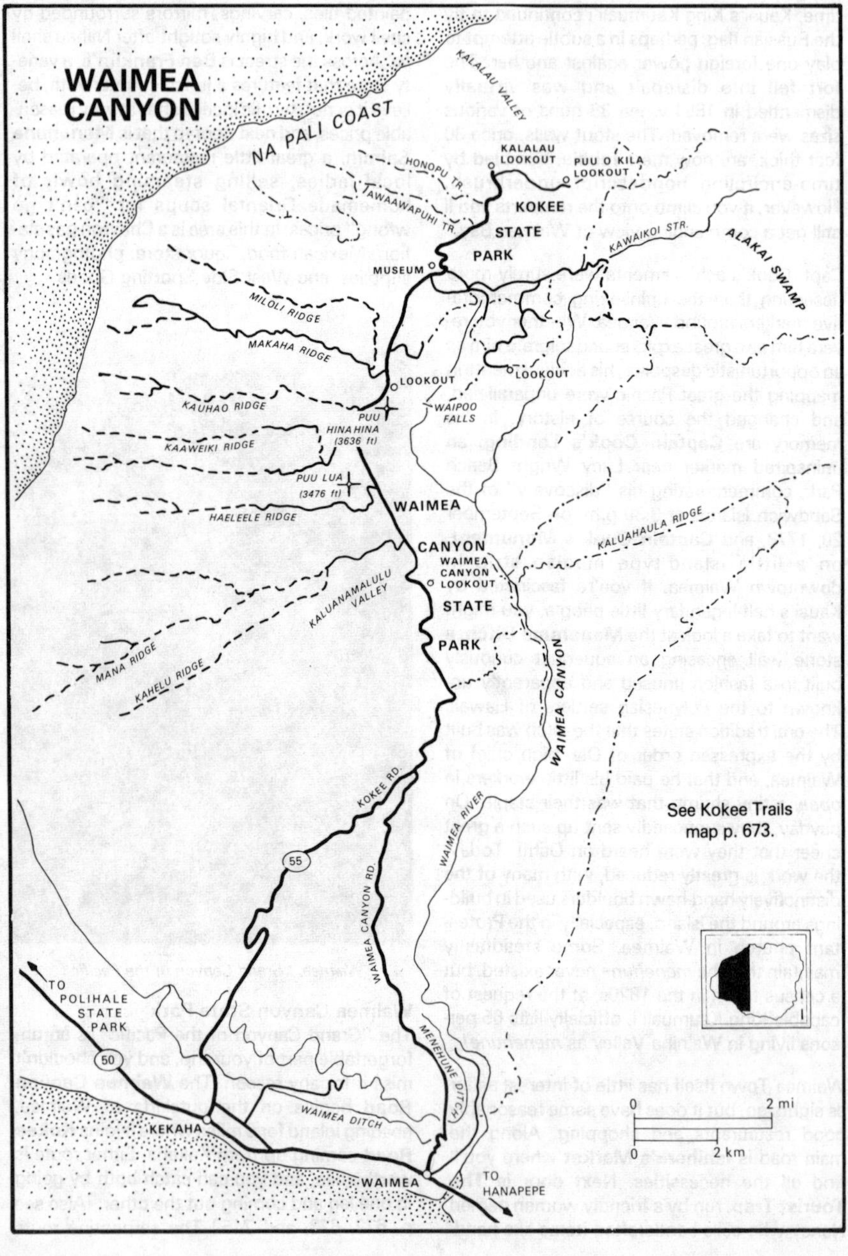
WAIMEA CANYON
NA PALI COAST
KALALAU VALLEY
KALALAU LOOKOUT
PUU O KILA LOOKOUT
HONOPU TR.
AWAAWAPUHI TR.
KOKEE STATE PARK
KAWAIKOI STR.
ALAKAI SWAMP
MUSEUM
MILOLI RIDGE
MAKAHA RIDGE
LOOKOUT
LOOKOUT
KAUHAO RIDGE
PUU HINAHINA (3636 ft)
WAIPOO FALLS
KAAWEIKI RIDGE
PUU LUA (3476 ft)
HAELEELE RIDGE
WAIMEA CANYON
KALUAHAULA RIDGE
WAIMEA CANYON LOOKOUT
KALUANAMALULU VALLEY
WAIMEA CANYON STATE PARK
MANA RIDGE
KAHELU RIDGE
WAIMEA CANYON
WAIMEA RIVER
KOKEE RD.
See Kokee Trails map p. 673.
55
WAIMEA CANYON RD.
TO POLIHALE STATE PARK
50
MENEHUNE DITCH
WAIMEA DITCH
KEKAHA
WAIMEA
TO HANAPEPE
0 2 mi
0 2 km

runs along a good but narrow road into Kauai's cool interior with plenty of fascinating vistas and turn outs along the way. The passenger, going up, gets the better view. Behind you, the coastal towns and their tall refinery stacks fade into the pale blue sea, while the cultivated fields are a study of green on green. Ever climbing, you feel as though you're entering a mountain fortress. The canyon yawns, devouring clouds washed down by draughts of sunlight. The colors are diffuse, blended strata of ordinary grays, royal purples, vibrant reds, russets, jet blacks, and school-girl pink. As you climb, every lookout demands a photo. You reach the thrilling spine, obviously different, where the trees on the red bare earth are gnarled and twisted. The road becomes a roller coast whipping you past raw beauty, immense and powerful. Drink deeply, contemplate, and move on into the clouds at the 2,000-foot level where the trees get larger again. Kokee's Trails come one after another. You pass Park HQ, then the **Kokee Natural History Museum,** gift shop, and lodge. The **Kokee Lodge Restaurant** serves a full breakfast and lunch, daily from 10:00 a.m., to 3:00 p.m., and dinner on Fri. and Sat. 6:00-9:00 p.m., but the cool weather calls especially for a slice of homemade pie and a steaming pot of coffee. Road ends at the Kalalau Valley Overlook. Walk a minute and pray that the clouds are cooperative, allowing lasers of sunlight to illuminate the hump-backed, green-cloaked mountains, silent and tortured, plummeting straight down to the roiling sea far, far below.

Kekaha

You enter Kekaha passing the homes of plantation workers trimmed in neat green lawns and shaded from the baking sun by palm and mango trees. Japanese gardens peek from behind fences. Along the main street are a gas station and **Kinipopo's Store,** your last chance for groceries, shave ice, and sundries. Cane trucks, like drones returning to the hive, carry their burdens into the ever-hungry jaws of the **C & H Sugar Company,** whose smoke stack owns the skyline. The turn off for Rt. 55 leading to Waimea Canyon, and Kokee 19 miles away, branches off in the center of town. Route 50 proceeds along the coast. When still in town, you pass **H.P. Faye Park** and its swimming pool. Then the golden sands of **Kekaha Beach Park** stretch for miles, widening as you head west, with pull-offs and shade-tree clusters now and again. The sun always shines, and the swimming and surfing are excellent (see p. 745). The sea sparkles, and the land flattens wide and long, with green cane billowing all around. Dry gulches and red buttes form an impromptu inland wall.

In 6 miles are the gates of **Barking Sands Airfield and Pacific Missile Range.** Here howl the dogs of war, leashed but on guard. You can use its beach if maneuvers are not in progress

The sugar mill is the economy of west Kauai.

by calling 335-4111. They're hot, shadeless, and pounded by unfriendly surf, but they afford the best view of **Niihau,** a purple Rorschach on the horizon, and the closest that you're ever likely to get to the "Forbidden Island." The beach has the largest sand dunes on the island, due to the ocean's shallowness between the 2 islands. Supposedly, if you slide down the dunes, made from a mixture of sand and ground coral, the friction will cause a sound like a barking dog.

Route 50 splits after you pass the missile range. Stay to the right till an HVB Warrior points to **Polihale State Park.** You go in by 4 miles of well-graded dirt cane road. At a stop sign at a crossroads, you're pointed to Polihale ("Home of the Spirits"), but the road gets rougher. When you arrive, the campgrounds are first; proceed left to a pavilion, picnic area, and toilets, (see p. 745). The swimming is dangerous but the hiking grand. Here the cliffs come down to the sea, brawny and rugged with the Na Pali Coast beginning around the far bend. Where the cliffs meet the sea is a ruin of **Polihale Heiau.** This is a powerful spot, where the souls of the dead made their leap from land into infinity. The priests of this temple chanted special prayers to speed them on their way, as the waters of life flowed from a "sacred spring" in the mountainside.

BEACHES AND PARKS

Kauai's southwest underbelly has the best beaches on the island. They're not only lovely to look at, but at most the surf is inviting and cooperative, and they lie in the island's sunbelt. At some you can camp, at all you can picnic, and a barefoot stroll is easy to come by just about anywhere along these 30 sun-drenched miles. For permits, issuing offices, and general information on **camping** see p. 670-671.

Poipu Beach Park

This is Kauai's best developed beach in the middle of the island's most developed area, so it can be crowded. The actual beach park is at the eastern end of Poipu, and if you walk west many half-moon crescents front the hotels and condos from the Waiohai Resort to the Sheraton Kauai. Poipu Beach Park provides a pavilion, tables, showers, toilets, playground, and lifeguards. The swimming, snorkeling, and bodysurfing are great. A sheltered pool rimmed by lava boulders is gentle enough for anyone, and going just beyond it provides the more exciting wave action often used by local surfers. Follow the rocks out to a point with a number of tidepools. Go around it for more beach and great snorkeling.

Continue east past the Poipu Kai Resort. In less than a mile is a wide sandy beach known as **Shipwreck Beach.** It's best to walk from Poipu, but if you want to drive a bit closer take Weliweli Road from Koloa to the very end. Hurricane Iwa deposited sand here making the beach wider and longer. The swimming and snorkeling are good, but as in all secluded beaches, use extra caution. There is no official camping here, but local people sometimes bivouac in the ironwoods at the east end. The only people who regularly frequent the beach are fishermen and a few nude sunbathers; sometimes, since Brennecke's Beach was roughed up by Iwa, surfers come for the big swells. If you continue walking eastward, more hidden beaches follow.

Salt Pond County Beach Park

The local people from around Hanapepe enjoy this popular beach park. It was heavily damaged by Hurricane Iwa, and has recently undergone an extensive facelift, with pavilions, tables, toilets, showers, and camping (county permit). The swimming and snorkeling are excellent, and a natural breakwater in front of the lifeguard makes a pool safe for tots. Surfers enjoy the breaks here, and a constant gentle breeze makes the area popular with windsurfers. To the left of the beach is a large shallow pond where natural sea salt is still harvested. Take Rt. 50 through Hanapepe until you come to Rt. 543 and make a right. Follow this road to the little Japanese cemetery on your left, where a sign directs you to the park. For more details see p. 740.

Pakala

Popular with the surfers, this beach is not an official park. Follow Rt. 50 west to mile marker no. 21, and a bunch of cars parked here indicates "surf's up." Walk down past the bridge to a well-worn pathway leading through a field. In a few minutes is the beach, a 500-yard horseshoe of white sand. Off to the left is a rocky promentory popular with local fishermen. The swimming is fair, and the reef provides good snorkeling, but the real go is the surf. The beach is also nicknamed "Infinity" because the waves last so long. They come rolling in graceful arcs to spill upon the beach, then recede in a regular, hypnotic pattern causing the next wave to break and roll perfectly. Sunset is a wonderful time to come here for a romantic evening picnic.

Lucy Wright County Beach Park

Just after you cross the Waimea River signs point to this 5-acre park, popular with the local folk. There's a picnic area, restrooms, showers, playground, and tent camping (county permit). Pick up supplies in Waimea. The park is situated around the mouth of the river which makes the water a bit murky. The swimming is fair if the water is clear, and the surfing is decent around the mouth of the river.

Kokee State Park

Tent camping is allowed at Kokee State Park with a permit, and the **Kokee Lodge** also provides self-contained cabins, furnished with stoves, refrigerators, hot showers, cooking and eating utensils, bedding, linens, and wood available for fireplaces. The cabins cost $25 per night (5-night maximum) and vary from one large room for 3, to 2-bedroom units that sleep 7. The cabins are tough to get on holidays, trout-fishing season (August to September), and during the wild plum harvest in June and July. For reservations write well in advance to Kokee Lodge, Box 819, Waimea, Kauai, HI 96796, tel. 335-6061. Please include a SASE, number of people, and dates requested. A $25 deposit is required for confirmation of reservation. Check in is noon, check out 10:00 a.m. The lodge is open Mon. to Thurs. 8:30 a.m. to 5:30 p.m., until 10:00 p.m. Fri. and Saturday. Get to Kokee either by taking Waimea Canyon Road from Waimea, or Kokee Road from Kekaha (see p. 741-743).

Kekaha Area Beaches

Route 50 dips down along the coast after you pass Kekaha, and immediately miles of white sand present themselves. If you want safe swimming, take a dip in the pool at **H.P. Faye Beach Park.** Farther along, you can pick your spot anywhere along the beach. The area is good for swimming and snorkeling during calm weather, and fair for surfing, although the reef can be quite shallow in spots. Kekaha Beach Park covers 30 acres: a pavilion, tables, toilets, and grills. Since there's no tourist development in the area, it's generally quite empty. Up the road is Barking Sands Military Base. You can visit the beach here, mostly for a walk and a good view of Niihau by calling the base in advance, tel. 335-4111. If war games aren't happening, you can even arrange to camp for a few days.

the beach at Polihale

Polihale State Park

This is a wonderful area at the end of the road (see p. 744). You can day trip to soak up the sights and you'll find a pavilion, showers, toilets, and grills. Both RV and tent camping are allowed with a state park permit. The camping area is on the left before you get to the pavilion. If you want seclusion, walk up the road here past the chain gate and then down to the beach. There are generally no hassles, but the rangers do come around, and you should have a permit because it's a long way back to Lihue to get one.

ACCOMMODATIONS

Lodging in the southwest mostly means staying in Poipu. Otherwise, avail yourself of facilities in the beach parks, the Kokee Lodge cabins, and at Kahili Mountain Park, sitting at the foot of the mountains off Rt. 50. Most available rooms are in medium- to high-priced condos, with the rest in first-class hotels, except for the Kauai YMCA that sits amongst all this grandeur and rents cheap bunks in a communal dormitory.

Inexpensive

The **Kauai YMCA** (women welcome!) is about the cheapest place in Hawaii. Walk east along the beach road past Brennecke's Restaurant and look for the Poipu WW II Memorial Building built in 1949 that is the main facility. One large dormitory room doubles as a general function room in the daytime. Pick your mattress from a large stack in the corner and claim a piece of the floor: amenities include the full kitchen and hot showers. Lodging is a mere $6 per night, which reduces to $4 per night if you purchase a $10 membership card. There's no restriction on length of stay, so if you're planning anything longer than 3 nights, you make out better buying the card. The facility is kept clean by the clientele in a cooperative effort. A full-time resident manager is in attendance, and there is usually no hassle with theft. For full information, write YMCA of Kauai, Box 1786, Lihue, HI 96766, or call between 8:00 a.m. and 4:00 p.m., tel. 742-1182 or 742-1200.

Kahili Mountain Park is a gem *if* you enjoy what it has to offer; it's like a camp for big people. To get there follow Rt. 50 west past the turn-off to Koloa, and look for a little sign pointing mountainside up a cane road. Ignore the "private" sign and continue to a gate made from an enormous ship's anchor chain. A plastic card inserted in a slot lowers the security chain. You get a card on arrival, or one is mailed to you after the park receives your reservation deposit. The surroundings are absolutely beautiful, and the only noise, except for singing birds, is an occasional helicopter flying into Waimea Canyon. The high meadow is surrounded by mountains, with the coast visible and Poipu Beach about 15 minutes away. In the middle of the meadow are a cluster of rocks, a mini replica of the mountains in the background. A spring-fed pond is chilly for swimming, but great for catching bass (poles provided) that make a tasty dinner. There are 3 types of accommodations: cabinettes, cabins, and deluxe cabins. The cabinettes are the most rustic, built exactly like Army tents with some even retaining a canvas roof. They're in a cluster facing a meadow and each is surrounded by flower beds. Inside are bunks on a ce-

cabinettes at Kahili Mountain Park

ment floor, running water, a cement tub used as a cooler (ice provided), a 2-burner stove, foodbox, and a *lanai* outside. All dishes and utensils are provided and even washed for you each morning if you leave them in the bus tray. Bathrooms and showers are in a central building with laundry facilities and a relaxing Japanese *ofuro* (hot tub). Cabinettes rent for $15 d, $4 extra person, $60 per week, or $65 for one with an electric refrigerator. The cabins are more than adequate with a full kitchen, bedrooms, private toilets, outdoor showers, priced reasonably at $32 d, $4 extra person. The one deluxe cabin is a secluded 2-bedroom, 2-bath affair with a beautiful view renting for $50 flat rate. Very substantial weekly and monthly discounts are offered. The park has been open for about 20 years and has recently been purchased by the Seventh-Day Adventist Church, which plans to build a school but retain the rental units. The present manager is John Fagel, and the grounds and the facility are beautifully kept by the original caretakers, Smitty, Ralph, and Veronica. For full information, write Kahili Mountain Park, Box 298, Koloa, HI 96756, tel. 742-9921.

Garden Isle Cottages are the least expensive apartment/cottages at Poipu. Tucked away at the west end along Hoona Road between Poipu Beach and the Spouting Horn, they sit on the beach surrounded by lush foliage, offering privacy. The cottages are operated by artists Robert and Sharon Flynn, whose original works highlight each of the units. All the studios to 2-bedroom apartments are self-contained and fully equipped. Prices range, s/d from $36-$48 for a studio, no kitchen, to $65-$100 for a 2-bedroom, $6 additional person for all. The cottages require a 2-night minimum, no maid service. Write Garden Isle Cottages, R.R. 1, Box 355, Koloa, HI 96756, tel. 742-6717.

Moderate

Although the prices in Poipu can be a bit higher than elsewhere on Kauai, you get a lot for your money. Over a dozen well-appointed modern condos are lined up along the beach and just off it, with thousands of units available. Most are a variation on the same theme: comfortably furnished, fully equipped, with a tennis court here and there, always a swimming pool, and maid service available on request. Most require a minimum stay of at least 2 nights, with discounts for long-term. The following condos and hotel have been chosen to give you a general idea of what to expect, and because of their locations. All are on the beach, listed from west to east. Prices average about $85 s/d for a one-bedroom apartment, up to $200 for a 3-bedroom, with extra persons ($8), charged only for groups of more than 4 and 6 people in the multiple-bedroom units. You can get excellent brochures of the Poipu area listing most of the accommodations available by writing to **Poipu Beach Resort Assoc.**, Box 730, Koloa, HI 96756, tel. 742-7444.

Poipu Kapili is a 3-story condo that looks more like "back East" bungalows. Across the road from the beach, most units having ocean views. The pool is located in the center of the property, and lighted tennis courts are free, racquets and balls provided. The bedrooms are huge, with ceiling fans and wicker headboards; kitchens are spacious with full stoves, dishwashers; each unit has its own private *lanai.* Monthly and weekly discounts available. Write Poipu Kapili Condominium, R.R. 1, Box 272, Koloa, HI 96756, tel. 800-367-7052, on Kauai tel. 742-6449.

The **Kiahuna Plantation Condominiums** (there's a hotel too) surround the lovely Kiahuna Gardens. The front office is like a small private home, where you register just like at a hotel. The large units, bright and airy featuring cross ventilation through louvered windows, have full bathrooms, kitchens, and enormous *lanai.* Apartments overlook both the Kiahuna and Muir gardens, and the impeccable grounds of the Sheraton next door. You get a lot for your money at the Kiahuna Plantation, with up to 5 and 7 people at no extra charge in the appropriate units. Write Kiahuna Plantation Condos, R.R. 1, Box 73, Koloa, HI 96756, tel. 800-367-7052, on Kauai, tel. 742-6411.

The **Poipu Shores** are at the east end of the beach, surrounded by other condos. They're slightly less expensive than the rest, allowing up to 6 people at no extra charge. Weekly maid service is provided free. All units are clean, spacious, and airy, with the area's best beaches a short stroll away. Write Poipu Shores, R.R. 1, Box 95, Koloa, HI 96756, tel. 800-367-5686, on Kauai, tel. 742-6522.

The **Poipu Beach Hotel**, owned by AMFAC, is friendly, with a family atmosphere. On the beach, each room has a *lanai* overlooking the sea, and money-saving kitchenettes. There's a large courtyard with pool, BBQ grills, and tennis next door. Inside are restaurants and cocktail lounges, with nightly entertainment. Rates begin at a reasonable $79 s/d for a standard, to $105 for a deluxe, up to $600 for a 4-bedroom cottage. Write Poipu Beach Hotel, Koloa, HI 96756, tel. 800-227-4700, on Kauai, tel. 742-1681.

Expensive

Plenty of expensive condos are available with every luxury imaginable, but the following are Poipu's premiere hotels. The Sheraton Kauai is a deluxe hotel, while the Waiohai is world-class super-deluxe.

The original beachfront **Sheraton Kauai** was roughed up by that pesky wind Iwa, but the new wing across the road weathered the storm beautifully and is carrying on in the hospitable Sheraton tradition. The main lobby is soothing and airy, while the buildings are constructed around a freshwater lagoon. *Koi* ponds hold not only multicolored carp, but small nondescript fish that eat mosquito larvae! The rooms are done with plush tan carpets, with a green color scheme, and tasteful prints on the walls. Refrigerators cost an additional $2. You either get a garden or ocean view, with the vistas and price rising as you go up to the fourth floor. There are restaurants and snack bars in the hotel, and an excellent Polynesian Review and dinner on Sun. evenings. Prices range from a standard $100 d, to a deluxe $165, additional persons $15. Write Sheraton Kauai, Box 303, Koloa, HI 96756, tel. 800-325-3535, on Kauai, tel. 742-1661.

The **Waiohai Resort** is a first-rate luxury hotel. It's low rise, with the wings aligned to form a W. AMFAC spared no expense to create a full-service hotel geared to comfort. Each room comes with a refrigerator and stocked wet bar. You simply tick off your drinks and pay when you check out. The bathrooms and dressing rooms are ultra posh. The main hallways, all open and breezy, are adorned with silk hangings, marble, teak, and brass. There are 3 pools, spas, a health club, and various boutiques. Across the road at the beach, the hotel has surfboards, snorkeling equipment, sailboards, and floating tricycles. For the very genteel, tea is served afternoons in the reading room that has a superb collection of books on Hawaiiana. Various workshops and classes deal with Hawaiian arts and culture offered at the hotel, while its **Tamarind Room** provides an elegant dining experience. Prices range from $125 for a standard room, to $720 for a deluxe suite. For information write Waiohai resort, R.R. 1, Box 174, Koloa, HI 96756, tel. 800-227-4700, on Kauai, tel. 742-9511.

FOOD

Inexpensive

The majority of really inexpensive places to eat along the southwest shore are found in the villages west of Koloa/Poipu (listed above at "Sights and Villages"). Their names and locations appear again so that you can cross-reference. Rich ice cream, featuring island flavors, and snacks are served at the **Hawaiian Trading Post** in Lawai. The **Brick Oven Pizza** in Kalaheo serves tasty pizza and sandwiches from 11:00 a.m. to 11:00 p.m. Sandwiches, including a hefty vegetarian, all for under $4. This restaurant is conveniently located along the highway, and by calling ahead, tel. 332-8561, you can have pick-up service for a day's outing in this part of the island. In Hanapepe, the **Leeward Diner** serves sandwiches for under $2, and inexpensive goodies are available from **Omoide's Deli and Bakery.** In Waimea, treat yourself to a steaming bowl of homemade soup from **Menehune Saimin,** or a better-than-you'd-expect plate lunch from the lunch counter at **Ben Franklin's.** The **Kokee Lodge** in the state park has reasonably priced snacks and dinners.

A few places in and around Koloa/Poipu serve budget-priced meals, but mostly they sell snacks and take-outs. At the following restaurants and stands, you can fill up for under $5 with tasty and nutritious foods.

Koloa Ice House is on the left along Koloa Road as you enter town. It seems more like a

Just inland from the resort areas cows graze in the foothills of the Hoary Head Mountains.

deli than a restaurant, but you can have sit-down meals. They feature ice cream, shave ice, and mud pie. Tempting treats also include sandwiches, cheeses, fresh juices, fancy pastry, even lox and bagels! Open daily 10:30 a.m. to 9:00 p.m., tel. 742-6063

Also as you enter Koloa is **Fez's Pizza**, specializing in gourmet deep-dish pizza, sandwiches, and spaghetti. Open daily from lunch until 11:00 p.m. They deliver to Poipu hotel/condos by calling, tel. 742-9096. Just up the street are **Lappert's Aloha Ice Cream** and **Koloa Coffee and Bake Shop.** Their names are their menus.

On your right as you enter Poipu is a small complex called the Poipu Plaza. At **Taqueria Nortenos** you can fill up on Mexican fast food for under $4. They make their tacos and burritos a bit differently from most Mexican food stands: a taco for $1.20 is simply rice and beans in a taco shell. If you want the standard cheese, tomato, and lettuce, you have to ask for it at no extra charge. The flavorful food is homemade but pre-cooked, awaiting in heating trays. Filling, good, but not special, the Taqueria Norteno is open daily 11:00 a.m. to 11:00 p.m., until 5:30 p.m. on Wednesdays.

Poipu Inn is an old standard. Located just off the beach on Hoone Rd., they're open daily from 6:00 a.m. to 6:00 p.m. Although they serve good breakfasts and sit-down dinners, the best deal is take-out sandwiches for under $2, and filling plate lunches of *mahi mahi,* teri chicken, and the like, complete with salad and potato for under $4.

Moderate

The good news? Reasonably priced restaurants abound in southwest Kauai; better yet, the food's delicious! Here are the best.

If you're passing through Hanapepe you must stop at one of its 2 old standbys, favorites of tourists and locals. The money you save might even make them worth a special trip from the Poipu area. Perhaps the best restaurant on the island for the money is the **Green Garden**. This family-owned restaurant has it all: great food, large portions, and *aloha* service. The new section of the restaurant is set up to hold busloads of tourists who arrive for lunch; go a little earlier, or a little later than noontime. The old room has a few plants, but the name is really held up by the decor; green walls, chairs, tables, place mats, bathrooms. If you see anything on the menu that you might want to mix and match, just ask. Substitutions are cheerfully made! The full meal selections, including beverage, are mostly under $5, with many under $4. The homemade pies alone are worth the trip. The Green Garden is along Rt. 50 just as you enter town, open daily for breakfast, lunch, and dinner from 7:00 a.m., Sun. 5:00-8:30 p.m., closed Tues. evenings, reservations for dinner at tel. 335-5422.

Past the Green Garden, on the left, look for **Conrad's** and **Wong's.** Although they occupy the same building, they are different restaurants with different menus. Both are very reasonably priced, but they too are a favorite with the tour buses, and can be crowded. When you go in to the cafeteria-style dining room, you're handed 2 separate menus. Feel free to order from each. Conrad's (formerly Mike's, his dad) has standard American fare with a Hawaiian twist. Most sandwiches are under $3, main course dinners under $5. Wong's specialties are Chinese and Japanese dishes, all under $7, with many around $5. The service is friendly, the portions large, but the cooking is mediocre, except for the pies. You won't complain, but you won't be impressed either. Open daily, for breakfast, lunch, and dinner; closed after 2:00 p.m. Mon., tel. 335-5066.

If you want pampering, keep walking past the **Koloa Broiler,** but if you want a good meal at an unbeatable price, drop in. At the Koloa Broiler *you* are the chef. You order top sirloin $7.95, beef kabob $6.95, or *mahi mahi* $5.95. Your uncooked selection is brought to your table; you take it to a central grill where a large clock and a poster of cooking times tells you how long your self-made dinner will take. The feeling is like being at a potluck BBQ, and you can't help making friends with the other *chefs.* There is a simple salad bar and a huge pot of baked beans from which you can help yourself. Waiters bring fresh-baked bread and a pitcher of ice water. Put your selection on the grill, fix yourself a salad, eat it and it's just about time to turn your BBQ. Just before it's done, toast some bread on the grill. The small bar attracts a good mixture of tourists and local people in a neighborhood bar-type atmosphere. Centrally located on Koloa Road, open daily for lunch and dinner, tel. 742-9122.

A newer restaurant in the area gaining a reputation for good food at reasonable prices is the **Koloa Fish and Chowder House.** This restaurant bills itself as having the largest selection of seafood on Kauai, and also serves prime rib and chicken. Specialties include clam and oyster chowder, *kiawe*-broiled catch of the day, and chocolate espresso. In Koloa, open daily for lunch and dinner, tel. 822-7488.

In Poipu try the **Aquarium Restaurant** off Malo Road, the area's only Italian Restaurant serving a variety of pasta dishes, fresh fish, and pizza to go. The name comes from the restaurant's fish tank, Kauai's largest freshwater aquarium. Open daily 4:00-10:00 p.m., tel. 742-9505. At Poipu's Kiahuna Shopping Village is **Keoki's Paradise** featuring a seafood and taco bar from 4:30 p.m. to midnight, and dinner from 5:30-10:00 p.m., tel. 742-7534.

Expensive

Exquisite dining can be enjoyed at various restaurants that have perfect positions along Poipu's beaches for catching the setting sun. Prices are high, but the surroundings are elegant and the service impeccable.

The Sheraton Kauai's main dining facility, the **Outrigger Room,** features full breakfasts, midday buffets, and intimate dinners. Fridays are special with seafood buffets. The Outrigger Room has long been known for its Polynesian Review and the sumptuous feast that accompanies it on Sun. and Wednesdays. The Sheraton also houses the **Lawai Terrace Steakhouse** and the **Drum Lounge** for cocktails and dancing.

The **Plantation Garden Restaurant** is located at the Kiahuna Plantation Resort. You're put in the mood with a walk through the lovely gardens into the waiting room filled with parlor furniture and a brass-rail bar with corkscrew stools—the original porch of the old plantation house. The restaurant is richly appointed, and tables are set with crystal and silver. The menu offers appetizers such as *escargot* for $5.95, light suppers like seafood crepes for $9.95, and seafood dinners with a small selection of beef from $13.95. Children's dinners are $7.95. Salads (regular, Caesar, or spinach), or soup is included with a basket of hot bread. Open daily, tel. 742-1695 for reservations, especially for window tables.

The **Tamarind Room** in the Waiohai Hotel is *the* most elegant restaurant on Kauai. The European chef does justice to the richly furnished formal dining room. Dining here is designed to be a total experience. No windows in the room, the beauty comes from the surroundings themselves. Enjoy tables set with silver and crystal on linen table cloths with all meals arriving under silver pineapple domes. Start with papaya bisque in a carved bowl of ice, exotically laced with creme de cacao, ginger, and cream. The duck in peppercorn sauce is a good entree, and passionfruit mousse is a fine dessert selection. The waiters are extremely attentive without being obtrusive. Each course is announced, and water glasses are replaced, not refilled. The wine list has almost 400 selections, most vintages coming from California's finest cellars. At meal's end, a cart filled with liqueurs arrives as the final touch. Your bill of at least $100 for 2 is sweetened with a complimentary box of fine chocolates, along with a red rose for the lady. Definitely make reservations, tel 742-9511.

Brennecke's Seaside Bar and Grill may have to take a back seat in the elegance department, but its view can't be beat. A large part of the restaurant is an open-air deck directly across from Poipu Beach Park. Until 5:00 p.m., they serve great mai tais for only $2. The menu is moderate to expensive. The burgers, broiled over *kiawe* are excellent and priced well. You can order garlic bread and a salad for under $5. Dinners of lobster, prime rib, and catch of the day (your best bet) range from $12 to $20 and come with *pasta primavera* instead of regular old potatoes. Open daily, tel. 742-7588.

Buffets And Brunches

Two Poipu feasts that have become deservedly famous are the Waiohai's Sunday Brunch, and the Sheraton's Polynesian Review. On Sun. mornings, the Waiohai's chefs are set free to create culinary delights, and they outdo themselves. In the hotel's Terrace Room, 5 huge banquet tables are laden with *sushi,* smoked salmon, seafoods galore, croissants, eggs, beef, chicken, fruits, juices, sweets, and mouth-watering pies. The presentation is spectacular. The chef-artists create vegetable flowers, ice sculptures and geometric designs. The eyes are as satiated as the appetite. The very popular brunch starts at 10:00 a.m., but the line forms by 9:00 a.m. Free coffee helps with the wait, and reservations are not accepted for parties of less than 10 people, tel. 742-9511. The brunch, priced at a very reasonable $14.95, lasts until 2:00 p.m., and the lines start getting shorter after 1:00 p.m., but to do justice to all that's offered, allow yourself at least 2 hours to dine.

The Sheraton Kauai's Polynesian Review is held in the Outrigger Room on Sun. and Wed. evenings, with seating from 6:00 p.m. The show starts at 8:00 p.m. when you'll be treated to dances and music from throughout the islands of Polynesia. The buffet is as varied as the people of Hawaii with dishes of *sashimi, kalua* pork, standing ribs of beef, Oriental favorites, and a full complement of fruits, salads, and pastries. The price for dinner and show is $21.95; for reservations tel. 742-1661.

ENTERTAINMENT

If, after a sunset dinner and a lovely stroll along the beach, you find yourself with "dancing feet," or a desire to hear the strains of your favorite tunes, Poipu won't let you down. Many restaurants in the area feature piano music or small combos, often with a Hawaiian flair.

You can ease into the night by listening to classical guitar music in the Waiohai's **Terrace Restaurant,** from 6:30-10:00 p.m. Also, if you've dined in the hotel's Tamarind Lounge, tinkling softly along with the crystal is a piano from 7:30 p.m. to midnight.

The Sheraton Kauai's **Drum Lounge** beats with the rhythms of Hawaiian tunes nightly from 5:00-6:30 p.m., while the dance floor sways nightly from 8:00 to midnight, and a bit later on weekends.

The Poipu Beach Hotel's **Mahina Lounge** picks up the beat with dance music every Wed. and Sun. from 9:30 p.m. to 1:00 a.m., and frequently imports Top 40 dance bands from throughout the islands and around the country. They're always listed in the local free tourist literature.

SHOPPING

From Koloa to Poipu, shops and boutiques are strung along the road like flowers on a *lei.* You can buy everything from original art to beach

Shops line the raised wooden sidewalk in Koloa Town.

towels. Jewelry stores, surf shops, gourmet stores, even a a specialty shop for sunglasses are just a few. Old Koloa Town packs a lot of shopping into a little area. Besides, it's fun just walking the raised sidewalks of what looks very much like a "Western town." Shopping in Poipu means little more than walking down the beach and peeking into the boutiques. Also some small shopping malls might have that "just right" gift. For food shopping and souvenir hunting in the villages along Rt. 50 from Puhi to Kekaha, refer to "Sights and Villages" above.

Food Stores

In Koloa, if you're after food **Big Save Supermarket** is east on Koloa Road, and just around the bend heading down Waikomo Road. **Sueoka's Store** downtown is a local grocery and produce market. Next door is the **Old Koloa Mill**, a gourmet food shop where you'll find a great selection of wine, cheese, pasta, beef, and big fat pickles. Open daily until 11:00 p.m.

Food shopping in Poipu is very limited. The only real market, a small one at that, is **Brennecke's Mini Mart**, across the street from Poipu Beach Park. If you're staying in a Poipu condo, you'll save money by making the trip to a larger market in one of the nearby towns.

Boutiques, Gifts, And Apparel

Koloa Town has some fine shopping along the main street and for a few hundred yards down Poipu Road. Look for: **Crazy Shirts** selling T-shirts and islandwear; **Koloa Gold**, and **Koloa Jewelry** offering rings, necklaces, and scrimshaw; **Paradise Clothing** for alohawear, and **Progressive Expressions** for surfboards, surf gear, and islandwear.

In Poipu the **Koloa Gallery**, tel. 742-7118, sells pearls, coral jewelry, and handcrafted tiles by local artists. Don't forget the **flea market** at the Spouting Horn. **Foto Freddie**, tel. 742-9240 does processing, and sells film of all kinds. The **Kiahuna Shopping Village** offers unique one-stop shopping in a number of shops including: **The Ship Store Gallery**, tel. 742-7123, for all things nautical, including sea-inspired art; **Traders of Kauai**, tel. 742-7224, featuring distinctive gifts, children's wear, and alohawear; **Tropical Shirts** for original air-brush designs on shirts and Ts; and **For Your Eyes Only**, tel. 742-1512, for distinctive sunglasses.

Ocean Surf, General Activities

The Koloa/Poipu area has many surf and sailing shops that rent sports equipment, diving gear, and sponsor boating excursions. **South Shore Activities**, tel. 742-6873, offers just about all you'll need for sun and surf in Poipu. They feature all activities from horseback riding to helicopter tours and represent National Car Rental in Poipu. They rent all kinds of ocean equipment, and provide lessons. **Brennecke's Ocean Sports**, tel. 742-6570, specializes in snorkel and scuba lessons, while renting surfboards, boogie boards, windsurfers, canoe rides, and charter boats. **Poipu Activities Center**, tel. 742-7431, is another one-stop rental and tour center, while **Fathom Five Divers** in Koloa, tel. 742-6991, is a complete diving center offering lessons, certification, and rentals. If you're into horseback riding try **CJM Stables**, tel. 338-1314, for rides along the beach and inland picnic rides.

SERVICES AND INFORMATION

Medical, Emergency, And Health Emergency—911.

In the Poipu area the **Kauai Medical Group**, tel. 742-1621, offers medical services in its Koloa clinic Mon. to Fri. 8:00 a.m. to 5:00 p.m., Sat. 8:00 a.m. to noon, and after hours by arrangement at tel. 245-6810. You can have a full workout, massage, and spa facilities at **Clark Hatch Physical Fitness Center**, tel. 742-6409, in the Waiohai Resort in Poipu.

The **American Educational Institute**, tel. 742-7244, has a unique way of mixing business with pleasure. They offer seminars in medical, dental, and legal malpractice as well as a general course in financial planning. You put the course to work immediately by learning how to get a tax break on your tuition and vacation expenses.

General Information

Rental cars are available in Poipu from **National**, tel. 742-6873 at South Shore Activities; **Hertz**, tel. 742-6011, at the Sheraton Kauai.

The Koloa Post Office is along Koloa Road, tel. 742-6565. The area's only gas station is the **Koloa Chevron**, tel. 742-6868, at the corner of Koloa and Poipu roads.

NIIHAU

The only thing forbidding about Niihau is its nickname, "The Forbidden Island." Ironically, it's one of the last real havens of peace, tranquility, and tradition left on the face of the Earth. This privately owned island, operating as one large cattle and sheep ranch, is manned by the last remaining pure Hawaiians in the state. To go there, you must have a personal invitation by the owners or one of the residents. Some people find this situation strange, but it would be no stranger than walking up to an Iowa farmhouse unannounced and expecting to be invited in to dinner. The islanders are free to come and go as they wish, and are given the security of knowing that the last real Hawaiian place is not going to be engulfed by the modern world. Niihau is a reservation, but a *free-will* one, that anyone who has felt "the world too much with them" could easily admire.

The Land And Climate

The 17-mile **Kaulakahi Channel** separates Niihau from the western tip of Kauai. The island's maximum dimensions are 18 miles long by 6 miles wide, with a total area of 73 square miles. The tallest point on the island, **Paniau** (1,281 feet), lies on the east-central coast. There are no port facilities on the island, but the occasional boats put in at **Kii** and **Lehua landings,** both on the northern tip. Since Niihau is so low and lies in the rain shadow of Kauai, it receives only 30 inches of precipitation per year, making it dry and arid. Oddly enough, low-lying basins, eroded from the single shield volcano that made the island, act like a catchment system. In them are the state's largest naturally occurring lakes, **Halalii** and the slightly larger **Lake Halulu,** at 182 acres. Two uninhabited islets, **Lehua,** just off the northern tip, and **Kaula,** a few miles off the southern tip, each barely covers ½ square mile, and join Niihau as part of Kauai County.

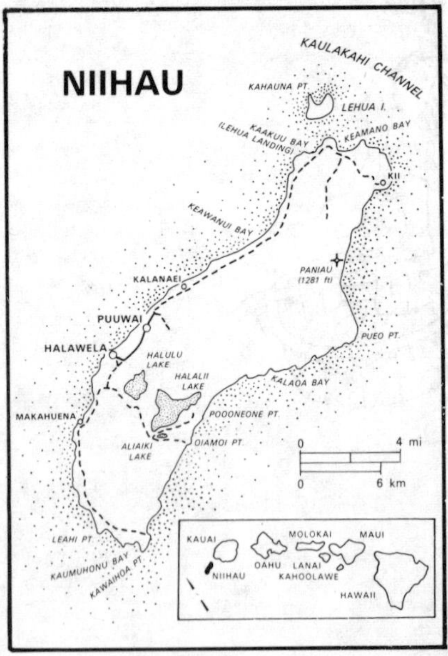

HISTORY

After Papa returned from Tahiti and discovered that her husband, Wakea, was playing around, she left him. The great Wakea did some squirming, and after these island-parents reconciled, Papa became pregnant and gave birth to Kauai. Niihau popped out as the afterbirth, along with Lehua and Kaula, the last of the low reef islands according to the creation chants found in the *Kumulipo.*

Niihau was never a very populous island because of the relatively poor soil, so the islanders had to rely on trade with nearby Kauai for many necessities including *poi.* Luckily, the fishing grounds off the island's coastal waters are the richest in the area, and they could always trade fish. The islanders became famous for Niihau mats, a good trade item, made from *makaloa,* a sedge that's plentiful on the island. Craftsmen also fashioned *ipu pawehe,* a geometrically designed gourd highly prized in the old days. When Capt. Cook arrived and wished to provision his ships, he remarked that the Niihau natives were much more eager to trade than those on Kauai, and he secured potatoes and yams that seemed to be in abundant supply.

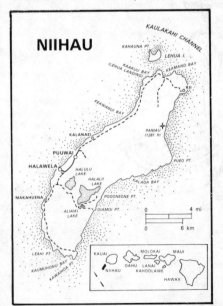

Kamehameha IV Sells
Along with Kauai, Niihau became part of the kingdom under Kamehameha. It passed down to his successors, and in the 1860s, Kamehameha IV sold it to the Robinson Family for $10,000. This Scottish family, which came to Hawaii via New Zealand, has been the sole proprietor of the island ever since, although they now live on Kauai. They began a sheep and cattle ranch, hiring the island's natives as workers. No one can say exactly why, but it's evident that this family felt a great sense of responsibility and purpose. Tradition passed down over the years dictated that islanders could live on Niihau as long as they pleased, but that visitors were not welcome without a personal invitation. With the native Hawaiian population decimated, the Robinsons felt that these proud people should have at least one place to call theirs and theirs alone. To keep the race pure, male visitors to the island were generally asked to leave by sundown.

Niihau Invaded
During WW II, Niihau was the only island of Hawaii to be occupied by the Japanese. A *Zero* pilot, after hitting Pearl Harbor developed engine trouble and had to ditch on Niihau. At first the islanders took him prisoner, but he somehow managed to escape and commandeer the machine guns from his plane. He terrorized the island, and the residents headed for the hills. One old woman who refused to leave was like a Hawaiian Barbara Fritchie. She told the Japanese to shoot her if he wished, but to please stop making a nuisance of himself, it wasn't nice! He would have saved himself a lot of trouble if he had only listened. Fed up with hiding, one huge *kanaka,* Benehakaka Kanahele, decided to approach the pilot with *aloha.* He was convinced the intruder would see the error of his ways. This latter-day *samurai* shot Mr. Kanahele for his trouble. Ben persisted and was shot again. An expression of pain, disgust, and disbelief at the stranger's poor manners spread across Ben's face, but still he tried pleading with the Japanese, who shot him for the third time. Ben had had enough, and grabbed the astonished pilot and flung him headlong against a wall, cracking his skull and killing him instantly. This incident gave rise to 2 wartime ditties. One went, "Don't shoot a Hawaiian three times or you'll make him mad." The other was a song whose title was, "You can't conquer Niihau, No how." Mr. Kanahele lived out his life on Niihau, and died in the 1960s.

Life Today
The only reliable connection that the islanders have with the outside world is a WW II vintage landing craft that they use to bring in supplies from Kauai. Until recently homing pigeons were used to send messages, but they have been replaced by 2-way radios. There's no communal electricity on the island, but people do have generators to power refrigerators and TVs. Transistor radios are very popular, and most people get around either on horseback or in pickup trucks. The population numbers around 230 people, 95% of whom are Hawaiian, with the other 5% being Japanese. There is one elementary school, in which English is used, but most people speak Hawaiian at home. The children go off to Kauai for high school, but after they get a taste of what the world at large has to offer, a surprisingly large number return to Niihau. After Hurricane Iwa battered the island a few years back, the state was very eager to offer aid. The people of Niihau thanked them for their concern, but told them not to bother, that they would take care of things themselves. Niihau was the only island to reject statehood in the plebiscite of 1959.

Today, some people attempt to accuse the Robinson family of being greedy barons of a medieval fifedom, holding the Niihauans as virtual slaves. This idea is utter nonsense. Besides the fact that the islanders have an open door, the Robinsons would make immeasurably more money selling the island off to resort developers than running it as a livestock ranch. As if the spirit of old Hawaii was trying to send a sign, it's interesting that Niihau's official *lei* is fashioned from *pupu,* a rare shell found only on the island's beaches, and its island-color is white, the universal symbol of purity.

Niihau Shell Work
The finest shell work made in Hawaii comes from Niihau. The tradition for making the shell work has been passed down over the generations. The shells themselves—tiny, and very rare *kahelelani* and *kamoa*—are abundant only

in the deep waters off the windward coast. Sometimes, the tides and winds are just right and they are deposited on Niihau's beaches, but rarely more than 3 times per year. Islanders then stop everything and head for the shore to painstakingly collect them. The shells are sorted according to size and color, and only the finest are kept: 80% are discarded. The most prized are so tiny that a dozen fit on a thumbnail. Colors are white, yellow, blue, and the very rare gold. The best-quality shells are free from chips or cracks, and after sorting, the shells are drilled. Various pieces of jewelry are fashioned, but the traditional pieces are necklaces and *lei.* These can be short single-strand chokers, or the lovely *pikake* pattern, a heavy double strand. The *rice* motif is always popular, and these are usually multi-stranded with the main shells clipped on the ends with various colored shells strung in as highlights. A necklace takes long painstaking hours, with every shell connected by intricate and minute knots. Usually the women of Niihau do this work. Clasps are made from cowrie shells found only on Niihau. No 2 necklaces are exactly alike. They sell by the inch, and the pure white and golden ones are very expensive, most handed down as priceless heirlooms. Although Niihau shellwork is available in fine stores all over the state, Kauai, because it's closest, gets the largest selection. If you're after a once-in-a-lifetime purchase, consider Niihau shells.

APPENDIX

MUSEUMS, LIBRARIES, ZOOS, GALLERIES AND GARDENS

Organization	Address and Telephone	Remarks
	OAHU	
Aloha Tower and Maritime Museum	Ala Moana Blvd., and Bishop St., Honolulu, HI tel. 536-6373 or 548-5713.	A landmark that said "Hawaii" to all who arrived by sea before planes took over. Great harbor and city views from top of tower. Visit *Hawaii Maritime Center* on 9th floor and famous double-hulled canoe *Hokule'a* and tall masted *Falls of Clyde,* berthed just next door at Pier 7.
USS *Arizona* Memorial and Submarine Museum	Arizona Memorial Dr, Pearl Harbor, HI 96818, tel. 422-2771.	A free tour of the sleek 184-foot white concrete structure that spans the sunken USS *Arizona.* Free Navy launches take you on the tour of "Battleship Row." Open Tues. to Sun., 8:00 a.m. to 3:00 p.m. No reservations, first come first served. Launches every 15 minutes. Visitor center offers graphic materials and movie reflecting the events of Pearl Harbor attack.
Army Museum Fort DeRussy	Box 8064, Honolulu, HI 96815, tel. 543-2639.	Official records, private papers, photos documenting activities of the U.S. Army in east Asia and the Pacific islands. Access to holdings is by appointment.
Bishop Museum and Planetarium	1525 Bernice St., Honolulu, HI 96819, tel. 847-3511.	Open daily 9:00 a.m. to 5:00 p.m., $4.75 for adults, $2.50 ages 6 to 17, under 6 free. The best collection in the world on Polynesia in general and Hawaii specifically. A true cultural treat. Should not be missed.

Children's Museum of Natural History	1201 Ala Moana Blvd., Honolulu, HI, Mon. to Fri. 9:00 a.m. to 4:00 p.m., Sat. 9:00 a.m. to 12:00 p.m.	Natural history and science exhibits.
East-West Center	1777 East-West Road, Univ. of Hawaii, Honolulu, HI 96848, tel. 948-8006	Cultural institute bringing together the peoples, art, history, and ways of East and West.
Episcopal Church in Hawaii	Queen Emma Square, Honolulu, HI 96813, tel. 536-7776.	Records and photos of church ministry in Hawaii from 1862.
Falls of Clyde Marine Museum	Pier 7, adjacent Aloha Tower, tel. 536-6373. Open daily 9:30 a.m. to 4:00 p.m.	Full-rigged sailing ship from last century.
Foster Botanical Garden	50 N. Vineyard Blvd. Open daily 9:00 a.m. to 4:00 p.m., tel. 531-1939.	Nine-acre oasis of exotic trees and rare plants.
Hawaii Chinese Historical Center	111 N. King St. Room 410, Honolulu, HI 96813, tel. 536-9302. Open 12 hours per week.	Rare books, oral histories, and photos concerning the history of Chinese in Hawaii.
Hawaii Medical Library, Inc.	1221 Punchbowl St., Honolulu, HI 96813, tel. 536-9302.	History of medicine in Hawaii.
Hawaii Pacific College Library	College information call 544-0200.	
Hawaiian Historical Society	560 Kawaiahao St., Honolulu, HI 96813, tel. 537-6271. Open Mon. to Fri., 10:00 a.m. to 4:00 p.m.	Extensive collection of 19th C. materials on Hawaiian Islands. 3,000 photos, 10,000 books, maps, microfilms. Adjacent to Hawaiian Mission Children's Society. Should be seen together and not missed.

Hawaiian Mission Children's Society	553 S. King St., Honolulu, HI 96813. tel. 531-0481.	Open Mon. to Fri., 10:00 a.m. to 4:00 p.m. Admission: $1.50 adults, $.75 children. Records, personal journals, letters and photos of early 19th C. Congregational missionaries to the Hawaiian Islands; archive of the Congregational Church in the Pacific. See HNL sites. Shouldn't be missed.
Hawaiian State Archives	Iolani Palace Grounds, Honolulu, HI 96813, tel. 547-2355. Open Mon. to Fri., 7:45 a.m. to 4:30 p.m.	Archives of the government of Hawaii. Private papers of Hawaiian royalty and government officials, photos, illustrations, etchings recording Hawaiian history. For anyone seriously interested in Hawaii. Shouldn't be missed.
Honolulu Academy of Arts	900 S. Beretania St., Honolulu, HI 96814, tel. 538-3693.	Object is to collect, preserve, and exhibit works of art (to conduct a public art education program related to the collection). Permanent and special exhibitions. Tours, classes, lectures, films.
Honolulu Botanical Gardens	50 N. Vine Yard Blvd., Honolulu, HI 96817, tel. 533-3406.	See Foster Botanical Gardens.
Honolulu Zoo	151 Kapahulu Ave., tel. 521-3487. Open daily 9:00 a.m. to 5:00 p.m.	Quiet respite from hustle of Waikiki. Includes a collection of tropical birds as well as pandas, zebras, and gibbon apes. Great for kids of all ages.
Iolani Palace	Box 2259 Honolulu, HI 96804, tel. 536-3552.	Iolani Palace Grounds. Perform all aspects of Historic research, restoration, and refurbishing of palace. The only royal palace in the U.S. Vintage artworks, antiques.
Kamehameha School	Kapalma Heights Road, Honolulu, HI 96813, tel. 842-8620.	Open Mon. to Fri., 7:30 a.m. to 4:00 p.m. Traditional school for children of Hawaiian descent. Rare books, periodicals, slides on Hawaiiana.

Paradise Park	3737 Manoa Rd., Honolulu, HI 96822, tel. 988-2141.	Exotic birds displayed in a tropical forest setting, includes trained birds presenting a performance.
Punahou School	1601 Punahou St., Honolulu, HI 96822, tel. 944-5823.	Collection available by special arrangment. Institutional archives of the oldest private school in Hawaii.
Queen Emma Summer Palace	2913 Pali Hwy., Honolulu, HI 96817, tel. 595-3167.	Restored historic home, built about 1848. Furniture and mementos of Queen Emma and her family. Some items belong to other members of the royal family.
Sea Life Park	Makapuu Point, Waimanalo, HI 96795, tel. 259-7933.	Varieties of Pacific marine plant and animal life, including several species of dolphins and whales. Feeding pool, Kaupa Village, turtle lagoon, restaurant, gift shop. See HNL sights.
Friends of Waipahu Cultural Garden Park	Box 103, Waipahu, HI 96797, tel. 677-0110.	Recreation of a plantation village in the style of a living museum.
USS *Bowfin,*	11 Arizona Memorial Drive, Pearl Harbor, HI 96818. Open daily from 9:30 a.m. to 4:30 p.m., tel. 423-1341.	Fully restored WW II submarine. Insight into the underwater war. Self-guided tours. Fascinating. Next door to *Arizona* Memorial. See HNL sights for more details.
Libraries	Oahu has more than a dozen libraries all over the island. The Central Administration number is 988-2194. Library for the blind and physically handicapped is at 402 Kapahulu Ave., tel. 732-7767.	

HAWAII

Bond Mission House	Hawi, HI 96719. Contact Lyman Bond at 889-5108 for an appointment.	Original, unrestored, off-the-beaten-track missionary house. See North Kohala sights for more information.
Thomas A. Jaggar Memorial Museum	Hawaiian Volcanoes National Park	Open daily 7:30 a.m. to 5:00 p.m. Natural history exhibits emphasize volcanology, but includes ethnology, zoology, and botany. A must-see.
Hulihee Palace	Box 1838 Kailua, HI 96740, tel. 329-1877. Downtown Kailua-Kona.	Exhibits of artifacts and furniture of 19th C. Hawaii, particularly items connected with members of the royal family.
Kamuela Museum	Box 507 Kamuela, HI 96743. Mr. and Mrs. Solomon, owners, curators, tel. 885-4724.	Open daily 8:00 a.m. to 5:00 p.m. Hawaiian artifacts from ancient Hawaii through the monarchy period, including ethnic groups arriving in the 19th century.
Kona Historical Society	Box 398, Captain Cook, HI 96704, tel. 323-3222.	Small collection of materials on the Kona section of the island. Founded 1976.
Liliuokalani Gardens Park.	See Hilo map for location.	Peace, quiet, amidst surroundings of a classical Japanese-style park.
Lyman House Memorial Museum	276 Haili St., Hilo, HI 96720, tel. 935-5021.	By appointment Saturdays. 5,600 publications, 10,000 photos, 600 newspapers. Inventory in process on correspondence, diaries, business records. Church school records. Maps and photos of island of Hawaii. Collection dates to 1832. One of the best private rock and mineral collections in the world.
Panaewa Zoo and Equestrian Center	25 Apuni St., Hilo, HI 96720, tel. 961-8311.	Exhibits of animal and plant specimens, educational and recreational facility.

Puuhonua O Honaunau National Historical Park	Box 129 Honaunali, HI 96726, tel. 328-2326.	Preserved and interpretive sights associated with temple of refuge. Excellent, park-like atmosphere. Shouldn't be missed. See South Kona sights for more information.
Libraries	There are libraries located in the main communities all over Hawaii. The central number in Hilo is 935-5407.	
	MAUI	
Alexander and Baldwin Sugar Museum	3957 Hansen Road, tel. 871-8050.	
Baldwin House	Front St., Lahaina, HI 96761. Open daily 9:30 a.m. to 5:00 p.m., tel. 661-3262.	Two-story home of medical missionary Dwight Baldwin. See Lahaina sights for details.
Brig *Carthaginian* Floating Museum	Lahaina Harbor, Lahaina. Open daily 9:00 a.m. to 5:00 p.m.	Replica of a 19th C. brig. Features whaling artifacts and exhibits of the humpback whale. See Lahaina sights for more information.
Hale Hoikeke Museum	2375 A Main, Wailuku, tel. 244-3326.	Hawaiian History Museum. Art Gallery featuring Kahoolawe artifacts and the renowned paintings of Edward Bailey.
Hale Pa'i Printshop Museum	Box 338, Lahaina, HI 96761, tel. 667-7040	Located on grounds of Lahainaluna school. See Lahaina sights. Operational relics of original printing press. Original Lahainaluna press publications, exhibit of Lahainaluna school past and present.
Hana Cultural Center	Box 27 Hana, HI 96713, tel. 248-8070.	Preserves and restores historical sites, artifacts, photos, documents etc. Construction of museum facilities in Hana.

Kula Botanical Gardens	Highway 377 to Upper Kula Road, tel. 878-1715.	Open daily 9:00 a.m. to 4:00 p.m. Excellent arrangments of tropical plants and flowers. Upcountry Maui.
Lahaina Arts Society	Box 991, Lahaina, HI 96761, tel. 661-0111.	To perpetuate Hawaiian culture, arts, crafts. Two galleries, annual scholarship, traveling exhibitions, helps maintain Lahaina district courthouse.
Lahaina Restoration Foundation	Box 991 Lahaina, HI 96761, tel. 661-3262.	James C. Luckey, director. Open Mon. to Fri., 10:00 a.m. to 4:00 p.m. Organization dedicated to the preservation of historical Lahaina. Sponsor restorations, archaeological digs and renovation of cultural and historical sites. Operate Baldwin Home, Brig *Carthaginian,* among others.
Maui Historical Society	Box 1018, Wailuku, HI 96793, tel. 244-3326.	Same as or part of Hale Hoikeke Museum. Promotes interest in and knowledge of history of Hawaii and Maui county. Six free lectures per year.
Whaler's Village Museum	Whaler's Village Shopping Center, Kaanapali, tel. 667-9564.	Whaling artifacts, 30-foot sperm whale skeleton set among gift shops. Self-guided learning experience while you shop.
Libraries	Maui's main library in Wailuku is at tel. 244-3945. Lanai Public Library, tel. 565-6996. Molokai Library at tel. 553-5483.	

KAUAI

Coco Palms Zoo	Coco Palms Hotel, Box 631 Lihue, HI 96766.	The Coco Palms is a must-see in itself. See Coco Palms for more information.
Grove Farm Homestead	P.O. Box 1631, Lihue, HI 96766, tel. 245-3202.	Open by appointment only. Records, business, and personal papers of early sugar planter George N. Wilcox. Definitely worth a visit. Personalized tours.
Hanalei Museum	Box 91, Hanalei, HI 96714, tel. 826-6783.	Local history. Aquariums with exotic reef fish.
Kauai Menehune Garden	tel. 245-2660.	Historical ancient Hawaiian garden.
Kauai Museum	4428 Rice, Lihue, HI 96766, tel. 245-6931.	Open Mon. to Fri. 9:30 a.m. to 4:30 p.m. Two buildings. Story of Kauai. Art and ethnic exhibits. Hawaiiana books, maps, prints, available at museum shop.
Kookee Natural History Museum	Box NN, Kekaha, HI 96752, tel. 335-9975.	Free. Open daily 10:00 a.m. to 4:00 p.m. Exhibits interpreting the geology, unique plants and animals of Kauai's mountain wilderness. Great to visit while visiting Waimea canyon.
Olu Pua Botanical Gardens	Kalaheo, HI, tel. 332-8182.	Open daily 8:30 a.m. to 5:00 p.m. Tours at 10:30 a.m. to 2:30 p.m. "Garden of a Thousand Flowers."
Paradise Pacifica Gardens	Wailua State Park, tel. 822-4911.	Open daily. International dinner and evening show nightly.
Waioli Mission House	Contact Director Barnes Riznik at tel. 245-3202. Waioli Corporation, Box 1631, Lihue, HI 96766.	
Libraries	The central library is at 4344 Hardy St., Lihue, HItel. 245-3617.	

BOOKLIST

INTRODUCTORY

Barrow, Terrence. *Incredible Hawaii.* Rutland, Vt.: Tuttle, 1974. Illus., Ray Lanternman. A pocket-sized compilation of oddities, little-known facts, trivia, and superlatives regarding the Hawaiian islands. Fun, easy reading, and informative.

Cohen, David, and Rick Smolan. *A Day in the Life of Hawaii.* New York: Workman, 1984. On December 2, 1983, 50 of the world's top photojournalists were invited to Hawaii to photograph a variety of normal life incidents occurring on that day. The photos are excellently reproduced, and are accompanied by a minimum of text.

Day, A.G., and C. Stroven. *A Hawaiian Reader.* New York: Appleton, Century, Crofts, 1959. A poignant compilation of essays, diary entries, and fictitious writings that takes you from the death of Captain Cook through the "statehood services."

Emphasis International. *On the Hana Coast.* Honolulu: Emphasis International Ltd., 1983. Text by Ron Youngblood. Sketches of the people, land, legends, and history of Maui's northeast coast. Beautifully illustrated with line drawings, vintage photos, and modern color work. Expresses true feeling and insight into people and things Hawaiian by letting them talk for themselves. An excellent book capturing what's different and what's universal about the people of the Hana district.

Friends of the Earth. *Maui, The Last Hawaiian Place.* New York: Friends of the Earth, 1970. A pictorial capturing the spirit of Maui in 61 contemporary color plates along with a handful of historical illustrations. A highly informative, as well as beautiful book printed in Italy.

Island Heritage Limited. *The Hawaiians.* Norfolk Island, Australia: Island Heritage Ltd., 1970. Text by Gavan Daws and Ed Sheehan. Primarily a "coffee table" picture book that lets the camera do the talking with limited yet informative text.

Judd, Gerritt P., comp. *A Hawaiian Anthology.* New York: MacMillan, 1967. A potpourri of observations from literati such as Twain and Stevenson who have visited the islands over the years. Also, excerpts from ordinary people's journals and missionary letters from early times down to a gleeful report of the day that Hawaii became a state.

Krauss, Bob. *Here's Hawaii.* New York: Coward, McCann Inc., 1960. Social commentary in a series of humorous anecdotes excerpted from this newspaperman's column from the late '60s. Dated, but in essence still useful because people and values obviously change very little.

Lueras, Leonard. *Surfing, The Ultimate Pleasure.* New York: Workman Publishing, 1984. An absolutely outstanding pictorial account of Hawaii's own sport—surfing. Vintage and contemporary photos are surrounded by well researched and written text. Bound to become a classic.

McBride, L.R. *Practical Folk Medicine of Hawaii.* Hilo, Hi.: Petroglyph Press, 1975. An illustrated guide to Hawaii's medicinal plants as used by the *kahuna lapa'au* (medical healers). Includes a thorough section on ailments, diagnosis, and the proper folk remedy to employ. Illustrated by the author, a renowned botanical researcher and former ranger at Volcanoes National Park.

Michener, James A. *Hawaii.* New York: Random House, 1959. Michener's fictionalized historical novel has done more to inform and misinform readers about Hawaii than any other book ever written. A great tale with plenty of local color and information that should be read for pleasure and not considered fact.

Piercy, LaRue. *Hawaii, This and That.* Hilo, Hi.: Petroglyph Press, 1981. Illus., Scot Ebanez. A 60-page book filled with one sentence facts and oddities about all manners of things Hawaiian. Informative, amazing, and fun to read.

Rose, Roger G. *Hawaii: The Royal Isles.* Honolulu: Bishop Museum Press, 1980. Photographs, Seth Joel. A pictorial mixture of artifacts and luminaries from Hawaii's past. Includes a mixture of Hawaiian and Western art depicting island ways. Beautifully photographed with highly descriptive accompanying text.

Wilkerson, James A., M.D., ed. *Medicine for Mountaineering.* 3rd ed. Seattle, Wa.: The Mountaineers, 1985. Don't let the title fool you. Although the book focuses on specific health problems that may be encountered while mountaineering, it is the best first-aid and general health guide available today. Written by doctors for the layman to use until help arrives, it is jam-packed with easily understandable techniques and procedures. For those intending extended treks, it is a must.

HISTORY/ POLITICAL SCIENCE

Albertini, Jim, et al. *The Dark Side of Paradise, Hawaii in a Nuclear War.* Honolulu: cAtholic Action of Hawaii. Well-documented research outlining Hawaii's role and vulnerability in a nuclear world. This book presents the anti-nuclear and anti-military side of the political issue in Hawaii.

Apple, Russell A. *Trails: From Steppingstones to Kerbstones.* Honolulu: Bishop Museum Press, 1965. This "Special Publication #53" is a special-interest archaeological survey focusing on the trails, roadways, footpaths, and highways and how they were designed and maintained throughout the years. Many "royal highways" from pre-contact Hawaii are cited.

Ashdown, Inez MacPhee. *Old Lahaina.* Honolulu: Hawaiian Service Inc., 1976. A small pamphlet-type book listing most of the historical attractions of Lahaina Town, past and present. Ashdown is a life-long resident of Hawaii and gathered her information firsthand by listening to and recording stories of ethnic Hawaiians and old *kamaaina* families.

———. *Ke Alaloa o Maui.* Wailuku, Hi.: Kamaaina Historians Inc., 1971. A compilation of the history and legends of sites on the island of Maui. Ashdown was at one time a "lady in waiting" for Queen Liliuokalani and has since been proclaimed Maui's "Historian Emeritus."

Bell, Roger. *Last Among Equals: Hawaiian Statehood and American Politics.* Honolulu: University of Hawaii, 1984. Documents Hawaii's long and rocky road to statehood, tracing political partisanship, racism, and social change.

Cameron, Roderick. *The Golden Haze.* New York: World Publishing, 1964. An account of Captain James Cook's voyages of discovery throughout the South Seas. Uses original diaries and journals for an "on the spot" reconstruction of this great seafaring adventure.

Daws, Gavan. *Shoal of Time, A History of the Hawaiian Islands.* Honolulu: University of Hawaii Press, 1968. A highly readable history of Hawaii dating from its "discovery" by the Western world down to its acceptance as the 50th state. Good insight into the psychological makeup of the influential characters that formed Hawaii's past.

Department of Geography, University of Hawaii. *Atlas of Hawaii.* 2nd ed. Honolulu: University of Hawaii Press, 1983. Much more than an atlas filled with reference maps, it also contains commentary on the natural environment, culture, sociology, a gazetteer, and statistical tables. Actually a mini encyclopedia.

Feher, Joseph. *Hawaii: A Pictorial History.* Honolulu: Bishop Museum Press, 1969. Text by Edward Joesting and O.A. Bushnell. An oversized tome laden with annotated historical and contemporary photos, prints, and paintings. Seems like a big "school book," but extremely well done. If you are going to read one survey about Hawaii's historical, social, and cultural past, this is the one.

Fuchs, Lawrence. *Hawaii Pono.* New York: Harcourt, Brace and World, 1961. A detailed, scholarly work presenting an overview of Hawaii's history, based upon psychological and sociological interpretations. Encompasses most socio-ethnological groups from native Hawaiians to modern entrepreneurs. A must for social historical background.

Handy, E.S., and Elizabeth Handy. *Native Planters in Old Hawaii.* Honolulu: Bishop Museum Press, 1972. A superbly written, easily understandable scholarly work on the intimate relationship of pre-contact Hawaiians and the *aina* (land). Much more than its title implies, should be read by anyone seriously interested in Polynesian Hawaii.

The Hawaii Book. Chicago: J.G. Ferguson, 1961. Insightful selections of short stories, essays, and historical and political commentaries by experts specializing in Hawaii. Good choice of photos and illustrations.

Hawaiian Children's Mission Society. *Missionary Album.* Honolulu: Mission Society, 1969. Firsthand accounts of the New England missionaries sent to Hawaii and instrumental in its conversion to Christianity. Down-home stories of daily life's ups and downs.

Heyerdahl, Thor. *American Indians in the Pacific.* London: Allen and Unwin Ltd., 1952. Theoretical and anthropological accounts of the influence on Polynesia of the Indians along the Pacific coast of North and South America. Fascinating reading, with unsubstantiated yet intriguing theories presented.

Ii, John Papa. *Fragments of Hawaiian History.* Honolulu: Bishop Museum, 1959. Hawaii's history under Kamehameha I as told by a Hawaiian who actually experienced it.

Joesting, Edward. *Hawaii: An Uncommon History.* New York: W.W. Norton Co., 1972. A truly uncommon history told in a series of vignettes relating to the lives and personalities of the first white men, Hawaiian nobility, sea captains, writers, and adventurers. Brings history to life. Absolutely excellent!

Lee, William S. *The Islands.* New York: Holt, Rinehart, 1966. A socio-historical set of stories concerning *malihini* (newcomers) and how they influenced and molded the Hawaii of today.

Liliuokalani. *Hawaii's Story By Hawaii's Queen.* Rutland, Vt.: Tuttle, 1964. A moving personal account of Hawaii's inevitable move from monarchy to U.S. Territory by its last queen, Liliuokalani. The facts can be found in other histories, but none provides the emotion or point of view as expressed by Hawaii's deposed monarch. A "must" read to get the whole picture.

Nickerson, Roy. *Lahaina, Royal Capital of Hawaii.* Honolulu: Hawaiian Service, 1978. The story of Lahaina from whaling days to present, spiced with ample photographs.

Smith, Richard A., et al., eds. *The Frontier States.* New York: Time-Life Books, 1968. Short and concise comparisons of the two newest states: Hawaii and Alaska. Dated information, but good social commentary and an excellent appendix suggesting tours, museums, and local festivals.

Takaki, Ronald. *Plantation Life and Labor in Hawaii, 1835-1920.* Honolulu: University of Hawaii Press, 1983. A perspective of plantation life in Hawaii from a multi-ethnic viewpoint. Written by a nationally known island scholar.

MYTHOLOGY AND LEGENDS

Beckwith, Martha. *Hawaiian Mythology.* Honolulu: University of Hawaii Press, 1970. Forty-five years after its original printing, this work remains *the* definitive text on Hawaiian mythology. Ms. Beckwith compiled this book from many sources, giving exhaustive cross-refrences to genealogies and legends expressed in the oral tradition. If you are going to read one book on Hawaii's folklore, this should be it.

Colum, Padraic. *Legends of Hawaii.* New Haven: Yale University Press, 1937. Selected legends of old Hawaii reinterpreted, but closely based upon the originals.

Elbert, S., comp. *Hawaiian Antiquities and Folklore.* Honolulu: Univerity of Hawaii Press, 1959. Illus. Jean Charlot. A selection of the main legends from Abraham Fornander's great work, *The Polynesian Race.*

Melville, Leinanai. *Children of the Rainbow.* Wheaton, Ill.: Theosophical Publishing, 1969. A book on higher spiritual consciousness attuned to nature, which was the basic belief of pre-Christian Hawaii. The appendix contains illustrations of mystical symbols used by the *kahuna.* An enlightening book in many ways.

Thrum, Thomas. *Hawaiian Folk Tales.* Chicago: McClurg and Co., 1907. A collection of Hawaiian tales from the oral tradition as told to the author from various sources.

Westervelt, W.D. *Hawaiian Legends of Volcanoes.* Boston: Ellis Press, 1916. A small book concerning the volcanic legends of Hawaii and how they related to the fledgling field of volcanism at the turn of the century. The vintage photos alone are worth a look.

NATURAL SCIENCES

Abbott, Agatin, Gordon MacDonald, and Frank Peterson. *Volcanoes in the Sea.* Honolulu: University of Hawaii Press, 1983. A simplified yet comprehensive text covering the geology and volcanism of the Hawaiian islands. Focuses upon the forces of nature (wind, rain, and surf) that shape the islands.

Boom, Robert. *Hawaiian Seashells.* Honolulu: Waikiki Aquarium, 1972. Photos, Jerry Kringle. A collection of 137 seashells found in Hawaiian waters, featuring many found nowhere else on Earth. Broken into categories with accompanying text including common and scientific names, physical descriptions, and likely habitats. A must for shell collectors.

Brock, Vernon, and W.A. Gosline. *Handbook of Hawaiian Fishes.* Honolulu: University of Hawaii Press, 1960. A detailed guide to most of the fishes occurring in Hawaiian waters.

Carlquist, Sherwin. *Hawaii: A Natural History.* New York: Doubleday, 1970. Definitive account of Hawaii's natural history.

Carpenter, Blyth, and Russell Carpenter. *Fish Watching in Hawaii.* San Mateo, Ca.: Natural World Press, 1981. A color guide to many of the reef fish found in Hawaii and often spotted by snorkelers. If you're interested in the fish that you'll be looking at, this guide will be very helpful.

Hamaishi, Amy, and Doug Wallin. *Flowers of Hawaii.* Honolulu: World Wide Distributors, 1975. Close-up color photos of many of the most common flowers spotted in Hawaii.

Hawaii Audubon Society. *Hawaii's Birds.* Honolulu: Hawaii Audubon Society, 1981. A field guide to Hawaii's birds, listing the endangered indigenous species, migrants, and introduced species that are now quite common. Color photos with text listing distribution, description, voice, and habits. Excellent field guide.

Hosaka, Edward. *Shore Fishing in Hawaii.* Hilo, Hi.: Petroglyph Press, 1984. Known as the best book on Hawaiian fishing since 1944. Receives the highest praise because it has born and bred many Hawaiian fishermen.

Hubbard, Douglass, and Gordon MacDonald. *Volcanoes of the National Parks of Hawaii.* Volcanoes, Hi.: Hawaii Natural History Assoc., 1982. The volcanology of Hawaii, documenting the major lava flows and their geological effect on the state.

Island Heritage Limited. *Hawaii's Flowering Trees.* Honolulu: Island Heritage Press. A concise field guide to many of Hawaii's most common flowering trees. All color photos with accompanying descriptive text.

Kay, E. Alison, comp. *A Natural History of the Hawaiian Islands.* Honolulu: University of Hawaii Press, 1972. A selection of concise articles by experts in the fields of volcanism, oceanography, meteorology, and biology. An excellent reference source.

Kuck, Lorraine, and Richard Togg. *Hawaiian Flowers and Flowering Trees.* Rutland, Vt.: Tuttle, 1960. A classic field guide to tropical and subtropical flora illustrated in watercolor. A "to the point" description of Hawaiian plants and flowers with a brief history of their places of origin and their introduction to Hawaii.

Merlin, Mark D. *Hawaiian Forest Plants, A Hiker's Guide.* Honolulu: Oriental Publishing, 1980. A companion guide to trekkers into Hawaii's interior. Full-color plates identify and describe the most common forest plants.

Merlin, Mark D. *Hawaiian Coastal Plants.* Honolulu: Oriental Publishing, 1980. Color photos and botanical descriptions of many of the plants and flowers found growing along Hawaii's varied shorelines.

Merrill, Elmer. *Plant Life of the Pacific World.* Rutland, Vt.: Tuttle, 1983. The definitive book for anyone planning a botanical tour to the entire Pacific basin. Originally published in the 1930s, it remains a tremendous work.

Nickerson, Roy. *Brother Whale, A Pacific Whalewatcher's Log.* San Francisco: Chronicle Books, 1977. Introduces the average person to the life of Earth's greatest mammals. Provides historical accounts, photos and tips on whalewatching. Well written, descriptive, and the best "first time" book on whales.

Stearns, Harold T. *Road Guide to Points of Geological Interest in the Hawaiian Islands.* Palo Alto: Pacific Books, 1966. The title is almost as long as this handy little book that lets you know what forces of nature formed the scenery that you see in the islands.

van Riper, Charles, and Sandra van Riper. *A Field Guide to the Mammals of Hawaii.* Honolulu: Oriental Publishing. A guide to the surprising number of mammals introduced into Hawaii. Full-color pages document description, uses, tendencies, and habitat. Small and thin, makes a worthwhile addition to any serious trekker's backpack.

TRAVEL

Birnbaum, Stephen, et al., eds. *Hawaii 1984.* Boston: Houghton Mifflin, 1983. Well-researched, informative writing, with good background material. Focuses primarily on known tourist spots with only perfunctory coverage of out-of-the-way places. Lacking in full coverage maps.

Bone, Robert W. *The Maverick Guide to Hawaii.* Gretna, La.: Pelican, 1983. Adequate, personalized writing style.

Fodor, Eugene, comp. *Fodor's Hawaii.* New York: Fodor's Guides, 1983. Great coverage on the cliches, but short on out-of-the-way places.

Hammel, Faye, and Sylvan Levy. *Frommer's Hawaii on $35 a Day.* New York: Frommer, Pasmantier, 1984. Hammel and Levy are good writers, but the book is top-heavy with info on Honolulu and Oahu and skimps on the rest.

Riegert, Ray. *Hidden Hawaii.* Berkeley: And/Or Press, 1982. Ray offers a "user friendly" guide to the islands.

Rizzuto, Shirley. *Hawaiian Camping.* Berkeley: Wilderness Press, 1979. Adequate coverage of the "nuts and bolts" of camping in Hawaii. Slightly conservative in approach and geared toward the family.

Smith, Robert. *Hawaii's Best Hiking Trails.* Also, *Hiking Kauai, Hiking Maui, Hiking Oahu,* and *Hiking Hawaii.* Berkeley: Wilderness Press, 1977 to 1982. Smith's books are specialized, detailed trekker's guides to Hawaii's outdoors. Complete with useful maps, historical references, official procedures, and plants and animals encountered along the way. If you're focused on hiking, these are the best to take along.

Stanley, David. *South Pacific Handbook.* 3rd ed. Chico, Ca.: Moon Publications, 1986. The model upon which all travel guides should be based. Simply the best book in the world for travel throughout the South Pacific.

Sutton, Horace. *Aloha Hawaii.* New York: Doubleday, 1967. A dated but still excellent guide to Hawaii providing sociological, historical, and cultural insight. Horace Sutton's literary style is the best in the travel guide field. Entertaining reading.

Thorne, Chuck. *The Diver's Guide to Maui.* Kahului, Hi.: Maui Dive Guide, 1984. A no-nonsense snorkeler's and diver's guide to Maui waters. Extensive maps, descriptions, and "straight from the shoulder" advice by one of Maui's best and most experienced divers. A must for all levels of divers and snorkelers.

Thorne, Chuck and Lou Zitnik. *A Divers' Guide to Hawaii.* Kihei, Hi.: Hawaii's Diver's Guide, 1984. An expanded divers' and snorkelers' guide to the waters of the 6 main Hawaiian islands. Complete list of maps with full descriptions, tips, and ability levels. A must for all levels of snorkelers and divers.

Wurman, Richard. *Hawaii Access.* Los Angeles: Access Press, 1983. The "fast food" publishers of travel guides. The packaging is colorful and bright like a burger in a styrofoam box, but there's little of substance inside.

COOKING

Alexander, Agnes. *How to Use Hawaiian Fruit.* Hilo, Hi.: Petroglyph Press, 1984. A full range of recipes using delicious and different Hawaiian fruits.

Fitzgerald, Donald, et al., eds. *The Pacific House Hawaii Cookbook.* Pacific House, 1968. A full range of Hawaiian cuisine including recipes from traditional Chinese, Japanese, Portuguese, New England, and Filipino dishes.

Gibbons, Euell. *Beachcombers Handbook.* New York: McKay Co., 1967. An autobiographical account of this world-famous naturalist as a young man living "off the land" in Hawaii. Great tips on spotting and gathering naturally occurring foods, survival advice, and recipes. Unfortunately the lifestyle described is long outdated.

Margah, Irish, and Elvira Monroe. *Hawaii, Cooking with Aloha.* San Carlos, Ca.: Wide World, 1984. Island recipes including *kalua* pig, *lomi* salmon, and hints on decor.

LANGUAGE

Boom, Robert, and Chris Christensen. *Important Hawaiian Place Names.* Honolulu: Boom Enterprises, 1978. A handy pocket-sized book listing most of the major island place names and their translations.

Elbert, Samuel. *Spoken Hawaiian.* Honolulu: University of Hawaii Press, 1970. Progressive conversational lessons.

Elbert, Samuel, and Mary Pukui. *Hawaiian Dictionary.* Honolulu: University of Hawaii, 1971. The best dictionary available on the Hawaiian language. The *Pocket Hawaiian Dictionary* is a condensed version of this dictionary which is less expensive and adequate for most travelers with a general interest in the language.

GLOSSARY

Words with asterisks (*) are used commonly throughout the islands.

*a'a**—rough clinker lava. *A'a* has become the correct geological term to describe this type of lava found anywhere in the world.

ahuapua—pie-shaped land divisions running from mountain to sea that were governed by *konohiki,* local *ali'i* who owed their allegiance to a reigning chief

aikane—friend; pal; buddy

aina—land; the binding spirit to all Hawaiians. Love of the land is paramount in traditional Hawaiian beliefs.

akamai—smart; clever; wise

akua—a god, or simply "divine." You'll hear people speak of their family or personal *amakua* (ancestral spirit). A favorite is the shark or the *pueo* (Hawaiian owl).

*ali'i**—a Hawaiian chief or nobleman

*aloha**—the most common greeting in the islands. Can mean both "hello" or "goodbye," "welcome" or "farewell." It also can mean romantic love, affection, best wishes.

aole—no

auwe—alas; ouch! When a great chief or loved one died, it was a traditional wail of mourning.

halakahiki—pineapple

*hale**—house or building; often combined with other words to name a specific place such as Haleakala (House of the sun) or Hale Pai (printing house).

*hana**—work. Combined with *pau* it means end of work or quitting time

hanai—literally "to feed." Part of the true *aloha* spirit. A *hanai* is a permanent guest, or an adopted family member, usually an old person or a child. This is an enduring cultural phenomenon in Hawaii, where a child from one family (perhaps that of a brother or sister, and quite often one's grandchild) is raised as one's own without formal adoption.

*haole**—a word that at one time meant foreigner, but now means a white person or Caucasian. Many etymological definitions have been put forth, but none satisfies everyone. Some feel that it signified a person without a background, because the first white men could not chant their genealogies as was common to Hawaiians.

*hapa**—half, as in a mixed-blooded person being referred to as *hapa haole*

*hapai**—pregnant; used by all ethnic groups when a *keiki* is on the way

*haupia**—a coconut custard dessert often served at *luau.*

*heiau**—a traditional Hawaiian temple. A platform made of skillfully fitted rocks, upon which structures were built and offerings made to the gods.

*holoku**—an ankle-length dress that is much more fitted than a *muumuu,* and which is often worn on formal occasions

hono—bay, as in Honolulu (Sheltered Bay)

ho'oilo—traditional Hawaiian winter that began in November

hoolaulea—any happy event, but especially a family outing or picnic

*hoomalimali**—sweet talk; flattery

*huhu**—angry; irritated

*hui**—a group; meeting; society. Often used to refer to Chinese businessmen or family members who pool their money to get businesses started.

hukilau—traditional shoreline fish-gathering in which everyone lends a hand to *huki* (pull) the huge net. Anyone taking part shares in the *lau* (food). It is much more like a party than hard work, and if you're lucky you'll be able to take part in one.

*hula**—a native Hawaiian dance in which the rhythm of the islands is captured by swaying hips and stories told by lyrically moving hands. A *halau* is a group or school of *hula.*

huli huli—barbecue, as in *huli huli* chicken

i'a—fish in general. *I'a maka* is raw fish.

*imu**—underground oven filled with hot rocks and used for baking. The main cooking feature at a *luau* used to steam-bake the pork and other succulent dishes. Traditionally the tending of the *imu* was for men only.

ipo—sweetheart; lover; girl- or boyfriend

kahili—a tall pole topped with feathers resembling a huge feather duster. It was used by an *ali'i* to announce his presence.

*kahuna**—priest; sorcerer; doctor; skillful person. *Kahuna* had tremendous power in old Hawaii which they used for both good and evil. The *kahuna 'ana'ana* was a feared individual because he practiced "black magic" and could pray a person to death, while the *kahuna lapa'au* was a medical practitioner bringing aid and comfort to the people.

kai—the sea. Many businesses and hotels employ *kai* as part of their name.

kalua—roasted underground in an *imu.* A favorite island food is *kalua* pork.

*kamaaina**—a child of the land; an old timer; a longtime island resident of any ethnic background; a resident of Hawaii or native son. Oftentimes hotels and airlines offer discounts called *"kamaaina* rates" to anyone who can prove island residency.

kanaka—man or commoner; later used to distinguish a Hawaiian from other races. Tone of voice can make it derogatory.

*kane**—means man, but actually used to signify a relationship such as husband or boyfriend. Written on a door it means "Men's Room."

*kapu**—forbidden; taboo; keep out; do not touch

*kaola**—any food that has been broiled or barbecued

*kaukau**—slang word meaning food or chow; grub. Some of the best food in Hawaii comes from the *"kaukau* wagons," trucks that sell plate lunches and other morsels.

kauwa—a landless, untouchable caste that was confined to living on reservations. Members of this caste were often used as human sacrifice at *heiau.* Calling someone *kauwa* is still considered a grave insult.

kava—a mildly intoxicating traditional drink made from the juice of chewed awaroot, spat into a bowl, and used in religious ceremonies.

*keiki**—child or children; used by all ethnic groups. "Have you hugged your *keiki* today?"

kiawe—an algaroba tree from S. America commonly found along the shore. It grows a nasty long thorn that can easily puncture a tire. Legend has it that the trees were introduced to the islands by a misguided missionary who hoped the thorns would coerce natives into wearing shoes. Actually, they are good for fuel, as fodder for hogs and cattle, and for reforestation—none of which you'll appreciate if you step on one of their thorns, or flatten a tire on your rental car!

kokua—help. As in "Your *kokua* is needed to keep Hawaii free from litter."

kona wind*—a muggy subtropical wind that blows from the south and hits the leeward side of the islands. It usually brings sticky hot weather, and is one of the few times when air conditioning will be appreciated.

konane—a traditional Hawaiian game, similar to checkers, played with pebbles on a large flat stone used as a board

koolau—windward side of the island

kukui—a candlenut tree whose pods are polished and then strung together to make a beautiful *lei.* Traditionally strung on the rib of a coconut leaf and used as a candle also.

kuleana—homesite; the old homestead; small farms. Especially used to describe the small spreads on Hawaiian Homes Lands on Molokai.

*Kumulipo**—ancient Hawaiian genealogical chant that records the pantheon of gods, creation, and the beginning of mankind

kupuna—a grandparent or old timer; usually means someone who has gained wisdom. The statewide school system now invites *kupuna* to talk to the children about the old ways and methods.

la—the sun. Combined with other words to be more descriptive such as, *La*haina (Merciless sun) or Haleaka*la* (House of the sun).

*lanai**—veranda or porch. You'll pay more for a hotel room if it has a *lanai* with an ocean view.

lani—sky or the heavens

*lau hala**—traditional Hawaiian weaving of mats, hats, etc. from the prepared fronds of the pandanus (screw pine)

*lei**—a traditional garland of flowers or vines. One of Hawaii's most beautiful customs. Given at any auspicious occasion, but especially when arriving or leaving Hawaii.

lele—the stone altar at a *heiau*

limu—edible seaweed of various types. Gathered from the shoreline, it makes an excellent salad. It's used to garnish many island dishes and is a favorite at a *luau.*

lomilomi—traditional Hawaiian massage; also, raw salmon made up into a vinegared salad with chopped onion and spices

*lua**—the toilet; the head; the bathroom

luakini—a human sacrifice temple. Introduced to Hawaii in the 13th C. at Wahaula Heiau on the Big Island.

luau*—a Hawaiian feast featuring *poi, imu,* baked pork, and other traditional foods. Good ones provide some of the best gastronomical delights in the world.

luna—foreman or overseer in the plantation fields. They were often mounted on horseback and were renowned either for their fairness or cruelty. They represented the middle class, and served as a buffer between the plantation workers and the white plantation owners.

*mahalo**—thank you; *mahalo nui,* "big thanks" or "thank you very much"

mahele—division. The "Great Mahele" of 1848 changed Hawaii forever when the traditional common lands were broken up into privately owned plots.

mahu—a homosexual; often used derisively like "fag" or "queer"

*mahimahi**—a favorite eating fish. Often called a dolphin, but a *mahimahi* is a true fish, not a cetacean.

maile—a fragrant vine used in a traditional *lei*. It looks ordinary but smells delightful.

*makai**—toward the sea; used by most islanders when giving directions

makaainana—a commoner, as opposed to an *ali'i;* a person "belonging" to the *aina* (land)

make—dead; deceased

*malihini**—newcomer; tenderfoot; a recent arrival

malo—the native Hawaiian loincloth. Never worn anymore except at festivals or pageants.

*mana**—power from the spirit world; innate energy of all things animate or inanimate; the grace of god. *Mana* could be passed on from one person to another, or even stolen. Great care was taken to protect the *ali'i* from having their *mana* defiled. Commoners were required to lie flat on the ground and cover their faces whenever a great *ali'i* approached. *Kahuna* were often employed in the regaining or transference of *mana*.

manauahi—free; gratis; extra

manini—stingy; tight. A Hawaiianized word taken from the name of Don Francisco Marin, who was instrumental in bringing many fruits and plants to Hawaii. He was known for never sharing any of the bounty from his substantial gardens on Vineyard Street in Honolulu, thus his name became synonymous with stinginess.

*mauka**—toward the mountains; used by most islanders when giving directions

mele—a song or chant in the Hawaiian oral tradition that records the history and genealogies of the *ali'i*

mauna—mountain. Often combined with other words to be more descriptive, such as Mauna Kea (White Mountain).

menehune—the legendary "little people" of Hawaii. Like leprechauns, they are said to have shunned mankind and possess magical powers. Stone walls said to have been completed in one night are often attributed to them. Some historians argue that they actually existed and were the aboriginals of Hawaii, inhabiting the islands before the coming of the Polynesians.

moa—chicken; fowl

*moana**—the ocean; the sea. Many businesses and hotels as well as places have *moana* as part of their name.

moe—sleep

moolelo—ancient tales kept alive by the oral tradition and recited only by day

*muumuu**—a "Mother Hubbard," a long dress with a high neckline introduced by the missionaries to cover the nakedness of the Hawaiians. It has become fashionable attire for almost any occasion in Hawaii.

nani—beautiful

nui—big; great; large; as in *mahalo nui* (thank you very much)

ohana—a family; the fundamental social division; extended family. Now used to denote a social organization with grassroots overtones as in the "Save Kahoolawe Ohana."

okolehau—literally "iron bottom"; a traditional booze made from *ti* root; *okole* means your "rear end" and *hau* means "iron," which was descriptive of the huge blubber pots that it was made in. Also, if you drink too much it'll surely knock you on your *okole*.

*ono**—delicious; delightful; the best. *Ono ono* means "extra or absolutely delicious."

opihi—a shellfish or limpet that clings to rocks and is gathered as one of the islands' favorite *pupu*. Custom dictates that you never remove all of the *opihi* from a rock; some are always left to grow for future generations.

opu—belly; stomach

pa'u—long split skirt often worn by women when horseback riding. Last century, an island treat was when *Pa'u* riders would turn out in their beautiful dresses at Kapiolani Park in Honolulu. The tradition is carried on today at many of Hawaii's rodeos.

*pahoehoe**—smooth ropey lava that looks like burnt pancake batter. *Pahoehoe* is now the correct geological term used to describe this type of lava found anywhere in the world.

pake—a Chinese person. Can be derisive, depending on tone in which it is used. It is a bastardization of the Chinese word meaning "uncle."

*pali**—a cliff; precipice. Hawaii's geology makes them quite common. The most famous are the *pali* of Oahu where a major battle was fought.

*paniolo**—a Hawaiian cowboy. Derived from the Spanish *espaniola*. The first cowboys brought to Hawaii during the early 19th century were Mexicans from California.

papale—hat. Except for the feathered helmets of the *ali'i* warriors of old Hawaii, hats were generally not worn. However, once the islanders saw their practical uses, and how fashionable they were, they began weaving them from various materials and quickly became experts at manufacture and design.

*pau**—finished; done; completed. Often combined into *pau hana* which means end of work or quitting time.

pilau—stink; bad smell; stench

pilikia—trouble of any kind, big or small; bad times

*poi**—a glutinous paste made from the pounded corn of taro which ferments slightly and has a light sour taste. Purplish in color, it's a staple at a *luau,* where it is called "one, two, or three finger" poi depending upon its thickness.

pono—righteous or excellent

pua—flower

*puka**—a hole of any size. *Puka* is used by all island residents when talking about a pinhole in a dinghy or a tunnel through a mountain.

punalua—the tradition of sharing mates in practice before the missionaries came. Western seamen took advantage of it, and this led to the spreading of contagious diseases and eventually to the ultimate demise of the Hawaiian people.

*punee**—bed; narrow couch. Used by all ethnic groups. To recline on a *punee* on a breezy *lanai* is a true island treat.

*pu pu**—an appetizer; a snack; hors d'oeuvres; can by anything from cheese and crackers to *sushi.* Oftentimes, bars or nightclubs offer them free.

pupule—crazy; nuts; out of your mind

pu'u—hill, as in Pu'u Ulaula (Red Hill)

*tapa**—a traditional paper cloth made from beaten bark. Intricate designs were stamped in using beaters, and natural dyes added color. The tradition was lost for many years, but is now making a comeback, and provides some of the islands' most beautiful folk art.

taro*—the staple of old Hawaii. A plant with a distinctive broad leaf that produces a starchy root. It was brought by the first Polynesians and was grown on magnificently irrigated plantations. According to the oral tradition, the life-giving properties of taro hold mystical significance for Hawaiians, since it was created by the gods at about the same time as mankind.

ti—a broad green-leafed plant that was used for many purposes, from plates to *hula* skirts (never grass), and especially used to wrap religious offerings presented at the *heiau*.

*tutu**—grandmother; granny; older woman; used by all as a term of respect and endearment.

*ukulele**—*uku* means "flea" and *lele* means "jumping," so literally "jumping flea"—the way the Hawaiians perceived the quick finger movements on the banjo-like Portuguese folk instrument called a *cavaquinho.* The *ukulele* quickly became synonymous with the islands.

*wahine**—young woman; female; girl; wife. Used by all ethnic groups. When written on a door it means "Women's Room."

wai—fresh water; drinking water

wela—hot. *Wela kahao* is a "hot time" or "making whoopy."

*wiki**—quickly; fast; in a hurry. Often seen as *wiki wiki* (very fast), as in "Wiki Wiki Messenger Service."

INDEX

Boldfaced page numbers indicate primary reference. For designated towns, beaches and special sights: (H) = Hawaii Island; (K) = Kauai; (L) = Lanai; (M) = Maui; (Mo) = Molokai; (N) = Niihau; (O) = Oahu

I

J

photo by Sandy Bisignani

ABOUT THE AUTHOR

Joe Bisignani is a fortunate man because he makes his living doing the two things that he likes best: traveling and writing. Joe has been with Moon Publications since 1979, and is the author of *Japan Handbook,* and *Maui Handbook.* When not traveling, he makes his home in northern California, where he lives with his wife Marlene and their daughter Sandra.

ABOUT THE ILLUSTRATORS

Diana Lasich Harper has been a contributing artist to several Moon books. After receiving a degree in art at San Jose State University, California, she moved to Hawaii where she lived for four years. Much of her time there was spent cycling, hiking and *always* drawing. From Hawaii, Diana moved to Japan where she lived for two years and studied wood block printing, *sumie,* and *kimono* painting. Her illustrations appear on pages 1, 9, 20, 21, 43, 47, 48, 74, 82, 90, 95, 99, 113, 124, 136, 155, 157, 159, 160, 164, 171, 175, 189, 225, 248, 288, 302, 325, 353, 389, 425, 427, 445, 453, 474, 484, 485, 522, 550, 652, 682, 698, 706.

Louise Foote lives on an experimental urban commune in Chico with her two lovely daughters. When not at Moon Publications drafting maps, she works as an archaeologist. Louise also renovates homes, and builds custom furniture. Sometimes, she turns her hand to illustrating, and her work appears on pages 11, 12, 14, 15, 16, 18, 19, 22, 23, 53, 80, 91, 92 141, 161, 172, 173, 178, 179, 180, 194, 195, 321, 324, 366, 430, 457, 458, 468, 498, 511, 527, 530, 533, 544, 559, 577, 593, 613, 626, 660, 661, 662, 693, 719, 732.

Mary Ann Abel was born and raised in a small town in West Virginia. She uses this background to infuse her work with what she values most: family and nature. Mary Ann is a member of the *Sunday Art Mart* in Honolulu, where she sells her artwork. She also displays at various "juried shows" in and around Honolulu, and currently, her work can be seen at the *Myonghee Art Gallery* in Waikiki. Mary Ann lives in Honolulu with her husband Richard and her daughters Robin and Nicole. Her illustrations appear on pages 69, 331, 374, 403, 450, 452, 459, 576, 582, 619, 642, 753, 756.

Sue Strangio Everett was born and raised in Chico, California where she attended Chico State University, majoring in Fine Art. For the past 12 years, she has refined and developed her skills, working primarily as a graphic artist. Sue is also accomplished in pottery design and glazing, silk screening, weaving, etching, stained glass work and pen and ink. While finding the patience to paint the cover from Joe Bisignani's sad little stick figures, she also drew the illustrations on pages 106, 134, 137, 165, 176, 181, 182, 411, 418, 431, 442, 596, 653.

Gary Quiring is a freelance photographer living in Chico, California. He has traveled extensively throughout the U.S., S.E. Asia, and Latin and South America, all the while photographing the people and their environments. While living on Maui, near the Seven Sacred Pools, he shot the photos that appear in this book. If you are interested in gaining access to his stock of transparencies, please contact: The Stockmarket, 1181 Broadway, N.Y., N.Y., 10001, tel. (212) 684-7878; or Gary Quiring, Rt. 2 Box 195, Chico, CA 95926. Besides in the color plates, Gary's b&ws appear on pages 146, 380.

Debra Fau is a born artist. She can't help it...she's French. Deb lives in Chico where she sings with a rock'n' roll band, does *batik,* tie-dye, and paintings. She keeps the wolf from the door by cocktail waitressing, where she's renowned for carrying the best tray in town. Her drawings appear on pages 7, 183, 322, 323, 333.

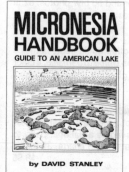

DID YOU ENJOY THIS BOOK?

Then you may want to order other MOON PUBLICATIONS' titles.

BLUEPRINT FOR PARADISE: How to Live on a Tropic Island by Ross Norgrove. Do you dream of living on a tropical island paradise? *Blueprint for Paradise* clearly and concisely explains how to make that dream a reality. Derived from his own and others' experiences, Norgrove covers: choosing an island, owning your own island, designing a house for tropical island living, transportation, getting settled, and successfully facing the natural elements. Breathtaking illustrations complete this remarkable guide. 202 pages. Available November 1987. **Code MN36** **$14.95.**

JAPAN HANDBOOK by J.D. Bisignani. Packed with practical money-saving tips on travel, food and accommodation. *Japan Handbook* is essentially a cultural and anthropological manual on every facet of Japanese life. 35 color photos, 200 b/w photos, 92 illustrations, 29 charts, 112 maps and town plans, an appendix on the Japanese language, booklist, glossary, index. 504 pages. **Code MN05** **$12.95**

INDONESIA HANDBOOK, 4th edition by Bill Dalton. The most comprehensive and contemporary guide to Indonesia. Discover the cheapest places to eat and sleep, ancient ruins and historical sites, wildlife and nature reserves, spiritual centers, arts and crafts, folk theater and dance venues. 12 color pages, hundreds of photos, illustrations, maps, charts, booklist, vocabulary, index. 900 pages. Available in February 1988.
Code MN01 **$12.95**

NEW ZEALAND HANDBOOK by Jane King. New Zealand is nature's improbable masterpiece, a world of beauty and wonder jammed into three unforgettable islands. Explore whitewater rapids, ski the slopes of a smoldering volcano, cast a flyrod in an icy stream, or have a bet on "the trots." 8 color pages, 99 b/w photos, 146 illustrations, 82 maps, index. 512 pages.
Code MN35 **$13.95.**

MAUI HANDBOOK by J.D. Bisignani. Boasting historic Lahina, sensitively planned Kaanapali resort, power center Haleakala, and precipitous Hana Road, Hawaii's Maui is one of the most enchanting and popular islands in all of Oceania. 6 color and 50 b/w photos, 62 illustrations, 27 maps, 13 charts, booklist, glossary, index. 235 pages.
Code MN29 **$8.95**

GUIDE TO JAMAICA: Including Haiti by Harry S. Pariser. No other guide treats Jamaica with more depth, historical detail, or practical travel information than *Guide to Jamaica.* 4 color pages, 51 b/w photos, 39 illustrations, 10 charts, 18 maps, booklist, glossary, index. 165 pages.
Code MN25 **$7.95**

GUIDE TO PUERTO RICO AND THE VIRGIN ISLANDS: Including the the Dominican Republic by Harry S. Pariser. Discover for yourself the delights of America's "51st states," from the wild beauty of St. John, an island almost wholly reserved as a national park, to cosmopolitan San Juan. 4 color pages, 55 b/w photos, 53 illustrations, 29 charts, 35 maps, booklist, glossary, index. 225 pages. **Code MN21** **$8.95**

GUIDE TO THE YUCATAN PENINSULA by Chicki Mallan. Explore the mysterious monolithic cities of the Maya, plunge into the color and bustle of the village market place, relax on unspoiled beaches, or jostle with the jet set in modern Cancun. 4 color pages, 154 b/w photos, 55 illustrations, 53 maps, 68 charts, appendix, booklist, vocabulary, index. 300 pages. **Code MN32** **$10.95**

ARIZONA TRAVELER'S HANDBOOK by Bill Weir. This carefully researched guide contains the facts and background to make Arizona accessible and enjoyable. It's all here—places to go, directions, hours, phone numbers, as well as motel, restaurant, and campground listings. 8 color pages, 250 b/w photos, 81 illustrations, 53 maps, 4 charts, booklist, index. 448 pages. **Code MN30** **$10.95**

ALASKA YUKON HANDBOOK: A Gypsy Guide to the Inside Passage and Beyond by David Stanley. The first true budget guide to Alaska and Western Canada. 37 color photos, 76 b/w photos, 86 illustrations, 70 maps, booklist, glossary, index. 230 pages. **Code MN07** **$7.95**

CALIFORNIA DOWNHILL by Stephen Metzger. Gives complete, detailed listings of all of California's 40 downhill ski areas, from the bunny slopes of Big Bear to the near-vertical faces of Squaw Valley—and everything in between. 15 color and 37 b/w photos, 21 illustrations, 30 maps, 41 charts, index. 144 pages. **Code MN31** **$7.95**

BACKPACKING: A HEDONIST'S GUIDE by Rick Greenspan and Hal Kahn. This humorous, handsomely illustrated how-to guide will convince even the most confirmed naturophobe that it's safe, easy, and enjoyable to leave the smoggy security of city life behind. 90 illustrations, annotated booklist, index. 199 pages. **Code MN23** **$7.95.**

MOONBOOKS MAKE GREAT GIFTS!

HAWAII HANDBOOK by J.D. Bisignani. Offers a comprehensive introduction to Hawaii's geography, vibrant social history, arts, and events. The travel sections inform you of the best sights, lodging and food, entertainment, and services. J.D. Bisignani has discovered bargains on excursions, cruises, car rentals, and airfares. Maps, charts, illustrations, color and b/w photos, index. 750 pages. **Code MN34** **$14.95**

A HAWAIIAN READER
Edited by A. Grove Day and Carl Stroven

BEST SOUTH SEA STORIES
Edited by A. Grove Day and Carl Stroven

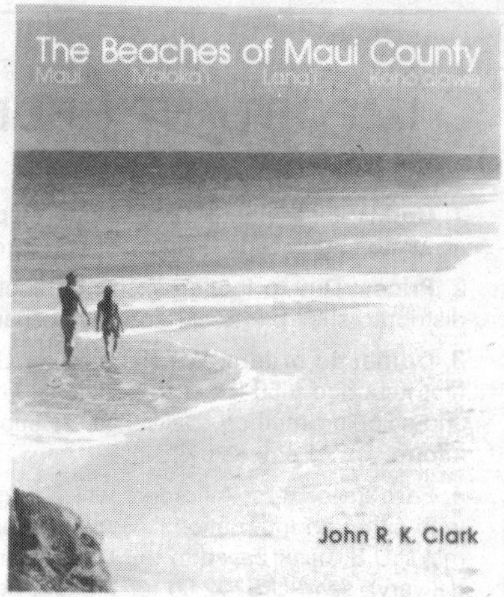

The Beaches of Maui Country
by John R. K. Clark
This guide covers every beach on the islands of Maui, Molokai, Lanai, Kahoolawe and Molokini. Discover for yourself these well-known and lesser-known beaches. Photos, illus., maps, tables. 172 pages.
CodeUH12 **$9.95**

REFERENCE MAPS TO HAWAII

The *Honolulu Advertiser* calls these University of Hawaii full color, topographic maps, "far and away the best (and most beautiful) maps of the Islands available today." These useful maps will greatly add to your enjoyment of the islands.

TITLE	SCALE	CODE/PRICE	DESCRIPTION
Kuaui	1:158,000	UH05**$2.25**	folded; incl. maps of Lihue, Kapaa
Hawaii (Big Island)	1:250,000	UH06**$2.50**	folded; incl. map of Hilo
Oahu	1:158,000	UH07**$2.50**	folded; incl. street maps of Honolulu, Kaneohe
Maui	1:150,000	UH08**$2.25**	folded; incl. street maps of Lahaina, Wailuku
Molokai & Lanai	1:158,000	UH09**$2.95**	folded; incl. Lanai and insets of Lanai City, Kaunakakai

IMPORTANT ORDERING INFORMATION

1. Codes: Please enter book and/or map codes on your order form. This will assure accurate and speedy delivery of your order.

2. Prices: Due to foreign exchange fluctuations and the changing terms of our distributors, all prices are subject to change without notice.

3. Domestic orders: We ship UPS or US Postal Service 1st class. Send $3.00 for first item and $.50 for each additional item. Please specify street or P.O. Box address, and shipping method. Deliveries are subject to availability of merchandise. We will inform you of any delay.

4. Foreign orders: All orders which originate outside the U.S.A. **must** be paid for with either an International Money Order or a check in U.S. currency drawn on a major U.S. bank based in the U.S.A. For International Surface Bookrate (8-12 weeks delivery), send U.S. $2.00 for the first book and U.S. $1.00 for each additional book.

5. Telephone orders: We accept Visa or Mastercharge payments.
MINIMUM ORDER U.S. $15.00. Call in your order: (916) 345-5413.
9:00 a.m. - 5:00 p.m. Pacific Standard Time.

6. Noncompliance: Any orders received which do not comply with any of the above conditions will result in the return of your order and/or payment intact.

MOONBELTS

A new concept in moneybelts. Made of heavy-duty Cordura nylon construction and strong water-resistant fabric, the *Moonbelt* offers maximum protection for your important papers. This pouch, designed for all-weather comfort, slips under your shirt or waistband, rendering it virtually undetectable and inaccessible to pickpockets. Many thoughtful features: 1-inch-wide nylon webbing, heavy-duty zipper, and a 1-inch high-test quick-release buckle. No more fumbling around for the strap or repeated adjustments, this handy plastic buckle opens and closes with a touch, but won't come undone until you want it to. Accommodates travelers cheques, passport, cash, photos. Size: 3½ x 8. Available in black or white.

$6.95

ORDER FORM

(See important ordering information opposite page)

Name: ______________________ Date: ______________

Street: ______________________________________

City: ____

State or Country: ______________ Zip Code: ________

Daytime Phone: _______________________________

Quantity	Full Book or Map Title	Code	Price
		Taxable Total	
		Sales Tax (6%) for California Residents	
		Shipping and Handling Costs	
		TOTAL	

SHIP TO: ☐ address above ☐ other ______________________

____

____

Make checks payable to:

MOON PUBLICATIONS 722 Wall St. Chico CA 95928 USA tel. (916) 345-5413

WE ACCEPT VISA AND MASTERCHARGE!

To order: CALL IN YOUR VISA OR MASTERCHARGE NUMBER, or send written order with your Visa or Mastercharge number and expiry date clearly written.

CARD NO. ☐ VISA ☐ MASTERCHARGE

☐☐☐☐☐☐☐☐☐☐☐☐☐☐☐☐

SIGNATURE ______________________ EXPIRATION DATE ____________

MINIMUM ORDER: US$15

MN34